W9-ANB-750

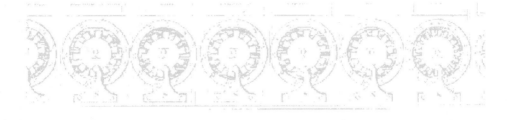

2nd edition

ENCYCLOPEDIA OF
PHILOSOPHY

6

volume

2nd edition

ENCYCLOPEDIA OF
PHILOSOPHY

DONALD M. BORCHERT

Editor in Chief

MACMILLAN REFERENCE USA
An imprint of Thomson Gale, a part of The Thomson Corporation

THOMSON

GALE

Detroit • New York • San Francisco • San Diego • New Haven, Conn. • Waterville, Maine • London • Munich

Encyclopedia of Philosophy, Second Edition

Donald M. Borchert, Editor in Chief

LIBRARY OF CONGRESS CATALOGING-IN-PUBLICATION DATA

Encyclopedia of philosophy / Donald M. Borchert, editor in chief.—2nd ed.
   p. cm.
     Includes bibliographical references and index.
     ISBN 0-02-865780-2 (set hardcover : alk. paper)—
     ISBN 0-02-865781-0 (vol 1)—ISBN 0-02-865782-9 (vol 2)—
     ISBN 0-02-865783-7 (vol 3)—ISBN 0-02-865784-5 (vol 4)—
     ISBN 0-02-865785-3 (vol 5)—ISBN 0-02-865786-1 (vol 6)—
     ISBN 0-02-865787-X (vol 7)—ISBN 0-02-865788-8 (vol 8)—
     ISBN 0-02-865789-6 (vol 9)—ISBN 0-02-865790-X (vol 10)
     1. Philosophy–Encyclopedias. I. Borchert, Donald M., 1934-

B51.E53 2005
103–dc22
                                     2005018573

This title is also available as an e-book.
ISBN 0-02-866072-2
Contact your Thomson Gale representative for ordering information.

Printed in the United States of America
10 9 8 7 6 5 4 3 2 1

contents

ENCYCLOPEDIA OF
PHILOSOPHY
2nd edition

MASARYK, TOMÁŠ GARRIGUE
(1850–1937)

Tomáš Garrigue Masaryk, a Czech statesman and philosopher, and president of Czechoslovakia from 1918 to 1935, was born in Hodonín, Moravia. His political career belongs to history; of interest to students of philosophy is the fact that he studied philosophy at the University of Vienna from 1872 to 1876 under Franz Brentano. He spent the year 1876–1877 at Leipzig, where Wilhelm Wundt was his teacher and Edmund Husserl and Richard Avenarius were fellow students. In 1879 Masaryk became *Privatdozent* at Vienna, submitting *Der Selbstmord als sociale Massenerscheinung* (Vienna, 1881) as his habilitation thesis. In 1882 Masaryk became professor of philosophy at the Czech University in Prague, where he soon made his mark as a politician and writer in Czech. *Základové konkretné logiky* (The foundations of concrete logic; Prague, 1885; German translation, *Versuch einer concreten Logik,* Vienna, 1887) and *Otázka sociální* (The social question; Prague, 1898; German translation, *Die philosophischen und sociologischen Grundlagen des Marxismus,* Vienna, 1899) were followed by books on Czech history and politics and by an extensive Russian

intellectual history, first published in German as *Russland und Europa* (2 vols., Jena, Germany, 1913; translated by Eden and Cedar Paul as *The Spirit of Russia,* 2 vols., London, 1919). World War I and the presidency of Czechoslovakia put an end to Masaryk's academic pursuits, but a book of memoirs, *Světová revoluce* (The world revolution; Prague, 1925; English translation, edited by H. W. Steed, *The Making of a State,* London, 1927) and *Hovory s T. G. Masarykem* (Conversations with T. G. Masaryk; 3 vols., Prague, 1931–1935) by Karel Čapek (English translations by M. and R. Weatherall, *President Masaryk Tells His Story,* London, 1934, and *Masaryk on Thought and Life,* London, 1938) reformulate his convictions impressively.

Masaryk was a practical philosopher who believed that philosophy should not only contemplate the world but also try to change it. He thus had little interest in problems of epistemology or cosmology. In his early life he reacted against German idealism and accepted British empiricism (David Hume) and French positivism (Auguste Comte). Later he argued for a type of realism that he called concretism. In every act of knowing, he believed, the whole man takes part. Concretism acknowledges not only reason but also the senses, the emotions, and the will—the whole experience of our consciousness. It is something like William James's radical empiricism without the exceptional experiences admitted by James. But Masaryk's main interest was in sociology and philosophy of history.

Masaryk's realism was combined with a deep religious belief—Masaryk was a theist who found the Unitarianism of his American wife congenial—and a strong conviction of the immutable difference between right and wrong. Masaryk's thinking centered on the crisis of civilization caused by the decay of religion. He diagnosed the diseases of modern man (indifference, suicidal mania, violence, war, etc.) and prescribed remedies for them. He believed that sociology is the foundation of any further cultural advance but that its method must not be purely genetic and descriptive. Teleology, or explanation by purpose, is legitimate. The aim of history is the realization of the ideal of humanity. Masaryk's humanism was not, however, merely humanitarianism, although he often spoke of democracy as another term for his ideal. In spite of his sympathies for the concrete demands of socialism, Masaryk remained an individualist who disapproved of all forms of collectivism. He criticized Karl Marx as a blind worshiper of determinist science. Nevertheless, Masaryk exalted the role of the right kind of science. In *Základové konkretné logiky,* his philosophically most ambitious book, he classified the sciences and showed how they are internally related and coordinated. The task of philosophy is to create a worldview based on the results of the sciences. Masaryk desired a new "Advancement of Learning" that would save man from intellectual and moral anarchy.

Masaryk assigned an important role in the realization of his ideal to his own nation, the Czech, and interpreted its history, remembering the Hussites and the Bohemian Brethren as a preparation for this task. He thoroughly criticized Russia for being a breeding ground for all the European diseases, particularly romanticism and materialism. Fëdor Dostoevsky, whom he both admired and rejected as a thinker, was a lifelong concern. Masaryk always expressed the deepest sympathies for the English and American tradition of empiricism and moralism and, in politics, turned his nation resolutely toward the Anglo-Saxon West. In 1918 he liberated the Czechs not only politically but also intellectually.

See also Avenarius, Richard; Brentano, Franz; Comte, Auguste; Dostoevsky, Fyodor Mikhailovich; Empiricism; Humanism; Hume, David; Husserl, Edmund; James, William; Marx, Karl; Philosophy of History; Positivism; Teleology; Wundt, Wilhelm.

Bibliography

For information on Masaryk as a thinker, see the bibliography and articles in *Festschrift Thomas G. Masaryk zum 80. Geburtstag,* 2 vols., edited by B. Jakowenko (Bonn, 1930); W. P. Warren, *Masaryk's Democracy* (Chapel Hill: University of North Carolina, 1941); and René Wellek, "Masaryk's Philosophy," in *Essays on Czech Literature* (The Hague: Mouton, 1963).

René Wellek (1967)

MASS

The mass of a body is its inertia or resistance to change of motion. More precisely, it is a property of the body that determines the body's acceleration under the influence of a given force. Mass can therefore be measured either by the amount of force necessary to impart to the body a given motion in a given time or by the acceleration produced by a given force.

The absolute metric unit of mass is the gram, which is the mass of a body whose velocity increases by one centimeter per second each second if acted upon by a force of one dyne. Other common units are the kilogram (1,000 grams) and the pound (453.592 grams). For velocities that are small as compared with the speed of light, the mass of a body is a constant, characteristic of the body and independent of its location—in contrast to weight, which varies with the body's place on Earth or in the universe.

Although fundamental to science and, together with length and time, the basis of all measurements in physics, the concept of mass was unambiguously defined only at the end of the nineteenth century. However, its rudimentary sources, systematically employed long before by Isaac Newton and to some extent already by Johannes Kepler, can be traced back to early Neoplatonic ideas concerning the inactivity of matter as opposed to the spontaneity of mind. The ancient metaphysical antithesis of matter and spirit served as a prototype of the physical contrast of mass and force.

CONCEPT OF INERTIAL MASS

Antiquity, and Greek science in particular, had no conception of inertial mass. Even the idea of quantity of matter (*quantitas materiae*), the antecedent of inertial or dynamic mass, was foreign to the conceptual scheme of Aristotelian natural philosophy. Paradoxically, it was Neoplatonism and its admixtures of Judeo-Christian doctrines, with their emphasis on the spiritual and immaterial nature of reality, that laid the foundations for the inertial conception of mass, which later became the basic notion of materialistic or substantial philosophy. To accentuate the immaterial, sublime source of all force and life in the intellect or God, Neoplatonism degraded matter to impotence and endowed it with inertia in the sense of an absolute absence of spontaneous activity. For Plotinus, Proclus, Philo, Ibn Gabirol, and the Platonic patristic authors, matter was something base, inert, shapeless and "plump," attributes that reappear in Kepler's characterization of matter as that which is too "plump and clumsy to move itself from one place to another."

The idea of a quantitative determination of matter different from, and ontologically prior to, spatial extension originated in scholastic philosophy in connection with the problem of the transubstantiation. The question of how accidents of condensation or rarefaction (volume changes) can persist in the consecrated *hostia* of the holy bread and wine of the Eucharist whereas the substances of the bread and the wine change into the Body and the Blood of Christ led Aegidius Romanus, a disciple of Thomas Aquinas, to the formulation of his theory of *duplex quantitas*. According to this theory matter is determined by two quantities; it is "so and so much" (*tanta et tanta*) and "occupies such and such a volume" (*et occupat tantum et tantum locum*), the former determination, the *quantitas materiae*, having ontological priority over bulk. Aegidius's early conception of mass as quantity of matter, expounded in his *Theoremata de Corpore Christi* (1276), was soon renounced and had little influence on the subsequent development of the concept of mass. It was primarily Kepler who ascribed to matter an inherent propensity for inertia in his search for a dynamical explanation of the newly discovered elliptical orbits of planetary motion; in need of a concept expressing the opposition intrinsic in matter to motory forces, Kepler formulated the inertial concept of mass. In his *Epitome Astronomiae Copernicanae* (1618) he declared that "inertia or opposition to motion is a characteristic of matter; it is stronger the greater the quantity of matter in a given volume."

A different approach to the same idea arose from the study of terrestrial gravitation. As soon as gravity was regarded no longer as a factor residing in the heavy body itself, as Aristotle taught, but as an interaction between an active principle, extraneous to the gravitating body, and a passive principle, inherent in matter, as Alfonso Borelli and Giovanni Baliani (author of *De Motu Gravium*, 1638) contended, the notion of inertial mass became a necessity for a dynamical explanation of free fall and other gravitational phenomena. Furthermore, Christian Huygens's investigations of centrifugal forces (*De Vi Centrifuga*, 1659; published in Leiden, 1703) made it clear that a quantitative determination of such forces is possible only if with each body is associated a certain characteristic property proportional to, but conceptually different from, the body's weight. Finally, the systematic study of impact phenomena, carried out by John Wallis, Sir Christopher Wren, and Huygens, enforced the introduction of inertial mass. With Newton's foundations of dynamics (*Principia*, 1687) these four categories of apparently disparate phenomena (planetary motion, free fall, centrifugal force, and impact phenomena) found their logical unification, through his consistent employment of the notion of inertial mass. Newton's explicit definition of this concept, however, as "the measure of quantity of matter, arising from its density and bulk conjointly" was still unsatisfactory from both the logical and the methodological points of view. It was probably the influence of Kepler or of Robert Boyle and his famous experiments on the compressibility of air that made Newton choose the notion of density as a primary concept in his peculiar formulation of the definition of mass, a formulation that was severely criticized in modern times, especially by Ernst Mach and Paul Volkmann.

LEIBNIZ AND KANT

Gottfried Wilhelm Leibniz's original conception of mass (1669), in contrast to Newton's, defined it as that property which endows primary matter with spatial extension and antitypy, or impenetrability. In his later writings, especially in his doctrine of monads, Leibniz associated mass with secondary matter and saw in it a property of a collection of substances (monads) resulting from their being a collection. Finally, recognizing the insufficiency of purely geometric conceptions to account for the physical behavior of interacting bodies, Leibniz departed from the Cartesian approach and accepted the dynamic, or inertial, conception of mass. The trend of Leibniz's ideas was brought to its final consequences by Immanuel Kant, with his rejection of the Newtonian *vis inertiae*, the dynamic opposition against impressed force. Refuting its legitimacy on the ground that "only motion, but not rest, can oppose motion," Kant postulated the law of inertia as corresponding to the category of causality ("every change of the state of motion has an external cause") and consequently defined mass as the amount of the mobile (*die Menge des Beweglichen*) in a given volume, measured by the quantity of motion (*Die metaphysischen Anfangsgründe der Naturwissenschaft*, 1786).

DEFINITION OF MASS

Under the influence of the Kantian formulation, often incompletely understood, and primarily owing to the fact that in spite of the universal use of the concept in science as well as in philosophy no clear-cut definition of mass was available, most authors defined mass as quantity of matter without specifying how to measure it. Toward the middle of the nineteenth century, with the rise of modern foundational research and the critical study of the principles of mechanics, the logical deficiency of such definitions became obvious. It was primarily Ernst Mach, preceded by Barré de Saint-Venant and Jules Andrade, who insisted on the necessity of a clear operational definition of mass. In an essay, "Über die Definition der Masse" (1867; published in 1868 in *Carl's Repertorium der Experimentalphysik,* Vol. 4, pp. 355–359), and in the *Science of Mechanics* (*Die Mechanik in ihrer Entwicklung, historisch-kritisch dargestellt,* Leipzig, 1883; translated by T. J. McCormack, La Salle, IL, 1942), Mach defined the ratio of the masses of two bodies that interact with each other but are otherwise unaffected by all other bodies in the universe as the inverse ratio of their respective accelerations ($m_1/m_2 = a_2/a_1$), thereby converting Newton's third law of action and reaction to a definition of mass. If a particular body is chosen as the standard unit of mass, the mass of any other body can be unambiguously determined by simple physical operations. The practical method of comparing masses by weighing is, of course, operationally still simpler but logically more complicated, since the notion of weight presupposes that of mass. Although Mach's definition is not quite unobjectionable, it has gained great popularity and is generally adopted in modern texts in science.

INERTIAL AND GRAVITATIONAL MASS

In addition to its inertial mass, every physical body possesses gravitational mass, which determines, in its active aspect, the strength of the gravitational field produced by the body and, in its passive aspect, the amount by which the body is affected by the gravitational field produced by other bodies. According to Newton's law of universal gravitation, the force of attraction is proportional to the inertial masses of both the attracting and the attracted bodies. The resulting proportionality of inertial and gravitational masses of one and the same body, experimentally confirmed by Newton, Friedrich Bessel, Roland von Eötvös, and others, remained in classical physics a purely empirical and accidental feature, whereas the strict proportionality between the active and the passive gravitational masses is a straightforward consequence of Newton's third law of action and reaction or, alternatively, of the very definition of inertial mass if the postulated interaction is of gravitational nature. In general relativity, however, the so-called principle of equivalence, which maintains the unrestricted equivalence between uniformly accelerated reference systems and homogeneous gravitational fields, implies the fundamental identity between inertial and passive gravitational masses. In addition, it can be shown that on the basis of general relativity the active gravitational mass of a body or dynamical system equals its inertial mass, so that in relativistic physics, in contrast to Newtonian physics, the identity of all three kinds of masses is a necessary consequence of its fundamental assumptions.

MASS AND ENERGY

Whereas general relativity led to an important unification of the concept of mass, special relativity already, with Albert Einstein's paper *Does the Inertia of a Body Depend upon Its Energy Content?* (1905; reprinted in *The Principle of Relativity,* New York, 1923), led to a vast generalization of the concept by showing the equivalence of mass and energy insofar as a body emitting radiative energy of an amount E loses mass to an amount of E/c^2, where c is the velocity of light. Subsequent research, especially in connection with energy transformations in nuclear physics, supported the general validity of the formula $E = mc^2$, according to which mass and energy are interconvertible and one gram of mass yields 9×10^{20} ergs of energy. It also became obvious that Antoine Lavoisier's law of the conservation of mass (1789) and Robert Mayer's (or Hermann Helmholtz's) law of the conservation of energy were only approximately correct and that it was the sum total of mass and energy that was conserved in any physicochemical process.

INFLUENCE OF THE ELECTROMAGNETIC CONCEPT

The way to these far-reaching conclusions of relativity had been prepared to some extent already by the introduction of the electromagnetic concept of mass at the end of the nineteenth century (by J. J. Thomson, Oliver Heaviside, and Max Abraham). It seemed possible on the basis of James Clerk Maxwell's electromagnetic theory to account for the inertial behavior of moving charged particles in terms of induction effects of purely electromagnetic nature. Walter Kaufmann's experiments (1902) on the deflection of electrons by simultaneous electric and magnetic fields and his determination of the slightly variable inertial mass of the electron seemed at the time to support the hypothesis that the mass of the electron, and ultimately the mass of every elementary particle, is of purely electromagnetic nature. Although such eminent theoreticians as H. A. Lorentz, Wilhelm Wien, and Henri Poincaré accepted these ideas, according to which the whole universe of physics is but an interplay of convection currents and their radiation, with physical reality stripped of all material substantiality, the electromagnetic conception of mass had to make way for the relativistic concept as outlined above. Certain aspects of the electromagnetic conception of mass did survive, however, and reappeared in modern field theories—in particular the fundamental tenet that matter does not do what it does because it is what it is, but it is what it is because it does what it does.

See also Aristotle; Boyle, Robert; Energy; Ibn Gabirol, Solomon ben Judah; Kant, Immanuel; Kepler, Johannes; Leibniz, Gottfried Wilhelm; Mach, Ernst; Maxwell, James Clerk; Neoplatonism; Newton, Isaac; Patristic Philosophy; Philo Judaeus; Plotinus; Poincaré, Jules Henri; Proclus; Thomas Aquinas, St.

Bibliography

Bainbridge, K. T. "The Equivalence of Mass and Energy." *Physical Review* 44 (1933): 123.

Comstock, D. F. "The Relation of Mass to Energy." *Philosophical Magazine* 15 (1908): 1–21.

Jammer, Max. *Concepts of Mass in Classical and Modern Physics.* Cambridge, MA: Harvard University Press, 1961; Mineola, NY: Dover, 1997.

Lampa, A. "Eine Ableitung des Massenbegriffs." *Lotos* 59 (1911): 303–312.

Mach, Ernst. *Die Geschichte und die Wurzel des Satzes von der Erhaltung der Arbeit.* Prague, 1872.

Pendse, C. G. "On Mass and Force in Newtonian Mechanics." *Philosophical Magazine* 29 (1940): 477–484.

Whittaker, E. T. "On Gauss' Theorem and the Concept of Mass in General Relativity." *Proceedings of the Royal Society,* A, 149 (1935): 384–395.

M. Jammer (1967)

MATERIALISM

Materialism is the name given to a family of doctrines concerning the nature of the world that give to matter a primary position and accord to mind (or spirit) a secondary, dependent reality or even none at all. Extreme materialism asserts that the real world is spatiotemporal and consists of material things and nothing else, with two important qualifications: first, space and time, or space-time, must also be included if these are realities rather than mere systems of relations, for they are not material things in any straightforward sense. Second, materialism is fundamentally a doctrine concerning the character of the concrete natural world we inhabit, and it is probably best to set to one side controversies over abstract entities such as numbers, or geometric figures, or the relations of entailment and contradiction studied in logic. A strictly extreme materialism would undertake to show that, to the extent that any of these were genuine realities, they are all material in nature, but the issues raised by abstract entities will not be pursued here. It is with extreme materialist views in the concrete realm that this entry is concerned, and in what follows, "materialist" is to be understood in that sense.

Philosophers and scientists have had various views regarding the constitution and behavior of material objects and over whether every material thing is a body, or whether forces, or waves, or fields of force are also realities in their own right. Thus, the cardinal tenet of materialism, "Everything that is, is material," covers a range of different claims.

To accommodate these differences, a material thing can be defined as a being possessing many physical properties and no other properties, or as being made up of parts all of whose properties are physical. The physical properties are position in space and time, size, shape, duration, mass, velocity, solidity, inertia, electric charge, spin, rigidity, temperature, hardness, magnetic field intensity, and the like. The phrase "and the like" is important, for it indicates that any list of physical properties is open-ended. A material thing is one composed of properties that are the object of the science of physics. And physics is a developing science, in which new properties are still being discovered. The question "What counts as a physical property?" thus has no determinate answer. In consequence, there are also no fully determinate answers for the questions "What is a material thing?" and "What does materialism claim?"

This is less serious for materialism than may at first appear, for there is a broad consensus on which properties—among those already known—are the physical ones. And new properties that emerge from research in the physical sciences are, generally speaking, readily identified as belonging among the physical ones rather than representing an anomalous, nonphysical development. It is known well enough what is involved in claiming that something is a material reality, and therefore it is understood well enough what is involved in the various versions of extreme materialism, all of which assert that everything there is, is material.

The psychological characteristics people ascribe to themselves and to one another—consciousness, purposiveness, aspiration, desire, and the ability to perceive, for example—are not considered to be physical properties. So materialism differs from panpsychism, the doctrine that everything material is also at least partly mental or spiritual. Materialism denies the world's basic entities possess these psychological properties. Materialists add that there is no second class of nonmaterial beings in possession of such psychological properties and no others; there are no incorporeal souls or spirits, no spiritual principalities or powers, no angels or devils, no demiurges and no gods (if these are conceived as immaterial entities). Hence, nothing that happens can be attributed to the action of such beings.

The second major tenet of materialism is, accordingly, "Everything that can be explained can be explained on the basis of laws involving only the relevant physical conditions." The differences among materialists over the types of effect material things can have on one another make this second tenet another slogan covering a variety of particular doctrines. Further, although materialists have traditionally been determinists, holding that there is a physical cause for everything that happens, this is not strictly required by materialism itself. Recently, the appeal of determinism has been weakened by the development and success of quantum theory, and many contemporary materialists are not committed to determinism. It should also be mentioned that metaphysical materialism in no way involves an overzealous disposition to pursue money and tangible goods, despite the popular use of "materialistic" to describe this interest.

NATURE AND APPEAL OF MATERIALISM

The enduring appeal of materialism arises from its alliance with those sciences that have contributed most to an understanding of the world humans inhabit. Investigations in the physical sciences have a materialist methodology; that is, they attempt to explain a class of phenomena by appeal to physical conditions alone. The claim of materialists is that there is no subject matter that cannot be adequately treated with a materialist methodology. This claim cannot be established by any scientific investigation; it can be established, if at all, only by critical reflection on the whole range of human thought and experience.

Early philosophers proceeded dogmatically, aiming to prove the material nature of the world by mere reflection on what must be. Contemporary materialists are much more modest, offering the claim as a speculative but reasonable generalization from the progress of the physical sciences.

Materialism has been, traditionally, a minority view, indeed a rather daring and scandalous one, but it has made considerable progress over the past century, particularly among educated European peoples. There seem to be three main reasons for this. First, the rise of what might be called "cosmic naturalism"; there has been a decline in those aspects of religious conviction that involve appeal to providential or satanic interventions in the course of events, so that pestilence or climate change, for example, are not attributed to nonmaterial, supernatural forces. Second, the rise of "medical materialism"; the discovery of the biochemical mechanisms involved in neural functioning, and their links to psychological processes, so that it is now taken for granted that thinking, feeling, and the will are subserved by the nervous system, and can be altered by making physical changes by the use of drugs or electrodes. A malfunction of the mind is taken to be a malfunction of the brain. This is a kind of pragmatic materialism—the physical aspects are accorded primacy. Third, the rise of "electronic materialism"; recent years have witnessed an astonishing expansion in the range and sophistication of the mental tasks that digital machines can perform. Not only remembering, recalling, and calculating, but pattern recognition, estimation processes, problem solving, and learning new skills, which hitherto have been the exclusive preserve of living, conscious beings, are now routinely performed by electronic devices that, unless panpsychism is true, are purely physical structures. This has formed the background for an increasingly common assumption that mental activity is a special kind of physical process, which is one critical aspect of materialism.

Materialism remains, nonetheless, a striking and apparently paradoxical doctrine, for it insists that the only differences between human beings and grains of sand prove to be matters of energy flow and structural complexity. People have continued to embrace materialism in the face of the difficulties with which it is beset because it offers a comprehensive, unified account of the nature of reality that is economical, intelligible, and consistent with the most successful of the sciences.

HISTORY OF MATERIALISM

CLASSICAL PERIOD. Materialism has been a theme in European speculative thought from the earliest periods for which there is any record.

Ionian philosophers in the tradition of Thales (sixth century BCE) attempted to account for the origin and present state of the world by appeal to changes in the state of a fundamental underlying substance (the *arche*), which in most cases was held to be of a physical nature. Parmenides of Elea (fifth century BCE) vigorously defended a thoroughgoing monism, maintaining that the world is One, unchanging, eternal, homogeneous, indivisible, indestructible, and without any interior void.

These two threads of thought are combined in the true materialism of Leucippus and his pupil Democritus, who flourished at Abdera in the fifth century BCE. Between them they worked out the first clear conception of matter, the first clear restrictions on the kinds of natural interactions in which material particles could participate, and the first clear program of explanation by appeal to these material interactions alone. The "Great Diakosmos," a lost work written by one or the other (or both), expounded their position. Their basic idea was that the fundamental stuff was of just one kind (matter) and that the fundamental entities were material atoms that were of course by no means unique, but otherwise had all the characteristics of Parmenides' One. These atoms are in constant motion in a void that surrounds them.

Insofar as it can be reconstructed, their doctrine embraced the following theses:

(1) Nothing exists but atoms and empty space.

(2) Nothing happens by chance (for no reason at all); everything occurs for a reason and of necessity. This necessity is natural and mechanical; it excludes teleological necessitation.

(3) Nothing can arise out of nothing; nothing that is can be destroyed. All novelties are merely new combinations or separations of atoms.

(4) The atoms are infinite in number and endlessly varied in form, but uniform in composition, being made of the same stuff. They act on one another by pressure or collision only.

(5) The great variety of things that we encounter in the world is a consequence of the variety in number, size, shape, and arrangement of the atoms that compose them.

(6) The atoms have been in confused random motion from all eternity. This is their natural state and requires no explanation. (Some scholars dispute the attribution of random motion to the atoms and credit the "Great Diakosmos" with advancing the doctrine of an eternal fall through infinite space, which was later presented by Epicurus.)

(7) The basic mechanism whereby complex bodies are formed is the collision of two atoms, setting up a vortex. In the vortex motion is communicated from the periphery toward the center. In consequence, heavy atoms move to the center, and there form a body, which is dense relative to the collection of light atoms around the periphery. The vortex continually embraces any new atoms that come near it in their random motion, and it thus begins a world.

This materialist philosophy requires a mechanical account of human sensation. The Leucippus-Democritus account seems to have been ingenious, speculative, and false. Sensation occurs in the human soul, which, like everything else, is composed of atoms. Objects perceptible by the distal senses sight, hearing, or smell, give off effluences, or images, composed of fine, smooth atoms. There are channels in the eyes, ears, and nose along which these effluent atoms pass to collide with the atoms of the soul and produce sensation. Differences of color, in the case of vision, or of pitch, in the case of sound, are due to the varying smoothness or roughness of the incoming image atoms. With the contact senses touch and taste, it is the size and shape of the atoms on the surface of the perceived object that act on soul atoms in the skin or tongue.

Sensory qualities (for example, sweetness, bitterness, temperature, and color) are thus not qualities of the object perceived, which is a collection of atoms, possessed only of physical properties such as size, shape, mass, and hardness. The sensory qualities are, rather, the effects of that collection of atoms on us, that is, on our soul atoms. Here is an early appearance of the distinction between primary and secondary qualities, a distinction every subsequent materialist has also found it necessary to make.

Empedocles (fifth century BCE) founded a medical school in Acragas (Agrigento) in Sicily. His aim was to account in a naturalistic manner for the special features of this world, particularly for the specially organized matter to be found in living creatures. The first appearance of the famous four elements—earth, air, fire, and water—is in his theory. Empedocles seems to have believed that each of these four elements comprised a different type of atom. The creation and dissolution of the macroscopic objects of this world is brought about by the combination and separation of these atoms by two fundamental forces, love and hate, or harmony and discord.

Under the influence of love and hate the world goes through an endless cycle from complete random separation of elements (the triumph of hate), through gradually increasing order, to a complete, calm, spherical, harmonious union (the triumph of love). Hate then begins to exert itself once more. Disintegration sets in, and ultimately the world returns to the state of complete separation of elements. The present state of the world lies between these two extremes. The existence of planetary systems and the origin of animals are thus explained as the influence of love.

Empedocles can be considered a true materialist only if love and hate are either inherent forces in the elemental atoms or themselves material elements with a cementing or corrosive effect on combinations of the other elements; however, he probably thought of them as blind, powerful gods. The rest of his system is similarly ambiguous. On the one hand, he believed in the transmigration of souls and adhered to some kind of Orphic mystery religion; on the other, he gave a mechanical account of sensation, held that the soul was composed of fiery atoms, and said that the blood around the heart is the thought of men. Empedocles' philosophy thus perpetuated the materialist tradition but not in a rigorous or consistent form.

The hostile misinterpretation of his ethics as unworthily hedonistic has made Epicurus (342–270 BCE) the most famous of classical materialists. In his middle age Epicurus came to Athens and founded a school where materialism was taught as the sole foundation of a good life, at once disciplined, calm, serene, and free from superstition.

He adopted the materialist metaphysics of the "Great Diakosmos" but gave a modified account of the origin of worlds. There are an infinite number of atoms falling vertically through an infinite space. In one construction of the Epicurean system the heavier, faster atoms occasionally strike the lighter, slower ones obliquely, giving them a slight lateral velocity. In another construction all atoms fall at uniform velocity, and the original deviations from parallel downward motion are left unexplained.

However caused, the original lateral deviations result in more collisions and deviations and the establishment of vortexes. From these vortexes ordered arrangements of atoms arise. The number of atoms and the time available are unlimited, so every possible arrangement of atoms must occur at some time or another. This world, with its marvelously organized living bodies, is thus just one of the infinite, inevitable arrangements into which the indestructible atoms must fall.

The only Roman author of note in the tradition of materialism is Lucretius (born c. 99 BCE), whose long didactic poem *De Rerum Natura* gives imaginative sparkle to the metaphysics of Epicurus. Lucretius adopted the second account of the fall of atoms through the void and appealed to some form of voluntary action to explain the original deviations from vertical descent. He thus introduced a nonmechanical source of motion, inconsistent with the remainder of his system.

Like Epicurus, Lucretius was motivated by a wish to free people from the burden of religious fear. He argued passionately and at length against the existence of any spiritual soul and for the mortality of humankind. These beliefs have been explicit features of materialism ever since.

SEVENTEENTH CENTURY. From the close of the classical period until the Renaissance the church and Aristotle so dominated European speculation that materialist theories virtually lapsed. The revival of materialism is attributable to the work of two seventeenth-century philosophers, Gassendi and Hobbes, who crystallized the naturalistic and skeptical movements of thought that accompanied the rediscovery of antiquity and the rise of natural science. Their most important forerunners were probably Telesio, Campanella, and Cyrano de Bergerac, all of whom attempted to combine materialistic views in physics with a psychology based on sensations.

Pierre Gassendi (1592–1655), who in the last part of his life taught astronomy at the Royal College in Paris, rejected the official Aristotelian philosophy of his time and set about the rehabilitation of Epicureanism. To bring the Epicurean system into closer conformity with Christian doctrine, he claimed that the atoms are not eternal but created. They are finite, not infinite, in number and are organized in our particular world by a providential determination of initial conditions.

Gassendi's materialism extended over physics and psychology, undertaking to account for all inanimate changes and for sensation on a materialist basis. He treated the coming into being of particular things as the accumulation of matter about a seed atom.

But his metaphysics was not, strictly speaking, materialistic, for outside the experienced world Gassendi admitted a creative and providential God and an immaterial and immortal intellect in man distinct from his corporeal soul. There are even some lapses in the physics, too, for Gassendi spoke of gravitation as some kind of movement for self-preservation and allowed that growth from seed atoms may be controlled by formative principles other than the natural motions of atoms.

Thomas Hobbes (1588–1679) was much more consistent and uncompromising. In 1629 he discovered Euclidean geometry and was captivated by its method. During the years that followed he strove to work out a rational philosophy of nature on the Euclidean model.

Hobbes's aim was to discover by cunning analysis of experience the fundamental principles expressing the true nature of everything. The truth of these principles would be manifest to right reason and could thus serve as axioms from which a comprehensive theory of the nature of the world could be deductively derived.

The resulting system is almost pure materialism. Hobbes hoped to use the new non-Aristotelian physics of the seventeenth century as the basis for a final, complete account of reality. From definitions of space and motion he derived the laws of uniform motion. From these, together with a notion of the interaction of bodies, he hoped to proceed to an account of change, thence to an account of sensible change, thence to a theory of the senses and appetites of people, and finally to his notorious civil philosophy.

No part of the universe is not a body, said Hobbes, and no part of the universe contains no body. Hobbes was a plenist, holding all space to be filled by an intangible material ether if nothing else. This doctrine followed directly from his definition of a body as anything existing independently of human thought and having volume. Thus, Hobbes considered God to be a corporeal spirit difficult to distinguish from his eternal, immutable, omnipresent, embodied space, the pervasive ether.

All change in the universe consists in the motion of bodies, so all change reduces to change of position and velocity. Further, nothing can cause a motion but contact with another moving body. The substance of anything is body, and "incorporeal substance" is therefore a contradiction in terms. Hobbes thereby disposed of angels, the soul, and the God of orthodox theology. He departed from strict materialism, however, in his introduction of "conatus" and "impetus" (which are not physical properties) into his account of the initiation of motion and measurement of acceleration. Conatus also enters into Hobbes's account of human sensation and action. Sensations are motions in a person's body, and changes of sensation are changes of that motion. Sensory qualities are

really within the perceiver, but by conatus a "phantasm" is projected from the observer onto the observed.

Hobbes was the first to take seriously the problems that language, thought, and logic pose for materialism. He developed a nominalist theory of language and took the subject matter of thought and inference to be phantasms of sense or abstractions from these phantasms. He held, for example, that to remember is to perceive one has perceived. But Hobbes did not make clear just what contact mechanism is at work in mental operations nor whether the phantasms are genuinely corporeal. Thus, in spite of his best efforts, it is doubtful that he developed a fully consistent materialism.

The influence of Gassendi and Hobbes was diminished by the prestige of their brilliant contemporary, Rene Descartes (1596–1650), who accepted a materialist and mechanical account of the inanimate world and the brute creation but insisted that men had immaterial, immortal spirits whose essential nature lay in conscious thought undetermined by causal processes. According to Descartes, there are in the world two quite different sorts of things, extended (material) substances and thinking (spiritual) substances, which are mysteriously united in the case of humankind. He thus crystallized the tradition of dualism (the doctrine that there are just two fundamentally different kinds of substance), which was until recently materialism's chief rival.

EIGHTEENTH CENTURY. In Epicurus and Lucretius one motive for working out a materialist philosophy was to provide an antidote for the all too prevalent religious terror of their times. With Hobbes, and again in eighteenth-century France, the corresponding motive was opposition to religious oppression. But in addition, rapid growth in physiological knowledge had given rise to the hope that a complete doctrine of man in purely physiological terms was possible and so generated a medical materialism that made the path of the metaphysicians smoother.

Ever since the time of Democritus, materialists had held that the soul consists of fine particles within the body. In the course of the eighteenth century this suggestion was taken up and amplified, and some attempt was made to give it an experiential basis.

An anonymous manuscript, the *Ame materielle*, written between 1692 and 1704, contains many ingenious explanations of mental function along Democritean lines. Pleasure and pain consist, respectively, of the flow of finer or coarser particles through the channels of the brain. The passions are a matter of the temperature of the heart. Reason consists in the ordering of the soul's fine particles, and the effect of wine in its course through the body is to dislodge some of these fine particles from their proper places. The manuscript is panpsychic in its expression, crediting the atoms with a rudimentary consciousness and will, but it is materialist in substance, for these qualities are not credited with any causal power. The doctrines advanced were purely hypothetical and, as we now know, false. The *Ame materielle* had successors in Dr. Maubec's *Principes physiques de la raison et les passions de l'homme* (1709), which again gave a materialist vision of man a panpsychic dress and opposed Descartes's view of the mind as a thinking substance. During the middle years of the century, Denis Diderot's many unsystematic writings took progressively a more materialistic turn. Diderot's *Le reve de d'Alembert* is a striking hypothetical account of heredity, growth, and the simpler forms of animal behavior in terms of internal motions of living bodies.

The most famous medical materialist is Jean de la Mettrie (1709–1751), a doctor with a philosophical bent whose radical views obliged him to leave a fashionable practice in Paris to live in Holland and Prussia. In *L'homme machine* (1943 [1748]) he presented a view of the human being as a self-moving machine.

After criticizing all views of the soul as a spiritual entity, La Mettrie proceeded to review all the commonsense evidence for the physical nature of mental activity. He cited the effects of bodily needs, aging, and sleep; he pointed to the analogy of the human body to much "lower" forms, which were not supposed to harbor spiritual minds. Anticipating Pavlov, he spoke of the mechanical basis of speech and of the possibilities of educating deaf-mutes and anthropoid apes. He explained learning to perceive and learning to make moral judgments by appeal to modifications of the brain. Human action is accounted for by the then new doctrine of the stimulus irritability of muscles. La Mettrie embarrassed those who held that the soul is a spiritual unity governing all vital functions by observing the continuing function of organs removed from bodies, the muscular activity of dead or decapitated animals, and the ability of a bisected polyp to grow into two complete ones. He explained conscious sensation and the mental capacities of which we are introspectively aware by means of a magic-lantern analogy, but this was unsatisfactory, for the status of the images involved was not made clear.

The details of La Mettrie's physiology, depending as they do on supposed movements of nervous filaments, are false. However, his program of seeking in neural changes the explanation of mental activity has endured, and his claim that appeals to the actions of a spiritual soul can furnish only pseudo-explanations has gained wide support.

Jean Cabanis (1757–1808), a French doctor, continued this line of thought and in 1802 published *Rapports du physique et du moral de l'homme*, the most notable innovation of which was to treat the brain as analogous with the digestive system, making sensory impressions its aliments and thoughts its product. The great metaphysical materialist of the period is Paul Heinrich Dietrich d'Holbach (1723–1789), a German nobleman living in Paris. His work the *Systeme de la nature* was published under a false name "Mirabaud," with a false imprint "London" (Amsterdam) in 1770. This "Bible of all materialism" is speculative philosophy in the grand style; in it the antireligious motive is again uppermost. Holbach maintained that nothing is outside nature. Nature is an uninterrupted and causally determined succession of arrangements of matter in motion. Matter has always existed and always been in motion, and different worlds are formed from different distributions of matter and motion. Matter is of four basic types (earth, air, fire, and water), and changes in their proportions are responsible for all changes other than the spatiotemporal ones that motion without redistribution can accomplish.

Mechanical causes of the impact type, such as collision or compression, are the only intelligible ones, hence the only real ones. Because human beings are in nature and part of nature, all human actions spring from natural causes. The intellectual faculties, thoughts, passions, and will can all be identified with motions hidden within the body. In action outward motions of the limbs are acquired from these internal movements in ways we do not yet understand.

Holbach based the intellectual faculties on feeling and treated feelings as a consequence of certain arrangements of matter. Introspected changes are all changes in our internal material state. Thus, in remembering, we renew in ourselves a previous modification. He treated personal characteristics and temperament in terms of a person's internal structure and interpreted so-called free action not as motiveless action (an absurdity) but as action that, although seeming to flow from a free choice, actually springs from an ultimately unchosen modification of the brain. Holbach's theory of mind is also interesting because in dealing with wit and genius, it suggests the first behavioral analyses of mental concepts. As consistency required, he held the soul to be mortal. The purity of Holbach's materialism is marred only by his admission of relations of sympathy, antipathy, and affinity among material particles, in addition to their unequivocally physical properties, the primary qualities, gravity, and inert force.

The revolution in chemistry that was effected by Joseph Priestley (1777) in England and Antoine-Laurent Lavoisier in France in the 1770s and 1780s was of importance for the later development of materialism, for it established chemistry as a strictly physical science. Since the beginning of the nineteenth century, all properly chemical explanations appeal only to material substances and their natural interactions. Such a chemistry has since been extended in biochemistry to cover all the processes of life, and the case for materialism has thereby been profoundly strengthened. Priestley himself nevertheless vigorously upheld an unorthodox version of Christianity, insisting that the existence of God and the resurrection of the body are not incompatible with a materialist and determinist view of the natural world.

NINETEENTH CENTURY. The philosophers of greatest influence in the nineteenth century—Kant, Fichte, Hegel, Schopenhauer, Lotze, and Mill, for example—were all of an idealist or phenomenalist bent. The dialectical materialism of Friedrich Engels and Karl Marx is not an extreme materialism of the kind discussed here.

Ludwig Buchner, a minor figure, deserves mention as the first to claim explicitly that materialism is a generalization from *a posteriori* discoveries. In *Kraft und Stoff* (1855) he claims that we have discovered (not proven *a priori*) that there is no force without matter and no matter without force.

There was during this period a continuation of inquiry and speculation on the physiological bases of mental function. Jacob Molescott (1852), Karl Vogt (1846, 1854), and Emil Du Bois-Raymond proceeded with the investigation of physiological processes along biophysical and biochemical lines. The most important developments were scientific findings that undermined the barrier between physical systems and living organisms and thus softened the natural resistances to materialistic theses.

In 1828 the synthesis of urea was achieved, and this refuted the idea that biochemistry was in some way special and distinct from chemistry. In 1847, Hermann Helmholtz established the conservation of energy in organic systems, making still less plausible any claims that living and nonliving systems could not possibly be comprehended in a single theory.

In 1859 Charles Darwin published his *Origin of Species*, in 1871 his *Descent of Man*. T. H. Huxley had produced *Man's Place in Nature* in 1863. These three works at last provided a plausible, empirically grounded case for two of the main planks of materialism, the claim that the organization of living things into forms admirably adapted for survival and reproduction can be explained without appeal to immanent or transcendent purposes, and the claim that humans are a part and product of the natural world. Since then biologists, physiologists, and pathologists have increasingly taken the truth of medical materialism for granted, couching their explanations in physicochemical terms without questioning the propriety or completeness of successful explanations in this form.

TWENTIETH CENTURY. The triumphant progress in the twentieth century of a materialistic biology and biochemistry has almost completely eliminated vitalist notions of living forms as governed by forces additional to, and distinct from, the purely physical forces operating on inanimate matter. The situation of earlier ages has been reversed; it now seems implausible to maintain that the vital functions of living organisms are different in kind from chemical (ultimately, physical) processes. In the attempt to demonstrate that something other than matter exists, it is on mind, rather than life, that the opponents of materialism now rely.

Early in the twentieth century, the behaviorist movement arose, in a development linked to the emergence of psychology as a distinct science in its own right, rather than a branch of the philosophy of mind. Many psychologists became disheartened by the difficulties involved in any introspective investigation of inner mental states, and turned to the study of behavior. In its analyses and explanations of human activities, behaviorist psychology relies as far as possible on publicly observable, physical phenomena of stimulus and response. Its aim was to expel the traditionally conceived inner, immaterial mind from psychology, and in this way was a profoundly materialistic development.

In the realm of the mind, a new challenge for immaterialists has also developed. The rise of cybernetics (the abstract theory of machines) and its applications in computing machinery threatens the idea of a special status for mental activity. The gathering and interpretation of information, the employment of stored information, successful and spectacular problem solving, even analogues of fatigue, overload, and confusion, hitherto all found only among complex living organisms, are now displayed by computing hardware, that is, by material structures all of whose operations can be explained in terms of physical properties alone.

Approaching the issue from the opposite direction, experimental study of the nervous systems of animals and of ourselves is showing, in ever-increasing detail, how artificially induced physical changes in the electrochemical state of the nervous system issue in changes in the subject's mental activity. Displays of emotion, performance in perception and recall, and anxiety and tension are being tied down to brain function in this way.

During the twentieth century, there were in fact three distinct movements of a materialistic stamp in the philosophy of mind. In the 1920s and 1930s some logical positivists, led by Rudolph Carnap (1932–1933) and Otto Neurath, espoused an epistemic materialism. They held that the meaning of any statement consists in the directly testable statements deducible from it (the protocol sentences). In order for language and meaning to be public and shared, these protocol sentences must be intersubjectively testable. However, because no statement about one individual's experience or thought or other inner psychological state can be tested by anyone else, only sentences referring to the physical properties of physical entities are intersubjectively testable in the required way. Now, because most statements about minds are incontestably meaningful, they must, despite appearances to the contrary, in fact refer to physical properties and entities, even though translations of them into physical terms cannot be provided. In this way the philosophy of language led to a behaviorist materialism.

The beginnings of translation into behavioral terms was offered for some psychological expressions—for example, "is happy"—by directing attention to the way in which the use of such expressions is taught. A key element in teaching such an expression is to point to people behaving happily. In this emphasis on the conditions under which an expression can be learned, the positivists anticipated the favorite strategy of Ludwig Wittgenstein (1953) and moved away from complete dependence on their general doctrines of meaning and verification.

During the middle years of the twentieth century, the analytic behaviorists, in particular Gilbert Ryle (1949) and his followers, offered to show that descriptions of states of mind are essentially dispositional, so that attributions of intention and intelligence, choice and desire, excitement and fear, and other mental states are all to be understood as attributions of a disposition to behave in a characteristic manner in appropriate circumstances. Dispositions are held by most thinkers to issue from some standing or recurrent underlying state, and with these analytic behaviorists the relevant states underlying human mental life were assumed to be states of the body. Their manifest intention to exorcise any spiritual soul—as Ryle would put it, any "ghost in the machine"—places them in the materialist tradition.

Wittgenstein, although he disdained the title behaviorist, belongs to the same group. He insisted that in any acceptable analysis of a mental concept the description of a person's state of mind must make reference only to publicly detectable features of the organism and its behavior. His many subtle discussions of mental concepts are all attempts to identify the patterns of behavior whose display would constitute being in a given state of mind. To attribute that state of mind to someone is to attribute a disposition to display the relevant pattern of behavior. The alternative analysis that interprets the various states of mind as states and processes in a spiritual soul is, according to Wittgenstein, not merely false, it is unintelligible.

On two key points the analytic behaviorists were not convincing. First, if mental states are dispositions to display particular patterns of behavior, they cannot be causes of the behavior in question. It cannot be that a man's anger made him shout, for the shouting is itself just an aspect of the anger. Nor can a woman's pride have made her stubborn. Yet this causal link between a mental state and the characteristic behavior pattern that springs from it, is at the heart of how we understand one another.

Second, some inner mental episodes, such as afterimages, pains, sudden unsought recollections, dreams, or flashes of insight, resist any plausible dispositional analysis. The mind does seem to be a collection of categorical states, items, or events in addition to a cluster of dispositions. The effort to correct both these weaknesses, first the denial of any categorical component, and later the denial of any causal power to the mind, was a significant factor in materialism's subsequent development.

The third group of twentieth-century materialists embraced a theory of mind known as central-state physicalism, from which contemporary materialism derives. The central-state physicalists held that although it may be that some mental states can be understood dispositionally, there are many mental states, items, or events that must be accorded a straightforwardly categorical status. These categorical mental states turn out to be, as a matter of contingent fact, states of the central nervous system. To introspective awareness they do not seem to be neural states, but the explanation for this is that the nervous system is presented to itself in an opaque or covert fashion.

The mind has many aspects, and mental life underpins almost every distinctively human capacity. Most of our distinctive capacities have been pointed to as showing that a living human being must be something more than a mere assemblage of atoms. To understand ourselves, we cannot do without the concepts of perception, belief, and intelligence; action, decision, and choice; motive, drive, and need; feeling, emotion, and mood; temperament and character. We will also need to treat of consciousness and self-consciousness. The task for materialists is to explain how merely material structures could exhibit all these mental attributes. In attempting this, two basic approaches were at first adopted, the behavioral and the topic neutral.

Behavioral strategy. The central-state physicalists were able to appropriate the earlier work of the behaviorists and accept that the attribution to an organism of some of the mental predicates (for example intelligence, equanimity, or ambition) is in reality the attribution of a disposition to behave in a characteristic way under suitable conditions. The organism displaying the behavior, the form the behavior takes, and the conditions under which it is manifested, are all specifiable in purely physical terms. Moreover, the remarkable subtlety and complexity of human behavior, which until the twentieth century appeared to surpass anything of which a mere machine could be capable, no longer has such immaterialist implications, for now the development of electronic machines suggests that the ability to duplicate human performance is possible. In particular, the self-monitoring features of conscious behavior can be displayed by material systems.

Topic-neutral strategy. Many mental states resist the behavioral strategy: being in pain, seeing a color, or feeling depressed, for example. For these, a different claim was made: To attribute such a state is to assert that there is present within the organism some state or process that typically arises from a particular kind of stimulus and/or typically issues in a characteristic kind of behavior. A burning pain, for example, is a state of a person typically arising from excessive heat on the skin, and characteristically issuing in applications of soothing cream to the affected part. Mental predicates of this kind have been called *topic-neutral* because they do not specify the nature of the inner state in question. The inner state is not described either as material or as immaterial. To say that someone is in pain, the argument runs, does not of itself imply that the experience belongs to a immaterial mind. It implies only that the person is in some central state or other, arising from the states and processes in the sensory

system (input), and issuing in certain behavior patterns (output). When we attempt to identify this central state, we find that the sensory system provides inputs to the organism's central nervous system, which in turn sets in train the muscular movements required for any type of behavior. If inner states admit of the topic-neutral treatment, they, too have no immaterialist implications.

Among early central-state physicalists, some, such as Paul K. Feyerabend (1963) and Hilary Putnam, claimed only that this is the most promising line for investigation to now take. Others, such as U. T. Place (1956), J. J. C. Smart (1959, 1963), and Herbert Feigl (1958), went further and held that any alternative dualist view is already frankly incredible.

CONTEMPORARY MATERIALISM

During the later years of the twentieth century, under the influence chiefly of David Armstrong (1968) and David Lewis (1972), the topic-neutral strategy was taken up and developed. The behavioral strategy became less prominent, as more and more mental attributions were interpreted as asserting that the organism was in an appropriate categorical state. And the role of the mental as the causal bridge between stimulus and response was taken up and emphasized. Mental states came to be regarded as theoretical constructs and assimilated to other theoretical entities more familiar from other sciences, as philosophers adopted a third strategy for accounting for mental descriptions in a material world.

CAUSAL/THEORETICAL STRATEGY. In a complete departure from the behaviorist viewpoint, which saw mentality as a matter of the outer effects of stimuli, the new position is that the really essential thing about any mental state is its causal role, as the crucial inner intermediary between input and response. The idea is that the activity of conscious living beings calls for explanation, and the most appropriate explanations will attribute to such organisms inner states, produced by environmental and remembered elements, and producing behavior that, in the light of the organism's beliefs, is best suited to fulfilling its purposes.

So the mind becomes an inner, theoretical entity, the that-which-best-accounts-for the phenomena of conscious behavior. The analogy was drawn with the gene in biology, that-which-best-accounts-for the phenomena of heredity, and with lightning, that-which-best-accounts-for flashes, thunder, and some kinds of storm damage.

Then, still following the analogy, the research question becomes that of finding which element in the world turns out to fill the theoretical role in question. Structures crucially involving the DNA molecule, as it turns out, best account for heredity. Electrical discharges, as it turns out, best account for the flashes, rumbles, and damage of electrical storms. This is a matter of the contingent identification of underlying structures and processes as the causal bases for patterns of observed phenomena. So with the mind: It is the central nervous system (brain, optic nerve, spinal chord, and some other components) that, as it turns out, fulfills the mind's causal role as the intermediary and clearinghouse between the inputs, many of which we know as experience, and the outputs that consist in purposive activity.

In this way functionalism, the dominant form of contemporary materialism, developed. It has two components. The first component is a theory of the mind, which asserts that the essential feature of the mind is its causal role, and identifies the different states of mind—beliefs, fears, plans, twinges, and so forth—in terms of their particular places in the whole mental causal scheme. This theory of the nature of mind lends itself to materialism, but is not itself materialist. It is topic-neutral, allowing for any of a number of views of what it is that provides the causal bridge between inputs and responses. The second component in functionalist materialism is the theoretical identification of the mind with the central nervous system. This is a contingent assertion about what minds turn out to be in this world. As such, it is vulnerable to various empirical developments, as all substantial empirical claims should be.

OBJECTIONS TO MATERIALISM

THE POSSIBILITY OF SCIENTIFIC REFUTATION.
Materialism is a strong version of naturalism. It asserts that everything whatsoever that occurs in this world is the result of the operation of physical forces in accord with physical laws. So a spectacular and unequivocal divine intervention in the course of nature, such as the Apocalypse and the Day of Judgment as described in the book of Revelation, would spell the end of materialism as a credible philosophy.

Less spectacular developments could have the same impact. The firm establishing of parapsychological powers (telepathy, clairvoyance, or psychokinesis) would do so, for by definition any paranormal phenomenon involves knowledge or action by a mind in defiance of physical law. So also would developments in neural science that uncovered variations in effectual states of mind without any appropriate change in states of the central nervous system. Or changes in the central nervous system

linked to changes in mental state, such as forming a new resolution, that systematically violate the probabilities for neural change that physical laws set forth and that defy any modification to accepted physical laws.

Materialism, being vulnerable in these ways, remains to that extent speculative. But whereas a watching brief needs to be kept over the progress of scientific investigations, it is fair to say that there is at present no serious threat from these quarters. The credibility of positive paranormal results has, if anything, diminished in the course of the past half century. And we are very far indeed from being able to assert that the activity of the brain is physically anomalous. Quite the contrary; so far, no apparent violations of physical law have been found.

THEOLOGY. Materialism not only holds that there are no supernatural interventions in the course of nature, but that there are no divine beings of any kind. To defend materialism on these points, one must first show that there is no valid deductive argument for the existence of a necessary being, then sustain the view that this world does not call for a divine creator as the best explanation for its existence and character.

Next, one must deny that religious experience reveals a supernatural realm, as vision provides access to a physical one. Adopting the skeptical empiricists' critique, one can argue that religious experience is not sufficiently uniform, widespread, and unanimous to warrant abandoning the natural modes of explanation that have served so well in all other enquiries, especially as supernatural hypotheses face peculiar difficulties when it comes to putting them to the test. The materialist position is strengthened by the promise of continued success in finding concrete natural explanations of religious experience through developments in sociology, psychology and physiology.

If these positions can be established, claims to the existence of God and the occurrence of miracles are established neither by argument nor in experience and so must be considered as interpretative hypotheses laid upon the experienced world. The materialist must again urge that in framing hypotheses, as in seeking explanations, there is no sufficient reason for deserting the natural for the supernatural. In such circumstances as these considerations of parsimony exclude all supernatural entities from any reasonable ontology.

Materialists must show that, contrary to the claims of Spiritualists and Buddhists, there is no sufficient reason to believe in survival of bodily death or in reincarnation. And indeed there are plausible arguments that both doctrines rest on untenable views of the self. These arguments do not impugn the possibility of bodily resurrection, but that is compatible with materialism.

METAPHYSICS. Materialism has in the past been assailed as incomplete. Even if, in a great advance on its predecessors, modern cosmology does provide explanations for the origin, persistence, and motion of the fundamental particles, it provides none for the initial conditions from which these derive. Nor does materialism make intelligible why each fundamental interaction has had one result and not another. The reply, now widely accepted, is that all chains of explanation must eventually come to a terminus and that to seek to go beyond contingent truths concerning the items and processes in this world is to go hunting a mare's nest.

THE MIND AND HUMAN EXPERIENCE. There is no doubt that our own conscious experience provides the greatest intuitive challenge to materialism. C. D. Broad in *The Mind and Its Place in Nature* (1925) formulates many people's reaction to the suggestion that mental events are physical events, such as molecular movements, taking place in our body:

> About a molecular movement it is perfectly reasonable to raise the question "Is it swift or slow, straight or circular and so on?" About the awareness of a red patch it is nonsensical to ask whether it is a swift or slow awareness, a straight or circular awareness, and so on. Conversely, it is reasonable to ask whether it is a clear or a confused awareness, but it is nonsense to ask of a molecular movement whether it is a clear or a confused movement. Thus the attempt to argue that "being a sensation of so and so" and "being a bit of bodily behavior of such and such a kind" are just two names for the same characteristic is evidently hopeless. (p. 623)

Indeed, this attempt is hopeless, but it is not one a materialist must make. We need to distinguish the process of being aware from the item of which we are aware. The two "names" that materialists claim to name the same thing are "subject S having sensation P" and "subject S undergoing bodily changes Q," and it has become clear since Broad wrote that what is or is not nonsensical is not an immediate deliverance of introspection, but an issue in the fashioning of concepts to improve theories of the world. As for P, which is the item of which S is aware—what Broad calls the sensation S has—there would be no absurdity if this could be dealt with by a topic-neutral strategy. We are aware that something is going on in us,

which deserves the description "red patch," but according to the topic-neutral strategy, the nature of what is going on is not part of what we are conscious of. The fact of the matter, according to the materialists, is that we have a covert presentation of bodily changes Q to the person S, who is having the sensation. Nevertheless, the two main stumbling blocks for functionalist materialism both concern the character of our inner life.

The qualia problem. The topic-neutral or causal/theoretical strategies may well be satisfactory for those inner states that have no special "feel" about them, such as deciding. We can decide to do something, and be aware that we have decided, but that awareness carries no special feel or twinge or glow with it. We are aware that something is going on in us, something that will have an impact on how we behave by bringing a new causal factor into our life. But that state, and our awareness of that state, reveal nothing about its nature as material or immaterial. Decisions and intentions are thus favorable candidates for a topic-neutral analysis—so, too, is doing mental arithmetic, where the process leads to changes in what one will say or do, but carries no other inner characteristics that one is aware of.

The case is otherwise, however, with sensations and feelings. To see a red patch is to be aware of an inner state that has a redness about it, that sets it apart from the green and blue patches we see. This difference is not obviously a difference in how we discriminate the two items, and react to them, as is brought out by the spectrum-shift arguments, which point out that although your outward color-vision behavior may match mine, you may see reds as I see pale pinks, or blues as I see greens.

To be in love is certainly to be in a state apt to issue in a characteristic pattern of behavior. But it is more than that; there is a complex of feelings involved that do not of themselves involve behavioral differences, but differences in consciousness, by comparison with those not in love.

To be angry, or in pain, or delighted, carry special sensations or feelings with them too. All such sensations or feelings are known as *qualia*, and the qualia problem is the problem of fitting them in to a materialist world view. It is notorious that when you are seeing something green, and therefore experiencing a sensation of green, there is no green physical surface anywhere inside you. The sharp pangs of pain are similarly elusive—the neural activities have been found that occur when pain is felt, but the painfulness of pain does not seem to be present among them.

Qualia seem to be an important part of being conscious. They seem to make a difference to how we speak and act, yet they stand outside the network of physical causation, neither taking energy in their production, nor having any force to apply to change the world. They challenge the deep materialist commitment to the physical closure of the natural world. If only physical items can have physical effects, then qualia cannot even produce our awareness of them, nor our capacity to describe them, which makes them paradoxical items indeed.

There have been attempts to account for them behavioristically, as dispositions to act and react in particular ways. Perhaps the most promising materialist suggestion is that the intrinsic qualities of sensations are in reality purely schematic and enable us only to distinguish one sensation from another. Inner states notoriously elude direct characterization. Our attempts to describe them often proceed by comparison with other sensations directly or ultimately picked out by reference to their stimulus and/or response. For example, we describe smells as of cinnamon or of rotten eggs (stimulus) and as appetizing or nauseating (response); we speak of pains as jabbing, burning, or like "pins and needles." Feelings of anger, shame, pride, and fear are all described in terms of bodily temperature.

If the sameness or difference of inner states but not their nature is given introspectively, sensations could well be states of the nervous system typically connected with stimulus and/or response, even though we are not aware of this. This strategy for dealing with qualia faces the problems of spectrum-shift arguments, because two sets of sensations, tastes for example, could be shifted relative to one another along a spectrum, yet perform equally well in informing us of the sameness or difference, and typical causes and effects, of our inner states.

The qualia problem was long emphasized by F. C. Jackson (1998) in a series of influential articles. His most recent stance is the "there must be a solution" solution: Somehow, qualia must be reconcilable with materialism, even if we cannot see how.

The insight problem. The second currently most acute problem for materialism concerns the nature of human insight and understanding. When we learn to speak a language, we acquire the ability to conduct a conversation satisfactorily; that is, to make appropriate responses to the speech of others, to initiate conversations using sounds the other recognizes and responds to. But to properly understand, more than linguistic competence is required. This was dramatized by John Searle (1992) in his "Chinese Room" argument: If someone who had no understanding of Chinese but who could recognize Chinese characters were shut away in a room, and provided with pieces of Chinese—questions and so forth—through a mailbox, that person could, using a computerized dictionary for example, choose appropriate Chinese-character responses. This is a linguistic competence that does not include understanding and is clearly deficient by comparison with the capacity of a genuine Chinese speaker. The missing component, understanding or insight, proves just as elusive as do the qualia to materialist studies of the nervous system.

PHILOSOPHY. Materialism faces several other more general objections, for the most part of a logical kind, that must be faced.

The argument from self-destruction. A popular argument for disposing of materialism is this:

All doctrines concerning the nature of the world are arrived at by inference.

Thus, *a fortiori*, materialism is so reached.

But if materialism is true, inference is a causally determined process in people's brains, and not a rational process.

Materialism is therefore a doctrine arrived at by non-rational causal processes.

Thus, if it is true, there can be no reason to think it so.

This argument has a long history, being found in Epicurus and developed and defended by J. B. S. Haldane (1932) and Karl Popper (1977). Nevertheless, it is invalid. That the course of a given process of inferring was determined by the structure of a brain does not entail that it was an unreasonable inference. Nor does it entail that there could be no ground for thinking it reasonable. We can see that this is so, by comparing reasoning in people with calculating in adding machines. The result reached is a causal consequence of the structure of the machine; it is nonetheless a correct one, and one we are entitled to rely on. Haldane later retracted his argument (1954).

Asymmetrical knowledge of physical and mental states. Another common argument against materialism points out that, although ordinary people can recognize thoughts and feelings and intentions, they are completely ignorant of processes in the central nervous system, and so the mental occurrences cannot be identified with any such physical events. Friedrich Paulsen, for example, argued to this effect in chapter one of his *Introduction to Philosophy* (1895 [1892]).

This argument is also, as it stands, invalid. It is like arguing that because the police know some of the characteristics of a man who committed a crime but do not know anything about John Smith, John Smith could not possibly be the man who committed the crime. A similar reply is provided by Place and Smart in articles cited in the bibliography.

The argument would be valid if another premise were added: In introspection the full nature of mental events is disclosed. But there is no good reason for thinking this premise is true.

A variation of this argument claimed that introspective knowledge of our own mental states is incorrigible, whereas no knowledge of anything physical is incorrigible, so mental states cannot be physical. This argument faded from view after Armstrong exposed its weakness: We can and do make mistakes about our own inner mental states.

The general nature of human reason. Keith Gunderson (1964) revived an argument of Descartes's to the effect that men are not machines, even cybernetic machines, and therefore not merely material. In all known machines the matching or surpassing of a human intellectual ability is a specific outcome of a specific structure. Each skill is a skill at some specific task and no other. But in human beings, intellectual skills are generalized and come in clusters; human reason is a tool for all circumstances. Thus, it is not proven that the human skill and that of the machine arise from a like inner structure. On the contrary, the reasonable conclusion is that the machine's skill and the human skill are to be explained in different ways—that is, a person is not any kind of machine.

The reply available to materialists is that this argument is premature. The simulation of human performance by material assemblages is in its infancy. There seems no reason to suppose a machine with generalized skills impossible.

Intentionality. Unlike the situation with anything physical, in the realm of the mind there are relations that can exist even in the absence of one of their terms. These are the intentional relations, which include intending, believing, hoping, fearing, and desiring. The argument from intentionality rests on this peculiarity and may be put this way:

A peculiarity of many mental states is their essential connection with an object. In intending, I must intend something, and in hoping, I must hope for something.

However, whereas when I kick something, the thing I kick must exist, the thing intended or the thing hoped for may or may not have any real existence.

In this way some mental states differ essentially from all physical states.

Thus, materialism cannot be true.

The materialist reply to this argument is that intentional "relations" are strictly speaking not relations but monadic states that are identified by reference to what would fulfill them or constitute their exercise. These are possible states or circumstances that, were they actual, would be material. It is a further question, however, whether the existence of mere, unactualized possibilities is compatible with a strict materialism.

Logical connections between distinct existences. The essential link between a mental state and the behavior to which it gives rise has also been seen to rule out materialism:

Where an intention is carried out, both the intention and the thing intended exist.

They are two different things.

Nevertheless, they are logically connected, because what was carried out makes the intention what it was.

But any two different physical items are only contingently connected.

Hence, mental states cannot be physical items.

Materialists urge in rebuttal that this is a consequence of the peculiarly causal character of mental states and has its counterpart in the uncontroversially physical realm.

Thus if we describe arsenic causally as a lethal poison, there is a logical connection between drinking the lethal poison arsenic and dying, even though the arsenic, the drinking, and the dying, are all distinct existences.

NONREDUCTIVE MATERIALISM

Despite the progress made in rebutting the classical objections to materialism, and despite the current popularity, in English-speaking philosophy, of functionalist physicalism as a philosophy of mind, uneasiness remains that materialism accords insufficient recognition to consciousness and its highest expressions—music, literature, love, and fine feeling generally, as well as culture, morality, and religious aspiration. In response to this, there have been some attempts at a softer materialism that tries to accord to the physical a primary but not exclusive place. While everything depends on the physical, it does not reduce to the physico-chemical, but rather supervenes upon it. The most thorough attempt in this direction is J. F. Post's *The Faces of Existence* (1987). A further step away from extreme materialism is taken in Nicholas Maxwell's *The Human World in the Physical Universe* (2001), which advocates a dual-aspect position while clinging to the central materialist claim that the universe is a closed system, in which the only causally effective forces are the physical ones.

See also Philosophy of Mind.

Bibliography

GENERAL HISTORIES OF MATERIALISM

Lange, Frederick Albert. *Geschichte des Materialismus* (1865). Translated by E. C. Thomas as *The History of Materialism*. London: Truebner, 1877–1892. This classic is by far the most important secondary source in the history of materialist theories. All English editions since the London edition of 1925 include an introduction by Bertrand Russell titled "Materialism."

Lewes, George Henry. *The Biographical History of Philosophy*. London: C. Knight, 1845. A lively and idiosyncratic history, with good comments on materialist philosophers.

Vitzthum, R. *Materialism: An Affirmative History and Definition*. Amherst, NY: Prometheus, 1995. Accessible work, emphasizing the scientific aspects of the development of materialism.

CLASSICAL PERIOD

Aristotle. *Metaphysica*. Translated by W. D. Ross as *Metaphysics* Oxford: Clarendon Press, 1924. Most easily accessible source for ancient world opinion on materialistic Greeks.

Burnet, John. *Early Greek Philosophy*. 4th ed. London: A & C Black, 1930.

Burnet, John. *Greek Philosophy; Thales to Plato*. London: Macmillan, 1914. Standard account of ancient philosophy.

Lucretius. *De Rerum Natura*. Classic presentation, in Latin verse, expanding and occasionally modifying the doctrines of Epicurus. Translated by Rolfe Humphries as *The Way Things Are*. Bloomington: Indiana University Press, 1969. Another edition, translated by R. E. Latham. Harmondsworth, England: Penguin, 1961.

SEVENTEENTH CENTURY

Brandt, Frithiof. *Den mekaniske Naturopfattelse hos Thomas Hobbes*. Translated by Vaughan Maxwell and Annie Fairstoll as *Thomas Hobbes' Mechanical Conception of Nature*. London: Librairie Hachette, 1928. Detailed and definitive.

Cyrano de Bergerac, Savinien de. *Etats et empires de la lune* and *Etats et empires du soleil*. 1657, 1662. Translated by Richard Aldington as *Voyages to the Moon and the Sun*. New York: Orion Press, 1962. These fictional works epitomize the seventeenth-century movement toward materialism.

Gassendi, Pierre. *Animadversiones in Decimum Librum Diogenis Laerti*. Lyons, France, 1649.

Gassendi, Pierre. *De Vita et Moribus Epicuri Libri Octo*. Lyons, France, 1647.

Gassendi, Pierre. *Philosophiae Epicuri Syntagma*. Lyons, France, 1649.

Gassendi, Pierre. *Syntagma Philosophicum*. Lyons, France, 1658. These four works appeared together in *Opera Omnia*. Lyons, France, 1658. Facsimile reprint Stuttgart-Bad-Cannstatt, frommann, 1964. In these four works Gassendi expounds and defends Epicurus (except where his views conflict with Catholic doctrine.)

Hobbes, Thomas. *English Works*, edited by William Molesworth. London: Bohn, 1839.

Hobbes, Thomas. *Latin Works*, edited by William Molesworth. London: Bohn, 1839.

Mintz, Samuel I. *The Hunting of Leviathan*. Cambridge, U.K.: Cambridge University Press, 1962. Narrates contemporary reactions to Hobbes.

Peters, Richard. *Hobbes*. Harmondsworth: Penguin, 1956. Interesting and comprehensible introduction.

Rochot, Bernard. *Les travaux de Gassendi sur Epicure et sur l'atomisme 1619–1658*. Paris: Librarie Philosophique, 1944. Most accessible modern treatment of Gassendi.

Spink, John S. *French Free-Thought from Gassendi to Voltaire*. London: University of London, Athlone Press, 1960.

EIGHTEENTH CENTURY

Cabanis, Pierre-Jean-Georges. *Rapports du physique et du moral de l'homme*. Paris, 1802. English translation by M. D. Saidi. Baltimore: Johns Hopkins Press, 1981.

Diderot, Denis. *Oeuvres completes*. Paris: Garnier Freres, 1875.

Holbach, Paul Heinrich Dietrich d'. *Systeme de la nature … par Mirabaud*. 1770. Translated by H. D. Robinson as *The System of Nature*. Edited by Denis Diderot. Boston: J. P. Mendum, 1853. Classic treatise.

La Mettrie, Julien Offray de. *L'homme machine*. 1748. Translated and edited by Ann Thom as *Machine Man*. Cambridge, U.K.: Cambridge University Press, 1996. There is also a critical edition with notes by Aram Vartanian. Princeton, 1960.

Maubec. *Principes de la raison et les passions de l'homme*. Manuscript held in the Bibliotheque nationale in Paris (B.N. n.a.f.r.14709).

Priestley, Joseph. *Disquisitions Relating to Matter and Spirit*. London: J. Johnson, 1777.

NINETEENTH CENTURY

Buchner, Ludwig. *Kraft und Stoff* (1855). Translated by J. Frederick Collingwood as *Force and Matter*. London, Truebner, 1884.

Darwin, Charles. *The Descent of Man*. New York: Appleton, 1871.

Darwin, Charles. *The Origin of Species*. London: John Murray, 1859. Classic treatise.

Moleschott, Jakob. *Der Kreislauf des Lebens*. Mainz, Germany: Von Zabern, 1857.

Passmore, John. *A Hundred Years of Philosophy*. London: Duckworth, 1957. Readable and authoritative guide.

Vogt, Karl. *Kohlerglaube und Wissenschaft*. Giessen, Germany: Ricker, 1855.

Vogt, Karl. *Physiologische Briefe*. Giessen, Germany, 1854.

TWENTIETH CENTURY

Armstrong, David M. *A Materialist Theory of the Mind.* London: Routledge and Kegan Paul, 1968. A modern classic, first systematic exposition of central-state physicalism.

Carnap, Rudolf. "Psychologie in physikalischer Sprache" (1932–1933). Translated by Frederick Schick as "Psychology in Physical Language," in *Logical Positivism*, edited by A. J. Ayer. Glencoe, IL: Free Press, 1959. Epistemic materialism.

Eliot, Hugh. *Modern Science and Materialism.* London: Longmans, Green, 1919.

Feigl, Herbert. "The 'Mental' and the 'Physical.'" In *Minnesota Studies in the Philosophy of Science.* Vol. 2, edited by Herbert Feigl et al. Minneapolis: University of Minnesota Press, 1958. Identifies mental states with brain processes.

Feyerabend, Paul K. "Materialism and the Mind-Body Problem." *Review of Metaphysics* 17 (1) (1963): 49–66. Claims materialism is the only plausible view.

Hook, Sidney, ed. *Dimensions of Mind: A Symposium.* New York: New York University Press, 1960. Deals with the relations of mind, body, and machinery from many points of view.

Lewis, David K. "Psychophysical and Theoretical Identifications." *Australasian Journal of Philosophy* 50 (1972): 249–258.

Nagel, Ernest. "Are Naturalists Materialists?" In his *Logic without Metaphysics.* Glencoe, IL: Free Press, 1957.

Popper, Karl, and John C. Eccles. *The Self and Its Brain.* New York: Springer International, 1977. Full-scale attempt at a Cartesian dualism. Includes discussion of the argument from self-refutation.

Place, U. T. "Is Consciousness a Brain Process?" *British Journal of Psychology* 47 (1956): 44–50. Pioneering paper in central state physicalism.

Ryle, Gilbert. *The Concept of Mind.* London: Hutchinson, 1949. Readable and influential advocacy of analytic behaviorism.

Skinner, B. F. *Science and Human Behavior.* New York: Macmillan, 1953. Major statement of methodological behaviorism.

Smart, J. J. C. *Philosophy and Scientific Realism.* London: Routledge and Kegan Pual, 1963. Amplification of Smart's materialism.

Smart, J. J. C. "Sensations and Brain Processes." *Philosophical Review* 68 (1959): 141–156. Classic and influential pioneering physicalist paper.

Wittgenstein, Ludwig. *Philosophical Investigations.* Oxford: Blackwell, 1953. Influential but difficult reappraisal of the logic of mental concepts.

CONTEMPORARY MATERIALISM

Braddon-Mitchell, David, and Frank Jackson. *The Philosophy of Mind and Cognition.* Oxford: Blackwell, 1996. Best modern introduction, with discussion of the qualia problem.

Chalmers, David J. *The Conscious Mind: In Search of a Fundamental Theory.* New York: Oxford University Press, 1996. Presents a moderate dualist position.

Churchland, Paul. *A Neurocomputational Perspective.* Cambridge, MA: MIT Press, 1989. Shows how information systems can exhibit mental powers.

Dennett, Daniel. *Consciousness Explained.* Boston: Little, Brown, 1991. Functionalist account of consciousness.

Gillett, Carl, and Barry Loewer, eds. *Physicalism and Its Discontents.* New York: Cambridge University Press, 2001. Sympathetic treatment of difficulties for materialism, with useful bibliography.

Jackson, Frank, ed. *Consciousness.* Aldershot, U.K.: Ashgate, 1998. Collection of articles, including some on qualia.

Kim, Jaegwon. *Mind in a Physical World.* Cambridge, MA: MIT Press, 1998.

Lycan, William G. *Consciousness and Experience.* Cambridge, MA: MIT Press, 1996. Functionalist view.

Lycan, Willaim G., ed. *Mind and Cognition, An Anthology.* 2nd ed. Malden, MA: Blackwell, 1999. Collection of influential articles.

Maxwell, Nicholas. *The Human World in the Physical Universe: Consciousness, Free Will, and Evolution.* Lanham, MD: Rowman & Littlefield, 2001. Presents a dual-aspect reconciliation of physical science and conscious experience.

McGinn, Colin. *The Problem of Consciousness.* Oxford: Blackwell, 1990. Argues the problem is beyond our competence to resolve.

Papineau, David. *Philosophical Naturalism.* Oxford: Blackwell, 1993. Concerns supervenience and physicalism.

Poland, Jeffrey. *Physicalism; The Philosophical Foundations.* Oxford: Clarendon, 1994. General and systematic presentation of the philosophy of materialism.

Post, John F. *The Faces of Existence.* Ithaca, NY: Cornell University Press, 1987. Propounds nonreductive materialism.

Rosenthal, David, ed. *The Nature of Mind.* New York: Oxford University Press, 1991. Collection of influential articles.

Searle, John. *The Rediscovery of the Mind.* Cambridge, MA: MIT Press, 1992. Antireductionist materialism.

Thau, Michael. *Consciousness and Cognition.* Oxford: Oxford University Press, 2002.

PHILOSOPHICAL OBJECTIONS

Armstrong, David M. "Is Introspective Knowledge Incorrigible?" *Philosophical Review.* 72 (1963): 417–432.

Broad, Charlie Dunbar. *The Mind and Its Place in Nature.* London: Harcourt, Brace, 1925. Readable review of various doctrines of the mind.

Ducasse, Curt John. *Nature, Mind, and Death.* La Salle, IL: Open Court, 1951. Dualist attack on materialism.

Foster, John L. *The Immaterial Self: A Defence of the Cartesian Dualist Conception of the Mind.* London: Routledge, 1991.

Gunderson, Keith. "Descartes, La Mettrie, Language and Machines." *Philosophy* 39 (1964): 193ff. Revives argument from the generalized nature of reason.

Haldane, J. B. S. *The Inequality of Man.* London: Chatto and Windus, 1932. Presents the argument from self-refutation.

Haldane, J. B. S. "I Repent an Error." *The Literary Guide.* (April 1954): 7 and 29. Retracts argument from self-refutation.

Lewis, C. S. *Miracles.* New York: Macmillan, 1947. Expounds argument against materialism as self-refuting.

Paulsen, Friedrich. *Einleitung in die Philosophie.* 1892. Translated by Frank Thilly as *An Introduction to Philosophy.* New York: Holt, 1895. Idealist attack on materialism.

Plantinga, Alvin. "Probability and Defeaters." *Pacific Philosophical Quarterly* 84 (3) (2003): 291–298. Argues that materialism is self-subverting.

Keith Campbell (1967, 2005)

MATERIALISM, DIALECTICAL

See *Dialectical Materialism*

MATERIALISM, HISTORICAL

See *Historical Materialism*

MATHEMATICS, FOUNDATIONS OF

The study of the foundations of mathematics comprises investigations, though probably not all possible investigations, that consist of general reflection on mathematics. The subject naturally proceeds by singling out certain concepts and principles as "fundamental" and concentrating attention on them, but of course the identification of fundamental concepts and principles is itself based on foundational research or may be revised in the light of it.

In this entry considerable emphasis will be placed on philosophical questions about mathematics, which undoubtedly belong to foundations. However, many, perhaps most, foundational investigations are mainly mathematical. In the last hundred years an important role has been played by mathematical logic. We shall not give a detailed exposition of mathematical logic, but we hope that our discussion will give an idea of the relation between the logical problems and results and the philosophical problems and an idea of some of the results of recent work in logic.

Two of the main qualities for which mathematics has always attracted the attention of philosophers are the great degree of systematization and the rigorous development of mathematical theories. The problem of systematization seems to be the initial problem in the foundations of mathematics, both because it has been a powerful force in the history of mathematics itself and because it sets the form of further investigations by picking out the fundamental concepts and principles. Also, the systematic integration of mathematics is an important basis of another philosophically prominent feature, its high degree of clarity and certainty. In mathematics systematization has taken a characteristic and highly developed form—the axiomatic method—which has from time to time been taken as a model for systematiza-

tion in general. We shall therefore begin our main exposition with a discussion of the axiomatic method.

Foundational research has always been concerned with the problem of justifying mathematical statements and principles, with understanding why certain evident propositions are evident, with providing the justification of accepted principles that seem not quite evident, and with finding and casting off principles which are unjustified. A natural next step in our exposition, then, will be to consider mathematics from an epistemological point of view, which leads us to examine mathematics as a primary instance of what philosophers have called a priori knowledge. In this connection we shall give some logical analysis of two very basic mathematical ideas, class and natural number, and discuss the attempts of Gottlob Frege and Bertrand Russell to exploit the intimate relation between these two ideas in order to prove that mathematics is in some way a part of logic. We shall also discuss Immanuel Kant's views on the evidence of mathematics and other conceptions of a priori knowledge. (The word *evidence* will often be used in this entry in a way that is unusual outside philosophical writings influenced by the German tradition, to mean "the property of being evident"—German, *Evidenz.*)

The growth of modern mathematics, with its abstract character and its dependence on set theory, has caused the problem of evidence to be focused on the more particular problem of platonism. It is in this development and the accompanying growth of mathematical logic that modern foundational research has centered.

Throughout the nineteenth century, mathematicians worked to make arithmetic and analysis more rigorous, which required axiomatization and an attempt to use the concepts of the theory of natural numbers as a basis for defining the further concepts of arithmetic and analysis. The manner in which this axiomatization and definition was undertaken was platonist, in the sense that both numbers and sets or sequences of numbers were treated as existing in themselves. The development of set theory by Georg Cantor provided a general framework for this work and also involved even greater abstraction and even stronger platonist assumptions.

The growth of mathematical logic introduced as further elements the axiomatization of logic (the basic step in which was completed by Frege in 1879), the effort to incorporate the axiomatization of logic into that of mathematics, and the accompanying tendency, on the part of Frege and Giuseppe Peano, to interpret rigorous axiomatization as formalization. Frege carried the development much further by undertaking to develop the whole of arithmetic and analysis in a formal system that is essentially a system of set theory.

At the turn of the twentieth century the entire development reached a crisis with the discovery of the paradoxes of set theory, which showed that the concept of class or set as it was then being used had not been sufficiently clarified. Much of the foundational research of the early twentieth century—and not only in the axiomatization of set theory—was directed at problems posed or believed to have been posed by the paradoxes.

In that period emerged three general viewpoints, each of which had its own program based on a distinctive attitude toward the question of platonism. The most radical was intuitionism, based on L. E. J. Brouwer's critique of the whole idea of platonism. In contrast to Brouwer, David Hilbert had a firm commitment to the patronizing tendency in mathematics, but he held epistemological views that were fundamentally in accord with Brouwer's critique of platonism. Making use of the fact that no matter how platonist the mathematics formalized, questions of provability in a formal system are meaningful from a narrow constructivist point of view, Hilbert's school sought to secure the foundations of platonist mathematics by metamathematical investigation of formalized mathematics—in particular, by a proof of consistency. This viewpoint was called formalism, although the designation is misleading, since Hilbert never maintained that even platonist mathematics could be simply defined as a "meaningless" formal system.

Proponents of the third viewpoint, logicism, whose leading figure was Russell, continued to believe in Frege's program of reducing mathematics to logic. Accepting this program involved taking some platonist assumptions as intuitively evident.

A great deal of work in mathematical logic was directed toward clarifying and justifying one or another of these points of view. We might mention Brouwer's (informal) results on the impossibility of constructively proving certain theorems in analysis, Arend Heyting's formalization of intuitionist logic, the development of finitist proof theory by Hilbert and his coworkers, and Russell and A. N. Whitehead's *Principia Mathematica* as a much further development of mathematics within a system of set theory.

Nonetheless, the trichotomy of logicism, formalism, and intuitionism has probably never been the best classification of points of view in foundations. It does not take account of one of the philosophically most important problems, that of predicativity, or of some mathematical

developments—such as the development of the semantics of logic by Leopold Löwenheim, Thoralf Skolem, Kurt Gödel, and Alfred Tarski—which were crucially important for later work. At any rate the schools no longer really exist. All of them had programs that encountered serious difficulties; further experience with set theory and the axiomatizations of Ernst Zermelo and Russell deprived the paradoxes of their apparently apocalyptic character; and specialized work in mathematical logic led more and more to the consideration of problems whose significance cut across the division of the schools and to looking at the results of the schools in ways which would be independent of the basic controversies. A decisive step in this development came in the early 1930s, with the discovery of Gödel's incompleteness theorem and the coming of age of formal semantics.

Some areas of the foundations of mathematics will be passed over here—in particular, we shall not go far into the significance of the fact that mathematics has applications to the concrete world, although historically the relation between mathematics and its applications has been very close, and the present sharp distinction between pure and applied mathematics is a rather recent development. For instance, we shall omit a special consideration of geometry. If the pre-twentieth-century view that geometry is a purely mathematical theory that nonetheless deals with actual space is correct, then the omission is unjustified. However, even the question whether this view still has something to be said for it is more intimately related to the philosophy of physics than to the problems on which we shall concentrate. Geometry as understood today by the pure mathematician, as the general study of structures analogous to Euclidean space, raises no philosophical problems different from those raised by analysis and set theory.

§1. THE AXIOMATIC METHOD

As we said, we shall begin our discussion with the axiomatic method. Consideration of the notion of an informal axiomatic system leads to the notions of formalization and formal system. Through this process, especially through the last step, mathematical theories become themselves objects of mathematical study. The exploitation of this possibility is perhaps the specifically modern move in the study of the foundations of mathematics and has led to an enormous enrichment of the subject in the last hundred years.

1.1. AXIOMATIZATION. Ever since Euclid, axiomatizing a theory has meant presenting it by singling out certain propositions and deducing further ones from them; if the presentation is complete, it should be the case that all statements which could be asserted in the theory are thus deducible. Axiomatization has also come to mean a similar reduction of vocabulary, in that certain notions should be taken as primitive and all further notions which are introduced in the development of the theory should be defined in terms of the primitive ones. In essence this is the conception of an axiomatized theory that prevails today, although it has been developed in different directions.

There are important ambiguities concerning the means of deduction and definition to be admitted in the development of the theory. Here informal axiomatics always makes use of some general background that can be used in developing the theory but is not itself included in the axiomatization. In modern mathematics this background typically includes logic and arithmetic and usually also analysis and some set theory. For example, in an axiomatic theory concerning objects of a certain kind, one permits oneself very quickly to make statements about sequences and sets of those objects, to introduce concepts defined in terms of the primitives of the theory by means of these general mathematical devices, and to make inferences that turn on laws of arithmetic, analysis, or set theory. Such notions often enter into the statement of the axioms themselves. We shall presently say more about the significance of this procedure.

It might seem natural to require provisionally that the means of deduction and definition be restricted to those of pure logic, for logic is supposed to contain those rules of correct inference which have the highest degree of generality and which must be applied in all sciences. We would then regard an axiomatization as only partial if deductions from it required the use of methods of the special sciences—in particular, branches of mathematics (likewise if, in addition to the primitives, notions other than purely logical ones entered into the definitions). An axiomatic theory would then consist of just those statements that are deducible by purely logical means from a certain limited set of statements and of the statements that can be obtained from these by definitions expressible purely logically in terms of the primitives.

It seems possible that such an axiomatic system was the objective toward which Euclid was striving. He evidently did not intend to allow himself general mathematical notions, such as arithmetical ones, for he included propositions involving such notions among his axioms and undertook to develop some of number theory from the axioms in Books VII–IX. Even some of Euclid's well-

known failures to achieve this degree of rigor—for example, his assuming in his very first proof that two circles with the center of each lying on the circumference of the other will have two points of intersection—might have arisen because he saw them as immediate deductions from the meaning of the concepts involved. Of course, a rigorous theory of definition would require definitions to be given or axioms to be explicitly stated in such a way that such deductions do proceed by mere logic.

A perfectly satisfactory axiomatization in this form certainly was not possible in Euclid's time; it probably had to wait for two developments that did not take place until the late nineteenth century, Frege's discovery and axiomatization of quantification theory and the Dedekind-Peano axiomatization of arithmetic. (Nonetheless, considerable progress was made prior to these developments.)

This remark points to a limitation of the conception we are considering, for it does not give a meaning to the idea of an axiomatization of logic itself, although such axiomatization has played a vital role in modern foundational studies. Appreciation of this point leads to the concept of a formal system, but before we consider this concept let us observe a consequence of the axiomatization of a theory.

1.2. THE ABSTRACT VIEWPOINT. Suppose a theory is so completely axiomatized that all concepts of the special theory which are used in statements and deductions are explicitly given as primitives and all special assumptions underlying the proofs are disengaged and either stated among or deduced from the axioms. This means that the validity of the deductions does not at all depend on the actual meaning of the primitive terms of the special theory. It follows that the formal structure determined by the primitive concepts and the axioms can have a more general application than they have in the given special theory, in the sense that we could by any choice of interpretation of the primitive terms obtain a deductive system of hypotheses concerning some subject matter, even though the hypotheses will in many cases be false.

This fact is of crucial importance in the study of axiom systems. We can then think of a *model* of an axiomatic theory as a system of objects and relations that provides references for the primitive terms so that the axioms come out true. We can think of axiomatization as having proceeded with a particular model in mind, but this need not have been the case; at any rate, interest attaches to the study of other possible models. (Although we may, in this discussion, allow means of deduction that go beyond pure logic, it ought to be the case that if a proposition is deducible from the axioms of the theory, then it must be true in all models of the theory. It might be reasonable to take this as a sufficient condition of deducibility, but if so it seems that the notion of model will have to have a relativity comparable to that of the notion of deducibility.)

For example, suppose we consider absolute geometry—that is, Euclidean geometry without the parallel postulate. Then any model either of Euclidean geometry or of the standard non-Euclidean geometries will be a model of absolute geometry. If the parallel postulate is deducible from the other axioms of Euclidean geometry—that is, from the axioms of absolute geometry— then it must be true in every model of absolute geometry. The construction of models for non-Euclidean geometries showed that this is not the case. We call an axiom of a system independent if it is not deducible from the others. Thus, if the theory obtained by dropping an axiom $\mathcal{A}$ has a model in which $\mathcal{A}$ is false, then $\mathcal{A}$ is independent.

Another possibility, which has been much exploited in modern mathematics, is to replace a system of primitive terms and axioms by what amounts to an explicit definition of a model of the axioms. Thus, suppose Euclidean geometry is formulated with two primitive predicates (following Alfred Tarski in "What Is Elementary Geometry?," 1959):

$$\text{``}\beta(x,y,z)\text{''},$$

meaning "x, y, and z are collinear, and y lies between x and z or $y = x$ or $y = z$," and

$$\text{``}\delta(x,y,z,w)\text{''},$$

meaning "x is the same distance from y as z is from w." (The variables here range over points, which in the informal theory must be thought of as a primitive notion.) Then we can define a *Euclidean space* as a triple $\langle S,B,D \rangle$, where S is a set of entities called "points," B a ternary relation on S, and D a quaternary relation on S, such that the axioms of Euclidean geometry hold. Then to any theorem proved from these axioms corresponds a statement of the form "Every Euclidean space is such that … ." A number of attempts to characterize mathematical structures axiomatically have led in a similar way to explicit definitions of abstract types of structure. This is regarded, for more than historical reasons, as a fruit of the axiomatic method. The search for an axiomatic basis for a mathematical theory is also the search for a formulation of the arguments in a fashion which will make them more generally applicable, giving them a generality which can be expressed in the definition of a general type of structure.

1.3. FORMALIZATION. Whereas one development of the axiomatic method tends to the replacement of axioms by definitions, another leads to the conception of a formal system. One result of the axiomatization of a theory was that the meaning of the primitive terms became irrelevant to the deductions. If we carry this abstraction from meaning to its limit, we can cover the case of axiomatizations of logic and resolve once and for all the question of what means of deduction are to be allowed. That is, we put into the construction of an axiom system a complete specification of all the means of inference to be allowed (for example, logic and basic mathematics) in the form both of further axioms and of rules of inference that allow us to infer from statements of certain given forms a statement of another given form. If this is done with utmost rigor, so that use can be made of only as much of the meaning of the terms as is specified in axioms and explicit definitions, then the system is specified simply in terms of the designs of the "linguistic" forms in which it is expressed. "Linguistic" is put in quotation marks because, invariably, much of the language has been replaced by an artificial syntax. We are left with a specification of certain strings of symbols as "axioms" and certain rules, each of which allows us to "infer" a new string from certain prior ones. The strings which we can obtain from axioms by successive application of the rules can be called *theorems*.

A proper explanation of the concept of a formal system requires somewhat more apparatus. The exactness of this procedure requires that the strings of symbols used be constructed out of preassigned material, which we can assume to be a finite list of symbols. Among the strings of these symbols we single out a subclass that we call formulae (or well-formed formulae, wffs), which are those strings to which, in an interpretation, we would give a meaning. (The non-wffs correspond to ungrammatical sentences.) Then a certain class of formulae is singled out as the axioms. The class of theorems can be defined as the closure of the axioms under certain operations; that is, rules of the following form are specified:

(R_i). If $\mathcal{A}_1, \cdots, \mathcal{A}_{r_i}$ are theorems and $\mathcal{R}_i(\mathcal{A}_1, \cdots \mathcal{A}_{r_i})$, then $\mathcal{B}$ is a theorem, where $\mathcal{R}_i$ is some relation on strings of the symbols of the system.

So the definition of *theorem* is an inductive definition with the clauses (R_i) and

every axiom is a theorem.

In this setting we can resolve another ambiguity of our original rough conception of axiomatization. The question arises concerning what conditions a class of statements must satisfy to be appropriate as the axioms of an axiomatic theory. Various epistemological desiderata, such as self-evident truth for the intended model, are put aside once we take the abstract point of view. Another requirement that has been found natural in the past is that both individual axioms and the class of axioms as a whole should have a certain simplicity. What there is in the way of general theory about the simplicity of individual axioms has not played much of a role in investigations of the foundations of mathematics, although much effort has been expended in replacing individual axioms with simpler ones or in finding systems of axioms which have particular advantages of "naturalness" for intended applications.

In order to characterize the important axiom systems which have been used in the past we shall have to place some limitation on the class of axioms. In the traditional cases the class has been finite. However, the formalization of such an axiomatic system can give rise to an infinite system—for example, if we take as axioms all instances of a certain schema.

The limitation which is used instead of a finite class of axioms is based on the fact that the notions of formula, axiom, and theorem are to be syntactically specified. Then the requirement is that there be a mechanical, or effective, procedure for deciding whether a given formula is an axiom and whether a given inference (of a formula from finitely many premises) is correct according to the rules of inference. This requirement is natural in the light of the idea that a proof of a statement in an axiomatic theory should contain all the mathematically significant information needed to show that the statement is indeed assertible in the theory. That would not be the case, it is argued, if something beyond mechanical checking were needed to determine the correctness of the proof. (It should be pointed out, however, that generalizations of the concept of formal system in which this condition is not satisfied are frequently used in mathematical logic.)

The notion of a formal system gives the highest degree of generality, in that there is no element of the symbolism whose interpretation is restricted. Indeed, it permits much of what we might want to say about an axiomatic theory to be formulated without reference to interpretation, since the formulae, axioms, and rules of inference are specified without reference to interpretation, and what is a theorem is then defined, again without such reference. An entire division of the theory of formal systems—what is usually called syntax—can thus be built up with no more than a heuristic use of interpretation. In particular, the intensional notions—concept, proposition, etc.—relied on so far in the informal exposition can be eliminated.

The concept of a formal system also brings to the formulation of the theory the highest degree of precision, at the cost of a still further idealization in relation to the concrete activities of mathematicians. Furthermore, the concept not only gives a refined formulation to axiomatizations and allows a mathematical study of axiom systems of a more general scope than was possible without it but also makes possible a precise formulation of differences about mathematical methods. Carrying the axiomatic method to this limit makes possible a new approach to a wide variety of questions about the foundations of mathematics.

Inasmuch as axiomatization is a rendering of a theory in a more precise formulation (if not a singling out of some particular aspect of the theory), the axiomatized theory cannot be identified in every respect with what has gone before. It can replace, however, what has gone before and actually has done so in many cases. The passage from axiomatization to formalization is in an important respect more radical than the various stages of informal axiomatization, and we can therefore regard a formalization of a theory as not so much a more precise formulation of the theory as an idealized representation of it. The process of replacing expressions of natural language by artificial symbols, which goes on in all mathematical development, is here carried to an extreme. For example, we lay down by a definition what are "formulae" and "proofs" in the system, whereas informally we rely for the notion of sentences on our more or less unanalyzed linguistic sense, and for proofs we rely on this sense, on mathematical tradition, and on intuitive logic. In particular, formulae and formal proofs are of unbounded length and complexity, without regard to the limits of what we can perceive and understand.

With this goes the fact that the basic general notions with which we operate in formulating and reflecting on theories—sentence, proposition, deduction, axiom, inference, proof, definition—are replaced in the formalized version by specifically defined, more or less simplified and idealized substitutes. In particular, although we "interpret" formalized theories, the relation between a sign or a formal system and its reference in some model is a "dead" correspondence, an aspect of a purely mathematical relation between two systems of objects. This enables one to avoid the intractable problems of how linguistic expressions come to have "meaning" and, with it, reference and is therefore an extremely valuable piece of abstraction. But it is an abstraction; moreover, it does not mean that the informal linguistic and intellectual apparatus disappears altogether, since it will still be used in the setting up and investigation of the formalized theory. In fact, one of the results of formalization is a sharper separation between what is within the theory and what belongs to discourse about it—that is, to the metatheory. If the metatheory is in turn axiomatized and then formalized, the same situation arises at the next-higher level.

The importance of this observation is difficult to assess, but it is relevant to a number of problems we shall discuss later—in particular, attempts to argue from results of mathematical logic to philosophical conclusions.

§2. EPISTEMOLOGICAL DISCUSSION

2.1. A PRIORI KNOWLEDGE. We shall now put the matter of axiomatization and formalization aside and consider mathematics from the point of view of general epistemology. The guiding thread of our discussion will be the fact that a powerful tradition in philosophy has regarded mathematics, or at least a part of it, as a central case of a priori knowledge. This means that reflection on mathematics has been at the center of philosophical discussion of the concept of a priori knowledge.

The characteristics of mathematics which have led to the conclusion that mathematics is a priori are its abstract character and accompanying enormous generality and its great exactitude and certainty, which, indeed, have traditionally been considered absolute. Thus, even before setting forth a developed logical analysis of the concept of number, we find that the effort to interpret "2 + 2 = 4" as a hypothesis that can be checked by observation runs into obvious obstacles. It is perhaps not so vital that the statement refers to abstract entities, numbers, which are not the sort of thing we observe. The concept of number certainly does apply to empirically given objects, in the sense that they can be counted and that the numbers thus attributed to them will obey such laws as "2 + 2 = 4." Therefore, the proposition could so far be taken as a law concerning such entities. Even then its range of application is so enormous, extending over the entire physical universe, that it seems evident that if it were taken as a hypothesis, it would be stated and used in a more qualified way, at least by critically minded scientists. In other words, the certainty that we attribute to elementary arithmetical propositions would be quite unwarranted if they were laws based on observation. Even in the case of math-

ematical principles to which we do not attribute this degree of certainty, such as the axiom of choice and the continuum hypothesis, the possible "contrary evidence" would arise from the deductive development of the theory involved (in the examples, set theory), not from observation.

Moreover, it seems that we ought to be able to conceive of a possible observation which would be a counterinstance. Although it is perhaps not evident that this is impossible, the ideas that come to mind lead either to descriptions of doubtful intelligibility or to the description of situations where it seems obviously more reasonable to assume some other anomaly (such as miscounting or the perhaps mysterious appearance or disappearance of an object) than to admit an exception to "2 + 2 = 4."

Another difficulty is that the concept of number must apply beyond the range of the concrete entities which are accessible to observation; such abstract entities as mathematical objects must be subject to counting, and this seems also to be the case for transcendent entities.

The foregoing considerations could be developed into decisive arguments only with the help of both a more developed formal analysis of number and a more detailed discussion of the relation between arithmetical laws and actual counting and perhaps also of the role of mathematics in empirical science. In any case, they do not tell against another form of the denial that arithmetic is a priori, the view that arithmetical laws are theoretical principles of a very fundamental sort, which we are therefore far more "reluctant to give up" in a particular situation than more everyday beliefs or impressions or even than fundamental theoretical principles in science. Such a view would nonetheless take it to be conceivable that in response to some difficulty in, say, particle physics a new theory might be formulated which modified some part of elementary arithmetic.

2.2. MATHEMATICS AND LOGIC. The above considerations show why it is necessary to add technical analysis to the epistemological discussion. We shall take as our guiding thread the attempt to show that mathematics—in particular, arithmetic—is a part of logic. This attempt has led to some of the most important results in the logical analysis of mathematical notions. The view that mathematics can be reduced to logic is one of the principal general views on the foundations of mathematics which we mentioned earlier; it goes generally by the name of logicism, and its classic expression is in the writings of Frege and Russell.

Even if successful, the reduction of mathematics to logic could not by itself give an account of how there can be a priori knowledge in mathematics, for it would only reduce the problem of giving such an account to the corresponding problem with regard to logic. Nonetheless, the a priori character of mathematics has traditionally been found perhaps slightly less certain than that of logic. The obvious fact that one of the primary tasks of mathematics is the deductive development of theories has been found to be one of the most powerful supports of the claim that mathematics is a priori. We can expect that a successful reduction of mathematics to logic will simplify the problem of a priori knowledge, and not only by replacing two problems by one. Logic is more unavoidable: We cannot get anywhere in thinking without using logical words and inferring according to logical rules. This would suggest that logic is in fact more basic than mathematics and more certainly a priori. (It would also suggest that philosophical treatments of logic are more liable to circularity.) Moreover, in the course of history philosophers have invoked sources of evidence for mathematics which are at least apparently special, such as Kant's pure intuition. Thus, a reduction of mathematics to logic might make superfluous certain difficult epistemological theories.

The claims of logicism are based in large part on mathematical work in axiomatics. A number of nineteenth-century investigations showed that the basic notions of analysis—for example, rational, real, and complex number—could be defined, and the basic theorems proved, in terms of the theory of natural numbers and such more general notions as class and function. At the same time, axiomatic work was done in the arithmetic of natural numbers, culminating in the axiomatization of Richard Dedekind (1888) and Peano (1889). The movement toward formalization began somewhat later, with the work of Frege and of the school of Peano.

Thus, the effort to reduce mathematics to logic arose in the context of an increasing systematization and rigor of all pure mathematics, from which emerged the goal of setting up a comprehensive formal system which would represent all of known mathematics with the exception of geometry, insofar as it is a theory of physical space. (But of the writers of that generation only Frege had a strict conception of a formal system.) The goal of logicism would then be a comprehensive formal system with a natural interpretation such that the primitives would be logical concepts and the axioms logical truths.

We shall be guided by Frege's presentation, although he did not go very far in developing mathematics within his system and of course the system turned out to be inconsistent. Nonetheless, it is already clear from Frege's work how to define the primitives and prove the axioms of a standard axiomatization of arithmetic. We shall begin with some discussions of the notions of number and class, which are crucial for the reduction and for the foundations of mathematics generally.

2.3. COUNTING AND NUMBER. In order to be clearer about the concept of number, we might start with the operation of counting. In a simple case of carefully counting a collection of objects, we perhaps look at and point to each one successively, and with each of these directions of the attention we think of or pronounce one of a standard series of symbols (numerals) in its place in a standard ordering of these symbols. We are careful to reach each of these objects once and only once in the process. We thus set up a one-to-one correspondence between the objects and a certain segment of the series of numerals. We say that the number of objects in the collection is _____, where the blank is filled by the last numeral of the series.

Before pursuing this matter further, let us examine the series of numerals itself. We have certain initial symbols and rules for constructing further symbols whose application can be iterated indefinitely. We could simplify the situation in actual language and suppose that there is one initial symbol, say "|," and a generating operation, concatenation of another "|," so that the numerals will be |, ||, |||, ||||, · · ·, It is not clear, however, that it is merely a matter of "practical convenience" that ordinary numerals are, in the long run, considerably more condensed: If a string of several million "|'s" were offered as a result of counting, one would have to count them to learn what the number was.

However, it is worth asking whether the pure notion of natural number requires more than the possibility of generating such a string of symbols. By "symbols" do we mean here blobs of ink? Only with certain reservations. The particular blobs which we have produced are not at all essential; if we write others—|, ||, |||, ||||, · · ·—they will do just as well. In fact, we could have chosen symbols of quite different forms and still have produced something equivalent for our purposes, such as +, ++, +++, · · ·, or something not consisting of marks on paper at all, such as sounds, which are, of course, actually used. As long as it is capable of representing to us the process of successive generation by which these sequences of symbols are produced, anything will do—any collection of perceptible objects that can be placed in one-to-one order-preserving correspondence with our first sequence of symbols.

Thus, the blobs of ink serve as the representatives of a quite abstract structure. This abstraction allows us (even on a subordinate level) to disregard some limitations of the blobs besides their particularity and accompanying boundedness to a particular place and time. They are constructed according to a procedure for generating successive ones, and what matters is the structure embodied in the procedure, not any particular limitations that might be encountered in carrying it out. On a sufficiently abstract level we say that we can continue to generate symbols indefinitely, although life is too short, paper and ink run out, the earth perhaps disintegrates, etc.

Here we have already taken the step of introducing abstract entities. In a weak form this could be represented as taking certain abstract equivalence relations between entities (e.g., marks on paper) as criteria of identity for new kinds of entities (e.g., symbols as types or, further, numbers). But we have already reached a point where more is involved, since the abstract entities which are represented by all the marks of a given equivalence class belong to a series which can be continued far beyond any practical possibility of constructing representatives. We can create a "pseudo-concrete" model by appealing to space, time, and theoretical physics, but then we are already depending on abstract mathematical objects. Given that we do think of numerals as referring to numbers, it is natural to introduce the apparatus not only of identity but also of quantification. Certain uses of such quantification, however, will involve still stronger presuppositions than we have uncovered up to now, and we shall discuss these when we consider platonism and constructivism.

2.4. AXIOMS OF ARITHMETIC. We have so far taken for granted that the natural numbers are obtained by starting with some initial element 0 and iterating an operation of "successor" or "adding 1." This is the basis for an especially simple axiomatization of the theory of natural numbers, that of Dedekind and Peano, in which the primitives are "0," "number" ("NNx"), and "successor" (which we shall give as a relation: "Sxy" means "y is successor of x"). Then the axioms are

(1) $\qquad\qquad NN0.$

(2) $\qquad NNx \supset (\exists!;y)(Nny \& Sxy).$

(3) $\qquad\qquad \neg S0x.$

(4) $\qquad\qquad Sxz \& Syz . \supset x = y.$

(5) $(F)[F0 \& (x)(y)(Fx \& Sxy . \supset Fy) . \supset (x)(NNx \supset Fx)].$

In (5), "(F)" may be read "for all properties F," but for the present we shall not discuss just what this means. We do not need to suppose that precisely what properties there are is determined in advance, but we have to acknowledge that if it is not determined what properties there are, then it may not be determined precisely what natural numbers there are.

We could think of the natural numbers as given by a kind of inductive definition:

(a) $\qquad\qquad NN0.$

(b) $\qquad\qquad$ If NNx, then $NN(Sx)$.

(c) Nothing is a natural number except by virtue of (a) and (b).

However, in this case we have to suppose that the successor relation is given in such a way that axioms (2), (3), and (4) are evident. We might think of "0" as represented by "|" and the successor function as represented by the addition of another "|" to a string. Then there is apparently an appeal to spatial intuition in regarding these axioms as evident. In that event the induction principle (5) will be in some way a consequence of (c). It could be regarded simply as an interpretation of (c), or one might argue, as Ludwig Wittgenstein apparently did at one time (see Friedrich Waismann, *Introduction to Mathematical Thinking*, Ch. 8), that the meaning of all natural numbers is not given to us by such specifications and our independent concept of "all" and that the induction principle functions as a criterion for a proposition's being true of all natural numbers.

2.5. THE CONCEPT OF CLASS (SET). Before we discuss further the notion of number it is necessary to give some explanation of the notion of class or set. We shall consider two explanations, one suggested by Cantor and one suggested by Frege.

2.5.1. *Frege's explanation.* Instead of the term *class* or *set*, Frege used the phrase "extension of a concept." Frege's usage is based on the tendency to regard the predicates of a language as standing in quantifiable places—

John is a Harvard man.

Henry is a Harvard man.

∴ John and Henry have something in common—

and the tendency to derive from general terms abstract singular terms, which are usually explained as referring to properties or attributes.

These two tendencies can be separated. Frege regarded predicates in context as in fact referring, but to concepts, not to objects. Concepts, like the predicates themselves, have argument places; Frege called both predicates and concepts "unsaturated" because only with the argument place filled by an object (in the case of a predicate, a proper name) could they "stand by themselves." A notation which expresses his conception is that of the second-order predicate calculus, in which the above conclusion might be symbolized (misleadingly) as $(\exists F)[F(\text{John}) \,\&\, F(\text{Henry})]$. An expression which is syntactically appropriate for denoting an object cannot denote a concept, and vice versa.

The extension of a concept, then, is simply an object associated with the concept in such a way that if two concepts apply to the same objects, they have the same extension—that is,

$$(6) \qquad \hat{x}Fx = \hat{x}Gx. \equiv (x)(Fx \equiv Gx),$$

where $\hat{x}Fx$ is the extension of the concept F. This is essentially Frege's famous axiom V (*Grundgesetze der Arithmetik*, Vol. I, p. 36; Frege's notion of concept can interpret the quantifiers in our axiom 5).

2.5.2. Cantor's explanation. Cantor characterized a set as "jedes Viele, welches sich als Eines denken lässt, d.h. jeden Inbegriff bestimmter Elemente, welcher durch ein Gesetz zu einem Ganzen verbunden werden kann" ("every many, which can be thought of as one, that is, every totality of definite elements which can be combined into a whole by a law"; *Gesammelte Abhandlungen*, p. 204). "Unter einer 'Menge' verstehen wir jede Zusammenfassung M von bestimmten wohlunterschiedenen Objekten m unserer Anschauung oder unseres Denkens (welche die 'Elemente' von M genannt werden) zu einem Ganzen" ("By a 'set' we understand any collection M of definite well-distinguished objects of our intuition or thought, which are called the 'elements' of M, into a whole"; p. 282).

It is virtually impossible to explain Cantor's idea of set without using words of the same general type, only vaguer ("collection," "multitude," *Inbegriff*). We can perhaps approach it by mentioning a few ways in which multitudes are thought of as unities: by being thought of by means of a predicate—that is, by being brought under a concept in Frege's sense—so that Frege's extensions could perhaps be regarded as sets, or by being in some way brought to the attention at once, even without the inter-

vention of language; in particular, a finite number of objects of perception can constitute a set. That the objects must be "determinate and well-distinguished" means that it must be determinate what the elements are, that identity and difference be well-defined for the elements, and that a set must be determined by its elements.

One is inclined in this connection to think of a set as "composed" of its elements, but this is not essential and might lead to confusion of a set with a spatiotemporal sum, but a portion of space or time (for example, a geometric figure) can be partitioned in a number of ways, so the sets of the parts will be different but the sum will always be the same.

The picture of finite sets can be extended in such a way that one might imagine an "arbitrary" infinite set independent of any predicate. Suppose it is to be a set S of natural numbers. We go through the natural numbers one by one deciding for each n whether n is a member of S ($n \in S$) or not. Although the determination takes infinitely long, it is determined for each n whether $n \in S$. (Or we might imagine its being done all at once by God.)

2.5.3. Difficulties in these conceptions. Both Cantor's and Frege's conceptions of sets have difficulties which did not come clearly to the consciousness of logicians and set-theorists until the discovery of the set-theoretical paradoxes, discussed below. We shall merely mention here a source of difficulty. In both theories a set or extension is supposed to be an object, capable of being itself a member of sets. Cannot this give rise to circularities—that is, that a set is formed from or constituted by certain objects, among them itself?. (Or, in Frege's terms, among the objects in the range of the quantifiers on the right side of formula 6 are $\hat{x}Fx$ and $\hat{x}Gx$ themselves, so that the identity condition for these objects, which from Frege's point of view was part of their essence, seems to depend on particular facts about them.)

We shall not say anything at the moment about the particular form the difficulties take or about how to resolve them. We shall continue to use second-order quantification somewhat vaguely; one can interpret the variables as ranging over Frege's concepts, in most cases over classes or even over intensional entities, as might have been suggested by our original word "property."

2.6. FREGE'S ANALYSIS OF NUMBER. We can now proceed to the main steps of Frege's argument for the thesis that arithmetic is a part of logic. Frege observed that a necessary and sufficient condition for, say, the number of F's (which we shall write as "$N_x Fx$") to be the same as the number of G's is that there should be a one-to-one correspondence of the F's and the G's. (In that case we say they are numerically equivalent.) This criterion, which is quite general—that is, not restricted to the case where there are only finitely many F's or G's—had already been exploited by Cantor to generalize the notion of cardinal number to infinite classes. It can be justified by our discussion of counting and number, above.

On the basis of a one-to-one correspondence between the F's and $\{1, \cdots, n\}$ we are prepared to say that the number of F's is n. But no such correspondence can then exist with $\{1, \cdots, m\}$ for any $m \neq n$, and if by the same criterion there are n G's, then by composition we can set up a one-to-one correspondence between the F's and the G's. If there are m G's for $m \neq n$, we cannot. So we say that there are n F's if and only if a one-to-one correspondence exists between the F's and $\{1, \cdots, n\}$, and in that case there are n G's if and only if there is a one-to-one correspondence between the F's and the G's. Writing "there are n F's" as "$(\exists x)_n Fx$," we have that if $(\exists n)[(\exists x)_n Fx]$,

(7) $N_x Fx = N_x Gx. \equiv$ the F's and the G's are numerically equivalent.

Since we have no independent criterion for the case where there are infinitely many F's, we take (7) to be true by definition in that case. We then have Frege's criterion.

Frege then defined a relation H as a one-to-one correspondence of the F's and the G's if and only if for every F there is exactly one G to which it bears the relation H and vice versa—in symbols,

(8) $(x)[Fx \supset (\exists! y)(Gy \mathbin{\&} Hxy)] \mathbin{\&} (y)[Gy \supset (\exists! x)(Fx \mathbin{\&} Hxy)]$,

where "$(\exists! x)(\cdots x \cdots)$" can be defined in first-order logic:

(9) "$(\exists! x)(\cdots x \cdots)$" for "$(\exists x)[\cdots x \cdots \mathbin{\&} (y)(\cdots y \cdots \supset y = x)]$".

Thus, numerical equivalence can be defined by a formula "$(\exists H)\mathscr{S}(H,F,G)$," where "$\mathscr{S}(H,F,G)$" is an abbreviation for a first-order formula, namely, the expansion of (8) in terms of (9).

The relation of numerical equivalence is an equivalence relation; Frege's idea was, in effect, to define cardinal numbers as the equivalence classes of this relation. This definition, however, requires a powerful use of the notion of extension which is allowed by his axiom (6). In other words, $N_x Fx$ is to be the extension of the concept concept numerically equivalent to the concept F—that is, we define

(10) "$N_x Fx$" for "$\hat{G}(\exists H)\mathscr{S}(H,G,F)$".

(In fact, in the *Grundgesetze*, Frege avoided applying the extension operator to a second-order variable by appeal to formula 6: G can be replaced by its extension. We define "$\hat{G}\mathscr{F}(G)$" as $\hat{y}(\exists G)[y = \hat{x}Gx . \mathscr{F}(G)]$".)

Formula (10) gives a definition of Cantor's general concept of cardinal number, so we can prove (7); no further use of axiom V is needed for the definition of the natural numbers and the proof of the axioms (1)–(5). We now define Peano's primitives—"0," "Sxy" ("y is the successor of x"), and "NNx" ("x is a natural number"):

(11) "0" for "$N_x(x \neq x)$,"

for then (7) yields $N_x Fx = 0 \equiv \neg(\exists x)Fx$.

Intuitively, $n + 1 = N_x(x = 0 \vee \cdots \vee x = n)$; this result will be reached if we define "Sxy" as follows:

(12) "Sxy" for "$(\exists F)\{y = N_w Fw \mathbin{\&} (\exists z)[Fz \mathbin{\&} N_w(Fw \mathbin{\&} w \neq z) = x]\}$".

Intuitively, the number of F's is one more than the number of G's if there is an F such that the number of the *rest* of the F's is precisely $N_x Gx$. Definition (12) implies that in this case $S(N_x Gx, N_x Fx)$.

The remaining primitive is defined by an ingenious device (already present in Frege's *Begriffsschrift*), which yields mathematical induction: we want to define "NNx" so that something true of 0 and of the successor of anything of which it is true is true of every natural number—that is,

(13) $F0 \mathbin{\&} (x)(y)(Fx \mathbin{\&} Sxy. \supset Fy) . \supset (x)NNx \supset Fx$.

But this will be immediate if we define "x is a natural number" as "x falls under every concept F which 0 falls under and which is such that any successor of whatever falls under it also falls under it"—that is,

(14) "NNx" for "$(F)\{F0 \mathbin{\&} (x)(y)(Fx \mathbin{\&} Sxy. \supset Fy) . \supset Fx\}$".

To prove the other axioms: (1) is immediate from (14); that S is one-to-one and that 0 is not the successor of anything follow from (12) together with (7).

2.7. DIFFICULTIES IN LOGICISM. The first difficulty with Frege's construction is certainly the use Frege made of the notion of extension. We have alluded to difficulties with the ideas of set theory; they affected Frege's system through Russell's deduction in 1901 of a contradiction from (6). (For Russell's initial exchange of letters with Frege, see van Heijenoort, 1967). We shall discuss Russell's paradox and other paradoxes and the difficulties of the concept of class below.

Nonetheless, it turns out that a reasonably secure system of set theory can be developed in any one of a number of ways that are more than sufficient for the definition of Peano's primitives and proof of his axioms. In fact, no part of the axiomatic apparatus of a system of set theory which gives rise to any doubts as to consistency is really necessary for this reduction; we can say that if the development in set theory of a branch of mathematics necessarily involves the stronger and more problematic parts of set theory, this is due to the nature of the branch of mathematics itself, not the reduction to set theory.

This success is not without loss for the development of arithmetic: it seems that in the more natural set-theoretical systems (the theory of types, Zermelo's set theory) no definition of "N_xFx" can be given with the same appearance of naturalness as in (10). The consequences of Russell's theory of types are more serious: The numbers must be duplicated at each type. What one usually ends up doing is identifying the numbers in a somewhat arbitrary way with a sequence of sets of the required order type.

Given that all this has been done, in what sense is the enterprise a reduction of arithmetic to set theory, and in what sense is it a reduction to logic? To take up the last question first, obviously the construction does not reduce arithmetic to logic unless the principles of the set theory involved can count as logical principles. The notion of class is not very far removed from concepts which played a role in traditional logic; from that point of view it is not at all evident why the first-order predicate calculus, which is already a considerable extension of the traditional formal apparatus, should count as logic and the theory of classes should not.

One difference is that whereas a valid formula of first-order logic will yield a truth if the quantifiers are interpreted to range over any domain of objects whatsoever, and without regard to its cardinal number in particular, set theory involves existence assumptions, so the domain over which the quantifiers range must be large enough to contain representatives for the sets whose existence is implied by the formula in question. In Frege's procedure these assumptions were embodied in the admission as a term of an abstract " $\hat{x}Fx$ " for any predicate "F," and simple nonparadoxical instances of (6) already require that Frege's universe contain infinitely many objects.

Frege, of course, regarded (6) as a logical principle, a view which was fairly well refuted by its inconsistency. It would be much more reasonable to regard set theory as logic if its existence assumptions all followed from a single general principle, such as (6). But the analysis of the foundations of set theory stimulated by the paradoxes points to the opposite conclusion: Any very definite system of existential postulates will prove incomplete in the sense that it is always possible to construct further existential postulates that are stronger (in the sense of first-order, or even second-order, logic). Moreover, these postulates assume a character not unlike principles of construction, so it is at least as natural to consider them hypothetical and analogical extensions of "constructions in pure intuition" as it is to consider them principles of logic. At any rate, if logic consists of the necessary principles of all coherent reasoning, then it seems evident that the stronger principles of set theory do not have this character; it is far from certain even that the weaker ones have it (perhaps even that all of first-order logic does). This being so, a reduction of arithmetic to set theory does little to increase the security and clarity of the foundations of arithmetic.

2.8. KANT'S VIEW. One of the purposes that Frege, Russell, and many later proponents had in mind in seeking to reduce arithmetic to logic was to show that no appeal to sensible intuition was necessary in arithmetic, as had been claimed by such empiricists as John Stuart Mill and by Kant in his theory of a priori intuition. Let us consider whether this purpose has been accomplished. Since Kant's view constitutes an independent effort to explain the a priori character of arithmetic, and since it is part of an extremely influential general philosophy, it deserves special mention.

Kant began by insisting that mathematical judgments (at least the most characteristic ones) were synthetic, rather than analytic. We shall not enter into the question of just what he meant by that. Provided that one remembers that the scope of logic was much narrower for Kant than it is for us, it is plausible to suppose that his claim that mathematical judgments are synthetic implies that the propositions of a mathematical theory cannot be deduced from logical laws and definitions. The case of Kant's principal example, the geometry of space, seems clear, given, for instance, the fact that there are consistent geometrical theories which differ with respect to certain fundamental principles, such as the parallel postulate. (Even here, however, one might claim that the difference in principles corresponds to a difference in the meanings of the primitive terms. In application to real space this comes down to the question of "conventionalism" in geometry. W. V. Quine is probably right in holding that one cannot, in general, decide the question whether such a difference is merely a difference of meaning.)

The case of arithmetic presents a certain similarity if we deny that set theory is logic. The proofs in the set-theoretic development even of such elementary arithmetical laws as "2 + 2 = 4" depend on existential axioms of these theories. However, this does not mean that we can come as close to clearly conceiving the falsity of these principles as we can for the principles of geometry. Although we can easily enough set up a domain in which the existence postulates will fail, it is not clear that this counts as conceiving that the numbers $0, 1, 2, \cdots$ should not exist.

Kant went on to maintain that the evidence of both the principles of geometry and those of arithmetic rested on the "form of our sensible intuition." In particular, he said that mathematical demonstrations proceeded by "construction of concepts in pure intuition," and thus they appealed to the form of sensible intuition. Mathematical proof, according to Kant, required the presentation of instances of certain concepts. These instances would not function exactly as particulars, for one would not be entitled to assert anything concerning them which did not follow from the general concept. Nonetheless, conclusions could be drawn which were synthetic, because the construction of the instance would involve not merely the pure concept as of an abstract structure but also its "schematism" in terms of the general structure of our manner of representing objects to ourselves.

Thus, geometric figures would obey the axioms of geometry even though these axioms were not provable by analysis of the concepts. At the same time, the constructions would serve to verify any existence assumptions involved. (Indeed, instead of existential axioms Kant spoke of postulates asserting the possibility of certain constructions.)

In the case of arithmetic Kant argued that in order to verify "7 + 5 = 12" one must again consider an instance, this time in the form of a set of five objects, and add each one in succession to a given set of seven. It seems that although the five objects may be quite arbitrary, even abstract, they will, if not themselves present to perception, be represented by symbols which are present and which exhibit the same structure. In fact, we find this structure even in the symbolic operations involved in the formal proofs of "7 + 5 = 12" either within a set theory or directly from axioms for elementary number theory—or even in the proof of the formula of *first*-order logic

$$(\mathbf{15})\, (\exists x)_7 Fx \,\&\, (\exists x)_5 Gx \,\&\, (x)\neg(Fx \,.\, Gx) \,.\, \supset (\exists x)_{12}(Fx \vee Gx),$$

which is the key to the proof of "7 + 5 = 12" in Frege's construction. We think of "$(\exists x)_n(Fx)$" expanded as follows:

$$\text{"}(\exists x)_0 Fx\text{" for "}\neg(\exists x)Fx\text{".}$$

$$\text{"}(\exists x)_{n+1}Fx\text{" for "}(\exists x)[Fx \,\&\, (\exists y)_n(Fy \,\&\, y \neq x)]\text{".}$$

The arguments for the claim that intuition plays an essential role in mathematics are inevitably subjectivist to a degree, in that they pass from a direct semantical consideration of the statements and of what is required for their truth to a more pragmatic consideration of the operations involved in understanding and verifying them (and perhaps even "using" them, in a broad sense) and to a metalinguistic reflection on formulae and proofs as configurations of symbols. Gottfried Wilhelm Leibniz had already emphasized the essential role of calculation with symbols in mathematics, and to Kant this role became an argument for the dependence of mathematics on sensible intuition.

We can see why the arguments must have this subjectivist character if we notice the complete abstractness of both set theory and arithmetic, which talk of objects in general in terms of logical operations (propositional combination, quantification) which are equally general. Even the specifically mathematical objects (sets and numbers) are subjected by the theory only to certain structural, relational conditions, so that they are not, as it were, individually identified by the theory. The content thus does not suggest any direct sensory verification; indeed, it seems that any proposition which is susceptible of such verification must contain some particular reference to space or time or to objects or properties which by nature occur only in space and time. Although it is Frege's construction and the development of set-theoretic mathematics which make this fact clear, Kant apparently was aware of it in the case of arithmetic, which he related closely to the pure categories and therefore to logic.

Nevertheless, it does not seem, at least in the light of philosophical and mathematical experience, that we can directly verify these propositions, or even understand them, independently of the senses. Determining the precise nature of the dependence of the operations of the mind in general on the senses is one of the central difficulties of all philosophies. But it is hard to maintain that we understand mathematical structures, or even the general notion of object which underlies them, without at least starting with a sensible representation, so that concrete explanations make use both of embodiments of the structures by perceptible objects and of reflection on symbolism. For instance, explanations of the notion of class can either make use of an appeal to language, as Frege's explanation does, or begin with the notion of a group of perceptible objects. (Indeed, it seems that even in the second case an appeal to language is sooner or later indispensable.)

Perhaps more decisive than these rather vague considerations is the fact that we cannot carry on any even fairly elaborate reasoning in mathematics without, as it were, placing ourselves at the mercy of a symbolic representation. Prior to the construction of a proof or calculation we do not know the answer to any substantial mathematical question. That the proof can be constructed, that the calculation turns out as it does, is, as it were, brute fact without which one cannot see any reason for the mathematical state of affairs being what it is. In *Über die Deutlichkeit der Grundsätze der natürlichen Theologie und der Moral*, Kant gave this as his principal reason for asserting that mathematics proceeds by representing concepts in intuition, and in the *Critique of Pure Reason* the idea is again suggested in the discussion of "7 + 5 = 12" and the remarks about "symbolic construction" in algebra.

One might argue that the existence of a natural number *n* is verified by actually constructing a sequence of numerals up to that point. Such a construction provides a representation for the numbers up to *n*. It is noteworthy that either it or a mental equivalent is necessary for a full and explicit understanding of the concept of the number *n*. This gives some plausibility to the view that the possibility of such a representation rests on the "form of our sensible intuition," since everything belonging to the content of the particular realization is nonessential. It is perhaps permissible to speak, as Kant did, of "pure intuition," because we are able to take the symbols as representing or embodying an abstract order. This conception could be extended to the intuitive verification of elementary propositions of the arithmetic of small numbers. If these propositions really are evident in their full generality, and hence are necessary, then this conception gives some insight into the nature of this evidence.

However, the above description already ceases to apply when we pass to the construction, by a general rule, of the sequence of natural numbers and therefore when we consider large numbers, which we must describe in terms of general rules. Besides the "factor of abstraction" signalized in our being able to use sensory representations in thinking about the abstract structures they embody, there is also a factor of higher generality and the accompanying possibility of iteration, so that the sequence of natural numbers extends far beyond those represented by numerals it is possible actually to construct. Here the sense of the notion of "form of intuition" is less clear. Kant's idea, however, must surely be that the larger numbers are conceived only as an extension of the structures of our actual experience. The fact that the forms in question are, according to Kant, those of space and time means that the abstract extension of the mathematical forms embodied in our experience parallels an extension of the objective world beyond what we actually perceive.

Kant connected arithmetic with time as the form of our inner intuition, although he did not intend by this to deny that there is no direct reference to time in arithmetic. The claim apparently was that to a fully explicit awareness of number goes the successive apprehension of the stages in its construction, so that the structure involved is also represented by a sequence of moments of time. Time thus provides a realization for any number that can be realized in experience at all. Although this view is plausible enough, it does not seem strictly necessary to preserve the connection with time in the necessary extrapolation beyond actual experience. However, thinking of mathematical construction as a process in time is a useful picture for interpreting problems of constructivity (discussed below).

Kant's view enables us to obtain a more accurate picture of the role of intuition in mathematics, but, at least as developed above, it is not really satisfying, because it takes more or less as a fact our ability to place our perceptions in a mathematically defined structure and to see truths about this structure by using perceptible objects to symbolize it. The great attraction of Kantianism comes from the fact that other views seem unable to do any better: Frege, for example, carried the epistemological analysis less far than Kant in spite of his enormously more refined logical technique.

2.9. CONVENTIONALISM. Attempts to avoid dogmatism completely while still affirming the existence of a priori knowledge in mathematics have been made on the basis of conventionalism, the characteristic logical positivist view of a priori knowledge. This view in effect rejects the question of evidence in mathematics: Mathematical statements do not need evidence because they are true by fiat, by virtue of the conventions according to which we specify the meanings of the words occurring in mathematics. Mathematics is therefore "without factual content" or even "empty."

Before we proceed to discuss this view we should distinguish it from two others which are associated with logical positivism, the view that mathematical statements are true by virtue of the meanings of the words in them and the view that they are analytic. The doctrine that mathematical statements are true by virtue of the meaning of the words they contain is somewhat vague and is likely to reduce to the doctrine that they are analytic, to conventionalism, or to something compatible with Kantianism or even with some form of direct realism. If there are objective relations of meaning which hold not merely by fiat, then there is as much need in this view for an account of the evidence of our knowledge of them as there is for the evidence of mathematics itself.

The view that mathematics is analytic has generally been associated on one side with logicism and on the other with conventionalism. The definitions of "analytic" that have been given have been such that logical truths were automatically analytic. If the thesis that mathematics is analytic was to say more than the thesis of logicism, the definitions had to be taken as explicating a concept which had a more direct epistemological significance, usually truth by virtue of meanings or truth by convention. (Once this has been done, the connection with logicism seems less important, in spite of the importance that the logical positivists attributed to it. Thus, one may explain the claim that the axioms of set theory are analytic by saying that they are "meaning postulates" in Carnap's sense, but one could argue equally well that the axioms of number theory are meaning postulates. Logicism was important to the logical positivists for other reasons: the reduction served as a methodological paradigm; it served the "unity of science.")

That the propositions of mathematics should be true by convention in a strong sense, that one should actually have set up conventions which determine that they should be true, seems possible only for "rational reconstructions" of mathematics by explicit construction of an axiom system and identification of the system with mathematics. If such a procedure could be carried out, there would still be room for discussion of the sense in which it showed that the mathematics practiced by those who are not interested in foundations is true by convention.

The usual conventionalist position appeals to rules specifying that certain propositions are to be true by convention or, more often, to rules of another sort (such as semantic rules of an interpreted formal system), from which it can be deduced that certain statements are true,

the nature of the premises being such that they can be called conventions governing the use of expressions. (For example, the truth of any statement that is a substitution instance of a theorem of the classical propositional calculus can be deduced from the information contained in the truth tables for the propositional connectives. Then if the truth tables are regarded as semantical rules specifying the meanings of the connectives, then the theorems of classical propositional logic thus become true by virtue of these rules.)

In the simplest case—that of simply laying down, by rules or in individual instances, that certain sentences are to be taken as expressing true statements—something more seems to be required to justify this procedure as attributing "truth" to "statements." No serious philosopher, however, has been content to leave the matter at that.

Nonetheless, the procedure of specifying by rules runs into a difficulty essentially independent of the form of the rules and the manner in which they are interpreted. This difficulty, which was pointed out forcefully by Quine early in his career (in "Truth by Convention") and is perhaps implicit in remarks by Frege, is that the passage from the general statements which are the actual explicit conventions to the truth by convention of specific statements involves inference. So something essentially logical is not, on the face of it, reduced to convention by the analysis. The inferences will assume properties of generality (for example, the properties of the universal quantifiers) and of the conditional, since the rules will in all probability be of the form of conditionals—for instance, they may say that if a statement satisfies certain conditions, then it is true by convention. In the example that we gave, one needs in addition the laws of contradiction and of excluded middle: Application of the truth tables already supposes that each statement has one, and only one, of the two truth-values.

Quine showed that the attempt to regard the rules by which this inference proceeds as themselves valid by convention leads to an infinite regress. For example, suppose a rule is *modus ponens:* from "p" and "$p \supset q$" infer "q". This could be stated as the convention:

(16) If A and C are true and C is the result of substituting A for "p" and B for "q" in "$p \supset q$", then B is to be true.

Now, suppose that for some A' and B' we have proved that A' and C' are true by convention, where

(17) C' is the result of substituting A' for "p" and B' for "q" in "$p \supset q$".

Then we have also

(18) A' is true;

(19) $A' \supset B'$ is true.

Therefore, by (16) and *modus ponens, B'* is true. However, in order to represent this inference as proceeding according to the convention, it is necessary to make another application of *modus ponens,* and so on.

The above argument would not prevent this form of conventionalism from being applied to further parts of mathematics, particularly to existential axioms. In view of the equivalences between derivability statements in logic and elementary propositions in number theory, as well as the above-mentioned element of brute fact in the existence of a derivation, it is not likely that such an approach will work for elementary number theory. But with the stronger axiom systems for set theory the view is on somewhat firmer ground, in that such axioms are often not justified by appeal to direct evidence and "pragmatic" criteria have played a role in the selection of axioms.

Nonetheless, the procedure also has much in common with the setting up of a hypothetical theory in science, and, indeed, as Alfred North Whitehead and Russell already emphasized, the axioms are subject to a sort of checking by their consequences, since some propositions deducible from them are decidable by more elementary and evident mathematical means. It is not evident that if a system of axioms is replaced by another because its consequences come into conflict with intuitive mathematics, the meaning of "set" has changed and the original axioms can be interpreted according to a previous meaning so as to remain true. Moreover, set theory proceeds on the assumption that the truth-value of statements is determinate in many cases where it is not determined by the axioms—that is, by the conventions.

Quine, in fact, now argues, apparently even in the case of elementary logic, that there is no firm ground for distinguishing between making such principles true by convention and adopting them as hypotheses ("Carnap and Logical Truth"). This is as much an extension of conventionalism to the whole of science as a rejection of it in application to mathematics.

2.9.1. *Wittgenstein's view.* At this point we must consider the possibility that a priori truths, even the elementary ones, are thought of as true by convention, not in the sense that they may be made so by an explicit convention actually set up but in the sense that the conventions are, as it were, implicit in our practice with the logical and mathematical vocabulary. It might still be argued that the

principles of mathematics are not in that way sufficiently distinguished from the principles of natural science or from other rather deep or fundamental principles that we firmly accept. But this objection could be met by a more detailed descriptive analysis of how logical and mathematical words are used.

However, this type of conventionalism must be careful not to slip into the situation of the more explicit conventionalism of requiring a necessary connection between general intentions and their application in particular statements which is not itself accounted for by the conventions. It appears that the only philosopher who has really faced these challenges has been Ludwig Wittgenstein, in his later period. In connection with Wittgenstein it would probably be better to speak of "agreement" than convention, since the reference to explicit conventions or to "decisions" seems metaphorical, as a picture which is contrasted with that against which he is arguing rather than as a fundamental theoretical concept. It is agreement in our actions—e.g., what we say follows from what— that is essential. We should also be cautious in attributing to Wittgenstein any explanatory theory of logical and mathematical knowledge, in view of his disclaimers of presenting a theory.

Even with these qualifications Wittgenstein's view seems highly paradoxical, for in order to avoid the above-mentioned pitfall the analysis in terms of agreement must extend even to the connection between general rules and their instances. This seems to be the point of the famous discussion of following a rule in Wittgenstein's *Philosophical Investigations.* What ultimately determines what is intended in the statement of a rule are facts of the type of what is actually accepted in the course of time as falling under it.

Wittgenstein (I, 185) gave the example of instructing someone in writing down the terms of the sequence of natural numbers $0, 2, 4, \cdots, 2n, \cdots$. At the start the instructor does not actively think that when the time comes the pupil is to write $1{,}000, 1{,}002, 1{,}004, \cdots$, rather than $1{,}000, 1{,}004, 1{,}008, \cdots$. Wittgenstein regarded it as conceivable that the pupil might do the second on the basis of a misunderstanding which we just could not clear up. Moreover, it is, as it were, just a fact of natural history that normally, in such a case, we accept the first and reject the second—indeed, continue in that way ourselves. It appears, further, that the same issue can arise for steps in the sequence which have been written before, since the recognition of symbols as tokens of an already understood type is itself an application of a rule (see I, 214).

Wittgenstein's criticism seems directed particularly against certain psychological ideas associated with platonism and Kantianism. The manner in which the steps of writing numerals are determined by the rule cannot be explained by appealing to one's understanding of the relations of abstract entities expressed in the rule or even to the intentions of the instructor. According to Wittgenstein the criterion of how the pupil does understand the rule lies in the steps which he in fact takes. And what makes them right or wrong is their agreement or disagreement with what we do.

The steps are indeed determined by the rule, in the sense that at each stage there is only one number we accept as correct, and the force of social custom directs us to expand the series in the way we do. But this does not mean that Wittgenstein considered his appeals to custom and training as constituting a fully satisfactory explanation of either the agreement that exists or the fact that we feel "compelled" by the rule, for it is because we are made as we are that we react to custom and training as we do.

The paradoxical nature of Wittgenstein's position can perhaps be brought out by considering the case of a complex mathematical proof which contains steps which no one has thought of before. The proof may lead to a quite unexpected conclusion. Yet each step is recognized by every trained person as necessary, and their combination to form the proof is entirely convincing. (This is, of course, not inevitably the case: proofs as published can be obscure or doubtful and can rest on principles about which there are difficulties.) In spite of the fact that it is in principle possible for an irresolvable disagreement to arise at each point, this does not happen: Irresolvable disputes among mathematicians are only about fundamental principles and about taste. Nonetheless, Wittgenstein, in *Remarks on the Foundations of Mathematics*, used the metaphor of decision in speaking of our acceptance of the proof and spoke of the proof as providing a new criterion for certain concepts; his terminology suggests change of meaning.

The vast extent of the agreement on which mathematics rests seems to have astonished Wittgenstein; indeed, it is hard to understand, on his view, how such agreement is possible and why contradictions arise so seldom. We may be faced here with natural facts, but they are facts which show an extremely regular pattern.

Wittgenstein devoted a good deal of attention in the *Remarks* to discussions of calculation and proof, their relation to mathematical truth, and the ways in which they resemble and differ from experiment. In a number of examples he revealed an outlook which resembles Kant's

in seeing a construction either of figures or of arrangements of formulae or propositions as essential to a proof. To the problem concerning how such a singular construction can serve to establish a universal and necessary proposition Wittgenstein suggested a quite different answer: In accepting the proof we accept the construction as a paradigm for the application of a new concept, so that, in particular, we have new criteria for certain types of judgments. (For example, if we have determined by calculation that $25 \times 25 = 625$, then a verification that there are 25×25 objects of a certain kind is also accepted as verifying that there are 625.) The same question arises in connection with the possibility of conflict in these criteria as arose in connection with agreement.

We shall close at this point our discussion of the a priori character of mathematics and the attempts to justify and explain it. In the sense that the concepts of mathematics are too general and abstract to refer to anything particular in experience, their a priori character is evident, at any rate after a certain amount of logical analysis of mathematical concepts. The a priori evidence of mathematics, on the other hand, is perhaps not raised, by our discussion, above the level of a somewhat vague conviction. In the case of the more powerful forms of set theory one is probably forced to admit that the evidence is less than certainty and therefore to admit that there is an analogy between the principles involved and the hypotheses of a scientific theory. In the case of arithmetic and elementary logic, however, this conviction can withstand the objections that might be posed, but in view of the difficulties we have discussed in relation to various accounts, it seems still not to have been analyzed adequately.

§3. PLATONISM AND CONSTRUCTIVISM

The discussion in the preceding section suggests that the problem of evidence in mathematics will appear to differ according to the part of mathematics being emphasized. The form which discussion of these differences has tended to take is a distinction between two broad methodological attitudes in mathematics, which we shall call platonism and constructivism. This section will be devoted to a discussion of these attitudes.

3.1. PLATONISM. We begin with platonism because it is the dominant attitude in the practice of modern mathematicians, although upon reflection they often disguise this attitude by taking a formalist position. Platonism is the methodological position that goes with philosophical realism regarding the objects mathematics deals with.

Mathematical objects are treated not only as if their existence is independent of cognitive operations, which is perhaps evident, but also as if the facts concerning them did not involve a relation to the mind or depend in any way on the possibilities of verification, concrete or "in principle."

This is taken to mean that certain totalities of mathematical objects are well defined, in the sense that propositions defined by quantification over them have definite truth-values. Thus, there is a direct connection between platonism and the law of excluded middle, which gives rise to some of platonism's differences with constructivism.

It is clear that there is a connection between platonism and set theory. Various degrees of platonism can be described according to what totalities they admit and whether they treat these totalities as themselves mathematical objects. These degrees can be expressed by the acceptance of set-theoretic existence axioms of differing degrees of strength.

The most elementary kind of platonism is that which accepts the totality of natural numbers—i.e., that which applies the law of excluded middle to propositions involving quantification over all natural numbers. Quite elementary propositions in analysis already depend on this law, such as that every sequence of rational numbers either tends to the limit 0 or does not, which is the basis for the assertion that any real number is either equal to 0 or not. We shall see that not even this assertion is immune to constructivist criticism.

What is nowadays called classical analysis advances a step further and accepts the totality of the points of the continuum or, equivalently, the totality of subsets of the natural numbers. The equivalence between these totalities and their importance in mathematics were brought out by the rigorous development and "arithmetization" of analysis in the nineteenth century. We recall that the theories of (positive and negative) integers and rational numbers can be developed from the theory of natural numbers by means of the notion of ordered pair alone and that this notion can in turn be represented in number theory. A general theory of real numbers requires general conceptions of a set or sequence of natural numbers to which those of a set or sequence of rational numbers can be reduced.

Following Paul Bernays ("Sur le platonisme dans les mathématiques") we can regard the totality of sets of natural numbers on the analogy of the totality of subsets of a finite set. Given, say, the numbers $1, \cdots, n$, each set is fixed by n independent determinations of whether a given number belongs to it or not, and there are 2^n possible ways of determining this. An "arbitrary" subset of the natural numbers is fixed by an infinity of independent determinations fixing for each natural number whether it belongs to the subset or not. Needless to say, this procedure cannot be carried out by a finite intelligence. It envisages the possibility of sets which are not the extensions of any predicates expressed in a language.

3.1.1. *Impredicative definitions.* The strength of the assumption of the totality of arbitrary subsets of the natural numbers becomes clear if we observe that it justifies impredicative definitions, definitions of sets or functions in terms of totalities to which they themselves belong. A predicate of natural numbers involving quantification over all sets of natural numbers will have a well-defined extension, which will be one of the sets in the range of the quantifier.

Such definitions have been criticized as circular (for example, by Henri Poincaré), but they do not seem so if we understand the sets as existing independently of any procedure or linguistic configuration which defines them, for then the definition picks out an object from a preexisting totality. The resistance that impredicative definitions met with arose partly because their acceptance clashes with the expectation that every set should be the extension of a predicate, or at least of a concept of the human mind.

Given any definite (formalized) notation, we can by Cantor's diagonal method define a set of natural numbers which is not the extension of a predicate in the notation. Thus, no procedure of generating such predicates by continually expanding one's notation can possibly exhaust the totality. And the idea that every set is the extension of a predicate has little sense if it is assumed that in advance of the specification of notations there is a totality of possible predicates which can be arrived at by some generating procedure.

If the statements of classical analysis are interpreted naively, then quite elementary theorems, such as that every bounded set of real numbers has a least upper bound, require impredicative definitions. Nonetheless, in *Das Kontinuum*, Hermann Weyl proposed to construct analysis on the basis of mere platonism with respect to the natural numbers. He proposed an interpretation under which the least upper bound theorem is true. Later interpretations have preserved more of the statements of classical analysis than Weyl's, and it is an involved technical question how much of it can be given a natural predicative interpretation (see below).

3.1.2. *Set theory and the paradoxes.* Set theory as developed by Cantor and as embodied in the present standard systems involves a higher degree, or variety of degrees, of platonism. The axiom system of Zermelo and its enlargement by Fraenkel (which is called the Zermelo-Fraenkel system), for example, allows the iteration of the process of forming the set of all subsets of a given set and the collection into a set of what has been obtained by iterated application of this or some other generating procedure. This latter allows the iteration into the transfinite. If we assume we have transfinite ordinal numbers, then we can generate a transfinite succession of "universes" U as follows: Let $\mathcal{P}(A)$ be the set of all subsets of the set A.

U_0 = a certain class, perhaps empty, of "individuals."

$$U_\alpha + 1 = \mathcal{P}(U_\alpha) \cup U_\alpha.$$

U_α = the union of all U_β, for $\beta < \alpha$, if α is a limit ordinal.

Then for certain ordinals α the U_α will form models for the different systems of set theory ($U_\omega + \omega$ for Zermelo's set theory, without Fraenkel's axiom of replacement).

The paradoxes of set theory imply that we must accept some limitations on forming totalities and on regarding them in turn as mathematical objects—that is, as sets. If, for example, the totality of sets is a well-defined set, then it seems that it will be reasonable to ask of each set x whether it is a member of itself ($x \in x$) or not and to form $\hat{x}(x \notin x)$, the set of all sets which are not members of themselves. This will satisfy

$$(y)[y \in \hat{x}(x \notin x) . \equiv y \notin y],$$

which implies

$$\hat{x}(x \notin x) \in \hat{x}(x \notin x) . \equiv . \hat{x}(x \notin x) \notin \hat{x}(x \notin x).$$

a contradiction. This is Russell's paradox, the most shocking, because the most elementary, of the paradoxes of set theory.

On the same basis one can ask for the cardinal number of the set of all sets, which we shall call S. Then $\mathcal{P}(S)$, the set of all subsets of S, will have a cardinal number no greater than that of S, because $\mathcal{P}(S) \subseteq S$. But by Cantor's theorem the cardinal number of $\mathcal{P}(S)$ is properly greater than that of S (Cantor's paradox, 1895).

If the totality O of ordinals is a set, then, since it is well-ordered, there will be an ordinal number γ that represents its order type. But then O will be isomorphic to the set of ordinals less than γ—that is, to a proper initial segment of itself. This is impossible: γ must be the great-

est ordinal, but there is no obstacle to forming $\gamma + 1$ (Burali-Forti's paradox, 1897).

These paradoxes do not imply that we have to stop or otherwise limit the process, described above, of generating larger and larger universes. On the contrary, we must never regard the process as having given us "all" sets. The totality of sets, and hence the totality of ordinal numbers, cannot be the terminus of a well-defined generating process, for if it were we could take all of what we had generated so far as a set and continue to generate still larger universes.

Thus, suppose we consider the arguments for the paradoxes applied to a particular U_α, as if it were the universe of all sets. The construction precludes $x \in x$, so $\hat{x}(x \notin x)$ is just U_α itself. But $U_\alpha \notin U_\alpha$ and hence is disqualified as a set. The same consideration applies to Cantor's paradox. Burali-Forti's paradox is avoided because the passage from U_α to $U_{\alpha+1}$ always introduces well-orderings of higher order types. Thus, for no α can U_α contain "all" ordinals, no matter how the ordinals are construed as sets. (A very natural way of construing them would be such that α occurs in $U_{\alpha+1}$ but not in U_β for any $\beta \leq \alpha$. But then only for certain ordinals will U_α contain an ordinal for each well-ordered set in U_α.)

For some time after they were first discovered, the paradoxes were viewed with great alarm by many who were concerned with the foundations of mathematics. In retrospect this seems to have been because set theory was still quite unfamiliar; in particular, the distinction between the customary reasonings of set theory and those that led to the paradoxes was not very clear. The opposition that set theory had aroused had not yet died down. However, the marginal character of the paradoxes has seemed more and more evident with time; the systems which were soon devised to cope with the paradoxes (Russell's theory of types and Zermelo's set theory, both published in 1908) have proved satisfactory in that they are based on a reasonably clear intuitive idea, and no one today regards it as a serious possibility that they (or the stronger Zermelo-Fraenkel system) will turn out to be inconsistent. This does not mean that the security and clarity of set theory are absolute; in the sequel some of the difficulties will become apparent.

The above-described sequence of universes uses general conceptions of set and ordinal but applies the characteristic move of platonism only one step at a time. It renounces what Bernays calls "absolute platonism," the assumption of a totality of all mathematical objects which can be treated as itself a customary mathematical object—for example, a set. Such a conception seems definitely destroyed by the paradoxes. The totality of sets can be compared with Kant's "Ideas of Reason": it is an "unconditioned" or absolute totality which just for that reason cannot be adequately conceived by the human mind, since the object of a normal conception can always be incorporated in a more inclusive totality. From this point of view there is an analogy between the set-theoretic paradoxes and Kant's mathematical antinomies.

If we assume that every set will appear in one of the U_α, we have a conception which is adequate for all of modern mathematics except, perhaps, the recent theory of categories. The conception is by nature imprecise: there are limitations on our ability to circumscribe both what goes into the power set of a given set and what ordinals there are. It is perhaps unreasonable to apply classical logic to propositions involving quantification over all sets, since such an application seems to presuppose that it is objectively determined what sets (and a fortiori, on this conception, what ordinals) there are. Nonetheless, this additional idealization does not seem to have caused any actual difficulties.

This way of conceiving sets combines two of Russell's early ideas for resolving the paradoxes—the theory of types and the theory of "limitation of size." What are rejected as sets are the most inclusive totalities, such as the entire universe. (Our talking of "totalities" while rejecting them as sets is not incompatible with our conception; as John von Neumann observed, all that is necessary is to prohibit them from belonging to further classes. Von Neumann's observation was the basis for some new set theories, the principal one being that of Bernays and Gödel.) Moreover, the sets are arranged in a transfinite hierarchy: One can assign to each set an ordinal, its type or, as it is now called, rank, which will be the least ordinal greater than the ranks of its members. We have thus a transfinite extension of the cumulative theory of types. But we have dropped the more radical idea from which Russell proceeded: that each variable of a system of set theory should range over objects of a specified type, and that "$x \in y$" is meaningless unless the range of "y" is of a type one higher than that of "x," so that, in particular, "$x \in x$" is meaningless.

3.1.3. *Predicativism.* In the first twenty-five years or so after the discovery of the paradoxes a number of more radical proposals for their elimination were presented. These generally amounted to some further attenuation of platonism. We shall first consider the program of eliminating impredicative definitions, which amounts to a restriction of platonism to the natural numbers. This was the outcome of the general views of Poincaré and Russell.

Russell's original theory, the ramified theory of types, which formed the basis of *Principia Mathematica*, was directed to the elimination of impredicative definitions, which he held to involve a "vicious circle" and to be responsible for the paradoxes. The effect was, however, nullified by his axiom of reducibility.

A greatly simplified version of the ramified theory is as follows: One has variables, each of which is assigned a natural number as its level, and the predicates of identity and membership. The logic is the usual quantification theory, except that in the rules for quantifiers allowance must be made for levels. Since the levels can be cumulative, we could have for the universal quantifiers the following:

(20) $\qquad (x^i)Fx^i \supset Fy^j$ if $j \le i$;

(21) From "$p \supset Fy^j$" infer "$p \supset (x^i)Fx^i$," where for "p" only something not containing free "y^j" can be substituted.

The axioms are those of identity, extensionality, and the following schema of class existence:

(22) If "F" represents a predicate which does not contain free x^{i+1}, any free variables of level $> i + 1$, or any bound variables of level $> i$,

$$(\exists x^{i+1})(y^i)(y^i \in x^{i+1} \equiv Fy^i).$$

One effect of this axiom is that a predicate involving quantification over objects of level n need not have an extension of level n. Therefore, the axiom does not assert the existence of any impredicative classes; in fact, it is compatible with the idea that classes are constructed by the construction of predicates of which they are the extensions.

Russell's actual theory combined that of a hierarchy of levels, applied in this case to "propositional functions," the objects over which the variables of a higher-order logic were to range, with the "no class" theory, the introduction of locutions involving classes by contextual definition in terms of propositional functions. In order to derive classical mathematics, however, he wanted to avoid dividing the classes into levels. This he did by postulating the axiom of reducibility, which asserts that for every propositional function there is a function of the lowest possible level (compatible with the nature of its arguments) extensionally equivalent to it. Russell admitted that this axiom was equivalent to the existence of classes, and he has never been satisfied with it. In effect, it yields even impredicatively defined classes and destroys the effect of the hierarchy of levels.

A formalization of mathematics on the basis of the ramified theory is the most natural formalization if a platonist theory of classes is repudiated but classical logic admitted. The construction of the natural numbers leads to the difficulty that the class quantifier needed to reduce induction to an explicit definition is no longer available. One must either assume the natural numbers or have a hierarchy of different concepts of natural number.

A ramified theory with the natural numbers as individuals and the Peano axioms would be a natural formalization of the mathematics allowed by platonism with respect to the natural numbers. But there is in principle no reason not to extend the hierarchy of levels into the transfinite. The question of the limits of predicative mathematics has become identical with the question of the transfinite ordinals that can be predicatively introduced.

We have said that quite elementary proofs in analysis already require impredicative definitions when naively interpreted. Nonetheless, from recent work it appears that a good deal of classical analysis is susceptible of a natural predicative interpretation, which, however, fails for some theorems. One can, on this basis, give a good approximation to classical analysis, but not to the whole of it. That part of mathematics which depends essentially on still more powerful set theory is completely lost. It seems that it would not be reasonable to insist on this limitation unless there were some quite powerful reason for rejecting platonism. We shall discuss some possible reasons later.

3.2. CONSTRUCTIVISM. We shall now consider the complete rejection of platonism, which we shall call constructivism. It is not a product of the situation created by the paradoxes but rather a spirit which has been present in practically the whole history of mathematics. The philosophical ideas on which it is based go back at least to Aristotle's analysis of the notion of infinity (*Physics*, Bk. III). Kant's philosophy of mathematics can be interpreted in a constructivist manner, and constructivist ideas were presented in the nineteenth century—notably by Leopold Kronecker, who was an important forerunner of intuitionism—in opposition to the tendency in mathematics toward set-theoretic ideas, long before the paradoxes of set theory were discovered.

Our presentation of constructivism relies heavily on the "intuitionism" of Brouwer, presented in many publications from 1907 on, but the ideas can also be found to some extent in other critics of platonism, including the French school of Émile Borel, Poincaré, and Henri Lebesgue, although in their work predicativity played a greater role than constructivity. These writers did not arrive at a very consistent position, but they contributed mathematically important ideas. L. E. J. Brouwer reached and developed a conclusion from which they shrank: that a thoroughgoing constructivism would require the modification of classical analysis and even of classical logic.

3.2.1. Intuitionism. Constructivist mathematics would proceed as if the last arbiter of mathematical existence and mathematical truth were the possibilities of construction. "Possibilities of construction" must refer to the idealized possibility of construction mentioned in the last section. Brouwer insisted that mathematical constructions are mental. The possibilities in question derive from our perception of external objects, which is both mental and physical. However, the passage from actuality to possibility and the view of possibility as of much wider scope perhaps have their basis in intentions of the mind—first, in the abstraction from concrete qualities and existence; second, in the abstraction from the limitations on generating sequences. In any case, in constructive mathematics the rules by which infinite sequences are generated are not merely a tool in our knowledge but part of the reality that mathematics is about.

Why this is so can be seen from the problem of assertions about the infinite. We have suggested that the generation of a sequence of symbols is something of which the construction of the natural numbers is an idealization. But "construction" loses its sense if we abstract further from the fact that this is a process in time which is never completed. The infinite in constructivism must be "potential" rather than "actual." Each individual natural number can be constructed, but there is no construction which contains within itself the whole series of natural numbers. To view the series *sub specie aeternitatis* as nonetheless determined as a whole is just what we are not permitted to do.

Perhaps the idea that arithmetic rests on time as a form of intuition lies behind Brouwer's insistence on constructivity interpreted in this way. One aspect of sensibility from which we do not abstract in passing from concrete perception to its form is its finite character. Thus, whatever one may think of the notion of form of intuition, Brouwer's position is based on a limitation, in principle, on our knowledge: Constructivism is implied by the postulate that no mathematical proposition is true unless we can in a nonmiraculous way know it to be true.

Because of its derivation from his own philosophical account of mathematical intuition Brouwer called his position, and the mathematics which he constructed on the basis of it, intuitionism. We shall use this name for a species of constructivism which answers closely to Brouwer's ideas.

In spite of the "potential" character of the infinite in mathematics, we shall not renounce assertions about all natural numbers or even, with some reservations, talk of infinite classes. A proposition about all natural numbers can be true only if it is determined to be true by the law according to which the sequence of natural numbers is generated. This Brouwer took to be equivalent to its possessing a proof. Thus, the intensional notions of "law" and "proof" become part of the subject matter of mathematics.

A consideration of existential propositions connects the broad philosophical notion of constructivity with the general mathematical notion. Roughly, a proof in mathematics is said to be constructive if wherever it involves the mention of the existence of something, it provides a method of "finding" or "constructing" that object. It is evident that the constructivist standpoint implies that a mathematical object exists only if it can be constructed; to say that there exists a natural number x such that Fx is to say that sooner or later in the generation of the sequence an x will turn up such that Fx. If x depends on a parameter y, this x must be determinable from y on the basis of the laws of the construction of the numbers and of the constructions involved in F. Proving $(\exists x)Fx$ means showing how to construct x, so one can say that the proof is not complete until x has been exhibited. (But then "proof" is used in an idealized sense.) To prove $(y)(\exists x)Fxy$ must involve giving a general method for finding x on the basis of y.

This point of view leads immediately to a criticism of the basic notions of logic, particularly negation and the law of excluded middle. That "$(x)Fx$" is true if and only if it can be proved does not mean that "$(x)Fx$" is a statement about certain entities called proofs in the way in which, on the usual interpretation, it is a statement about the totality of natural numbers. According to Brouwer we can assert "p" only if we have a proof; the hypothesis that $(x)Fx$ is the hypothesis that we have a proof, and it is a reasonable extrapolation to deny that we can say more about what "$(x)Fx$" asserts than is said in specifying what is a proof of it. The explanation of "$\neg(x)Fx$" as "$(x)Fx$ cannot be proved" does not satisfy this condition. Brouwer said instead that a proof of "$\neg p$" is a construction which obtains an absurdity from the supposition of a proof of "p."

An immediate consequence of this interpretation is that the law of excluded middle becomes doubtful. Given a proposition "p," there is no particular reason to suppose that we shall ever be in possession either of a proof of "p" or of a deduction of an absurdity from "p." Indeed, if the general statement of the law of excluded middle is taken as a mathematical assertion, a proof of it will have to yield a general method for the solution of all mathematical questions. Brouwer rejected this possibility out of hand.

It is evident that such a point of view will lead to changes in quite basic parts of mathematics. Many instances of the law of excluded middle, where the propositions involved can be shown constructively to be systematically decidable, will be retained. But Brouwer rejected even very elementary instances in classical analysis. Let the sequence r_n of rational numbers be defined as follows: if there is no $m \leq n$ such that the mth, $(m + 1)$st, $(m + 2)$d terms of the decimal expansion of π are each 7, then $r_n = 1/2^n$; if there is such an m, then $r_n = 1/2^k$, where k is the least such m. Then r_n constructively defines a real number r. But a proof of either $r = 0$ or $r \neq 0$ would tell us whether or not there are three 7's in the decimal expansion of π. Thus, we cannot assert either $r = 0$ or $r \neq 0$.

For a satisfactory constructivist theory of analysis, an analysis is needed of the notion of an arbitrary set or sequence of natural numbers. Brouwer's analysis gives additional distinctiveness to intuitionism. Such a sequence is thought of as generated by a succession of independent determinations or "free choices," which may be restricted by some law. Obviously the succession of choices must be thought of as never being complete. In the absence of a law a statement about a sequence can be true only if it is determined to be true by some finite initial segment of the sequence. The consequence of this is that a function defined for all sequences of natural numbers whose values are integers must be continuous. It also leads to sharper counterexamples to the law of excluded middle: It is absurd that for all sequences α, either $(x)(\alpha(x) = 0)$ or $\neg(x)(\alpha(x) = 0)$. We can also sharpen the result of the preceding paragraph and state generally that not every real number is equal to or different from 0.

The intuitionist point of view thus leads to a distinctive logic and to a distinctive theory of the foundations of analysis. The latter contains another distinctive principle, the bar theorem, obtained by analyzing the requirement that if a function is defined for all sequences, there must be a constructive proof of this fact. It is roughly equivalent to the proposition that if an ordering is well-founded, transfinite induction holds with respect to it. Nonetheless, intuitionism is far from having shown itself capable of the same rich development as classical mathematics, and it is often very cumbersome. Important as it is in itself, it does not provide a sufficient motive for renouncing platonism.

3.2.2. *Finitism.* So far our account of constructivism has been based entirely on Brouwer's intuitionism. However, intuitionism is not the only possible constructivist development of mathematics. Indeed, it makes some quite powerful assumptions of its own. As we have said, the intuitionists make the notions of construction and proof a part of the subject matter of mathematics, and the iteration of logical connectives, especially, renders it possible to make quite elaborate and abstract statements involving construction and proof. Thus, intuitionist mathematics seems to rest not merely upon intuition but upon rather elaborate reflection on the notion of intuitive construction. (It also does not obviously exclude impredicativity, since what counts as a proof of a given proposition can be explained in terms of the general notion of proof.) A constructivist might feel that intuitionism leads from the Scylla of platonist realism to the Charybdis of speculative idealism.

A weaker and more evident constructive mathematics can be constructed on the basis of a distinction between effective operation with forms of spatiotemporal objects and operation with general intensional notions, such as that of proof. Methods based on operation with forms of spatiotemporal objects would approximate to what the mathematician might call elementary combinatorial methods or to the "finitary method" which Hilbert envisaged for proofs of consistency. Formal systems of recursive number theory, in which generality is expressed by free variables and existence by the actual presentation of an instance or (if the object depends on parameters) a function, will accord with this conception if the functions admitted are sufficiently elementary—for example, primitive recursive functions. In such formalisms any formula will express a general statement each instance of which can be checked by computation. For this reason classical logic can be used. Moreover, the concept of free choice sequence can be admitted so that some analysis can be constructed.

The precise limits of this conception are perhaps not clear, although it is evident that some constructive arguments are excluded. The conception does not allow full use of quantifiers but probably does allow a limited use of them.

3.2.3. *The Hilbert program.* If one accepts the idea that from a philosophical point of view constructivist conceptions are more satisfactory than platonist conceptions—more evident or more intelligible—one is not necessarily constrained to abandon classical mathematics. The way is still open to investigating classical mathematics from a constructive point of view, and it may then prove to have an indirect constructive sense and justification.

Such an investigation was the objective of the famous program of Hilbert, which was the third main animating force—with logicism and intuitionism—in foundational research in the period before World War II. The possibility arises first from the fact that classical mathematics can be formalized (though not completely; we shall consider this fact and its implications later). Once it has been formalized, one can in principle drop consideration of the intended meaning of the classical statements and simply consider the combinations of the symbols and formulae themselves. Thus, if the proof of a certain theorem has been formalized in a system S (say Zermelo-Fraenkel set theory), it is represented as a configuration of symbols constructed according to certain rules. Whether a configuration is a proof can be checked in a very elementary way.

The concepts by which a formal system is described belong, in effect, to finitist mathematics. For example, the consistency of the system is the proposition that no configuration which is a proof will have a last line of a certain form—for example, $\mathcal{A}$ & $\neg\mathcal{A}$. Nonetheless, although in the mathematical study we abstract from the intended interpretation, this interpretation certainly guides the choice of the questions in which we are interested.

Hilbert sought to establish classical platonist mathematics on a firm foundation by formalizing it and proving the consistency of the resulting formalism by finitist means. The interest of the question of consistency depends on the fact that the formulae of the system represent a system of statements; that is, even if the meanings of the platonist conceptions are highly indeterminate, statements in terms of them are introduced according to an analogy with "real" (i.e., finitist) statements which is intended to preserve at least the notions of truth and falsity and the laws of logic.

In fact, Hilbert had a further motive for his interest in consistency: the fact that platonist mathematics is an extension of an extrapolation from finitist mathematics. Certain elementary combinatorial notions are also embodied in the formalism; formulae involving them express "real statements." Hilbert thought of the other formulae as expressing "ideal statements"—analogous to the ideal elements of projective geometry—introduced to give greater simplicity and integration to the theory. Within the system they have deductive relations to the real statements. It would be highly undesirable that a formula of the system should be seen by elementary computation to be false and yet be provable. One might hope to prove by metamathematical means that this would not happen. In the central cases a proof of consistency is sufficient to show that it would not. Thus, suppose we extend a quantifier-free recursive number theory by adding quantifiers and perhaps also second-order quantifiers. A proof of the consistency of the resulting system will show that no false numerical formula (stating a recursive relation of particular integers) will be provable. In fact, it will yield a constructive proof of any formula of the original system provable in the extension, in this sense showing the use of "ideal" elements to be eliminable. Since Hilbert it has been pointed out (chiefly by Georg Kreisel) that many further results relevant to the understanding of nonconstructive mathematics from a constructivist point of view can be obtained from consistency proofs.

Hilbert hoped to settle the question of foundations once and for all, which for him meant establishing the platonist methods of set theory on a firm basis. His hope was founded on two expectations: that all of mathematics (at least all of analysis) could be codified in a single formal system and that the consistency of this system could be proved by methods so elementary that no one could question them. He was disappointed of both these expectations as a result of Gödel's incompleteness theorems (1931). Work on the program has nonetheless continued, with the limitations that one has to work with formalisms which embody only part of the mathematics in question and that the proofs must rely on more abstract, but still constructive, notions; and the work in finitist proof theory has achieved valuable results, some of which will be discussed later.

§4. MATHEMATICAL LOGIC

Our remaining considerations on the subjects of the two preceding sections fit best into an independent discussion of mathematical logic as a factor in the study of the foundations of mathematics. Before World War II an important part of the work in logic was directed toward establishing, in the service of some general position such as logicism or intuitionism, a more or less final solution to the problems of foundations. Certain particular results, and probably also a more diffuse evolution of the climate of ideas, have discouraged this aim. Today nearly all work in mathematical logic, even when motivated by philosophical ideas, is nonideological, and everyone

acknowledges that the results of this work are independent of the most general philosophical positions.

Starting from the axiomatic method in a more general sense, mathematical logic has become the general study of the logical structure of axiomatic theories. The topics selected from the great variety of technical developments for discussion here are Gödel's incompleteness theorems, recursive function theory, developments related to Hilbert's program, foundations of pure logic, and axiomatic set theory.

4.1. GÖDEL'S INCOMPLETENESS THEOREMS.
Research in mathematical logic took quite new directions as a result of the discovery by Kurt Gödel, in 1930, of his incompleteness theorems. According to the first theorem (as strengthened by J. B. Rosser in 1936) any formalism S that is sufficiently powerful to express certain basic parts of elementary number theory is incomplete in the following sense: A formula $\mathcal{A}$ of S can be found such that if S is consistent, then neither $\mathcal{A}$ nor $\neg\mathcal{A}$ is provable in S. The conditions are satisfied by very weak systems, such as the first-order theory Q whose axioms are the Peano axioms for the successor function and the recursion equations for addition and multiplication. (This system is formalized in first-order logic with equality, having successor, addition, and multiplication as primitive function symbols. The axioms are versions of our axioms (1)–(4), recursion equations for addition and multiplication, and an axiom which says that every number not equal to 0 is the successor of something.) They are satisfied by extensions of systems that satisfy them and therefore by the full elementary number theory Z (the first-order version of the Dedekind-Peano axiomatization, obtained from Q by adding induction: in place of the second-order axiom (5) one adds all results of substituting a predicate of the formalism for "F" in (7), by analysis, and by axiomatic set theories in which number theory can be constructed. They are also satisfied by formalizations of intuitionist theories. Evidently adding further axioms offers no escape from this incompleteness, since the new theories will also satisfy the conditions of the theorem.

One of the conditions necessary for some general statements of the theorem is that which we mentioned earlier, that proofs can be checked mechanically. This must be interpreted more precisely in terms of one of the concepts of recursive function, discussed below.

The technique of Gödel's proof is of great interest and has since found wide application. It consists of a mapping of the syntax of the theory into the theory itself, through assigning numbers to the symbols and formulae of the system. Any syntactical relation will then be equivalent to some relation of natural numbers. For the crucial relation "$\mathscr{X}$ is a proof in S of the formula $\mathscr{A}$" the corresponding relation $P(x,a)$ can be expressed in the theory, and certain things about it can be proved in S. Then the undecidable formula $\mathscr{A}$ is a formula which has a number k such that what $\mathscr{A}$ says (about numbers) is equivalent to the unprovability of the formula number k, i.e., $\mathscr{A}$. (1) Then if only true formulae are provable, $\mathscr{A}$ is unprovable. But then $\mathscr{A}$ is true. Therefore, (2) by the same assumption $\neg\mathscr{A}$ is also unprovable. This appeal to the notion of truth was replaced in Gödel's detailed argument by the condition that S be consistent for (1) and ω-consistent for (2). By changing the formula Rosser showed that the assumption of ω-consistency could also be replaced by that of consistency.

The proof that if S is consistent, then $\mathscr{A}$ is unprovable is finitist. If S and the mapping of its syntax into S satisfy some further conditions, the argument can be formalized in S. This yields the second theorem of Gödel. If S is consistent, then the formula which, under the above mapping, corresponds to the consistency of S is unprovable in S.

The first theorem implies not only that mathematics as a whole cannot be codified in a single formal system but also that the part of mathematics that can be expressed in a specific formal notation cannot be so codified. This fact undermines most attempts at a final solution to the problem of foundations by means of mathematical logic. The second theorem was a blow to the Hilbert program in particular. The methods that the Hilbert school envisaged as finitary could apparently be codified in first-order number theory Z; indeed, that they can be so codified seems fairly certain, even though the notion of finitary methods is not completely precise. Therefore, not even the consistency of Z is provable by finitary means. Moreover, the consistency of stronger and stronger systems requires stronger and stronger methods of proof.

There has been much discussion of the broader philosophical implications of Gödel's theorem. We shall not enter into the discussion of such questions as whether the theorem shows the falsity of any mechanistic theory of mind. It should be remarked that there are a number of connections between the surpassing of any given formal system by possible means of proof and the inexhaustibility phenomena in the realm of mathematical existence. Gödel's argument can be viewed as a diagonal argument parallel to that by which Cantor proved that no countable set of sets of natural numbers can exhaust all

such sets. Peano's axioms are categorical if the range of the quantifiers in the induction axiom (5) includes all classes of natural numbers, but in the context of a formal system one can use only the fact that induction holds for classes definable in the system, of which there are only countably many. In set theory the addition of axioms asserting the existence of very large classes can make decidable previously undecidable arithmetical formulae.

4.2. RECURSIVE FUNCTION THEORY. A number of problems in mathematical logic require a mathematically exact formulation of the notion of mechanical or effective procedure. For most purposes this need is met by a concept of which there are various equivalent formulations, arrived at by several writers. The concept of (general) recursive definition, introduced in 1931 by Jacques Herbrand and Gödel, was the first. A function of natural numbers which is computable according to this conception (the "computation" consists of the deduction of an evaluation from defining equations by simple rules) is called a general recursive, or simply a recursive, function. Other formulations are that of λ-definability (Alonzo Church), computability by Turing machine (A. M. Turing), algorithms (A. A. Markov), and different notions of combinatorial system (Emil Post and others).

The concept of recursive definition has proved essential in decision problems. Given a class of mathematical problems defined by some parameter, is there an effective algorithm for solving each problem in the class? As an example consider the tenth problem of Hilbert: Given a polynomial with integral coefficients, is there a general method that tells us whether it has a zero among the integers? If such a question can be resolved in the affirmative, the resolution can generally be reached on the basis of the intuitive conception of an algorithm: If one can invent the procedure, then it is generally clear that the procedure is effective. But to give a negative answer to such a question one needs some idea of the possible effective procedures. The development of recursive function theory has made possible a large number of results asserting the nonexistence of decision procedures for certain classes of problems. This way of interpreting the results depends on a principle known as Church's thesis, which says that the mathematical conception of an effectively computable function in fact corresponds to the intuitive idea—i.e., that a number-theoretic function is (intuitively) effectively computable if and only if it is recursive.

An important type of decision problem is that concerning provability in formal systems. Given a formal system S, is there an algorithm for deciding whether a given formula $\mathcal{A}$ is a theorem of S? If there is, then S is said to be decidable. Although quite interesting examples of decidable systems exist, the systems to which Gödel's first incompleteness theorem applies are undecidable. In fact, Gödel's type of argument can also be used to prove that first-order logic is undecidable (as by Church in 1936).

Another important aspect of recursive function theory is the classification of sets and functions according to different principles related to recursiveness. One such principle, stated in terms of the complexity of possible definitions by recursive predicates and quantifiers (the Kleene-Mostowski hierarchy), not only is of wide application in logic but is closely related to older topological classifications. One can single out the arithmetical sets (those sets definable from recursive predicates by quantification over natural numbers alone), the hyperarithmetical sets (a certain transfinite extension of the arithmetical hierarchy—in effect, those sets definable in ramified analysis with levels running through the recursive ordinals), and the analytic sets (those sets definable from recursive predicates by quantification over numbers and functions, or sets, of natural numbers). The recursive ordinals, singled out by Church and Kleene, can most readily be characterized as the order types of recursive well-orderings of the natural numbers.

The theory of recursive functions is evidently valuable for explicating different notions of constructivity and for comparing classical and constructive mathematics. A constructive proof of a statement of the form "$(x)(\exists y)Fxy$" should yield an effective method of obtaining y from x. For example, Kleene and his collaborators have shown that any statement provable in formalized intuitionist number theory and analysis has a property called "realizability," which amounts roughly to interpreting "$(x)(\exists y)Fxy$" as asserting the existence of a recursive function giving y in terms of x. Although it is also intuitionistically meaningful, the construction gives a classical interpretation of the intuitionist formalisms. It also allows a sharpening and extension of Brouwer's counterexample technique. Certain classically provable formulas can be shown not to be realizable and therefore not to be provable in the intuitionist formalisms Kleene considers.

A problem arises with regard to the relation between the concept of recursive function and the fundamental concepts concerning constructivity—for instance, the concept of intuitionism. One cannot interpret Church's thesis as explicitly defining "effectively computable function" and therefore as giving the meaning of the intuitionist quantifiers. For by definition a function is general recursive if there is a set of equations from which for each possible argument one can compute the value of the function for that argument, a statement of the form "$(x)(\exists y)Fxy$." If this is interpreted constructively, the proposed definition is circular. The relation between "function constructively proved to be everywhere defined" and "general recursive function" is still not clear. One can ask whether every intuitionistically everywhere-defined number-theoretic function is general recursive or whether every (classically) general recursive function can be proved constructively to be such. Neither question has yet been resolved.

4.3. DEVELOPMENT OF THE HILBERT PROGRAM.

For the study of constructivity it is also important to study more restricted types of recursive definition that can be seen by definite forms of argument to define functions. This is particularly important for the extended Hilbert program.

Gödel's second incompleteness theorem meant that the consistency even of elementary number theory Z could not be proved by the methods envisaged by Hilbert. A number of consistency results of the sort envisaged by Hilbert have since been obtained by stronger constructive methods. Gödel and Gentzen proved independently (and finitistically) that if intuitionistic first-order arithmetic is consistent, then so is classical first-order arithmetic. The proofs were based on a quite simple method of translating classical theories into intuitionist theories which is of wide application—for example, to pure logic. One renders an atomic formula P by $\neg\neg P$ (in elementary number theory, equivalent to P itself). If $\mathcal{A}$, $\mathcal{B}$ are translated into $\mathcal{A}°$, $\mathcal{B}°$, respectively, then $\mathcal{A} \vee \mathcal{B}$ is translated by $\neg\neg(\mathcal{A}° \vee \mathcal{B}°)$, $(\exists x)\mathcal{A}$ by $\neg\neg(\exists x)\mathcal{A}°$, $\mathcal{A} \supset \mathcal{B}$ by $\neg(\mathcal{A}° \& \neg \mathcal{B}°)$, $\mathcal{A} \& \mathcal{B}$ by $\mathcal{A}° \& \mathcal{B}°$, $\neg\mathcal{A}$ by $\neg \mathcal{A}°$, and $(x)\mathcal{A}$ by $(x)\mathcal{A}°$. Evidently the translation not only proves relative consistency but also gives each provable formula an intuitionist meaning according to which it is intuitionistically true. If $\mathcal{A}$ is a quantifier-free formula of number theory, or if it is composed with conjunction, negation, and universal quantification only, then if it is provable in Z, it is intuitionistically provable. This translation can easily be extended to ramified analysis. Since intuitionistically the consistency of the intuitionist systems follows from their soundness under the intended interpretation, the consistency of the classical systems has been intuitionistically proved.

A sharper result was obtained in 1936 by Gerhard Gentzen. New proofs, with various advantages and refinements, have since been found by several workers.

Gentzen proved the consistency of Z by adding to finitist arithmetic the assumption that a certain recursive ordering of natural numbers, of order type ϵ_0 (the least ordinal greater than ω, ω^ω, ω^{ω^ω}, $\cdots$), is a well-ordering. This assumption could be proved in intuitionist ramified analysis using set variables only of level 1 but could not in elementary number theory.

Gentzen's result has made it possible to extract further information about the power of elementary number theory. Kreisel obtained information about the relation between elementary number theory and certain quantifier-free arithmetics and also obtained a characterization of the functions which can be proved in Z to be general recursive.

A corresponding result for ramified analysis for finite levels was obtained by Lorenzen in 1951 and sharpened by Kurt Schütte. It was extended by Schütte to transfinite levels.

On the basis of these results we can say that constructive consistency proofs are available for all of predicative mathematics. In well-defined senses they are the best possible results (for instance, the above-mentioned ordinal ϵ_0 cannot be replaced by a smaller one). Nonetheless, efforts to give such a proof for impredicative classical analysis, not to speak of axiomatic set theory, have proved fruitless.

Results of quite recent research have shed considerable light on this situation. Clifford Spector (1962) proved the consistency of classical analysis relative to a quantifier-free theory (Gödel 1958) of primitive recursive functionals of arbitrary finite types, enriched by a new schema for defining functionals by "bar recursion." This amounted to generalizing Brouwer's bar theorem to arbitrary finite types. Such generalized bar recursion has not found a constructive justification, but the method has led to consistency proofs by the original bar theorem for subsystems of analysis which are, according to a reasonable criterion, impredicative.

Kreisel (1963) has shown that intuitionist analysis, with the bar theorem and a strong schema of "generalized inductive definitions" included, does not suffice to prove the consistency of classical analysis. Such a proof requires an essential extension of constructive methods beyond the established intuitionist ones.

Solomon Feferman and Schütte have given an analysis of the notion of predicativity according to which established intuitionist methods go beyond predicative ones. According to their conception, inductive definitions

such as that of the class O of numbers representing the recursive ordinals are impredicative.

What has been the fate of the Hilbert program? Put most broadly, its objective was to secure the foundations of platonist mathematics by a constructive analysis of classical formal systems. The incompleteness phenomena have made it impossible, in dealing with stronger and stronger systems, to avoid the introduction of more and more abstract conceptions into the metamathematics. However interesting the information obtained about the relation between these conceptions and the platonist ones, it is not evident that these conceptions are in all respects more secure. Moreover, in the present state of research it is not certain that strong enough constructive methods can be found even to prove the consistency of classical analysis.

This state of affairs is unfavorable to those methodological views seeking to restrict mathematics to the methods which have the greatest intuitive clarity. It is evident that such methods will not suffice to resolve certain mathematical questions whose content is extremely simple, namely those concerning the truth of certain statements of the form "$(x)Fx$," where "F" stands for a primitive recursive predicate of natural numbers. Proponents of the views in question seem forced to admit that even such questions can be objectively undetermined.

4.4. FOUNDATIONS OF LOGIC. An important result concerning pure logic obtained in finitist metamathematics is a theorem, or cluster of related theorems—including Herbrand's theorem (1931) and Gentzen's theorem (1934)—to the effect that the proof of a formula of first-order logic can be put into a normal form. In such a normal-form proof the logical complexity of the formulae occurring in the proof is in certain ways limited in relation to the complexity of the conclusion; for instance, no formula can contain more nested quantifiers than the conclusion. The proof is, as it were, without detours, and *modus ponens* is eliminated. As a consequence, a quantifier-free formula deduced from quantifier-free axioms can be proved by propositional logic and substitution, which implies all the consistency results proved by the Hilbert school before the discovery of Gödel's theorem. Gentzen's theorem also applies to intuitionist logic and to other logics, such as modal logics.

These theorems, which are the fundamental theorems of the proof theory of quantification theory, are closely related to the fundamental theorem of its semantics, Gödel's completeness theorem. Every formula not formally refutable has a model—in fact, a model in which the quantifiers range over natural numbers; i.e., there are denumerably many individuals. This can be strengthened to the following: If S is any set (finite or infinite) of formulae of first-order logic, it has a denumerable model unless some finite subset of S is inconsistent—that is, unless the conjunction of the subset's members is formally refutable (Skolem-Löwenheim theorem).

This theorem has some quite startling consequences: in particular, it applies if S is the set of theorems of some system of set theory. Then if the system is consistent, S has a denumerable model even though S may contain a theorem which asserts.the existence of nondenumerable sets. That is not a contradiction: If n represents a nondenumerable set in the model, there will indeed be only countably many m's such that $m \in n$ is true in the model, but the assertion "n is nondenumerable" will be true in the model because the model will not contain an object representing the function that enumerates the objects m for which $m \in n$ is true in the model. The model is denumerable only from "outside."

This is an example of a model which is nonstandard in that it differs in some essential way from the intended one. The Skolem-Löwenheim theorem also implies the existence of nonstandard models for systems of number theory. In fact, there is a nonstandard model even for the set S of all true formulae of elementary arithmetic. The number sequence cannot be characterized up to isomorphism by any countable set of first-order formulae.

The existence of denumerable models of set theory illustrates how essential the platonist conception of set, particularly of the set of subsets of a given set, is to set theory. If there is no more to the platonist conception than is specified in any particular formal system, then apparently the cardinal number of a set cannot be objectively determined. Indeed, the cardinal number of a set depends on what mappings there are and therefore on what sets there are.

The acceptance of this relativity has been urged by many, including Skolem. A fully formalist conception would give rise even to the relativity of the natural numbers themselves.

The completeness theorem and the construction of nonstandard models are fundamental tools in a now rapidly developing branch of logic called model theory. This subject can be viewed as a development of logical semantics, but what is perhaps distinctive about the point of view underlying recent work is that it regards a model of a formal theory as a type of algebraic structure and, in general, that it integrates the semantic study of formal systems with abstract algebra. Model theory takes mathematical logic a long way from the philosophical issues with which we have been mainly concerned, in particular by taking for granted a strong form of platonism. The leaders of this development have, in fact, emphasized the application of metamathematical methods to problems in ordinary mathematics.

There are other investigations concerning the foundations of pure logic. For example, we have mentioned that there can be no decision procedure for quantification theory. Nonetheless, there is interest in the question of what subclasses of formulae are decidable. As a striking result in this direction we might mention the proof of A. S. Kahr, E. F. Moore, and Hao Wang (1962) that the existence of models of formulae of the form "$(x)(\exists y)(z)M(x,y,z)$" (or, equivalently, the provability of formulae of the form "$(\exists x)(y)(\exists z)M(x,y,z)$" where "$M(x,y,z)$" is an arbitrary quantifier-free formula, is undecidable. The development of appropriate concepts of model and completeness proofs for modal logics and intuitionist logic has come to fruition in recent years. In the case of the completeness of intuitionist logic, the situation is unclear. E. W. Beth (1956) has given a construction of models in terms of which he proves classically the completeness of intuitionist quantification theory. On the other hand, Kreisel has shown that the completeness of intuitionist logic cannot be proved by methods available in present intuitionist formal systems and, indeed, that it is incompatible with the supposition that all constructive functions of natural numbers are recursive.

4.5. AXIOMATIC SET THEORY. We shall not undertake here to survey the different axiomatic systems of set theory. We shall, however, mention some developments in the metamathematics of set theory, developments concerning the axiom of choice and Cantor's continuum problem.

The axiom of choice asserts (in one formulation) that for every set A of nonempty sets no two of which have a common element, there exists a set B which contains exactly one element from each of the sets in A. This axiom became prominent when Zermelo used it in 1904 to prove that every set can be well-ordered. Although it was much disputed, it came to be applied more and more, so that entire theories of modern abstract mathematics depend essentially on it. Naturally the question arose whether it was provable or refutable from the other axioms of various systems of set theory. A. A. Fraenkel (1922) showed that it could not be proved from Zermelo's axioms, provided that the axioms allowed individuals—that is, objects which are not sets—in the range of the quantifiers.

The continuum problem appears to be an elementary problem in the arithmetic of cardinal numbers: Is there a cardinal between $\aleph_0$, the cardinal of the integers, and $2^{\aleph_0}$, that of the continuum; stated otherwise, does the continuum contain subsets of cardinal number different from that of the continuum and that of the integers? If the answer is negative, then $2^{\aleph_0} = \aleph_1$, the first cardinal larger than $\aleph_0$, and the cardinal of the first noncountable well-ordering. Cantor's conjecture that $2^{\aleph_0} = \aleph_1$ is called the continuum hypothesis.

Gödel, in 1938, proved that the axiom of choice and a generalization of the continuum hypothesis are consistent with the other axioms. The argument applies to a number of different systems, including the Zermelo-Fraenkel system (ZF). What is proved (finitistically) is that if, say, ZF is consistent, it is likewise consistent with a new axiom, the axiom of constructibility, which implies the axiom of choice and the generalized continuum hypothesis. For the constructible sets, which are the sets obtained by extending the ramified hierarchy of types through all the ordinals, can be proved in the system to satisfy all the axioms plus the axiom of constructibility, which says that every set is constructible. In terms of models, any model of ZF contains a subclass that is a model in which all sets are constructible. The constructible sets are of interest on their own account; Gödel has remarked that the idea behind them is to reduce all impredicativities to one special kind, the existence of large ordinals. However, he does not consider the axiom of constructibility plausible.

Thus, it has been known for some time that the axiom of choice and the continuum hypothesis are not refutable from the other axioms. More recently, Paul J. Cohen proved that they are not provable either. That is, if, say, ZF is consistent, it remains so by adding the negation of the axiom of choice or by adding the axiom of choice and the negation of the continuum hypothesis. Starting from Gödel's ideas, Cohen developed a quite new method for constructing models, which has led very quickly to a large number of further independence results.

The situation with respect to the axiom of choice and the continuum problem raises anew the question of how definite our idea of a set is, whether or not such a question as the continuum problem has an objectively determinate answer. Most mathematicians today find the axiom of choice sufficiently evident. But the continuum hypothesis—perhaps because of its more special character and because of the fact that the analogy of the infinite

to the finite on which the conception of the set of all subsets of a given set is based does not suggest a justification of it—is left much more uncertain by considerations of intuitive evidence or plausibility. The role of the Skolem-Löwenheim theorem in Gödel's and Cohen's constructions might encourage the idea that the continuum hypothesis is in fact undetermined. Gödel himself believes that it is false and hopes that an axiom will be found which is as evident as the axiom of choice and which suffices to refute the continuum hypothesis. At present no one seems to have a good idea of what such an axiom would be like. It would have to be of a different character from the usual strong axioms of infinity, to which the method of Gödel's consistency proof applies.

The question of the continuum hypothesis is thus very close to the general epistemological question concerning platonism. If the general conceptions of set and function are given in some direct way to the mind, if, to echo René Descartes, the idea of the infinite is in one's mind before that of the finite, there is no reason to expect a comparatively simple question like the continuum problem to be unanswerable. If, on the other hand, the platonist conceptions are developed by analogies from the area where we have intuitive evidence, if they are "ideas of reason" which, without having an intuition corresponding to them, are developed to give a "higher unity" which our knowledge cannot obtain otherwise, then it would not be particularly surprising if the nature of sets were left indeterminate in some important respect and, indeed, could be further determined in different, incompatible ways.

SUPPLEMENT (2005)

The period since 1967 has seen considerable work in all areas of the foundations of mathematics. This is most notable on the mathematical side. These developments will be discussed before turning to philosophical work.

§5. MATHEMATICAL LOGIC

Of the extensive work since the 1960s, that dealing with formalized axiomatic theories is most central to the foundations of mathematics, although there might now be more debate than earlier about the centrality of the axiomatic method. For some time mathematical logic has been divided into Proof theory, Model theory, Computability (recursion) theory, and Set theory (see the entries on those subjects), although of course there are important interconnections. Model theory and computability theory are more purely mathematical, although their methods are important for the other two areas, and some applications (such as nonstandard analysis) are of foundational interest.

One upshot of work in Proof theory is that strong subsystems of classical analysis (second-order arithmetic) have been analyzed by means that are in some sense constructive but much more powerful and abstract than was envisaged in the early history of the subject. A possibly clearer foundational gain was achieved by another proof-theoretic program, which can trace its roots to Hermann Weyl's (1918) attempt to reconstruct classical analysis predicatively. The work of Harvey Friedman, Stephen Simpson, and others, surveyed in Simpson (1998), showed that many standard theorems of analysis (and of other branches of mathematics) can, if suitably formulated, be proved in weak systems. The method of Reverse mathematics (q.v.) made it possible to calibrate exactly what axiomatic power was needed to prove a particular theorem.

The most striking developments have been in set theory, where Paul Cohen's proof in 1963 of the independence of the axiom of choice and the continuum hypothesis touched off an explosion of research. Cohen's method of forcing proved of wide applicability. In the following years, many more independence results were found in all areas of set theory and its applications. In particular, many classical conjectures were shown both consistent with and independent of the standard axiom system ZFC (or ZF in cases where the axiom of choice sufficed to prove a statement).

This body of work might suggest to a philosopher a vast indeterminacy in the concept of set or of the universe of sets, a random-seeming collection of logical relations among statements independent of ZF or ZFC. However, there is more order than this picture would suggest. The existence of important independent statements would suggest seeking new axioms, and in fact progress has been made by developing the consequences of two kinds of new axioms: strong axioms of infinity (axioms asserting the existence of certain large cardinals) and special cases of the axiom of determinacy.

The large cardinal axioms that have been studied have turned out to be linearly ordered by consistency strength (see §6 of the entry on Set theory), and this has made it possible to determine the consistency strength of other independent statements. In particular this is true of the game-theoretic axiom of determinacy. The assumption PD that the latter holds for projective sets of real numbers (roughly those definable by quantification over

reals) implied solutions to the classical problems of descriptive set theory, the study of these sets. PD (and more) was shown to follow from strong large cardinal axioms.

Although this result left the continuum problem untouched, it did show that a program of investigating new axioms along lines proposed by Kurt Gödel in the 1940s could settle an important class of open problems. The large cardinal axioms implying PD have the desirable feature that their consequences in second-order arithmetic cannot be altered by forcing. W. Hugh Woodin's (2001) approach to the continuum problem (see §6 of the entry on Set theory) aims to extend this result to a higher level. But it is not regarded even by Woodin himself as a definitive solution, and even the question whether the continuum hypothesis has a determinate truth-value remains open.

§6. APPROACHES TO PHILOSOPHY OF MATHEMATICS

In 1967 philosophy of mathematics was largely ancillary to logic, and discussion centered either on logical results or on the earlier foundational programs that had contributed to the development of mathematical logic. Since then it has become more a subject in its own right. It has been influenced by the general tendencies moving the philosophy of science away from logic. In particular, historical studies have assumed a larger role, and many such studies have been of developments not close to logic.

In the earlier entry, the philosophical problems discussed concern the analysis of basic mathematical concepts (such as natural number) and the identification and justification of mathematical principles. The term *foundations* naturally suggests that focus. But the philosophy of mathematics can and does contain inquiries of other kinds. It has been charged with concerning itself only with elementary mathematics. This charge is not correct; for example, identifying the axioms required for conclusions in set theory is a matter of high-level mathematical research, and in general the justification of axioms is not independent of knowledge of the theories developed from them.

But it is true that an inquiry into basic concepts and principles will be selective in its attention to the elaboration of mathematics in current and earlier research. And one may well seek philosophical understanding of aspects of mathematical practice of a different kind. One influential strand of work of this kind is that inaugurated by Imre Lakatos, particularly in his book *Proofs and Refutations* (1976). Lakatos studied a classic theorem of Leonhard Euler (1707–1783) relating the number of vertices, faces, and edges of a polyhedron and brought to light difficulties that had been found with proofs of it over a period of time and the refinements of the statement of the theorem that had resulted. An underlying idea was that mathematical knowledge is more fallible than a certain traditional picture has it, for a different reason from those that might be suggested by difficulties with basic principles. For reasons of space, this sort of inquiry will not be pursued here, but it should be recognized that this strand of philosophy of mathematics has grown relative to the whole since 1967.

§7. LOGICISM AND THE NEO-FREGAN PROGRAM

In §2, much attention is paid to the project of reducing arithmetic to logic and the analysis of number. Logicism in its earlier forms has not been revived, but a kind of neologicism has become an active program. It was observed that the axioms of arithmetic could be derived in second-order logic from the criterion (7) in §2.6, with numerical equivalence defined as in (8). (This is briefly sketched after (12), but the most difficult case, the proof that every natural number has a successor, is omitted.) (7) thus formulated has come (misleadingly) to be called Hume's principle (HP). The second-order theory with the number operator N_xFx and HP as a nonlogical axiom is called Frege arithmetic (FA). In 1983 Crispin Wright gave the proof that the Dedekind-Peano axioms of second-order arithmetic are provable in FA using Frege's definitions, but this was in essentials proved by Gottlob Frege and has come to be called Frege's theorem. Intuitively, Frege uses the definition of N_xFx in terms of extensions only to derive HP, and then the work is done by that principle. Richard G. Heck Jr. showed in 1993 that this was essentially true of Frege's proofs in *Grundgesetze*. Several logicians showed that FA is consistent if second-order arithmetic is.

Wright's neo-Fregean proposal is to take FA as basic arithmetic. It is a logical construction of arithmetic only if the notion of cardinal number is a logical notion and HP is a principle of logic. As a proof that arithmetic is a part of logic the construction seems to be question-begging. Still, it generated a lot of discussion by Wright and others of the status of abstraction principles like HP, which take an equivalence relation of entities of one kind as a criterion of identity for entities of another kind. Wright's initial idea seems to have been that HP is something close to a definition, although it is not an explicit definition and does not meet the usual standard for a

contextual definition, that it should enable the term introduced to be eliminated by paraphrase of contexts in which it occurs. A fatal difficulty for this idea is that HP can be true relative to a domain of individuals only if the domain is infinite. Wright and his collaborators continued to argue that HP is analytic. Others have doubted that a principle that implies the existence of an infinite sequence of objects could be analytic. Another difficulty is that Frege's inconsistent axiom V is an abstraction principle, and other abstraction principles that seem plausible are either inconsistent or can be satisfied only in a finite domain.

The program of axiomatizing parts of mathematics by abstraction principles is of independent logical interest, and work has been done on analysis, and preliminary work on set theory. Kit Fine (2002) carried out an extensive analysis of abstraction principles, to distinguish those that introduce inconsistency from those that do not.

§8. PLATONISM

Since World War II, the view that classical mathematics is seriously threatened by the known paradoxes or by other unknown ones has virtually disappeared. Platonism as described in §3 has been widely accepted as a mathematical method. Taking the language of classical mathematics at face value, as implying the existence of abstract mathematical objects, even forming uncountable and still larger totalities, and allowing reasoning using both the law of excluded middle and impredicative definitions, is probably a default position among philosophers and logicians. This can be called default platonism. It is in relation to such a view, whether accepting it or rejecting it, that much of the work in the philosophy of mathematics since 1967 has concentrated on ontological problems. How might this position be rejected?

§9. CONSTRUCTIVISM

In §3.2, platonism is contrasted principally with constructivism. Intuitionism and other forms of constructivism did not accept the reasoning characteristic of classical mathematics, in the case of intuitionism the law of excluded middle.

A significant development in this area is the argument in favor of intuitionist logic based on considerations of the philosophy of language presented by Michael Dummett (1973). This has, however, had more influence on discussions of realism as a general philosophy than on the foundations of mathematics specifically. Important metamathematical work on intuitionistic theories was done especially in the 1960s and 1970s. An important development is the development of intuitionistic-type theories that are of much greater expressive power than traditional intuitionistic theories. That of Per Martin-Löf (1984) is the most developed. But although intuitionistic logic has proved to have wide application, intuitionism has declined significantly as a general approach to mathematics, competing with classical mathematics. Another constructive approach to mathematics, pioneered by Errett Bishop (1967), has been developed by several mathematicians. Although it has been more active in the last generation than intuitionism, philosophers have been more interested in the latter, perhaps justifiably because what is philosophically interesting about the Bishop approach is shared with intuitionism, and L. E. J. Brouwer and other intuitionists did more to develop philosophical arguments for their position.

§10. NOMINALISM

The term *platonism* is also used so that the view contrasts with nominalism. Since 1980 or so that opposition has been more prominent among philosophers, especially in North America. This is perhaps fundamentally due to the great influence of scientific naturalism on all theoretical parts of philosophy.

The traditional way in which nominalism rejects default platonism is by not taking the language of mathematics at face value and seeking to paraphrase it in such a way that commitment to abstract mathematical objects is avoided. Programs of this kind have been pursued especially since the 1980s, but it has proved essential to enlarge traditional nominalist resources in at least one of two ways: allowing points and possibly regions of space-time as physical or allowing modality. It is then possible to reconstruct a considerable amount of classical mathematics, at least if one accepts a controversial thesis of George Boolos (1998) that his reading of the language of monadic second-order logic by means of the English plural does not involve commitment to such entities as sets, classes, concepts, or pluralities. What has been achieved in this sort of reconstruction is surveyed in John P. Burgess and Gideon Rosen, *A Subject with No Object* (1997).

A bolder proposal was made by Hartry H. Field (1980, 1989): Where he parted from default platonism was in rejecting the view that statements of classical mathematics, taken at face value with regard to meaning, are true and even that mathematics aims at truth. He sought to account for the apparent objectivity of mathematics by viewing it instrumentally, as a device for making inferences within scientific theories. The role of truth is taken over by conservativeness: Given a nominalistic scientific theory T, a mathematical theory M is conservative if adding its resources to those of T does not enable the derivation of conclusions in the language of T that were not already derivable. This committed him to giving nominalistic versions of scientific theories, and (with the previously mentioned assumption about points and regions of space-time) he was able to give such a version of the Newtonian theory of gravitation. Difficulties stand in the way of carrying out this program for modern physical theories.

§11. STRUCTURALISM

Two related intuitions about modern mathematics are widely expressed: that it is the study of (abstract) structures and that mathematical objects have no more of a nature than is expressed by the basic relations of a structure to which they belong. The structuralist view of mathematical objects is a development of the second intuition. Its relation to default platonism is ambiguous. Some versions, which can be called eliminative structuralism, reject one part of that view, taking the language of mathematics at face value, by proposing paraphrases that eliminate reference to mathematical objects or at least to the most typical mathematical objects. Others take the structuralist idea as an explication of what the reference to objects in standard mathematical language amounts to. This noneliminative type of structuralism offers an ontological gloss on default platonism rather than a modification or rejection of it.

A simple case of an eliminative structuralist analysis is a translation of the language of second-order arithmetic into that of pure second-order logic. Suppose A is a sentence of second-order arithmetic. Since arithmetical operations such as addition and multiplication are second-order definable, it can be assumed that A contains as only primitives N (natural number), S (successor), and 0. The structure of the natural numbers is characterized by a second-order sentence with these primitives, the conjunction P of these axioms. If A is provable, the sentence $P \rightarrow A$ is provable by pure logic. If A is true, it is valid in the standard semantical sense. One can regard $P \rightarrow A$ (or the result of replacing $N, S, 0$ by variables) as a translation of A that eliminates reference to numbers. The translation has the difficulty that if there is no structure satisfying the axioms, then $P \rightarrow A$ and $P \rightarrow \neg A$ are both vacuously true. The translation seems to presuppose that P is satisfiable.

One version of structuralism would allow sets as basic objects. This would be a natural way of developing the first intuition, understanding structures as set-theoretic constructs. But a general structuralist view of mathematical objects would naturally aim not to exempt sets from structuralist treatment. At this point modality has been introduced. In the previous example, the assumption that it is possible that there are N, S, and 0 satisfying P is sufficient, since $P \to A$ can be strengthened to $\Box(P \to A)$. The modal structuralism of Geoffrey Hellman (1989) is a version of eliminative structuralism relying on this idea. It includes a detailed treatment of set theory. (An approach had been sketched earlier by Hilary Putnam [1967].)

What these constructions accomplish depends on the status of second-order logic, a question that arises also for the neo-Fregean program and for nominalism. Concerning this there has been much debate. Regarding set theory, there is the additional problem that the presupposition of the possibility of the structure is of a structure of such large cardinality that it could not be witnessed by objects that are in any sense concrete or physical, so that the claim of the construction to eliminate reference to mathematical objects can be questioned.

Other versions of structuralism are suggested by remarks of Willard Van Orman Quine (1969) and of some earlier writers. Noneliminative structuralisms have been worked out in some detail by Michael D. Resnik (1997), Stewart Shapiro (1997), and Charles Parsons (1990). Concerning these views, there is debate about the status of structures, as well as about questions about identity.

§12. ROBUST PLATONISM?

A more robust type of platonism is expressed in Gödel's remark that "the set-theoretical concepts and theorems describe some well-determined reality, in which Cantor's conjecture must be either true or false" (1964, p. 260). Such a view would be supported by whatever general considerations support philosophical realism. But something more is demanded, a certain clarity and unambiguity of set-theoretical concepts and quantification over sets. Gödel wished to argue that the continuum hypothesis (CH) must be either true or false, even though he was unable to determine which. What might reinforce his claims would be a development (such as the work of Woodin [2001]) that determines the truth-value of CH. However, the assumptions of such a result might then be incorporated into a less robust platonist view. Perhaps the greater value of Gödelian realism is as a regulative principle: one is more likely to find answers to mathematical questions if one assumes at the outset that there are answers to be found.

That decisive philosophical arguments can be given for such a realistic stance is unlikely. An alternative is to say that default platonism applied to mathematics as it develops represents the limit of what one should claim about the determinateness of the reality described by mathematical theories. This would be the application to mathematics of the naturalistic stance recommended by Quine in many writings, but without his privileging of empirical science. Such a view was advanced by Hao Wang (1974) and more recently by Penelope Maddy (1997).

Gödel's confidence in set-theoretic concepts has not been universally shared; in particular Solomon Feferman (1998, 1999) has defended a skeptical view, influenced by the earlier predicativist tradition.

§13. EPISTEMOLOGICAL PROBLEMS

In the 1967 entry, the epistemological discussion centered on the question whether mathematics can be shown to be *a priori*. It seems that there has been no decisive advance on this question, so others will be concentrated on here.

Paul Benacerraf (1973) raised in rather abstract terms a problem about mathematical knowledge: If default platonism is true, how can one have mathematical knowledge? One response would be to start from the fact that one evidently does have mathematical knowledge and then question the assumptions that generate the problem. One assumption made in Benacerraf's original formulation, the causal theory of knowledge, is relatively easy to reject. To demand a causal relation between objects referred to in a proposition for knowledge of that proposition seems to stack the deck in advance against abstract objects, and the causal theories that were current when he wrote have not stood up well in general epistemology. But one can see the problem in more general terms: Can one give an epistemology for mathematics that is naturalistic? The most fruitful approach might then be to examine actual mathematical knowledge and to consider what sort of explanation of it makes sense and whether it then meets some standard of naturalism.

No explicit program of this kind has been carried far. One place where one might naturally look for naturalistic explanation is psychology, and there has been a considerable amount of research on the development of concepts of number in young children. Although the questions are often framed in terms of the concept of set, it is not clear that that is essential or that ontology is at all central to the formulation of the problems. It can be argued that mathematical ontology only arises at a more advanced state of the development of mathematical competence than the children investigated have reached.

When one does consider even the mathematics taught in elementary college courses, then what one has to go on is history and the reflection of mathematicians (and sometimes philosophers) on the justification of their claims. That some basic statements and inferences are rationally evident seems an inescapable assumption. Examples would be simple logical inferences and the most elementary axioms of set theory, such as the pairing axiom. It does not mean that this evidence does not get crucial reinforcement from the development of theories based on these evident starting points or that the latter can never be revised in the light of the further development of knowledge. Other assumptions might become evident when an edifice of knowledge has been built up; that might be true of higher-level set-theoretic axioms such as power set and choice. What possible explanations of rational evidence would count as naturalistic is a question that has not been much explored. But now any grounds for holding that no acceptable explanation is possible would have to rely on *a priori* presuppositions.

A less abstract and perhaps more interesting epistemological question arises particularly for higher set theory. It is suggested by the indispensability argument mentioned earlier. Whatever one thinks of rational evidence in general, it is already diminished when one reaches the usual axioms for the mathematics applied in science, as is indicated by the issues about the law of excluded middle raised by Brouwer, and those about impredicativity raised by Poincaré (1908) and Weyl (1918, 1919). However, a long history of successful application convinces one, for example, that the classical mathematics of the continuum is necessary for science and at least as well established as basic physics itself. This is the claim made by the indispensability argument, and it had been suggested earlier by Bertrand Russell and then Gödel that axioms could derive their evident character from the theory they give rise to. Among the applications of mathematics, however, are those within mathematics. Gödel's view apparently was that much of mathematics (including some higher set theory) could be seen to be evident in an *a priori* way, not contaminated by evidence derived from application in empirical science. However, particularly in higher set theory axioms could obtain additional justification through the theories constructed on their basis, and such justification would be possible for stronger axioms, such as the stronger large cardinal

axioms that have been proposed, where a convincing intrinsic justification is not available.

Gödel's view and the indispensability argument have in common that the justification of mathematical axioms can rest at least to a certain degree on their consequences. However, for Gödel this is compatible with the status of mathematics as rational knowledge independent of experience, whereas for the main proponents of the indispensability argument, Quine and Putnam (1971), it is not. The indispensability argument clearly runs out before higher set theory. Empirical science makes no use of it, and indeed it has been argued that from the proof theorist's point of view the mathematical theories that are applied in science are weak.

Since few are satisfied with intrinsic justifications for the strongest axioms of infinity, and little such justification is claimed for determinacy axioms, the accepted solution to the classical problems of descriptive set theory rests on assumptions whose justification depends on the theory they give rise to (see Martin 1998). The same would have to be admitted for any solution to the continuum problem that can be expected in the forseeable future.

§14. HISTORICAL STUDIES

Practically every aspect of the history of the foundations of mathematics has seen some intensive scholarly study in the period since 1967. With respect to Immanuel Kant, a decisive development was Michael Friedman's *Kant and the Exact Sciences* (1992), which integrated Kant's philosophy of mathematics with his philosophy of physics and gave the strongest version of the logical view of the role of intuition in mathematics pioneered by Evert Willem Beth (1959) and Jaakko Hintikka (1974). Younger scholars have followed up Friedman's work, often criticizing aspects of it. In particular they have explored the relation of Kant's thought about mathematics to the mathematics of his own time and earlier and to the philosophy of his immediate predecessors.

One strand of work on Frege, of which Boolos and Heck (see Demopoulos 1995) have been the leaders, has worked out perspicuously the mathematical content of Frege's work, particularly in *Grundgesetze*. Another strand has emphasized his conception of logic and how it differs from our own conception of logic. A third has drawn connections of Frege to nineteenth-century developments in mathematics, particularly geometry.

The foundations of mathematics as an object of special study arose from the revolution in mathematics in the nineteenth century, particularly developments in its second half: the rigorization of the methods of analysis, the beginning of set theory and of abstract methods, the rise of modern logic, and the role assumed early in the twentieth century by the paradoxes. Every aspect of this development has been the subject of scholarly study. The same holds of later developments such as Russell's logic, Brouwer's intuitionism, the Hilbert program, and the work of the Vienna Circle. Space does not permit describing this work, but in the bibliography selective references have been given.

See also Aristotle; Brouwer, Luitzen Egbertus Jan; Cantor, Georg; Carnap, Rudolf; Church, Alonzo; Constructivism and Conventionalism; Descartes, René; First-Order Logic; Frege, Gottlob; Geometry; Gödel, Kurt; Gödel's Theorem; Hilbert, David; Infinity in Mathematics and Logic; Intuitionism and Intuitionistic Logic; Kant, Immanuel; Knowledge, A Priori; Logic, History of; Logical Paradoxes; Mill, John Stuart; Modal Logic; Neo-Kantianism; Neumann, John von; Nominalism, Modern; Peano, Giuseppe; Poincaré, Jules Henri; Proof Theory; Quantifiers in Formal Logic; Quine, Willard Van Orman; Realism and Naturalism, Mathematical; Russell, Bertrand Arthur William; Second-Order Logic; Set Theory; Structuralism, Mathematical; Tarski, Alfred; Turing, Alan M.; Types, Theory of; Weyl, (Claus Hugo) Hermann; Whitehead, Alfred North; Wittgenstein, Ludwig Josef Johann.

Bibliography

TEXTBOOKS

Boolos, George, John P. Burgess, and Richard C. Jeffrey. *Computability and Logic*. 4th ed. New York: Cambridge University Press, 2002. The first edition of this book (by Boolos and Jeffrey) was published in 1974.

Enderton, Herbert B. *A Mathematical Introduction to Logic*. 2nd ed. San Diego: Harcourt/Academic Press, 2001. The first edition of this book was published in 1972.

George, Alexander, and Daniel J. Velleman. *Philosophies of Mathematics*. Oxford, U.K.: Blackwell, 2002.

Shapiro, Stewart. *Thinking about Mathematics*. New York: Oxford University Press, 2000.

Shoenfield, Joseph R. *Mathematical Logic*. Reading, MA: Addison-Wesley, 1967. Reprinted Urbana, IL: Association for Symbolic Logic, 2001.

COLLECTIONS OF PAPERS

Benacerraf, Paul, and Hilary Putnam, eds. *Philosophy of Mathematics: Selected Readings*. 2nd ed. (with revised selection). Cambridge, U.K.: Cambridge University Press, 1983.

Ewald, William, ed. *From Kant to Hilbert: A Source Book in the Foundations of Mathematics*. 2 vols. Oxford, U.K.: Clarendon Press, 1996.

Gödel, Kurt. *Collected Works*, 5 vols. Edited by Solomon Feferman et al. New York: Oxford University Press, 1986–2003. Vol. I, *Publications 1929–1936*, 1986. Vol. II, *Publications 1938–1974*, 1990. Vol. III, *Unpublished Essays and Lectures*, 1995. Volumes. IV and V, *Correspondence*, Oxford: Clarendon Press, 2003.

Hart, W. D., ed. *The Philosophy of Mathematics*. New York: Oxford University Press, 1996.

Shapiro, Stewart, ed. *The Oxford Handbook of Philosophy and Mathematics and Logic*. New York: Oxford University Press, 2005.

Van Heijenoort, Jean, ed. *From Frege to Gödel: A Source Book in Mathematical Logic, 1879–1931*. Cambridge, MA: Harvard University Press, 1967.

§1. The Axiomatic Method

1.1. Axiomatization

Beth, Evert Willem. *The Foundations of Mathematics: A Study in the Philosophy of Science*. Amsterdam, Netherlands: North-Holland, 1959. Parts II and III.

Euclid. *The Thirteen Books of Euclid's Elements*, 3 vols. 2nd ed. Translated by Thomas L. Heath. New York: Dover, 1956. The first edition of this book was published in 1908.

1.2. The abstract viewpoint

Hilbert, David. *Grundlagen der Geometrie*. 10th ed. Stuttgart, Germany: Teubner, 1968. Translated as *Foundations of Geometry* (Chicago: Open Court, 1971). The first German-language edition of this book was published in 1899.

Tarski, Alfred. "What Is Elementary Geometry?" In *The Axiomatic Method*, edited by Leon Henkin, Patrick Suppes, and Alfred Tarski. Amsterdam, Netherlands: North-Holland, 1959.

1.3. Formalization

Church, Alonzo. *Introduction to Mathematical Logic*. Princeton, NJ: Princeton University Press, 1956.

Hilbert, David, and Paul Bernays. *Grundlagen der Mathematik*, 2 vols. 2nd ed. Berlin: Springer, 1968–1970. The first edition of this book was published in 1934–1939.

Kleene, Stephen Cole. *Introduction to Metamathematics*. New York: Van Nostrand, 1952.

Tarski, Alfred. *Introduction to Logic*. New York: Oxford University Press, 1941.

§2. Epistemological Discussion

2.2 Mathematics and logic

Frege, Gottlob. *Grundgesetze der Arithmetik*, 2 vols. Hildesheim, Germany: Olms, 1962. Partly translated by Montgomery Furth as *The Basic Laws of Arithmetic: Exposition of the System* (Berkeley: University of California Press, 1964). The first German-language edition of this book was published in 1893. Vol. 2, 1903.

Frege, Gottlob. *Die Grundlagen der Arithmetik*. Edited by Christian Thiel. Hamburg, Germany: Meiner, 1986. Translated by J. L. Austin as *The Foundations of Arithmetic: A Logico-mathematical Enquiry into the Concept of Number*. 2nd ed. (Oxford, U.K.: Blackwell, 1953). The first German-language edition of this book was published in 1884.

Russell, Bertrand. *Introduction to Mathematical Philosophy*. London: Allen and Unwin, 1919.

Russell, Bertrand. *The Principles of Mathematics*. 2nd ed. London: Allen and Unwin, 1937. The first edition of this book was published in 1903.

Whitehead, A. N., and Bertrand Russell. *Principia Mathematica*, 3 vols. 2nd ed. Cambridge, U.K.: Cambridge University Press, 1925–1927.

2.4. Axioms of arithmetic

Dedekind, Richard. *Was sind und was sollen die Zahlen?* 3rd ed. Braunschweig, Germany: Vieweg, 1911. The first edition of this book was published in 1888. Translation in Ewald.

George and Velleman, above.

Hilbert and Bernays, above.

Kleene, *Introduction*, above.

Peano, Giuseppe. *Arithmetices principia nova methodo exposita*. Turin, Italy: Bocca, 1889. Translation in van Heijenoort.

Waismann, Friedrich. *Introduction to Mathematical Thinking*. New York: Ungar, 1951.

2.5 The concept of class (set)

Benacerraf and Putnam, above. Papers in part IV of 2nd ed. on the concept of set.

Cantor, Georg. *Contributions to the Founding of the Theory of Transfinite Numbers*. Chicago: Open Court, 1915. Translation of papers written from 1895 to 1897.

Cantor, Georg. "Foundations of a General Theory of Manifolds." In Ewald 1996. (With some other short texts.) Translation of a paper of 1883.

Cantor, Georg. *Gesammelte Abhandlungen*. Edited by Ernst Zermelo. Hildesheim, Germany: Olms, 1962. The first publication of this book was in 1932.

Fraenkel, A. A., Yehoshua Bar-Hillel, and Azriel Lévy. *Foundations of Set Theory*. 2nd ed. Amsterdam: North-Holland, 1973.

Gödel, Kurt. "The Present Situation in the Foundations of Mathematics." In Gödel 1986–2003, Vol. III, 45–53.

2.6 Frege's analysis of number

Frege, Gottlob. *Begriffschrift*. Hildesheim, Germany: Olms, 1964. The first publication of this book was in 1879. Translation in van Heijenoort.

Frege, Gottlob. The Foundations of Arithmetic, above.

Frege, Gottlob. Grundgesetze der Arithmetik, above.

George and Velleman, chapter 2.

2.7. Difficulties in logicism

Carnap, Rudolf. "Die logizistische Grundlegung der Mathematik." *Erkenntnis* 2 (1931): 91–105. Translation in Benacerraf and Putnam.

Poincaré, Henri. *Science et méthode*. Paris: Flammarion, 1908. Translated by Francis Maitland as *Science and Method* (New York: Nelson, 1914).

Wittgenstein, Ludwig. *Remarks on the Foundations of Mathematics*. Rev. ed. Translated by G. E. M. Anscombe. Edited by G. H. von Wright, R. Rhees, and G. E. M. Anscombe. Cambridge, MA: MIT Press, 1978.

2.8 Kant's view

Kant, Immanuel. *Kritik der reinen Vernunft*. Riga, Russia: N.p., 1781. Translated by Paul Guyer and Allen W. Wood as *Critique of Pure Reason* (New York: Cambridge University Press, 1998). See especially Introduction (in 2d ed.), Transcendental Aesthetic, Axioms of Intuition, and Discipline of Pure Reason in Dogmatic Use.

Kant, Immanuel. "Untersuchung über die Deutlichkeit der Grundsätze der natürlichen Theologie und der Moral" (1764). In *Gesammelte Schriften*, Vol. 2, 272–301. Berlin: G. Reimer, 1902. Translated by David Walford in *Theoretical Philosophy, 1755–1770* (New York: Cambridge University Press, 1992).

2.9 Conventionalism

Carnap, Rudolf. *Logische Syntax der Sprache*. Vienna, Austria: Springer, 1934. Translated as *Logical Syntax of Language* (London: Routledge and Kegan Paul, 1937).

Carnap, Rudolf. *Meaning and Necessity*. 2nd ed. Chicago: University of Chicago Press, 1956.

Gödel, Kurt. "Is Mathematics Syntax of Language?" In Gödel 1986–2003, Vol. III, 334–362. The introduction by Warren Goldfarb (324–334) questions the interpretation of Carnap as a conventionalist.

Quine, W. V. "Carnap and Logical Truth" (1960). In *The Ways of Paradox and Other Essays*. 2nd ed. Cambridge, MA: Harvard University Press, 1976.

Quine, W. V. "Truth by Convention" (1936). In *The Ways of Paradox and Other Essays*. 2nd ed. Cambridge, MA: Harvard University Press, 1976.

Wittgenstein, Ludwig. *Lectures on the Foundations of Mathematics, Cambridge, 1939*. Edited by Cora Diamond. Ithaca, NY: Cornel University Press, 1976.

Wittgenstein, Ludwig. *Philosophical Investigations*. 2nd ed. Translated by G. E. M. Anscombe. Oxford, U.K.: Blackwell, 1958.

Wittgenstein, Ludwig. Remarks on the Foundations of Mathematics, above.

§3. Platonism and Constructivism

3.1. Platonism

Bernays, Paul. "Sur le platonisme dans les mathématiques." *L'enseignement mathématique* 34 (1935): 52–69. Translation in Benacerraf and Putnam.

Church, Alonzo. "Comparison of Russell's Solution of the Semantical Antinomies with That of Tarski." *Journal of Symbolic Logic* 41 (1976), 747–760. Gives a precise formulation of the ramified theory of types, taking account, as §3.1.3 does not, of its intensional aspect.

Feferman, Solomon. "Systems of Predicative Analysis." *Journal of Symbolic Logic* 29 (1964): 1–30. Part 1 surveys work on predicativity up to 1963.

Gödel, Kurt. "Russell's Mathematical Logic" (1944). In Gödel 1986–2003, Vol. II, 119–141.

Gödel, Kurt. "What Is Cantor's Continuum Problem?" (1947, 1964), In Gödel 1986–2003, Vol. II, 254–270.

Russell, Bertrand. "Mathematical Logic as Based on the Theory of Types" (1908). In *Logic and Knowledge: Essays 1901–1950*, edited by Robert Charles Marsh. New York: Macmillan, 1956.

Weyl, Hermann. "Der *circulus vitiosus* in der heutigen Begründung der Analysis." *Jahresbericht der Deutschen Mathematiker-Vereinigung* 28 (1919): 85–92. Translated as appendix to *The Continuum*.

Weyl, Hermann. *Das Kontinuum*. Leipzig, Germany: Veit, 1918. Translated as *The Continuum* (Kirksville, MO: Thomas Jefferson University Press, 1987).

§3.2 Constructivism

Gödel, Kurt. "Über eine bisher noch nicht benützte Erweiterung des finiten Standpunktes." *Dialectica* 12 (1958): 280–287. Translated in Gödel 1986–2003, Vol. II, 240–251. Note also the expanded English version (1972) in the same volume.

Heyting, Arend. *Intuitionism: An Introduction.* Amsterdam, Netherlands: North-Holland, 1956.

Hilbert, David. "Die Grundlagen der Mathematik." *Abhandlungen aus dem mathematischen Seminar der Hamburgischen Universität* 6 (1928): 65–85. Translation in van Heijenoort.

Hilbert, David. "Über das Unendliche." *Mathematische Annalen* 95 (1926): 161–190. Translation in van Heijenoort.

Hilbert and Bernays, above.

Tait, W. W. "Finitism." In *The Provenance of Pure Reason.* New York: Oxford University Press, 2005. This article originally appeared in the *Journal of Philosophy* (1981).

Troelstra, A. S. *Principles of Intuitionism.* Berlin: Springer, 1969.

Weyl, Hermann. *Philosophy of Mathematics and Natural Science.* Princeton, NJ: Princeton University Press, 1949.

4.1. Gödel's incompleteness theorems

Gödel, Kurt. "Über formal unentscheidbare Sätze der *Principia Mathematica* und verwandter Systeme I." *Monatshefte für Mathematik und Physik* 38 (1931): 173–198. Translated in Gödel 1986–2003, Vol. I, 144–195.

Smullyan, Raymond M. *Gödel's Incompleteness Theorems.* New York: Oxford University Press, 1992.

Gödel's incompleteness theorem is treated in each of the general works on mathematical logic cited above and in many other works.

4.2. Recursive function theory

Kleene, *Introduction*, above.

Rogers, Hartley, Jr. *Theory of Recursive Functions and Effective Computability.* New York: McGraw-Hill, 1967.

4.3. Development of the Hilbert program

Gentzen, Gerhard. *Collected Papers.* Edited by M. E. Szabo. Amsterdam, Netherlands: North-Holland, 1969.

Gentzen, Gerhard. "Die Widerspruchsfreiheit der reinen Zahlentheorie." *Mathematische Annalen* 112 (1936): 493–565. Translated in Gentzen 1969.

Gödel, Kurt. "Zur intuitionistischen Arithmetik und Zahlentheorie." *Ergebnisse eines mathematischen Kolloquiums* 4 (1933): 34–38. Translated in Gödel 1986–2003, Vol. I, 286–295.

Kreisel, Georg. "Hilbert's Programme." *Dialectica* 12 (1958): 346–372.

Kreisel, Georg. "On the Interpretation of Non-finitist Proofs." *Journal of Symbolic Logic* 16 (1951): 241–267; 17 (1952): 43–58.

Schütte, Kurt. *Proof Theory.* New York: Sprinter-Verlag, 1977.

Spector, Clifford. "Provably Recursive Functionals of Analysis." In *Recursive Function Theory, Proceedings of Symposia in Pure Mathematics*, Vol. 5, 1–27. Providence, RI: American Mathematical Society, 1962.

Takeuti, Gaisi. *Proof Theory.* 2nd ed. Amsterdam, Netherlands: North-Holland, 1987. This edition contains important appendices by other authors.

4.4. Foundations of logic

Bell, J. L., and A. B. Slomson. *Models and Ultraproducts.* Amsterdam, Netherlands: North-Holland, 1969.

Gentzen, Gerhard. "Untersuchungen über das logische Schliessen." *Mathematische Zeitschrift* 39 (1934): 176–210, 405–431. Translated in Gentzen 1969.

Gödel, Kurt. "Die Vollständigkeit der Axiome des logischen Funktionenkalküls." *Monatshefte für Mathematik und Physik* 37 (1930): 349–360. Translated in Gödel 1986–2003, Vol. I, 102–123.

Herbrand, Jacques. *Écrits logiques.* Edited by Jean van Heijenoort. Paris: Presses Universitaires de France, 1968. Translated as *Logical Writings* (Dordrecht, Netherlands: D. Reidel, 1971).

Prawitz, Dag. *Natural Deduction: A Proof-Theoretical Study.* Stockholm, Sweden: Almqvist and Wiksell, 1965.

Skolem, Thoralf. *Selected Works in Logic.* Edited by J. E. Fenstad. Oslo, Norway: Universitetsforlaget, 1970. Some of the important papers are translated in van Heijenoort with significant introductions.

Tarski, Alfred. *Logic, Semantics, Metamathematics: Papers from 1923 to 1938.* 2nd ed. Translated by J. H. Woodger. Edited by John Corcoran. Indianapolis, IN: Hackett, 1983. The first edition was published in 1956.

4.5. Axiomatic set theory

Cohen, Paul J. "The Independence of the Continuum Hypothesis." *Proceedings of the National Academy of Sciences, USA* 50 (1963): 1143–1148; 51 (1964): 105–110.

Cohen, Paul J. *Set Theory and the Continuum Hypothesis.* New York: Benjamin, 1966.

Kunen, Kenneth. *Set Theory: An Introduction to Independence Proofs.* Amsterdam, Netherlands: North-Holland, 1980.

Scott, Dana. "A Proof of the Independence of the Continuum Hypothesis." *Mathematical Systems Theory* 1 (1967), 89–111. A lucid presentation using the alternate method of Boolean-valued models.

§5. Mathematical Logic

Barwise, Jon, ed. *Handbook of Mathematical Logic.* Amsterdam, Netherlands: North-Holland, 1977.

Kanamori, Akihiro. *The Higher Infinite.* 2nd ed. Berlin: Springer, 2003.

Simpson, Stephen G. *Subsystems of Second-Order Arithmetic.* Berlin: Springer, 1998.

Woodin, W. Hugh. "The Continuum Hypothesis." *Notices of the American Mathematical Society* 48 (2001): 567–576, 681–690.

See the bibliographies of Computability theory, Model theory, Proof theory, and Set theory.

§6. Approaches to the Philosophy of Mathematics

George, Alexander, and Daniel J. Velleman. *Philosophies of Mathematics.* Oxford, U.K.: Blackwell, 2002.

Grosholz, Emily, and Herbert Breger, eds. *The Growth of Mathematical Knowledge.* Dordrecht, Netherlands: Kluwer Academic, 2000.

Lakatos, Imre. *Proofs and Refutations.* New York: Cambridge University Press, 1976.

Shapiro, Stewart. *Thinking about Mathematics.* New York: Oxford University Press, 2000.

§7. Logicism and the Neo-Fregean Program

Boolos, George. *Logic, Logic, and Logic*. Cambridge, MA: Harvard University Press, 1998.

Demopoulos, William, ed. *Frege's Philosophy of Mathematics*. Cambridge, MA: Harvard University Press, 1995.

Fine, Kit. *The Limits of Abstraction*. New York: Oxford University Press, 2002.

Hale, Bob, and Crispin Wright. *The Reason's Proper Study*. Oxford, U.K.: Clarendon Press, 2001.

Wright, Crispin. *Frege's Conception of Numbers as Objects*. Aberdeen, Scotland: Aberdeen University Press, 1983.

§9. Constructivism

Bishop, Errett. *Foundations of Constructive Analysis*. New York: McGraw-Hill, 1967.

Bishop, Errett, and Douglas Bridges. *Constructive Analysis*. Berlin: Springer, 1985.

Dummett, Michael. "The Philosophical Basis of Intuitionistic Logic" (1973). In *Truth and Other Enigmas* (London: Duckworth, 1978).

Martin-Löf, Per. *Intuitionistic Type Theory*. Naples, Italy: Bibliopolis, 1984.

Troelstra, A. S., ed. *Metamathematical Investigation of Intuitionistic Arithmetic and Analysis*. Berlin: Springer, 1973.

Troelstra, A. S., and D. van Dalen. *Constructivism in Mathematics*, 2 vols. Amsterdam, Netherlands: North-Holland, 1988.

§10. Nominalism

Burgess, John P., and Gideon Rosen. *A Subject with No Object: Strategies for Nominalist Reconstruction of Mathematics*. Oxford, U.K.: Clarendon Press, 1997.

Field, Hartry H. *Realism, Mathematics, and Modality*. Oxford, U.K.: Blackwell, 1989.

Field, Hartry H. *Science without Numbers*. Princeton, NJ: Princeton University Press, 1980.

Malament, David. Review of *Science without Numbers*, by Hartry H. Field. *Journal of Philosophy* 79 (1982): 523–534.

§11. Structuralism

Hellman, Geoffrey. *Mathematics without Numbers*. Oxford, U.K.: Clarendon Press, 1989.

Parsons, Charles. "The Structuralist View of Mathematical Objects." *Synthese* 84 (1990): 303–346.

Putnam, Hilary. "Mathematics without Foundations." *Journal of Philosophy* 64 (1967): 5–22.

Quine, W. V. *Ontological Relativity and Other Essays*. New York: Columbia University Press, 1969.

Resnik, Michael D. *Mathematics as a Science of Patterns*. Oxford, U.K.: Clarendon Press, 1997.

Shapiro, Stewart. *Philosophy of Mathematics: Structure and Ontology*. New York: Oxford University Press, 1997.

§12. Robust Platonism?

Feferman, Solomon. "Does Mathematics Need New Axioms?" *American Mathematical Monthly* 106 (1999): 99–111.

Feferman, Solomon, et al. "Does Mathematics Need New Axioms?" *Bulletin of Symbolic Logic* 6 (2000): 401–446.

Feferman, Solomon. *In the Light of Logic*. New York: Oxford University Press, 1998.

Maddy, Penelope. *Naturalism in Mathematics*. Oxford, U.K.: Clarendon Press, 1997.

Maddy, Penelope. *Realism in Mathematics*. Oxford, U.K.: Clarendon Press, 1990.

Tait, W. W. "Truth and Proof: The Platonism of Mathematics." *Synthese* 69 (1986): 341–370.

Wang, Hao. *From Mathematics to Philosophy*. London: Routledge and Kegan Paul, 1974.

§13. Epistemological Problems

Benacerraf, Paul. "Mathematical Truth." *Journal of Philosophy* 70 (1973): 661–679.

Hauser, Kai. "Is Cantor's Continuum Problem Inherently Vague?" *Philosophia Mathematica* (III) 10 (2002): 257–285.

Maddy, Penelope. "Indispensability and Practice." *Journal of Philosophy* 89 (1992): 275–289.

Martin, Donald A. "Mathematical Evidence." In *Truth in Mathematics*, edited by H. G. Dales and G. Oliveri, 214–231. Oxford, U.K.: Clarendon Press, 1998.

Parsons, Charles. "Reason and Intuition." *Synthese* 125 (2000): 299–315.

Putnam, Hilary. *Philosophy of Logic*. New York: Harper and Row, 1971.

Putnam, Hilary. "What Is Mathematical Truth?" In *Mathematics, Matter, and Method*. 2nd ed. New York: Cambridge University Press, 1979.

§14. Historical Studies

Boolos, George. *Logic, Logic, and Logic*, above. Section on Frege Studies.

Demopoulos, William, ed. *Frege's Philosophy of Mathematics*, above.

Dummett, Michael. *Frege: Philosophy of Mathematics*. Cambridge, MA: Harvard University Press, 1991.

Ewald, William B., ed. *From Kant to Hilbert*, above.

Ferreiros, José. *Labyrinth of Thought: A History of Set Theory and Its Role in Modern Mathematics*. Basel, Switzerland: Birkhäuser, 1999.

Friedman, Michael. *Kant and the Exact Sciences*. Cambridge, MA: Harvard University Press, 1992.

Goldfarb, Warren. "Frege's Conception of Logic." In *Future Pasts: The Analytic Tradition in Twentieth-Century Philosophy*, edited by Juliet Floyd and Sanford Shieh, 25–41. New York: Oxford University Press, 2001.

Goldfarb, Warren, and Thomas Ricketts. "Carnap's Philosophy of Mathematics." In *Science and Subjectivity*, edited by David Bell and Wilhelm Vossenkuhl. Berlin: Akademie-Verlag, 1992.

Gödel, Kurt, *Collected Works*, above. Introductory notes by various writers.

Hallett, Michael. *Cantorian Set Theory and Limitation of Size*. Oxford, U.K.: Clarendon Press, 1984.

Heck, Richard G., Jr. "The Development of Arithmetic in Frege's *Grundgesetze der Arithmetik*" (1993) and other essays reprinted in Demopoulos.

Hintikka, Jaakko. *Knowledge and the Known. Historical Perspectives in Epistemology*. Dordrecht, Netherlands: Reidel, 1974.

Kneale, William, and Martha Kneale. *The Development of Logic*. Oxford, U.K.: Clarendon Press, 1962.

Mancosu, Paolo, ed. *From Brouwer to Hilbert: The Debate on Foundations of Mathematics in the 1920s*. New York: Oxford University Press, 1998.

Parsons, Charles. "Platonism and Mathematical Intuition in Kurt Gödel's Thought." *Bulletin of Symbolic Logic* 1 (1995): 44–74.

Posy, Carl J., ed. *Kant's Philosophy of Mathematics: Modern Essays*. Dordrecht, Netherlands: Kluwer Academic, 1992.

Ricketts, Thomas. "Logic and Truth in Frege." *Aristotelian Society Supplementary Volume* 70 (1996): 121–140.

Shabel, Lisa. "Kant on the 'Symbolic Construction' of Mathematical Concepts." *Studies in the History and Philosophy of Science* 29 (1998): 589–621.

Shabel, Lisa. "Kant's Philosophy of Mathematics." In *The Cambridge Companion to Kant and Modern Philosophy*. Edited by Paul Guyer. New York: Cambridge University Press, forthcoming.

Sieg, Wilfried. "Hilbert's Programs, 1917–1922." *Bulletin of Symbolic Logic* 5 (1999): 1–44.

Sieg, Wilfried, and Dirk Schlimm. "Dedekind's Analysis of Number: Systems and Axioms." *Synthese* forthcoming.

Sutherland, Daniel. "Kant on Arithmetic, Algebra, and the Theory of Proportion." *Journal of the History of Philosophy* forthcoming.

Tait, William. *The Provenance of Pure Reason*. New York: Oxford University Press, 2005. See especially essays 5 and 10–12.

Van Heijenoort, Jean, ed. *From Frege to Gödel: A Source Book in Mathematical Logic, 1879–1931*. Cambridge, MA: Harvard University Press, 1967.

Charles Parsons (1967, 2005)

MATHER, COTTON
(1663–1728)

Cotton Mather, scholar, clergyman, and author, was the oldest son of Increase Mather, one of the leading figures in the Puritan theocracy in Massachusetts. The younger Mather was so precocious that he entered Harvard College at the age of twelve and was graduated at fifteen. Because he stammered, he felt unqualified to preach and therefore began to study medicine. After a few years, however, he overcame his speech handicap and became the assistant to his father at the Second Church, Boston. Ordained in 1685, he remained in the service of the Second Church for the rest of his life.

Mather was disappointed in many of the major quests of his life. Partly because he associated himself politically with the unpopular royal governor, Sir William Phips, partly because of the diminished prestige of the Puritan clergy, and partly because of his own often unpleasant personal qualities he lost the power to wield significant influence in public affairs. When he greatly desired to succeed his father, who retired in 1701 as president of Harvard College, he was not selected. Convinced that Harvard no longer represented the true Calvinist faith, he threw himself energetically into the foundation of Yale College, but its presidency was not offered to him until 1721, when he declined the position because of his age.

Mather's intellectual attitudes during his earlier years were extremely narrow, for he moved within the confines of a strict Puritan worldview; later, however, he became more tolerant of the differing beliefs of others. Finally, especially in his *Christian Philosopher* (1721), he moved close to the natural religion characteristic of the Age of Reason. He interpreted the theological doctrine of divine Providence in philosophical terms by asserting that the order of the universe was planned for man's good by an all-wise, all-good God. Man's appreciation of natural Beauty and his application of reason to observations drawn from nature are sufficient to prove the existence and beneficence of God. His scientific communications to the Royal Society of London led to his election as a fellow in 1713, one of the first Americans to be so honored. He was one of the earliest in the colonies to advocate inoculation against smallpox, and he ably defended his position in several pamphlets. The change in his mental attitude thus epitomizes the alteration in the intellectual life that pervaded his milieu.

Nowhere is this duality more apparent than in Mather's involvement in the witchcraft epidemic in Salem. He attempted to make a "scientific" study of the cases, but he came to the conclusion that they could be treated by prayer and fasting. He warned the judges in witchcraft trials to proceed very cautiously against the suspects and to be particularly careful in admitting "spectral evidence," yet in his *Wonders of the Invisible World* (1693) he argued that the verdicts in the Salem trials were justified. By 1700, however, he changed his mind about the fairness of the trials. In regard to the suspicion of witchcraft, as in other respects, Mather stood uneasily between traditional faith and the new scientific outlook.

See also Philosophy of Religion, History of; Scientific Method.

Bibliography

Mather's most important works (of more than 450 published) are *Magnalia Christi Americana, or the Ecclesiastical History of New England* (London, 1702); *Essays to Do Good* (Boston, 1710; originally titled *Bonifacius*, Boston, 1710); and *Christian Philosopher* (London: E. Matthews, 1721). Kenneth B. Murdock has edited, with introduction and notes, *Selections from Cotton Mather* (New York: Harcourt Brace, 1926; new ed., 1960).

Discussion of Mather may be found in Ralph P. and Louise Boas, *Cotton Mather, Keeper of the Puritan Conscience* (New

York and London: Harper, 1928); Barrett Wendell, *Cotton Mather, the Puritan Priest* (New York: Dodd Mead, 1891; new ed., with introduction by Alan Heimert, New York: Harcourt Brace, 1963); and Otho T. Beall and Richard Shryock, *Cotton Mather, First Significant Figure in American Medicine* (Baltimore: Johns Hopkins Press, 1954).

OTHER RECOMMENDED WORKS

An Edition of Paterna, Cotton Mather's Previously Unpublished Autobiography, Complete, with Introduction and Notes. Edited by Ronald A. Bosco. Diss., University of Maryland, 1975.

Diary of Cotton Mather. Salem, MA: Higginson, 1997.

Mather Microfilm: Part I, The Papers of Cotton Mather. Boston: Massachusetts Historical Society, 1973.

The Papers of Cotton Mather. Boston, MA: Massachusetts Historical Society; Worcester, MA: American Antiquarian Society, 1981.

Paterna: The Autobiography of Cotton Mather. Delmar, NY: Scholars' Facsimiles & Reprints, 1976.

Scheick, William J., ed. *Two Mather Biographies: Life and Death and Parentator.* Cranbury, NJ: Associated University Presses, 1989.

Selected Letters of Cotton Mather. Compiled with commentary by Kenneth Silverman. Baton Rouge: Louisiana State University Press, 1971.

The Witchcraft Delusion in New England; Its Rise, Progress, and Termination, as Exhibited by Dr. Cotton Mather in The Wonders of the Invisible World, and by Mr. Robert Calef in His More Wonders of the Invisible World. Compiled by Samuel Gardner Drake. New York: B. Franklin, 1970.

J. L. Blau (1967)
Bibliography updated by Michael J. Farmer (2005)

MATTER

The term "matter" and its cognates ("material," "materialist," "materialistic," and the like) have played active parts in philosophical debate throughout intellectual history. Natural philosophers have studied material objects and contrasted them with such immaterial agencies as energy and fields of force; metaphysicians and mathematical philosophers have distinguished the material or tangible aspects of things from their formal or intangible aspects, their physical properties from their geometrical ones. Again, the terms "matter" and "material" have played a humble part not only in science but also in moral philosophy and even theology. Matter has thus been placed in opposition to life and mind, soul and spirit, and a preoccupation with worldly pleasures and bodily comforts, as opposed to the "higher" pleasures of the mind, has been condemned as "materialistic" and unworthy of spiritual beings. In thinking about matter, accordingly, the question of how far—if at all—these various distinctions can

actually be justified and reconciled must always be borne in mind.

This question immediately poses a historical problem, for ideas about matter have not been static. On the contrary, they have been subject to continual development, and it is highly doubtful whether one can isolate a single concept of matter shared by, say, Anaximander and Thomas Aquinas, Democritus and René Descartes, Epicurus and Albert Einstein. Thus, for instance, a seventeenth-century philosophical thesis about the relations between mind and matter must be interpreted in relation to seventeenth-century ideas about physics and chemistry. Such a thesis can be transplanted into the intellectual environment of the twentieth century only by taking into account changes in the fundamental concepts of science during the intervening years. We must therefore consider how the concept of matter has been progressively refined and modified in the course of intellectual history.

GREEK PHILOSOPHY

As far as we can judge from the surviving texts and the testimony of Aristotle, the idea of a constituent or material ingredient (*hyle*) common to things of all kinds was a central concept of the Ionian school of philosophy. The Ionian philosophers, beginning with Thales of Miletus, disagreed about the nature of this common ingredient. Some likened it to water, others to air or breath, others to fire; some insisted that it could have no properties analogous to those of any familiar substance but must be entirely undifferentiated or unlimited. Yet they agreed, at any rate, in their statement of the basic philosophical problem: "What universal, permanent substance underlies the variety and change of the physical world?"

It would be a mistake, however, to think of the Ionians as materialists in the modern sense. As they conceived it, the universal material of things was far from being brute, inorganic, passive, mindless stuff intrinsically devoid of all higher properties or capabilities. Water, for instance, was, for them, not a sterile, inorganic chemical but a fertilizing fluid, and in their system it was quite open to consideration whether the basic stuff of the world might not be provided by either spirit (pneuma) or mind (nous). At this initial stage in philosophical speculation, indeed, the questions preoccupying philosophers cut across many of the distinctions that later generations were to treat as fundamental.

We first find these distinctions being drawn explicitly and insisted on by the Athenian philosophers, following the examples of Plato and Aristotle. For instance, Plato and his fellow mathematicians at the Academy explained the properties of homogeneous material substances in one way, those of organized, functional systems in another. Like the Sicilian philosopher Empedocles, they classified material substances into four contrasted states or kinds—solid (earth), aeriform (air), liquid (water), and fiery (fire)—but they added a novel mathematical theory to account for the contrasted properties of these four kinds of substance. Each kind, they supposed, had atoms of a distinct geometrical shape, and they hypothetically identified these shapes with four of the five regular convex solids—tetrahedron, cube, octahedron, and icosahedron—whose mathematical properties had been studied by Plato's associate Theaetetus. (The fifth solid, the dodecahedron, they associated with the twelve constellations of the outer heavens.) The characteristic properties of organisms, on the other hand, they explained in functional rather than material terms. The form of any bodily organ must be accounted for as reflecting its role in the life of the organism; this form should be thought of as created specifically to perform a particular function as effectively as the available materials permitted.

Aristotle went further. He distinguished sharply between the material substance of which an object was composed and the form imposed on it, and he questioned whether the characteristic properties of any substance or system could be usefully explained in either atomistic or geometrical terms. In order to understand the properties and behavior of any individual object, it was first necessary to recognize it as an object of a particular kind. Each kind of object existing in nature had properties determined by its own special form or essence, so that any universal primary stuff (*hyle*) must be devoid of any particular distinguishing characteristic. For Aristotle and his followers the problem of distinguishing substances became primarily a matter of taxonomy, of qualitative classification, rather than a quantitative, physicochemical problem. Weight, from this point of view, was just one possible quality among others. Aristotle's views went beyond those of Plato in one other respect that was to have profound implications for cosmology. He drew a clear distinction between the sublunary world, whose objects were composed of the four terrestrial elements—earth, air, fire, and water—and could be created and destroyed, and the superlunary or celestial world of the outer heavens, whose inhabitants were composed of the quintessence (fifth essence) and exempted from change and decay. Of all terrestrial things only the souls of rational beings in any way shared this immutability.

LATER CLASSICAL AND MEDIEVAL PERIODS

Subsequent philosophers—whether in Hellenistic Alexandria (200 BCE–550 CE), the Islamic centers of learning (650–1150), or the newly founded universities of western Europe (950–1500)—introduced a number of variations into the debate about matter without adding any fundamentally new themes. For both the Stoics and the Epicureans, ideas about matter were closely associated with religious beliefs. Epicurus and his followers—notably, the Roman poet Lucretius—developed the more fragmentary speculations of Democritus and Leucippus about the atomic structure of matter into a complete philosophical system. But the atoms of the Greek philosophers differed from those of nineteenth-century European science in three crucial respects. First, they had an indefinitely large range of sizes and shapes instead of a limited number of fixed forms, one for each chemical "element." Next, they interacted only by direct contact or impact rather than by exerting forces of attraction or repulsion on one another. And, finally, they existed in special varieties—atoms of magnetism, of life, of mind, and of soul—to explain all sorts of activities—physical, biological, psychological, and even spiritual. The collisions and conjunctions of these atoms were regarded by Epicurus as an autonomous physical process, for his fundamental aim was to attack any belief in external interference by divine agencies in the affairs of the natural world.

The Stoics, such as Zeno of Citium and Chrysippus, rejected atoms in favor of three kinds of continuous physical medium or spirit (pneuma) for both scientific and religious purposes. The pneuma was an integrative agency, analogous to a field of force, capable of maintaining a stable pattern of properties and behavior in a physical system; in addition, it was capable of existing in separation from the solid and liquid frame of the "body" and could probably be identified with the soul. Instead of rejecting the traditional deities, like the Epicureans, the Stoics reinterpreted them as incorporeal agencies comparable to the pneuma. Yet though the Stoics and the Epicureans differed about many things, they agreed that every agency capable of producing physical effects—even the mind—must be regarded as a material body (soma). As a result for Lucretius pure mind was composed of very smooth and mobile atoms; for Chrysippus it consisted of undiluted fire.

The alchemical philosophers, for their part, introduced an experimental element into the study of matter. Beginning with the Democritean Bolos of Mendes (c. 200

BCE), going on through Maria the Jewess and Zozimos of Alexandria (second and third centuries CE), the alchemists exploited the traditional craft techniques of the Middle Eastern metallurgists, dyers, and jewelers and attempted to find ways of separating and isolating the essences or spirits in things. In this way they were led to contrast volatile and chemically active substances, such as alcohol and ether (spirits), with solid and passive ones, such as earths and *calces* (bodies). The association of the soul and the body in living creatures was thus treated as analogous to the association of volatile and gaseous with solid and earthy substances in a chemical compound. When freed from this association, incorporeal spirits naturally tended to rise toward the heavens and corporeal bodies to sink to the earth, a fact that apparently harmonized with the traditional Aristotelian contrast between the celestial and terrestrial worlds.

Nevertheless, philosophers and theologians in the strictly orthodox Aristotelian tradition rejected Stoic, Epicurean, and alchemical ideas as being excessively materialistic. In their view the soul was not in any way a subject for chemical or quasi-chemical speculation. The forms or essences of things were not themselves composed of any material stuff, even of the highly tenuous kinds conceived by the Stoics and alchemists. Accordingly, for Thomas Aquinas and the other philosophers of the high Middle Ages, the relation between matter and form was a problem in metaphysics or theology rather than one in natural philosophy.

NEW THEORIES: 1550–1750

Thus, the revival of the physical sciences during the Renaissance started from a position in which no single doctrine about the nature of matter was clearly established and generally accepted. All supporters of the new mechanical philosophy were attracted to an atomistic or corpuscular view of matter, but most of them took care to dissociate themselves from the original atomistic doctrines of Democritus and Epicurus, which were still suspected of having atheistical implications. Thus, Johannes Kepler explained the crystalline structure of snowflakes by reference to a geometrical theory of atoms modeled on that of Plato, Galileo Galilei embraced atomism as a physical embodiment for the points of geometry, and Descartes treated all matter as corpuscular in structure, at the same time denying the theoretical possibility of a void or vacuum. All of them regarded such mechanical interactions as collisions as the basic model for physical processes and sought to build up a theory of forces

(dynamics) capable of explaining the established generalizations about the motions of physical objects.

However, attempts to work out an effective and comprehensive system of physical theory without going beyond the categories of atomism inherited from the Greeks encountered a number of difficulties. These sprang ultimately from the dual axiom that any agency capable of producing physical effects must be composed of a corresponding type of material object and that these objects could influence one another only by direct mechanical action, which required that the bodies be in contact. To deny the first half of this axiom implied accepting the notion of nonmaterial physical agencies; to deny the second implied accepting action at a distance. Both these notions were widely rejected as being incompatible with sound natural philosophy.

The immediate outcome of this dual axiom was to commit the advocates of the new mechanical corpuscular philosophy to a proliferation of new kinds of atom—for instance, magnetic, calorific, and frigorific corpuscles—introduced to account for the corresponding physical phenomena of magnetism, heat, cold, and so on. Although some philosophers, including Descartes, saw the possibility of cutting down the types of atoms—for example, by explaining heat as a consequence of the internal agitation of the material atoms composing hot bodies—even Descartes felt bound to accept that light, magnetism, and the like were carried by subtle fluids made up of corpuscles of insensible weight. Matter, he declared, came in three kinds, of which only "third matter" was subject to gravity and thus had any weight.

An indirect but even more profound outcome of the corpuscularian axiom was to support Descartes's fundamental division between mind and matter as absolutely distinct substances. The least plausible element in traditional atomism had been its psychology. Christian theology had added its own objections to any explanation of mental activity that regarded the mind as composed of atoms, no matter how light or mobile, for this, it was generally agreed, came perilously close to denying the immortality of the soul. The new physical science of the seventeenth and eighteenth centuries accordingly limited its aim. The realm of nature consisted of material bodies interacting mechanically by contact and impact and could be studied by science. The realm of spirit—including, at least, the intellectual activities of human beings—was a distinct and separate object of speculation to which the categories of physical science were not directly relevant. Much of the debate in subsequent epistemology can be traced to this point.

Accordingly, for two hundred years beginning around 1700, the concept of matter kept a central place in physical theory but was set aside as irrelevant to the study of mind. In physics the first major break with traditional ideas came through the work of Sir Isaac Newton. By his theories of dynamics and gravitation, Newton established a sharp distinction between material objects in a strict sense, whose mass conferred on them both inertia and weight, and forces, which were a measure of the way in which material objects interacted rather than a special kind of material thing. In the case of gravity, as he showed in his *Philosophiae Naturalis Principia Mathematica* (1687), these forces had to be supposed capable of acting over distances of many million miles, though Newton himself was inclined to believe that some invisible mechanical link existed by which the sun, for instance, exerted its gravitational action on the planets. In the later editions of his *Opticks* (especially those published after Gottfried Wilhelm Leibniz's death in 1716) he extended this idea to explain other physical phenomena. Electrical, magnetic, and chemical action also, he argued, might prove to be manifestations of forces of attraction and repulsion acting across the spaces between the massive corpuscles of bodies. Thus, the traditional system of atoms and the void was amended to become a theory of material corpuscles interacting by centrally directed forces.

CLASSICAL PHYSICS

Newton's program for natural philosophy made its way only slowly to begin with, but it met with no grave check until the late nineteenth century. At first, his insistence on mass as the essential property of matter was not found universally convincing. Others continued to regard extension, impenetrability, weight, or the capacity to produce physical effects as the indispensable criterion. As a result, throughout the eighteenth century there was an element of cross-purposes in debates about the corporeal nature of, for example, light and fire. Two developments particularly helped to clarify the intellectual situation and established the Newtonian categories as the basis of physical science. First, Antoine Lavoisier and his followers—notably, John Dalton—demonstrated that the phenomena of chemistry as well as those of physics could be unraveled on the assumption that all genuine material substances possessed mass and were composed of corpuscles or atoms. Second, the mathematical work of Leonhard Euler and his successors transformed Newton's account of forces of attraction and repulsion into the modern theory of fields of force.

After 1800, then, physical scientists went ahead rapidly with the experimental and mathematical work that culminated in the so-called classical physics and chemistry of the late nineteenth century. In this system the agents responsible for physical action were divided into two sharply contrasted categories. On the one hand, there was matter; this consisted of massive atoms that combined to form molecules in accordance with the principles of chemical combination. The mechanical energy associated with the motion of the molecules within any body accounted for its temperature; the fields of force between them explained gravitational, electric, and magnetic attraction and repulsion. On the other hand, there were those agencies—such as light and radiant heat—that apparently lacked both mass and weight and that were transmitted in the form of waves across the empty space between the material atoms. Gravitation apart, these various agencies turned out, as was shown by James Clerk Maxwell's electromagnetic theory of light, to be all of one general kind. By combining the established theories of the electrical and magnetic fields of force into a single mathematical system having the same degree of generality as Newton's dynamics, Maxwell demonstrated that electromagnetic waves would share the known properties of light and radiant heat and would move across space with the same velocity that had actually been measured in the case of light. This interpretation gained greatly in strength when Heinrich Hertz used an intermittent electrical spark to produce artificial electromagnetic waves, the so-called radio waves.

Though devoid of mass, these various forms of radiation nevertheless carried energy. Numerically, the sum total of all forms of energy in any isolated system (like the sum total of the masses of all the material bodies involved) was apparently conserved unchanged throughout all physical and chemical changes. As a result it seemed for several decades that the whole of natural philosophy could successfully be built on the central distinction between matter and energy and on the two independent axioms of the conservation of mass and the conservation of energy. Thus, Newton's program for physical science came close to being finally fulfilled in classical physics and chemistry.

TWENTIETH-CENTURY RECONSIDERATIONS

This intellectual equilibrium was short-lived. As Sir John Squire put it:

> Nature and all her Laws lay hid in Night.
> God said "Let Newton be, and all was Light."

It could not last. The Devil, shouting "Ho!
Let Einstein be," restored the *status quo*.

To do Einstein justice, the difficulties in the classical system that he resolved had been considered residual embarrassments for some time, and many of the conceptual changes for which he argued have since established themselves as indispensable features of physical theory. Still, they did undoubtedly have the effect of blurring the sharp distinctions and tidy certitudes of nineteenth-century science.

The effect of these conceptual changes on our concept of matter has been profound. Physicists have been compelled to reconsider and modify all the fundamental planks in the program enunciated for natural science by the mechanical philosophers of the seventeenth century. To begin with, Einstein displaced the seventeenth-century model of mechanical action as the universal pattern for intelligible physical processes by a new model based on electromagnetic theory. The embarrassments facing physicists in the 1890s arose, he showed, from a mathematical conflict between Maxwell's theory of electromagnetism and the mechanics of Galileo and Newton. Einstein circumvented these difficulties in his theory of relativity by giving priority to the theory of electromagnetic fields and by amending the principles of Newtonian mechanics to conform to the Maxwellian pattern. As a result the attitudes of a representative late nineteenth-century physicist, such as William Thomson, Lord Kelvin (who declined to accept Maxwell's theories, declaring that he could embrace a physical explanation of a phenomenon wholeheartedly only if he could make a mechanical model to demonstrate it), have since come to seem excessively narrow.

As a result of this initial change, however, certain other fundamental elements in classical physics have had to be called in question. The absolute distinction between matter and energy, for instance, has gone by the board. It now appears that any quantity of energy (E) is in certain respects equivalent to a proportional quantity of mass ($m = E/c^2$, where c is Maxwell's constant, equal to the measured velocity of electromagnetic radiation); that for theoretical purposes the twin conservation principles of nineteenth-century physics and chemistry should be joined in a single axiom, according to which the sum total of energy and mass (combined according to the formula $E + mc^2$) was conserved in all physical processes; and that in appropriate circumstances a quantity of electromagnetic energy can be transformed into the corresponding quantity of matter or vice versa. This implication was confirmed in the 1930s from a detailed study of individual actions between atomic nuclei and other particles, and it was dramatically reinforced by the explosion of the first atomic bombs, whose energy was derived from the marginal loss of mass involved in the nuclear fission of such heavy elements as uranium.

Meanwhile, the earlier contrast between matter, which was assumed to exist in discrete atomic units, and radiation, which traveled in the form of continuous waves, was under criticism for quite different reasons. First, Max Planck showed that bodies exchanged light-energy in the form of bundles or wave-packets. Einstein, going further, argued that electromagnetic energy always existed in the form of these photons. Then, in the early 1920s, Louis de Broglie put forward the idea that the subatomic particles into which Niels Bohr and Ernest Rutherford had analyzed the fundamental material units of earlier chemistry might themselves manifest some of the properties of wave-packets. This was confirmed in 1927, when it was shown that a beam of electrons passed through a crystal lattice produced a diffraction pattern just as a beam of light of the corresponding wavelength and velocity would have done. By the 1960s it began to appear that matter-particles might differ from the energy-packets of light or other kinds of radiation only in having part of their energy frozen in the form of inertial mass.

Finally, the theory of quantum mechanics, first formulated between 1926 and 1932 by Werner Heisenberg, Erwin Schrödinger, and P. A. M. Dirac, has radically undercut one last presupposition, which had underlain physical science since the time of Galileo. From 1600 on, the fundamental units of matter—whether called corpuscles, particles, or atoms—had been regarded as intrinsically brute, inert, and passive. They might be constituted in such a way that they are capable of exerting forces on one another by virtue of their relative motions and positions, but one had to seek the ultimate source of this capacity—as of their motion—in God who created them. (This was one point on which Newton, Descartes, and Maxwell all agreed.) Since 1926 the final unit of analysis in physics has ceased to bear any serious resemblance to these inert corpuscles. Instead, the quantum physicists begin with certain wave functions or eigenfunctions, which characterize the activity of, say, an electron or an atom as much as they do its structure and position. Just as mass has ceased to be entirely distinct from energy, so the particles of Newton's physics have ceased to be absolutely distinct from the forces of attraction and repulsion acting between them. On the contrary, according to the principles of contemporary physical theory, every kind of fundamental particle—whether of matter or energy—should be associated with a corresponding mode of interaction and force field. Photons, electrons, mesons, nucleons—all these have a dual aspect, being characterized partly by their inertial mass or intrinsic energy and partly by their pattern of interaction with the environment. One outstanding and at present unsettled question is whether the transmission of gravitational forces, from which the whole notion of a field began, also involves the propagation of particles ("gravitons") at a finite speed. If it proves that "gravitons" do in fact exist and travel at the same speed as photons, this will tie up one of the more notorious loose ends of mid-twentieth-century physics.

IMPLICATIONS OF NEW THEORIES

Today almost all the axioms of earlier natural philosophy have been qualified, if not abandoned. Mass has ceased to be the essential, unalterable characteristic of all physical objects and now appears to be one variant of the wider category of energy. No longer can any determinate amount of this energy be localized with absolute precision (Heisenberg's principle), and we are left with a picture of a natural world whose fundamental elements are not so much passive bricks as units of activity. This transformation—as Samuel Sambursky has argued—involves a reaction against the axioms of seventeenth-century physics as radical as the Stoics' rejection of the atomism of Epicurus. Indeed, Sambursky points out, there is a strong parallel between the two reactions. As in the Stoic theory, physicists today also consider matter essentially active rather than passive and explain its behavior as the outcome of patterns of energy and excitation associated with any given state or condition.

The full implications of this change for our other ideas are beginning to become apparent only now. In biology, at any rate, a considerable change has come about since 1950 by the extension of physical theories about molecular structure into the fields of genetics, embryology, and bacteriology. Here the intimate association of structure and function characteristic of modern subatomic theory is reproduced in the association of specific biological activities with particular configurations (and, thus, eigenfunctions) of the complex molecules involved. The extensions of the new ideas about matter into the theory of organic development and human behavior are still at a speculative stage.

This much can, however, be said. During the centuries that have elapsed since the revival of natural philosophy at the Renaissance, the concept of matter has changed its character quite fundamentally. In the present state of scientific thought, accordingly, all earlier questions about, for instance, the relation of matter, life, and mind need to be entirely reconsidered. When, for instance, Descartes classified matter and mind as distinct substances, he was putting the concept of mind and mental activities in opposition to a concept of matter as inert extension, a concept that is now discredited. To that extent the extreme dualism of Descartes's philosophy has been not so much refuted by later science as made irrelevant; its categories no longer fit our situation.

Similarly, other long-standing debates concerning, for example, the reality of the material world or the relation between material objects and our sensations will need to be reappraised in the light of changes in our concept of matter. But this is a task for the future.

See also Anaximander; Aristotle; Atomism; Bohr, Niels; Chrysippus; Descartes, René; Dynamism; Empedocles; Energy; Epicurus; Einstein, Albert; Ether; Galileo Galilei; Heisenberg, Werner; Hertz, Heinrich Rudolf; Kepler, Johannes; Lavoisier, Antoine; Leucippus and Democritus; Mass; Maxwell, James Clerk; Newton, Isaac; Plato; Renaissance; Schrödinger, Erwin; Thales of Miletus; Thomas Aquinas, St.; Zeno of Citium.

Bibliography

In general, this article follows the argument of Stephen Toulmin and June Goodfield, *The Architecture of Matter* (London: Harper and Row, 1962), in which the development of the concept of matter is fully analyzed but discussed without serious technicalities. For the various periods covered here the reader is referred to the following works.

GREEK PHILOSOPHY

S. Sambursky, *The Physical World of the Greeks* (London: Routledge and Paul, 1956), is an outstanding survey for the general reader. W. K. C. Guthrie, *A History of Greek Philosophy*, Vol. 1 (Cambridge, U.K.: Cambridge University Press, 1962), and G. S. Kirk and J. E. Raven, *The Presocratic Philosophers* (Cambridge, U.K.: Cambridge University Press, 1957), are up-to-date scholarly discussions of the Ionian natural philosophers. F. M. Cornford, *Plato's Cosmology* (London: K. Paul, Trench, Trubner, 1937), is the most convenient existing version of the *Timaeus*, in which Plato's views about matter are expounded. J. H. Randall Jr., *Aristotle* (New York: Columbia University Press, 1960), provides an illuminating account of that philosopher's scientific ideas; it is useful for the nonspecialist.

LATER CLASSICAL AND MEDIEVAL PERIOD

S. Sambursky's *The Physics of the Stoics* (London: Routledge and Paul, 1959) and *The Physical World of Late Antiquity* (London, 1962) complete the story begun in his *Physical World of the Greeks* (see above). Cyril Bailey, *The Greek*

Atomists and Epicurus (Oxford, 1928), and A. J. Hopkins, *Alchemy, Child of Greek Philosophy* (New York: Columbia University Press, 1934), are scholarly but readable: Both books remain stimulating and full of interest. E. J. Holmyard, *Alchemy* (London, 1957), and A. C. Crombie, *Medieval and Early Modern Science* (Garden City, NY: Doubleday, 1959), are readable popular surveys.

NEW THEORIES: 1550–1750

H. T. Pledge, *Science since 1500* (London: H. M. Stationery Office, 1939; reprinted, New York: Harper, 1959), and A. R. Hall, *From Galileo to Newton* (London, 1963), are general histories, both of which include useful material on the new theories. Mary B. Hesse, *Forces and Fields* (Edinburgh, 1961); Marie Boas, *Robert Boyle and Seventeenth Century Chemistry* (Cambridge, U.K.: Cambridge University Press, 1958); Hélène Metzger, *Les doctrines chimiques* (Paris, 1923) and *Newton, Stahl, Boerhaave* (Paris: F. Alcan, 1930); I. Bernard Cohen. *Franklin and Newton* (Philadelphia: American Philosophical Society, 1956); and E. J. Dijksterhuis, *The Mechanization of the World Picture,* translated by C. Dikshoorn (Oxford: Clarendon Press, 1961), are scholarly books dealing in a penetrating way with more detailed aspects of the subject.

CLASSICAL PHYSICS

Edmund Whittaker, *History of the Theories of Aether and Electricity,* 2 vols. (Edinburgh, 1951–1953), and Mary B. Hesse, *Forces and Fields* (see above), are the best specialist surveys. For the general reader Charles C. Gillispie, *The Edge of Objectivity* (Princeton, NJ: Princeton University Press, 1960), N. R. Campbell, *What Is Science?* (London: Methuen, 1921; reprinted, New York: Dover, 1952), Albert Einstein and Leopold Infeld, *The Evolution of Physics* (New York: Simon and Schuster, 1938), and George Gamow, *Biography of Physics* (New York, 1963), may be selected from many others as being particularly useful.

TWENTIETH-CENTURY RECONSIDERATIONS

A great many books of general interest have been published about the twentieth-century transformation in physical theory. Apart from Einstein and Infeld, op. cit., and Gamow, op. cit., one of especial merit is Banesh Hoffmann, *The Strange Story of the Quantum* (New York: Harper, 1947). Many of the physicists directly involved have written interestingly about the changes—notably, Werner Heisenberg, *Philosophical Problems of Nuclear Science* (London: Faber, 1952). The analogy between Stoic matter theory and wave mechanics is pursued in Sambursky, *The Physics of the Stoics* (see above).

Stephen E. Toulmin (1967)

MATTER AND PROBLEMS OF PERCEPTION

See *Appearance and Reality; Illusions; Perception; Phenomenalism; Primary and Secondary Qualities; Realism; Sensa*

MATTHEW OF ACQUASPARTA
(c. 1237–1302)

Matthew of Acquasparta, the Italian Franciscan scholastic philosopher and theologian, was born in Acquasparta, near Todi in Umbria, possibly of the illustrious Bentivenghi family. In 1254 he entered the Franciscan order, and about 1268 he began studies at the University of Paris, where he was profoundly influenced by Bonaventure's system. Matthew was lector in the Studium Generale at Bologna (at least for the year 1273–1274), and in 1276 he became master in theology at Paris. From 1279 to 1287, he was lector Sacri Palatii in Rome, succeeding John Peckham. He was general of the order from 1287 to 1289. In 1288 he was made cardinal, and in 1291 he was named bishop of Porto and Santa Rufina. Matthew died at Rome, where he is buried in the church of Ara Coeli.

DOCTRINE

Matthew taught and wrote during the time of conflict between the Augustinian–Franciscan doctrinal tradition and the rising Thomistic Aristotelianism. In this far-reaching controversy he proved himself to be exceptionally well-versed in Augustine's doctrines and in general a faithful follower of Bonaventure. Although he incorporated a few Aristotelian elements, Matthew's system in its entirety shows that he was among the purest adherents of Augustinianism in the last quarter of the thirteenth century. He had a calm, balanced mind, a sober style, and an exact manner of formulating his ideas. In discussion he was generally modest and perceptive. With these qualities he often achieved, at least in his *Quaestiones Disputatae de Fide et de Cognitione,* a level comparable to that of the greatest thinkers of his age.

In his theory of knowledge Matthew taught that our intellect knows the individual object not only by reflection, as St. Thomas Aquinas held, but also by a direct perception, which precedes the formation of an abstract idea. By virtue of this perception, the intellect forms a *species singularis* of the concrete object with all the richness of detail it possesses in reality. In this way the mind prepares for knowledge of the essence of the object. Similarly, the soul knows its own existence and habits not only by reasoning and by reflection but also by a direct and intimate intuition. In *Quaestiones Disputatae de Cognitione,* Matthew presented a personal solution to the controversial question of the activity of the knowing subject. Rejecting the impressionism of Bonaventure and Thomas Aquinas, the innatism of Thomas of York and

Roger Bacon, and the pure activism of William of Auvergne and John Peckham, Matthew defended a semi-activism, not an occasionalism. Whereas according to pure activism the *species intentionalis* is completely (matter and form) caused by the knowing subject, according to Matthew the matter comes from the object, the form from the subject. This opinion, however, was soon contested by Roger Marston as contradicting both Aristotle and Augustine.

Matthew defended the theory of divine illumination almost in the same manner as did Bonaventure. The purely human faculties for knowing the extramental world do not give us either clear understanding or certainty. We need the aid of the divine *rationes aeternae* (divine ideas) to illuminate our mind during the process of knowledge. God is not simply the creator of human intelligence; he also conserves it and concurs in each of its actions. This collaboration of God by means of the divine illumination is possible because man in his mind bears a special likeness to his creator. Our intellect is illumed by the divine light that contains the eternal ideas and is the ground of all created beings. The divine light is not the object itself of our knowledge but the moving principle that leads us to the true knowledge of the created world. Following the Augustinian doctrine, Matthew believed that the object of knowledge never determines the election of the will.

Among Matthew's other philosophical theses, the following are worthy of mention. Matthew, like Bonaventure, rejected the possibility of a creation from eternity; the spiritual beings (souls and angels) are necessarily composed of matter and form, because if they were composed simply of essence and existence (as Thomas Aquinas taught), this would not account for their contingency. Also, the process of coming to existence must be explained by the Augustinian theory of the *rationes seminales*. The "being body" (*esse corporale*) constitutes a plurality of forms. The two elements of the beings, matter and form, are together the cause of individuality. Matthew upheld the Ontological Proof of the existence of God; he also argued that the knowledge of God that we attain through faith is compatible with scientific knowledge. Matthew was particularly interested in problems concerning the relations between the natural order and the supernatural order.

IMPORTANCE

Matthew is undoubtedly to be ranked among the great scholastic thinkers. His importance, however, lies not so much in the originality of his thought as in the fact that he is, after Bonaventure, the ideal representative of Augustinianism. The only philosophers that are known to have been directly influenced by him are Roger Marston and Vitalis of Furno.

See also Aristotelianism; Aristotle; Augustine, St.; Augustinianism; Bacon, Roger; Bonaventure, St.; Marston, Roger; Medieval Philosophy; Ontological Argument for the Existence of God; Peckham, John; Thomas Aquinas, St.; Thomas of York; William of Auvergne.

Bibliography

PRIMARY SOURCES

Matthew's most important philosophical works are *Introitus ad S. Scripturam* (1268–1269), in *Bibliotheca Franciscana Scholastica Medii Aevi*, Vol. I (Quaracchi, 1903; 2nd ed., 1957), pp. 3–21; *Introitus ad S. Theologiam* (probably 1271–1272), ibid., pp. 22–33; *Commentarius in I, II, et III Sententiarum* (1271–1272), unedited manuscript at Quaracchi; *Quaestiones Disputatae* (1267–1287), which is almost complete in *Bibliotheca Franciscana Scholastica Medii Aevi*, Vols. I–II, XI, XVII–XVIII (Quaracchi, 1903–1961); *Quaestiones de Anima VI*, in *Archives d'histoire doctrinale et littéraire du moyen âge*, edited by A.-J. Gondras, Vol. XXIV (Paris, 1958), pp. 203–352; *Quaestiones Disputatae de Anima XIII*, edited by A.-J. Gondras, *Études de philosophie médiévale* 50 (1961); VI Quodlibeta, about 90 questions (1276–1279), unedited manuscript at Quaracchi; *Concordantiae Super IV Libros Sententiarum*, unedited manuscript at Quaracchi.

SECONDARY SOURCES

Beha, H. M. "Matthew of Acquasparta's Theory of Cognition." *Franciscan Studies* 20 (1960): 161–204; 21 (1961): 1–79, 383–465.

Bettoni, E. "Rapporti dottrinali fra M. d'Acquasparta e G. Duns Scoto." *Studi francescani* 15 (1943): 113–130.

Bonafede, G. "Il problema del 'lumen' nel pensiero di Frate M. d'Acquasparta." *Rivista rosminiana* 31 (1937): 186–200.

Doucet, V. *Matthaei ab Aquasparta, Quaestiones Disputatae de Gratia*. Quaracchi, 1935. See pp. 11*–163* for a general introduction.

Pacchierini, L. *La dottrina gnoselogica de M. d'Acquasparta*. Naples, 1949.

Pegis, A.-C. "Matthew of Aquasparta and the Cognition of Non-being." In *Scholastica Ratione Historico-Critica Instauranda*, 463–480. Rome: Pontificum Athenaeum Antonianum, 1951.

Simoncioli, F. "Il concetto di legge in M. d'Acquasparta." *Studi francescani* 56 (1959): 37–50.

A. Emmen, O.F.M. (1967)

MAUPERTUIS, PIERRE-LOUIS MOREAU DE
(1698–1759)

Pierre-Louis Moreau de Maupertuis, the French scientist and philosopher, was born in Saint-Malo, Brittany. Elected in 1723 to the Académie des Sciences (and to the Royal Society in 1728), he first became known for his work in geometry. The expedition that he led to Lapland in 1736 to measure a degree of meridian near the pole helped finally to prove that Earth was an oblate spheroid. With his early introduction of Newtonian theories into France, Maupertuis became a leading exponent among the *philosophes* of the ideal of experimentalism as opposed to the overly deductive method in science associated with the Cartesian tradition. In 1744 Frederick II of Prussia asked him to reorganize the Berlin Academy of Sciences and later appointed him as its president (1746–1759). The remainder of his career was intimately linked to the activities of this group, and the growth of the academy into an important center of research owed much to his efforts.

PRINCIPLE OF LEAST ACTION

Maupertuis's famous principle of least action, which contributed signally to the systematization of mechanics, was formulated in "Recherche des loix du mouvement" (1746) as follows: "Whenever any change occurs in nature, the quantity of action employed for this is always the smallest possible"—the "quantity of action" being proportional to the product of the mass of a body and its velocity and the distance traversed. Among the heated controversies provoked by this notion, Samuel Koenig's unfair (although understandable) attribution of it to Gottfried Wilhelm Leibniz brought about a scandalous quarrel and lifelong enmity between Maupertuis and Voltaire. But all this proved irrelevant to the historic value of the principle of least action, which, clarified progressively by the applications it found in the works of Leonhard Euler, Joseph Lagrange, William Hamilton, Hermann Ludwig von Helmholtz, and others, emerged ultimately as a basic concept in the mathematical analysis of dynamic systems.

COSMOLOGICAL ARGUMENT.
In the *Essai de cosmologie* (1750), Maupertuis's extension of the principle of least action to the much debated problems of theodicy offered a compromise solution between the radical antifinalism of contemporary materialists and the naive finalism of those who saw God's wisdom in every manifestation of design in nature, however trivial or self-contradictory. By claiming that an actual mathematical equation showed God's regulation of nature through the parsimony of kinetic means employed in the production of all physical events, Maupertuis succeeded in giving an original and seemingly scientific version of the Cosmological Argument. But his assumption that there is logical necessity as such in the existence of mechanical laws, which was consistent with the example of René Descartes and Leibniz, typified a rationalist attitude that, though prevalent at the time, was already undermined by those who, like David Hume, alleged a merely empirical necessity for physical causation. Although Maupertuis's distrust of metaphysical reasoning led him to present his cosmological argument not as demonstrably certain, but only as the best that the imperfect human intellect was capable of, it remained perhaps less plausible than ingenious, particularly since it was affirmed without sufficient regard either to the epistemological difficulties it incurred or to the possible nontheological interpretations of its underlying minimal concept. Coming late in a current of thought that was to yield before long to new orientations in philosophy, the *Essai de cosmologie* had a limited historical impact. It was, in fact, in a form essentially free of teleological meanings that the principle of least action exercised its considerable influence on the development of physicomathematical science.

BIOLOGY: THE STRUCTURE OF MATTER

A different science, biology, inspired Maupertuis's next major work (1751), the *Dissertatio Inauguralis Metaphysica de Universali Naturae Systemate* (known also as the *Système de la nature*). Study of the problem of heredity had led Maupertuis to reject, in the *Vénus physique* (1745), the then reigning doctrine of preformation and to favor instead a theory of epigenesis using the law of attraction. But he had subsequently found this theory inadequate and had despaired altogether of accounting mechanistically for the origins and nature of life. In the *Dissertatio Inauguralis*, therefore, he sought to explain the formation of living things by supposing that all the elementary particles of matter are individually endowed in a proportionately elementary degree with "desire, aversion, and memory," by virtue of which they combine to form organic entities.

Such a notion, no less than that of least action, betrays a marked Leibnizian background in Maupertuis's thinking, despite his outspoken criticism of the metaphysics of Leibniz. It is true, nevertheless, that Maupertuis did not assign the metaphysical status of the monads to his "percipient particles" but, rather, presented them as part of a general biological hypothesis; he accounted for the elemental coexistence of physical and psychic properties in nature by reference to a common unknowable substance. Thus, the philosophical basis of his biological theorizing may be described as either an "atomistic dualism" or a "corpuscular psychism," sustained by a phenomenological accord between matter and its presumed psychic qualities. These ideas were misinterpreted in materialistic terms by Denis Diderot and contributed indirectly to the eventual success of naturalism in biology. Since Maupertuis's metabiological conception was also intended to explain the structural transformations of the various species by a process of genetic mutation, it merged, in that respect too, with an important current of evolutionist speculation that grew in France after about 1750.

EPISTEMOLOGY

The views of Maupertuis in epistemology can be judged from a number of his writings. While, like Étienne Bonnot de Condillac and most of the *philosophes*, he agreed with John Locke that sensation is the source of all our knowledge, his position was appreciably more sophisticated, probably because of his encounter with the Berkeleian critique. If this critique did not quite win him over to subjectivism, he at least became convinced that experience offers no more than the disjointed fragments of a merely phenomenal reality and that the substance presumed to excite in the mind the perceptions that in turn are projected cognitively toward the natural world remains itself beyond objective determination. Maupertuis ascribed even the evidence of mathematics not to any intrinsic veracity of such knowledge but to the fact that it is based on the repetition (*réplicabilité*) of certain simple ideas that consist of identical units and are abstracted from the heterogeneous totality of sensory impressions. In the same spirit, his *Réflexions philosophiques sur l'origine des langues et la signification des mots* (1748) raises the equally crucial question of the linguistic prefigurations of sense experience, from which scientific reasoning is unable completely to escape.

ETHICS

Maupertuis's principal excursion into ethics, *Essai de philosophie morale* (1749), tried somewhat overambitiously to reconcile the Stoic, Epicurean, and Christian schools but succeeded only in reaching an eclectic view characterized by the author's own pessimism concerning the chances of human felicity. It offered, however, an early instance of the application of arithmetic to the problem of happiness by its attempt to express, in the analogy of statics, the equations of a "hedonistic calculus."

IMPORTANCE

Generally, the thought of Maupertuis pursued the aim, shared by many of his contemporaries, of linking philosophy more concretely than in the past with the content of the particular sciences. Instead of presenting an overall logical coherence, his work contributes various philosophical essays reflecting the different points of departure dictated by his primarily scientific interests. The cosmological thesis, speculative biology, and moral opinions of Maupertuis remained largely separate from each other; moreover, Maupertuis himself was often in the curious but historically symptomatic predicament of searching earnestly for metaphysical solutions while disbelieving in their possibility. Having elaborated the principle of least action and the notion of percipient particles of matter in a rather ambiguous zone between metaphysics proper and scientific theory, it is not surprising that he should have suffered much unmerited neglect from historians both of philosophy and of science. But it is now recognized that Maupertuis had a significant, even if secondary, role in the maturing of modern physics and biology alike, as well as in the transition of philosophical thinking from classical metaphysics to the critical position adopted by Immanuel Kant.

See also Condillac, Étienne Bonnot de; Cosmological Argument for the Existence of God; Descartes, René; Geometry; Hamilton, William; Helmholtz, Hermann Ludwig von; Hume, David; Kant, Immanuel; Leibniz, Gottfried Wilhelm; Meier, Georg Friedrich; Pessimism and Optimism; Scientific Method; Voltaire, François-Marie Arouet de.

Bibliography

WORKS BY MAUPERTUIS

Lettres. 1752. Place of publication unknown.

Examen philosophique de la preuve de l'existence de Dieu. In *Memoirs of the Berlin Academy of Sciences.* 1756.

Oeuvres. 4 vols. Lyons, 1756.

WORKS ON MAUPERTUIS

Abelé, Jean. "Introduction à la notion d'action et au principe de l'action stationnaire." *Revue des questions scientifiques* 119 (1948): 25–42.

Bachelard, Suzanne. *Les polémiques concernant le principe de moindre action au XVIIIᵉ siècle.* Paris: Université de Paris, Palais de la Découverte, 1961.

Beeson, David. *Maupertuis: An Intellectual Biography.* Oxford: Voltaire Foundation, 1992.

Brunet, Pierre. *Étude historique sur le principe de la moindre action.* Paris, 1938.

Brunet, Pierre. *Maupertuis, étude biographique* and *Maupertuis: l'oeuvre et sa place dans la pensée scientifique et philosophique de XVIIIᵉ siècle.* 2 vols. Paris: Blanchard, 1929. An authoritative study of Maupertuis's life and thought.

Crombie, A. C. "Maupertuis, précurseur du transformisme." *Revue de synthèse* 78 (1957): 35–56.

Feher, Marta. "The Role of Metaphor and Analogy in the Birth of the Principle of Least Action of Maupertuis (1698–1759)." *International Studies in the Philosophy of Science* 2 (1988): 175–188.

Gossman, L. "Berkeley, Hume and Maupertuis." *French Studies* 14 (1960): 304–324.

Guéroult, Martial. "Note sur le principe de la moindre action chez Maupertuis." In *Dynamique et métaphysique leibniziennes,* 215–235. Strasbourg, 1934.

Maglo, Koffi. "The Reception of Newton's Gravitational Theory by Huygens, Varignon, and Maupertuis: How Normal Science May Be Revolutionary." *Perspectives on Science* 11(2) (2003): 135–169.

Ostoya, Paul. "Maupertuis et la biologie." *Revue d'histoire des sciences* 7 (1954): 60–78.

Terrall, Mary. *The Man Who Flattened the Earth: Maupertuis and the Sciences in the Enlightenment.* Chicago: The University of Chicago Press, 2002.

Vartanian, Aram. "Diderot and Maupertuis." *Revue Internationale De Philosophie* 38 (1984): 46–66.

Aram Vartanian (1967)
Bibliography updated by Tamra Frei (2005)

MAXWELL, JAMES CLERK
(1831–1879)

James Clerk Maxwell, the British physicist, came from a well-known Scottish family, the Clerks; his father adopted the name Maxwell on inheriting an estate originally belonging to that family. Maxwell was educated at Edinburgh University and the University of Cambridge, becoming a fellow of Trinity College in 1855. In 1856 he won the Adams Prize at Cambridge for an essay in which he demonstrated that the rings of Saturn would be unstable if they were continuously solid or fluid and that they must be composed of discrete and separated parts. Maxwell was professor of natural philosophy at Marischal College in Aberdeen from 1856 to 1860 and professor of natural philosophy and astronomy at King's College in London from 1860 to 1865. His first paper on electromagnetism appeared in 1856; his electromagnetic field theory with the derivation of the velocity of light was first published in 1861–1862 and in more rigorous form in 1865; and he began work on the kinetic theory of gases in 1860. From 1865 to 1871 Maxwell remained at his country estate in Scotland where he worked on his *Treatise on Electricity and Magnetism,* which summarized the subject and his contributions thereto. In 1871 he became the first occupant of the Cavendish chair of experimental physics at Cambridge, supervised the construction of the Cavendish Laboratory, and later guided the first research done there. During this period he edited the works of Henry Cavendish. During his lifetime Maxwell also did research on color vision, mechanics, and other topics, and although his fame rests on his theoretical achievements, his experimental work was noteworthy.

THE ELECTROMAGNETIC FIELD

Maxwell's greatest contribution to fundamental physics was his concept of the electromagnetic field, a concept that underwent much modification both in the course of his own researches and at the hands of his successors. In modern terms, a field—such as the electric field—is a condition in the space surrounding charged bodies that determines the force that a unit electric charge would experience if it were placed at any point. In field theory all actions are regarded as transmitted from point to point by the contiguous modification of the field between the points, and the field is regarded as the seat of energy. Contemporary physics is dominated by the field-theoretic viewpoint, whether or not it is reinterpreted in terms of quantum theory.

Maxwell aimed at embodying in mathematical notation the ideas of Michael Faraday and, in particular, Faraday's fruitful concept of lines of force. In this Maxwell was inspired by the work of William Thomson (later Lord Kelvin), who had demonstrated the mathematical analogy between the problems of heat flow and of the distribution of static electricity. Maxwell developed similar analogies in his first paper on the subject, "On Faraday's Lines of Force" (1855–1856), drawing separate analogies for different aspects of electromagnetism: between electrical and fluid currents, and between electric or magnetic lines of force and fluid currents. While suggestive, such an endeavor was of course not a unified theory. "I do not think," he wrote, "that we have any right at present to understand the action of electricity, and I hold that the chief merit of a temporary theory is, that it shall guide experiment, without impeding the progress of the true theory when it appears." The beginning of the paper is of interest as a statement of method; Maxwell points out the pitfalls of commitment to a mathematical formula, in which case "we entirely lose sight of the phenomena to be explained," or to a physical hypothesis, the irrelevant parts of which are liable to carry one beyond the truth. He advocates instead the use of physical analogy, "that partial similarity between the laws of one science and those of another which makes each of them illustrate the other."

In his "On Physical Lines of Force" (1861–1862), Maxwell's electromagnetic field theory appears for the first time, presented as a deduction from a detailed model of the ether. Magnetic lines of force are represented as molecular (microscopic) vortices in this ether, the matter of the ether whirling around in planes normal to the direction of the lines of force, so that the latter is the direction of the axes of the vortices. Maxwell found that in this fashion he could represent the properties of lines of force needed for magnetostatics, that is, that the lines should tend to contract along their length and repel each other laterally. But how can neighboring vortices spin in the same sense, since their neighboring boundaries move in opposite directions, and how are these motions initiated and communicated through the ether? Maxwell assumed a layer of tiny idle wheels between each pair of vortex cells in the ethereal substance. These wheels can rotate freely, so that a uniform magnetic field is represented by the vortex cells all spinning at the same rate and in the same sense, and the interspersed wheels rotating in place in the opposite sense. The idle wheels can also move from place to place in a conductor, but they are constrained to rolling contact without slipping with the neighboring vortices. The translatory motion of the wheels is identified with the electric current and used to explain the manner in which a magnetic field is created by an electric current (Hans Christian Ørsted's discovery); it also is used to account for electromagnetic induction. Furthermore, in a dielectric, including the vacuum, the wheels are not free to move in translation, but can only be displaced slightly against the elastic forces of the material of the cells. This action of displacement is the displacement current that forms the new term Maxwell added to previous results, while transforming all of them into his theoretical language. Maxwell then proceeded to calculate the velocity of propagation of transverse waves in his elastic ether. The speed of these waves was proportional to the ratio between the electromagnetic and electrostatic units of charge.

The factor of proportionality between the speed of the waves and the ratio of the units depended in this calculation on the specific model chosen for the ether; the argument showing the two terms to be equal cannot be regarded as very satisfactory. In "A Dynamical Model of the Electromagnetic Field" (1865), the electromagnetic field equations are presented directly without recourse to the ether model, and the relation between velocity of waves and ratio of electrical units is derived directly from the equations. Since, according to Wilhelm Weber and Friedrich Kohlrausch (1857), the ratio between the units was 3.11×10^8 meters/sec., whereas, according to Armand Fizeau, the speed of light was 3.15×10^8 meters/sec., Maxwell drew the important conclusion that light consisted of waves in the electromagnetic ether. This finally gained general acceptance when Heinrich Hertz generated electromagnetic waves by electrical means and showed that they had all the properties of light except that they were of much lower frequency, a result of the conditions of generation.

In his later papers Maxwell no longer relied on specific models of the ether. In the *Treatise* he wrote:

> The attempt which I then [in "On Physical Lines of Force"] made to imagine a working model of this mechanism must be taken for no more than it really is, a demonstration that mechanism may be imagined capable of producing a connexion mechanically equivalent to the actual connexion of the parts of the electromagnetic field. The problem of determining the mechanism required to establish a given species of connexion between the motions of the parts of a system always admits of an infinite number of solutions.

Nevertheless, he still regarded the underlying phenomena as motions and stresses in the mechanical ether, maintaining that the energy of magnetism "exists in the form of some kind of motion of the matter in every portion of space," apparently of a vortical character. Maxwell's views differ from those of the twentieth century in the following ways: The electromagnetic field was not regarded as a separate dynamic entity from matter, that is, a material ether; ordinary matter was treated macroscopically, phenomenologically, rather than from the atomic point of view; and the role of charge in the theory was ambiguous. Late in the nineteenth century H. A. Lorentz combined Maxwell's field theory with Continental conceptions of atomicity of charge to establish the classical theory of the dualism of matter and field.

KINETIC THEORY OF GASES

Also of fundamental importance was Maxwell's work on the kinetic theory of gases. In deriving the experimental gas laws, previous investigators had made the simplified assumption that all the gas molecules moved with the same speed. In "Illustrations of the Dynamical Theory of Gases" (1860), Maxwell first derived the equilibrium distribution of the velocities of the molecules: the components of the velocity along a given direction are distributed according to Carl Friedrich Gauss's error law. This paper also contained the startling result, later demonstrated experimentally, that the viscosity (internal friction) of a gas should be independent of its density. Maxwell wrote two other pathfinding papers on the kinetic theory; their main subject was the derivation of the transport coefficients of a gas (coefficients of diffusion, viscosity, and thermal conductivity) and, in the last of them, the discussion of radiometric phenomena.

Maxwell's work on the kinetic theory may be regarded as constituting the first important introduction of statistical reasoning into physics and the first steps in the development of statistical mechanics, later continued by Ludwig Boltzmann and Josiah Gibbs. In statistical mechanics the use of statistics is not a manifestation of any indeterminism in the purported fundamental laws of nature, as it is in quantum physics; rather it is the reflection of our ignorance of the exact motions of the enormous number of molecules in any macroscopic system. The very immensity of this number (there are about 6×10^{23} hydrogen atoms in one gram of hydrogen) and the minuteness of the individual molecules give assurance that in ordinary experiments the measurable properties will be statistical in character and thus will be exactly the properties singled out by a statistical theory.

Maxwell's demon, a hypothetical being that apparently could reverse the tendency of isolated systems toward increase of disorder or entropy and so would violate the second law of thermodynamics, appears in his *Theory of Heat* (London, 1872, pp. 308–309). The thermal equilibration of neighboring vessels containing gas, representing a state of maximum disorder, could be destroyed by a being capable of seeing the individual molecules of the gas who acts so as to let only the faster molecules in one container pass through a small hole into the other, and the slower ones in the latter to pass in the reverse sense. Since the temperature is determined by the mean energy of motion of the molecules, this process would result in the gas in one vessel becoming warmer than that in the other, without any interference from outside the system. The demon has been exorcised by L. Brillouin and others (see Brillouin's *Science and Information Theory*, New York, 1956, Ch. 13). To obtain the information about an approaching molecule that the demon needs in order to decide whether or not to open the hole,

the demon must absorb at least one quantum of light, the energy of which is reasonably greater than the mean energy of the quanta of thermal radiation that are always present. The absorption of this quantum demonstrably leads to a greater increase in entropy in the total system (including the demon) than the decrease obtained by properly manipulating the hole.

See also Boltzmann, Ludwig; Energy; Ether; Faraday, Michael; Gibbs, Josiah; Matter; Motion; Philosophy of Physics; Quantum Mechanics.

Bibliography

The *Scientific Papers of James Clerk Maxwell,* including his semipopular lectures but not the *Treatise* and other books, appear in two volumes edited by W. D. Niven (Cambridge, U.K.: Cambridge University Press, 1890). See in particular his Bradford address, "Molecules," Vol. II, pp. 361–377, in which he expresses most lucidly his religious and metaphysical position. The *Treatise on Electricity and Magnetism,* 3rd ed., edited by J. J. Thomas, was published in 1892 at Oxford. The standard biography is Lewis Campbell and William Garnett, *The Life of James Clerk Maxwell* (London: Macmillan, 1882).

Arthur E. Woodruff (1967)

MAYA

See *Indian Philosophy*

MCCOSH, JAMES
(1811–1894)

James McCosh, an influential representative of "commonsense realism," was born in southern Ayrshire, Scotland. He was educated at Glasgow and Edinburgh universities. McCosh was licensed for the ministry in 1834 and served as a pastor of the Established Church of Scotland until 1850, when he was appointed professor of logic and metaphysics at Queen's College of Belfast. In 1868 he came to America to serve as president of the College of New Jersey (now Princeton University), a position he held until 1888.

McCosh's philosophical outlook was in its largest features inherited from the "Scottish school" of Thomas Reid, Dugald Stewart, and others. On one side this meant the denial that our beliefs about the external world rest on any dubious inferences, causal or otherwise, from immediately presented ideas. Those beliefs are rather the natural, noninferential accompaniments of sensation, and their general reliability cannot sensibly be questioned. On another (and for McCosh, more important) side, commonsense philosophy meant apriorism. In *The Intuitions of the Mind, Inductively Investigated* (London and New York, 1860), McCosh undertook to enumerate certain fundamental principles (such as principles of causation and moral good) that belong to the constitution of the mind. Although persons are not necessarily or normally aware of these very general truths, their particular cognitions and judgments are regulated by them. In saying that these principles are to be discovered "inductively" McCosh did not mean that they are inductive generalizations. Certainly one is led to these principles by reflection on experience. But once before the mind, the principles are recognized as self-evidently and necessarily true. McCosh's realism, unlike that of H. L. Mansel and William Hamilton, was relatively free of the influence of Immanuel Kant. Thus, in *An Examination of Mr. J. S. Mill's Philosophy* (London and New York, 1866), McCosh defended Hamilton's intuitional philosophy against Mill's criticism but took care to disassociate himself from the former's "agnostic" view that man's knowledge is limited to the finite.

The most original aspect of McCosh's philosophy was his effort to accommodate evolution and Christian theism. In one of his earliest works, *The Method of the Divine Government, Physical and Moral* (Edinburgh, 1850), he opposed the view that God's design exhibits itself entirely in the lawful development of nature. Such a view, he thought, amounted to a denial of divine providence. Divine government proceeds instead by a combination of law and particular, spontaneous interventions. When *The Origin of Species* appeared (1859), McCosh found it natural to identify his "special providences" with Charles Darwin's "chance variations." In *Christianity and Positivism* (New York and London, 1871) he argued that evolution, properly understood, is not only compatible with a divine design but in fact magnifies the Designer. Unlike Darwin, McCosh found nothing abhorrent in the notion that God employs the struggle for survival as a technique of creation. He was confident that success in that struggle was a matter of moral rather than physical strength.

McCosh's writings enjoyed considerable popularity, particularly among the evangelical clergy who found in them a way of dealing with the difficulties raised by science and science-inspired philosophies.

See also Common Sense; Darwin, Charles Robert; Darwinism; Hamilton, William; Kant, Immanuel; Mansel, Henry Longueville; Mill, John Stuart; Realism; Reid, Thomas; Stewart, Dugald.

Bibliography

Apart from those already mentioned, McCosh's chief works are *The Supernatural in Relation to the Natural* (New York: R. Carter, 1862); *The Scottish Philosophy, Biographical, Expository, Critical, from Hutcheson to Hamilton* (London, 1874); and *First and Fundamental Truths, Being a Treatise on Metaphysics* (New York: Scribners, 1889). An extensive bibliography by Joseph H. Dulles is appended to the autobiographical *The Life of James McCosh*, edited by William Milligan Sloane (New York: Scribners, 1896).

Douglas Arner (1967)

MCDOUGALL, WILLIAM
(1871–1938)

William McDougall, a British-American proponent of hormic psychology, was born in Chadderton, England, the second son of a chemical manufacturer. He was educated at schools in England and Germany, and at Manchester and Cambridge universities, where he received first-class honors in biology. In 1897 he qualified in medicine at St. Thomas's Hospital, London. While working there with Charles Scott Sherrington, he read William James's *Principles of Psychology,* and returned to Cambridge to study psychology on a fellowship from St. John's College. He joined the Cambridge Anthropological Expedition (1899) to Torres Straits, collaborating with W. H. R. Rivers in sensory researches and with Charles Hose in anthropological studies, which resulted in *The Pagan Tribes of Borneo* (London, 1912). He worked at Göttingen with G. E. Müller and subsequently joined the psychology department of University College, London, under James Sully, where he published researches supporting Thomas Young's theory of color vision against those of H. L. F. von Helmholtz and Ewald Hering (*Mind* 10 [1901]: 52–97, 210–245, 347–382). In London, and in Oxford from 1904 as Wilde reader in mental philosophy, McDougall worked on reflexes, inhibition, and psychophysical relationships. In *Physiological Psychology* (London, 1905) he combined James's view of instinctive action and emotion as objective and subjective aspects of the excitement of inherited perceptual dispositions with Sherrington's theory of the nervous system as integrator of reflex and instinctive-impulsive actions. McDougall explained subjectivity and purposiveness through R. H. Lotze's "psychoneural parallelism," postulating psychic currents induced in etherlike soul-stuff by neural activity.

McDougall first outlined his hormic psychology in *An Introduction to Social Psychology* (London, 1908). He derived human behavior from instincts, which are innate psychophysical dispositions with specific cognitive, affective, and conative aspects (for example, perception of danger, fear, flight). In adult humans, instincts operate indirectly through socially acquired patterns, the sentiments, in which object(s) and instinct(s) have become enduringly associated. Sentiments increasingly remote from innate instincts are exemplified, for instance, by parental love, family feeling, patriotism. In the growth of character the developing sentiments become hierarchically ranged round a master sentiment (or ruling passion) whose nucleus in a stable character is the self-regarding sentiment.

In *Body and Mind* (London, 1911), subtitled *A History and Defense of Animism,* McDougall reviewed psychophysical theories. To explain heredity and evolution, memory and learning, the "body-memory" of growth and repair, and parapsychological evidences of personal survival, he now discarded Lotzean parallelism, and declared himself, unfashionably, a dualist, interactionist, vitalist, animist, and Lamarckian.

In World War I McDougall enlisted as a French army ambulance driver but was drafted into the Royal Army Medical Corps. His command of a British shellshock unit provided the limited clinical material for his *Abnormal Psychology* (see below). In 1920 he became professor of psychology at Harvard, and in 1927 professor of psychology at Duke University. His American period was one of immense literary productivity. *The Group Mind* (New York, 1920) essayed to complete McDougall's social psychology by applying the hormic theory to "national mind and character." It was a work of subjective sociopolitical criticism rather than of objective scientific psychology, and resembled his many books of polemic and propaganda on national and international policy, from *Is America Safe for Democracy?* (New York, 1921) to *World Chaos* (London and New York, 1931). In these he advocated racial eugenics, a subsidized intellectual aristocracy, and a world air police, to defend the finest (explicitly North European–American) type of civilization.

In *An Outline of Psychology* (New York and London, 1923), *An Outline of Abnormal Psychology* (New York and London, 1926), and *Character and the Conduct of Life* (New York and London, 1927), McDougall elaborated his theory of personality built from sentiments that are powered by instincts, themselves channels of biological purposive energy (horme). The self-regarding sentiment governs conduct according to guidelines formed through identifications with admired persons or abstract ideals. Within the self-regarding sentiment, moral sentiments (conscience) control crude instinctive impulses, and thus, in McDougall's view, individual free will is truly exercised. The ordered hierarchy of sentiments completes the integration of personality. In *Abnormal Psychology,* McDougall reproached both Sigmund Freud and Carl Jung for neglecting the integration of personality—at that time Freud's "superego" and Jung's "self" were not yet formulated.

McDougall's theory still had to explain the occurrence of autonomous complexes apparently outside the hierarchy, and of dissociated activities and "multiple" personalities. Rejecting Freud's determinism, McDougall considered these unconscious mental functions purposive and goal-seeking. He then combined his personality theory with a revised view of body-mind relationships in an elaborate monadic theory based upon that of Gottfried Wilhelm Leibniz. Every personality is integrated as a converging hierarchy of monads, each "potentially a thinking striving self, endowed with true memory." A supreme monad "which each of us calls 'myself'" exercises control by telepathic communication through the hierarchy. Failure of integration allows pathological conflicts, automatisms in sleep or hypnosis, or even revolt of a subordinate monad as a dissociated personality.

McDougall left open the question whether monads might be perceptible through the senses, and he considered the monadic theory to be consistent with either a monistic or a dualistic psychophysical theory. To reconcile a presumably purposive mind with an apparently causally determined body, he suggested that there might be two types of monad, one goal-seeking and the other cause-following, that were somehow interconnected, or one single series of monads with two aspects, causalistic and finalistic. Thus McDougall reconciled his theory both with causal-mechanistic schemes of neurophysiological levels (Sherrington) and with more purposive views, neurological (Henry Head, *Studies in Neurology,* London, 1920) and psychological (hormism). However, he too hastily equated biological purpose (horme) with individual goal-seeking will, and acquired self-control with the capacity for choice and responsibility in conduct.

Once a noted experimental physiologist, McDougall later based hormic psychology increasingly upon his purposivist metaphysical beliefs, little upon verifiable observation or experiment. His great experimental work at Duke was designed to test Chevalier de Lamarck's hypothesis of evolution by inheritance of acquired characteristics. Eventually, after ten years and twenty-three animal generations, McDougall reported an apparently inherited facilitation of learning in laboratory rats. Subsequent workers have not confirmed his results.

A lucid and persuasive writer, McDougall wielded great if temporary influence, and guided many English-reading students toward dynamic, biological, and social psychology. His weaknesses were his fondness for intellectual and verbal solutions to empirical problems, and his temptation to premature systematization. Admiration tinges the epigram that, had the Creator but paused to consult William McDougall, there had been no need of redemption.

See also Darwinism; Freud, Sigmund; Helmholtz, Hermann Ludwig von; James, William; Jung, Carl Gustav; Lamarck, Chevalier de; Leibniz, Gottfried Wilhelm; Lotze, Rudolf Hermann; Macrocosm and Microcosm; Panpsychism; Psychology; Racism; Vitalism.

Bibliography

ADDITIONAL WORKS BY MCDOUGALL

Psychology, the Study of Behavior. London: Williams and Norgate, 1912.

Ethics and Some Modern World Problems. New York and London, 1924.

The Battle of Behaviourism. London: Kegan Paul, 1928. Written with J. B. Watson.

Modern Materialism and Emergent Evolution. New York: Van Nostrand, 1929.

Psycho-analysis and Social Psychology. London: Methuen, 1936.

WORKS ON MCDOUGALL

Greenwood, Major, and May Smith. "William McDougall." In *Obituary Notices of Fellows of the Royal Society,* Vol. III, 39–62. London, 1939–1941. Contains a complete bibliography.

Nicole, J. Ernest. *Psychopathology.* London, 1930; 3rd ed., 1942. Chs. 15, 16, 21.

Woodworth, R. S. *Contemporary Schools of Psychology.* New York: Ronald Press, 1931. Ch. 6.

J. D. Uytman (1967)

MCDOWELL, JOHN
(1942–)

John McDowell, a professor of philosophy at the University of Pittsburgh, was born in Boksburg, South Africa. After receiving his bachelor's from the University College of Rhodesia and Nyasaland he was awarded a Rhodes scholarship to New College, Oxford, where he earned a second bachelor's in 1965 and a master's in 1969. In 1966 he became a fellow of University College, Oxford, where he remained until he joined the faculty at the University of Pittsburgh in 1986. McDowell is a fellow of both the British Academy and the American Academy of Arts and Sciences.

With the rise of modern science there emerged a view of the world that is radically different from that of everyday life, a view sometimes described as "the view from nowhere." This new view was made possible, McDowell argues, by a new clarity regarding natural scientific understanding. Modern natural science explains things not by giving reasons to show that they are somehow better that way but by subsuming them under discoverable physical laws; it understands things by locating them within the realm of law as it contrasts with what Wilfrid Sellars calls the space of reasons. Because modern scientific understanding focuses on explanation by appeal to (physical) laws rather than to reasons, the world as revealed in the view from nowhere is "disenchanted," empty of meaning and value, indeed, of all distinctively human significance. One of the most pervasive themes in McDowell's work (whether in the philosophy of language, the philosophy of mind, metaphysics, epistemology, or ethics) is that philosophers since René Descartes have mistakenly assumed that respectable philosophy must begin with the view from nowhere, and thereby with a conception of nature as the realm of law, rather than with the everyday view from here and its much richer conception of nature.

Consider an ordinary sign, say a stop sign. In day-to-day life one knows how to follow such a sign. But how, the philosopher asks, can one follow the rule expressed by the sign given that what is presented is itself a mere thing, merely a piece of painted metal? It can seem natural to answer that the sign expresses a rule, tells one how to go on, only under an interpretation, that independent of an interpretation of that bit of matter as a stop sign, the sign just stands there. But this cannot be right, McDowell argues following Ludwig Wittgenstein, because any interpretation—say an utterance of the sound *stop*—will be similarly inert unless provided with an interpretation. The right response is to reject the assumption that what is presented is a mere thing. One can learn to conceive the sign as a mere thing independent of all human concerns, just as one can learn to conceive nature in a way that is independent of sensory experience. (One can learn to take the view from nowhere.)

But that capacity is essentially late; it cannot be understood except against the backdrop of one's everyday ability to follow rules such as that expressed in a stop sign.

Indeed, thinking of a sign as a mere thing is itself a matter of rule-following: from the perspective afforded by the view from nowhere, the sign tells one how it is to be thought, namely, as a particular bit of stuff shaped in a certain way. Although the view from nowhere involves pure cognition rather than bodily action, one needs in that case as well the notion of going on in light of a conception of correctness, of thinking one way rather than another on the basis of an understanding of the thing about which one thinks.

Knowing how to follow a rule is at least in some cases a perceptual skill, the ability to see an expression of the rule (e.g., a stop sign) as telling one how to go on. In his masterwork *Mind and World* (1994) McDowell argues more generally that experience, conceived as the capacity to take in manifest facts (e.g., to see that things are thus and so), is an essential component in any adequate conception of cognition. According to his diagnosis the modern unquestioned assumption that natural scientific understanding is the only acceptable mode of access to nature leads philosophers to begin with the mistaken idea that the space of reasons within which thought operates is dualistically opposed to nature. As a result, modern philosophy falls into an oscillation between two equally unsatisfactory conceptions of cognition: on the one hand, an empty coherentism that eschews the notion of experience altogether, and on the other hand, what Sellars calls the "Myth of the Given," the idea that brute impacts of the sort described in physics might provide a perceiver with reasons for belief.

Rejecting the assumption that generates the oscillation, McDowell urges that what is needed instead is the Kantian conception of experience as inextricably involving both sensibility and understanding. Because experience so conceived is at once passive, that is, receptivity in operation, and conceptually articulated, it can serve rationally to constrain one's thought about what is the case, and thereby to explain the empirical contentfulness of thought. As McDowell also argues, the capacity for experience so conceived is essentially second nature; it is acquired only in the course of one's acculturation into natural language, where natural language is itself to be understood as a repository of tradition, the embodiment of the possibility of an orientation to the world.

In his writings on ethics McDowell argues that modern philosophers have a fundamentally distorted conception of practical reason grounded in their scientistic understanding of nature and that this conception has blinded them to the insights of the ancient Greeks. The capacity to act virtuously, he argues following Aristotle,

essentially involves the capacity to take in objective moral facts, where this latter capacity—like the capacity to take in nonmoral facts—is acquired in the course of one's acculturation. It follows that the rationality, and so the desirability, of a life of virtue cannot be established from the outside, independent of how a virtuous person sees things. Critical reflection in ethics, as in any other domain, is Neurathian, possible only from within the tradition one inherits.

Although mostly written in the form of essays, McDowell's work systematically addresses many of the deepest philosophical perplexities that can arise on reflection about human being in the world and the nature and place of language in human life. His writings provide a diagnosis and a cure for the ills of modernity, and a rich, subtle, and profoundly moral vision of what it is to be human.

See also Aristotle; Descartes, René; Ethics, History of; Metaethics; Philosophy of Language; Philosophy of Mind; Rule Following; Sellars, Wilfrid.

Bibliography

WORKS BY MCDOWELL

Plato. *Theaetetus.* Oxford, U.K.: Clarendon Press, 1973. A translation with extensive notes.

Mind and World. Cambridge, MA: Harvard University Press, 1994. The text of McDowell's 1991 Locke Lectures, with a long afterword.

"Having the World in View: Sellars, Kant, and Intentionality." *Journal of Philosophy* 95 (9) (1998): 431–491. A revised version of McDowell's 1997 Woodbridge Lectures.

Meaning, Knowledge, and Reality. Cambridge, MA: Harvard University Press, 1998. A collection of essays in the philosophy of mind, the philosophy of language, metaphysics, and epistemology.

Mind, Value, and Reality. Cambridge, MA: Harvard University Press, 1998. A collection of essays in ethics, the philosophy of mind, and metaphysics.

WORKS ON MCDOWELL

De Gaynesford, Maximilian. *John McDowell.* Cambridge, U.K., and Malden, MA: Polity Press, 2004.

Smith, Nicholas H., ed. *Reading McDowell: On Mind and World.* London and New York: Routledge, 2002. A collection of essays, with responses by McDowell.

Stjernberg, Fredrik, ed. *Theoria* 70 (2/3) (2004). A special issue devoted to essays on McDowell's work, with responses by McDowell.

Thornton, Tim. *John McDowell.* Chesham, U.K.: Acumen, 2004.

Danielle Macbeth (2005)

MCGILVARY, EVANDER BRADLEY

(1864–1953)

Evander Bradley McGilvary, an American realist philosopher, was born in Bangkok, Siam. He received his B.A. from Davidson College in 1884, his M.A. from Princeton in 1888, and his Ph.D. from the University of California in 1897. He was appointed assistant professor of philosophy in California and then Sage professor of ethics at Cornell (1899–1905). From 1905 to 1924 he was professor of philosophy and head of the department at the University of Wisconsin, and in the year 1912–1913 he was the president of the American Philosophical Association. He was the Howison lecturer in 1927, the Mills lecturer in 1928, and the Carus lecturer in 1939.

PHILOSOPHICAL ORIENTATION

McGilvary's "first impulse" toward philosophy was a reaction against the theology in which he was schooled. He came under the Hegelian influence of George Howison at California, and his writings from 1897 to 1903 reflect this influence. But McGilvary, like other Hegelians of his time, eventually found Hegelianism unacceptable. From the start McGilvary held the view that every part of the world is what it is by virtue of its organic relation to every other part. And when he broke with Hegelianism, he took with him this theory of relations and the characteristically Hegelian view that two antagonistic ideas always suggest a third that synthesizes the truth of each.

Realist philosophers in America during the first two decades of the twentieth century were struggling to formulate an epistemology that would do justice both to those elements in experience that are clearly in the objective world and to those dependent upon the experiencing organism. Taking William James's thesis that "the world is as it is experienced," the non-Hegelian new realists developed a monistic realism, but it always threatened to become panobjectivism. In reaction the critical realists set forth a dualistic realism that always threatened to become pansubjectivism. In his "perspective realism" McGilvary sought to combine the truth of new realism with the truth of critical realism. He, too, took James's thesis as his starting point and sought to combine epistemological monism with epistemological dualism and the theory of external relations with the theory of internal relations. McGilvary's synthesis of the objective and the relative—like John Dewey's and A. N. Whitehead's—was dubbed "objective relativism" by A. E. Murphy.

To effect the synthesis of monism and dualism, McGilvary developed his theory of perspectives. It is summarized in the first three postulates of perspective realism: (1) "In our sense-experience there is presented to us in part the real world in which we all in common live"; (2) "Every particular in the world … is what it is only because of its context"; (3) "In the world of nature any 'thing' at any time is, and is nothing but, the totality of the relational characters, experienced or not experienced, that the 'thing' has at that time in whatever relations it has at that time to other 'things.'" McGilvary first hinted at such a theory in 1907, but he did not systematically state it until twenty years later, and in 1939 it became the core of his Carus lectures, *Toward a Perspective Realism*. This work is the key to understanding McGilvary's philosophy, and it grew out of his early thinking about the nature of consciousness.

THE NATURE OF CONSCIOUSNESS

McGilvary believed that the question of the precise nature of consciousness was the fundamental question of philosophy. Like other realists, he agreed with James that consciousness is a relation. Since it was his view that things are what they are only in their relations to other things, he could not agree with realists who claimed that this relation was external. Consciousness, he held, is that relation by which anything becomes an experience. It is a unique kind of "togetherness" of, or between, things. It is neither a spatial nor temporal togetherness, nor is it any other distinguishable relation. The peculiar relation of feeling binds external objects together into an experiential unity we call "consciousness," "awareness," or "experiencing."

McGilvary thought this togetherness may have been what Immanuel Kant meant by the synthetic unity of apperception. It has a unique center of reference in the body of the experiencing organism. This centering gives to the relation of togetherness a character and coloring all its own. Hence, consciousness exists in individualized instances, like other relations, yet each instance produces an individuality generically different from that of any other individualized relation. Each instance is its own kind of betweenness.

As he developed this theory, McGilvary increasingly described consciousness in terms of perspectives. In addition to the familiar perceptual perspectives of space and time, he said, consciousness is characterized by intellectual, moral, and aesthetic perspectives. All these perspectives have both a physical and an "epiphysical," a dynamic and an "epidynamic," causal and noncausal quality. The most distinctive characteristic of these perspectives is the absence of energy transaction between their station point (the organism) and objects in the perspective. The peculiar "epidynamic" relatedness of a perspective does not "go over" to the object or do anything to it. Yet it does "go over" in the way any other relation "goes over" from one term to another. It is a conditioning relatedness that is not itself a cause of the physical existence of its objects, nor is it itself an object in the relation complex. Thus, a perspective (seeing, for example) is not an act of the organism on its object. If it were, it would be difficult to understand how an organism can see now what antedates the seeing, such as a star that may have exploded aeons ago. Like the verb "to relate," the verb "to see" does not name an act performed on the objects seen, any more than "having" a grandfather is an act performed on him. Physical objects become a field of vision when light from them stimulates an organism through its eyes, just as grandparents become grandparents only when a grandchild is born.

The organism, then, is a condition of vision, and as such it is not one of the members or terms in the relationship, just as common parents are a condition for the relationship of brotherhood but are not members in that relationship. Seeing the star that no longer exists is no more difficult for McGilvary to explain than how being an ancestor of a president of the United States is a quality that comes to belong to persons who die before the event that permits ascribing that characteristic to them. In the same way the perspective realist can hold that the physical object that initiated the series of physical conditions that ended in a perception of attributes occupying the position of that object still does not have those attributes. These attributes, however, can be considered part of the real world resulting from a real and natural relation between the organism and external objects. Not all physical qualities, then, are causally conditioned. Sense qualities, for example, can be considered part of their object but are not causally related to the organism that senses them.

It is the same for McGilvary with memory or knowledge of the past. The pastness of an event is not independent of all external standpoints. The pastness of consciousness is retro*spective,* a particular kind of perspectivity, but not retro*active.* Consciousness also is prospective, another kind of perspectivity, but not active on the future. This is the "epiphysical" or "epidynamic" quality of the consciousness relation that distinguishes it from other physical, dynamic, causal relations that act on their objects. Perspectives do not exist if that means being in space and time. Nor do they subsist. The being of a perspective is its being between—"inter-sistence," McGilvary called it—and each perspective is its own kind of "inter-sistence."

But it is not clear whether McGilvary thought that each perspective is an instance of consciousness and whether perspectives go to make up what we call consciousness. Nor does he show us how to distinguish between what the organism contributes to the perspective, as its station point, and what is there independent of the organism. At times he said nothing is there independent of the organism, for the organism is the necessary condition of any perspective. But when Dewey said that the logical forms of our knowledge cannot be read back into nature (because they come into being only when inquiry is instituted and are only modes of operating upon subject matter), McGilvary disagreed. He argued that any logical form that serves to solve a problematic situation serves that purpose because it is actually the form of the subject matter under investigation, not of the subject matter as it was immediately experienced when inquiry started but as successful inquiry shows the subject matter to have been in the natural world.

It is doubtful, then, that McGilvary, like the other objective relativists, was any more successful than other realists in doing justice to the objective and the relative found in experience.

McGilvary's few articles on ethics present familiar positions, but none of them is developed systematically, nor did McGilvary apply his perspective realism beyond epistemological and ontological problems.

See also Consciousness; Dewey, John; Hegelianism; Howison, George Holmes; James, William; Murphy, Arthur Edward; Realism; Whitehead, Alfred North.

Bibliography

WORKS BY MCGILVARY

"Pure Experience and Reality: A Re-assertion." *Philosophical Review* 16 (May 1907): 266–284.

"The Physiological Argument against Realism." *Journal of Philosophy* 4 (October 1907): 589–601.

"Realism and the Physical World." *Journal of Philosophy* 4 (December 1907): 683–692.

"Experience and Its Inner Duplicity." *Journal of Philosophy* 6 (April 1909): 225–232.

"Experience as Pure and Consciousness as Meaning." *Journal of Philosophy* 8 (September 1911): 511–525.

"The Relation of Consciousness and Object in Sense Perception." *Philosophical Review* 21 (March 1912): 152–173.

"A Tentative Realistic Metaphysics." In *Contemporary American Philosophy*, edited by G. P. Adams and W. P. Montague, 2 vols. New York: Macmillan, 1930. Vol. II, pp. 109–132.

"The Revolt against Dualism." *Philosophical Review* 40 (May 1931): 246–265.

"Perceptual and Memory Perspectives." *Journal of Philosophy* 30 (June 1933): 109–132.

Toward a Perspective Realism. La Salle, IL: Open Court, 1956. His 1939 Carus lectures and his only book.

Between 1918 and 1926 McGilvary published only two book reviews. His publications after 1926 display a new interest in and command of mathematical physics. Two of these papers are reprinted in his book. In all he published 48 articles and 23 reviews in addition to 81 articles in *The New International Encyclopedia* (New York, 1902).

WORKS ON MCGILVARY

Murphy, Arthur E. "McGilvary's Perspective Realism." *Journal of Philosophy* 56 (February 1959): 149–165. Reprinted in *Reason and the Common Good,* edited by W. H. Hay et al. Englewood Cliffs, NJ: Prentice-Hall, 1963.

Oliver, Donald W. "The Logic of Perspective Realism." *Journal of Philosophy* 35 (April 1938): 197–208.

Thomas Robischon (1967)

MCTAGGART, JOHN MCTAGGART ELLIS
(1866–1925)

John McTaggart Ellis McTaggart, a British metaphysician, was born in London, the son of Francis and Caroline Ellis. (His father later took the name McTaggart to fulfill a condition for inheriting a bequest.) He attended school at Clifton and went on to Trinity College, Cambridge, where he took first-class honors in the moral science tripos in 1888. He was made a fellow of Trinity in 1891. The next year he paid a visit to New Zealand, where his widowed mother lived, and there he met Margaret Elizabeth Bird, whom he married in 1899, during a second visit to New Zealand. Thereafter he resided at Cambridge. Active in the affairs of his college and the university, he was a busy and successful teacher from 1897 until he retired in 1923. He died suddenly in January 1925.

McTaggart's philosophy is a peculiar and quite personal variety of Hegelian idealism. Ultimate reality, he held, is spiritual: It consists entirely of individual minds and their contents. He understood this in a way that excludes space, time, and material objects from reality. What appear to us as being these things are really minds and parts of the contents of minds, but we "misperceive" these entities in a systematic way, and this misperception is the source of the whole apparent universe. Despite the unreality of time, McTaggart argued, there is an important sense in which it is true to say that individual persons are immortal, and that they are reincarnated in a succession of (apparent) bodies. He also held that in reality persons stand in relations either of direct perception, and consequently love, or of indirect perception, and consequently affection, to one another. Love is, indeed, the basically real emotional state. There is, however, no God in this heavenly city, for McTaggart did not think there is any reason to believe that there is or even can be an overarching mind that includes individual minds like ours but is still in some sense an individual mind itself. McTaggart was, in addition, a determinist, though he held that determinism is not incompatible with the existence of valid judgments of moral obligation.

On these basic points McTaggart never changed his mind. He argued in support of them both in his early writings on G. W. F. Hegel and in his great systematic work, *The Nature of Existence*. The main difference between his earlier and his later work is that in the former the arguments are dialectical in a Hegelian manner, whereas in the latter they are more straightforwardly deductive.

WRITINGS ON HEGEL

McTaggart's commentaries on Hegel are all more or less critical of Hegel, and none is entirely reliable as pure exegesis. Two deal primarily with Hegelian methodology. The essays on the dialectic defend Hegel's method against what McTaggart took to be common misunderstandings and criticisms and offer an account of the way in which the Absolute Idea works to move thought from stage to stage. The *Commentary on Hegel's Logic* is a detailed and very careful examination of the validity of each step in the logical development of the categories. McTaggart frequently found Hegel to be mistaken or confused about his transitions and in some cases offered alternative modes of development.

The essays on cosmology are among McTaggart's most interesting work. He here discussed, more fully than anywhere else, a number of concrete topics—such as the moral criterion, sin, the organic nature of society, and the relations between Christianity and Hegelianism—in the light of his metaphysical position. He brought out his differences, not only with Hegel, but with many of the British Hegelians as well. And in the concluding chapter he presented with great clarity and power what is essentially his mature view of the relations between selves in ultimate reality.

SOME DOGMAS OF RELIGION

In *Some Dogmas of Religion* McTaggart examined, in a careful but nontechnical manner, a number of dogmas that are especially relevant to Christianity. (By *dogma* he meant "proposition having metaphysical significance.") He argued that dogmas of some sort are essential to any religion and that we must have reasoned proof of a dogma before we can be justified in believing in it. Then, without claiming to give conclusive arguments (for these would involve a whole metaphysical system) he argued in favor of immortality, preexistence, and determinism, criticized the belief in a personal and omnipotent God, and attacked some of the arguments that have been alleged to support this belief. Finally, he tried to show that there is much less connection than is frequently held to be between the truth of theism and improved chances for personal happiness.

NATURE OF EXISTENCE

McTaggart's metaphysical system is presented in two parts. In the first, contained in Volume I of *The Nature of Existence*, he gave an extended argument to show that whatever exists must be of a certain nature and must, therefore, satisfy a certain requirement, to be explained below. In the second part, occupying Volume II, he examined various types of entities that our present experience shows us as existing to determine whether these entities can satisfy the requirement; he attempted to account for the apparent existence of those entities that do not really exist; and he evaluated the practical importance of the results he had thus reached.

The argument of Volume I is almost entirely a priori. McTaggart appealed to experience for only two propositions: that something exists, and that what exists has parts. His argument proceeds through the following stages: First, McTaggart offered a proof of the principle of the Identity of Indiscernibles. Second, he argued that every substance must have a "sufficient description," that is, a description that uniquely identifies the substance and contains no reference to substances that are only identified (as by pointing or by the use of purely referring expressions), not described.

He next moved to the assertion that every substance, without exception, must be divisible into parts that are themselves substances, and hence into parts within parts to infinity. The crucial argument is then presented. The principle that every substance must have a sufficient description together with the principle that every substance is infinitely divisible into further substances would entail a contradiction unless the substances in question were such that from the nature of any existing substance there follow sufficient descriptions of all of its parts within parts to infinity. This can occur, McTaggart showed, if the substance stands in a certain extremely complex relation to its parts, which he called the relation of "Determining Correspondence"; it can occur, he held, in no other way. Hence, whatever exists—and we know that something does exist—must satisfy the conditions necessary for it to stand in Determining Correspondence relations to its parts.

In Volume II McTaggart denied the existence of material objects, space, judgments, inferences, sense data, and certain other mental contents, on the ground that entities of these types cannot satisfy the conditions required for them to stand in Determining Correspondence relations. His denial of the existence of time, however, rests on a quite different argument. This argument is McTaggart's most widely discussed contribution to philosophy. Briefly, it is as follows: Temporal positions and events may be ordered either as earlier-later or as past-present-future. Ordered the first way, they form what McTaggart called a *B*-series; ordered the second way they form an *A*-series. In the first stage of the argument McTaggart tried to show that the *A*-series characteristics "past," "present," and "future" are essential to the existence of time. He assumed it to be admitted that change is essential to time, and he argued that unless the *A*-series characteristics can change, nothing can change. The *B*-series characteristics cannot change, for if an event is ever earlier than another, it is always earlier; and neither can the other characteristics of events change, for if it is ever true that an event is, for instance, the death of a queen, then it is always true that this event is the death of a queen. Hence, without the *A*-series there cannot be time, and in the second stage of the argument McTaggart tried to show that a vicious infinite regress is involved in affirming the existence of a series ordered by *A*-series characteristics. Each member of such a series must have all the *A*-series characteristics, he said, but those characteristics are incompatible. If we try to remove the contradiction by saying that each member possesses all the characteristics *at different times*, we are presupposing the existence of different moments of time at which the *A*-series characteristics are possessed. But each of these moments, to be temporal, must itself possess all of the *A*-series characteristics, which, again, is impossible; the attempt to relieve this contradiction by appeal to yet another set of moments only gives rise to another set of contradictions, and so on.

McTaggart's complicated and difficult account of the relations between appearance and reality centers on the concept of a *C*-series, analogous to the *B*-series in having its members related by an asymmetrical and transitive relation, but timeless. The model for the *C*-series relationship is the concept of "inclusion," and the terms that are included in and inclusive of each other are perceptions, that is, parts of spirits. McTaggart argued that reality must be structured so as to form a set of related inclusion series that, however, are misperceived as temporal series. He drew the further conclusion that time had a first moment and will have a last moment.

McTaggart went on to discuss the question of the value of the universe, both in its prefinal stages and at the stage when the appearance of time has ceased. Taking both "good" and "evil" to stand for simple, unanalyzable characteristics, and arguing that only what is spiritual can have value, he found that in the prefinal stages the relative proportions of good and evil will fluctuate considerably, though we can be confident that on the whole the proportion of good will steadily increase. In the final stage we will exist in a "timeless and endless state of love" far more profound and powerful than anything we now have any inkling of. We shall, McTaggart said, "know nothing but our beloved, those they love, and ourselves as loving them," and this will be our ultimate and unshakable satisfaction. If McTaggart's metaphysics thus concludes with a vision that he himself was not unwilling to call mystical, it is at least a vision that springs from one of the most brilliantly conceived and carefully executed attempts any philosopher has ever produced to grasp the nature of reality in purely rational terms.

See also Hegel, Georg Wilhelm Friedrich; Time.

Bibliography

WORKS BY MCTAGGART

Studies in the Hegelian Dialectic. London: Cambridge University Press, 1896; 2nd ed., Cambridge, 1922.

Studies in Hegelian Cosmology. London: Cambridge University Press, 1901; 2nd ed., Cambridge, 1918.

Some Dogmas of Religion. London: Arnold, 1906; 2nd ed., London, 1930.

A Commentary on Hegel's Logic. London: Cambridge University Press, 1910.

The Nature of Existence. 2 vols. Vol. I, London: Cambridge University Press, 1921; Vol. II, edited by C. D. Broad. London: Cambridge University Press, 1927.

Essays in *Philosophical Essays*, edited by S. V. Keeling. London: Arnold, 1934.

Human Immortality and Pre-existence. New York: Kraus Reprint, 1970.

Philosophical Studies, edited by S. V. Keeling. South Bend, IN: St Augustine's Press, 2000.

WORKS ON MCTAGGART

C. D. Broad delivered an obituary address to the British Academy that contains an admirable summary of McTaggart's work. It was published in the society's *Proceedings* for 1927 and reprinted in the second edition of *Some Dogmas of Religion*, as well as in Broad's *Ethics and the History of Philosophy* (London: Routledge, 1952). *John McTaggart Ellis McTaggart*, by G. Lowes Dickinson (London: Cambridge University Press, 1931), contains more information about McTaggart's life, in addition to interesting reminiscences and a chapter by S. V. Keeling on McTaggart's metaphysics. The standard commentary is C. D. Broad's exhaustive *Examination of McTaggart's Philosophy* (Vol. I, London: Cambridge University Press, 1933; Vol. II, in two parts, London: Cambridge University Press, 1938). This work is discussed at length by R. L. Patterson in *The Philosophy of C. D. Broad* (New York: Tudor, 1959). (For discussion of McTaggart on time, see the bibliography for the *Time* entry.)

OTHER RECOMMENDED WORKS

Airaksinen, Timo. *The Ontological Criteria of Reality: A Study of Bradley and McTaggart.* Turku, Finland: Turun Yliopisto, 1975.

Cesarz, Gary L. *Substance and Relations in McTaggart's Philosophy: A Re-examination of His Basic Principles.* PhD diss., University of New Mexico, 1988.

Farmer, David John. *Being in Time: The Nature of Time in Light of McTaggart's Paradox.* Lanham, MD: University Press of America, 1990.

Gale, Richard M. *The Language of Time.* London, Routledge & Kegan Paul; New York, Humanities Press, 1968.

Geach, P. T. *Truth, Love, and Immortality: An Introduction to McTaggart's Philosophy.* Berkeley: University of California Press, 1979.

Mellor, D. H. *Real time.* Cambridge, U.K., and New York: Cambridge University Press, 1981.

Rochelle, Gerald. *Behind Time: The Incoherence of Time and McTaggart's Atemporal Replacement.* Aldershot, Hants, U.K.; Brookfield, VT: Ashgate, 1998.

Rochelle, Gerald. *The Life and Philosophy of J. McT. E. McTaggart, 1866–1925.* Lewiston, NY: E. Mellen, 1991.

Schulz, James Allen. *McTaggart's Theory of Substance.* PhD diss., Northwestern University, 1974.

J. B. Schneewind (1967)
Bibliography updated by Michael J. Farmer (2005)

MEAD, GEORGE HERBERT
(1863–1931)

George Herbert Mead, the American pragmatist philosopher, was born in South Hadley, Massachusetts. He received his BA from Oberlin College in 1883 and did graduate work at Harvard in 1887–1888, where he studied under Josiah Royce and William James. From 1888 to

1891 he studied psychology and philosophy in Europe. He was married in 1891 and in the same year was appointed instructor at the University of Michigan. In 1892 he joined the staff of the University of Chicago and later became chairman of its philosophy department.

A major figure in American pragmatism, Mead has also had a large influence on psychologists and social scientists. Many thinkers, including Alfred North Whitehead and John Dewey, regarded Mead as a creative mind of the first magnitude. He published relatively few papers, however, and died before he was able to develop his many original ideas into an integrated philosophy. Large segments of his books were collated from his unfinished manuscripts and from his students' notes and hence are repetitious, unsystematic, and difficult.

Mead's main philosophic themes may be classified as follows: (1) the emergence of mind and self from the communication process between organisms (often termed his "social behaviorism"), discussed in *Mind, Self and Society*; (2) the psychological genesis of scientific categories in purposeful acts, discussed in *The Philosophy of the Act*; and (3) the social conception of nature and the location of reality in the present, discussed in *The Philosophy of the Present*.

SOCIAL BEHAVIORISM

Mead's thought stemmed from the impact of Darwinism on nineteenth-century ideas. Man was regarded as an organism functioning in accordance with natural laws. This approach opposed traditional philosophy and theology and sought to understand human nature by the methods of experimental science. The theory of evolution also gave impetus to the conception of the universe as a process rather than as a set of fixed, unalterable essences that remain invariant over time. In psychology the process concept was expressed in functionalism, which sought to comprehend all mental phenomena not as structures, traits, or attributes of the mind but as relations between the organism and its environment. These ideas were taken up by behavioristic psychology, which dismissed introspection as unscientific and confined itself to experimental data, particularly the responses of organisms to stimuli under varying conditions.

Mead challenged many of the crudities of behaviorism. In rejecting introspection, this school tended to regard it as a nonexistent phenomenon, since it could not be studied experimentally. Mead's social behaviorism sought to widen behaviorism to include the introspectively observed phenomena of consciousness. For Mead stimulus and response are meaningful only when viewed as aspects of communication; they cannot be studied in abstraction from the social process in which actions occur. Furthermore, organisms do not merely respond mechanically and passively to stimuli. Rather, the individual purposefully selects its stimuli. Mead here opposed associationism; the organism is a dynamic, forceful agent, not a mute receptacle for ideas that are later associated. For Mead organism and environment mutually determine each other. Mind emerges from this reciprocal determination.

Mead's naturalistic conception of introspection was based on the viewpoint that an idea is the early, inner stage in an ongoing act directed toward an environmental goal. The mistake of the behaviorists was to study merely one part of the complete act, the last, overt stage, thereby ignoring the initial phase of the act, which occurs privately, within the organism.

According to Mead actions occur within a communicative process. The initial phase of the overt stage of an act constitutes a gesture. A gesture is a preparatory movement that enables other individuals to become aware of the intentions of the given organism. The rudimentary situation is a conversation of gestures, in which a gesture on the part of the first individual evokes a preparatory movement on the part of the second, and the gesture of the second organism in turn calls out a response in the first person. On this level no communication occurs. Neither organism is aware of the effect of its own gestures upon the other; the gestures are nonsignificant. For communication to take place, each organism must have knowledge of how the other individual will respond to his own ongoing act. Here the gestures are significant symbols.

Communication is also based on the fact that actions are organized temporally. The consequences of behavior (final phases of the act) are present in imagery during the early phases of the action and control the nature of the developing movement. There are usually several alternative ways of completing a movement that has been started. Since the final phases of the act control the ongoing movement, the organism can select one of these alternative ways of conjoining means with the end. In this manner rational conduct is possible. Where organisms use significant symbols, the role of the other individual controls the ongoing act. In advance of our completion of a social action, we anticipate the response of the other individual. Since our behavior is temporally organized, the imported role of the other may cause us to select a course of action that is different from what we originally intended.

Mind is the ability of an organism to take the role of the other toward its own developing behavior. Reflexivity, the ability of a person to reflect upon himself, is the necessary condition for the emergence of mind within the social process. With reflexivity the social act is imported within the individual and serves to alter the person's ongoing acts. A complete social act can be carried out internally without external movements necessarily occurring. Mead denotes the internalized role of the other as the "me." Each organism has an "I," which is a capacity for spontaneity. The "I" is expressed when the individual alters his ongoing response or creates a new response to the "me." Individuality and originality arise from the inner conversation between the "I" and the imported role of the other. An inner forum comes to exist, consisting of a dialogue between the "I" and the "me." This inner rehearsal of projected actions constitutes introspection, or thinking.

In the organized group situation, such as is exemplified in games, the individual learns to take into himself the entire social organization which now exerts internal control over his ongoing acts. The "generalized other" is the group's attitudes imported into the individual. It is here that social institutions enter into an individual's thinking as a determinative factor and cause him to develop a complete self. Now the inner forum becomes an inner dialogue between the person and the group.

The religious experience occurs in situations where each person becomes closely identified with the other members of the group. In common efforts, such as in teamwork, where a sense of closeness develops among everyone involved, a feeling of exaltation arises. Here Mead refers to a "fusion" of the "I" and the "me."

Mead's social psychology is similar to the psychoanalytic theories of Sigmund Freud and Harry Stack Sullivan in that it conceives personality as arising from the internalization of the roles of other persons and relates inner conflict to the tension between the spontaneous forces of the person and the introjected demands of society. The temporal organization of the act, stressed by Mead, is also a key concept in automatic control machinery and digital computers, where the later stages of a process feed back upon the earlier phases, modifying the ongoing process.

PHILOSOPHY OF SCIENCE

Mead sought to find the psychological origin of science in the efforts of individuals to attain power over their environment. The notion of a physical object arises out of manipulatory experience. Perception is coordinated with the ongoing act: When we approach a thing we wish to manipulate, the imagery of handling that thing is present in the distance perception. Here again there is a temporal organization of the act, in that the later phase of the action, the contact experience, is present in the earlier stage when we are merely perceiving the distant object. Perception involves the readiness of the organism to manipulate the thing when the intervening distance has been traversed. The reality of a thing is in the consummatory phase of the act, the contact experience, and this reality is present in the experience of perceiving that thing at a distance.

There is a social relation to inanimate objects, for the organism takes the role of things that it manipulates directly or that it manipulates indirectly in perception. For example, in taking (introjecting or imitating) the resistant role of a solid object, an individual obtains cognition of what is "inside" nonliving things. Historically, the concept of the physical object arose from an animistic conception of the universe.

Contact experience includes experiences of position, balance, and support, and these are used by the organism when it creates its conceptions of the physical world. Our scientific concepts of space, time, and mass are abstracted from manipulatory experience. Such concepts as that of the electron are also derived from manipulation. In developing a science we construct hypothetical objects in order to assist ourselves in controlling nature. The conception of the present as a distinct unit of experience, rather than as a process of becoming and disappearing, is a scientific fiction devised to facilitate exact measurement. In the scientific worldview immediate experience is replaced by theoretical constructs. The ultimate in experience, however, is the manipulation and contact at the completion of an act.

COSMOLOGY

The Philosophy of the Present develops the conception that reality always exists in a present. However, as it is experienced, the present involves both the past and the future. A process in nature is not a succession of instantaneous presents or a sequence of spatial points. Instead there is both spatial and temporal duration, or continuity.

The developing action is the basis of existence. It is true that as we look back the present is determined by the past. But each new present, as it passes into the next present, is a unique emergent. A new future also arises as the result of the emerging present. Hence, we are always reconstructing our pasts and restructuring our future.

Novelty stretches out in both directions from the present perspective.

Every object in the universe is seen from the perspective of a particular individual. What is seen from one person's perspective may be different from that which is seen by another individual. Mead was not solipsistic, however, for although a person sees nature only from his own perspective, he is able to import within himself the perspectives of others. Reality is the integration of different perspectives. Mead made use of the theory of relativity to project his theory of sociality and mind into nature. Sociality is the ability to be in more than one system at a time, to take more than one perspective simultaneously. This phenomenon occurs in emergence, for here an object in the process of becoming something new passes from one system to another, and in the passage is in two systems at the same time. During this transition, or transmutation, the emergent entity exists on two levels of nature concomitantly.

Mead's philosophy has been compared with that of Martin Buber. Although their approaches stem from different traditions, both thinkers have a social conception of nature and conceive of the self as arising from a social matrix. Certain affinities between Mead and Edmund Husserl have been suggested, in that the mind's reflexive examination of itself is an effort to describe the constitution and foundation of experience.

See also Behaviorism; Buber, Martin; Darwinism; Dewey, John; Evolutionary Theory; Experience; Freud, Sigmund; Husserl, Edmund; James, William; Natural Law; Pragmatism; Royce, Josiah; Whitehead, Alfred North.

Bibliography

WORKS BY MEAD

The Philosophy of the Present, edited by Arthur E. Murphy. Chicago: Open Court, 1932. Mead's Carus Lectures. Prefatory remarks by John Dewey.

Mind, Self and Society from the Standpoint of a Social Behaviorist, edited by Charles W. Morris. Chicago: University of Chicago Press, 1934. Based on Mead's lectures in social psychology. Introduction by Morris. Contains a listing of Mead's writings.

Movements of Thought in the Nineteenth Century, edited by Merritt H. Moore. Chicago: University of Chicago Press, 1936. Notes from course lectures.

The Philosophy of the Act, edited by Charles W. Morris, in collaboration with John M. Brewster, Albert M. Dunham, and David L. Miller. Chicago: University of Chicago Press, 1938. Unpublished papers and lecture notes. Introduction by Morris.

The Social Psychology of George Herbert Mead, edited by Anselm Strauss. Chicago: University of Chicago Press, 1956. Introduction by Strauss.

The Social Psychology of George Herbert Mead, Part Six: Self, edited by Anselm Strauss. Chicago, University of Chicago Press, 1965.

Movements of Thought in the Nineteenth Century, edited by Merrit H. Moore. Chicago: University of Chicago Press, 1967.

George Herbert Mead: Essays on His Social Philosophy, edited by John w. Petras. New York: Teachers College Press, 1968.

On Social Psychology: Selected Papers. Rev. ed, edited by Anselm Strauss. Chicago: University of Chicago Press, 1972.

Miller, David L. *George Herbert Mead: Self, Language, and the World.* Austin: University of Texas Press, 1973.

Selected Writings, edited by Andrew J. Reck. Chicago: University of Chicago Press, 1981.

The Individual and the Social Self: Unpublished Work of George Herbert Mead, edited by David L. Miller. Chicago: University of Chicago Press, 1982.

George's Page: A Document Repository for the Work of George Herbert Mead with Resources to Support Research on His Contribution to Social Psychology, edited by Lloyd Ward and Robert Throop. St. Catherines, ON: The Mead Project, Dept. of Sociology, Brock University, 1998–.

Essays in Social Psychology, edited by Mary Jo Deegan. New Brunswick: Transaction Publishers, 2001.

WORKS ON MEAD

Cook, Gary A. *George Herbert Mead: The Making of a Social Pragmatist.* Urbana: University of Illinois Press, 1993.

Joas, Hans. *G. H. Mead: A Contemporary Re-examination of His Thought.* Cambridge, MA: MIT Press, 1985.

Lee, Grace Chin. *George Herbert Mead: Philosopher of the Social Individual.* New York: King's Crown Press, 1945. Includes bibliography of secondary literature.

Natanson, Maurice. *The Social Dynamics of George Herbert Mead.* Washington, DC: Public Affairs Press, 1956. Discusses affinities with Husserl's phenomenology. Includes bibliography. Introduction by Horace M. Kallen.

Pfuetze, Paul E. *The Social Self.* New York: Bookman Associates, 1954. Comparisons between Mead, Buber, and psychoanalysis.

William H. Desmonde (1967)
Bibliography updated by Michael J. Farmer (2005)

MEANING

What is it for a sentence—or a substantial expression, such as a word or phrase—to have a particular "meaning" in a given language? While it is widely agreed that the meaning of a sentence, phrase, or word must have something to do with the way that the expression is used by speakers of the language, it is not at all obvious how to move from that vague idea to a precise answer to our question. One problem is that utterances of a given sentence might be used to convey all manner of messages, many of which would be far removed from what we intuitively regard as the literal linguistic meaning of the sentence. Any account of meaning in terms of use must find a way to avoid having every innovative or idiosyncratic feature of use registered as an aspect of meaning. There are two ideas about linguistic meaning that might help with this problem. One is the idea that linguistic meaning is a matter of convention. The other is the idea that linguistic meaning is compositional; that is, the linguistic meaning of a sentence depends in a systematic way on the meanings of the words and phrases from which the sentence is constructed.

LINGUISTIC MEANING IS CONVENTIONAL

To define the meaning of a sentence as the message or messages that the sentence is, or can be, used to convey is inadequate, because too inclusive. In order to exclude the innovative or idiosyncratic features of language use, we might reach for the notion of a rule of language: What it is for a sentence to mean that p is for there to be a rule saying that the sentence is to be used (or may be used) to convey the message that p. However, if a rule is something that is formulated explicitly (in language), then the proposal may just reintroduce the notion of linguistic meaning; and that would be unsatisfactory if the project is to define or analyze the notion of linguistic meaning in other terms. So, instead of the notion of an explicitly formulated rule we can make use of the notion of a convention, defined as a rationally self-perpetuating regularity (Lewis, 1969). The resulting proposal is that what it is for a sentence S to mean that p in the language of a given population is for there to be a convention in that population to use utterances of S to convey the message that p.

LINGUISTIC MEANING IS COMPOSITIONAL

The term *theory of meaning* can be applied to two very different kinds of theory. On the one hand, there are semantic theories that specify the meanings of the expressions of some particular language; on the other hand, there are metasemantic theories that analyze or explain the notion of meaning. We should expect the idea that meaning is compositional to be reflected in semantic theories. The way in which the meanings of sentences depend on the meanings of words and phrases should be revealed in a semantic theory by having the meaning specifications for whole sentences derived logically from more basic principles that specify the meanings of words and phrases.

Many features of the messages conveyed by the use of a sentence will not be seen simply as the results of contributions to meaning made by the words in the sentence—contributions that would be repeated in other sentences—but rather as the products of interaction between the meaning of the sentence and other background assumptions. (The study of this interaction is called pragmatics. See Davis, 1991.) It is true, for example, that a letter of reference that says only, "Mr. X's command of English is excellent, and his attendance at tutorials has been regular" is likely to convey the message that Mr. X is not a talented philosopher (Grice, 1975). But this message is not the logical product of the meanings of the words and phrases used. Rather, the letter writer is able to convey that message by relying on shared assumptions about what information would be relevant in the circumstances. (See Grice's early [1961] proposals about pragmatics.)

TWO APPROACHES TO THE STUDY OF MEANING

These ideas, that meaning is conventional and compositional, can be seen at work in two important approaches to the study of linguistic meaning, on which this article focuses. One is Herbert Paul Grice's program for analyzing the concept of literal linguistic meaning in terms of psychological notions such as belief and intention (Grice, 1989). The other is Donald Davidson's project of illuminating the notion of meaning by considering how to construct compositional semantic theories for natural languages (Davidson, 1984).

GRICE'S ANALYTICAL PROGRAM

The Gricean analytical program can be regarded as having two stages (for overviews, see Avramides, 1989; Neale, 1992). The first stage aims to characterize a concept of speaker's meaning that corresponds, roughly, to the idea of conveying, or attempting to convey, a particular message (Grice, 1957, and other papers, 1989). The second stage then aims to use the concept of speaker's meaning, along with the notion of a convention, to build an analysis of literal linguistic meaning. (In fact, Grice himself did not introduce the notion of convention, but used a slightly different idea. See Grice, 1989; Lewis, 1969, 1975; Schiffer, 1972.)

The basic idea of the first stage of the program is that an agent who is attempting to convey a message—perhaps the message that it is time for tea—makes an utterance (which might or might not be linguistic in nature) with the intention that the hearer should come to believe that it is time for tea and should believe it, at least in part, in virtue of recognizing that this is what the utterer intends him or her to believe. The analysis of speaker's meaning was refined and complicated in the face of counterexamples (Grice, 1989; Strawson, 1964; Schiffer, 1972), but it retained the crucial feature of not itself importing the notion of literal meaning. This feature is shared by the analysis of convention as a rationally self-perpetuating regularity, and so the prospects are good that the analysis of meaning resulting from Grice's program can meet the requirement of noncircularity.

PROBLEMS WITH GRICE'S PROGRAM. Grice's program does, however, face a number of serious objections. One problem concerns the application of the program to sentences that are never used at all—perhaps because they are too long or too implausible. Clearly, the Gricean analysis of literal meaning cannot be applied directly to these sentences. If we want to say that there is, nevertheless, a fact of the matter as to what unused sentences mean, then we seem bound to appeal to the meanings of the words and phrases from which unused sentences are built. But now we come to the most serious problem for the program, namely, how to analyze the notion of meaning as it applies to subsentential expressions.

Parties to a convention know what the relevant regularity is, and their belief that they and others have conformed to the regularity in the past gives them a reason to continue conforming to it. Thus, the Gricean program involves crediting speakers of a language with knowledge about regularities of use. While this is plausible in the case of the use of complete sentences, it is problematic when we move to subsentential expressions. Words and phrases are used in complete sentences, and they make a systematic contribution to the meanings of the sentences in which they occur. Regularities of use for words and phrases are regularities of contribution to the messages that sentences are used to convey. But spelling out in detail how words and phrases (and ways of putting them together) contribute to the meanings of complete sentences is a highly nontrivial project. So, it is not plausible that every speaker of a language knows what these regularities of contribution are.

The problem for the Gricean program is that it seems bound to attribute to ordinary language users knowledge that they do not really have. It may be that we can deal with this problem by invoking some notion of tacit (Chomsky, 1986) or implicit (Dummett, 1991, 1993) knowledge (Loar, 1981). But the dominant consensus—and the view of one of the most authoritative exponents

of Grice's program (Schiffer, 1987)—is that the project of analyzing literal meaning in terms of intentions and beliefs cannot be completed.

DAVIDSON AND TRUTH-CONDITIONAL SEMANTICS

Any metasemantic theory can be used to provide conditions of adequacy on semantic theories. Thus, consider the Gricean metasemantic proposal:

Sentence S means that p in the language of population G if and only if (iff) there is a convention in G to use utterances of S to convey the message that p.

And suppose that a semantic theory for a particular language L delivers as one of its meaning specifications:

Sentence S1 means (in L) that wombats seldom sneeze.

Then, according to the metasemantic proposal, one necessary condition for the correctness of the semantic theory is that there should be a convention in the population of L-speakers to use utterances of S1 to convey the message that wombats seldom sneeze.

This kind of transposition can be carried out in the opposite direction too. Any condition of adequacy on semantic theories can be reconfigured as a partial elucidation of the concept of meaning—or of whatever other concept plays a key role in the semantic theory—and a great deal of philosophical work on the concept of meaning proceeds by considering constraints on semantic theories. Davidson's work (1984) provides an important example of this approach.

THE TRUTH-CONDITIONAL FORMAT. As we introduced the notion, a semantic theory is a theory that tells us what expressions mean. It is natural to suppose, then, that the key concept used in a semantic theory will be the concept of meaning, and that the format of the meaning specifications for sentences will be either:

The meaning of sentence S = m

or else:

Sentence S means that p

according as meanings are or are not regarded as entities. But Davidson (1967) rejects both these formats, and argues instead for the truth-conditional format:

Sentence S is true if and only if p.

His argument comes in two steps.

The first step is intended to rule out the idea that, to each word, each phrase, and each sentence, there should be assigned some entity as its meaning. This step proceeds by showing that, under certain assumptions about the assignment of entities, all true sentences would be assigned the same entity. (The argument that is used here is sometimes called the Frege argument.) Clearly, no such assignment of entities could be an assignment of meanings, since not all true sentences have the same meaning. However, it is possible to resist this first step by arguing that an assignment of meanings would not conform to the assumptions that are needed to make the Frege argument work.

Even though the first step is controversial, the second step in Davidson's argument remains important for anyone who begins by favoring the format:

Sentence S <u>means that</u> p.

We said that, given the compositionality of meaning, we should expect that, in a semantic theory, the meaning specifications for whole sentences will be derived from more basic principles that specify the meanings of words and phrases. But Davidson points out that the logical properties of the "means that p" construction raise problems for the formal derivation of meaning specifications for sentences. In contrast, the truth-conditional format is logically well understood. And from the work of Alfred Tarski on certain formal languages (1944, 1956) we can carry over methods for deriving truth-condition specifications for sentences from axioms that assign semantic properties to words and phrases.

CONDITIONS OF ADEQUACY. If what a semantic theory tells us about each sentence of a language is to be cast in the truth conditional format:

Sentence S is true if and only if p

then what are the conditions of adequacy on semantic theories? We have already seen an adequacy condition on the internal structure of a semantic theory; namely, that it should reveal how the truth conditions of complete sentences depend on the semantic properties of words and phrases. But what conditions must the truth condition specifications themselves meet, in order to be correct?

Tarski imposed, in effect, the condition that the sentence that fills the "p" place should translate (or else be the very same sentence as) the sentence S. (This is Tarski's Convention T [1956].) This condition of adequacy can be transposed into a partial elucidation of the concept of truth in terms of the concept of translation. The concept of translation is sufficiently closely related to the concept of meaning that we can move from here to a partial elucidation of truth in terms of meaning:

If a sentence S means that p then S is true iff p.

But we cannot shed any light on the concept of meaning itself without bringing in extra resources.

The key notion that Davidson introduces is that of "interpretation." We imagine using the deliverances of a semantic theory to help interpret the linguistic behavior of speakers. For these purposes, we can abstract away from the details of the format, and use deliverances in the schematic form:

Sentence S _____ p

to license the redescription of utterances of a sentence S as linguistic acts of saying or asserting that p. Now, by providing a way of understanding speakers' specifically linguistic behavior, a semantic theory can play a part in the project of interpreting, or making sense of, them. So, any constraints on the project of overall interpretation of people can be reconfigured as partial elucidations of the key concepts used in semantic theories.

Two suggestions for overarching constraints on interpretation emerge from Davidson's work. One possible constraint is that speakers should be so interpreted that what they say and believe about the world turns out to be by and large correct. This is the "principle of charity" (Davidson, 1967, 1973). The other possible constraint—widely reckoned to be more plausible—is that speakers should be so interpreted that what they say and believe about the world turns out to be by and large reasonable or intelligible. This is sometimes called the "principle of humanity" (see Wiggins, 1980).

In the imagined project of interpretation, the deliverances of a semantic theory are used in schematic form. For these purposes, at least, it does not matter whether the semantic theory uses the "means that p" format or the "is true if and only if p" format. So we can, if we wish, say that the constraints on interpretation shed light on the concept of meaning and thence—by way of the connection between meaning and truth—on the concept of truth.

MEANING AND USE

We began from the vague idea that meaning has something to do with use, and have focused on two approaches to the study of meaning, both of which lay stress upon such notions as conveying the message that *p*, saying that *p*, and asserting that *p*. Both approaches take the basic way of specifying the meaning of a sentence to involve a "that *p*" clause, and both permit the straightforward connection between meaning and truth. However, there are other ways to develop the idea of a link between meaning and use. For example, we might regard knowing the meaning of a sentence as knowing how to use it appropriately. Or we might say that knowing the meaning of a sentence is knowing under what circumstances a speaker would be warranted in using the sentence to make an assertion. Many of these ways of linking meaning with use do not lead to specifications of meaning by way of a "that *p*" clause, and so do not support the direct transfer of elucidation from the concept of meaning to the concept of truth. It is to metasemantic theories of this kind that the term "use theory of meaning" is usually applied. Use theories of meaning are often coupled with the claim that there is nothing substantive to be said about the concept of truth (see Field, 1994; Horwich, 1990, 1995).

See also Chomsky, Noam; Davidson, Donald; Dummett, Michael Anthony Eardley; Frege, Gottlob; Grice, Herbert Paul; Intention; Philosophy of Language; Pragmatics; Reference; Semantics; Strawson, Peter Frederick; Tarski, Alfred; Truth.

Bibliography

Avramides, A. *Meaning and Mind: An Examination of a Gricean Account of Language.* Cambridge, MA: MIT Press, 1989.

Chomsky, N. *Knowledge of Language: Its Nature, Origin, and Use.* New York: Praeger, 1986.

Davidson, D. *Inquiries into Truth and Interpretation.* New York: Oxford University Press, 1984.

Davis, S. *Pragmatics: A Reader.* New York: Oxford University Press, 1991.

Dummett, M. *The Logical Basis of Metaphysics.* Cambridge, MA: Harvard University Press, 1991.

Dummett, M. *The Seas of Language.* Oxford: Clarendon Press, 1993.

Field, H. "Deflationist Views of Meaning and Content." *Mind* 103 (1994): 249–285.

Grice, H. P. "The Causal Theory of Perception." *Proceedings of the Aristotelian Society,* supp. vol. 35 (1961): 121–152. Reprinted in Grice, 1989.

Grice, H. P. "Logic and Conversation." In *Syntax and Semantics,* Vol. 3: *Speech Acts,* edited by P. Cole and J. Morgan, 41–58. London, 1975. Reprinted in Grice, 1989.

Grice, H. P. "Meaning." *Philosophical Review* 66 (1957): 377–388. Reprinted in Grice, 1989.

Grice, H. P. *Studies in the Way of Words.* Cambridge, MA: Harvard University Press, 1989.

Horwich, P. "Meaning, Use and Truth." *Mind* 104 (1995): 355–368.

Horwich, P. *Truth.* Oxford: Blackwell, 1990.

Lewis, D. *Convention.* Cambridge, MA, 1969.

Lewis, D. "Languages and Language." In *Language, Mind and Knowledge,* edited by K. Gunderson. Minneapolis: University of Minnesota Press, 1975.

Loar, B. *Mind and Meaning.* Cambridge, U.K.: Cambridge University Press, 1981.

Neale, S. "Paul Grice and the Philosophy of Language." *Linguistics and Philosophy* 15 (1992): 509–559.

Schiffer, S. *Meaning* (1972). Oxford: Clarendon Press, 1988.

Schiffer, S. *The Remnants of Meaning.* Cambridge, MA: MIT Press, 1987.

Strawson, P. F. "Intention and Convention in Speech Acts." *Philosophical Review* 73 (1964): 439–460.

Tarski, A. "The Concept of Truth in Formalized Languages." In *Logic, Semantics, Metamathematics,* edited by A. Tarski, 152–278. Oxford: Clarendon Press, 1956.

Wiggins, D. "What Would Be a Substantial Theory of Truth?" In *Philosophical Subjects,* edited by Z. van Straaten, 189–221. Oxford: Clarendon Press, 1980.

Martin Davies (1996)

MEASUREMENT AND MEASUREMENT THEORY

Metrology in general and measurement theory in particular, have grown from various roots into fields of great diversity in the natural and social sciences, engineering, commerce, and medicine. Informally, and in its widest empirical sense, a measurement of a property, exhibited by stereotype objects in variable degrees or amounts, is an objective process of assigning numbers to the objects in such a way that the order-structure of the numbers faithfully reflects that of degrees or amounts of the measured property. Measuring instruments with pointers and calibrated scales for reading are the basic empirical means by which numerical assignments are realized. Abstractly, a particular way of assigning numbers as measures of extents of a property in objects is called a *quantity scale.* In the natural sciences, the results of measurement on a quantity scale are expressed in the form of denominate numbers, each comprised of a numerical value (magnitude) and a physical unit. Nominalists support the view that the results of measurement are not denominate numbers but numerals and perhaps other symbols.

CLASSICAL TEMPERATURE MEASUREMENT

To illustrate this morass of preliminary definitions, consider classical temperature measurement. Temperature is a local thermodynamic property of physical substances, linked to the transfer of thermal energy (heat) between them. From the standpoint of statistical mechanics, heat in a physical substance is a macroscopic manifestation of the random motion of the constitutive atoms or molecules. An increase of temperature in the substance matches the increase of rate of molecular motion, so that temperature can be rigorously conceived as a measure of the kinetic energy of molecules.

It is important to emphasize that classical temperature measurement does not depend on any of these deep underlying physical theories. In 1592 Galileo Galilei was able to measure temperature in a theory-independent way, using the contraction of air that drew water up a calibrated tube. Approximately a century later, Daniel G. Fahrenheit invented the mercury-in-glass thermometer, again without understanding energy conservation laws that were discovered and firmly established only after 1850. These remarks, however, are not all that obvious and must be taken with a grain of salt. Precise construction of thermometers and their calibration certainly relies on theories of heat and the correct representation of (freezing and boiling) reference points. Immediately a foundational question arises: Is measurement theory-laden? The answer to this question is subtle and depends on how measurement is modeled. Because modeling of numerical quantification of measurable properties makes no commitments to and assumptions about quantitative laws and substantive scientific theories, a straight answer must be in the negative. However, measurement theory addresses many issues that go well beyond the construction of quantity scales, including prominent relationships among quantity scales of measurable properties, studied by well-established scientific theories.

From the inception of quantifying temperature and other variable properties, the concept of measurement has proved to be a steady source of methodological difficulties. For example, it would be false to conclude that today it was twice as warm as yesterday because today the local temperature at noon was balmy ninety degrees and it was only forty-five degrees yesterday. The inference may appear correct because on the Fahrenheit scale indeed there is 90°F = 2 × 45°F. But to the opposite effect, a meteorologist equipped with a Celsius thermometer observed at the same site that the temperature today was 32.2°C and it was 7.2°C yesterday, inferring that today's temperature was approximately 4.6 times higher than yesterday. Based on the familiar conversion formula $b°C = 5/9(a°F - 32)$ from Fahrenheit to the Celsius scale, the meteorologist quickly obtains the equalities 32.2°C = 90°F and 7.2°C = 25°F, further corroborating that today's

temperature on the Celsius scale is not twice as high as it was yesterday. Simple physical experiments show that it is not meaningful to make scale-independent comparative statements of the form above —"yesterday was n times as warm as today," if the temperature is measured traditionally on an *interval* scale (including Celsius, Fahrenheit, Reaumur, and Rankine) in the sense of Stanley Smith Stevens (1960) and the definition recalled below. Science has little use for observational statements whose truth depends on the choice of quantity scales. In all cases of quantitative observation, the main interest is in those measurement data that are invariant under scale transformations. Louis Narens discusses many other examples of a similar nature in his *Theory of Meaningfulness* (2002).

A performance of any empirical observation is usually a complex activity that is impossible and (fortunately) unnecessary to report completely. The structure of a measurement-based observation that an experimenter is able to extract and analyze formally with some success is best captured by a measurement model. For example, in the simplest and best-known physical situation of temperature measurement, the experimenter assumes that the temperature-bearing entities (e.g., substances in vessels) can, at least conceptually, be identified and distinguished one from another, and then appropriately labeled or described. As common in other branches of mathematics, the experimenter next conceives of collecting such labels or mathematical descriptions of substances into a set, to be called a *measurement domain* and denoted M. Because this domain furnishes a mathematical basis for modeling the scale structure of measurable properties, care must be exercised in its selection. To simplify the preceding pedantic language in what follows the discussion will often refer to M as a domain of substances, objects, or events, when in actuality we mean a set of their mathematical labels or descriptions.

Galileo and Fahrenheit were able to order effectively many substances at given time instances in accordance with their exhibited degrees of the temperature property, here denoted t, without recourse to any antecedently established thermodynamical theories. This suggests that the scaling model of temperature measurement should be based on a designated comparative relation $\leq_t$, where the associated atomic formula "$x \leq_t y$" is meant to express that substance y is at least as warm as substance x, for all substances x and y belonging to the underlying domain M.

THE MEASUREMENT MODEL

The resulting deceptively simple *measurement model*, commonly symbolized by the ordered pair $(M, \leq_t)$, captures the ordering of substances with respect to degrees of their temperature property t at a specified time instant. It should be clear that a similar model can be used to characterize the comparison of substances with respect to their mass property. In many measurement-theoretic applications, the foregoing comparative relation $\leq_t$, henceforth abbreviated to $\leq$, enjoys the following pair of measurability properties for all elements x and y in the given domain M:

(i) *Transitivity*: If $x \leq y$ and $y \leq z$, then $x \leq z$.

(ii) *Connectedness*: $x \leq y$ or $y \leq x$.

We associate with every comparative relation $\leq$ a canonical *indiscernibility* equivalence relation $\approx$, defined by

$$x \approx y \text{ iff } x \leq y \text{ and } y \leq x$$

for all x and y in M. Here the notation "iff" is a standard abbreviation for "if, and only if." Under the foregoing intended interpretation, the atomic formula "$x \approx y$" encodes the fact that substances x and y have the same degree of temperature. It should be obvious that the relation $\approx$ partitions the domain M into equivalence classes of substances, where each class contains precisely those substances whose degrees of temperature coincide.

At this point we may ask: What are measurement models good for and how do we know that they are adequate? In measurement theory, measurement models have four basic functions: upholding *numerical representation*, specifying the *uniqueness* of representation, and capturing quantitative and qualitative *meaningfulness*.

REPRESENTATIONAL ROLE OF MEASUREMENT MODELS. In their *representational* role, measurement models provide a mathematical basis for numerical quantification of extents, degrees, or amounts of measurable properties of objects. For example, in the case of temperature measurement, the possibility of numerical quantification of the variable temperature property t comes down to the existence of a *quantity scale*, rendered precise by a real-valued function, denoted $\Phi: M \rightarrow R$, that assigns to each substance x in M a unique real number $\Phi(x)$ in R (interpreted as the degree of temperature of substance x) in such a way that the numerical order in the host field $(R, \leq)$ of real numbers agrees with the comparative relation $\leq$ specified in the measurement model. Formally, we have the order-embedding representational condition

$$x \leq y \text{ iff } \Phi(x) \leq \Phi(y)$$

for all x, y in M. In general, there is no guarantee that an order-embedding function Φ exists. A major task of representational measurement theory is to find a body of empirically meaningful constraints—constraining the structure of $(M, \leq)$, usually called the *representation axioms*, such that they are necessary and sufficient for the existence of a quantity scale (order-embedding function) Φ. The preceding transitivity and connectedness properties are usually included in the collection of representation axioms, but generally they are not sufficient for the existence of a quantity scale. In essence, this is the way the experimenter expects to achieve a theoretically justified passage from qualitative observations (x is t-er than y) to quantitative data that may be processed further by various computational and statistical means. It should be clear that the foregoing low-complexity measurement model is totally ineffective in characterizing the measurement of television violence, unemployment, and many other highly complicated attributes studied in the social sciences.

Not surprisingly, quantity scales (if they exist) are seldom unique. We have already seen that two arbitrary temperature measurement scales $\Phi': M \rightarrow R$ (e.g., for Celsius degrees) and $\Phi: M \rightarrow R$ (e.g., for Fahrenheit degrees) are always linked via functional composition of the form $\Phi'(x) = f(\Phi(x))$ for all substances x, where $f: R \rightarrow R$ is an affine (positive linear) *permissible transformation*, specified by $f(r) = ar + b$ with $a > 0$ for all real numbers r. From the standpoint of algebra, the totality of permissible transformations between temperature quantity scales forms a numerical affine group. In general, a property is said to be measured on an *interval* scale provided that its family of permissible transformations is the affine group. Along similar lines, a property is measured on a *ratio* scale just in case its family of permissible transformations is the similarity group of all functions $f: R \rightarrow R$, specified by $f(r) = ar$ with $a > 0$ for all real numbers r. So the apparent relativism and arbitrariness in the choice of measurement methods and accompanying quantity scales are factored out by invoking pertinent scale-transformations. In addition to guaranteeing the existence of a quantity scale, representation axioms specify the correct group of permissible transformations between scales. Thus if the experimenter intends to draw conclusions about objective temperature values, he or she must consider the associated affine group of scale-transformations and ensure that they preserve all numerical relationships of interest.

DETECTION OF MEANINGLESS OBSERVATIONAL STATEMENTS. Measurement models are instrumental in detecting meaningless observational statements; meaningfulness has long been a favorite of measurement theorists. We begin with the simplest characterization. Given a binary numerical relation ρ on the real line R, we say that ρ is *quantitatively meaningful* for the measurement model $(M, \leq)$ just in case for all quantity scales Φ', Φ: $M \rightarrow$ R the equivalence

$$\Phi'(x) \, \rho \, \Phi'(y) \text{ iff } \Phi(x) \, \rho \, \Phi(y)$$

holds for all elements x and y in M. It is easily seen that this definition automatically generalizes to n-place relations. For example, for any pair of temperature scales Φ' (e.g., Celsius) and Φ (e.g., Fahrenheit) the equivalence

$$\Phi'(x) - \Phi'(y) < \Phi'(z) - \Phi'(w) \text{ iff } \Phi(x) - \Phi(y) < \Phi(z) - \Phi(w)$$

holds for all substances x, y, z, and w. The concept of quantitative meaningfulness is extremely useful in determining the applicability of statistical concepts (including sample averages and standard deviation) in the world of measurement data.

There is a closely related concept of qualitative meaningfulness that is based on the notion of automorphism. Recall that an order-embedding map α: $M \rightarrow M$ of the domain of a measurement model $(M, \leq)$ to itself is called a measurement automorphism precisely when it is one-to-one and onto. Briefly, a binary relation ρ on the measurement domain M is said to be qualitatively meaningful for the model $(M, \leq)$ provided that for each measurement automorphism α: $M \rightarrow M$ and for all x and y in M the equivalence

$$x \, \rho \, y \text{ iff } \alpha(x) \, \rho \, \alpha(y)$$

holds. Less formally, a binary relation ρ on M is measurement-theoretically meaningful for $(M, \leq)$ if the exact identity of ρ-related objects is irrelevant. The only thing that matters is that the objects in M possess the measured property in equal amounts. In general, quantitative and qualitative meaningfulness are not coextensive. The notion of qualitative meaningfulness is important in delineating the class of model-definable relations. It is easy to check that the omnipresent indiscernibility relation $\approx$ is qualitatively meaningful for $(M, \leq)$.

REPRESENTATION AXIOMS. Finally, in addition to securing a quantity scale and its uniqueness (up to permissible transformations), representation axioms of a measurement model can also be viewed as capturing the overall *empirical content* under consideration, encountered in testing the measurement model's adequacy. In this context, measurement axioms are usually classified into *rationality* (design) axioms (including transitivity)—assumed to be automatically true under the intended interpretation; *structural* (technical) axioms (e.g., the Archimedean axiom), crucial in establishing powerful representation theorems; and various testable *empirical* axioms, characterizing (often in a highly idealized way) specific measurement methods.

To appreciate the striking simplicity of measurement models, it is important to realize that these models represent the observational structure of a measurable property in such a way that most of the empirical detail of the actual observation is ignored. Here the experimenter is interested only in a basic abstraction that is based on comparisons of extents of given measurable properties, sufficient for a suitable order-preserving numerical quantification.

REPRESENTATIONAL THEORY OF MEASUREMENT

Measurement theory in general (as a branch of applied mathematics) and representational measurement theory in particular, are mainly based on work summarized in *Foundations of Measurement* (vol. 1, 1971) by David Krantz and others; *Foundations of Measurement* (vol. 2, 1989) by Patrick Suppes and others; and in *Foundations of Measurement* (vol. 3, 1990) by Duncan Luce and others. These authors use a model-theoretic (semantic) conception of empirical theories. In brief, instead of conceiving measurement theory as a deductively organized body of empirical claims, the semantic conception views a theory as a way of specifying a class of set-theoretic relational structures that represents various aspects of reality. The principal objectives of measurement theory are the study of set-based models of measurable properties of empirical objects, maps between them, and the representation of measurement models in terms of convenient numerical structures, with special regards to the relationships between the latter and affiliated quantitative theories of empirical objects.

Representational measurement theory studies many species of measurement models. In his *Physics: The Elements*, Norman Campbell (1920) noted that in modeling *extensive* properties (including, e.g., length, area, volume, mass, and electric charge), the above specified order-theoretic measurement model $(M, \leq)$ has a powerful algebraic enrichment, typically symbolized by $(M, \leq, \circ)$, where $\circ$ is a binary composition operation on M, satisfying the following partially testable empirical conditions for all x, y, z, and w in M:

(i) *Commutativity*: $x \circ y \approx y \circ x$.

(ii) *Associativity*: $(x \circ y) \circ z \approx x \circ (y \circ z)$.

(iii) *Monotonicity*: $x \leq y$ iff $x \circ z \leq y \circ z$.

(iv) *Positivity*: $x \leq x \circ y$ and not $x \circ y \approx x$.

(v) *Strongly Archimedeanness*: If $x \leq y$ and not $x \approx y$, then for any z and w there exists a positive integer n such that $n \cdot x \circ z \leq n \cdot y \circ w$, where $n \cdot x$ is defined inductively by setting $1 \cdot x = x$ and $(n + 1) \cdot x \approx n \cdot x \circ x$.

In the case of length measurement, the measurement domain M consists of suitable and to some extent idealized length-bearing entities (e.g., straight, rigid rods) that can be properly identified and distinguished one from another. Because length measurement is modeled within a classical framework, relativistic reminders that length is not an intrinsic property of rods but something relational—relative to inertial reference frames—will not be of concern.

To measure length in a basic way, independently of any application of laws, the experimenter *operationalizes* the comparative "at least as long as" relation $\leq$ by placing two rods side by side in a straight line, with one end of the rods coinciding, and observing which one extends at the other end. In this manner the experimenter has an effective way of determining whether the relational formula "$x \leq y$" holds for virtually any pair of rods x and y in M. Of course if rod x is a physical part of rod y or is equal to y, then the validity of "$x \leq y$" is accepted by default. The composition $x \circ y$ of rods x and y is understood to be the rod obtained by the operation of placing rods x and y end to end in a straight line. Thus we take the abutted combination of rods x and y to be the whole composite rod $x \circ y$.

We know from David H. Krantz and others (1971, p. 73) that the representation axioms above are necessary and sufficient for the existence of a real-valued, order-embedding, additive scale function $\Phi: M \rightarrow R$, satisfying the representational condition

$$\Phi(x \circ y) = \Phi(x) + \Phi(y)$$

for all x, y in M. We see that the representation axioms not only justify a numerical quantification of amounts or extents of measurable properties, they capture the structure of the associated extensive measurement process itself.

In his basic concepts of measurement Brian Ellis (1966) addresses the question whether the preceding interpretation of composition operation $\circ$ is intrinsic to physical measurement of length or is perhaps just a convenient convention. Ellis points out that the representation axioms listed above remain valid even if the experimenter uses an orthogonal concatenation of rods. Specifically, this time the composite rod $x \circ' y$ is obtained somewhat artificially as a rod formed by the hypotenuse of the right triangle, whose sides are the rods x and y. Thus here the experimenter is abutting x and y perpendicularly rather than along a straight line. Not surprisingly, because the operational peculiarities of respective compositions in a straight line versus orthogonally are not visible in the representation axioms, the corresponding enriched measurement models $(M, \leq, \circ)$ and $(M, \leq, \circ')$ are measurement-theoretically indiscernible. Ellis holds a conventionalist view of measurement, in the sense that measurable properties do not exist independently of their methods of measurement.

The technical problem of "$x \circ x$" is circumvented by using an unlimited supply of copies of x (so that $x \circ x \approx x \circ y$, where $x \approx y$) or by passing to a partial composition operation. Ontological objections against using models with infinitely many objects are obvious. Another problem is whether the comparative relation $\leq$ and composition $\circ$ of a measurement model $(M, \leq, \circ)$ are directly observable. Scientific realists in particular argue that in general the representation axioms treat the empirical structures of measurement models as something decisively theoretical.

There are several ways to develop a general theory of *derived* measurement. In some ways the most natural place to start is with the notion of fundamental measurement, covered earlier. A measurable property is said to be *fundamental* or *basic* provided that its measurement does not depend on the measurement of anything else. Simply, a measurement theorist starts with a measurement model $(M, \leq, \circ)$ of a basic property together with the characterizing representation axioms and then proves the existence and uniqueness of the quantity scale. No other measurement models are needed.

In contrast, a *derived* measurable property is measured in terms of other previously established quantity scales and measurement models. A classical example in physics is density, measured as a ratio of separate measurements of mass and volume. To avoid conceptual confusion, it is not suggested that a fundamental measurement of density is impossible. When mass and volume are known, there are offsetting advantages to working with a derived notion of density. Another question is whether any measurement is truly basic.

A BRIEF HISTORY OF MEASURING DEVICES

It is invariably difficult to trace the origins of measurement devices. Weights and measures were among the earliest tools, invented and used in primitive societies. Ancient measurements of length were based on the use of parts of the human body (e.g., the length of a foot, the span of a hand, and the breath of a thumb). Time was measured by water clocks, hourglasses, and sundials.

The earliest weights were based on objects frequently weighed (e.g., seeds, beans, and grains). Comparisons of capacities of containers were performed indirectly by filling gourds and vessels with plant seeds—which were later counted—and water. These *qualitative* measurement methods, used in conjunction with crude balance scales, formed a basis of early commerce. There was an enormous proliferation of local and national measurement systems and units (e.g., Egyptian around 3000 BCE; Babylonian around 1700 BCE; Greek in 500 BCE; and Roman around 100 BCE). Romans adapted the Greek system that was later adopted with local variations throughout Europe as the Roman Empire spread. As these methods of associating numbers with physical objects were growing, it became possible to compare the objects *abstractly* by comparing the associated numbers and to combine them by manipulating numbers. In the presence of standardized units accepted by the whole community it became possible to replace accidental comparatives of the form "five times the width of my finger" with more universal but still unit-dependent "3.75 inches."

In England in the early thirteenth century, measures and weights (strongly influenced by the Roman system) quickly evolved along the lines of strict standardization. In France, standardization of measures and weights came several centuries later. In 1670 Gabriel Mouton, a French priest, proposed the establishment of a decimalized metrology of weights and measures. The unit of length that was finally decided on was one ten-millionth part of a meridional quadrant of the earth. Weight of a cubic decimeter of distilled water at maximum density temperature of 4°C was adopted as the kilogram. (During the second half of the twentieth century there was a shift away from standards based on particular artifacts toward standards based on stable quantum properties of systems.) The adoption of the metric system in France and generally in Europe was slow and difficult, until the International Bureau of Weights and Measures, formed in 1875, recommended the universal adoption of the MKS metric system in European countries that was subsequently signed in seventeen states. In the modern SI (Système International d'Unites) version of the metric system, there are seven base units (length, mass, time, temperature, electric charge, luminous intensity, and phase angle) from which all other units of measurement are derived.

One impressive feature of modern science is the rapidity with which new measuring instruments are being developed. For example, in the case of time measurement, and starting from imprecise ancient water clocks and hourglasses, people in the Middle Ages built town clocks (maintained by hand) to display local time. In 1656 Christian Huyghens built the first accurate pendulum clock; less than a century later John Harrison presented the first nautical chronometer. In 1928 Joseph Horton and Warren Morrison built the first quartz crystal oscillator clock. And finally, in 1950, Harold Lyons developed an atomic clock based on the quantum mechanical vibrations of the ammonia molecule. Cesium atomic clocks measure time with an accuracy of 10^{-15} seconds.

Experimental science has progressed thanks in great part to the speedy development of highly accurate measuring devices in nearly all branches of science, engineering, and medicine. The symbiotic relationship between theoretical research and measurement methodology continues to be a fundamental factor in the development of science. Philosophically, measurement is important because it provides empirical foundations for the construction of quantitative scientific theories, necessary for reliable prediction and explanation of vast categories of empirical phenomena.

See also Decision Theory; Experimentation and Instrumentation; Quantum Mechanics; Suppes, Patrick.

Bibliography

Campbell, Norman. *Physics: The Elements*. Cambridge, U.K.: Cambridge University Press, 1920.

Ellis, Brian David. *Basic Concepts of Measurement*. London: Cambridge University Press, 1966.

Heisenberg, Werner. *The Physical Principles of the Quantum Theory*. Translated into English by Carl Eckart and Frank C. Hoyt. Chicago: University of Chicago Press, 1930.

Krantz, David H., R. Duncan Luce, Patrick Suppes, and Amos Tversky. *Foundations of Measurement*. Vol. 1: *Additive and Polynomial Representations*. New York: Academic Press, 1971.

Luce, R. Duncan, David H. Krantz, Patrick Suppes, and Amos Tversky. *Foundations of Measurement.* Vol. 3: *Representation, Axiomatization and Invariance.* New York: Academic Press, 1990.

Narens, Louis. *Theories of Meaningfulness.* Mahwah, NJ: Erlbaum, 2002.

Stevens, Stanley Smith. "On the Theory of Scales of Measurement." In *Philosophy of Science*, edited by Arthur Danto and Sidney Morgenbesser, New York: Meridian, 1960.

Suppes, Patrick, David H. Krantz, R. Duncan Luce, and Amos Tversky. *Foundations of Measurement.* Vol. 2: *Geometrical, Threshold and Probabilistic Representations.* New York: Academic Press, 1989.

Zoltan Domotor (2005)

MEDIAVILLA, RICHARD OF

See *Richard of Mediavilla*

MEDICAL ETHICS

A basis for medical ethics can be found in the Hippocratic oath. These ethics, in sum, emphasize that doctors should keep confidences, soothe their patients' suffering, and not overstep their medical abilities. The limitations of physicians set the limits of the code. With fewer limits, there are more issues to discuss: surrogate motherhood; allocation of expensive but lifesaving modalities; an emphasis on privacy and autonomy and an evaluation of the medical system itself. A caveat is necessary. The discussion of medical ethics that follows is based on the present day American system of medical practice. While much of the ethics and ethos of medicine crosses cultures, other issues may not. For example, particular questions concerning paternalism especially related to truth telling are often culture specific. Also, the American legal system, at least according to some, encourages malpractice suits against physicians leading to interesting questions about how best to practice medicine.

A standard set of topics in medical ethics are: abortion, euthanasia, confidentiality, truth telling, medicolegal jurisprudence, genetics and medicine, allocation, experimentation and informed consent, suffering, and guilt. Each area can be associated with a basic question.

Issues in medical ethics tend to arise not from questions about moral theory but from practical and clinical concerns. Failure to take this fact into account can lead to analyses that bear little resemblance to principles or rules that can be applied in clinical practice. One important difference between typical questions that arise from moral theory and those that arise in medical contexts is the lack of disinterest that one usually finds in medical contexts where a disinterested perspective is probably unrealistic. One cannot be disinterested in a beautiful but possibly battered infant. One cannot be disinterested in the pain and suffering of a terminally ill patient in virtually unmitigatable pain who asks to be allowed to die. But even if disinterested, a physician need not, therefore, be uninterested or uncaring. Indeed, physicians almost always have emotional investment in cases such as these. Whether they should or should not is another issue (a question that concerns medical education and human nature), but they do.

Even so, the moral principles appealed to are traditional ones. Do not cause pain unnecessarily. Keep promises and tell the truth, except when obvious harm will result from doing so. Do not interfere with the lives of people unless they ask for this sort of help. Do not be so selfish that the good of others is never considered. Thus, despite the glittering high technology of the modern day hospital, the dramatic emergency room, the life and death feeling of the neonatal intensive care unit, the vulnerability often felt in the examining room, medical ethics is still ethics. What follows is a description of some central issues in medical ethics.

PATERNALISM AND THE GEORGETOWN MANTRA

To say that A acts paternalistically toward B involves five beliefs on the part of A about the action aimed at B: (1) It is done for the good of B; (2) A is qualified to perform the act; (3) the action violates a specifiable moral rule; (4) the most important factor is the good of B; (5) B believes that no outside help is needed. Justifying a paternalistic action requires that it be clear that B would be irrational not to want the action forced and that A be willing to accept as a general rule something such as, "In all cases like this, a paternalistic action is allowable" (see Bernard Gert's and Charles Culver's *The Justification of Paternalism*; for an overview of the issue see the entry under *paternalism* in the Stanford Encyclopedia of Philosophy, available from http://plato.stanford.edu/entries/paternalism/).

The four part approach to medical ethics, often referred to (after the home of its proponents) as the Georgetown mantra suggests that all medical ethics decisions can be seen from the standpoint of playing off autonomy, beneficence, non-maleficence, and justice one against the other with the goal being, in each case, to get just the right balance. The four parts represent principles: respect persons rights to decide for themselves; help those in need; avoid harming others; fair treatment, given what is owed. The mantra, popularized in *The Principles of Bioethics* by Tom Beauchamp and James Childress, was presented as a midlevel set of principles between theory, from which they were derivable, and practice. Whether using an approach based on the four principles overemphasized the application of principles to the detriment of, and need for, an overarching theoretical approach, is an ongoing debate, one especially relevant to the pedagogy of medical ethics (see Koppelman [1999]).

Because physicians make ethical decisions to some extent based on their medical school courses in medical ethics, pedagogy has always played an important role in medical ethics. Initially, most medical ethics courses were based on extrapolations from an analytic approach to ethics. There are at least two other approaches. One stresses phenomenology, the other stresses the view that patients are best understood in terms of their unfolding stories or narratives thus diminishing the role of analytic type approaches to medical ethics. The use of literature in teaching medical ethics is a natural consequence of seeing medical ethics in this manner. This essay shall discuss neither the narrative approach to medical ethics, the phenomenological approach, nor the pedagogy of medical training (on the narrative approach, see Howard Brody's *Stories of Sickness* and A.H. Hawkins's *Literature, Medical Ethics, and Epiphanic Knowledge*; for the phenomenological approach, see Zaner [1981]); for pedagogy, see the journal, *Academic Medicine*; for a critique of some uses of literature as well as a defense of an analytic approach to medical ethics, see Zucker [2006]).

THE DOCTOR-PATIENT RELATIONSHIP

The issue of paternalism is closely related to questions about the norms governing the doctor-patient relationship. Different models have been proposed to characterize this relationship. Most are based on some version of a contract and so rights are important. The business model: Here the patient gives up rights (privacy, for example) and money. For this, the patient receives service (health care). The engineering model: the doctor as a mechanic. Just as one leaves an automobile with the mechanic after trying to describe the problem, the patient tells the mechanic-physician what seems to be wrong and, in effect, leaves. Here, once the physician knows the problem, the patient is treated more like an automobile and less like a person. The patient trades the right to be treated like a person for a tune-up from the doctor—in the hope that this is the best route to running smoothly.

The priest to supplicant model: The doctor has access to important information to which the patient has no access. On this model, getting better is like having one's soul saved by a priest. Staying within the church requires that you follow the rituals required of you by the priest. Getting better requires that you follow the doctor's instructions. On this view, self-help programs would be discouraged. On the collegial model, the stress is on the partnership between the physician and patient. They are partners with a common goal: the health of the patient. On this model, each side trusts the other; each has confidence in the other. The physician suggests treatment, the patient agrees or says why not, so that a compromise can be reached.

The covenant model is not based on a contract. It stresses the dedication of the physician to the goals of medicine. Among the highest of these goals are eliminating disease and alleviating pain. The covenant model focuses on trust, concern, and sympathy. It emphasizes the caring relationship. To many, the appeal to such ideals characterizes the medical profession.

These medical models are ambiguous in the following sense. Are they descriptive or normative? These models are not meant to be an exact replica of reality. Rather, each is, to some extent, heuristic; meant to highlight an aspect of doctor-patient relations making them easier to analyze (on doctor patient models, see E. J. and L. L. Emanuel's *Four Models of the Physician-Patient Relationship*).

ABORTION

The ethical questions concerning abortion have to do with the justification of killing in a medical context. The first line of defense permitting abortion is the claim that what is killed is not the sort of thing that is (or should be) protected by traditional rules against killing. A second line of defense is seeing abortion as a help to the pregnant woman who wants the abortion. It is even possible to see abortion as a help to a fetus whose life, if not aborted, would be one of pain, degeneration, and death (e.g., infants with Tay-Sachs disease). A third line of defense views abortion as a public health issue. That is, history shows that some pregnant women will seek abortions. If abortions were illegal or very difficult to get, only the rich would be able to get safe abortions. This would be unfair as well as pose health risks to the poor. In a situation, where abortion is contemplated as an option, the question from medicine's standpoint, whether explicit or implicit, is: What is the moral status of a fetus (see entry on "Abortion")?

EUTHANASIA

There are situations where a physician might be asked (desire) to let a patient die, might be asked (desire) to help a patient to die, or might be asked (desire) to outright kill a patient. The usual reasons are unmitigatable pain (except through rendering the patient unconscious); irrevocable loss of meaningful consciousness (permanent vegetative state); irrevocable loss of some ability held so dear to the patient that death is preferable (see entry on "Euthanasia").

While it may be rational to prefer death to constant, unremitting pain, it still may be unethical for a physician to allow such a patient to die (by withdrawing or never starting life-sustaining therapy) when that patient can be kept alive. It should be noted that sometimes, the pain referred to is not so much the pain of physiology gone awry as it is the emotional distress caused by the loss of quality of life. That is, a return to baseline may not be possible and, to some people, a new and restricted life is not worth living.

The blunter version of the euthanasia question is: Should a physician kill a patient under any of these circumstances even with the permission of the patient, even where the patient begs to be killed or allowed to die? Writing a prescription for a lethal drug dose and giving it to a patient knowing that it will be used to commit suicide is considered physician assisted suicide. Some consider it a violation of medical ethics. Even if care is taken in establishing the legal and moral rules for physician assisted suicide, this can still be seen as irrelevant to the ethical evaluation. Appeal to the medical tradition does not support assisted suicide as a legitimate form of practice but there is no reason to think that tradition must be obeyed, that no new traditions can be initiated. The clearest example of traditions changing is the shift toward autonomy and consent in medicine—paternalism certainly had been the rule.

It has been argued that medicine has no room at all for intentional killing or letting patients die (see Thomasma and Pellegrino [1993]). The argument can be supported by religion but it need not be. The argument can be based on the nature of the medical profession and what most patients come to expect from physicians. The argument—by no means an uncontested one—is that letting physicians kill patients (or allowing physicians to let patients die) would erode patients' trust that nothing will be done to them that is not in their best interests. The argument goes on to claim that allowing physicians to kill some patients will create nagging suspicion: Will I be next?

The profession of medicine is dedicated to preserving life and make it better. Therefore, medicine should not aim at ending life. Here there is a clash between individual patient rights and physician rights to discharge what may be seen as the obligations of the profession.

The Council on Ethical and Judicial Affairs of the American Medical Association (AMA) updated its Do Not Resuscitate (DNR) guidelines to include two reasons for withholding Cardio-Pulmonary Resuscitation (CPR): (1) The action would be medically futile; (2) the patient has requested no CPR. The guidelines also suggest that physicians talk to their patients about the possibilities of cardiac arrest and the need for CPR. The idea is to have an informed patient taking an active part in the decision-making. Physicians—the AMA guidelines say—are obligated to honor the wishes of the patient (or named surrogate) except where it is clear to the physician that the CPR would be futile. The definition of *futile* is: (a) unlikely to restore cardiac or respiratory function; or (b) unlikely to achieve stated patient goals.

The guidelines allow the physician to enter DNR in the record because of futility but only if the patient or surrogate is fully informed. *Fully* includes explaining why and what the alternatives are if the patient still wants CPR. Of course, sometimes it is not the patient who wants everything done. Sometimes, it is a family member.

Part (b) of the AMA suggested definition of futility (viz., not likely to achieve stated patient goals) would allow for a patient to demand CPR for just a few hours more of life when that, but only that, was likely to occur. This can be seen as counterproductive in that it is a waste of resources and offers false hope to patients (Lo [1991] offers a standard defense of this view). Judging a hope false on allocation grounds may well beg a question against the role of autonomy in medical practice.

CONFIDENTIALITY AND TRUTH TELLING

Confidentiality goes hand-in-hand with privacy and truth telling. During a visit, a physician may ask personal questions such as "Are you sexually active?" Physicians expect truthful answers. Truthfulness is insured by the tacit understanding that answers will be kept private and used only to help the patient. Where the clear well-being of a third party (or parties) is jeopardized by keeping a confidence, there is at least the presumption that the confidence can be violated (on this, see *Tarasoff v. The Regents of the State of California*). Contagious diseases are just one kind of example. People with seizure disorders and drivers of public vehicles who have high blood pressure would not have their driver licenses suspended if physicians never reported this information. These sorts of cases bring up a related question.

Should a physician be put in a situation where privacy and confidentiality are likely to be compromised? Physicians working for industry or for government can be in a situation where they are expected to reveal what would otherwise be kept confidential. In cases like these, what counts as a confidence is determined by the sort of physician one is. Physicians doing health exams for insurance companies or school boards cannot keep certain conditions private. Physicians working for factories are expected to identify malingerers. Should these be seen as violations of confidentiality? Do they undercut the very professionalism of the physician? A true malingerer does hurt everybody by collecting undeserved benefits. But should it be the role of any physician to protect the economic interest of a company and its workers?

Physicians who work for the armed services or as team physicians in organized sports can find themselves in the odd situation of patching someone up in order to have that person go back into battle or back onto the playing field only to risk more injury. Some physicians in the armed forces may find themselves as consultants to interrogators. The justification here is that in this capacity the physicians are behavioral scientists and therefore freed of their usual ethical obligations because those obligations are based on clinical medicine (see Bloche and Marks [2005] for an analysis of this type situation). Are such physicians in conflict with the higher goals implicit in the covenant view of the doctor-patient relationship? Put another way, is the covenant view of the doctor-patient relation, even if meant merely as normative, a realistic normative picture? What are realistic values for the medical profession? This question is the crux of medical ethics.

"Should physicians ever not tell the truth?" is a question related to the justification of paternalism. The usual context for questioning the necessity of truth telling is along the lines of withholding some information that the physician knows the patient (or a third party) would like to know (e.g., your son has a sexually transmitted disease [STD]); or deflecting a question such as "What do you think it is, doctor?" because the doctor thinks the answer is not one that the patient really wants to hear. Where truth telling and confidentiality conflict, confidentiality almost always will take precedence. Whether it should, is another question. The nondirective counseling favored by most genetic counselors may sometimes be open to being interpreted as withholding truthful replies.

MEDICO-LEGAL JURISPRUDENCE

There is no issue in medical ethics that does not have a legal version of it—a case brought to court. The theory behind most decisions is personal injury law. In medical malpractice, one must show damage that was caused by care that was less than standard.

There have been many cases that can be considered to be landmarks. *Tarasoff v. The Regents of the State of California*, decided in 1976, found that a psychiatrist was negligent in not warning a third party that she might be at risk from a patient. This decision changed the form of consent in psychiatry and clinical psychology limiting the confidentiality that can be offered a patient in therapy. Less dramatic but almost as far reaching is *Helling v. Carey*, which helped determine standards of care against which to judge physicians; on surrogate motherhood; *in the Matter of Baby M*; on abortion, *Roe v. Wade*; on brain death and persisitent vegetative state, *In the Matter of Karen Quinlan, An Alleged Incompetent* and *Cruzan v. Director, Mo. Health Dpeartment*; on privacy, *Griswold v. Connecticut*; on informed consent, *Canterbury v. Spence*.

Medical malpractice has an allocation aspect to it. Some specialties are sued much more than others. The usual reasons cited are the high-risk patients seen and the high expectations of many of these patients (here is an overlap of consent and malpractice; appropriate consent should include a realistic statement of expected outcomes). Rather than continue paying for high malpractice coverage to insurers and rather than risk what they take to be unfair assaults on their integrity, specialists will retire early or relocate to areas with low malpractice rates. Legislation proposed to limit awards in malpractice cases can be seen as trying to limit suits filed. But such legislation can also be viewed as aiding insurance companies who cover physicians (as well as aiding less than fully competent physicians).

GENETICS AND MEDICINE (GENOMIC MEDICINE)

Until the recent successes of the human genome project, issues in medical genetics revolved around genetic counseling and a what now might be termed proto-genetic engineering. Patients, sometimes referred to as clients in the genetic counseling context, almost always ask: Why did this happen to me? Should I have another child? What do you think this is? Directive counseling would answer these questions explicitly, sometimes before they were asked. Nondirective counseling deflected them as best as possible. The justification for the nondirective approach is that any directive counseling smacked of paternalism, at the least, and eugenics, the attempt to change the gene pool through selective breeding of humans, at the worst. The nondirective approach grew out of the fact that advances in genetics that made genetic counseling a viable specialty coincided with the connection made between the eugenics movement in the United States and the use of eugenics in Nazi Germany. Eugenics is implicit in any directed program of genetic counseling and prenatal diagnosis along with selective abortion, thus the preference for nondirective counseling (negative eugenics weeds out unwanted genetically controlled traits; positive eugenics encourages the proliferation of desired genetically controlled traits).

The major question connected to genetics via the Human Genome Project is in what ways would we like to be better—and just how much better? And not just for us, for our progeny. Talk about what the good life is and even how best to reach it has a long history. But now there is promise that it is attainable via genetic engineering, that we will be able to choose or redesign our genes so that we will have more control over our ability to live the good life. Nurture plays a role but having the possibility of controlling the raw material of nature gives us a head start on nurture. We can be taller, shorter, thinner, more muscular, more musical, more mathematical, and so on. Again, even a head start is better than the level playing field—if these are our goals. John Rawls proposed that because what he termed *natural assets* are not distributed according to moral worth, a principle of redress was needed as a way to compensate people slighted by the natural lottery. Such a principle of redress would have to be implicit in the control over the natural lottery (on this whole topic, see Buchanan, Brock, and Daniels [2000] as well as Rawls [1971]).

Cloning humans, cloning stem cells, methods for prenatal genetic selection (including genetically engineering our progeny) raise issues that reflect those from abortion, euthanasia, privacy, and allocation. Answering: "What sort of person do we want our child to be?" or "What sort of people do we want in general and how much should we spend to get them?" are variations of age-old ethical issues. If some genetic changes are actually crucial to what we are as humans, then there are issues of defining personhood involved.

ALLOCATION

Allocation issues are divided into microallocation (who gets what) and macroallocation (how should health care itself be distributed). These two questions straddle the line between economics, social and political philosophy,

and ethics. The question is one of a proper distribution of goods, where some baseline version of health is a minimal good and maximum health is the maximum good. Any decision of how to distribute these goods will also determine in part what we take the profession of medicine to be. Given that resources—time and money, as well as organs, fetal tissue, hospitals, operating rooms, and so on—are limited, it is difficult to decide how to distribute health care in a just manner. Why should some people get more and better health care than others? It certainly does happen. Is it because of planning or is it just the luck of the draw? Should something as important as health care be left to luck? The question is how to deal with the reality and the necessity.

Daniel Callahan (2000) has argued that many of our worst allocation problems are traceable to what he terms the research agenda of medicine, an agenda to cure everything to extend life as a goal in and of itself. Daniel Callahan thinks medicine should have another major goal. He offers three alternative principles. First, research should focus on premature death, ones before sixty-five, according to the U.S. government. Callahan gives a looser formulation. He says: "[any death is premature if it occurs] before a person has lived long enough to experience a typical range of human possibilities and aspirations: to work, to learn, to love, to procreate, and to see one's children grow up and become independent adults" (Callahan 2000, p. 654).

Second, research should aim at reducing poor quality of life at the last stages of life. Third, clinicians should be persuaded that helping a patient to a peaceful death is just as important as fighting for life to the end, against all odds. Callahan says that as ideals, helping a patient to a peaceful death and fighting for life against all odds are of equal value because, in the end, we all die. It is here that this perspective on allocation overlaps euthanasia issues.

A program of allocation based on autonomy and tolerance in a laissez-faire driven economy, where economics plays an important role in health care means some people will get less health care and suffer for it. In such situations, one would be forced to say (after H.T. Engelhardt in his Shattuck Lecture of 1984) that this is unfortunate but not unfair. If, however, justice demands more of an equitable distribution of needed goods, and health is one such good, then the unfortunate begins to blend into the unfair.

The lifeboat offers an interesting model for both macro and micro allocation. How many lifeboats should any ship carry? In a crowded lifeboat, should anyone have to go overboard to save the majority? What is the best strategy for saving the majority, for getting the most moral result? How is such a decision to be made? Should there be prearranged rules, should there be deviations allowed (many toddlers aboard, no sailors), should the rules be made during times of stress (a storm, rising seas)? For a lifeboat case, see *United States v. Holmes*.

FREE AND INFORMED CONSENT IN CLINICAL AND EXPERIMENTAL MEDICINE

The gold standard for medical experimentation is the randomized, double-blind, and placebo controlled experiment with a statistically predetermined cutoff point. There is no such thing in clinical studies or in science in general as definitive results, per se. All results are definitive enough, against a background of assumptions and goals. Design and ethics go together. A poorly designed experiment will waste resources and, where there is risk, will put subjects at risk for no good reason. Consent is an ethically necessary part of any experiment. The consent must be free and informed. Subjects cannot be under so much emotional or physical pressure that they feel that they must consent. They must believe it when told that their deciding not to enter a study will not affect their treatment. This freedom from felt coercion overlaps the informed in free and informed consent because it is unlikely that someone under the previously mentioned stresses would (or could) fully understand the information given. The benefit from an experiment must at least promise some gain to the subject or future patients proportional to whatever is the risk of harm. The gain may be limited only to the knowledge that one has helped some future people.

To highlight some issues, consider work done by Dr. Saul Krugman at Willowbrook. Many children at the Willowbrook State School in New York developed hepatitis because of poor sanitary conditions. Newly admitted children were separated from other children, kept in clean quarters but fed the virus collected from infected children. Careful follow-up on these children revealed that there were two strains of hepatitis, one more communicable than the other. In defense of the experiment, it was pointed out that children were likely to get hepatitis anyway and that as subjects they received better care than they would otherwise. Parents had given consent but the reward for consent was immediate admission instead of a long wait (Munson 2003). Willowbrook exemplifies clashes between a physician's obligations to society—clean up Willowbrook; obligation to patients—find a cure or preventive for hepatitis; obligation to science—

find out more about hepatitis, even if a cure is not imminent. It also highlights consent issues. How can one get truly free and informed consent for these subjects or their parents? Recent experiments utilizing genetic therapy have been halted because of excess morbidity and deaths. In these instances, there was great risk, but taking the risk was the only route to possible freedom from disease.

Free and informed consent is part of any clinical encounter as well. The principles insuring free and informed consent for subjects also apply to patients in everyday clinical situations. Patients must be treated with up-to-date therapies that are aimed specifically at their condition. Treating a contagious disease affects others but does not affect the principle that it is the patient in front of the physician who ought to be the target for therapy. Patients must be told what they are asked to accept as therapy and why. They must believe that they can ask questions as well as ask for a second opinion without jeopardizing their treatment. And, of course, risk in therapy must be proportional to gain. An often overlooked point is that some patients do not want much, if any, information. In such cases, doctors have to gauge just how little information they can safely (medically and legally) refrain from giving verbally (where consent forms are needed, information is written, and the question would be how carefully and explicitly the material should be explained to the patient).

PAIN AND SUFFERING

Sometimes, medicine can do no more than to alleviate pain. Sometimes, physicians cannot even diagnose the underlying problem. But if they can relieve pain, they have discharged what might be called a minimum obligation. This is the sort of obligation that is captured in the old saying "Above all, do no harm." Sometimes the only way to pursue this end is by listening to a patient ask, and ruminate on, the Jobian question, "Why is this happening to me?" Perhaps this aspect of medical ethics is the one that takes it furthest from traditional philosophy.

See also Bioethics; Euthanasia; Genetics and Reproductive Technologies.

Bibliography

American Medical Association Council on Ethical and Judicial Affairs. *Code of Medical Ethics*, sec. 2.035. Chicago: AMA Press, 1997.

Annas, G., and M. Grodin, eds. *The Nazi Doctors and the Nuremberg Code: Human Rights in Human Experimentation*. New York: Oxford University Press, 1992.

Annas, G. *American Bioethics: Crossing Human Rights and Health Law Boundaries*. New York: Oxford University Press, 2004.

Annas, G. *Standard of Care, the Law of American Bioethics*. New York: Oxford University Press, 1993.

Annas, George. "Culture of Life Politics at the Bedside—the Case of Terri Schiavo." *New England Journal of Medicine* (2005).

Beauchamp, T., and J. Childress. *Principles of Biomedical Ethics*. 5th ed. New York: Oxford University Press, 2001.

Beaufort de, I. "Patients in a Persistent Vegetative State—A Dutch Perspective." *New England Journal of Medicine* (2005).

Bloche, G., and J. Marks. "Doctors and Interrogators at Guantanamo Bay." *New England Journal of Medicine* (2005).

Boyle, P., and K. O'Rourke, eds. *Medical Ethics: Sources of Catholic Teachings*. Washington, DC: Georgetown University Press, 1999.

Brody, Howard. *Stories of Sickness*. 2nd ed. New York: Oxford University Press, 2002.

Buchanan, A., D. Brock, and N. Daniels. *From Chance to Choice: Genetics and Justice*. Cambridge, U.K.: Cambridge University Press, 2000.

Callahan, Daniel. "Death and the Research Imperative." *New England Journal of Medicine* 342 (2000): 654–656.

Charon, R. ed. *Stories Matter—the Role of Narrative in Medical Ethics*. Philadelphia: Taylor and Francis, 2002.

Code of Medical Ethics 2004–2005. Chicago: American Medical Association Press, 2004.

Cohen, C., ed. *New Ways of Making Babies: The Case of Egg Donation (Medical Ethics Series), National Advisory Board on Ethics in Reproduction*. Bloomington: Indiana University Press, 1996.

Emanuel, E. J., and L. L. Emanuel. "Four Models of the Physician-Patient Relationship." *Journal of the American Medical Association* 267 (16) (1992): 2221–2226.

Engelhardt, H. T. *The Foundations of Bioethics*. 2nd ed. New York: Oxford University Press, 1996.

Engelhardt, H. T. "Shattuck Lecture—Allocating Scarce Medical Resources and the Availability of Organ Transplantation; Some Moral Presuppositions." *New England Journal of Medicine* 311 (1984): 66–71.

Frame, J. *Medical Ethics: Principles, Persons, and Problems (Christian Perspectives)*. Phillipsburg, NJ: Presbyterian and Reformed, 1988.

Hawkins, A. H. "Literature, Medical Ethics, and Epiphanic Knowledge." *The Journal of Clinical Ethics* (5) (1994): 283–290.

Hilyard, B. *U.S. Supreme Court and Medical Ethics: From Contraception to Managed Health Care (Paragon Issues in Philosophy)*. St. Paul, MN: Paragon House, 2004.

Hoffmaster, B., B. Freedman, and G. Fraser. *Clinical Ethics, Theory, and Practice*. Clifton, NJ: Humana Press, 1989.

Holmess, H., and L. Purdy. *Feminist Perspectives in Medical Ethics*. Bloomington: Indiana University Press, 1992.

Jonsen, A., M. Siegler, and W. Winslade. *Clinical Ethics: A Practical Approach to Ethical Decisions in Clinical Medicine*. 4th ed. New York: McGraw-Hill, 2002.

Kass, L., and J. Wilson. *The Ethics of Cloning*. Washington DC: AEI Press, 1998.

Katz, Jay, ed. *Experimentation with Human Beings; The Authority of the Investigator, Subject, Professions, and State in the Human Experimentation Process*. New York: Russell Sage Foundation, 1972.

Koppelman, L., ed. *Building Bioethics—Conversations with Clouser and Friends on Medical Ethics*. Dordrecht, Netherlands: Kluwer Academic Publishers, 1999.

Kuhse, H., P. Singer, eds. *Bioethics*. Malden, MA: Blackwell, 1999.

La France, A. *Bioethics: Health Care, Human Rights, and the Law*. New York: Matthew Bender, 1999.

Lo, B. "Unanswered Questions about DNR Orders." *Journal of the American Medical Association* 265 (1991): 1874–1875.

Magnus, D., G. McGee, and A. Caplan, eds. *Who Owns Life?*. Amherst, New York: Prometheus, 2002.

Marquis, D. "Why Abortion is Immoral?" *The Journal of Philosophy* 86 (4) (1987).

Munson, R. *Intervention and Reflection: Basic Issues in Medical Ethics*. 7th ed. Belmont, CA: Wadsworth, 2003.

Pence, G. *Classic Cases in Medical Ethics: Accounts of Cases That Have Shaped Medical Ethics, with Philosophical, Legal, and Historical Backgrounds*. New York: McGraw-Hill, 2003.

Pellegrino, E. and D. Thomasma. *The Virtues in Medical Practice*. New York: Oxford University Press, 1993.

Plomer, A. *The Law of Ethics and Medical Research: International Bioethics and Human Rights*. New York: McGraw-Hill Humanities/Social Sciences/Language, 2003.

Rachels, James. "Active and Passive Euthanasia." *New England Journal of Medicine* 292 (1975): 78–80.

Rawls, John. *A Theory of Justice*. Cambridge, MA: Harvard University Press, 1971.

Rispler-Chaim, V. *Islamic Medical Ethics in the Twentieth Century (Social, Economic, and Political Studies of the Middle East and Asia)*. Leiden, Netherlands: Martinus Nijhoff, 2003.

Steinberg, A., and F. Rosner. *Encyclopedia of Jewish Medical Ethics: A Compilation of Jewish Medical Law on All Topics of Medical Interest*. Nanuet, NY: Feldheim, 2003.

Steinbrook, Robert. "Physician-Assisted suicide in Oregon—An Uncertain Future." *New England Journal of Medicine* 346 (2002): 460–464.

Thomasma, D., and P. Marshall. *Clinical Medical Ethics: Cases and Readings*. Boston: University Press of America, 1995.

Thompson, L. "Human Gene Therapy: Harsh Lessons, High Hopes." *FDA Consumer Magazine* (2000).

Tomlinson, T., and H. Brody. "Futility and the Ethics of Resuscitation." *Journal of the American Medical Association* 264 (1990): 1276–1280.

Veatch, R., ed. *Cross-Cultural Perspectives in Medical Ethics*. 2nd ed. Boston: Jones and Bartlett, 2000.

Veatch, R. *Medical Ethics (Jones and Bartlett Series in Philosophy)*. Boston: Jones and Bartlett, 1997.

Widdershoven, G. "Beyond Autonomy and Beneficence: The Moral Basis of Euthanasia in the Netherlands." Available from http://www.ethical-perspectives.be/viewpic.php?LAN=E&TABLE=EP&ID=52.

Zaner, R. *The Context of Self: A Phenomenological Inquiry Using Medicine As a Clue*. Athens: Ohio University Press, 1981.

Zucker, A. "Medical Ethics as Therapy." *Medical Humanities* (2006).

Arthur Zucker (2005)

MEDIEVAL AND EARLY CHRISTIAN PHILOSOPHY

In addition to the general article *Medieval Philosophy*, the Encyclopedia features the following articles having discussions of early Christian and medieval schools and movements: *Apologists*; *Augustinianism*; *Averroism*; *Byzantine Philosophy*; *Carolingian Renaissance*; *Chartres, School of*; *Gnosticism*; *Ockhamism*; *Patristic Philosophy*; *Saint Victor, School of*; *Scotism*; and *Thomism*. Particular aspects of early Christian and medieval thought are discussed in the Encyclopedia's general entries, including *Ethics, History of*; *Islamic Philosophy*; *Jewish Philosophy*; *Logic, History of*; *Metaphysics, History of*; *Mysticism, History of*; *Semantics, History of*; and *Universals, A Historical Survey*. See also *Christianity*; *Illumination*; and *Liber de Causis*. See "Medieval Philosophy" and "Christianity" in the index for entries on important figures in this area.

MEDIEVAL PHILOSOPHY

"Medieval philosophy" began with the African Christian Augustine of Hippo (354–430), whose life and writings reflected the unsettled state of the declining Roman Empire long before the commencement of the Middle Ages proper. His rich and many-sided works display the Platonic otherworldliness of his theories of knowledge and world history. According to Augustine's vision, the true cosmic plan unfolds in the history of the City of God, and the local accidents of the Earthly City are of little account in comparison. Correspondingly, true wisdom and virtue are obtainable only in the light of the Christian faith and by the prevenience of divine grace; human nature, grossly corrupted since the Fall, is in need of a correspondingly complete divine remaking. Whereas for Plato and Aristotle the fulfillment of human capacities required the possession of a high degree of sophisticated intelligence, for Augustine such fulfillment depended on rightness of the will and the affections. These two features, a radical view of the transforming power of grace and a voluntaristic accent, may be regarded as the kernel of Augustinianism, at least insofar as it affected subsequent thought. The tremendous influence of Augustine on medieval thought is matched by that of Ancius Manlius Severinus Boethius, whose grandiose plan was to transmit to the Latin West the works of Plato and Aristotle—a plan rudely cut short by his execution in 524. However, he accomplished the translation of Aristotle's logical works into Latin; his commentaries on some of them, and on the Neoplatonist Porphyry's introduction (*Isagoge*) to the *Categories* of Aristotle, were immensely influential in shaping the technical Latin vocabulary and turns of expression that prevailed in the Middle Ages, so much so that any appreciation of medieval thought must inevitably be inadequate without a thorough acquaintance with Boethius's logical output.

The intervention of the Dark Ages presented Western scholars with a gigantic task of rethinking and reconstruction. During these centuries of insecurity and uprootedness there was little intellectual endeavor, apart from the exceptional work of the Neoplatonist John Scotus Erigena in the ninth century. The logical, theological, and classical inheritance slumbered insecurely within the libraries of threatened Western monasteries. When Anselm of Canterbury (1033–1109) began to exploit Boethian logic in order to render his Christian faith intelligible, he had no immediate predecessor who in any way approached his stature as a thinker. Author of the Ontological Argument and fully alive to the power of linguistic analysis as a tool for clarifying conceptual problems, Anselm was the father of Scholasticism. Working within an Augustinian framework, Anselm and other logical theologians of the eleventh and twelfth centuries attempted to bring into order and coherence the body of doctrine to which they were committed by Holy Writ, dogmatic pronouncements, and the works of earlier authoritative church writers. The formidable dimensions of the enterprise were well known to them, as is shown in the lists of clashing antitheses made explicit in the *Sic et Non* (For and Against) of the ill-fated logician Peter Abelard (1079–1142). A systematic collection of authoritative opinions, the *Sentences*, upon which all subsequent medieval thinkers exercised their logical and philosophical ingenuity in the form of commentary, was compiled by Peter Lombard (c. 1095–1160).

While the Latin West, employing a predominantly logical Aristotelianism, was engaged in the tasks described above, as well as in controversy on the topic of universals, the more advanced Islamic civilization spreading from the Middle East possessed the whole body of Aristotle's works. These received development, commentary, and a Neoplatonic flavor at the hands of a series of subtle thinkers, among whom were al-Fārābī (c. 873–950), Avicenna (980–1037), and Averroes (c. 1126–c. 1198). From about the middle of the twelfth century on, Latin translations of their works became available; and through these, as well as through translation directly from the Greek, Western thinkers eventually knew all of Aristotle's writings.

The Jewish philosophers Solomon ben Judah ibn Gabirol (c. 1021–1058 or 1070) and Moses Maimonides (1135–1204) also contributed to the intellectual ferment of the thirteenth century, which was accompanied by the establishment of universities within which members of the recently founded orders of Dominican and Franciscan friars were soon competing with secular masters for professorships. Generally speaking, the Dominicans, following the lead of Thomas Aquinas (c. 1224–1274), attempted to assimilate Aristotle by adopting a framework within which divine grace was seen as completing and fulfilling human nature, rather than dramatically abrogating it in the Augustinian manner. Consequently, the Thomistic tradition represented a separation, at least in principle, of philosophy from theology and a more optimistic view of human nature, society, and the civil state, coupled with opposition to those Latin Averroists who were prepared to compartmentalize their thought to the extent of claiming that on certain points philosophy (Aristotle, as interpreted by Averroes) demonstrated conclusions incompatible with their personal Christianity. Those who preferred to remain within the Augustinian stream, especially St. Bonaventure (c. 1217–1274), John Duns Scotus (c. 1266–1308), and William of Ockham (c. 1285–1349), nevertheless increasingly absorbed elements of the new Aristotelianism. Concerned as they were with the sense in which theology could be a science (a form of knowing), Duns Scotus and William of Ockham evinced a tendency to bring epistemological considerations more to the forefront of their work.

NATURE OF SCHOLASTICISM

ARISTOTELIAN EMPIRICISM: MATTER, FORM, AND SUBSTANCE. Medieval philosophy and logic are aspects of an effort to resolve conceptual puzzles (often, but not always, theologically inspired) and to underpin such resolutions with a satisfactory theory of how things are and why they are as they are. The dominant theory, although subjected to multiple variations and modifications during the medieval period, was basically Aristotelian and therefore involved an ultraempiricist effort (not always successful) to resist the abrogation of the pretheoretical commonsense aspect of the world by the theoretical. Before the consideration of any theory, whether scientific or metaphysical, human beings are inevitably confronted with a world populated by a multiplicity of diverse kinds and sorts of beings that are subject to generation, change, and death. These diverse beings are understood to the extent that "why?" questions about them or their kinds can be answered; they are the objects of evaluation insofar as they or their qualities, quantities, states, or relations are characterized as good, bad, and so on.

In accordance with the nonabrogatory policy, a technical vocabulary is required such that the pretheoretical picture does not forfeit its basic sense by relativization to a more fundamental theory that demands radical revision of that picture. For example, an ultraempiricist account of how things are must always leave place for the attribution of a literal (and not merely metaphorical) sense to questions regarding the "makings" of sense objects, states of affairs, or processes. The term *matter* represents an attempt to guarantee such a literal sense—it is the general reply to the always sensible question (in the context mentioned) "What is it made out of?" The detailed replies to such questions—"wood," "stone," "bones and flesh," "clay," "cloth," and so forth—all mention makings or materials out of which something is made, physical antecedents that are among the necessary conditions of a thing's being.

In the same context, however, explanations of why things are as they are can be given by reference to the kinds or sorts to which those things belong; for example, "Horses are self-moving because they are animals, and all animals are self-moving." Here a feature of a particular sort of being (horse) is explained by reference to its general kind (animal), and it is the notion of "form" (with its alternative medieval vocabulary, "nature," "essence," "quiddity") that represents a reminder of the fact that things fall into distinguishable sorts (species) that can in turn be subsumed under broader kinds (genera). Since truistic explanations can be given in terms of sorts and kinds, the form or essence is said to be the principle of the intelligibility, or explanation-worthiness, of things; and such general definitions as "Man is rational animal" are said to hold true in regard to the formal aspect of things. Whether or not the definitions are true of things in a scientific sense is of little import to the philosophical notion of form: Its point is to ensure the nonabrogation, by a general theory of how things are, of the pretheoretical picture of the diversity of things; realization of this point may lie behind Aquinas's agnosticism concerning the scientific value of such formal definitions.

It is plain that the replies to questions about the makings (matter) of things still involve a formal aspect, since not only are explanations in terms of the definitions of wood, stone, and the other sorts of material mentioned still possible, but it is also possible sensibly to ask what the wood or stone is made out of, or what "stuff" endures when wine becomes vinegar. In order to do justice to such possibilities—and to the pretheoretical conviction that in processes of change the successive sorts that occur are not totally new creations but rather a sequence of diverse activizations of a common substratum—the notion of "prime" matter is employed; this is matter as mere substratum, totally devoid of any formal aspect. Prime matter was viewed schematically, by a kind of extrapolation, as pure susceptibility upon which the various formal actualities supervene, and was said to be by some medievals the principle of individuation, whereby form, the principle of intelligibility and generality, is concretized to the particularity of the various individual "this-es" that belong to a given sort. Thus, one might say that a horse is an *equinizing* of prime matter, a stone is a *petrifying* of prime matter, and so on; this use of verblike nouns helps to bring out the fact that form is act, or actuality, as opposed to the mere susceptibility of prime matter. These verblike nouns are constant, since it never makes sense to say of a horse, for example, that is it more horse or less horse (using "more" and "less" in a nonquantitative sense). Some actualizations, however, are variable, such as whiteness; one can say of a white object that it is (or becomes) more white or less white.

The real correlates of certain of the constant actualizations are called substances, objects that are pretheoretically recognized as being constantly what they are over the whole span of their existence. A horse does not become a horse, and on ceasing to be a horse, it simply ceases to be, whereas a white object can be something that becomes white in varying degrees and may cease to be white, but it is not on that account said to cease to exist. When adjectival terms such as *white* are used to denote subjects in sentences, such as "A white thing is coming down the road," it always makes sense (although in many instances it may be superfluous) to ask a question like "What is the thing that is white and is coming down the road?" This is true because such terms leave open the possibility of asking a question regarding the nature of the "something else" (*aliquid aliud*, as Aquinas has it) that is qualified (in this instance by the whiteness). When the "something else" is a substance, such as "horse," the possibility of a further question having a similar sense, but with the substance name in place of the adjective, vanishes. For example, one would not ask, "What is the thing that is a horse and is coming down the road?" Thus, this notion of substance is unlike that with which John Locke was concerned; for him it did make sense, even when a substantial sentence subject had been used, to carry on with requests for information about what he called a "something besides."

TECHNICAL LANGUAGE, MEANING, AND UNIVERSALS. Much of medieval philosophical and logical discourse involved the endowment of old words with new senses, as part of the artificialization of natural language that is characteristic of the Schoolmen, who, according to Locke, "covered their ignorance with a curious and inexplicable web of perplexed words." The Scholastics were in fact to some extent aware of the exigencies of discourse of this sort, which constitutes a kind of halfway house between the sort of philosophy that is careful to use only a completely jargon-free natural language, and the sort that is prepared to use the resources of some totally artificial language (such as those of modern symbolic logic) as a set of coordinates whereby sense and senselessness may be distinguished. When discussing the technical sense of "in" in sentences such as "Qualities inhere *in* substances," Boethius had distinguished no fewer than nine ways in which the word *in* could be used. It was clear to him that the *man* of the technical sentence "Man is a species" does not play the same role as does the name *man* in "Socrates is a man"; if it did, then one should be able to use these two sentences as premises whence "Socrates is a species" (which is false or nonsensical) could be inferred.

How, then, are such terms as *man, animal, genus,* and *species*, as they occur in sentences like "Man is a species" and "Animal is a genus," to be understood? These are sentences of a sort that must occur in the discussion of the principles of those definitions described as efforts to do justice to the formal aspect of things. Interpretation of such sentences as consisting of two names joined by *is* naturally leads to the question, transmitted by Boethius when commenting on Porphyry, of what the things are that these names name. Are the things named by such specific or generic names extramental entities additional to individual human beings and animals? An affirmative answer represents one medieval form of the option for a "realist" position in the problem of universals, and throughout the period thinkers were divided on this topic. Certain early medieval antirealists, such as Roscelin and Garland the Computist, developed a solution that had been suggested by Boethius: Words such as *species* and *genus*, said Boethius, may be interpreted as "names of names" (*nominum nomina*), so that "Man is a species" should be analyzed as "'Man' is a species," with *species* naming the word *man* and indicating that it is predicable specifically of many individuals. Herein lies one of the roots of the logical doctrine developed during the thirteenth and fourteenth centuries, the doctrine of *suppositio*.

Roscelin and Garland went further than Boethius and regarded *man* in "Man is a species" not as a mentioned name (a mentioned significant utterance) but as a mere utterance (*vox*) undergoing mention; thus St. Anselm accused Roscelin of having reduced universals to the "breath of an utterance" (*flatus vocis*). Other antirealists, observing that this extreme nominalism (as it is usually called) failed to account for the success of language as a representation of the formal aspect of things, adopted an intermediate position, according to which the universal is a natural (as opposed to a merely conventional) mental sign, or concept; such a position was designed to secure the objective reference of the universal while avoiding commitment to the plethora of extra entities demanded by realism. Abelard, Aquinas, and Ockham may be credited with having held, each in his own way, a doctrine of this type.

EXTENT OF THE ARTIFICIALIZATION OF LANGUAGE. There are several facets of the general medieval concern with the study of meaning. In the writings of Anselm of Canterbury, for example, there is an immensely powerful and pervasive realization that the overt, apparent, or grammatical form of an utterance need not show its implicit, true, or logical form—a realization whose revival has been most prominently reinitiated in our own age by Bertrand Russell. Again and again Anselm's writings contain the contrast between forms of speech that are allowed by the loose texture of ordinary language (*usus loquendi*) and the forms to which a strict attention to the exact sense (*significatio per se*) commits one; the loose texture is methodically explored, and the results of this exploration are applied to the elucidation of difficulties raised by forms of speech found in Holy Writ and ordinary language. In their technical explanations Anselm and his successors felt compelled to make innovations that violated the grammar of the natural language (Latin) in which they wrote; for instance, in expressing the objective counterparts of assertions concerning the meaning of adjectival (as opposed to substantival) words, Anselm used the novel formula "Literate is literacy," which in its Latin version (*Grammaticus est grammatica*) is about as full of scandals, from the point of view of ordinary Latin grammar, as any three-word sentence could be.

Naturally the classicists of the time, like their counterparts of the sixteenth century, took alarm at these monstrous impurities of language; a classicist rearguard action is shown in the *Metalogicon* of John of Salisbury (c. 1115–1180), who at one point explicitly argues against mixtures of abstract and concrete of the kind put forth by Anselm. A better-known example of this technical development, resulting in nonsense in respect to ordinary language, is found in Aquinas's assertion that a man *is* neither his humanity nor his existence, whereas God *is* both his essence (divinity) and his existence; these claims involve a like mixture of concrete and abstract nouns that in nontechnical speech just cannot be connected by the same "is" (or "is not").

BREAKDOWN OF COMMUNICATION. The semiartificial language of the Scholastics was excessively clumsy, and, in the absence of the precise definitional control that goes with a totally artificial language, required for its tolerably safe employment an intuitive power extending beyond the ordinary; even when this has been achieved, the history of the period demonstrates that there is no guarantee that communication will be maintained. For example, skill in the use of such language probably reached its peak in the writings of Duns Scotus, the Subtle Doctor. He rejected the theory that matter is the principle of individuation on the grounds that this attribution leaves the individual lacking in total intelligibility and even makes problematic the possibility of an omniscient being's (God's) radical understanding of the individual object. He therefore posited that individuation is performed not by a material, but by a formal, principle; for example, by "Socrateity" in respect of the individual Socrates, and in general by the "thisness" (*haecceitas*) appropriate to each individual "this." We have already observed the connection between form and intelligibility presupposed in this operation, an operation that raises a further phase of the universals controversy and at the same time exemplifies the breakdown in communication.

Ockham criticized the Scotist thing-centered formal distinction (*distinctio formalis a parte rei*) alleged to hold between the universal nature in question (humanity in the case of a human being) and the individuating formal principle (Socrateity) that makes the individual into *this* individual. Ockham was at a loss to see how this distinction could be thing-centered (*a parte rei*) and yet not commit its proponent to the admission of extra entities (humanity, Socrateity) over and above, and distinct from, individuals, in spite of the fact that the existence of universals as extra entities of this sort was denied by Scotus.

It has already been suggested that form may be best expressed by means of verblike nouns (*equinizing, petrifying*); hence, the abstract nouns often used to express formal principles could be viewed as being more verblike than namelike—a position taken by Aquinas from Boethius and apparently recognized by other Scholastics.

If this view is accepted, then the statement that the Socrateity of Socrates is distinct from his humanity may be interpreted, using appropriate verblike forms, as asserting that *Socratizing* is not identical with *humanizing*, an analysis that yields a true thing-centered distinction and yet does not send one on a vain search for extra named entities over and above the man Socrates; this offers at least one way in which the Scotist contention may be consistently understood.

But Ockham assumed, in effect, that any distinction that holds in respect of things (a "real" distinction) can only be like that which holds between, for example, Socrates and Plato and that is expressed by a sentence such as "Socrates is not Plato," wherein "Socrates" and "Plato" are names (as opposed to the verblike *Socratizing* and *humanizing*). When, therefore, Ockham encountered the further Scotist tenet that although a thing-centered formal distinction holds between Socrateity and humanity (for example), it is nevertheless not the case that a real distinction holds between the two, he assumed that "Socrateity" and "humanity" could be treated in the same way as such names as Socrates, Plato, Cicero, and Tully, and that even as the negation of a real distinction between Tully and Cicero amounts to a statement of their real identity as the same individual object, so also the denial of a real distinction between Socrateity and humanity amounts to a statement of real identity of this sort. In point of fact, however, once the verblike nature of the form-expressing words *Socrateity* and *humanity* has been grasped, it becomes clear that a denial of a real distinction between Socrateity and humanity should be understood as the rejection of any attempt to treat those form expressions as though they were pure names. The whole weight of Ockham's subsequent attack, aimed as it was at the consequence that the Scotists were in such contexts stating the denial of a real identity (one framed in terms of names, as opposed to verbs) is therefore totally misplaced.

The same blindness, combined with the theological premise that God is omnipotent, and hence can effect anything that does not involve a contradiction, also played havoc with other distinctions patiently established by earlier thinkers. For example, the distinction between essence and existence, some of whose associated theses were described above as embodying novel uses of words, was attacked on the grounds that the essence of a thing (a man's humanity) and its existence are (if a *real* distinction holds between them) two things distinct in the way that Socrates and Plato are two distinct things. In consequence, the Ockhamists considered themselves licensed to assert that the admission of a *real* distinction between essence and existence has as a consequence the possibility of God's omnipotence producing something's essence without at the same time producing its existence, or vice versa, however, this is patently absurd, and therefore (they concluded) there is no real distinction between essence and existence.

In the presence of such misplaced criticism it is obvious that scholastic thought could have been better expressed in a fully artificial language, armed with precise definitions and a greater capacity for generating and identifying new parts of speech than that of the semiartificial language that was used.

REACTION AGAINST TECHNICAL ARTIFICIALIZATION. Although the artificialization of natural language for the expression of technical truths beyond the capacity of natural language proceeded apace from the time of Anselm, the final major philosophical reaction, brought about by communication difficulties, was in the opposite direction. Ockham's attitude to the contrast between ordinary and technical discourse was the polar opposite of Anselm's attitude at the opening of the period. For Anselm, accounts of meaning could and did call for the use of, or have as consequences, technical assertions that were either nonsense from the point of view of ordinary usage, or at least involved radical departures therefrom—and his successors were similarly venturesome.

Ockham, although likewise constantly conscious of the contrast between ordinary speech and the technical forms of speech used by his predecessors, nevertheless placed propriety of expression on the side of ordinary speech, and not on the technical side, except in those instances where the novel locutions of his forerunners could be explained away or disarmed as mere stylistic ornament. His lists of sentences that are false if taken literally (*de virtute sermonis*) because words are not therein used properly (*secundum proprietatem sermonis*) are catalogs of the sort of technical assertions that for Anselm and following thinkers had been a necessary consequence of the special requirements of logical and philosophical discourse, and that for them enshrined propriety to a degree to which the looseness of ordinary speech could not aspire. This reversal of attitude, symptomatic of the breakdown of communication in terms of semiartificial language, did not, of course, immediately prevail, it was combated at great length, for instance, by John Wyclyf (c. 1320–1384). Nevertheless, Ockham's attitude, reinforced by Renaissance philology, ultimately triumphed and was represented in the strictures of Locke on "the frivolous use of uncouth, affected, and unintelligible terms" that made philosophy "unfit or uncapable to be brought into well-bred company and polite conversation."

ETHICS AND POLITICS. Augustine's severe view of the effects of the Fall of man resulted in a largely negative view of the civil state. He held that save in the ideal case of a Christian commonwealth, earthly states are merely coercive institutions that would not exist had man not fallen, and serve simply to issue punishments and remedies for the corruption of human nature. Correspondingly, divine grace is seen by Augustine as playing a dramatically elevating part in the reformation and reordination of the will. However, the thirteenth-century revival of full Aristotelianism, coupled with the Thomist view of grace as a completion rather than an abrogation of nature, allowed that civil subordination was natural to man, would exist even if the Fall had not taken place, and hence could not be written off as an extraneous penal imposition; the state possesses a positive value in its own right.

Aquinas's enormously detailed philosophical anthropology constituted the foundation of his version of Aristotelian humanist ethics and politics, to which he attempted to give a Christian completion; it cited the perfection and fulfillment of human nature in the intellect rather than in the will: Accordingly, he viewed law as essentially a rule of right reason, rather than as a species of will-based command. This doctrine was in conflict with the teachings of the Augustinian voluntarists such as Ockham, whose view has endured through Thomas Hobbes and John Austin down to modern times. Aquinas's system of rationally based natural law as a measure of the value of human actions in general, and of human law in particular, was in opposition to the absolutist tendencies evident in the coalescence of revived Roman law with Augustinianism, which were to come to final fruition in the sovereign nation-state of our own era. The distinction between the righteous prince (who remains within the bounds of the law) and the tyrant (who puts himself above the law) had been trenchantly enunciated by John of Salisbury, was supported by the non-Roman medieval legal tradition, and clearly presupposes limits to the powers of the chief legal authority.

It is clear that Aquinas's natural-law theory supports this limiting attitude and justifies resistance to tyranny; he was therefore faced with the task of coming to terms with those features of Roman law (to be emphasized in the Renaissance) according to which the prince is above the laws. This he did by distinguishing between the coercive power (*vis coactiva*) and the directive, or rationally qualifying, power (*vis directiva*) of law: In respect of the first the prince is above the law, but in respect of the second he is voluntarily subject to it. In his theory of law Aquinas directly influenced Richard Hooker, to whom Locke admitted his indebtedness.

It is in connection with Aquinas's defense of the right of resistance, as well as in his prima facie puzzling assertions on the relation of the papacy to civil power, that we may best see how he attempted to resolve the perennial problem of the relation between political principle and political fact through the use of exceptive (*nisi forte ...*) clauses. Instead of rigidly carrying through principle to the bitter end and at all costs, without any regard for concrete or historical facts (in the manner, one might say, of Plato in the *Republic*), Aquinas suggested that the most rational course would be to make appropriate accommodations with local conditions, if necessary by recourse to empirically based anticipation of the results of political action. For example, it follows from natural law that tyranny may rightly be resisted by force; this justification of rebellion may be acted upon, said Aquinas, except perhaps (*nisi forte*) when the facts of the case make it plain that the revolution will generate worse evils than the tyranny that it is designed to displace. Again, in religious matters he declared that the ecclesiastical power is to be obeyed rather than the civil, and in civil matters the lay power is to be obeyed rather than the ecclesiastical, except perhaps (*nisi forte*) in the special case of the two powers' being amalgamated in one person, such as the Roman pontiff.

Commentators discussing this last example, and not armed with a realization of the significance of its exceptive (*nisi forte*) structure, have inferred from it that Aquinas here committed himself to an extreme papalist position that would endow the pope with the fullness of spiritual and temporal power. However, once the significance of that structure has been gathered from the many other available textual examples, the conclusion may be drawn that Aquinas taught the separation of these powers as a matter of principle, yet he also observed the local fact that insofar as the pope is a temporal ruler of papal territory, he, exceptionally, holds both spiritual and temporal power. A like adaptability may be seen in Aquinas's concession that the secondary precepts of natural law are mutable in accordance with changing historical conditions and in his recommendation that laws should be tailored to fit the type of population for which they are intended; to attempt to legislate a people into full virtue is futile.

Augustinianism in general, and the Augustinian theory of law as essentially will-based command, received impetus and encouragement from the archbishop of Paris's condemnation in 1277 of certain Aristotelian theses of Arabic philosophical complexion, a condemnation that also bore upon some Thomist positions. The tendency of Averroism had been toward a pantheism that diminished the freedom of God in the act of creation. Aquinas's claim that moral evaluation consists of rational assessments based upon the intrinsic nature of the cases in question was also susceptible of being interpreted as constituting a restriction on divine omnipotence. Accordingly, Duns Scotus and Ockham, in varying degrees, claimed that the rules governing the attribution of Tightness or wrongness to human actions were contingent in relation to the absolute power of God; the consequent contingency of connection between deed and merit has caused some historians to assume that in Augustinian thought one may find the basis of Martin Luther's doctrine of justification by faith alone, as well as a source for the legal aspects of the Hobbesian theory of sovereignty.

SCIENCE AND PHILOSOPHY. Although the nonabrogatory policy of medieval philosophy outlined above served well enough to ensure that philosophers took seriously the fully human realm of reasons, purposes, hopes, and so forth, thus avoiding the split between the thinker as a human being and the thinker as a philosopher, the extrapolation of that policy's attendant ultraempiricism to sciences such as physics and cosmology tended to a greater or lesser extent to inhibit their development as practical tools. A prime and early example of such ultraempiricist inhibition is to be found in the refusal of the second-century astronomer Ptolemy to consider a sun-centered planetary system because it so obviously is at variance with things as we find them to be, a refusal that was espoused by most but not all medieval philosophers. On this point Ptolemy was in agreement with the physics-based cosmology of Aristotle, but in general he represented a rival tradition, that of the mathematicians, who were usually regarded by the medievals as devisers of ingenious fictions that served merely to "save the observed appearances." Mathematical theories were accordingly believed to lack the necessity attributable to the vast and coherent background of Aristotelian physics and metaphysics, and this attitude prevailed until the time of Galileo Galilei.

However, there was some support for the development of mathematical physics, insofar as it relies on thought experiments as opposed to exact experiment, in the very competent medieval enlargements on a point whose root lay ultimately in Aristotle's *Categories*; there, when attempting to differentiate between substances (such as man, tree, stone) and qualities (such as whiteness, roundness, hardness), Aristotle pointed out that the latter are susceptible of degree, while the former are not. To this remote starting point much of modern mechanics owes its origin, for through speculation on the various kinds, rates, and degrees of "intension" and "remission" of qualities, the ideas of constant motion and acceleration and deceleration (uniform or nonuniform), and their relations to time and distance were thoroughly explored by fourteenth-century philosophers, such as those of Merton College, Oxford. Nicholas Oresme (c. 1325–1382) related these aspects of motion to their graphical expressions and anticipated infinitesimal calculus and coordinate geometry. Herein lies the starting point of certain segments of Galileo's mechanics.

See also Abelard, Peter; al-Fārābī; Anselm, St.; Aristotelianism; Aristotle; Artificial and Natural Languages; Augustine, St.; Augustinianism; Austin, John; Averroes; Averroism; Avicenna; Boethius, Anicius Manlius Severinus; Bonaventure, St.; Duns Scotus, John; Erigena, John Scotus; Galileo Galilei; Hobbes, Thomas; Ibn Gabirol, Solomon ben Judah; Islamic Philosophy; Jewish Philosophy; John of Salisbury; Logic, History of; Luther, Martin; Maimonides; Mathematics, Foundations of; Neoplatonism; Ontological Argument for the Existence of God; Oresme, Nicholas; Pantheism; Peter Lombard; Plato; Porphyry; Realism; Roscelin; Russell, Bertrand Arthur William; Scotism; Socrates; Sovereignty; Thomas Aquinas, St.; Thomism; Universals, A Historical Survey; William of Ockham; Wyclyf, John.

Bibliography

SOURCES, TEXTS, COMMENTARIES, TRANSLATIONS

Al-Farabi. *Al-Farabi's Commentary and Short Treatise on Aristotle's De interpretatione.* Translated by F. Zimmermann. London, 1981.

Al-Farabi. *Al-Farabi's Philosophy of Plato and Aristotle.* Translated by M. Mahdi. Ithaca, 1969; rev. ed. 2001.

Albert the Great. *Opera Omnia.* Edited by P. Jammy. 21 vols. Lyon, 1651.

Albert the Great. *Summa Theologiae.* Edited by D. Siedler. Munster, 1978.

Anselm of Canterbury. *Opera Omnia.* Edited by F. Schmitt. 6 vols. Stuttgart-Bad Cannstatt, 1968.

Aquinas, Thomas. *S. Thomae Aquinatis Doctoris Angelici Opera Omnia.* Rome, 1882.

Aquinas, Thomas. *Summa contra Gentiles.* Translated by A. Pegis et al. 5 vols. Notre Dame, IN, 1975.

Aquinas, Thomas. *Summa Theologiae.* Edited by T. Gilby et al. 61 vols. London, 1964–1980.

Augustine.*Against the Academicians and The Teacher.* Translated by P. King. Indianapolis, 1995.

Augustine. *Confessions.* Translated by H. Chadwick. Oxford, 1991.

Augustine. *Confessions.* Text, translation, and commentary by J. O'Donnell. Oxford, 1992.

Augustine. *De genesi ad litteram.* Translated by J. Taylor. New York, 1982.

Augustine. *Of True Religion.* Translated by J. Burleigh. Chicago, 1964.

Augustine. *On Christian Doctrine.* Translated by D. Robertson. Indianapolis, 1958.

Augustine. *On the Free Choice of the Will.* Translated by T. Williams. Indianapolis, 1993.

Augustine. *On the Trinity.* books 5–8, Translated by G. Matthews. Cambridge, 2002.

Augustine. *The City of God against the Pagans.* Translated by H. Bettenson. London, 1972.

Averroes. *On the Harmony of Religion and Philosophy.* Translated by G. Hourani. London, 1976.

Averroes. *Middle Commentary on Aristotle's De anima.* Edited by and translated by A. Ivri. Provo, UT, 2002.

Boethius. *De Consolatione philosophiae.* Edited by C. Moreschini. Munich, 2000.

Boethius. *The Consolation of Philosophy.* Translated by J. Relihan. Indianapolis, 2001.

Bonaventure. *Opera Omnia.* 10 vols. Ad Claras Aquas, 1882–1902.

Bonaventure. *Saint Bonaventure's Disputed Questions on the Mystery of the Trinity.* Translated by Z. Hayes. St. Bonaventure, NY, 1979.

Maimonides, Moses. *Ethical Writings of Maimonides.* Translated by R. Weiss and C. Butterworth. New York, 1975.

Maimonides, Moses. *The Guide to the Perplexed.* Translated by S. Pines. 2 vols. Chicago, 1963.

Scotus, John Duns. *Opera omnia.* Edited by C. Balic et al. Vatican City, 1950–.

Scotus, John Duns. *God and Creatures: The Quodlibetal Questions.* Translated by F. Alluntis and A. Wolter. Princeton, NJ, 1975.

Scotus, John Duns. *Questions on the Metaphysics of Aristotle.* Translated by G. Etzkorn and A. Wolter. St. Bonaventure, NY, 1997.

Scotus, John Duns. *Philosophical Writings.* Translated by A. Wolter. Edinburgh, 1962.

William of Ockham. *Opera philosophica et theological.* 17 vols. Edited by G. Gál et al. St. Bonaventure, NY, 1967–1988.

William of Ockham. *Philosophical Writings.* Translated by P. Boehner, rev. F. Brown. Indianapolis, IN, 1990.

HISTORIES

Armstrong, A. H. ed. *The Cambridge History of Later Greek and Early Medieval Philosophy.* Cambridge, 1967.

Gilson, E. *History of Christian Philosophy in the Middle Ages.* London, 1955.

Nasr, S. H. and O. Leaman, eds. *History of Islamic Philosophy.* 2 vols. London, 1996.

Schmidtt, C. B. and Q. Skinner, eds. *The Cambridge History of Renaissance Philosophy.* Cambridge, 1988.

Leaman, O. and D. Frank, eds. *History of Jewish Philosophy.* London, 1997.

STUDIES

Augustine

Brown, P. *Augustine of Hippo.* Berkeley, CA, 1967; rev. ed., 2000.

Gilson, E. *The Christian Philosophy of St. Augustine.* New York, 1960.

Kirwan, C. *Augustine.* London, 1989.

Rist, J. *Augustine: Ancient Thought Baptized.* Cambridge, 1994.

Boethius

Marenbon, J. *Boethius.* New York, 2003.

Al-Farābī

Druart, T.-A. "Le sommaire du livre des 'Lois' de Platon (Gawami' Kitab al-Nawamis li-Aflatun) par Abu Nasr al-Farabi." *Bulletin d'Etudes Orientales* 50 (1998) 109–55.

Galston, M. *Politics and Excellence: The Political Philosophy of Alfarabi.* Princeton, 1990.

Mahdi, M. *Alfarabi and the Foundations of Islamic Political Philosophy.* Chicago, 2001.

Ibn Sina

Gutas, D. *Avicenna and the Aristotelian Tradition. Introduction to Reading Avicenna's Philosophical Works.* Leiden, 1988.

Wisnovsky, R. *Aspects of Avicenna.* Princeton, 2002.

Anselm of Canterbury

Southern, R. *Saint Anselm: A Portrait in a Landscape.* London, 1990.

Peter Abelard

Marenbon, J. *The Philosophy of Peter Abelard.* Cambridge, 1997.

Peter Lombard

Colish, M. *Peter Lombard.* 2 vols. Leiden, 1994.

John of Salisbury

Wilks, M. *The World of John of Salisbury.* Oxford, 1984.

Ibn Rushd

Endress, G. and J. Aertsen, eds. *Averroes and the Aristotelian Tradition. Sources, Constitution, and Reception of the Philosophy of Ibn Rushd (1126–1198).* Leiden, 1999.

Renan, E. *Averroès et l'averroïsme.* Paris, 1852; 3rd rev. ed. 1866; repr. 1997.

Moses Maimonides

Buijs J. *Maimonides: A Collection of Critical Essays.* Notre Dame, IN, 1988.

Hyman, A. ed. *Maimonidean Studies.* 4 vols. New York, 1991–1996.

Kraemer, J. ed. *Perspectives on Maimonides: Philosophical and Historical Studies.* London, 1996.

Albert the Great

Weisheipl, J. *Albertus Magnus and the Sciences.* Toronto, 1980.

Bonaventure

Gilson, E. *The Philosophy of St. Bonaventure.* New York, 1938.

Thomas Aquinas

Benez, D. *The Primacy of Existence in Thomas Aquinas.* Translated by B. Llamzon. Chicago, 1966.

Finnis, J. *Aquinas.* Oxford, 2000.

MacDonald, S. and E. Stump, eds. *Aquinas' Moral Theory.* Ithaca, NY, 1999.

McInerny, R. *Ethica Thomistica.* Rev. ed. Washington, DC, 1997.

O'Connor, D. *Aquinas and Natural Law.* London, 1967.

Wippel, J. *The Metaphysical Thought of Thomas Aquinas: From Finite Being to Uncreated Being.* Washington, DC, 2000.

John Duns Scotus

Adams, M. ed. *The Philosophical Theology of John Duns Scotus.* Ithaca, NY, 1990.

Cross, R. *The Physics of Duns Scotus.* Oxford, 1998.

William of Ockham

Adams, M. *William Ockham.* 2 vols. Notre Dame, IN, 1987.

Other studies

Alverny, M.-T. "Le Cosmos symbolique du XIIe siècle." *Archives d'Histoire Doctrinale et Littéraire du Moyen Age.* 20 (1953) 31–81.

Black, A. *Political Thought in Europe 1250–1450.* Cambridge, 1992.

Craig, W. *The Problem of Divine Foreknowledge and Future Contingents from Ockham to Suarez.* Leiden, 1988.

D'Ancona Costa, C. *La Casa della sapienza. La transmissione della metafisica greca e la formazione della filosofia araba.* Milan, 1996.

Davidson, H. *Alfarabi, Avicenna, and Averroes, on Intellect: Their Cosmologies, Theories of the Active Intellect and Theories of Human Intellect.* New York, 1992.

Gracia, J. *Introduction to the Problem of Individuation in the Early Middle Ages.* Munich, 1984; 2nd ed. 1988.

Grant, E. ed. *A Source Book in Medieval Science.* Cambridge, MA, 1974.

Grant, E. *God and Reason in the Middle Ages.* Cambridge, 2001.

Grant, E. *The Foundations of Modern Science in the Middle Ages: Their Religious, Institutional, and Intellectual Contexts.* Cambridge, 1966.

Gutas, D. *Greek Thought, Arabic Culture: The Greco-Arabic Translation Movement in Baghdad and Early 'Abbasid Society (2nd–4th/8th–10th Centuries).* London, 1998.

Jacobi, K. ed. *Argumentationstheorie: Scholastische Forschungen zu den logischen und semantischen Regeln korrekter Folgerns.* Leiden, 1993.

Knuuttila, S. *Modalities in Medieval Philosophy.* London, 1993.

Lovejoy, A. *The Great Chain of Being: A Study of the History of an Idea.* Cambridge, MA, 1936.

Maier, A. *Studien zur Naturphilosophie der Spätmittelalter.* 5 vols. Rome, 1952–1968.

McGrath, A. *Iustitia Dei.* 2 vols. Cambridge, 1986.

Miethke, J. *De potestate papae. Die päpstliche Amtskompetenz im Widerstreit der politischen Theorie von Thomas von Aquin bis Wilhem von Ockham.* Tübingen, 2000.

Pasnau, R. *Theories of Cognition in the Later Middle Ages.* Cambridge, 1997.

Skinner, Q. *The Foundations of Modern Political Thought.* 2 vols. Cambridge, 1978.

Desmond Paul Henry (1967)
Bibliography updated by Scott Carson

MEDITATION IN INDIAN PHILOSOPHY

Meditation as a distinct practice in Indian philosophy appears in a variety of texts from the third century before the common era as well as in sculptural depictions that date from 3500 BCE. The quintessential manual on meditation, the *Yoga Sūtra*, was composed by approximately 200 CE and includes philosophical positions and meditation techniques from the Sāṃkhya, Jaina, and Buddhist traditions.

Early depictions of meditating figures were found in the excavations of Mohenjodaro and Harappa, Indus Valley cities that date from 3500 BCE Sculptures and steatite seals show people with half-closed eyes sitting in the lotus posture. In some seals, animals surround a meditating figure, indicating a shamanic, totemic origin of this tradition.

The earliest text of Indian literature, the *Ṛg Veda*, which dates from at least 1500 BCE, mentions longhaired ascetics and, amidst hundreds of hymns extolling various gods and goddesses, lays out the philosophical foundations for later traditions of meditation. *Ṛg Veda* (1:164.20) describes two birds in the same tree, one eating sweet berries while the other merely witnesses. This theme repeats itself in the *Muṇḍaka Upanishad* (3:l:l) and the *Śvetaśvatara Upanishad* (4:6) and is expressed in the *Bhagavad Gītā* themes of the lower nature subject to constant change and activity (*prakrti*) and the higher nature or inner true self (*puruṣa* or *ātman*). The worldview presented in this early metaphor delineates two major modalities of engagement with the world. One aspect freely and unreflectively participates in and contributes to the world. The other aspect remains aloof and transcendent, as a spectator or onlooker.

Sāṃkhya philosophy, articulated by the philosopher Ishvarakrishna in the early centuries of the common era, delineates a cosmology based on this dynamic tension between the processes of activity and witnessing. The realm of activity includes psychological states (*bhāva*), operations of the mind (*manas*), sense and motor capacities (*indriya*), as well as the subtle and gross elements (*bhūta*) that manifest as discrete, concrete objects. By understanding and harnessing the karmically influenced outflows that arise when the witnessing consciousness becomes intrigued and defined by the particularity found in the manifest realm of activity, one gains mastery over and release from compulsive behavior, resulting in liberation (*kaivalyam*). This philosophy undergirds the system of Yoga, which presents a variety of meditation techniques to accomplish the goal of liberation. Yoga also appears within non-Vedic traditions such as Jainism, Buddhism, Sufism, and Sikhism.

THE YOGA SŪTRA

The *Yoga Sūtra* of Patañjali (c. 200 CE) defines Yoga as the restraint of the fluctuations of the mind (*yogaś-citta-vṛtti-nirodha?*). The application of Yoga allows for the gradual diminishment of karmic influences, referred to as seeds (*bīja*) or residues (*saṃskāra*). Yoga specifies five aspects of defilement that must be controlled: ignorance, egoism, attraction, repulsion, and a desire for life to continue. By following the practices of Yoga, including meditation, karma dissipates. The practitioner reshapes his or her identity, abandoning attachment to fixed behaviors. By drawing inward, one reaches deeper self-understanding and approaches a state of lucidity and purification.

Numerous meditation practices can be found in the texts of Yoga, Buddhism, Jainism, and Sikhism. Different objects of meditation are listed, including fixing one's attention on Īśvara through the use of mantra. Patañjali defines Īśvara, sometimes referred to as a deity, as a special soul or *purusa* who has never been tainted by the actions of karma. By fashioning such an ideal through the imagination, one can then strive to emulate this rarefied being. For a Jaina, this state of Īśvara is symbolized through the twenty-four great teachers (Tīrthaṅkāra). For a Buddhist, Lord Buddha serves the same function. In the Hindu bhakti or devotional tradition, fixing one's attention on any one of a variety of deities can result in karmic purification, with Krishna and Rama being the most frequently worshipped Vaisnava deities and Siva and Ganesh and the Goddess Kāli the object of devotion for Saivites. For the Sikhs, the highest soul cannot be named and exists outside time (*akal*). However, the ten Sikh gurus, beginning with Guru Nanak, serve as objects with worship because of their teachings. Patañjali, through his concept of chosen deity (*iṣṭa devatā*), suggests that the meditative procedures engaged in order to purify oneself carry more significance than the actual object of one's meditation.

Several other practices are listed in the *Yoga Sūtra* that do not require the presence of an inspirational, theistic object of devotion. They include becoming one-pointed in one's activities, regulating one's breath, experiencing inner radiance, reflecting on an auspicious dream, or "meditation as desired" (1:39). Patañjali puts forward a progressive technique, where one begins with a gross, outward object (*vitarka*) and then takes it inward, seeing its relationship with and grounding in one's men-

tal constructs. One then moves on to more subtle aspects of one's psychological conditioning (*vicāra*), focusing on the patterns of past karma that tend to govern one's personality. By applying meditation techniques of focusing and calming the mind, and by probing into the root causes of one's motivations, one gradually gains the ability to move into a seedless state of pure being, referred to as *nirbīja samādhi*.

ETHICS

Ethics plays a crucial role in the meditation systems of India. Buddhists refer to these practices as perfections. Yogis and Jainas share a list of common vows. By holding to nonviolence (*ahiṃsā*) one engenders an atmosphere of well-being that brings calm and solace to others. By holding to truth, one's word corresponds to reality. Through not stealing, one gains appreciation of all that exists without seeking to appropriate or horde it for oneself. By abandoning sexual obsession, one makes the world safe from one's designs and manipulations. By giving up the acquisition of things, one can learn to understand one's motivations and past predilections. These five vows, common to nearly all India's meditative paths, allow for the deconstruction of destructive habits and the active construction of a safe, ethically-grounded world. For the Buddhists and the Yogis, a purified person naturally exhibits enlightened behavior and is friendly (not jealous) toward successful people, compassionate (not scornful) toward those who suffer, happy (not envious) for those who are meritorious, and retain their equanimity (do not become hateful) in regard to those who lack virtue.

PRACTICE

Meditation enables the practitioner to avoid the repetition of behavior that can be harmful to oneself and others. Indian philosophy, particularly as found in Buddhism, Sāṃkhya, and Yoga, claims that due to desire or thirst (*kāma/tṛṣṇa*) one engages in actions (karma) prompted by the residues of past actions (*saṃskāra*) that lead to repeated difficulty, darkness, and even despair (*duḥkha*). By the application of meditation and meditative ethical practices, one can cultivate an alternate way of being (*prati-pakṣa-bhāvanā*)rooted in purity. By withdrawing the outward flows of the mind and the senses and reversing the tendency to be defined by external objects and realities, one can become free of psychological entanglements and social expectations, achieving the status of a solitary hero, in charge of one's own reality. The word Jina, an epithet for Vardhamana Mahavira, the twenty-fourth and most recent Tīrthaṅkāra of the Jaina tradition, indicates that he was a great vanquisher, one who conquered his past karma to establish himself as a model for others to emulate. Similarly, the enlightenment of the Buddha is cloaked with martial symbolism, with Siddhartha defeating the evil Mara in a great test of wills.

Meditation results in the accumulation of powers, ranging from enhanced language-learning abilities and physical beauty to memory of one's past lives. Through focusing on the interior energy of the body, one gains intimacy with the various subtle energy centers (*cakras*) that correlate with locations along the spine. These include vortexes of the earth-connected eliminative function, sexuality, and power found in the respective areas of the anus, the sexual organs, and the solar plexus. Above these three lower functions, one finds the seat of compassion in the heart, an array of emotions in the area of the throat, the third eye representing insight between the eyebrows, and in the area above the skull, a magnificent lotus. Through meditation techniques associated with Tantra and popularized from the eighth century forward, one systematically advances from the lower *cakras* toward the higher ones, bring about the ascent of a force known as the *kundalini*. However, whether the philosophy originates from Yoga, Buddhism, or Jainism, all traditions state that the powers (*siddhi*) must not distract one from the ultimate goal of self-purification.

Indian systems of meditation mandate the presence of a qualified teacher guru in order to engage in this variety of techniques. A well-qualified guru, in addition to knowing the mechanics, guides the student through the pitfalls of self-aggrandizement and periodic disappointment. Discovering one's past history can be fraught with frightful memories; the guru assists the disciple in this process of self-discovery. The Jaina tradition of past-life stories and the Buddha's narration of his past births in the Jataka tales, demonstrate that human action derives from ignorant, self-serving motivations, unless one has made a commitment to strive for purification. As shown in the paradigmatic case of the life of the Buddha, a realization of the fleeting nature of reality will often prompt a potential meditator to seek out instruction on how to achieve and maintain peace of mind. In the case of the Buddha, he studied various techniques for six years under two different renowned teachers before he entered into *nirvāṇa* and subsequently decided to teach others how to overcome their own personal difficulties through meditation. Guru Nanak (1469–1539), living in a time of great strife between Hindus and Muslims, underwent a miraculous transformation that prompted him to develop a new way of meditation that transcended both traditions. Modern day Yoga and meditation practices offer pathways of self-cultivation through the purification of the body, the emotions, and one's way of being situated in the world. These traditions all trace their origins back to an original teacher, whether Swami Vivekananda or Krishnamacarya for many schools of Yoga or to the Buddha himself for Buddhist meditators.

The philosophical texts on meditation in each of the traditions outline different paths and offer different catalogues of the karma that must be overcome. The *Yoga Sūtra* and its commentaries outlines five states of mind, five afflictive karma categories, seven levels of *samadhi*, a threefold path and an eightfold path of practice, and a tenfold ethical system. The core texts of Buddhism set forth an eightfold path and a fivefold assessment of the nature of reality that further subdivides into either seventy-five or one hundred constituent features. The Theravada texts outline nine meditations on objects with form and four formless meditation states. The *Tattvārtha Sūtra*, the foundational meditation text of Jainsim, describes 148 forms of karma known as *prakrtis* and a fourteen-step analysis of states of increasing purification.

Meditation constitutes an important aspect of Indian philosophy. It requires an active engagement of the world through ethics. It requires the cultivation of a body that can sit for long periods of time. It also requires protracted states of introspection in order to gain mastery over the mind. Meditation comprises a comprehensive system of purification that, regardless of the particular theological context or philosophical point of view, serves to diminish negative karma and bring about states of equanimity.

See also Brahman; God in Indian Philosophy; Knowledge in Indian Philosophy; Liberation in Indian Philosophy; Mind and Mental States in Indian Philosophy; Negation in Indian Philosophy; Self in Indian Philosophy; Truth and Falsity in Indian Philosophy.

Bibliography

Chapple, Christopher Key, and Eugene P. Kelly, Jr., trs. *The Yoga Sūtra of Patanjali: An Analysis of the Sanskrit with Accompanying English Translation*. New Delhi: Sri Satguru Publications, 1990.

King, Winston. *Theravāda Meditation: The Buddhist Transformation of Yoga*. University Park: Pennsylvania State University Press, 1980.

Ñāṇamoli, Bhikku, tr. *The Path of Purification (Vissudhimagga) of Buddhaghosa*. Comombo: Semage, 1964.

Roebuck, Valerie J., tr. *The Upaniṣads*. London: Penguin Books, 2003.

Sargeant, Winthrop, tr. *The Bhagavad Gītā*. Albany: State University of New York Press, 1990.

Tatia, Nathmal, tr. *That Which Is: Tattvārtha Sūtra*. San Francisco: HarperCollins, 1994.

Christopher Key Chapple (2005)

MEGARIANS

The Megarians flourished during the fourth and the early third centuries BCE. They derived their name from their connection with Megara on the Isthmus (a city one day's walk west of Athens). They constituted a 'philosophical school' only in a weak sense: no shared lifestyle, no rigid body of doctrine. Since no work of any Megarian has survived, knowledge of them must rely on fragments and reports of other authors.

The earliest Megarian was Euclides of Megara. Diogenes Laertius (2.106) reports that Euclides' followers "were called 'Megarians,' then 'Eristics,' and later 'Dialecticians.'" Modern scholars traditionally understood this report as indicating that a single school had three successive labels. However, in 1977 David Sedley argued that the three labels designated three distinct groups of philosophers that were influenced to some extent by Euclides but, far from constituting a single school, were in competition with one another. Sedley's reconstruction has won widespread, although not universal, scholarly approval. The present entry will cover all those thinkers who have traditionally been regarded as Megarians, including Eristics and Dialecticians, except the Dialecticians Diodorus and Philo, who have separate entries.

Euclides of Megara was probably born after 450 BCE and died before 365 BCE. A pupil of Socrates, he also studied Parmenides' writings. He is mentioned by Plato in the *Phaedo* (59b–59c), where he is portrayed as present at Socrates' death, and in the *Theaetetus* (142a–143c), where he is described conversing with Terpsion, another early Megarian. After Socrates' death, Plato and some of his companions fled Athens to stay for awhile with Euclides at Megara. Euclides authored six dialogues: *Lamprias, Aeschines, Phoenix, Crito, Alcibiades*, and a *Discourse on Love*. We know little of Euclides' philosophical views. He claimed that the good is one although it is called by many names (such as 'wisdom,' 'God,' and 'mind'), and that the contrary of the good is mere nonbeing: he thus seems to have borrowed Socratic views in ethics and combined them with Eleatic monism. He attacked proofs by opposing their conclusions, not their premises (he probably did this by reducing to absurdity the conclusions, wherein an influence of the methods of Zeno of Elea can be detected), and he rejected arguments from parallel cases.

Euclides had numerous pupils: Dionysius of Chalcedon, Dioclides of Megara, Thrasymachus of Corinth, Ichthyas, and Clinomachus of Thurii, who founded the Dialectical school. According to Diogenes Laertius (2.112), Clinomachus was "the first who wrote about assertibles, predicates, and the like." Later, in Stoic logic, assertibles and predicates are two of the main types of sayables, incorporeal items that are signified by utterances of linguistic expressions and are themselves neither thoughts nor linguistic expressions (specifically, assertibles and predicates are what is signified, respectively, by utterances of declarative sentences and predicative expressions). It is unclear how much of the Stoic views about assertibles and predicates was already held by Clinomachus, but it cannot be ruled out that the basics were already in place.

According to some sources, one of Euclides' pupils was named 'Bryson.' Modern scholars disagree on whether there was exactly one thinker answering to this name, and whether he is the same as the one who introduced a method for squaring the circle which was criticized by Aristotle.

Later Dialecticians were Polyxenus (to whom the authorship of a 'third man' argument against forms is ascribed) and Eubulides of Miletus. Since he taught Demosthenes and wrote a defamatory book against Aristotle, Eubulides was probably born in the second half of the fourth century BCE. According to Diogenes Laertius (2.108), he fathered seven arguments: the Liar, the Disguised, the Electra, the Veiled, the Heaper, the Horned, and the Baldhead. These arguments, in question-and-answer form, were extensively discussed by later Hellenistic philosophers.

It is not clear whether Eubulides' version of the Liar had already the devastating self-referential character of modern versions. For instance, we cannot rule out that Eubulides' version was presented roughly as follows: The questioner makes an obviously false statement, adds the remark 'I am speaking falsely,' and then asks whether he is speaking truly or falsely—both answers can be regarded as correct with regard to different statements made by the questioner. Note that all ancient versions of the Liar turn on the sentence 'I am speaking falsely' (modern versions instead turn on 'This sentence is false' or variants thereof). The Heaper heaps questions concerning heaps: 'Does one grain constitute a heap?' 'Do two grains constitute a heap?' 'Do ten thousand grains constitute a heap?'

One is likely to answer the first question negatively, and then, on the assumption that the addition of a single grain cannot transform what is not yet a heap into one, is induced to answer negatively each of the following.

The Baldhead was probably an alternative formulation of the same puzzle. On the basis of Lucian (*Vitarum Auctio*, 22–23), we can plausibly reconstruct the Veiled as follows: 'Do you know your father?—Yes.—If I set a veiled man before you and I ask you whether you know him, what do you answer?—That I do not know him.—But the veiled man is your father. So, you both know and do not know your father.' The Disguised and Electra were probably variants of the Veiled. On the basis of Diogenes Laertius (7.187), we can plausibly reconstruct the Horned as follows: 'If you have not lost something, do you still have it?—Yes.—Have you lost horns?—No.—Then you still have horns.'

Pupils of Eubulides were Euphantus of Olinthus, Apollonius, surnamed 'Cronus' (his pupil Diodorus inherited this surname from him), and Alexinus of Elis, whose fondness of controversy earned him the nickname 'Elenxinus' ('Refuter'). Some sources describe Alexinus as a Dialectician, others as an Eristic. Active around 300 BCE, he wrote a book *On Education* and works against other thinkers, Aristotle and Zeno of Citium among them. Alexinus attacked Zeno by taking arguments of his and constructing unpalatable 'parallels,' namely arguments that were isomorphic to Zeno's and had plausible premises but absurd conclusions. For instance, Zeno had offered the following argument: 'What is rational is better than what is not rational; but nothing is better than the universe; therefore, the universe is rational' (Sextus Empiricus, *Adversus Mathematicos*, 9.104).

Alexinus constructed the following parallel: 'What is poetic is better than what is not poetic; but nothing is better than the universe; therefore the universe is poetic' (Sextus Empiricus, *Adversus Mathematicos*, 9.108). Zeno was thereby left with two options: either claim that his argument is valid whereas Alexinus's parallel is not, or claim that all the premises of his argument are true whereas at least one of Alexinus's parallel is not. The first option was hard to follow because the two arguments are extremely similar (in fact, neither of them is valid in first-order logic as it stands, but becomes such if an uncontroversial premise is added: 'Something is rational' in the case of Zeno's argument, 'Something is poetic' in the case of Alexinus's parallel). Sextus Empiricus (*Adversus Mathematicos*, 9.109–110) reports that Zeno's followers chose the second option: they insisted that all the premises of Zeno's argument are true but one of Alexinus's parallel is not.

Little is known of Panthoides, a Dialectician who flourished around 300–280 BCE. The last Megarian about whom we are relatively well informed is Stilpo of Megara, who probably lived between 360 and 280 BCE. According to Diogenes Laertius (2.113), "so far did he excel everyone else in inventiveness and sophistry that nearly the whole of Greece was looking at him and Megarizing." He had many pupils, Zeno of Citium and Menedemus of Eretria among them, and wrote many dialogues. According to Plutarch (*Adv. Colotem*, 23, 1120a), Stilpo claimed that what is predicated must be identical with what it is predicated of. For example, goodness cannot be predicated of a man because it is not identical with him, nor can running be predicated of a horse because it is not identical with it. Stilpo's attack on predication recalls a position criticized by Plato in the *Sophist* (251a–c), and therefore lends plausibility to identifying Plato's target with some Megarian earlier than Stilpo. Stilpo attacked forms. One of his arguments can perhaps be reconstructed on the basis of Diogenes Laertius (2.119) and Alexander of Aphrodisias (*Commentary on Aristotle's Metaphysics*, 84, 7–14). Suppose that individual perceptible men and the form Man were the only men. It is surely true that man speaks. But who is then the man who speaks? Nobody: for it is none of the particular perceptible men (for why should it be this one rather than this one?), and it is not the form Man (for forms do not speak). If we want to avoid denying that man speaks, we must give up the assumption that individual perceptible men and the form Man are the only men, and therefore introduce a 'third man.' This seems to undermine our motivation for assuming there is the form Man.

According to Diogenes Laertius (2. 115), when Demetrius Poliorcetes had taken Megara and wanted Stilpo to list the items he had lost, "he said that he had lost nothing of his own: for nobody had subtracted his learning, and he still had reason and knowledge." This anecdote suggests that for Stilpo the only human goods are moral and intellectual attainments, which are inalienable (a view close to that of the Cynics).

In the *Metaphysics* (9. 3, 1046b29–32), Aristotle attributes to unnamed Megarians the view that a thing has the capacity to do something when and only when it is actually doing it. For example, whenever the builder is building, he also has the capacity to build, but when he is not building, he lacks the capacity to build. We are unable to link this view to any specific Megarian, and the ideas about modality we can ascribe to Diodorus Cronus and Philo do not chime with it.

See also Alexander of Aphrodisias; Cynics; Diodorus Cronus; Diogenes Laertius; Hellenistic Thought; Parmenides of Elea; Philo of Megara; Plato; Plutarch of Chaeronea; Socrates; Sextus Empiricus; Stoicism; Zeno of Citium; Zeno of Elea.

Bibliography

COLLECTIONS OF FRAGMENTS

Döring, K. *Die Megariker. Kommentierte Sammlung der Testimonien.* Amsterdam: Grüner 1972.

Giannantoni, Gabriele. *Socratis et Socraticorum reliquiae.* 4 vols. Naples: Bibliopolis, 1990.

SECONDARY LITERATURE

Döring, K. "Gab es eine Dialektische Schule?" (Was there a Dialectical School?). *Phronesis* 34 (1989): 293–310.

Makin, Stephen. "Megarian Possibilities." *Philosophical Studies* 83 (1996): 253–276.

Montoneri, Luciano. *I Megarici: Studio storico-critico e traduzione delle testimonianze antiche.* Catania, Italy: University of Catania, 1984.

Müller, Robert. *Introduction à la pensée des Mégariques.* Paris: Vrin, 1988.

Müller, Robert. *Les Mégariques: fragments et témoignages.* Paris: Vrin, 1985.

Schofield, Malcolm. "The Syllogisms of Zeno of Citium." *Phronesis* 28 (1983): 31–58.

Sedley, David. "Diodorus Cronus and Hellenistic Philosophy." *Proceedings of the Cambridge Philological Society* 203 (1977): 74–120.

Zeller, Eduard. *Die Philosophie der Griechen in ihrer geschichtlichen Entwicklung dargestellt.* 5th ed. Leipzig, Germany: Reisland, 1920—1923, 2.1, p. 244–275.

Paolo Crivelli (2005)

MEIER, GEORG FRIEDRICH
(1718–1777)

Georg Friedrich Meier was a German philosopher and aesthetician. A pupil of Alexander Gottlieb Baumgarten, Meier succeeded Baumgarten as extraordinary professor at the University of Halle in 1740 and became a full professor in 1748, holding that position until his death.

Meier, a prolific writer, developed and commented on Baumgarten's doctrines as an extension and revision of Wolffianism and went far beyond Baumgarten in the reform of Wolffianism. His treatises, used as textbooks in many universities, were perspicuous, sophisticated, and modern renderings of Wolffian doctrine; by their thorough discussion of basic concepts and attention to details they give one of the best insights into the Wolffian system and its problems. Christian Wolff's and Baumgarten's ideas were rendered more fluid by Meier's work, establishing connections between disparate problems and establishing new distinctions. Meier's style was closer to the style of the "popular philosophers" than to that of orthodox Wolffians, and he made little use of the Wolffian mathematical method in philosophy.

Meier's *Vernunftlehre* introduced into the traditional frame of Wolffian logic lengthy psychological and methodological discussions like those of the Pietist philosophers A. F. Hoffmann and C. F. Crusius. He also presented a detailed typology of concepts. In a marked departure from Wolff, he stressed the limits of the human understanding, devoting an entire work to the subject (*Betrachtungen über die Schranken der menschlichen Erkenntniss*).

Meier's *Metaphysik*, although in general rather close to Baumgarten, shows the same individual features. For instance, in empirical psychology Meier advocated a subjectivism like that of Crusius. He held that the nature of our understanding determines what we can or cannot think. This determination, like the principle of *cogitabilis* in Crusius, is the foundation of the principle of identity.

Meier devoted several pamphlets to the immortality of the soul, which he held could not be theoretically demonstrated. Any a priori proof of God's existence must be completed by an a posteriori one. And in general Meier would not extend the power of reason much beyond basic truths and human experience.

Meier's most typical work was his *Anfangsgründe aller schönen Künste und Wissenschaften* (Principles of All Beautiful Arts and Sciences). He was opposed to the classical thesis that art imitates nature. He stressed the importance of sensitivity (the "lower faculty") and the indispensability of a knowledge of the beautiful within one's whole outlook on the world. Besides Baumgarten, whose views it is difficult to extricate from Meier's because of their close collaboration, Meier was influenced by the Swiss critics Johann Jakob Bodmer and Johann Jakob Breitinger and by English aestheticians. Like Baumgarten, he gave the term *aesthetics* a broad interpretation and, like Baumgarten's, his work contains an extensive discussion of scientific methodology.

See also Aesthetics, History of; Baumgarten, Alexander Gottlieb; Crusius, Christian August; Identity; Scientific Method; Wolff, Christian.

Bibliography

PRINCIPAL WORKS BY MEIER

Anfangsgründe aller schönen Künste und Wissenschaften. 3 vols. Halle, 1748–1750.

Gedanken über die Religion. Halle, 1749.

Vernunftlehre. Halle, 1752.

Philosophische Sittenlehre. 5 vols. Halle, 1753–1761. A much extended version of Baumgarten's *Ethica Philosophica.*

Metaphysik. 4 vols. Halle, 1755–1759.

Betrachtungen über die Schranken der menschlichen Erkenntniss. Halle, 1775.

WORKS ON MEIER

Bergmann, E. *Die Begründung der deutschen Aesthetik druch A. G. Baumgarten und G. F. Meier.* Leipzig: Röder and Schunke, 1911.

Böhm, Hans. "Das Schönheitsproblem bei G. F. Meier." *Archiv für die gesamte Psychologie* 56 (1926).

Langen, S. G. *G. F. Meier.* Halle, 1778.

Makkreel, Rudolf. "The Confluence of Aesthetics and Hermeneutics in Baumgarten, Meier, and Kant." *Journal of Aesthetics and Art Criticism* 54(1) (1996): 65–75.

Giorgio Tonelli (1967)
Bibliography updated by Tamra Frei (2005)

MEINECKE, FRIEDRICH
(1862–1954)

Friedrich Meinecke, the German historian and political philosopher, was small in stature and somewhat frail but remained mentally very vigorous and intellectually prolific until his death at the age of ninety-two. His great charm and influence were due partly to his erudition, partly to his modesty, and partly to two conflicting tendencies in his thinking that he continually sought to reconcile.

One of these tendencies was his patriotism and loyalty to Germany's best traditions of the past. As a boy he had been thrilled by the sight of the victorious German troops marching home through the Brandenburg Gate after the Franco-Prussian War. Later he admired the skill with which Otto von Bismarck established the long-desired unification of his country and saw with pride Germany's industrial and commercial expansion into a great power. After studying under the Prussian nationalist historian J. G. Droysen, Meinecke became an archivist and published in rapid succession several valuable historical works, including accounts of the German uprising against Napoleon Bonaparte and a two-volume biography of Hermann von Boyen, one of the leading figures in the reorganization and liberalization of Prussia in the early nineteenth century. In 1893 he was appointed an editor of the leading German historical journal, *Historische Zeitschrift,* a post that he filled with distinction for forty years until ousted by the Nazis.

The second tendency in Meinecke's thinking asserted itself in 1901 when he became deeply occupied with the problems of European political philosophy. In that year he was promoted to a teaching position at the University of Strassburg, later moving to Freiburg. Here in these two cities in the beautiful Rhine valley Meinecke's eyes were opened to the charm of the countryside. His talks with the Roman Catholic population and scholars and his contact with French culture widened his outlook and quickened his philosophical interests. These were his happiest years. In 1914 he was appointed to a permanent professorship at Berlin.

Meinecke's dual preoccupation with liberal culture and with Prussia found expression in a perceptive account of German development. *Weltbürgertum und Nationalstaat* (1908) examines the views of many cosmopolitan liberals and political leaders and, at the same time, analyzes the characteristics and pretensions of the Prussian state, which had been exaggerated by G. W. F. Hegel. It was supplemented by some two dozen articles written by Meinecke in the following years and reprinted in *Preussen und Deutschland* (1918).

Can reason of state justify the employment of might against right? May a state properly do things that are ethically forbidden to the ordinary citizen? Does it enjoy a code of morals above and beyond that of the private individual? Meinecke's classic treatment of these old but perennial questions, *Die Idee der Staatsräson in der neueren Geschichte* (1924), examines meticulously the actions of various European rulers and statesmen and the writings of numerous political theorists from Niccolò Machiavelli to Heinrich von Treitschke. Meinecke comes to the conclusion that, since power is the essence of its existence, the state is justified in using such means as are necessary to maintain and even extend its power, but that this power is limited by the state's obligation to protect the rights of its citizens and to promote their cultural and material welfare. It is, however, practically impossible to draw a precise line between state egoism and ideal morality.

Meinecke always preferred to till a small area where he could closely observe concrete facts and deal with them in a rigorously critical scientific manner. For Leopold von Ranke and Jakob Burckhardt he had the highest regard. He rejected the grandiose theoretical constructions of Karl Lamprecht, Oswald Spengler, and Arnold Toynbee. If he could be said to have had any one primary underlying thought, it would be that of individuality—the unique individual character of every event, person, social group, nation-state, or idea. In addition he believed in evolution—the capacity of every individuality for development either by growth or decay. Hence his preoccupation with Machiavelli, Cardinal Richelieu, Freiherr vom Stein, Friedrich Schleiermacher, Wilhelm von Humboldt, Johann Wolfgang von Goethe, Joseph Maria von Radowitz, Bismarck, and Adolf Hitler. Meinecke's conceptions of individuality and evolution contributed to the new way of historical thinking, now known as "historicism," which developed in the age of Johann Gottfried Herder and Goethe and which Meinecke minutely unfolded in *Die Entstehung des Historismus* (1936). Historicism dealt a sharp blow to unquestioning belief in absolute values, optimistic positivism, religious creeds, and natural law. It opened wide the floodgates of relativism. Meinecke, however, was not unaware of the aberrations resulting from historicism and tried to counteract them by repeatedly insisting that the only sure and safe guide to morality and conduct is the individual's own conscience.

With the advent to power of the Nazis, Meinecke was forced to retire from active teaching, and under their tyranny he suffered spiritual agony and physical hardship. He might have escaped abroad as did so many others; but he remained in the country hoping to hasten Hitler's downfall and by his own advice and influence to help to lead Germany back to its older and better traditions. He was a close personal friend of General Beck and had some inkling of the plots to get rid of Hitler, but did not participate actively in them. His last contribution to an understanding of German history and his own interpretation of it was his little volume *Die deutsche Katastrophe* in 1946. Later, when the University of Berlin fell under communist control he took the lead in founding the new Free University in West Berlin, of which he was appropriately chosen rector.

See also Burckhardt, Jakob; Goethe, Johann Wolfgang von; Hegel, Georg Wilhelm Friedrich; Herder, Johann Gottfried; Historicism; Humboldt, Wilhelm von; Machiavelli, Niccolò; Political Philosophy, History of; Schleiermacher, Friedrich Daniel Ernst; Spengler, Oswald; Toynbee, Arnold Joseph.

Bibliography

WORKS BY MEINECKE

The principal works of Friedrich Meinecke are *Weltbürgertum und Nationalstaat* (Munich and Berlin, 1908; 7th ed., 1929); *Preussen und Deutschland* (Munich and Berlin, 1918); *Die Idee der Staatsräson in der neueren Geschichte* (Munich and Berlin: Oldenbourg, 1924), translated by D. Scott as *Machiavellism: The Doctrine of Raison d'État and Its Place in Modern History* (London: Routledge and Kegan Paul, 1957); and *Die Entstehung des Historismus,* 2 vols. (Munich and Berlin: Oldenbourg, 1936). *Die deutsche Katastrophe* (Wiesbaden: Brockhaus, 1946), translated by Sidney B. Fay as *The German Catastrophe* (Cambridge, MA: Harvard University Press, 1950, and Boston, 1962), written at the moment of Germany's utter defeat and deepest despair, contains Meinecke's penetrating reflections on the preceding hundred years, the causes of the Nazi disaster, and his faith in the future. Two short autobiographical volumes are *Erlebtes, 1862–1901* (Leipzig: Koehler and Amelang, 1941) and *Strassburg-Freiburg-Berlin, 1901–1914* (Stuttgart: Koehler, 1949). A six-volume edition of part of his works was published for the Friedrich Meinecke Institute of the University of Berlin between 1957 and 1962; this edition contains a volume of his correspondence and a reprint, with valuable editorial introductions and notes, of his more important writings. See also Meinecke's *Cosmopolitanism and the National State,* translated by Robert B. Kimber (Princeton, NJ: Princeton University Press, 1970); *Historism: The Rise of a New Historical Outlook,* translated by J. E. Anderson (London: Routledge and Kegan Paul, 1972); and *The Age of German Liberation, 1795–1954,* edited by Peter Paret, translated by Paret and Helmuth Fischer (Berkeley: University of California Press, 1977).

WORKS ABOUT MEINECKE

One of the best books on Meinecke and historicism is Walther Hofer, *Geschichtsschreibung und Weltanschauung: Betrachtungen zum Werk Friedrich Meineckes* (Munich: Oldenbourg, 1950). A bibliography of writings by and about Meinecke may be found in the *Historische Zeitschrift,* Vol. 174, 503–523.

ADDITIONAL SOURCES

Pois, Robert A. *Friedrich Meinecke and German Politics in the Twentieth Century.* Berkeley: University of California Press, 1972.

Sterling, Richard W. *Ethics in a World of Power: The Political Ideas of Friedrich Meinecke.* Princeton, NJ: Princeton University Press, 1958.

Wolfson, Philip J. "Friedrich Meinecke (1862–1954)." *Journal of the History of Ideas* 17 (1956): 511–525.

Sidney B. Fay (1967)
Bibliography updated by Philip Reed (2005)

MEINONG, ALEXIUS
(1853–1920)

Alexius Meinong studied under Franz Brentano at the University of Vienna from 1875 through 1878 and taught at the University of Graz from 1882 until his death. In 1894 he established at Graz the first laboratory for experimental psychology in Austria. Some of his psychological writings fall within this area, but most pertain to what Brentano called descriptive psychology. The philosophical works, referred to below, also pertain to descriptive psychology.

Meinong's most important contributions to philosophy concern the theory of objects, the theory of assumptions, the theory of evidence, and the theory of value. He also discussed, at considerable length, the nature of the emotions and their relation to intellectual phenomena, imagination, abstraction, wholes and other "complex objects," relations, causality, possibility, and probability.

THEORY OF OBJECTS

The two basic theses of Meinong's theory of objects (*Gegenstandstheorie*) are (1) there are objects that do not exist and (2) every object that does not exist is yet constituted in some way or other and thus may be made the subject of true predication. Traditional metaphysics treats of objects that exist as well as of those that merely subsist (*bestehen*) but, having "a prejudice in favor of the real," tends to neglect those objects that have no kind of being at all; hence, according to Meinong, there is need for a more general theory of objects.

Everything is an object, whether or not it is thinkable (if an object happens to be unthinkable then it is something having at least the property of being unthinkable) and whether or not it exists or has any other kind of being. Every object has the characteristics it has whether or not it has any kind of being; in short, the *Sosein* (character) of every object is independent of its *Sein* (being). A round square, for example, has a *Sosein*, since it is both round and square; but it is an impossible object, since it has a contradictory *Sosein* that precludes its *Sein*.

Of possible objects—objects not having a contradictory *Sosein*—some exist and others (for example, golden mountains) do not exist. If existence is thought of as implying a spatiotemporal locus, then there are certain subsistent objects that do not exist; among these are the *being* of various objects and the *nonbeing* of various other objects. Since there are horses, there is also the being of horses, the being of the being of horses, the nonbeing of the nonbeing of horses, and the being of the nonbeing of the nonbeing of horses. And since there is no Pegasus, there is the nonbeing of Pegasus, as well as the being of the nonbeing of Pegasus and the nonbeing of the being of Pegasus.

Meinong's theory must be distinguished from both Platonic realism, as this term is ordinarily interpreted, and the reism, or concretism, of Brentano and Tadeusz

Kotarbiński. (Meinong noted that since his view is broader than realism, it might properly be called objectivism.) Thus, the Platonic realist could be said to argue: "(*P*) Certain objects that do not exist have certain properties; but (*Q*) an object has properties if and only if it is real; hence (*R*) there are real objects that do not exist." The reist, or concretist, on the other hand, reasons from not-*R* and *Q* to not-*P*; that is, he derives the contradictory of Plato's first premise by taking Plato's second premise along with the contradictory of Plato's conclusion. But Meinong, like Plato and unlike the reist, accepted both *P* and *R*; unlike both Plato and the reist, he rejected *Q* by asserting the independence of *Sosein* from *Sein*; and therefore, again unlike both Plato and the reist, he said that the totality of objects extends far beyond the confines of what is merely real (*das Universum in der Gesamtheit des Wirklichen noch lange nicht erschöpft ist*).

This doctrine of *Aussersein*—of the independence of *Sosein* from *Sein*—is sometimes misinterpreted by saying that it involves recourse to a third type of being in addition to existence and subsistence. Meinong's point, however, is that such objects as the round square have no type of being at all; they are "homeless objects," to be found not even in Plato's heaven. Bertrand Russell objected that if we say round squares are objects, we violate the law of contradiction. Meinong replied that the law of contradiction holds only for what is real and can hardly be expected to hold for any object, such as a round square, that has a contradictory *Sosein*.

Russell's theory of descriptions is often thought to constitute a refutation of the doctrine of *Aussersein*; actually, however, his theory merely presupposes that Meinong's doctrine is false. According to Meinong, the two statements "The round square is round" and "The mountain I am thinking of is golden" are true statements about nonexistent objects; they are *Sosein* and not *Sein* statements. The distinction between the two types of statements is most clearly put by saying that a *Sein* statement (for example, "John is angry") is an affirmative statement that can be existentially generalized upon (we may infer "There exists an *x* such that *x* is angry") and a *Sosein* statement is an affirmative statement that cannot be existentially generalized upon; despite the truth of "The mountain I am thinking of is golden," we may not infer "There exists an *x* such that I am thinking about *x* and *x* is golden." Russell's theory of descriptions, however, presupposes that every statement is either a *Sein* statement or the negation of a *Sein* statement and hence that there are no *Sosein* statements. According to Russell, a statement of the form "The thing that is *F* is *G*" may be paraphrased as "There exists an x such that x is F and x is G, and it is false that there exists a y such that y is F and y is not identical with x." If Meinong's true *Sosein* statements, above, are rewritten in this form, the result will be two *false* statements; hence Meinong could say that Russell's theory does not provide an adequate paraphrase.

An impossible object, as indicated above, is an object having a *Sosein* that violates the law of contradiction. An *incomplete object*, analogously, is one having a *Sosein* that violates the law of the excluded middle. Of the golden mountains, which most readers will think of on reading the paragraph above, it will be neither true nor false to say that they are higher than Mount Monadnock. And some objects are even more poorly endowed. For example, if I wish that your wish will come true, then the object of my wish is whatever it is that you happen to wish; but if, unknown to me, what you wish is that my wish will come true, then this object would seem to have very little *Sosein* beyond that of being our mutual object. Meinong said that such an object is a *defective object* and suggested that the concept may throw light upon some of the logical paradoxes.

The theory of complexes—that is, the theory of wholes and other such "objects of higher order"—upon which Meinong wrote at length, also falls within the theory of objects.

None of the objects discussed above is created by us, nor does any of them depend in any way upon our thinking. Had no one ever thought of the round square, it would still be true *of* the round square that it does not exist; the round square need not be thought of in order not to exist. We draw these objects, so to speak, from the infinite depths of the *Ausserseienden*, beyond being and not-being.

THEORY OF ASSUMPTIONS

Meinong's theory of assumptions, or suppositions, is set forth in *Über Annahmen* ("On Assumptions"; first ed., Leipzig, 1902; 2nd ed., Leipzig, 1910). The theory is best understood by contrasting it with two theses held by Brentano, to which Meinong's theory may be said to be a reaction. The first of Brentano's theses is that of reism, or concretism, referred to above: Every object is a concrete thing; there are no objects such as the being of horses or the nonbeing of unicorns; the object of a judgment, therefore, is not a proposition, fact, or state of affairs; it is, rather, a certain concrete thing that the judgment may be said either to accept or to reject. And according to the second of Brentano's theses, there are basically only two types of intellectual attitudes we can take with respect to

any object: We can simply think about the object, in which case it is the object of a thought or idea, or we can take an intellectual stand with respect to the object, either accepting it or rejecting it, in which case it becomes the object of a judgment. Meinong rejected both these theses of Brentano.

The object of a judgment, according to Meinong, is not a concrete thing; it is an "objective" (*Objektiv*). "That there are horses," for example, designates an objective—an object of higher order, containing horses as a kind of constituent. (Thus, the nonexisting, nonsubsisting round square is a constituent of that subsisting objective that is the nonbeing of the round square.) Assumptions, like judgments, take objectives as their objects.

What Meinong intended by his term *assumption* (*Annahme*) is most clearly exemplified in deliberation: "Suppose I were to do A. What would happen then? And now suppose I were not to do A. What would happen then?" Assumptions belong to a category falling between ideas and judgments. Like mere ideas, they do not themselves involve commitment, belief, or conviction; therefore, as such, they do not involve any possibility of error. Like judgments, they are concerned with objectives (in the above example, with what is designated by "I shall do A"), which are either true or false (it is either true or false that I shall do A); and, like judgments, assumptions involve either affirmation ("Suppose I do A") or denial ("Suppose I do not do A"), but affirmation or denial without commitment.

Meinong argues that only by reference to assumptions can we understand such phenomena as the nature of inference, our apprehension of negative facts, communication in general, desire, art, and the nature of play and of games. *Über Annahmen*, which is probably Meinong's best book, contains important material on these and many other topics.

THEORY OF EVIDENCE

The concept of evidence involves three dichotomies: (1) direct and indirect; (2) a priori and a posteriori; and (3) "evidence for certainty" and "evidence for presumption." Meinong's conception of the first two dichotomies is similar to that of Brentano. Thus there are axioms of mathematics and logic and the theory of objects, which are directly evident and a priori; and there are facts of "inner perception"—for example, the fact that I am making such-and-such an assumption, or the fact that I take something to be a tree—which are directly evident and a posteriori. (Any psychological process that "presents" an object to us, as memory may be said to present certain objects of the past, is also a process that "presents itself"; "self-presentation" is thus the source of that evidence which is direct, certain, and a posteriori.) These directly evident judgments may confer evidence upon certain other judgments, which are then said to be indirectly evident.

For Meinong, paradigm cases of what is a priori evident would be expressed by "Round squares are both round and square" and "red is different from blue." Every a priori judgment has four characteristics: It is grounded in the nature of its object (*gegenständlich begründet*); it is certain; it is necessary; and it does not take into consideration the question whether its object exists. (Brentano had said that every a priori judgment is a judgment to the effect that a certain type of object does not exist.)

An evident presumption (*Vermutung*) may be directly evident but not certain. The concept is needed, according to Meinong, in order for us to understand memory, perception, and induction. In each of these three cases we have a source of knowledge that cannot be impugned as such but may on occasion mislead us. A particular memory judgment, for example, may not be certain, but it may be evident, especially if it is supported by other memory judgments, by perceptual judgments, or by inductive inferences from such judgments; analogously, this holds for any particular perceptual judgment or any particular inductive conclusion. Such items of a posteriori knowledge may be compared with the cards in a pack, "no one of which is capable of standing up by itself, but several of which placed together can serve to hold each other up. Or, for something more solid, consider a stack of weapons in the field." A consequence of this theory of evident presumptions is that a false judgment may yet be evident, a consequence that Brentano took to be absurd. Evidence does not guarantee truth; but, according to Meinong, evidence resembles truth in that if a judgment is evident, then its being evident—its *Evidentsein*—as well as the *Evidentsein* of this *Evidentsein*, and so on ad infinitum, is also evident.

An essential part of Meinong's epistemology is his theory of "emotional presentation" There is an analogy between the way in which we come to know, say, that the temperature is high and the way in which we come to know that the temperature is agreeable. Meinong proposed, as a "heuristic principle," that we try to carry the analogy as far as possible. If it is by means of a subjective feeling that we perceive the temperature to be agreeable, it is also by means of a subjective sensation that we perceive the temperature to be high. In neither case is the subjective experience the object of the presentation; in neither case is our apprehension a matter of inference or of reasoning from effect to cause. "The sense in which the sky is said to be 'beautiful,' for example, is precisely that in which it is said to be 'blue.' But the experience by means of which the first property is presented plays an important role in our psychical life in addition to that of enabling us to grasp something else. This fact is reflected in our language; we refer to the one experience directly, but in the other case we must go round about, by way of the object that is presented, and use some such expression as 'experience of blue.'" Meinong noted that the traditional arguments against a "subjectivistic" or "psychologistic" interpretation of ordinary sense perception apply equally to any such interpretation of emotional presentation.

THEORY OF VALUE

In the final version of his theory of value, Meinong made use of the theory of emotional presentation considered above, as well as of Brentano's doctrine of correct and incorrect emotion—that is, the doctrine according to which emotions, like judgments, may be said to be correct or incorrect, justified or unjustified, and according to which certain things may thus be said to merit or be worthy of certain emotions.

The basic concept of value theory is not that of desire, interest, or utility, but that of value feeling (*Wertgefühle*). Value feelings take objectives as their objects, more particularly, objectives consisting of the being or nonbeing of certain objects. One type of value feeling is *Seinsfreude*, pleasure or joy in the existence or being of a certain object; another type is *Seinsleid*, displeasure or sorrow with respect to the existence or being of a certain object. But the feelings of joy and sorrow may also be directed toward nonexistence and nonbeing; hence there are four fundamental types of value feeling, which may be illustrated by reference to the nature of good and evil. The good is that which merits *Seinsfreude* if it exists and *Nichtseinsleid* (sorrow with respect to its nonexistence) if it does not exist; evil, on the other hand, merits *Seinsleid* if it exists and *Nichtseinsfreude* (joy with respect to its nonexistence) if it does not exist. Meinong noted that human beings are not consistent in their emotional reactions. For example, as far as our health and ordinary comforts are concerned, we experience considerable *Nichtseinsleid* when they are absent, but not the appropriate amount of *Seinsfreude* when they are present.

Our actions have moral qualities other than those of being good, bad, or indifferent. Meinong introduced four moral categories, which he explicated by reference to good and bad. Actions that are good may be either meritorious or simply required; those that are bad may be either excusable or inexcusable. (Meinong's terms are, respectively, *verdienstlich, correct, zulässig,* and *verwerflich.*) One may say of any act that performance is meritorious if and only if nonperformance is bad but excusable; nonperformance is meritorious if and only if performance is bad but excusable; performance is required if and only if nonperformance is inexcusable; and nonperformance is required if and only if performance is inexcusable. Given this "law of omission" (*Unterlassungsgesetz*), Meinong's concepts of meritorious, required, excusable, and inexcusable, respectively, approximate what are sometimes called the supererogatory, the obligatory, misdeeds that are venial, and misdeeds that are not venial. According to one of Meinong's followers (Ernst Schwarz), these four moral concepts are related to the concept of justified or correct emotion in the following way: The meritorious is that which it is incorrect to blame and incorrect not to praise; the required is that which it is incorrect to blame, correct to praise, but not incorrect not to praise; the merely excusable is that which it is incorrect to praise, correct to blame, and not incorrect not to blame; and the inexcusable is that which it is incorrect to praise and incorrect not to blame.

See also Brentano, Franz; Epistemology, History of; Ethical Objectivism; Kotarbiński, Tadeusz; Logical Paradoxes; Nonexistent Object, Nonbeing; Plato; Platonism and the Platonic Tradition; Propositions; Psychology; Realism; Russell, Bertrand Arthur William; Value and Valuation.

Bibliography

WORKS BY MEINONG

Meinong summarized his principal philosophical conclusions in *Die deutsche Philosophie der Gegenwart in Selbstdarstellungen,* edited by Raymund Schmidt (Leipzig, 1921), Vol. I, pp. 91–150. His purely psychological writings can be found in the first volume of *Gesammelte Abhandlungen* (2 vols.; Leipzig: Barth, 1913–1914).

Theory of Objects

Meinong's theory of objects is discussed in "Über Gegenstandstheorie" (1904); this article was reprinted in Vol. II of his *Gesammelte Abhandlungen* and translated as "The Theory of Objects" in *Realism and the Background of Phenomenology,* edited by Roderick M. Chisholm (Glencoe, IL: Free Press, 1960). The theory is discussed also in *Über die Stellung der Gegenstandstheorie im System der Wissenschaften* (Leipzig, 1907) and, indeed, in almost all Meinong's writings after 1904.

Epistemology

His most important epistemological writings are *Zur erkenntnistheoretischen Würdigung des Gedächtnisses* (1886), reprinted in Vol. II of *Gesammelte Abhandlungen; Über die Erfahrungs-grundlagen unseres Wissens* (Berlin, 1906); *Über Möglichkeit und Wahrscheinlichkeit* (Leipzig: Barth, 1915); and *Über emotionale Präsentation* (Vienna, 1917).

Value Theory

Meinong's principal writings in value theory are *Psychologischethische Untersuchungen zur Werththeorie* (Graz: Leuschner and Lubensky, 1894) and the posthumously published *Zur Grundlegung der allgemeinen Werththeorie* (Graz: Leuschner and Lubensky, 1923).

WORKS ON MEINONG

Among the most useful writings on Meinong are Bertrand Russell, "Meinong's Theory of Complexes and Assumptions," three articles in *Mind* 13 (1904): 204–219, 336–354, and 509–524; J. N. Findlay, *Meinong's Theory of Objects and Values* (2nd ed., Oxford: Clarendon Press, 1963); G. Dawes Hicks, "The Philosophical Researches of Meinong," in *Critical Realism* (London: Macmillan, 1938); and Konstantin Radakovic et al., *Meinong-Gedenkschrift* (Graz: "Styria" Steirische Verlagsanstalt, 1952).

Important material on all aspects of Meinong's philosophy can be found in *Philosophenbriefe: Aus der wissenschaftlichen Korrespondenz von Alexius Meinong mit Fachgenossen seiner Zeit,* edited by Rudolf Kindinger (Graz: Akademischen Druck- u. Verlagsanstalt, 1965).

OTHER RECOMMENDED WORKS

Barber, Kenneth F. *Meinong's Hume Studies: Translation and Commentary.* PhD diss., University of Michigan, 1967.

Grossmann, Reinhardt. *Meinong.* London; Boston: Routledge & K. Paul, 1974.

Lambert, Karel. *Meinong and the Principle of Independence: Its Place in Meinong's Theory of Objects and Its Significance in Contemporary Philosophical Logic.* Cambridge, U.K., and New York: Cambridge University Press, 1983.

Schubert Kalsi, Marie-Luise. *Alexius Meinong's Elements of Ethics: With Translation of the Fragment Ethische Bausteine.* Dordrecht; Boston: Kluwer Academic Publishers, 1996

Sylvan, Richard. *Exploring Meinong's Jungle and Beyond: An Investigation of Noneism and the Theory of Items.* Canberra: Research School of Social Sciences, Australian National University, 1980.

Works by Meinong

Gesamtausgabe. Herausgeber: Rudolf Haller und Rudolf Kindinger. Graz, Austria: Akademische Druck- u. Verlagsanstalt, 1968–1978.

Abhandlungen zur Werttheorie. Rudolf Kindinger. Graz, Austria: Akademische Druck- u. Verlagsanstalt, 1968.

Abhandlungen zur psychologie. Rudolf Kindinger. Graz, Austria: Akademische Druck- u. Verlagsanstalt, 1969.

On Emotional Presentation. Evanston, IL: Northwestern University Press, 1972.

Über philosophische Wissenschaft und ihre Propädeutik; Über die Stellung der Gegenstandstheorie im System der Wissenschaften; Über die Erfahrungsgrundlagen unseres Wissens; Zum Erweise des allgemeinen Kausalgesetzes. Graz: Akademische Druck- u. Verlagsanstalt, 1973.

On Assumptions. Berkeley: University of California Press, 1982.

Meinong Reconstructed versus Early Russell Reconstructed: A Study in the Formal Ontology of Fiction. PhD diss., Indiana University, 1986.

Uber Gegenstandstheorie; Selbstdarstellung. Hamburg: F. Meiner, 1988.

Alexius Meinong und Guido Adler: Eine Freundschaft in Briefen. Amsterdam; Atlanta, GA: Rodopi, 1995.

Roderick M. Chisholm (1967)
Bibliography updated by Michael J. Farmer (2005)

MELANCHTHON, PHILIPP
(1497–1560)

Philipp Melanchthon, the German reformer, was born at Bretten, Baden, and died at Wittenberg. He was a grand-nephew of the great humanist Johannes Reuchlin, who encouraged him in his studies and deeply influenced his outlook. After studying at Heidelberg and Tübingen, Melanchthon, on Reuchlin's recommendation, became professor of Greek at Wittenberg. Because of his persuasiveness in interpreting the humanist spirit, this appointment marked the beginning of a new era in German education. At Wittenberg, Melanchthon collaborated closely with Martin Luther. He helped him both in translating the Bible and in giving systematic shape to the new theology that until that time had existed in a highly subjective form. Melanchthon's task was to reduce this theology to exact form and to set it forth as an integrated and persuasive system. In 1521 Melanchthon published his *Loci Communes Rerum Theologicarum,* a work that in its various editions was one of the most influential manuals of Protestant theology.

During the rest of his career, Melanchthon was much occupied with controversy and debate. In many of the famous conferences of the Reformation era, his influence was thrown on the side of moderation and peace. He was closely identified with some of the most important formularies of the period, such as the Augsburg Confession.

Such activities involved even a man of conciliatory spirit in vigorous debate, and Melanchthon's position in the history of thought is largely determined by the controversies in which he took part. Two of these demand consideration.

The Adiaphoristic controversy was concerned with "indifferent matters"—that is, religious practices or theological beliefs on which flexibility or compromise might be permissible. Melanchthon was unfairly charged with including among the "adiaphora" such major questions as justification by faith. Melanchthon did not minimize the importance of essentials, but he was inclined to veil them beneath a conscious indefiniteness of expression. This deliberate obscurity extended to many matters that were intensively canvassed in the sixteenth century. He was willing to concede that good works are necessary to salvation, but not in the way in which the connection had traditionally been taught. He was prepared to recognize seven sacraments, but only if most of them were regarded as rites that have no inherent efficacy in securing salvation. Later he retreated from the permissive position he had adopted on the "adiaphora" and maintained a strict interpretation of the doctrines set forth in the *Loci Communes.*

More acute and more important was the controversy about synergism. Here the central issue was the relation between God's grace and man's will in regeneration. In his early period, Melanchthon, strongly influenced by Luther and deeply impressed by the experience of dependence upon God, severely restricted the role of man's will. To defend free will was to rob God's grace of its unique supremacy. But Melanchthon naturally tended to adopt a mediating outlook, and ethical issues were of great importance to him. Desiderius Erasmus, in his controversy with Luther concerning free will, had advanced views that served to modify Melanchthon's position. Melanchthon was now prepared to recognize the part played in conversion by man's will. The position that he reached (called synergism) precipitated a violent debate. Melanchthon's own statements were ambiguous and lacking in precision. His supporters (Johan Pfeffinger and Viktorin Strigel, for instance) and his opponents (Nikolaus von Amsdorf and Matthias Flacius Illyricus) were very explicit indeed. Synergism, however, can best be understood as an ethical protest against attitudes that paralyze the conscience and leave the church powerless in its struggle against moral chaos. Melanchthon's concern with God's moral purity led him to the belief that the problems of evil and of human responsibility have been aggravated by an extreme doctrine of predestination. He therefore abandoned the decree of eternal reprobation. The cause of sin lies in man himself; the hardening of his heart is due to his own perversity. Man has a real measure of responsibility for his spiritual condition. Man's will, therefore, can cooperate with God's grace, and does so. The human will, of course, is never the primary cause of man's regeneration—the Spirit of God and the preaching of the Word always maintain the initiative—but man's will is specifically granted a place, and unless there is consent on man's part there can be no effective regeneration. Melanchthon guarded himself against the charge of Pelagianism, but nevertheless he was accused of yielding to this heresy. The violence of the controversy was due to the seriousness of the issues involved. A wide range of theological views had to be reexamined, and every aspect of the Christian doctrine of man and of salvation was involved. The controversy was finally silenced by the Formula of Concord, which ruled against the Melanchthonist position.

See also Erasmus, Desiderius; Evil, The Problem of; Logic, History of; Luther, Martin; Pelagius and Pelagianism; Reformation.

Bibliography

WORKS BY MELANCHTHON

"Works." In *Corpus Reformatorum,* edited by K. G. Bretschneider and E. Bindseil, Vol. I–XXVIII. Brunswick, Germany, 1834–1860.

Supplementa Melanchthoniana. Leipzig: Haupt, 1910.

The Loci Communes of Philipp Melanchthon. Translated by C. L. Hill. Boston, 1944.

WORKS ON MELANCHTHON

Hammer, W. *Die Melanchthonforschung im Wandel der Jahrhunderte,* 3 vols. Gütersloh, Germany: Gerd Mohn, 1967–1981.

Hartfelder, K. *Philipp Melanchthon als Preceptor Germaniae.* Berlin: Hofmann, 1889.

Hildebrandt, Franz. *Melanchthon, Alien or Ally?* Cambridge, U.K.: Cambridge University Press, 1946.

Kusukawa, Sachiko. *The Transformation of Natural Philosophy: The Case of Philip Melanchthon.* Cambridge, U.K.: Cambridge University Press, 1995.

Richards, J. W. *Philipp Melanchthon: The Protestant Preceptor of Germany.* New York, 1898.

Wengert, Timothy. *Human Freedom, Christian Righteousness: Philip Melanchthon's Exegetical Dispute with Erasmus of Rotterdam.* Oxford: Oxford University Press, 1998.

Gerald R. Cragg (1967)
Bibliography updated by Christian B. Miller (2005)

MELISSUS OF SAMOS

(fifth century BCE)

Melissus of Samos, the Greek Eleatic philosopher, led the Samian fleet against the Athenians and defeated them (Plutarch, *Pericles* 26, quoting a lost work of Aristotle). The date of the battle was 441–440 BCE, and this is the only reliable date in the biography of Melissus. He was said to have been a pupil of Parmenides, but this may be an inference from his work, which gives ample evidence of dependence on Parmenides.

Portions of Melissus's book titled *On Nature or What Exists,* written in prose, were quoted and preserved by the Aristotelian commentator Simplicius. The total length of these fragments is a little under one thousand words—enough to provide evidence of the content and quality of Melissus's argument. No other fragments survive. The pseudo-Aristotelian treatise *On Melissus, Xenophanes and Gorgias* (c. first century CE) adds nothing useful.

Melissus's argument, as revealed by the fragments, was similar to Parmenides' in method and results, although it differed in some details. The starting point is the contradictoriness of descriptions of change. Any change ultimately implies the generation of something from nothing or its destruction into nothing, and Melissus, with Parmenides, held both of these to be impossible on the ground that "nothing" is absolutely nonexistent and unthinkable. Hence, what exists must have existed always and must continue to exist (Melissus seems to view eternity as a continual existence through time, whereas Parmenides thought of a timeless present).

From the eternity of what exists, Melissus deduced its spatial infinity. He argued that if what exists did not come into existence, it had no beginning or end, and being without beginning or end, it must be limitless or infinite. He seemed not to have noticed the ambiguity of "beginning" and "end" (or else his defense of the move from time to space has been lost); this is presumably the basis of Aristotle's criticism of the argument (*De Sophisticis Elenchis* 167b13 and 168b35), although he does not make it quite explicit.

From the spatial infinity of what exists, Melissus deduced its unity. If there are two things in existence, each must limit the extent of the other; there cannot be more than one limitless thing in existence. Thus, Melissus chose a different route to the monism of Parmenides—indeed, according to most interpreters of Parmenides, this route was closed to him since, unlike Melissus, he held that what exists is spatially limited. But this is a dubious interpretation of Parmenides.

Next, Melissus argued that if what exists is one, it cannot have parts and must therefore be incorporeal because any solid body has actual or imaginable parts. Moreover, what exists cannot vary in density since this, according to Melissus, could come about only if one area contained less of being—and hence more of nonbeing—than another, and nonbeing is absolutely nonexistent. For similar reasons there is no motion, since there is no "give" anywhere in the plenum (this is an argument against motion that may not have been used by Parmenides). Every form of change—whether of size, order, or quality—means the coming into existence of something that previously was nothing, or the annihilation of something that exists, and these are ruled out by the first stage of Melissus's argument.

In the eighth fragment Melissus applies his own criteria of existence to the plural beings of the sensible world. If these things, such as air and fire, exist, then they must be just what our senses tell us they are and nothing else. But our senses tell us that they do change into something else. Our senses must therefore be wrong about this; hence, we can conclude that they were wrong initially in telling us that things are many and not one. The sensible world is therefore illusion.

Melissus was the least important of the Eleatics. Zeno's arguments proved more influential than his, and Parmenides was the original genius who pioneered the way. If Melissus has any claim to special historical importance that is not shared by the other Eleatics, it is perhaps that by applying Eleatic criteria to the plural beings posited by his opponents, he produced a formula (in Fr. 8) that led Leucippus directly to the concept of atoms. In the absence of complete texts it is wiser to refrain from pronouncing on Melissus's originality. Aristotle criticized both Parmenides and Melissus for bad arguments (*Physics* 186a6) and was more severe on Melissus, but perhaps that was because Melissus's clear style made him an easier target.

See also Aristotle; Change; Eternity; Infinity in Mathematics and Logic; Leucippus and Democritus; Parmenides of Elea; Plutarch of Chaeronea; Space; Zeno of Elea.

Bibliography

Fragments of Melissus's writings in Greek with German translations have been published in Diels-Kranz, *Fragmente der Vorsokratiker,* 10th ed., Vol. I (Berlin, 1960); English translations, in J. Burnet, *Early Greek Philosophy,* 4th ed. (London: A. and C. Black, 1930).

Selected texts with English translation and commentary are in G. S. Kirk and J. E. Raven, *The Presocratic Philosophers* (Cambridge, U.K.: Cambridge University Press, 1957); the commentary should be treated with caution, especially on the subject of infinity and Melissus's relation with the Pythagoreans. The same is true of J. E. Raven, *Pythagoreans and Eleatics* (Cambridge, U.K.: Cambridge University Press, 1948).

See also Harold Cherniss, *Aristotle's Criticism of Presocratic Philosophy* (Baltimore: Johns Hopkins Press, 1935), and G. E. L. Owen, "Eleatic Questions," in *Classical Quarterly* 10 (1960).

ADDITIONAL SOURCES

Barnes, J. *The Presocratic Philosophers,* 2nd ed., 180–185, 194–230, 298–302. London: Routledge and Kegan Paul, 1982.

Bicknell, P. "Melissus' Way of Seeming." *Phronesis* 27 (1982): 194–201.

Booth, N. B. "Did Melissus Believe in Incorporeal Being?" *American Journal of Philology* 79 (1958): 61–65.

Burnet, J. *Greek Philosophy. Thales to Plato,* 4th ed., 320–329. London, 1930.

Cherniss, H. *Aristotle's Criticism of Presocratic Philosophy,* 2nd ed., 61–72, 402–403. New York: Octagon, 1964.

Curd, P. *The Legacy of Parmenides: Eleatic Monism and Later Presocratic Thought,* 202–204, 206–216, 224–227. Princeton, NJ: Princeton University Press, 1998.

Furley, D. *The Greek Cosmologists,* Vol. 1: *The Formation of the Atomic Theory and Its Earliest Critics,* 110–114. Cambridge, U.K.: Cambridge University Press, 1987.

Furley, D. "Melissus of Samos." In *Ionian Philosophy,* edited by K. Boudouris, 114–122. Athens, 1989.

Guthrie, W. K. C. *A History of Greek Philosophy,* Vol. 2: *The Presocratic Tradition from Parmenides to Democritus,* 101–121. Cambridge, U.K.: Cambridge University Press, 1965.

Jouanna, J. "Rapports entre Mélissos de Samos et Diogène d'Apollonie, à la lumière du traité hippocratique De natura hominis." *REA* 67 (1965): 306–323.

Kirk, G. S., J. E. Raven, and M. Schofield. *The Presocratic Philosophers,* 2nd ed., 390–401. Cambridge, U.K.: Cambridge University Press, 1983.

Loenen, J. H. M. M. *Parmenides, Melissus, Gorgias: A Reinterpretation of Eleatic Philosophy.* Assen: Royal VanGorcum, 1961.

Owen, G. E. L. "Plato and Parmenides on the Timeless Present." *Monist* 50 (1966): 317–340. Reprinted in *The Pre-Socratics,* edited by A.P. D. Mourelatos, 271–292, Garden City, NY: Anchor Press, 1974, and in G. E. L. Owen, *Logic, Science and Dialectic. Collected Papers in Greek Philosophy,* edited by M. Nussbaum, 27–44, Ithaca, NY: Cornell University Press, 1986.

Reale, G. *Melisso. Testimonianze e frammenti. Introduzione, traduzione e commento.* Biblioteca di Studi Superiori. Filosofia antica, 50. Florence: Nuova Italia, 1970.

Sedley, D. "Parmenides and Melissus." In *The Cambridge Companion to Early Greek Philosophy,* edited by A. A. Long, 125–131. Cambridge, U.K., and New York: Cambridge University Press, 1999.

Solmsen, F. "The 'Eleatic One' in Melissus." *Verslagen en Mededeelingen der Koninklijke Akademie van Wetenschappen* (Amsterdam) n.s. 32 (8) (1969): 219–233.

Vitali, R. *Melisso di Samo, "sul mondo o sull' essere": Una interpretazione dell'Eleatismo.* Urbino, Italy: Argalìa, 1973.

Vlastos, G. Review of J. E. Raven, *Pythagoreans and Eleatics.* *Gnomon* 23 (1953): 29–35.

David J. Furley (1967)
Bibliography updated by Richard D. McKirahan (2005)

MEMORY

Remembering is one of the most characteristic and most puzzling of human activities. In particular, personal memory—the ability mentally to travel back into the past, as leading psychologist Endel Tulving puts it—often has intense emotional or moral significance: It is perhaps the most striking manifestation of the peculiar way human beings are embedded in time, and of humans' limited but genuine freedom from their present environment and immediate needs. Memory has been significant in the history of philosophy as much in relation to ethics and to epistemology as in theories of psyche, mind, and self.

The philosophy of memory is a fascinating, diverse, and underdeveloped area of study, which offers difficult but rewarding connections not only with psychology and the cognitive sciences, but also with the social sciences and political theory, and with literature and the arts. Outside philosophy, interest in memory increased massively and disproportionately in the late twentieth century in both the neurocognitive sciences and the humanities, driven both by internal developments within disparate disciplines and by wider social and cultural concerns about trauma and recovered memories, about the politics of forgetting and collective responsibility, about memory loss in an aging population, and about the manipulation, control, ownership, and protection of individual memory. The widespread and troubled fascination in Western culture with this last set of concerns in particular, and with challenging associated questions about moral psychology and personal identity, is suggested by the success of films like *Bladerunner* (1982), *Memento* (2000), and *Eternal Sunshine of the Spotless Mind* (2004).

As a result, just as in other areas of the philosophy of mind, it has become increasingly difficult to cordon off a set of questions about memory, or methods for its study, which are uniquely or primarily philosophical. Some philosophers treat memory as a case study in philosophy of science, asking for example whether the psychology of memory might be reducible to the neuroscience of memory. Others begin with the phenomenology of memory, the ordinary experiences and practices of remembering; others still inquire into cross-cultural or historical differences in these practices. It seems likely, further, that psychopharmacological influences on memory, and their potential misuse, will make memory a central topic in the emerging fields of neuroethics and philosophy of psychiatry. This entry covers more traditional philosophical issues about the nature of memory, but includes some consideration of the need for a broader framework that can encompass the neural, embodied, psychological, and social aspects of remembering.

FORMS OF REMEMBERING

When a person is remembering, there are many different activities he or she may be engaged in, and the expression of the individual's memory can take many different forms. One reminisces with old allies about shared experiences; one finally calls to mind that obscure fact; one mindlessly cycles off down the lane, despite not having been on a bike for years; one sits alone and ruminates on one joyful or agonizing moment long ago; one gathers with others to commemorate a significant occasion; one writes or fashions something in memory of a person or an event; a photo, an odd memento, or a long-forgotten melody suddenly immerses a person in the emotions of another time.

It is not easy to pinpoint just what is common across this range of activities, and some philosophers have argued that not all of them involve true memory. But the present-day consensus in both philosophy and psychology is that there are at least three distinct forms of remembering that can helpfully be detected in the variety of ordinary experience.

First, in remembering specific events or episodes from an individual's personal past he or she draws on *personal memory* (also known as *experiential* or *event memory*): For example, one remembers walking down by the river with a friend that spring afternoon. Psychologists often call this *episodic memory*, or sometimes *autobiographical memory*.

A different form of memory is naturally expressed with a "that" complement: One remembers that Aristotle was Alexander's tutor. This *factual* or *semantic memory* is akin to simple belief, and the remembered facts can be about events in the remote past, or indeed the future, as well as personally experienced events. One can factually remember details one has been told about one's early life, for example, for which one has no personal memory, no sense at all of what the past experiences were like.

In English, and many other languages, people sometimes contrast things that they "just know" from what they genuinely (personally) remember, thus treating personal memory as the basic or essential kind of memory. But in other contexts people are happy to talk also of remembering facts, and to attribute their general beliefs about the world to "memory" in a broader sense.

Personal/episodic remembering and factual/semantic remembering are both forms of *declarative memory*, in which individuals seek to hook up to reality, to represent the world or the past. Although remembering activities often have quite different functions as well, under normal circumstances such memories aim at truth. This is so even though, as both scientific and common-sense psychology increasingly suggest, people do not always get there. The point is not that memory necessarily or even reliably achieves this aim, but that one's ordinary practices include a general commitment to its reliability in doing so. For example, an individual may or may not in fact have walked by the river with a friend that spring afternoon, and Aristotle may or may not actually have been Alexander's tutor. But if one is sincerely expressing that personal memory, or that factual memory, one is (among other things) making a claim about what happened.

In these declarative forms of memory, the content of one's memory can in principle —at least in central cases—be articulated. But when a person wonders if a friend remembers how to play the flute, or how to drive a car, the person is asking not about the friend's personal or factual memories, but about his or her skills or embodied memories. Philosophers have often talked here of *habit memory*, while psychologists identify these cases as types of *procedural memory*, where this category is also taken to include more basic/primitive forms of conditioning and associative learning.

Procedural memory has been sharply divided from declarative memory for a number of reasons: Perhaps most important is the case of H.M., an epileptic patient who suffered terrible amnesia after brain surgery in the 1950s. H.M., who had lost his hippocampus and other brain structures now known to be central to declarative memory, was no longer able to lay down event memories, so that he would forget everything minutes after its occurrence, and lose any clear sense of time passing. Yet H.M. was still able to learn new games, and to improve his performance at new perceptual-motor skills, despite having no idea each time that he had ever tried them before.

Procedural memory is philosophically important for a number of reasons, although habits and skilled activities have been little studied. For example, neither philosophers nor psychologists have a clear grip on the various ways that personal memory and other high-level cognitive processes interact with remembered embodied skills. Competition and coordination between the different memory systems can both occur. On the one hand, skilled performers in dance or sport know that their motor habits often run best in a groove, when not consciously or verbally controlled: yet the skills involved are robust and flexible, unlike more primitive forms of procedural memory, and can sometimes be directly shaped by mood, context, verbal instruction, and conscious decision.

These conceptual, grammatical, and experiential distinctions between personal, factual, and habit memory have in contemporary cognitive psychology been developed into theories of distinct memory systems. There is considerable disagreement about the psychological status of these systems, and about whether the distinction between episodic and semantic memory, in particular, should be characterized by reference merely to the kind of information in question, or by an essential phenomenological difference. Since there is little agreement more generally about what a psychological system or module is, or about the nature of any putative natural kinds in psychology, these debates about memory systems are likely to be resolved only in conjunction with progress on broader questions in philosophy of psychology.

PERSONAL MEMORY

An individual's capacity to conjure up experiences, emotions, and events from long in the past involves the same kind of memory as the mundane ability to keep track of just what he or she has been doing, feeling, and thinking in the last day or week. Personal remembering does not seem to be distinguished from other related activities—imagining, dreaming, factual remembering, for example—by the level of sensory detail or vividness which it involves: some memories, after all, are both faint and fragmentary, while some scenes of fantasy can be richly imagined. Memory capacities, even in their normal and reliable functioning, are both fallible and selective: human beings don't need either total or precise recall to maintain sufficient coherence and continuity of self over time, for personal memory works in part through an ongoing condensing, editing, and summarizing of life experiences, on which people draw in specific autobiographical narratives. One's narratives or other memory expressions can be public or private, and they can be more or less under one's control, either smoothly tailored to specific audiences or emerging in involuntary fragments.

Personal remembering is a context-sensitive activity from the start. As young children build on their earlier abilities to understand typical sequences of events, their capacity to remember particular past experiences is supported and shaped by adults. Joint attention to the shared past emerges in an interactive social environment, as children come to see that there can be different perspectives on the same past time. Spontaneous self-conscious thought about the personal past is a gradual development out of these memory-sharing practices, which can vary considerably in nature, frequency, and significance across contexts and cultures. One condition for the full emergence of such self-conscious thought about his or her own past experiences, which may be surprisingly late, is that the child picks up the causal connections between events in time, and within the child's own history. Some grasp of the temporal asymmetry of experience is needed to understand that, in principle at least, remembered events can be integrated on a connected temporal dimension. Children's personal memory, then, is a highly sophisticated achievement closely linked not only to their emerging self-awareness and understanding of other minds, but also to their recognition that they cannot change the past, and that their current and future actions are unique and irrevocable.

Because early personal remembering is socially situated in this way, it is also tightly meshed with emotional and social/moral development. Key social practices, such as promising and forgiving, and some central complex emotions, such as grief, love, and regret, depend essentially on personal memory and on one's grasp of temporal relations. The point here is not just that the fallible but more-or-less reliable operation of memory in two or more people is needed to give those people current informational access to the past times at which their paths have crossed. Memory's affective tone and influence means that, in addition to its role in retaining the past, it also has a forward-looking function, as Richard Wollheim argued in his *Thread of Life* (1984): Remembering can keep what happened in the past alive, giving it significance for one's ongoing relationships and projects. According to this view, memory is not just a means for checking on the continuity of the self over time, but also itself partly produces or creates personal identity: As Wollheim puts it, the past affects people in such a way that they become creatures with a past.

The particular ways in which, through memory, individuals deal with events and experiences that are no longer present varies according to context and aim. Most dramatically, for example, legal contexts impose demands and standards on the memory narratives witnesses must produce that differ greatly from the norms operating in other remembering activities. But questions about the reliability of memory and about its mechanisms arise in many different circumstances just because memory, with its orientation to truth, is in these ways intimately

involved in both personal identity and significant social practices. Two connected lines of thought have raised the most serious concerns about people's access to the past in remembering: philosophical views about representations and memory traces, and psychological accounts of the constructive nature of remembering.

THEORIES OF MEMORY

People can, sometimes, remember past events and experiences in the absence of immediate external cues or prompts to memory. It is natural, then, to think that somehow individuals carry around with them what they will need in order to remember when circumstances are right. Even one's ordinary conception of memory, C. B. Martin and Max Deutscher argued in their influential causal analysis *Remembering* (1966), requires the existence of an appropriate causal link between one's past experience and one's present remembering. Although the notion of the "memory trace" has appeared in many strange metaphors and theories in the history of philosophy and the history of science, it need be no richer than this idea of a state that causally connects experience and remembering in a certain way. This causal analysis embeds the theory of memory in the broader *representational theory of mind* which has come to characterize mainstream philosophy of cognitive science; however the bare invocation of memory traces is compatible with many quite different views about their nature and operation.

However, even this basic view about memory traces, in the eyes of its critics, engenders serious problems about the nature of a person's access to the past. If the past is thus truly lost, so that a person can only make contact with it by examining certain representations in the present, critics complain, there is a real danger of scepticism, to be countered by affirming that the person is in fact aware of the past directly in memory. The ensuing, long-running debate between representative realists or indirect realists, who accept memory representations, and direct realists or phenomenologists who reject them, is exactly parallel to that found in theories of perception. Although the dichotomous nature of this debate no longer fits the range of positions available, and many quite different views are often condensed by critics into a monolithic target, there is some common ground.

Contemporary trace theorists tend to work in a broadly materialist framework, and do not in general think of traces as *direct* objects of awareness from which the nature of the past is consciously inferred at the personal level of psychological analysis. If complex nonconscious processes, operating subpersonally on representations which may themselves be partial and context-sensitive, are involved in the shaping and constructing of the contents of memory, this does not mean that the experience of remembering is indirect. On this point, the positive direct realist contribution is convincing: Remembering, under normal circumstances, is a kind of immersion in which one has a pre-reflective confidence.

But this idea that an individual typically inhabits the memory, rather than judging and assessing it for plausibility and coherence, is in fact entirely compatible with the existence and involvement of subpersonal mechanisms operating on enduring but modifiable traces. Such mechanisms can be typically reliable even if they are fallible in particular instances. To raise a general skeptical worry again at this point against the invocation of memory representations would be unrealistically to demand incorrigible access to the past, to seek a blanket guarantee of accuracy in memory. Such blunt certainty about memory was expressed, for example, by the eighteenth-century Scots philosopher Thomas Reid, the most ardent critic of philosophies of "ideas" or "traces," who wrote that "those things really did happen which I distinctly remember" (Reid, *Essays*, 1849, p. 444). But this renders the indisputable evidence—both everyday and scientific—of errors in memory quite mysterious, and thereby threatens to erode commonsense realism about the past.

Theorists who posit memory traces are also criticized for adherence to what is seen as an arbitrary metaphor of "storage," unfortunately entrenched in the philosophy of memory since Plato's *Theaetetus*. The bare retention of capacities or dispositions to act or respond in certain ways, the critics complain, implies nothing about the means by which such capacities are retained: Storage is a mistakenly concrete way of thinking, as if each memory had to be stashed away separately, like sacks of grain in a storehouse or fixed entries in an archive. Ludwig Wittgenstein, for example, mocked the static but inaccessible inner records he identified in the psychological theories of his time: In notes of 1935–1936, he wondered "whether the things stored up may not constantly change their nature" (Stern 1991, p. 204).

In some invocations of memory representations, each trace has indeed been treated as distinct, with each single remembered item mapped on to one storage element. Such atomist or localist representational schemes make control over the contents of memory easier to imagine or achieve: The remembered items are passive, and must be manipulated or altered by an external executive. In this separation of data from process, ordinary

digital computers exemplify the localist memory scheme: But what is "stored" in human memory displays more intrinsic dynamics than this, tending in some contexts naturally to interfere, blend, and generalize without deliberate or voluntary control. But just as such computers do not exhaust possible computational devices, so localist representational schemes are not essential to the general framework of memory traces. Both historical theories of memories as patterned flows of "animal spirits" through the pores of the brain, and contemporary connectionist models in cognitive science employ distributed (rather than localist) representation: What can be distinctly remembered need not be held distinctly or independently, since each item is spread or "superposed" across many elements in a system or network. This entry examines the implications of these distributed models of memory after setting them in the context of recent developments in cognitive psychology and the cognitive sciences.

REMEMBERING AND THE COGNITIVE SCIENCES

The recent history of the sciences of memory offers a sharp contrast and corrective to the stereotyped image of cognitive science as a scientistic quest to reduce the human mind to the dull mechanism of digital computers. Memory research was one of the first areas to be taken out of the lab in the 1980s and 1990s, as psychologists sought to address the kinds of memory that matter in everyday life (such as autobiographical memory), and to find ecologically valid methods of studying such memories outside artificial isolated situations. The difficulty facing philosophers or scientists with an urge toward synthesis is not that psychological results are irrelevant to wider concerns about memory, but that the daunting diversity of methods and traditions even within cognitive psychology makes it hard to see how different levels of explanation might relate to one another. There are issues of considerable interest for the philosophy of science in understanding the connections between neuroscientific and cognitive-psychological descriptions and methods; and, equally, robust and philosophically intriguing research traditions on autobiographical memory in developmental, personality, and social psychology. This entry briefly examines ideas about the constructive nature of remembering that seem to have direct relevance to concerns about truth in memory.

Remembering is a multifaceted activity that takes place in the present, and so the best explanatory frameworks for understanding it will attend closely to the context of recall, rather than simply investigating the nature of encoded traces. Memories are often compiled or constructed for particular purposes when needed, not held fully formed. There is room for considerable internal plasticity in memory traces, which are (on the connectionist model) always composites shaped by the entire history of their network. The most dramatic work on construction in memory has come not from connectionist modeling, however, but from the research on suggestibility and false memory by Elizabeth Loftus and her colleagues (2003). Misleading information from external sources can be incorporated into personal recollection. Confident, entrenched childhood "memories" of spilling a bowl of punch at a wedding, for example, or of gazing long at an exceptionally colorful mobile in the days after birth, can be elicited artificially in certain circumstances. This work is partly motivated by a wish to confirm the possibility of false confessions, in which individuals may come sincerely and passionately to believe that they have committed horrible crimes in the past; but the mechanisms in play are just the ordinary and normally robust processes of shaping and generalizing memories to make them fit. Although Loftus has adopted the high moral tone of a crusade, ongoing careful investigation of individual differences and integration of these results with social and personality psychology promises a much richer picture of the conditions which make different kinds of distortion more likely.

Again, the point of this research is not to show, implausibly, that reliability in memory is impossible or unlikely. Psychologists assume that understanding the mechanisms of distortion will also throw light on the processes involved in veridical remembering. Reliability and accuracy are not transparent notions here. Pre-reflective confidence in personal memories can, and in certain contexts should, coexist with attention to the other evidence about the past which is often available, and care for the defeasible but subtle and robust capacities to winnow evidence that individuals have developed in the rich and complex social context of early memory-sharing and memory-using practices.

SOCIAL MEMORY AND SHARED MEMORY

The general constructive picture of remembering can be accepted while acknowledging that external influences—particularly social influences—on memory need not inevitably lead to error. As Sue Campbell argued in her powerful philosophical responses to the "memory wars," there are vital features of relational interaction with others that contribute positively to practices of good remembering, both in development and in adult social life: To treat the true unit of memory as the isolated individual, free from the distorting influence of other people, is to miss the value we often appropriately place on negotiating the past—both the personal past and the shared past—in company.

Indeed a need for attention to shared remembering and social remembering in both psychology and philosophy can be motivated from within the broadly constructivist framework itself. It is because one's internal memory is partial and context-sensitive, and does not naturally retain information in distinct and unchanging form between experience and recollection, that one relies so pervasively and—in the main— successfully on external social and technological scaffolding. A challenge for psychologists is to find ways to study shared memories that do not focus solely on the conformity induced or sought by powerful external authorities; and a challenge for philosophers is to construct a social ontology of memory by which to understand the diverse ways in which people manage to hook their incomplete inner systems of traces with the vast social and cultural resources in which cognition is situated.

Mark Rowlands (1999) and Rob Wilson (2004), for example, have suggested specific ways in which external symbol systems—in their many distinct historical and cultural forms—allow individuals to leave information and skills out in the world, saving on the resources and capacity required for biological memory. Drawing on the more precise invocations of terms like *social memory* and *collective memory* in the contemporary social sciences, this distributed cognition framework suggests that researchers can study the transmission of particular representations across different individuals and media, and the specific forms of interplay between group dynamics and individual recall. It also promises to throw better light on the influential work on memory by the French sociologist Maurice Halbwachs (1980).

Halbwachs's notion of the collective memory is often cited by contemporary social scientists and historians as deeply anti-psychological, or as sociologically determinist: but in fact his work focuses on the incomplete or shrouded nature of the individual's memory, which (outside of dreams) must be sculpted and completed within a social framework, which provides the context and the means for the construction of a specific recollection. Philosophical analysis can potentially be of immense service to empirical disciplines like cognitive anthropology and historical theory in the study of memory by showing how case studies of remembering activities in particular times and places might be embedded in robust broader theories of memory. So in addition to the long-standing philosophical concerns about truth and the self previously outlined, it is likely that philosophical attention will increasingly engage, through topics like memory, with the urgent challenge of connecting the cognitive sciences and the social sciences.

See also Cognitive Science; Computing Machines; Moral Psychology; Personal Identity; Philosophy of Mind; Plato; Reid, Thomas; Time, Consciousness of; Wittgenstein, Ludwig Josef Johann.

Bibliography

Bartlett, Frederic. *Remembering: A Study in Experimental and Social Psychology*. Cambridge, U.K.: Cambridge University Press, 1932.

Bursen, Howard. *Dismantling the Memory Machine*. Dordrecht: Reidel, 1978.

Campbell, John. "The Structure of Time in Autobiographical Memory." *European Journal of Philosophy* 5 (1997): 105–118.

Campbell, Sue. *Relational Remembering: Rethinking the Memory Wars*. Lanham, MD: Rowman and Littlefield, 2003.

Campbell, Sue. "Models of Mind and Memory Activities." In *Moral Psychology: Feminist Ethics and Social Theory*, edited by Peggy DesAutels and Margaret Urban Walker. Lanham, MD: Rowman & Littlefield, 2004.

Carruthers, Mary. *The Book of Memory*. Cambridge, U.K.: Cambridge University Press, 1990.

Casey, Edward S. *Remembering: A Phenomenological Study*. Bloomington: Indiana University Press, 1987.

Connerton, Paul. *How Societies Remember*. Cambridge, U.K.: Cambridge University Press, 1989.

Deutscher, Max. "Remembering 'Remembering.'" In *Cause, Mind, and Reality*, edited by J. Heil, 53–72. Dordrecht: Kluwer, 1989.

Draaisma, Douwe. *Metaphors of Memory: A History of Ideas about the Mind*. Translated by Paul Vincent. Cambridge, U.K.: Cambridge University Press, 2000.

Draaisma, Douwe. *Why Life Speeds Up as You Get Older: How Memory Shapes Our Past*. Translated by Arnold and Erica Pomerans. Cambridge, U.K.: Cambridge University Press, 2004.

Engel, Susan. *Context Is Everything: The Nature of Memory*. New York: W. H. Freeman, 1999.

Foster, Jonathan K., and Marko Jelicic, eds. *Memory: Systems, Process, or Function?* New York: Oxford University Press, 1999.

Hacking, Ian. *Rewriting the Soul: Multiple Personality and the Sciences of Memory*. Princeton, NJ: Princeton University Press, 1995.

Halbwachs, Maurice. *On Collective Memory*. Translated by F. J. and V. Y. Ditter. New York: Harper & Row, 1980.

Hamilton, Andy. "False Memory Syndrome and the Authority of Personal Memory-Claims: A Philosophical Perspective." *Philosophy, Psychiatry, and Psychology* 5 (1998): 283–297.

Hoerl, Christoph. "Memory, Amnesia, and the Past." *Mind and Language* 14 (1999): 227–251.

Hoerl, Christoph, and Teresa McCormack, eds. *Time and Memory: Philosophical and Psychological Perspectives*. New York: Oxford University Press, 2001.

Hyman, Ira E., and Elizabeth F. Loftus. "Errors in Autobiographical Memory." *Clinical Psychology Review* 18 (1998): 933–947.

Krell, David Farrell. *Of Memory, Reminiscence, and Writing: On the Verge*. Bloomington: Indiana University Press, 1990.

Loftus, Elizabeth F. "Our Changeable Memories: Legal and Practical Implications." *Nature Reviews Neuroscience* 4 (2003): 231–234.

Malcolm, Norman. *Memory and Mind*. Ithaca, NY: Cornell University Press, 1977.

Margalit, Avishai. *The Ethics of Memory*. Cambridge, MA: Harvard University Press, 2002.

Martin, C. B., and Max Deutscher. "Remembering." *Philosophical Review* 75 (1966): 161–196.

Martin, M. G. F. "Perception, Concepts and Memory." *Philosophical Review* 101 (1992): 745–763.

McClelland, James L., and David E. Rumelhart. "A Distributed Model of Human Learning and Memory." In *Parallel Distributed Processing: Explorations in the Microstructure of Cognition*. Vol. 2, edited by J. L. McClelland and D. E. Rumelhart, 170–215. Cambridge, MA: MIT Press, 1986,

Misztal, Barbara. *Theories of Social Remembering*. Maidenhead: Open University Press, 2003.

Neisser, Ulric. "The Ecological Study of Memory." *Philosophical Transactions of the Royal Society B: Biological Sciences* 352 (1997): 1697–1701.

Nelson, Katherine. "Self and Social Functions: Individual Autobiographical Memory and Collective Narrative." *Memory* 11 (2003): 125–136.

Owens, David. "The Authority of Memory." *European Journal of Philosophy* 7 (1999): 312–329.

Owens, David. "A Lockean Theory of Memory Experience." *Philosophy and Phenomenological Research* 56 (1996): 319–332.

Reid, Thomas. "Essays on the Intellectual Powers of Man." In *The Works of Thomas Reid*, edited by W. Hamilton. Edinburgh: McLachlan, Stewart, & Co., 1849.

Ricoeur, Paul. *Memory, History, Forgetting*. Translated by Kathleen Blamey and David Pellauer. Chicago: Chicago University Press, 2004.

Rowlands, Mark. *The Body in Mind: Understanding Cognitive Processes*. Cambridge, U.K.: Cambridge University Press, 1999.

Rubin, David C. *Memory in Oral Traditions: The Cognitive Psychology of Epic, Ballads, and Counting-Out Rhymes*. New York: Oxford University Press, 1995.

Schacter, Daniel. *Searching for Memory: The Brain, the Mind, and the Past*. New York: Basic Books, 1996.

Schacter, Daniel. *The Stranger Behind the Engram: Theories of Memory and the Psychology of Science*. Hillsdale, NJ: Lawrence Erlbaum, 1982.

Schechtman, Marya. "The Truth about Memory." *Philosophical Psychology* 7 (1994): 3–18.

Sorabji, Richard. *Aristotle on Memory*. London: Duckworth, 1972.

Stern, David G. "Models of Memory: Wittgenstein and Cognitive Science." *Philosophical Psychology* 4 (1991): 203–218.

Sutton, John. *Philosophy and Memory Traces: Descartes to Connectionism.* Cambridge, U.K.: Cambridge University Press, 1998.

Tulving, Endel. "Episodic Memory: from Mind to Brain." *Annual Review of Psychology* 53 (2002): 1–25.

Tulving, Endel, and F. I. M. Craik, eds. *The Oxford Handbook of Memory.* New York: Oxford University Press, 2000.

Warnock, Mary. *Memory.* London: Faber, 1987.

Wilcox, Stephen, and Stuart Katz. "A Direct Realist Alternative to the Traditional Conception of Memory." *Behaviorism* 9 (1981): 227–239.

Wilson, Robert A. *Boundaries of the Mind.* Cambridge, U.K.: Cambridge University Press, 2004.

Wollheim, Richard. *The Thread of Life.* Cambridge, U.K.: Cambridge University Press, 1984.

John Sutton (2005)

MENASSEH (MANASSEH) BEN ISRAEL

(1604–1657)

Menasseh (Manasseh) ben Israel, the Jewish scholar, philosopher, and theologian, was probably born in Madeira. His father, a victim of the Spanish Inquisition, escaped with his family to La Rochelle and then to Amsterdam, where Menasseh studied in the growing Jewish community. At eighteen he became a teacher and preacher. Although very successful in his rabbinical career, Menasseh could not support his family with his salary and so became a printer, establishing Holland's first Hebrew press. He printed his own first published work, an index to the *Midrash Rabbah* (1628). Most of his subsequent works are in Spanish, Portuguese, or Latin.

Menasseh's vast erudition in Jewish and Christian theology and philosophy and classical and contemporary literature attracted notice in 1632, when the first part of his *El Conciliador* appeared in Frankfurt (the second, third, and fourth parts appeared in Amsterdam, 1641–1651; the book was translated into English by E. H. Lindo, London, 1842). This work attempted to reconcile the apparent conflicts and contradictions in the Bible and brought Menasseh into the company of Gerhard Johannes and Isaac Vossius, Hugo Grotius, and many other scholars, who came to regard him as the leading expositor of Jewish thought to the Christian world. He corresponded with Christian and Jewish scholars everywhere, and many came to Amsterdam to confer with him.

Menasseh ben Israel was greatly interested in the Jewish and Protestant kabbalistic, mystical, and Messianic views of his time and was involved with some of the strangest seventeenth-century visionaries. This led to his most famous work and the best-known episode of his career. A Portuguese Jew from South America told him of finding some of the lost tribes of Israel in the jungles there. Using this material and other "data," Menasseh ben Israel published his *Hope of Israel* in Latin, Spanish, and English (1650), in which he argued that because the Israelites were spread almost everywhere on Earth, the Messianic age was at hand. If the Jews were readmitted to England, then all might be ready for the Messiah. Several influential Puritans, including Oliver Cromwell, held similar views, and they invited Menasseh ben Israel to London to discuss the readmission of the Jews. Menasseh ben Israel stayed in England from 1655 to 1657, but after much controversy no official solution emerged, although the unofficial readmission of Jews to England did begin. Disappointed, Menasseh ben Israel died shortly after leaving England.

Although his works are not of the first rank, Menasseh ben Israel was extremely influential in developing and disseminating a modernized form of Jewish learning and in making Christian scholars aware of then-current streams of Jewish thought.

See also Grotius, Hugo; Jewish Philosophy; Kabbalah.

Bibliography

The Hope of Israel appeared in Spanish in 1650 (Amsterdam) and was translated by Menasseh ben Israel into Latin the same year. An English translation by M. Wall appeared in London in 1650. The latest English edition was published in London in 1901.

Cecil Roth, *A Life of Menasseh ben Israel* (Philadelphia: Jewish Publication Society of America, 1934), contains an excellent bibliography of works by and about Menasseh ben Israel. Also consult the articles "Manasseh ben Israel" in *Jewish Encyclopedia* (London and New York, 1904), Vol. VIII, pp. 282–284, and *Dictionary of National Biography* (Oxford, 1959–1960), Vol. XII, pp. 898–899.

OTHER RECOMMENDED TITLES

Coppenhagen, J. H., ed. *Menasseh ben Israel (1604–1657): A Bibliography.* Jerusalem: Misgav Yerushalayim, 1990.

Méchoulan, H., and R. H. Popkin. *Menasseh ben Israel and His World,* edited by Y. Kaplan. Leiden: Brill, 1989.

Roth, C. *A Life of Menasseh ben Israel.* Philadelphia: Jewish Publications Society, 1934.

Richard H. Popkin (1967)
Bibliography updated by Oliver Leaman (2005)

MENCIUS
(fourth century BCE)

Mencius, a Chinese philosopher, is often regarded as the most important Confucian thinker after Confucius. He lived in the Warring States period, during which China was divided into different states with their own rulers, often waging war against each other. He traveled from state to state to convert rulers to the teachings of Confucius. At the same time, he also combated other influential movements of thought, especially those associated with Mozi and Yang Zhu (fifth to fourth century BCE). One's main access to his thinking is through the *Mengzi* (Mencius), probably compiled by his disciples or disciples of his disciples. The text was subsequently edited and shortened by Zhao Qi in the second century CE, and this is the version of the text available today.

Elaborating on Confucius's teachings, Mencius highlighted four ethical attributes: *ren* (benevolence, humaneness), *yi* (propriety), *li* (observance of rites), and *zhi* (wisdom). *Ren* has to do with love or concern for others and involves a reluctance to cause harm and the capacity to be moved by the suffering of others. The scope of such concern includes not just human beings but also certain kinds of animals, and there is a gradation in *ren* in that one has special concern for and obligations to those closer to oneself. *Ren* results from cultivating the special love for parents that everyone shares as an infant and the affective concern for others shown in the well-known Mencian example of one's commiseration for the infant on the verge of falling into a well.

The earlier use of *yi* refers to a proper regard for oneself and distancing oneself from disgrace, involving such things as not brooking an insult. Mencius retained this use of *yi*, but disgrace for him is measured not by ordinary social standards but by ethical standards, and *yi* has to do with a firm commitment to such standards. One regards what falls below such standards as potentially tainting oneself and insists on distancing oneself from such occurrences even at the expense of death. One example is that of a beggar starving to death, who would reject food given with abuse despite the resulting loss of life. According to Mencius everyone shares responses of this kind, which provide the starting point for cultivating *yi*.

Li originally referred to rites of sacrifice and later to rules of conduct governing ceremonial behavior as well as behavior in other social contexts. Mencius continued to use *li* in this way, and in addition used it to refer to an ethical attribute having to do with the observance of *li*. This

attribute involves a general disposition to follow *li*, as well as a mastery of the details of *li* that enables one to follow *li* with ease. It also involves one's observing *li* with the proper attitude and mental attention, such as reverence in interacting with others or sorrow in mourning.

In early Chinese thought, *xin*, which refers to the physical heart, is regarded as the site of both cognitive and affective activities. It is translated as "heart" or "mind," and sometimes as "heart/mind." *Xin* can form certain directions, which can take the form of long-term goals in life or more specific intentions. The fourth ethical attribute, *zhi*, involves having proper directions of the heart/mind, which in turn requires an ability to assess situations without adhering to fixed rules of conduct. This discretionary judgment may lead one to deviate from established rules of *li*, and may also guide one's behavior in situations in which no general rule is applicable.

For Mencius, these four ethical attributes result from people cultivating four kinds of predispositions of the heart/mind. These include commiseration, the sense of shame, a reverential attitude toward others, and the sense of right and wrong. He referred to these as the four "sprouts" or "beginnings" and regarded the four ethical attributes as growing from these predispositions in the way that a plant grows from a sprout. Besides commiseration and the sense of shame, he also regarded love for parents and obedience to elder brothers as the starting point for cultivating *ren* and *yi*, respectively. His view that the heart/mind has these ethical predispositions provides the basis for his response to the Moist and Yangist challenges.

Mozi advocated the doctrine of indiscriminate concern for everyone. He did not believe that human beings have the appropriate predispositions to begin with and thought that one could restructure one's motivations accordingly after endorsing this doctrine. In the absence of such predispositions, the practice of indiscriminate concern seems humanly impossible, a point seized on by Mozi's opponents. By contrast, Mencius thought that human beings have ethical predispositions that relate to the ethical ideal in the way that a sprout relates to a full-grown plant. Such predispositions contain within them a direction of growth and provide the appropriate emotional resources that one can draw on to achieve the ideal.

The Yangists advocated nourishing *xing* (nature), a term referring to the direction of growth or development of a thing. They understand the *xing* of human beings in biological terms, such as living to an old age, and regarded it as the proper direction of development for humans. Mencius rejected the biological conception of *xing*, instead, *xing* is constituted by the ethical direction implicit in the predispositions of the heart/mind. The view that *xing* has an ethical direction is expressed in his well-known slogan that *xing* (human nature) is good.

Although the heart/mind has the relevant ethical predispositions, they need to be nourished for them to flourish, and one should also guard against the various factors that can potentially harm their growth. Mencius often highlighted the senses as something that can lead one astray. The senses operate automatically—when they come into contact with their ideal objects, they are just pulled along unreflectively by these objects. By contrast, the heart/mind can reflect on what is proper and can halt any course of action it regards as improper. The heart/mind should constantly exercise these capacities to ensure that one progresses in an ethical direction.

One may also be led astray by erroneous doctrines, such as Mohist and Yangist teachings, which Mencius explicitly opposed. One may also be led astray by problematic desires. For example, in a series of dialogues between Mencius and King Xuan of the state of Qi, the king referred to his great desire to expand territories and his feverish desires for wealth, women, and display of valor. These desires not only led the king to harsh policies but also led him to rationalizations about his inability to be caring toward his people. Mencius's response was to try to steer the king toward seeing that a more caring policy toward the people is not only compatible with the king's desires but actually enables their attainment in a higher form. For example, a king who seeks to be invincible can do so by practicing *ren* government, thereby drawing the allegiance of the people. He will become invincible not in the sense of superior military strength, but in the sense of being without opposition.

While Mencius's teachings competed for influence with other kinds of Confucian teachings for several hundred years after his time, he eventually came to be regarded as the true transmitter of Confucius's teachings. Zhu Xi included the *Mengzi* as one of the Four Books, which became canonical texts of the Confucian tradition. Mencius also came to be regarded as the greatest Confucian thinker after Confucius himself, and his teachings have been influential on the development of Confucian thought in the Song (960–1279), Ming (1368–1644), Qing (1644–1912) Dynasties, and up to modern times.

See also Chinese Philosophy; Confucius; Mozi; Yang Zhu; Zhu Xi (Chu Hsi).

Bibliography

Chan, Alan K. L., ed. *Mencius: Contexts and Interpretations.* Honolulu: University of Hawaii Press, 2002.

Graham, A. C. "The Background of the Mencian Theory of Human Nature." In *Studies in Chinese Philosophy and Philosophical Literature*, 7–66. Albany: SUNY Press, 1990. Originally published in the journal *Tsing Hua Journal of Chinese Studies* 6 (1967).

Graham, A. C. *Disputers of the Tao: Philosophical Argument in Ancient China.* La Salle, IL: Open Court, 1989.

Lau, D. C., trans. *Mencius.* London: Penguin, 1970.

Legge, James, trans. *The Works of Mencius.* 2nd ed. Oxford, U.K.: Clarendon Press, 1895.

Nivison, David S. *The Ways of Confucianism: Investigations in Chinese Philosophy.* La Salle, IL: Open Court, 1996.

Shun, Kwong-loi. *Mencius and Early Chinese Thought.* Stanford, CA: Stanford University Press, 1997.

Kwong-loi Shun (2005)

MENDELSSOHN, MOSES
(1729–1786)

Moses Mendelssohn, the greatest Jewish philosopher in the eighteenth century, was born in Dessau, the son of a poor Jewish copyist of sacred scrolls. His first studies were devoted to the Bible, the Talmud, and Maimonides' *Guide for the Perplexed.* He followed his teacher Rabbi David Fränkel to Berlin in 1745, where he learned to read German and Latin while living in great poverty. In 1750 he became a tutor in the household of the Jewish silk manufacturer Isaak Bernhard; he was later a bookkeeper and ultimately a partner in Bernhard's firm. In Berlin Mendelssohn became a close friend of G. E. Lessing, C. F. Nicolai, and Thomas Abbt. After 1755 his reputation as a philosopher and critic grew rapidly throughout Germany. By his contemporaries he was regarded as eminently kind and virtuous, and because of his wisdom and ugliness he was called "The Jewish Socrates." Lessing is said to have modeled the character of Nathan in his drama *Nathan der Weise* upon Mendelssohn. In 1763 Mendelssohn's *Abhandlung über die Euidenz in den metaphysischen Wissenschaften* (Essay on Evidence in Metaphysical Science; Berlin, 1764) won a prize from the Berlin Academy, and he was later elected to the academy, although his appointment was never confirmed.

In spite of his Jewish extraction, Mendelssohn's development as a philosopher was notably German in character; he was influenced mainly by Gottfried Wilhelm Leibniz, Christian Wolff, Alexander Baumgarten, G. F. Meier, his Berlin friends, and among foreign philosophers, by John Locke, the earl of Shaftesbury, Edmund

Burke, Jean Baptiste Dubos, and Pierre-Louis Moreau de Maupertuis.

Mendelssohn was a typical "popular philosopher." He was empirically minded, refrained from final systematizations of his theories, wrote in an easy and attractive style, and was mainly interested in aesthetics, psychology, and religion (although he also discussed methodological and metaphysical questions). His contribution to the emancipation of the Jews was significant. Because of the continuous evolution of his ideas, a summary of his views can only cover the general trends of his thought. He exerted a great influence not only upon his closest friends but upon his whole generation in Germany, and upon Immanuel Kant in particular.

Aesthetics and psychology were, in Mendelssohn's mind, closely interrelated. He continued the work of Baumgarten and Meier, but amalgamated their doctrines with the tenets of English and French aesthetics translated into the terminology of German psychology. Generally attributed to Mendelssohn is the first clear distinction between Beauty and metaphysical perfection: He held that Beauty was an inferior, subjective kind of perfection. Metaphysical perfection consists in unity in a multiplicity. Aesthetic perfection arises out of the limits of human understanding. Man is unable to conceive, as God can, the real, supreme unity in the enormous variety of things. He must therefore content himself with introducing an artificial unity (uniformity) into some objects in order to be able to perceive them as wholes; and this is beauty.

In this way, Mendelssohn began a trend away from Baumgarten's and Meier's aesthetic objectivism toward a subjective aesthetics that soon dominated German aesthetics: A beautiful object is not necessarily perfect in itself, but must be perfect in its capacity to be perceived. The perception of Beauty strengthens the representative activity of the soul and makes it more perfect, thus causing a feeling of pleasure. The perception of Beauty causes intuitive knowledge; in its highest stage it becomes the "aesthetic illusion" in which, for example, fable appears as reality. Mendelssohn's conception of Beauty permitted him to explain the pleasurable effect of tragedy and of the sublime, whose distinction from Beauty he was the first in Germany to explain clearly. In tragedy, murder is the representation of a morally and metaphysically imperfect event, but its representation may be subjectively perfect. Mendelssohn, clearly under the influence of Burke, held that in the sublime, the pleasure in awareness of immensity of distance, size, or number is mixed with some pain because of our inability to comprehend it completely. In both cases, aesthetic pleasure is the result of the "mixed feeling" (*vermischte Empfindung*) arising in our soul: Even if some element of the perception is unpleasant, the perception as a subjective whole is pleasurable.

Mendelssohn's study of the perception of Beauty led him to introduce a doctrine of mental faculties that was later adopted in modified form by Kant and others. Mendelssohn held that aesthetic feelings must be attributed to a faculty different from intellect and desire, a faculty that he called the faculty of approval (*Billigungsvermögen*). The beauty of an object escapes us if we subject it to a process of analysis and definition; therefore, experience of the beautiful cannot be an object of knowledge. A beautiful object gives us aesthetic pleasure even if we do not possess the object; thus, the approval of Beauty must be distinct from desire. Metaphysical perfection, unlike Beauty, is both known by intellect and an object of desire.

Beauty is produced by genius. Genius does not imitate nature, but "idealizes" it; that is, it exhibits natural objects as God would have created them if his aim had been aesthetic and not metaphysical perfection. Genius is independent of rules because it establishes its own rules. A genius's procedure is instinctive.

Mendelssohn believed that both the existence of God and the immortality of the soul could be demonstrated. Although his *Morgenstunden oder Vorlesungen über das Daseyn Gottes* (Morning Hours, or Lectures on the Existence of God; Berlin, 1785) was written in awareness of Kant's previously published *Kritik des reinen Vernunft,* in it Mendelssohn accepted both the Ontological Argument and the Argument from Design.

Mendelssohn's *Phädon oder über die Unsterblichkeit der Seele (Phaedo,* or on the Immortality of the Soul; Berlin, 1767) was a dialogue on immortality in imitation of Plato's *Phaedo.* The soul is a simple substance and therefore indestructible. The soul might nevertheless lose its consciousness, but the divine wisdom and goodness of God would not allow this to happen.

Mendelssohn's plans to publish a work commemorating Lessing, who had died in 1781, prompted Friedrich Heinrich Jacobi to write to Mendelssohn asking whether he knew that Lessing was a Spinozist. The resulting quarrel, which soon involved Johann Georg Hamann, Johann Gottfried Herder, and Johann Wolfgang von Goethe as well as Mendelssohn and Jacobi, is discussed in the entry "Pantheismusstreit."

Mendelssohn had been challenged in 1769 by the Swiss physiognomist and religious writer Johann Kaspar Lavater either to demonstrate the falsity of Christian revelation or to become a convert to Christianity. Mendelssohn's answer was that the deism of the Enlightenment, which he had developed into a universal religion of reason, was in fact identical with Judaism. In his *Jerusalem oder über religiöse Macht und Judentum* (Jerusalem, or on Religious Power and Judaism; 2 vols., Berlin, 1783), Mendelssohn supported religious and political toleration, and advocated separation of church and state and civil equality for the Jews. He always fought against both advocates of anti-Semitism and conservative Jews for a cultural and political union of Christians and Jews.

See also Pantheismusstreit.

Bibliography

WORKS BY MENDELSSOHN

Philosophische Gespräche. Berlin, 1755.
Briefe über die Empfindungen. Berlin, 1755.
Betrachtungen über die Quellen und die Verbindungen der schönen Künste und Wissenschaften. Berlin, 1757.
Moses Mendelssohn an die Freunde Lessings. Berlin, 1786.
Werke. 7 vols, edited by E. G. B. Mendelssohn. Leipzig, 1843–1844.
Gesammelte Schriften, edited by D. Elbogen, J. Guttmann, and E. Mittwoch. Berlin: Akademie-Verlag, 1929–.
Jerusalem. Translated by Allan Arkush. Hanover, NH: University Press of New England, 1983.
Philosophical Writings. Translated and edited by D. Dahlstrom. Cambridge, U.K.: Cambridge University Press, 1997.

WORKS ON MENDELSSOHN

Altmann, Alexander. *Moses Mendelssohn: A Biographical Study.* Tuscaloosa: University of Alabama, 1973.
Arkush, Allan. *Moses Mendelssohn and the Enlightenment.* Albany: State University of New York Press, 1994.
Bamberger, F. *Die geistige Gestalt M. Mendelssohns.* Frankfurt, 1929.
Cahn, N. *M. Mendelssohns Moralphilosophie.* Giessen, 1921.
Cassirer, Ernst. "Die Idee der Religion bei Lessing und Mendelssohn." In *Festgabe zum zehn jährigen Bestehen der Akademie für die Wissenschaft des Judentums,* 22–41. Berlin, 1929.
Cohen, B. *Über die Erkenntnislehre M. Mendelssohns.* Giessen, 1921.
Goldstein, L. *M. Mendelssohn und die deutsche Aesthetik.* Königsberg, 1904.
Hoelters, Hans. *Der Spinozistische Gottesbegriff bei M. Mendelssohn und F. H. Jacobi, und der Gottesbegriff Spinozas.* Bonn, 1938.
Kayserling, Moses. *Moses Mendelssohn, sein Leben und sein Wirken.* Leipzig, 1862; 2nd ed., 1888.
Morgan, Michael. "Mendelssohn." In *History of Jewish Philosophy,* edited by D. Frank and O. Leaman. London: Routledge, 1997.
Pinkus, F. *M. Mendelssohns Verhältniss zur englischen Philosophie.* Würzburg, 1929.

Richter, L. *Philosophie der Dichtkunst, M. Mendelssohns Aesthetik.* Berlin, 1948.
Ritter, J. H. *Mendelssohn und Lessing.* 2nd ed. Berlin: Steinthal, 1886.
Sander, D. *Die Religionsphilosophie Moses Mendelssohns.* Erlangen, 1894.
Zarek, O. *M. Mendelssohn.* Amsterdam: Querido, 1936.

Giorgio Tonelli (1967)
Bibliography updated by Oliver Leaman (2005)

MENTAL CAUSATION

There is mental causation whenever a mental state, event, process, or activity has a causal effect. The pursuit of our lives seems replete with mental causation. It may thus seem as obvious that it occurs as we pursue our lives. But how mental causation is possible is not obvious. And therein lies a philosophical tale. Any attempt to explain how it occurs must engage the mind-body problem.

René Descartes (1596–1650) maintained that there is body-to-mind causation when we perceive our surroundings, and mind-to-body causation when we act. But one of the most serious charges leveled again his substance dualism, according to which the mind is an immaterial substance that is not extended in space, is that it leaves unexplained *how* mental states and events (etc.) have causal effects on our bodies. Descartes held that the locus of mind-body causal interaction is in the brain (specifically, in the pineal gland). His contemporary, Princess Elisabeth of Bohemia, asked how states of, or changes in, a substance not extended in space (the mind) could causally affect states of, or changes in, a substance extended in space (the brain or pineal gland), and declared such causal interaction too incredible to believe. The absence of a satisfactory answer to her "how-question" contributed to the demise of Cartesian substance-dualism (Watson 1987).

Many contemporary philosophers hold that to have a mind is not to possess an immaterial substance, but rather to possess certain capacities, such as the capacity to think and/or to feel. Brains serve somehow as the material basis of such capacities. (Whether an artificial brain could so serve is the question of whether artificial intelligence is possible.) But because of the many apparent differences between mental and physical properties, some philosophers, while rejecting Cartesian substance dualism, nevertheless embrace Cartesian property dualism. They hold that while there are no immaterial substances, mental properties are distinct from physical properties, and are related to certain of them by irreducible laws of nature. This view faces the question of how an individual's having a mental property could exert any causal influence on the course of events. Given the absence of a reality underlying both mental and physical reality, an individual's having a mental property would have to exert a direct causal influence on its initial effects in the brain, one unmediated by any mechanism.

The year 1870 marked more than a century of increasingly detailed investigation of human physiology. In that year, Ewald Herring declared at his lecture to the Imperial Academy of Sciences in Vienna that brain physiologists should make "the unbroken causative continuity of all material processes an axiom of [their] system of investigation" (translated and quoted in Butler 1910, pp. 64–65). It remains an axiom of neurophysiology. The fact that there are no "gaps" in physiological brain processes for mental events to fill led Thomas Huxley (1874) to maintain we are "conscious auotmata": conscious events accompany certain physiological brain events as dual effects of other physiological events, but are causally inert. Trained as a medical doctor, William James (1890) appropriated the term *epiphenomena*, a medical term for symptoms of diseases, for mental phenomena that while caused, lack causal efficacy. James Ward (1903) coined the term *epiphenomenalism* for the view that mental phenomena have no causal effects.

The view that mental phenomena are epiphenomena has a dense air of paradox. Epiphenomenalists maintain that we are merely under the illusion that there is mental causation. But, on their view, the illusion could not give rise to our belief in mental causation, for that would require mental causation. Moreover, on pain of inconsistency, they cannot take themselves to have been led to the doctrine by theoretical reasoning, for their being so led would involve mental causation. Indeed, reasoning itself seems to be a causal process. It should thus come as no surprise that virtually no contemporary philosophers who acknowledge the reality of the mental espouse the view that no mental states or events have causal effects. But the question of how they have effects remains.

Some philosophers combine the rejection of Cartesian substance dualism with the rejection of mental and physical event dualism, while nevertheless embracing Cartesian property dualism. C. D. Broad (1925) examined a dual-aspect theory of events, according to which physiological events in "the mind-brain" (1925, p. 439) have two independent aspects, one mental, the other physiological, the two linked by contingent fundamental laws. In discussion of the view, he formulated epiphenomenalism as a disjunctive doctrine: "mental events

either (a) do not function at all as cause factors; or that (b) if they do, they do so in virtue of their physiological characteristics, and not in virtue of their mental characteristics" (p. 473). If, rather than being accompanied by mental events, certain physiological events have mental characteristics, and so are mental events, then it seems, on the evidence, that they function as cause factors in virtue of their physiological characteristics, but not their mental ones. The mental qua mental seems causally inert.

Donald Davidson (1970) proposed the doctrine of anomalous monism: every particular mental event is a physical event, but there are no strict psychological or psychophysical laws, and mental characteristics are irreducible to physical characteristics. He did not, however, embrace Cartesian property dualism, which is committed to fundamental psychophysical laws. Moreover, he regarded talk of properties as pleonastic; strictly speaking, there are only predicates, not properties. He held that since mental events (i.e., events mental predicates are true of) are causes or effects, they fall under strict physical laws, and so are physical events because physical predicates that figure in the relevant strict laws are true of them. Still the causal relation, he emphasized, is extensional: if two events are causally related, they are so related however they are described. There is no qua-causation.

Many philosophers hold that properties are distinct from predicates, and indeed that predicates apply to things only in virtue of the properties that things have. And they hold that although the causal relation is indeed extensional, it is nevertheless the case that events enter into causal relations in virtue of certain of their properties. The weighs-less-than relation is extensional: If a weighs less than b, then it does so however a and b are described. Still a weighs less than b in virtue of something about each of them, namely their respective weights—their respective masses in the gravitational context in question. Anomalous monism entails the denial of token epiphenomenalism. But its proponents must answer the charge of commitment to type epiphenomenalism, the thesis that no events are causally related in virtue of falling under mental types (McLaughlin 1989, 1994; Kim 1993; Sosa 1993; see also Davidson 1993).

In the early twentieth century, the atomic view of matter was vindicated, and in the 1930s a quantum mechanical explanation of chemical bonding was provided, dispelling the idea that there are fundamental chemical forces; and later monumental advances in organic chemistry and molecular biology led to the demise of any form of vitalism (McLaughlin 1992). It is now generally held, on empirical grounds, that: for any (caused) microphysical event P there is a distinct microphysical event P^* that causally determines the objective probability of P (if determinism is true, that probability will be 1).

This thesis has been called by various names in the literature, including "the closure of the physical." Given this thesis, if Cartesian property dualism is correct, then it seems that an individual's having a mental property could have microphysical effects only if it causally overdetermined those effects. Such overdetermining psychophysical causal transactions would be fundamental in that they would be unmediated by any mechanism. While that may fall within the realm of logical possibility, it is hard to see how the view that it actually occurs could be justified (Kim 1998).

Many contemporary philosophers hold that there is a stronger dependence of mental properties on microphysical properties than Cartesian property dualism allows. There is no received formulation of the dependency. But one leading view is that it is captured by the following *supervenience* thesis: any minimal physical duplicate of the actual world is a duplicate *simpliciter* of it (Jackson 1998). A physical duplicate of the actual world is any world that is exactly like the actual world in every microphysical respect, in respect to its worldwide pattern of distribution of microphysical properties and relations, its worldwide pattern of distribution of microphysical objects, its microphysical laws of nature, and so on. A minimal physical duplicate of the actual world is any physical duplicate of it that contains nothing other than what is metaphysically required to be a physical duplicate of it.

While the supervenience thesis is incompatible with Cartesian property dualism, it does not entail that every property is a microphysical property. The thesis entails that any minimal physical duplicate of the actual world will have exactly the same worldwide pattern of distribution of properties as the actual world. But, as should be made clear below, that does not require that every property be a microphysical property. Indeed, one can embrace the supervenience thesis while holding a kind of property pluralism, according to which not only mental properties, but properties that figure in the laws of the special sciences—economics, psychology, biology, and even most of chemistry—are not microphysical properties. Some proponents of the supervenience thesis are property pluralists and hold, in addition, (token) event and state pluralism, on the grounds that events and states are property exemplifications. They thus hold that mental events, and events within the domains of the special sciences, are not microphysical events. Let us label this kind of "nonreductive physicalism," which combines the supervenience thesis with property and event pluralism, "NRP."

NRP theorists acknowledge that every event is such that its objective probability is causally determined by some microphysical event occurring across some cross section of its backward light cone. But they deny that this excludes higher-level events from being causes. Some defend this denial by distinguishing causation from causal determination (Yablo 1992). They hold that to be causally related, events must be appropriately proportional, and that microphysical events are typically disproportional to the higher-level events they causally determine, and are thus disqualified as causes of those events. On this view, when the turning of a key causes a lock to open, some microphysical event will causally determine that the lock opens. But it will not be a cause of the lock's opening. The reason is that it contains too much superfluous detail to be suitably proportionate to the opening of the lock. Had the key turning occurred without that microphysical event, the lock would still have opened. The key turning thus "screens off" the microphysical event vis-à-vis the lock's opening. Of course, in the counterfactual situation that is stipulated, some other microphysical event will underlie the key turning and cause the microphysical event underlying the lock's opening. But it is claimed that is so because higher-level causal transactions are implemented by lower-level ones, and ultimately by microphysical ones.

One charge against this view is that it mistakes causal explanation for causation. Any microphysical event that causally determines the opening of the lock causes it. Nevertheless, an explanation of why the lock opened in terms of a microphysical cause would be an extremely poor one indeed in a typical context since it would contain far too many details that are superfluous to understanding why the lock opened. But whether that charge can be justified remains a matter of dispute. The dispute turns on controversial issues about the nature of causation and the individuation of events.

Many NRP theorists hold that every event is caused by some microphysical event that determines its objective probability. They maintain, nevertheless, that higher-level events are causes. One concern about this view is that if higher-level events were causes, then their effects would include microphysical events. If my decision to walk into the next room causes me to walk into the next room, a result will be that many of the physical particles making up my body at the time of the decision will end up in the next room. The decision would be a cause (though not of course a sufficient cause) of the movements of the particles. Such "downward causation" is regarded by some philosophers as untenable (Kim 1998). NRP theorists respond that while the movements of the particles are in a sense causally overdetermined, such overdetermination is not the objectionable sort to which the interactionist Cartesian property dualist is committed. For the psychophysical causal interactions are not fundamental: They are implemented by causal transactions between microphysical events. Mechanics can ignore them. Still some critics charge that the fact that the microphysical event was brought about by another microphysical event leaves no work for the decision to do in bringing it about (Kim 1998). Some NRP theorists reply that this sort of worry is based on a productive conception of causation, and that we should eschew such a conception as unrealistic (Loewer 2002). They maintain that this sort of overdetermination can be accommodated by a kind of regularity account of causation (Melynk 2003), or a kind of counterfactual account of causation (Loewer 2002). This strand of the debate also leads to issues concerning causation and event individuation.

Given the supervenience thesis, any minimal physical duplicate of the actual world would have the same world-wide pattern of distribution of mental events and special science events as the actual world. Why is that the case if mental and special science events are not microphysical events? The leading NRP answer is that all mental and special science events are *realized* by microphysical events and such realization guarantees this result. While there is no received view of realization, the leading notion is the functionalist notion, according to which the realization relation is the relation of role-occupancy: a realization is a role-player. This idea, however, has been implemented in two different ways (see Block 1980). Role-functionalism implements it one way; filler-functionalism implements it in another (see McLaughlin forthcoming).

According to role-functionalism, every event token of a mental type M is a higher-order event token, an event of participating in some event or other that occupies a certain role R, which includes a causal role. Events that occupy R realize M events, that is, realize events that are exemplifications of M. On this view, higher-order events are never identical with lower-order events. Thus, even if mental events are always realized by microphysical events, no mental event is a microphysical event; similarly, for special science events. This event pluralism is compatible with the supervenience thesis because the basic roles could be filled by microphysical events that fill them in virtue of microphysical laws and conditions.

But NRP theorists would nevertheless face a problem in embracing role-functionalism, for there is a serious question of whether higher-order events have causal effects. While every second-order event is realized by a first order event that has causal effects, a serious question remains whether second-order events themselves have effects. The role-functionalist idea seems most plausible for abilities, but abilities themselves seem not to have causal effects, rather their bases or realizations do. The role-functionalist idea has, however, also been interestingly applied to constituted dispositional states, such as water-solubility, water-absorbency, fragility, ductability, and the like (Jackson, Pargetter, and Prior 1982; Prior 1985). For something to be water-soluble is (arguably) for it to be in some state that, under appropriate conditions, would cause it to begin to dissolve when immersed in a liquid. The state that has the causal role of producing the maninfestation of the disposition (dissolving) is the basis (realization) of the disposition. (Being composed of sodium chloride is one such basis; but the dispositional property is multiply realizable.) It is, however, the basis of water-solubility that causes the substance to dissolve when immersed in water, not the disposition—*if* the disposition is indeed a second-order state (other accounts of such states are possible). On this role-functionalist conception, the substance's being water-soluble seems to just be the fact that there is some state of it that would (in appropriate circumstances) result in its dissolving were it immersed in water.

The concern, then, is that if (token) mental states and events were functional states and events (i.e., higher-order states and events), they would have no causal effects (Jackson 1996, McLaughlin forthcoming). That would not exclude them from being causally explanatory. The claim that a substance dissolved in water because it is water-soluble provides some information about the causal chain leading to its dissolving (see Prior 1985). But the NRP theorist is after higher-level causation, not just causal explanation. Thus, the NRP theorist must respond to this concern with a compelling account of causation according to which functional states indeed have causal effects. Suffice it to note that the claim that functional states are inefficacious does not presuppose a productive conception of causation (see Lewis 1986).

According to filler-functionalism, an event is of mental type M if and only if it occupies or plays a certain role R, where R includes a causal role. On this view, an event token *realizes* role R by occupying the role—by filling it. For an event to be of type M is just for it to fill the role. Thus, if E occupies R, then E is thereby of type M. Since the role includes a causal role, filler-functionalists reject token-epiphenomenalism. Note that if, on a particular occasion, event token E is the occupant of R, then "E is the M event" will be a contingent statement of identity, like "Benjamin Franklin is the inventor of bifocals." (The description "the M event" will, like the description "the inventor of bifocals," be nonrigid: it will pick out different things in some possible worlds from those that it picks out in others.)

It may well be that tokens of various types of events can occupy role R, and thus be realizations of M; if so, then M is multiply realizable. Moreover, events of some type N can realize M, even when N itself is multiply realizable. That will be the case when an event is of type N if and only if it fills a role R*, which includes R as a proper sub-role (Shoemaker 1994). If, on a particular occasion, an event realizes M in virtue of being an N event, and realizes N in virtue of being a C event, then, on that occasion, the C event is the N event, the N event is the M event, and so the C event is the M event.

Notice, then, that, when conjoined with the thesis that every mental event is realized by some microphysical event, filler-functionalism entails that every mental event is a microphysical event. And indeed the filler-functionalist explanation of why any minimal physical duplicate of the actual world will have the same worldwide pattern of distribution of mental (and special sciences) events as the actual world is that the only basic fillers of the roles are microphysical events, which fill them solely in virtue of microphysical laws and conditions. Events are of different orders only relative to types. (Moreover, the ordering here, it has been pointed out, is not one of scale [Kim 1998].) The filler-functionalist account of realization will not serve the NRP theorist's purposes. On the filler view, every event is a microphysical event, and it is ultimately in virtue of microphysical event types that events enter into causal relations. Mental event types are not microphysical event types, both because of actual multiple microphysical realization, and because of the logical possibility of realization without microphysical realization. Nevertheless, they are relevant to whether events of one sort cause events of another since they implicitly type events in terms of patterns of causal relations. And that may very well make them indispensable to certain causal explanations. But whether such a view is correct turns, of course, not only on the nature of causation and the individuation

of events, but also on the nature of mental (and special science) properties.

Problems remain, moreover, that are specific to the mental. Some philosophers maintain that neither a role nor a filler-functionalist view is tenable for mental states with qualitative or phenomenal characters: states such that it is like something for the subject of the state to be in the state (e.g., the state of feeling pain). And some embrace Cartesian property dualism for phenomenal mental properties ("qualia"; Chalmers 1996, Kim 2005). They thus reject the psychophysical supervenience thesis. They hold that there could be an exact physical duplicate of the actual world that, unlike the actual world, is entirely devoid of phenomenal consciousness (a "zombie world"; Chalmers 1996). But they do not deny the closure of the physical. And they acknowledge that they may thus very well have to hold that an individual's having a phenomenal property has no causal effects. Suffice it to note that even this restricted epiphenomenalism has an air of paradox. It entails, for instance, that our feeling of pains never cause our pain-behavior, or even our beliefs that we are in pain.

Moreover, even if Cartesian property dualism is rejected for all mental properties, problems remain. Intentional mental states are explanatory, in part, by virtue of their propositional contents. For example, the content that *there is a snake in the room* figures essentially in both the rationalizing explanation, "He decided not to enter because he believed there was a snake in the room," and the nonrationalizing explanation, "He began to quiver because he feared that there was a snake in the room." The leading theories of content, however, are externalist theories, according to which the content of a mental state fails to supervene on intrinsic states of the subject (Putnam 1975, Burge 1979). On these views, two intrinsic duplicates (e.g., an inhabitant of Earth and her *doppelgänger* on Twin Earth) could be in intentional states with different contents. Indeed, according to some externalist theories, content depends on historical context (Dretske 1988), and according to others, on social context (Burge 1979). Some philosophers maintain that such highly relational properties are causally irrelevant to behavior, and so must play a noncausal explanatory role. But some philosophers defend the view that intentional states cause behavior, despite being essentially extrinsic (Yablo 1999). Others claim that wide content is causally explanatory because it provides information about the causal history of the agent's behavioral dispositions (Dretske 1988). And others contend that intentional states have an externalist or wide content in virtue of having a "narrow content" in a causal environmental context, and that it is narrow content that is causally relevant to behavior (Jackson 1996). There are other views as well that are as yet less explored. Suffice it to note that these content issues too are matters of ongoing philosophical investigation.

See also Anomalous Monism; Artificial Intelligence; Broad, Charlie Dunbar; Cartesianism; Consciousness; Content, Mental; Davidson, Donald; Descartes, René; Dualism in the Philosophy of Mind; Elisabeth, Princess of Bohemia; Functionalism; Huxley, Thomas Henry; James, William; Kim, Jaegwon; Mind-Body Problem; Nonreductive Physicalism; Philosophy of Mind; Putnam, Hilary; Qualia; Supervenience.

Bibliography

Block, N. *Readings in Philosophy of Psychology*. Vol. I. Cambridge, MA: Harvard University Press, 1980.

Broad, C. D. *The Mind and Its Place in Nature*. New York: Harcourt Brace, 1925.

Burge, T. "Individualism and the Mental." *Midwest Studies in Philosophy* 4 (1979): 73–121.

Butler, S. *Unconscious Memory*. London: A. C. Fifield, 1910.

Chalmers, D. J. *The Conscious Mind*. New York: Oxford University Press, 1996.

Descartes, René. *Meditions on First Philosophy* (1641). Edited by Stanley Tweyman. Ann Arbor: Caravan Books, 2002.

Davidson, Donald. "Mental Events." In *Experience and Theory*, edited by L. Foster and J. W. Swanson. University of Massachusetts Press and Duckworth, 1970. Reprinted in Donald Davidson, ed. *Actions and Events*. Oxford: Clarendon Press, 1980.

Davidson, Donald. "Thinking Causes." In *Mental Causation*, edited by John Heil and Alfred Mele. Oxford: Clarendon Press, 1993.

Dretske, F. *Explaining Behavior: Reasons in a World of Causes*. Cambridge, MA: MIT Press, 1998.

Huxely, T. H. "On the Hypothesis That Animals are Automata, and Its History." *Fortnightly Review* 16 (1874): 555–580. Reprinted in Huxley, *Collected Essays*, Vol. 1. New York: J. A. Hill, 1904.

Jackson, F. "Epiphenomenal Qualia." *Philosophical Quarterly* 32 (1982): 127–136.

Jackson, F. *From Metaphysics to Ethics*. Oxford: Oxford University Press, 1998.

Jackson, F. "Mental Causation: The State of the Art." *Mind* 105 (1996): 377–413.

Jackson, F., R. Pargetter, and E. Prior. "Functionalism and Type-Type Identities." *Philosophical Studies* 42 (1982): 209–225.

James, W. *The Principles of Psychology* (1890). Cambridge, MA: Harvard University Press, 1983.

Kim, J. *Mind in a Physical World: An Essay on the Mind-Body Problem and Mental Causation*. Cambridge, MA: MIT Press, 1998.

Kim, J. *Physicalism, or Something Near Enough*. Princeton, NJ: Princeton University Press, 2005.

Kim, J. *Supervenience and Mind: Selected Philosophical Essays*. New York: Cambridge University Press, 1993.

Lepore, E., and B. Loewer. "Mind Matters." *Journal of Philosophy* 84 (1987): 630–642.

Lewis, D. "An Argument for the Identity Theory." *Journal of Philosophy* 63 (1966): 17–25.

Lewis, D. "Events." In *Philosophical Papers* II, edited by D. Lewis, 241–269. Oxford: Oxford University Press, 1986.

Loewer, B. "Comments on Jaegwon Kim's Mind and the Physical World." *Philosophy and Phenomenological Research* LXV (2002): 655–662.

Macdonald, C., and G. Macdonald. "How to be Psychologically Relevant." *Debates on Psychological Explanation*. Vol. I, 60–77. Oxford: Blackwell, 1995.

McLaughlin, B. P. "Type Epiphenomenalism, Type Dualism, and the Causal Priority of the Physical." *Philosophical Perspectives* 3 (1989): 209–235.

McLaughlin, B. P. "The Rise and Fall of British Emergentism." In *Emergence or Reduction?*, edited by A. Beckermann, H. Flohr, and J. Kim, 49–93. Berlin and New York: Walter de Gruyter, 1992.

McLaughlin, B. P. "On Davidson's Response to the Charge of Epiphenomenalism." In *Mental Causation*, edited by John Heil and Alfred Mele, 27–40. Oxford: Clarendon Press, 1993.

McLaughlin, B. P. "Epiphenomenalism." In *A Companion to the Philosophy of Mind*, edited by S. Guttenplan, 277–289. Oxford: Blackwell, 1994.

McLaughlin, B. P. "Is Role-Functionalism Committed to Epiphenomenalism?" *Journal of Consciousness Studies*. Forthcoming.

Melnyk, A. *A Physicalist Manifesto*. Cambridge, U.K.: Cambridge University Press, 2003.

Prior, E. *Dispositions*. Scots Philosophical Mongraphs. Aberdeen: Aberdeen University, 1985.

Putnam, H. "The Meaning of 'Meaning,'" In *Mind, Language and Reality*, edited by H. Putnam, 215–271. Cambridge, U.K.: Cambridge University Press, 1975.

Shoemaker, S. *Identity, Cause, and Mind: Philosophical Essays*. Cambridge, U.K.: Cambridge University Press, 1994.

Sosa, E. "Davidson's Thinking Causes." In *Mental Causation*, edited by edited by J. Heil and A. Mele. Oxford: Clarendon Press, 1993.

Ward, S. L. "The Conscious Automism Theory." Lecture XIII of *Naturalism or Agnosticism*, vol. 2, 34–64. Adam and Charles Black, 1895/1903.

Watson, R. A. *The Breakdown of Cartesian Metaphysics*. Atlantic Highlands, NJ: Humanities Press, 1987.

Yablo, S. "Mental Causation." *Philosophical Review* 101 (1992): 245–280.

Yablo, S. "Wide Causation." *Philosophical Perspectives* 11 (1999): 251–281.

Brian P. McLaughlin (1996, 2005)

MENTAL CONTENT

See *Content, Mental*

MENTAL IMAGERY

See *Imagery, Mental*

MENTAL-PHYSICAL DISTINCTION

The distinction between the mental and the physical is central both to commonsense thinking about the world and to many philosophical, scientific, and religious theories. Perhaps it is as important to human thought as the distinction between fact and value, and between the empirical and the a priori. This entry will focus both on the role of the distinction in analytic philosophy and on various proposals about how it is to be understood.

The mental/physical distinction plays a role in two main areas of philosophy. First, in philosophy of mind, many arguments and issues are formulated in terms of it. Philosophers who advance physicalist theories about the mind argue that phenomenal consciousness (for example) is a physical phenomenon similar in kind to electricity or sexual reproduction; dualists deny this, saying that what we have here are two fundamentally different sorts of thing or two different characteristics of things. Second, in the philosophy of science and related parts of metaphysics, there is the issue of how to formulate the picture of the world that is presented to us by modern science. Many contemporary philosophers assume that this picture is in essence a physicalist one, and mean by this that the world-\view implicit in modern science bears important affinities with the materialism (also known as physicalism) of the seventeenth and eighteenth centuries, in particular that of La Mettrie and Hobbes. A natural assumption is that to properly evaluate whether the worldview of modern science really *is* a kind of physicalism, and to fully understand the related dispute in philosophy of mind between physicalism and dualism, one would need to clarify the mental/physical distinction. So what exactly *is* it?

There seems to a tacit general understanding of the mental/physical distinction but no rigorous idea of how it is to be drawn *exactly*—the implicit understanding has not been made explicit. That we understand the distinction in some sense is indicated by the fact that we spontaneously sort various features or characteristics of people or animals into two lists, the mental and the physical. So, to focus on a particular person Jones, we have on the mental side the fact that he knows where his car keys are, has itchy feet, wants tickets to the opera, and so on.

On the physical side, we have the fact that he weighs 170 pounds, is currently located in Detroit, Michigan, is moving in such and such a direction with such and such a speed, and so on. The problem comes when we try to say in any detail what the occurrences of "and so on" mean. What precisely places a feature in the mental list, and what distinguishes those on the mental list from those on the physical? What groups *weighing 170 pounds* together with *being currently located in Detroit, Michigan*, and sets it apart from *having itchy feet*? Or take some other property of Jones not mentioned so far: for example, that his brain is releasing certain hormones into his bloodstream—is *it* mental or physical? If, as it seems natural to say, it is physical, what makes it so?

There is no shortage of proposals in the literature about what makes it so, and more generally about how to understand the mental/physical distinction, but all of them face problems, and none commands widespread assent. What immediately follows is a brief catalogue. The first, and historically the most important, proposal is that of Descartes (1641). Descartes said that being physical (or material) is just being extended in space; likewise, he said, the essence of the mind is to think, to engage in the activity of thinking. Descartes went on to argue that, if this is the way to draw the mental/physical distinction, dualism in philosophy of mind is true. This clarification of the distinction is straightforward, but it also has a number of drawbacks. First, we think of matter as something that *occupies* space, rather than being identical to space—but Descartes notoriously makes no room for such a distinction. Second, there are intuitively physical forces—such as the force of gravity—that would not be classified as physical from Descartes' point of view. Third, the idea that the essence of the mind is to think apparently excludes mental states that are sensory rather than cognitive and those that do not involve some sort of mental activity.

The second proposal—one might view it as an updated version of Descartes—draws the mental/physical distinction by appealing to two ways in which we find out about the world: introspection and perception. On this view, something is mental just in case we can find out about it, at least in principle, by introspection, whereas something is physical just in case we can find out about it, at least in principle, by perception. But this proposal faces difficulties also. One problem is that many things that seem intuitively physical are not directly available to perception even in principle—for example, subatomic particles. One might weaken the criterion and say that something is physical just in case we can find out about it *either* by perception *or* by inference from perception. But

ENCYCLOPEDIA OF PHILOSOPHY
2nd edition

the problem now is that the mental states of other people are such that we can find out about *them* by inference from perception; hence the weakened account entails the physicality of those mental states. Another problem with this second proposal is that it is not clear what the category of introspection is. Introspection seems to be the faculty by which we find out about our own *mental* goings-on—but this drains the idea of content.

The third proposal, prominent in the work of Thomas Nagel (1974, 1986), explains the mental/physical distinction as a special case of the contrast between the subjective and the objective. One obvious problem here is that the distinction between the subjective and objective is itself unclear; it is no advance to take *subjective* to mean "mental." But Nagel himself interprets the distinction as concerning different conditions of understanding: An objective truth or fact is one that can be understood from more than one point of view, whereas a subjective truth or fact is one that can be understood from at most one point of view. One objection to this is that there are psychological phenomena that are objective in Nagel's sense; presumably, the psychological properties attributed to humans by theoretical as opposed to folk psychology are as objective as any anything else. (These properties are not available to introspection either—and this causes a problem for the previous proposal, too.) A second objection is that the distinction between mental and physical is now a distinction *within* the realm of things that can be understood. But it is quite unclear that something is physical only if it is understandable.

The two proposals we have just considered inherit from Descartes the idea that we need criteria *both* for the mental and the physical. But contemporary philosophers have also explored the more cautious idea that one might define directly what it is for something to be physical, leaving aside the question of what it is for something to be mental. Hence, the fourth proposal is that something is physical just in case it is the sort of thing that physical theory tells us about or perhaps is entailed by the sort of thing physical theory tells us about. The basic objection to this view is Hempel's dilemma (Hempel 1969; see also Crane and Mellor 1990). Hempel's dilemma is that if the physical theory in question is contemporary physics, this proposal entails that physicalism is obviously false—after all, nobody believes that contemporary physics is complete; on the other hand, if the physical theory in question is some idealized or future physics, then the proposal entails that physicalism is empty—after all, who knows what some idealized or future physics will include? Some (for example, Smart 1974) respond by asserting that it is

rational to believe that contemporary physics is complete. Although there is something right about this—surely it *is* rational to believe contemporary physics—the implicit suggestion that we should *define* the physical in terms of contemporary physics is implausible. Medieval impetus physics (for example) is a false and outmoded theory, but the property that objects have according to it—namely, impetus—is a physical property nonetheless.

According to a fifth proposal—sometimes called the paradigm physical object view—something is physical just in case it is the sort of thing required by or entailed by a complete account of the intrinsic nature of paradigmatic physical objects and their constituents (Block 1980; see also Feigl 1967). The basic idea of this view is that we have some paradigms of physical objects—trees, stones, planets, toasters—and that the physical is whatever you need to explain them. One problem with this view is that it is circular—it explains the physical in terms of physical objects. (The same problem afflicts the previous proposal, which defines the physical in terms of physical theories.). Another problem for this view is that if physical objects turned out very different from how they appear—if, for example, they had a spiritual essence—physicalism and idealism would on this view be indistinguishable.

Perhaps it is unsurprising on reflection that the proposals just reviewed run into difficulties; they are all attempts at saying something positive about what the physical consists in. The sixth proposal is the negative one of saying that *physical* just means "nonmental" (for example, Levine 2001). One problem with this idea is that it assumes some criterion or mark of what it is to be mental; for example, that something is mental just in case it has phenomenal character or intentionality or both. And someone might question or reject both proposals either singly or in combination. But the more serious problem for the *via negativa* is that, construed as a definition of the physical, it gets things quite wrong. A vitalist, for example, thinks that living things instantiate properties—*élan vital*—which are both nonmental and nonphysical. However, while vitalism might be as false and outmoded as medieval impetus physics, it is not self-contradictory.

In view of the fact that every extant proposal about how to clarify the mental/physical distinction faces problems, it is natural to wonder whether there *is* any clear distinction here at all. Perhaps this is a distinction that we draw in ordinary thought but is something that should be done away with in serious scientific or philosophical descriptions of the world. That is the proposal that a number of people have found themselves drawn to, including Chomsky (2000).

One response to this sort of scepticism is that it is driven by overly high standards of clarity. True, it is hard to clarify the mental/physical distinction, but this difficulty does not mean that there is no such distinction—for the same thing might be said for many interesting distinctions and concepts. A different (but consistent) response asks us to look again at why we wanted a clarification of the mental/physical distinction in the first place. If the answer is intellectual curiosity, the Chomksian view is as reasonable as any other. But Chomskian skepticism gains much of its power from the further idea that various intellectual projects in philosophy of mind and science *make no sense unless* the mental/physical distinction can be clarified. But in fact it is not clear that this is so. Earlier we noted that various projects in philosophy of mind and science are formulated in terms of the mental/physical distinction. But it does not follow that the distinction is *essential* to these projects. If the mental/physical distinction can be shown to play only an illustrative or inessential role in these projects, then skepticism about the distinction itself—whether or not it is warranted—will not be as consequential as it would otherwise appear to be.

See also Chomsky, Noam; Descartes, René; Dualism in the Philosophy of Mind; Hempel, Carl Gustav; Hobbes, Thomas; Idealism; La Mettrie, Julien Offray de; Nagel, Thomas; Philosophy of Science, History of; Philosophy of Science, Problems of; Physicalism.

Bibliography

Block, N. "Troubles with Functionalism." In *Readings in the Philosophy of Psychology*, vol. 1, edited by N. Block. Cambridge, MA: Harvard University Press, 1980.

Chomsky, Noam. *New Horizons in the Study of Language and Mind*. Cambridge, U.K.: Cambridge University Press, 2000.

Crane, T., and D. H. Mellor. "There Is No Question of Physicalism." *Mind* 99 (1990): 185.

Descartes, Rene. "Meditations on First Philosophy." In *The Philosophical Writings of Rene Descartes*, edited by John Cottingham. Cambridge, U.K.: Cambridge University Press, 1985. First published in 1641.

Feigl, H. *The "Mental" and the "Physical."* Minneapolis: University of Minnesota Press, 1967. First published 1958.

Hempel, C. "Reduction: Ontological and Linguistic Facets." In *Essays in Honor of Ernest Nagel*, edited by S. Morgenbesser, P. Suppes, and M. White. New York: St. Martin's Press, 1969.

Levine, J. *Purple Haze*. New York: Oxford University Press, 2001.

Nagel, T. *The View from Nowhere*. New York: Oxford, 1986.

Nagel, T. "What Is It Like to Be a Bat." *Philosophical Review* 4 (1974): 435–450.

Smart, J. J. C., "The Content of Physicalism." *Philosophical Quarterly* 28 (1974): 239—241.

Daniel Stoljar (2005)

MENTAL REPRESENTATION

"Mental representations" are the coin of contemporary cognitive psychology, which proposes to explain the etiology of subjects' behavior in terms of the possession and use of such representations. "How does a subject manage to move through her darkened bedroom without stumbling over the furniture? She has an accurate mental representation of the room's layout, knows her initial position in the room, and is able to use this representation, in roughly the way a mariner uses a chart, to navigate through the room." "How does a sighted subject manage to recover information, available in the retinal image, about 'what's where' in her environment? She computes a series of representations, using information present in the retinal image, that eventuates in a three-dimensional representation of the distal objects present in the subject's visual field." "Why do native speakers of English have difficulty recognizing the grammaticality of so-called garden-path sentences such as 'The horse raced past the barn fell'? In recovering the meaning of a sentence, a speaker first constructs a representation of the syntactic structure of the sentence. In the case of garden-path sentences, the parsing processes that construct this representation mistakenly take the sentence's subject noun phrase to be a complete sentence, thus concluding that the entire sentence is ungrammatical." Cognitive ethologists offer similar explanations of many animal behaviors: Foraging red ants are said to practice a form of dead reckoning to maintain a representation of their current location relative to their nest, which they use to find their way back; migratory birds are said to navigate using representations of various sorts (celestial, magnetometric, topographic, etc.) that are either innate or learned as juveniles.

If, as these explanations apparently assume, mental representations are real entities that play a causal role in the production of a subject's behavior, then presumably it makes sense to ask about the form in which the information contained in these representations is encoded. This question has been the focus of considerable debate, especially with respect to mental imagery. Descriptionalists argue that, subjective impressions to the contrary notwithstanding, all mental representation, including mental imagery, is descriptional in form; mental representations are said to represent in a way similar to the ways linguistic descriptions represent. Descriptionalists subscribe to a language of thought hypothesis, according to which all human cognition is conducted in a quasi-linguistic medium. Pictorialists, by contrast, argue at least some mental representations, notably those involved in mental imagery, represent in ways similar to the ways pictures represent. The issues in dispute here are not straightforwardly empirical. Neither party believes that we literally have descriptions or pictures in our heads; rather, their claims are about similarities to the respective ways that pictures and descriptions represent. But it is precisely these similarity claims that render this debate obscure. What are the respective ways that pictures and descriptions represent, and what are the salient similarities such that if they hold they would justify characterizing mental representations as being of one form rather than the other? It is not obvious that there is a definitive answer to either of these questions.

To describe the representations to which psychological and ethological explanations appeal as mental is not to imply that their possessors are conscious of them; typically the representations are nonconscious or subconscious. Nor is it to imply that these representations are nonphysical; there is no commitment here to dualism. Psychologists and ethologists presume that the representations to which their explanations appeal are neurologically realized, physical structures. The point of describing the representations as mental is simply to emphasize the particular explanatory role that these representations play in these explanations. The explanations undertake to explain a kind of purposive behavior on the part of a subject, in which the particular behavior exhibited by the subject is typically modulated in a characteristic fashion, not only by the goal or purpose of the behavior, but also by the environment in which the behavior is exhibited. Thus, for example, our subject's movement through her darkened bedroom is modulated by her knowledge of the current layout of the room. The mental representations that figure in these explanations serve two distinct explanatory roles: (1) They explain why a subject behaves in one way rather than another—she behaves as she does because she currently has this particular representation rather than another, and this representation is causally efficacious in the etiology of her behavior—and (2) they explain how the subject's behavior manages to be modulated (in characteristic ways) by her environment. Mental representations are able to play this dual explanatory role by virtue of possessing both physico-formal and semantic (intentional) properties that are linked in such a way as to ensure that a subject's environment can modulate

her behavior. Basically, the cognitive processes that make use of mental representations are causally sensitive to the physico-formal properties of these representations that encode their semantic properties in much the way that sound-reproduction processes are sensitive to the physico-formal properties of records, tapes, and CDs.

Commonsense psychological explanations of behavior standardly appeal to beliefs, desires, intentions, and other so-called propositional attitudes (e.g., "Jones went to the refrigerator because he wanted a beer and believed there to be one there"). Behaviorists and eliminativists have challenged the legitimacy of these explanations, arguing that propositional attitudes either do not exist or do not figure in the etiology of behavior. Impressed with the prominent explanatory role of mental representations in cognitive psychological and ethological explanations, many philosophers of mind, notably Jerry Fodor, have proposed establishing the materialistic respectability of these explanations by appeal to the notion of mental representation. Their strategy is to explicate propositional attitudes in terms of mental representations. They defend a doctrine called the representational theory of mind (RTM), which holds that possessing a propositional attitude (e.g., believing that it is sunny today) is a matter of having a mental representation that (1) expresses the propositional content of that attitude (viz., that it is sunny today) and (2) plays a causal-functional role in the subject's mental life and behavior characteristic of the attitude in question (viz., the characteristic role of beliefs in modulating goal-satisfying behavior). More formally, for any organism O, any attitude A toward the proposition P, there is a mental representation MR such that MR means that (expresses the proposition that) P and a relation R (which specifies the characteristic causal-functional role of the MRs that are associated with a given A); and O bears attitude A to P if and only if O stands in relation R to MR. So formulated, RTM is silent as to the form of the mental representations that express the propositional contents of attitudes; proponents of RTM, however, invariably assume that these representations are syntactically structured entities, composed of atomic constituents (concepts) that refer to or denote things and properties in the world. More colorfully, these representations are sentences in the language of thought. The structure and meaning of these sentential representations purportedly explain the particular semantic and causal properties that propositional attitudes exhibit.

RTM is clearly realist in its construal of propositional attitudes: It purports to explain, not only what they are, but also how they could have both the causal and semantic properties that common sense attributes to them (viz., of being causally efficacious in the production of other thoughts and of behavior, and of being semantically evaluable, as, e.g., true or false). RTM is equally realist in its construal of mental processes, which, it holds, are causal sequences of the tokenings of mental representation. These sequences are said to be proof-theoretic in character, with the sequential states in a thought process functioning like premises in an argument. Thought processes are, like arguments, generally truth preserving.

Proponents of RTM claim to find strong empirical support for the doctrine in the apparent explanatory (and predictive) successes of cognitive science, whose theories are heavily committed to the existence of mental representations. Critics tend to dismiss this claimed support, arguing that what is at issue is not whether there are mental representations but whether there are mental representations with the particular properties demanded by RTM. Critics argue that propositional-attitude contents cannot always be paired with mental representations in the way that RTM requires: A subject may bear a certain attitude to a proposition but lack, among the many mental representations that cognitive scientific theories attribute to her, any mental representation of that particular proposition. Thus, for example, more than one critic has pointed out that, while David Marr's computational theory of early vision (see his *Vision* [1982]) attributes to the visual system the assumption that objects in the visual field are rigid in translation, the theory does not attribute to the visual system an explicit representation of that assumption; rather, the assumption is implicit in the operation of visual processes. Proponents, for their part, have tended to dismiss such counterexamples as "derivative" cases, arguing that RTM nonetheless holds for what they term the "core" cases of propositional attitudes. Such a response presumes that there is a non–question-begging characterization of the class of core cases. It also presumes that the class so characterized includes those propositional attitudes that figure in the commonsense psychological explanations that RTM is intended to vindicate. It remains an open question whether either of these presumptions can be met.

Other critics of RTM have challenged the doctrine's apparent commitment to "classical" cognitive architectures that presume a principled distinction between mental representations, on the one hand, and the computational processes that are defined over these representations, on the other. These critics point out that connectionist computational models of cognition do not preserve such a distinction, so that, if, as these critics pre-

sume, cognitive architecture is connectionist rather than classical, then RTM is untenable. Not surprisingly, proponents of RTM have been in the forefront of efforts to demonstrate that cognitive architecture is not connectionist.

Still other critics of RTM have focused on the semantics of the postulated mental representations, arguing that, if RTM is to provide a materialistic vindication of explanations that appeal to propositional attitudes, it must be possible to provide a "naturalistic" semantics, a theory of content, for these representations. By such a semantics these critics understand a materialistic account, invoking no intentional or semantic notions, of how it is possible for mental representations to have the semantic properties that they do (of being about things in the world, of being truth valued, etc.). There is general agreement among critics and proponents alike that none of the proposed naturalistic semantics is adequate, but, where critics see in these failures the symptoms of RTM's untenability, proponents see the beginnings of a difficult but eventually successful research project. There is disagreement among critics as to the import for cognitive science itself of there possibly being no naturalistic semantics for mental representations. Some argue that it would impugn the claimed explanatory role of mental representations; others argue that it would not. Whatever the upshot of these arguments, the untenability of RTM would not in and of itself impugn the explanatory role of mental representations in cognitive science, since that commitment to mental representations does not entail RTM. One can perfectly well be a representationalist in the way that most cognitive scientists are without also being a proponent of RTM.

See also Cognitive Science; Connectionism; Eliminative Materialism, Eliminativism; Imagery, Mental; Language of Thought; Mental Causation; Philosophy of Mind.

Bibliography

Block, N., ed. *Imagery.* Cambridge, MA: MIT Press, 1981. A collection focusing on debate between descriptionalists and pictorialists regarding mental imagery.

Crane, T. *Mechanical Mind: A Philosophical Introduction to Minds, Machines, and Mental Representation.* London: Routledge, 2003.

Devitt, M. *Coming to Our Senses: A Naturalistic Program for Semantic Localism.* Cambridge, U.K.: Cambridge University Press, 1996.

Dretske, F. *Naturalizing the Mind.* Cambridge, MA: MIT Press, 1995.

Dretske, F. *Perception, Knowledge and Belief.* Cambridge, U.K.:
Cambridge University Press, 2000.

Field, H. "Mental Representation." *Erkenntnis* 13 (1978): 9–61.

Fodor, J. A. *Concepts: Where Cognitive Science Went Wrong.*
Oxford: Oxford University Press, 1998.

Fodor, J. A. *The Elm and the Expert.* Cambridge, MA: MIT
Press, 1994.

Fodor, J. A. "Fodor's Guide to Mental Representation." *Mind* 94
(1985): 55–97.

Fodor, J. A. "The Persistence of the Attitudes." In
Psychosemantics. Cambridge, MA: MIT Press, 1987.

Gunther, Y., ed. *Essays on Nonconceptual Content.* Cambridge,
MA: MIT Press, 2003.

Jackendoff, R. *Languages of the Mind: Essays on Mental
Representation.* London: Bradford, 1995.

Marr, D. *Vision.* San Francisco: Freeman, 1982.

Matthews, R. "Is There Vindication through
Representationalism?" In *Meaning in Mind: Fodor and His
Critics,* edited by B. Loewer and G. Rey. Oxford: Blackwell,
1991.

Matthews, R. "Troubles with Representationalism." *Social
Research* 51 (1984): 1065–1097.

McDowell, J. *Mind and World.* Cambridge, MA: Harvard
University Press, 1994.

Pylyshyn, Z. "The Explanatory Role of Representations." In
Computation and Cognition. Cambridge, MA: MIT Press,
1984.

Pylyshyn, Z. *Seeing and Visualizing: It's Not What You Think.*
Cambridge, MA: MIT Press, 2003.

Sterelny, K. *The Representational Theory of Mind: An
Introduction.* Oxford: Blackwell, 1991.

Stich, S. *Deconstructing the Mind.* Oxford: Oxford University
Press, 1996.

Stich, S., and T. Warfield, eds. *Mental Representation: A Reader.*
Oxford: Blackwell, 1994. An excellent collection of papers
on theories of content for mental representation; includes
Field (1978) and Fodor (1985).

Strawson, G. *Mental Reality.* Cambridge, MA: MIT Press, 1994.

Thau, M. *Consciousness and Cognition.* Oxford: Oxford
University Press, 2002.

Tye, M. *Consciousness, Color, and Content.* Cambridge, MA:
MIT Press, 2000.

Robert J. Matthews (1996)
Bibliography updated by Alyssa Ney (2005)

MERCIER, DÉSIRÉ JOSEPH
(1851–1926)

Désiré Joseph Mercier, a Thomist philosopher and Roman Catholic cardinal, was born in the Walloon section of Brabant, Belgium. At the end of his secondary education, Mercier decided to study for the priesthood; he studied philosophy and theology at the Malines Seminary for five years and subsequently at the University of Louvain. Ordained in 1874, he received the licentiate (equivalent to the current doctorate) in theology in 1877.

The same year he was named professor of philosophy at the Malines Seminary, where he taught logic and psychology for the next five years.

The famous encyclical, *Aeterni Patris,* of Pope Leo XIII, urging the restoration of scholastic, particularly Thomistic, philosophy, was published in 1879. In 1882 a chair of Thomistic philosophy was established at Louvain, and Mercier was named to this post.

For the next several years, Mercier taught courses in the various branches of philosophy, always attempting to relate Thomism to contemporary issues; in the course of this effort, Mercier became convinced that the task of making Thomism a living philosophy would require the combined efforts of many specialists. Hence, he conceived the notion of establishing a special institute of philosophy, with the aim not only of offering courses in Thomistic thought but also of providing the staff and facilities for a genuine research center. After considerable difficulty the Institute of Philosophy was established in 1889 as an integral part of the University of Louvain, with Mercier as its first president. The Philosophic Society of Louvain (still active) was founded by Mercier in 1888; in 1894 this organization founded the philosophical quarterly *Revue néo-scolastique* (still published under the title of *Revue philosophique de Louvain*), with Mercier as its editor.

From 1893 to 1906, Mercier's life was intimately bound up with that of the institute. His teaching activity continued; he published widely; and in the face of many difficulties, he worked incessantly to build and maintain the quality of the institute. His success in this area is measured by the fact that Louvain quickly became an internationally recognized center for philosophical work, attracting students from all over the world.

In 1906 Mercier's career in philosophy was interrupted by his being named archbishop of Malines; he was made cardinal the following year. From this time until his death, Cardinal Mercier's immense energies were directed toward the organizational and pastoral duties of his office. The seven volumes of his *Oeuvres pastorales* (Louvain, 1911–1928) give some indication of the extent of his writings on pastoral, religious, and theological matters. Chief among his interests were social, political, and scientific questions affecting religious life, the liturgy, and church unity. In 1921, at Malines, he initiated the "conversations" with members of the Anglican Church, which continued at intervals until his death.

World War I broke out during Cardinal Mercier's episcopate, and he became a national and international leader in resisting German imperialism and in articulating the moral rights of peoples and nations during times of war. His death was the occasion of worldwide tributes to Mercier's immense moral stature and influence as an outstanding philosopher, ecclesiastic, and citizen of the world.

MERCIER'S PHILOSOPHY

An examination of the life of Cardinal Mercier makes it evident that one dimension of his importance for the history of philosophy must be related to his key role in organizing and developing the Institute of Philosophy at Louvain. It becomes equally evident, however, that this dimension cannot be divorced from his originality and depth as a philosopher. Moreover, the significance of Mercier as a philosopher can be fully seen only in the context of the state of philosophy among Roman Catholic thinkers and teachers in Catholic institutions in the latter half of the nineteenth century, on the one hand, and in the light of Mercier's response to and understanding of the papal encyclical *Aeterni Patris,* on the other. Although there were scattered efforts at a renewal of Thomistic thought during this period, philosophy in Catholic circles was by and large eclectic and superficial. Little serious effort had been made to meet either the challenge of Immanuel Kant or the positivism of Auguste Comte and the skepticism of David Hume and the British empiricists. Consequently, Catholic philosophy was generally in serious disrepute.

It is in this setting that the publication of *Aeterni Patris* must be viewed. This encyclical has been misinterpreted by Catholic and non-Catholic thinkers alike as calling for a return to the letter of thirteenth-century thought and as representing ecclesiastical approval, even sanction, of a particular philosophical doctrine. Recent scholarship has amply demonstrated the falsity of both these views and shows Leo XIII's intent to have been a renewal and articulation of a philosophy organically linked to a great philosophical tradition and compatible with Christian faith but rethought in relation to contemporary problems and issues (see J. Collins in *Leo XIII and the Modern World,* edited by Edward T. Gargan, New York, 1961, pp. 181–209).

No one seems to have caught the spirit of this intent or to have grasped the urgency and challenge of the intellectual crisis of the time more accurately than Cardinal Mercier. Perhaps this can best be seen by a brief exposition of Mercier's thought in three crucial areas: the nature of the philosophical endeavor in itself and in its relation to revealed truth and theology, the relation of Thomistic

thought to modern philosophy, and the relation of philosophy to the discoveries of modern science.

For Mercier, philosophy is essentially an effort of reason reflecting on the data of experience. Included in this view is a strong affirmation that philosophy must take its point of departure and find its ultimate grounding in the evidence of the real, objective world, in contradistinction to all forms of idealism and theories of innate ideas. The role of reason is likewise strongly emphasized by Mercier, especially in his opposition to positivism. For him, philosophy must be scientific in the classical Aristotelian sense; the mind is capable of going beyond the contingent order of the factually given and of finding real, general necessity and order underlying the sensibly grasped world. Hence, Mercier makes a strenuous effort to reestablish the viability of a realistic metaphysics in the face of the Kantian critique and the severe limitations placed on reason by Comtian positivism. The doctrine of abstraction and the legitimate use of the analytic and synthetic activity of the mind constitute the operative principles in this effort. Nevertheless, philosophy for Mercier is a highly personal endeavor that must always remain open and be capable of organic growth in the light of new evidence. Thus, Thomistic philosophy is held by him as "neither an ideal which one is forbidden to surpass nor a barrier fixing the limits of the activity of the mind"; rather, it is a source of philosophical inspiration that provides a framework for entering into genuine dialogue with the contemporary situation.

Mercier is in fundamental agreement with St. Thomas Aquinas in expressing confidence in the impossibility of real contradiction between revealed doctrine and philosophically established truth. Revealed truth functions for him as an extrinsic negative norm, but it provides neither the motivation for adherence to a philosophical truth nor a source of evidence or knowledge for the philosopher in his proper task. Thus, Mercier emphasizes the essential autonomy, the rigorously rational character, the intrinsic openness, and the need for internal growth of philosophy.

In his writings Mercier is manifestly impatient with the general tendency of his immediate predecessors among Roman Catholic philosophers to opt for one of two general positions—a superficial eclecticism or a dogmatic and naive realism based on common sense. In sharp contrast to these positions, Mercier felt it absolutely essential to examine the whole of modern philosophy with great sympathy and to integrate its sound insights into an integral and rethought Thomism. This principle did not, however, prevent Mercier from being highly critical of the various contemporary philosophical positions. His polemical writings are directed against fideism, traditionalism (the view that human reason without the aid of revelation necessarily falls into error), voluntarism, sentimentalism, pragmatism, Cartesianism, positivism, and Kantian critical philosophy. He argued strenuously against the Cartesian principle of universal methodic doubt and against Cartesian dualism, undertaking to show that the Thomistic doctrine of the substantial unity of man could overcome the difficulties to which this dualism gives rise.

Positivism and Kantian philosophy, however, occupied most of Mercier's attention, and it was in relation to these views that Mercier developed his own epistemology (in *Critériologie générale,* 1899), which represents one of his most original contributions to the renewal of Thomistic thought. Against the positivist theories of H. A. Taine, John Stuart Mill, Herbert Spencer and Comte, which he undertook to refute in detail, Mercier insistently affirmed the primacy of the criterion of reason and the absolute value of "ideal judgments." Although the positivists of his day were his principal adversaries, Kant was probably the modern philosopher whom he most admired. His understanding of Kant was limited, however, to the interpretation of his times, and his criticism centers on what he considered to be the psychological subjectivism, hence relativism, of Kant. In the final analysis, then, he feels that both Kantian critical philosophy and positivism lead to skepticism and agnosticism. His response was an attempt to establish a realistic metaphysics on the basis of a sophisticated epistemological critique and a development of a theory of certitude. In his own systematic thought, it is not clear that Mercier fully succeeded in formulating what he intended—that is, a middle term between empiricism and rationalism—for his effort begins with a vigorous defense of the absolute certitude of ideal judgments, and from this position he attempts to establish the degree of certitude proper to judgments of experience. In choosing this starting point, Mercier is forced to infer the reality of the external world on the basis of an ideal principle of causality. Nevertheless, it remains a fact that Mercier's epistemology in its attempt to establish a viable, realistic metaphysics represented a major advance in Thomistic thought.

Apart from his epistemology the most original and commanding dimension of Mercier's thought concerned the relation between philosophy and science. In this area he strongly advocates the necessity for philosophy to be intimately acquainted with the findings of modern science. His own efforts in this area were devoted to a synthesis of the new science of psychology and traditional philosophy; the detail with which he undertook to understand the work of such contemporary psychologists as Wilhelm Wundt and the developments in medical psychology were radically new for his time. Although he clearly held that science and philosophy represent two different modes of thought and although he attributed some real autonomy to science, Mercier probably did not fully appreciate the theoretical component of science (this is hardly surprising given the state of the psychological sciences and the philosophy of science in his day). Hence, his synthesis represents an attempt to understand the facts and laws established by science in the light of metaphysical principles. Once again, however partial Mercier's particular solution to this problem may be, it represents a major advance over the earlier tendency of scholastic philosophy to develop in complete isolation from contemporary thought.

Mercier's own philosophical work represents, then, a vigorous and sustained effort to rethink traditional Thomistic thought in the light of contemporary thought on all fronts; moreover, the spirit of this effort was embraced by colleagues whom Mercier chose to staff the Institute of Philosophy. The true philosophical importance of Mercier must be judged by the caliber of philosophical research and writing that has emanated from the Louvain Institute from his day to the present.

See also Cartesianism; Comte, Auguste; Empiricism; History and Historiography of Philosophy; Hume, David; Kant, Immanuel; Mill, John Stuart; Neo-Kantianism; Positivism; Pragmatism; Rationalism; Taine, Hippolyte-Adolphe; Thomas Aquinas, St.; Thomism; Voluntarism; Wundt, Wilhelm.

Bibliography

WORKS BY MERCIER

For a complete bibliography of Mercier's writings, see *Revue néo-scolastique* 28 (1926): 250–258. Mercier wrote extensively for this and other philosophical journals, and much of his polemical writing appears in articles. His major books were written primarily as textbooks and frequently appeared in several mimeographed forms before publication; the published books were revised and frequently reprinted.

The following are his principal works: "La psychologie expérimentale et la philosophie spiritualiste," in *Bulletin de la Classe des Lettres et des Sciences Morales et Politiques et de la Classe des Beaux-Arts* (Brussels, 1900), which was translated by E. J. Wirth as *The Relation of Experimental Psychology to Philosophy* (New York: Benziger, 1902); *Psychologie,* 2 vols. (Louvain and Paris, 1892; 11th ed., 1923); *Logique* (Louvain and Paris, 1894; 7th ed., 1922);

Métaphysique générale ou ontologie (Louvain and Paris, 1894; 7th ed., 1923); *Les origines de la psychologie contemporaine* (Louvain and Paris, 1897; 5th ed., 1922), which was translated by W. H. Mitchell as *Origins of Contemporary Psychology* (New York, 1918); *Critériologie générale* (Louvain and Paris, 1899; 7th ed., 1918).

Mercier collaborated with M. de Wulf and D. Nys in writing *Traité Elémentaire de philosophie,* 2 vols. (Louvain and Paris, 1905; 5th ed., 1920), translated by T. L. Parker and S. A. Parker as *A Manual of Modern Scholastic Philosophy,* 3rd ed., 2 vols. (London: K. Paul, Trench, Trubner, 1928).

STUDIES ON MERCIER

The definitive personal and intellectual biography of Mercier is by L. de Raeymaeker, *Le Cardinal Mercier et l'Institut Supérieur de Philosophie de Louvain* (Louvain: Publications Universitaires de Louvain, 1952), which also contains a detailed account of the founding and history of the institute. The best critical study of Mercier's thought is in G. Van Riet, *L'epistémologie thomiste* (Louvain: Editions de l'Institut Supèrieur de Philosophie, 1946), pp. 135–178. Also to be noted is L. Noel, "Le psychologue et le logicien," *Revue néoscolastique* 28 (1926): 125–152. Probably the best biography in English is by J. Gade, *The Life of Cardinal Mercier* (New York: Scribners, 1934).

Alden L. Fisher (1967)

MEREOLOGY

"Mereology" (from Greek *meros,* "part") is the theory (often formalized) of part, whole, and cognate concepts. The notion of part is almost ubiquitous in domain of application, and for this reason Edmund Husserl assigned its investigation to formal ontology. Aristotle observed that the term *part* was used in various ways, as for a sub-quantity, a physical part (leg of an animal), a part in definition (animal is part of man), a part in extension (man is part of animal). Part concepts had obvious applications in geometry and were among Euclid's undefined terms. Several senses of "part" are expressible using the preposition "in," but not all uses of "in" express parthood.

Until the twentieth century it was generally assumed that the concept of part was sufficiently clear not to require elucidation, but gradually the need for a formal treatment became apparent. Euclid's maxim that the whole is greater than the part appeared to be contradicted by infinite classes, for example. In 1901 Husserl proposed a general theory of part and whole and distinguished several kinds of parts, notably dependent and independent parts. Explicit formal theories of part and whole were developed around 1914 to 1916 by Alfred North Whitehead and Stanisław Leśniewski, who worked independently of each other. They had different motivations: Whitehead wanted an empirical basis for geometry,

whereas Leśniewski wished to offer a paradox-free class theory. Mereology was later formulated within first-order predicate logic by H. S. Leonard and Nelson Goodman, who called it "the calculus of individuals." Mereology has often been employed by nominalists as a partial substitute for set theory, but it is not intrinsically a nominalistic theory: Part relations are definable via endomorphisms in many mathematical domains.

The most natural basic concept of mereology is that of a (proper) part to its (larger) whole. A coincident of an object is the object itself or something that shares all parts with it. An ingredient of an object is a part or coincident of it. Two objects overlap if and only if they share an ingredient, and they are disjoint if and only if they do not. The relation of part to whole has some minimal formal properties: It is (1) existence entailing; (2) asymmetrical; (3) transitive; and (4) supplementative. That means (1) that if one thing is part of another, if either the part or the whole exists, so does the other; (2) that if one thing is part of another, the second is not part of the first; (3) that a part of a part of a whole is itself a part of the whole; and (4) that if an object has a part, it has another part disjoint from the first. Principles (3) and (4) have occasionally been doubted, (4) unconvincingly. Some meanings of "part" are not transitive; for example, a hand is said to be part of the body, but an arbitrary chunk of flesh is not, and for such concepts counterexamples to (3) may sound plausible, but only because they restrict the general (and transitive) concept, to mean, for example, organ, functional part, immediate part, assembly component.

Beyond such minimal properties mereologists often make further assumptions. Very often it is assumed that objects with the same ingredients are identical: Such a mereology is extensional. Extensionality makes good sense for homogeneous domains such as regions of space or masses of matter, but some objects of distinct sorts seem to be able to coincide, at least temporarily, without identity. Another assumption often made is that any two objects make up a third, indeed that any nonempty collection of objects constitutes a single object, their mereological sum. The minimal properties together with extensionality and this general-sum principle constitute the classical mereology of Leśniewski and Leonard/Goodman: It is as rich in parts as an extensional theory can be, differing algebraically from Boolean algebra only in lacking a null element. It does, however, have an ontologically maximal object or universe, the sum of all there is, which by extensionality is unique. Whitehead denied that there was a universe: For him every object is part of something greater, so he rejected the sum principle. Whitehead also denied there are atoms, that is, objects without parts: For him, every object has a part. This antiatomism, together with supplementarity, ensures that every object has non-denumerably many parts. Whitehead thus denies geometrical points, and his method of extensive abstraction is directed to logically constructing substitutes for points out of classes of extended objects, an idea also carried through by Alfred Tarski. As the examples indicate, the issue whether atomism or antiatomism holds is independent of general mereology. Formally, the best worked-out forms of mereology are those of Leśniewski and his followers; they have shown that any of a wide range of mereological concepts may be taken as sole primitive of the classical theory.

Beyond extensional mereology attention has focused on the combination of mereological notions with those of space, time, and modality. Thus, Whitehead and a number of more recent authors combine mereological with topological concepts to define such notions as two regions' being connected, or their abutting (externally or internally), using mereology as its modern authors intended, as an alternative framework to set theory. When time is considered, matters become more complex. Some objects have temporal parts, including phases, and perhaps momentary temporal sections. States, processes, and events (occurrents) are uncontroversial cases of objects that are temporally extended, but many modern metaphysicians apply the same analysis to ordinary things such as bodies and organisms, giving them a fourth, temporal dimension, though this view is not uncontested. Whether or not continuants (spatially extended objects with a history but not themselves temporally extended) are thus reduced to occurrents, a number of chronomereological concepts may be defined and applied, such as temporary part, initial part, final part, permanent part, temporary overlapping, growth, diminution, and others, though their formulation will vary as applying to occurrents or continuants.

Embedding mereological notions within a modal framework likewise opens up a wider range of concepts such as essential part, accidental part, dependent part, accidental overlapping. Combining these in their turn with temporal notions allows the definition of concepts such as accidental permanent part, essential initial part, and so on. In general, where mereological notions are enriched with others, their interactions become multifarious and lose the algebraic elegance of the classical theory while gaining in applicability and usefulness.

In modal mereology much attention has been paid to R. M. Chisholm's thesis of mereological essentialism,

which states that every part of a continuant is both essential and permanent to that continuant (though, conversely, a part may outlast the whole and need not have it as whole). Chisholm's position is presaged in Gottfried Wilhelm Leibniz and Franz Brentano. Since it appears to be contradicted by everyday experience of such things as rivers, mountains, organisms, and artifacts, it is natural for Chisholm to regard such mereologically fluctuating things as not "real" continuants but as *entia successiva*, supervenient upon successions of continuants for which mereological essentialism holds.

The ubiquity and importance of mereological concepts ensure them a growing place within cognitive science and formal representations of commonsense knowledge, and there is no doubt that mereology is firmly established as a part of formal ontology.

See also Aristotle; Brentano, Franz; Chisholm, Roderick; Cognitive Science; Goodman, Nelson; Husserl, Edmund; Leibniz, Gottfried Wilhelm; Leśniewski, Stanisław; Metaphysics; Tarski, Alfred; Whitehead, Alfred North.

Bibliography

Chisholm, R. M. *Person and Object: A Metaphysical Study.* London: Allen and Unwin, 1976.

Husserl, E. "On the Theory of Wholes and Parts." In *Logical Investigations*, 2 vols. London: Routledge, 1970.

Leonard, H. S., and N. Goodman. "The Calculus of Individuals and Its Uses." *Journal of Symbolic Logic* 5 (1940): 45–55.

Leśniewski, S. "On the Foundations of Mathematics." In *Collected Works.* Dordrecht: Kluwer Academic, 1992.

Simons, P. M. *Parts: A Study in Ontology.* Oxford: Clarendon Press, 1987.

Whitehead, A. N. "Principles of the Method of Extensive Abstraction." In *An Enquiry concerning the Principles of Natural Knowledge.* Cambridge, U.K.: Cambridge University Press, 1919.

Peter Simons (1996)

MERLEAU-PONTY, MAURICE
(1908–1961)

Maurice Merleau-Ponty, a French philosopher associated with existential phenomenology, was the youngest philosopher ever to be appointed to the chair once occupied by Henri Bergson at the Collège de France. Merleau-Ponty was born in Rochefort-sur-Mer on March 14, 1908. His father died early in his childhood; he and his brother and sister were raised by his mother. He attended the Lycée Louis-le-Grand and then the École Normale Supérieure earning his aggregation in 1930. He taught in lycées and then was mobilized in the Fifth Infantry Regiment, and served as a second lieutenant from 1939 until demobilization in 1940. During the occupation he participated in the Résistance. After the liberation in 1945 he taught at the Université de Lyon; during this time he, together with Jean-Paul Sartre, founded the avant-garde journal, *Les temps modernes*. In was also in 1945 that his major work, the *Phenomenology of Perception* was published.

Merleau-Ponty is known primarily for developing an ontology that recognizes the philosophical significance of the human body and for his success in overcoming the dualism that has plagued European philosophy from its inception, but these endeavors also include significant contributions to post-structuralist linguistics, political theory, developmental psychology, and aesthetics. His early interest in the resonance between the emergent school of gestalt psychology and the phenomenology of Edmund Husserl and Martin Heidegger led to a radical reassessment of transcendental philosophy. He died abruptly on May 3, 1961, at the age of fifty-three, leaving his last major manuscript, *Le visible et l'invisible*, unfinished. Claude Lefort has edited the extant text, four chapters and an appendix, and published it together with extensive working notes dated from January 1959 to March 1961.

THE LIVED BODY

Merleau-Ponty revolutionized European thinking about the body—which since ancient Greece had taken it to be either insignificant or a detriment to knowledge—by demonstrating its constitutive role in the process of human understanding. He showed, for example, that it is through bodily motility that the various adumbrations or perspectival views of an object can be synthesized into a unitary whole. Human understanding of objective space, the three-dimensional Cartesian grid of depth, breadth, and height, is an abstraction from lived space—space articulated by the body's capacity to move purposively, to grasp things, to maintain the equilibrium that allows for stable visual coordinates, and to interrogate its environment. Furthermore, the body's ability to perceive the world is grounded in the body's double role as sensor and sensed, capable of being both subject and object of experience: One could not touch an object were one not oneself, as body—an object capable of being touched; nor could one see were her or his eyes not themselves objects located within the surroundings to which they are sensitive. The classical dualism, which views the body and other worldly objects as disjunct from the mind as the subject or agency of disembodied thought, is replaced with Merleau-Ponty's model of corporeal intentionality in which the body is revealed as having an intelligence of its own, manifest in reflex as in habitual activities, which allows it to interact with the world at a level prior to the reflexivity of deliberate conceptualization.

REVERSIBILITY THESIS

The transcendental role of the body, its ability to project its organizational schemas into the world, is inseparable from the body's own status as physical object subject to the worldly forces impinging upon it. These roles are inseparable, but not coincident. There is a divergence of the body as sensing from the body as sensed: The finger that touches the thumb or is touched by it does not form an identity with the thumb; rather the two bodily parts coexist in an ambiguous relationship of reversibility within the encompassing matrix of bodily being-in-the-world. Finger and thumb can reverse roles, the erstwhile sensor becoming the sensed, just as the hand that feels the table can sense itself being touched by the table. Yet neither of these roles would be possible were it not for the other.

THE FLESH OF THE WORLD

Merleau-Ponty takes the reversibility of subject and object roles in the case of human flesh as emblematic of a global manner of being which he designates as chiasm or intertwining. The term *flesh* is generalized to encompass worldly being as such. The world is taken as an arena of interaction in which every entity is what it is in relation to every other. This is not a pan-animism, but rather an attempt to rectify the post-Socratic reduction of nature to inert materiality in a movement of thought which is as consonant with the ancient concept of *physis* as it is with the contemporary notion of world as ecosystem. The figure of the chiasm, the intersection marking the point at which things touch each other as they cross, refers to the dynamics of worldly unfolding or global temporality in which the interaction of things brings about change. The brute or savage being of the world, the factuality of its transcendence, is counterbalanced with the relatedness of its denizens apparent in the relatively abiding structures human intelligence organizes under the heading of science. Humans are that aspect of the flesh of the world that is capable of the reflective relationship of conceptualization or understanding, but other aspects of the world betray other forms of corporeal reflexivity in the complex of interaction that encompasses organic cycles, weather systems, geological formations, and so forth as each of these contributes and responds to all the others.

VISIBLE AND INVISIBLE

Merleau-Ponty's thesis of the primacy of perception evolves from the middle phase of his thinking when he published the *Phenomenology of Perception* and set forth the view that "the perceived world is the always presupposed foundation of all rationality, all value and all existence" to later phases in which this thesis had to be expanded to accommodate the findings of extensive analyses of language based on his unique interpretation of the philosophical significance of Saussurean semiotics. There is controversy regarding his later thinking on the relative primacy of language and perception, but general agreement that the relationship between the two is that of intertwining: language, conceived as sign system, may be conceived as an invisible nexus of relations that is apparent in the visible world and is itself perceptible in speech and writing. The controversy centers on two questions regarding origins or foundations. Does the invisible structure of language reflect organization perceived in the world or does it constitute that nexus of relations? The second question challenges the legitimacy of asking the first: Is it possible to separate perception from language in such a way that one could even ask about the primacy of one with respect to the other?

Merleau-Ponty regards language as flesh, akin to the flesh of the body in its reflexivity—its relatedness to itself and world—but "less heavy, more transparent." In general, the structure of the visible-invisible relation can be defined as *asymmetrical reversibility*: Just as the object one touches can be seen although its tactile aspect remains invisible as such, so can the hidden or horizonal aspects of a given theme be brought into focal vision but only through the loss of its horizonality.

POLITICS

Merleau-Ponty's thinking in general is dynamic and emergent; it is unified by an elusive paradigm he would never have captured even if he lived longer than he did. Nowhere is this questing more apparent than in his political thought. He was always a critical reader of Marx—although he refrained from revisionism as long as he could—and was highly suspicious of the Communist revolution, although he initially endorsed its humanist goals. When Merleau-Ponty died at the height of his powers, he was working toward what may be called an ethics of expression and reversibility, and the direction of this thought can be seen articulating itself as early as his chapter on "Freedom" in the *Phenomenology of Perception*.

The issue that dominated left-wing politics in France—indeed, Europe at large and the USSR—had to do with the tension between party leadership and domination, on the one hand, and the emergence of an increasingly self-conscious proletariat anxious to take up the reins of history, on the other. Was the role of the Central Committee to take charge? Or to take its bidding from the workers of the world? Was the dialectical movement of history objectively determined by materiality? Or subjectively articulated in contests at the level of ideality?

Merleau-Ponty refused to take sides, but sought to undercut the polarity and find a means to embrace the truths to be found on both ends of the spectrum. "The world," he writes, "is already constituted, but also never completely constituted; in the first case we are acted upon, in the second we are open to an infinite number of possibilities. But this analysis is still abstract, for we exist in both ways *at once*. There is, therefore, never determinism and never absolute choice, I am never a thing and never bare consciousness. … It is impossible to determine precisely the 'share contributed by the situation' and the 'share contributed by freedom'" (p. 453). In short, it is through the expression of his situation on the part of the individual worker and his recognition of others in the same plight that solidarity is formed and action can be undertaken. The worker can benefit from guidance from above, but the task of gaining freedom and overcoming the forces that resist it cannot be displaced on to others, else the worker is reduced to slavery again, this time at the hands of his or her liberators.

This idea of circumscribed freedom was in direct opposition to the thesis of radical freedom then espoused by Merleau-Ponty's colleague and cofounder of *Les temps modernes*, Jean-Paul Sartre. This conflict at the level of ideas came to a head in the early 1950s with the disclosure of the atrocities being committed by Stalin in Russia. How to respond? Sartre maintained solidarity with the Communist Party; Merleau-Ponty distanced himself from both, and resigned from the editorial staff of the journal in 1953. The political writings in *Sense and Non-Sense* (1964 [1948]) were written before this break, and the critical reflections on Marxism (including a chapter on "Sartre and Ultrabolshevism") titled *Adventures of the Dialectic* was published in 1955. In the later *Humanism and Terror* (1969 [1947]), Merleau-Ponty sought to put the dialectical thinking of Hegel and Marx in historical perspective, transcend it, and point in a new direction. His conclusion constitutes another step in the direction of the ethics of expression and reversibility mentioned above. "To seek harmony with ourselves and others, in a word, truth, not only in … solitary thought but through the experience of concrete situations and in a living dialogue with others apart from which internal evidence cannot validate its universal right, is the exact contrary of irrationalism, since it accepts our incoherence and conflict with others as constants but assumes we are able to minimize them. It rules out the inevitability of reason and well as that of chaos" (1969 [1947], p. 187).

In his last and unfinished work, *The Visible and the Invisible* (1968 [1964]), Merleau-Ponty returns to the subject of dialectical thought, espouses the thought that ideality and materiality intertwine in a movement of history that can move in the direction of minimizing conflict, but explicitly repudiates the formalism that informs the work of Hegel, Marx, and Sartre in a misguided attempt to impose an abstract structure on the unpredictable and messy historical process in which situated human freedoms collide and intertwine. It is also in this work that he begins to articulate the notion of reversibility, his own response to the Husserlian doctrine of foundation (*Fundierung*).

PSYCHOLOGY

From the earliest of his writing until the last, Merleau-Ponty maintained the thesis of the irreducibility of the figure-ground or theme-horizon structure articulated by gestalt theory. This thesis holds that perception and cognition are fundamentally relational, hence stand in opposition to such standpoints as that of sense-data theory based on the notions of perceptual atoms, elemental simples, or discrete qualia.

In the *Phenomenology of Perception*, Merleau-Ponty offers an extended case study of Schneider, a World War I soldier debilitated by a shrapnel wound in the occipital region of his brain. The point of the study is to demonstrate the inadequacy of the standpoints of empiricism or physicalism, on the one hand, and intellectualism or transcendentalism, on the other, to provide an accurate description of Schneider's afflictions, which are neither purely physiological nor purely intentional but involve a degeneration of the lived body resulting in aberrant forms of substitution behavior in such domains as sexual responsiveness, existential spatiality, motility, expression, and memory.

Merleau-Ponty is unique among phenomenologists in reinterpreting Freudian notions regarding the unconscious in a positive way and integrating them within his own body of theory. This appropriation involved some

modification, to be sure, specifically that of asserting a continuity between conscious and unconscious aspects of human experience at the level of prereflective horizonality. Merleau-Ponty steers a middle course between Freud's relatively mechanistic account of such phenomena as repression, which attributes it to an autonomous function of censorship and dissemblance, and Jean-Paul Sartre's relatively voluntaristic account, which attributes repression to an act of self-deception on the part of a consciousness recoiling from the implications of its own freedom. Merleau-Ponty interprets behavior traditionally subsumed under the heading of repression in terms of a process of habituation operating at prepersonal or unreflective levels in which the body's response to worldly events becomes sedimented as a style of contending with a domain of existence permeated with negative significance. Thus, the aphonia and anorexia of a girl whose family has forbidden her to see her lover is understood, neither as a reversion to an infantile phase of oral sexuality, as Freud would have it, nor as a recoil from responsibility in the mode of magical transformation, as Sartre would have it, but as a refusal of coexistence, a withdrawal from the communal world of eating and talking, which acquires the autonomy of a habit exacerbated by former habitualities favoring oral modes of responding to the world.

In addition to his interests in gestalt psychology and Freudian psychoanalysis, Merleau-Ponty was also well-acquainted with the work done by his sometime colleague Jean Piaget in developmental psychology and the work of Jacques Lacan, a contemporary known for his reinterpretation of Freudian themes along semiological lines. There are frequent references to Piaget in *The Structure of Behavior* (1963 [1942]) and the *Phenomenology of Perception*, and an extended response to Lacan's seminal thinking on the mirror stage in a late essay titled "The Child's Relations with Others." Perhaps Merleau-Ponty's greatest contribution to psychological theory lies in his articulation of an ontological framework capable of consolidating the findings of thinkers across the full spectrum of ideologies from eidetic analysis to experimental and behavioral research: He unremittingly refused to endorse the radical distinctions between the a priori and the a posteriori, between transcendental and empirical approaches, which have functioned to isolate the various schools through polarized opposition.

AESTHETICS

Merleau-Ponty revivifies the ancient Greek sense of the term *aesthetics* by focusing on the perceptual foundations of art rather than concerning himself with judgments of taste. In accordance with his thesis of the primacy of perception, he regards the artist as one who seeks to respond to the world as it manifests itself perceptually rather than to superimpose preconceived conceptual structures upon the world. For example, classical Renaissance painting attempts to render depth on a two-dimensional surface by applying the laws of perspective. Such laws reduce depth to a mere rotation of breadth, seeing it from the side, and overlook the existential or lived aspect of depth as the dimension of exploration and mystery. In classical painting the eye of the artist is fixed and static, whereas in perception the artist's body is spatially mobile and not delimited to an instant of time.

Cézanne, Merleau-Ponty's favorite exemplar, renders depth in his paintings of Mont St. Victoire by using broad, blurred strokes in the foreground, clearer ones in the mid-ground, and an ethereal mistiness in the distance. In his still life paintings, table tops, vases, carafes of wine, and the like are portrayed as a moving eye would see them, not as a photograph would array them from a single point. The painting of galloping horses titled *Derby at Epsom* by Theodore Géricault shows the quadrupeds with their legs extended forward and backward, a distortion of the actual positions of legs in equine movement that succeeds in imparting motion to the animals rather than suspending them awkwardly in the air as a fixed frame, instantaneous representation would. The distortion is actually truer to what people perceive in the extended duration of the lived moment.

Artists have the ability to see what theoretical presuppositions lead people to overlook, and this allows them to bring the invisible to visibility, hence to bring the painting to life. Artists paint what they see rather than what they know of an object. Renoir visually interrogates the water he sees in the Mediterranean sea at Cassis to enable him to paint *The Bathers* in a pool in a sylvan setting. He sees the play of light through the fluid surfaces of the dynamic element that is invisible to the eye of the observer who can only see what he or she thinks is actually there. Artists train themselves to see the speck of light on the glistening surface of eyes that are, themselves, seeing. It is the invisibility of that speck of light to Fra Lippo Lippi, for example, who paints the eye as he thinks it truly is anatomically, that makes the persons in his portraits appear moribund.

The reversibility of seer and seen crosses as in a chiasm with the reversibility of the invisible and the visible. Artists attuned to their own visibility can paint their subjects seeing them and thereby depict the subjectivity of the subject that remains invisible to those who think that in perceiving others people see only their material bodies. Perception, however, is—or can be—truer to living bodies than Cartesian philosophy that reduces human flesh to *res extensa* and conceives *res cogitans* as invisible.

See also Aesthetic Experience; Aesthetics, History of; A Priori and A Posteriori; Art, Representation in; Bergson, Henri; Cartesianism; Dialectical Materialism; Empiricism; Freedom; Freud, Sigmund; Gestalt Theory; Hegel, Georg Wilhelm Friedrich; Heidegger, Martin; Humanism; Husserl, Edmund; Lacan, Jacques; Marxist Philosophy; Marx, Karl; Nomos and Phusis; Perception; Perception, Contemporary Views; Phenomenology; Physicalism; Piaget, Jean; Qualia; Rationality; Sartre, Jean-Paul; Unconscious.

Bibliography

PRINCIPAL WORKS BY MERLEAU-PONTY

Humanisme et terreur, Essai sur le problème communiste. Paris: Gallimard, 1947. Translated by John O'Neill as *Humanism and Terror: An Essay on the Communist Problem* (Boston: Beacon Press, 1969).

"La conscience et l'acquisition du langage." *Bulletin de psychologie* 236 (18) (1964): 3–6. Translated by Hugh J. Silverman as *Consciousness and the Acquisition of Language* (Evanston, IL: Northwestern University Press, 1973).

"La Nature": Notes, cours du collège de France. Compiled and with notes by Dominique Séglard. Paris: Editions du Seuil, 1995. Translated by Robert Vallier as *"Nature": Course Notes from the Collège de France* (Evanston, IL: Northwestern University Press, 2003).

La prose du monde. Paris: Gallimard, 1969. Translated by John O'Neill as *The Prose of the World* (Evanston, IL: Northwestern University Press, 1973).

La structure du comportement. Paris: Presses universitaires de France, 1942. Translated by Alden L. Fisher as *The Structure of Behavior* (Boston: Beacon Press, 1963).

Le visible et l'invisible. Edited by Claude Lefort. Paris: Gallimard, 1964. Translated by Alphonso Lingis as *The Visible and the Invisible* (Evanston, IL: Northwestern University Press, 1968).

Les aventures de la dialectique. Paris: Gallimard, 1955. Translated by Joseph Bien as *Adventures of the Dialectic* (Evanston, IL: Northwestern University Press, 1973).

Phénoménologie de la perception. Paris: Gallimard, 1945. Translated by Colin Smith as *Phenomenology of Perception* (London; New York: Routledge, 1962).

Résumés de cours, Collège de France, 1952–1960. Paris: Gallimard, 1968. Translated by John O'Neill as *Themes from the Lectures at the Collège de France, 1952–1960* (Evanston, IL: Northwestern University Press, 1970).

Sens et non-sens. Paris: Gallimard, 1948. Translated by Hubert L. Dreyfus and Patricia Allen Dreyfus as *Sense and Non-Sense* (Evanston, IL: Northwestern University Press, 1964).

Signes. Paris: Gallimard, 1960. Translated by Richard C. McCleary as *Signs* (Evanston, IL: Northwestern University Press, 1964).

WORKS ON MERLEAU-PONTY IN ENGLISH

Dillon, M. C. *Merleau-Ponty's Ontology.* 2nd ed. Evanston, IL: Northwestern University Press, 1997.

Johnson, Galen. *The Merleau-Ponty Aesthetics Reader.* Evanston, IL: Northwestern University Press, 1993.

Madison, G. B. *The Phenomenology of Merleau-Ponty.* Athens: Ohio University Press, 1981.

Silverman, Hugh J., and James Barry, eds. *Texts and Dialogues.* Atlantic Highlands, NJ: Humanities Press, 1992.

M. C. Dillon (2005)

MERSENNE, MARIN
(1588–1648)

Marin Mersenne, a French mathematician, philosopher, and scientist, was one of the most influential figures of the scientific and philosophical revolutions of the seventeenth century. Although he is remembered primarily for his relationship with René Descartes, he was a significant figure in his own right and also, through his immense correspondence, publications, and personal acquaintances, a key figure in coordinating and advancing the work of the new philosophers and scientists.

He was born at Oizé, France, and studied at Le Mans and later at the Jesuit college of La Flèche, from 1604 to 1609. (Descartes, eight years his junior, was there from 1604 to 1612, but their friendship began later, around 1623.) He next studied in Paris and then entered the pious and austere order of the Minims. After further theological studies Mersenne taught philosophy at a convent in Nevers until 1619, when he was sent back to Paris by his order. He remained there until his death in 1648, except for some trips to The Netherlands, Italy, and the French provinces. His Parisian monastic cell was the center of the European scientific world, as scholars, scientists, philosophers, and theologians often made their way to Mersenne's quarters.

MERSENNE'S PUBLICATIONS

From 1623 to 1625 Mersenne published several enormous polemical works attacking all sorts of Renaissance outlooks and figures, ranging from atheists, deists, kabbalists, astrologers, and numerologists to Pyrrhonists. These writings include the *Questiones Celeberrimae in Genesim* (1623), *L'impiété des deists, athées et libertins de ce temps, combatuë, et renversée* (1624), and *La vérité des sciences contre les septiques ou Pyrrhoniens* (1625). The last

work, more than a thousand pages long, was the culmination of this phase of Mersenne's career and the beginning of the scientific phase that was to continue until his death. Thereafter, his writings were on all sorts of scientific and mathematical subjects (including the famous *Harmonie universelle* [1636–1637] on the theory of music, harmonics, and acoustics) and were compendiums of the knowledge in these areas.

Mersenne became involved in the publication of fundamental works of his friends or correspondents, such as Galileo Galilei's *Mechanics* (translated by Mersenne), the objections to Descartes's *Meditations* (gathered by Mersenne), Herbert of Cherbury's *De Veritate* (in a translation by Mersenne), Thomas Hobbes's *De Cive* (the publication of which was arranged by Mersenne), and François de La Mothe Le Vayer's *Discours sceptique sur la musique* (published in Mersenne's *Questions harmoniques*). He also carried on a monumental correspondence that provides a magnificent running record of the intellectual revolution of the time. Mersenne was actively interested in an enormous range of scientific and pseudoscientific questions, from the most complex ones in physics, mathematics, and Hebrew philology to such ones as "How high was Jacob's ladder?" and "Why do wise men earn less money than fools?"

His major philosophical contributions were his massive refutation of skepticism, *La vérité des sciences,* and his later discussions of the nature of scientific knowledge. *La vérité des sciences* is a dialogue between a skeptic, an alchemist, and a Christian philosopher (Mersenne). The skeptic uses his arguments to show that alchemy is not a true science. When he broadens his attack to encompass all claims to knowledge of the real nature of things, Mersenne's Christian philosopher offers his own resolution to the skeptical crisis, starting with a detailed examination of Sextus Empiricus's *Outlines of Pyrrhonism.* He repeatedly contends that although the Pyrrhonian arguments may show that one cannot know the real nature of things, one can gain knowledge of the apparent, phenomenal world in terms of how it seems to one and how the various appearances are related. Although one's sense experiences vary and although one cannot tell what objects are really like, one can find laws that enable one to connect and, thus, to predict experiences. Although one cannot find any absolutely certain first principles, one can discover enough indubitable ones to enable one to construct systematic information about one's experienced world. "This limited knowledge suffices to serve us as the guide for our actions." One is able to know something—namely, the sciences of phenomena—and this has adequate pragmatic value for one in this life. Francis Bacon was trying to find out too much and was raising too many insoluble skeptical problems with his Idols. Instead, the ultimate answer to skepticism was to show how much one could and did, in fact, know. The last 800 pages of the work is a listing of what is known in mathematics and mathematical physics—until the Pyrrhonist gives in. He has been conquered not by being refuted but by being shown what sort of knowledge one can have once one grants that knowledge about reality is unattainable.

"CONSTRUCTIVE OR MITIGATED SKEPTICISM"

Mersenne was willing to accept the skeptic's claims but was unwilling to see them establish that nothing can be known. Instead, he saw an epistemological skepticism as the prelude to a "constructive or mitigated skepticism" which would allow a scientific and systematic development of the truths of the sciences of the empirical world. The rest of Mersenne's life was devoted to his religious duty, exploring in phenomenalistic terms what could be known about the world God had made. Mersenne's immense contribution to the scientific revolution was the result of his positive views. Although he had originally portrayed skepticism as one of the greatest menaces to humankind, he continued to insist in his scientific tracts that one can gain no certain knowledge about reality but can study only the surfaces of things as they appear to one and employ mathematics as a hypothetical system about things. Like his close friend Pierre Gassendi (in whose arms he died), Mersenne saw scientific endeavors as a via media between complete skepticism and dogmatism. Mersenne tended to emphasize the antiskeptical aspect of this view, whereas Gassendi tended to emphasize the anti-dogmatic one.

In his formulations of the new science Mersenne was probably the first to use a mechanical model to account for the world that one experiences and to develop a thoroughgoing phenomenalism (although hardly as well worked out as Gassendi's) adequate to state the findings and assumptions of modern science. Mersenne's lifelong devotion to science and scientists can apparently be attributed to their common quest for more information and understanding of the phenomenal world. Hence, Mersenne could see in Descartes a major contributor to the scientific revolution but could see nothing important in his metaphysical revolution. Descartes, Hobbes, Herbert of Cherbury, Gassendi, Blaise Pascal, Galileo, and others were, for Mersenne, together in seeking the truth of the sciences, although some of them still had illusions

that more truth than that could be discovered. For Mersenne, science had no metaphysical foundations and needed none. "Until it pleases God to deliver us from this misery," one can find no ultimate knowledge, but one can, if one is not destructively skeptical, proceed to gain and use scientific knowledge.

See also Bacon, Francis; Descartes, René; Galileo Galilei; Gassendi, Pierre; Herbert of Cherbury; Hobbes, Thomas; La Mothe Le Vayer, François de; Pascal, Blaise; Scientific Revolutions; Sextus Empiricus; Skepticism, History of.

Bibliography

WORKS BY MERSENNE

Correspondance du P. Marin Mersenne. 17 vols., edited by Paul Tannery, Cornélis de Waard, and René Pintard. Paris: G. Beauchesne, 1933–1988.

L'impiété des déistes, athées et libertins de ce temps. Stuttgart, Germany: Frommann, 1975.

Questions inouyes, Questions harmoniques, Questions théologiques, Les méchaniques de Galilée, Les préludes de l'harmonie universelle. Paris: Fayard, 1985.

La vérité des sciences contre les sceptiques ou pyrrhoniens, edited and annotated by Dominique Descotes. Paris: Champion, 2003.

Traité de l'harmonie universelle, edited by Claudio Buccolini. Paris: Fayard, 2003.

WORKS ABOUT MERSENNE

Chappell, Vere. *Grotius to Gassendi.* New York: Garland, 1992.

Dear, Peter. *Mersenne and the Learning of the Schools.* Ithaca, NY: Cornell University Press, 1988.

Lenoble, Robert. *Mersenne, ou, La naissance du mécanisme.* Paris: J. Vrin, 1943.

Popkin, Richard H. *History of Scepticism: From Savonarola to Bayle.* Rev. ed. New York: Oxford University Press, 2003.

Sorell, Tom. *The Rise of Modern Philosophy: The Tension between the New and Traditional Philosophies from Machiavelli to Leibniz.* Oxford, U.K.: Clarendon Press, 1993.

Vickers, Brian. *Occult and Scientific Mentalities in the Renaissance.* New York: Cambridge University Press, 1984.

Richard Popkin (1967, 2005)

MESLIER, JEAN
(1664–1729)

Jean Meslier, perhaps the least restrained freethinker of the French Enlightenment, is also one of the most notorious examples of apostasy. As curé of the village of Etrépigny in Champagne from 1689 to his death, Meslier lived in complete obscurity, attending to his pastoral duties. But under the innocuous exterior of the humble

Catholic priest, there seethed a violent hatred and passionate disavowal of the religion that it was his ironic profession to serve. Having resolved sometime in the 1720s to compose his only work, the *Testament,* with the aim of keeping it secret until his death, he felt free to vent fully the anti-Christian, atheistic, revolutionary—indeed, anarchistic—sentiments that he had been obliged to suppress beneath a lifelong mask of prudent duplicity. The available biographical facts are unfortunately too meager to clarify this extraordinary personality. It is known, however, that on one occasion Meslier's abhorrence of injustice and persecution brought him into bitter conflict with the local nobility and, indirectly, almost into rebellion against the archbishop of Rheims, who, siding (as might be expected) with feudal privilege in the dispute, had castigated the morally outraged but powerless curate.

EDITIONS OF THE *TESTAMENT*

The three autograph originals of the *Testament* addressed by its author to posterity were succeeded, in eighteenth-century France, by a profusion of manuscript copies that circulated briskly in the philosophical underworld of forbidden literature. The prolixity and other stylistic shortcomings of the work resulted, however, in its being edited in the form of various abridgments that proved more suitable for dissemination. The most important of these summaries was, without question, the *Extrait des sentiments de Jean Meslier,* prepared by Voltaire and published in 1762. This first printed version of the apostate priest's opinions was often reprinted, especially under the rubric of Baron d'Holbach's *Le bon sens du curé Meslier*—a combination of one of his own atheistic tracts and of the *Extrait*—which saw many editions well into the nineteenth century. The integral text of the *Testament* was not published until 1864.

THOUGHT

Meslier's entire critique follows from the assumption that religion is basically a political means whereby those in power consolidate their control over the vastly greater number of weak and poor members of society. All religious dogmas, beliefs, and rituals, supposedly devised by the ruling class as instruments of government, are considered to be nothing but errors and superstitions serving to dupe and paralyze the victims of tyranny, holding them in ignorant fear and keeping them from any effective action to alleviate their misery by overthrowing their oppressors.

Meslier thought primarily in terms of economic exploitation, asserting that the opulence and power of the few are, thanks to the protection of civil and religious laws, acquired and maintained at the expense of the near destitution of the people. There is little doubt that, in adopting this general view, he was motivated by deep feelings of sympathy for the sufferings of the poor, with whom he came into daily contact. His condemnation of Christianity therefore had at its root the eminently Christian virtue of pity for the downtrodden and helpless, joined, however, to a fiercely un-Christian zeal to right secular wrongs.

Although Meslier condemned all religions, he attacked Christianity in particular. The bulk of the *Testament* is devoted to fastidious refutations of the many different types of argument by which the "truth" of Christian revelation was presumed demonstrable. Meslier examines and rejects, in turn, the validity of faith, the historicity of miracles, the authenticity of Scripture, the authority of tradition, the accuracy of biblical prophecies, the testimony of martyrdom, the morality of eternal rewards and punishments, and the meaningfulness of such dogmas as the Trinity, the Incarnation, and transubstantiation. The *Testament* is, indeed, a compendium of the historical, exegetical, textual, and logical objections concerning the essentials of the Christian creed discussed in the critical and apologetic literature from the time of Pierre Bayle through the early decades of the eighteenth century. Meslier was conversant with this literature, and although there is relatively little in his criticism that is entirely new with him, the forcefulness, breadth, and intransigence of his "case against Christianity," together with its politicoeconomic basis, give his work a unique character.

Moreover, Meslier did not stop at exposing the fallacies of Christian belief and the social abuses of institutional religion but boldly pursued his train of thought to the affirmation of a materialistic system in which all phenomena can be traced to a physical basis and are subject to the laws of mechanics. He advocated atheism as the only outlook consistent with the interests of the majority of humankind in its struggle against the lust for domination of the unscrupulous few. Among the sources of the *Testament,* special importance should be given to Michel Eyquem de Montaigne's skeptical treatment of time-honored social practices, to the philosophy of Benedict de Spinoza, and to the Epicurean-Cartesian vision of a mechanistic, naturalistic universe in which the supernatural—particularly the doctrines of divine creation and spiritual immortality—no longer found any place.

INFLUENCE

The impact of Meslier's ideas still has to be studied carefully. During the eighteenth century it was merely his negation of Christianity that proved appealing, and his socioeconomic protest, with its overtones of popular revolution, went largely unheeded. Contrary to the philosophes' estimate of Meslier as compatible with middle-class *bon sens,* some Marxists have been able to see in him an audacious spokesman for the economically repressed class of peasants and urban workers and the advocate of socialistic and egalitarian reform of society. But even if this was the true spirit of Meslier's thought, it did not play its intended role, for his influence was largely assimilated into the mainstream of Enlightenment ideology, with its predominantly bourgeois, liberal, and deistic polemic directed at Christianity. Seen in retrospect, the principal weakness of Meslier's anti-Christian *summa* is his oversimplification of the extreme psychological and cultural complexity of the religious phenomenon and its social applications. Moreover, his ardent wish forever to abolish injustice and wretchedness from the world by the expedient (in his own words) of "hanging and strangling with the bowels of the priests all the nobles and rulers of the earth" was no less utopian than fanatical. Nevertheless, Meslier's indignant and savage denunciation of religion was meaningful at the historical moment that inspired and shaped it, when the Roman Catholic Church of France, owing to its official status and immense riches, actually had a vested interest in the perpetuation of political and economic institutions related to the feudal oppression and exploitation of the people.

See also Bayle, Pierre; Cartesianism; Clandestine Philosophical Literature in France; Enlightenment; Epicureanism and the Epicurean School; Holbach, Paul-Henri Thiry, Baron d'; Montaigne, Michel Eyquem de; Religion and Politics; Spinoza, Benedict (Baruch) de.

Bibliography

Marchal, Jean. *L'étrange figure du curé Meslier.* Charleville, France, 1957.

Morehouse, Andrew. *Voltaire and Jean Meslier.* New Haven, CT: Yale University Press, 1936.

Petitfils, E. *Un socialiste-révolutionnaire au commencement du XVIIIe siècle, Jean Meslier.* Paris, 1908.

Porchnev, B. F. *Jean Meslier, et les sources populaires de ses idées.* Moscow, 1955.

Spink, J. S. *French Free-Thought from Gassendi to Voltaire.* London: University of London, Athlone Press, 1960.

Le testament de Jean Meslier. 3 vols, edited by Rudolf Charles. Amsterdam, 1864.

Wade, I. O. *The Clandestine Organization and Diffusion of Philosophical Ideas in France from 1700 to 1750.* Princeton, NJ: Princeton University Press, 1938.

Aram Vartanian (1967)

METAETHICS

Judgments to the effect that certain things (or certain classes of things) are good or bad, right or wrong, or just or unjust, are first-order ethical judgments. Metaethics addresses second-order questions about the meaning and status of moral judgments, for example, "What does it mean to say that something is good or bad, or right or wrong?", "Are moral judgments statements that purport to be true or false?", and "In what sense, if any, can moral judgments be true or false (or correct or incorrect)?" Metaethical questions have been discussed throughout the history of philosophy, but systematic work on metaethics began early in the twentieth century with the publication of G. E. Moore's *Principia Ethica* (1993).

The first half of this entry discusses theories about the meaning of moral judgments, specifically, Moore's theory, the Franz Brentano–A. C. Ewing (1899–1973) theory, emotivism, Richard Hare's prescriptivism, Philippa Foot's theory normative relativism, and Allan Gibbard's (1942–) expressivism. The second half addresses the question of whether moral judgments are objectively true or false; it explains and assesses (some of) the main arguments for and against the view that moral judgments are objectively true or false. Questions about the truth of moral judgments are distinct from questions about moral knowledge. If moral judgments are not true or correct, then there is no such thing as moral knowledge. Moral knowledge is possible only on the assumption that there is something *to know* (i.e., moral truths). However, the view that there are objective moral truths does not imply that we have knowledge of them; it is compatible with moral skepticism, the view that there are objective moral truths but we cannot know what they are.

I. THEORIES OF MEANING

Twentieth-century work on metaethics begins with questions about the meaning of moral judgments.

1. MOORE'S OPEN QUESTION ARGUMENT. In *Principia Ethica* Moore claims that the concepts of intrinsic goodness and badness are the most fundamental moral concepts. He says that the concepts of right and wrong can be defined in terms of "good" and "bad." Moore

writes: "To assert that a certain line of conduct is, at a given time, absolutely right or obligatory, is obviously to assert that more good or less evil will exist in the world, if it be adopted than if anything else be done instead" (Moore 1993, p. 77). Moore argues that goodness (the property denoted by the word "good") is indefinable. By this he means that the property of goodness cannot be analyzed into constituent properties or elements. Goodness is a simple, ultimate property like the property of being yellow as opposed to a complex property such as the property of being a horse. Being a horse is analyzable in terms of other constitutive properties such as having a head, a heart, four legs, four hooves, and so on. Moore defends the claim that goodness is a simple, unanalyzable property with his "open question argument." This argument can be summarized as follows: Consider any definition of good or goodness according to which goodness is identical with a complex property (P). It will always make sense to ask if P is good (it is an open question whether P is good since it is not self-contradictory to deny that P is good). However, it makes no sense to ask whether P is P (this is not an "open question"—it is self-contradictory to deny that P is P). Therefore, goodness cannot be identical with P.

Moore considers several specific definitions of good, which he subjects to the open question argument. He considers the view that good means pleasure, the view that good means what we desire, and the view that good means what we desire to desire. Clearly the question "Is pleasure good?" is not equivalent to the question "Is pleasure pleasant?" The statement "That which we desire to desire is good" is not equivalent to the statement "That which is good is good." Moore's open question test seems to work very nicely for these and many other definitions of good, but he gives no reason to think that *every possible definition of goodness* fails his open question test. Another serious problem with Moore's argument is that he assumes that goodness cannot be identical with a property P unless the statement that P is good is analytic or true by definition. It is analytic (true by definition) that pleasure is pleasant, but it is not analytic that pleasure is good. Many contemporary philosophers contend that this assumption has been refuted. According to Hilary Putnam (1975) and Saul Kripke (1972), certain natural properties are identical with each other even though statements to the effect that the properties are identical are not analytic (not true by definition). For example, water is H_2O (the property of being water is identical with the property of being H_2O) even though the statement that water is H_2O is not true by definition.

2. MOORE'S POSITIVE VIEWS. Moore is a *cognitivist* (i.e., he holds that moral judgments are statements that ascribe properties to things). By contrast, *noncognitivism* is the view that moral judgments are not statements that ascribe properties to things. Moore claims that goodness is a simple, unanalyzable property. Goodness is not a natural property like redness that can be perceived or apprehended through the five senses. Nonetheless, Moore claims that we can have direct intuitive knowledge of this property. This view is problematic. It is open to debate whether any such property exists. The quality of goodness that Moore posits is elusive; it is difficult to know what he is referring to. Many people, on careful introspection, report that they do not intuit any such property. Another serious problem for Moore's view is that it seems to be unable to account for the fact that moral judgments give or purport to give us reasons to act in certain ways as opposed to others. To say that something is intrinsically good implies that we have reasons to choose or prefer it. But it is unclear why this should be so if Moore's theory is true. It is not clear why we should care whether or not our actions produce or fail to produce instances of the nonnatural properties that Moore postulates and claims are identical to the properties of goodness and badness. (Even if they exist, it is not clear that these nonnatural properties are "reason providing" in the way that something must be in order to be the property of goodness or badness.)

Moore's open question argument is one of the most influential arguments in the history of philosophy. Noncognitivist ethical theories, such as emotivism and prescriptivism, arose in a context of philosophical debate in which it was widely assumed that: (a) Moore has shown that goodness is indefinable, and (b) Moore's own positive view is untenable—"good" does not refer to a simple nonnatural property that we directly intuit. Some philosophers concluded that moral terms do not refer to any properties at all and that moral judgments are not statements that ascribe properties to things.

3. BRENTANO AND EWING. Brentano (1969) and Ewing (1947) agree with Moore that moral terms refer to "nonnatural" properties, but they give a very different description of the nature of those properties. They hold that the most fundamental moral properties are nonnatural *relational* properties of "fittingness" or "appropriateness" that hold between objects/ properties and attitudes toward them. Ewing holds that the relation of fittingness is unanalyzable and that our apprehension of it is self-evident. In *The Definition of Good* he says: "Certain characteristics are such that the fitting response to whatever

possesses them is a proattitude, and that is all there is to it" (Ewing 1947, p. 172). According to Brentano, to be good is to be an appropriate (fitting) object of love, and to say that one thing is better than another is to say that it is correct to prefer it to the other. Ewing holds that to say that something is good means that it ought to be the object of a favorable attitude. This theory arguably avoids the second objection to Moore's theory noted above. According to Brentano and Ewing, it is part of the meaning of moral judgments (e.g., judgments to the effect that something is good or bad, or right or wrong) that they claim to give us reasons to have favorable or unfavorable attitudes about certain things and reasons to choose certain things over others.

4. EMOTIVISM. Emotivism is the view that moral judgments are *expressions* of attitudes rather than statements that ascribe properties to things. Favorable (unfavorable) moral judgments about something express favorable (unfavorable) attitudes about it. "Lincoln was a good man" means roughly "Yea Lincoln." So understood, emotivism denies the obvious phenomenon of moral disagreement. Suppose that you claim that Stalin was a good man and I claim that he was a bad man. If moral judgments were mere expressions of attitudes, then this could not constitute a disagreement. We might both agree that you like Stalin and I dislike him. Similarly, it is not a disagreement if you express your fondness for a particular flavor of ice cream and I express my distaste for that same flavor.

Alfred Ayer (1952) and Charles Stevenson (1944) defend more sophisticated versions of emotivism. According to Ayer, to make a moral judgment is to express an attitude with the intention of influencing the attitudes or actions of other people: "Lincoln is a good man" means roughly "Yea Lincoln, catch the wave." In cases of moral disagreement, each party is attempting to alter the attitudes of the other. Stevenson holds that moral disagreement involves a disagreement in attitudes (the parties to the disagreement have incompatible attitudes about something), and each party is attempting to change the attitudes of the other party about the thing in question. Stevenson says that "*X* is good" means roughly "I approve of *X*; do so as well."

These revised versions of emotivism still do not afford a satisfactory account of moral disagreement. In cases of moral disagreement, people not only disagree in their attitudes and try to cause others to *share their attitudes*, they assert that their own attitudes are correct or justified and that the attitudes of those who disagree with

them are mistaken. If two people disagree about whether or not Stalin was a good man, each claims that the other's attitudes about Stalin are mistaken or inappropriate.

Ayer on moral reasoning. Moral disputes often involve disagreements about factual questions. Ayer says that, to the extent that moral disagreements involve disagreements about "factual" questions, they can be rationally debated. For example, we can rationally debate whether the institution of capital punishment deters murder and whether it frequently results in the execution of innocent people. Sometimes, however, moral disagreements are based on differences in basic moral principles. Utilitarians believe that we should always do whatever will have the best consequences. Some people are unconditional pacifists. They believe that killing people is always wrong no matter what, even if killing saves many lives and produces much better consequences than not killing. Utilitarians and unconditional pacifists accept incompatible basic moral principles. According to Ayer, when people disagree about matters of basic principle, their disagreements cannot be rationally debated or rationally resolved. (Gibbard's *Wise Choices and Apt Feelings*, discussed below, is a recent development of emotivism.)

5. HARE'S PRESCRIPTIVISM. One of the notable features of this theory is that Hare offers a systematic reply to Ayer's claims about the limits of moral reasoning. Hare claims that moral judgments are prescriptions that are universalizable and overriding. Prescriptions are commands, or imperatives, for example: "Don't lie!" and "Shut the door!" Since commands are not statements that are true or false, prescriptivism is a noncognitivist theory. To say that moral judgments are universalizable means that if one makes a moral judgment about a particular case, then one must make the same judgment about any cases that are similar to it in all morally relevant respects. (If I say that it is morally permissible for me to lie to my customers in a certain situation, then I am committed to the view that it would be permissible for others to lie to me in relevantly similar situations.) To say that moral judgments are overriding means that a person who makes moral judgments takes the prescriptions expressed by them to override any conflicting nonmoral considerations, such as considerations of prudence, etiquette, and the law. According to Hare statements of the form: "It is morally wrong all things considered for you to do *X*, but, nevertheless, you would be justified in doing *X*," are self-contradictory. On Hare's view it is also inconsistent to say that it is morally wrong (all things considered) for you to do *X* but still command or advise you to do *X*.

In response to Ayer's claims about the limits of moral reasoning, Hare would say that sometimes we can argue against another person's moral judgments by showing that they are *inconsistent*. Hare claims that requirements of consistency severely constrain the kinds of moral judgments we can make. Suppose that a dishonest plumber claims that it is morally permissible (or even obligatory) for him to defraud his customers and bill them for unneeded repairs that cost them thousands of dollars. To be consistent, he must say that it would be morally permissible (obligatory) for others to defraud him and those he cares about in relevantly similar (hypothetical and/or actual) cases. Since moral judgments are prescriptive, he is committed to prescribing that others defraud him and those he loves in relevantly similar circumstances. Consistency also requires that he refrain from objecting if others defraud him and those he loves in such cases.

In *Freedom and Reason*, Hare considers the case of a Nazi who claims that it is his moral duty to kill Jews. To be consistent, the Nazi must hold that others should kill him if he is Jewish. Suppose that we show the Nazi that, unbeknownst to him, he and his wife are Jewish. To be consistent, the Nazi must say (and *mean*) "All right, send me and my family to an extermination camp." Since moral judgments are overriding, the Nazi cannot consistently make any commands or pleas to the contrary. Hare thinks that few people can be consistent Nazis. Hare allows that a Nazi could be consistent if he or she so hates Jews that he or she sincerely holds that, (in Hare's words): "'Jews are such an abomination that I and my whole family, if we were Jews, should be sent to the gas chamber'" (Hare 1963, p. 172). One can be a consistent Nazi if one is willing to have one's moral principles applied against one's own interests and the interests of those one loves.

Hare gives no reason to think that the Nazi's distinctive moral views are false or mistaken, just that it is difficult to be a consistent Nazi. This concession bodes ill for Hare's theory of moral reasoning since if it cannot establish the correctness of the view that the Nazi's actions are wrong, it is doubtful that it can establish the correctness of *any* ethical judgments. However, Hare is too quick to concede the limits of his arguments in this case. It may be possible to be a consistent Nazi provided that one has a very great hatred of Jews and desires their extermination more than the continuation of one's own life and the lives of one's loved ones. The obvious question to ask here is whether such hatred is rational, and it seems that it is not. Such hatred depends on numerous false beliefs about the characteristics of Jews and their responsibility for the ills of the world. A Nazi could be consistent provided that she

is willing to have her principles applied against herself and her loved ones, but a Nazi could not be *both* consistent and adequately informed about matters relevant to her moral convictions. (See Hare's *Moral Thinking* [1981] for a later development of his views.)

As Hare himself notes, his consistency arguments apply only to people who make moral judgments. They do not apply to amoralists who refrain from making moral judgments. Hare's consistency arguments cannot show why we should not be amoral. Even more worrisome for Hare's purposes is that people who employ alternative normative concepts are able to endorse horrendous acts such as the extermination of the Jewish people. Suppose that a Nazi rejects the concepts of morally right and wrong actions in favor of a "Code of Honor" according to which it is "honorable" to kill Jews. Hare's theory does not give us any basis for criticizing such views.

This last possibility raises an important and somewhat neglected set of issues. There are many different alternative normative concepts (e.g., concepts of moral obligation and right and wrong, concepts of virtue, and concepts of honor). People are free to employ any of these concepts and order their lives in accordance with them; people are also free to reject any of these concepts. Philosophers who write about metaethics need to say much more about the *choices* we make in accepting and rejecting various normative concepts. They also need to say much more about the question of how, if it all, we can justify the choices we make in accepting/wielding certain concepts rather than others. (See Friedrich Nietzsche [1967, 1988], Hare [1981], Simon Blackburn [1993], John Mackie [1977], and Bernard Williams [1985] for discussions that shed light on these issues; also see the discussions of Foot, Gibbard, and "Incommensurability" below.)

6. FOOT AND THICK MORAL CONCEPTS. Both emotivism and prescriptivism imply that the concepts of good and bad and right and wrong have no fixed descriptive meaning. One can consistently apply these terms to any things (or any actions). For example, it is perfectly consistent to say that it is morally obligatory to clasp and unclasp one's hands every half hour or to say that bringing it about that the number of hairs on one's head is an even number is a great intrinsic good. These are sincere coherent ethical judgments provided that the person who makes them has the attitudes they express or is willing to consistently universalize the prescriptions that they express. Foot (1978) argues that this is a serious mistake

because there are limits to the things to which "good" and other moral terms can be consistently applied. She thinks that emotivism and prescriptivism make a mistake that is comparable to the sort of mistake one would make if one said that being proud of something consists simply in having a certain sort of attitude about it and that, in principle, *anything* could be the object of one's pride.

Pride is not just a feeling, a welling up in one's chest that one can have about anything. The object of one's pride must be: (a) one's own somehow, and (b) an achievement or something that one takes to be good. Even if I puff up my chest and feel it welling up as I look at the sky, it is not correct to say that I am (feeling) proud of the sky unless there is some background belief that explains why I think that it is somehow *mine*. Foot claims that something can be called a "good action" only if it satisfies one of the following conditions: (a) It is the fulfillment of a special duty derived from a role or promise or (b) it exemplifies a virtue. It follows that we cannot say that twiddling one's thumbs four times each day, for instance, is a morally good action in the absence of special reasons for thinking that it fulfills a duty or exemplifies a virtue.

Foot's own analysis of the meaning of moral judgments is a combination of noncognitivism and (naturalistic) cognitivism. She claims that moral judgments have both evaluative meaning (they express attitudes and guide actions) and descriptive meaning. Moral concepts that have both kinds of meaning are called "thick" concepts. Emotivism and prescriptivism claim that the concepts of right and wrong and good and bad are "thin" concepts. Thin normative concepts have no fixed descriptive meaning, only evaluative meaning.

Foot's theory aptly describes the meaning of the terms we use to refer to moral virtues and vices. Terms such as "generous," "cowardly," and "honest" are thick concepts—they have both evaluative and descriptive meaning. The words "generous" and "honest" commend or express favorable attitudes about the things to which they are applied. There are clear descriptive criteria for using such terms. It is a misuse of language to apply them to things that do not satisfy those criteria. It would be a misuse of the word "generous" to apply it to someone who never gives any tangible goods or time or effort to other people even though that person has a great deal of money and leisure time and many opportunities to help others in need. Foot's theory helps us to frame some important questions: "In ordinary language, are the terms 'good' and 'bad' and 'right' and 'wrong' thick or thin concepts?" "If these concepts are thin concepts, should we

dispense with them in favor of thick concepts?" Foot seems to think that the concepts of good and bad and right and wrong are thick concepts. By contrast, some proponents of "virtue ethics," including Williams (1985), think that the concepts of good and bad and right and wrong are thin concepts. However, they think that these thin concepts should be dropped or greatly downplayed in favor of the thick concepts that refer to virtues and vices.

Thick concepts mandate particular evaluations of certain kinds of things. Many thick concepts encapsulate objectionable evaluations (e.g., ethnic slurs). The word "n___" only applies to people of African origin; it cannot be correctly applied to Chinese or Europeans. The word "n___" also expresses contempt for Africans. Those who do not think that Africans, qua Africans, are worthy of contempt do not use the word "n___" (or do not use the word nonironically). (Similar comments apply to all other "ethnic slur terms.") Honor is another example of a thick concept that many people have reasonably chosen to abandon because they reject the evaluations implicit in its use. Given certain concepts of honor, it is dishonorable for me to not to challenge you to a duel to the death if you insult me or show me disrespect. Given other concepts of honor, it is dishonorable for me not to kill my sister if she is raped. These examples make it clear that, for any thick concept that we employ, we should be open to criticisms of the evaluations implicit in that concept and consider the possibility that they are mistaken and cease employing the concept. Thus, it is at least arguable that we need higher-level thin concepts in terms of which to assess the evaluations implicit in the thick concepts we use and encounter.

7. NORMATIVE RELATIVISM. This theory is defended by many anthropologists, including Ruth Benedict (1887–1948) and William Sumner (in Moser and Carson 2001). They claim that "*X* is morally right" means roughly "*X* is approved of by my society." This view is open to very serious objections. It implies that statements such as "Slavery is morally wrong, even though my society approves of slavery" are self-contradictory. But such statements are not self-contradictory. A person can criticize or dissent from the moral standards of her own society without contradicting herself. Normative relativism also implies that many ostensible moral disagreements between members of different societies are not genuine disagreements. Suppose that I am a member of a society that approves of the institution of slavery and you are a member of a society that disapproves of slavery. I claim that slavery is just and morally permissible. You object

and claim that slavery is unjust and impermissible. Surely this is a moral disagreement; what I say contradicts what you say. But, according to normative relativism, there is no disagreement in this case. My statement is perfectly consistent with your statement, and both statements are *true*—it is true that my society approves of slavery and true that your society disapproves of slavery.

8. GIBBARD'S EXPRESSIVISM. This theory is a recent development of emotivism that incorporates elements of the Brentano–Ewing theory. Gibbard (1990) analyzes moral judgments as claims about the rationality (or aptness) of feelings of guilt and anger. What a person does is *morally wrong* if and only if it is rational for him to feel guilty for having done it and for others to be angry at him for having done it. He defends an expressivist/emotivist analysis of rationality. According to Gibbard, to say that something (an act, belief, or feeling) is rational is to express one's acceptance of norms that permit it. Unlike Moore, Hare, and Foot, Gibbard does not claim to be offering an analysis of the ("ordinary language") meaning of moral terms. Rather, he describes his theory as a *proposal* about how to use normative concepts. Evidently, not every society has a normative system that includes norms for guilt and anger. Thus, on Gibbard's narrow construal of "morality," not every society has a moral code. Gibbard raises important questions about our choices between alternative normative concepts. Among other things, he asks about the value of morality (narrowly construed): Would we be better off with a normative code in which norms for guilt and anger didn't play a central role? Gibbard offers an answer to Nietzschean criticisms about the value of morality. He says that moral norms help coordinate guilt and anger. Guilt assuages anger and thereby helps promote peace between human beings. Normative codes that do not include norms for guilt will not be able to assuage anger and promote reconciliation between human beings as well as *moral* codes.

II. MORAL TRUTH, MORAL REALITY

We now turn to questions about moral truth and moral reality. In what sense, if any, can moral judgments be true or false or correct or incorrect? Are moral judgments objectively true or false in the way that we take ordinary "factual" statements to be? Is there a moral reality or something else in virtue of which moral judgments are true or false (or correct or incorrect)? We cannot answer these questions simply by appealing to theories of meaning. When we ask whether moral judgments are true or false, we are not simply asking about what we mean or *claim* when we make moral judgments. We are asking whether there is anything that backs up our moral judgments and makes them true or correct.

COGNITIVISM, NONCOGNITIVISM, AND THE TRUTH OF MORAL JUDGMENTS. Cognitivists hold that moral judgments are statements that *purport* to be true. This is compatible with the view that there are no moral facts (no moral reality) that back up our moral judgments and make (some of) them true or correct. Mackie (1977) holds such a view, which he calls an "error theory" of morality. Mackie is a cognitivist who claims that moral judgments are statements that assert or presuppose the existence of objective values. However, he claims that since objective values do not exist, *all moral judgments are false.*

Noncognitivists hold that moral judgments are not statements that purport to be true or false. Strictly speaking, noncognitivists cannot say that moral judgments are true or false. However, they can still say that moral judgments possess something that closely resembles truth or falsity. Emotivists can say that moral judgments are reasonable or unreasonable depending on whether the emotions or attitudes they express are reasonable or unreasonable. (At the very least attitudes and emotions can be unreasonable if they are based on false beliefs.) Prescriptivists can also make sense of something resembling the idea of moral truth. In *Moral Thinking*, Hare claims that there are certain moral judgments that an informed, consistent person must endorse, provided that he or she makes any moral judgments at all. These are judgments that we can reject only by opting out of moral discourse altogether.

MORAL OBJECTIVISM. Our ordinary notion of truth is a notion of *objective truth*. If something is true, then it is *true for everyone* (and true for everyone, everywhere, at all times). (Thus, it is misleading to use the word "truth" as many relativists do when they claim that the truth of moral judgments is "relative to" different people so that a moral judgment that is "true for" one person may not be "true for" another.) Let us use the term "objectivism" to refer to the view that moral judgments are objectively true or false (or objectively correct or incorrect in some sense that closely resembles truth or falsity). We should distinguish between the view that there is an objectively correct answer to *every* moral question and the view that there are objectively correct answers to *some*, but not all, moral questions. Call the former view "unqualified objectivism" and the latter view "qualified objectivism." Call the view that there are no objectively correct answers to any moral questions "unqualified nonobjectivism."

Unqualified objectivism implies that for any moral question, for example: "Was it right for Ms. Jones to have an abortion in April 1999?" there is an objectively correct answer and that anyone who gives a conflicting answer is mistaken. Qualified objectivism holds that there are some moral questions about which there are objectively correct answers and other moral questions about which there are no objectively correct answers. Unqualified nonobjectivism implies that, for any moral question, there is no objectively correct answer to that question.

MORAL REALISM. Statements such as "the earth is less than 100,000,000 miles from the sun" are true in virtue of facts that hold independently of what we believe or desire. *Moral realism* is the view that there are moral facts in virtue of which moral judgments are objectively true or false and that these facts are logically independent of the beliefs, attitudes, emotions, or preferences of rational beings and independent of the beliefs, attitudes, emotions, or preferences that rational beings would have in hypothetical situations (e.g., the moral beliefs that someone would have if she or he were fully informed about relevant facts). Moral nonrealism is the view that there are no independent moral facts. The truth of moral realism would guarantee the truth of moral objectivism, but one can be a moral objectivist without being a moral realist. Immanuel Kant, Roderick Firth (1917–1987), and Michael Smith (1954–) (see below) are moral objectivists but not moral realists. Hare's *Moral Thinking* also defends nonrealist moral objectivism.

IIA. ARGUMENTS AGAINST MORAL OBJECTIVISM

We now turn to arguments against moral objectivism.

1. DISAGREEMENT. Moral disagreement is widespread among ostensibly sane and rational people. Consider the following argument:

(1) There is disagreement among rational people about the answers to all (some) moral questions.

(2) If there is disagreement among rational people about the answer to a question, then there is no objectively correct or objectively true answer to that question.

Therefore, unqualified (qualified) nonobjectivism is true. (There are no moral questions [there are only some moral questions] for which there is an objectively correct answer.)

The cogency of this argument depends on the account of moral truth or correctness that the objectivist gives. If moral realism is true, then there are moral facts in virtue of which moral judgments are objectively true that are independent of what we believe. So, if moral realism is true, then moral objectivism is true, and the phenomenon of moral disagreement among rational people is not a serious objection to moral objectivism. Similarly, disagreement between reasonable people does not constitute any kind of objection to the view that ordinary historical judgments are objectively true or false. Consider the question: "Did Lee Oswald fire any of the shots that killed President Kennedy?" Rational people disagree about the answer to this question, and, at the present time, it may be impossible to know for certain what the answer is. In spite of the disagreement, there is an objective fact of the matter—either Oswald fired some of the fatal shots or else he did not. However, the phenomenon of ethical disagreement among ostensibly rational and well-informed people constitutes a serious argument against attempts to defend moral objectivism by appeal to theories of rationality because such theories claim that objective moral truths are constituted by the *agreement* of rational people. One standard rejoinder to the objection about disagreement is the claim that "*ideally* rational" or "*fully* rational" people would not have moral disagreements. (See the discussion of the ideal observer theory below.)

Digression: Disagreement vs. incommensurabilit. Moral disagreement should not be confused with moral incommensurability. Two people can disagree about whether an act is right or wrong only if they share the concepts of right and wrong action. Often, the differences between the moral views of different societies constitute cases of incommensurability rather than disagreement. Many philosophers and cultural anthropologists (including Nietzsche and Gertrude Anscombe) claim that the concept of moral obligation is unique to Judaism, Christianity, Islam, and the civilizations that developed from those religions. If this is true, then it is doubtful that Genghis Khan (c. 1167–1227) and his warriors possessed our concept of a moral obligation and morally right and wrong actions. I condemn the Mongol destruction of Iraq in the thirteenth century as a morally wrong action. Many or most of the Mongols who took part in this did so in good conscience, but it would probably be incorrect to say that they thought that what they did was morally right (they could not have this belief unless they employed the concepts of right and wrong actions). Even though we do not disagree about the *moral rightness* of this action, there is surely some kind of disagreement here. My moral judgments and the attitudes they endorse are contrary to many of Genghis Khan's attitudes; Genghis Khan clearly approves of (and thinks it correct to approve of) actions that I disapprove of and condemn as morally wrong.

2. THE APPEAL TO TOLERANCE.

This argument goes roughly as follows: "We should be respectful and tolerant of other people's moral views; however, moral objectivism implies that many people's views are mistaken and thus not worthy of respect or toleration." This argument is widely accepted and motivates many people to reject moral objectivism, but, on examination, it is a very weak argument that few philosophers take seriously. First, endorsing moral objectivism does not commit one to being intolerant of the moral views of others. If I am an unqualified objectivist, then I think that there are objectively correct answers to every moral question. However, my being an objectivist does not entail that I claim to know what those answers are. Nor does my being an objectivist entail that I think that the views of others who disagree with me are worthy of disrespect or suppression. An objectivist can claim that objectively true moral principles require tolerance and respect for the views of others. Second, nonobjectivism does not imply that we should be tolerant. Nonobjectivists can endorse first-order moral principles that permit or require them to be intolerant of the views of others. All that follows from nonobjectivism is that one's moral judgments, *whatever they happen to be*, are not objectively true or false or objectively correct or incorrect.

3. MORAL EXPLANATIONS AND MORAL FACTS.

Gilbert Harman argues that it is unnecessary to posit the existence of moral facts in order to explain phenomena. Thus, moral facts are superfluous entities—there is no reason to suppose that they exist.

> [O]bservation plays a role in science that it does not play in ethics. The difference is that you need to make assumptions about certain physical facts to explain the occurrence of the observations that support a scientific theory, but you do not seem to need to make assumptions about any moral facts to explain the occurrence of the so-called moral observations I have been talking about. In the moral case, it would seem that you need only make assumptions about the psychology or moral sensibility of the person making the moral observation. In the scientific case, theory is tested against the world.
>
> (HARMAN 1977, P. 6)

Among the phenomena that moral facts might explain are the moral judgments we make and the moral sentiments we feel (e.g., feelings of guilt and indignation). According to Harman, these phenomena are fully explained by our psychology and the fact that we accept certain moral principles; we do not need to assume the existence of moral facts or assume that those principles are true. Harman gives the following example: Someone tortures an animal. You believe that this action is wrong and you feel moral indignation. Harman says that we do not need to postulate moral facts in order to explain *your* belief and *your* indignation. They are explained by the fact that you were taught certain moral principles and have a certain psychological make up. Your *accepting* the moral principles in question is necessary to explain your beliefs and your indignation, but *we* do not need to assume that your moral principles are *true*. By contrast, in science, we can justify the postulation of entities by their ability to explain our observations of the world. The postulation of atoms helps to explain such things as Geiger counters and nuclear bombs. (Nicholas Sturgeon offers an influential reply to this argument. See below.)

IIB. ARGUMENTS IN FAVOR OF MORAL OBJECTIVISM

Most contemporary philosophers who defend moral objectivism do so on one of the following three grounds:

1. THE APPEAL TO MORAL REALISM.

As explained earlier, the truth of moral realism would guarantee the truth of moral objectivism. Some versions of moral realism claim that moral properties are "nonnatural" properties. Such theories are widely criticized on the grounds that the entities that they postulate do not exist or that those entities cannot plausibly be identified with moral properties (see above). In light of these criticisms of nonnaturalist versions of moral realism, recent attempts to defend naturalistic versions of realism are particularly noteworthy.

Sturgeon's naturalistic realism. Sturgeon claims that moral facts are constituted by natural facts. Sturgeon holds that moral properties are identical with natural properties, but he does not take statements asserting the identity of moral properties and natural properties to be analytic. He claims that his view is invulnerable to Moore's open question argument. Sturgeon also attempts to answer Harman's argument about explanation. He defends his theory on the grounds that moral facts help explain certain phenomena. Sturgeon offers the following example: Hitler's moral depravity helps explain why he started World War II and ordered the Holocaust. If Hitler had not been morally depraved, he would not have started World War II, and he would not have ordered the Holocaust.

Harman's thesis implies that the supposed moral fact of Hitler's being morally depraved is irrelevant to the explanation of Hitler's doing what he did. To assess this claim, we need to conceive a situation in which Hitler was *not* morally depraved and consider the question whether in that situation he would still have done what he did. My answer is that he would not, and this answer relies on a (not very controversial) moral view: that in any world at all like the actual one, only a morally depraved person could have initiated a world war, ordered "the final solution," and done any number of other things Hitler did. That is why I believe that if Hitler had not been morally depraved, he would not have done those things and hence that the fact of his moral depravity is relevant to an explanation of what he did (Sturgeon "Moral Explanations," in Sayre-McCord 1988, p. 249). Sturgeon's arguments have generated a very lively debate. (Criticisms by Terrance Horgan and Mark Timmons (1951–) are particularly noteworthy.)

2. THEORIES OF RATIONALITY. Many nonrealists claim that there are objective moral facts that are constituted by facts about what it is rational for people to believe or desire or "will." Kant, Hare, and Christine Korsgaard defend such views. Kant holds that moral truths (truths about what is right and wrong) are truths about what we can rationally and consistently will. For Kant moral truths are truths of reason.

The ideal observer theory (IOT) uses the idea of an ideally rational moral judge or ideal observer as a standard for the truth of moral judgments. According to Firth's version of the IOT, a favorable moral judgment about X ("X is good/right") is (objectively) true provided that all ideal observers would feel approval for X. An unfavorable moral judgment about X ("X is bad/wrong") is (objectively) true provided that all ideal observers would feel disapproval for X (Hospers and Sellars, pp. 200–221). In *Ethical Theory*, Richard Brandt (1959) defends a different version of the IOT. Brandt says that a moral judgment X is objectively true provided that all ideal observers would accept or believe X. (David Hume and Adam Smith also defend versions of the IOT.) Firth ascribes the following characteristics to an ideal observer:

(1) Omniscience or knowledge of all nonmoral facts;

(2) omnipercipience, or the ability to imagine vividly any events or states of affairs, including the experiences of others;

(3) disinterestedness, that is, not having any interests or desires that involve essential reference to particular persons or things;

(4) dispassionateness, that is, not having any emotions that are directed upon objects because they are believed to have essentially particular features;

(5) consistency;

(6) normality "in other respects."

Firth thinks that all ideal observers would feel approval and disapproval for the same things. Given this, and given his version of the IOT, unqualified moral objectivism is true. Brandt thinks that ideal observers would agree about the answers to some, but not all, moral questions. He thinks that the IOT commits us to qualified objectivism. If both Firth and Brandt are mistaken and ideally rational moral judges could disagree in their attitudes or judgments about *every moral question*, then the IOT commits us to unqualified nonobjectivism.

Ideal observers are characterized as "informed" or "fully informed." Brandt says that ideal observers must possess all information "relevant to" the issues they judge. Firth notes difficulties in determining which facts are and are not relevant to answering a given moral question. He contends that there is no way to determine which facts are and are not relevant to a given moral question without presupposing answers to controversial moral questions that the IOT is supposed to provide rather than presuppose. Because of this he feels compelled to say that an ideal observer is *omniscient* with respect to all nonmoral facts. There is an unintended irony in Firth's characterization of an ideal observer as a *human being* who is omniscient "but otherwise normal." Humans are very far from being omniscient. It is not clear that it makes sense to talk about how you or I would react if we were omniscient. An omniscient being would have to be God or some kind of deity. If we press this point, then the IOT starts to look a lot like a divine will theory of morality.

Michael Smith's *The Moral Problem* (1994) defends a theory that closely resembles the IOT. With qualifications, Smith holds that to say that an action is morally right means that we have normative reason to do it. What a person has normative reason to do is what he or she *would desire to do* if fully rational (being fully rational includes having no false beliefs and having all relevant true beliefs). Smith stresses that what I have normative reason to do (in my actual circumstances) depends on what my fully rational self would want (or advise) my actual self to do. (Smith's theory is sometimes called an "ideal advisor theory.") Smith thinks that his theory implies that there are (objective) moral facts. On his account, the judgment "it is right for *S* to do *X*" is objectively true provided that we would *all desire* that *S* do *X* if we were fully rational. Smith thinks that an *ideally rational* process of reflection and debate between people who initially disagree in their desires about what people should do is likely to yield (complete) agreement.

According to Smith, thick moral concepts such as "honesty" and "treachery" reveal considerable agreement about what is right and wrong. The common use of such concepts reveals that nearly everyone agrees that acts of treachery are wrong (other things equal) and that acts of honesty are right (other things equal). Smith also argues that much seemingly intractable moral disagreement has its origins in (unreasonable) appeals to religious authority. (Others take a very different view about the relevance of religion to these issues; see below.) Smith says that the case for moral objectivism ultimately depends on the outcome of (first-order) debates in normative ethics. In order to determine "whether or not there *really are* moral facts," we must "engage in normative ethical debate and … see where the arguments that we give ultimately lead us" (Smith 1994, p. 202). "The real question is whether we will, by engaging in such debate, come up with answers to moral questions that secure the free agreement of those who participate" (Smith 1994, p. 201).

3. THE APPEAL TO GOD'S WILL. Some hold that God's will constitutes the objective standard for the truth of moral judgments. The view that God created human beings for certain purposes is one way of making sense of the widely held view that ethical theories should be based on theories of human nature or the "telos" of human life. The most well-known theory that attempts to base (objective) morality on God's will is the divine command theory. The traditional divine command theory (TDCT) holds that God's commands constitute the ultimate standard of right and wrong. What makes an act morally obligatory is that God commands it; what makes an act morally permissible is that God permits it; what makes an act is morally wrong is that God forbids it.

There are a several standard objections to the TDCT. These objections are widely regarded as fatal or decisive. (1) The TDCT implies that nothing anyone does can be morally obligatory or morally wrong unless God exists and commands and forbids us to do certain things. How-ever, certain actions would be right or wrong even if God did not exist. (2) The TDCT implies that *any act* would be right if God commanded us to do it. But certain acts (e.g., acts of cruelty or murder) would be wrong even if God commanded us to perform them. (3) The TDCT implies that what is wrong/obligatory is wrong/obligatory *because* God forbids/commands it. The TDCT does not allow us to say that *God forbids murder because murder is wrong*. Rather, the TDCT implies that *murder is wrong because God forbids it*. Thus, the TDCT implies that God has no reason to command one thing rather than another, and God's arbitrary commands cannot be the basis for genuine moral obligations.

These may be fatal objections to the TDCT. However, it does not follow that all theories that attempt to make God's will the basis for an objective morality are subject to fatal objections. Robert Adams (1937–) has formulated a modified version of the TDCT that avoids all of the objections to the TDCT. Adams's modified TDCT can be stated roughly as follows:

> If there is a loving God then: (1) an action is obligatory if, and only if, a loving God commands it; (2) an action is morally permissible if, and only if, a loving God permits it; and (3) an action is morally wrong if, and only if, a loving God forbids it. If there does not exist a loving God, then the rightness or wrongness of actions is determined in some other way.

Adams (1987) holds that if there is a loving God, then right and wrong are determined by God's commands; if there does not exist a loving God, then right and wrong are determined in some other way. Thus, Adams's theory avoids the first objection. Adams's modified TDCT also avoids the second objection. It does not imply that we would be morally obligated to obey God's commands if God commanded cruelty. If God commanded cruelty for its own sake, he would thereby show himself to be unloving. Adams's theory does not imply that we would be obligated to follow the commands of a cruel or unloving God. Adams cannot say that God commands what he commands *because* it is morally right (independently of being commanded by God). But Adams is *not* committed to the view that God's commands are arbitrary or that God has no reason to command one thing rather than another. Adams can say that God commands what he commands because of his loving nature and because he is omniscient. (See Linda Zagzebski's *Divine Motivation Theory* [2004] for a very different sort of religiously based moral theory.)

Suppose that there exists an omniscient loving God who created human beings for certain purposes. Suppose *also* that moral realism is false and there are no independent moral facts to which God's will must conform on pain of error. Given all of this, it is plausible to regard God's will and purposes as objective standards of morality; God's standpoint for assessing things is arguably more authoritative than that of a maximally rational human being. If moral realism is false and God does not exist, then the most promising basis for defending moral objectivism is by appeal to a theory of rationality.

See also Anscombe, Gertrude Elizabeth Margaret; Ayer, Alfred Jules; Brandt, R. B.; Brentano, Franz; Constructivism, Moral; Emotive Theory of Ethics; Error Theory of Ethics; Ethical Naturalism; Ethical Relativism; Ethics; Ethics, History of; Foot, Philippa; Hare, Richard M.; Harman, Gilbert; Hume, David; Ideal Observer Theories of Ethics; Internalism and Externalism in Ethics; Intuitionism, Ethical; Kant, Immanuel; Kripke, Saul; Mackie, John Leslie; Moore, George Edward; Moral Realism; Moral Skepticism; Nietzsche, Friedrich; Noncognitivism; Objectivity in Ethics; Projectivism; Putnam, Hilary; Rationalism in Ethics (Practical Reason Approaches); Smith, Adam; Stevenson, Charles L.; Sumner, William Graham; Williams, Bernard.

Bibliography

Adams, Robert. *The Virtue of Faith*. Oxford: Oxford University Press, 1987.

Ayer, A. J. *Language, Truth, and Logic*. 2nd ed. New York: Dover, 1952.

Blackburn, Simon. *Essays in Quasi-Realism*. Oxford: Oxford University Press, 1993.

Brandt, Richard. *Ethical Theory*. Englewood Cliffs, N.J.: Prentice-Hall, 1959.

Brandt, Richard. *A Theory of the Good and the Right*. Oxford: Oxford University Press, 1979.

Brentano, Franz. *The Origin of Our Knowledge of Right and Wrong*, edited by Roderick Chisholm. Translated by Roderick Chisholm and Elizabeth Schneewind. New York: Humanities Press, 1969.

Ewing, A. C. *The Definition of Good*. New York: Macmillan, 1947.

Foot, Philippa. *Virtues and Vices*. Berkeley: University of California Press, 1978.

Gibbard, Allan. *Wise Choices, Apt Feelings*. Cambridge, MA.: Harvard University Press, 1990.

Hare, R. M. *Freedom and Reason*. Oxford: Oxford University Press, 1963.

Hare, R. M. *The Language of Morals*. Oxford: Oxford University Press, 1952.

Hare, R. M. *Moral Thinking*. Oxford: Oxford University Press, 1981.

Harman, Gilbert. *The Nature of Morality*. Oxford: Oxford University Press, 1977.

Horgan, Terrance, and Mark Timmons. "Troubles on Twin Moral Earth: Moral Queerness Revived." *Synthese* 92 (1992): 221–260.

Hurka, Thomas. *Perfectionism*. Oxford: Oxford University Press, 1993.

Korsgaard, Christine, with G. A. Cohen, et al. *The Sources of Normativity*, edited by Onora O'Neill. Cambridge, U.K.: Cambridge University Press, 1996.

Kripke, Saul. *Naming and Necessity*. Cambridge, MA: Harvard University Press, 1972.

Mackie, J. L. *Ethics: Inventing Right and Wrong*. Middlesex, U.K.: Penguin, 1977.

Moore, G. E. *Principia Ethica*. 2nd ed. Cambridge, U.K.: Cambridge University Press, 1993.

Nietzsche, Friedrich. *On the Genealogy of Morals*. In *On the Genealogy of Morals and Ecce Homo*, translated by Walter Kaufmann. New York: Vintage Books, 1967.

Nietzsche, Friedrich. *The Twilight of the Idols and the Anti-Christ*. Translated by R. J. Hollingdale. Middlesex, U.K.: Penguin, 1968.

Putnam, Hilary. "The Meaning of 'Meaning.'" In *Mind, Language, and Reality: Philosophical Papers*. Vol II. Cambridge, U.K.: Cambridge University, Press 1975.

Ross, W. D. *The Foundations of Ethics*. Oxford: Clarendon Press, 1939.

Ross, W. D. *The Right and the Good*. Oxford: Clarendon Press, 1930.

Sidgwick, Henry. *The Methods of Ethics*. 7th ed. New York: Dover, 1966.

Smith, Michael, *The Moral Problem*. Oxford: Blackwell's, 1994.

Stevenson, Charles L. *Ethics and Language*. New Haven, CT: Yale University Press, 1944.

Warnock, G. J. *The Object of Morality*. London: Methuen, 1971.

Williams, Bernard. *Ethics and the Limits of Philosophy*. Cambridge, MA: 1985.

Zagzebski, Linda. *Divine Motivation Theory*. Cambridge, U.K.: Cambridge University Press, 2004.

ANTHOLOGIES

All of the following anthologies contain extensive bibliographies:

Darwall, Stephen, Allan Gibbard, and Peter Railton, eds. *Moral Discourse and Practice*. Oxford: Oxford University Press, 1997.

Hospers, John, and Wilfrid Sellars, eds. *Readings in Ethical Theory*. 2nd ed. Englewood Cliffs: Prentice-Hall, 1970.

Moser, Paul K., and Thomas Carson, eds. *Moral Relativism: A Reader*. Oxford: Oxford University Press, 2001.

Sayre-McCord, Geoffrey, ed. *Essays on Moral Realism*. Ithaca, NY: Cornell University Press, 1988.

Thomas L. Carson (2005)

METAMATHEMATICS

See *Mathematics, Foundations of*

METAPHOR

"Metaphors" have an emotive force and aesthetic dimension that have long been recognized. What has made metaphor so compelling to contemporary philosophers, however, has been its importance to cognition. Aesthetics and philosophy of religion are no longer the sole province of the study of metaphor. Instead, most of the research is located in philosophy of language, philosophy of science, and cognitive science. The ubiquity of metaphor and its contribution to all forms of discourse, the apparent anomaly of metaphor in light of standard accounts of language, and the increased interest by philosophers in providing theories for natural (rather than formal or artificial) languages have made an account of metaphor an important criterion of adequacy for theories of language. The limits of literality have similarly been felt in accounts of science and cognition. Max Black's (1962) seminal work connecting the use of scientific models to metaphors opened an area of inquiry now pursued by psychologists and cognitive scientists as well as philosophers of science. Some philosophers join questions of the role of metaphor in science to debates concerning scientific realism (Boyd, 1979; Hesse, 1970). The work emanating from theories of language and theories of science and cognition converge in concerns about meaning change, computer modeling of discovery processes, linguistic competencies, creativity, and religious discourse (Soskice, 1985).

While many questions remain, a few issues have been settled. The view of metaphor as an isolated word or phrase that is an occasional, unsystematic, and deviant phenomenon in language valued for its rhetorical force but disdained for its ability to mislead or be used in place of proper argument has been challenged. Metaphors have come to be understood as syntactically complex (Black, 1962; Tirrell, 1991) attributions that may or may not be grammatically deviant (Stern, 1985). In the tradition of I. A. Richards (1936) and Black, metaphors are generally taken to implicate entire conceptual domains or semantic fields (Kittay, 1987) through which a metaphor is interpreted, extended, and even systematically integrated into the language (Lakoff and Johnson, 1980). They either exploit some similarity between the metaphorically used term (the vehicle or source) and the concept spoken of (the topic or target) or create or intimate a similarity. While the similarity appealed to in earlier discussions pertained to intrinsic properties or properties associated with vehicle and topic, similarity has increasingly come to mean a relational or structural similarity—akin to models and analogies—between the contexts or domains (Black, 1962; Goodman, 1968) implicated in the metaphor.

While earlier debates concerned metaphor's cognitive value, current debates accept its cognitive function and ask if this function is properly assigned to metaphoric meaning and whether it is a distinctive form of cognition not reducible to other forms such as the capacity to recognize similarity and make comparisons. The outcome of the debate is important to the nature of language, of thought, and of epistemic enterprises such as science. If metaphors have meaning, then a theory of language must explain how such meaning is determined, and any account of mind in which linguistic capacity plays a central role for cognition must similarly explain how cognitive faculties make use of, and make possible, metaphorical thought. Similarly, if the use of metaphorical language in knowledge domains such as science is not reducible to literal language, then we need metaphor in order to understand and explain what is knowable. Furthermore, if we need metaphor to access scientific knowledge, as well as for aesthetic or evocative purposes, then the domains such as art and religion may be more akin to science—or related in more interesting ways—than we have presumed (Fleischacker, 1994). But if metaphors perform their cognitive function without generating a distinctive meaning, then theories of language that are based on literal language suffice; metaphoric contributions to cognition are assimilable to other, already understood or accepted cognitive abilities; the cognitive role of metaphor would be valuable only as heuristic (although, in the case of combinatorially complex problems, the heuristic contribution of metaphor itself may be irreplaceable), and we maintain a clear delineation between the scientific and the poetic.

The position propounding metaphoric meaning and the cognitive irreducibility of metaphor was staked out by Black and has been buttressed by arguments and evidence gathered by philosophers of science, cognitive psychologists, philosophers of language, and linguists. However, the parsimony of the opposing position, and its elegant articulation by Donald Davidson (1978), continues to make it attractive, despite the counterintuitive claim that metaphors have no meaning and the weighty evidence of metaphor's importance in all cognitive endeavors.

Philosophers claiming that metaphors have meaning generally begin by accepting some version of the interaction theory of metaphor but have utilized the resources of many different semantic theories (e.g., possible-world semantics [Bergman, 1982; Hintikka and Sandu, 1994], semantic-field theory [Kittay, 1987], cognitive semantics

[Gibbs, 1994; Lakoff and Johnson, 1980; Sweetser, 1990], a componential semantics [Levin, 1977], a Wittgensteinian semantic, and David Kaplan's semantics for demonstratives [Stern, 1985]). Some use speech-act theory, claiming that metaphors are a feature of speaker meaning rather than sentence meaning (Searle, 1981) or that metaphors are, in the end, elliptical similes after all (Fogelin, 1988).

Newer comparison theories, versions of the theory that metaphors are elliptic similes or implicit comparisons and so do not have a distinctive meaning, explore the notion of figurative rather than literal similarity (Glucks and Keysar, 1990; Ortony, 1979). Some of these approaches offer a causal theory, opposing it to a semantic theory, claiming that metaphors cause us to make comparison by "intimating similarities" and have a causal effect of creating intimacy among speaker and listener (Cohen, 1978; Cooper, 1986). Questions remain concerning the relation between metaphor and literal language (e.g., Can the distinction be drawn in a clear fashion? Is the interpretative process the same or different? Is language originally metaphorical or literal?) and other nonliteral languages (see Hintikka and Sandu, 1994; Jakobson, 1960).

The importance of metaphor in science was stressed by Mary Hesse (1970), who developed the understandings of metaphors as systematic analogies in which the "neutral"—that is, unexplored analogical relations—provide a distinctive source for predictive claims. Dedre Gentner (1982), a cognitive psychologist, along with her associates has identified features, such as systematicity and higher-order relations, that make some metaphors more productive for cognitive purposes than others.

Noting the affinity between metaphor and analogy has permitted a number of researchers in philosophy and psychology to make headway with computational approaches to metaphor—a promising tool for testing theories of metaphor and for understanding the extent to which accounts of metaphor are amenable to formal and precise accounts (Holyoak and Thagard, 1989; Steinhart and Kittay, 1994). Making use of advances in our understanding of metaphor, theorists have explored the role of metaphor in creativity, in language acquisition and concept formation, and in both the consolidation and the breakdown of habituated patterns of thought such as cultural prejudice. These latter developments (which have especially been taken up by feminist philosophers and other social critics) bring the question of the cognitive role of metaphor full circle, reconnecting it to its rhetorical force.

See also Aesthetics, History of; Aesthetics, Problems of; Black, Max; Cognitive Science; Davidson, Donald; Goodman, Nelson; Hintikka, Jaako; Kaplan, David; Philosophy of Language; Philosophy of Religion; Philosophy of Science, History of; Philosophy of Science, Problems of.

Bibliography

Bergman, M. "Metaphorical Assertions." *Philosophical Review* 91 (1982): 229–245.

Black, M., ed. *Models and Metaphors*. Ithaca, NY: Cornell University Press, 1962.

Boyd, R. "Metaphor and Theory Change: What Is 'Metaphor' a Metaphor For?" In *Metaphor and Thought*, edited by A. Ortony. Cambridge, U.K.: Cambridge University Press, 1979.

Cohen, T. "Metaphor and the Cultivation of Intimacy." *Critical Inquiry* 5 (1978): 3–12.

Cooper, D. *Metaphor*. Oxford: Blackwell, 1986.

Davidson, D. "What Metaphors Mean." In *On Metaphor*, edited by S. Sacks. Chicago: University of Chicago Press, 1979.

Fleischacker, S. "Frustrated Contracts, Poetry, and Truth." *Raritan* 13 (4) (Spring 1994): 47–70.

Fogelin, R. *Figuratively Speaking*. New Haven, CT: Yale University Press, 1988.

Gentner, D. "Are Scientific Analogies Metaphors?" In *Metaphor: Problems and Perspectives*, edited by D. S. Maill. Atlantic Highlands, NJ: Humanities Press, 1982.

Gibbs, R. *The Poetics of Mind: Figurative Thought, Language, and Understanding*. Cambridge, U.K.: Cambridge University Press, 1994.

Glucksberg, S., and B. Keysar. "Understanding Metaphorical Comparisons: Beyond Similarity." *Psychological Review* 97 (1990): 3–18.

Goodman, N. *Languages of Art*. Indianapolis: Bobbs Merrill, 1968.

Hesse, M. *Models and Analogies in Science*. Notre Dame, IN: University of Notre Dame Press, 1966.

Hintikka, J., and G. Sandu. "Metaphor and Other Kinds of Nonliteral Language." In *Aspects of Metaphor*, edited by J. Hintikka. Dordrecht: Kluwer Academic, 1994.

Holyoak, K. J., and P. Thagard. "Analogical Mapping by Constraint Satisfaction." *Cognitive Science* 13 (1989): 295–355.

Jakobson, R. "Closing Statement: Linguistics and Poetry." In *Style in Language*, edited by T. A. Sebeok. Cambridge, MA: Technology Press of MIT, 1960.

Kittay, E. F. *Metaphor: Its Cognitive Force and Linguistic Structure*. Oxford: Clarendon Press, 1987.

Lakoff, G., and M. Johnson. *Metaphors We Live By*. Chicago: University of Chicago Press, 1980.

Levin, S. R. *The Semantics of Metaphor*. Baltimore: Johns Hopkins University Press, 1977.

Ortony, A. "The Role of Similarity in Similes and Metaphors." In *Metaphor and Thought*, edited by A. Ortony. Cambridge, U.K.: Cambridge University Press, 1979.

Richards, I. A. *The Philosophy of Rhetoric*. Oxford: Oxford University Press, 1936.

Searle, J. "Metaphor." In *Philosophical Perspectives on Metaphor*, edited by M. Johnson. Minneapolis: University of Minnesota Press, 1981.

Soskice, J. M. *Metaphor and Religious Language.* Oxford: Clarendon Press, 1985.

Steinhart, E., and E. F. Kittay. "Generating Metaphors from Networks: A Formal Interpretation of the Semantic Field Theory of Metaphor." In *Aspects of Metaphor*, edited by J. Hintikka. Dordrecht: Kluwer Academic, 1994.

Stern, J. "Metaphor as Demonstrative." *Journal of Philosophy* 82 (1985): 677–710.

Sweetser, E. *From Etymology to Pragmatics: The Body-Mind Metaphor in Semantic Structure and Semantic.* Cambridge, U.K.: Cambridge University Press, 1990.

Tirrell, L. "Reductive and Nonreductive Simile Theories of Metaphor." *Journal of Philosophy* 88 (1991): 337–358.

Eva F. Kittay (1996)

METAPHOR [ADDENDUM]

This addendum confines itself to general accounts of the nature of verbal metaphor, setting aside work on such more specialized questions as whether metaphors are paraphrasable and such more general and speculative questions as whether the nonverbal arts provide convincing examples of nonverbal metaphor.

SEMANTIC TWIST THEORIES

Semantic twist theories follow Beardsley in holding that a metaphor is a sentence in which a relation of tension or incongruity obtains among the standing meanings of its constituent words and phrases, a tension which is relieved when some of these meanings (those of what Max Black called the *focus*) change or "twist" so as to come into harmony with the others (those of the *frame*). Semantic twist theories have been devised to fit many different conceptions of meaning and of verbal incongruity (Kittay 1989, Ricoeur 1979, Skulsky 1992). Such theories have trouble accounting for sentences one takes to be metaphors despite the availability of a completely apt and pertinent literal reading, sentences one might call *twice-apt*. An example is the joke epitaph a friend composed for Thomas Hobbes: *This is the true philosopher's stone.*

PRAGMATIC TWIST THEORIES

Pragmatic twist theories (Grice 1989, Searle 1979, Sperber and Wilson 1985/6) hold that when we indulge in metaphor, we use words and phrases with their standard literal meanings to *say* one thing, yet we are taken to *mean—taken as intending to convey*—something else. To put it another way, *our sentence as used by us* means one

thing, *we in using it* mean something else—where both "things" are straightforwardly propositional in character. Only by attributing some special meaning to *us* can listeners portray *our utterance* as an intelligible, cooperative contribution to a shared conversational enterprise. Metaphor becomes a mode of overt insinuation, akin to conversational implicature, loose talk, and indirect speech acts. (Theories of this second kind likewise have difficulty accounting for twice-aptness.)

COMPARATIVISM

A new and more robust form of comparison theory (Fogelin 1988) holds that a metaphor "A is (a) B" is an elliptically presented comparison of its primary subject (A) to its secondary subject (B, or Bs in general), where this comparison is to be taken in a distinctively *figurative* manner, as a *simile*. Whether one takes it literally or figuratively, a comparison "A is like (a) B" is true just in case A shares sufficiently many of (a) B's most salient properties. Understanding metaphor becomes a matter of identifying a distinctively figurative way of deciding which properties of (a) B count as salient for present conversational purposes and how many of them count as sufficiently many.

BRUTE FORCE THEORIES

Brute force theories (Davidson 1984, White 1996) hold that in metaphor no words go missing and neither words nor speakers mean anything out of the ordinary. Instead, an utterance that would otherwise be pointless or unaccountable produces what Richard Moran (1989) calls a "framing effect": listeners are induced to view or consider or experience a primary subject A in a special light afforded by the sheer mention, in the midst of a discourse devoted to A, of the secondary subject B.

CONCEPTUAL THEORIES

Conceptual theories (Lakoff 1993, Fauconnier and Turner 2002) hold that verbal metaphor is a manifestation of pervasive modes of thinking wherein people "map" one conceptual domain (e.g., love affairs with their successive stages) onto another (e.g., journeys with their successive stops) or "blend" the systems of terms in which they conceive two different domains.

SEMANTIC ACCOUNTS

An assortment of recent semantic theories (Stern 2000, Walton 1993, Hills 1997) rehabilitate metaphorical truth and metaphorical sentence content outside the confines of verbal opposition theories by drawing on more general accounts of pretense, presupposition, and demonstrative thought.

See also Beardsley, Monroe C.; Black, Max; Events in Semantic Theory; Hobbes, Thomas; Presupposition; Semantics.

Bibliography

Cavell, Stanley. "Aesthetic Problems of Modern Philosophy." In *Must We Mean What We Say? A Book of Essays*. New York: Scribners, 1969.

Cohen, Ted. "Notes on Metaphor." *Journal of Aesthetics and Art Criticism* 34 (3) (1976): 249–259.

Davidson, Donald. "What Metaphors Mean." In *Inquiries into Truth and Interpretation*, 245–264. Oxford: Clarendon Press, 1984.

Derrida, Jacques. "White Mythology." In *Margins of Philosophy*, translated by Alan Bass. Chicago: University of Chicago Press, 1982.

Fauconnier, Gilles, and Mark Turner, *The Way We Think: Conceptual Blending and the Mind's Hidden Complexities*. New York: Basic Books, 2002.

Fogelin, Robert J. *Figuratively Speaking*. New Haven, CT: Yale University Press, 1988.

Gibbs, Raymond J. *The Poetics of Mind: Figurative Thought, Language, and Understanding*. New York: Cambridge University Press, 1994.

Goatly, Andrew. *The Language of Metaphors*. London: Routledge, 1997.

Grice, H. Paul. "Logic and Conversation." In *Studies in the Ways of Words*. Cambridge, MA: Harvard University Press, 1989.

Hills, David. "Aptness and Truth in Verbal Metaphor." *Philosophical Topics* 25 (1) (1997): 117–153.

Kittay, Eva Feder. *Metaphor: Its Cognitive Force and Linguistic Structure*. Oxford: Clarendon Press, 1989.

Lakoff, George. "The Contemporary Theory of Metaphor." In *Metaphor and Thought*. 2nd ed., edited by Andrew Ortony. Cambridge, U.K.: Cambridge University Press, 1993.

Moran, Richard. "Seeing and Believing: Metaphor, Image, and Force." *Critical Inquiry* 16 (1) (1989): 87–112.

Ortony, Andrew. *Metaphor and Thought*, 2nd ed. Cambridge, U.K.: Cambridge University Press, 1993.

Ricoeur, Paul. "The Metaphoric Process as Cognition, Imagination, and Feeling." In *On Metaphor*, edited by Sheldon Sacks. Chicago: University of Chicago Press, 1979.

Searle, John R. "Metaphor." In *Expression and Meaning*. Cambridge, U.K.: Cambridge University Press, 1979.

Skulsky, Harold. *Language Recreated: Seventeenth-Century Metaphorists and the Act of Metaphor*. Athens: University of Georgia Press, 1992.

Sperber, Dan and Deirdre Wilson, "Loose Talk." *Proceedings of the Aristotelian Society* 86 (1985/6), 153-171.

Stern, Josef. *Metaphor in Context*. Cambridge, MA: MIT Press, 2000.

Walton, Kendall L. "Metaphor and Prop Oriented Make-Believe." *European Journal of Philosophy* 1 (1) (1993): 39–57.

White, Roger M. *The Structure of Metaphor: The Way the Language of Metaphor Works*. Oxford: Blackwell, 1996.

David Hills (2005)

METAPHYSICS

Physics is the scientific investigation of the fundamental nature of physical being. Metaphysics—at least within that tradition that traces itself back to Aristotle's eponymous treatise—is the philosophical investigation of the even more fundamental nature of being as such. Metaphysics is concerned with the contours of the categories of entity postulated or presupposed by any possible, acceptable, account of the world, whether of the physical world or of any other aspect of the world. The task of metaphysics is to lay out a complete, coherent ontology, embracing all that is necessary to capture the correct account of the world in any of the special inquiries—whether they be empirical, mathematical, modal, or moral.

THE CHANGING METHODS OF METAPHYSICS

Traditionally, metaphysics was practiced as a top-down, a priori discipline, with Euclidean geometry as its model. The metaphysician begins with self-evident principles of a highly general nature, together with appropriate definitions, and proceeds to draw out the necessary consequences.

This approach is clearly exemplified in the work of two prominent eighteenth-century metaphysicians, Gottfried Wilhelm Leibniz and Benedict (Baruch) de Spinoza. Leibniz spun metaphysical gold out of the dross of the *principles of noncontradiction* and sufficient reason: His entire *Monadology* (1965), replete with an infinite collection of possible worlds, with the actual world (the best of all possible worlds) consisting of a myriad of mutually reflecting, simple, mind-like substances. Spinoza was even more self-consciously imitating Euclid, but his conclusions are almost diametrically opposed to those of Leibniz. Spinoza's ontology comprises exactly one substance (God-or-Nature), of which the mental and the physical realms are two aspects, and everything about the one Substance is absolutely necessary—only the actual is really possible.

In the light of its lofty aim, the conflicting conclusions of its practitioners, and their exaggerated claims to have achieved the aim with completeness and certainty, it is perhaps unsurprising that the discipline of metaphysics, so practiced, has been regularly contested. Empiricists, led by David Hume, have often attacked a priori metaphysics, contrasting its lackluster or conflicting results with the astonishing successes of empirical sciences, on the one hand, and of mathematics on the other.

At the end of the eighteenth century, Immanuel Kant, in response to Hume's critique, attempted a partial vindication of a priori metaphysics. According to Kant, metaphysics can play a legitimate role as handmaid to science and a less straightforward role in upholding ethics. Through an analysis of the cognitive needs of thinking, sensing beings, it can establish the presuppositions of Newtonianism—Euclidean space, absolute time, deterministic causation, and enduring interacting substances obeying conservation laws. In addition, if a metaphysical hypothesis—the existence of God or the freedom of the will—is required for the smooth and effective operation of morality, then that may be legitimately adopted as though it were true, as a postulate of practical rationality. Kant's compromise evidently failed to rein in the metaphysical spirit, his work unleashing a century's worth of metaphysical system-building in an increasingly problematic idealist tradition.

In the late nineteenth century, the appetite for idealist metaphysics began to fade. A realist assault on this tradition was launched by Alexius Meinong, Bertrand Russell, Gottlob Frege, and George Moore, and their style of argumentation, as much as the content of their conclusions, was influential in shaping the twentieth century's more circumspect approach to metaphysics. Rather more radically a group of scientifically minded thinkers—inspired by Ludwig Wittgenstein's *Tractatus* (1922), rallying under the banner of Logical Positivism and brandishing a verificationist criterion of meaning—declared all metaphysical discourse completely meaningless. They argued that sentences that cannot be either verified by observation or proven by pure logic and are not merely beyond our knowing but are strictly speaking, *meaningless*. Echoing Hume, they denied any legitimate space for metaphysics between a posteriori science and a priori logic. The shortcomings of Logical Positivism were rapidly exposed (mostly by its adherents and fellow empiricists such as Karl Popper), but its offspring—ordinary language philosophy—cast over the metaphysical enterprise a pall that did not lift until the 1960s. Metaphysics, cautiously revived by heirs of both movements (albeit with notable differences in methodology detailed below), is once again a flourishing discipline in the early twenty-first century.

Contemporary metaphysics is characterized by a bottom-up approach rather than the traditional top-down approach. The contemporary metaphysician begins with a problem or puzzle, often generated by some basic data or the consequences of such data. The different sources of this basic data characterize two broad traditions. One tradition—championed by Moore, mediated midcentury by philosophers such as P. F. Strawson, Arthur Prior, and Roderick Chisholm and embraced by contemporary philosophers such as Frank Jackson—takes as prime data the deliverances of everyday discourse and commonsense, so called "Moorean facts": for example, that I have two hands; that there is a piece of cheese in my left hand and a stick of chalk in my right; that the chalk and the cheese are distinct things; that cheese and chalk have the same color, and so on.

A different tradition, traceable back through the empiricists (such as Russell and Rudolph Carnap), mediated by Willard Quine, and embraced by philosophers such as John Smart, John Mackie, and David Armstrong, is less impressed with commonsense data. It takes the serious data to be constituted by the presuppositions and deliverances of extraordinarily successful scientific theories: that there is no role for the flow of time in a fundamental account of the world; that the fundamental laws are probabilistic rather than deterministic; that simultaneity is relative to motion; and that space–time may be non-Euclidean. The presuppositions and deliverances of the mathematical disciplines essential to science are also treated as serious data: for example, that there numbers, and an infinite class of such; that there are functions from numbers to numbers and that the infinite class of such functions is vastly bigger than the infinite class of numbers; that there can be no complete axiomatization of mathematical truth, and so on.

The two traditions overlap, of course, as exemplified in the work of prominent metaphysicians like David Lewis. Lewis (1981, 1986) draws extensively on both kinds of data, seeking an ontology compatible with and explanatory of both. However, if that's not possible, the data from the sciences usually trump those of commonsense.

To say that contemporary metaphysics is bottom-up is not to saddle it with a crude inductivism—the fallacious inference of general theories from finite data. The task of the contemporary metaphysician is not so much to *prove* an ontology, either from high-level first principles or from lower-level data, as to *propose* an ontology to accommodate and explain the data, to resolve apparent conflicts by explaining away the appearance of such, or explain why the data are misleading. The methodology is less like that of pure mathematics and more like that of science—conjecture and refutation—with the difference being the kind of data that require accommodation or furnish a counterexample.

Given a finite amount of data, the number of potentially adequate metaphysical theories seems limited only by the imagination of practicing metaphysicians. To decide between theories we need more than data accommodation. Metaphysicians typically subscribe to *Occam's Razor*—the injunction to refrain from multiplying entities beyond necessity. The *Razor*, read as an endorsement of ontological abstemiousness, is sometimes considered a license to slash entities without regard for a complementary principle—the injunction to refrain from eliminating entities that are necessary. Necessary for what? For accommodating and explaining the data. The upshot of these two principles is, then, that a theory must explain the data; and, of two theories that both explain the data, the theory with fewer ontic commitments is to be preferred.

So, we begin with a domain of discourse—such as mind, or mathematics, or morality—and note that, on the surface at least, it supplies data that posit or presuppose an ontology. Our ordinary mind-talk, for example, presupposes mental states (experiences, thoughts, desires, emotions) along with physical states, and a rich network of causal interactions between them. Mathematics posits numbers, classes, functions, spaces, and a rich array of other abstract objects. Morality presupposes goods and evils, rights and obligations, virtues and vices. But there is often a problem with the entities posited or presupposed. For example, if the mind is something over and above the physical, how can it causally interact with the physical without violating physical laws? And if it is difficult to understand how the mind could affect physical states, it is even more difficult to see how numbers, existing outside space and time, could affect the mind. Whence, then, our knowledge of numbers? Finally, a good would have to be something the mere recognition of which would engage the will, and nothing (some will aver) could do that. The question arises, then, whether such things as minds, numbers, and goods should be counted among the indispensable building blocks of the universe. Is it coherent to postulate them? Are they consistent with the rest of what we know? And even if it is coherent, do we really need them to accommodate the data? Can they be explained, or explained away, in a complete, consistent account of the world? Already with the posing of such seemingly unavoidable questions, the enterprise of metaphysics is up and running.

A SPECTRUM OF METAPHYSICAL APPROACHES

Whenever entities are posited to explain the data provided by some domain of discourse, three broad responses, differing in ontological commitment, are possible. At one end of the spectrum we have *realism*, at the other, *antirealism*; between, we have *determinationism*. Each can be divided into two subcategories.

The realist with respect to a domain accepts both the discourse and the data at face value; affirms the necessity of the entities postulated to explain the data, and adds that the entities really are basic—they are additional to (or "over and above") whatever else there may be. Realism comes in two broad varieties. Transcendent realism locates the posited entities outside the spatiotemporal, causal order. By contrast, immanent realism locates the entities within the spatiotemporal, causal order, typically ascribing them an indispensable causal role.

Most realists about numbers and other abstract entities have been of the transcendent variety, but recently, some number-realists have embraced immanence, espousing a role for abstract entities in the causal network. A transcendent realist theory of value is also usually ascribed to Plato—with the Form of the Good, like all the Forms, eternal and unchanging, existing "over and above" the transient realm of particular contingent beings. It is not hard to find naturalist theories of value that ascribe them a causal role, but as we will see below, there is an important sense in which naturalism about value is not fully realist—it does not posit value "over and above" the natural realm. A version of immanent value realism holds, like Platonic realism, that value is real, that it is something "over and above" the purely natural realm, but adds that value plays a causal role with respect to the motivational states of sensitive beings.

At the other end of the spectrum we have antirealism. The antirealist repudiates the entities in question, maintaining that the discourse that delivers the data is fundamentally misleading. But the data can be misleading in one of two very different ways. The data are recorded and delivered in what appear to be genuine, truth-bearing (or assertoric) claims. What masquerades as truth-bearing claims, however, might really be something else, and the nonassertoric antirealist says just that. Rather than being truth-bearing assertions, they might be expressions of desire, or moves in a language game, or instruments in the derivation of genuinely truth-bearing assertions. In ethics, nonassertoric antirealism is *noncognitivism*; in the philosophy of science, *instrumentalism*; in the philosophy of math, *formalism*; in the philosophy of mind, the *intentional stance theory*; and so on. Nonassertoric antirealism allows apparent reference to the purported entities while denying there are any such.

The assertoric antirealist, by contrast, accepts that the discourse consists of genuine truth-bearing assertions but rejects those assertions as untrue. In the metaphysics of the mind, this constitutes *eliminativism* concerning the entities. In the metaphysics of morality, it is known as the *error theory*. An increasingly popular variant of assertoric antirealism, especially with respect to abstract entities such as numbers, is *fictionalism*. The fictionalist thinks that the relevant claims are untrue but also thinks that there is a point in continuing the discourse just as though they were.

Between realism and antirealism lie a collection of approaches that share a doctrine of *determination*. Like the realist, the determinationist acknowledges the discourse and the data that suggest the disputed entities. Like the antirealist, however, the determinationist denies that the disputed entities are basic, holding that the truth about the higher level is fully determined by the truth about ontologically more fundamental entities. Determinationism also comes in two varieties, *reductive* and *nonreductive*. The reductionist holds either that the disputed entities are reducible to more basic entities (entity reduction) or that all the facts about the disputed entities are reducible to facts about undisputed entities (fact reduction).

A necessary and sufficient condition for entity education is that the (apparently) higher-level entities are identical to lower-level entities, that properties of the reducible entities are identical to properties of the lower-level entities, and consequently that truths about the reducible entities turn out to be truths about the entities to which they reduce. The reduced entities are nothing but the lower-level entities to which they are reduced. Thus, for example, *logicism* claims that numbers are reducible to classes: The number zero, for example, is simply identical to the empty class; the number one is identical to the class of all singleton classes, and so on. The identity theory of the mind claims that mental states are identical to physical states of the brain. The ethical naturalist claims that moral properties (such as the rightness of actions) are identical to natural properties (such as maximizing expected happiness).

A classic example of reduction without entity reduction can be found in Russell's justly famous theory of descriptions. In his *Principles of Mathematics*, Russell embraced Meinong's theory of nonexistent objects: that there are genuine objects—*possibilia* like the golden mountain and the King of France, and *impossibilia* like the round square—which have a range of features (the golden mountain is made of gold) but which lack the crucial feature of existence. In "On Denoting"—which set the tone for twentieth century analytic philosophy—Russell repudiated this ontology by showing that phrases that apparently denote such possibilia are not really denoting phrases at all. They do not denote particulars, and *they do not denote anything else*. Russell shows us a way of dispensing with nonexistent objects, but unlike the eliminativist, he does not repudiate the data or the discourse that suggest them. Rather, he shows how to translate the data into facts about properties. Nonexistents disappear from Russell's ontology theory, but the data that suggested them are fully accommodated. This is a kind of reduction without being a reduction of the problematic entities. It is a reduction of the *facts* about the purported entities while the entities are repudiated or "analyzed away." Let's reserve the term *fact reduction* for those cases in which every fact about some purported entities is equivalent to a fact about some other entities; there is no entity reduction, and the purported entities are repudiated.

Finally, we have nonreductive determinationism, which has gained considerable currency through the notion of supervenience in philosophy of mind. All determination theories affirm that there can be no difference in one kind of entity without a difference in another, more basic kind. For example, a widely held view is that there can be no difference in the moral without some difference in the natural. Another is that there can be no difference in the mental without some difference in the physical. The higher-level entities are thus determined by the lower-level entities. What is characteristic of a supervenience theory as such is that it posits this determination, does not repudiate the higher-level entities, but also denies the reducibility of the higher-level entities to the lower-level entities.

Supervenience is naturally located between reductionism and realism. The supervenience theorist agrees with the realist and the fact reductionist that the higher-level entities cannot be reduced to the lower-level entities but agrees with the entity reductionist that the higher-level entities are not ontologically basic. There is thus a sense (weaker than the reductionist sense) in which supervening entities are "nothing over and above" the basic entities, but there is also a sense in which the supervening entities, while falling short of the independently real, enjoy some kind of autonomy denied reducible entities.

Those sympathetic to physicalism (viz., there is nothing over and above the physical) but skeptical that mental state kinds are identical to physical state kinds are attracted to the thesis of the nonreductive supervenience of the mental. Those sympathetic to naturalism (viz., there is nothing over and above the purely natural) but skeptical that moral properties are identical to natural properties are attracted to the nonreductive supervenience of the moral on the natural.

Supervenience theories share considerable common ground with *emergence* theories—lately enjoying something of a revival—and it is interesting that supervenience is popular in domains (such as philosophy of mind and philosophy of biology) where emergence theories also seem a promising compromise between realism and reductionism.

Whether or not there is logical space for nonreductive determinationism has not yet been satisfactorily settled. Like other attempts to forge middle paths between two clear alternatives, a supervenience theory embodies a certain instability, suggesting to some that, in the end, the supervenience advocate will either be forced to embrace the reductionism eschewed or lapse into a form of realism.

One particularly important determination theory is worth singling out for special attention since it has played a pivotal role in the history of metaphysics—namely, determination by the mental (or *mind-dependence*). Broadly speaking, this is *idealism*, and it is a perennially attractive option—indeed, so attractive that idealism has often been taken to be *the* rival to realism. Bishop George Berkeley famously claimed that physical objects are nothing but (are identical to) congeries of experiences. The notorious problem of maintaining the intermittently observed tree in the quad in uninterrupted existence led Berkeley to posit an *omniobserver*, someone to keep a perpetual eye on things. A different response to this problem moves beyond actual experiences to various potential experiences. Physical differences that go undetected may be *detectable* by observers under suitable hypothetical conditions. (*If* you were in the quad, or having in-the-quad experiences, *then* you would have tree experiences.) An idealist could add those conditional states to the determination base. This move, from Berkeleian idealism to phenomenalism, might be a move from entity reduction to fact reduction, or it might be a move from entity reduction to supervenience. If physical objects "disappear" in the final analysis leaving behind the truths that

appear to be about them, then we have fact reduction. If physical objects are not identified with anything else, reference to physical objects as genuine entities remains, and the totality of facts about such objects is determined by the actual and conditional facts about experiences, then we have a version of supervenience.

Faced with the fact that actual minds have various cognitive shortcomings, the idealist may also want to tidy up both actual and potential mental states in various ways. The physical facts are held to be determined not by the actual mental states of existing observers but by the mental states that *ideal observers* would have if they were ideally placed. Hence, variations on the basic idealist theme of mind dependence include *positivism*, *ideal limit* theories of truth, and related accounts such as *internal realism*. Many who regard Berkeleian idealism about the physical world as deeply implausible have embraced some version of idealism in other domains—with respect to mathematical entities, theoretical entities, God, possibilities, colors, values, and universals. This three-fold classification helps explain why there is a certain amount of confusion in debates about realism since *antirealism* and *nonrealism* (the disjunction of antirealism and determinationism) and are not usually defined or carefully distinguished.

A PROBLEM IN METAPHYSICS: UNIVERSALS AND PARTICULARS

These patterns of opposition and compromise—realism versus antirealism, with determination seeking a middle way—have played out across the metaphysical spectrum. They find a particularly clear expression, however, in a problem of central concern to metaphysics since its very inception—the problem of universals and particulars, a problem the intrinsic interest of which proves prefatory to its myriad applications. For one's attitude toward universals and particulars has profound implications for one's attitude to a host of other problems—those of abstract entities, change, time, causation, identity, possibility, value, and morality.

Consider a stick of chalk (*A*), a wedge of cheese (*B*), and a chunk of chocolate (*C*). *A* is chalk and *B* is not chalk—it follows that *A* and *B* are not identical. This is an application the principle of the *indiscernibility of identicals*, often associated with Leibniz: If entity *X* is identical to entity *Y*, then anything true of *X* is also true of *Y*. This in turn is a consequence of the *principle of non contradiction*: that no proposition can be both true and false. So much seems straightforward, yet this sort of easy observation intersects with a second, equally obvious fact, to create a puzzle: *A* is yellow and *B* is yellow. How can *A* and *B*, clearly distinct, be *the same*—that is, yellow? How can they be both the same and not the same? That's puzzling.

Whenever we strike an apparent contradiction (*A* and *B* are the same and are not the same), it is natural to make a distinction. *A* and *B* are not *numerically* the same (they are two) but they are *qualitatively* the same (they instantiate the property *yellowness*). Properties are instantiated by particulars one at a time—they are *monadic* universals. But there are also universals that characterize couples and triples. *Resemblance*, for example, is not a property that particulars have or lack. Resemblance involves pairs—it is a *dyadic* relation. And *betweenness*, which characterizes triples, is a *triadic* relation, and so on. The problematic data can be accommodated, and the apparent inconsistency explained away, by an ontology that posits two radically different categories of being—particulars and universals—and a relation of instantiation (itself a universal) holding between particulars and universals.

Responses to this two-tiered ontology have traditionally been categorized as either *nominalist* or *realist*, with a third category—*conceptualist*—sometimes thrown rather awkwardly into the mix. The six-fold schema set out above suggests that the space of possibilities is much richer. With respect to universals, one might be antirealist (assertoric or nonassertoric), determinationist (reductive or nonreductive), or realist (transcendent or immanent). Further, any of those positions might be combined with one of the six distinct approaches to particulars. So in all there are thirty-six possible combinations, not just two or three. For example, one might be a transcendent realist about both universals and particulars, or an immanent realist about one and a reductionist about the other, or a reductionist about both universals and particulars (invoking some third category of entity to which both reduce), and so on. Not all of these combinations have been embraced, but many have. For the purposes of illustrating the approaches and the arguments that characterize them, a few of the more commonly held positions are sketched.

REALISM ABOUT PARTICULARS, NONREALISM ABOUT UNIVERSALS

A particular, unlike a universal, lacks the mysterious capacity to be "fully present" in distinct particulars. We feel we understand particulars, perhaps because we are experientially acquainted with them. We do seem to be acquainted with concrete particulars—such as bits of chalk, cheese, and chocolate. But there are other purported entities that strike us as particular rather than universal that are not like these—for example, numbers, classes, propositions, and possibilities. And there are others that are difficult to categorize—such as space and time.

Particularism embraces realism about particulars—there are particulars, and particulars are not reducible to anything more basic—and adds that the *only* basic entities are particulars. It is thus a one-tier ontology with both considerable simplicity and commonsense in its favor. Particularism affirms that anything at all (universals, numbers, classes, possibilities, causation, space, time) is either eliminable or reducible to particulars. *Concrete* particularism is more austere, restricting fundamental being to concrete particulars, the paradigms of which are physical objects. The concrete particularist is a realist about concrete particulars and is typically an immanent realist, assigning particulars both spatiotemporal location and a role in the causal order. There are versions of transcendent realism about particulars although typically transcendent particulars will be abstract rather than concrete (for example, numbers, classes, and possibilities).

In what follows particularism is combined with five different versions of nonrealism about universals. These five accounts have all been called "nominalisms," but the nomenclature is not particularly perspicuous. Sometimes nominalism connotes *concrete particularism*; at others, the broader doctrine of *particularism*. Sometimes it connotes *antirealism* about universals; at others, *determinationism*. *Predicate nominalism*, which holds that there are just particulars and the words (names) we call them by, is perhaps the clearest candidate for the title. *Mereological nominalism* combines concrete particularism with reduction of universals. *Conceptualism*, sometimes called "concept nominalism," is a version of idealism—reduction of universals to mental particulars. *Extensionalism*, sometimes called "class nominalism," is a reduction of universals not to concrete particulars but to classes of concrete particulars. Finally, *resemblance theories* are determinationist and may be of either the reductive or nonreductive kind. The determination base includes concrete particulars and resemblances between them.

PREDICATE NOMINALISM AS AN ELIMINATIVIST PARTICULARISM. The most austere version of nominalism—often called *word* or *predicate nominalism*—is naturally construed as concrete particularism combined with eliminativism about universals. It holds that there are concrete particulars and there are the predicates (words) we apply to them, and that is all. Simply put: Things are yellow because we call them "yellow." We call things by the same name—*A* and *B* are both called "yellow"—but there is no need to postulate a universal of yellowness instantiated by all things so called. (Distinct people are called "Brian," but we do not postulate a universal *Brianness*.)

The predicate nominalist repudiates universals rather than reducing them to particulars but accommodates the data by means of the following equivalences:

A is yellow ⇔ *A* is called "yellow."

B is yellow ⇔ *B* is called "yellow."

C is brown ⇔ *C* is called "brown."

On the left-hand side we have some Moorean facts, which apparently presuppose concrete particulars (*A*, *B*, *C*) and universals (yellowness; brownness). However, the right-hand side supplants reference to a property with reference to a predicate. Since it is implausible to identify yellowness with the predicate "yellow," the position is plausibly construed as denying the universal yellowness: There is a word "yellow," we call a bunch of things "yellow," and if we call them "yellow," they are yellow (end of story).

Some criticisms of word nominalism are worth sketching because they involve argument kinds that crop up repeatedly in this area. The word nominalist's explanation of the data seems backwards. Distinct things are not made yellow by virtue of being called "yellow;" they are called "yellow" because they are one color, conventionally dubbed "yellow." If we call a person "Brian," then for any other similar person—for example, his identical twin—it is a matter of separate convention whether we also call him "Brian." But if we call a color sample on a chart "yellow," and another sample is qualitatively indistinguishable from that, the original convention covers the second color sample, and we call it "yellow," too.

Secondly, since there are only concrete particulars, words must also be concrete particulars. How many words are there on the following line?

yellow, yellow

There are two answers: two and one. There are two concrete words but only one dictionary entry at issue. We must distinguish between *word-tokens* and *word-types*. On the one hand, word-tokens are spatially located, unrepeatable, concrete particulars. A word-type, on the other hand, has distinct word-tokens as instances. Word-types look very like universals. Elimination of one universal—yellowness—has only been achieved at the cost of accepting another—the word-type "yellow."

To eliminate this word-type, the nominalist might deploy the complex predicate "called 'tokens of the word-type "yellow."'" But this launches a regress, for the same problem resurfaces for applications of this new predicate. Universals are eliminated at one level only to have them pop up in the shape of word-types at the next. Only if word-types at all levels are eliminable in favor of word-tokens will universals be exorcised, but that would require an infinite supply of word-tokens, and there are just not enough to go around. The nominalist might invoke *possible* word-tokens here, but that would launch the nominalist beyond the actual world into the problematic outer space of possibility—not a happy place for nominalists to venture.

Finally, chalk is *called* "yellow," but the cheese is also *called* "yellow." *Calling* involves many distinct particular-word pairs—it seems to be a dyadic relation linking particulars and word-tokens, and relations are universals. If one tries to eliminate this relation in favor of another word, we are again launched on a tiresome regress.

There is an alternative construal of predicate nominalism according to which yellowness is eliminated in favor of a different property—*being called "yellow."* But this would be neither elimination of universals (since both properties have an equal claim to being universals) nor a reduction of universals to particulars. It is simply a proposal to economize within the class of universals itself. As Lewis noted in a different context (possibility), it is not just the number of entities that fall within an ontological category that matters to ontic simplicity, but more importantly, it is the number of basic ontological categories countenanced. If there is something unsatisfactory about the *category* of universal, then whether you admit one, or a million, or an infinite array is immaterial—your attempt to eliminate universals fails.

MEREOLOGICAL NOMINALISM AS ENTITY REDUCTION. Predicate nominalism is an eliminativist version of concrete particularism, but there are reductionist versions too—*mereological nominalism*, for example. Mereology is the theory of the part–whole relation. Some particulars are parts of other particulars. The top of the pen and the body of the pen are both proper parts of the pen, and the pen is the mereological sum of the body and the top. The pen continues to exist even when the top is removed and its parts are separated. Perhaps the chalk and the cheese are also parts of a particular, a spatially scattered whole made partly of chalk and partly of cheese.

Starting with A, B, and C, there are at least four such distinct, albeit overlapping, mereological sums—$(A+B)$, $(B+C)$, $(A+C)$ and $(A+B+C)$—yielding at least seven distinct concrete particulars in total. Note that sameness of parts entails sameness of whole: $((A+B)+A)$, for example, has just two parts, A and B, and so is identical to $(A+B)$. If there are n basic (nonoverlapping) concrete particulars, then, assuming the principle of *unrestricted mereological composition* (that every sum of concrete particulars is itself a concrete particular), there are 2^n-1 concrete particulars. The principle is controversial, but one way of characterizing concrete particularism is this: The principle of unrestricted composition places an upper bound on the collection of entities.

Let $S(F)$ be the mereological sum of all particulars to which predicate F applies—$S(yellow)$ is the sum of all yellow things. Plausibly, something is yellow if and only if it is a part of $S(yellow)$. This suggests the following analysis:

X is $F \Leftrightarrow X$ is a part of $S(F)$

Note that the analysis assumes that for any predicate F, the sum of all things with F is also a concrete particular. However, it does not assume unrestricted composition—for there may be collections of particulars to which no single predicate applies. This mereological analysis, if adequate, might allow us to identify the property F-ness with $S(F)$, a concrete particular.

Mereological nominalism accommodates quite a lot of data about properties such as *water* and *yellow*. But take two related properties such as *water* and *single H_2O molecule* that involve the part–whole relation—a quantity of water has parts that are single H_2O molecules. Mereological particularism entails that for something to be water, it has to be a part of $S(water)$, and for something to be a single H_2O molecule, it has to be part of the $S(single \ H_2O \ molecule)$. But these two sums are *identical*—sum all quantities of water, and sum all single molecules of water, and you arrive at the same whole. So mereological nominalism entails that to be water just is to be a single molecule of water—and that, unfortunately for the theory, is just false.

CONCEPTUALISM AS IDEALISM ABOUT UNIVERSALS.

The attraction of conceptualism is that it reduces universals to something concrete, particular, and also mind-friendly: *concepts*. Concepts are things that the mind can get a handle on whereas universals may be problematic in that respect. The beginning idea is that the cheese is yellow if and only if the cheese falls under the concept of yellow. Quite generally, where $C(F)$ is the concept of F, we have:

X is $F \Leftrightarrow X$ falls under $C(F)$.

We can thus explain the data by appealing to a concept—an apparently familiar mental particular—rather than a mind-independent universal.

Our mental vocabulary (such as belief, thought, desire) suffers a pervasive state-content ambiguity. *My belief that the cheese is yellow* might be my state of believing, as in: "My belief that the cheese is yellow, given my aversion to yellow cheese, made me refuse it." But it might also be the content of my belief, as in: "My belief is just the same as yours: that the cheese is yellow." Our believings are distinct entities, but what we believe here is the same. Believings are mind-dependent (which believings there are depends on who believes what), but the common content of distinct believings does not depend on what you or I believe.

Concepts also suffer the state-content ambiguity—there are concept-graspings and there are the concepts grasped. Concepts in the state-sense are mind-dependent (which concept-graspings exist depends on who is grasping what), but the contents of such graspings do not appear to be mind-dependent.

The conceptualist may eschew concepts as contents of graspings in favor of a myriad different and individual graspings. But your grasping of yellow has something in common with mine. What is that? If we apply conceptualism to this datum then, as with predicate nominalism, we are launched on a regress and there will not be enough particular concept graspings to accommodate all the data.

EXTENSIONALISM: REDUCTION OF UNIVERSALS TO CLASSES.

For every predicate F that may or may not apply to a particular, there is the class of all and only the particulars to which F applies in fact, the extension of F—$E(F)$. In our example, class $\{A,B\}$ is the extension of *yellow*, $\{C\}$ the extension of *brown*. Something is yellow if and only if it is in the class of yellow things. So the following is an apparently necessary equivalence:

X is $F \Leftrightarrow X$ is a member of $E(F)$.

This suggests identifying F-ness with its extension, $E(F)$. (After abandoning concrete particularism, Quine adopted extensionalism.)

Extensionalism is sometimes called "class nominalism," but the postulation of classes marks a real departure from concrete particularism. Classes may be particular, but they are not concrete. Classes are "over and above" the concrete particulars that are their members, and Nelson

Goodman's criterion explains why. Starting with *A, B, C* there are at most seven concrete particulars. However, there are many more classes. There are seven nonempty classes of particulars. Each one pairs off with a mereological sum—{*A,B*} with *A+B*, {*A*} with *A*, and so on—but we cannot identify these classes with the corresponding concrete particulars. Classes are individuated by membership: They are identical if and only if they have exactly the same members (the principle of extensionality). So the singleton class {*A*} is a distinct entity from its sole member *A*. A piece of cheese is not a class consisting of a piece of cheese. Quite generally a class is not the mereological sum of its members.

Once we acknowledge classes of classes, the hierarchy of classes "over and above" the concrete particulars, *A, B, C* explodes into a vast and infinitely intricate structure, one massively exceeding the modest seven-member ontology of mereological sums countenanced by the concrete particularist. The two-membered class {{*A,B*},*A*}, for example, is distinct from the two-membered class {*A,B*}. The former has a member {*A,B*} that the latter lacks. Contrast this with ((*A+B*)+*A*) and (*A+B*)—the same concrete particular.

Extensionalism, a radical departure from nominalism, thus has plenty of resources—but does it have enough to do justice to the data? Being a chordate is the property of being a heart-bearing animal; being a renate, the property of being a kidney-bearing animal. These are distinct properties. As it happens, these two properties have the same extension. Extensionalism thus entails that they are one and the same property. As generous as the ontology of classes is, it is not generous enough. This *coextension problem* is a classic example of an argument against a reduction thesis. The reduction base is shown to be insufficiently rich to capture all relevant entities.

A different criticism suggests that there are too many classes as well. A universal involves sameness. There are, however, "arbitrary" collections of concrete particulars exhibiting no genuine sameness. If the sameness of *A* and *B* (yellowness) reduces to the fact that both are members of {*A,B*}, why does not the fact that *A* and *C* are both members of {*A,C*} yield a genuine sameness there? The class theorist could bite this bullet and accept that all classes are universals. (Bullet-biting is a rather common response to recalcitrant data.) A different response would be to block the counterexample by declaring that only certain "natural" classes are genuine or have what it takes to be universals. (This response exhibits an ad hocness that is arguably worse than bullet-biting.)

An explanatory asymmetry argument against extensionalism is often deployed. It is claimed that *A*'s being yellow *explains A*'s membership of the class of yellow particulars, not the other way around. This claim contradicts the extensionalist's claim that these facts are really one and the same. The extensionality principle, however, entails that if *X* is a member of a class *C*, then *that very class* could not have lacked *X*—any class *C** that lacks *X* is *necessarily* distinct from *C*. That *A* is a member of {*A,B*} is necessary. That *A* is yellow is, by contrast, contingent. No contingent fact explains a necessary fact, and so the argument fails. Even though it fails, it suggests a different argument. It follows, by the indiscernibility of identicals, that a contingent fact (such as *A*'s being yellow) cannot be a necessary fact (such as *A*'s being a member of {*A.B*}). But extensionalism entails they are the same fact. Call this the *necessary extension* problem.

The coextension and necessary extension problems are closely related. The reason chordate and renate cannot be identified with the class that is their common extension is that their extensions *might* well have differed from each other. And that presupposes that they have their extensions contingently, not necessarily. Since chordate and renate differ in their possible extensions, one way of modifying extensionalism would be to expand the reduction base to include possibilia. Two accounts have predominated. One embraces possible but nonactual particulars and takes the extension of property *P* to be the class of actual and nonactual particulars that have *P*. (This presupposes that particulars are world-bound—no particular appears in more than one possible world.) Another is to include possible but nonactual *worlds* with common or overlapping domains of particulars. In each possible world *W*, the property *P* has an extension in *W*. The property *P* thus induces a function *F(P)* from worlds to extensions—and a reductionist might identify *P* with the function *F(P)*. These accounts are both reductionist, presupposing different accounts of possibility. They go well beyond the domain of concrete particulars entertained by traditional extensionalists, and they are both known as *intensional* accounts of universals.

Despite the richness of the framework of worlds and functions, however, it may still not be rich enough to capture all the data. Being *triangular* is the property of being a plane figure with three angles. Being *trilateral* is the property of being a plane figure with three sides. Because each logically necessitates the other, these properties induce the very same function from worlds to classes of concrete particulars (or classes of possibilia), and so even these intensionalist accounts render them identical. If they are not identical, then we need something more discriminating than functions from worlds to classes of particulars with which to identify them.

RESEMBLANCE THEORIES: REDUCTION AND SUPERVENIENCE. An important group of theories claim that property facts are determined by facts about resemblance. A crude version of the resemblance theory invokes paradigms, and resemblance to such paradigms—namely, where $P(F)$ is a specified paradigm of F:

$$X \text{ is } F \Leftrightarrow X \text{ resembles } P(F).$$

The shortcomings of the paradigm account are numerous. It entails, for example, that the designated paradigm of yellowness is *necessarily* yellow (since everything necessarily resembles itself). It also entails that anything resembling $P(F)$ in any respect at all is F. A far more promising account draws on the notion of *similarity circle*—a class such that all the members of the class resemble every member of the class, and nothing outside the class also resembles every member of the class. Provided that there is sufficient variety in particulars, similarity circles carve out what are, intuitively, the genuine universals without the necessity for privileging any particular. This might be regarded as a reduction of universals to classes of particulars plus resemblances, but it can also be regarded as a supervenience thesis: Properties supervene on a basis consisting of resemblance and the domain of particulars. There can be no difference in properties without some difference in the structure of resemblances—same resemblance structure, same properties.

As Russell famously noted, any account that grounds properties in resemblance faces a problem. Resemblance is a relation between particulars and as such seems to be a universal. It might be considered an ontological saving to reduce myriad universals to one, but as noted in the context of word nominalism, what is important is the number of nonempty ontological *categories*.

This criticism of resemblance theories can be generalized to any attempt to reduce universals to something "else." Suppose we reduce property P to some entity Reduct(P): the class of Ps; the mereological sum of Ps; the concept of P; the similarity circle that corresponds to P, and so on. The reductionist says that for X to be P is for X to bear some suitable relation R to Reduct(P). But the reductionist is then forced either to admit one universal—the relation R—or to apply the theory to R itself, launching an unhappy regress.

Resemblance theorists might employ the tu quoque, charging that the realist faces a similar regress. Assume realism: For X to be yellow is for X to instantiate (I) the universal yellowness (Y). But then, for X to instantiate Y is for a certain triple—X,Y,I—to stand in a relation, I^*. I^* cannot be I. For one thing I, is a dyadic relation, and I^* is a triadic relation. For another, this would involve a relation taking itself as one of its own *relata*. So I^* is distinct from I. We can repeat the argument to obtain a third relation I^{**}, and so on. So the realist is thus as much involved in a regress as any of the reductionist rivals.

The realist might appeal to the category response: The regress is damaging to the particularist because it shows that the category of relation cannot be done away with. That's an internal inconsistency. But the realist about universals does not object to that category being nonempty, and even an infinite class of distinct instantiation relations constitutes no embarrassment for realism as such. Of course, a realist who wants to keep the number of universals down to a small or finite collection might be embarrassed.

Finally, the resemblance theorist may run out of the kind of variety in actual objects required to set properties apart. (Renate and chordate are still coextensive.) To increase the variety and block a coextension objection, the resemblance theorist might take a now familiar tack—embracing relations of resemblance between *possible* as well as actual particulars. As with the related attempts to deflect counterexamples by invoking possibilia, this constitutes a significant and not entirely unproblematic expansion of the reduction base. Certainly it violates the original nominalistic spirit that inspired it.

REALISM ABOUT BOTH PARTICULARS AND UNIVERSALS

One explanation for this apparent failure to eliminate or reduce universals is realism—that universals are neither eliminable, nor reducible, nor supervenient. That this is no proof of realism is obvious—we may not have exhausted all possible alternatives. However, realism about universals conjoined with realism about particulars does explain these failures, as well as providing an explanation of the ubiquitous Moorean facts of predication.

TRANSCENDENT REALISM ABOUT UNIVERSALS. What is often called *ante rem* realism, or Platonic realism, is a transcendent realism: that irreducible universals exist of necessity, beyond contingency in general, and beyond the contingent causal network in particular. One powerful explanatory principle, typically embraced by transcendent realists (Plato perhaps) states that any meaningful predicate, whether simple or complex, applies to things in virtue of designating a genuine universal. So not only contingent predicates such as "black" and "raven" designate universals, so, too, do predicates that apply of necessity (such as "self-identical"); predicates that apply to nothing (such as "unicorn"); predicates that apply to nothing of necessity (such as "self-distinct"); and finally, not only simple predicates (such as "black" and "raven") designate universals, but so do complex predicates (such as "black raven," "not black," "black or raven," "black if and only if a raven," and so on). Since predicates apply to universals themselves (e.g., *yellowness is a pretty color*), universals are instances of other universals. This *unrestricted transcendent realism* makes the domain of universals a largely a priori affair.

Perhaps the greatest threat to unrestricted transcendent realism is Russell's paradox. Particulars have properties (such as being honest or cowardly), but properties also have properties (honesty is virtue, chalkiness is a universal, a piece of chalk is not a universal), and those properties have properties in turn (virtue is good, being a universal is something all universals have in common, being a particular is a universal not a particular).

By unrestricted realism the two predicates—*being a universal* and *being a concrete particular*—designate two universals, *U* and *P*. All universals have *U* in common. *U* is a universal, and so *U* itself has *U*. *U* is *self-predicating*. However, *P* is not a concrete particular (it is a universal), and so *P* is *non-self-predicating*. Given unrestricted realism, the meaningful predicate *non-self-predicating* designates a universal, *N*. Each universal either has *N* or lacks *N*. If *N* has *N*, then *N* is non-self-predicating—but then *N* does not self-predicate and so *N* lacks *N* (contradiction). If *N* lacks *N*, then *N* is not non-self-predicating; that is, *N* is self-predicating, and so *N* has *N* (contradiction again).

Russellian paradoxes can be constructed for just about any account of universals, including the most austere version of predicate nominalism. (The predicate "short" is called "short," but the predicate "long" is not called "long." Call the former "self-predicating" and the latter "non-self-predicating." Is the predicate "non-self-predicating" called "non-self-predicating"? Paradox ensues.) Russellian paradoxes are thus too pervasive, the realist might claim, for them to be peculiarly damaging to realism. Still, short of embracing paradoxes, the realist has an obligation to deflect them.

Any adequate realist answer to Russellian paradoxes must involve some restriction on the predicates: namely, not every apparently meaningful predicate necessarily designates a universal. Russell's theory of types is a classic restriction. Type theory stratifies entities. Simplifying somewhat: particulars are type-0 entities, properties of particulars are type-1 entities, properties of (type-1) properties are type-2 entities, and so on. A type-0 entity may either have or lack a type-1 property, and a type-1 property may have or lack a type-2 property, but no property either has or lacks a property of the same type. A property is always one type higher than the highest type of entity to which it can be sensibly applied or denied. Thus, the question of whether a universal *P* has or lacks *itself* does not arise. It is neither true nor untrue that *P* lacks *P*. The very attempt to apply *P* to itself is a *category* error (like the attempt to apply the color green to the number 7), and so the predicates "self-predicating" and "non-self-predicating" are literally *meaningless*. (The notion of a category error took on a life of its own long after Russell's theory of types lost the attention of most philosophers.) The paradox is blocked because there are no universals of self-predication or of non-self-predication.

The chief worry about a type theory is that it rules itself out as unsayable—to state it one must violate its strictures. Take the claim *no universal can be applied to, or denied of, a universal of the same type*. This makes a perfectly general claim about all universals. What type does the universal of being a universal (*U*) belong to? It cannot consistently be assigned a level. It is this problem that undergirds the famous theme of Wittgenstein's *Tractatus*, that philosophy consists of things that can be shown but cannot be said.

IMMANENT REALISM ABOUT UNIVERSALS. An important group of restricted realist theories trace their ancestry to Aristotle. Not every predicate picks out a universal, and it is a contingent matter, to be settled a posteriori, what universals there are. *In rebus* realism is a version of immanent realism. It begins with the simple idea that universals exist only in their instances. If a universal is not instantiated, it does not exist. Consequently, a predicate must apply to a particular for it to designate a genuine universal. This *instantiation condition* prohibits universals such as unicornhood. It also rules out various truth-functional combinations of universals. Even if *black* and *raven* are both universals, the predicate "not black and a raven" does not designate a universal (since all ravens are black).

Armstrong, a prominent advocate of immanent realism, places two further conditions on a predicate for it to designate a universal. Firstly, the predicate must apply in virtue of a *genuine identity* in the particulars. Even if *yellow* and *raven* are both universals, the disjunctive predicate "yellow or a raven" does not pick out a universal, despite being instantiated, because there is no qualitative identity exemplified by a yellow submarine and a black raven. Secondly, Armstrong draws on a condition inspired by the Eleatic Stranger in Plato's *Sophist*, who makes the intriguing suggestion (known as the *Eleatic Principle*) that the mark of being is causal power. Armstrong requires that to be real, a universal must feature in causal laws. (Universals must do some work for their living.)

The Eleatic Principle gives natural science a crucial role in delineating the ultimate constituents of being. Interestingly, it also suggests an immanent realism that denies the instantiation condition. Michael Tooley has argued, within the same immanent realist framework, that there could be properties that play a genuine role in the causal order, because they enter into basic causal laws, but that could remain uninstantiated. If causal power is the mark of the real, it would be hard to deny them ontic standing, but if so, they are not *in rebus* universals—they exist independently of their exemplification by particulars. Clearly, there is wide scope for other, quite different versions of both transcendent and immanent realism about universals.

REALISM ABOUT UNIVERSALS, REDUCTIONISM ABOUT PARTICULARS

If one embraces realism about universals, then, for the sake of simplicity, it would be worthwhile exploring the reduction or particulars to universals. Every particular X comes along with a bundle (or a class) of properties, $B(X)$—the class of all the properties it has. Further, an object X has property P if and only if P is a member of $B(X)$. This suggests that we embrace just one entity (the bundle) rather than two (the particular and its bundle). The bundle theory identifies a particular with the bundle of its properties.

This bundle theory faces problems analogous to the reduction of universals to classes of particulars—both too many classes and not enough classes. Firstly, there are too many classes. The class {golden, mountain} does not pick out any actual concrete particular—the golden mountain does not exist. This fact, however, may not be considered entirely undesirable. Meinong famously argued that metaphysics needs to accommodate data pertaining to the nonactual as well as to the actual. To explain the nonexistence of the golden mountain, the golden mountain must be an object with a specific nature, a nature that it possesses of necessity. If being

golden and mountainous were contingent properties of the golden mountain, then who is to say that Kilimanjaro is not the golden mountain? The bundle theory thus dovetails nicely with this theory of possible objects.

The bundle theorist still owes us an account of the distinction between concrete existent particulars (Kilimanjaro) and merely possible particulars (the golden mountain). Meinong thought that it is their completeness that sets them apart. Kilimanjaro is complete—for every property, Kilimanjaro either has it or lacks it. The golden mountain is incomplete—it is a mountain, and it is made of gold, but for many properties (e.g., *more than 1 mile high*), it neither has the property nor lacks it. But this will not do—we could specify complete bundles of properties that do not correspond to any concrete particular.

Are there enough bundles of properties to accommodate all particulars, or does the bundle theory face a coextension problem? A bundle theory of particulars entails the Identity of indiscernibles (the converse of the indiscernibility of identicals): If X and Y are qualitatively identical (share all properties), then X and Y are numerically identical. This principle would be trivially true provided conditions such as *being identical to X* were genuine properties. But the bundle theorist cannot start with properties that presuppose antecedently given particulars. The bundling properties would have to be purely qualitative. But then it does seem possible for distinct particulars to share all their purely qualitative properties. (Quantum theory, for example, entails that it is possible for two bosons to share their fundamental quantum states—including the state corresponding to location.) That is incompatible with the bundle theory.

An essential property of a particular is a property without which that particular would not exist. It is controversial whether there are essential properties, and if so, which properties of any given particular are essential. However, there is widespread agreement that not every property of a particular is essential to it. At least some properties are such that an item could lose them without going out of existence. The bundle theory suffers an analogue of the necessary extension problem. Classes by their nature are necessary, eternal, and unchanging. So the bundle theory would appear to entail *super-essentialism*: that every property of a particular is essential to it; that if a particular lost a property, it would cease to be.

REJECTING REALISM ABOUT UNIVERSALS AND PARTICULARS

The space of possibilities is not restricted to reduction in one of two directions. Universals and particulars might both be reduced to some third, more basic, kind of entity. One prominent example of such an approach is *trope theory*.

A trope (this patch of brownness, that instance of sweetness) is a particularized universal—a particular instantiation of a universal by a particular. Put like that, of course, tropes apparently presuppose both particulars and universals. They appear to be nonbasic entities. But it is a characteristic move in metaphysics to take as ontologically basic something that has hitherto been assumed to be derivative and reverse the ontological order.

Tropes have the advantage of incorporating both particularity and qualitative character in their nature and are thus promising building blocks. The proposal is that particulars and universals are both classes of tropes, albeit different kinds of classes: Particulars are classes of *co-located* tropes—tropes occupying the same space and time—and universals are classes of *exactly resembling* tropes. A particular X has property P just in case the class of co-located tropes that make up X overlaps with the class of resembling tropes that constitute P.

Trope theory has the advantages of simplicity and comprehensiveness. Further, it avoids the co-extension problem that besets extensionalism. No redness trope is identical to a roundness trope. So even if *redness* and *roundness* always go together (they are always co-located) the class of all roundness tropes is a distinct class from that of redness tropes.

Trope theory retains the necessary extension problem. Classes have their members by necessity, but a concrete particular does not have its properties by necessity. By identifying predication with the intersection of two classes, trope theory implies that all predications are necessary. Again, such problems may be avoidable by invoking possible worlds, but only at the cost of expanding the reduction base to something that makes the resulting reduction rather costly in terms of ontological resources.

THE FUTURE OF METAPHYSICS

The proposed schema for locating metaphysical theories is applicable in all of the various domains of the discipline, and the argument patterns for realism, antirealism, and determinationism bear important similarities across those domains. The basic data might involve claims about time, causation, possibility, the fundamental truths of arithmetic, mental states, spatial relations, value, morality, and so on. Theorists will take the data and lay out an ontology to explain them, or explain them away, either taking the surface ontology at face value, explaining it in terms of something more basic, or occasionally eliminating it altogether.

The modern metaphysician, aware of the underdetermination of theory by data, rarely expects or demands that the arguments conclusively establish any metaphysical proposal. Rather, the metaphysician will examine each metaphysical proposal on its explanatory merits, assessing first its explanatory adequacy with respect to the existing data, searching for new data to test and probe the proposal, and then turning to the more inherently contestable issues of theoretical elegance, economy, and overall coherence with other metaphysical theories. Inevitably, a considerable degree of fallibility and uncertainty remains. Still, that acknowledged, the future of metaphysics is no less secure than the future of science: Human beings can and will continue to probe the fundamental nature of the world right up to the limits of their cognitive abilities. Their doing so will, inescapably, implicate them in the enterprise of metaphysics.

See also Aristotle; Armstrong, David M.; Berkeley, George; Carnap, Rudolf; Chisholm, Roderick; Frege, Gottlob; Gödel, Kurt; Goodman, Nelson; Hume, David; Kant, Immanuel; Leibniz, Gottfried Wilhelm; Lewis, David; Mackie, John Leslie; Meinong, Alexius; Metaphysics, History of; Metaphysics, Nature of; Moore, George Edward; Newton, Isaac; Plato; Popper, Karl Raimund; Prior, Arthur Norman; Quine, Willard Van Orman; Russell, Bertrand Arthur William; Smart, John Jamieson Carswell; Spinoza, Benedict (Baruch) de; Strawson, Peter Frederick; Wittgenstein, Ludwig Josef Johann.

The Encyclopedia contains two additional general articles on this subject: *Metaphysics, History of*, and *Metaphysics, Nature of*. It also features the following articles: *Absolute, The*; *Apeiron/Peras*; *Appearance and Reality*; *Arche*; *Being*; *Categories*; *Causation: Metaphysical Issues*; *Chance*; *Chaos Theory*; *Continuity*; *Cosmos*; *Determinism, A Historical Survey*; *Dialectic*; *Emanationism*; *Essence and Existence*; *Eternal Return*; *Eternity*; *Hen/Polla*; *Idealism*; *Identity*; *Infinity in Theology and Metaphysics*; *Logos*; *Macrocosm and Microcosm*; *Materialism*; *Monad and Monadology*; *Monism and Pluralism*; *Naturalism*; *Nature, Philosophical Ideas of*; *Nomos and Phusis*; *Nothing*; *Nous*; *Ontology*; *Panpsychism*; *Personal Identity*; *Personalism*; *Persons*; *Pessimism and Optimism*; *Possibility*; *Relations, Internal and External*; *Solipsism*; *Substance and Attribute*; *Time*; *Unconscious*; *Universals, A Historical Survey*; *Vitalism*; *Voluntarism*; *Why*.

Differing schools of metaphysical thought are represented in the articles *Aristotelianism*; *Augustinianism*; *Cartesianism*; *Hegelianism*; *Neoplatonism*; *Ockhamism*; *Platonism and the Platonic Tradition*; *Scotism*; *Spinozism*; *Stoicism*; *Thomism*.

Bibliography

Aristotle. "Metaphysics." In *The Complete Works of Aristotle: The Revised Oxford Translation*, edited by J. Barnes, 1552–1728. Princeton, NJ: Princeton University Press, 1984.

Armstrong, D. M. *A Theory of Universals*. Cambridge, U.K.: Cambridge University Press, 1978.

Ayer, A. J. *Language, Truth, and Logic*. New York: Oxford University Press, 1936.

Berkeley, G. *Three Dialogues Between Hylas and Philonous*. Oxford: Oxford University Press, 1998.

Bradley, F. H. *Appearance and Reality*. London: Swan Sonnenschein, 1893.

Brentano, F. *Psychology from an Empirical Standpoint*, edited by O. Kraus. Translated by A. C. Rancurello, D. B. Terrell, and L. L. McAlister. London: Routledge, 1973.

Carnap, R. *Der Logische Aufbau der Welt*. Leipzig: Felix Meiner Verlag, 1928.

Carnap, R. *Meaning and Necessity*. Chicago: University of Chicago Press, 1947.

Carnap, R. "The Elimination of Metaphysics through Logical Analysis of Language." In *Logical Empiricism at its Peak: Schlick, Carnap, and Neurath*, edited by S. Sarkar, 10–33. New York: Garland, 1996.

Chisholm, R. M. *Person and Object: A Metaphysical Study*. La Salle: Open Court, 1976.

Churchland, P. M. "Eliminative Materialism and the Propositional Attitudes." *Journal of Philosophy* 78 (1981): 67–90.

Davidson, D. "Mental Events." In *Experience and Theory*, edited by L. Foster and J. W. Swanson, 79–101. London: Duckworth, 1970.

Dennett, D. C. *The Intentional Stance*. Cambridge, MA: MIT Press, 1987.

Duhem, P. M. M. *The Aim and Structure of Physical Theory*. Translated by P. Wiener. Princeton, NJ: Princeton University Press, 1954.

Feyerabend, P. "Mental Events and the Brain." *Journal of Philosophy* 40 (1963): 295–296.

Field, H. H. *Science without Numbers: A Defence of Nominalism*. Oxford: Blackwell, 1980.

Gödel, K. "Some Basic Theorems on the Foundations of Mathematics and Their Philosophical Implications." In *Collected Works. Vol. III*, edited by S. Feferman, et al., 304–323. Oxford: Oxford University Press, 1995.

Goodman, N. "A World of Individuals." In *The Problem of Universals*, edited by I. M. Bochenski, A. Church, and N. Goodman, 13–32. Notre Dame, IN: University of Notre Dame Press, 1956.

Goodman, N. "Predicates Without Properties." *Midwest Studies in Philosophy* 2 (1977): 212–213.

Hegel, G. W. F. *Phenomenology of Spirit*. Translated by A. V. Miller, Oxford: Oxford University Press, 1977.

Jackson, F. *From Metaphysics to Ethics*. Oxford: Oxford University Press, 1997.

Kant, I. *Prolegomena to Any Future Metaphysics*. Translated by L. W. Beck. Indianapolis: Bobbs-Merrill, 1950.

Kim, J. *Supervenience and Mind: Selected Philosophical Essays*. New York: Cambridge University Press, 1993.

Leibniz, G. W. *Monadology*. In *Monadology and Other Philosophical Essays*. Translated by P. Schrecker and A. M. Schrecker. New York: Bobbs-Merrill, 1965.

Lewis, D. *On the Plurality of Worlds*. Oxford: Blackwell, 1986.

Lewis, D. *Parts of Classes*. Oxford: Blackwell, 1991.

Mackie, J. L. *Ethics: Inventing Right and Wrong*. Harmondsworth, NY: Penguin, 1977.

Maddy, P. *Realism in Mathematics*. Oxford: Oxford University Press, 1990.

Meinong, A. "On the Theory of Objects." In *Realism and the Background of Phenomenology*, edited by R. Chisholm, 76–117. Glencoe, IL: Free Press, 1960.

Montague, R. *Formal Philosophy: Selected Papers of Richard Montague*. New Haven, CT: Yale University Press, 1974.

Moore, G. E. *Philosophical Studies*. New York: Harcourt, Brace, 1922.

Oddie, G. *Value, Reality, and Desire*. Oxford: Oxford University Press, 2005.

Parsons, T. *Nonexistent Objects*. New Haven, CT: Yale University Press, 1980.

Plato. *The Dialogues of Plato*. Translated and edited by B. Jowett. Oxford: Clarendon Press, 1953.

Popper, K. *Conjectures and Refutations: The Growth of Scientific Knowledge*. London: Routledge, 1963.

Post, J. F. *The Faces of Existence: An Essay in Nonreductive Metaphysics*. Ithaca: Cornell University Press, 1987.

Priest, G. *Beyond the Limits of Thought*. Oxford: Clarendon Press, 2002.

Prior, A. N. *Papers on Time and Tense*. Oxford: Clarendon Press, 1968.

Putnam, H. *Reason, Truth and History*. Cambridge, U.K.: Cambridge University Press, 1981.

Quine, W. v. O. *From a Logical Point of View*. Cambridge, MA: Harvard University Press, 1953.

Rodriguez-Pereyra, G. *Resemblance Nominalism: A Solution to the Problem of Universals*. Oxford: Oxford University Press, 2002.

Ryle, G. *The Concept of Mind*. London: Hutchinson's University Library, 1949.

Russell, B. "On Denoting." *Mind* 14 (1905): 479–493.

Russell, B. *The Principles of Mathematics*. Cambridge, U.K.: Cambridge University Press, 1903.

Russell, B. *The Analysis of Matter*. London: Routledge, 1927.

Schlick, M. "Form and Content: An Introduction to Philosophical Thinking." *Moritz Schlick: Philosophical Papers. Vol. II*, edited by H. L. Mulder and B. F. B. van de Velde-Schlick. Translated by P. Heath. Dordrecht: Reidel, 1979.

Smart, J. J. C. *Philosophy and Scientific Realism*. London: Routledge & Kegan Paul, 1963.

Spinoza, B. "Ethics." In *The Collected Writings of Spinoza, Vol. 1*. Translated by E. Curley. Princeton, NJ: Princeton University Press, 1985.

Strawson, P. F. *Individuals, an Essay in Descriptive Metaphysics*. London: Methuen, 1959.

Tichy, P. "An Approach to Intensional Analysis." *Noûs* 5 (1971): 273–297.

Tooley, M. *Causation*. Oxford: Oxford University Press, 1987.

Tooley, M., ed. *Metaphysics. Vols. 1–5*. New York: Garland, 1999.

Williams, D. C. "The Elements of Being." *Review of Metaphysics* 7 (1953): 3–18; 171–192.

Van Cleve, J. "Three Versions of the Bundle Theory." *Philosophical Studies* 47 (1985): 95–107.

Wittgenstein, L. *Tractatus Logico-Philosophicus*. London: Routledge & Kegan Paul, 1922.

Zalta, E. *Abstract Objects: An Introduction to Axiomatic Metaphysics*. Dordrecht, Holland: Reidel, 1983.

Graham Oddie (2005)

METAPHYSICS, HISTORY OF

The word *metaphysics* derives from the Greek *meta ta physika* (literally, "after the things of nature"), an expression used by Hellenistic and later commentators to refer to Aristotle's untitled group of texts that we still call the *Metaphysics*. Aristotle himself called the subject of these texts first philosophy, theology, or sometimes wisdom; the phrase *ta meta ta physika biblia* ("the books after the books on nature") is not used by Aristotle himself and was apparently introduced by the editors (traditionally by Andronicus of Rhodes in the first century BCE) who classified and cataloged his works. Later, classical and medieval philosophers took this title to mean that the subjects discussed in the *Metaphysics* came "after the things of nature" because they were further removed from sense perception and, therefore, more difficult to understand; they used Aristotle's frequent contrast of things "prior and better known to us" with things "prior and better known in themselves" to explain why the treatises on first philosophy should come "after the books on physics." In medieval and modern philosophy "metaphysics" has also been taken to mean the study of things transcending nature—that is, existing separately from nature and having more intrinsic reality and value than the things of nature—giving *meta* a philosophical meaning it did not have in classical Greek.

Especially since Immanuel Kant *metaphysics* has often meant a priori speculation on questions that cannot be answered by scientific observation and experiment. Popularly, "metaphysics" has meant anything abstruse and highly theoretical—a common eighteenth-century usage illustrated by David Hume's occasional use of *metaphysical* to mean "excessively subtle." The term has also been popularly associated with the spiritual, the religious, and even the occult. In modern philosophical usage *metaphysics* refers generally to the field of philosophy dealing with questions about the kinds of things there are and their modes of being. Its subject matter includes the concepts of existence, thing, property, event; the distinctions between particulars and universals, individuals and classes; the nature of relations, change, causation; and the nature of mind, matter, space, and time. In the eighteenth and nineteenth centuries *metaphysics* was used broadly to include questions about the reality of the external world, the existence of other minds, the possibility of a priori knowledge, and the nature of sensation, memory, abstraction, and so on. In present usage these questions are included in the study of epistemology.

THE CLASSICAL PERIOD

The history of metaphysics in Western philosophy (taking "metaphysics" in the contemporary sense) began with speculations by the Ionian cosmologists in the sixth century BCE about the origin of the physical universe, the matter or stuff from which it is made, and the laws or uniformities everywhere present in nature. Our knowledge of these early cosmologists comes mostly from Aristotle and other classical authors; the main figures were the Milesians (Thales, Anaximander, and Anaximenes), Pythagoras, and Heraclitus.

PARMENIDES. The beginning of metaphysics, however, is most conveniently dated from Parmenides (fl. c. 475 BCE), since some of the typical characteristics of metaphysics as a distinct philosophical inquiry are present in, or at least suggested by, his surviving writings. These characteristics are, first, the conception of philosophy as an attempt to understand the universe by means of a logical investigation that is a priori, appealing to meanings of terms rather than to the evidence of the senses. This method is in contrast to the method of natural science, which relies on sense perception. Second is a more or less explicit use of very general principles viewed as sufficient to arrive at a true account of reality. Such principles were, for example, noncontradiction and something like a principle of sufficient reason, which is expressed in Parmenides' poem: "Also, what necessity impelled it, if it did spring from Nothing, to be produced later or earlier? Thus it must Be absolutely, or not at all." Philosophy was therefore conceived as a deductive science like mathematics. Third is the paradoxical contrast between apparent reality and true reality and the association of the truly real with singleness and unchangingness.

Of these features of Parmenides' writings, the first is fundamental; it can be taken as a defining characteristic of metaphysics. Like the natural scientist, the metaphysician gives an account of the universe; unlike the scientist, he does not base his account on observations and experiments, at least not on any special observations and experiments made for the purpose. His account is based primarily on analysis of concepts; if he does appeal to the evidence of the senses, he appeals to something generally familiar, not to new evidence he is adding to knowledge. Parmenides himself apparently believed he had done all that could be done by way of a philosophical account of the universe. His account consists in pointing to what he believed were the logical consequences of saying "It is." He dismissed everything else either as poetic imagery with no claim to truth or as empirical science; he indiscriminately referred to both as opinion. His position was not naive; it is not easy to see how a metaphysician can give an account of reality based on logic alone unless reality in some sense has the features of necessity and vacuous generality belonging to logical truths. And doctrines similar to Parmenides' logical monism have frequently reappeared in the history of metaphysics—for example, in Neoplatonism, in Benedict de Spinoza, and in nineteenth-century Hegelianism. There is more than a superficial resemblance between Parmenides' Being, the Neoplatonists' One, Spinoza's God or nature, and G. W. F. Hegel's Absolute as understood by a metaphysician like F. H. Bradley. Perhaps the underlying reasoning is that recognizing that metaphysics gives an account of the world based on analysis of concepts rather than on empirical evidence, these philosophers have felt that logic alone should be sufficient basis for making assertions about the world; since whatever is logically true is thought to be necessarily and always true, they have concluded that the world itself must be unchanging and in some sense necessarily what it is.

LATER PRE-SOCRATICS. Parmenides apparently believed he had said all that a metaphysician could say about the world. Accordingly, his followers Melissus and especially Zeno are more critical than constructive—a trait shown by many later metaphysicians who are more often concerned to demonstrate what they take to be logical failures in the ordinary or scientific understanding of

reality than to give a positive account of reality. We learn from Plato's *Parmenides* that Zeno's paradoxes of motion were meant to support Parmenides' system by showing contradictions in the ordinary concept of change. (When does the arrow move? Not now, because at any given instant it is in one place and hence not moving; not at some other time, because if it is moving, it must be moving now.)

Parmenides' general effect, however, was to interest philosophers in following what seemed to be the logical implications of their assumptions. An example is Anaxagoras, who apparently argued from the assumption that reality is many and changing to the conclusion that the things we ordinarily call real are composed of unendingly smaller parts similar to the whole things, that "all things are together," that "everything contains a part of every other thing," and that although there are rearrangements of things, nothing is ever really created or destroyed. Like his contemporaries Empedocles and the atomists Leucippus and Democritus, Anaxagoras did rely on observation and experiments to give an account of nature, but the surviving fragments suggest that his cosmology was arrived at largely by a priori reasoning in the way Parmenides' was, although the resulting account of reality is the opposite of Parmenides' account. And in the same way that something like Parmenides' logical monism is repeated in Neoplatonism, in Spinoza, and in nineteenth-century Hegelianism, something like Anaxagoras's logical pluralism is repeated in Gottfried Wilhelm Leibniz's theory of monads and Bertrand Russell's logical atomism. The common feature of this kind of system is that on logical grounds reality is described as composed of elements viewed as the limit of an unending process of division; the least parts of things are, so to speak, real infinitesimals—things smaller or simpler than any given thing one can mention. The atomism of Leucippus, Democritus, and, later, Lucretius is, by contrast, primarily a physical theory. These thinkers believed that the existence of atoms can be shown empirically; their atoms have finite sizes and such recognizable physical properties as shape and motion and, perhaps, weight, and the theory anticipates Galileo Galilei and Isaac Newton rather than Leibniz and Russell.

PLATO. In Plato's *Phaedo* Socrates is made to say he once studied Anaxagoras but gave up this study and all empirical investigations of nature, deciding instead to "have recourse to conceptions and examine in them the truth of realities." Anaxagoras, Parmenides, and others had also had recourse to conceptions in contrast to the evidence of the senses; what is new in the *Phaedo* is the theory of

Ideas or Forms, which historians of philosophy sometimes ascribe to Plato (c. 427–347 BCE) and sometimes to Socrates himself. For Plato, at least, ideas exist independently of the things we see and touch; moreover, they are considered the source of existence of things we see and touch, somewhat as a man is the cause of his shadow or of his reflection in a mirror or a pool of water. Popularly, Plato's metaphysics means the theory of Ideas in this sense, and in this way the theory has had a great influence in the history of thought. Plato's own evaluation, however, was considerably more critical than that of many of his followers. The theory of Ideas in this form is presented in the *Phaedo* as a hypothesis that cannot be known to be true; in the *Parmenides* its logical weaknesses are pointed out; in the *Timaeus* it is used as part of a "probable" or "likely" cosmology. Nevertheless, Plato does consistently argue for the existence of mind or soul as a kind of entity distinct from, and in some sense prior to, physical objects. This thesis is developed, notably in the *Phaedo,* where the theory of Ideas is used as a step in proving the immortality of soul, in the *Phaedrus,* and in Book X of the *Laws.* In these contexts Plato argues that since bodies cannot move themselves (apparent self-motion is reduced to one part's moving another) whereas soul can, the ultimate source of observed motions must be soul or mind. In the *Laws* this argument is used to prove the existence of the gods, who are understood as sources of observed motions and changes in the visible universe.

Plato's technical contributions to metaphysics are contained in the difficult later dialogues, especially the *Parmenides* and *Sophist.* Both dialogues purport to be a criticism of Eleatic philosophy, by Parmenides himself in the *Parmenides* and by an "Eleatic stranger" in the *Sophist.* In the *Parmenides* Parmenides is represented as illustrating the method of dialectic by scrutinizing his own hypothesis that "the One exists" and deducing the logical consequences both of asserting and of denying this hypothesis. The point is that what follows depends on how the hypothesis is understood—in particular, on how one understands unity and existence. If, for example, unity is thought to be in no way compatible with plurality, a thing that has unity can hardly have anything else. Thus, it cannot have spatial extension, for it would then have a right and a left, an up and a down. The more straightforward *Sophist* classifies philosophers into materialists and idealists according to their criteria of reality. A general criterion of reality as power is suggested, and a number of concepts of equal generality with that of being are introduced and discussed—sameness, difference, rest, and motion. The apparent paradox in negation is explained by distinguishing absolute nonbeing (*A* does

not exist) from relative nonbeing (*A* is non-*B*) or otherness and by distinguishing the existential is (*A* exists) from the is of predication (*A* is characterized by *B*). In the *Timaeus* the generic concepts are used in the mythical account of the construction of the physical universe by a godlike artisan using an ideal pattern as a blueprint.

ARISTOTLE. Aristotle (384–322 BCE) is indirectly the source of the term *metaphysics*; he is also the source of a systematic list of metaphysical issues, a technical language in which these issues are stated, and a metaphysical system that has had followers down to the present and has proved immensely fruitful. In part, the importance of this system has been in serving as an object of criticism, although this function has been served by Plato as much as by Aristotle and Aristotle himself illustrates Plato's importance as an object of criticism in the history of metaphysics.

The problems of "first philosophy," or metaphysics, listed by Aristotle in books Beta and Kappa of the *Metaphysics* are partly about metaphysics itself: Does its subject matter include all the basic concepts and assumptions of all the special sciences? Does it include the principles of logic? Is there metaphysical knowledge in contrast to opinion? These questions ask, in effect, whether metaphysics is a superscience proving the assumptions made by the special sciences and also the assumptions it itself uses—whether, in short, it is a logically self-contained body of knowledge contrasting with the logically incomplete special sciences. This concept of metaphysics was held, for example, by René Descartes, but on the whole Aristotle rejected this view. Metaphysics is less the capstone of a hierarchy of sciences than a discussion of problems left over by the special sciences. Physics, for example, assumes there is motion, but it is not part of the metaphysician's job as Aristotle saw it to prove this assumption; at most, he should explain it or defend it from criticism. Aristotle thought of metaphysics as explaining things we already know to be true rather than as giving reasons for the assumptions we make in the sciences and everyday life, thereby providing the underpinnings of science and common sense.

Some of the problems of metaphysics listed by Aristotle are questions about the kinds of things there are. In addition to physical objects perceived by the senses, do such abstractions as Plato's Ideas or the mathematician's numbers, points, lines, and so on also exist? Are all existing things particulars, or do universals like man or whiteness exist, too? Do particulars of the same kind have anything in common, and if so, what and how? Are physical objects something more than the material parts that compose them, and if so, what?

For Aristotle, however, the most fundamental questions of metaphysics concerned the concepts of being and unity. Are being and unity properties of things (since everything both is and is one thing), or are they entities or substances of some kind (as Parmenides seemed to have thought)? If being and unity are things in their own right, what kind of things are they? These questions are suggested by Plato's *Parmenides* and *Sophist*. Aristotle's answers are his most important contribution to metaphysics. In the *Sophist* Plato suggested a general definition of being as power but gave little by way of an explicit analysis of this sense of being, which does not correspond to the use of the word in ordinary language. Such an explicit analysis is the center of Aristotle's metaphysics; his contribution can be summarized as the view that although there are many ways in which things are and are one (and there are therefore many senses of being and unity) and although these ways are irreducibly distinct, they nevertheless depend on one basic kind of being. Being is neither an attribute nor a thing and cannot therefore be defined in the ways *triangular* or *horse* can be defined. But we can pick out a basic sense of being, illustrated in such statements as, "This is a horse" or "This is a man," and show how the other senses of being depend on it. "Being a horse," "being a man," and, in general, "being an *X*" in the basic sense of being means to have attributes and therefore to be a subject of thought and discourse without in turn being an attribute of something else; "being a horse" is not, for Aristotle, an attribute of some more basic subject of thought and discourse. Primarily, what there is, is this horse, this man, and so on when we are speaking of an individual; secondarily, what there is, is horse, man, and so on understood as species or kinds of things. Qualities, dates, locations, motions, relations, and the like are attributed to the things that exist in the basic sense; they themselves do not have independent existence and "are" only in a derivative and borrowed sense of being.

Aristotle's analysis of being is the heart of his metaphysics; it is not the whole of it or the part most stressed by his later followers. What is often referred to as Aristotle's metaphysics is his account of the universe. Roughly, it states that there are a large but finite number of things that for the most part (with exceptions such as the sun, the only thing of its kind, and biological "mistakes" resulting from mutation and crossbreeding) belong to definite kinds—for example, plant and animal species. In most cases the individual members of these kinds or classes are born and die, but the classes themselves do not change. Some things—for example, the stars—exist forever and apart from uniform motions do not change at all. There is an ultimate prime mover that is the source of all observed motion and change but is itself completely immaterial and therefore completely motionless and changeless. This set of ideas is in the *Metaphysics*, and the pluralism and some theory of natural kinds do follow from Aristotle's analysis of being. But the theory of prime movers and the Unmoved Mover is also in the *Physics* as a scientific—that is, demonstrable—account of the physical universe; it is not therefore a true part of his metaphysics, which is dialectical (arguing from common opinion and logic) rather than scientific.

The central chapters of the *Metaphysics* elucidate and defend the claim that such commonsense things as this horse, this man, and so on are the fundamental subjects of discourse. Aristotle upheld this claim against (1) the view that the ultimate material parts of things are the ultimate subjects of discourse (so that "This is a horse" would be understood as "These material elements have horselike attributes"); (2) the view that Platonic Ideas are the ultimate subject of discourse (where "This is a horse" is understood as "The horse is exemplified by these sensible qualities"); and (3) the view that the basic sense of being is illustrated in, for instance, "There is a horse in the barn"—the view according to which "there is" means "it is true that" or "it is a fact that." For Aristotle to be is to be an individual, and the being of a thing is primarily its nature or identifying features rather than the fact that it is. Aristotle hardly even recognized the sense of being involved in such sentences as "There are good men, and there are wicked men," which can be read as "Among all the things that are, some are—that is, have the identifying features of—good men; others are wicked men." Such sentences suggest that what exists primarily are featureless particulars, which can be referred to collectively as "the things that exist," not commonsense things.

In general, the question "What is being?" became for Aristotle "What is an individual?," a horse, a man, a house, and so on being understood as paradigms of an individual. And, positively, the central argument of the *Metaphysics* is that an individual is primarily the distinguishing features by which we identify and classify it. Aristotle himself believed that these classifications are learned through experience; he was a realist in the sense that he thought the groups and classes of things are there to be learned by observation and are not simply mental constructions. Therefore, there is a sense in which we learn empirically what being is. But metaphysics is not itself an empirical study of being; Aristotle did not, for instance, think of metaphysics as a science of high-level generality describing the properties that all beings (individuals) have.

Aristotle's *Metaphysics* in its present form—and there is no reason to think it ever had a very different form—is barely readable in large stretches. Other parts read like outmoded astronomy; still other parts read like rather tedious lexicography. The devastating criticism of Plato is largely borrowed from Plato himself. However, the *Metaphysics* gives a surprisingly coherent set of answers to the questions it raises, and the questions themselves are those that metaphysicians still ask.

NEOPLATONISM. The Neoplatonists in the late classical period were metaphysicians of great power and originality. They were also of great importance in the development of metaphysics since they formed a link between ancient and medieval philosophy. The main figure of this movement, Plotinus (c. 204–270), associated metaphysics with mysticism and personal asceticism. The mystical and religious side of his philosophy was stressed by his disciple and editor Porphyry (c. 232–304), and such later Neoplatonists as Iamblichus and Proclus gave a further religious and even occult and superstitious emphasis to the movement. But the intellectual power of the movement is shown in as late a philosopher as Ancius Manlius Severinus Boethius (c. 480–524), and through Boethius Neoplatonism had a very strong influence on medieval philosophy and, therefore, indirectly on modern philosophy.

Plotinus. Plotinus's philosophy is a paradigm case of a metaphysical system according to one common conception of metaphysics. It asserts the unreality or half reality of the things of everyday experience; the illusory character of change, motion, and even space and time; the superior reality of soul or mind over matter. It conceives of goodness and intelligence as substantial things and stresses personal mysticism and an ascetic way of life. The line of thought by which Plotinus arrived at this position is not easy to follow, but, briefly, it seems to have been somewhat as follows. Whatever is, is one thing (even a collection of things is said to "be" only when counted as one thing—a collection); the answer to the question "What is being?," understood as a request for a description of being, is therefore unity or singleness. But unity or singleness cannot be described any further, although a direct, intuitive experience of it is in some sense possible. Since being is equivalent to unity and since things can have unity to a greater or lesser degree, we can speak of

degrees of being. Although unity is itself ineffable, it does duplicate itself in a kind of descending series of things—in goodness and intelligence—in a lesser way in disembodied spirits, in a still lesser way in human souls, least of all in physical objects and their properties and relations. The emanation of successively less real things from unity is to be understood in a logical rather than a physical sense. Speaking accurately, unity or singleness (the One) is not a cause at all, although it can be described metaphorically, for example, as an inexhaustible fountain of being bringing existence to all the things that are by its continuous overflow. Plotinus's writings are full of these metaphors, but he recognized them as metaphors, and the underlying position is rigorously argued, granting the not implausible identification of being with unity or singleness.

Plotinus's line of thought begins with the assumption that being and unity are properties that things have—properties of utmost generality, to be sure, but still properties in the same way that black or being four-legged are properties of a horse. Combined with this seems to be the Platonic assumption that properties are not simply modifications of particulars or ways that particulars exist; properties are entities in their own right that particular things instance or exemplify. The first of these two assumptions is clearly made in the *Isagoge*, Porphyry's short introductory treatise on Aristotle's *Categories*. In Porphyry's account—and in this account he is presumably expressing a typically Neoplatonic point of view—the theory of categories or types of predication is a theory of kinds of predicates: genus, species, difference, property (that is, essential property), and accident. These kinds of predicates (the predicables) are distinguished from individuals. But even expressions designating individuals are predicates of a sort according to Porphyry; such expressions as "Socrates," "this man here," and "this thing here" are attributes, differing from the predicables because they are "only said of a single thing" whereas the predicables "are said of several things." The distinction is between attributes belonging to several things and attributes belonging to only one thing. But of individuals themselves, in contrast to attributes, nothing is said; they can apparently be characterized only indirectly, as the ultimate subjects of predication.

This account of predication makes the distinction between thing and property peripheral to metaphysics. The important distinction is between relatively less general and relatively more general attributes, culminating in the most general attributes, being and unity. Porphyry spoke of substance as "the most general genus" and in a sense the only real genus, since unlike animal, for example, which is a genus relative to man but only a special case relative to "living thing," substance is not itself a special case of some higher genus. Neoplatonic metaphysics is largely an analysis, similar to Plato's *Parmenides*, of these ultimate genera; the main force of Plotinus's writings is the argument that the ultimate genera cannot be described in any ordinary way but are in some sense manifest in lower orders of being. Neoplatonism thus easily lends itself to religious interpretation; in the late classical world it actually was a theological system associated with a religious way of life competing with Christianity.

THE MIDDLE AGES

Porphyry's *Isagoge*, translated into Latin by Boethius in the sixth century, gave philosophers some basic tools and stimulated speculation on two questions in particular: (1) What is a thing considered just by itself, as a bare existent, apart from all its attributes? (2) Do attributes exist (or subsist) separately from human thought and discourse and from the things that are said to have attributes? The first question, implicit in Porphyry's account of predication, is roughly the problem of distinguishing essence from existence, what a thing is from the fact that it is. The second question (really, group of questions) was explicitly raised but not answered by Porphyry; it is the problem of universals much discussed throughout medieval philosophy.

For Aristotle the contrast between what a thing is and the fact that it is, is at best peripheral to metaphysics. Aristotle recognized that the question "Does *X* exist?" is distinct from "What is *X*?," but he attached no metaphysical importance to the distinction. Particular questions of the form "Does *X* exist?" are decided by sense perception or by proof; there is no general metaphysical question about the nature of existence ("thatness") in contrast to essence ("whatness"). The metaphysician is concerned with what things are rather than with their existence or nonexistence. Aristotle's position was that what things are—that is, their being—is primarily what is contained in their definitions; the definition of a thing describes its essence, which is equivalent to its species (the traits that identify it as the kind of thing it is) which is in turn identified with its genus, differentia, and essential properties. But when, as in Porphyry, genus (mammal), difference (solid-hoofed), species (horse), property (neighs), and accident (gray) are indiscriminately called attributes of the thing itself, it is natural to ask what it is that has these attributes or what it is that gives this collection of attributes an actual rather than a merely possible existence.

The problem of universals dominated metaphysics in the early Middle Ages; it was discussed by metaphysicians from Boethius in the sixth century to Roscelin and Peter Abelard in the twelfth century. The main philosophical tradition during this period was the Augustinian tradition, represented by Boethius himself, John Scotus Erigena (c. 810–c. 877), St. Anselm (1033–1109), William of Champeaux (d. c. 1120), St. Bonaventure (c. 1217–1274), and many others. This tradition favored realism; species and genera like horse and animal were thought to exist not only apart from human thought and discourse (epistemological realism) but also apart from particular horses and animals. Species and genera were regarded as paradigms, archetypes, or exemplars of particular things; as such, they exist in the mind of God and are used by him as models in creating nature. As in St. Augustine and Plato, the fundamental contention is that particulars cannot be recognized and identified as one of a general type unless we first have independent knowledge of the type; the inference is that these general types must exist apart from, and in some sense prior to, the particulars exemplifying them.

St. Anselm's proof of God's existence (anticipated by St. Augustine), has had an important history in its own right; it is also an illuminating example of Christian Platonism in the early Middle Ages. The argument cannot be appreciated apart from its context of religious meditation, but it can be picked out and studied (as it has been by philosophers to this day) as a kind of supreme test case of Platonic (or Neoplatonic) metaphysical assumptions. Briefly, the argument is that (1) we have a concept of a supreme being (a being "than which nothing greater can be conceived") so that (2) the Supreme Being "exists in the understanding." Since (3) it is greater to exist in reality than merely in the understanding, it is contradictory to say the Supreme Being exists only in the understanding; hence, we can infer that (4) the Supreme Being does exist in reality. Kant's objection seems decisive. The existence (as contrasted with the concept of existing) of the Supreme Being cannot be a part of our concept of the Supreme Being. If it were, our concept would be the Supreme Being, not its concept. But the argument seems inevitable if one assumes, as the Neoplatonists did, that existence is an attribute that things have and, in consequence of having it, are, as things are red in consequence of having the attribute redness. Combined with the assumption that attributes have an independent existence, this line of thought leads to the conclusion that existence or being is itself an existing thing; the existence of things in nature is thought of as being due to their receiving a part of the inexhaustible thing, being, somewhat as an illuminated object receives its light from a source of illumination. Furthermore, it seems to follow that existence must itself necessarily exist as an analytic consequence of what it is (just as "Redness is red" seems to state an analytic necessity). Given these assumptions, the Ontological Argument for God's existence, as Kant later called it, is at least a strong temptation; the argument has had a history identical with the history of logical monism in metaphysics, from Parmenides to Hegel and beyond, as well as a close association with Christian theology.

REVIVAL OF CLASSICAL PHILOSOPHY

Although the realism-nominalism controversy occupied philosophers in the eleventh and twelfth centuries, new ways of thinking in metaphysics were being prepared by translations of Greek and Arabic texts into Latin, especially translations of Aristotle and his Arabian commentators. In the early Middle Ages there was very little firsthand knowledge of the Greek philosophers. Plato's *Timaeus, Phaedo,* and *Meno* were known, but the important later dialogues, including *Parmenides* and *Sophist,* were not. The Greek texts had been preserved, however, and, especially after the capture of Constantinople by crusaders in 1204, were slowly recovered in the West. In the thirteenth century William of Moerbeke made a literal Latin translation of Proclus's *Commentary on the Parmenides*; the commentary contained the text of the *Parmenides* through the first hypothesis, thereby giving philosophers some firsthand knowledge of that important dialogue.

Aristotle was even less known and understood in the early Middle Ages. Only his logic, the text of *De Interpretatione,* and the other logical treatises in Neoplatonized versions through Boethius were known. As late as the thirteenth century, two Neoplatonic texts—the "Theology of Aristotle" (actually a compilation from Plotinus's *Enneads,* IV–VI) and the *Liber de Causis* (a work based on Proclus's *Elements of Theology*)—were wrongly attributed to Aristotle. However, Aristotle's writings had been translated into Syriac by Nestorian Christians in the fifth century and from Syriac into Arabic in the ninth century; Latin translations of Arabic texts were made in the twelfth century and directly from Greek texts by Robert Grosseteste and William of Moerbeke in the thirteenth century. By the end of the thirteenth century most of Aristotle was translated into Latin and was generally available to philosophers. In effect, Aristotle was a new philosopher who appeared on the scene and dominated it as if he were a contemporary; the *Metaphysics* was the

stimulus for such metaphysicians as Albert the Great, St. Thomas Aquinas, John Duns Scotus, William of Ockham, and others in the thirteenth and fourteenth centuries.

THOMAS AQUINAS. Thomas Aquinas's metaphysics is an attempt to explain the distinctions between essence and existence, necessary and contingent existence, and particulars and universals, using the language and much of the metaphysical outlook of Aristotle. For Thomas commonsense things like horses and houses do exist in a literal and straightforward sense apart from human observers and also apart from God and paradigms of things in the mind of God. The existence of these commonsense things is not an attribute that they receive from outside; it is not like the light the earth receives from the sun. The existence of finite things in nature is an intrinsic act of existing that these things exercise. But Thomas also held that the ordinary things we experience exist contingently in the sense that their existing is not an analytic consequence of what they are; it is not something they do by nature. There must therefore be a cause (in a metaphysical, not a physical, sense of "cause") of their existence; this must be a necessary being, identified with God, who exists by his own nature. Contingent beings, like horses and houses, are obviously contingent because being composed of matter, their existence is finite—they begin to exist and cease to exist. Matter also accounts for the individuality of things; things that are identical insofar as what they are, or, in other words, things that have the same nature, are still different things because the matter of which they are composed is different. God, on the contrary, is immaterial and, hence, one and unchanging. Thomas, like the Neoplatonists, associated finitude, contingency, plurality, and change with matter. He differed from the Neoplatonists chiefly in his view that finite things—in particular, human persons—exist in their own right (by virtue of a delegated power, as it were) and do not merely participate in the existence of a higher order of being. In this view Thomas agreed with Christian theology and was close to Aristotle.

DUNS SCOTUS. John Duns Scotus (c. 1266–1308) seems to have agreed with Thomas that being is not an attribute or a thing in some sense shared by all the things said to be. On the other hand, he criticized Thomas's contrast of essence with existence, arguing that whatever we are aware of must be an essence in some sense, including even individuality or "thisness," which he treats as an attribute of individuals ("this horse here"), distinguishing them from indeterminate beings ("a horse" or "the horse" in general).

WILLIAM OF OCKHAM. William of Ockham (c. 1285–1349) held that general or indeterminate expressions like "a horse" or "the horse" do not correspond to general beings either in the mind or in reality but refer indifferently to individual horses. He was therefore conventionally called a nominalist in contrast to Duns Scotus, a realist. But William of Ockham's main point seems to be that logical distinctions between universal, particular, and singular are not distinctions between kinds of things—not an enumeration of what there is—but are, rather, ways of referring to the one and only one kind of thing that does exist—namely, the commonsense things we encounter in everyday experience. For this reason William was probably closer to Aristotle's own view than either Thomas or Duns Scotus; unlike them his explicit aim was to state Aristotle's original position as accurately as he could. But William's successors—notably, John of Mirecourt and Nicholas of Autrecourt—pushed William's views in a direction that anticipated Hume and even twentieth-century logical positivism. We can talk meaningfully only about what we are acquainted with through the senses, and we are acquainted only with particulars, so that all discourse about things refers ultimately only to particulars. The existence of a particular is never an analytic necessity or an analytic consequence of the existence of some other; hence, all meaningful statements about things are only probable.

DESCARTES TO KANT

DESCARTES. The revival of metaphysics in the seventeenth century begins with René Descartes (1596–1650), who has been traditionally considered the originator of modern philosophy. The ideas most commonly associated with Descartes are not original with him. In St. Augustine's writings can be found the *cogito ergo sum* argument and the view that our own existence is the ultimate certainty since we can be certain of it while the existence of all other things is in doubt. The argument that nothing less than God could have produced the idea of God in the human mind can also be found in St. Augustine. The Ontological Argument had a famous history in the Middle Ages, and the view that physical objects have only geometrical attributes of shape and motion was held by early Greek atomists. The concept of mind as a substantial thing more or less externally attached to the body is hardly original with Descartes. But to say this is to say only that Descartes used a good deal of material from old ruins in his work of "building from the foundation" in metaphysics in order "to establish a firm and abiding superstructure in the sciences."

Descartes was most original in his conception of philosophical method and philosophical truth. No metaphysical assertion is to be believed unless (1) it is understood with the kind of clarity and distinctness that mathematical propositions have and (2) its truth is either so intrinsically obvious that, like the postulates of geometry, it cannot be doubted or it is proved with the same rigor with which theorems are proved in geometry. Descartes's philosophy can be viewed in large part as an effort to reduce the second criterion to the first—that is, to show that at least in the case of metaphysical propositions, if we understand them clearly and distinctly, we are thereby certain of their truth. These claims made for his or any other metaphysical assertion were revolutionary and most influential. As Descartes and his followers understood them, they amounted to a demand that metaphysics be scientific, understanding by the word *scientific* being subject to a kind of rigorous intellectual discipline best illustrated in mathematics and the exact physical sciences.

SPINOZA. Benedict de Spinoza (1632–1677), following one interpretation of Descartes's demand for clarity and distinctness in metaphysics, thought of metaphysics as a deductive account of the universe to be developed from a few definitions—notably, the definition of substance as a being that requires nothing outside itself to be or to be conceived—and self-evident assumptions. His inferences are that there must logically be one and only one substance, uncreated and everlasting; there are an infinite number of attributes of the one substance, only two of which, thought and extension, are known to us; attributes are faces of the one substance—self-contained ways of describing it—rather than properties inhering in it the way we commonly think of colors as inhering in physical objects; the universe, described in terms of the attribute extension, is a mechanical system in which all happenings are links in a chain of physical causation; an equally complete causal determinism holds when the universe is conceived in terms of the attribute thought.

LEIBNIZ. Gottfried Wilhelm Leibniz (1646–1716) was also a follower of Descartes in the sense that he agreed with the demand for a rigorously scientific metaphysics and for clear and distinct ideas in contrast to scholastic verbiage. But while Leibniz agreed that metaphysical assertions are true if clearly and distinctly understood, he interpreted this to mean that metaphysical truths (and truths of reason generally, in contrast to contingent truths of fact) are logically necessary; their denial involves a self-contradiction. Leibniz understood clarity and distinctness in a logical rather than a psychological sense; for him "the true mark of a clear and distinct notion of an object is the means we have of knowing therein many truths by *a priori* proofs." And we know a truth by an a priori proof when "by the help of definitions or by the resolution of concepts" we "reduce" it to an explicit tautology of the form "*A is A*" or "*A is not non-A.*"

Leibniz's metaphysical system is, in effect, an effort to get a clear and distinct idea of the universe in his own rather special sense of clarity and distinctness. And his technical writings in metaphysics consist largely of a series of somewhat different a priori proofs of a number of metaphysical assertions, including the following: There are an infinite number of substances, each of which is logically complete in that it contains in some sense all the properties it ever has exhibited or will exhibit; no two substances exhibit exactly the same properties ("identity of indiscernibles"); a complete description of any one substance would be a description of the entire universe "from a point of view"; space and time are relations among things, not things in their own right; the appearance of causal relations between things is illusory, reflecting God's deliberate prearrangement rather than any real influence exerted by one thing on another. In proving these assertions, Leibniz relied on a principle of sufficient reason stating, in effect, that there is always a rational explanation for a fact. But the principle of sufficient reason is not really a description of the universe for Leibniz. What it really expresses is the idea that in principle any truth can be given an a priori proof; the underlying thought is that when any statement is understood with perfect clarity and distinctness, it will be seen to be an explicit tautology.

LOCKE. Spinoza and Leibniz are usually grouped with Descartes as rationalists, as contrasted with British empiricists, represented in the seventeenth century by John Locke (1632–1704). But in an important way Locke, too, was a follower of Descartes; he was also mainly interested in replacing scholastic jargon with clear and distinct ideas and opening the way for the sciences. Locke's main contribution to metaphysics lies in his critical discussion of substance and essence. Descartes had laid it down as an indubitable common notion that "nothing is possessed of no attributes, properties, or qualities," so that "when we perceive any attribute, we therefore conclude that some existing thing or substance to which it may be attributed, is necessarily present." Locke did not deny that this is a valid inference; he does not question the distinction between thing and property. But he asked what we know (or, as he phrased it, "What is our idea") of a thing

beyond its attributes, powers, and so forth. His answer was that we have no clear and distinct idea at all; we know only what the common notion itself says—namely, that if there are attributes, there must be something underneath that has them. We have no clear idea what is underneath or what "underneath" means in this context. We know only the attributes, powers, and so on (indiscriminately called qualities by Locke) of things, not the things in themselves.

Here, however, Locke was criticizing only the notion of substance as substratum underlying properties. And this is a concept of substance minimized by Aristotle and never stressed by metaphysicians. Thomas Hobbes, for example, argued that the accidents of body, such as shape or hardness, are the very "manner of our conception of body." To ask for a description of body apart from its accidents would be, for Hobbes, a senseless request. Locke's more important and original criticism concerns the notion of essence—the notion of what a thing is in contrast to what it is made of, how big it is, its location, its age, and the like. Locke argued at length that the distinction is a useless one; the question "What is X?" can be answered only by enumerating X's observed properties, and (most important) we cannot see any logical necessity for the coexistence of just these and not some other combination of properties. We do not therefore have any knowledge of real essences except in cases where we ourselves construct the thing in question, as in mathematics. Locke reasoned, roughly, that we know the attributes and powers of things only through the simple sense impressions we have of them. Since, for the most part at least, there are no noticeable necessary connections between simple sense impressions, we cannot explain why things appear as they do but can only describe how they do appear. Locke never denied there is a reason for things' having just the attributes and powers they have and not some others, but he denied our ability ever to have clear and distinct ideas of these reasons. The effect of Locke's view is to deny the possibility of metaphysical knowledge when metaphysics is conceived of in the way Francis Bacon, for example, conceived of it, as a very general but still empirical and even experimental study of the formal causes of things, as distinguished from natural science, which studies material and efficient causes.

BERKELEY AND HUME. Locke never questioned the distinction between ideas of things and the qualities in things that cause ideas, and he thought we have at least a "relative and obscure" idea of a thing in contrast to its qualities. But George Berkeley (1685–1753) questioned both distinctions, partly on grounds of fact but more especially on grounds of a general theory of meaning. For Berkeley the grammatical distinction between subject and predicate has no counterpart in a distinction between things and properties; we can talk meaningfully only about what we are acquainted with, and we are acquainted only with individual colors, sounds, tastes, and the like. Since these individual colors, sounds, and tastes have characteristics that are admittedly mental, such as pleasantness and painfulness, and are relative to the human observer in various ways, Berkeley concluded we can talk meaningfully only about mental entities or, as he called them, following the usage of Descartes and Locke, ideas in the mind. In this way Berkeley arrived at phenomenalism (things exist exactly as they appear to the senses) and idealism (things exist only as objects of conscious perception; their being consists in being perceived). Berkeley was not thoroughgoing in these positions; he thought it meaningful to talk about other minds and about God even though we cannot directly perceive such phenomena.

These qualifications, however, were swept aside in the thoroughgoing phenomenalism of David Hume (1711–1776). Hume criticized the notion of a mind as distinguished from the ideas said to be in the mind for the same reasons that Berkeley criticized the notion of matter. According to Hume, the notion of existence itself signifies nothing beyond a greater or less degree of force and vivacity attaching to sense impressions and mental images. Our beliefs in the continuous existence of physical objects and the presence of causal connections between them are explained as effects of habitual associations of ideas for which there is, strictly speaking, no evidence. Although Hume is usually and correctly called an empiricist in contrast to speculative metaphysicians like Leibniz or Spinoza, there is a sense in which he was as much a rationalist as his contemporary Christian Wolff. Hume assumed that the ultimate subject of thought and discourse must be something we are directly conscious of, that we are directly conscious only of individual sensations (or their more or less faint copies), and that whenever we can discriminate one sensation or feeling from another, these exist separately and hence count as different things. These assumptions amount to a theory of empiricism, but they are not themselves empirical assertions. Nor, on the other hand, are they necessary truths in Leibniz's sense—propositions whose denial involves a self-contradiction. In effect, they demonstrate how Hume understood Descartes's demand for clarity and distinctness in metaphysics and are analogous to Leibniz's principle of sufficient reason, which expressed his understanding of the same demand. For Leibniz clarity and distinctness meant, in the end, reduction to an explicit tautology; for Hume clarity and distinctness meant, in the end, reduction to directly verifiable assertions about sensations and feelings.

KANT. By the time of Hume's death, in 1776, the difficulties and ambiguities in Descartes's program for metaphysics were apparent. Cartesianism inspired both the speculative constructions of Spinoza, Nicolas Malebranche, Leibniz, and others and the critical and—at least, on the surface—increasingly skeptical philosophies of Locke, Berkeley, and Hume. This, at least, was the view taken by Immanuel Kant (1724–1804). It led Kant to ask whether metaphysics could be scientific—whether metaphysical knowledge is even possible and if not, how the questions that gave rise to metaphysics in the past could be answered. In discussing these problems, Kant made a very penetrating analysis of metaphysics as a discipline and a set of assertions and as a "human propensity"; Kant's contribution, apart from his own system, was to raise questions about what metaphysical assertions, as distinguished from scientific assertions, are, about the sense in which they claim truth, and about the grounds on which they are to be believed or disbelieved.

From Kant's point of view the history of metaphysics (insofar as metaphysics had claimed to be a science) had been a story of dogmatism versus skepticism. Dogmatists like Leibniz have held that metaphysics can, on the basis of purely logical or conceptual considerations, answer with absolute certainty questions about the origin of the universe, the existence of God, and the immortality of the soul. "Dogmatists," as Kant used the word, can be materialists, panpsychists, or dualists, monists or pluralists. What they share is a confidence that a metaphysician can give an account of the nature of reality using a priori reasoning. Skeptics, on the other hand, are empiricists; for them there are no universal and necessary truths of fact and reasoning alone, in contrast to observing and experimenting, is of no use whatsoever in answering questions about the existence or natures of things. For Kant this alternating dogmatism and skepticism was the effect of alternating overconfidence and lack of confidence in the abilities of the human mind. Accordingly, his critical philosophy is an effort to show what human knowledge is like and what its limits must necessarily be.

Dogmatic metaphysics in Kant's sense is not mere ad hoc speculation; it is an understandable and correctable misuse of basic concepts. The dogmatic metaphysician rightly sees that we actually use concepts like substance (in contrast to accidents) or causation (in contrast to mere succession). He also correctly saw that we are a priori certain of such things as the irreversibility of time or the impossibility of two physical objects' occupying the same space. But he uncritically concluded that we have a power other than sense perception of knowing what things are like, whereas the true conclusion is that we ourselves determine in advance what any object of knowledge must be like. The questions we ask about things and the answers we look for are determined by our own a priori forms of perceiving (space and time) and of judging (every attribute must belong to some substance, every event must have some cause and so on). Mistaking these a priori forms of perceiving and judging for descriptions of things-in-themselves, the dogmatic metaphysician is led to speak of ultimate subjects and first causes. In Kant's view these speculations are misguided and even meaningless. But metaphysical ideas, such as an ultimate subject or a first cause, do have a regulative use in encouraging us never to be satisfied with what we actually know at any given time. And Kant did not infer that the beliefs that metaphysicians have tried to prove—beliefs in personal immortality or in the existence of God—are illusory. These beliefs are not like belief in perpetual motion machines; they can be justified and can even be supported by arguments—but by moral arguments, not speculative arguments. Dogmatic metaphysics can thus be explained and even in a sense vindicated. It cannot be taken seriously as a source of knowledge, however.

METAPHYSICS SINCE KANT

Kant's own metaphysical position was idealistic. Aristotle's categories reappear somewhat altered in Kant's philosophy as forms of judgment. The most immediate and obvious effect of Kant's thought can be seen in the idealistic systems of his younger German contemporaries and successors, Johann Gottlieb Fichte (1762–1814), Friedrich Schelling (1775–1854), Arthur Schopenhauer (1788–1860), and, above all, Georg Wilhelm Friedrich Hegel (1770–1831).

HEGEL. Among the idealists, however, it was Hegel whose metaphysical outlook has probably had more general intellectual influence than that of any other single recent philosopher. Kant's critical idealism assumes a clear-cut contrast between what is given in experience (sense impressions) and the forms we use to arrange and interpret what is given. In general, Kant assumed a clear distinction between what is directly perceived and what is inferred or constructed by the mind. Hegel's absolute idealism consists largely in denying this contrast; for him the underlying notion of a plurality of separately existing particulars, uniquely located in space and time (conceived as containers in which things are unambiguously placed), was a false, even a logically incoherent notion. He appears to have arrived at this conclusion from the assumptions that things-in-themselves cannot be distinguished meaningfully from things as we know them and that things as we know them gradually take shape in our consciousness and become defined only in contrast to other things. On this basis he concluded that all things shade off into their opposites and that the connections between things we establish in thought are as much a part of the things as their so-called inherent properties. Hegel was thus led to the monistic position that there is only one kind of substance and only one truly substantial entity. His idealism is an evolutionary pantheism in which the only self-subsistent reality is spirit; it contrasts not only with materialism in the traditional sense but with any metaphysical position associating reality with some kind of hard definiteness.

Outside of philosophy proper Hegel's influence was apparent mainly in inspiring a view of things as phases of a living and growing history; institutions, languages, ideas, even philosophies themselves, were seen as quasi-living and even quasi-personal phenomena whose histories were to be sympathetically grasped and appreciated rather than appraised by themselves on the basis of a priori standards. This widely held view has been encouraged by Hegel's absolute idealism, in which reality is associated with self-expression and all-inclusiveness, not with given things or facts. Within philosophy Hegel's influence can be seen in the many evolutionary idealisms of the nineteenth and early twentieth centuries. It can also be seen in the more rigorous and critical thought of Hegelians like F. H. Bradley (1846–1924) and J. M. E. McTaggart (1866–1925). Bradley in particular stressed the negative side of Hegelianism, finding logical antinomies in the ordinary concepts of things, properties, relations, causation, and space and time. McTaggart, on the other hand, attempted to rephrase Hegelianism as a clear and straightforward speculative system. This tradition is continued by such contemporary metaphysicians as Brand Blanshard.

METAPHYSICS AND PRAGMATISM. Largely through the influence of German idealism and especially of Hegel, metaphysics in the nineteenth century generally meant a priori cosmology and, in particular, an idealist cosmology contrasted and even opposed to the alleged mechanistic and materialist assumptions of science. Auguste Comte's positive—that is, nonmetaphysical—philosophy did not attack metaphysics as such; it attacked speculative philosophy as a way of providing substitutes for religious beliefs. Popularly, metaphysics was associated with religion, idealism, and spiritualism and opposed to science, which was associated with empiricism and materialism. But this concept of metaphysics, although still popular, was only a temporary alignment in the history of metaphysics and was strongly challenged even in the nineteenth century.

A notable example is the American philosopher C. S. Peirce (1839–1914). Peirce was a Hegelian to the extent that he believed there are no self-identical particulars that can be unambiguously located or identified. Reality is indeterminate both in the sense that it is characterized by novelty and unpredictability and in the sense that things are not just what they are but shade off continuously into other things; reality is an evolutionary process that is in some sense rational. But for Peirce this outlook is required by reflection on experience and the sciences, metaphysics itself being an observational science whose job is "to study the most general features of reality and real objects" and whose backward condition is due chiefly to the fact that "its leading professors have been theologians." Science and experience force us to give up the concept of definite, unambiguous facts and fixed a priori assumptions; science is a community of inquirers sharing methods and a kind of moral and intellectual discipline rather than a body of knowledge or a set of assumptions (as Kant, for example, had thought). Metaphysics for Peirce was an attempt to describe how reality must seem to men imbued with science; reality is what will eventually be agreed on by the community of inquirers; general laws and relations among things are real since these, rather than particular facts, are the objects of scientific research. Peirce's concept of metaphysics influenced John Dewey (1859–1952), and largely through Dewey it has had considerable importance in recent American philosophy. Like Peirce, Dewey hoped metaphysics could be a descriptive account of generic traits exhibited in all experience.

LOGICAL POSITIVISM. The mainstream of metaphysics in the nineteenth and early twentieth centuries was idealistic; metaphysicians responded to Kant by constructing systems meant to extend or deepen Kant's critical idealism. But another response was to question dogmatic metaphysics more profoundly than Kant himself. This more radical questioning was begun by such nineteenth-century philosophers of science as Ernst Mach (1839–1916), who criticized the notion that general concepts of science (for example, force) described unob-

served entities or that scientific laws are more than convenient formulas for summarizing observations.

This line of criticism has been most forcefully and systematically carried out by twentieth-century logical positivism. For the logical positivists metaphysics has a special meaning; an assertion is metaphysical if it purports to make a statement of fact but fails to do so—and therefore fails to have a meaning—since no observations count as evidence for or against it. This special use of metaphysics should be understood in the context of the belief of logical positivists that traditional questions of metaphysics do have a point, but a point that traditional formulations of the questions obscure. They are not questions about things at all but about language—in particular, about the types of words and sentences and the logical vocabulary needed to express the findings of the sciences.

The hope of some logical positivists was that if traditional metaphysical questions were translated into questions about the language of science, the answers would be immediately and clearly seen. If, for example, "Does non-being exist?" is phrased as "Are sentences of the form 'X is not an F' ever true?," the answer is obviously "Yes." But it became increasingly clear that in the construction of languages expressing the findings of the sciences problems analogous to traditional metaphysical problems occur. For example, some positivists suggested that sentences such as "Two plus two equals four" owe their truth to linguistic usage rather than to a necessary connection between things, perceived by reason, as past metaphysicians often assumed. Critics pointed out, however, that since it is an empirical fact that we use language as we do, the substitution of "true by virtue of linguistic convention" for "necessary truth" threatens to make "Two plus two equals four" a merely empirical statement. Thus, a distinction is needed between what we merely do not say and what our language will not allow us to say. This does not, of course, mean that nothing was gained over traditional metaphysics, but it does mean that the achievement of logical positivism has been to elucidate or reconstruct traditional metaphysical issues rather than give a method for easily solving them. Accordingly, logical positivists now tend to accept metaphysics in its conventional sense, as the name of a legitimate part of philosophy, along with the special use of metaphysical to refer to pseudoinformative assertions that in reality are meaningless.

ORDINARY-LANGUAGE PHILOSOPHY. The logical positivists were strongly influenced by Bertrand Russell's view that much of traditional metaphysics resulted from a superficial and hasty analysis of ordinary language as well as by the view of Russell and Peirce that past failures of metaphysicians were due to a narrowly restricted logic that prevented them from analyzing ordinary language correctly. The notion that traditional metaphysics resulted from a superficial understanding of ordinary language has been developed independently of logical positivism (although sometimes popularly confused with it) by Ludwig Wittgenstein, Gilbert Ryle, and a large number of contemporary British and American philosophers. Like the logical positivists the ordinary-language philosophers agree that traditional metaphysical questions are in some sense intelligible but need to be radically reformulated; unlike the positivists they are not concerned with rephrasing them as questions about the language of science. They want to show, rather, how metaphysical questions can be solved (or dissolved) by exhibiting the less obvious but essential presuppositions that give linguistic expressions the meanings they actually have in ordinary discourse. Positively, ordinary-language philosophers use linguistic analysis (for example, naming, referring, describing, and so on) to deal with traditional metaphysical issues, and like logical positivists they accept metaphysics in this positive sense as a legitimate area of philosophy.

PHENOMENOLOGY AND EXISTENTIALISM. Both logical positivism and ordinary-language philosophy could be viewed as extensions of Kant's criticism of dogmatic metaphysics; they both sharply contrast with Hegelianism and, in general, with the more or less speculative metaphysical systems inspired by Kant's idealism. A third major development in nineteenth-century and twentieth-century metaphysics, represented by phenomenologists and existentialists, agreed with Hegelians that metaphysics is not an observational science in any ordinary sense and also agreed with analytically minded philosophers that a priori reasoning cannot establish anything about the nature of reality. Accordingly, these philosophers sought new and unconventional ways of experiencing or encountering reality. This response is shown by more conventional metaphysicians like Henri Bergson (1859–1941), who stressed the inability of spatializing and static conceptual thinking to represent correctly the reality of immediate experience, especially its temporal flow, or by Alfred North Whitehead (1861–1947), who stressed imaginative feeling and emotion as a way of gaining access to the inner natures of things. Phenomenologists hold that common sense and science presuppose a more primitive experience that can be grasped by a deliberately naive description of how things actually appear to us; existentialists argue that the subject of metaphysics is a reality that cannot be described in an emotionally neutral way but is in some sense possessed or encountered in personal commitment to a cause or in facing the certainty of one's own death. Phenomenology and existentialism have been combined by systematic philosophers like Martin Heidegger and Jean-Paul Sartre, whose systems attempt to express an intuitive understanding of time, contingency, and particularity as these are experienced in human life.

PHILOSOPHICAL ANALYSIS. In the English-speaking world at least, the most original and important contributions to metaphysics at the present time come from analytic philosophers largely influenced by logical positivism or ordinary-language philosophy. These philosophers see the present situation in metaphysics somewhat as Aristotle did when he reviewed the history of metaphysics up to his own time. In a sense, Aristotle thought, everything had been said, but in a sense nothing had been said because the early philosophers were vague and inarticulate. Contemporary metaphysicians, however, are in a better position to review and analyze the history of their subject than was Aristotle, partly because the history itself is so much richer and partly because contemporary insights make the work of past metaphysicians more intelligible.

See also Albert the Great; Analysis, Philosophical; Anaximander; Anaximenes; Anselm, St.; Aristotle; Augustine, St.; Bergson, Henri; Berkeley, George; Blanshard, Brand; Boethius, Anicius Manlius Severinus; Bonaventure, St.; Bradley, Francis Herbert; Comte, Auguste; Descartes, René; Dewey, John; Duns Scotus, John; Erigena, John Scotus; Existentialism; Fichte, Johann Gottlieb; Galileo Galilei; Grosseteste, Robert; Hegel, Georg Wilhelm Friedrich; Heidegger, Martin; Heraclitus of Ephesus; Hobbes, Thomas; Hume, David; Iamblichus; Idealism; Kant, Immanuel; Leibniz, Gottfried Wilhelm; Leucippus and Democritus; Locke, John; Logical Positivism; Mach, Ernst; McTaggart, John McTaggart Ellis; Melissus of Samos; Metaphysics, Nature of; Neoplatonism; Newton, Isaac; Ontological Argument for the Existence of God; Parmenides of Elea; Peirce, Charles Sanders; Phenomenology; Plato; Plotinus; Porphyry; Pragmatism; Proclus; Pythagoras and Pythagoreanism; Russell, Bertrand Arthur William; Ryle, Gilbert; Sartre, Jean-Paul; Schelling, Friedrich Wilhelm Joseph von; Schopenhauer, Arthur; Spinoza, Benedict (Baruch) de; Thales of Miletus; Thomas Aquinas, St.; Whitehead,

Alfred North; William of Champeaux; William of Moerbeke; William of Ockham; Wittgenstein, Ludwig Josef Johann; Wolff, Christian; Zeno of Elea.

Bibliography

GENERAL WORKS

Copleston, F. C. *A History of Philosophy*, 7 vols. London: Burns, Oates and Washbourne, 1946–. A careful, detailed work requiring close study; probably the most comprehensive and scholarly general history available. Includes excellent bibliographies and sections on metaphysics in chapters on individual philosophers.

De George, Richard T., ed. *Classical and Contemporary Metaphysics: A Source Book.* New York: Holt, Rinehart and Winston, 1962. A book of readings emphasizing contemporary authors but also including selections from classical texts.

Gilson, Étienne. *Being and Some Philosophers*, 2nd ed. Toronto: Pontifical Institute of Mediaeval Studies, 1952. A challenging essay on the history of metaphysics argued with great subtlety by an outstanding Roman Catholic philosopher.

Kaufmann, Walter, ed. *Philosophic Classics*, 2 vols. Englewood Cliffs, NJ: Prentice-Hall, 1994. A comprehensive sourcebook for the history of philosophy, with some excellent introductory essays.

Lovejoy, Arthur O. *The Great Chain of Being.* Cambridge, MA: Harvard University Press, 1936. Traces some main themes of metaphysics from the Greeks to the nineteenth century; a wide-ranging essay in the history of ideas rather than the conventional history of philosophy.

Smith, T. V., ed. *Philosophers Speak for Themselves*, 4 vols. Chicago: University of Chicago Press, 1956. A collection of readings from Thales to Kant.

Whitehead, A. N. *Adventures of Ideas.* New York: Macmillan, 1933. Suggestive and sometimes profound nontechnical essays on movements in science and philosophy by a great twentieth-century metaphysician.

PRE-SOCRATICS

Burnet, John. *Early Greek Philosophy*, 4th ed. New York, 1930. Lucid and authoritative; contains translations of some important fragments.

Freeman, Kathleen. *Ancilla to the Pre-Socratic Philosophers.* Cambridge, MA: Harvard University Press, 1948. English translations of the surviving pre-Socratic writings collected in Hermann Diel's monumental *Fragmente der Vorsokratiker.*

PLATO

Cornford, F. M. *Plato and Parmenides.* New York: Liberal Arts Press, 1957. Translations with running commentaries of Parmenides' *Way of Truth* and Plato's *Parmenides*; for advanced students.

Cornford, F. M. *Plato's Theory of Knowledge.* New York: Liberal Arts Press, 1957. Translations with running commentaries of Plato's *Theaetetus* and *Sophist.*

Lynch, William F. *An Approach to the Metaphysics of Plato through the Parmenides.* Washington, DC: Georgetown University Press, 1959. An attempt to see the *Parmenides* as a straightforward assertion of "basic positions in Platonic metaphysics."

Ryle, Gilbert. "Plato's *Parmenides.*" *Mind* 48 (1939): 129–151, 302–325. Article by a leading contemporary British ordinary-language philosopher; suggests a modern reading.

Vlastos, Gregory. "The Third Man Argument in the *Parmenides.*" *Philosophical Review* 63 (3) (1954): 319–349. Technical but clear and acute analysis of the third-man argument against the theory of ideas in the first half of the *Parmenides.*

ARISTOTLE

Aristotle. *Metaphysics.* Translated by Richard Hope. New York: Columbia University Press, 1952. With an analytical index of technical terms; a useful edition for advanced students. Index contains Greek terms with Latin equivalents.

Brumbaugh, Robert S. "Aristotle's Outline of the Problems of First Philosophy." *Review of Metaphysics* 7 (3) (1953). A brief but very helpful analysis of the organization of the *Metaphysics.*

Owens, Joseph. *The Doctrine of Being in the Aristotelian Metaphysics.* Toronto: Pontifical Institute of Mediaeval Studies, 1951. Highly technical but original and forcefully argued interpretation of the *Metaphysics.*

NEOPLATONISM

Bréhier, Émile. *The Philosophy of Plotinus.* Translated by Joseph Thomas. Chicago: University of Chicago Press, 1958. Readable sympathetic account of Plotinus and his school by a modern French historian of philosophy.

Porphyry. *Isagoge.* Translated by J. Tricot. Paris: J. Vrin, 1947. A translation into French of the complete text, with introduction and notes.

EARLY MIDDLE AGES

Anselm. *Proslogium and Monologium.* Translated by S. N. Deane. La Salle, IL: Open Court, 1962.

Malcolm, Norman. "Anselm's Ontological Arguments." *Philosophical Review* 69 (1) (1960): 41–62. A closely reasoned analysis of Anselm's argument and medieval and modern criticisms.

LATE MIDDLE AGES

Copleston, F. C. *Aquinas.* Harmondsworth, U.K.: Penguin, 1955. Clearly written, relatively simple introduction to Thomas; contains a useful bibliography.

Moody, Ernest A. *The Logic of William of Ockham.* New York: Sheed and Ward, 1935. A scholarly study of William of Ockham and medieval logic and metaphysics; difficult but searching and persuasive.

Thomas Aquinas. *Concerning Being and Essence.* Translated by George C. Leckie. New York: Appleton, 1937. Difficult but important treatise on a basic distinction in Thomistic metaphysics.

SEVENTEENTH CENTURY

Aaron, R. I. *John Locke.* London, 1955.

Balz, A. G. A. *Descartes and the Modern Mind.* New Haven, CT: Yale University Press, 1952.

Beck, Leslie J. *The Method of Descartes.* Oxford: Clarendon Press, 1952.

Descartes, René. *Selections.* Edited by R. M. Eaton. New York, 1927.

Hampshire, Stuart. *Spinoza.* Harmondsworth, U.K.: Penguin, 1987. An excellent exposition and criticism with a general concluding chapter on the nature of metaphysics.

Jackson, Reginald. "Locke's Distinction between Primary and Secondary Qualities." *Mind* 37 (1929): 56–76. Explains and criticizes Locke's contrast between ideas in the mind and qualities in things and between primary and secondary qualities.

Leibniz, Gottfried Wilhelm. *The Monadology and Other Philosophical Writings.* Edited by Robert Latta. London, 1948.

Leibniz, Gottfried Wilhelm. *New Essays concerning Human Understanding.* Translated, with notes, by Alfred G. Langley, 3rd ed. La Salle, IL, 1949. A standard edition containing some very interesting but little-known essays by Leibniz in an appendix.

Locke, John. *An Essay concerning Human Understanding.* New York: Dover, 1958.

Whitehead, A. N. *Science and the Modern World.* New York: Macmillan, 1925. Early chapters contain a brilliant critique of seventeenth-century and eighteenth-century science and philosophy.

EIGHTEENTH CENTURY

Kant, Immanuel. *Prolegomena to Any Future Metaphysics.* Edited by Lewis White Beck. New York: Liberal Arts Press, 1951. A good introductory text by a leading authority on Kant; contains a useful bibliography.

Smith, N. K. *Immanuel Kant's Critique of Pure Reason,* 2nd ed. New York, 1933. A classic translation of Kant's major work.

Warnock, G. J. *Berkeley.* Harmondsworth, U.K.: Penguin, 1953. An exceptionally good introductory work; highly critical of some of Berkeley's leading arguments.

METAPHYSICS SINCE KANT

Ayer, A. J., ed. *Logical Positivism.* Glencoe, IL: Free Press, 1959. A collection of the most important and influential papers in the logical positivist movement; includes an unusually complete bibliography covering the entire range of twentieth-century analytic philosophy.

Findlay, J. N. *Hegel.* New York: Humanities Press, 1964. A very clearheaded sympathetic exposition of Hegel's system.

Passmore, John. *A Hundred Years of Philosophy.* London: Duckworth, 1957. A useful and very well written survey of philosophy since 1860; emphasizes metaphysics and theory of knowledge in English-speaking countries.

Royce, Josiah. *The Spirit of Modern Philosophy.* Boston and New York, 1926. Lectures on post-Kantian philosophy, especially nineteenth-century German idealism.

White, Morton. *Toward Reunion in Philosophy.* Cambridge, MA: Harvard University Press, 1956. A forceful and lively essay on main issues in recent British and American philosophy; Part I is devoted to recent metaphysics.

Wolheim, Richard. *F. H. Bradley.* Harmondsworth, U.K.: Penguin, 1959. An introduction to Bradley; quite critical but closely and skillfully argued.

Roger Hancock (1967)

METAPHYSICS, HISTORY OF [ADDENDUM]

THE CRITIQUE OF METAPHYSICS

In the years just before and after World War II a decidedly negative attitude toward metaphysics pervaded the analytic tradition. Before the war the logical positivists appealed to their empiricist criterion of significance to conclude that taken at face value as claims about the non-linguistic world, metaphysical statements are literally meaningless. After the war ordinary language philosophers were not much kinder in their assessment of metaphysical claims. Here, Ludwig Wittgenstein led the charge with his claim that metaphysical statements are nothing more than nonsense born of linguistic confusion; but even ordinary language philosophers who found the Wittgensteinian critique overblown thought defenders of traditional metaphysics naöve if not totally misguided. Then, in the space of just a single year, two books appeared that did much to soften these pervasive antimetaphysical prejudices: P. F. Strawson's *Individuals: An Essay in Descriptive Metaphysics* (1959) and Willard Van Orman Quine's *Word and Object* (1960). Although each of these books was written by a philosopher whose roots were squarely within one of the two traditions that had been so critical of metaphysics, both were avowedly metaphysical works, and both exerted enormous influence on succeeding generations of philosophers.

STRAWSON

For Strawson, metaphysics is an inquiry into the most general features of our thought about the world, what Strawson calls our conceptual framework. Revisionary metaphysicians find that framework philosophically problematic and seek to replace it with a superior framework; whereas descriptive metaphysicians have the more humble goal of describing the conceptual framework we actually employ. Strawson himself had been a leading figure in the ordinary language tradition that identified philosophy with conceptual analysis; but he denies that descriptive metaphysics is simply a form of conceptual analysis. It is both more general and more comprehensive than conceptual analysis, and it seeks to identify the presuppositions of the various uses of language that constitute the subject matter for conceptual analysis.

The topics that Strawson discusses in *Individuals* are those that provide the focus for traditional metaphysics: the individuation and persistence of particulars, the relationship between material bodies and the frameworks of space and time, the mind-body problem, and the problem of universals. Nonetheless, Strawson's approach to these topics is colored by his ordinary language roots. He asks about the identification and reidentification of particulars, the attribution of psychological and physical predicates, and the underpinnings of the subject-predicate distinction. But not only is the methodology of *Individuals* rooted in the ordinary language tradition. Its substantive conclusions serve to vindicate the commonsense picture of the world that gets expressed in ordinary language; nor is this surprising since the book is supposed to be an exercise in descriptive metaphysics. Accordingly, the material bodies of everyday experience are taken to be the ontologically basic particulars; psychological and physical properties are construed as irreducibly different; the notion of a person is treated as a primitive concept not susceptible of any form of reductive analysis; and the distinction between particulars and the universals they instantiate is treated as ontologically fundamental.

QUINE

The metaphysical framework at work in Quine's *Word and Object* could hardly be more different. By Strawson's standards Quine is a revisionary metaphysician. In Quine's book the commonsense metaphysics Strawson defends gives way to an austere ontological scheme geared to accommodate the core insights of what Quine takes to be the most successful scientific theory: physics. Accordingly, we have the view that time is just another dimension along with the three spatial dimensions; familiar particulars are construed as space-time worms; we have a strictly materialist account of thought and experience; talk of meanings, properties, and propositions along with the appeal to the modal notions of necessity and possibility are rejected; and the only abstract entities we countenance are the classes or sets of the mathematician.

Furthermore, while Strawson pays close attention to the ways words function in ordinary language, Quine is an heir to the logical positivist tradition and employs the technical tools of formal logic in formulating and justifying his metaphysical theory. As Quine sees it, simply by endorsing the claims of physics one is committed to the metaphysical framework he defends. Here, he relies on an account of ontological commitment he developed in works before *Word and Object*. According to that account, to determine the ontological commitments associated with endorsing a certain body of discourse, one translates the sentences making up that body into the language of first-order logic. If we call the sentences resulting from

that translation *S1 … Sn*, then we can say that in accepting the original body of discourse, one commits oneself to the existence of all those entities that must exist if *S1 … Sn* are to come out true.

So if, by this criterion, one discovers that a given statement commits one to the existence of entities of a certain sort, then, provided one accepts that statement, one is required to include entities of the relevant sort in one's ontological framework; or, better, one is so required unless one can show that the commitment is only apparent; and one succeeds in showing that if one can come up with a plausible paraphrase of the original statement that, by Quine's test, is innocent of any commitment to entities of the kind in question. The underlying theme of *Word and Object* is that there is no plausible paraphrase of the sentences making up physical theory that shows them to be free of the metaphysical commitments expressed in the ontology of *Word and Object*.

RECENT BRITISH METAPHYSICS

The work of Strawson and Quine led to a revival of traditional metaphysics. The change was gradual, and it tended to take different forms on the two sides of the Atlantic. In Britain the influence of Strawson's approach was especially strong. Strawson's view that metaphysics is concerned with the structure of our thought about the world led to a style of metaphysics where the emphasis is on our conceptual practices and the presuppositions of those practices. Given the centrality of the idea of conceptual structures in terms of which we talk and think about the world, it is not surprising that British metaphysicians over the past four decades or so have been deeply concerned with questions about the relationship between our thought and the world that thought is about. Pivotal here has been the opposition between what Michael Dummett (1978) calls realists and antirealists. Whereas Dummett's realists want to claim that there is a mind-independent world, correspondence to which makes our statements and beliefs true, his antirealists question the idea of a reality whose constitution is independent of our conceptual activities and the conceptual structures we bring to bear in inquiry, and they hold that what we call truth is some epistemic property like that of being supported by adequate evidence.

RECENT METAPHYSICS OUTSIDE BRITAIN

During the 1960s and 1970s metaphysical discussion outside Britain was heavily influenced by Quine. While they tended to endorse Quine's account of ontological commitment, many philosophers from this period were uncomfortable with the austere metaphysical framework he had defended in *Word and Object*. A major area of concern was Quine's unwillingness to accept properties and propositions. He had argued that whereas sets have clear-cut identity conditions (a set α is identical with a set β just in case α and β have the same members), no such identity conditions are possible for properties and propositions. Critics such as Roderick M. Chisholm (1976) replied that we have no option but to accept abstract entities like these. The existence of properties, they said, is presupposed by our talk of similarity, by subject-predicate discourse, and by talk involving abstract singular terms like *wisdom*, *triangularity*, and *mankind*; and they argued that propositions are required to serve as the objects of our beliefs.

But in endorsing properties and propositions philosophers from this period found themselves confronted with important metaphysical questions. Familiar objects, we say, have properties, but what exactly is the relationship between an object and its properties? What is called the bundle theory provided one answer to this question. On this theory there is nothing more to an individual than the properties associated with it; familiar objects are just bundles of properties. But if that is so, it should be impossible for numerically different individuals to share all their properties. Critics of the bundle theory such as Gustav Bergmann (1967) and David Armstrong (1989) argued that since this is not impossible each familiar object incorporates a constituent over and above its properties, a constituent unique to that object. This individuating constituent was variously called a bare particular or a thin particular and was construed as the literal bearer of the properties copresent with it.

The notion of a proposition gave rise to other problems. Propositions, we think, are not just true or false; they can be necessarily true or necessarily false, contingently true or contingently false, and possibly true or possibly false. Now, Quine had notoriously rejected talk of modality. Modality, he said, is mired in obscurity. To make sense of modal notions, critics such as Saul Kripke (1972), David Lewis (1986), and Alvin Plantinga (1974) appealed to the Leibnizian notion of a possible world. The idea was, first, that our world (the actual world) is just one of many possible worlds and, second, that what is unique about modal discourse is that it takes the full range of possible worlds and not just the actual world as its subject matter. These theorists did not all agree about the nature and status of possible worlds, but they did agree in endorsing the Leibnizian idea that to say that a proposition is necessarily true is to say that it is true in all possible worlds and to say that it is possibly true is to say that it is true in some possible world. This approach to modality proved tremendously fruitful. Not only did the framework of possible worlds shed light on talk of propositional necessity and propositional possibility, but it proved helpful as well in clarifying a whole variety of otherwise puzzling phenomena like the distinction between essence and accident, the concept of meaning, counterfactual conditionals, the concept of causation, and the notion of a law of nature.

The influence of these possible worlds metaphysicians was felt throughout philosophy, and by the 1980s metaphysics had come back into its own. For metaphysicians trained in that decade and after, the positivist and ordinary language attacks on metaphysics were quaint episodes from a distant past. These younger metaphysicians were not in the least apologetic about their discipline. Indeed, they were anxious to develop and defend comprehensive metaphysical theories. The result has been a tremendously active period in which all of the topics on the traditional metaphysical agenda have come under debate. Questions about universals, the structure and individuation of ordinary objects, and possible worlds and modality continue to be discussed; but in recent years metaphysicians have dealt with a much broader range of questions including those about the nature of time and space-time, the nature of identity and existence, the existence and structure of events, persistence through time, material constitution, the nature of fictional entities, freedom of the will, causality, and the nature of the mental.

See also Metaphysics; Metaphysics, Nature of.

Bibliography

Armstrong, David. *Universals: An Opinionated Introduction*. Boulder, CO: Westview Press, 1989.

Bergmann, Gustav. *Realism: A Critique of Brentano and Meinong*. Madison: University of Wisconsin Press, 1967.

Chisholm, Roderick M. *Person and Object: A Metaphysical Study*. La Salle, IL: Open Court, 1976.

Dummett, Michael. *Truth and Other Enigmas*. Cambridge, MA: Harvard University Press, 1978.

Kim, Jaegwon, and Ernest Sosa. *Metaphysics: An Anthology*. Malden, MA: Blackwell, 1999.

Kripke, Saul. *Naming and Necessity*. Cambridge, MA: Harvard University Press, 1972.

Lewis, David. *On the Plurality of Worlds*. Oxford, U.K.: Blackwell, 1986.

Loux, Michael J. *Metaphysics: A Contemporary Introduction*. 2nd ed. New York: Routledge, 2001.

Loux, Michael J. *Substance and Attribute: A Study in Ontology*. Dordrecht, Netherlands: D. Reidel, 1978.

Loux, Michael J., and Dean W. Zimmerman. *Oxford Handbook of Metaphysics*. New York: Oxford University Press, 2003.

Plantinga, Alvin. *The Nature of Necessity*. Oxford, U.K.: Clarendon Press, 1974.

Quine, Willard Van Orman. *From a Logical Point of View: Nine Logico-philosophical Essays*. Cambridge, MA: Harvard University Press, 1953.

Quine, W. V. *Word and Object*. Cambridge, MA: MIT Press, 1960.

Strawson, P. F. *Individuals: An Essay in Descriptive Metaphysics*. London: Methuen, 1959.

Van Inwagen, Peter. *Material Beings*. Ithaca, NY: Cornell University Press, 1990.

Van Inwagen, Peter. *Metaphysics*. Boulder, CO: Westview Press, 1993.

Michael J. Loux (2005)

METAPHYSICS, NATURE OF

Almost everything in metaphysics is controversial, and it is therefore not surprising that there is little agreement among those who call themselves metaphysicians about what precisely it is that they are attempting. In beginning a discussion of the nature and validation of metaphysical arguments and theories, the best course we can follow is to list some of the standing preoccupations and ambitions of metaphysicians. For this purpose we need to make the assumption that there is a distinct class of metaphysical philosophers, a class into which such thinkers as Plato, Thomas Aquinas, René Descartes, Benedict de Spinoza, and G. W. F. Hegel would fall and from which purely critical or analytic philosophers like the later G. E. Moore would be excluded. It has to be admitted, however, that the line between metaphysical and nonmetaphysical philosophy is exceedingly hard to draw, for many metaphysicians from Plato on have been expert in the supposedly nonmetaphysical pursuit of analyzing or clarifying ideas, while few self-styled analysts have contrived to stick to pure analysis without the open or covert advocacy of a metaphysical point of view.

Setting these difficulties aside, we may note three main features of metaphysics as traditionally practiced. First, metaphysicians have constantly aspired to say what there is in the world or to determine the real nature of things; they have been preoccupied, that is, with the concepts of existence and reality. Their interest in these concepts springs from a double source: from the reflection that the surface show of things often misrepresents them, with the result that we are set the task of determining their real as opposed to their apparent constitution, and from the need to specify what ultimately different kinds of things there are in the world, a need that presses itself on our attention when we wonder whether, for example, minds or numbers are independent existents. The first of these tasks might seem to belong to the scientist rather than the philosopher, for science, too, makes constant use of the distinction between the apparent and the real; we shall indicate in the next paragraph why metaphysicians have not been ready to accept this proposal for lightening their labors.

Second, metaphysics has been commonly presented as the most fundamental and also the most comprehensive of inquiries. It claims to be fundamental because questions about what there is or about the ultimate nature of things underlie all particular inquiries. If you are to assess the results of mathematical investigations, for instance, you need to determine the ontological status of mathematical objects, and according to the theory, this is a task for the metaphysician. The claim of metaphysics to be comprehensive is more difficult to justify. One possible line of support for it, followed by Aristotle, is found in the reflection that questions about existence and reality, along with those about potential and actual being and about causation that are also raised by metaphysicians, cut across the boundaries of particular sciences and arise in connection with every sort of subject matter. Thus, metaphysics is comprehensive just because of its extreme generality. But there is another way in which the claim to comprehensiveness has been advanced. It has been customary to say that whereas sciences like physics and mathematics are departmental studies each of which deals only with a part or particular aspect of reality, metaphysics, by contrast, is concerned with the world as a whole. This explains why philosophers have been unwilling to accept the suggestion that scientists might be left to determine the true nature of things. A scientific theory purports to explain, for example, the real constitution of matter or the fundamental mechanisms of the human body but not to draw the distinction between appearance and reality in an entirely general way, not to tell us, to give an instance, whether matter is the ultimate reality, as materialists suppose, or whether it is itself a manifestation of spirit, as Hegel tried to argue.

This contrast between metaphysics and the particular sciences is sometimes developed in yet another way, again, as will be apparent, to the great advantage of metaphysics. It is said that inquiries in the individual sciences are carried out under assumptions it is the business of metaphysics to make explicit and either to justify or to correct. Metaphysics, by contrast, proceeds without assumptions and is thus fully self-critical where the particular sciences are in part credulous. This line of argument goes back to Plato, who tells us that mathematicians postulate the existence of "odd and even numbers" and "three kinds of angles," and implies that these "hypotheses," taken as "starting points" or "bases" in mathematics, could find their justification and thus lose their hypothetical character in the comprehensive "synoptic" study Plato called dialectic. The dialectician is a man who leaves nothing unquestioned, and just because of this the results of all other inquiries must be seen as no more than provisional; they await ratification or correction from the dialectician. The apparently arbitrary and obviously vague character of this suggestion has not prevented its having a continued appeal to philosophers. Even today, we sometimes hear it said that we need not be unduly disturbed by, for example, the findings of physiologists and psychologists, since the proponents of these sciences work under assumptions it is the business of philosophers to uncover and correct in the light of their knowledge of the whole man (for an argument on these lines see J. S. Haldane, *The Philosophy of a Biologist,* Oxford, 1935).

If metaphysics is to make good its claim to be uniquely self-critical, its propositions must be shown to be exempt from intellectual challenge as those of no other study are. Descartes, in fact, tried to offer such a demonstration. He argued first that such commonsense assertions as "There is a table under the window" were in every case open to theoretical doubt: However much I seemed to perceive a table, it might be that I was under perceptual illusion or was dreaming. Next, he maintained that even propositions whose truth appeared to be evident, such as those of mathematics, could not be accepted as necessarily in order. An evil demon could be deceiving me into thinking them clear and distinct when they did not really deserve this description. But matters were different when we came to the fundamental metaphysical truth "I think, therefore I am." This truth was such that in the very act of doubting it, one reaffirms it. To doubt is to think, and in thinking that I might not exist, I make clear that I do. Hence, there is at least one truth about whose correctness I could not be in error, and this is a truth of metaphysics. But Descartes was not content to stop at this point. He went on to argue that if I, a being with obvious limitations, certainly exist, then just as certainly there exists a perfect being whose nature is such that he would never deceive me into thinking that true which is not in fact so, once I have satisfied myself that it is by the test of clear and distinct perception. The effect of this move was to provide a guarantee for the findings of the sciences, which were otherwise open to "hyperbolical" doubt. We

could henceforth be assured on metaphysical grounds that whatever was clearly and distinctly perceived was true. As for the propositions of metaphysics itself, their truth was guaranteed by their connection with the *cogito,* which, as we have seen, could not be intelligibly questioned.

The interest of these arguments for our present purpose lies not in their details but in the basic claims they involve. The propositions of metaphysics, according to Descartes, are intellectually impregnable, and in this respect they contrast not only with the beliefs of common sense but also with the pronouncements of the sciences, at least when these are considered apart from their metaphysical guarantee. But from where can they derive their unique certainty? The only possible answer is from their being the products of reason when that faculty is put to work in the fullest and freest way. The result will be that metaphysics is not only the most fundamental of studies; it is also one that relies for its results on the efforts of reason alone.

METAPHYSICS AND THE SUPERSENSIBLE

Thus far, we have observed three main features in the projected science of metaphysics. It claims to tell us what really exists or what the real nature of things is, it claims to be fundamental and comprehensive in a way in which no individual science is, and it claims to reach conclusions that are intellectually impregnable and thus possess a unique kind of certainty. Now, many critics of metaphysics have suggested that these claims could be justified only if metaphysics were a factual science providing us, on the strength of rational insight, with knowledge of things or aspects of reality that lie beyond the range of the senses. Nor is this view without support from practicing metaphysicians. Plato drew a contrast between "things seen" and "things unseen" and argued that only things unseen were proper objects of knowledge. From his time on there was a standing tendency to identify the province of the metaphysician with what was vaguely called the supersensible, or the realm of the intellect. Aristotle, for example, distinguished between sensible and insensible substance and assigned the investigation of insensible substance to "first philosophy," or metaphysics. Medieval and early modern philosophers thought of God, the "being of beings," as an entity without bodily extension or shape and for that reason considered him outside the province of the empirical sciences. More generally, it was widely believed that behind the phenomena that present themselves in everyday experience, there lie realities whose existence and properties can be established only by use of the intellect and that can hence be described as noumena, or intelligible objects. In this view, the proper concern of metaphysics was to give us news about noumena.

From the eighteenth century on much ingenuity has been displayed in showing the untenability of this position. The idea that there might be a science that was at once factual and purely intellectual drew its firmest support from the example of mathematics. David Hume suggested, however, that the concern of the mathematician was not with matters of fact and existence but solely with "relations of ideas": His aim was only to make explicit what was already implicit in the premises from which he started. The propositions of mathematics were indeed necessary truths, but by the same token they gave no information about the world. If an inquiry was to pronounce on matters of fact, its method must be empirical, not conceptual, and this meant that its results could not possibly claim to be intellectually impregnable, for anything established on the strength of experience might need to be amended or even withdrawn in the light of further experience. There were no final empirical truths.

A natural reply to this is to argue that even if every factual inquiry must begin from experience, it need not necessarily terminate there. Why should not the metaphysician argue from the characteristics of things sensible to the existence and the nature of things supersensible, as, for instance, Thomas Aquinas and John Locke thought they could? Immanuel Kant was much concerned about the proper answer to this question. He allowed—and here he showed more sympathy with metaphysicians than empiricists then or now—that such concepts as cause and substance, which figure prominently in supposed inferences from the phenomenal to the noumenal, have a necessary character; in Kant's terminology they are a priori, as opposed to empirical, concepts. But he denied as stoutly as Hume that they can therefore be used to carry us beyond the range of possible experience. The question "What brought that about?" is a necessary question, one we cannot rationally refuse to ask, but the answer to such questions must always be sought within experience. If we try, as, for example, Descartes did, to maintain that there must be a First Cause, a necessary being entirely different from the contingent things with which we are familiar, we cease to attach any clear meaning to the concept of cause, for, as Hume saw, it is an essential part of the idea of cause that a cause precede its effect. We can talk about causes as long as we remain within the sphere of the temporal; once we step outside it, the concept loses its determinate char-

acter. And what is true of cause here is also true of substance and other metaphysical notions. We can give sense to the concept of substance if we understand it as the permanent that persists through change, but if we eliminate the reference to time, we are left with no more than the logical notion of that which is always a subject and never a predicate, an idea that in its pure form is too indeterminate to be put to metaphysical or, indeed, any other use.

Another attack on metaphysics as the supposed science of intelligible reality was made by the logical positivists. It is a mark of those propositions that belong to accredited sciences like mechanics or genetics, they argued, that we know in principle how to test them; we can see what difference it makes that they are true rather than false. But if a metaphysician comes along and tells us that what really exists is not trees or tables but, say, monads, what tests can we apply to determine the truth of his statement, and what difference does it make if it is true? By definition monads are entities that could never be encountered within experience, nor is their presence supposed to have particular empirical consequences like that of electrons and similar unobservables postulated by natural scientists. Thus, a metaphysical thesis will be compatible with any state of affairs whatsoever, just as the propositions of logic and mathematics are. But if this is so, how can it possibly be maintained that metaphysics gives us information about the world, even the unseen world? The news it purports to bring can only be news from nowhere.

These highly general refutations of a particular conception of metaphysics have seldom been found convincing by metaphysicians. One reason for this is that they fail to come to grips with individual metaphysical arguments, for example, with the *cogito*. Another is that they appear to prejudge the case against this sort of metaphysics. Why, for example, should it be supposed that a metaphysical thesis must make an empirical difference? Another cause of their failure to carry conviction, however, may be found in the fact that many metaphysicians have worked with a different concept of their subject, one that does not involve it in the claim that it provides information or rivals the empirical sciences. This conception will be considered below.

METAPHYSICS WITHOUT ONTOLOGY

We have already seen that metaphysicians have wanted to say both that their propositions possess a peculiar certainty and that they are significant as a purely analytic proposition is not. In Kantian terminology they pretend to the status of synthetic a priori truths. Now, many critics of metaphysics have made the assumption that a proposition could be synthetic a priori only if it at once stated a truth of fact and was established by conceptual means alone, a combination they regard as impossible. Facts must be established empirically; pure thinking can lead to the knowledge only of analytic truths. But if we look at Kant's alleged synthetic a priori judgments, particularly those he called principles of the understanding, we see that they make no claim to state facts, even very general facts. A principle like the principle of causality is not a very wide empirical truth, mysteriously known in a nonempirical way; it is, on the contrary, the expression of a rule of procedure that serves to tell us not what properties things have but how to interpret them. Kant supposed that principles of this sort had a special sort of necessity, though they did not logically compel; they owed this, he thought, to the fact that they are prescribed by the human mind as principles specifying what is to count as objective in our experience. Thus, we take it to be a feature of what is objectively there that no quality is present except in a determinate degree, that nothing ever goes entirely out of existence (all change is transformation), that nothing happens except for a reason, and so on.

Kant himself intended this doctrine to have limited application. He thought of the principles of the understanding as prescribing the form of the phenomenal world that we know by means of the senses and investigate in the natural sciences. In his view there were other aspects of experience, in particular the activities of the moral agent, in regard to which they had no legislative force. But it is possible to think of an extension of Kant's doctrine and imagine a set of principles that would prescribe the form not just of one department of experience, but of experience as a whole. A set of principles of this kind would tell us how to organize the data of our experience in such a way that we could give a unitary account of them; it would thus help us make sense of the scheme of things entire. Possessed of concepts of this sort, we could hope to resolve the apparent inconsistencies of science and common sense, together with the more serious conflicts between science and religion and science and morality. We should then be masters of an overall point of view enabling us to see things synoptically or have a set of ideas that would allow us to differentiate the real nature of the universe from its merely superficial aspects. We should, in short, be in possession of a metaphysics.

There can be no doubt that many of the classical metaphysical systems can be thought of as conforming to this schema. In the system of Aristotle, for instance, the key concepts are teleological, and their articulation is to be found in the doctrine of the four causes. It is axiomatic in Aristotle's thought that everything serves a purpose; Aristotle's ambition is to find the point of each phenomenon and thus specify its place in the articulation of the whole. He attempted to carry through his program not only at the biological level, the most obvious source of the concepts involved, but also above and below it—in moral, political, and social life, on the one hand, and in physical science, on the other. His success in these spheres is unequal, but that does not affect the general character of the enterprise.

The popular philosophy of materialism, again, can be seen as an attempt to make sense of the world as a whole on the basis of a distinctive set of first principles. The primary thought of the materialist might be expressed in the axiom that there is nothing that cannot be satisfactorily explained in natural terms; belief not merely in the competence, but also in the omnicompetence, of natural science is a prominent item in his credo. The materialist sees the world as a vast mechanism; whatever happens is the result of natural causes, and all other phenomena must be assessed and understood on this basis. Thus, the phenomena that characterize religious and moral life can be taken in psychological and social terms as things whose causes are ultimately natural, though scarcely in the terms favored by those who engage in them. Religion, as Sigmund Freud said, is an illusion but not an unintelligible illusion; science can account for it, as it can account for everything else.

Finally, Hegelianism made a conscious attempt to produce a metaphysics that constitutes an overall reading of experience. The central concept here is the concept of spirit; it is alleged that everything can be understood in terms of this concept once we take account of the fact that spirit cannot fulfill its potentialities except by working on and against something not itself—in Hegel's peculiar language, "its own other." Thus, we can make sense of the existence of a world of nature in this system; it is there to subserve the purposes of spirit. We can make sense of the social world, too, for many of the characteristics of mind are intelligible only when people are aware of one another and know that others are aware of them. Self-respect and self-contempt would be cases in point.

Each of the systems mentioned could be said to rest on a basic idea or intuition, an idea articulated in a series of concepts taken as definitions of reality and applied, with greater or less success, to the whole range of experience. To appreciate the force of such a system, we need to grasp the basic idea as well as understand the articulated concepts; we have to see the world as the metaphysician in question saw it. The deviser of a metaphysical theory thus becomes a man with a vision of the scheme of things entire. It is important to add, however, that he is not merely a man with a vision, in which case he would be indistinguishable from a philosophical poet. He needs to work his vision out in a theory; he needs to argue his case both by adducing those facts that immediately support it and by explaining those that on the face of things do not.

It seems clear that most of the standard claims for metaphysics can be understood with this account of the matter. Since the first principles of a metaphysical system have prescriptive force, exactly as Kant's principles of the understanding had in regard to the world of nature, they can be properly thought to compel every rational thinker. Their certainty is not the certainty of logic, and yet it exceeds that of any individual statement of fact, for facts are descried only within a framework that these principles provide. Again, even if a system of this kind does not tell us precisely what there is, it nevertheless pronounces on the real character of the world as opposed to the surface show. According to the materialist, for instance, there seem to be features of experience that transcend the natural realm, but in the end it turns out that this is not so. Everything, including men's thoughts and actions, can be accounted for satisfactorily in natural terms. That a scheme of this kind is comprehensive, wider than that of any particular science, goes without saying; that it is fundamental because it is concerned with the coordination of ways of thinking in widely differing spheres is also obvious. True, there is no straightforward counterpart in this type of theory for the criticism by metaphysics of the assumptions of the particular sciences: Metaphysics not being a source of knowledge in itself, it cannot be claimed that other studies are dependent on it as, say, chemistry is dependent on physics. But this circumstance will not prevent this type of metaphysician from putting his own construction on the results of the sciences, as the example of Hegelianism shows. He may have no warrant to question such results, but all the same he may insist on interpreting them in his own way when he offers his reading of experience as a whole. Hegel was doubtless too brusque in his treatment of Isaac Newton and John Dalton, but it does not follow that the whole project for a philosophical treatment of natural phenomena is a mistake.

ARGUMENT AND TRUTH IN METAPHYSICS

If metaphysics answers the description given above, a description that would fit many if not quite all of the best-known metaphysical systems, two questions immediately arise. First, we may be asked what sort of a study metaphysics is in this account. Is it a priori or empirical, and to what sorts of argument does it appeal? Second, there is the question what criteria to use in choosing among metaphysical systems. Seeing that many systems are possible, are there any objective ways of deciding that one system embodies the true or the proper way to look at the world?

ARGUMENT. The answer to the first query is that metaphysics, according to this account, is neither a priori nor empirical, though it makes constant use of both deductive and probable reasoning. A metaphysician is concerned to advocate, articulate, and apply a set of basic interpretative principles, categorical principles we might call them, and principles of this kind cannot be grounded in either conceptual considerations or an appeal to empirical fact. They cannot be supported conceptually since no contradiction is involved in disputing them; they cannot be deduced from facts since they claim to apply with unrestricted validity, no matter what data turn up in experience. They may indeed be suggested by experience and commonly are, but that is not to say that they can be shown to be acceptable or unacceptable by simple empirical methods. Apart from anything else there are no absolutely neutral data to which we can appeal when supporting or attacking a metaphysical theory. For though it is the case that every metaphysician has the duty of explaining all the facts as he sees them, he also has the privilege of being able to decide what really is to count as fact. To see the importance of this we have only to reflect on the different views of religious phenomena taken by materialists and their opponents.

However, though it is true that a metaphysical theory on this account can be established neither deductively nor inductively, deductive and inductive argument both bulk large in metaphysical discussion. Like any other thinker the metaphysician is much concerned with consequences and consistency. He often wants to make the point that since p is true and p implies q; which in turn implies r, we are logically committed to r or to contending that since q is false and p implies q, p must also be false. The very fact that a metaphysician has a theory to put forward means that he must be preoccupied with the logical connections between the concepts that constitute his system. To say this, however, is not to deny his preoccupation with fact or with probable arguments. Unlike an empirical scientist he establishes no new facts, but all the same he has a double interest in fact. First, he is concerned, more than any specialized inquirer, to see similarities in widely different areas of fact, a process that is relevant to both the formulation and the application of his theory and that involves him in much reasoning by analogy. Second, he needs to pay constant attention to the state of factual knowledge in working out and pressing home his central insight. He promises, after all, to make sense of all the data of experience, and he must consequently take continuous account of these data. The legend that metaphysicians are indifferent to fact has no foundation; on the contrary, they have a primary interest in facts of all sorts even though they do not originate any factual propositions. The extent to which advances in cybernetics have been discussed in recent years by philosophers interested in the truth of materialism affords an apt and striking illustration of this point.

TRUTH. We saw that one charge made against metaphysics as a doctrine of what there is was that no decisive considerations can be adduced either for or against such a theory; the monads of Gottfried Wilhelm Leibniz and the Forms of Plato make no empirical difference. In this respect are things any better in our revised form of metaphysics? It must be confessed that the initial appearance is not favorable. We have emphasized that the first principles of such a system are neither analytic nor empirical; the temptation to conclude that they must accordingly be no more than arbitrary prescriptions, representing a point of view taken up for no good reasons, is strong. And though we have also urged that metaphysicians of this sort have a special interest in fact, the force of that contention is considerably weakened by the admission that they claim the right to decide for themselves what really is fact. If we arm them with this veto—and it is hard to see how they could be refused it—the question of metaphysical truth seems wholly intractable.

It could be, however, that we are setting an impossible standard for metaphysics in requiring it to possess a decision procedure as clear-cut as those of mathematics and the natural sciences. One reason that we can get a straight answer about the acceptability of a theory in physics is that physics works on principles that it does not question (such as that every natural happening will have a sufficient natural explanation). In metaphysics, by contrast, we are concerned with the comparison and assessment of precisely this type of principle. As the widest and most general of all forms of thinking, metaphysics can appeal to no fixed criteria beyond itself except to the requirements of internal consistency that any theory must satisfy. Nor is it true that every reputable branch of knowledge possesses obvious and easily applicable decision procedures. If, for example, we compare metaphysics with history instead of physics, we may begin to see that there are areas of study where dispute and disagreement play a prominent part and that still can claim to proffer understanding and enlightenment. Once we pass beyond the mere ascertaining of fact, there are many histories written from many points of view and resting on many judgments about what is historically important; it is not really possible to hope for a final decision about which, if any, is correct or even about the relative merits of any two equally sophisticated interpretations. However, we do not conclude from this that history is a pointless pursuit rational men would do well to avoid. We realize that a study like history can enlarge the mind and educate the understanding even when it does not add to the sum of public knowledge.

A comparison with metaphysics that is in some respects even closer is provided if we consider the interpretation of a literary text. The data the literary critic confronts—I am thinking of someone who offers a reading of a controversial literary work like *Hamlet* or *Faust*—are "harder" than in the case of metaphysics, but this does not prevent the appearance of a wide variety of conflicting theories. And it happens that there are no accepted criteria for deciding among the various theories; all that each critic can do, in the last resort, is explain his way of looking at the text, marshal the points in its favor, and invite the reader to test the matter for himself. But we need not conclude from this that it will be a matter of luck or, perhaps, of psychology which theory will win the reader's approval. At the end of the day, he can be entirely convinced of the authenticity of one particular reading, and he can be persuaded that it offers more enlightenment, covers the central points more impressively, and does better justice to the evidence than its rivals. He may not be able to produce knockdown grounds in favor of his choice, but that is not to say that he has made it for no reason at all.

Metaphysical argument is like literary argument in that it reaches no apparent end; it is like it again in terminating, insofar as it ever does terminate, in an insight that is more personal than public. The old dream of a demonstrated metaphysics whose propositions were even more certain than those of mathematics could scarcely be further from realization. But it would be wrong on that account to think that the concepts of truth and falsity have no application in metaphysics. At the lowest estimate we can describe one system of metaphysics as more illuminating than another. We must, however, decide for ourselves what is really illuminating and what is not. As in the case of the humanities in general, we cannot just learn the truth from another.

CONTEMPORARY ANTIMETAPHYSICS

Theories that profess to deal with "the world as a whole," however they are meant to be taken, are today more often objects of suspicion than of interest, thanks to the influence of G. E. Moore and the later work of Ludwig Wittgenstein. Moore himself never attacked metaphysics explicitly, and indeed his early work, both in logic and in moral philosophy, showed pronounced metaphysical leanings of a generally Platonic kind. But the "Defence of Common Sense" with which he came to be most prominently associated was evolved as a counterblast to views put forward by contemporary metaphysical philosophers, views that, as Moore saw them, could be maintained only by someone prepared to disregard what he evidently knew to be true. When F. H. Bradley, for instance, argued that time is not real, Moore thought this an absurd paradox since the reality of time is taken for granted in any statement containing a temporal expression. If time is not real, it cannot be true that yesterday was Friday or that I had my breakfast before leaving for work. Moore's procedure here, which is to call the metaphysician's bluff by reminding him of what in an off-duty moment he will himself acknowledge that he knows, was generalized by some of his followers into an all-round exposé of metaphysics, which they represented as necessarily consisting of paradoxes and evident falsehoods. For this purpose the thesis that everything is material did not differ from its rival that everything is spirit; both were, when taken seriously, obviously false. There might be a point in maintaining such a thesis (it could be a revealing paradox, according to John Wisdom, or serve a deep-seated psychological purpose, according to Morris Lazerowitz), but in no sense could it express what was really the case.

Moore and his followers assume here that there can be only one correct description of a situation and that in matters like dating or temporal precedence it is known to all of us. It is not obvious that this view is correct, for it could be, as Bradley thought, that a description that was valid and serviceable at the commonsense level would need to be superseded when wider considerations were taken into account. One way of putting Bradley's view is to say that metaphysics claims to offer a conceptual scheme in terms of which we can give a description of the world that is ultimate and comprehensive, but that it also recognizes the existence of many subordinate and more limited schemes, each of which has its point in the characterization of appearances. The Bradleian doctrine of degrees of truth and reality is obviously relevant here, and it cannot be said that Moore gives it very serious consideration. But even if this point had to be granted, the respectability of metaphysics might still be in doubt, for the whole notion of an ultimate description of the world is itself suspect thanks to the work of Wittgenstein.

According to Wittgenstein, a principal source of philosophical error has been the idea that the primary function of language is to describe. The truth is, rather, that we engage in many different "language games," each of which serves its own purpose and each of which is authentic at its own level. There can be no question of ruling any such game out of court; the fact that it is played is sufficient evidence that it is appropriate. Nor are different sets of language users rivals; it could not be said, for instance, that physics gives a truer picture of the world than common sense or that the naïvetés of everyday moral language are corrected by the psychologist. If we keep these diverse languages apart, we see that each has its own point and utility. The idea of a finally correct language that would embrace and replace them all is clearly the height of absurdity, and, hence, metaphysics in its revised form is no more acceptable than was metaphysics in the shape of news from nowhere.

But this analysis, too, is built on questionable assumptions. First, is it really clear that language games or areas of linguistic activity are as distinct as Wittgenstein says they are? The point is by no means clear as far as the language games of science and common sense are concerned, for most scientists and many plain men think that the scientific account of the physical world gives a truer picture of it than that embodied in the ordinary man's everyday beliefs. Nor can we agree without further argument with the thesis that sufficient authentication is found for a language game when we note that it is played. There are, after all, games and games. In a form of game much played in the ancient world, elaborate formulas to appease the god of the sea were devised by those about to embark. As a result, a certain way of talking commanded a wide use and approval. But could that fact alone be invoked to show that it was legitimate? Surely, we should want to object that however much such language was used, its use could not be legitimate if in fact there was no god of the sea or if he exercised no influence on whether seafarers reached their destinations safely. To do this, however, is to make the propriety of a language game subject to the tenability of the factual assumptions on which it rests. Although this is not to maintain that the only use of language is to describe (which would be absurd), it is to claim a certain priority for the language game in which we say how things are.

Metaphysics as we have expounded it is concerned with resolving conceptual conflicts by finding a way of speaking that will enable us to express the true nature of the world. If we possess such a way of speaking, we have a yardstick by which to measure the ultimate tenability, as opposed to the immediate use, of particular language games—the languages of religion, science, law, and so on. It is not self-evident that each of these is in order as it is, and though the fact that they are constantly used and understood is enough to show that they serve some purpose, it does not in itself show that they are suited for the purposes those who use them have in mind. These games are indeed played, but they could, for all that, be played on false pretenses. To decide whether they are, we must have recourse to metaphysics.

METAPHYSICS AS ANALYSIS

Even if the foregoing account of the nature of metaphysics were accepted as generally unobjectionable, there are many philosophers who would deny that it covers everything metaphysicians have attempted or are attempting to do. In particular, it fails to accommodate an activity pursued by many contemporary analytic and linguistic philosophers that has a clear affinity with the work of some of the classical metaphysicians. The classical metaphysicians were led to ask what there is partly because of puzzles about the status of numbers and qualities. Plato had produced arguments to show that these must be independently real, and Aristotle elaborated the doctrine of categories as an answer to them. Now, there are plainly parallels to this controversy in contemporary philosophy, both in the discussions among logicians about names and descriptions (which revive the ancient dispute about the relative priority of universals and particulars) and in the arguments about the relation of the mind and body that have recently been so prominent in British and American philosophy. What is notable about these issues, as opposed to those mentioned above, is that matters of fact appear to have no relevance to their solution. If we can solve them at all, we can solve them only by thinking.

This contrast is both genuine and important; there certainly are philosophical activities that are traditionally connected with metaphysics and that cannot be subsumed either under the schema given above or under that which it was meant to replace. These activities are in essence logical or analytic, and insofar as it is confined to them, metaphysics is indistinguishable from analysis. But there is no reason to confine metaphysics to such inquiries. That metaphysicians have been speculative theorists as well as ontologists in the restricted modern sense is almost too obvious to need mention; to decide, as some

commentators do, that the speculation can be set aside as regrettable and the ontology played up is at best arbitrary. Nor is it true that we can make an entirely clear-cut distinction between the two. If we look at recent work on the mind-body problem, for instance, we see that much of it is indeed logical in a wide sense of that word but that considerations of substance also come in, for example, when we discuss the nature of consciousness or of thought bearing in mind the properties and possibilities of thinking machines. An all-important motive that impels men to persist with these questions is the need to take account once more of the claims of materialism against a background in which new scientific and technical discoveries seem to lend increased support to those claims. However fascinating logical problems may be, interest in them cannot be long sustained without some external stimulus. It is such a stimulus that metaphysics of the broad kind argued for above may be expected to provide.

See also Appearance and Reality; Aristotle; Being; Bradley, Francis Herbert; Categories; Descartes, René; Dialectic; Existence; Freud, Sigmund; Hegel, Georg Wilhelm Friedrich; Hegelianism; Hume, David; Kant, Immanuel; Language, Philosophy of; Leibniz, Gottfried Wilhelm; Locke, John; Logical Positivism; Materialism; Metaphysics, History of; Monad and Monadology; Moore, George Edward; Ontology; Plato; Spinoza, Benedict (Baruch) de; Thomas Aquinas, St.; Time; Wisdom, (Arthur) John Terence Dibben; Wittgenstein, Ludwig Josef Johann.

Bibliography

CLASSICAL WORKS

Aristotle. *Works,* Vol. VIII, *Metaphysics,* edited by J. A. Smith and W. D. Ross. Oxford, 1928. See especially Γ 1–2; E 1; Λ 1–2, 6. Compare also W. D. Ross, *Aristotle's Metaphysics,* Vol. I. Oxford, 1924. See pp. lxxvii ff.

Baumgarten, A. G. *Metaphysica.* Halle, 1739.

Bradley, F. H. *Appearance and Reality,* Oxford, 1893. See especially the preface and introduction.

Descartes, René. *Meditations on First Philosophy* (1641). In *The Philosophical Works of Descartes,* translated by E. S. Haldane and G. R. T. Ross, 2 vols. New York, 1931. See especially "Reply to Second Objections."

Hegel, Georg Wilhelm Friedrich. *Phenomenology of Mind* (1807). Translated by J. B. Baillie, 2nd ed. New York: Macmillan, 1931.

Hume, David. *Enquiry concerning Human Understanding.* London, 1748. There are many modern editions.

Hume, David. *A Treatise of Human Nature* (1739–1740), edited by L. A. Selby-Bigge. Oxford, 1888; 1941.

Kant, Immanuel. *Critique of Pure Reason* (1781). Translated by N. Kemp Smith. London, 1929.

Kant, Immanuel. "Inaugural Dissertation" (1770). In *Kant's Inaugural Dissertation and Early Writings on Space,* translated by J. Handyside. Chicago: Open Court, 1929.

Kant, Immanuel. *An Inquiry into the Distinctness of the Principles of Natural Theology and Morals* (1764). In *Kant's Critique of Practical Reason,* edited by L. W. Beck. Chicago, 1949.

Kant, Immanuel. *Prolegomena to Every Future Metaphysics* (1783). Translated by P. G. Lucas. Manchester, U.K., 1953.

Plato. *Republic.* Translated by A. D. Lindsay. London: Deat, 1976. See especially VI–VII.

Plato. *Sophist.* In *Plato's Theory of Knowledge,* edited by F. M. Cornford. London: K. Paul, Trench, Trubner, 1935. See especially 253ff.

Wolff, Christian. *Philosophia Prima Sive Ontologia.* Frankfurt, 1729; edited by J. Ecole, Hildesheim, 1962.

MODERN WORKS

Ayer, A. J. *Language, Truth and Logic.* London: Gollancz, 1936. Lively brief account of the logical positivist criticism of metaphysics. See also the introduction to the second edition (1945) for replies to objections.

Broad, C. D. "Critical and Speculative Philosophy." In *Contemporary British Philosophy,* edited by J. H. Muirhead, Vol. I. London: Allen and Unwin, 1924. An influential article.

Carnap, Rudolf. "The Elimination of Metaphysics through Logical Analysis of Language." In *Logical Positivism,* edited by A. J. Ayer. Glencoe, IL: Free Press, 1959. An important and influential article; originally published in 1932.

Carnap, Rudolf. *Philosophy and Logical Syntax.* London: Kegan Paul, 1935.

Collingwood, R. G. *An Essay on Metaphysics.* Oxford: Clarendon Press, 1940. Written in reaction to Ayer but also of independent interest.

Emmet, D. M. *The Nature of Metaphysical Thinking.* London: Macmillan, 1945.

Lazerowitz, Morris. *The Structure of Metaphysics.* London: Routledge and Paul, 1955. Mainly influenced by Moore.

Moore, G. E. "The Conception of Reality." In his *Philosophical Studies.* London: Routledge, 1922. Sharp criticism of Bradley.

Moore, G. E. "A Defence of Common Sense." In his *Philosophical Papers.* London: Allen and Unwin, 1959.

Moore, G. E. *Some Main Problems of Philosophy.* London: Allen and Unwin, 1953. Expounds at length the doctrine of "A Defence of Common Sense"; written in 1911.

Pears, D. F., ed. *The Nature of Metaphysics.* London: Macmillan, 1957. A series of modern discussions of metaphysics.

Walsh, W. H. *Metaphysics.* London, 1963.

Wittgenstein, Ludwig. *The Blue and Brown Books: Preliminary Studies for the Philosophical Investigations.* Oxford: Blackwell, 1958.

Wittgenstein, Ludwig. *Philosophical Investigations.* Oxford: Blackwell, 1953.

Wittgenstein, Ludwig. *Tractatus Logico-Philosophicus.* London: Routledge, 1922.

W. H. Walsh (1967)

METAPHYSICS, NATURE OF [ADDENDUM]

What is metaphysics? An answer to this question requires a specification both of the *scope* of metaphysics—that is, of the nature of the questions that metaphysicians raise and attempt to answer—and of the *methods* that they employ in this enterprise.

THE SCOPE OF METAPHYSICS

As regards scope, a natural answer is that metaphysics is concerned with the investigation of the ultimate nature of reality, where this involves the attempt, first, to arrive at the most fundamental truths about what exists, and, second, to provide an account of the concepts that are involved in such fundamental truths. This characterization immediately gives rise to the question of the relation between metaphysics and science. The goal of physics, surely, is to arrive at the ultimate truth concerning the nature of the physical world. Similarly, the goal of psychology is to determine the ultimate nature of minds and mental states. How, then, do the sciences leave any room for the discipline of metaphysics?

This is a crucial question. But if one considers the issues that metaphysicians address, a clear answer will emerge. First of all, then, a central part of metaphysics involves offering accounts of concepts that are essential to scientific theories in general but of which no account is offered within any of the sciences themselves. These will include such concepts as those of particulars, properties, relations, persisting entities, events, states of affairs, causation, and laws of nature, and, with regard to these concepts, metaphysicians will ask, for example, whether causal relations logically supervene on noncausal states of affairs and whether laws of nature logically supervene upon the total history of the universe.

Second, philosophers attempt to establish necessary truths involving some of those concepts. Some of these possible necessary truths—such as the claim that any particular must have some intrinsic properties—may very well have no bearing upon scientific theories. Others, however, certainly do so. Thus, for example, the thesis that any particular must have some categorical properties implies that some current scientific theories are incomplete since they attribute propensities to objects without supplying any categorical basis. Or, more dramatically, other metaphysical theses—such as the much-discussed proposition that it is impossible for a cause to be either earlier than or simultaneous with its effect—are on a collision course with some scientific theories that have been advanced. So, for example, this claim entails that tachyons cannot exist and that positrons cannot be electrons traveling backward in time. It also means that the General Theory of Relativity, in allowing for causal and temporal loops, is allowing for something that is logically impossible. Or, again, if a cause cannot be simultaneous with its effect, then the mathematical formulation of Newton's Second Law of Motion—$F = ma$—is not satisfactory since it fails to assign different times to the force and the acceleration that it causes.

Third, science is typically silent on questions that have no bearing on the experimental content and predictions of scientific theories. A vivid illustration here is provided by the philosophy of time. For, contrary to what Putnam and others have claimed, current scientific theories such as the Special Theory of Relativity do not settle the issue between tensed and tenseless accounts of the nature of time. Metaphysicians are, then, addressing a perfectly legitimate question when they ask whether a tensed view of time is right, or a tenseless view, and this is clearly not a question that physics attempts to answer.

Fourth, physics and the other sciences involve presuppositions for which they offer no justification. In particular, it is assumed that there is an external world and that it is a material world. Metaphysics, by contrast, makes no such assumption, and so treats it as a question to be investigated and, hopefully, answered whether there is a material world or whether, instead, the basic concrete particulars are mental entities so that some form of idealism is true.

Fifth, physics, in attempting to arrive at theories that will provide explanations of physical events, takes for granted the idea that the world of physical events is causally closed so that the only causes of physical events are other physical events. Our ordinary experience, on the other hand, appears to provide considerable support for the view that experiences involve qualitative properties, or qualia, that, in the first place, are not reducible to the fundamental entities, properties, and relations postulated in physics, and that, in the second place, appear to enter into the causation of some physical events. It is very natural to think, for example, that when a person sees something and says that it is red, that there was a property of qualitative redness that the person was aware of and that that property played a causal role in producing that person's utterance. Metaphysicians, accordingly, working in the philosophy of mind, view it as a controversial matter whether the causation of physical events involves only the entities, properties, relations, and states of affairs that are the stuff of physics. In addition, the idea that the world of

physical events is causally closed rules out libertarian free will, and again, a metaphysician will insist, correctly, that until this issue is examined and settled, the assumption that physical events have only physical causes is not a justified assumption.

Sixth, the sciences rely upon induction in the form of the method of hypothesis or inference to the best explanation. The question of the justification of such methods—or of induction in general—is, of course, a question within epistemology. However, the answer to this epistemological issue may very well turn upon questions in metaphysics. So, for example, some philosophers have argued that, on the one hand, if laws are merely certain sorts of cosmic regularities, then one can never be justified in believing that any exceptionless, nonprobabilistic law obtains, and, on the other hand, that such beliefs can be justified given a metaphysically stronger conception of laws—such as the view that they are second-order relations between universals. A justification of the methods of science may depend, accordingly, upon the answers to important metaphysical questions.

Seventh, one of the crucial questions concerning the nature of reality is whether the natural world was brought into existence by God, or, at least, by some sort of immaterial being, possibly of a much more limited sort. Scientifically-based arguments have, of course, been offered both for and against the existence of an immaterial creator, but the evaluation of such arguments continues to be something that falls outside of the scope of science as presently practiced.

Finally, the sciences are concerned exclusively with the existence of contingent entities and states of affairs whereas metaphysics is not. For while questions about whether there are properties that are not reducible to those of physics, about whether the world of physical events is causally closed, about whether humans have libertarian free will, and, most would say, about whether God exists, are questions about contingent matters, metaphysics is also concerned about the existence of various things such that, if they do exist, it appears that their existence is necessary rather than contingent. Do numbers and other mathematical entities exist? Does the null set exist? Do other set-theoretical entities not involving any contingent entities exist? Is there a Platonic realm consisting of transcendent or uninstantiated universals? Do objective values exist—perhaps, as Plato thought—also in the same realm as transcendent universals? Is there a world containing intentional entities—such as concepts, propositions, or nonconcrete possible worlds? In conclusion, then, it seems clear that there are an enormous number of very important issues that are concerned with the ultimate nature of reality and that do not fall within the scope of science.

THE METHODS OF METAPHYSICS

Metaphysical claims vary in their modal status: Some, if true, are contingent truths while others, if true, are necessary truths. One would expect, then, that quite different methods must be employed in these different cases. In fact, however, the variety is considerably greater than this suggests. Let us consider, then, some of the more important methods that philosophers use in the attempt to arrive at knowledge of metaphysical truths.

DIRECT ACQUAINTANCE WITH MENTAL ENTITIES.

Consider disputes in present-day philosophy of mind concerning the existence and nature of qualitative properties of experiences, or qualia. Philosophers who affirm the existence of qualia appeal, for example, to logical possibilities of zombies and inverted spectra. Arguably, however, such appeals involve the idea that there are properties that one is directly aware of—properties that would be absent in the case of zombies and differently correlated with physicalistic properties in the case of inverted spectra. At bottom, accordingly, there seems to be an appeal to the idea of direct acquaintance with instances of properties and relations.

The idea of direct acquaintance is least controversial when invoked in support of properties and relations that can be completely given in experience. Many philosophers, however, maintain that one can also be directly acquainted with mental states that involve intentionality—such as thoughts, beliefs, preferences, emotions, and so on—while some philosopher claim that one can also be directly acquainted with a self that enjoys those various mental states.

DIRECT PERCEPTION OF NONMENTAL ENTITIES.

If it exists, direct acquaintance provides one with noninferential knowledge—or, at least, noninferentially justified beliefs—concerning mental states of oneself. Many philosophers argue, however, that the scope of noninferential knowledge is not restricted to one's own current mental states. Thus it is claimed, for example, that one can have noninferentially justified beliefs about events that happened yesterday—which will therefore allow one to set aside Bertrand Russell's suggestion that perhaps the world came into being five minutes ago. Or, one can have noninferential knowledge about the existence of external, material objects, and so know that one is not a brain in

vat and that idealism is not true. Or, one can be directly acquainted with objective moral values, such as the non-natural properties of George Edward Moore, or with mathematical entities, such as the natural numbers, or with supernatural minds, such as God.

None of these claims is, of course, uncontroversial. Indeed, some of them are highly contentious. The point is simply that in trying to get clear about what legitimate methods are available to the metaphysician, the idea of noninferential knowledge of contingent states of affairs—an idea often associated with such notions as direct awareness, direct acquaintance, and direct perception—deserves serious examination.

INDUCTIVE METHODS.

However broad the scope of noninferential knowledge may be, it is surely true that many important metaphysical propositions concerning contingent matters of fact are such that they cannot be known in that way: They must, on the contrary, be justified on the basis of other justified beliefs. Consider, for example, the thesis that humans have immaterial, immortal souls, or the thesis that the mind is identical with the brain, or the thesis that the theoretical entities postulated by physics are real.

How do metaphysicians proceed in such cases? It is hard to see any alternative to the inductive methods employed within science where one employs such notions as hypotheticodeductive method, crucial experiments, and inference to the best explanation.

Thus, one possibility is to try to arrive at plausible entailments of the relevant proposition that can be experimentally tested. So, for example, the proposition that humans have immaterial minds would certainly seem to entail conclusions concerning what will happen in cases of brain damage. If this is so, one can then determine whether those predictions hold true. Here, as elsewhere, of course, if the predictions turn out to be false, one can modify the theory so that one has a theory that no longer has those entailments. But then considerations of simplicity and ad hocness, which are appealed to within science, will become relevant.

In some cases, one may not be able to construct an experimental test since one is dealing with theories that are experientially equivalent. Consider, for example, the problem of deciding between Berkeley's theory of reality and the view that there is a mind-independent, physical world. In such cases philosophers have sometimes been tempted to embrace the view that there are competing, interpretative, conceptual schemes between which there is no rational way of deciding. But here it is important to notice that one can equally well have competing scientific theories that are observationally equivalent—a fact that does not mean that there cannot be rational grounds for preferring one theory to the other. Two theories may, for example, differ radically with regard to simplicity, and one may be able to show, within a sound, inductive logic, that the simplicity of a theory is directly related to the a priori probability that the theory is true.

Many metaphysical propositions, however, are not concerned with contingent matters of fact. What methods are available, then, when one is dealing with propositions that, if true, are necessary?

ANALYTIC DERIVATION. One fundamental method for establishing metaphysical truths that are necessary is by showing that they are analytically true statements, where this is a matter of showing that they follow from logical truths in the narrow sense via substitution in accordance with relevant definitions.

But how are the definitions to be assessed? Here there are at least two fundamental criteria: one positive and one negative. As regards the negative criterion, a definition must not be exposed to counterexamples, so a very important task in evaluating a definition is to see whether it is possible to construct counterexamples to the definition. If it appears to satisfy this negative criterion, then the next question is whether the definition enables one to derive what seem to be the fundamental necessary truths involving the concept in question.

THE SEARCH FOR TRUTHMAKERS. Another important technique that metaphysicians use in attempts to establish necessary truths is that of asking what sorts of facts or states of affairs could suffice to make relevant statements true. Thus, David Lewis (1986), for example, argued for the existence of a plurality of possible worlds by attempting to show that, on the one hand, such concrete worlds can serve as truthmakers for statements about what is logically possible, logically necessary, and logically impossible, and, on the other hand, that nothing else, including ersatz possible worlds, can do so. If this is right, and if, as is surely the case, at least some modal statements are true, then it follows that there is a plurality of concrete worlds.

Another illustration is provided by laws of nature. Thus, it is possible first of all to describe worlds that contain fewer and fewer instances of some basic law of nature that obtains in our world, and then, second, to argue that even if there were no instances, the law in question *could* still obtain. If this is so, then the truthmakers for nomo-

logical statements cannot be cosmic regularities, and other possibilities will have to be canvassed—such as states of affairs involving either dispositions that are never manifested or second-order relations between universals.

THE APPEAL TO INTUITIONS. A third important method that philosophers employ in attempting to arrive at necessary truths is that of appealing to intuitions. Where a metaphysical truth, if necessary, appears to be an analytic truth, the appeal to intuition would not seem to be a satisfactory terminus since it provides no account of why the proposition that seems to be necessarily true is true whereas an analytic derivation would do precisely that.

Many philosophers hold, however, that there are a priori necessary truths that are not analytic. So, for example, there are propositions concerning apparently simple, incompatible properties, such as the proposition that nothing can be both red and green at the same place at the same time. In addition, if ethical statements have cognitive content, then it is natural to think that there are basic moral statements that would be true in any possible world and thus which are necessary—such as the proposition that pain is intrinsically bad and the proposition that the killing of innocent persons is prima facie seriously wrong. But if this is right, then, if it can plausibly be argued that such propositions are not analytically true, there may be no alternative to the view that the truth of such propositions is known by means of some sort of direct, intellectual intuition, however uninformative such an account may seem.

See also Berkeley, George; Epistemology; Lewis, David; Metaphysics; Metaphysics, History of; Philosophy of Mind; Moore, George Edward; Putnam, Hilary; Russell, Bertrand Arthur William.

Bibliography

Armstrong, David M. *Universals and Scientific Realism.* 2 vols. Cambridge, U.K.: Cambridge University Press, 1978.

Armstrong, David M. *A World of States of Affairs.* Cambridge, U.K.: Cambridge University Press, 1997.

Campbell, Keith. *Contemporary Metaphysics: An Introduction.* Encino, CA: Dickenson, 1976.

Carroll, John W. *Readings on Laws of Nature.* Pittsburgh, PA: University of Pittsburgh Press, 2004.

Jubien, Michael. *Contemporary Metaphysics.* Malden, MA: Blackwell, 1997.

Lewis, David. *On the Plurality of Worlds.* Oxford: Blackwell, 1986.

Kim, Jaegwon, and Ernest Sosa, eds. *A Companion to Metaphysics.* Malden, MA: Blackwell, 1995.

Kim, Jaegwon, and Ernest Sosa, eds. *Metaphysics: An Anthology.* Malden, MA: Blackwell, 1999.

Loux, Michael, and Dean W. Zimmerman, eds. *The Oxford Handbook of Metaphysics.* Oxford: Oxford University Press, 2003.

Putnam, Hilary. "Time and Physical Geometry." *Journal of Philosophy*, 64 (8) (1967): 240–247.

Sosa, Ernest, and Michael Tooley, eds. *Causation.* Oxford: Oxford University Press, 1993.

van Inwagen, Peter, and Dean W. Zimmerman, eds. *Metaphysics: The Big Questions.* Malden, MA: Blackwell, 1998.

Michael Tooley (2005)

METEMPSYCHOSIS

See *Reincarnation*

METHOD IN PHILOSOPHY

See *Philosophy*

METHODOLOGY

See *Scientific Method*

MEYERSON, ÉMILE

(1859–1933)

Émile Meyerson, a French epistemologist and philosopher of science, was born in Lublin, Poland (at that time Russia). He was educated in Germany, where, after completing his classical studies, he studied chemistry under Robert Wilhelm Bunsen. In 1882 he settled in Paris; following a disappointing experience with industrial chemistry, he served as foreign editor of the Havas news agency and later as director of the Jewish Colonization Association for Europe and Asia Minor. After World War I he became a naturalized French citizen.

Meyerson never held an official teaching position. But a group of philosophers and other scholars, attracted by his celebrated erudition, formed an eager and attentive audience. He was especially well versed in the history of the sciences (chiefly, but not exclusively, the physico-chemical sciences) from their origins to their most recent developments. His command of language, his clarity of thought, and his extraordinary capacity for work served him well. Both his writings and his person gave an impression of great robustness—"solid as a Roman wall," as André Lalande once remarked.

Meyerson's philosophy was offered not as a philosophy of nature but as a "philosophy of the intellect." He set himself the tasks of disentangling the principles that govern the advance of thought and of extracting from reason the kernel that constitutes the *intellectus ipse*. This search for the a priori, he held, this new critique of pure reason, should not itself be conducted in an a priori manner. It had to proceed empirically—not directly, through a psychological analysis of the activity of thought, but indirectly, through reflection on the products of thought. These products may be true or false, so long as they bear witness to a serious effort of the intellect. From this point of view, the history of the sciences provides unique documentation. Thus it is that, of Meyerson's three major works, the first (*Identité et réalité*, Paris, 1908) is almost exclusively epistemological; but in the second, *De l'explication dans les sciences* (Explanation in the sciences; 2 vols., Paris, 1921), and especially in the third, *Du cheminement de la pensée* (The ways of thought; 3 vols., Paris, 1931), the scope is widened to encompass the whole of knowledge. In the last two works it is shown that the mind works always and everywhere in the same fashion, and this catholicity of reason proves that it does indeed include a portion that is a priori.

Each of Meyerson's works begins with an attempt to dispel the positivist bias that weighed so heavily on his years of apprenticeship. Science requires the concept of thing; science searches for explanation. It is not content simply to bind together by laws the phenomena given us in sense experience in order only to predict and control them. Science tends to dissolve the qualitative datum—but only to reach behind it for a more lasting and more objective, substantial *real.* Science not only seeks to know the how, but also to understand the why. Its aim is speculative. Its theories are not merely edifices built of laws; they claim to reveal to us the innermost causes of things. Realism and causalism are two fundamental tendencies that, taken together, govern the entire activity of the scientist. For the scientist, "phenomenism" and "legalism," when he submits to them, are only provisional stages. His ambition is to get to the bottom of things, his ultimate purpose is an ontological one.

In what does explanation consist? It is at this point that the Meyersonian theory proper begins. In every domain, whether it be philosophy, science, or everyday life, to explain is to identify. Causality is nothing but a form of logical identity. We understand a change only when it becomes evident to us that, at bottom, nothing has happened, that the entire effect was already present in the cause—or at least that the change has been reduced to the minimum, to a simple displacement. The old adage *causa aequat effectum,* mechanistic theories, and chemical equations all manifest this identifying tendency. As the Eleatic paradoxes attest, we are troubled even by change of place and by the mere passage of time. Reason is satisfied only to the degree that it succeeds in eliminating time. The principle of inertia, the reversibility of mechanical phenomena, the conservation of matter and energy, the permanence and immutability of the ultimate elements, show in what direction we insistently turn as we strive for intelligibility.

Yet in a world thus rigidly set, there still remains a qualitative diversity that is the source of new attempts at identification: the elimination of "secondary qualities," the explanation of apparent differences in terms of combinations of quite similar elements from which all but geometrical properties have been removed. Thus the world is fully intelligible to us only if we succeed in assimilating it, in the final analysis, to homogeneous space. Being, like becoming, tends to turn into its opposite when our reason seeks to explain it.

But reality resists this persistent will to identify. Carnot's principle defeats any hope of eliminating time. It proves that the irreversibility of the course of time is not a subjective illusion, that the future is not interchangeable with the past, in brief, that something really does happen. Furthermore, in denying sense qualities any place in the physical world, mechanism has not thereby made them disappear. The heterogeneity of the data of sense exists unexplained and indeed inexplicable from a mechanistic point of view. In addition, atomic discontinuity puts an obstacle in the way of geometrization. Reality rejects the identity to which reason would reduce it. The real is only partly intelligible; it contains elements that are irreducible, and hence irrational. It is in fact the presence of these irrational elements, contradicting the rationalist idealism of the philosophers, that can serve to define the real in opposition to the structures erected by our thought. Thus while reason may well move from success to success in the quest for identity that essentially motivates its activities, it can never win a definitive victory. In the end, it is condemned to defeat.

Indeed, how could matters be otherwise? There is something odd and almost absurd about this endeavor of reason, for its complete success would betoken its ultimate failure. To explain reality fully would amount precisely to denying it as real, to dissolving it into a motionless and undifferentiated space, that is, into nothingness. A perfect explanation of the world would end up in acosmism. And the conflict would be met with again even if the object studied were only an ideal one, as in the case of mathematical speculation. Reasoning, even that which is apparently formal, is never tautological. Thought, at work, advances; it does not just repeat interminably that *A is A.* Meyerson came to emphasize more and more reason's need for something diverse to assimilate, and he tended to define reason not so much by its end, identity, as by its activity, identifying. Reason is thus essentially divided against itself. This is the epistemological paradox.

Meyerson later extended these views to other domains, from scientific reason to philosophical reason, from the modern physicist to primitive man and the medieval thinker; but they were first suggested to him by reflection upon classical science. Have the revolutions in physics served to confirm or contradict them? In *La déduction relativiste* (Paris, 1925), Meyerson easily showed that relativity theory was inspired throughout by the same ideal of objectivization and geometrization. Like Parmenides's sphere or René Descartes's world, Albert Einstein's universe is resorbed into space. However, quantum physics, because it sets bounds to continuity and objectivity, contains something "unassimilable." Meyerson believed, nonetheless, that quantum theory, in the interpretation given it by the Copenhagen school, was a passing "aberration," and that as soon as the physicists recognized the possibility of doing so, they would hasten to return to traditional views—a conjecture that was in part subsequently verified.

If the detail is rich, the broad outlines of Meyerson's philosophy are simple and clear. It enjoyed great prestige about 1930. Since then, it has been somewhat overshadowed by the philosophy of the scientific theorists of the Copenhagen school, although Louis de Broglie retains the high estimate of it stated in his preface to Meyerson's *Essais.* Meyerson's philosophy has also been neglected because of the general shift of interest among contemporary philosophers from epistemological to existential problems.

See also Descartes, René; Einstein, Albert; French Philosophy; Identity; Lalande, André; Parmenides of Elea; Zeno of Elea.

Bibliography

Meyerson's writings include the small work *Réel et déterminisme dans la physique quantique* (Paris: Hermann,

1933) and a posthumously published collection, *Essais* (Paris: J. Vrin, 1936). An English translation of *Identité et réalité* by Kate Loewenberg appeared under the title *Identity and Reality* in London and New York in 1930.

See also André Lalande, "L'épistémologie de M. Meyerson," in *Revue philosophique de la France et de L'étranger* 96 (1922): 259–280; Léon Brunschvicg, "La philosophie d'Émile Meyerson," in *Revue de métaphysique et de morale* 33 (1926): 39–63; George Boas, *A Critical Analysis of the Philosophy of Émile Meyerson* (Baltimore: Johns Hopkins Press, 1930); Jacob Loewenberg, "Meyerson's Critique of Pure Reason," in *Philosophical Review* 41 (1932); Albert E. Blumberg, "Émile Meyerson's Critique of Positivism," in *Monist* 42 (1932): 60–79; André Metz, *Meyerson, une nouvelle philosophie de la connaissance*, 2nd ed. (Paris, 1934); Thomas R. Kelly, *Explanation and Reality in the Philosophy of Émile Meyerson* (Princeton, NJ: Princeton University Press, 1937), with bibliography; *Bulletin de la Société française de philosophie* (April 1961), an issue devoted to Meyerson in celebration of the centenary of his birth.

Robert Blanché (1967)
Translated by Albert E. Blumberg

MICHAEL SCOT

See *Scot, Michael*

MICROCOSM

See *Macrocosm and Microcosm*

MIDDLETON, CONYERS
(1683–1750)

Conyers Middleton was an English historian and clergyman; he entered Trinity College, Cambridge, in 1700. He took orders in the Church of England and became a fellow of his college, but he had to resign his fellowship at the time of his first marriage in 1710. He held various livings but never obtained any considerable preferment in the church. The course of Middleton's life unfortunately provides several grounds for questioning his integrity and ingenuousness.

Middleton's first major publication was *A Letter from Rome, showing an exact conformity between Popery and Paganism* (London, 1729). His theme was certainly not entirely original. It can, for instance, be traced to Part IV of Thomas Hobbes's *Leviathan* (1651), and there is even some suspicion of plagiarism at the expense of a little-known French treatise, *Conformité des cérémonies modernes avec les anciennes* (Leiden, 1667). What was remarkable was the force and skill with which Middleton traced the relics of the worship of Vesta in the cult of the Virgin and deployed passages from the Christian Fathers that excoriated as heathen such practices as the erecting of votive tablets or the use of holy water.

Daniel Waterland, in his *Scripture Vindicated* (London, 1731–1732), had attacked the deist Matthew Tindal's *Christianity as Old as the Creation* (London, 1730). In 1731 Middleton published an anonymous *Letter to Waterland,* in which he urged that it was unwise to insist on the literal truth of every sentence in the Bible, and in particular ridiculed bits of the book of Genesis. His authorship was discovered, and during the ensuing uproar the public orator of Cambridge was heard to cry for a book burning. Middleton next wrote a very profitable *Life of Cicero*; in this instance the charge of plagiarism seems to have been borne out.

After writing an *Introductory Discourse* (1747), Middleton published *A Free Enquiry into the Miraculous Powers, which are supposed to have subsisted in the Christian Church from the Earliest Ages, through several successive Centuries* (London, 1748). Coincidentally, David Hume's first *Enquiry,* containing the section "Of Miracles," which later became notorious, was published in the same year. Many years later, in *My Own Life* (London, 1777), Hume confessed his chagrin: "On my return from Italy, I had the mortification to find all England in a ferment, on account of Dr. Middleton's *Free Enquiry,* while my performance was entirely overlooked and neglected."

There was every reason to compare the two books, for the tendency of both was to undermine belief in the miraculous. But whereas Hume was raising methodological difficulties about the possibility of providing adequate historical proof of such occurrences, especially in a religious context, Middleton was concerned primarily with the historical evidence actually available. His argument was addressed in the first instance to those, including the great majority of educated Protestants, who believed both that the occurrence of miracles was a guarantee of religious truth and that the age of miracles was now past. This position was obviously precarious, for where precisely was the crucial dividing line to be drawn? Middleton directed his onslaught at this weak point. It was, as Leslie Stephen said, "incomparably the most effective of the whole deist controversy." Although Middleton himself never ventured to question the miracle stories of the New Testament, he attacked the credibility of similar accounts in the early Christian church. In a series of damaging quotations, he displayed the credulity of the Fathers, including some of the most respected, such as St.

Augustine, and even cited passages in which others seem to have been deliberately approving pious frauds. The impact of Middleton's attack would have been smaller on a position that was less inherently precarious. Arguments of this kind would not have been effective, for instance, with Protestant "enthusiasts" such as the Wesleys or with the Roman Catholics, who insisted that the age of miracles was not past. As a historian, Middleton displayed the faults characteristic of his period, particularly the naive view that stories must be either wholly and straightforwardly true or else just lies. His importance lies in the contributions he made toward undermining the arbitrary barriers between secular and sacred history.

See also Augustine, St.; Hobbes, Thomas; Hume, David; Miracles; Tindal, Matthew.

Bibliography

Apart from the works of Middleton mentioned in the text, see Sir Leslie Stephen's article on Middleton in the *Dictionary of National Biography* (London and New York, 1909), Vol. XIII. pp. 343–348, as well as his *History of English Thought in the Eighteenth Century* (3rd ed., New York: Putnam, 1902), Ch. 4.

Antony Flew (1967)

MIDDLETON, RICHARD OF

See *Richard of Mediavilla*

MIKHAILOVSKII, NIKOLAI KONSTANTINOVICH
(1842–1904)

Nikolai Konstantinovich Mikhailovskii (Mikhailovsky), the Russian philosopher, social thinker, and literary critic, was a theorist of Russian Populism and an exponent of a form of positivism first advanced by his contemporary, Pëtr Lavrov. Mikhailovskii was born near Meshchovsk, Russia, the son of a landowner of moderate means. After his parents' death, he was enrolled in the St. Petersburg Mining Institute in 1856. Expelled in 1861 for leading student protests against the government, he became a writer on social and literary topics for progressive St. Petersburg reviews. From 1869 to 1884 he edited *Otechestvennyye zapiski* (Annals of the fatherland), at that time the chief organ of Russian radicalism. Mikhailovskii was

periodically banished from the capital by the tsarist authorities, but he sufficiently tempered the expression of his views to avoid imprisonment and permanent exile. He remained an influential radical spokesman until his death in St. Petersburg.

Mikhailovskii's humanistic, democratic outlook took shape early in his career, under the influence of John Stuart Mill, Pierre-Joseph Proudhon, and the Russian thinkers Aleksandr Herzen and Vissarion Belinskii. The most direct and extensive philosophical influence on Mikhailovskii was that of Lavrov, whose combination of an antimetaphysical positivism with an emphasis on the "subjective," moral demands of the human consciousness provided Mikhailovskii with his basic philosophical orientation. In his numerous philosophical essays, chief of which is *Chto takoe progress?* (What is progress?; 1869–1870), Mikhailovskii strongly developed the ethical foundation and the individualism of this orientation and defended it against the views of Herbert Spencer, Auguste Comte, Charles Darwin, and later against those of Karl Marx and Friedrich Engels.

In opposition to Spencer, Mikhailovskii argued that human progress cannot be understood "objectively," or nonteleologically, and that in general the phenomena of man's historical and social life can only be approached through a "subjective method" that takes into account the feelings and aims of the individual and makes moral evaluations. Mikhailovskii protested the stunting of the individual by the division of labor in modern industrial society, maintaining that the goal of progress should be a more homogeneous social order in which each individual would be able to develop his diverse abilities comprehensively and harmoniously. Against the social Darwinists he maintained that in human society a struggle for survival is neither inevitable nor desirable, and he asserted that as the division of labor was eliminated, economic competition would yield to cooperation. During the last quarter of the nineteenth century, Mikhailovskii was a leading exponent of Russian Populism—a form of agrarian socialism that emphasized the *obshchina*, or peasant village commune.

Like Comte, Mikhailovskii viewed historical progress as occurring in three stages. Adhering to the "subjective method," however, he distinguished these stages by reference to their teleology. In the objectively anthropocentric stage man sees himself as the end or purpose of nature. In the eccentric stage he still finds ends in nature but no longer regards himself as their unique focus. In the subjectively anthropocentric stage man finally realizes that ends or purposes do not inhere in nature but are produced by him; the individual dispenses with supernaturalism and metaphysics of every sort and relies on his own active energies for the promotion of his moral ideals.

Mikhailovskii's doctrines, and in particular his emphasis on the autonomous moral individual, brought him into sharp conflict with nascent Russian Marxism. In the 1890s his critiques of Marxism were extensively attacked by both Georgii Plekhanov and V. I. Lenin.

See also Belinskii, Vissarion Grigor'evich; Comte, Auguste; Darwin, Charles Robert; Engels, Friedrich; Herzen, Aleksandr Ivanovich; Lavrov, Pëtr Lavrovich; Lenin, Vladimir Il'ich; Marx, Karl; Marxist Philosophy; Mill, John Stuart; Plekhanov, Georgii Valentinovich; Positivism; Proudhon, Pierre-Joseph; Russian Philosophy; Spencer, Herbert.

Bibliography

WORKS BY MIKHAILOVSKII

Dostoevsky, A Cruel Talent. Translated by Spencer Cadmus. Ann Arbor, MI: Ardis, 1978.

Polnoe sobranie sochinenii (Complete works). 10 vols, edited by E. Kolosov. 4th ed. St. Petersburg, 1906–1914.

Selections from "What Is Progress?" and from other essays in *Russian Philosophy*, 3 vols. Edited by James M. Edie, James P. Scanlan, Mary-Barbara Zeldin, and George L. Kline. Chicago: Quadrangle, 1965.

Literaturnaia kritika i vospominaniia (Literary criticism and memoirs). Moscow: Iskusstvo, 1995.

WORKS ON MIKHAILOVSKII

Billington, James H. *Mikhailovsky and Russian Populism.* Oxford: Clarendon Press, 1958.

Kanevskaya, M. *N. K. Mikhailovsky's Criticism of Dostoevsky: The Cruel Critic.* Lewiston, NY: Edwin Mellen Press, 2001.

Zen'kovskii, V. V. *Istoriia Russkoi Filosofii.* 2 vols. Paris: YMCA Press, 1948–1950. Translated by George L. Kline as *A History of Russian Philosophy.* 2 vols. New York: Columbia University Press, 1953.

James P. Scanlan (1967)
Bibliography updated by Vladimir Marchenkov (2005)

MIKI KIYOSHI
(1897–1945)

Miki Kiyoshi, a Japanese philosopher of history and leading intellectual in the stormy years before World War II, was born in Isseimura, Hyogo prefecture. He was a student of Nishida Kitarō and of Hatano Seiichi at Kyoto University. He developed an early interest in the philosophy of history and studied in Germany (1922–1924) under Heinrich Rickert and Martin Heidegger, absorbing also some socialist ideas. In 1927 he accepted a chair of philosophy at Hōsei University, Tokyo, but he had been rejected as a teacher by his alma mater for dubious reasons—he had a love affair with a widow, in his day a more than sufficient reason to be excluded from a state university. Feeling resentment, and moved by the social climate of the time, he became Japan's first spokesman for philosophical Marxism. His essays on historical materialism (1927–1930) created a stir in academic circles and in the general public. His Marxism, however, was strongly colored by Heidegger's *Anthropologie* and by Blaise Pascal's conception of man, two views he had studied as a youth. His later works are not at all Marxist. In 1930 he was briefly imprisoned for contributing money to leftist causes; as a result he had to give up his teaching career and make a living as a social critic. During the crucial years before World War II, as ultranationalism became pervasive, Miki at first held to liberal principles without compromise. In 1936, he joined the Shōwa Research Society, which was led by Prince Konoe Fumimaru and which strove to moderate though not to oppose the mounting militarist trend. As the Shōwa became more and more nationalistic, Miki, though liberal at heart, had to compromise. For opposing Japan's entry into World War II and for aiding prosecuted leftists, he was returned to prison toward the war's end, and there he died.

Miki's best works are *Rekishi tetsugaku* (Philosophy of history; Tokyo, 1932) and *Kōsōryoku no ronri* (The logic of the power of imagination; Tokyo, 1939). In the first work Miki's starting-point is the subjective existential and sensible experience of life. From this he proceeds to formulate the structure of "history-in-the-making." Fundamental experience of life, he says, creates selfhood, the historical subject that is the only maker of history, since in selfhood there are not subjective and objective factors, but only lived experience. *Kōsōryoku no ronri* reflects Miki's use of Immanuel Kant's *Einbildungskraft* ("imaginative power") as it was revived by Heidegger and also reveals the evolution of Miki's thought away from the logos as social rationality that dominated *Rekishi tetsugaku* and toward a major role for pathos, the subjective inspiration that in Japan led to ultranationalist feelings. Miki was perhaps hinting that rationality was losing ground to ultranationalist passion. At any rate, for Orientals, the logic of the imagination, with its creation of myths and of what Miki calls "forms" of technocultural systems, is said to have some advantages, such as artistic inventiveness and creativity, over conceptual knowledge and usual logic. Miki uses terms borrowed from his master Nishida, the originator of the Oriental "logic of field."

See also Hatano Seiichi; Heidegger, Martin; Historical Materialism; Japanese Philosophy; Kant, Immanuel; Marxist Philosophy; Nishida Kitarō; Pascal, Blaise; Rickert, Heinrich.

Bibliography

For works in Japanese, see *Miki Kiyoshi Choshaku-shū* (Miki Kiyoshi's collected works), 16 vols. (Tokyo, 1945–1951), and Miyagawa Tōru, *Miki Kiyoshi* (Tokyo, 1958). For works in English see Gino K. Piovesana, "Miki Kiyoshi: Representative Thinker of an Anguished Generation," in *Studies in Japanese Culture,* edited by Joseph Roggendorf (Tokyo: Sophia University, 1963), pp. 141–161.

Gino K. Piovesana, S.J. (1967)

MILETUS, SCHOOL OF

See *Pre-Socratic Philosophy*

MILHAUD, GASTON
(1858–1918)

Gaston Milhaud, a French philosopher, came to philosophy by way of mathematics, which he taught for nearly ten years in the lycées before becoming a professor of philosophy at the University of Montpellier. In 1909 he went to the University of Paris, where the chair of history of philosophy in its relationship to the sciences was created especially for him.

His courses on Antoine Augustin Cournot and Charles Renouvier were published (*Études sur Cournot,* Paris, 1927; *La philosophie de Charles Renouvier,* Paris, 1927). Under the influence of Paul Tannery, his works on the history of science were at first devoted to Greek science: *Leçons sur les origines de la science grecque* (Paris, 1893) and *Les philosophes géomètres de la Grèce* (Paris, 1900). Later they were extended to include modern science. Examples are *Études sur la pensée scientifique chez les Grecs et chez les modernes* (Paris, 1906); *Nouvelles Études sur l'histoire de la pensée scientifique* (Paris, 1911); and *Descartes savant* (published posthumously, Paris, 1923).

Milhaud was both a historian and an epistemologist. With Henri Poincaré, Pierre Duhem, and Édouard Le Roy he belongs to that group of French scholars who around 1900, following the path opened for them by Émile Boutroux, denounced scientific dogmatism, using as a basis the precise analysis of past and contemporary examples in history of science. They emphasized the role of spiritual initiative, and thus the element of contingency, in the construction of scientific theories. Milhaud himself generally avoided the dangerous words *convention* and *commodité* used by Le Roy and Poincaré. He spoke, rather, of free creations, of the activity of the mind, and of the spontaneity of reason (*Le rationnel,* Paris, 1898). In his thesis, *Essai sur les conditions et les limites de la certitude logique* (Paris, 1894), he maintained that certitude, which is founded on the principle of noncontradiction, is limited to the domain of pure mathematics. He believed that it was thus possible to establish a radical break between the realm of mathematical knowledge and the realm of knowledge of the real world.

However, almost immediately thereafter (2nd ed., 1897), he regretted having shown himself to be too much the logician: "I see today that even in the extreme example of absolute rigor dreamed of by the mathematician, the living and dynamic identity of thinking always takes precedence over the static immobility of the principle of identity." The fundamental concepts and principles of all sciences result from rational decisions that simultaneously transcend both experience and logic, in the sense that they are not determined by either external or internal necessities. Positivism is, therefore, outmoded. A "fourth stage" consists of the liberation of thought from the obstacles imposed on it by the dogmatism of Auguste Comte (*Le positivisme et le progrès de l'esprit,* Paris, 1902). Nonetheless, scientific contributions are not arbitrary, and they have a universal value, in that they have matured on a basis of fact and have gradually imposed themselves upon the mind as a network of relations in which logical exigencies are composed and harmonized with the demands of a practical and aesthetic order.

See also Boutroux, Émile; Comte, Auguste; Cournot, Antoine Augustin; Duhem, Pierre Maurice Marie; French Philosophy; Le Roy, Édouard; Mathematics, Foundations of; Philosophy of Science, History of; Poincaré, Jules Henri; Positivism; Renouvier, Charles Bernard.

Bibliography

For selections from Milhaud, see R. Poirier, *Philosophes et savants français,* Vol. II, *La philosophie de la science* (Paris, 1926), pp. 55–80. A. Nadal, "Gaston Milhaud," in *Revue d'histoire des sciences* 12 (1959): 1–14, has a bibliography.

Robert Blanché (1967)

MILL, JAMES

(1773–1836)

James Mill, a British historian, economist, psychologist, utilitarian philosopher, and father of John Stuart Mill, was born in Scotland but spent most of his adult life in London. His father was a shoemaker, but his mother was ambitious for James to get a good education and to rise to a higher rank in society. He attended the University of Edinburgh, supported by the patronage of Sir John Stuart (1759–1815), for whom John Stuart Mill was named. Mill distinguished himself as a Greek scholar, receiving his MA in 1794. He then studied divinity and was licensed to preach in 1797. He gave some sermons, but by this time he was an agnostic, basing his disbelief in a benevolent deity, according to his son, on the degree of evil in the universe. He did some tutoring in Scotland, but in 1802 he moved to London where he sought to make a living as a writer and editor. He contributed to a wide assortment of newspapers and journals, and, from 1803 to 1806, he edited the *St. James Chronicle* and the *Literary Journal*. The latter was an ambitious periodical that professed to give a summary view of all the leading departments of human knowledge. In 1805 he married Harriet Burrow, and their first child, born in 1806, was John Stuart Mill.

In 1808 Mill made the acquaintance of Jeremy Bentham (1748–1832), the founder of the utilitarian tradition in modern philosophy. Mill adopted Bentham's utilitarian philosophy and used it as the foundation for his writings on government, education, freedom of the press, and other topics. In 1806 Mill began an ambitious project: to write *The History of British India*, emphasizing the social conditions and movements rather than battles and rulers. This was not completed until 1818, but it immediately became the definitive work on the subject and led to Mill being offered a position at India House, from which the East India Company managed British interests in India. He rose to the position of head of the office and served there until his death.

Mill was not only a "disciple" of Bentham. He was a friend and for a time financially dependent on Bentham's support. At times he and his family lived in houses owned by Bentham, and he and his family spent several summers at Bentham's summer houses. On these summer visits Bentham depended on Mill to be his conversational companion. Mill also edited some of Bentham's writings.

One of Mill's life works, and that for which he is now most famous, is the education that he gave his son John Stuart Mill. From infancy John Stuart was tutored by his father, seven days per week, studying in the room where James was writing the *History of British India* and other articles to support the family. At the end of each day they would take a walk at which time John Stuart would report to his father what he had learned, and he was severely reprimanded if he had not gotten it right. At age three John Stuart was learning Greek from vocabulary cards; so he had already learned English. At age eight he began Latin. By the time that he was twelve he had read, in Greek and Latin, enormous tomes of classical literature, as reported in John Stuart Mill's *Autobiography* (1873).

James Mill was active in promoting the Benthamite philosophy in current politics. He was one of the founders of what came to be known as "philosophical radicalism," a force to the left of the two major parties, the Tories and Whigs. The group included such well-known persons as Francis Place (1771–1854), a successful tailor and organizer of London demonstrations by working people; David Ricardo (1772–1823), the economist, who was probably Mill's best friend; and John Austin (1790–1859), the utilitarian jurist. The radicals advocated extension of suffrage to all tax payers, if not universal suffrage; the secret ballot in elections; the removal of tariffs on imported grain and, in general, free trade; and other legislation for the benefit of the mercantile and working classes.

WRITINGS

Mill wrote on a wide variety of topics for a number of periodicals. These show the breadth of his interests and expertise. Subjects included money and exchange, Spanish America, China, General Francisco de Miranda (1750–1816), the East India Company, liberty of the press, Bentham's law reforms, education, prison discipline, slavery, and religious toleration. In 1805 he published a translation of C. F. Villers's *History of the Reformation*. In 1807 he wrote *Commerce Defended*, an answer to a book that claimed that Britain could be independent of commerce. He wrote a number of articles for the supplement to the fifth edition of the *Encyclopaedia Britannica*, which appeared from 1816 to 1823. Some of these articles were later published independently, the most important being those on "Jurisprudence," "Prisons," "Education," and "Government." Mill's *History of British India*, in three volumes, was finished and published in 1818. In 1821 Mill published *Elements of Political Economy*, which he intended as a "schoolbook" based on his teaching Ricardian economic theory to John Stuart Mill. From 1824 to 1826 he contributed to the *Westminster Review*, a periodical started as an organ of the Radicals to answer the *Quarterly Review* of the Tories and the *Edinburgh Review* of the Whigs. In 1829 appeared his

Analysis of the Phenomena of the Human Mind, in two volumes, putting forward his "associationist" psychological theories. His last major work was the *Fragment on Mackintosh*, published in 1835 after a delay caused by Sir James Mackintosh's (1765–1832) death. In it he presents his ethical views in opposition to those of Mackintosh.

PHILOSOPHY

Mill's philosophy is empiricist, assuming that all knowledge ultimately comes from sense experience, including muscular contractions and sensation from bodily organs. He believed that the inductive method, which had been fruitful in the physical sciences, would be equally effective in philosophy. In *Analysis of the Phenomena of the Human Mind* Mill, using the method of introspection, attempts to give a complete analysis of mental phenomena, resolving them into the primitive feelings from which they are derived by association. "Feeling," according to him, includes every phenomenon of the mind. One's experience is either a knowledge of feelings separately or a knowledge of the order in which they follow each other. Some philosophers had claimed that there are feelings not derived from sensations, but Mill thinks that this is a mistake. He follows David Hume in distinguishing between impressions and ideas. "Ideas" are copies of previous "impressions." Impressions, for Mill, are caused by the external world acting in some way on the mind. The philosopher can only classify the various modes in which they present themselves. One's consciousness reveals simply a series of "sensations" and "ideas." The mind is a stream of these phenomena. The connections of ideas are due to association in either "synchronous" or "successive" order.

When Mill turns to an analysis of sensations and ideas exciting to action, he again attempts to resolve them into simple laws. A desire is an idea of a pleasant sensation; an aversion, an idea of a painful sensation; each having tacit reference to a future time. One associates these pains and pleasures with their causes, coming to desire the causes, and one associates these with one's own actions as possible causes. In this theory of action Mill is a psychological hedonist, but he is not a psychological egoist, in one meaning of that term. Although the pleasure or pain is the agent's own pleasure or pain, it may be associated with the pleasure or pain of another person, such that one desires that person's pleasure or pain. This can even be generalized to a love for humanity, such that one has pleasure at the thought of anyone's pleasure. Thus, it can be possible to be motivated to seek the greatest happiness of everyone, the utilitarian criterion of right action. Mill held, however, that actions are right when they are foreseen to produce the greatest happiness, whether or not this is the motive of the action. But the motive to produce the greatest happiness is important in admiring or despising the character of the agent.

At the same time that Mill recognizes the possibility of altruistic action, of an agent finding pleasure in the sacrifice of his or her own good to the greater good of others, he does not rely on this motive in his political philosophy. He argues from the predominance of selfish interests in his arguments for representative democracy. In his article "Government" he starts from the utilitarian premise that the end of government, as of all conduct, is the greatest happiness. He claims that this can be achieved by assuring for all persons the greatest possible quantity of the produce of their labor. Thus, he defends property, if it reflects this objective. Government is people uniting to delegate to a few the power necessary for protecting this legitimate property. The difficult problems of government relate to the means of preventing these few from themselves having an interest contrary to that of the many. The key is representation. The community as a whole cannot desire its own misery, and, although it cannot act as a whole, it can act through representatives. If these representatives can be prevented by adequate checks from misusing their powers, good government is possible. He believes that responsible representation is possible if election is for brief periods, perhaps annual; by secret ballot; and if the right to vote is extensive enough to prevent the class of electors from having an interest contrary to the whole community. One problem that he addresses is that the people do not understand their own interests. His answer is that ignorance is curable, whereas government by a minority class is sure to be bad.

In *Fragment on Mackintosh* Mill engages in a polemic against a moral sense ethical theory, even one based on associationist psychology and a greatest happiness principle. Mackintosh agrees that the criterion of right and wrong is the greatest happiness, but he claims that the moral sense is a feeling produced by the contemplation of right and wrong that becomes an independent unit, no longer resolved into its origin. It becomes a particular faculty, necessary to discern right and wrong. On the contrary, Mill says that no particular faculty is necessary to discern utility. To say that conduct is right is the same thing as to say that it produces greatest happiness. If the moral sense orders conduct opposed to the general happiness, it is so far bad. If it never orders such conduct, then it is superfluous. Mackintosh uses the example of Fletcher of Saltoun to illustrate his point. Fletcher would have sacrificed his life to save his country, but would not do any-thing base to save his country. Mill attacks this. If you refuse to save your country because you think the means base, your morality is immoral. All general rules, he says, imply exception, but only when they conflict with the supreme rule. If a rule for increasing utility diminishes utility in a given case, then it must be broken in that case.

INFLUENCE

Mill was a significant contributor to the liberalism of nineteenth-century Britain. His articles calling for expansion of suffrage, freedom of the press, freedom of religion, free trade, abolition of slavery, state-supported education, and legal and prison reform no doubt had an influence on his contemporaries and the next generation. He was significant in popularizing Bentham's and Ricardo's views. His psychological theories were a foundation on which Alexander Bain and other psychologists sought to use associationism as one element in a more complete psychology. His most significant influence, however, was by way of his son, John Stuart Mill, who reflects, although he significantly revises, the philosophy of his father.

See also Austin, John; Bain, Alexander; Bentham, Jeremy; Democracy; Empiricism; Ethics, History of; Hume, David; Liberalism; Mill, John Stuart; Utilitarianism.

Bibliography

WORKS BY MILL

A Fragment on Mackintosh. London: Baldwin and Cradock, 1835.

Analysis of the Phenomena of the Human Mind (1829). 2 vols. New York: A. M. Kelley, 1967.

The Collected Works of James Mill. New York: Routledge, 1992a.

Political Writings, edited by Terence Ball. New York: Cambridge University Press, 1992b.

WORKS ABOUT MILL

Bain, Alexander. *James Mill: A Biography* (1882). New York: A. M. Kelley, 1967.

Halévy, Elie. *The Growth of Philosophic Radicalism.* Translated by Mary Morris. London: Faber and Gwyer, 1928.

Stephen, Leslie. *The English Utilitarians* (1900). 3 vols. New York: A. M. Kelley, 1968.

Henry R. West (2005)

MILL, JOHN STUART
(1806–1873)

John Stuart Mill, the English philosopher, economist, and administrator, was the most influential philosopher in the English-speaking world during the nineteenth century and is generally held to be one of the most profound and effective spokesmen for the liberal view of man and society. In the belief that men's opinions are the dominant influence on social and historical change, Mill tried to construct and to propagate a philosophical position that would be of positive assistance to the progress of scientific knowledge, individual freedom, and human happiness. Despite numerous flaws in his theories, he succeeded in providing an alternative to existing views on morals and politics and their foundations that was both specific and cohesive enough to give a markedly liberal tendency to social and political opinion, and also sufficiently tolerant and inclusive to gain it access to an extraordinarily large and diverse public. Mill cannot be ranked among the greatest of pure philosophers, either for his originality or for his synthesizing power. His work in logic, however, broke new ground and gave a badly needed impetus to the study of the subject, while his reformulations of classical British empiricism and Benthamite utilitarianism gave these positions a relevance and continuing vitality that they would not otherwise have had.

Although Mill's views on economics will not be discussed in the present article, an excellent summary of them is contained in the article on Mill by F. Y. Edgeworth in Palgrave's *Dictionary of Political Economy.*

LIFE

John Stuart Mill was born in London, the son of James and Harriet Burrow Mill. Outwardly his life was not eventful. He was educated by his father and never attended school, although for a short time he read law with John Austin. In 1823 he became a clerk in the East India Company, where his father was a high official, and worked there until 1858. Eventually he became chief of his department, a post involving considerable administrative responsibility. In 1831 he was introduced to Harriet Taylor, the wife of a successful merchant and mother of several children. Friendship between Mill and Mrs. Taylor rapidly developed into deep though Platonic love, and for the next twenty years they saw each other constantly, despite the increasing social isolation this involved. Mill was convinced that Mrs. Taylor was a great genius: He discussed all of his work with her and attributed to her an enormous influence on his thought. Her husband died in 1849, and three years later she married Mill. In 1858, while the Mills were on a tour of France, Harriet died in Avignon. Mill bought a house nearby so that he could always be near her grave.

In 1857 Mill had written a brilliant defense of the East India Company for the parliamentary debate on renewal of the company's charter. When renewal was not granted, Mill retired, refusing an offer of a position in the government as an official for Indian affairs. In 1865 he was invited to stand for election to Parliament as an independent member for Westminster. He accepted, and although he refused to campaign, contribute to expenses, or defend his views, he won, and served until the next election, in 1868, when he was defeated. Thereafter he spent his time alternately in London and in Avignon, admired and sought after by many, accessible to few. He died after a very brief illness, attended by his wife's daughter Helen, who had looked after him since her mother's death.

EDUCATION AND PHILOSOPHICAL RADICALISM.

Until 1826 Mill's thought was completely controlled by his father. James Mill gave him one of the most formidable educations on record, starting him on Greek at the age of three and Latin at eight. By the age of fourteen he had read most of the major Greek and Latin classics, had made a wide survey of history, and had done intensive work in logic and mathematics. He had also been prepared for acceptance of the central tenets of philosophical radicalism, a set of economic, political, and philosophical views shared by the group of reformers who regarded Jeremy Bentham and James Mill as their intellectual leaders. When at the age of fifteen John Stuart Mill read Bentham's *Traité de législation,* it had the effect on him of a religious revelation. It crystallized his thoughts and fixed his aim in life—to be a reformer of the world. Guided by his father, he threw himself into the work of the radicals; he edited Bentham's manuscripts, conducted a discussion group, wrote letters to the press and articles critical of laws, judicial decisions, and parliamentary debates and actions.

DEPRESSION AND CHANGE OF VIEWS.

Late in 1826, Mill suffered a sudden attack of intense depression, which lasted for many months. The attack led him to reconsider the doctrines in which he had been raised and to seek other than Benthamite sources of thought. He believed that his capacity for emotion had been unduly weakened by strenuous training in analytic thought, with the result that he could no longer care for anything at all. In the poetry of William Wordsworth he found something of a cure—an education of the feelings that helped to balance the education of intellect given to him by his father. In 1828 he met Gustave d'Eichthal, a French follower of Comte de Saint-Simon, who sent him an early essay by

Auguste Comte and a great deal of Saint-Simonian literature. He also met John Sterling, a disciple of Samuel Taylor Coleridge. Mill came to admire both the Saint-Simonians and the Coleridgeans, and he attempted to incorporate into his own thinking what he took to be sound in their doctrines. In 1829 he published nothing at all, but by the following year he had reached a philosophical position that seemed to him far more adequate than the older Benthamism. He never again changed his philosophical views so radically.

COMTE AND SAINT-SIMON.

The historical standpoint of the Saint-Simonians, as well as the appreciation of the value of old institutions emphasized by Coleridge, impressed Mill as important additions to Benthamism, which, he thought, simply neglected such factors. He accepted the outlines of the Saint-Simonian–Comtian philosophy of history, and particularly its theory that in social change there is an alternation between "critical" periods, in which society destroys outmoded forms of life and tends toward disintegration, and "organic" periods, in which new forms of common life are evolved and social cohesion is reestablished. He agreed also with the French view that in his own times society had come to the end of a critical period. From Coleridge he learned to think of the cultured class as the leader of opinion in a nation. He also came to believe that the problem he had in common with other intellectuals was that of assisting the world, and especially England, to emerge from the critical period and progress toward a new organic period. Unless this was done, he thought, the tendency toward disintegration might possibly grow too strong to be controlled.

Three important consequences followed from this. First, merely negative remarks upon institutions, laws, and political arrangements were no longer sufficient. Although much remained that needed to be changed, it was necessary now to replace what had been destroyed with something better. Second, the views of those who defended the old and outmoded could no longer be dismissed, in Benthamite fashion, as mere lies used in defense of vested interests. What is now outmoded must, at one stage of historical development, have served a valuable purpose; otherwise it could not have survived. Those who defend it are those who see the good still in it; hence we must seek for the truth in their views, and not merely reject the falsity. The particular vice plaguing social thought is not the tendency to make mistakes of fact or faulty inferences from facts, but the great ease with which data can be overlooked: in a word, one-sidedness. Hence, if we are to obtain sound social views, our greatest need is for a complete survey of data, and this is possible to achieve only if we can appreciate the truth that our opponents have learned. For each man is naturally one-sided and can overcome this only by education and effort. Third, the tactics of a reformer must be adapted to the period in which he lives. In particular, during a critical period there is no point in promulgating an entire system: no one will listen, and the ideas will not serve to improve social cohesion. One must proceed cautiously, piecemeal, educating one's public as one goes. One must—especially in England, Mill held, where any appearance of system is abhorrent—confine oneself to particular issues, only slowly insinuating more general principles; or else work only from points on which there is general agreement, so as to avoid any shocking appearance of novelty.

This set of views dictated the program that Mill followed for the next twenty or more years. He did not abandon his early epistemology or ethical beliefs, but in developing them he always tried to emphasize their inclusiveness and their constructive power, rather than their critical and destructive powers. He refrained (with one major exception) from publishing a systematic account of his ideas, but wrote instead occasional essays dealing with fairly specific issues, in which he always tried to bring out the value of the books he was criticizing. (These tactics are largely responsible for the common view of Mill as a wavering, halfhearted, muddled thinker, appreciative of what others had to say but holding no clear opinions of his own.) He defended what he held to be sound views on philosophy, but he did not explicitly link these views together, except in his *System of Logic*, which was an entirely different case. Methods of investigation, Mill held, could be relatively neutral as regards political and moral opinion. Since these methods could be discovered from analysis of subjects like physical science, in which there was widespread agreement on results, there was a good chance of obtaining general agreement on the methods. The methods could thus serve as a cohesive, rather than a disruptive, social force.

THE *SYSTEM OF LOGIC*

Mill's *Logic* is in fact by no means neutral with regard to substantive issues. It is the first major installment of his comprehensive restatement of an empiricist and utilitarian position. It presents (sometimes, to be sure, only as "illustration") a fairly complete outline of what would now be called an "empiricist" epistemology, although Mill himself used "empiricist" in a deprecatory sense to mean "miscellaneous information," as contrasted with "scien-

tific knowledge." It begins the attack on "intuitionism" that Mill carried on throughout his life, and it makes plain his belief that social planning and political action should rely primarily on scientific knowledge, not on authority, custom, revelation, or prescription. The *Logic* had a rapid and wide success. Adopted as a text first at Oxford and eventually at Cambridge, it was also read by many outside the universities, including workmen. Its success can be explained in part by its enormous superiority to any book then existing in the field, but credit must also be given to its clear and unmistakable relevance to social problems (and to religious questions: it was attacked as atheistic by some of its earliest reviewers).

With the publication of the *Logic*, Mill took a major step toward showing that the philosophy of experience, which had hitherto been identified primarily as a skeptical position, could offer at least as much in the way of constructive thinking as any other kind of view. His treatment of deductive inference was far more sympathetic to formal logic than that of previous empiricists; and by arguing that, with care, certainty could be attained even in inductive reasoning, he made it plain that empiricism was not committed to a Humean standpoint. Mill held that the philosophy of experience was more likely than any other to encourage the development of society along liberal lines. He therefore held that it was a matter of considerable importance to show that empiricism was a viable alternative to the less progressive views—notably, Scottish commonsense philosophy and German idealism—which were then dominant. The *Logic* succeeded in doing this.

The *Logic* is primarily a discussion of inferential knowledge and of the rules of inference. (The discussion of noninferential, or as Mill also called it, immediate or intuitive, knowledge belongs, in Mill's view, to metaphysics.) It contains six books. In the first two, Mill presented an empiricist theory of deductive inference, and, since mathematics is the chief deductive science, a discussion of the nature of the truth of mathematics, especially of its axioms. In Book III, Mill discussed induction, its grounds, its methods, and its results. Book IV, titled "Of Operations Subsidiary to Induction," contains chapters on observation and description, abstraction, naming, and classification. Book V is a discussion of fallacies. Book VI contains Mill's attempt to extend the methods of the physical sciences, as derived in Book III, to what were then called "moral sciences," that is, psychology and sociology. He argued for the possibility of a science of human nature and action, and assessed the value of the various methods for attaining it. He concluded with a chapter on the logic of morality, discussing primarily the relation between rules for actions and the factual statements that serve as their foundations.

No adequate summary of the contents of the *Logic* can be given here, but some of Mill's leading views may be indicated.

DEDUCTIVE REASONING. Mill's argument in Book I of the *Logic* is intended to show the mistake of those who say that deductive inference (as found, for example, in the syllogism) is entirely useless because it involves a petitio principii, but at the same time to make it clear that deduction in general is never the source of new knowledge. Mill agreed that the conclusion of a syllogism may not contain more than is contained in the premises and that "no reasoning from generals to particulars can, as such, prove anything, since from a general principle we cannot infer any particulars, but those which the principle itself assumes as known."

It is useless to defend deduction by saying that it shows us what was "implicit" in our premises, unless we can go on to explain how something can be implicitly contained in what we already know. Mill's solution to this problem and his explanation of the value of rules of deduction rest on his view that "all inference is from particulars to particulars." When we reason "All men are mortal; Jones (not yet dead) is a man; so Jones is mortal," our real evidence for the assertion that Jones will die is our knowledge that Smith, Peters, Wilkins, and many other individuals who resemble Jones in many respects did die. We infer from their deaths to his. The general premise that all men are mortal is not itself our evidence. It is rather a note, or register, of the particular evidence on which the conclusion really depends, together with the prediction that what we have found in cases that we have already observed will also hold in similar cases not yet observed. The real inference, Mill thought, comes in constructing the general proposition on the basis of observation of particular cases. Deduction is to be understood as a way of interpreting the note that has been made of our previous inference. It is valuable because misinterpretation is very easy; but it no more gives us new information than do propositions that are true by definition. Such propositions, which Mill called "verbal," only pull out of a word what was previously put into it; and in the same way, a syllogism simply retrieves from a general proposition a particular one that was previously assumed to be in it. Since there is no real progress of thought in deduction, deductive inference is merely *apparent* inference. Induction is the only procedure that gives us nonverbal general

propositions that go beyond what has actually been observed. Hence, only in induction do we make *real* inferences.

Mathematical knowledge is no exception to this. Taking geometry first, as the deductive science par excellence, Mill argued that its conclusions are necessary only in the sense that they necessarily follow from the premises from which they are deduced. But the premises themselves—ultimately, the axioms—are grounded on observation and are generalizations from what we have always experienced. (The definitions are in a somewhat different position, although an experiential element is involved in the belief that the entities they define, such as a geometric point or line, really exist.) That two straight lines do not enclose a surface is evident to us every time we look at two straight lines that intersect. The laws of psychology, operating on such experiential data, are sufficient to explain the production in us of the belief that such lines cannot possibly enclose a surface: hence we need not appeal to intuition or to some other nonexperiential source to explain the belief. Even the inconceivability of the denial of the axioms of geometry does not show, Mill argued, that they are not based on experience. For inconceivability is psychological, and the fact that we cannot think of something does not show that that thing cannot exist. Mill went on to offer an account of the way in which arithmetic and algebra are founded on experience. Here the essential point is that groups of four items, for example, may be rearranged into, or formed from, two groups of two items each, or a group of three items together with a group of one item. Seeing that this is always so, we come, through the operation of psychological laws, to believe that 2 + 2, or 3 + 1, *must* be the same as 4. Algebra is simply a more abstract extension of this sort of belief.

With these explanations Mill hoped to show how mathematics can yield propositions that are not merely verbal and that are certainly true of the world of experience, but that do not depend on any nonexperiential sources of knowledge. His account has never been accepted by philosophers as it stands, but there have been some attempts, among thinkers influenced by pragmatism, to work out a philosophy of mathematics along lines analogous to Mill's.

INDUCTIVE REASONING AND SCIENTIFIC EXPLANATION. In Mill's view, induction is clearly of central importance, since it is the only possible source of substantive general propositions. While the details of his theory are complicated, its main lines may be concisely indicated. All methodical and critical induction rests on the fundamental principle of the uniformity of nature; namely, that what has happened once will happen again, if circumstances are sufficiently similar. Mill thought that this is a factual proposition that is itself derived by a primitive and natural process of induction: we first note a few limited regularities and predict that they will hold in the future. After our predictions come true, we spontaneously generalize, saying that since some events have been found to occur in repeating patterns, all events will be found to occur in repeating patterns. Belief in the uniformity of nature is thus derived from, and resolvable into, belief in the existence of less sweeping patterns of occurrences, or into particular causal laws. Mill defined "cause of a phenomenon" as "the antecedent, or concurrence of antecedents, on which it is invariably and unconditionally consequent." Like the "axiom" of the uniformity of nature, the principle that every occurrence has a cause is confirmed by all our experience. It is, in fact, simply a more precise way of stating the principle of the uniformity of nature. The hope of science is to formulate propositions about specific sequences of phenomena that can be relied on to the same degree as the law of causation. And the problem of methodical induction—which is the core of the problem of scientific reasoning—arises when it is discovered that the simplest method of induction (that of assembling positive instances of a sequence of phenomena and generalizing directly from them) often leads to general propositions that turn out to be false. We then seek ways of obtaining better results. The fundamental technique is to obtain evidence which will allow us to argue as follows: Either A is the cause of a, or else there are some events which have no cause; and since we are certain that every event has a cause, we may be certain that A causes a.

According to Mill, there are four inductive methods: the method of agreement, the method of difference, the method of residues, and the method of concomitant variations. He also discussed a combination of the first two, calling it the joint method of agreement and difference. We use the first two methods in this way. If we find that A under circumstances BC is followed by abc, while under circumstances DE it is followed by ade, then A cannot be the cause either of bc or of de, since they sometimes do not occur when A occurs (and hence by the definition of "cause," cannot be caused by it). But a occurs under both sets of conditions; hence it could be the effect of A: This illustrates the method of agreement. To ascertain if something other than A might be the cause of a we use the method of difference. Will BC without A be followed by a? If not, we have so far confirmed our view that A causes

a, for, in the cases we have examined, A is always followed by a and a never occurs without being preceded by A. Hence, by the definition of "cause," A is, so far as our evidence goes, the cause, or part of the cause, of a—or else there are events without any regular cause.

Science does not rely upon induction and experiment alone. It is only infrequently, Mill thought, that we will find genuine causal laws, that is, absolutely invariable sequences. More frequently we will find regularities that hold as far as a limited experience shows but which, we have reason to believe, might well not hold under quite different circumstances. These "empirical laws" are not to be considered basic laws of nature. Much of the practical application of science depends on them, but we cannot claim to have truly scientific knowledge until we can deduce empirical laws from basic laws of nature, showing why the combination of circumstances and laws renders inevitable the limitations within which the empirical laws hold. This makes clear the aim of science: to discover laws of nature and empirical laws, and to connect them, in a deductive system, in such a way as to show how the unrestricted laws would give rise to the regularities reported by the empirical laws. The various sciences are differentiated by the ways in which these two types of laws must be discovered and connected. In some sciences it is possible to discover laws of nature directly, deduce what the empirical laws must be, and then proceed to verify the deductions by checking against experimental data. In others, empirical laws are discovered first, and laws of nature are presented as hypotheses to explain them. These alleged laws of nature are then tested by deducing further empirical laws from them and testing these deductions. In any science, however, explanation comes to an end when laws of nature are reached: These are simply ultimate facts that are to be accepted.

THE MORAL SCIENCES. In the last book of the *Logic*, Mill argued that the phenomena of individual or social human life are no exception to the law of causation, and that consequently it must be possible to determine what are the natural laws of human behavior. He investigated the various modes of inquiry used in the different physical sciences to determine which are most suited to this sort of investigation, and he sketched an outline of what a completed science of man will be. Here as elsewhere, Mill thought that "however complex the phenomena, all their sequences and coexistences result from the laws of the separate elements." Since the separate elements in this instance are men, it is the basic laws of psychology from which, when the science is completed, all the laws and regularities concerning social phenomena must be deduced. Because of the enormous number of interacting elements, however, the complexity of social action is so great that no direct deduction of its regularities from basic psychological laws will be possible. In order to make this deduction it will be necessary first to construct a science of human character that will cover both the development of human character and the tendencies to action of different types of persons. From the laws of this science, which Mill called "ethology," we may hope eventually to get sociological laws. Even then, however, we will at best obtain statements of tendencies toward action, for the enormous number of factors involved in determining social action will not allow any more accurate predictions. Still, Mill held, "knowledge insufficient for prediction may be most valuable for guidance" in practical affairs. His chief interest lay in the possibility of obtaining scientific guidance for the direction of political decisions.

How far, then, had social science actually progressed? Mill thought that the basic laws of psychology were by then well established: they were the laws put forward by psychologists of the associationist school, among whom James Mill was preeminent. But the science of ethology, which John Stuart Mill had hoped to found himself, eluded him, and he gave up work on it shortly after he published the *System of Logic*. Although the absence of the intermediate laws that this science was designed to contribute made impossible the completion of sociology, Mill thought that at least one basic law of social change had been discovered and substantially proven: Comte's law of three stages. One element, Mill argued, is more important than any other single factor in causing change in society: "This is the state of the speculative faculties of mankind, including the nature of the beliefs which … they have arrived at concerning themselves and the world by which they are surrounded. … the order of human progression in all respects will mainly depend on the order of progression in the intellectual convictions of mankind." Comte had shown that opinion always passes through the same three phases. Men first try to understand their universe in theological terms, then in metaphysical terms, and finally in scientific or, as he called them, positive terms. He had also shown that correlated with these three stages of opinion are types of social organization, which change as opinions change. This generalization, for Mill, was enormously important to our understanding of history and to our practical decisions, and up to that time it was the sole example of a well-founded sociological law. But Mill had high hopes that, with work, much progress could be made in constructing a social science; and he looked forward to a time when

"no important branch of human affairs will be any longer abandoned to empiricism and unscientific surmise."

EPISTEMOLOGY AND METAPHYSICS

With respect to metaphysics in the contemporary sense of systematic knowledge transcending experience, Mill claimed to have none; and his epistemology consists largely of an account of experiential knowledge in which he intended to show why nothing beyond such knowledge is either possible or necessary. Mill presented an empiricist theory of our knowledge of the external world and of persons which is equally free of the skepticism of David Hume and the theology of George Berkeley. He consequently covered quite thoroughly a good deal of the ground that was gone over again in the discussions among empiricists and logical positivists in the second and third decades of the twentieth century.

AIM AND METHOD. Mill held that we must know some things intuitively, without inference, if we know anything at all, and he rejected skepticism as failing to make a relevant distinction between knowledge and doubt ("In denying all knowledge it denies none"). For if all knowledge were inferential, there would be no firm starting point for inference, and we should be led into a vicious infinite regress of premises. But because whatever can be known only by intuition is beyond the realm of rational discussion and experimental test, such intuitive knowledge is not easily distinguished from dogmatic opinion. Hence, it was Mill's aim to reduce to an absolute minimum the number of points at which intuitions are required. In the *Logic* he argued that no intuitions are necessary for mathematics, logic, or the procedures of natural science. In the *Examination of Sir William Hamilton's Philosophy* (1865), he pursued these questions further and explicitly took up the questions he had claimed to avoid in the earlier work—especially those concerning the foundations and nature of our knowledge of bodies and of minds.

Mill argued that we cannot tell by intuition or by introspection what we know intuitively. In order to distinguish what is directly given to consciousness from what is there as a result of inference, we must try to investigate the *origins* of the present contents of our minds. And again, this cannot be done directly, because the minds of infants are not accessible to us. Hence, Mill concluded, "the original elements can only come to light as a residual phenomena, by a previous study of the modes of generation of the mental facts which are confessedly not original." This is the psychological method that was originated by John Locke. In using it, Mill attempted always to show how experience, acting in accordance with known laws of psychology, can explain all of our knowledge. If successful, such accounts make unnecessary (and therefore unwarranted, according to sound scientific methodology) any appeal to extraordinary faculties or to nonexperiential sources of knowledge.

MATTER AND MIND. Mill attempted to explain our belief in the existence of matter and in the existence of our own and other minds by using a psychological method. The "Psychological Theory of the Belief in an External World," as he called it, postulates first, a mind capable of expectation (that is, of forming the conception of possible sensations that would be felt if certain conditions were realized), and second, the psychological laws of association. The claim is that these two factors, operating on experienced sensations and reminiscences of them, would generate not only a belief in an external world but, in addition, a belief that this belief was immediate or intuitive. Mill argued first that by an external object we mean only something that exists whether it is thought of or not, that stays the same even if the sensations we get from it change, and that is common to many observers in a way that sensations are not. One's concept of the external world, Mill said, is made up only to a slight degree, at any moment, of actual sensations, but to a large degree of possible sensations—not of what I am sensing, but of what I would sense *if* I moved, or turned my head, and so forth. These possible sensations, moreover, are thought of as being in groups: numbers of them would be present if I did this, numbers of others if I did that. Contrasted with any particular actual sensation, these groups of possible sensations seem stable and permanent. Moreover, there is not very much regularity in the sequences of our actual sensations, but there is considerable regularity associated in our minds with the groups of possible sensations: We will regularly get this sensation following that one if we do this following that. Hence ideas of cause and power, which (as had been argued in the *Logic*) depend on regularity and succession, are associated with the groups of possible sensations, and not with the actual sensations. At this stage we begin to refer any actual sensation to some group of possible sensations, and even to think of the possibilities as the cause or root of the actual sensation. The groups of possibilities, having permanence and causal power, are so different from fleeting actual sensations that they come to be thought of as being altogether different from them. When it finally becomes clear that the permanent possibilities are publicly observable, we have a concept answering in all respects to our definition

of externality. Hence, Mill said, matter "may be defined, a Permanent Possibility of Sensation"; this is all, he held, that the plain man believes matter to be, and indeed, Mill shared this belief. Mill's aim, however, was not so much to defend the belief, as to account for it. And his account, which appeals only to psychological laws known to operate in many other kinds of cases, is simpler than accounts that would make the belief in matter an original part of our mind or an intuitive belief: Consequently, he held, it is a better account.

Mill went on to ask how far a similar theory is adequate to account for mind. The theory will work, he thought, to a large extent, since we know nothing of our mind but its conscious manifestations, and since we know other minds only through inference from the similarities of other bodies and their actions to ours. But memory and expectation pose a fatal difficulty. They involve a belief in something beyond their own existence, and also the idea that I myself have had, or will have, the experience remembered or expected. Hence, if the mind is really a series of feelings, it is an extraordinary series, for it is one that is "aware of itself as a past and future." And if it is not this paradoxical series, it is something more than a series—but what that can be we have no idea. Mill concluded that at this point we are "face to face with that final inexplicability at which … we inevitably arrive when we reach ultimate facts," and all we can do is accept the facts as inexplicable. Hence, mind is not simply a permanent possibility of sensation.

Sensations and feelings—the data of experience—are, then, intuitively known; the fact of memory (a consequence of which Mill thought to be expectation) is also known directly; and the kind of link between past and present involved in memory (which Mill took to be the central inexplicable reality about the self) is known directly. Aside from these, there is only one additional inexplicable fact, and that is belief—the fact that there is a difference between contemplating, or imagining, or supposing, and actually believing. Mill rejected his father's analysis of belief, but could develop no adequate account of his own.

ETHICS

According to Mill, agreement on moral beliefs is the most important single factor making for cohesion in society, and where it is lacking society cannot be unified. In his own times he saw and recognized the significance of the first serious widespread breakdown of belief in the Christian moral scheme. He thought it a task of first importance to provide an alternative view of morality that would be both acceptable to those who still clung, in part, to their older views, and capable of redirecting these older moral attitudes into newer paths. He was a utilitarian in ethics: that is, he held that an action is right if, and only if, it brings about a greater balance of good over bad consequences than any other act open to the agent, and he also believed that only pleasure is intrinsically good and only pain intrinsically bad. Bentham and James Mill had held a similar position, but John Stuart Mill modified their view in a number of ways, attempting always to show that utilitarianism need not be a narrow or selfish view and that it did not force one to rely, for social progress, purely on impersonal institutional arrangements and thereby compel one to leave human personality out of account. By arguing that the utilitarian could appreciate the wisdom embodied in traditional morality as well as offer rational criticism of it, and that he could also accept and account for the high value of self-sacrifice and could make the development and perfection of individual character the key obligation of morality, Mill sought to rebut the most frequent criticisms of the Benthamite morality and thereby make it more generally acceptable. Although his ethical writings (especially *Utilitarianism*) have been much criticized, they contain the most influential philosophical articulation of a liberal humanistic morality that was produced in the nineteenth century.

In his ethical writings, Mill pursued the attack on intuitionism that was so constant a feature of his other work. This issue is especially important with regard to moral problems. Intuitionism, he said in the *Autobiography,* is "the great intellectual support of false doctrines and bad institutions" because it enables "every inveterate belief and every intense feeling … to dispense with the obligation of justifying itself by reason…. There never was such an instrument devised for consecrating all deep-seated prejudices." The intuitionists supposed, Mill believed, that only their view could account for (1) the uniqueness of moral judgments, (2) the rapidity with which the plain man passes moral judgments, and (3) the authority to be given to commonsense moral judgments. To the first point, Mill answered with the theory that moral feelings may have unique properties, just as water has, and yet may still be derived, by a chemical compounding process, from simpler elements that do not have those properties. Hence, so far there is no need to say that these feelings are caused by unique intuitions. To the second point he replied that rapidity of judgment may be due to habit and training as well as to a faculty of intuition. And with regard to the third point, which is the crucial one, he argued that the utilitarian can give at least as

good an account as the intuitionist of the authority of common sense in moral matters. Rules such as those that enjoin the telling of truth, the paying of debts, the keeping of promises, and so forth (Mill called these "secondary rules") were taken by him to indicate, not widespread intuitions, but the results of hundreds of years of experience of the consequences of actions. These rules, based on so much factual knowledge, are of considerable value in helping men to make correct decisions when time or data for a full calculation of the results in a particular case are lacking. The wisdom of the ages, thus embodied in the rules and precepts of commonsense morality, is an indispensable supplement to the limited knowledge and almost inevitable one-sidedness of any single person. It is for these reasons, utilitarians claim, that these rules and precepts have a certain cognitive authority. There is no need to appeal to a faculty of intuition to explain the authority, and therefore such an explanation is, from a scientific point of view, unwarranted.

Mill thus gave a prominent place to moral directives other than the utilitarian principle. But he was basically an act-utilitarian, believing that each particular obligation depends on the balance of pleasure and pain that would be produced by the act in question. The utilitarian principle is so abstract, Mill thought, that it is unlikely to be actually used, except in cases where two secondary rules come into conflict with each other. But it serves the invaluable function of providing a rational basis for the criticism of secondary rules (this is brought out especially well in the essay on justice, Ch. 5 of *Utilitarianism*), and there was no doubt in Mill's mind that there can never be a right act that contravenes the principle. This is true even with regard to the rule (to which Mill gave so much emphasis) dictating the development and perfection of individual character. It often seems that Mill placed more stress on individuality, or self-realization, than on general welfare, and critics frequently claim that he contradicted himself by saying that both of these constitute the sole highest good. But there is no contradiction in his views, for he held that self-development is the best way for an individual to work for the common good.

Mill's concern with the problem of free will sprang from his view of the importance of self-development. (He presented this view both in the *Logic* and in the *Examination of Hamilton*.) The doctrine of necessity, which he had been taught to believe, seemed to him to make a man a creature of his environment, and this doctrine depressed and disturbed him for many years. When he realized that the desire to improve oneself could be a powerful motive and that actions dictated by this desire, although not contravening the law of causation, are properly said to be due to oneself rather than to one's environment, he felt "as if an incubus had been raised off him." He thought that this view enabled him to make determinism compatible with his emphasis on the individual's responsibility for his own character.

Two aspects of Mill's *Utilitarianism* have been attacked more frequently than any others. The first is his attempt to broaden utilitarianism by making a distinction between *kinds* of pleasure, so that an act producing a smaller amount of a more valuable kind of pleasure might be obligatory, rather than an act producing a larger amount of a less valuable kind of pleasure. This line of reasoning has been said to involve him in flagrant contradictions, or else to be sheer nonsense.

The second aspect is his attempt to give some sort of reasoned support to the utilitarian principle itself, which led G. E. Moore to accuse him of committing the "naturalistic fallacy." Moore thought Mill was trying to give a conclusive proof of a first moral principle, but he was mistaken. Throughout his life, Mill consistently held that no such proof of the principle was possible, either deductively or inductively. There is, however, no agreement as to the manner in which Mill attempted, in the fourth chapter of *Utilitarianism,* to support his first principle so that he would not be open to the same reproach of dogmatism that he had made against the intuitionists. Mill's remarks here are extremely unclear. His problem arises because, while he insisted that there must be a factual basis for moral judgments, he held that moral judgments are different in kind from factual propositions and therefore cannot be strictly derived from them. Although he failed to solve this problem, he at least propounded it in precisely the form in which it has perplexed (not to say obsessed) recent moral philosophers.

SOCIAL AND POLITICAL PHILOSOPHY

Mill was more aware than were the older Benthamites of the importance of nonrational and noninstitutional factors to an understanding of society, and was consequently less disposed to rely on legal and governmental reforms for the improvement of it. He believed in democratic government, but he was convinced that it could not work well unless the citizens who lived under it were reasonably well educated, tolerant of opposing views, and willing to sacrifice some of their immediate interests for the good of society. He was profoundly worried about the tendency of democracies to suppress individuality and override minorities: Indeed, this, and not the problem of forcing those who control government to work for the

interests of the people, seemed to him the crucial problem of his times. Hence, in his writings on social and political philosophy, his central concern was to show the importance of personal freedom and the development of strong individual character and to devise ways of encouraging their growth.

ECONOMIC THEORY. With regard to economic theory Mill at first supported a general policy of laissez-faire, but increasing awareness of the uselessness to the individual of political freedom without economic security and opportunity led him to reexamine his objections to socialism. By the end of his life he had come to think that as far as economic theory was concerned, socialism was acceptable. His reservations about it sprang from his fear that it would give overwhelming strength to the tendencies of the age toward suppression of individuality.

ON LIBERTY. Mill thought that his essay *On Liberty* was the most likely of all his works to be of enduring value. In it he maintained the view, which he had expressed as early as 1834, that "the sole end for which mankind are warranted, individually or collectively, in interfering with the liberty of action of any of their number, is self-protection." Mill argued for this view especially in regard to freedom of thought and discussion. "We can never be sure," he wrote, "that the opinion we are endeavoring to stifle is a false opinion; and if we were sure, stifling it would be an evil still": These are the lines of his defense, which rests ultimately on his assessment of the importance of sociological knowledge to the direction of social action and on his view of the peculiar difficulties in obtaining it. In the third chapter, Mill argued at length for the importance of "individuality," which, he held, comes from, or indeed is identical with, continued effort at self-development. Even eccentricity is better, he held, than massive uniformity of personality and the stagnation of society that would result from it. Mill's strong emphasis on this point stems from his conviction, here strongly influenced by Alexis de Tocqueville, that the chief danger of democracy is that of suppressing individual differences and of allowing no genuine development of minority opinion. Democratic tyranny would be far worse, he held, than aristocratic or despotic tyranny, since it would be far more effective in utilizing the most efficient of means of social control, the pressure of public opinion. Against this the only reliable safeguard would be the development of personalities strong enough to resist such pressures.

REPRESENTATIVE GOVERNMENT. In more specifically political matters the same concerns are evident. Mill defended representative democracy, but not solely on the grounds used by the older Benthamites. Representative government, he held, is ideally the best form of government because it does more to encourage the growth and development of individuality than any other form of government. By leading people to participate in the processes of governing, representative government makes them more active, intelligent, and well rounded than even the best-intentioned of despotisms could. It thereby gives them vitally important moral training, by cultivating their public sympathies, strengthening their habit of looking at social questions from an impersonal point of view, and aiding their identification of personal interests with the interests of society. Care must be taken, however, to get a true democracy, one in which minorities as well as majorities are represented. For this reason Mill enthusiastically endorsed Thomas Hare's scheme of proportional representation. He also favored plural voting, which would allow educated and responsible persons to have more influence than the uneducated, by giving the former several votes. Mill's view of the function of the representative also shows his concern to get as much intelligence as possible into government. A properly educated constituency, he held, would be able and willing to select the best men available; and since those elected would be better informed and wiser on particular issues than the electorate, it would be absurd to bind the representatives to anything but a very general agreement with the beliefs and aims of the electors.

INDIVIDUALS AND SOCIETY. Mill is frequently criticized for overlooking the organic elements in society and for thinking of society as a mere aggregate of units in which each unit is what it is regardless of its membership in the whole. Mill certainly held this view as far as the most fundamental laws of psychology are concerned. But his view of individual character involves new considerations. Individuals, he held, are radically affected by their membership in society and inevitably formed by the customs, habits, morality, and beliefs of those who raise them. There is, however, no impersonal assurance, metaphysical or otherwise, that the individual will feel himself an organic member of any group. He will do so, Mill thought, only if he is educated to do so. Mill cannot be accused of underestimating the importance of ensuring that men are so educated, and it is not clear that an organic theory has anything better to offer on a practical level.

RELIGIOUS VIEWS

Mill maintained for the most part a determined silence on religious questions. Although he had written "On Nature" and "The Utility of Religion" by 1858, and although he lived during a period of increasingly free discussion of all possible religious subjects, he thought that the British public would not listen patiently to what he had to say on these questions and that he could not publish his views without alienating readers and losing public influence. And this, as he made quite clear in his correspondence with Auguste Comte, he was determined not to do. Despite his precautions, however, he was generally taken to be atheistic, and he was sometimes criticized for not openly stating the views that, so it seemed, he insinuated but did not defend. The consternation of his followers and the delight of his opponents was therefore considerable when it became apparent from the posthumously published *Three Essays on Religion* (1874) that Mill did not entirely condemn religious aspirations and hopes and even thought that there might be some faint possibility of the existence of rational support for a religious view of the world. Admirers felt betrayed, and religious critics proclaimed that Mill's secular education and materialistic position here issued in collapse and evident moral and intellectual bankruptcy.

GOODNESS OF GOD. Mill's most famous pronouncement on religion occurs not, however, in the *Three Essays,* but in the *Examination of Hamilton.* Discussing the use made by one of Hamilton's philosophical followers, Henry Mansel, of Hamilton's view that we cannot know the Absolute, Mill particularly criticized Mansel's theory that even the moral terms we apply to God do not mean what they mean when we apply them to men. Mill objected to this theory in the name of logic: If terms are not to be used in their usual sense, they ought not to be used at all. But, more strongly, he went on to say that a being, no matter how powerful, whose acts are not sanctioned by the highest human morality conceivable, is not deserving of worship. If Mill were convinced of the existence of such a being he would not worship him. "I will call no being good," Mill proclaimed, "who is not what I mean when I apply that epithet to my fellow creatures, and if such a being can sentence me to hell for not so calling him, to hell I will go."

NATURE. Of the *Three Essays,* the first two, at least, show no reversal or collapse of Mill's views. In "On Nature" Mill argued that the maxim "Follow Nature" is of no use as a guide to action. For "Nature" either means "everything that happens, good as well as bad," in which case it offers no guidance whatsoever; or it means "what happens without any human interference," and in that case the maxim is self-contradictory. Nature in the second sense, Mill went on to argue, offers at least as much evil to our observation as good; it is rather a challenge to amendment than an ideal for imitation. From this, two conclusions follow. First, it is our job to improve nature, especially human nature; for it is only insofar as men have intervened to change things that the world has become civilized, safe, and happy, even to the limited extent that it has. Human virtues are not natural: They are preeminently the results of cultivation. Even justice is an artificial virtue, Mill said, and the idea of natural justice does not precede, but follows, it. Second, in view of the suffering and ugliness presented by much of the natural world, the only religious view that is at all tenable is one which holds that the deity is not omnipotent, that "the Principle of Good *cannot* at once and altogether subdue the powers of evil," and that, consequently, men should think of themselves as the far from useless helpers of a limited but benevolent God.

UTILITY OF RELIGION. In "The Utility of Religion," Mill argued that much of the social usefulness attributed to religion is actually due to the influence of a widely accepted and instilled moral code, and to the force of public opinion guided by that code. The belief in the supernatural origin of morality may once have helped it to gain acceptance, but is no longer needed, or indeed, even effectual, in maintaining this acceptance. The effect of religion on individuals springs largely from our need to have ideal conceptions that move us to action. "The essence of religion is the strong and earnest direction of the emotions and desires towards an ideal object, recognized as of the highest excellence, and as rightfully paramount over all selfish objects of desire." But a religion of humanity, Mill argued, can have this effect to an even greater extent than a supernatural religion. The religion of humanity would cultivate our unselfish feelings and would free us from any need for intellectual juggling or willful blindness with regard to its tenets, since it would rather point out than deny the evil in the world and urge us to work to remove it.

GOD. Thus, the first two essays of the *Three Essays* together suggest that the alternative to a supernatural religion is not simple acceptance of Nature, but the construction of an alternative way of living based on education and convention; and these themes are to be found throughout Mill's thought. The third essay, "Theism," drafted from 1868 to 1870, which assesses arguments in support of a supernatural religious view, seems to make more concessions to traditional religiosity than the other essays; but even these are slight. In this essay, Mill dis-

cussed the possibilities of rational support for supernatural beliefs. Dismissing all a priori reasoning, he found only the Argument from Design at all convincing, and this argument gives us at best "no more than a probability" that some intelligent creator of the world exists. For the same evidences that thus support the existence of a creator also go to show that he was not omnipotent and do not prove that he was omniscient. Mill suggested that we think of a limited deity faced with the independent existence of matter and force. To this picture of a Platonic demiurge, Mill thought we are entitled to add that benevolence may have been one (although surely not the only) moral attribute of the creator. But Mill emphasized strongly the importance of the work of man in improving the world. "If man had not the power," he said, "by the exercise of his own energies for the improvement both of himself and of his outward circumstances, to do for himself and other creatures vastly more than God had in the first instance done, the Being who called him into existence would deserve something very different from thanks at his hands."

IMMORTALITY AND MIRACLES. Mill argued that there is no evidence for the immortality of the soul and none against it. After a lengthy discussion of Hume's arguments on this point he found that roughly the same is true of miracles. But in each case he pointed out that there is room for *hope*: One may, if it is comforting and encouraging, hope that the soul is immortal and that the revelations attested by miracles are true. And it is this point more than any other in the essay that upset Mill's admirers. For while he concluded that the proper rational attitude to supernatural religion is skepticism rather than belief or positive disbelief and that "the whole domain of the supernatural is thus removed from the region of Belief into that of simple Hope," he also held that it may be valuable and justifiable to encourage religious hopes. This, he said, can be done without impairing the power of reason; and indulgence in such hopes may help some men to feel that life is more important and may strengthen their feelings for others. Furthermore, to construct a picture of a person of high moral excellence, such as Christ, and form the habit of seeking the approval of this person for one's acts, may aid that "real, though purely human, religion, which sometimes calls itself the Religion of Humanity, and sometimes that of Duty." Critics may wish to call these views objectionable, but in Mill at least they are not inconsistent. They hark back to his early discovery of the importance of cultivating the feelings and develop the further implications of his idea of the moral importance of educating the emotions. His assessment of the degree to which scientific support can be given to a supernaturalist theory by evidences of design, low though it is, may seem far too high; but his interest in the theory of a limited deity with whom we must cooperate to bring about improvement in the world is hardly great enough or personal enough to lend credence to the accusations that he had undergone an emotional collapse.

See also Bentham, Jeremy; Bradley, Francis Herbert; British Philosophy; Causation; Coleridge, Samuel Taylor; Comte, Auguste; Empiricism; Hamilton, William; Liberty; Locke, John; Logic, History of; Mansel, Henry Longueville; Mill, James; Mill's Methods of Induction; Moore, George Edward; Saint-Simon, Claude-Henri de Rouvroy, Comte de; Utilitarianism.

Bibliography

WORKS BY MILL

Mill's works have not yet been collected. Even the projected University of Toronto Press edition of his Works will probably not contain all of them. Mill's own *Bibliography,* edited by M. MacMinn, J. R. Hainds, and J. M. McCrimmon (Evanston, IL, 1945), is not quite complete.

Mill's books (all of which were published in London, unless otherwise noted) are as follows: *System of Logic,* 2 vols. (1843; 8th ed., 1872); *Essays on Some Unsettled Questions of Political Economy* (1844; written 1830–1831); *Principles of Political Economy,* 2 vols. (1848; 7th ed., 1871; variorum ed., W. J. Ashley, ed., 1909); *On Liberty* (1859); *Dissertations and Discussions,* periodical essays, 2 vols. (1859), 4 vols. (1875); *Considerations on Representative Government* (1861); *Utilitarianism,* reprinted from *Frasers Magazine,* 1861 (1863); *An Examination of Sir William Hamilton's Philosophy* (1865; 6th ed., 1889); *Auguste Comte and Positivism* (1865); *Subjection of Women* (1869; written in 1861); *Autobiography* (1873; more complete edition, J. J. Coss, ed., New York, 1924).

Among Mill's shorter writings of philosophical interest (most reprinted in *Dissertations and Discussions*) are the following: "Whately's Elements of Logic," *Westminster Review* (1828); "The Spirit of the Age," in the *Examiner* (1831), included in *The Spirit of the Age,* edited by F. Hayek (Chicago, 1942); "Prof. Sedgwick's Discourse" (1835); "Civilization" (1836); "Bentham" (1838); "Coleridge" (1840); "M. de Tocqueville on Democracy in America" (1840); "Bailey on Berkeley's Theory of Vision" (1842); "Michelet's History of France" (1844); "Dr. Whewell on Moral Philosophy" (1851); "Bain's Psychology" (1859); "Austin on Jurisprudence" (1863); "Plato" (1866); "Inaugural Address to the University of St. Andrews" (1867); "Berkeley's Life and Writings," *Fortnightly Review* (1871); "Grote's Aristotle" (1873); "Chapters on Socialism," *Fortnightly Review* (1879), reprinted as *Socialism,* edited by W. D. P. Bliss (Linden, MA, 1891).

Of Mill's literary essays, the best known are "What Is Poetry?" and "The Two Kinds of Poetry," in *Monthly Repository* (1833), reprinted in part in *Dissertations and Discourses* as "Thoughts on Poetry and Its Varieties."

WORKS ON MILL

Life

For Mill's life, see his *Autobiography*; F. E. Mineka, ed., *Earlier Letters,* 2 vols. (Toronto, 1963); H. S. R. Elliott, ed., *Letters,* 2 vols. (1910); J. Stillinger, ed., *Early Draft of John Stuart Mill's Autobiography* (Urbana: University of Illinois Press, 1961). See F. Hayek, ed., *John Stuart Mill and Harriet Taylor* (1951), for their correspondence. See also the standard M. St. John Packe, *The Life of John Stuart Mill* (1954); A. Bain, *John Stuart Mill* (1882); and W. L. Courtney, *Life of John Stuart Mill* (1886); H. O. Pappe, *John Stuart Mill and the Harriet Taylor Myth* (Melbourne, 1960); A. W. Levi, "The Writing of Mill's Autobiography," in *Ethics* 61 (1951).

Among many estimates of Mill's life and character are those by R. H. Hutton, reprinted in *Criticism on Contemporary Thought and Thinkers,* Vol. 1 (1894); J. Martineau, in *Essays* 3 (1891); J. Morley, in *Critical Miscellanies* 2 (1877); B. Russell, in *Proceedings of the British Academy* (1955); W. Ward, in *Men and Matters* (1914).

General Works

For general commentary on the thought of Mill see Sir Leslie Stephen, *English Utilitarians,* Vol. 3 (1900); R. P. Anschutz, *Philosophy of John Stuart Mill* (Oxford, 1953); Karl Britton, *John Stuart Mill* (1953).

Logic

See O. A. Kubitz, *Development of John Stuart Mill's System of Logic,* Illinois Studies in the Social Sciences, VIII (Urbana, IL, 1932); R. Jackson, *Deductive Logic of John Stuart Mill* (Oxford, 1941); W. Whewell, *Of Induction, with especial reference to Mr. J. Stuart Mill's System of Logic* (1849), and see E. A. Strong, "W. Whewell and John Stuart Mill," *Journal of the History of Ideas* (1955). Classic criticisms include: T. H. Green, "The Logic of John Stuart Mill," *Works,* Vol. II (1886); F. H. Bradley, *Principles of Logic* (Oxford, 1883), Bk. II, Part II, Chs. 1–3; W. S. Jevons, "John Stuart Mill's Philosophy Tested," reprinted in *Pure Logic* (1890).

Metaphysics

Among older studies of interest are: W. L. Courtney, *The Metaphysics of John Stuart Mill* (1879); C. M. Douglas, *John Stuart Mill: A Study of His Philosophy* (Edinburgh and London: Blackwood, 1895); J. McCosh, *An Examination of Mr. John Stuart Mill's Philosophy* (London and New York, 1866); and John Grote, *Exploratio Philosophica* (Cambridge, U.K.: Deighton Bell, 1865; 2 vols., 1900). Few recent discussions center explicitly on Mill.

Ethics and Utilitarianism

E. Halévy, *La formation du radicalisme philosophique,* 3 vols. (Paris: F. Alcan, 1901–1904), translated into English by Mary Morris as *Growth of Philosophic Radicalism* (London: Faber and Gwyer, 1928), is the basic study of the development of Benthamite doctrine; see also E. Albee, *History of English Utilitarianism* (1900) and J. Plamenatz, *The English Utilitarians* (Oxford: Blackwell, 1949). Especially valuable older critical works are John Grote, *Examination of the Utilitarian Philosophy* (Cambridge, U.K., 1870) and F. H. Bradley, *Ethical Studies* (Oxford, 1876), Ch. 3. Recent discussions start from the criticisms of G. E. Moore,

Principia Ethica (London: Cambridge University Press, 1903), Chs. 1 and 3. Compare J. Seth, "Alleged Fallacies in Mill's Utilitarianism," in *Philosophical Review* 17 (1908); E. W. Hall, "The 'Proof' of Utility in Bentham and Mill," in *Ethics* 9 (1949); J. O. Urmson, "Interpretation of the Moral Philosophy of John Stuart Mill," in *Philosophical Quarterly* 3 (1953). I. Berlin's lecture, "John Stuart Mill and the Ends of Life" (London, 1962), is more general.

Political Philosophy

See G. H. Sabine, *History of Political Theory*, 3rd ed. (New York: Holt, Rinehart and Winston, 1961); M. Cowling, *Mill and Liberalism* (Cambridge, 1963). J. F. Stephen, *Liberty, Equality, Fraternity* (1873) is an interesting early attack; others are summarized in J. C. Rees, *Mill and His Early Critics* (Leicester, U.K., 1956). B. Bosanquet, *Philosophical Theory of the State* (1899) and D. G. Ritchie, *Principles of State Interference* (1891) present representative criticism. J. H. Burns, "John Stuart Mill and Democracy," in *Political Studies* 5 (1957), traces the development of Mill's views. For criticisms of Mill's views on sociological method, see K. Popper, *Open Society and Its Enemies*, 2 vols. (London: Routledge, 1945), Ch. 14, and P. Winch, *Idea of a Social Science* (London: Routledge and Kegan Paul, 1958), especially Ch. 3.

J. B. Schneewind (1967)

MILL, JOHN STUART [ADDENDUM]

The most important development in John Stuart Mill scholarship of the past half century is the publication of the *Collected Works of John Stuart Mill* in thirty-three volumes (1963–1991), with John M. Robson as general editor. This is a monumental publication by the University of Toronto Press, which will provide data for Mill scholars in years to come. The seven volumes of letters and many volumes of essays, speeches, and journals, show that most of his writing was not on narrowly philosophical topics: Much of it was on concrete political issues of his day. There are four volumes of newspaper writings. The *Collected Works* also makes available all of the revisions in successive editions of his major works, such as *System of Logic* (Vols. VII–VIII) and *Principles of Political Economy* (Vols. II–III, and it makes available out-of-print works such as his *An Examination of Sir William Hamilton's Philosophy* (Vol. IX). The exhaustive index in the final volume enables scholars to find Mill's views on various topics scattered throughout his writings.

Another development is the publication of a periodical devoted to utilitarian studies. *The Mill Newsletter* began publication in 1965 by the University of Toronto Press under the editorship of John M. Robson. It carried long and short articles, news of new and forthcoming books and articles, and a continuing bibliography of works on Mill. In 1989 it merged with *The Bentham Newsletter* to become *Utilitas: A Journal of Utilitarian Studies*, now being published by Cambridge University Press. It has provided a vehicle for Mill scholarship including but not limited to his philosophy.

The most substantial studies of the totality of Mill's philosophy are *John Stuart Mill*, by John Skorupski (1989) and the collection of essays that he edited in *The Cambridge Companion to Mill* (1998). In the former, Skorupski gives a critical but sympathetic account of Mill's philosophy of language, his philosophy of science, his philosophy of mathematics, and his epistemology and metaphysics as well as a discussion of his moral and political philosophy. In *The Cambridge Companion to Mill*, the same areas are addressed by various contributors. Mill's radical empiricist theory of mathematical truth has been dismissed by most philosophers of mathematics since his time. But the essay by Philip Kitcher (Skorupski 1998, pp. 57–111) gives it a sympathetic interpretation.

The most widely read philosophical works of Mill continue to be his essays *Utilitarianism* (Mill 1963–1991, vol. X, p. 203–206) and *On Liberty* (Mill 1963–1991, vol. XVIII, p. 215–310). Debates concerning utilitarianism in the last half century, such as the distinction between act-utilitarianism and rule-utilitarianism and the plausibility of each, have included controversies over the interpretation and plausibility of Mill's position on these issues. Also, those attacking or defending liberalism have inevitably included references to Mill's essay as one of the most representative statements of the liberal position. With the development of feminist philosophy, his essay *The Subjection of Women* (Mill 1963–1991, vol. XXI, p. 259–348) has also received renewed attention as an early feminist statement, sometimes dismissed as the *liberal feminist* position, but sometimes defended against its critics.

Two controversial topics in Mill's utilitarianism continue to receive a focus of attention: his distinction between pleasures on grounds of superiority or inferiority of quality as well as quantity and his alleged *proof* of the principle of utility. In the early part of the twentieth century, the first of these was generally regarded as either inconsistent with his hedonism or as nonsense, and the second was regarded as a classic case of fallacious reasoning. In the last half century, these have been defended, although not always in the same ways. Some "friends" of Mill have tried to reduce the distinction of qualities to a quantitative distinction; others have insisted that Mill is correct in recognizing the phenomenal diversity of pleasurable experiences. But even among the latter there is disagreement about whether Mill is correct in correlating the distinction with the distinctively human, as opposed to nonhuman animal, faculties and whether qualitatively distinct pleasures are consistently preferred by those who are qualified by experiences of both. Important works on these topics are found in books by Wendy Donner (1991) and Henry West (2004). Donner emphasizes that those qualified by experience to judge the qualities of pleasure are not simply those who have experienced different pleasures but those whose experience has been developed by education and enlightenment. Mill's *proof* has been the subject of numerous interpretations and controversy. It is no longer dismissed as a collection of fallacies, but whether it is a sound argument with plausible assumptions is still a matter of great debate. West defends it as a sound argument.

The consistency between Mill's apparently hedonistic utilitarianism and his essay *On Liberty* has been another topic of extensive discussion. Here again, more recent discussion has been more friendly to Mill but with differences in interpretation. Some commentators have claimed consistency for him by a reinterpretation of his utilitarianism to make it nonhedonistic, with a conception of happiness that essentially involves the free exercise of rational capacities. Others have seen in Mill's psychological assumptions, with a complex phenomenal account of pleasure, including *higher* and *lower* and the necessity for self-development as a necessary condition for the higher pleasures, a basis for consistency that remains hedonistic. Mill's *On Liberty* attempts to distinguish between conduct that concerns others and that concerns only oneself. Strictly construed, very little conduct concerns only oneself. Studies of *On Liberty* by C. L. Ten (1980), John Gray (1983, rev. ed. 1996), and J. C. Rees (1985) have reinterpreted the distinction in terms of conduct concerning the *interests* of self or others. Mill is seen to be holding the view that there is a right to liberty, which is a right to autonomy. There is controversy, however, over the substance of this right and also over the *harm principle* which limits it.

Whether Mill was a rule-utilitarian was one of the questions that generated the distinction between act-utilitarianism and rule-utilitarianism. The essay by J. O. Urmson (1953) interpreting Mill as a rule-utilitarian has been challenged and supported by citations from Mill texts both pro and con. A middle position, argued by Fred R. Berger (1984) and others, is that Mill endorsed a strategy for achieving the greatest happiness that was in practice rule-utilitarian but that Mill seemed to think that if all hidden utilities were taken into consideration, there would be no conflict between the two positions. Acts that violate useful rules weaken the rules and undermine the rule-abiding character of the agent. Acts that form part of a collection of acts that have bad consequences can theoretically be assigned a fraction of those bad consequences. Whether these moves are adequate to remove the conflict is suspect.

Perhaps most significant as a way of resolving the conflict in favor of a rule-utilitarian interpretation has been the attention drawn to the importance of sanctions in Mill's theory of morality. Most commentators make a distinction between act-utilitarianism as a criterion of right action and act-utilitarianism as a decision procedure for action. It is generally recognized that Mill rejected act-utilitarianism as a decision procedure in all cases, but some commentators, such as Roger Crisp (1997), still hold that he was an act-utilitarian with regard to the criterion of right action. Essays by David Lyons and by L. W. Sumter (in Cooper, et. al. 1979, 1–19 and 99–114), and in the study by West (2004) claim that Mill cannot be regarded as either an act-utilitarian or a rule-utilitarian but that his moral theory is more complex than either. Lyons's essays on various aspects of Mill's ethics are reprinted in *Rights, Welfare, and Mill's Moral Theory* (Lyons 1994).

In Chap. V of *Utilitarianism*, Mill has a theory of rights correlative to some but not all morally significant actions, and he restricts the morally obligatory to those actions for which punishment has utility; in *August Comte and Positivism*, (Mill 1963–1991, vol. X, p. 337–339), he clearly states a theory of morally meritorious action that goes beyond what is morally required. These would indicate that Mill's moral theory has a structure that is more complicated than any simple act- or rule-formulation.

Mill's contribution to the development of psychological theory is the subject of an important study by Fred Wilson (1990), who interprets Mill as a pioneer in turning psychology into an empirical science. A major study of Mill's economic theory is by Samuel Hollander (1985). Geoffrey Scarre has published a study of Mill's metaphysical views (1989).

Michael St. John Packe's *The Life of John Stuart Mill* (1954) continues to be the standard biography of the details of the Mill's life. But Nicholas Capaldi (2004) has recently written a thorough intellectual biography, arguing that Mill combined a Coleridgean/Germanic romanticism with his Benthamite Enlightenment heritage.

Mill continues to have his critics. H. J. McCloskey finds fault with nearly everything in Mill's philosophy (1971), and his liberalism has been attacked by Gertrude Himmelfarb (1974). McCloskey, however, does recognize that Mill's philosophy of language anticipated Ludwig Wittgenstein's notion of *family resemblances* in his rejection of Plato's essentialism.

See also Epistemology; Ethics; Logic, History of: Modern Logic: The Boolean Period: The Heritage of Kant and Mill; Metaphysics; Philosophy of Language; Plato; Social and Political Philosophy.

Bibliography

Alican, Necip Fikri. *Mill's Principle of Utility: A Defence of John Stuart Mill's Notorious Proof*. Amsterdam: Rodopi, 1994.

Anderson, Susan Leigh. *On Mill*. Belmont, CA: Wadsworth, 2000.

Berger, Fred R. *Happiness, Justice, and Freedom: The Moral and Political Philosophy of John Stuart Mill*. Berkeley: University of California Press, 1984.

Capaldi, Nicholas. *John Stuart Mill: A Biography*. Cambridge, U.K.: Cambridge University Press, 2004.

Cooper, Wesley E., Kai Nielsen, and Steven C. Patten, eds. *New Essays on John Stuart Mill and Utilitarianism. Canadian Journal of Philosophy* Supp. Vol. 5. Guelph, ON: Canadian Association for Publishing in Philosophy, 1979.

Crisp, Roger. *Routledge Philosophy Guidebook to J. S. Mill's "Utilitarianism"*. London: Routledge, 1997.

Donner, Wendy. *The Liberal Self: John Stuart Mill's Moral and Political Philosophy*. Ithaca, NY: Cornell University Press, 1991.

Duncan, Graeme Campbell. *Marx and Mill: Two Views of Social Conflict and Social Harmony*. Cambridge, U.K.: Cambridge University Press, 1973.

Gray, John. *Mill on Liberty: A Defence*. Rev. ed. London: Routledge and Kegan Paul, 1996.

Habibi, Don A. *John Stuart Mill and the Ethic of Human Growth*. Dordrecht: Kluwer, 2001.

Himmelfarb, Gertrude. *On Liberty and Liberalism: The Case of John Stuart Mill*. New York: Knopf, 1974.

Hollander, Samuel. *The Economics of J. S. Mill*. 2 vols. Toronto: University of Toronto Press, 1985.

Kitcher, Philip. "Mill, Mathematics, and the Naturalist Tradition." In *The Cambridge Companion to Mill*, edited by John Skorupski. Cambridge U.K.: Cambridge University Press, 1998.

Laine, Michael. *Bibliography of Works on John Stuart Mill*. Toronto: University of Toronto Press, 1982.

Lyons, David, *Rights, Welfare, and Mill's Moral Theory*. New York: Oxford University Press, 1994.

McCloskey, H. J. *John Stuart Mill: A Critical Study*. London: Macmillan, 1971.

Mill, John Stuart. *Collected Works of John Stuart Mill*. 33 vols., edited by J. M. Robson. Toronto: University of Toronto Press, 1963–1991.

The Mill Newsletter. Vols. 1–23. Toronto: University of Toronto Press, 1965–1989.

Morales, Maria. *Perfect Equality: John Stuart Mill on Well-Constituted Communities*. Latham, MD: Rowman & Littlefield, 1996.

Packe, Michael St. John. *The Life of John Stuart Mill*. London: Secker & Warburg, 1954.

Rees, J. C. *John Stuart Mill's "On Liberty"*. Oxford: Clarendon, 1985.

Riley, Jonathan. *Liberal Utilitarianism: A Social Choice Theory and J. S. Mill's Philosophy*. Cambridge, U.K.: Cambridge University Press, 1988.

Ryan, Alan. *J. S. Mill*. London: Routledge and Kegan Paul, 1974.

Ryan, Alan. *The Philosophy of John Stuart Mill*. 2nd ed. New York: Macmillan, 1988.

Scarre, Geoffrey. *Logic and Reality in the Philosophy of John Stuart Mill*. Dordrecht: Kluwer, 1989.

Schwartz, Pedro. *The New Political Economy of J. S. Mill*. London: Weidenfeld and Nicolson, 1973.

Semmel, Bernard. *John Stuart Mill and the Pursuit of Virtue*. New Haven: Yale University Press, 1984.

Skorupski, John, ed. *The Cambridge Companion to Mill*. Cambridge, U.K.: Cambridge University Press, 1998.

Skorupski, John. *John Stuart Mill*. London, New York: Routledge, 1989.

Ten, C. L. *Mill on Liberty*. Oxford: Oxford University Press, 1980.

Thomas, William. *Mill*. Oxford: Oxford University Press, 1985.

Thompson, Dennis F. *John Stuart Mill and Representative Government*. Princeton, NJ: Princeton University Press, 1976.

Urmson, J. O. "The Interpretation of the Moral Philosophy of J. S. Mill." *The Philosophical Quarterly* 3 (1953): 33–39.

Utilitas: A Journal of Utilitarian Studies 1– (1989–).

West, Henry R. *An Introduction to Mill's Utilitarian Ethics*. Cambridge, U.K.: Cambridge University Press, 2004.

Wilson, Fred. *Psychological Analysis and the Philosophy of John Stuart Mill*. Toronto: University of Toronto Press, 1990.

Henry R. West (1996, 2005)

MILLER, DICKINSON S.
(1868–1963)

Dickinson S. Miller was an American ethical philosopher and epistemologist who published both under his own name and under the pseudonym R. E. Hobart. He was born in Philadelphia and studied at the University of Pennsylvania, Clark University, the universities of Berlin and Halle, Hobart College, and Harvard University. He held a doctorate in philosophy from Halle and a D.Sc. from Hobart.

At Harvard, Miller was a student of William James, who became his longtime friend and with whom he often discussed and argued points of philosophy. James was instrumental in getting Miller an appointment as associate professor of philosophy at Bryn Mawr College in 1893, the year after Miller's graduation from Harvard.

Miller left Bryn Mawr in 1898 to become first an instructor and then a professor of philosophy at Harvard. He subsequently joined the Columbia faculty, where he remained until the 1920s. He had also received a D.D. at Berkeley (California) Divinity School and in 1911 started to teach apologetics at the General Theological Seminary in New York City.

In his later days he lived for several years (1927–1932) close to his friend the critical realist Charles Augustus Strong, in Fiesole, near Florence, Italy. Strong appreciated Miller's company, especially because of Miller's neorealistic tendencies as opposed to Strong's different epistemological outlook. Their discussions were lively and interminable. George Santayana occasionally joined them, coming to Florence from Rome. Miller was a visitor during 1926 at the Vienna circle of logical positivists; although mostly a silent listener at the circle's sessions, he was an intensely interesting and challenging discussant in individual conversations. During his last twenty-five years he lived in Boston.

Miller's was an extremely penetrating and constructively critical mind. In a number of remarkable articles he addressed himself mainly to such topics as direct realism, the philosophy of mind, and also the controversy between William James and E. A. Singer on behaviorism. Especially interesting is "Is Consciousness 'A Type of Behavior'?" (1911), mainly about the "automatic sweetheart" puzzle. In 1951, Miller wrote "'Descartes' Myth' and Professor Ryle's Fallacy," a sharp critique of Gilbert Ryle's logical behaviorism. He also wrote on David Hume's views on causality and induction, on various topics in moral philosophy, and most notably, on the free-will–determinism issue. Miller's article provocatively titled "Free Will as Involving Determination and Inconceivable without It" (1934), published, for obscure reasons, under the name R. E. Hobart, has become a locus classicus of the free-will controversies. With remarkable lucidity and perspicacity Miller brought up to date the essentials of the point of view of Hume and J. S. Mill. He argued that once we realize the clear distinctions between causality and compulsion and between indeterminism and free will, the traditionally vexing problem disappears, and a fully adequate account of human freedom, responsibility, reward, and punishment can be given. Miller's views on religion and theology were extremely liberal and modern, close to the outlook of Unitarianism (in fact, he occasionally served as a Unitarian minister in the Boston area).

Miller's contributions to the epistemological controversies of his time may now seem a bit old-fashioned, but they are worthy of renewed attention because the same issues are still being debated, albeit in a different style and terminology.

See also Behaviorism; Epistemology; Ethics, History of; Hume, David; James, William; Logical Positivism; Mill, John Stuart; Ryle, Gilbert; Santayana, George.

Bibliography

WORKS BY MILLER

"Is Consciousness 'A Type of Behavior'?" *Journal of Philosophy* 8 (1911): 322–327.

"The Pleasure-Quality and the Pain-Quality Analysable, Not Ultimate." *Mind* 38 (1929): 215–218.

"Is There Not a Clear Solution of the Knowledge-Problem?" *Journal of Philosophy* 34 (1937): 701–712; 35 (1938): 561–572.

"An Event in Modern Philosophy." *Philosophical Review* 54 (1945): 592–606.

"Hume's Deathblow to Deductivism." *Journal of Philosophy* 46 (1949): 745–762.

"'Descartes' Myth' and Professor Ryle's Fallacy." *Journal of Philosophy* 48 (1951): 270–280.

Under the Name R. E. Hobart

"Hume without Scepticism." *Mind* 39 (1930).

"Free Will as Involving Determinism and Inconceivable without It." *Mind* 43 (1934): 1–27.

Herbert Feigl (1967)

MILLIKAN, RUTH GARRETT
(1933–)

Born December 19, 1933, and raised in Swarthmore, Pennsylvania, where her father taught physics, Millikan received her Ph.D. from Yale University in 1969. She began her career as a self-described "faculty housewife," raising four children before publishing her first book. Internationally recognized, Millikan has made significant contributions to philosophy of biology, animal cognition, philosophy of language, mind, and ontology. A unifying theme is the importance of the fact that humans are products of evolution. (Millikan's mother held a Ph.D. in paleontology—perhaps influencing Millikan's orientation to Darwinism.) A student of Wilfred Sellars, Millikan rejects epistemic *givens* and takes *meaning* talk to have the function of helping speakers bring their use into conformity with others; unlike other Sellarsians, Millikan sees the sort of function that underwrites intentional content everywhere, not just in linguistic creatures. Her first book (Millikan 1984) is a detailed articulation of teleosemantics, a Darwinian account of both mental representations and language.

Millikan's work reaches far beyond her account of intentionality, as a small sample of her conclusions shows—among them: that dogs have perfectly good concepts, that some thoughts have two *directions of fit* at once, that understanding language is a form of direct perception. Difficult to summarize, Millikan's program can nonetheless be seen to be framed by three questions: In the philosophy of mind, What is it for one's *thoughts* to be of something?; in epistemology, What is it for one to *know what* one is thinking of?; and in metaphysics, What makes for the *objective samenesses* in the world that one's thoughts are of? Her interlocking answers form a picture of human cognition that challenges tradition on several scores, even as she seeks to defend tradition in the form of scientific realism and the correspondence theory of truth.

THOUGHT

What one's thoughts are of is, according to Millikan, determined by their historically selected function. All intentional items (bee dances, linguistic forms, perceptions, desires, fears, and so forth) have such *proper functions*, and what any particular intentional item is about, its content, is determined by such functions. (That individual words or token mental states have proper functions and that their content owes to proper functions are claims that have encountered vigorous opposition.) Specifically, a *proper function* of a feature F of an organism O is a task whose performance by earlier instances of F in other organisms of O's kind in O's lineage accounts for the proliferation of F in O's kind here and now. Importantly, there are nonbiological cases of proper function—for example, customs, hammers, and nails—so the relevant notions of *task* and *lineage* must be understood broadly. The *content* of a representation type R is given by the connection between instances of R and worldly circumstances, recurrent exploitation of which by consumers of R has contributed to their proliferation over time.

What makes *mental representations*, such as thoughts, beliefs, and desires, distinct from other information-bearing items, such as bee dances? Mental representations are representations that "when they perform their proper function, their referents are identified" (Millikan 1984, p. 13). By *identified*, Millikan means that the referent is represented as being the same thing again. For

example, Clarence's visual perception that a spider is crawling up his leg is an intentional state with a job to do, and such states exist in us because historically selected for performance of that job. The function of his thoughts is to coordinate information he already has about the spider with new information he is acquiring as well as with his subsequent action, trying to brush the self-same spider off his leg. For Clarence's thoughts to be of the spider, then, they must meet the additional requirement of functioning to create this sort coordination of information. The capacity to think of the same *as being the same*, or "coidentifying" (Millikan 2000), is an important accomplishment, distinctive of advanced cognition.

Millikan here joins company with P. F. Strawson and Gareth Evans in claiming that some form of reidentificatory capacity is necessary for thought about the objective world. Unlike Strawson or Evans, Millikan takes her insight about coidentification to have dramatic consequences for self-knowledge.

SELF-KNOWLEDGE

What sort of access do we have to our own thoughts? Millikan is a content externalist—just as the meanings of one's words are not settled by one's intentions, the content of one's thoughts are also determined by facts outside one's ken. To know what one is thinking of, then, is not an a priori matter. Some find this consequence troubling and seek to reconcile content externalism with first-person authority. But Millikan (1993) embraces this result, and argues that a still more radical conclusion follows from her functional account of cognition, namely, that *nothing* is epistemically "given" to thinkers. In particular, "meaning rationalism"—the doctrine that sameness and difference of meaning, univocity, and meaningfulness are all a priori accessible—is false. (It is a good question just who qualifies as a *meaning rationalist*—some argue, pace Millikan, that even Gottlob Frege not.) Millikan's rejection of meaning rationalism has several startling consequences: We can have no a priori access to logical possibility; there is nothing rationally wrong with believing contradictions; the validity of inferences is not an a priori property; and the very idea of a Fregean *mode of presentation* must be discarded. In short, like meaning, rationality ain't in the head.

Millikan's radical anti-individualism about meaning and rationality might be opposed by more moderate externalisms. And her attack on the very idea of modes of presentation meets with resistance from those who see a genuine explanatory role for modes, even within naturalistic accounts of the mind.

ONTOLOGY

Coidentification is the heart of thought because the goals of organisms are served by coidentifying. But the goals of organisms would only be thus served if there were genuine coidentifiables in the objective world. Millikan's ontology is decidedly realist. Her functional take on concepts has her carving nature at different joints than others might, however. For Millikan, empirical concepts are of *substances*, that is, *coidentifiables*. The category *substance* includes real kinds (e.g., *mouse*), individuals (e.g., *Mama*), event types (e.g., *breakfast again*), and numerous other stuffs and types (e.g., *ice, Starbucks Coffee House*). At an important level of abstraction, there is no genuine ontological distinction to be made among these things.

SUMMARY

In briefest summary: Millikan's program for understanding the nature of representation—which is to say, for understanding ourselves—is impressive for its combination of detail and scope.

See also Evans, Gareth; Frege, Gottlob; Philosophy of Biology; Philosophy of Language; Philosophy of Mind; Sellars, Wilfrid; Strawson, Peter Frederick.

Bibliography

WORKS BY MILLIKAN

Language, Thought and Other Biological Categories: New Foundations for Realism. Cambridge, MA: MIT Press, 1984.

White Queen Psychology: And Other Essays for Alice. Cambridge, MA: MIT Press, 1993.

"On Unclear and Indistinct Ideas." In *Philosophical Perspectives*, Vol. 8: *Logic and Language.* Edited by J. Tomberlin, pp. 75–110. Ascadero, CA: Ridgeview, 1994.

"Images of Identity." *Mind* 106 (423) (1997): 499–519.

On Clear and Confused Ideas: An Essay about Substance Concepts. Cambridge, U.K.: Cambridge University Press, 2000.

Varieties of Meaning. Cambridge, MA: MIT Press, 2002.

WORKS ABOUT MILLIKAN

Brandom, R. *Making It Explicit: Reasoning, Representing and Discursive Commitment.* Cambridge, MA: Harvard University Press, 1994.

Burge, T., and C. Peacocke. "Our Entitlement to Self-Knowledge." *Proceedings of the Aristotelian Society* XCVI (1995): 91–158.

Evans, G. *The Varieties of Reference.* Oxford: Oxford University Press, 1982.

Fodor, J. "A Theory of Content II: The Theory." *A Theory of Content and Other Essays.* Cambridge, MA: MIT Press, 1990, 65–77.

Lawlor, K. "Confused Thought and Modes of Presentation." *Philosophical Quarterly* 55 (218) (2005): 21–36.

Sainsbury, M. "Fregean Sense." In *Logica*. Edited by Timothy Childers, Petr Kolásr, and Vladimir Svoboda. pp. 261–276. Prague: Filosofia, 1997.

Strawson, P. F. *Individuals: An Essay in Descriptive Metaphysics.* London: Methuen, 1959.

Strawson, P. F. *Subject and Predicate in Logic and Grammar.* London: Methuen, 1974.

Krista Lawlor (2005)

MILL'S METHODS OF INDUCTION

John Stuart Mill, in his *System of Logic* (Book III, Chapters 8–10), set forth and discussed five methods of experimental inquiry, calling them the method of agreement, the method of difference, the joint method of agreement and difference, the method of residues, and the method of concomitant variation. Mill maintained that these are the methods by which we both discover and demonstrate causal relationships, and that they are of fundamental importance in scientific investigation. Mill called these methods "eliminative methods of induction." In so doing, he was drawing an analogy with the elimination of terms in an algebraic equation—an analogy that is rather forced, except with respect to the various methods that are classed under the heading of method of difference. As will be demonstrated, it is perhaps best to use the term "eliminative methods" with reference to the elimination of rival candidates for the role of cause, which characterizes all these methods.

ILLUSTRATIONS OF THE METHODS

The general character of Mill's methods of experimental inquiry may be illustrated by examples of the two simplest ones, the methods of agreement and of difference. Mill's canon for the method of agreement is this: "If two or more instances of the phenomenon under investigation have only one circumstance in common, the circumstance in which alone all the instances agree is the cause (or effect) of the given phenomenon."

For example, if a number of people who are suffering from a certain disease have all gone for a considerable time without fresh fruits or vegetables, but have in other respects had quite different diets, have lived in different conditions, belong to different races, and so on, so that the lack of fresh fruits and vegetables is the only feature common to all of them, then we can conclude that the lack of fresh fruits and vegetables is the cause of this particular disease.

Mill's canon for the method of difference is this: "If an instance in which the phenomenon under investigation occurs, and an instance in which it does not occur, have every circumstance in common save one, that one occurring in the former; the circumstance in which alone the two instances differ, is the effect, or the cause, or an indispensable part of the cause, of the phenomenon."

For example, if two exactly similar pieces of iron are heated in a charcoal-burning furnace and hammered into shape in exactly similar ways, except that the first is dipped into water after the final heating while the second is not, and the first is found to be harder than the second, then the dipping of iron into water while it is hot is the cause of such extra hardness—or at least an essential part of the cause, for the hammering, the charcoal fire, and so on may also be needed. For all this experiment shows, the dipping alone might not produce such extra hardness.

The method of agreement, then, picks out as the cause the one common feature in a number of otherwise different cases where the effect occurs; the method of difference picks out as the cause the one respect in which a case where the effect occurs differs from an otherwise exactly similar case where the effect does not occur. Both are intended to be methods of ampliative induction, that is, methods by which we can reason from a limited number of observed instances to a general causal relationship: The intended conclusion is that a certain disease is always produced by a lack of fresh fruits and vegetables, or that dipping iron into water while it is hot always hardens it, if it has been heated and hammered in a particular way. And the other three methods are intended to work in a similar manner.

These methods have been criticized on two main counts: First, it is alleged that they do not establish the conclusions intended, so that they are not methods of proof or conclusive demonstration; and second, that they are not useful as methods of discovery. Such criticisms have been used to support the general observation that these methods play no part, or only a very minor part, in the investigation of nature, and that scientific method requires a radically different description.

In order to estimate the force of such criticisms, and to determine the real value of the eliminative methods, Mill's formulation need not be discussed in detail. Instead, one need only determine what would be valid demonstrative methods corresponding to Mill's classes, and then consider whether such methods, or any approximations of them, have a place in either scientific or commonsense inquiry.

METHODS OF AGREEMENT AND OF DIFFERENCE

To avoid unnecessary complications, let us assume that the conclusion reached by any application of the method of agreement or of difference is to have the form "Such-and-such is a cause of such-and-such kind of event or phenomenon." For a formal study of these methods and the joint method we could regard a cause as a necessary and sufficient condition of the effect—or, in some cases, as a necessary condition only, or as a sufficient condition only—where to say that X is a necessary condition for Y is just to say that wherever Y is present, X is present, or briefly that all Y are X; and to say that X is a sufficient condition for Y is just to say that wherever X is present Y is present, or briefly that all X are Y.

In general we shall be looking for a condition that is both necessary and sufficient for the phenomenon, but there are variants of the methods in which we look for a condition that is merely necessary or merely sufficient. In practice, however, we are concerned with conditions that are not absolutely necessary or sufficient, but that are rather necessary and/or sufficient in relation to some *field*, that is, some set of background conditions, which may be specified more or less exactly. We are concerned, for example, not with the cause of a certain disease in general, but with what causes it in human beings living on the earth, breathing air, and so forth. Again, we are concerned not with the cause of hardness in general, but with that of a greater-than-normal hardness in iron in ordinary circumstances and at ordinary temperatures. The field in relation to which we look for a cause of a phenomenon must be such that the phenomenon sometimes occurs in that field and sometimes does not. We may assume that this field is constituted by the presence of certain qualities or at least of some general descriptive features, not by a specific location.

The *observation* that supports the conclusion is an observation of one or more instances in each of which various features are present or absent. An instance may be one in which the phenomenon in question occurs, which we may call a *positive instance*, or one in which the phenomenon does not occur, which we may call a *negative instance*.

To reason validly, however, from any such observation to a general causal conclusion, we require an additional general premise, an *assumption*. We must assume that there is some condition which, in relation to the field, is necessary and sufficient (or which is necessary, or which is sufficient) for the phenomenon, and also that this condition is to be found within a range of conditions that is restricted in some way. For these methods fall within the general class of eliminative forms of reasoning, that is, arguments in which one possibility is confirmed or established by the elimination of some or all of its rivals. The assumption will state that there is a cause to be found and will limit the range of candidates for the role of cause; the task of the observation will be to rule out enough of the candidates initially admitted to allow some positive conclusion.

POSSIBLE CAUSES. It follows from the above that the assumption must indicate some limited (though not necessarily finite) set of what we may call *possible causes*. These are the factors (Mill calls them *circumstances* or *antecedents*) that, it is initially assumed, may be causally relevant to the phenomenon. Any possible cause, any factor that may be causally relevant in relation to the field in question, must, like the phenomenon itself, be something that sometimes occurs and sometimes does not occur within that field.

But are we to assume that a possible cause acts singly, if it acts at all? If the possible causes are *A, B, C,* etc., the phenomenon is *P,* and the field is *F,* are we to assume that the cause of *P* in *F* will be either *A* by itself or *B* by itself, and so on? Or are we to allow that it might be a conjunction, say *AC,* so that *P* occurs in *F* when and only when *A* and *C* are both present? Are we to allow that the necessary and sufficient condition might be a disjunction, say (*B* or *D*), so that *P* occurs in *F* whenever *B* occurs, and whenever *D* occurs, but only when one or other (or both) of these occurs? Again, are we to allow that what we have taken as possible causes may include counteracting causes, so that the actual cause of *P* in *F* may be, say, the absence of *C* (that is, the negation not-*C*, or $\overline{C}$) or perhaps $B\overline{C}$ so that *P* occurs in *F* when and only when *B* is present and *C* is absent at the same time?

There are in fact valid methods with assumptions of different sorts, from the most rigorous kind, which requires that the actual cause should be just one of the possible causes by itself, through those which progressively admit negations, conjunctions, and disjunctions of possible causes and combinations of these, to the least rigorous kind of assumption, which says merely that the actual cause is built up out of these possible causes in some way.

CLASSIFICATION OF THESE METHODS. There will be, then, not one method of agreement, one method of difference, and one joint method, but a series of variants of each. A complete survey could be made of all possible

methods of these types, numbered as follows: A number from 1 to 8 before a decimal point will indicate the kind of assumption. Thus, it is assumed that there is an actual cause that is

(1) one of the possible causes;

(2) one of the possible causes or the negation of a possible cause;

(3) a possible cause or a conjunction of possible causes;

(4) a possible cause or a disjunction of possible causes;

(5) a possible cause or the negation of a possible cause, or a conjunction each of whose members is a possible cause or the negation of a possible cause;

(6) a possible cause, or the negation of a possible cause, or a disjunction each of whose members is a possible cause or the negation of a possible cause;

(7) a possible cause, or a conjunction of possible causes, or a disjunction each of whose members is a possible cause or a conjunction of possible causes;

(8) a possible cause, or the negation of a possible cause, or a conjunction each of whose members is a possible cause or the negation of one; or a disjunction each of whose members is a possible cause or the negation of one, or a conjunction each of whose members is a possible cause or a negation of one.

The first figure after the decimal point will indicate the sort of observation, as follows:

(1) a variant of the method of agreement;

(2) a variant of the method of difference;

(3) a variant of the joint method;

(4) a new but related method.

The second figure after the decimal point will mark further differences where necessary, but this figure will have no constant significance.

The complete survey cannot be given here, but a few selected variants will be considered, numbered in the manner set forth above.

POSITIVE METHOD OF AGREEMENT. Let us begin with an assumption of the first kind, that there is a necessary and sufficient condition *X* for *P* in *F*, that is, that for some *X* all *FP* are *X* and all *FX* are *P*, and *X* is identical with one of the possible causes *A, B, C, D, E.* (It may be noted that a condition thus specified may sometimes not be what we would ordinarily regard as the cause of the phenomenon: We might rather say that it *contains* the real cause. However, in our present account we shall call such a condition the cause; it is explained below how the cause of a phenomenon may be progressively located with greater precision.)

We obtain a variant of the method of agreement (1.12) by combining with this assumption the following observation: A set of one or more positive instances such that one possible cause, say *A*, is present in each instance, but for every other possible cause there is an instance from which that cause is absent. This yields the conclusion that *A* is necessary and sufficient for *P* in *F*.

For example, the observation might be this:

	A	B	C	D	E
I_1	*p*	*a*	*p*	·	*a*
I_2	*p*	*p*	*a*	*a*	·

where *p* indicates that the possible cause is present, *a* that it is absent, and a dot that it may be either present or absent without affecting the result. I_1 and I_2 are positive instances: I_1 shows that neither *B* nor *E* is necessary for *P* in *F*, I_2 that neither *C* nor *D* is necessary, and hence, given the assumption, it follows that *A* is necessary and sufficient.

Since this reasoning eliminates candidates solely on the ground that they are not necessary, there is another variant (1.11) that assumes only that there is some necessary condition for *P* in *F* identical with one of the possible causes, and (with the same observation) concludes that *A* is a necessary condition for *P* in *F*.

Negative method of agreement. Besides the positive method of agreement, in which candidates are eliminated as not being necessary because they are absent from positive instances, there are corresponding variants of a negative method of agreement in which candidates are eliminated as not being sufficient because they are present in negative instances. This requires the following observation: A set of one or more negative instances such that one possible cause, say *A*, is absent from each instance, but for every other possible cause there is an instance in which it is present. For example:

	A	B	C	D	E
N_1	*a*	*p*	·	·	·
N_2	*a*	·	*p*	*p*	·
N_3	*a*	·	·	·	*p*

If the assumption was that one of the possible causes is sufficient for *P* in *F*, this observation would show (1.13) that *A* is sufficient, while if the assumption was that one of the possible causes is both necessary and sufficient, this observation would show (1.14) that *A* is necessary and sufficient.

METHOD OF DIFFERENCE. For the simplest variant of the method of difference (1.2) we need this observation: a positive instance I_1 and a negative instance N_1 such that of the possible causes present in I_1, one, say *A*, is absent from N_1, but the rest are present in N_1. For example:

	A	B	C	D	E
I_1	*p*	*p*	*p*	*a*	·
N_1	*a*	*p*	*p*	·	*p*

Here *D* is eliminated because it is absent from I_1, and hence not necessary, and *B, C,* and *E* are eliminated because they are present in N_1 and hence not sufficient. Hence, given the assumption that one of the possible causes is both necessary and sufficient for *P* in *F*, it follows that *A* is so. (Note that since it would not matter if, say, *E* were absent from I_1, the presence of the actual cause in I_1 need not be the only difference between the instances.) We may remark here that the method of difference, unlike some variants of the method of agreement, requires the assumption that there is some condition that is both necessary and sufficient for *P*. It is true, as we shall see later with variants 4.2 and 8.2, that the "cause" detected by this method is often not itself a necessary condition, or even a sufficient one; but the assumption needed is that *something* is both necessary and sufficient.

JOINT METHOD. The joint method may be interpreted as an indirect method of difference, that is, the job done by I_1 above may be shared among several positive instances, and the job done by N_1 among several negative instances. That is, we need (for 1.3) the following observation: a set S_i of one or more positive instances and a set S_n of one or more negative instances such that one of the possible causes, say *A*, is present throughout S_i and absent throughout S_n, but each of the other possible causes is either absent from at least one positive instance or present in at least one negative instance. Given that one of the possible causes is both necessary and sufficient, this yields the conclusion that *A* is so.

SIMPLE VARIANTS OF THESE METHODS. With an assumption of the second kind (that the requisite condition is either a possible cause or a negation of a possible cause) we need stronger observations. Thus, for variants of the positive method of agreement (2.11 and 2.12) we need this: two or more positive instances such that one possible cause (or negation), say *A*, is present in each instance, but for every other possible cause there is an instance in which it is present and an instance from which it is absent. This is needed to rule out, as candidates for the role of necessary (or both necessary and sufficient) condition, the negations of possible causes as well as the possible causes other than *A* themselves.

For the corresponding variant of the method of difference (2.2) we need this: a positive instance I_1 and a negative instance N_1 such that one possible cause (or negation), say *A*, is present in I_1 and absent from N_1, but each of the other possible causes is either present in both I_1 and N_1 or absent from both. For example:

	A	*B*	*C*	*D*	*E*
I_1	*p*	*p*	*a*	*a*	*p*
N_1	*a*	*p*	*a*	*a*	*p*

Since *B* is present in N_1, *B* is not sufficient for *P* in *F*; but since *B* is present in I_1, not-*B* is not necessary for *P* in *F*; thus neither *B* nor not-*B* can be both necessary and sufficient. Similarly, *C*, *D*, *E*, and their negations, and also not-*A*, are ruled out, and thus the necessary and sufficient condition must be *A* itself. This is the classic difference observation described by Mill, in which the only (possibly relevant) difference between the instances is the presence in I_1 of the factor identified as the actual cause; but we need this observation (as opposed to the weaker one of 1.2) only when we allow that the negation of a possible cause may be the actual cause.

The joint method needs, along with this weaker assumption, a similarly strengthened observation: That is, each of the possible causes other than *A* must be either present in both a positive and a negative instance or absent from both a positive and a negative instance, and then this variant (2.3) still yields the conclusion that *A* is both necessary and sufficient.

(What Mill and his followers describe as the joint method may be not this indirect method of difference, but rather a double method of agreement, in which a set of positive instances identifies a necessary condition and a set of negative instances identifies a sufficient condition. Such a combination is redundant with an assumption of either of the first two kinds, but not when the assumption is further relaxed.)

MORE COMPLEX VARIANTS. We consider next an assumption of the third kind, that the requisite condition is either a possible cause or a conjunction of possible causes. (This latter possibility seems to be at least part of what Mill meant by "an intermixture of effects.") This possibility does not affect the positive method of agreement, since if a conjunction is necessary, each of its conjuncts is necessary, and candidates can therefore be eliminated as before. But since the conjuncts in a necessary and sufficient condition may not severally be sufficient, the negative method of agreement as set forth above will not work. The observation of (1.13 or) 1.14 would now leave it open that, say, *BC* was the required (sufficient or) necessary and sufficient condition, for if *C* were absent from N_1 and *B* from N_2, then *BC* as a whole might still be sufficient: It would not be eliminated by either of these instances. This method now (in 3.14) needs a stronger observation, namely, a *single* negative instance N_1 in which one possible cause, say *A*, is absent, but *every* other possible cause is present. This will show that no possible cause or conjunction of possible causes that does not contain *A* is sufficient for *P* in *F*. But even this does not show that the requisite condition is *A* itself, but merely that it is either *A* itself or a conjunction in which *A* is a conjunct. We may express this by saying that the cause is $(A\underline{\ldots})$, where the dots indicate that other conjuncts may form part of the condition, and the dots are underlined, while *A* is not, to indicate that *A* *must* appear in the formula for the actual cause, but that other conjuncts may or may not appear.

The corresponding variant (3.2) of the method of difference needs only the observation of 1.2; but it, too, establishes only the less complete conclusion that $(A\underline{\ldots})$ is a necessary and sufficient condition of *P* in *F*. For while (in the example given for 1.2 above) *B*, *C*, *D*, and *E* singly are still eliminated as they were in 1.2, and any conjunctions such as *BC* which, being present in I_1, *might* be necessary, are eliminated because they are also present in N_1 and hence not sufficient, a conjunction such as *AB*, which contains *A*, is both present in I_1, and absent from N_1, and might therefore be both necessary and sufficient. Thus this assumption and this observation show only that *A* is, as Mill put it, "the cause, or an indispensable part of the cause." The full cause is represented by the formula $(A\underline{\ldots})$, provided that only possible causes that are present in I_1 can replace the dots.

In the corresponding variant of the joint method (3.3), we need a *single* negative instance instead of the set S_n, for the same reason as in 3.14, and the cause is specified only as $(A\underline{\ldots})$.

With an assumption of the fourth kind (that the requisite condition is either a possible cause or a disjunction of possible causes), the negative method of agreement (4.13 and 4.14) works as in 1.13 and 1.14, but the positive method of agreement is now seriously affected. For with the observation given for 1.12 above, the necessary and sufficient condition might be, say, (B or C), for this disjunction is present in both I_1 and I_2, though neither of its disjuncts is present in both. Thus the observation of 1.12 would leave the result quite undecided. We need (for 4.12) a much stronger observation, that is, a single positive instance in which A is present but all the other possible causes are absent together; but even this now shows only that the cause is (A or...). This assumption (that the cause may be a disjunction of possible causes) allows what Mill called a "plurality of causes," for each of the disjuncts is by itself a "cause" in the sense that it is a sufficient condition; and what we have just noted is the way in which this possibility undermines the use of the method of agreement.

The method of difference, on the other hand (4.2), still needs only the observation of 1.2; this eliminates all possible causes other than A, and all disjunctions that do not contain A, either as being not sufficient because they are present in N_1 or as not necessary because they are absent from I_1. The only disjunctions not eliminated are those that occur in I_1 but not in N_1, and these must contain A. Thus this observation, with this assumption, shows that a necessary and sufficient condition is (A or...), that is, either A itself or a disjunction containing A, where the other disjuncts are possible causes absent from N_1. This, of course, means that A itself, the factor thus picked out, may be only a sufficient condition for P.

The joint method with this assumption (4.3) needs a *single* positive instance, but can still use a set of negative instances and it specifies the cause as (A or...).

As the assumptions are relaxed further, the method of agreement requires stronger and stronger observations. For example, in 6.12, which is a variant of the positive method with an assumption allowing that the necessary and sufficient condition may be a disjunction of possible causes or negations, the observation needed is a set S_i of positive instances such that one possible cause, say A, is present in each, but that for every possible combination of the other possible causes and their negations there is an instance in which this combination is present (that is, if there are n other possible causes, we need 2^n different instances). This observation will eliminate every disjunction that does not contain A, and will show that the requisite necessary and sufficient condition is (A

or...), and hence that A itself is a sufficient condition for P in F. A corresponding variant of the negative method of agreement (5.14) shows that (A...) is a necessary and sufficient condition, and hence that A itself is necessary—a curious reversal of roles, because in the simplest variants, the positive method of agreement was used to detect a necessary condition and the negative one a sufficient condition.

In the method of difference, however, the observation of 1.2 (or, where negations are admitted, that of 2.2) continues to yield results, though the conclusions become less complete, that is, the cause is less and less completely specified. For example, in 8.2, where we assume that there is a necessary and sufficient condition for P in F which may be one of the possible causes, or a negation of one, or a conjunction of possible causes or negations, or a disjunction of possible causes or negations or of conjunctions of possible causes or negations—which in effect allows the actual condition to be built up out of the possible causes in any way—the observation of 2.2 establishes the conclusion that the requisite condition is (A... or...). that is to say, it is either A itself, or a conjunction containing A, or a disjunction in which one of the disjuncts is A itself or a conjunction containing A. Since any such disjunct in a necessary and sufficient condition is a sufficient condition, this observation, in which the presence of A in I_1 is the only possibly relevant difference between I_1 and N_1, shows even with the least rigorous kind of assumption that A is at least a necessary part of a sufficient condition for P in F—the sufficient condition being (A...).

The joint method, as an indirect method of difference, ceases to work once we allow both conjunctions and disjunctions; but a double method of agreement comes into its own with this eighth kind of assumption. In 8.12, as in 6.12, if there are n possible causes other than A, the set of 2^n positive instances with A present in each but with the other possible causes present and absent in all possible combinations will show that (A or...) is necessary and sufficient, and hence that A is sufficient. Similarly in 8.14, as in 5.14, the corresponding set of $2^{>n}$ negative instances will show that (A...) is necessary and sufficient and hence that A is necessary. Putting the two observations together, we could conclude that A is both necessary and sufficient.

A new method, similar in principle, can be stated as follows (8.4): If there are n possible causes in all, and we observe 2^n instances (positive or negative) which cover all possible combinations of possible causes and their negations, then the disjunction of all the conjunctions found in the positive instances is both necessary and sufficient for P in F. For example, if there are only three possible causes, A, B, C,

A	B	C	P
p	p	p	a
p	p	a	p
p	a	p	p
p	a	a	a
a	p	p	a
a	p	a	p
a	a	p	a
a	a	a	a

and we have the observations listed in the accompanying table, then ($A B \overline{C}$ or $A \overline{B} C$ or $\overline{A} B \overline{C}$) is a necessary and sufficient condition for P in F. For if these are the only possibly relevant conditions, each combination of possible causes and negations for which P is present is sufficient for P, and these are the only sufficient conditions for P, since in all the relevantly different circumstances P is absent; but the disjunction of all the sufficient conditions must be both necessary and sufficient, on the assumption that there is some condition that is both necessary and sufficient.

MANY VALID METHODS. We thus find that while we must recognize very different variants of these methods according to the different kinds of assumptions that are used, and while the reasoning that validates the simplest variants fails when it is allowed that various negations and combinations of factors may constitute the actual cause, nevertheless there are valid demonstrative methods which use even the least rigorous form of assumption, that is, which assume only that there is some necessary and sufficient condition for P in F, made up in some way from a certain restricted set of possible causes. But with an assumption of this kind we must be content either to extract (by 8.2) a very incomplete conclusion from the classical difference observation or (by 8.12, 8.14, the combination of these two, or 8.4) to get more complete conclusions only from a large number of instances in which the possible causes are present or absent in systematically varied ways.

AN EXTENSION OF THE METHODS. An important extension of all these methods is the following: Since in every case the argument proceeds by eliminating certain candidates, it makes no difference if what is *not* eliminated is not a single possible cause but a cluster of possible causes which in our instances are always present together or absent together, the conclusion being just as we now have it, but with a symbol for the cluster replacing A. For example, if in 2.2 we have, say, both A and B present in I_1 and both absent from N_1, but each possible cause either present in both or absent from both, it follows that the cluster (A,B) is the cause in the sense that the actual cause lies somewhere within this cluster. A similar observation in 8.2 would show that either A, or B, or AB, or (A or B) is an indispensable part of a sufficient condition for P in F.

METHOD OF RESIDUES

The method of residues can be interpreted as a variant of the method of difference in which the negative instance is not observed but constructed on the basis of already known causal laws.

Suppose, for example, that a positive instance I_1 has been observed as follows:

	A	B	C	D	E
I_1	p	p	a	p	a

Now if we had, to combine with this, a negative instance N_1 in which B and D were present and A, C, and E absent, we could infer, according to the kind of assumption made, by 2.2 that A was the cause, or by 8.2 that (A... or...) was the cause, and so on. But if previous inductive inquiries have already established laws from which it follows that given $\overline{A} B \overline{C} D \overline{E}$ in the field F, P would not result, there is no need to observe N_1; we already know all that N_1 could tell us, and so one of the above-mentioned conclusions follows from I_1 alone along with the appropriate assumption.

Again, if the effect or phenomenon in which we are interested can be quantitatively measured, we could reason as follows. Suppose that we observe a positive instance, say with the factors as in I_1 above, in which there is a quantity x_1 of the effect in question, while our previously established laws enable us to calculate that with the factors as in N_1 there would be a quantity x_2 of this effect; then we can regard the difference $(x_1 - x_2)$ as the phenomenon P which is present in I_1 but absent from N_1. With an assumption of kind (1) or (2) or (4) or (6)—that is, any assumption that does not allow conjunctive terms in the cause—we could conclude that the cause of P in this instance I_1 was A alone, and hence that A is a sufficient condition for P in F. With an assumption of kind (1) or (2) we could indeed infer that A is both necessary and sufficient, but with one of kind (4) or (6) we could conclude only that a necessary and sufficient condition is (A or...).

To make an assumption of any of these four kinds is to assume that the effects of whatever factors are actually relevant are merely additive, and this lets us conclude that the extra factor in I_1, namely A, by itself produces in relation to F the extra effect (x_1-x_2). But with an assumption of kind (3) or (5) or (7) or (8), which allows conjunctive terms, and hence what Mill calls an "intermixture of effects," we could only infer that the cause of (x_1-x_2) in this instance was (A...). With the other factors that were present in both I_1 and N_1, A was sufficient to produce this differential effect, but it does not follow that A is sufficient for this in relation to F as a whole. (Though Mill does not mention this, such a use of constructed instances along with some observed ones is in principle applicable to all the methods, not only to the method of difference in the way here outlined.)

METHOD OF CONCOMITANT VARIATION

The method of concomitant variation, like those already surveyed, is intended to be a form of ampliative induction; we want to argue from a covariation observed in some cases to a general rule of covariation covering unobserved cases also. To interpret this method we need a wider concept of cause than that which we have so far been using. A cause of P in the field F must now be taken, not as a necessary and sufficient condition, but as something on whose magnitude the magnitude of P, in F, functionally depends. For our present purpose this means only that there is some true lawlike proposition which, within F, relates the magnitude of the one item to that of the other. The *full cause*, in this sense, will be something on which, in F, the magnitude of P wholly depends, that is, the magnitude of P is uniquely determined by the magnitudes of the factors that constitute the full cause.

A full investigation of such a functional dependence would comprise two tasks: first, the identification of all the factors on which, in F, the magnitude of P depends, and second, the discovery of the way in which this magnitude depends on these factors. The completion of the first task would yield a mere list of terms, that of the second a mathematical formula. Only the first of these tasks can be performed by an eliminative method analogous to those already surveyed.

We should expect to find concomitant variation analogues of both the method of agreement and the method of difference, that is, ways of arguing to a causal relationship between P and, say, A, both from the observation of

cases where P remains constant while A remains constant but all the other possibly relevant factors vary, and also from the observation of cases where P varies while A varies but all the other possibly relevant factors remain constant. And indeed there are methods of both kinds, but those of the second kind, the analogues of the method of difference, are more important.

As before, we need an assumption as well as an observation, but we have a choice between two different kinds of assumption. An assumption of the more rigorous kind would be that in F the magnitude of P wholly depends in some way on the magnitude of X, where X is identical with just one of the possible causes A, B, C, D, E. Given this, if we observe that over some period, or over some range of instances, P varies in magnitude while one of the possible causes, say A, also varies but all the other possible causes remain constant, we can argue that none of the possible causes other than A can be that on which the magnitude of P wholly depends, and thus conclude that X must be identical with A, that in F the magnitude of P depends wholly on that of A. (But *how* it depends, that is, what the functional law is, must be discovered by an investigation of some other sort.)

An assumption of the less rigorous kind would be that in F the magnitude of P wholly depends in some way on the magnitudes of one or more factors X, X', X'', etc., where each of the actually relevant factors is identical with one of the possible causes A, B, C, D, E. Given this, if we again observe that P varies while, say, A varies but B, C, D, E remain constant, this does not now show that B, for example, cannot be identical with X, etc.; that is, it does not show that variations in B are causally irrelevant to P. All it shows is that the magnitude of P is not *wholly* dependent upon any set of factors that does not include A, for every such set has remained constant while P has varied. This leaves it open that the full cause of P in F might be A itself, or might be some set of factors, such as (A,B,D) which includes A and some of the others as well. All we know is that the list must include A. This observation and this assumption, then, show that a full cause of P in F is (A, ...); that is, that A is an actually relevant factor and there may or may not be others. Repeated applications of this method could fill in other factors, but would not *close* the list. (And, as before, it is a further task, to be carried out by a different sort of investigation, to find *how* the magnitude of P depends on those of the factors thus shown to be actually relevant.)

To close the list, that is, to show that certain factors are actually irrelevant, we need to use an analogue of the method of agreement. If we assume, as before, that the full cause of P in F is some set of factors (X, X', X'', etc.), but also that P is *responsive* to all these factors in the sense that for any variation, in, say, X while X', X'', etc. remain constant P will vary, and that X, X', X'', etc. are identical with some of the possible causes A, B, C, D, E, then if we observe that P remains constant while, say, A, C, D, and E remain constant but B varies, we can conclude that B is causally irrelevant, that none of the X's is identical with B.

USES AND APPLICATIONS OF THE ELIMINATIVE METHODS

We have so far been considering only whether there are demonstratively valid methods of this sort; but by stating more precisely what such methods involve, we may incidentally have removed some of the more obvious objections to the view that such methods can be applied in practice. Thus, by introducing the idea of a *field*, we have given these methods the more modest task of finding the cause of a phenomenon in relation to a field, not the ambitious one of finding conditions that are absolutely necessary and sufficient. By explicitly introducing the possible causes as well as the field, we have freed the user of the method of agreement from having to make the implausible claim that the user's instances have only one circumstance in common. Instead, the user has merely to claim that they have in common only one of the possible causes, while admitting that all the features that belong to the field, or that are constant throughout the field, will belong to all the instances, and that there may be other common features too, though not among those that he has initially judged to be possibly relevant.

Similarly, the user of the method of difference has only to claim that no *possibly relevant* feature other than the one he has picked as the cause is present in I_1 but not in N_1. Also, we have taken explicit account of the ways in which the possibilities of counteracting causes, a plurality of causes, an intermixture of effects, and so on, affect the working of the methods, and we have shown that even when these possibilities are admitted we can still validly draw conclusions, provided that we note explicitly the incompleteness of the conclusions that we are now able to draw (for example, by the method of difference) or the much greater complexity of the observations we need (for example, in variants of the method of agreement or method 8.4).

ELIMINATIVE METHODS AND INDUCTION. By making explicit the assumptions needed and by presenting the eliminative methods as deductively valid forms of argument, we have abandoned any pretense that methods

such as these in themselves solve or remove the "problem of induction." Provided that the requisite observations can be made, the ultimate justification of any application of one of these methods of ampliative induction will depend on the justification of the assumption used; and, since this proposition is general in form, it will presumably have to be supported by some other kind of inductive, or at least nondeductive, reasoning. But we must here leave aside this question of ultimate justification.

ELIMINATIVE METHODS AND DETERMINISM. Some light, however, can be thrown on the suggestion frequently made that causal determinism is a presupposition of science. If these eliminative methods play some important part in scientific investigation, then it is noteworthy that they all require deterministic assumptions: They all work toward the identification of a cause of a given phenomenon by first assuming that there is some cause to be found for it. However, it has emerged that what we require is not a single universally applicable principle of causality, namely, that every event has a cause, but something at once weaker in some ways and stronger in other ways than such a principle. The principle assumed is that the particular phenomenon P in the chosen field F has a cause, but that a cause of P in F is to be found within a range of factors that is restricted in some way. We have also found that different concepts of a cause are required for concomitant variation and for the other methods. The complaint that the phrase "uniformity of nature" cannot be given a precise or useful meaning, incidentally, has been rebutted by finding in exactly what sense our methods have to assume that nature is uniform.

EMPLOYMENT OF THE METHODS. Such assumptions are in fact regularly made, both in investigations within our already developed body of knowledge and in our primitive or commonsense ways of finding out about the world. In both these sorts of inquiry we act on the supposition that any changes that occur are caused; they do not "just happen." In a developed science, the causal knowledge that we already have can limit narrowly the range of possibly relevant causal factors. It can tell us, for this particular phenomenon, what kinds of cause to be on the lookout for, and how to exclude or hold constant some possibly relevant factors while we study the effects of others.

In more elementary discoveries, we restrict the range of possibly relevant factors mainly by the expectation that the cause of any effect will be somewhere in the near spatiotemporal neighborhood of the effect. The possible causes, then, will be features that occur variably within the field in question in the neighborhood of cases where the effect either occurs, or might have occurred, but does not.

USE OF METHOD OF DIFFERENCES. As an example of the above, singular causal sequences are detected primarily by the use of variants of the method of difference. Antoine-Henri Becquerel discovered that the radium he carried in a bottle in his pocket was the cause of a burn by noticing that the presence of the radium was the only possible relevant difference between the time when the inflammation developed and the earlier time when it did not, or between the part of his body where the inflammation appeared and the other parts.

Similar considerations tell us that a certain liquid turned this litmus paper red: The paper became red just after it was dipped in the liquid, and nothing else likely to be relevant happened just then. The situations before and after a change constitute our negative and positive instances respectively, and we may well be fairly confident that this is the only possibly relevant factor that has changed. We do not and need not draw up a list of possible causes, but by merely being on the lookout for other changes we can ensure that what would constitute a large number of possible causes (identified as such by their being in the spatiotemporal neighborhood) are the same in I_1 as in N_1.

Repeating the sequence—for example, dipping another similar piece of litmus paper into the liquid—confirms the view that the liquid caused the change of color. But it is not that in this case we are using the method of agreement; the repetition merely makes it less likely that any other change occurred to cause the change of color simultaneously with each of the two dippings, and this confirms our belief that the instances are what the use of the method of difference would require.

Since, in general, it will not be plausible to make an assumption more rigorous then one of kind (8), the conclusion thus established will only be that this individual sequence is an exemplification of a *gappy* causal law, of the form that (*A... or...*) is necessary and sufficient for *P* in *F*. But this is exactly what our ordinary singular causal statements mean: To say that this caused that says only that this was needed, perhaps in conjunction with other factors that were present, to produce the effect, and it leaves it open that other antecedents altogether (not present in this case) might produce the same effect.

General causal statements, such as "The eating of sweets causes dental decay," are to be interpreted similarly as asserting gappy causal laws. Anyone who says this would admit that the eating of sweets has this effect only in the presence of certain other conditions or in the absence of certain counteracting causes, and he would admit that things other than the eating of sweets might produce tooth decay. And such a gappy causal law can be established by the use of method 8.2, or the method of concomitant variation, or by statistical methods that can be understood as elaborations of these. Such general causal statements are, however, to be understood as asserting gappy causal laws, not mere statistical correlations: Anyone who uses such a statement is claiming that in principle the gaps could be filled in.

USE IN DISCOVERING EFFECTS. The use of the above methods is not confined to cases where we begin with a question of the form "What is the cause of so-and-so?" We may just as well begin by asking "What is the effect of so-and-so?"—for example, "What is the effect of applying a high voltage to electrodes in a vacuum tube?" But we are justified in claiming that what is observed to happen is an effect of this only if the requirements for the appropriate variant of the method of difference are fulfilled.

USE OF METHOD OF AGREEMENT. The simpler variants of the method of agreement can be used to establish a causal conclusion only in a case in which our previous knowledge narrowly restricts the possible causes and justifies the belief that they will operate singly. For example, if the character of a disease is such as to indicate that it is of bacterial origin, then the microorganism responsible may be identified through the discovery that only one species of microorganism not already known to be innocent is present in a number of cases of the disease. Otherwise, the observation of what seems to be the only common factor in a number of cases of a phenomenon can be used only very tentatively, to suggest a hypothesis that will need to be tested in some other way.

Where, however, we have a very large number of extremely diverse instances of some effect, and only one factor seems to be present in all of them, we may reason by what is in effect an approximation to method 8.12. The diverse instances cover at least a large selection of all the possible combinations of possibly relevant factors and their negations. Therefore it is probable that no condition not covered by the formula (*A* or...) is necessary, and hence, if there is a necessary and sufficient condition, (*A* or ...) is such, and hence *A* itself is a sufficient condition of the phenomenon.

Similarly, by an approximation to 8.14, we may reason that the one possibly relevant factor that is found to be absent in a large number of very diverse negative instances is probably a necessary condition of the phenomenon (that is, that its negation is a counteracting cause).

USE OF METHOD OF CONCOMITANT VARIATION. The method of concomitant variation, with statistical procedures that can be considered as elaborations of it, is used in a great many experimental investigations in which one possibly relevant factor is varied (everything else that might be relevant being held constant) to see whether there *is* a causal connection between that one factor and the effect in question. (Of course, what we regard as a single experiment may involve the variation of several factors, but still in such a way that the results will show the effects of varying each factor by itself: Such an experiment is merely a combination of several applications of concomitant variation.)

FURTHER USES. The "controlled experiment," in which a control case or control group is compared with an experimental case or experimental group, is again an application of the method of difference (or perhaps the method of residues, if we use the control case, along with already known laws, to tell us what would have happened in the experimental case if the supposed cause had not been introduced.)

An important use of these methods is in the progressive location of a cause. If we take "the drinking of wine" as a single possible cause, then an application of 8.2 may show that the drinking of wine causes intoxication: That is, this factor is *a* necessary element in *a* sufficient condition for this result. But we may then analyze this possible cause further and discover that several factors are included in this one item that we have named "the drinking of wine," and further experiments may show that only one of these factors was really necessary: The necessary element will then be more precisely specified. But the fact that this is always possible leaves it true that in relation to the earlier degree of analysis of factors, the drinking of wine was a necessary element in a sufficient condition, and the discovery of this (admittedly crude) causal law is correct as far as it goes and is an essential step on the way to the more accurate law that is based on a finer analysis of factors.

CRITICISM OF THE METHODS

The sort of example presented above helps to rebut one stock criticism of these methods, which is that they take for granted what is really the most important part of the procedure, namely, the discovery and analysis of factors. Any given application of one of these methods does presuppose some identification of possible causes, but it will not be completely vitiated by the fact that a finer analysis of factors is possible. Besides, the use of the methods themselves (particularly to discover singular causal sequences and hence the dispositional properties of particular things) is part of the procedure by which factors are further distinguished and classified. Also, the assumptions used, especially with regard to the range of possible causes allowed, are corrigible, and in conjunction with the methods they are self-correcting. A mistaken assumption is likely to lead, along with the observations, to contradictory conclusions, and when this happens we are forced to modify the assumption, in particular, to look further afield than we did at first for possibly relevant factors.

A fundamental and widely accepted objection to the claim that these methods form an important part of scientific method is that science is not concerned, or not much concerned, with causal relations in the sense in which these methods can discover them. It may be conceded that the formulation and confirmation of hypotheses and theories of the kind that constitute the greater part of a science such as physics is a scientific procedure quite different from the actual use of these methods. Even the discovery of a law of functional dependence is, as was noted, a task beyond what is achieved by our method of concomitant variation. It may also be conceded that many sciences are concerned largely with the simple discovery of new items and the tracing of processes rather than with causal relationships. Further, it was noted that these methods logically *cannot* be the whole of scientific procedure, since they require assumptions which they themselves cannot support.

In reply to this objection, however, it can be stressed, first, that a great deal of commonsense everyday knowledge, and also a great deal of knowledge in the more empirical sciences, is of causal relations of this sort, partly of singular causal sequences and partly of laws, especially of the incomplete or gappy form at which these methods characteristically arrive.

Second, it is largely such empirical causal relations that are explained by, and that support, the deeper theories and hypotheses of a developed science. But if they are to be used thus, they must be established independently.

Third, although descriptions of the eliminative methods of induction have often been associated with a kind of ground-floor empiricism that takes knowledge to be wholly concerned with empirical relations between directly observable things, qualities, and processes, the methods themselves are not tied to this doctrine but can establish causal relations between entities that are indirectly observed. For example, as long as there is any way, direct or indirect, of determining when a magnetic field is present and when there is an electric current in a wire, the methods can establish the fact that such a current will produce a magnetic field.

Finally, even where such causal relations are not the main object of inquiry, in investigation we constantly make use of causal relations, especially of singular causal sequences. In measuring, say, a voltage, we are assuming that it was the connecting of the meter across those terminals that caused this deflection of its needle, and the precautions that ensure that this is really so are to be explained in terms of our methods.

In fact, these methods are constantly used, explicitly or implicitly, both to suggest causal hypotheses and to confirm them. One should not, of course, expect any methods of empirical inquiry to establish conclusions beyond all possibility of doubt or all need of refinement, but in using these methods we can frequently say at least this: We have reason to suppose that for an event of this kind in this field there is some cause, and if the cause is not such-and-such, we cannot see what else the cause might be.

See also Deduction; Determinism, A Historical Survey; Empiricism; Induction; Mill, John Stuart.

Bibliography

WORKS ON INDUCTION

The classical study of eliminative induction remains that of J. S. Mill, *A System of Logic* (London, 1843), Book III, Chs. 8–10. Mill acknowledges that his study owes much to John Herschell, *A Preliminary Discourse on the Study of Natural Philosophy* (London: Longman, Rees, Orme, Brown, and Green, 1831), Part II, Ch. 6, and both are fundamentally indebted to Francis Bacon, *Novum Organum* (London: Joannem Billium, 1620), Book II. Since Mill, the literature has become extensive, but mostly in textbooks rather than in original works on logic or philosophy. There have been many worthwhile treatments of eliminative induction that are far above the textbook level—notably those of John Venn, *Empirical Logic* (London, 1889), Ch. 17; Christoff von Sigwart, *Logic*, 2nd ed. (Freiburg, 1893), translated by Helen Dendy as *Logic* (London: Sonnenschein, 1895), Vol. II, Part II, Ch. 5; and H. W. B. Joseph, *An Introduction to Logic* (Oxford: Clarendon Press, 1906), Ch. 20. But there are only a small number of writers who, either by criticizing Mill or developing his account, have added something new and

substantial to either the logic or the philosophy of eliminative induction.

CRITICISMS OF MILL'S METHODS

Mill's most important critics are William Whewell, *The Philosophy of Discovery* (London, 1860), Ch. 22; W. S. Jevons, *The Principles of Science* (London: Macmillan, 1874), Chs. 11, 19, and 23; F. H. Bradley, *The Principles of Logic* (London: K. Paul, Trench, 1883), Book II, Part II, Ch. 3; and M. R. Cohen and Ernest Nagel, *An Introduction to Logic and Scientific Method* (New York: Harcourt Brace, 1934), Ch. 13.

ELABORATIONS ON MILL'S METHODS

The main writers who have tried to develop Mill's ideas on the logical side are W. E. Johnson, *Logic* (Cambridge, U.K., 1924), Part II, Ch. 10; C. D. Broad, "The Principles of Demonstrative Induction" in *Mind* 39 (1930): 302–317 and 426–439; and G. H. von Wright, *A Treatise on Induction and Probability* (London: Routledge and Paul, 1951). Broad, following Johnson, undertakes a demonstrative reconstruction of Mill's methods and tries to extend eliminative methods to reasonings that terminate in quantitative laws. Von Wright's is the most thorough treatment so far published and studies the conditions under which "complete elimination" can be achieved even with what are here called the "less rigorous" kinds of assumptions. His account, however, seems somewhat unclear.

FURTHER STUDIES

The only major addition to the pure philosophy of induction is that of J. M. Keynes, *A Treatise on Probability* (London: Macmillan, 1921), Part III. Three more recent books that contain some discussion of it are J. O. Wisdom, *Foundations of Inference in Natural Science* (London: Methuen, 1952), Ch. 11; S. F. Barker, *Induction and Hypothesis* (Ithaca, NY: Cornell University Press, 1957), Ch. 3; and J. P. Day, *Inductive Probability* (London: Routledge and Paul, 1961), Sec. 5.

J. L. Mackie (1967)

MILTON, JOHN
(1608–1674)

John Milton, the English poet, author, and political writer, was born in London, the son of a prosperous scrivener. He was educated at St. Paul's School in London and Christ's College, Cambridge. After receiving an M.A. in 1632, he spent six years in study at his father's estate in Horton. In 1638 and 1639 he traveled to Italy, where he met Galileo Galilei, and on his return to London he found employment as a tutor. He wrote five pamphlets (1641–1642) attacking episcopacy, and his unhappy marriage in 1642 lent intensity to his subsequent tracts on divorce. In 1644 he published the tract *Of Education,* as well as *Areopagitica,* his famous attack on censorship of the press. His pamphlet justifying regicide, *Tenure of*

Kings and Magistrates (1649), probably brought him the post of secretary for foreign tongues to the Council of State. He wrote several defenses of the revolutionary government, but after 1652 total blindness forced him to withdraw gradually from public life. He turned to the completion of his theological treatise, *De Doctrina Christiana,* and his *History of Britain* and to the fulfillment of his poetic ambitions. Despite a brief return to public controversy in 1659 and 1660, Milton was treated leniently by the Restoration government. His epic, *Paradise Lost,* was published in 1667; *Samson Agonistes* and *Paradise Regained* appeared together, in one volume, in 1671. He died in 1674, survived by his third wife.

APPROACH AND METHOD

Milton was essentially a religious and ethical thinker, and his views are a striking blend of Christian humanism and Puritanism. The fullest statement of his position is *De Doctrina Christiana,* which was complete in all but certain details by 1660.

Milton believed that the Bible is divine revelation, plain and perspicuous in all things necessary to salvation. In matters of religion Scripture is the only outward rule or authority, and conscience, illuminated by the spirit of God, the only guide within. This scrupulous biblicism, however, is linked (as in Socinianism) with a strong emphasis on reason. Conscience, even when illuminated by the spirit, operates in rational terms rather than through mystical insight, so that "right reason" becomes the guide to Scripture. At the heart of this view, authorizing yet limiting the role of reason, is the doctrine that Scripture is an accommodation of God's will to the limited understanding of man. God has made in the Bible as full a revelation of himself as man is capable of receiving, and the safest approach is thus to form in the mind "such a conception of God, as shall correspond with his own delineation and representation of himself." This view eliminates speculations of a transcendental kind, reserving an area of mystery into which reason may not trespass; at the same time it encourages reason to assimilate biblical revelation to the categories of ethics. Thus, the theological treatise, like *Paradise Lost,* is a theodicy; its aim is to discover a view of God that is both worthy of him and consistent with revelation.

THEOLOGY

Milton's aim led him to some unorthodox conclusions, the most striking of which is his rejection of the doctrine of the Trinity. Embracing a loosely Arian position, he insisted on the unity of God and the consequent subordi-nation of the Son and the Holy Spirit to the Father. The Son is the first of the creatures, and although he is the perfect image of the Father and even made of the same substance, he is not of one essence with the Father. The Spirit, a rather supernumerary figure, was created at a later date than the Son. Milton maintained that the doctrine of the Trinity is a purely manmade mystery, with no scriptural foundation; it defies logic and degrades our conception of deity.

There was a second deviation from orthodoxy in the direction of monism. Milton rejected the Augustinian doctrine of the creation of the world ex nihilo and presented a theory of creation *de Deo.* Drawing support from both Scripture and reason, he argued that the universe was made out of the substance of God. This view, he claimed, is not only more logical than the alternative position, but in its assertion of the goodness of matter it underlines more emphatically the benevolence of the creator. The same antiascetic impulse is present in Milton's theory of body and soul; he argued that the higher comprehends the lower, that spirit contains matter, and that the body should thus be seen not as the prison house of the soul but as integral to it: "The whole man is soul, and the soul man." From this conclusion two corollaries proceed: first, the human soul is not created immediately by God but is propagated from father to son in a natural order; second, the whole man dies, body and soul, and does not live again until the end of time. Milton's view of spirit and matter probably encouraged both his rejection of traditional Eucharistic theory and his radical endorsement of divorce and polygamy.

FREE WILL. The doctrines we have examined, which are departures from the main traditions of Christianity, were designed to avoid dualism and to make theology conform to the canons of logical thought. A second group of doctrines emerged as a defense of free will against Calvinism. Milton rejected the orthodox Calvinist view of predestination and reduced the decree of predestination to a general offer of salvation to all men who are willing to believe. Other Arminian views reinforced his conviction that man is free to pursue or refuse salvation. Milton wished to show that regeneration is a matter neither of faith nor of works but of works of faith. Faith, it is true, is a gift of God, but every man is given sufficient grace to put a saving faith within his reach. Finally, the object of a saving faith is God the Father rather than Christ, so that such a faith is possible beyond the bounds of the Christian religion.

ETHICS

The relation of the individual to the community absorbed Milton's attention during two decades of public controversy (1640–1660). His tracts, written in response to the disturbing events of the period, received force and direction from his lasting concern with liberty. Reason is "but choosing"; it is the power of ethical action, and man must therefore be free to choose between good and evil. Only by knowing evil and rejecting it can one become virtuous, for, as Milton remarked in *Areopagitica*, "That which purifies us is trial, and trial is by what is contrary." Prescriptive morality, enforced by church or state, prevents both the real understanding of truths already known and the discovery of new truths.

Milton defended the autonomy of reason by appealing from manmade authorities—positive law, canon law, custom, or tradition—to the law of nature. The work of John Selden probably encouraged him to develop a distinction between the primary law of nature, given to Adam at the creation, and the secondary law, the imperfect remnants of the primary law in fallen man. Secondary law allows for the "hardness of heart" that was introduced by the Fall and thus prescribes for such aspects of man's fallen state as war, servitude, divorce, and private property. In *De Doctrina Christiana*, however, Milton stressed the importance of the primary or unwritten law of nature that was "given originally to Adam, and of which a certain remnant, or imperfect illumination, still dwells in the hearts of all mankind; which, in the regenerate, under the influence of the Holy Spirit, is daily tending towards a renewal of its primitive brightness." This law teaches whatever is intrinsically good and agreeable to right reason, and in making it the final authority, Milton gave his ethic a religious orientation.

Thus, Milton's ethical position was that of the Christian humanist. Grace, he believed, comes to perfect nature, not to destroy it; by means of grace reason is illuminated and natural virtue sanctified. In this emphasis he resembled the Cambridge Platonists, writers like Benjamin Whichcote, John Smith, and Nathanael Culverwel, who sought to unify man's natural and religious experience by insisting that reason is "the candle of the Lord." Milton also resembled these philosophers in his habit of drawing upon Platonic writings, particularly on Plato's myths, in order to enrich his treatment of reason and the passions. Although his stress on the Bible prevented classical philosophy from making a direct contribution to his theology, Platonism nonetheless played a major and continuous part in shaping his ethical idealism.

The influence of Puritanism, as well as of humanism, led Milton to stress the importance of liberty. Believers are a "royal priesthood," and those who force the conscience of the individual are guilty of forcing the spirit of God. Central to Milton's conception of Christian liberty is the distinction between the Mosaic law, a law of bondage that extorts servile obedience through fear, and the Gospel, which offers a free, elective, and spiritual service based on man's filial relation to God. Spiritual regeneration, moreover, brings about a renewal of man's natural powers; the understanding is restored in large measure to its primitive clearness, the will to its primitive liberty. This strong emphasis on inner law led Milton to the antinomian view that Christ, by his life and death, abrogated the whole Mosaic law, the moral parts as well as the judicial and ceremonial parts. The sum of the law—love God and love your neighbor—remains and must be fulfilled by following the spirit, or the "internal scripture" (*De Doctrina Christiana*, I, xxvii). At this point, in spite of a continuing emphasis on reason, Milton had moved toward a position similar to the Quaker doctrine of inner light.

CHURCH AND STATE

Despite his early support of Presbyterianism, Milton soon came to believe that "*New Presbyter* is but *Old Priest* writ large." He defended the growth of religious sects on the ground that God requires unity of spirit rather than unity of doctrine, and he denied both the claim of the church to exercise secular power and that of the state to wield ecclesiastical power. His final view was that a particular church is a purely voluntary association of believers. Ministers should be elected by their congregations and supported by free offerings, and no ceremonial observances, such as the Sabbath, should be made obligatory. Despite his separation of the powers of church and state, however, Milton could not follow his more radical contemporaries in divorcing civil good from the good of religion. Although he denied the magistrate "compulsive" powers in matters of religion, he left him the "defensive" function of protecting Protestant Christianity from the threat of open "popery and idolatry."

Milton's view of the state varied in accordance with the changing conditions in which he was called upon to defend the revolutionary party. A basic line of his argument founds the state upon a social contract. Men are born free, but the effects of the Fall cause them to agree to a common league to bind one another from mutual injury. The people are thus the sovereign power in the state and have the right to revoke the power that they

have delegated. When it became apparent that the Puritan party represented a small part of the nation, Milton resorted to a further argument that was not entirely consistent with the social contract theory. The revolutionary party, he maintained, was guided by providence and consisted of those most worthy to rule and to interpret the good of the people. The minority must force the majority to be free.

POETRY

The themes and preoccupations of Milton's prose gain in power when expressed in the "more simple, sensuous, and passionate" language of poetry. All the major poems center on the theme of temptation and move toward a clarification of true heroism. Temptation works through passion, in its simplest form through sensuality and anger but more subtly through specious reasoning and the lure of evil means to good ends. The definition of true heroism involves the exposure of such false forms as the romantic sensuality of Comus in the early "Masque" (1634) or Satan's courage of despair in the late epics. *Paradise Lost,* which was written to justify God's ways to man by dramatizing man's freedom and responsibility, ends with Adam setting out to imitate the spiritual heroism of the Son of God—revealed to him in a vision—and thus to achieve a "paradise within" that will be "happier far" than the outward paradise he has lost. Samson, in *Samson Agonistes,* also achieves a victory over himself through suffering and discovers that freedom is enjoyed only in the service of God. *Paradise Regained,* which has as its subject the temptation of Jesus in the wilderness, presents Milton's final and most complete study of heroism. Avoiding the temptations to distrust and presumption, the Son rejects Satan's offers of worldly power and authority and realizes the spiritual sense in which he is Messiah.

ARTS AND SCIENCES

In his literary theory Milton emphasized the importance of genres and of decorum and urged the power of literature to create moral order in the individual and the society. (See his preface to Book II of *The Reason of Church Government,* the preface to *Samson Agonistes,* and the invocations to Books I, III, and IX of *Paradise Lost.*) His view of education (*Of Education*) was humanistic in its stress on languages and classical texts, its dislike of scholasticism, and its ethical aim. He showed no deep interest in the new science, and he used the traditional science in his poetry because it was for him a better source of metaphor. As a historian he had a critical sense of the value of evidence, but his view of history moved from millenarian optimism to the pessimism that informs the survey of history in the last two books of *Paradise Lost.*

See also Arius and Arianism; Culverwel, Nathanael; Determinism and Freedom; Galileo Galilei; Humanism; Liberty; Plato; Platonism and the Platonic Tradition; Smith, John; Socinianism; Whichcote, Benjamin.

Bibliography

WORKS BY MILTON

The definitive edition of the text is *The Works of John Milton,* edited by Frank Allen Patterson et al., 18 vols. (New York: Columbia University Press, 1931–1938), with an index, 2 vols. (New York, 1940). A supplement to the Patterson edition, *A Variorum Commentary on the Poems of John Milton,* with Merritt Y. Hughes as the general editor, was also published by Columbia University Press (New York, 1970).

There are editions of the poetry and selected prose by Frank Allen Patterson, *The Student's Milton* (New York: F. S. Crofts, 1930; rev. ed., 1933); Merritt Y. Hughes, *Complete Poems and Major Prose* (New York: Odyssey Press, 1957); and others. Editions of the poetry include those by James Holly Hanford, *Poems* (New York, 1937; 2nd ed., 1953); Harris Francis Fletcher, *Complete Poetical Works* (Boston, 1941); and Helen Darbishire, *Poetical Works,* 2 vols. (Oxford, 1952–1955).

Scholarly introductions provide continuous commentary on the prose in the closely annotated *Complete Prose Works,* edited by Donald M. Wolfe et al. (New Haven, CT: Yale University Press, 1953–1982), 8 volumes.

WORKS ON MILTON

General Criticism

Douglas Bush provides a penetrating review of Milton's life and works in *English Literature in the Earlier Seventeenth Century* (Oxford: Clarendon Press, 1945; rev. ed., 1962); a survey of the scholarship is found in James Holly Hanford, *A Milton Handbook,* 4th ed. (New York: F. S. Crofts, 1946). The standard biography is still David Masson's *The Life of John Milton,* 6 vols. (London: Macmillan, 1859–1880; rev. ed., with index, 1881–1896).

Milton's Thought

Pioneer work is found in Denis Saurat's stimulating if erratic *Milton: Man and Thinker* (London: Dent, 1925; rev. ed., 1944) and in the more literary *Milton* (London, 1930) by E. M. W. Tillyard. G. N. Conklin considers theological method in *Biblical Criticism and Heresy in Milton* (New York: King's Crown Press, 1949), and the growth and significance of Milton's theology are examined authoritatively by Maurice W. Kelley in *This Great Argument* (Princeton, NJ: Princeton University Press, 1941). On Milton's political and ethical views, see A. S. P. Woodhouse, "Milton, Puritanism and Liberty," in *University of Toronto Quarterly* 4 (1934–1935): 483–513; William Haller, *The Rise of Puritanism* (New York: Columbia University Press, 1938) and *Liberty and Reformation in the Puritan Revolution* (New York: Columbia

University Press, 1955); Arthur Barker, *Milton and the Puritan Dilemma, 1641–1660* (Toronto: University of Toronto Press, 1942; reprinted, 1955); Michael Fixler, *Milton and the Kingdoms of God* (London: Faber and Faber, 1964); Ernest Sirluck, "Milton's Political Thought: The First Cycle," in *Modern Philology* 61 (1964): 209–224.

Other aspects of Milton's thought are covered in Kester Svendsen, *Milton and Science* (Cambridge, MA: Harvard University Press, 1956); Howard Schultz, *Milton and Forbidden Knowledge* (New York: Modern Language Association of America, 1955); Walter C. Curry, *Milton's Ontology, Cosmogony and Physics* (Lexington: University of Kentucky Press, 1957); and Irene Samuel, *Plato and Milton* (Ithaca, NY: Cornell University Press, 1947). Further criticism is listed in a selective bibliography by Douglas Bush, op. cit.; in the bibliographies by David H. Stevens, *A Reference Guide to Milton, from 1800 to the Present Day* (Chicago: University of Chicago Press, 1930); Harris Francis Fletcher, *Contributions to a Milton Bibliography, 1800–1930* (Urbana: University of Illinois, 1931); and Calvin Huckabay, *John Milton: A Bibliographical Supplement, 1929–1957* (Pittsburgh: Duquesne University Press, 1960); and the annual bibliographies of *Studies in Philology* and *PMLA*.

H. R. MacCallum (1967)

MIMESIS

Mimesis has been a cardinal concept for those traditions of aesthetics, from antiquity to the present, that focus on the status and value of artistic representation. The semantics of the Greek term *mimēsis* cover much more than simple imitation; its senses include resemblance, dramatic impersonation, and other species of correspondence or likeness. The idea of mimesis came to designate the relationship between certain art forms (poetry, dance, music, painting/sculpture) and the aspects of reality they are capable of depicting or evoking. Although some strands of mimeticist thinking appeal to standards of verisimilitude and mirroring, it is mistaken to reduce all models of mimesis to a single canon of realism.

Plato's highly influential approach to mimesis is less straightforward than usually claimed. From *Cratylus* to *Laws*, he applies the language of mimesis to numerous relationships of ontological and/or semantic dependence (even, in *Timaeus*, e.g., 39e, the whole material universe's dependence on a divine prototype). Mimetic entities match, but never reproduce, their exemplars; the relationship can be construed as "qualitative," not "mathematical" (*Cratylus* 432). In representational art, moreover, those exemplars may be (partially) imaginative/fictive: witness, for example, the idealized painting that furnishes a metaphor for philosophy at *Republic* 472d. When, in *Republic* 10, Socrates notoriously critiques the mirror-like limitations of mimetic poetry and painting, locating artistic images at two removes from "the truth," his argument does not convict all mimesis of worthlessness but provocatively challenges lovers of art to identify a moral justification that transcends pleasure at merely simulated appearances (and the emotions they can excite). As *Sophist* 235d–6c, distinguishing *eikastic* (objective) from *phantastic* (viewer-dependent) mimesis, shows, Plato does not ascribe a uniform rationale to all artistic representation. At a psychological and cultural level, arguments such as *Republic* 392c–401a suggest that the impact of mimesis necessarily reflects the qualities of the supposed reality it projects.

Aristotle explicitly accepts that the contents of mimetic art, both musicopoetic and visual, can legitimately vary between the actual, the putative, and the ideal (*Poetics* 25). Regarding mimesis as an instinctual factor in the human need to model and understand the world, he embeds it in an anthropology of cognition that stretches from children's play to philosophy (*Poetics* 4). He also appreciates the powerful emotional effects of mimetic works on their audiences, a point equally illustrated by the *Poetics* and by the treatment of music as mimetic (i.e., affectively expressive) in *Politics* 8.5; for him, the passions, when well induced, are a medium of ethical judgment. Furthermore, Aristotle has a dual-aspect conception of mimesis that allows him to distinguish—more than Plato had done—between internal (work-centered) and external (truth-related) criteria of mimetic value. The resulting aesthetics is, importantly, neither formalist nor moralist.

Hellenistic and later Greek philosophers continued to grapple with epistemological and ethical issues raised by mimesis. Especially notable is Neoplatonism's ambivalent engagement with the concept; Plotinus, for instance, who discerned mimetic relationships hierarchically structuring all reality, disparaged much actual art yet allowed some artistic mimesis, *qua* creative intuition, to grasp the authentic forms of nature (*Enneads* 5.8.1). The legacy of this and other ancient versions of mimesis was revived in the Renaissance; it has remained a vital element in debates about the complex position of representational art between the poles of truth and fiction, realism, and imagination.

See also Art, Representation in.

Bibliography

Halliwell, Stephen. *The Aesthetics of Mimesis: Ancient Texts and Modern Problems*. Princeton, NJ: Princeton University Press, 2002.

Janaway, Christopher. *Images of Excellence: Plato's Critique of the Arts*. Oxford: Clarendon Press, 1995.

Sörbom, G. *Mimesis and Art*. Stockholm: Svenska Bokförlaget, 1966.

Stephen Halliwell (2005)

MINAGAWA KIEN
(1734–1807)

Minagawa Kien, a Japanese Confucianist, painter, and writer, was born in Kyoto. At the age of twenty-eight, having established himself as a Confucianist, he became the official scholar for Lord Matsudaira Nobumine. His literary skill made him an outstanding figure in Kyoto circles; he had a following of three thousand. For a Confucianist his life was unusually dissipated. His era was a time of moral decline, but this was eventually checked by several edicts. The 1790 edict against "heterodox doctrines" affected Minagawa and he reformed his habits, though his ideas did not change.

Minagawa's philosophical reputation has recently grown among Japanese philosophers because of his positivist approach to Confucian studies. He is considered an eclectic because he upheld neither the official Zhu Xi school of Neo-Confucianism nor the rival Wang Yangming school. Minagawa was analytic and positivist, which made him a kind of forerunner of Western philosophy in Japan. This assessment stems largely from two of Minagawa's works, *Ekigaku kaibutsu* (The learning of the book of changes on the discovery of things) and *Meichū rokkan* (Six chapters on categories).

Ekigaku kaibutsu starts from the Chinese classic *I Ching,* the "Book of Changes" or "Book of Divination," which despite its esoteric nature stimulated Minagawa and other Confucianists to make a study of celestial phenomena. *Ekigaku kaibutsu* clearly manifests his lifetime search for the nature of things. However, for him "things" are mainly human affairs seen from the ethicopolitical point of view, and their "discovery" or investigation is in relation to the ruling of the realm.

Meichū rokkan analyzes the origins of basic concepts or categories. Starting with words, Minagawa shows that they are abstract expressions of reality itself. He believes that we grasp reality objectively through its manifestation in words. This rather naive realist epistemology is an attempt to penetrate the nature of things without employing *ri*, Zhu Xi's abstract "principle," or the "innate knowledge" of Wang Yangming. Among Minagawa's categories, significant ones are learning or science (*gaku*) and

wisdom (*tetsu*). Although he did not wholly grasp modern science or philosophy, he came very close.

Another topic of interest to Minagawa is the samurai class, which he criticizes in many of his writings. He hoped the samurai would survive as the intellectual and moral leaders of the ordinary people.

See also Chinese Philosophy; Japanese Philosophy; Positivism; Wang Yangming; Wisdom; Zhu Xi (Chu Hsi).

Bibliography

For Minagawa's works see *Nihon Tetsugaku Shisō Zensho* (Library of Japanese philosophical thought), edited by Saigusa Hiroto (Tokyo, 1957), Vol. I, pp. 109–119, and Saigusa Hiroto, *Nihon Yuibutsuronsha* (Japanese materialists; Tokyo, 1956), pp. 95–107.

Gino K. Piovesana, S.J. (1967)

MIND

See *Idealism; Mind-Body Problem; Other Minds; Personal Identity; Psychology; Reason; Thinking*

MIND AND MENTAL STATES IN BUDDHIST PHILOSOPHY

A fundamental idea of all nonmaterialist Indian schools of philosophy, whether orthodox ones that follow the Vedas or heterodox ones such as Buddhist and Jaina that do not, is the cultivation of mind and mental states. Techniques of *yoga* in Hindu tradition aim at attaining a conscious state in which ordinary mental activities, such as perception and imagination, are suspended. Classical yoga, as expounded by Patanjali's *Yogasutra* (Woods, 1927), is widely influential in the Hindu tradition.

ORTHODOX AND HETERODOX SCHOOLS

In Buddhism, *citta, mano,* and *vinnana* are three of the main terms to do with mind and mental states. These terms are highly nuanced but are roughly translatable as heart, mind, and consciousness, respectively. These are best understood as processes, not substances, and none are permanent. The *Majjhima Nikaya* (Middle length sayings), *Digha Nikaya* (Long discourses), *Samyutta Nikaya* (Kindred sayings), and *Anguttara Nikaya* (Gradual sayings) are the basic four collections of *suttas* (discourses) expounding the early Buddhist position, and *Vissudhimagga* (The path of purity) is a salient text.

Indian schools of philosophy include three heterodox (*nastika*) schools, which do not accept the Vedas as divine revelation. These three schools (Carvaka, Jainism, and Buddhism), each in their different ways, put more emphasis upon experience than revelation. The three schools represent a continuum on metaphysical matters from most materialistic (Carvaka) to least materialistic (Buddhism). Jainism at midpoint asserts a material, adhesive soul that gets darkened with negative karmic particles due to wrong actions such that many *jivas* (souls) cannot retain their natural luminosity.

According to ancient Indian materialism (Carvaka school), perception is the basic *pramana* (valid means of knowing), and accordingly, matter is the only reality because it alone is perceived. Here the soul is understood as a living body with the quality of consciousness. But how could materialists show that consciousness does not exist independently of body? Orthodox schools as well as the other two heterodox schools, Jainism and Buddhism, found materialistic reductionism of the mental to the physical unconvincing.

JAINISM. Jainism is especially well known for two doctrines: the view that all judgments of non-omniscient beings need to be qualified—that is, the "somehow view" (*syadvada*); and non-injury to sentient beings—that this, the nonviolence view (*ahimsa*). According to Jainism, consciousness is the essence of the *jiva*, and human consciousness is limited so that ordinary judgments of nonomniscient beings must be qualified by *syat* (somehow) to express conditional knowing. Only one of the *Tirthankaras*, that is, those who cross over to liberation, have omniscience in regard to salvific knowledge. In Jainism the *jiva* is self-luminous and illuminates other things, filling out the body like a radiant, eternal light within it. Jains believe that the *jiva* can attain complete freedom (*kaivalya*). When the *jiva* is in a state of ignorance or bondage, it is because its vision is obscured due to karmic particles adhering to it. So, although Jainism has a spiritual, ethical outlook that aspires to personal self-transformation, its metaphysics of the soul holds that the soul is material, of the shape of the body, and is afflicted by karmic particles. When these are thrown out of the *jiva* due to penance or good works, the *jiva* can see clearly. Harming living beings is one thing that causes karmic particles to cloud the soul's vision. In ethics, Jains think that the passions impeding liberation are anger, pride,

infatuation, and greed. These sorts of passions bind the *jiva* to matter. Since there is consciousness in all parts of the body, the soul is coextensive with the body. Potentially, all souls are equal since all have the capacity for liberation (*kaivalya*).

BUDDHISM. Another of the heterodox schools, Buddhism, holds that right concentration of mind through four stages is the way to *nirvana* (enlightenment). The first stage is on reasoning and investigation regarding the truths; here there is the joy of pure thinking. The second stage of concentration is unruffled meditation, freedom from reasoning, and the arising of the joy of tranquillity. The third stage of concentration is detachment from even the joy of tranquillity; here there is indifference even to such joy and a feeling of bodily ease. The fourth stage of concentration is detachment from this bodily ease: At the fourth *jhana* (level of consciousness in meditation), there is perfect equanimity and the attainment of nirvana. At this level the psychic powers (*abhinna*) are said to develop. Overall, *sila, samadhi,* and *panna* (morality, concentration, and wisdom, respectively) form the essentials of the eight-fold noble path in Buddhism (right view, right intention, right speech, right action, right livelihood, right minfullness, right effort, right contemplation, right concentration). In Buddhism there is no permanent substance (*svabhava*) either in humankind or in deities, for experience shows that all things are impermanent, nonsubstantial, and unsatisfactory. The doctrine of *anatman* (no self, or nonsubstantiality) implies that there is no substance of a permanent, blissful, center of consciousness anywhere in the universe.

The doctrinal context of *jhana* is four noble truths: suffering, its arising, passing away, and the path to its passing away. The cessation of suffering occurs through meditation. The *jhanas* were instrumental in Buddha's enlightenment in that *jhanas* prepare one for higher insights (*abhinna*), are associated with liberating wisdom (*panna*), and are the spiritual endowment of the fully liberated person (*tathagata*). *Jhanas* have their own internal dynamic, contributing to purification and liberation of mind. In developing *jhanic* insight, one focuses on experience, eliminates ignorance, and achieves wisdom. There are really two systems: tranquillity and insight. The development of serenity or tranquillity meditation (*samatha bhavana*) is one system; the other is the development of insight meditation (*vipassana bhavana*) is the other. The former is also called development of concentration (*samadhi bhavana*); the latter is also called the development of wisdom meditation (*panna bhavana*). The practice of serenity meditation aims at developing a calm, concentrated, unified state of consciousness to experience peace and wisdom. Insight meditation requires development of *samadhi*, and serenity is useful for this too, so the two systems work together. *Jhana* belongs inherently to the serenity side. Translation of *jhana* is difficult, with absorption coming closest. *Jhanas* involve total absorption in the object.

CONCEPTUAL STRUCTURES IN BUDDHISM

ORALITY AND MENTALITY. Oral tradition and group recitation of sutras marked the very beginnings of Buddhism of the Pali Nikayas (collections of *suttas* in different texts, e.g., *Majjhima Nikaya*). Despite the strong tradition of text, commentary, and subcommentary, Buddhism initially developed from oral tradition, as did Hinduism. In contrast with the European and North American preoccupation with journal articles and books as vehicles for intellectual debate, the power of the spoken word remains very much a part of Buddhism. This power of the spoken word can be seen, for example, in the Indo-Tibetan tradition of debate and the Sino-Japanese *kung-an* and *koan* traditions of perspectival shifts while becoming one with the *koan*.

It is clear is that Buddhism did not begin with manuscripts. It is not a religion as in the monotheistic (Judeo–Christian–Islamic) tradition but developed out of a forest tradition of meditation in which monks stayed in orchards, deer parks, mango groves, and forests, periodically reciting the words of the Buddha aloud in group recitation. Eventually, councils and canons of texts emerged. It was not so at first, and it is reasonable to believe that the authority of individual experience is at the heart of early Buddhism rather than hierarchy and the authority of promulgated texts.

MIRACLES OF INSTRUCTION, CONVERSION, AND MINDFULNESS. An unrepeatable event, violation of law of nature, and any extraordinary event are senses of *miracle* ordinarily recognized in Anglo-American philosophy of religion as a starting point for discussion. In Buddhism, the miracle of instruction is the starting point. Traditionally, one has to come and sit down by the side of the teacher. Texts show that *dhamma* (truth, doctrine) teaching sometimes includes a miracle, where conversion occurs and miracle becomes part of the experience of a Buddhist practitioner.

Oral recitation makes of oneself a holy scripture as the embodiment of truth: Truth is not so much a property of abstract disembodied proposition as it is embod-

ied in the lives of those who practice Buddhism. Belief in the Buddha, the doctrine, and the Sangha (order of monks and nuns) is the recited *three refuges* formula for being Buddhist. Both confidence and knowledge are operative in Buddhism, both *belief in* and *belief that*. Buddhism did not emphasize authority of the guru or pundit but the authority of one's own experience, so there is no *blind faith*.

The baseless faith of the Brahmins is contrasted with the rational faith of the Buddhists. Brahmins are depicted as a string of blind people, each relying on the other but none of them seeing things as they really are. Buddhism is, by contrast, self-reliance, with several stages of confidence or faith. There is initial faith in coming to hear whether there is anything in the Buddhist doctrine, then there is path faith that is compatible with doubt and struggle, and then there is the achievement of a realized nonbacksliding faith; realized faith is the wisdom of knowing and seeing for oneself as things really are.

MIND AND MORALITY. By mind all things are made, all things are made by mind: Thus begins the *Dhammapada* (The path of purity), a popular Buddhist text. Morality is intimately connected with mentality on the Buddhist view, and intention is far more important than consequences in assessing *sila*, or morality. It would go too far to say that consequences are totally irrelevant to Buddhists: Following the first precept of harmlessness shows a concern with outcomes as well.

Buddhism defies categorization in Aristotelean, Utilitarian, and Kantian categories, not because of this conceptual confusion but because of its distinctive voice. Buddhism is most importantly about wisdom, not knowledge alone, and it is also about compassion, which is one of the ways to enlightenment. Although Mahayana Buddhism emphasized altruism and Theravada Buddhism had comparatively little to say about kindness and compassion, it is clear that there are Pali Canon texts that commend kindness, and value it as a means of attaining nirvana (Gombrich 1998). *Metta*, *karuna*, and *mudita* (loving kindness, compassion, and sympathy) are valued, ethically related mental states in even the earliest stratum of Buddhism, just as *priti* (joy) is a characteristic of Buddhist monks.

MEDITATION AND CONFIRMATION OF PRE-EXISTING BELIEFS. There is an epistemological basis for belief in propositions concerning *kamma* and *punabb-hava* (rebirth; literally, "again becoming"). This emphasis on one's own experience extends even to epistemology, where the *pramana* (valid means of knowing) of experience and, to a limited extent, inference based on experience, are emphasized instead of testimony, comparison, and divine revelation. The epistemological basis of belief in karma and rebirth is said in the texts and by modernist interpreters such as K. N. Jayatilleke (1963), K. N. Upadhyaya (1998), and D. J. Kalupahana (1992), to rest on meditational experience at the fourth *jhana*.

Some in Buddhism hold that knowing and seeing rebirth provides *empirical justification* for belief in karma and rebirth. These same thinkers believe that Buddhism has no metaphysics. However, first, it is dubious that memory, bodily continuity, or self-awareness will work as meaning conditions for the reidentification of the same person across lives. Second, metaphysics is not the same as speculation, and Buddhism can be antispeculative and still have metaphysical commitments to beliefs such as rebirth.

It is tempting to think of Buddhism as empiricism since it is described in the Pali texts as a *come and see* (*ehipassika*) doctrine, but while its claims may, in a weak sense, be experientially verifiable if true, they are not falsifiable if false. Hence they are not verifiable in a sufficiently robust sense to distinguish Buddhism from other path faiths and to count as *empirical verification*. What is at work, instead, is *experiential confirmation*. In addition, the mind and senses are not separated in Buddhism but are together the *six gateways* to knowledge so that there is no sharp cleavage between empiricism and rationalism, as there is in European and North American thought. All that can be had in Buddhism is experiential confirmation, as in the cases of other worldviews, such as that of Christianity. Psychological certainty is not identical to logical certainty. Experiential justification may be entirely convincing on a personal basis yet fall short of the objectivity involved in establishing the truth of observation, sentences that are testable and repeatable at will.

CONTINUITY, PERSONAL IDENTITY, AND NAMA-RUPA. The strength of a cord does not always depend on something running end to end, as in Buddhism where there is continuity of process but no speculative belief about a permanent substance underlying it all. In Buddhism, *vinnana* (consciousness) develops (rather than descends) in the womb in the rebirth process across lives. There is no one term that provides a link between lives in early Buddhism. Perhaps *sankhara* (dispositions) comes closest.

A view that superficially looks like the Buddhist one is Hume's *phenomenalist* view of the self. Here, the self is a bundle of perceptions. Hume famously says that all perceptions are distinct existences and that the mind never recognizes any necessary connections between these perceptions. However, one does not find exactly this view in Buddhism. Hume had a problem with combining the two assumptions about distinct existence of perceptions and no necessary connections, but early Buddhism's problem is not Hume's problem: To ask what keeps the perceptions of a person together in early Buddhism is to make what from an early Buddhist view is the unwarranted assumption of the distinct existence of perceptions.

Namarupa may be understood as that which appears (appearance or phenomenon) in its interrelationship with *nama*, or that which one uses to get a handle on an appearance (the concept). So *namarupa* is the reality formed by the unity of concept and phenomenon; it is conceptualized reality or the process of ordinary experiencing. Inadequate are "mind and body" or "name and form" as translations (Ross Rheat, in Potter: 1996 VII 45). It is evident that *namarupa* provides no evidence for substantialist mind-body dualism in early Buddhism. As Surendranath Dasgupta rightly observes (1922), matter and mind dualism and opposition are absent from Buddhism, Upanishads, and Samkhya schools of philosophy. Overall, Buddhism—which differs from Hume on the point of distinct existences—on the issue of *self*, is closer to Process philosophy than to either Humean empiricism or Cartesian rationalist dualism.

"LIFE AFTER DEATH": ETERNAL LIFE AND ENDLESS LIFE. In macro view the *punabbhava* rebirth realms, that is, humans, gods, animals, hungry ghosts, purgatory beings, and titans, may be viewed ontologically or psychologically. Viewed ontologically, in the Buddhist metaphysical view of the process of rebirth, the ordinary case is that one is reborn. There is also the extraordinary case of the *Tathagata* (the *thus gone* liberated one, e.g., Buddha Sakyamuni) who passes away in *parinibbana* (final enlightenment) having achieved *nibbana* (enlightenment) in this very life. Yet, no early Buddhist text gives a theory about what, if anything, happens after death in the case of the *Tathagata*. Afterlife views are regarded as speculative and discussing them not conducive to enlightenment. The antispeculative emphasis informs the Ten Speculative Questions (speculative questions that the Buddha would not commit to answering because they involve knowledge claims that go beyond experience) set aside by Buddha. The deathless (*amata*) may be viewed simply as the elimination of obsession, hate, and confusion in everyday life of the Buddhist practitioner.

Heaven (*devaloka*), the world of the gods, is simply another rebirth station. What is translated, *devaloka* is neither a permanent resting place nor a monotheist's beatific vision. From it some *devas* (the shining ones) may be reborn elsewhere, including as humans, before attaining final liberation.

The Buddhist goal is stopping the wheel of birth and death rather than attaining endless life. The emphasis is on attaining eternal life in the here and now by purifying ones heart and living well. In this conceptual scheme in which impermanence, nonsubstantiality, and suffering play key roles, the idea of striving after an immortality viewed as endless life would be not simply be unattainable but logically incoherent.

Accordingly, terms for mind and mental states in Buddhism are not terms for a permanent stuff or substance that is independent of conditions. Saying so does not deny continuity across lives. There is continuity without self-same substance. There is a stream of consciousness depending for its continuance on union of male and female, proper timing, and presence of *gandhabba* (cupid). Without these three conditions, there is no rebirth.

NIRVĀṆA. That Buddhist rebirth is not Hindu transmigration is evident from the anatta doctrine of Buddhism juxtaposed with the atman doctrine of Hinduism. At the level of meditation, there is considerable overlap of technique; however, such that an attempt to forge a complete disjunct between these two traditions will distort both history and practice. Buddha was born a Hindu and is considered by Hindus as an avatara of Vishnu. For polemical and practical purposes of building a Sangha, Buddhist texts routinely depict Buddhists triumphing over Jains and Brahmins in debate. So there is a distinctive Buddhist mentality such that Buddhism will never be rightly described as assimilable to Hinduism without remainder.

Early Buddhist texts are not perfectly consistent in the use of terms for the state of consciousness called enlightenment or being awake. However, a frequent finding is that *nibbana* (enlightenment) while alive is distinguished from *parinibbana* (final enlightenment) after death of a *Tathagata*. This distinction is subject to a range of textual emphases and resultant interpretations. The simplest, most clear way to draw the distinction is to say that enlightenment in life is the destruction of *raga, dosa,* and *moha* (obsession, hate, and confusion) in everyday life; that final enlightenment is death of one who has already been enlightened in life.

That dying is, but death is not, an experience in life is itself a conceptual truth. Hence, it is not logically possible to experience death and describe it, and there are no mental states to be ascribed to *the Tathagata after death*. Asked whether the Tathagata exists, does not exist, both, or neither, Buddha refused to assent to any of these. Buddha's silence shows that the matter of final enlightenment (*parinibbana*) is beyond experience.

See also Aristotle; Ayer, Alfred Jules; Brahman; Buddhist Epistemology; Cartesianism; Hume, David; Kant, Immanuel; Knowledge in Indian Philosophy; Liberation in Indian Philosophy; Meditation in Indian Philosophy; Mysticism, the Indian Tradition; Negation in Indian Philosophy; Philosophy of Language in India; Self in Indian Philosophy; Truth and Falsity in Indian Philosophy; Utilitarianism.

Bibliography

Carter, John Ross, trans. *The Dhammapada*. New York: Oxford University Press, 2000

Collins, Steven. *Selfless Persons: Imagery and Thought in Theravada Buddhism*. New York: Cambridge University Press, 1990.

Dasgupta, Surendranath. *A History of Indian Philosophy*. Vol. I. Cambridge, U.K.: Cambridge University Press, 1922. p. 95.

Gombrich, R. F. *Kindness and Compassion as Means to Nirvana*. Amsterdam: Royal Netherlands Academy of Arts and Sciences, 1998.

Griffiths, Paul J. *On Being Buddha: The Classical Doctrine of Buddhahood*. Albany: State University of New York Press, 1994.

Griffiths, Paul J. *On Being Mindless: Buddhist Meditation and the Mind-Body Problem*. Delhi: Sri Satguru, 1999.

Gunaratna, Henapola. *Path of Serenity and Insight*. Delhi: Motilal Banarsidass, 1985.

Hamilton, Sue. *Early Buddhism: A New Approach: The I of the Beholder*. Surrey, U.K.: Curzon Richmond, 2000.

Herman, Arthur L. *The Problem of Evil and Indian Thought*. Delhi: Motilal Banarsidass, 1976.

Hoffman, Frank J. *Rationality and Mind in Early Buddhism*. Delhi: Motilal Banarsidass, 1987.

Hoffman, Frank J., and Mahinda Deegalle, eds. *Pali Buddhism*. Richmond, U.K.: Curzon Press, 1996.

Hoffman, Frank J., and Godabarisha Mishra, eds. *Breaking Barriers: Essays in Asian and Comparative Philosophy in Honor of Ramakrishna Puligandla*. Fremont CA: Asian Humanities Press, 2003.

Horner, I. B. *Women in Primitive Buddhism: Laywomen and Alms Women*. Delhi: Motilal Banarsidas, 1999.

Jayatilleke, K. N. *Early Buddhist Theory of Knowledge*. London: Allen & Unwin, 1963.

Kalupahana, David J. *History of Buddhist Philosophy*. Honolulu: University of Hawaii Press, 1992.

Lamotte, Etienne. *History of Indian Buddhism: From the Origins to the Saka Era*. Translated from the French by Sara

Webb-Boin under the supervision of Jean Dantinne. Louvaine-la-Neuve: Universite Catholique de Louvain Institut Orientaliste, 1988.

Matilal, B. K. *Logic, Language, and Reality: Indian Philosophy and Contemporary Issues.* Delhi: Motilal Banarsidass, 1999.

Mohanty, J. N. *Classical Indian Philosophy.* Lanham: Rowman & Littlefield, 2000.

Potter, Karl, ed. *Encyclopedia of Indian Philosophy.* Vol. VII. Delhi: Motilal Banarsidass, 1996.

Puligandla, Ramakrishna. *An Encounter with Awareness.* Wheaton, IL: Theosophical Publishing House, 1981.

Smart, Ninian. *Doctrine and Argument in Indian Philosophy.* London: Allen & Unwin, 1964.

Upadhyaya, K. N. *Early Buddhism and the Bhagavad-Gita.* Delhi: Motilal Banarsidass,1998.

Warder, Anthony Kennedy. *Indian Buddhism.* Delhi: Motilal Banarsidass, 2000.

Frank J. Hoffman (2005)

MIND-BODY PROBLEM

In Genesis 3:19, God tells Adam, "dust thou art, and unto dust thou shalt return," reminding Adam that he was fashioned from the dust of the earth. Modern science tells us that the earth was formed from the dust of the sun and that we are composed of materials formed from star dust. We are, however, also possessed of mind: We can think, feel, and exercise our will—as did Eve when she ate the forbidden fruit of the tree of knowledge of good and evil. The ancient mind-body problem is how the mind or soul or spirit is united with the body. It has now been known for several centuries that our minds are related to our bodies via their relation to a certain bodily organ, the brain. The ancient problem led to the mind-brain problem: How are our minds related to our brains? Are they one thing or two? And if two, how are the two united? But the fundamental problem is: What is the place of mental phenomena in nature?

The doctrine that the soul is distinct from the body, existing prior to it and after bodily death, is found in the writings of Plato. (In the *Phaedo*, one argument of Socrates for immortality is that the soul is not made of parts, and so cannot come apart.) The Platonic idea of a soul independent of the body was embraced by Augustine of Hippo, a major figure in the development of the Christian doctrine of an immaterial, immortal soul. But as to how soul and body are united, Augustine could only marvel: "The manner in which spirits are united to bodies is altogether wonderful and transcends the understanding of men" (*On the City of God*, XXI, 10 Haldane 1994, p. 335).

René Descartes tried to lay the foundation for a science of nature according to which all bodies are located in a physical realm—a substance, *res extensa*, which pervades all of space— and all interactions among them are governed by mechanistic laws. But mind (*res cogitans*), he argued, lacks spatial extension (and even location at a spatial point) and so is not subject to the mechanistic laws of the physical realm, thus leaving the will free. Minds, moreover, are substances and so capable of existence independently of physical substance; thus, immortality of the mind is possible. Descartes argued that it is certain that he is his mind since doubt itself requires a doubter and thus a thinking subject, an *I*. And he argued that he is not his body since he can clearly and distinctly conceive of his existing without a body and that it is thus possible for him to exist disembodied.

He nevertheless also acknowledged in *Meditations on First Philosophy* (1641): "there is nothing nature teaches me more expressly, or more sensibly than that I have a body, which is ill disposed when I feel pain, which needs to eat and drink when I have feelings of hunger and thirst, etc. … I am joined to it very closely and indeed so compounded and intermingled with my body, that I form, as it were, a single whole with it" (Cottingham et. al. 1985, p. 59). On his view, what unites body and mind is causation, from body to mind (as in perception), and from mind to body (as in action), with the pineal gland in the brain being the primary locus of such interaction. In correspondence with Descartes, Princess Elisabeth of Bohemia pressed the issue of how states of, or changes in, a substance not in space could causally affect states of, or changes in, something in space, and declared such causal interaction too incredible to believe. Descartes was never able to provide a satisfactory answer to her how-question, and in a candid moment remarked: "It does not seem to me that the human mind is capable of conceiving quite distinctly and at the same time both the distinction between mind and body, and their union" (Kenny 1970, p. 142).

Nicholas Malebranche denied mind-body causal interaction, maintaining that God is the only causal agent (Nadler 1999). Were a certain a type of brain state *B* and mental state *M* to co-occur, then that would be because God, who is continually engaged in acts of creation of the world, only causes an instance of one of them when he causes an instance of the other; *B* and *M* would thus co-occur are a result of being dual-effects of God's acts of creation. This brand of *parallelism* is called *occasionalism*. Of course, if God is without spatial extension or location, then Elisabeth's how-question will recur for God's causal interaction with the physical world. But it was thought that how-questions come to an end where the ways of God are concerned. Gottlieb Leibniz held a version of parallelism, *preestablished harmony*, according to which there is no causal interaction among substances, any regularities among them being the result of God's having actualized a world in which those regularities hold. And he held a kind of *idealism*, according to which all substances are monads, which have only states of perception and appetite (Sleigh 1999). Benedict (Baruch) Spinoza rejected Descartes's claim that the mind is a substance, arguing that only God or Nature (*Deus, sive Natura*) is capable of independent existence, and took all mentality and physicality to be different modes of God or Nature. On his view, a kind of pantheism, we are each finite modes of God or Nature, and our mind and body are identical modes though conceived of under two different kinds of attributes: bodily and mental (Garrett 1999). He thus held a kind of *dual-aspect theory*. Thomas Hobbes, an atheist, held a version of *materialism*, reminiscent of the ancient atomism of Democritus and Lucretius—Lucretius wrote of atoms moving in an infinite void—according to which all that exists is matter in motion (Gert 1999). He tried to show how mental processes are just mechanical brain processes, maintaining that thinking is just computation, thereby anticipating the computational view of mental processes prevalent in contemporary cognitive science.

There is something deeply commonsensical about Descartes's interactionism. It seems that bodily sensations such as aches, pains, itches, and tickles cause us to moan, wince, scratch, or laugh and do so by causing brain states that result in bodily movements. In deliberate action, we act on our desires, motives, and intentions in trying to carry out our purposes; and acting on them seems to involve their causing brain states, which cause our muscles to contract, and so our bodies to move, thereby affecting our environment. Perception of the environment seems to involve physical to mental causal transactions: What we perceive causes us to undergo a sense experience. Thus, when we see the scenes before our eyes, for instance, those scenes cause our visual experiences via their effects on our brains. Descartes's substance dualism, however, seems untenable.

But suppose that minds have not just temporal location but spatial location as well. (It is worthwhile pausing to note that according to the theory of general relativity, nothing can be in time without being in space.) Indeed, suppose that they are located where appropriately biologically functioning brains are but that they are nevertheless neither identical with brains nor composed of material particles, being entirely devoid of matter and lacking physical properties such as mass or charge. The spatiotemporal coincidence of minds and brains would be no violation of the principle that two physical objects cannot occupy exactly the same place at exactly the same time since, by hypothesis, minds are not physical objects. They are entirely disembodied even though they are spatiotemporally coincident with appropriately functioning brains. They are a kind of fundamental energy field coincident with such brains. On this conception might minds causally contribute to the animation of their coincident brains and the brains in turn causally influence them?

This sort of view was a subject of debate in the late nineteenth and early twentieth century, as were debates in biology concerning whether there are wholly immaterial entelechies that are spatiotemporally coincident with organisms and which generate a vital force that causally contributes to guiding the development of organisms and sustaining their integrity (McLaughlin 2003). This view of mentality offers no conception of the nature of minds beyond the negative one that they lack any physical properties save spatiotemporal location and the positive one that they are the seat of mental capacities and abilities, the bearers of mental properties, and what undergo mental change. No hint is offered as to how they could be the seat of mental capacities or abilities—of how such abilities and capacities could be exercised within them. No hint is offered as to what their operations might be, as they are entirely devoid of material constituents. Such matters must be taken as primitive; such how-questions are unanswerable.

Many philosophers have argued that to have a mind is not to bear a relation to an object (physical or otherwise) that is the mind but, rather, to have certain capacities and abilities, such as the capacity to think and to feel and the ability to will. We ourselves have these capacities and abilities. We ourselves are the bearers of mental properties, undergo mental events, and engage in mental activity. Moreover, we are embodied. It does not follow that we are identical with our bodies or some part of them such as our brains. A clay statue may fail to be identical with the lump of clay with which it is spatially coincident. They may fail to be identical because they have different temporal properties (perhaps the lump existed before being shaped into a statue) and because they have different modal properties (the lump can survive being squashed while the statue cannot). Rather, the lump may materially constitute the statue (Pea 1997). On a four-dimensionalist conception of objects, however, the lump and statue are space-time worms that have spatiotemporal segments that are identical (Sider 2001). Perhaps we are materially constituted by our bodies (or brains) but fail to be identical with them since they, unlike us, lack mental properties. They may also have different temporal properties from us. If we could exist in a disembodied form after the death and disintegration of our bodies and their organs, then, of course, we are not identical with our bodies or brains.

But it is also true that we are not identical with our bodies or brains if they can continue to exist after we have ceased to exist. We may cease to exist at brain death; but at brain death, the brain still exists. Albert Einstein's brain was removed from his skull shortly after his death with the hope that it would yield insight into his prodigious intelligence. But if he ceased to exist upon the death of his brain, then he was not his brain; and it was not he who was removed from the skull of his corpse. Einstein with his famous equation $E=mc^2$, taught us that mass and energy are interconvertible. (Some contemporary New Age Spiritualists would tell us that Einstein's unique energy was released from the matter of his brain upon the expiration of his body, and so that he continues on decoupled from any body. Why any energy released would be Einstein is left entirely obscure, however; and the question of how his mentality was linked to his brain while it was carrying out its normal biological functions remains unanswered. Suffice it to note here that the study of matter-energy in space-time is the subject of physics. We will return to physics shortly.)

Our biologically functioning brains serve somehow as the basis of our capacities to think and to feel and of our volition. Another topic of debate in the late nineteenth and early twentieth centuries was whether, despite the nonexistence of any immaterial object that is the mind, the brain serves as only the causal basis of mental capacities and abilities. On this conception, when we exercise our mental capacities and abilities, mental events (and states) occur within our brains. But they are not identical with occurrences of any kinds of nonmental brain events such as physiological ones; and, indeed, mental events are linked to brain occurrences of other kinds only spatiotemporally and causally: They may accompany them and be causes or effects of them. Since, on this conception, mental events occur within the brain, it might be claimed that they thereby count as physical since the brain is a physical object. But that seems merely a verbal issue. The dualist will claim the important point is that types of mental events are not identical with any other types of brains events and that the only (relevant) relations that token mental events bear to tokens of other kinds of brain events are spatiotemporal and causal. The chief concern raised about this view was whether mental events exert any causal influence on other brain events.

Ewald Herring, in his 1870 lecture at the Imperial Academy of Sciences in Vienna, declared that physiologists should make "the unbroken causative continuity of all material processes an axiom of [their] system of investigation" (Butler 1910, pp. 64–65). He took this position on the grounds that, on the evidence, there seem to be no *gaps* in the physiological processes in the brain to be filled by mental events. The relationship between mental and physiological events, he maintained, should be left as a question for philosophy; brain physiologists can safely bracket it. The fact that there seem to be no gaps in physiological causal chains for mental events to occupy led Thomas Huxley (1874) to maintain that we (and other animals) are *conscious automata*: conscious events accompany certain physiological brain events as dual effects of other physiological events but are themselves causally inert. Trained as a medical doctor, William James (1890) appropriated the term *epiphenomena*, a medical term for symptoms of diseases, for mental phenomena that while caused, lack causal efficacy. James Ward (1903) coined the term *epiphenomenalism* for the view that mental phenomena have no causal effects. The claim that conscious phenomena are epiphenomena is, however, deeply perplexing. If they are, then our belief that we are in pain is never caused by our feeling of pain. And our experience of control over some of our bodily movements cannot give rise to our belief that we are in control of them, for that, too, would require mental causation.

During this period concern was also raised about whether mental causation would violate the law of conservation of energy. (Leibniz had argued earlier that Descartes was committed to minds affecting the motion of material particles in the pineal gland in violation of the conservation laws of momentum and kinetic energy; his mechanics, however, required contact forces, and was eclipsed by Isaac Newton's mechanics, which rejected that requirement [Woolhouse 1985, Papireau 2001].) One response made to the concern about conservation of energy is that causation may very well not require energy transfer; it does not, for instance, on a regularity theory of causation, according to which causation is subsumption under a law of nature, or on a conditional theory of causation, according to which one event causes another if, had the first not occurred, the second would not have occurred either (Broad 1925, ch. III).

Another point made in response was that the conservation of energy principle is silent about the causes of motion, stating only that energy must be conserved within the total system (Broad 1925, ch. III). (Given general relativity, it is mass-energy that is conserved within the total system.) Unlike on Descartes's conception of the mental, on the conception under consideration, mental events occur within the total system of space-time. Indeed, it seems logically possible that certain mental properties are fundamental force-generating properties, just as in classical mechanics the masses of bodies generate the gravitational force, and the electrical charges of bodies generate the electrostatic force.

Perhaps our will involves such a force. There could be a force that is exerted only when matters becomes so configured as to constitute a brain in which certain sorts of mental properties are realized, and that affects the behavior of material particles in ways that causally contribute to bodily behavior that we regard as being under the (partial) control of our volition. Perhaps, further, this *configurational force* is fundamental, affecting the behavior of bodies in ways unanticipated by laws governing matter at lower-levels of complexity. If so, then in the framework of classical mechanics, there would be a mental force law on a par with the inverse square laws—the law of gravity and Coulomb's law.

In the framework of nonrelativistic quantum mechanics, mental energy would contribute to determining the value of the Hamiltonian of Erwin Schröedinger's equation. Since mechanics is a branch of physics, it might be claimed that if mechanics has to take mental properties into account, then the properties would thereby count as physical. But the dualist would regard that as a merely verbal point and note that the important point is that mental properties would be fundamental, irreducible force-generating properties. It should be noted, however, that while such configurational forces could be accommodated within Newtonian mechanics and are compatible with Schröedinger's equation, the role of mental properties would by no means be straightforward on the view in question. By hypothesis, the configurational forces would be exerted only when certain enormously complex microstructural properties were realized by minute physical structures of portions of the brain. On the dualist hypothesis in question, mental properties are distinct from any microstructural properties—at most, accompanying them as a matter of fundamental law. But, then, mechanics would, arguably, have to advert only to the microstructural properties in question, taking them

to be the configurational force-generating properties (McLaughlin 1992).

Another view discussed during the period in question is that every mental event is a physiological event but that mental properties are not physiological properties (Lewes 1985, Alexander 1920, Broad 1925). If mental events are physiological events, then they have causal effects. And the mistake made by theorists who found no gaps to be filled by mental events would be that they failed to realize that certain physiological events are mental events in that they fall under mental event types. This view faces the following issue: What is it about a physiological event in virtue of which it falls under a mental event type (or exemplifies a mental property)? Suppose that physiological event P falls under mental event type M and that physiological event P^* does not. It seems, then, that there must be some difference between P and P^* in virtue of which P is and P^* is not an event of type M. The issue is what that difference is. George Henry Lewes (1875) seems to have anticipated a functionalist answer of a kind sometimes given today (See Lewis 1966): He spoke of the role of the physiological event in the organism. But the most widely discussed answer during the period in question was that there are fundamental, irreducible laws of nature linking physiological properties with mental properties (Alexander 1920, Broad 1925).

Thus, the reason P is and P^* is not an instance of M is that P is an instance of a physiological event type that is linked via a fundamental noncausal law of nature to M while P^* falls under no such physiological type. Charles Dunbar Broad (1925–) called this view *emergent materialism*, and he called such laws of nature *transordinal laws*. (Transordinal laws were later denigrated as *nomological danglers* [Feigl 1950].) The guiding idea was that through the course of evolution, complex structures are formed that have genuinely new kinds of properties that are fundamental and thus irreducible. The emergent properties of wholes are linked to properties of their parts and relations among their parts only by fundamental laws. Emergent materialism is thus a kind of dual-aspect theory according to which the mental and physiological aspects of events are linked only by fundamental laws. On this view mental events are causes. But Broad raised the issue of whether they enter into causal relations only in virtue of their physiological properties and so not in virtue of their mental properties (Broad 1925, p. 473). If so, then emergent materialism is committed to a kind of property or type epiphenomenalism (McLaughlin 1989).

In the twentieth century science made truly momentous advances. The atomic theory of matter was vindicated, a quantum mechanical explanation of chemical bonding was provided—dispelling the idea that there are fundamental chemical forces—and organic chemistry and molecular biology made giant strides leading to the demise of any form of vitalism. There seem to be no fundamental mental forces of nature, no mental energy on par with electromagnetic energy, no mental force fields. At least mechanics has as yet no need of such hypotheses. It is now thought that all the fundamental forces are ones that are exerted below the level of the atom: the gravitational force, the electromagnetic force, the weak force, and the strong force. There is some hope for unification, but no role is envisioned for the mental. Of course, current microphysics may well be false; there is at present no quantum theory of gravity. It is, moreover, at least logically possible that our current physics is profoundly mistaken and that the physics in fact true of our world is a kind of Cartesian physics in which mentality plays a fundamental role. But that seems just a fantasy. It is fairly widely assumed that whatever revisions lie ahead for physics, they will not substantially change the dialectic as concerns the mind-body problem.

The mind-body problem is fundamentally the problem of the place of mental phenomena in nature. Contemporary philosophical discussions of the mind-body problem typically proceed under the (often) tacit assumptions that: We are wholly constituted by atoms and more fundamental physical particles, all of which are ingredients of beings entirely devoid of mentality; any fundamental forces at work in us are also at work in many such beings; and that for any (caused) microphysical event P, there is a distinct microphysical event P^* that causally determines the objective probability of P (if determinism is true, that probability will be 1). The last— which, unlike the others, is often explicitly stated—is sometimes called *the closure of the microphysical* though it goes under other names as well.

Of course, one way of responding to the question of the place of an alleged mental phenomenon in nature is by denying that there actually is any such phenomenon. One can be an *eliminativist* about it. Most contemporary philosophers are eliminativists concerning not only nonspatial, immaterial minds, but also spatiotemporally located immaterial minds: They deny that there are any such things. And they do so for much the same reasons mentioned earlier. Moreover, most contemporary philosophers deny that there are sense data, essentially private mental objects of which only the subject can be aware. Nevertheless, most hold that there are mental properties, capacities, abilities, states, events, and

processes. And discussion mainly focuses on their place in nature.

There are many unresolved questions. One central issue concerns the manner in which biologically functioning brains serve as a basis for our capacities to think and to feel and our ability to will: Are they merely a causal basis, or are they rather a constitutive basis? Other issues include whether freedom of the will is compatible with the manner in which they are, such a basis, and with the closure of the microphysical; whether there could be other kinds of material bases for mental capacities and abilities (e.g., silicon-based brains); and what the conditions for personal identity are given the fact of our material embodiment. And there are, as well, theological questions such as whether immortality may somehow be possible despite the fact of our material embodiment. (Might it be possible through the resurrection of the body?)

Among our mental capacities is the capacity to reflect on our own mental lives. Indeed, it is because we have such a capacity that we are able to formulate the mind-body problem. We are not only conscious (as are most kinds of animals), but self-conscious as well. The place in nature of our capacities for self-consciousness must be found. Engagement with the mind-body problem, moreover, requires theoretical reasoning. We form beliefs on the basis of others that provide reasons for them. And we engage in practical reasoning when we deliberate about courses of action (e.g., whether to finish reading the present article). Our capacities for theoretical and practical reasoning must also be located in nature.

The exercise of mental capacities and abilities involves mental states and events (including mental acts). The fundamental problem of the place of mental states and events in nature is that, on the one hand, they have or are instantiations of properties that seem sui generis, and on the other hand, they occur in space-time (arguably, within our skulls) and seem to enter into causal relations with other states and events, including microphysical ones (as, for example, when we deliberately move our bodies across the room with the result that physical particles in our bodies come to be on the other side of the room). The apparently sui generis properties primarily include those of intentionality and phenomenal consciousness.

Properties of intentionality divide into two broad kinds: modes of representation and representational contents. Beliefs, desires, hopes, and intentions, for example— so called *propositional attitudes*—are representational. They have an intentional (representational) mode—

belief, desire, hope, intention—and they have an intentional (representational) content, a content that is (semantically) satisfied or not, depending on the way the world is. States of phenomenal consciousness have phenomenal characters (*qualia*): It is like something for the subject of such a state to be in the state (Nagel 1974). States of phenomenal consciousness include bodily sensations, sense experiences, acts of mental imagery, felt emotions, and occurrent thoughts. Thus, for instance, it is like something for a subject to feel pain, or to visually experience red, or to visualize a sunset. Emotions such as fearing that *P* and being joyous that *P* have contents, and their characteristic manifestations in phenomenal conscious—feelings of fear and feelings of joy—have phenomenal characters. An occurrent thought such as thinking to oneself that it will rain tomorrow will have a representational content and a phenomenal character as well (even if not a distinctive, characteristic one). (Suffice it to note that the relationship between intentionality and phenomenal consciousness and whether one is primary are highly controversial issues.)

Many contemporary philosophers of mind are engaged in the project of trying to naturalize either intentional properties or phenomenal characters—that is to say, to locate them in nature conceived as fundamentally microphysical. It has been argued that such naturalization projects are doomed to failure where intentional properties are concerned because such properties are identifiable only by their place in a network of normative, rational relations and are thus irreducible, having *no echo* in the physical sciences (Davidson 1970). But even some philosophers who are optimistic about the prospects of naturalizing intentional properties maintain that the attempt to naturalize phenomenal consciousness may face insuperable difficulties. Huxley mused: "How it is that anything so remarkable as a state of consciousness comes about as a result of irritating nervous tissue, is just as unaccountable as the appearance of the Djinn, when Aladdin rubbed his lamp" (Huxley 1986, p.193). Indeed, it has been claimed that "consciousness is what makes the mind-body problem really intractable" (Nagel 1974, p. 435); that it is "the hard nut of the mind-body problem" (McGinn 1989, p. 394); that it is "the hard part of the mind-body problem" (Strawson 1994, p. 93); and that phenomenal character poses "the hard problem" of consciousness (Chalmers 1996, p. xiii).

Some philosophers have maintained that the link between phenomenal characters and physicality is so mysterious that it is reasonable to hypothesize that the particles—the star dust—from which we are composed must have as yet undiscovered *protomental* properties, which, though their mode of combination somehow constitute phenomenal characters (James 1890; Nagel 1979). Physics, however, has as yet found no need of this *panpsychism* hypothesis. Moreover, if the protomental properties are not themselves phenomenal characters and are objective in nature, then the concern arises that their link with phenomenal characters would also be mysterious. In any case, so mysterious has the connection between phenomenal character and physicality seemed that some philosophers have maintained that we are cognitively closed to the sorts of concepts required for understanding the place of phenomenal characters in nature and thus that the matter transcends human understanding (McGinn 1989).

There are a variety of different naturalizing projects, and some are incompatible with others. However, there have been attempts to state a commitment shared by them all. One leading formulation of such a shared commitment is the following global supervenience thesis: Any minimal physical duplicate of our world is a duplicate *simpliciter* of it (Jackson 1998). A physical duplicate of our world (the actual world) is any possible world that is exactly like our world in every microphysical respect, in respect to its world-wide pattern of distribution of microphysical properties and relations, its world-wide pattern of distribution of microphysical objects, its microphysical laws of nature, and so on. A minimal physical duplicate of our world is any physical duplicate of it that contains nothing other than what is metaphysically required to be a physical duplicate of it. Proponents of different naturalizations programs will offer different explanations of why mental phenomena do not yield a counterexample to the supervenience thesis.

Philosophers, however, who maintain that mental properties of certain sorts are emergent properties, fundamental constituents of nature, linked to other properties only by contingent fundamental laws of nature, will deny the supervenience thesis. Since the laws in question (Broad's *transordinal laws*) are contingent and fundamental, it is possible for them to fail to hold even though all of the actual microphysical laws of our world hold. Such philosophers are committed to there being a possible world that is a minimal physical duplicate of our world yet not a duplicate *simpliciter* of it because the world is devoid of the mental properties in question (or instantiations of them). For example, someone who holds that phenomenal characters are fundamental in nature will claim there is a possible world that is a minimal physical duplicate of our world yet, unlike our world, is devoid of phenomenal consciousness—*a zombie world* (Chalmers 1996)—and thus not a duplicate *simpliciter* of our world. And, similarly, someone who held that intentional properties are fundamental will be committed to their being a possible world that is a minimal physical duplicate of our world but which fails to be a duplicate *simpliciter* of our world since it is devoid of intentionality.

Any world that is a minimal physical duplicate of our world will be one in which exactly the same microphysical causal transactions occur as do in our world. If either normative intentional properties or phenomenal characters yield counterexamples to the supervenience thesis, then such properties make no difference to what microphysical causal transactions occur in our world. And they could make a difference to whether certain causal transactions occur in our world only if those transactions fail to be implemented by microphysical ones. Such, it seems, are the facts of our world.

Whether intentionality and phenomenal consciousness can be naturalized—whether they can be located in nature conceived of as fundamentally microphysical—are the fundamental issues of the contemporary mind-body problem. These are issues of intensive, ongoing debate.

See also Augustine, St.; Broad, Charlie Dunbar; Cartesianism; Computationalism; Descartes, René; Dualism in the Philosophy of Mind; Einstein, Albert; Elisabeth, Princess of Bohemia; Functionalism; Hobbes, Thomas; Huxley, Thomas Henry; James, William; Leibniz, Gottfried Wilhelm; Leucippus and Democritus; Lucretius; Malebranche, Nicholus; Mental Causation; Newton, Isaac; Plato; Reductionism in Philosophy of Mind; Self-knowledge; Socrates; Spinoza, Benedict (Baruch) de; Supervenience.

Bibliography

Alexander, S. *Space, Time, and Deity, the Gifford Lectures at Glasgow, 1916–1918.* 2 vols. London: Macmillan, 1920.

Broad, C. D. *The Mind and Its Place in Nature.* New York: Harcourt Brace, 1925.

Butler, S. *Unconscious Memory.* London: A. C. Fifield, 1910.

Chalmers, D. J. *The Conscious Mind: In Search of Fundamental Theory.* New York: Oxford University Press, 1996.

Cottingham, J. "Descartes, Rene." In *Cambridge Dictionary of Philosophy.* Edited by R. Audi, 223–227. Cambridge, U.K.: Cambridge University Press, 1999.

Crane, T. *Elements of Mind.* Oxford: Oxford University Press, 2001.

Descartes, R. *The Philosophical Writings of Rene Descartes*, Vols. 1 and 2. Edited and translated by J. Cottingham, R. Stootoff, and D. Murdoch. Cambridge, U.K.: Cambridge University Press, 1985.

Davidson, D. "Mental Events." In *Experience and Theory.* Edited by L. Foster and J. W. Swanson. Amherst: University of Massachusetts Press, 1970.

Feigl, H. "The 'Mental' and the 'Physical.'" In *Concepts, Theories, and the Mind-Body Problem: Minnesota Studies in the Philosophy of Science Volume II.* Edited by H. Feigl, M. Scriven, and G. Maxwell, 370–497. Minneapolis: University of Minnesota Press, 1958.

Garrett, D. "Spinoza, Baruch." In *Cambridge Dictionary of Philosophy.* Edited by R. Audi, 870–874. Cambridge, U.K.: Cambridge University Press, 1999.

Gert, B. "Hobbes, Thomas." In *Cambridge Dictionary of Philosophy.* Edited by R. Audi, 386–390. Cambridge, U.K.: Cambridge University Press, 1999.

Haldane, J. "Medieval and Renaissance Philosophy of Mind." In *A Companion to Philosophy of Mind.* Edited by S. Guttenplan, 333–338. Oxford: Blackwell, 1994.

Huxely, T. H. "On the Hypothesis that Animals are Automata, and its History." *Fortnightly Review* 16 (1874): 555–580. Reprinted in T. H. Huxley, *Collected Essays, Vol. 1, Methods and Results.* 4th ed. London: Macmillan, 1904.

Huxley, T. H. *Lessons in Elementary Physics.* London: Macmillan, 1986.

Jackson, F. *From Metaphysics to Ethics.* Oxford: Oxford University Press, 1998.

James, W. *The Principles of Psychology.* Cambridge, MA: Harvard University Press, 1890.

Kim, J. *Mind in a Physical World: An Essay on the Mind-Body Problem and Mental Causation.* Cambridge, MA: MIT Press, 1998.

Kim, J. *Physicalism, or Something Near Enough.* Princeton, NJ: Princeton University Press, 2005.

Kenny, A., ed. and trans. *Descartes: Philosophical Letters.* Oxford: Oxford University Press, 1970.

Lewes, G. H. *Problems of Life and Mind.* Vol. 2. London: Kegan Paul, Trench, Turbner, 1875.

Lewis, D. "An Argument for the Identity Theory." *Journal of Philosophy* 63 (1966): 17–25.

McCann, E. "Philosophy of Mind in the Seventeenth Century." In *A Companion to Philosophy of Mind*, edited by S. Guttenplan. Oxford: Blackwell, 1994.

McGinn, C. "Can We Solve the Mind-Body Problem?" *Mind* 98 (1989): 349–466.

McGinn, C. *The Character of Mind.* Oxford: Oxford University Press, 1982.

McLaughlin, B. P. "The Philosophy of Mind." In *Cambridge Dictionary of Philosophy*, edited by R. Audi, 684–694. Cambridge, U.K.: Cambridge University Press, 1999.

McLaughlin, B. P. "The Rise and Fall of British Emergentism." In *Emergence or Reduction?*, edited by A. Beckermann, A, H. Flohr, and J. Kim, 49–93. Berlin: Walter de Gruyter, 1992.

McLaughlin, B. P. "Type Epiphenomenalism, Type Dualism, and the Causal Priority of the Physical." *Philosophical Perspectives* 3 (1989): 209–235.

McLaughlin, B. P. "Vitalism and Emergence." In *Cambridge History of Philosophy 1870–1945*, edited by T. Baldwin, 631–639. Cambridge, U.K.: Cambridge University Press, 2003.

Nadler, S. "Malebranche, Nicolas." In *Cambridge Dictionary of Philosophy*, edited by R. Audi, 531–532. Cambridge, U.K.: Cambridge University Press, 1999.

Nagel, T. "Panpsychism." In *Mortal Questions*. Cambridge, U.K.: Cambridge, 1979.

Nagel, T. "What Is it like to be a Bat?" *Philosophical Review* LXXXIII (4) (1974): 435–450.

Papineau, D. "The Rise of Physicalism." In *Physicalism and Its Discontents*. Edited by C. Gillett and B. Loewer, 3–36. Cambridge, U.K.: Cambridge University Press, 2001.

Plato. *Phaedo*.

Rea, M., ed. *Material Constitution*. Latham, MD: Rowman & Littlefield, 1997.

Sider, T. *Four Dimensionalism*. Oxford: Oxford University Press, 2001.

Sleigh, R. C. "Leibniz, Gottfried Wilhelm." In *Cambridge Dictionary of Philosophy*, edited by R. Audi, 491–494. Cambridge, U.K.: Cambridge University Press, 1999.

Strawson, G. *Mental Reality*. Cambridge, MA: MIT Press, 1994.

Van Cleve, J. "Emergence vs. Panpsychism: Magic or Mind Dust?" *Philosophical Perspectives*. Vol. 4, edited by in J. E. Tomberlin, 215–226. Atascadero, CA: Ridgeview, 1990.

Ward, S. L. "The Conscious Automaton Theory." Lecture XII. *Naturalism or Agnosticism*, Vol. 234–264. London: Adam and Charles Black, 1896–1898.

Woolhouse, R. "Leibniz's Reaction to Cartesian Interaction." *Proceedings of the Aristotelian Society* 86 (1985): 69–82.

Brian P. McLaughlin (2005)

MIRACLES

The term "miracle," like the word *nice*, is often used to refer primarily to the responses of the user. In this usage, a miracle is merely some event that astounds the speaker, with perhaps some presumption that others will or should react to it in the same way; just as in the parallel case *nice* means simply "agreeable to me," with perhaps again some suggestion that all right-minded people will feel the same. But the senses of "miracle" that are of philosophical and methodological interest are stronger and less subjectively oriented. Although they include the idea that wonder is called for as at least part of the appropriate response, the crux as well as the ground for the wonder is that a miracle should consist in an overriding of the order of nature. A miracle is something that would never have happened had nature, as it were, been left to its own devices.

This idea of overriding is essential; however, it is certainly subject to various variations and additions. Some writers, for instance, insist that the word *miracle* should be used in such a way that it becomes necessarily true that a miracle can be worked only by God or by his specially deputed agents. Others even build into their very definition of *miracle* some reference to the purposes for which Authority is supposed to be prepared to consider making such an exception. Certainly, most theist theologians are also at great pains to maintain that a miraculous event could not properly be considered a violation, since it would not really represent any infringement, of the fundamental hierarchical order. "It is not against the principle of craftsmanship (*contra rationem artificii*) if a craftsman effects a change in his product, even after he has given it its first form" (Thomas Aquinas, *Summa contra Gentiles*, III, 100). But these very labors to show that and how such "violations" need involve no ultimate irregularity still admit and presuppose the essentially overriding character of the miraculous. There would be no point in trying to show in this way that a miracle must ultimately be no violation of regularity unless it were taken for granted that it apparently is such a violation.

This point is fundamental, and it needs to be stressed more heavily today than in the past. For in addition to the traditional theist reluctance to ascribe to the Deity anything savoring of unseemly irregularity, it is nowadays usual to encounter a certain shyness about any apparent repudiation of scientifically accepted modes of explanation. Thomas Aquinas, earlier in the chapter referred to above, gave a perfectly clear and unequivocal definition of *miracle* that makes no bones at all about the crux of the matter, namely, that "those things are properly called miracles which are done by divine agency beyond the order commonly observed in nature (*praeter ordinem communiter observatum in rebus*)." Again, in the twentieth century, Dr. Eric Mascall, remaining in the same forthright tradition, insisted in his article in *Chambers' Encyclopaedia* that the word *miracle* "signifies in Christian theology a striking interposition of divine power by which the operations of the ordinary course of nature are overruled, suspended, or modified."

MIRACLES AND NATURAL ORDER

To seize the fundamental point that a miracle is an event that violates the "ordinary course of nature" is to appreciate that the notion of a miracle is logically parasitical on the idea of an order to which such an event must constitute some sort of exception. This being so, a strong notion of the truly miraculous—a notion involving something more than the notions of the merely marvelous, the significant, or the surprising—can only be generated if there is first an equally strong conception of a natural order. The inevitable tension between the ideas of rule and of exception thus gives concepts of the miraculous an inherent instability. It is perhaps relevant to notice how this tension has been felt in the history of ideas. Where there is as yet no strong conception of a natural order, there is little room for the idea of a genuinely miraculous event as distinct from the phenomenon of a prodigy, of a wonder, or of a divine sign. But once such a conception of a natural order has taken really firm root, there is a great reluctance to allow that miracles have in fact occurred or even to admit as legitimate a concept of the miraculous.

An interesting early case of this is provided by Benedict de Spinoza in his *Tractatus Theologico-Politicus,* in which he tried to reconcile his vision of a natural order (*Deus sive natura*) with an acceptance of the Bible as in some sense a privileged document. He did this partly by admitting the limitations of observatory powers of the men of biblical days, but mainly by urging that conventional interpreters of the Bible read far more miracles into it than it contains, because they constantly read poetic Hebrew idioms literally. Today, more and more theologians seem to be noticing the exact words used by the New Testament writers in describing the sorts of alleged events that, in more scientific ages, have been characterized (and perhaps dismissed) as miraculous. These words are τερατὰ ("wonders," or "prodigies"), δυναμεῖς ("powers"), σημεία ("signs"); and, particularly in St. Paul, χαρισματὰ ἰαμάτων ("graces of healing") and ἐνεργήματα δυνάμεων ("effects of powers"). None of these words seems to carry any entailments about the overriding of a natural order. On the other hand, once a really strong conception of natural order has arisen, its adherents tend to dismiss out of hand all stories of putative occurrences in the belief that if they allowed that these occurrences had taken place at all, they would have to admit them to have been miraculous. One may refer here to R. M. Grant's recent *Miracle and Natural Law in Graeco-Roman and Early Christian Thought* (Amsterdam, 1952) and to William E. H. Lecky's classic study *History of the Rise and Influence of Rationalism in Europe* (London, 1890). The former summarizes its own thesis as follows: "Credulity in antiquity varied inversely with the health of science and directly with the vigor of religion" (p. 41). This, however, was later qualified by the important observation that "at least in some respects Christians were far less credulous than their contemporaries, at least in the period before Augustine" (p. 120). Lecky traced a development in which stories of the ostensibly miraculous, from being accepted as a chief guarantee of the authenticity of the Christian revelation, become instead "a scandal, a stumbling block, and a difficulty" (Vol. I, p. 143). In the nineteenth century the radical biblical critic David Strauss announced in the introduction to his *Das Leben Jesu* (2 vols., Tübingen, 1835; translated by Mary Ann Evans as *Life of Jesus Critically Examined,* London, 1848), "We may summarily reject all miracles, prophecies, narratives of angels and demons, and the like, as simply impossible and irreconcilable with the known and universal laws which govern the course of events." And in the twentieth century there was even a bishop of the Church of England capable of saying of the author of Mark, "He was credulous inasmuch as the miracles, as they are narrated, cannot, in the light of our modern knowledge of the uniformity of nature, be accepted as historical facts" (F. W. Barnes, *The Rise of Christianity,* London and New York, 1947, p. 108).

DILEMMA OF HOLDING STRONG RULES WHILE ADMITTING EXCEPTIONS. The spokesman for the occurrence of the miraculous faces a dilemma that arises from the very essence of the concept he espouses. It is tempting, but wrong, for the believer in the miraculous to think that he can afford to gloat over any little local difficulties and embarrassments that may from time to time beset the forward march of science. But insofar as a miracle involves an alleged overriding of a law of nature, he too is committed to showing the subsistence of a natural order. Exceptions are logically dependent upon rules. Only insofar as it can be shown that there is an order does it begin to be possible to show that the order is occasionally overridden. The difficulty (perhaps an insoluble one) is to maintain simultaneously both the strong rules and the genuine exceptions to them. The oscillations in the history of thought are to be understood by reference to this tension (amounting perhaps to a contradiction) that is inherent in the concept of the miraculous, and it is on this same tension that the various logical and methodological problems also center.

LOGICAL AND METHODOLOGICAL PROBLEMS

It is with logical and methodological problems that we are primarily concerned. The classical, and by far the best, approach is by way of the notorious section X, "Of Miracles," in David Hume's *Enquiry concerning Human Understanding* (1748). This and Section XI of this *Enquiry,* both of which were parts of a single coordinated case, constitute Hume's answer to what was, in his day, the stock program of Christian apologetic. This program had two stages: the first was an attempt to establish the existence and certain minimal characteristics of God by appealing only to natural reason and experience, the second was an attempt to supplement this rather sketchy religion of nature with a more abundant revelation. This program, in its characteristically eighteenth-century form, received its archetypal fulfillment in Archdeacon William Paley's *Natural Theology* (London, 1802) and also in his *Evidences of Christianity* (London, 1794). In the eighteenth-century form, the weight of the first part of the case was borne primarily by the Argument to Design. If from a watch we may infer a watchmaker, then the orderliness of the universe entitles us to infer, by parity of reasoning, a Maker of the universe. The second part of the case rested on the claim that there is ample historical evidence to show that the biblical miracles, including the crucial physical resurrection of Jesus bar Joseph, did in fact occur, and that this in turn proved the authenticity of the Christian revelation.

Paley's style of systematic rational apologetic has no doubt gone out of fashion, at least among Protestants. But Hume's challenges to the whole idea of a substantial natural theology and to the project of establishing the authenticity of any alleged revelation by proving that its claims have been supported by miracles are not, and are not likely to become, dead issues. For in 1870 the third session of the First Vatican Council defined as constitutive dogmas of the Roman Catholic religion both of the positions that Hume had challenged. The relevant passage of the canon dealing with the second reads, "If anyone shall say ... that miracles can never be known for certain, or that the divine origin of the Christian religion cannot properly be proved by them: let him be cast out" (*si quis dixerit ... aut miracula certo cognosci numquam posse nec iis divinam religionis christianae originem rite probari: anathema sit*; H. Denzinger, ed., *Enchiridion Symbolorum*, 29th ed., Sec. 1813, Freiburg im Breisgau, 1953).

PROBLEM OF SUPERNATURAL REVELATION. Hume's main contention was thus, in his own words, that "a miracle can never be proved so as to be the foundation of a system of religion." For him, all other questions about the miraculous were, officially at least, merely incidental to this basic tenet. He defined a "miracle" as "a transgression of a law of nature by a particular volition of the Deity, or by the interposition of some invisible agent." This definition has been attacked on various counts, but the criticism is misconceived, for two reasons. First, this was in fact the way in which the opponents whom Hume had in mind defined the term "miracle." Thus, Dr. Samuel Clarke, in his famous Boyle lectures (*The Works of Samuel Clarke*, Vol. II, London, 1738, p. 701), had defined "miracle" as "a work effected in a manner ... different from the common and regular method of providence, by the interposition either of God himself, or of some intelligent agent superior to men." Second, if, as Clarke and the orthodox tradition would have it, the occurrence of a miracle is to serve "for the proof or evidence of some particular doctrine, or in attestation of the authority of some particular person," then surely a miracle must be conceived in this way. It is only and precisely insofar as it is something really transcendent—something, so to speak, that nature by herself could not contrive—that such an occurrence could force us to conclude that some supernatural power is being revealed.

In this context it would be worse than useless to appeal to revelation for criteria by which genuinely miraculous events may be identified, and thus distinguished from the unusual, the untoward, or the merely ordinary. For if the occurrence of a miracle is to serve as the endorsement of a revelation, then we have to find some means entirely independent of that revelation by which the endorsement itself may be recognized. Exactly the same point applies, of course, if, with what is now a rather fashionable school of apologetic, it is urged that miracles are not essentially overridings, but signs. If a sign is to signify to the unbeliever, then there must be some means independent of the doctrinal system itself by which the signs may be identified and read. As has been suggested already, there is much to be said for trying to interpret the records of τέρατα and σημεῖα in the New Testament in terms of some notion of sign, rather than as miracle stories proper. But it is necessary to insist on two facts that seem to be often overlooked—namely, that part of the price that must be paid for this method of interpretation is the sacrifice of the use of these stories as independent evidence of the genuinely revelatory character of the doctrines; and that such a sacrifice presumably entails the rejection of at least one defined dogma of the Roman Catholic Church, and hence of the truth of Roman Catholicism as a theological system.

A similar but different point applies if a relativistic definition of "miracle" is adopted, as was done, for instance, by John Locke. In his *Discourse of Miracles* (written 1702, published posthumously), he defined the word *miracle* as "a sensible operation, which, being above the comprehension of the spectator, and in his opinion contrary to the established course of nature, is taken by him to be divine." It was also done, in a slightly different way, by St. Augustine, who insisted that "nature is the will of God" (*Dei voluntas rerum natura est*), and hence that "a portent is not contrary to nature, but contrary to our knowledge of nature" (*Portentum ergo fit non contra naturam, sed contra quam est nota natura*; *De Civitate Dei*, XXI, 8). To operate with a relativistic notion of this sort is necessarily to be deprived of the possibility of arguing that a miracle is a miracle regardless of whatever anyone may happen to know or to believe about it, and hence to rob the attempt to base an apologetic on the occurrence of miracles of whatever initial plausibility it might otherwise possess. For the occurrence of events that are merely inexplicable *to us,* and *at present,* provides no good ground at all for believing that doctrines associated with these occurrences embody an authentic revelation of the transcendent. There is, of course, no particular reason why Locke himself should have been disturbed about this. The case of Augustine, however, is more interesting, for he is a recognized saint and one of the four great doctors of the church. And yet insofar as he held to a relativistic notion of a miracle, he was safeguarding the vital doctrine of the total dependence of the whole creation—but at the price of subverting a sort of apologetic which it has since become essential for Roman Catholics to believe in as a possibility.

PROBLEM OF IDENTIFYING AN EVENT AS MIRACULOUS. Up to this point it has been insisted that if the occurrence of a miracle is to serve—as Clarke and the orthodox tradition would have it—"for the proof or evidence of some particular doctrine, or in attestation of the authority of some particular person," then in a traditional sense, miracles must be conceived of as involving the overriding of some natural order that is at least partly autonomous. The importance of this crucial point is often overlooked. Another immediately consequential point, however, is overlooked perhaps even more often, namely, that if an occurrence that is miraculous in the traditional sense is to serve as evidence for anything, it must be possible to identify it as being miraculous. Furthermore, as was urged above, if its occurrence is to serve as an endorsement of some doctrinal system, the method of identification must be logically independent of that system. The difficulty of meeting this last requirement is often concealed by the acceptance of what seems, for many people, to be an almost unquestionable assumption. Protagonists of the supernatural, and opponents too, take it for granted that we all possess some natural (as opposed to revealed) way of knowing that and where the unassisted potentialities of nature (as opposed to a postulated supernature) are more restricted than the potentialities that, in fact, we find to be realized or realizable in the universe around us.

This is a very old and apparently very easy and tempting assumption. It can be found, for instance, in Cicero's *De Natura Deorum,* and hence presumably much earlier, in Cicero's Greek sources. Nevertheless, the assumption is entirely unwarranted. We simply do not have, and could not have, any natural (as opposed to revealed) criterion that enables us to say, when faced with something that is found to have actually happened, that here we have an achievement that nature, left to her own unaided devices, could never encompass. The natural scientist, confronted with some occurrence inconsistent with a proposition previously believed to express a law of nature, can find in this disturbing inconsistency no ground whatever for proclaiming that the particular law of nature has been supernaturally overridden. On the contrary, the new discovery is simply a reason for his conceding that he had previously been wrong in thinking that the proposition, thus confuted, did indeed express a true law; it is also a reason for his resolving to search again for the law that really does obtain. We certainly cannot say, on any natural (as opposed to revealed) grounds, that anything that actually happens is beyond the powers of unaided nature, any more than we can say that anything that any man has ever succeeded in doing transcends all merely human powers. For our evidence about the powers of nature in general, and of men in particular, is precisely and only everything that things and people do. For a scientist to insist that some recalcitrant fact constitutes an overriding of a still inviolably true law of nature is—to borrow Rudolf Carnap's mischievous analogy—as if a geographer were to maintain that the discrepancies between his maps and their objects show that there is something wrong with the territories concerned.

The insistence of the scientist, insofar as he is simply a scientist, on always seeking strictly universal laws is itself rooted in the fundamental object of the whole scientific quest: if scientists are to find comprehensive explanations, they must discover universal laws. A scientist's refusal to accept the idea that in any single case nature has been overridden by supernatural intervention is grounded partly on precisely the above-mentioned lack of any natural (as opposed to revealed) criterion for distinguishing natural from supernatural events, and partly on his commitment—which is chiefly what makes him a scientist—to continue always in the search for completely universal laws, and for more and more comprehensive theories. In view of this, it need be neither arbitrary nor irrational to insist on a definition of a "law of nature" such that the idea of a miracle as an exception to a law of nature is ruled out as self-contradictory.

The seductive but erroneous idea that we do possess some natural means for the identification of the supernatural is one that, in some respects, parallels the notion that it is logically possible to derive prescriptive norms from knowledge of what is, in some purely descriptive sense, natural. In each case there are adherents for whom the division between natural and supernatural, or between natural and unnatural, is nothing but an incoherent muddle. Likewise, in each case there are others who, in support of their choice, are prepared to deploy some more or less elaborate structure of theoretical justification.

PROBLEM OF EVIDENCE. All of this argumentation, although both relevant and (in spirit at least) thoroughly Humean, has little in common with the line of argument Hume chose to develop in the section "Of Miracles." Although this line of argument is equally methodological, it treats the question of miracles as it arises in the field of history rather than as it might impinge upon natural science. Hume was primarily concerned not with the question of fact but with that of evidence. The problem was how the occurrence of a miracle could be proved, rather than whether any such events ever had occurred. Consequently, even if Hume was successful, the way would still remain clear for people to believe in miracles simply on faith. In his own mordant way, Hume himself was happy to allow for this, but he always insisted that "a wise man proportions his belief to the evidence."

This concentration on the evidential issue means that Hume's thesis, however offensively expressed, is nevertheless at bottom defensive. Hume hoped that he had discovered "a decisive argument … which must at least silence the most arrogant bigotry and superstition, and free us from their impertinent solicitations … an argument which … will … with the wise and learned, be an everlasting check to all kinds of superstitious delusion…." These words were very carefully chosen. The whole argument was directed to the wise—to those, that is, who insist on proportioning their belief to the evidence. It did not show that the substantive claims of the bigoted and superstitious are in fact false. It was intended to serve as a decisive check on any attempt to solicit the assent of rational men by producing proof of the occurrence of the miraculous. In particular, the object was to interdict the second movement of the standard apologetic attack as outlined above.

If for present purposes a certain amount of misguided psychologizing is ignored, the following would appear to be the gist of Hume's "everlasting check." There is, he remarked, "no species of reasoning more common, more useful, and even necessary to human life than that derived from the testimony of men and the reports of eye-witnesses and spectators." Yet all testimony must ulti-

mately be subject to assessment by the supreme court of experience. Certainly there are, as Hume observed, "a number of circumstances to be taken into consideration in all judgments of this kind." Yet "the ultimate standard by which we determine all disputes … is always derived from experience and observation." (Of all people, Hume, as the author of that most famous paragraph in the *Treatise of Human Nature*, should have said not "*is*," but "*ought*" always to be so derived.)

The weight of the testimony required must depend on the apparent credibility of the events reported. If the events are in some way marvelous and rare, then the testimony for them has to be treated with more circumspection than the witness to everyday occurrences. But supposing that the testimony is for events that, had they occurred, would have been genuinely miraculous: we are then confronted with a paradoxical dilemma, proof balanced against proof. However overwhelming the testimony might have appeared were it not being considered as evidence for a miracle, in this peculiar case the testimony must always be offset against a counterproof. In Hume's own words, "A miracle is a violation of the laws of nature; and as a firm and unalterable experience has established these laws, the proof against a miracle, from the very nature of the fact, is as entire as any argument from experience can possibly be imagined."

In the first part of section X, Hume argued generally from the concept of the miraculous—from, as he put it, "the very nature of the fact." In the second he deployed several more particular assertions about the corruptions to which testimony is liable, urging that such corruptions are exceptionally virulent where any religious issue is involved. He also added a further consideration relevant to any attempt "to prove a miracle and make it a just foundation for any … system of religion."

This consideration was expressed badly and was entangled in one or two inessential errors and confusions. But a letter makes clear Hume's intent. The point is that if the occurrence of some sort of miracle is to serve as a guarantee of the truth of a system of religion, then there must not have been any similar miracle under the auspices of a rival system, the truth of which would be incompatible with the truth of the first. Consequently, insofar as we are considering a miracle not as a putative bald fact but as a possible endorsement of the authenticity of a revelation, we have to throw into the balance against the testimony for the miracles of any one candidate revelation all the available testimony for all the miracle stories presented by all the rival systems that are inconsistent with the first. In its appeal to a necessary conflict of evidence, this argument resembles the paradoxical dilemma expounded above.

MIRACLES AND THE PHILOSOPHY OF HISTORY

Enough already has been said to suggest that there is more to Hume's check than a trite insistence that since the occurrence of a miracle must be very improbable, it would have to be exceptionally well evidenced in order to be believed. C. S. Peirce was in possession of the vital clue (which he seems never to have exploited fully) when he remarked, "The whole of modern 'higher criticism' of ancient history in general, and of Biblical history in particular, is based upon the same logic that is used by Hume" (*Values in a Universe of Chance*, edited by P. P. Wiener, New York, 1958, pp. 292–293). When we follow this clue, it becomes obvious that Hume himself saw "the accounts of miracles and prodigies to be found in all history, sacred and profane" as presenting a methodological problem. This section on miracles constitutes the outer ring of Hume's defenses against the orthodox religious apologetic. But at the same time it is also part of his contribution to an understanding of the presuppositions and the limitations of critical history.

This fact seems not to have been appreciated as it should have been. There is, for instance, no reference to Hume's section "Of Miracles" in R. G. Collingwood's *The Idea of History* (Oxford, 1946); and neither Collingwood nor F. H. Bradley seems to have had any idea of the extent to which Bradley's own essay, "The Presuppositions of Critical History" (*Collected Papers*, Vol. I., Oxford, 1935), echoed arguments first developed by Hume. It is worthwhile to consider possible causes of this neglect. In part it is to be attributed to the insistence (at one time universal) on treating section X, "Of Miracles," as though it were a separate and disingenuous essay, irrelevantly inserted into the first *Enquiry* simply to cause scandal and thereby push up sales. This perverse and gratuitously offensive notion has misled interpreters to overlook some extremely relevant remarks in Part I of section VIII which concern the inescapably uniformitarian presuppositions of both the natural and the social sciences. Even those who have succeeded in appreciating section X as a very considerable piece of argumentation have been inclined to pigeonhole it as being a contribution to the philosophy of religion only. Certainly Hume's argument does, in the first instance, belong to the philosophy of religion; and this, of course, is how Hume presented it. Yet, as we have already seen, it also has a place in the philosophy of science. The fact that Hume appreciated this is perhaps suggested by his proposal that if, against all reasonable expectation, there were to be sufficient historical evidence to establish that the "miracle" of a universal eight-day eclipse had occurred in January 1600, "then our present philosophers [scientists], instead of doubting the fact, ought to receive it as certain; and ought to search for the causes whence it might be derived." It is surely significant that in this one context, and inconsistently with his own official definition of *miracle*, he spoke not of "a violation of the laws of nature," but rather, and more weakly, of "violations of the usual course of nature."

The same nodal argument which thus has a place in both the philosophy of religion and the philosophy of science belongs equally in the philosophy of history. For what Hume was contending (with certain lapses and hesitations) is that the criteria by which we must assess historical testimony, and the general presumptions which alone make it possible for us to interpret the detritus of the past as historical evidence, must inevitably rule out any possibility of establishing, upon purely historical grounds, that some genuinely miraculous event has indeed occurred. Hume concentrated on testimonial evidence because his conception of the historian, later illustrated in his own famous *History of England*, was of a judge assessing with judicious impartiality the testimony set before him. But the same Humean principles can be applied more widely to all forms of historical evidence.

The fundamental propositions are first, that the present detritus of the past cannot be interpreted as historical evidence at all, unless we presume that the same basic regularities obtained then as today; and second, that in trying his best to determine what actually happened, the historian must employ as criteria all his present knowledge, or presumed knowledge, of what is probable or improbable, possible or impossible. In his first work, the *Treatise of Human Nature* (II, iii, i), Hume had argued that it is only on such presumptions that we can justify the conclusion that ink marks on old pieces of paper constitute testimonial evidence. Early in the first *Enquiry*, in the first part of section VIII, he urged the inescapable importance of having such criteria. In a footnote to section X, he quoted with approval the reasoning of the famous physician De Sylva in the case of a Mlle. Thibaut: "It was impossible she could have been so ill as was proved by witnesses, because it was impossible she could, in so short a time, have recovered so perfectly as he found her."

FLAWS IN HUME'S ACCOUNT. Two very serious faults in Hume's presentation of his argument may obscure the force and soundness of De Sylva's reasoning, as well as the fact that this sort of application of canons to evidence is absolutely essential to the very possibility of critical history.

The first fault is a rather wooden dogmatism of disbelief. For against all his own high, skeptical principles, Hume tended to take it for granted that what in his own day he and all his fellow men of sense firmly believed about the order of nature constituted not just humanly fallible opinion, but the incorrigible last word. He was thus betrayed into categorically dismissing as downright impossible certain reported phenomena that the later progress in the study of abnormal psychology and of psychosomatic medicine has since shown to have been perfectly possible. But the moral to be drawn from these lapses into dogmatism is not that Hume was mistaken in insisting that the critical historian must apply canons of possibility and probability to his evidence, but that he failed to appreciate that all such canons are themselves subject to criticism and correction.

The second major fault in Hume's treatment is both more serious and more excusable. He was unable to provide an adequate account of the logical character of a law of nature. Hence, he could not offer any sufficiently persuasive rationale for employing, as canons of exclusion in historical inquiry, propositions that express, or that are believed to express, such natural laws. The way may thus seem to be open for a historian who holds different presuppositions, yet still remains truly a historian, to endorse as veridical stories of events that, had they occurred, would have been truly miraculous. (For a sustained study of such attempts to have it both ways, see T. A. Roberts, *History and Christian Apologetic,* London, 1960.)

This problem of the logical nature of natural laws has, of course, many more aspects than those that immediately concern us here. But it is important first to emphasize that it is at least as much a problem for Hume's immediate opponents as for Hume. For it is his opponents who need a strong sense of "miracle," in which the miraculous can be distinguished from the merely marvelous. It is tempting, but entirely wrong, for the spokesman for the miraculous to think that he can afford to triumph over Hume's difficulties without being himself committed in any way to producing his own account of the character of laws of nature—an account that shall be more satisfactory as an analysis and yet, at the same time, consistent with the things the spokesman himself wants to say about the miraculous. His dilemma, to repeat, is that he needs to be able to accommodate simultaneously both the strong laws and the spectacular transgressions.

NOMOLOGICAL PROPOSITIONS. Casting back to the reasoning of De Sylva, it can now be seen that (and how) it constitutes a paradigm of critical history. For it is only and precisely by presuming that the laws that hold today held in the past and by employing as canons all our knowledge—or presumed knowledge—of what is probable or improbable, possible or impossible, that we can rationally interpret the detritus of the past as evidence and from it construct our account of what actually happened. But in this context, what is impossible is what is physically, as opposed to logically, impossible. And "physical impossibility" is, and surely has to be, defined in terms of inconsistency with a true law of nature. Or rather, since this sense of "impossible" is prior to the development of science proper, it might be said that what is physically impossible is whatever is inconsistent with a true nomological proposition.

Both causal propositions and those expressing laws of nature fall under the genus nomological. Although Hume himself concentrated on the causal species, what he said can easily be extended. In his view, when we say that *A* is the cause of *B*, the main thing we are saying is that *B*'s are constantly conjoined with *A*'s—never as a matter of fact *A* and not *B*, or, in modern terminology, *A* materially implies *B*. Of course, he went on, people think they are asserting not a mere constant conjunction, but some real connection, and in a way this is right. The fact is, according to Hume, that there *is* a connection, but that it is a psychological one: we have formed a habit of associating the idea of an *A* with the idea of a *B*.

Yet this account of causal propositions cannot be adequate. All causal propositions entail subjunctive conditionals. (A subjunctive conditional, appropriately enough, is a proposition of the form, "If it were … it would.") Thus, "*A*'s are the only things which cause *B*'s" entails "If *A* were not to occur (or to have occurred) *B* would not occur (or have occurred)." But no variation on the material implication theme, with or without benefit of associationist psychological speculation, can be made to entail any such subjunctive conditional. Furthermore, the same essential inadequacy afflicts any extension of a Humean analysis to cover nomologicals in general. For a nomological is, by the above definition, a contingent proposition that entails some contingent subjunctive conditional.

The essential difference between the contingent "All *X* are ϕ" and the equally contingent "Any *X* must be ϕ" is that the former can be expressed as a material implication, "Not both X and not ϕ," whereas the latter cannot be so expressed, because it is a nomological, entailing such subjunctive conditionals as "If there were to have been an X (which in fact there was not) it would have been a ϕ." The nomological goes far beyond the statement of a mere conjunction of X and ϕ as a matter of fact. It asserts also a (contingent) connection between X and ϕ. For although the nomological is no more logically necessary than the corresponding material implication, it says not merely that, as it happens, a constant conjunction has been, is being, and will be maintained, but also that it would be and would have been maintained regardless of what anyone did or might have done. To assert the nomological is to assert that the conjunction is one that can be relied upon. It is for this reason that experimental evidence is so essential to our knowledge of nomologicals: the obvious and ultimately the only satisfactory test of the reliability of a law is to subject it to strains. It is for the same reason that a knowledge of nomologicals provides, at least in principle, a guarantee of repeatability. To say that the conjunction of B's with A's is reliable is to say that any time anyone likes to produce an A he will thereby bring about a B.

THE HISTORIAN'S APPROACH. In the light of the above discussion, we can again consider the question of historical evidence for the miraculous. The critical historian, confronted with some story of a miracle, will usually dismiss it out of hand, asking first only whether it can be used as evidence, not for the occurrence reported, but for something else. To justify his procedure he will have to appeal to precisely the principle Hume advanced: the "absolute impossibility or miraculous nature" of the events attested must, "in the eyes of all reasonable people … alone be regarded as a sufficient refutation." Our sole ground for characterizing the reported occurrence as miraculous is at the same time a sufficient reason for calling it physically impossible. Contrariwise, if ever we became able to say that some account of the ostensibly miraculous was indeed veridical, we can say it only because we now know that the occurrences reported were not miraculous at all.

OBJECTIONS TO THE HISTORIAN'S APPROACH. To this representation of the procedure of the critical historian there are two main objections. First, it will be argued that such an approach to what purports to be historical evidence for the miraculous is irrationally dogmatic, for in this instance the historian seems to be represented as dismissing all evidence that conflicts with his own fundamental prejudices and as defending a closed system in which his professional predilections are guaranteed against falsification by a "Heads-I-win: Tails-you-lose" argument. This is a very understandable objection. It is made more plausible by the regrettable fact that there have been, and still are, many historical writers whose actual procedures correspond rather too closely to this suggested representation. Also it is, of course, true that the dilemmas generated by the tension implicit in the concept of the miraculous must necessarily seem to their victims to have a "Heads-you-win: Tails-I-lose" aspect. Nevertheless, the critical historian is not committed to the sort of bigoted dogmatism the present objection attributes to him.

Nomological laws and reports of miracles. As Hume was insisting from first to last, the possibility of miracles is a matter of evidence and not of dogmatism. For, to proceed beyond Hume, the nomological proposition that provides the historian's canon of exclusion will be open and general and of the form "Any X must be ϕ." The proposition reporting the (alleged) occurrence of the miracle will be singular, particular, and in the past tense; it will have the form "This X on that particular occasion was not ϕ." Propositions of the first sort can in principle be tested at any time and in any place. Propositions of the second sort cannot any longer be tested directly. It is this that gives propositions of the first sort the vastly greater logical strength that justifies their use as criteria of rejection against the latter. It will indeed be only and precisely insofar as we have evidence sufficient to warrant our assertion of the general nomological that excludes the particular historical proposition that we shall have sufficient reason to claim that the event it reports would have been genuinely miraculous.

The logic of evidence. Suppose that in some particular case the evidence for a miracle appears extremely strong. Then perhaps the historian may ask himself whether the nomological proposition that precludes this event is after all true. It could, in principle at any rate, be further tested. If, as is possible, it were shown to be false after all, then perhaps the event so strongly evidenced did indeed occur. But by the same token, that event could now no longer be described as truly miraculous. This, surely, is what has happened in the case of so many of the reports of astonishing psychosomatic cures, which Hume himself, in his capacity as a historiographer, too rashly dismissed. (Consider, for example, his contemptuous rejection of the stories of faith healings by the Emperor Vespasian and of the many cures associated with the tomb of the Jansenist Abbé Paris, all in section X of his first *Enquiry.*) Alternatively, the nomological proposition might survive even our further tests. Hume should be the last one to deny that it must remain always conceivable—logically, that is, as opposed to physically possible—that the event in question did in fact occur. Yet in this case, no matter how impressive the testimony might appear, the most favorable verdict that history could ever return must be the agnostic, and appropriately Scottish, "not proven."

Need for canons of evidence. The second objection to the above representation of the procedure of the critical historian suggests that there is something arbitrary or at least optional about the appeal to canons provided by some of our knowledge, or presumed knowledge, of what is probable or improbable, possible or impossible. Once again there is some ground for this objection. Certainly we can choose whether or not we will try to act as critical historians. But once that fundamental choice is made, there is nothing arbitrary and nothing optional about insisting on the employment of these canons. For the essential aim of the historian is to get as near as he can to a full knowledge of what actually happened, and why. To do this he must find and interpret evidence, for belief unsupported by evidence may be true, but it cannot constitute knowledge. Yet to interpret the detritus of the past as evidence, and to assess its value and bearing as such, we must have canons. And for a rational man, these canons can only be derived from the sum of his available knowledge, or presumed knowledge. It is not the insistence on the systematic employment of these always corrigible canons that is arbitrary; what is arbitrary is to pick and choose in the interests of your ideological predilections among the available mass of miracle stories, or to urge that it is (psychologically) impossible that these particular witnesses were lying or misinformed and hence that we must accept the fact that on this occasion the (biologically) impossible occurred. If one once departs in such arbitrary ways from these canons of critical history, then anything and everything goes. (For examples of precisely this sort of arbitrariness, see M. C. Perry, *The Easter Enigma,* London and New York, 1959.)

Possible justifications for belief in miracles. Nothing that has been said in this article decisively closes the door on faith. We have been concerned only with questions about the possibilities of having good reasons for belief in the miraculous. Again, nothing has been said to preclude the production of nonhistorical and nonscientific considerations that might, either by themselves or with the aid of historical or scientific evidence, justify our belief that certain miracles did indeed occur. Perhaps one might

develop some defensible system of rational theology that would provide criteria both for identifying particular occurrences as miraculous and for separating the true miracle stories from the false. Hume tried to rule this out also, of course, in section XI of his *Enquiry,* and elsewhere. But it has been no part of our present task to examine arguments against natural theology. Finally, it is perfectly possible to develop a new concept and to apply to it the term "miracle." There is never anything to keep anyone from simply changing the subject.

See also Augustine, St.; Bradley, Francis Herbert; Carnap, Rudolf; Cicero, Marcus Tullius; Clarke, Samuel; Collingwood, Robin George; Eliot, George; Hume, David; Locke, John; Natural Law; Nature, Philosophical Ideas of; Paley, William; Peirce, Charles Sanders; Revelation; Spinoza, Benedict (Baruch) de; Strauss, David Friedrich; Teleological Argument for the Existence of God; Thomas Aquinas, St.

Bibliography

HISTORICAL STUDIES

Grant, R. M. *Miracle and Natural Law in Graeco-Roman and Early Christian Thought.* Amsterdam, 1952.

Lecky, W. E. H. *History of the Rise and Influence of Rationalism in Europe.* London, 1865. Chs. 1–3. These chapters carry on approximately from where Grant leaves off.

Stephen, Leslie. *English Thought in the Eighteenth Century,* 3rd ed. London, 1902. Vol. I. Contains the classic account of the entire controversy of which Hume's "Of Miracles" formed a part.

LOGICAL AND METHODOLOGICAL STUDIES

Augustine. *The City of God,* XXI, 8.

Hume, D. *An Enquiry concerning Human Understanding,* VIII–XI.

King-Farlow, J. "Miracles: Nowell-Smith's Analysis and Tillich's Phenomenology." *International Philosophical Quarterly* 2 (1962). Although this article appeared in a Jesuit journal, it seems to accept most of the sort of methodological criticism presented in the present article. The bibliography of recent Roman Catholic literature on the subject is especially valuable.

Lewis, C. S. *Miracles.* London and New York, 1947. Mozley (see below), Tennant (see below), and Lewis all give Anglican views, of which Tennant's is perhaps the most liberal and Lewis's the most conservative. The latter employs a theoretical structure of the type referred to in the discussion of the problem of identifying the supernatural in order to uphold the possibility of miracles. For a discussion and development of the ideas touched on in that section, see the exchanges between H. H. Dubs, A. Lunn, and P. Nowell-Smith in the *Hibbert Journal* (1950–1952).

Mill, J. S. *A System of Logic,* III, 4 and 25.

Mozley, J. B. *On Miracles.* London, 1865.

Roberts, T. A. *History and Christian Apologetic.* London: S.P.C.K., 1960.

Smith, G. D., ed. *The Teaching of the Catholic Church,* 2nd ed. London, 1952.

Spinoza, B. *Tractatus Theologico-Politicus,* VI.

Tennant, F. R. *Miracle and Its Philosophical Presuppositions.* Cambridge, U.K.: Cambridge University Press, 1925.

Thomas Aquinas. *Summa contra Gentiles,* III, 98–107.

ILLUSTRATIONS OF MAIN METHODOLOGICAL POINTS

Huxley, T. H. "Agnosticism and Christianity." In *Lectures and Essays.* London, 1902. An attack on Newman (see below).

Middleton, Conyers. *A Free Inquiry into the Miraculous Powers which are supposed to have subsisted in the Christian Church from the earliest ages through several successive centuries.* London: R. Manby and H.S. Cox, 1749. A pivotal work in the great eighteenth-century controversy described by Stephen.

Morrison, F. *Who Moved the Stone?* New York: Century, 1930. A gripping, if very unsophisticated, study of New Testament evidence.

Newman, J. H. "Essay on the Miracles Recorded in Ecclesiastical History." In *The Ecclesiastical History of M. L'Abbé Fleury.* Oxford, 1842. This essay by the future cardinal deserves to be read alongside Middleton's *Free Inquiry* (see above).

Perry, M. C. *The Easter Enigma.* London: Faber and Faber, 1959. An attempt to apply the findings of psychical research to the interpretation of the New Testament documents. It illustrates both an admirably undogmatic flexibility about what in fact is and is not possible and a certain inconsistency in applying the canons of critical history.

Schweitzer, Albert. *The Quest for the Historical Jesus, from Reimarus to Wrede.* London: Black, 1910. A classic history of a historiographical subject. It is interesting to note that the work contains no reference to Hume.

Thomson, J. M. *Miracles in the New Testament.* London: Edward Arnold, 1912. An important but neglected work by a historian who later achieved distinction in the field of secular history.

West, D. J. *Eleven Lourdes Miracles.* London: Duckworth, 1957. A study of the best evidence by a psychiatrist and sometime research officer of the Society for Psychical Research.

Antony Flew (1967)

MIRACLES [ADDENDUM]

Consistent with standard eighteenth-century accounts by Christian apologists, English deists, and skeptics like David Hume, a miracle is still usually thought of as an event with religious significance that is in some sense contrary to the laws of nature. There is no consensus about the best definition. Thus, in their investigations concerning the credibility of miracles, philosophers often have recourse to paradigmatic cases of purported miracles such as the resurrection of Jesus from the dead.

Most philosophers endorse a conception of miracles consistent with the possibility of a violation of the laws of nature. J. L. Mackie (1982) calls a miracle "a supernatural intrusion into the normally closed system that works in accordance with the laws of nature." Richard Swinburne (1970) holds that a miracle is "a non-repeatable counter-instance to a law of nature." A counterinstance to a given law of nature will either be a miracle or will require the formulation of some new alternative law. The second option will be unattractive to the degree that the new law fails to predict the phenomena supporting the original law and/or gives what most likely are false predictions, thus playing havoc with regularities of science. In that event, it would be better to postulate the occurrence of a miracle than to modify our formulae for the laws of nature.

A miracle may, in principle, be identifiable. But is belief in miracles ever epistemically justified? Hume argued that it is not, but his interpreters have disagreed about the specific nature and the overall success of his argument. The controversy centers on Hume's "general maxim" about testimony on behalf of a miracle, which states the following:

> That no testimony is sufficient to establish a miracle, unless the testimony be of such a kind, that its falsehood would be more miraculous, than the fact, which it endeavours to establish; and even in that case there is a mutual destruction of arguments, and the superior only gives us an assurance suitable to that degree of force, which remains, after deducting the inferior. (Hume 1975, 115–116)

J. L. Mackie (1982) perceived a need for three specific improvements on Hume's argument: (1) decisions about the value of specific testimonial evidence must always be more provisional than Hume acknowledged; (2) a more accurate conception of inductive generalization is needed than what Hume assumed in his conception of a well-established law of nature; and (3) Hume misunderstood the potential exponential increase in probability conferred by multiple witnesses to an event. But, on balance, with these provisos in place, Hume's argument, Mackie concluded, succeeds in showing that the "intrinsic improbability" of a miracle is too great to be overturned by any degree of testimonial support.

More recently, several of Hume's interpreters have favored the translation of Hume's maxim into the language of the Bayesian probability calculus. This reformulation is desirable if there is to be a more precise exposition of the maxim and of its use in Hume's argument against miracles. Since Hume's informal statement of his maxim in English harbors ambiguities about conditional probabilities, this is easier said than done.

Let M be some miracle statement; let t(M) be testimony to the occurrence of M; let E be the evidence of "constant and uniform experience" confirming the laws of nature; and let K be background evidence. On a probabilistic reading, the first part of Hume's maxim mentions two probabilities—the probability of the event (M) that some testimony t(M) seeks to establish, and the probability of the falsehood of the testimony, t(M) & ~M—and indicates that the first probability must be greater than the second if the testimony is to make the miracle statement credible. For Bayesian purposes, this relation needs to be translated into a comparative probability statement reflecting conditional probabilities. Everything depends on how each probability statement is rendered.

Jordan Howard Sobel concludes that Hume's maxim, when rendered in the language of probability theory, furnishes the critic with a powerful means of arguing against miracles. One probabilistic reading he has favored is the following:

$$\Pr (M/E \& K) > \Pr [\sim\! M \& t(M))/E \& K]$$

as if the antecedent probability of the miracle given the laws of nature—$\Pr (M/E \& K)$—should count as the crucial thing. If this probability is less than 0.5, as it surely is, then the miracle statement lacks credibility.

Sobel (1987) has also proposed the following alternative reading of Hume's maxim:

$$\Pr [M \& t(M)/E \& K] > \Pr [\sim\! M \& t(M)/E \& K]$$

This version differs from the first in proposing an estimation of the prior probability of the *conjunction* of M & t(M) and in stipulating that this probability must be greater than the falsehood of the testimony.

John Earman (2000) identifies one general problem with Hume's maxim and objects to Sobel's rendition of it. First, Hume needs a maxim that specifies a *sufficient* condition for the actual occurrence of a miracle to be more likely than the falsehood of testimony for a miracle. But he specifies only a *necessary* condition.

Second, Earman argues that neither of the two probabilities alluded to in the maxim is captured in the right way by Sobel's translation. Both probabilities should be conditioned on t(M), the testimony to the miracle. This is because Hume is assuming a situation where the one seeking to determine the credibility of a miracle state-

ment is aware of existing testimony to the occurrence of a miracle. The investigator is not concerned with the prior probability of testimony, or, for that matter, with the prior improbability of the miracle. The probability of the falsehood of the testimony should therefore be rendered

$$\Pr [\sim\! M/t(M) \& E \& K]$$

This makes sense of the plausible idea that the probability of falsehood is best determined by "the percentage of cases where no miracle occurs on occasions when the witness testifies to a miracle" (Earman 2000, 41). And the probability of the event some testimony seeks to establish should instead be represented as follows:

$$\Pr [M/t(M) \& E \& K]$$

The resulting probabilistic reading of Hume's maxim is as follows:

$$\Pr [M/t(M) \& E \& K] > \Pr [\sim\! M/t(M) \& E \& K]$$

This formula is tautologous and unexceptional. It doesn't have the consequence that either Hume or Sobel intend; it does not deliver an a piori argument against the credibility of miracle statements. It turns out, Earman argues, that this rendition of the first part of Hume's maxim also spells trouble for the coherence of the second part, because it would then appear to be counseling an illicit double counting of countervailing factors in the evidence.

The upshot of Earman's analysis is that there is no way to deploy Hume's maxim in an argument against miracles without a careful exploration of the details of historical evidence concerning a miracle statement and testimonial evidence offered in support of it. This Hume failed to do. Earman himself stops short of carrying out this investigation and is, in effect, agnostic about the occurrence of miracles.

While there seems to be no a priori philosophical argument against the credibility of miracle statements, there are philosophical resources for estimating the value of historical evidence, such as that developed by New Testament historians for the resurrection (see, for example, N. T. Wright [2003]). Richard Swinburne (2003) goes further, estimating the value of background evidence for theism together with specific historical evidence for the resurrection of Jesus. The background evidence, he argues, provides good reason to expect a miracle or two, reducing the weight that must be carried by specific historical evidence in order to establish the actual occurrence of a miracle. In turn, the historical evidence tends to confirm the theistic hypothesis because it indicates the fulfillment of the expectation generated by the background evidence and is itself additional evidence for the existence of God.

The philosophical study of the concept of miracle has led to a fruitful exploration of more general issues, such as the metaphysics of causation, the epistemology of testimonial evidence, and, in the philosophy of science, the proper conception of a law of nature.

See also Deism; Earman, John; Hume, David; Laws of Nature; Mackie, John Leslie.

Bibliography

Earman, John. *Hume's Abject Failure: The Argument against Miracles.* Oxford: Oxford University Press, 2000.

Geivett, R. Douglas, and Gary R. Habermas, eds. *In Defense of Miracles.* Downers Grove, IL: InterVarsity Press, 1997.

Hume, David. *Enquiries concerning Human Understanding and concerning the Principles of Morals.* Reprinted from the 1777 edition with Introduction and Analytical Index by L. A. Selby-Bigge; with text revised and notes by P. H. Nidditch. 3rd ed. Oxford: Clarendon Press, 1975.

Mackie, J. L. "Miracles and Testimony." Chapter 1 in *The Miracle of Theism: Arguments for and Against the Existence of God.* Oxford: Clarendon Press, 1982.

Sobel, J. H. "On the Evidence for Testimony for Miracles: A Bayesian Interpretation of David Hume's Analysis." *Philosophical Quarterly* 3 (1987): 166–86.

Sobel, J. H. "Hume's Theorem on Testimony Sufficient to Establish a Miracle." *Philosophical Quarterly* 41 (1991) 229–237.

Swinburne, Richard. *The Concept of Miracle.* London: Macmillan, 1970.

Swinburne, Richard. *The Resurrection of God Incarnate.* Oxford: Clarendon Press, 2003.

Wright, N. T. *The Resurrection of the Son of God.* Minneapolis, MN: Fortress Press, 2003.

R. Douglas Geivett (2005)

MIRANDOLA, COUNT GIOVANNI PICO DELLA

See *Pico Della Mirandola, Count Giovanni*

MIURA BAIEN
(1723–1789)

Miura Baien, a Japanese Confucianist who in the era of Tokugawa rule most closely approached Western philosophy, was born in Ōita prefecture on the island of Kyūshū.

After the usual training in Chinese classics, Miura went to Nagasaki and learned astronomy, physics, medicine, and economics and developed a great admiration for Western experimental methods. This explains in part his rationalism in opposition to the general reliance on the authority of the classics. He devoted his life to scholarship, refusing several offers to serve feudal lords. To help the poor he organized a relief society based on communal principles. Miura's encyclopedic knowledge also included economics. In *Kagen* (The origin of price) he discussed currency like his contemporary Adam Smith. Miura wrote "if bad money finds wide circulation, good money will go into hiding," a statement similar, in words at least, to Gresham's law.

Miura's main philosophical works are three: *Gengo* (Abstruse words), an exposition of logic; *Zeigo* (Superfluous words), an exposition of the philosophy of nature; and *Kango* (Presumptuous words), an exposition of ethics. *Gengo* is highly esteemed as original because in it he expounds his ideas of *jori*, or the logic of "things" (an abstract concept covering everything). This logic is based not on ancient authority but on rational or experimental grounds. Miura built his logic according to the laws of nature and things. In these he saw a unity and order of antithetic natural elements. He called his dialectic *hankan gōitchi*, or "synthesis of the contraries." This dialectic is both a logical device and the inner reality of things. Things, which are always in the process of becoming, pass from unity to multiplicity and back again, through antithesis and synthesis. His merits as the forerunner of modern trends in science and philosophy notwithstanding, Miura had rather staid political and theological ideas. His criticism of Christianity, in *Samidare-shō*, focuses on the idea that a foreign religion that puts God before devotion to one's lord and one's father cannot be tolerated.

See also Chinese Philosophy; Japanese Philosophy; Nature, Philosophical Ideas of; Philosophy of Economics; Smith, Adam.

Bibliography

Miura's works are available in Japanese in *Baien zenshū* (The collected works of Miura Baien), 2 vols. (Tokyo, 1912). See also G. K. Piovesana, "Miura Baien, and His Dialectical and Political Ideas," in *Monumenta Nipponica* 20 (1965): 389–443, which contains a translation of Miura's letter "Answer to Taga Bokkyō." See also W. T. de Bary, Ryusaku Tsunoda, and Donald Keene, eds., *Sources of Japanese Tradition* (New York: Columbia University Press, 1958), pp. 489–497; N. S. Smith, "An Introduction to Some Japanese Economic Writings of the 18th Century," in *Transactions of the Asiatic Society of Japan,* 2nd series, 11 (1934): 80–88; and

L. Hurvitz, "The *Samidareshō*," in *Monumenta Nipponica* 8 (1953): 289–326; 9 (1953): 330–356.

Gino K. Piovesana, S.J. (1967)

MODAL INTERPRETATION OF QUANTUM MECHANICS

The term *modal interpretation* is ambiguous. It is a proper name that refers to a number of particular interpretations of quantum mechanics. And it is a term that singles out a class of conceptually similar interpretations, which includes proposals that are not generally referred to as modal ones.

This ambiguity was already present when Bas C. van Fraassen coined the term in the 1970s by transposing the semantic analysis of modal logics to quantum logic. The resulting modal interpretation of quantum logic defined a class of interpretations of quantum mechanics, of which van Fraassen developed one instance in detail, called the Copenhagen modal interpretation. In the 1980s Simon Kochen and Dennis Dieks developed independently an interpretation of quantum mechanics that became known as *the* modal interpretation, turning the term into a proper name. In the 1990s further research produced new proposals, broadening attention to the class of modal interpretations.

The development of modal interpretations can be positioned as attempts to understand quantum mechanics as a theory according to which some but not all observables of physical systems have definite values. Quantum mechanics predicts the outcomes of measurements of observables pertaining to systems and is typically silent about whether these observables have values themselves. Attempts to add to quantum mechanics descriptions of systems in which all quantum-mechanical observables have values became deadlocked in the 1960s: Kochen and Ernst Specker's no-go theorem proved that such descriptions are inconsistent if these values have to comply to the same mathematical relations as the observables themselves; John S. Bell's inequalities showed that the descriptions easily lead to nonlocal phenomena at odds with relatively theory (Redhead 1987). Modal interpretations add descriptions to quantum mechanics according to which only a few *preferred observables* have values, and avoid in this way specifically the Kochen-Specker theorem.

A second common element is that modal interpretations do not ascribe one state to a system, as quantum mechanics does, but two: a dynamical state and a value state. By doing so another peculiarity of quantum mechanics is overcome, namely that states of systems evolve alternately by *two* mutually incompatible laws: the Schrödinger equation that yields smooth state evolution in between measurements, and the projection postulate that yields discontinuous evolution at measurements. In modal interpretations dynamical states of systems evolve with the Schrödinger equation only, and value states evolve typically discontinuously. A particular modal interpretation is now characterized by the value states it assigns to systems; value states fix the preferred definite-valued observables and their values.

Finally there is the claim that modal interpretations stay close to quantum mechanics. The dynamical states that modal interpretations assign can be taken as the states that quantum mechanics assigns, the only difference being that the former do not evolve by the projection postulate. Modal interpretations may thus be said to incorporate quantum mechanics instead of replacing it, as some hidden-variables theories do.

QUANTUM-MECHANICAL HILBERT-SPACE MATHEMATICS

In quantum mechanics the state and observables of a physical system are represented by mathematical entities defined on a Hilbert space associated with the system. A Hilbert space H contains vectors $|\psi\rangle$, and if it is an n-dimensional space, there exist sets $\{|e_1\rangle, |e_2\rangle, \ldots |e_n\rangle\}$ of n vectors that are pair-wise orthogonal. Such a set is called a basis of the space, which means that any vector $|\psi\rangle$ in H can be decomposed as a weighted sum of the elements of the basis: $|\psi\rangle = \sum_i c_i |e_i\rangle$. The Hilbert space associated with two disjoint physical systems consists of the tensor product $H_1 \otimes H_2$ of the Hilbert spaces associated with the separate systems. If $\{|e_1\rangle, \ldots |e_n\rangle\}$ is a basis of H_1 and $\{|f_1\rangle, \ldots |f_m\rangle\}$ a basis of H_2, then any vector $|\Psi\rangle$ part of $H_1 \otimes H_2$ can be decomposed as a sum $|\Psi\rangle = \sum_{i,j} C_{ij} |e_i\rangle \otimes |f_j\rangle$ (a double summation).

Linear operators A on a Hilbert space are linear mappings within that space. The operator that projects any vector on the vector $|\psi\rangle$ is called a projector and is written as $|\psi\rangle\langle\psi|$. In quantum mechanics the state of a system is represented by such a projector, or by a density projector W which is a complex sum $\sum_i \lambda_i |\psi_i\rangle\langle\psi_i|$ of projectors. An observable pertaining to a system (e.g., its momentum or spin) is represented by a self-adjoint operator A. Self-adjoint operators and density operators can be decomposed in terms of their eigenvalues a_i and projectors on their pair-wise orthogonal eigenvectors $|a_i\rangle$, that is, $A = \sum_i a_i |a_i\rangle\langle a_i|$. (Complications due to degeneracies, phase factors, and infinities are ignored.)

PARTICULAR MODAL INTERPRETATIONS

In all interpretations named modal, the dynamical state of a system is represented by a density operator W on the system's Hilbert space. This dynamical state evolves with the Schrödinger equation and has the usual quantum-mechanical meaning in terms of measurement outcomes: If observable A is measured, its eigenvalue a_i is found with probability $p(a_i) = \langle a_i|W|a_i\rangle$.

The value state of a system is represented by a vector $|v\rangle$ and determines the values of observables by the rule: A has value a_i iff $|v\rangle$ is equal to the eigenvector $|a_i\rangle$ of A. This rule leaves many observables without values; a specific value state is an eigenvector of only a few operators, which then represent the preferred observables. Particular modal interpretations fix the value states of systems differently.

In van Fraassen's (1973, 1991) Copenhagen modal interpretation $|v\rangle$ is a vector in the support of the dynamical state (which implies that W can be written as a convex sum of $|v\rangle\langle v|$ and other projectors). Van Fraassen is more specific about value states after measurements. If an observable A of a system is measured, the dynamical state of the composite of system and measurement device may become $|\Psi\rangle\langle\Psi|$, with $|\Psi\rangle = \sum_i c_i |a_i\rangle\otimes|R_i\rangle$. The vectors $|a_i\rangle$ are eigenvectors of the measured observable, and the $|R_i\rangle$'s are eigenvectors of a device observable that represents the outcomes (the pointer readings). The value states after this measurement are, according to van Fraassen, with probability $|c_i|^2$ simultaneously given by $|a_i\rangle$ for the system and by $|R_i\rangle$ for the measurement device, respectively.

The decomposition $|\Psi\rangle = \sum_i c_i |a_i\rangle\otimes|R_i\rangle$ is mathematically special because it contains one summation (as said, a decomposition of a vector $|\Psi\rangle$ in a product space $H_1\otimes H_2$ relative to bases of the separate Hilbert spaces has usually a double summation). This special single-sum decomposition is called the bi-orthogonal decomposition of $|\Psi\rangle$, and a theorem (Schrödinger 1935) states that every vector $|\Psi\rangle$ in $H_1\otimes H_2$ determines exactly one basis $\{|e_1\rangle, \ldots |e_n\rangle\}$ for H_1 and one basis $\{|f_1\rangle, \ldots |f_m\rangle\}$ for H_2 for which its decomposition becomes such a bi-orthogonal decomposition.

Kochen (1985) and Dieks (1989) use this decomposition to define value states in their modal interpretation:

If two disjoint systems have a composite dynamical state $|\Psi\rangle\langle\Psi|$ and the bi-orthogonal decomposition of the vector $|\Psi\rangle$ is $|\Psi\rangle = \sum_i c_i |e_i\rangle\otimes|f_i\rangle$, then the value states are with probability $|c_i|^2$ simultaneously $|e_i\rangle$ for the first system and $|f_i\rangle$ for the second. Kochen adds a perspectival twist to this proposal, absent in Dieks's earlier writing: For Kochen the first system witnesses the second to have value state $|f_i\rangle$ iff it has itself value state $|e_i\rangle$ (which is the case with probability $|c_i|^2$) and the second system then witnesses, conversely, the first to have value state $|e_i\rangle$.

The Kochen-Dieks proposal applies to two systems with a composite dynamical state represented by a projector $|\Psi\rangle\langle\Psi|$ only. The spectral modal interpretation by Pieter Vermaas and Dieks (1995) generalizes this proposal to n disjoint systems with an arbitrary composite dynamical state W. This composite state fixes the dynamical states of all subsystems. Let $W(x)$ be the dynamical state of the x-th system part of the composite and let it have an eigenvalue-eigenvector decomposition $W(x) = \sum_i w_i(x)|w_i(x)\rangle\langle w_i(x)|$. The value state of this x-th system is then $|w_i(x)\rangle$ with probability $w_i(x)$. Vermaas and Dieks gave, moreover, joint probabilities that the disjoint systems have simultaneously their value states $|w_i(1)\rangle$, $|w_j(2)\rangle$, etcetera.

In the spectral modal interpretation a composite system, say, system 1+2 composed of the disjoint systems 1 and 2, has an eigenvector $|w_k(1+2)\rangle$ of its dynamical state $W(1+2)$ as its value state. The atomic modal interpretation by Guido Bacciagaluppi and Michael Dickson (1999) fixes the value states of such composite systems differently. Bacciagaluppi and Dickson assume that there exists a set of disjoint atomic systems, for which the value states are determined similarly as in the spectral modal interpretation, and propose that the value states of composites of those atoms are tensor products of the value states of the atoms: the value state of the composite of atoms 1 and 2 is $|w_i(1)\rangle\otimes|w_j(2)\rangle$ iff the value states of the atoms are $|w_i(1)\rangle$ and $|w_j(2)\rangle$, respectively.

THE CLASS OF MODAL INTERPRETATIONS

The class of modal interpretations comprises those proposals according to which only a few observables have values, and that can be formulated in terms of dynamical and value states. The interpretations by Richard Healey (1989) and by Jeffrey Bub (1997) have this structure quite explicitly and are therefore often called modal ones (Healey's proposal has a number of similarities with the Kochen-Dieks proposal; in Bub's the value state of a system is an eigenvector of an observable fixed independently of the system's dynamical state). One may argue that David Bohm's mechanics (1952) is also a modal interpretation.

RESULTS

The development and application of modal interpretations have led to mixed results. The maximum set of observables that can have values by modal interpretations without falling prey to the Kochen-Specker theorem has been determined (Vermaas 1999). Bub and Rob Clifton showed that this set is the only one that satisfies a series of natural assumptions on descriptions of single systems (Bub, Clifton, and Goldstein 2000). The evolution of value states, which determines the description of systems over time, can be given (Bacciagaluppi and Dickson 1999). This evolution was, however, shown not to be Lorentz-covariant for the spectral and atomic modal interpretations and, to a lesser extent, for Bub's interpretation, revealing that the assumption that only a few quantum-mechanical observables have values, still may lead to problems with relatively theory (Dickson and Clifton 1998, Myrvold 2002).

Moreover, even though this assumption yields consistent descriptions of single systems, joint descriptions of systems were still proved to be problematic. First, it is commonly assumed in quantum mechanics that the observable of a system 1 represented by the operator A defined on H_1, and the observable of a composite system 1+2 represented by the operator $A_1 \otimes I_2$ on $H_1 \otimes H_2$ (I_2 is the identity operator on H_2) are one and the same observable. The Copenhagen, Kochen-Dieks, and spectral modal interpretations have the debatable consequence that these observables should be distinguished (Clifton 1996). Second, the spectral modal interpretation cannot give joint probabilities that systems 1, 2, ... , and their composites, 1+2, ... , have simultaneously their value states $|w_i(1)\rangle$, $|w_j(2)\rangle$, $|w_k(1+2)\rangle$, etcetera (Vermaas 1999, ch. 6).

These negative results motivated in part the formulation of the atomic modal interpretation but can also be avoided by adopting Kochen's perspectivalism, which implies that one accepts constraints on describing different systems simultaneously. Finally, the Kochen-Dieks, spectral, and atomic modal interpretations have problems with properly describing measurements, doubting their empirical adequacy. David Albert and Barry Loewer (1990) argued that after a measurement, the dynamical state of the system-device composite need not be $|\Psi\rangle\langle\Psi|$ with $|\Psi\rangle = \sum_i c_i |a_i\rangle \otimes |R_i\rangle$, and that the mentioned interpretations then need not yield descriptions in which the device displays an outcome (Bacciagaluppi and Hemmo 1996).

ASSESSMENT

These results allow critical conclusions about particular modal interpretations and raise doubts about the viability of the class of modal interpretations. Three remarks can be made about this assessment.

First, an evaluation of the results may depend on what one expects from interpretations. If interpretations are to provide descriptions that allow realist positions about quantum mechanics, the inability of, say, the spectral modal interpretation to give joint probabilities that systems have simultaneously value states, proves this interpretation problematic. But if interpretations, in line with van Fraassen's view, are to yield understanding of what quantum mechanics means, this inability of the spectral modal interpretation is an interesting conclusion about how quantum-mechanical descriptions of systems differ from those of other physical theories. The result that some modal interpretations may be empirical inadequate, is, however, fatal independently of one's expectations for interpretations.

Second, the set of particular modal interpretations that is analyzed so far does not exhaust the class of modal interpretations. Research therefore continues (e.g., Bene and Dieks 2002).

Third, these results are relevant to the project of interpreting quantum mechanics in general. Existing and new interpretations, modal or not, according to which only some observables have definite values, are constrained by the negative results and can now be assessed as such; and existing and new interpretations may benefit from the positive results about modal interpretations.

See also Bell, John, and Bell's Theorem; Bohm, David; Quantum Mechanics; Van Fraassen, Bas.

Bibliography

Albert, David Z., and Barry Loewer. "Wanted Dead or Alive: Two Attempts to Solve Schrödinger's Paradox." In *Proceedings of the 1990 Biennial Meeting of the Philosophy of Science Association*. Vol. 1., edited by Arthur Fine, Micky Forbes, and Linda Wessels. East Lansing, MI: Philosophy of Science Association, 1990.

Bacciagaluppi, Guido, and Michael Dickson. "Dynamics for Modal Interpretations." *Foundations of Physics* 29 (1999): 1165–1201.

Bacciagaluppi, Guido, and Meir Hemmo. "Modal Interpretations, Decoherence and Measurement." *Studies in History and Philosophy of Modern Physics* 27 (1996): 239–277.

Bene, Gyula, and Dennis Dieks. "A Perspectival Version of the Modal Interpretation of Quantum Mechanics and the

Origin of Macroscopic Behavior." *Foundations of Physics* 32 (2002): 645–671.

Bohm, David. "A Suggested Interpretation of Quantum Theory in Terms of 'Hidden Variables.'" *Physical Review* 85 (1952): 166–193.

Bub, Jeffrey. *Interpreting the Quantum World*. Cambridge, U.K.: Cambridge University Press, 1997.

Bub, Jeffrey, Rob Clifton, and Sheldon Goldstein. "Revised Proof of the Uniqueness Theorem for 'No Collapse' Interpretations of Quantum Mechanics." *Studies in History and Philosophy of Modern Physics* 31 (2000): 95–98.

Clifton, Rob. "The Properties of Modal Interpretations of Quantum Mechanics." *British Journal for the Philosophy of Science* 47 (1996): 371–398.

Dickson, Michael, and Rob Clifton. "Lorentz-Invariance in Modal Interpretations." In *The Western Ontario Series in Philosophy of Science*. Vol. 60, *The Modal Interpretation of Quantum Mechanics*, edited by Dennis Dieks and Pieter E. Vermaas. Dordrecht, Netherlands: Kluwer, 1998.

Dieks, Dennis. "Quantum Mechanics Without the Projection Postulate and Its Realistic Interpretation." *Foundations of Physics* 19 (1989): 1397–1423.

Healey, Richard A. *The Philosophy of Quantum Mechanics: An Interactive Interpretation*. Cambridge, U.K.: Cambridge University Press, 1989.

Kochen, Simon. "A New Interpretation of Quantum Mechanics." In *Symposium on the Foundations of Modern Physics*, edited by Pekka Lahti and Peter Mittelstaedt. Singapore: World Scientific, 1985.

Myrvold, Wayne C. "Modal Interpretations and Relativity." *Foundations of Physics* 32 (2002): 1773–1784.

Redhead, Michael. *Incompleteness, Nonlocality, and Realism: A Prolegomenon to the Philosophy of Quantum Mechanics*. Oxford: Clarendon Press, 1987.

Schrödinger, Erwin. "Discussion of Probability Relations Between Separated Systems." *Proceedings of the Cambridge Philosophical Society* 31 (1935): 555–563.

van Fraassen, Bas C. *Quantum Mechanics: An Empiricist View*. Oxford: Clarendon Press, 1991.

van Fraassen, Bas C. "Semantic Analysis of Quantum Logic." In *The University of Western Ontario Series in Philosophy of Science*. Vol. 2, *Contemporary Research in the Foundations and Philosophy of Quantum Theory*, edited by C. A. Hooker. Dordrecht, Netherlands: Reidel, 1973.

Vermaas, Pieter E. *A Philosopher's Understanding of Quantum Mechanics: Possibilities and Impossibilities of a Modal Interpretation*. Cambridge, U.K.: Cambridge University Press, 1999.

Vermaas, Pieter E., and Dennis Dieks. "The Modal Interpretation of Quantum Mechanics and Its Generalization to Density Operators." *Foundations of Physics* 25 (1995): 145–158.

Pieter E. Vermaas (2005)

MODALITY, PHILOSOPHY AND METAPHYSICS OF

Some things are true; some are false. Some are true, but might have been false. Some are true but could not have been false. Some are false, but might have been true. Some are false but could not have been true. Thus, there are at least these different modes of truth and falsity: necessity and possibility. A truth bearer—a proposition, a statement, or an interpreted sentence—is necessarily true if and only if (iff) it is not possible that it be false; it is possibly true iff it is not necessary that it be false. A contingency is what is possibly true as well as possibly false. The study of the ways in which truth and falsity interact with necessity and possibility is the subject of modal logics.

If there are modal distinctions to be made about truth bearers—because, say, while the sum of seven and five could not fail to be twelve, there might have been twelve planets orbiting the sun even though there are not—arguably there are modal distinctions to be made regarding the attributes objects possess. While Socrates could have failed to be snub-nosed, he could not have failed to be human or perhaps a person. Modality as it pertains to the bearers of truth is *de dicto* modality; modality that concerns the way in which an object possesses an attribute is *de re*. Conventionally, $\square$ and $\lozenge$ express necessity and possibility, respectively.

KINDS OF NECESSITY

Necessities may be distinguished according to their scope or, perhaps, their subject matter. Some concern the limits of meaning and inference and are systematized by formal logical systems. Classical logicians maintain that meaning and inference are best understood in terms of a two-valued logic according to which truth bearers may take only the values of true or false and that exactly one of a truth bearer and its negation is true. These ideas are encoded by, though not strictly equivalent to, the laws of excluded middle, $P \lor \neg P$, and noncontradiction, $\neg(P \& \neg P)$. Where objects and their attributes are concerned, there are analogous laws: Each thing either has or lacks a given attribute and neither both has and lacks the same attribute, formally represented as $\forall x(Fx \lor \neg Fx)$ and $\forall x \neg(Fx \& \neg Fx)$. Some nonclassical logics have correspondingly different foundational laws. Such laws of logic are treated as necessary truths, though usually they are stated without any *de dicto* modal qualifier. Logical truths, the truths that follow validly from the axioms of logic, are the logical necessities. Whatever is consistent with the laws of logic are the logical possibilities and if the falsity of something follows from the laws of logic, then it is a logical impossibility.

Disputes about which of the many logical systems is the single correct system that formalizes valid inference are, then, disputes about what the logical necessities are. Disputes about whether there is a single such correct system are disputes about whether there is a plurality of sets of logical necessities, one corresponding to each system of logic. Broader notions of logical necessity are sometimes given by adding linguistic or conceptual truths. Analytic or conceptual necessities are those that follow from the laws of logic plus the linguistic or conceptual truths. That all bachelors are unmarried is a favorite example of such an analytic truth.

Laws of nature and their associated counterfactual conditionals are often thought to be necessary in one sense and contingent in another. There are many true universal generalizations and many unbroken sequences of types of events. Not all of these, however, form part of some scientific theory; some generalizations and patterns are accidental. Those that are not accidental and constitute the fundamentals of a scientific theory are the laws of nature and whatever follows from those laws are the natural necessities. Whatever is consistent with the laws of nature are the natural possibilities. It is sometimes useful to make distinctions among the natural necessities and separate the physical, chemical, biological, psychological, and perhaps other necessities.

The natural necessities are not logical truths, however. Orthodoxy has it that logical truth is known *a priori*, without any specific experiences, while scientific truth is knowable only *a posteriori*, on the basis of experience. That empirical investigation is required for scientific knowledge is taken to show that the natural necessities are contingent; they might have been otherwise. Certainly, they are not analytic and cannot be known simply by reflecting on their contents. If one takes the most central laws of physics to be the axioms of physics, then what follows from those laws are the physical necessities. That the basic physical laws are required to infer the physical necessities demonstrates more conclusively that the physical necessities are not logical truths and, so, are not logical necessities. If laws of nature are necessary in some legitimate sense, then the meaning of □ when applied to laws of nature must differ from its meaning when it is applied to laws of logic.

Somewhat more controversial is the idea that there is an intermediate modality between the logical and the natural: the metaphysical. Like natural necessities, meta-physical necessities are not logical truths and yet, unlike the natural necessities, the central metaphysical principles are to be known *a priori* even if knowledge of some particular metaphysical necessities requires some empirical knowledge. While there is no contradiction in denying such metaphysical principles, their proponents maintain that they are, nevertheless, necessary and that they express limits on genuine possibilities for existence. Accordingly, logical possibilities that fail to be metaphysical possibilities would be merely formal possibilities.

Thus, if there are two distinct attributes that are essentially related, then while there is no contradiction in asserting that an object could possess the one without the other, it would be, strictly speaking, impossible for any object to possess the one without the other. There might be attributes such that if an object even possibly possesses it, then that object possesses that attribute essentially. Arguably, if something is a concrete object such as a brick, then it must be concrete and could not be an abstract object such as the power set of the real numbers. Those who embrace this intermediate modality think that metaphysical principles state nontrivially what is at least part of the essence of an object—that without which it could not be—and, so, they are known as essentialists or sometimes Aristotelian essentialists since Aristotle advocated a form essentialism.

While the philosophy of modality is dominated by controversies about whether there are the three modalities mentioned and, if so what their relations are, there are others of interest. If one takes up the general pattern used earlier and recognizes that a common way to characterize the content of a modality is to formulate a set of axioms and define a sense of □ so that it applies to all and only whatever follows from those axioms, then there are indefinitely many kinds of modality. For each formally characterized system of logic there is a candidate for logical necessity, not all of which are equivalent. Such a plurality cascades down through any modality that relies on logical consequence for its own characterization.

Among the most commonly discussed of the other modalities are the epistemic, doxastic, and moral necessities. Epistemic necessity can be thought of as whatever follows from what is known and the scope of the known can be specific to an individual or to a community. Doxastic necessity is what follows from what is believed. Moral necessities are the relevant moral obligations and duties. Whether any of the modalities mentioned is nothing but a special form of any of the others is a substantial question, but the only clear connection, given the way they have been characterized, is that all the nonlogical modalities tacitly embed the logical. The axiom-theorem structure demands this, making each of them an extension of the logical and not a special case of it.

SOURCES OF NECESSITY

For any recognized kind of necessity there is the substantive question of what accounts for the fact that some truths, and not some others, are necessary in the relevant sense. As with other forms of discourse, there are deep philosophical questions about whether one has any knowledge involving modality. These questions have at least two forms. The first form is a standard challenge from the skeptic who does not deny, in this context, that there are necessary truths but who denies either that one has any knowledge of which truths are necessary or that nonskeptics are entitled to their knowledge claims according to their own standards of knowledge. The second form comes from the modal antirealist, one who either denies that there are any modal truths or who claims that modal truth is so closely bound to cognizers that statements involving modality lack significant objectivity, making them more like statements of taste or preference than statements of fact. Modal noncognitivists maintain that modal discourse is used not to make assertions but to, perhaps, express an attitude or a commitment toward some nonmodal truths. David Hume (1739) adopted a kind of noncognitivism about the relation of cause and effect. Simon Blackburn (1986) and Crispin Wright (1980, 1989) advanced contemporary defenses of versions of modal antirealism.

Realist interpretations of modal discourse treat some statements involving modality as true in some person-independent manner. If modal truth is to be a species of truth more generally then, thinks the realist about modal discourse, modal truth must concern sufficiently determinate and objective facts. This is the question of what grounds modal truth or, perhaps, what the truth conditions are for modal claims. Common suggestions have been that something is possible iff it is conceivable, iff it implies no contradiction, iff it is true in at least one mathematical model, or iff it is true in at least one possible world.

The success conditions for a theory of modality depend on the purpose of that theory. Any successful theory should be extensionally adequate; it should declare as necessary all and only what is necessary. Philosophical theories are often put forward as being more than merely extensionally adequate, sometimes because they are intended as linguistic or conceptual analyses. A conceptual analysis would state not only the appropriate biconditionals that fix the extension of *necessary*, it would do so in such a way that analyzed the meaning of that term. Successful conceptual analyses must not only be extensionally adequate, they must also be noncircular by avoiding the use of what is to be analyzed in the analysis or definition. Analyses of modal notions would need to avoid analyzing *necessary* in terms of any modal notions like *necessary*, *possible*, or their cognates. When empirical confirmation of the extensional adequacy of a theory is impossible to obtain, conceptual analyses are attractive. The conceptual analysis guarantees extensional adequacy because the analysis given means nothing more and nothing less than that for which it is a theory. Theories not intended as conceptual analyses must involve some other warrant for the thesis that the theory is extensionally adequate.

If proposed as an analysis, a conceivability theory faces difficulties regarding both extensional adequacy and circularity. If it is formulated in terms of conceivers who are not perfect conceivers, then extensional adequacy is not guaranteed; there may be possibilities of which no one is capable of conceiving or else conceivers may be capable of conceiving what is impossible without noticing that it is impossible. Formulating the theory in terms of what is merely conceivable, whether by an ideal or fallible conceiver, renders the analysis circular because the semantic analysis of *possible* is given in terms of what it is possible to conceive. Formulating it in terms of what is actually conceived by an omniscient being avoids this circularity but brings metaphysical commitments that few want to make on the basis of their philosophy of modality alone.

The logical positivists wished to maintain that logical and mathematical truths were necessary, but they resisted all substantive metaphysics as distinct from the ontologies of the sciences. Alfred J. Ayer (1936) developed a version of conventionalism about modality. By dividing propositions into the classes of those that concern ideas or concepts only and those that concern facts, Ayer maintained that only propositions regarding ideas were both necessary and knowable *a priori*. They make no claims about the empirical world and, so, are not subject to empirical falsification and are either necessarily true or necessarily false. These propositions are analytically true or analytically false according to Ayer because they are true or false due solely to the definitions or analyses of their constituent symbols, both logical and nonlogical. It is necessarily true that all bachelors are unmarried not because of the way the world is but because of what is meant by *all*, *bachelors*, *unmarried*, and tacitly, *if, then*.

Willard Van Orman Quine provided what has become the received critique of attempts to ground necessary truth and falsehood in the facts of language. In "Two Dogmas of Empiricism" (1951) Quine argued that there is no hard and fast distinction between propositions that are about the world and those that are not and, so, that no proposition is immune from refutation on partly empirical grounds. Thus, he argued that there is no interesting analytic-synthetic distinction on which the positivist program depends. In "Truth by Convention" (1948) he argued that stipulations regarding the meanings of expressions cannot be a general source of necessity, since at most they can transform obvious logical truths into more convenient but less obvious truths.

So, it is a logical truth that all unmarried males are unmarried and if bachelors just are, by definition, unmarried males, then the logical truth plus the definition of *bachelor* is sufficient for the truth of "all bachelors are unmarried." However, this transforming work of definitions requires something to begin with that is already necessarily true: the relevant logical truth. Linguistic conventions are unable to account for the necessity of the logical truths. Rudolf Carnap (1954) tried to solve this problem by avoiding the semantic foundation of meaning, thus avoiding Quine's critique, and by relying on syntactic facts of grammar and rules of logical proof. He understood logical truth as what is derivable from the null class of sentences.

While not relying on meanings, the standard problems regarding extensional adequacy and circularity arise. Standard understandings of logical systems have it that there are infinitely many sentences that may be derived from the null set, not all of which have been derived. Framing the theory in terms of what has actually been derived renders the account extensionally inadequate, while framing it in terms of facts of derivability renders it circular. A successful form of the linguistic theory of modality might retreat from the positivist's rejection of all metaphysics and appeal to facts about concepts or propositions in a Platonic Heaven of abstract objects. Alternatively, there could be a stipulation by a kind of ostention according to which *necessary* is stipulated to apply to some already established classes of truths, say logical, mathematical, and analytic truths. This would give one a kind of conventional basis for necessity, but not for the truth of what is by this convention called *necessary*. This account assumes that there are logical, mathematical, and analytic truths before the stipulation. While each account avoids the problems posed for Ayer's (1936) and Carnap's, they do not deliver what the positivists

wanted: a general theory that demonstrates why logical, mathematical, and analytic truths are completely immune from empirical refutation while at the same time avoiding all metaphysics that they found philosophically distasteful. Alan Sidelle (1989) attempted to present a more defensible version of conventionalism.

POSSIBLE WORLDS AND MODAL LOGIC

Before and during the time that the positivists were developing their philosophical approach to modality and Quine (1948, 1951) was subjecting it to critical scrutiny, elementary first-order predicate logic was being extended with the use of modal operators, most famously by Clarence Irving Lewis (1918) and Lewis and Cooper Harold Langford (1932). Unlike the developments of nonmodal logics up to that time, about which there was widespread agreement that alternative axiom systems were equivalent, there were many inequivalent axiomatic systems of modal logic. Worse, standard first-order logics had been provided with mathematical semantic foundations from which the systems of proof could be shown to be adequate for proving all theorems of first-order logic and for never permitting the derivation of any nontheorems. Modal logics lacked a similar semantic framework. The many inequivalent systems made it impossible, on formal grounds alone, to determine which logic was the proper formalization of modal concepts that, in turn, caused some to wonder whether modal concepts were sufficiently respectable to be given systematic treatment.

Part of the difficulty arose because the modal expressions in formal languages, $\square$ and $\lozenge$, were treated like the negation symbol, $\neg$. Thus, if P were a sentence of the formal language, $\neg$P, $\square$P, and $\lozenge$P would also be sentences of the language. Like negation, the modal operators could be used in quantified sentences of the language, so that if $\forall xFx$ and $\exists xFx$ were sentences of the language, $\square\forall xFx$, $\forall x\square Fx$, $\square\exists xFx$, and $\exists x\square Fx$ would be as well. The *de dicto* use of modality in $\square\forall xFx$ and $\square\exists xFx$ seemed innocent enough to those who were not convinced by Quine's (1951) critique of analyticity. More troublesome were the *de re* forms, $\forall x\square Fx$ and $\exists x\square Fx$. In stating that everything is necessarily or essentially F and that something is necessarily or essentially F, these sentences seem to make metaphysical claims, about which the positivists had succeeded in raising suspicion.

In 1963 Saul Kripke made prominent some developments in the semantics of modal logic. The central idea was to mimic an important aspect of the formal semantics for first-order logic. The mathematics of model theory that had enabled logicians to define what it is for an argument to be formally valid involved appealing to a domain of objects, mathematical models, that were customarily thought to be abstract objects. In these models, one could define the extensions of predicates, intuitively the sets of objects that possessed the relevant attributes or that stood in the relevant relations to each other. Logical notions like validity could be defined in terms of these mathematical models.

Kripke and others saw that if this model-theoretic framework were extended, a similar formal semantics could be given for modal logics. Whereas standard models had concerned only everything that does exist, the extension of this approach was simply to take as the domain everything that exists not only in the actual world but also everything that exists in every possible world. The second key idea was to treat the modal operators like quantifiers. If $\square$ was treated as $\forall$ and $\lozenge$ as $\exists$, then $\square P$ could be thought of as a expressing the claim that P is true in every possible world and $\lozenge P$ could be thought of as expressing the claim that P is true in at least one such world, whether this world or not. A historical overview of developments of this general approach before Kripke's elegant presentation can be found in B. J. Copeland (1996).

POSSIBLE WORLDS AND METAPHYSICS

Those proposing this possible worlds semantics for modal logic thought of the structure quite abstractly. The suggestion to think of the main domain as the set of all possible worlds was merely a heuristic to illuminate the intuitive idea behind the abstract structure of the semantics. It was David Lewis (1973) who recommended taking this heuristic to have metaphysical significance. He argued that modal claims can be paraphrased with claims about possible worlds. Many agreed with this much, but resisted Lewis's genuine modal realism," according to which each world in this plurality was as robust and concrete as one thinks of this world. In some of these worlds there are donkeys that talk and in some there are blue swans. So, while those concerned with the semantics of modal logic were concerned with providing a formal mathematical structure according to which important logical notions like logical consequence could be precisely characterized, Lewis was concerned with the issue of the grounds for the truth values of modal claims. So, for Lewis, $\square P$ is true iff P is true in all the worlds; otherwise, not.

The formal apparatus involved an accessibility relation over this set of worlds and that relation could have variable extension. This permitted Lewis (1973) to assess counterfactual conditionals in terms of what happens not merely in some world or other, but what happens in close or sufficiently similar worlds. Thus, in some circumstances I could have done otherwise because in an appropriately similar world one similar to me does otherwise.

Lewis's (1973) genuine modal realism served as the focus of much discussion about the philosophy and metaphysics of modality, although the position has had relatively few adherents. The possible worlds theorist was able to take the mathematical results about modal logic and to find in them the grounds for modal truth. Initial discussions of the possible worlds framework, however, focused on reasons for thinking that while the framework should be adopted, Lewis's metaphysics of possible worlds should be resisted.

One serious problem for the genuine modal realist is epistemological. Suppose that there really is a plurality of concrete worlds and that it is facts about these worlds that make true or false one's modal assertions. How can this account of the truth conditions for modal claims be squared with the often-unstated starting point in the philosophy of modality: that one possesses some knowledge of modal truth that is not merely trivial? One thinks that one knows that there could be talking donkeys, blue swans, and many more things that do not actually exist. One also thinks one knows the truth of some counterfactual conditionals, such as that were the sun to cease to exist, then the earth would cool rapidly and that were a thin pane of ordinary glass to be struck by a flying rock, it would break. If the modal facts, however, really are facts about other worlds, how could one have gained any of this knowledge?

A second apparent problem is that the possible worlds framework looks ill suited to the task of philosophical analysis of modal idioms. If one says that $\lozenge P$ is true iff P is true in every possible world, then the analysis certainly appears to be extensionally adequate, but at the cost of circularity. If one says, rather, that $\lozenge P$ is true iff P is true in every world that there is, then obvious circularity is avoided at the cost of no longer exhibiting the extensionally adequacy of the analysis.

The epistemological problem was addressed by those who proposed accounts of the nature of possible worlds in terms of objects that, it was maintained, one already had reason to accept. Instead of thinking of truth in possible worlds as truth in or about concrete maximal spatiotemporal wholes, it was argued that truth in possible worlds is really truth in maximal states of affairs (Plantinga 1974), truth in world stories—maximal consistent sets of propositions (Adams 1974), or truth about properties of a special kind—ways the world might have been (Stalnaker 1976). Each theory was actualist in that it recognized only objects that actually exist or, to use the vocabulary of possible worlds, each recognized only objects that exist in the actual world. To that extent each of these alternatives had the advantage of locating the ground for modal truths in this world and not another. That there was a useful solution to the general form of the epistemological problem posed for Lewis's (1973) genuine modal realism depends on whether the central feature of the problem was that the modally relevant facts inhabited or constituted worlds distinct from one's own.

Arguably, the central feature of the problem was that it was hard to wed the metaphysics of concrete worlds with plausible accounts of the nature of knowledge. Lewis's account of worlds permitted no physical or causal contact with features of other worlds. To avoid this general problem, some mutually favorable accounts of the natures of states of affairs, propositions, or properties on the one hand and knowledge on the other hand are required. To the extent that these entities are abstract and to the extent that abstract entities are not spatiotemporally or causally located, these actualist theories do not solve this epistemological problem. To the extent that spatiotemporal connectedness is not necessary for access to, say, propositions, then the genuine modal realist could, perhaps, take advantage of an alternative account of knowledge to avoid this particular problem.

Lewis (1986) recognized that his theory of modality could not serve as the basis for a proper analysis of modal notions, if he could not analyze the concept of a possible world. If he could not, possible truth would be analyzed in terms of possible worlds that, while involving some philosophical advance perhaps, does not constitute a full analysis of modal concepts in nonmodal terms. Lewis (1986) argued that each world is a maximal spatiotemporally connected whole; objects inhabit the same world when they spatiotemporally connect to each other. On the reasonably safe assumption that these spatiotemporal notions are not themselves modal, obvious circularity is avoided.

Extensional adequacy must still be secured. Lewis (1986) tries to secure it by somewhat contentious means. He appeals to a Humean principle of recombination to support the thesis that there are sufficiently many possible worlds. Recombination is the denial of necessary connections between distinct existences. So long as the objects occupy distinct spatiotemporal locations, anything could exist with anything else or, strictly speaking, a duplicate of anything could exist with a duplicate of anything else. This basis for plenitude is more contentious than was the avoidance of obvious circularity because it depends on the more controversial Humean principle. Essentialists reject that principle as do those who maintain that laws of nature are metaphysically necessary.

There may yet be some hidden circularity or other theoretical impropriety as argued by Scott A. Shalkowski (1994, 2004). Of course, if there is a plurality of concrete worlds in which sufficiently much of what one takes to be possible is true, then knowing this would be sufficient warrant for declaring that possible truth just is truth in some world or other. It is knowing that there is this match between one's apparent modal knowledge and the internal workings of the worlds in the plurality that is difficult to secure in a nonquestion-begging way. Were philosophical analysis sufficient to justify not only that there are possible worlds, but that they are concrete and sufficiently plentiful for the required correlation, then all would be well for the genuine modal realist. John Divers and Joseph Melia (2002), however, argued that analysis is inadequate to establish that there are sufficiently many worlds. The danger, then, is that the grounds for genuine modal realism as a full theory of modality are question-begging or else inadequate. Furthermore, they argue that the framework may not even be extensionally adequate because there may be no complete set of all possible worlds.

Some objections to genuine modal realism concerned whether the conditions it provides really are adequate to grounding the modal claims one thinks one is entitled to make. For example, one knows that in some instances one could have behaved otherwise than one did. Strictly speaking, though, I am a world-bound individual. I inhabit only this spatiotemporal whole and not another. However, it is what goes on in other worlds that is supposed to account for the fact that I could have behaved otherwise. I could have behaved otherwise because some world contains a counterpart of me that does, in a suitably similar situation, behave otherwise. This is Lewis's counterpart theory (1968, 1986).

Kripke (1972/1980) argued that counterpart theory is inadequate precisely because the modal claim under consideration concerns what I could do. How does what someone else somewhere else does make it the case that I could have followed that alternative course of action? That someone else in this space-time does something else does not make it the case that I could have done the same, so someone else in another space-time seems no more relevant.

Though Kripke's (1972/1980) objection has intuitive appeal, arguably it is question-begging. Lewis (1986) develops counterpart theory so that the identity of individuals across worlds, transworld identity, just is a matter of having a counterpart in those other worlds. Just as there are philosophical issues about in what identity over time consists, there are philosophical issues about in what identity in modal contexts consists. According to some theories of identity over time, an object that lives for a hundred years is constituted by distinct temporal parts. There is, therefore, precedent for something like counterpart theory. What counts as a counterpart of an object in a distinct world is a matter of relevant similarity, where relevance is determined by, for example, the counterfactual conditional to be assessed. Similar remarks apply to Alvin Plantinga's (1974) objection from numerical identity.

D. M. Armstrong (1989) argued for a somewhat less ontologically ambitious modal realism: combinatorialism. According to combinatorialism possible worlds are recombinations of individuals, properties, and relations of the actual world. Like Lewis (1968), Armstrong relies on a Humean principle of recombination. A recombination of actual objects and actual properties and relations constitutes a nonactual possible world. One difference is that Lewis formulates his principle in terms of duplicates of objects, whereas Armstrong does so in terms of the objects themselves. Where Lewis has no need to countenance qualitatively indiscernible worlds as distinct, Armstrong does. That an object, a, is F and that another, b, is exactly like a except that it is G instead of F, provides for a recombination exactly like the actual world save that in this recombination it is b that is F and a that is G. This seems to involve a commitment to haecceitism, the view that there are nonqualitative differences between worlds. Though this seems to be a natural consequence of his basic combinatorial insight, Armstrong rejects haecceitism.

The are two important issues that confront the combinatorialist. First, some principled, nonmodal restriction on the principle of recombination must be given, since if there is no such restriction, impossible worlds will result and the theory will be extensionally inadequate. With no restriction, there is a recombination in which some object is both wholly red and wholly green, thus rendering it false that ◊P is true iff P is true in at least one of the combinatorialist's worlds. Armstrong (1989)

attempts restrictions that arise naturally from his own theory of universals in an attempt to solve this problem.

More significant is the problem of alien properties. It is plausible that there could be objects that possess properties that no actual object possesses and that cannot be constructed from any properties that actual objects possess. Unless one is prepared to claim that one's world is maximally qualitatively rich, this consequence is unwelcome. Those who, like Armstrong (1989), wish to acknowledge the existence only of properties that are exhibited, must concede that this is a feature of the theory, in spite of strong reasons to the contrary. For other than special pleading, what reason is there for thinking that this world does not stand to another world in the relation of relative-impoverishment with respect to properties as some simpler worlds stand in relation to this one? Those who adopt a more Platonistic theory of properties and recognize uninstantiated abstract properties avoid this problem of alien properties, but at the cost of needing to solve the epistemological problems regarding one's knowledge of properties rather than one's knowledge of the genuine modal realist's worlds.

FICTIONALISM AND MODALISM

One development that at least initially promises to retain the advantages of genuine realism without this epistemological trouble is modal fictionalism. Strictly speaking, while it is possible that there be talking donkeys, there are none. However, it is also literally true that according to the fiction of possible worlds, there are worlds in which there are talking donkeys. Gideon Rosen (1990) suggested that ◊P is true iff according to the fiction of possible worlds, P or some appropriate paraphrase is true in some possible world. Possible worlds are taken to be useful fictions in the same way that scientists have found ideal gases and frictionless planes to be theoretically useful. Whether fictionalism gains any theoretical advantage over modal realism depends on the content of the operator "according to the fiction of possible worlds." It is natural to think that this should be interpreted as something like: "if the fiction of possible worlds were true, then," which is apparently modal.

Whether this is a problem for fictionalism is a matter of its point. If it is to possess all the advantages that Lewis (1986) claimed, specifically an account of all modal truth, then if the fictional operator is modal, fictionalism fails. The fictionalist also confronts a problem with incompleteness. No modal realist has given a complete specification of the contents of each world, so strictly speaking the modal fictionalist is confronted with truth value gaps for the modal claims about which the modal realist has been silent. The realist can be content with this silence since the realist need not be committed to anyone being modally omniscient. That there are gaps in the fictionalist account is a departure from orthodoxy that must be warranted by significant argument.

Kit Fine (1977), Christopher Peacocke (1978), and Graeme Forbes (1989) suggested a modalist approach that rejects the call for a reductive theory of modality in nonmodal terms. If anything, the explanation goes in the opposite direction: something is true in a possible world iff it is possibly true. For the modalist, reality is irreducibly modal and this is exhibited by the attempts to translate the whole of the possible worlds theory into a modal language, expanding the basic modal language to include an actuality operator as well as indices for the operators to permit the tracking of modal contexts. For example, if one permits oneself w_1, to be a variable ranging over worlds, $w^\star$ to stand for the actual world, and E to be a two-place predicate by which one can express that an object exists in a world, then the possible worlds translation of "There could have been more things than there actually are" is:

$$\exists w_1[\forall w \forall x(Exw^\star \rightarrow Exw_1) \,\&\, \exists y(\neg Eyw^\star)].$$

Where $\lozenge_1$ permits one to express a given possibility, A expresses actuality, and A_1 expresses what is actual in a specific possibility, the modalist translation for this is:

$$\lozenge_1\{[\square \forall x(AEx \rightarrow A_1 Ex)] \,\&\, \exists y \neg AEy\}.$$

Melia (1992) argued that the modalist translation is not a reduction of possible worlds discourse at all, but merely a notational variant of the possible worlds statement. Even if it is granted that one has a firm grasp on the modalist's basic modal and actuality operators, once the subscripts are added and one operator is placed within the scope of others, one has no intuitive grasp of their meanings in those contexts. The only way to understand them, indeed the way the modalist explains them, is by reference to the possible worlds semantics. Contrary to the modalist claims, this makes it appear as though possible worlds discourse, not the modalist's, is semantically basic and more perspicuous.

Some assumed that modalism is to be recommended only if it can reduce possible worlds discourse in modal terms. However, why, exactly, should the modalist provide translations of all possible worlds claims? What must be determined is what, if any, possible worlds claims are merely artifacts of the possible worlds framework. It is no reason to give up modalism if it cannot accommodate mere artifacts of the possible worlds framework that is, ultimately, rejected as a literal account of modal metaphysics. For instance, according to Lewis's (1968) developments, each world is as it is. It is not essential that a world be that way, but it is essential that that specific world be that particular way. Being that way is precisely what distinguishes that world from all others. Modalists are not bound to make this essentialist claim part of their theory. So long as the modalist can say all that one has either theory-neutral or modalist grounds for asserting, the failure to translate all the modal realist's claims should not count against modalism.

Though modalism is not wedded to essentialism, Fine (1977) argued not only that reality is irreducibly modal but also that *de re* modality is more basic than *de dicto*, defending the most general aspects of essentialism defended by Kripke (1972/1980) and Hilary Putnam (1975). These works brought essentialism back into philosophical discussion among analytic philosophers. Each was concerned with the semantics for proper names and natural kinds terms. Once necessity, analyticity, and *a priority* were clearly separated from each other, some essentialist theses—such as that the origins/genealogy are essential to some objects and that substances have their chemical constitution essentially—became more plausible. Fine extended this so that *de dicto* modality, concerned as it is with the necessary truth and falsehood of some propositions, is explained by *de re* modal facts about the natures of truth bearers or concepts or logical functions. This provides essentialism with an explanatory role so that if objects, whether concrete or abstract, have properties without which they would not be those very objects, then modal truth is on a par with nonmodal truth. Truth, whether modal or nonmodal, depends on being. The modalist simply maintains that being is irreducibly modal.

MODALITY AND METAPHYSICS

In the end, the philosophy and metaphysics of modality rests on metaphilosophical foundations. Many of the objections to the various positions have been piecemeal, showing that a theory has some consequence that is supposed to be intolerable. Lewis (1986) made quite clear that the case for genuine modal realism was a philosophical inference to the best explanation, not a single silver bullet–like argument. He claimed that when all things were considered his theory possessed the best balance of theoretical virtues and vices. Other theories might rely on less controversial ontologies or they may avoid some other counterintuitive consequences of modal realism.

Nevertheless, when all things are taken into account, Lewis thinks that his theory is the best package. Those willing to engage Lewis on his own terms must provide comparable details about the relative merits and difficulties of an alternative to properly undercut the warrant that Lewis thinks that he has given for modal realism.

An alternative is to question the appropriateness of inference to the best explanation in metaphysical contexts. That argument form is typically associated with contexts in which prior experience showed that one kind of event or fact—the activity of mice—explained another—the disappearance of cheese. When one confronts another instance of missing cheese and one has been unable to observe rodents, the inference to the activity of mice might well be appropriate. In metaphysics there is no analogue to prior experience. If the legitimacy of an argument form is not knowable *a priori*, some *a posteriori* basis is needed for thinking that the argument is appropriate to a given context of application. One knows that statistical inferences are appropriate under some conditions and not others because of what one knows from empirical investigation of the world. In the absence of some general reason to think that a metaphysical theory is more likely to be true when it is the conclusion of an inference to the best explanation, the application of an inference form may be warranted in some empirical contexts but unwarranted in metaphysical contexts. Thus, warrant for a specific theory of modality depends on deeper considerations about forms of argument appropriate to metaphysics.

See also Metaphysics; Modality and Language.

Bibliography

Adams, Robert Merrihew. "Primitive Thisness and Primitive Identity." *Journal of Philosophy* 76 (1) (1979): 5–26.

Adams, Robert Merrihew. "Theories of Actuality." *Noûs* 8 (1974): 211–231.

Armstrong, D. M. *A Combinatorial Theory of Possibility*. New York: Cambridge University Press, 1989.

Ayer, Alfred J. *Language, Truth, and Logic*. London: V. Gollancz, 1936.

Blackburn, Simon. "Morals and Modals." In *Fact, Science, and Morality*, edited by Graham Macdonald. Oxford, U.K.: Blackwell, 1986.

Brock, Stuart. "Modal Fictionalism: A Response to Rosen." *Mind* 102 (1993): 147–150.

Carnap, Rudolf. *The Logical Syntax of Language*. London: Routledge, 1954.

Chihara, Charles. *The Worlds of Possibility: Modal Realism and the Semantics of Modal Logic*. Oxford, U.K.: Clarendon Press, 1998.

Copeland, B. J., ed. *Logic and Reality: Essays on the Legacy of Arthur Prior*. Oxford, U.K.: Clarendon Press, 1996.

Divers, John. *Possible Worlds*. London: Routledge, 2002.

Divers, John, and Joseph Melia. "The Analytic Limits of Genuine Modal Realism." *Mind* 111 (2002): 15–36.

Fine, Kit. "Essence and Modality." In *Philosophical Perspectives. Vol. 8, Logic and Language*. Atascadero, CA: Ridgeview, 1994.

Fine. Kit. "Plantinga on the Reduction of Possibilist Discourse." In *Alvin Planting*, edited by James Tomberlin and Peter van Inwagen. Dordrecht, Netherlands: D. Reidel, 1985.

Fine, Kit. Postscript to *Worlds, Times, and Selves*. London: Duckworth, 1977.

Forbes, Graeme. *The Languages of Possibility*. Oxford, U.K.: Basil Blackwell, 1989.

Forbes, Graeme. *The Metaphysics of Modality*. Oxford, U.K.: Clarendon Press, 1985.

Forrest, Peter, and D. M. Armstrong. "An Argument against David Lewis' Theory of Possible Worlds." *Australasian Journal of Philosophy* 62 (1984): 164–168.

Gendler, Tamar-Szabo, and John Hawthorne, eds. *Conceivability and Possibility*. New York: Oxford University Press. 2002.

Hume, David. *A Treatise of Human Nature*. Bks. I and II. 2 vols. London, 1739. Bk. III, London, 1740. Modern editions are by L. A. Selby Bigge (Oxford, 1888 and 1896) and by A. D. Lindsay (London and New York, 1911, 2 vols).

Kripke, Saul A. "A Completeness Theorem in Modal Logic." *Journal of Symbolic Logic* 24 (1959): 1–14.

Kripke, Saul A. "Naming and Necessity." In *Semantics of Natural Language*, edited by Donald Davidson and Gilbert Harman. Dordrecht, Netherlands: D. Reidel, 1972. Published with additions as *Naming and Necessity*. Cambridge, MA: Harvard University Press, 1980.

Kripke, Saul A. "Semantic Analysis of Modal Logic." *Zeitschrift für Mathematische Logik und Grundlagen der Mathematik* 9 (1963): 67–96.

Kripke, Saul A. "Semantic Considerations on Modal Logic." *Acta Philosophica Fennica* 16 (1963): 83–94.

Lewis, Clarence Irving. *A Survey of Symbolic Logic*. Berkeley: University of California Press, 1918.

Lewis, Clarence Irving, and Cooper Harold Langford. *Symbolic Logic*. New York: Century, 1932.

Lewis, David. "Anselm and Actuality." *Noûs* 4 (1970): 175–188.

Lewis, David. *Counterfactuals*. Cambridge, MA: Harvard University Press, 1973.

Lewis, David. "Counterpart Theory and Quantified Modal Logic." *Journal of Philosophy* 65 (1968): 113–126.

Lewis, David. *On the Plurality of Worlds*. Oxford, U.K.: Blackwell, 1986.

Linsky, Leonard, ed. *Reference and Modality*. London: Oxford University Press, 1971.

Loux, Michael J., ed. *The Possible and the Actual*. Ithaca, NY: Cornell University Press, 1979.

Lycan, William G. "Armstrong's New Combinatorialist Theory of Modality." In *Ontology, Causality, and Mind: Essays in Honour of D. M. Armstrong*, edited by John Bacon, Keith Campbell, and Lloyd Reinhardt. New York: Cambridge University Press, 1993.

Lycan, William G. *Modality and Meaning*. Dordrecht, Netherlands: Kluwer Academic, 1994.

Marcus, Ruth Barcan, *Modalities: Philosophical Essays*. New York: Oxford University Press, 1993.

McGinn, Colin. "Modal Reality." In *Reduction, Time, and Reality*. New York: Cambridge University Press, 1981.

Melia, Joseph. "Against Modalism." *Philosophical Studies* 68 (1992): 35–56.

Pap, Arthur. *Semantics and Necessary Truth*. New Haven, CT: Yale University Press, 1958.

Peacocke, Christopher. "Necessity and Truth Theories." *Journal of Philosophical Logic* 7 (1978): 473–500.

Plantinga, Alvin. *The Nature of Necessity*. Oxford, U.K.: Clarendon Press, 1974.

Plantinga, Alvin. "Two Concepts of Modality: Modal Realism and Modal Reductionism." In *Philosophical Perspectives. Vol. 1, Metaphysics*, edited by James E. Tomberlin, 189–231. Atascadero, CA: Ridgeview, 1987.

Plantinga, Alvin. *Essays in the Metaphysics of Modality*. New York: Oxford University Press, 2003.

Prior, Arthur, and Kit Fine. *Worlds, Times, and Selves*. Amherst: University of Massachusetts Press, 1977.

Putnam, Hilary. "The Meaning of 'Meaning.'" *Minnesota Studies in the Philosophy of Science* 7 (1975): 131–193.

Quine, W. V. O. *From a Logical Point of View*. New York: Harper and Row, 1953.

Quine, W. V. O. "Truth by Convention." In *Philosophical Essays for A. N. Whitehead*, edited by O. H. Lee. New York: Longmans, 1948.

Quine, W. V. O. "Two Dogmas of Empiricism." *Philosophical Review* 60 (1951): 20–43.

Quine, W. V. O. *The Ways of Paradox*. New York: Random House, 1966.

Rosen, Gideon. "Modal Fictionalism." *Mind* 99 (1990): 327–354.

Rosen, Gideon. "A Problem for Fictionalism about Possible Worlds." *Analysis* 53 (1993): 71–81.

Shalkowski, Scott A. "Logic and Absolute Necessity." *Journal of Philosophy* 101 (2004): 55–82.

Shalkowski, Scott A. "The Ontological Ground of the Alethic Modality." *Philosophical Review* 103 (1994): 669–688.

Sidelle, Alan. *Necessity, Essence, and Individuation: A Defense of Conventionalism*. Ithaca, NY: Cornell University Press, 1989.

Stalnaker, Robert. "Possible Worlds." *Noûs* 10 (1976): 65–75.

Van Inwagen, Peter. *Ontology, Identity, and Modality*. New York: Cambridge University Press, 2001.

Van Inwagen, Peter. "Two Concepts of Possible Worlds." *Midwest Studies in Philosophy* 11 (1986): 185–213.

Wright, Crispin. "Necessity, Caution, and Scepticism." *Proceedings of the Aristotelian Society Supplement* 63 (1989): 203–238.

Wright, Crispin. *Wittgenstein on the Foundations of Mathematics*. Cambridge, MA: Harvard University Press, 1980.

Scott A. Shalkowski (2005)

MODALITY AND LANGUAGE

See Appendix, Vol. 10

MODALITY AND QUANTIFICATION

Quantified modal logics combine quantifiers ($\forall$ for *all*, and $\exists$, for *some*) with an intensional operator $\square$ (for such expressions as 'necessarily' and 'Ralph believes that'). Quantifying into intensional contexts (or quantifying in, for short) occurs when a quantifier binds an open variable that lies within the scope of $\square$, as in sentences with the form $\exists\square Fx$. Systems of quantified modal logic (QML) routinely include formulas of this kind, but Willard Van Orman Quine (1963) famously argues that quantifying in is incoherent.

Here is a quick summary of his main line of reasoning. Consider (1)–(3), an apparent counterexample to the law of substitution for identity:

(1) 9 equals the number of planets

(2) Necessarily 9 is greater than 7

(3) Necessarily the number of planets is greater than 7

Although (3) is the result of the substituting 'the number of planets' for '9' in (2), and both (1) and (2) are true, (3) is presumably false. Quine calls term positions where substitution fails opaque contexts and argues that terms occupying them do not play their normal referring roles. Both '9' and 'the number of planets' refer to nine, so something other than the terms' referents must explain why the truth values of (2) and (3) differ. Presumably, the difference is in the manner of referring to or describing nine. Now note that the standard truth condition for $\exists$ says that (4) is true if and only if (iff) the open sentence (5) is true of some object:

(4) $\exists x$(necessarily, x is greater than 7)

(5) Necessarily, x is greater than 7

However, (5) results from putting 'x' for either '9' in (2) or 'the number of planets' in (3), and (2) and (3) were sensitive to the manner in which nine is described. Since 'x' does not describe anything at all, information needed to make sense of (5) being true of an object is now missing. As Quine puts it, what object is (5) true of? Presumably, it is nine, that is, the number of planets. However, the number of planets appears not to satisfy (5), since (3) was false.

Arthur F. Smullyan (1948) was one of the first to respond to Quine's argument. He notes that when 'the number of planets' is translated away according to Bertrand Russell's theory of definite descriptions, (1)–(3) does not constitute a violation of the law of substitution (LS). On the analysis that matches the intuition that (3) is false, it is not possible to derive the translation of (3) from (2) and the translation of (1) in predicate logic, even given LS. If one adopts the position that any purported failure of substitution for an expression is a good reason to treat it as a definite description, then there are no terms in opaque contexts in the first place, and Quine's reasoning does not get off the ground. However, this solution, Quine notes, is limited to those cases where Russell's technique can be plausibly applied.

Alonzo Church (1943) and Rudolf Carnap (1947) propose a different tactic. Presuming that variables of quantification range over concepts rather than objects, Quine's complaint that satisfaction of (5) by an object is unintelligible does not apply. However, Quine finds quantification over concepts ontologically disreputable; and furthermore, citing an alternative treatment of quantification would not rebut an argument concluding the incoherence of quantifying in for quantification over objects, a result damaging enough to QML.

There are a number of different strategies for responding to Quine's objection in the case of quantifying over objects. One popular tactic, exemplified in David Kaplan's "Quantifying In" (1969), involves selecting a privileged class of terms (for Kaplan, the so-called vivid names). Although the truth values of (3) and (2) are sensitive to the ways nine is described, one argues that there is no corresponding indeterminacy in (5) because one of these ways is privileged. Presuming '9' is privileged, (2), and not (3), is used to resolve the status of (5). Since (2) is true, (5) is true of nine, and the fact that that (3) is false is irrelevant.

In note 3 of "Quantifying In" (1969) Kaplan suggests another way to circumvent Quine's objections to (5) without using privileged terms. The idea is (roughly) to revise the truth condition for ∃ so that ∃x(necessarily, x is greater than 7) is T iff some object satisfies the open sentence (6):

(6) x bears the property of being necessarily greater than seven

Since 'x' in (6) lies outside the scope of 'necessarily', substitution holds in this position, and Quine's worries

no longer apply. (Something like this tactic is used by Quine himself in "Quantifiers and Propositional Attitudes" [1955] to analyze quantification into belief contexts.)

Kaplan's (1969) strategy is reflected in a solution implicit in the earliest published QML. The system (developed by Ruth Barcan Marcus [1946]) includes the axiom $\forall x \forall y(x = y \rightarrow \Box x = y)$, which is now known to correspond to the condition that variables are rigid designators, that is, they pick out the same object in every possible world. Under these circumstances (5) is equivalent to (6), and so (6) can be used to make sense of (5).

Kit Fine's "The Problem of De Re Modality" (1989) makes yet another contribution to the problem. Here a formal definition of satisfaction by objects for open sentences like (5) is provided in cases where 'necessarily' indicates logical or analytic necessity.

In "A Backward Look at Quine's Animadversions on Modalities" (1990) Marcus records how the force and variety of such criticisms of Quine's argument led him to a strategic retreat. He conceded that quantifying in is at least coherent, but raised a different objection. Quine perceived early on that attacks on his argument appear to pay a serious price. Appeals to privileged ways of describing things, to rigid designators, or to the cogency of (6) boil down to having to make sense of the idea that some objects bear necessary properties that other objects do not. Quine complains that this amounts to an unacceptable form of essentialism. What sense can it make to assert of an object itself (apart from any way of describing it) that it has necessary properties?

An influential response to this worry appears in the early pages of "Naming and Necessity" (1972), where Saul Kripke undermines Quine's presumption that it only makes sense to attribute necessary properties to an object under a description. Here, the focus shifts from brands of logical or analytical necessity, which were the main concern when Quine first wrote, to metaphysical or physical necessity. Kripke defends the view that objects in themselves do have essential properties. For example, molecules of water are necessarily composed of hydrogen and oxygen, because water just is H_2O.

Kripke and others rescued some brands of essentialism from the negative reputation it had when Quine first wrote. However, one need not respond to Quine by arguing for the coherence of a robust essentialism. In "Opacity" (1986) Kaplan argues that the essentialism produced by quantifying in is so weak as to be entirely innocuous. Terence Parsons, in "Essentialism and Quantified Modal

Logic" (1969), reports the technical result that sentences of QML that express a controversial essentialism will not be theorems, nor will they be derivable from any collection of premises expressing (nonmodal) facts.

Parsons (1969) and others point out that while quantifying in allows one to assert essentialist claims, this hardly qualifies as a reason for abandoning it. QML should provide an impartial framework for analyzing and evaluating argumentation on all philosophical positions, however misguided. That quantifying in provides resources to express (even the most obnoxious) essentialism is a point in its favor. In any case, Quine's complaint that QML is essentially essentialist amounts to a retraction of the view that quantifying in is (literally) incoherent, for if that were true, quantifying in would not entail essentialism, it would express nothing at all.

It is important to note that Quine's main argument against quantifying in would appear to apply equally well to expressions for propositional attitudes such as "Ralph believes that," for these also create opaque contexts. However, in the case of belief, the situation is different, since charges of essentialism are out of place. In "Intensions Revisited" (1981) Quine explores failings for belief that are analogs to essentialism for necessity.

Despite attacks on Quine's main argument, many still accept the conclusion that quantifying in is incoherent. Graeme Forbes (1996) notes that adherents of this view face a new puzzle, posed by strong intuitions in favor of the intelligibility of English sentences like those represented by ∃x(Ralph believes that x is a spy). So those adherents need an alternative analysis of the logical form of propositional attitude sentences that avoids quantifying in, one Forbes sets out to provide. A tension Quine faces here is that explanations placating intuitions that quantifying in is coherent for belief will provide tools that resolve his worries about necessity.

QML has come a long way in the sixty years since Quine first launched his attack on it. Possible worlds semantics has flourished, bringing a wealth of technical results. For example, soundness and completeness have been proven for a variety of systems that allow quantifying in but reject LS in modal contexts. Theorems are also available on exactly how and where essentialist features arise in QML (e.g., see Fine 1978, 1981). Though work in modal semantics employs ideas that are anathema to Quine (notably the notion of a possible object), it provides tools for better understanding worries about quantifying in. An interest in answering Quine's objections to QML has motivated many of these developments. So,

oddly, Quine's legacy has enriched what he hoped to disinherit.

See also Modal Logic.

Bibliography

QUINE'S SEMINAL ARTICLES ON QUANTIFYING IN

"Notes on Existence and Necessity." *Journal of Philosophy* 40 (1943): 113–149.

"Quantifiers and Propositional Attitudes." In *Reference and Modality*, edited by Leonard Linsky, 101–111. New York: Oxford University Press, 1955.

"Reference and Modality." In *From a Logical Point of View*. New York: Harper and Row, 1963.

"Three Grades of Modal Involvement." In *The Ways of Paradox and Other Essays*. Cambridge, MA: Harvard University Press, 1966.

SOME OTHER IMPORTANT WORKS ON QUANTIFYING IN

Barcan, Ruth. "A Functional Calculus of First Order Based on Strict Implication." *Journal of Symbolic Logic* 2 (1946): 1–16.

Carnap, Rudolf. *Meaning and Necessity*. Chicago: University of Chicago Press, 1947.

Church, Alonzo. "Review of Quine." *Journal of Symbolic Logic* 8 (1943): 45–52.

Fine, Kit. "Model Theory for Modal Logic." *Journal of Philosophical Logic* 7 (1978): 125–156, 277–306; 10 (1981): 293–307.

Fine, Kit. "The Problem of De Re Modality." In *Themes from Kaplan*, edited by Joseph Almog, John Perry, and Howard Wettstein. New York: Oxford University Press, New York, 1989.

Forbes, Graeme. "Substitutivity and the Coherence of Quantifying In." *Philosophical Review* 105 (1996): 337–372

Kaplan, David. "Opacity." In *The Philosophy of W. V. Quine*, edited by Lewis Edwin Hahn and Paul Arthur Schilpp, 229–289. LaSalle, IL: Open Court, 1986.

Kaplan, David. "Quantifying In." In *Words and Objections*, edited by Donald Davidson and Jaakko Hintikka. Dordrecht, Netherlands: D. Reidel, 1969.

Kripke, Saul. "Naming and Necessity." In *Semantics of Natural Language*, edited by Donald Davidson and Gilbert Harman, 253–355. Dordrecht, Netherlands: D. Reidel, 1972.

Marcus, Ruth Barcan. "Essentialism in Modal Logic." *Noûs* 1 (1967): 91–96.

Marcus, Ruth Barcan. "A Backward Look at Quine's Animadversions on Modalities." In *Perspectives on Quine*, edited by Robert B. Barrett and Roger F. Gibson. Cambridge, MA: Blackwell, 1990.

Parsons, Terence. "Essentialism and Quantified Modal Logic." *Philosophical Review* 78 (1969): 35–52.

Quine, W. V. O. "Intensions Revisited." In *Theories and Things*. Cambridge, MA: Harvard University Press, 1981.

Smullyan, Arthur F. "Modality and Description." *Journal of Symbolic Logic* 13 (1948): 31–37.

James W. Garson (2005)

MODAL LOGIC

Traditionally, the modes implicit in modal logic are the modes of truth and ultimately the modes of being: necessary, possible, impossible, and contingent. While the study of the formal properties of those notions is still an important part of modal logic, other interpretations have been added over the years, such as temporal, epistemic, and deontic. Furthermore, more recently, other formal languages have been suggested, which, although not modal logic in a strict sense, are closely related to it, such as dynamic logic.

BRIEF HISTORY

Modern modal logic began in 1912 when Clarence Irving Lewis published a paper in *Mind*, in which he recommended that the logic of *Principia Mathematica* be supplemented with what he called intensional connectives. Among the latter was a binary connective of strict implication for which he introduced a new symbol, a "fishhook" to distinguish it from the "horseshoe" of the material conditional. Thus, $\phi \prec \psi$ and $\phi \supset \psi$ would both be read "if ϕ then ψ," but Lewis specifically intended for the former to model the elusive notion of entailment. Other connectives were possibility, for which he used the symbol $\diamond$ (a diamond), and necessity, for which F. B. Fitch would later suggest $\square$ (a box): thus, $\diamond\phi$ and $\square\phi$ were read "it is possible that ϕ" and "it is necessary that ϕ," respectively. The interest in strict implication declined somewhat after it was discovered that there are paradoxes of strict implication in parallel with those of material implication in classical logic. Lewis's legacy was not lost, however. On the one hand, philosophers like Alan Ross Anderson and Nuel Belnap went on to develop logics of entailment and relevance, a tradition that has proved hardy. On the other hand, since necessity and possibility seem more interesting than strict implication—$\phi \prec \psi$ is in any case analyzable as either $\square(\phi \supset \psi)$ or $\neg \diamond (\phi \wedge \neg\psi)$— later logicians preferred to do their modal logic in terms of those concepts.

Lewis's original ambition was to find the logic of strict implication. Much to his surprise he later found himself confronted by a veritable embarrassment of riches: an ever increasing number of modal logics—not only his own famous quintuple of systems S1, S2, S3, S4, and S5 (his own tentative favorite was S3, the so-called Survey system) but also many, in fact, infinitely many others. Since he never translated his semantic intuitions into a formal structure, the differentiation between different proposals became a problem. Some help in this regard arrived in the form of the concept of a matrix, essentially a set of truth-values (usually but not necessarily finitely many) plus a truth-value table for each connective. This idea, which was due to Jan Łukasiewicz, was then generalized into the notion of an algebra (essentially a set with operators) and taken into modal logic by Alfred Tarski and his collaborators. The advent of algebraic logic revitalized modal logic. Two works from this period are particularly noteworthy. One was the first formal result in modal logic worth the name, J.C.C. McKinsey's algebraic characterization of S2 and a proof that it is decidable. The other was a paper in 1951 by Bjarni Jónsson and Tarski foreshadowing the next major development: the era of possible-worlds semantics.

Since the term *possible-worlds semantics* is today used pretty much synonymously with the term *Kripke semantics*, it is germane to ask: Who invented Kripke semantics? In fact, this question has been the object of much discussion, some heated. When the new semantics emerged at the end of the 1950s, Rudolf Carnap had laid the ground work; his states really played the role that possible worlds would later play, even if he only worked with descriptions of them. What Carnap did not have, and which turned out to make all the difference, was the accessibility relation (this concept is explained later on). The accessibility relation did appear in the Jónsson-Tarski paper mentioned earlier, and it now seems likely that Arthur Prior and C. A. Meredith had also discovered it in the early 1950s. But it was Saul A. Kripke, along with Stig Kanger and Jaakko Hintikka, who first published accounts in which the accessibility relation was a central concept and its versatility recognized. That Kripke's work overshadowed the work by Kanger and Hintikka and proved so much more influential than theirs is perhaps not surprising, given the clarity and mathematical maturity Kripke's papers and the systematic development of his theory.

After Kripke's early work followed a period of increasingly formal concern. Not surprisingly, the philosophers have focused on the philosophy of modal logic, including modal metaphysics, while the mathematicians have pursued the mathematics of modal logic, including model theory, algebra, and even category theory. Another significant development has been the expanding use of modal logic in theoretical computer science: with energy and inventiveness—but of course guided by their own interests—computer scientists have, within a short time, transformed modal logic.

SYNTAX

This entry only considers classical modal logic, that is, logic that extends classical logic. Historically, even though for a long time it is modal predicate logic that has been of particular interest to philosophers, propositional modal logic has received much more attention from formal logicians, probably because agreement on what constitutes a generally accepted conceptual framework for research was reached much earlier in the latter area.

PROPOSITIONAL LOGIC. To the set of the usual truth-functional connectives, add two new connectives: a box operator $\Box$ and a diamond operator $\Diamond$. After Tarski, a theory, in a technical sense, is a set of formulas (called theses of the logic) that contains all classical two-valued tautologies and is closed under *modus ponens* (if ϕ and $\phi \supset \psi$ are theses of the logic, then so is ψ). Similarly, a logic, in the technical sense used here, is a theory that is closed under uniform substitution (if $\phi(\chi/P)$ results from a formula ϕ by replacing all occurrences of a certain propositional letter P with a formula χ, then $\phi(\chi/P)$ is a thesis of the logic if ϕ is). A normal modal logic is a logic that contains as theses all instances of the schema $\Diamond\phi \equiv \neg\Box\neg\phi$ as well as of the so-called Kripke schema $\Box(\phi \supset \psi) \supset (\Box\phi \supset \Box\psi)$ and, in addition, is closed under the rule of necessitation (if ϕ is a thesis, then so is $\Box\phi$). A great number of normal modal logics have been studied, many of them definable in terms of further schemata, for example,

(D) $\Box\phi \supset \Diamond\phi$,

(T) $\Box\phi \supset \phi$,

(4) $\Box\phi \supset \Box\Box\phi$,

(5) $\neg\Box\phi \supset \Box\neg\Box\phi$,

(G) $\Diamond\Box\phi \supset \Box\Diamond\phi$,

(H) $(\Diamond\phi \wedge \Diamond\psi) \supset (\Diamond(\phi \wedge \psi) \vee \Diamond(\phi \wedge \Diamond\psi) \vee \Diamond(\psi \wedge \Diamond\phi))$,

(W) $\Box(\Box\phi \supset \phi) \supset \Box\phi$.

To bring some order into the bewildering multiplicity of modal logics, E. J. Lemmon suggested $KX_1, \dots, X_n$ as a code name for the smallest normal modal logic that contains all substitution instances of schemata $X_1, \dots, X_n$. In this notation, one may identify K as the smallest normal logic, KT as the Gödel/Feys/von Wright logic, and KT4 and KT45 as the logics S4 and S5, respectively. The logics KD, KD4, and KD45, of special interest to deontic and doxastic logic, are sometimes called weak T, weak S4, and weak S5, respectively. The logics KT4G and KT4H are better known as S4.2 and S4.3, respectively, and the logic

K4W as the Gödel/Löb logic GL. The set of all normal logics, ordered by set inclusion, forms a lattice of immense complexity, as do sets of more inclusive classes of nonnormal modal logics. The efforts to explore these structures continue but are increasingly a concern for mathematicians rather than for philosophers.

PREDICATE LOGIC. Modal predicate logic does not exhibit the relative orderliness or maturity of its propositional relative. Philosophical questions such as the proper treatment of individuals persist. Quantification, in particular into opaque contexts—that is, contexts within the scope of modal operators—has been a main problem, as evidenced by Quine's unrelenting criticism over a lifetime. A formal beginning was made by Ruth Barcan Marcus, after whom two central formulas have been named—the Barcan formula (BF) and the converse Barcan formula (CBF):

(BF) $\forall x\Box\phi \supset \Box\forall x\phi$,

(CBF) $\Box\forall x\phi \supset \forall x\Box\phi$

Other examples of formulas that were much discussed in early literature are

$$\forall x\forall y(x = y \supset \Box(x = y)),$$

$$\forall x\forall y(x \neq y \supset \Box(x \neq y)),$$

$$a = b \supset \Box(a = b),$$

$$a \neq b \supset \Box(a \neq b),$$

where a and b are individual constants. Various authors have held different views on which of these, if any, are valid. It would seem that to take a stand in such matters is to rely on implicit semantic ideas, however sketchy. It was accordingly an important step when at last, thanks to Kripke and others, formal semantics were articulated.

SEMANTICS

The development of modal logic, both material and formal, preceded in steps. Propositional logics were studied extensively before predicate logicians had been able to work out a generally accepted common ground. Till this day, the area of modal propositional logic is more definitive than the relatively more unsettled area of modal predicate logic.

PROPOSITIONAL LOGIC. The possible-worlds semantics, introduced by Kripke in the early 1960s, may be cast in the following form (which differs from Kripke's original formulation in terminology and, to some extent, in substance). A frame is a pair (U, R), where U, the universe of discourse or simply the universe of the frame, is a non-empty set of elements that are often called possible worlds but that may more neutrally be called points, and R is a binary relation in U, called the accessibility relation or sometimes the alternativeness relation or even the alternative relation. If two points u, v of U are related by R (i.e., if $(u, v) \in R$), then one says that v is accessible from u or that v is an alternative to u. A valuation in U is a function V assigning to each propositional letter P a subset $V(P)$ of U. A model is a structure (U, R, V) where (U, R) is a frame and V is a valuation in U. Truth in modal logic is doubly relative: to a model and to a point in the model. Thus, if $\mathfrak{M} = (U, R, V)$ is a model, u a point in U and ϕ a formula, one may inductively define the notion of ϕ being true at u in $\mathfrak{M}$, schematically $u \vDash^{\mathfrak{M}} \phi$, as follows:

$u \vDash^{\mathfrak{M}} P$ iff $u \in V(P)$, if P is a propositional letter;

$u \vDash^{\mathfrak{M}} \neg\phi$ iff not $u \vDash^{\mathfrak{M}} \phi$,

$u \vDash^{\mathfrak{M}} \phi \wedge \psi$ iff $u \vDash^{\mathfrak{M}} \phi$ and $u \vDash^{\mathfrak{M}} \psi$,

$u \vDash^{\mathfrak{M}} \phi \vee \psi$ iff $u \vDash^{\mathfrak{M}} \phi$ or $u \vDash^{\mathfrak{M}} \psi$,

and similar conditions for other truth-functional connectives:

$u \vDash^{\mathfrak{M}} \Box\phi$ iff, for all points v, if $(u,v) \in R$ then $v \vDash^{\mathfrak{M}} \phi$,

$u \vDash^{\mathfrak{M}} \Diamond\phi$ iff there is some point v such that $(u, v) \in R$ and $v \vDash^{\mathfrak{M}} \phi$.

(Readers may note the roles played in this definition by R and V: The latter is needed to get the definition started, the former to evaluate formulas beginning with a modal operator; the truth-functional connectives are taken care of by the usual truth tables.) A formula is valid in a frame if it is true at every point in every model definable on that frame; and it is valid in a class of frames if it is valid in each one of the frames of the class.

There is a sense in which this semantics fits modal logic. The set of formulas that are valid in a given class of frames will always be a normal modal logic and can be called the logic determined by that class of frames. A logic is sound with respect to a class of frames if every thesis of the logic is valid in that class, and it is complete with respect to the class if every formula that is valid in the class is a thesis of the logic; hence a logic is determined by a class of frames if and only if it is both sound and complete with respect to that class. It is an interesting fact, and no doubt one reason for the popularity of Kripke semantics, that many of the logics defined in the philosophical literature are determined by simply defined classes of

frames. For example, T, S4, and S5 are determined by the class of frames whose accessibility relations are reflexive, reflexive and transitive, and reflexive, symmetric, and transitive, respectively. Similarly, KD, KD4, and KD45 are determined by the class of all frames whose accessibility relations are serial, serial and transitive, and serial, transitive and euclidean, respectively. (A binary relation R is serial if, for every element u in its field there is some element v, not necessarily distinct from u, such that $(u, v) \in R$, euclidean if, for all elements u, v, w in its field, if $(u, v) \in R$ and $(u, w) \in R$ then $(v, w) \in R$.) At the extremes are the smallest normal modal logic K and the inconsistent logic, which are determined by, respectively, the class of all frames and the empty class of frames.

The way in which Kripke's semantics seems to fit modal logic led some authors, for example, Lemmon, to conjecture that all normal modal logics are complete, that is, determined by some class of frames. However, that the fit is less than perfect was proved in 1971 by Kit Fine and S. K. Thomason, who exhibited, independently of one another, instances of incomplete normal modal logics.

PREDICATE LOGIC. Among several possible versions of semantics for modal predicate logic, the following is essentially a modified version of Kripke's semantics for first-order modal logic from 1963. For simplicity, assume a formal language for predicate logic containing predicate letters and individual constants (but, for example, no descriptions or functional operators); thus, the terms of this language are individual variables or individual constants. To generalize the central concepts *frame* and *model* used in propositional modal logic, several new notions must be introduced. To begin with, besides a universe U of points (possible worlds) and an accessibility relation R, as before, one needs a nonempty set D of objects and a function E defined on U that takes values in the set of subsets of D. One can refer to D as the domain and to E as the existence function, to the elements of D as possible individuals and to the elements of E_u as individuals existing at u or individuals actual at u (where u is a point in U). Altogether, a structure (U, R, D, E), where U, R, D, E are as specified, is a frame. Next, one can say that I is an interpretation (in D with respect to U) if it is a family of functions I_u, where u ranges over U, such that I_u assigns a set of n-tuples of elements of D to each n-ary predicate letter and an element of D to each individual constant. If $\mathfrak{F} = (U,R,D,E)$ is a frame, then $\mathfrak{M} = (\mathfrak{F},I) = (U,R,D,E,I)$ is a model (on $\mathfrak{F}$) if I is an interpretation in D with respect to U.

The following observation shows the sense in which the present concept of model is a generalization over that of propositional semantics: Nullary predicate letters behave in the present setting as propositional letters do in the propositional case. To see this, let P be a nullary predicate letter. By the definition, the interpretation of P is a set of 0-tuples, hence $I_u(P)$ is either $\emptyset$ (the empty set) or $\{\emptyset\}$ (the singleton set whose only member is the one and only 0-tuple). If one arbitrarily identifies $\{\emptyset\}$ with truth and $\emptyset$ with falsity, one thereby also in effect identifies the set $\{u \in U : I_u(P) = \{\emptyset\}\}$ with the proposition expressed by P in $\mathfrak{M}$. Thus, the interpretation plays a role in the predicate case similar to that of the valuation in the propositional case, albeit a much bigger role.

Besides all this, one needs yet another concept to define truth-conditions: something to take care of the quantifiers. An assignment (in a set D) is a function from the set of individual variables of one's formal language to D. Notice that if A is an assignment in D and x is a variable, then $A(x)$ is an element of D but perhaps not of E_u, if u is an arbitrary point in U. If $\mathfrak{M} = (U, R, D, E, I)$ is a model and A is an assignment in D, then the denotation of t in $\mathfrak{M}$ under A is a function $\|t\|_A^{\mathfrak{M}}$ defined on U as follows:

$$\|t\|_A^{\mathfrak{M}}(u) = \begin{cases} I_u(t), & \text{if } t \text{ is an individual constant,} \\ A(t), & \text{if } t \text{ is an individual variable.} \end{cases}$$

The truth of a formula ϕ in a model $\mathfrak{M}$ under an assignment A at a point u, in symbols $u \vDash_A^{\mathfrak{M}} \phi$, may now be defined:

$u \vDash_A^{\mathfrak{M}} P(t_0, \ldots, t_{n-1})$ iff $(\|t_0\|_u^{\mathfrak{M}}, \ldots, \|t_{n-1}\|_u^{\mathfrak{M}}) \in I_u(P)$, if P is an n-ary predicate letter,

$u \vDash_A^{\mathfrak{M}} \forall x \, \phi$ iff $u \vDash_B^{\mathfrak{M}} \phi$, for all assignments B such that $B(x) \in E_u$ and, for all variables y, if $x \neq y$ then $A(y) = B(y)$.

The remaining clauses of the definition (for the truth-functional connectives and the modal operators) are as before. In particular,

$u \vDash_A^{\mathfrak{M}} \Box \phi$ iff, for all v, if $(u, v) \in R$ then $v \vDash_A^{\mathfrak{M}} \phi$.

As in the propositional case, one associates truth with models and validity with frames. Thus, one can say that a formula is true in a model if it is true under all assignments at all points in the model. By the same token, one can say that a formula is valid in a frame if it is true in all models on the frame.

Some object languages contain constant predicates besides predicate letters. Common examples of such predicates are the unary E (the existence predicate) and the binary = (the identity predicate) with corresponding truth-conditions:

$u \vDash_A^{\mathfrak{M}} Et$ iff $\|t\|_A^{\mathfrak{M}}(u) \in E_u$, if t is a term,

$u \vDash_A^{\mathfrak{M}} t = t'$ iff $\|t\|_A^{\mathfrak{M}}(u) = \|t'\|_A^{\mathfrak{M}}(u)$, if $t = t'$ are terms,

The meaning of E and = depends neither on the interpretation I nor the assignment A; for this reason E and = may be called logical constants. Notice that if the identity predicate is available, the existence predicate is definable: Provided that t is distinct from x, if t is a variable, $E(t) \equiv \exists x(x = t)$ is a valid schema.

The following remarks apply to this particular modeling. All instances of the Barcan formula (BF) are valid in all and only frames satisfying the condition of decreasing domains, that is,

for all u and v, if $(u, v) \in R$ then $E_u \supseteq E_v$.

Similarly, all instances of the converse Barcan formula (CBF) are valid in all and only frames that satisfy the condition of increasing domains, that is

for all u and v, if $(u, v) \in R$ then $E_u \subseteq E_v$.

Of the other predicate logical formulas discussed earlier, $\forall x \forall y(x = y \supset \Box(x = y))$ and $\forall x \forall y(x \neq y \supset \Box(x \neq y))$ are valid, while neither $a = b \supset \Box(a = b)$ nor $a \neq b \supset \Box(a \neq b)$ is valid. This reflects an important difference between how individual variables and individual constants are treated in this modeling: In spite of their name, the denotation of individual constants may vary from point to point in the universe, whereas the denotation of variables, their name notwithstanding, remains fixed throughout the universe. Here is obviously a niche to be filled! Suppose one introduces a new syntactic category of names and requires that the interpretation of a name n be constant over the universe of points; formally, $I_u(n) = I_v(n)$, for all $u, v \in U$. Then, if m and n are any names, $m = n \supset \Box(m = n)$ and $m \neq n \supset \Box(m \neq n)$ are both valid. The proposed modification amounts to treating the elements of the new category of names as what is now known, after Kripke, as rigid designators.

Among other modelings for modal predicate logic, David Lewis's counterpart theory should be mentioned.

According to the Kripke paradigm, an individual may exist in more than one possible world (with respect to the formal modeling defined above, it is possible that E_u and E_v should overlap, in a model, even if $u \neq v$). For Lewis, however, each individual inhabits its own possible world; but it may have counterparts in other possible worlds. This approach has also been influential, both in philosophical and in mathematical quarters.

INTERPRETATIONS

The original interpretation of modal logic—the official interpretation, if one prefers—was of course the one that led to its construction: the interpretation in terms of necessity and possibility. But over time there have been many others.

THE ALETHIC INTERPRETATION. In formal philosophy, as in formal conceptual analysis generally, there is a constant interplay between intuition and formalism. Efforts to explicate pretheoretical notions lead to a formalism, for example, an axiom system in a formal language or a set theoretical modeling. Once a formalism is in place, it takes on a life of its own: Not only may it undergo a formal development but it can also be interpreted, sometimes in ways that are not foreseen. Reflections on such interpretations lead to refined, sometimes revised, intuitions. The latter in turn may inspire more sophisticated formalisms. And so it goes. The formalism described earlier in this entry is a product of such interplay, having arisen principally as a result of efforts to understand what Georg Henrik von Wright called the alethic modalities necessity and possibility. Not surprisingly, questions persist about to what extent this formalism is a successful explication of one's informal understanding of necessity and possibility.

Formal semantics for modal logic is, by itself, philosophically neutral. The elements of the universe of a modal logical frame, which from a formal point of view are just points in a logical space, must be given a substantial meaning by philosophers who wish to use them outside the realm of pure abstraction. In tense logic the points will be points of time, in epistemic logic perhaps epistemic situations, and so on. Under the alethic interpretation they are often referred to as possible worlds, an ordinary language word with no clear content. Indeed, the question as to what a possible world is has exercised philosophers since the beginning of the Kripke era. Answers—besides those rejecting the entire modal logical enterprise—have been numerous. Lewis argued for an extreme modal realism according to which possible worlds are concrete alternative universes existing in parallel with the actual world. Other philosophers, like Kripke, Alvin Plantinga, Robert Stalnaker, and David M. Armstrong also argued for one kind of modal realism or other but have taken them to be abstract entities. Still other philosophers regarded possible-worlds talk as a kind of convenient fiction or refer to linguistic conventions. The debate continues.

An exact and expressive formalism has the advantage that old informal questions falling within its range of interpretation can be addressed anew. One such question is the venerable distinction between *de dicto* and *de re*. To take Willard Van Orman Quine's well-worn example, consider the claim that the number of planets is necessarily greater than seven. Is it true? There seem to be two different ways of understanding this claim. To bring them out, one can translate them into an ad hoc, quasi-formal language:

(1) $\exists x((x = \text{the number of planets}) \wedge \Box(x > 7))$,

(2) $\Box \exists x((x = \text{the number of planets}) \wedge (x > 7))$.

Statement (1) is said to be *de re*, statement (2) *de dicto*. It may be argued that they say different things (presumably, most would agree that the former is true but that the latter is false). The former seems to "say of an object" (the *res*, the number of planets) that, by necessity, it has a certain property ("being greater than seven"). By contrast, the latter statement says that a certain statement is necessarily true (the *dictum*, namely, that the number of planets, whatever that number may be, is greater than seven). This example illustrates the important interaction between quantifying and modalizing: It is one thing to put a modal operator in front of a closed sentence, as in (2), it is another, arguably more problematic, to quantify into the scope of a modal operator, as in (1). The old topic of essences is obviously not far away.

Another distinction, which has been argued by Kripke, is that between logical modalities and metaphysical modalities (there may also be others, such as physical modalities). Logical necessity implies metaphysical necessity, but the converse is not true. For example, "Phosphorus is identical with Hesperus" (assuming the names *Phosphorus* and *Hesperus* are regarded as rigid designators) and "The chemical composition of water is H_2O" (again assuming that *water* and H_2O are rigid designators) have been offered as examples of statements that are metaphysically, but not logically, necessary.

The (epistemological) distinction between *a priori* and *a posteriori* also comes in here. In Kripke's theory, the two examples given in the preceding paragraph exemplify statements that, although metaphysically necessary, are nevertheless *a posteriori*. By contrast, given certain assumptions, "The Paris meter is one meter long" may be an example of a statement that is true *a priori* but is not metaphysically necessary.

TWO EARLY MATHEMATICAL INTERPRETATIONS. In the 1930s two technical interpretations of modal logic were made by the two greatest logicians of the twentieth century. One was the so-called provability interpretation, due to Kurt Gödel, according to which $\Box\phi$ is interpreted as "ϕ is provable" or "ϕ is provable in S," where S is a certain formal system. This interpretation was never forgotten, but it attracted major attention only relatively recently. The other interpretation, due to Tarski, is in terms of topology: Let C and I denote the closure CX and the interior IX, respectively, of any subset X of a topological space U. Tarski noted that the closure operator and the interior operator behave in a way analogous to the way the possibility operator and the necessity operator behave in S4. For example, if ϕ and ψ correspond to X and Y, respectively, then the formulas $\diamond(\phi \lor \psi) \equiv (\diamond\phi \lor \diamond\psi)$, $\diamond\phi \equiv \diamond\diamond\phi$, $\phi \equiv \top$, and $\phi \equiv \bot$ correspond to the equations $C(X \cup Y) \equiv CX \cup CY$, $CX = CCX$, $X = U$ and $X = \emptyset$. More generally, Tarski proved that an equation in topological terms is true in all topological spaces if and only if the corresponding formula is a thesis of S4. Like Gödel's interpretation, Tarski's interpretation, which is related to the development of the theory of closure algebras, was seminal.

THE TEMPORAL INTERPRETATION. A long-standing interest in the work of early Greek logicians combined with a passion for modal logic led Arthur Norman Prior, in the 1950s, to the idea of a modal logic of time. He dubbed his creation tense logic since one of his original motivations was to throw light on the grammatical notion of tense. In the beginning Prior was led to study frames (U, R) in which R is a linear relation on U (i.e., reflexive, transitive, and connected). Under that interpretation, the interpretation of the modal operators $\Box$ and $\diamond$ in effect becomes "always in the future" and "some time in the future." One focus for his early interest was the frame $(\mathbb{N}, \leq)$, where $\mathbb{N}$ is the set of natural numbers, which he associated with Diodorus Cronus. Trying to axiomatize the set of formulas valid in this frame—the Diodorean logic, as he called it—Prior successively made three conjectures. The first was that it is S4. This conjecture was disproved by Hintikka, who pointed out that all instances of the schema

(H) $(\diamond\phi \land \diamond\psi) \supset (\diamond(\phi \land \psi) \lor \diamond(\phi \land \diamond\psi) \lor \diamond(\psi \land \diamond\phi))$

are theses of the Diodorean logic but not all of S4. Prior's response was the new conjecture that it is S4.3, that is, the logic whose Lemmon code is KT4H. However, Michael Anthony Eardley Dummett showed that all instances of the schema

(Dum) $\Box(\Box(\phi \supset \Box\phi) \supset \Box\phi) \supset (\diamond\Box\phi \supset \Box\phi)$

are theses of the Diodorean logic but not all of S4.3. Prior's third conjecture was that the Diodorean logic is S4.3Dum. This final conjecture turned out to be correct, proved by R. A. Bull and, independently, by Kripke.

In general, Prior allowed the temporal ordering to be irreflexive. He also introduced operators for past time as well as for future time. Thus, the basic operators of tense-logic are the diamond operators F and P, with readings "it will be the case (some time in the future) that" and "it was the case (some time in the past) that," and the box operators G and H with the reading "always in the future" and "always in the past." Their truth-conditions in a frame $(U, <)$, where $<$ is at least a strict partial ordering (i.e., irreflexive and transitive), are:

$u \models^{\mathfrak{M}} F\phi$ iff $v \models^{\mathfrak{M}} \phi$, for some point v such that $u \leq v$,

$u \models^{\mathfrak{M}} P\phi$ iff $v \models^{\mathfrak{M}} \phi$, for some point v such that $v \leq u$.

$u \models^{\mathfrak{M}} G\phi$ iff $v \models^{\mathfrak{M}} \phi$, for all points v such that $u \leq v$,

$u \models^{\mathfrak{M}} H\phi$ iff $v \models^{\mathfrak{M}} \phi$, for all points v such that $v \leq u$.

Tense logic is in effect a kind of bimodal logic: It is natural to think of a tense-logical frame as a frame with two accessibility relations, one for the future and one for the past. What is special to tense logic is that those two relations are inverses of one another (and, consequently, all instances of the schemata PG$\phi \supset \phi$ and FH$\phi \supset \phi$ are valid).

The temporal operators mentioned are not the only ones possible. A particularly important pair of operators studied by Hans Kamp are SINCE and UNTIL:

$u \models^{\mathfrak{M}} \phi$ SINCE θ iff there is some $w \in U$ such that $w < u$ and $w \models^{\mathfrak{M}} \theta$ and, for all $x \in U$, if $w < x < u$ then $x \models^{\mathfrak{M}} \phi$,

$u \models^{\mathfrak{M}} \phi$ UNTIL θ iff there is some $w \in U$ such that $u < w$ and $w \models^{\mathfrak{M}} \theta$ and, for all $x \in U$, if $u < x < w$ then $x \models^{\mathfrak{M}} \phi$.

(In the literature, ϕ SINCE θ and ϕ UNTIL θ are often written $S(\theta, \phi)$ and $U(\theta, \phi)$, respectively.) Kamp proved that in certain contexts, for example, over $(\mathbb{R}, <)$ (where $\mathbb{R}$ is the set of reals and $<$ is the natural strict linear order) his operators suffice for temporal completeness; that is, in those contexts, all operators corresponding to first-order conditions on the temporal relation can be defined in terms of SINCE and UNTIL and truth-functional connectives. But in general there is no temporal completeness in this sense.

Still another important tense-logical operator is NOW, which refers to a designated, fixed point of reference. A language involving that operator requires a somewhat modified truth-definition: Where before the definition is with respect to a model and a point, it will now be with respect to a model and two points, which one might call the current point and the point of reference—the former is variable, the latter is fixed throughout the definition. The clauses pertaining to the old operators, which only involve the current point, are obvious. The novel clause is

$$(u, t) \vDash^{\mathfrak{M}} \text{NOW } \phi \text{ iff } (t, t) \vDash^{\mathfrak{M}} \phi.$$

THE EPISTEMIC INTERPRETATION. The possibility of epistemic logic (the logic of knowledge) and doxastic logic (the logic of belief) was realized by von Wright, who coined the terms, but it was Hintikka who set the field going. Hintikka associated, with each agent a, two operators $\mathbf{K}_a$ and $\mathbf{B}_a$, reading "a knows that ϕ" for $\mathbf{K}_a\phi$ and "a believes that ϕ" for $\mathbf{B}_a\phi$. By the same token, the formal counterparts of "for all that a knows, ϕ" and "ϕ is consistent with everything a believes" are $\neg\mathbf{K}_a\neg\phi$ and $\neg\mathbf{B}_a\neg\phi$. Already Hintikka's new notation was useful. To know that someone Qs is not the same as knowing someone who Qs, but Hintikka's notation makes this patent—$\mathbf{K}_a\exists x Q x$ has to mean something different from $\exists x \mathbf{K}_a Q x$ (compare the distinction between *de dicto* and *de re* mentioned earlier). Discussion about logical relationships was also facilitated. For example, is it reasonable to regard the type (4) schema $\mathbf{K}_a\phi \supset \mathbf{K}_a\mathbf{K}_a\phi$ (positive introspection, the KK-thesis) and the type (5) schema $\neg\mathbf{K}_a\phi \supset \mathbf{K}_a\neg\mathbf{K}_a\phi$ (negative introspection) as valid for rational knowledge? (Hintikka's own inclination was to accept the former but reject the latter.) Another example of the applicability of Hintikka's logic was to the puzzle known after George Edward Moore as Moore's paradox. Suppose I am ignorant of the fact, say, that it is currently raining in Cambridge, England, but that I am sufficiently informed of my own beliefs to be aware of my ignorance. Then someone who knows me may say, truly, "It is raining, but you don't believe it." But, as observed by Moore, it would be distinctly odd of me to agree, saying, "Yes, it is raining, but I don't believe it." Hintikka accounts for the oddness by suggesting that a belief operator $\mathbf{B}_a$ must satisfy certain

minimum conditions to count as an operator expressing rational belief. For example, it would be enough if the logic of $\mathbf{B}_a$ was at least as strong as the normal modal logic KD4, for in that logic a sentence $\phi \wedge \neg\mathbf{B}_a\phi$ may be consistent, but a sentence $\mathbf{B}_a(\phi \wedge \neg\mathbf{B}_a\phi)$ is always inconsistent (or, in Hintikka's terminology, doxastically indefensible).

Knowledge and belief about knowledge and belief has been an issue of late, of interest not only to philosophers but also to computer scientists and game theorists. It may be that everyone in a group of agents knows that ϕ, but this does not mean that ϕ is common knowledge in the group (a concept first studied by David Lewis); for that to be the case it is also required that everyone knows that everyone knows that ϕ, knows that everyone knows that everyone knows that ϕ, and so on. Interestingly, this concept can be axiomatized. If G is a nonempty, finite set of agents—for simplicity, assume that $G = \{1, \ldots, n\}$—write $\mathbf{E}_G\phi$ for "every member of G knows that ϕ" and $\mathbf{C}_G\phi$ for "it is common knowledge among the members of G that ϕ." Assuming that $\mathbf{K}_i$ is an S4-operator, for each $i \in G$, the logic of the two new operators may be characterized by requiring $\mathbf{C}_G$ also to be an S4-operator and adding the following conditions:

$$\mathbf{E}_G\phi \equiv (\mathbf{K}_1\phi \wedge \cdots \wedge \mathbf{K}_n\phi),$$

$$\mathbf{C}_G\phi \supset \mathbf{E}_G\phi,$$

$$(\phi \wedge \mathbf{C}_G(\phi \supset \mathbf{E}_G\phi)) \supset \mathbf{C}_G\phi.$$

THE DEONTIC INTERPRETATION. When von Wright published his seminal paper "Deontic Logic" in 1951, he in effect delivered a discipline just waiting to be born. The next decades saw a great number of papers and books written on this topic, but it is probably fair to say that the results are less definitive than those of several other subfields of modal logic. The basic idea is to study operators $\mathbf{O}$, $\mathbf{P}$, and $\mathbf{F}$ with the informal readings "it is obligatory that ϕ" for $\mathbf{O}\phi$, "it is permitted that ϕ" for $\mathbf{P}\phi$, and "it is forbidden that ϕ" for $\mathbf{F}\phi$. In so-called standard deontic logic (STD), $\mathbf{O}$ is treated as the box operator and $\mathbf{P}$ as the diamond operator of a normal logic; $\mathbf{F}$ may then be defined by a condition such as $\mathbf{F}\phi \equiv \mathbf{O}\neg\phi$ or $\mathbf{F}\phi \equiv \neg\mathbf{P}\phi$ (to be compared with the validities $\mathbf{P}\phi \equiv \neg\mathbf{O}\neg\phi$ and $\mathbf{O}\phi \equiv \neg\mathbf{P}\neg\phi$). STD—not a precise concept—provides the schema (D) $\mathbf{O}\phi \supset \mathbf{P}\phi$. One schema that for obvious reasons would be inappropriate in a deontic logic is (T), but weaker schemata such as $\mathbf{O}\mathbf{O}\phi \supset \mathbf{O}\phi$ and $\mathbf{O}(\mathbf{O}\phi \supset \phi)$ are sometimes included in STD.

Efforts to apply STD to even fairly simple everyday situations will often fail, as shown by the existence of so-called paradoxes, a topic much discussed in the literature.

Best known among the latter are perhaps the paradoxes of William David Ross, Roderick Chisholm, and James W. Forrester. (Ross's paradox was originally formulated within the logic of imperatives, but it is equally relevant for deontic logic.) A person is under an obligation to see to it that (ϕ) a letter is posted. Should he or she do it by seeing to it that (ψ) the letter is burned? Since $\phi \supset (\phi \vee \psi)$ is a tautology, $\mathbf{O}\phi \supset \mathbf{O}(\phi \vee \psi)$ is a thesis of STD. Evidently, according to STD the person should see to it that the letter is posted or burned; Ross found this conclusion bizarre. In Chisholm's paradox there are two things A and B that you may or may not do: Whether (ϕ) you do A is logically independent of whether (ψ) you do B. On the one hand, it ought to be the case that you do B if you do A ($\mathbf{O}(\phi \supset \psi)$). On the other hand, if you do not do A, then neither ought you to do B ($\neg\phi \supset \neg\mathbf{O}\psi$). Furthermore, even though A is something you ought to do ($\mathbf{O}\phi$), you will not do it ($\neg\phi$). In STD this description of a situation, regrettable perhaps but otherwise unremarkable, leads to contradiction. Forrester's paradox is subtler: suppose there is something one must not do, but that if one nevertheless does it, then one should do it in such and such a way. Again, STD comes to grief.

Among the many problems still not resolved in modern deontic logic—Hector–Neri Castañeda's work and his distinction between propositions and practitions notwithstanding—is the age-old question about the relationship between Seinsollen (ought to be) and Tunsollen (ought to do). It is interesting that von Wright, the father of the discipline, originally had intended for his deontic operators to take as arguments, not propositions, but actions; he seems to have changed his mind for technical reasons. With the advent of dynamic logic, it is nowadays possible to reconsider this option.

OTHER INTERPRETATIONS. The techniques of modal logic have been applied to a number of other areas of philosophical interest: imperatives, action, preference, place, even questions. Many of the more interesting applications make use of several modalities. For example, Kanger's theory of rights, which builds on Wesley Newcomb Hohfeld's famous analysis, combines concepts from deontic logic and the logic of action.

EXTENSIONS OF MODAL LOGIC

CONDITIONAL LOGIC. The analysis of conditionals has occupied philosophers for generations. Not all the resulting analyses belong to the field of modal logic, but there is a natural sense in which the conditional logics of Robert Stalnaker and David Lewis may be seen as gener-

alizations of classical modal logic. This is obvious if one employs a notation suggested by Brian Chellas: writing $[\phi]\psi$ and $\langle\phi\rangle\psi$ where Lewis had $\phi \; \square\!\!\rightarrow \; \psi$ ("if it were the case that ϕ, then it would be the case that ψ") and $\phi \; \diamond\!\!\rightarrow \; \psi$ ("if it were the case that ϕ, then it might be that ψ"), respectively. By this device, one moves from the language of traditional modal logic, where there is one box operator $\square$, to a language in which there are as many box operators $[\phi]$ as there are well-formed formulas ϕ. Corresponding to the minimal normal modal logic K is the minimal normal conditional logic in which every box operator satisfies the Kripke schema and the rule of necessitation, and which is also closed under the rule of congruence (if θ^* is the result of replacing all occurrences of ϕ in θ by an occurrence of ψ, then $\theta \equiv \theta^*$ is a thesis if $\phi \equiv \psi$ is). Lewis's logic VC of counterfactuals is the smallest normal conditional logic that contains all instances of the schemata:

$$[\phi]\phi,$$

$$\langle\phi\rangle\psi \supset \langle\psi\rangle\top,$$

$$\phi \supset (\psi \supset [\phi]\psi),$$

$$\phi \supset ([\phi]\psi \supset \psi),$$

$$[\phi \wedge \psi]\theta \supset [\phi](\psi \supset \theta),$$

$$\langle\phi\rangle\psi \supset ([\phi](\psi \supset \theta) \supset [\phi \wedge \psi]\theta).$$

Stalnaker's logic is obtained by requiring that also all instances of the schema

$$\langle\phi\rangle\theta \equiv [\phi]\theta$$

be theses.

DYNAMIC LOGIC. Looking for a useful way to formalize reasoning about programs, Vaughan Pratt, a computer scientist, arrived at what is nowadays known as dynamic logic, a formalism similar to modal logic; in fact, dynamic logic may be viewed as a generalization of modal logic in the same way as Chellas-formulated conditional logic may be seen as a generalization of modal logic. With each program α Pratt associated a box operator $[\alpha]$ and a diamond operator $\langle\alpha\rangle$, reading $[\alpha]\phi$ as "after every terminating computation according to α, ϕ" and $\langle\alpha\rangle\phi$ as "after some terminating computation according to α, ϕ." The resulting logic, originally called the modal logic of programs, evidently contains two basic categories of expressions, terms (for programs), and formulas (for propositions). A further complication over modal logic is the existence of term operators for the so-called regular operations. Thus, if α and β are programs, then $\alpha + \beta$ is the program consisting of α or β (the latter concept is of course of interest only in the context of nondeterministic automata) while α ; β is the program consisting of α immediately followed by β, and α* is the program consisting of α some finite number of times, possibly 0 (again, of interest only in a nondeterministic context). Finally, Pratt allowed a test program: ?ϕ is a program that, if run, fails if ϕ is false but otherwise returns to status quo. An axiomatization of PDL (propositional dynamic logic) is obtained by requiring each box operator [α] to be a normal modal operator and adding the following axiom schemata:

$$[\alpha + \beta]\phi \equiv ([\alpha]\phi \wedge [\beta]\phi),$$

$$[\alpha ;\beta]\phi \equiv [\alpha][\beta]\phi,$$

$$[\alpha^*]\phi \supset \phi,$$

$$[\alpha^*]\phi \supset [\alpha]\phi,$$

$$[\alpha^*]\phi \supset [\alpha^*][\alpha^*]\phi,$$

$$(\phi \wedge [\alpha^*](\phi \supset [\alpha]\phi)) \supset [\alpha^*]\phi,$$

$$[?\phi]\chi \equiv (\phi \supset \chi).$$

OTHER INTERPRETATIONS. Some of the generalizations of modal logic that have been made over the last few decades have an origin far from modal logic. Dynamic logic is one example that has already been mentioned. Another example is description logic, which is a family of formalisms used by computer scientists to represent knowledge that is already expressed in a certain regimented form; only after extensive work did those practitioners realize that what they were doing could be seen as a version of multimodal logic, that is, modal logic with several normal operators.

An example closer to ordinary modal logic is hybrid logic, a way of doing modal logic actually anticipated by Prior. Here, the object language of traditional modal logic is augmented by the introduction of concepts belonging to semantics, a device that can greatly increase the expressive strength of the formal language. One such augmentation is to allow a new category of syntactic objects, called nominals, a special set of propositional constants whose semantic interpretation is as singleton sets; in other words, nominals represent propositions that are true at exactly one point in the universe of a model. If i is a nominal and ϕ an ordinary formula, then (i $\supset \phi$) $\vee$ (i $\supset \neg\phi$) and $\diamond$(i $\wedge \phi$) $\supset \Box$(i $\supset \phi$) exemplify formulas valid in every frame. By contrast i $\supset \Box\neg$i is an example of a formula valid in exactly the class of frames (U, R) in which

R is irreflexive. This is a striking fact, for irreflexivity is notoriously not expressible in ordinary modal logic—the logic determined by the class of all frames with irreflexive accessibility relations is the same as the logic determined by the class of all frames, that is, K.

Like description logic, hybrid logic is actually a family of logics with different object languages. This proliferation of languages bears witness to the many different uses to which modal logic is nowadays being put. In this regard it is interesting to note a certain trade-off between more restrictive and more permissive options: in general, the more expressive a language is, the more endangered are desirable properties like completeness and decidability. Some philosophers may find the multifariousness of present-day computer science–driven modal logic bewildering. At any rate, we have come a long way from the beginning of modal logic when C. I. Lewis sought, and for a while thought he had found, the one and only logic of strict implication.

See also A Priori and A Posteriori; Armstrong, David M.; Carnap, Rudolf; Chisholm, Roderick; Diodorus Cronus; Dummett, Michael Anthony Eardley; Gödel, Kurt; Hintikka, Jaakko; Kripke, Saul; Lewis, Clarence Irving; Lewis, David; Logic, History of; Łukasiewicz, Jan; Marcus, Ruth Barcan; Mathematics, Foundations of; Modality, Philosophy and Metaphysics of; Moore, George Edward; Plantinga, Alvin; Prior, Arthur Norman; Provability Logic; Quine, Willard Van Orman; Ross, William David; Tarski, Alfred; Wright, Georg Henrik von.

Bibliography

ORIGINAL WORKS

Carnap, Rudolf. *Meaning and Necessity: A Study in Semantics and Modal Logic.* Chicago: University of Chicago Press, 1947.

Hintikka, Jaakko. *Knowledge and Belief: An Introduction to the Logic of the Two Notions.* Ithaca, NY: Cornell University Press, 1962.

Jónsson, Bjarni, and Alfred Tarski. "Boolean Algebras with Operators: Part I." *American Journal of Mathematics* 73 (1951): 891–939.

Kanger, Stig. "Provability in Logic." PhD diss., Stockholm University, 1957.

Kripke, Saul A. "Semantical Analysis of Modal Logic: I. Normal Modal Propositional Calculi." *Zeitschrift für Mathematische Logik und Grundlagen der Mathematik* 9 (1963): 67–96.

Kripke, Saul A. "Semantical Analysis of Modal Logic: II. Nonnormal Modal Propositional Calculi." In *The Theory of Models*, edited by J. W. Addison, L. Henkin, and A. Tarski, 206–220. Amsterdam, Netherlands: North-Holland, 1965.

Kripke, Saul A. "Semantical Considerations on Modal Logic." *Acta Philosophica Fennica* 16 (1963): 83–94.

Lewis, Clarence Irving. *A Survey of Symbolic Logic*. Berkeley: University of California Press, 1918.

Lewis, Clarence Irving, and Cooper Harold Langford. *Symbolic Logic*. New York: Century, 1932.

Lewis, David. *Counterfactuals*. Cambridge, MA: Harvard University Press, 1973.

McKinsey, J. C. C. "A Solution of the Decision Problem for the Lewis Systems S2 and S4 with an Application to Topology." *Journal of Symbolic Logic* (1941): 117–134.

Montague, Richard. "Logical Necessity, Physical Necessity, Ethics, and Quantifiers." *Inquiry* 4 (1960): 259–269.

Prior, Arthur. *Past, Present, and Future*. Oxford, U.K.: Clarendon Press, 1967.

Prior, Arthur. *Time and Modality*. Oxford, U.K.: Clarendon Press, 1957.

von Wright, Georg Henrik. "Deontic Logic." *Mind* 60 (1951a): 1–15.

von Wright, Georg Henrik. *An Essay in Modal Logic*. Amsterdam, Netherlands: North-Holland, 1951b.

SURVEY ARTICLES

Blackburn, Patrick, Frank Wolter, and Johan van Benthem. *Handbook of Modal Logic*. Forthcoming.

Gabbay, D. M., and F. Guenthner. *Handbook of Philosophical Logic. Vol. 2, Extensions of Classical Logic*. Dordrecht, Netherlands: D. Reidel, 1984.

Gabbay, D. M., and F. Guenthner. *Handbook of Philosophical Logic*. Vols. 3, 4, and 7. 2nd ed. Dordrecht, Netherlands: Kluwer Academic, 2001–2002.

Gochet, P., and P. Gribomont. "Epistemic Logic." In *Handbook of the History and Philosophy of Logic*, edited by D. M. Gabbay and John Woods. Forthcoming.

Goldblatt, Robert. "Mathematical Modal Logic: A View of Its Evolution." *Journal of Applied Logic* 1 (2003): 309–392.

TEXTBOOKS

Chellas, Brian F. *Modal Logic: An Introduction*. New York: Cambridge University Press, 1980.

Fitting, Melvin, and Richard L. Mendelsohn. *First-Order Modal Logic*. Dordrecht, Netherlands: Kluwer Academic, 1998.

Goldblatt, Robert. *Logics of Time and Computation*. CSLI Lecture Notes. Vol. 7. Chicago: Chicago University Press, 1987.

Hughes, G. E., and M. J. Cresswell. *A New Introduction to Modal Logic*. New York: Routledge, 1996.

Krister Segerberg (2005)

MODEL THEORY

In 1954 Alfred Tarski proposed the name *theory of models* for the study of "mutual relations between sentences of formalized theories and mathematical [structures] in which these sentences hold." This definition hides a program that was to apply metamathematical results (particularly the Compactness Theorem of first-order logic) in

what Abraham Robinson in 1950 had called "the development of actual mathematics." Anatolii I. Mal'tsev had launched this program in the Soviet Union in 1940, but communications were bad in this period and the program started afresh in the late 1940s with Tarski in the United States and Robinson in Britain. Mathematical model theory in the sense of this program has been remarkably successful, particularly in its applications to group theory and geometry, and it has far outgrown Tarski's initial definition of the theory of models.

Tarski's definition rested on the fact that one can use formal languages to define classes of structures. For mathematical applications it has turned out to be just as important that one can use formal languages to define sets and relations within a single structure. But at its base, model theory is more general even than this. Arguably it stands in the same relation to the traditional theory of definitions as modern proof theory stands to the traditional theory of syllogisms.

Most sentences are true in some contexts and false in others. If S is a sentence, then by an *interpretation* of S we mean a parcel of information about some possible context, which is enough to make S either true or false in that context. Suppose I is an interpretation of S. If I makes S true, we call I a *model* of S and we say that S is *true in I*. "Truth-in-a-model" is honest to goodness truth, no less than (say) being true at 3 o'clock.

The sentence S defines a class of interpretations, namely the class of its models. A simple example is the mathematical equation

$$x^2 + y^2 = 1$$

where x and y are variables ranging over real numbers. An interpretation of this equation consists of a pair of real numbers b,a where x is to name a and y to name b. Under this interpretation the sentence is true if and only if the point b,a lies on the circle C of radius 1 around the origin in the cartesian plane. So the circle C is the class of models of the equation. This example assumes that we have specified what form an interpretation of the equation should take. In concrete applications of model theory one begins with such a specification.

The sentence S can come from a natural language or a formal one. The range of information that might appear in interpretations is vast. They can specify the time of utterance, the time spoken of, the place, the speaker's identity, salient objects in the context (to give reference to "the previous owner", "the latter symbol", "Peter", etc.). They can also supply meanings for words that have none. But mathematical model theory concerns itself almost entirely with interpretations of a kind called *structures*. A structure supplies a set of objects, called the *domain* or *universe* of the structure. Besides giving a domain, a structure interprets expressions by attaching them to elements of the domain, or to set-theoretic objects built up from elements of the domain. For example a mathematical model theorist, to interpret the sentence

The mome raths outgrabe.

would probably supply two sets X and Y, together with the information that X is the set of things that count as mome raths and Y is the set of things that count as having outgribben. This interpretation is a model of the sentence if and only if X is a subset of Y.

When the sentence S comes from a formal language of logic, one can describe precisely how the truth value of S depends on the sets or objects used to interpret symbols of S. Tarski's model-theoretic definition of truth and satisfaction is a paradigm for this kind of description. The model-theoretic truth definition was an adaptation of the truth definition that Tarski gave in 1933 for formal languages. In that earlier definition Tarski assumed that all symbols needing an interpretation already had one (in general a set-theoretic one), and so the definition was strictly not model-theoretic. But truth definitions that run along similar lines to Tarski's, for example the definitions of truth underlying Richard Montague's semantics for fragments of English, are called "model-theoretic"; probably the use of set theory and recursion on the complexity of formulas are the features that this name brings to mind.

As a discipline, model theory takes no stand at all on whether there are possible worlds or on what objects there are in the universe. If you believe in possible worlds you can study interpretations that involve possible worlds; if you don't, you probably won't. There are branches of model theory where one puts strong limits on the kinds of interpretation that are allowed: For example in *recursive model theory* the structures are built up from computable functions of natural numbers. But since structures are set-theoretic objects, most mathematical model theorists make free use of the axioms of Zermelo-Fraenkel set theory, including the Axiom of Choice.

One should distinguish between model theory and "mathematical modeling". Modeling a phenomenon usually involves constructing a formal theory rather than a set-theoretic structure. But there are overlaps. For example abstract state machines, introduced by the model theorist Yuri Gurevich, are set-theoretic structures used to model parallel computation. In another direction, papers in Morgan and Morrison discuss the relations between theories and structures in scientific research, with particular reference to physics and economics.

FIRST-ORDER MODEL THEORY

First-order model theory is the most developed part of model theory, and other parts of model theory tend to be generalizations or analogues of the first-order case. We begin with some preliminary definitions that rest on first-order logic.

DEFINING STRUCTURES, TRUTH, AND SATISFACTION. First we define signatures. A *signature* is a collection of symbols as follows:

(1) *Relation symbols*, usually

$$P, Q, R, R_0, R_1, R_2, \ldots.$$

(2) *Individual constant symbols*, or more briefly *constants*, usually

$$a, b, c, c_0, c_1, c_2, \ldots.$$

(3) *Function symbols*, usually symbols such as

$$F, G, H, F_0, F_1, F_2, \ldots.$$

Each relation symbol and each function symbol in a signature has an *arity*, which is a positive integer. If a symbol has arity n, we say that the symbol is *n-ary*. We normally require that no symbol occurs in more than one of these three kinds, and that no relation or function symbol occurs with more than one arity. We say that a signature σ is a *reduct* of a signature τ (and that τ is an *expansion* of σ) if every constant in σ is also a constant in τ, every relation symbol of σ is also a relation symbol in τ with the same arity, and likewise for the function symbols in σ.

Let σ be a signature. A σ-*structure* is an ordered pair $A = \langle \text{dom}(A), f_A \rangle$ as follows:

$\text{dom}(A)$ is a nonempty set, known as the *domain* of A.

f_A is a function whose domain is the set of symbols in the signature σ.

For each constant c of σ, $f_A(c)$ is an element of $\text{dom}(A)$; we write this element as c_A.

For each relation symbol R of σ, $f_A(R)$ is an n-ary relation on $\text{dom}(A)$, where n is the arity of R; we write this relation as R_A.

For each function symbol F of σ, $f_A(F)$ is an n-ary function $F_A : \mathrm{dom}(A)^n \to \mathrm{dom}(A)$, where n is the arity of F.

By a *structure* we mean a σ-structure for some signature σ.

If A is a τ-structure and σ is a reduct of τ then we can make A into a σ-structure by removing the symbols not in σ; the resulting σ-structure is written $A|\sigma$ and called a *reduct* of A. Likewise A is an *expansion* of $A|\sigma$.

By the *elements* of a structure A we mean the elements of $\mathrm{dom}(A)$. (For example a structure A and its reduct $A|\sigma$ have the same elements.) By the *cardinality* of A we mean the cardinality of $\mathrm{dom}(A)$.

For each signature σ there is a corresponding first-order language $L(\sigma)$ as in the entry "First-Order Logic". Since each first-order language L is of the form $L(\sigma)$ for a unique signature σ, we can also refer to σ-structures as L-structures. We borrow the following facts and definitions from the entry "First-Order Logic", under the assumption that L is a first-order language and A is an L-structure.

If ϕ is a sentence of L then ϕ is either true or false in A. If ϕ is true in A, we write $A \vDash \phi$ and we call A a *model* of ϕ. If ϕ is false in A we write $A \nvDash \phi$.

By a *theory* in L we mean a set T of sentences of L. By a *model* of T we mean a model of all the sentences in T. We say that T is *consistent* if T has a model; otherwise it is *inconsistent*.

Let T be a theory in L and ϕ a sentence of L. We say that ϕ is a *consequence* of T, and that T entails ϕ, in symbols

(1) $$T \vDash \phi,$$

if every L-structure that is a model of T is also a model of ϕ. The theory T is said to be *complete* if for every sentence ϕ of L, either ϕ or $\neg\phi$ is a consequence of T. The expression (1) is called a *sequent*; it is *valid* if T does entail ϕ.

We write $\phi(x_1, \dots, x_n)$ for a formula of L whose free variables are all among $x_1, \dots, x_n$. If $a_1, \dots, a_n$ are elements of A, we write

$$A \vDash \phi[a_1, \dots, a_n],$$

pronounced "a_1 to a_n satisfy ϕ in A", if ϕ is true in A when each free variable x_i is interpreted as a name of a_i. This notion can be defined set-theoretically without relying on the semantic notion "name of".

These fundamental facts and definitions allow us to use first-order sentences in order to define classes of structures, and to use first-order formulas in order to define classes of elements in structures.

DEFINING CLASSES OF STRUCTURES. We write $\mathrm{Mod}(T)$ for the class of all L-structures that are models of the theory T. If A is an L-structure, we write $\mathrm{Th}(A)$ for the set of all sentences ϕ of L which are true in A; $\mathrm{Th}(A)$ is known as the *complete first-order theory* of A. If **K** is a class of L-structures, we write $\mathrm{Th}(\mathbf{K})$ for the set of those sentences of L which are true in every structure in **K**. We say that two L-structures A and B are *elementarily equivalent*, in symbols $A \equiv B$, if $\mathrm{Th}(A) = \mathrm{Th}(B)$. Elementary equivalence is an equivalence relation on the class of L-structures. We say that two theories S and T in L are *equivalent* if $\mathrm{Mod}(S) = \mathrm{Mod}(T)$; this is an equivalence relation on the class of theories in L.

Theorem 1 *The notions* Mod *and* Th *are related as follows:*

1. *If* $T \subseteq U$ *then* $\mathrm{Mod}(T) \supseteq \mathrm{Mod}(U)$.

2. *If* $\mathbf{J} \subseteq \mathbf{K}$ *then* $\mathrm{Th}(\mathbf{J}) \supseteq \mathrm{Th}(\mathbf{K})$.

3. $\mathbf{K} \subseteq \mathrm{Mod}(\mathrm{Th}(\mathbf{K}))$ *and* $\mathrm{Th}(\mathbf{K}) = \mathrm{Th}(\mathrm{Mod}(\mathrm{Th}(\mathbf{K})))$.

4. $T \subseteq \mathrm{Th}(\mathrm{Mod}(T))$ *and* $\mathrm{Mod}(T) = \mathrm{Mod}(\mathrm{Th}(\mathrm{Mod}(T)))$.

These facts are all immediate from the definitions.

The theory $\mathrm{Th}(\mathrm{Mod}(T))$ is called the *deductive closure* of the theory T; it consists of all the consequences of T. A theory is said to be *deductively closed* if it is its own deductive closure. By 3 of Theorem 1, a theory is deductively closed if and only if it is of the form $\mathrm{Th}(\mathbf{K})$ for some class **K** of structures. (In some older literature, deductive closure was included in the definition of "theory".)

A class of structures of the form $\mathrm{Mod}(\{\phi\})$, where ϕ is a single sentence, is said to be *first-order definable*, or an EC class. A class of structures of the form $\mathrm{Mod}(T)$, where T is a theory, is said to be *first-order axiomatisable*, or *generalised first-order definable*, or an EC_Δ class. A class **K** of L-structures is said to be *closed under elementary equivalence* if every L-structure elementarily equivalent to a structure in **K** is also in **K**.

We pause for some examples.

Example 1: Equivalence relations. We use the signature with one binary relation symbol E; call this signature σ. We write Exy for $E(x,y)$. An equivalence relation is a σ-structure that is a model of the following finite theory, which we shall call T_{eq}:

$\forall x\, Exx$ (reflexive)

$\forall x \forall y\, (Exy \rightarrow Eyx)$ (symmetric)

$\forall x \forall y \forall z\, (Exy \wedge Eyz \rightarrow Exz)$ (transitive)

Example 2: Fields. The following example has been central in the development of model theory. We adopt a signature with constants 0 and 1, binary function symbols $+$ and $\cdot$ and a 1-ary function symbol $-$. This signature is appropriate for talking about rings, so it is known as the *signature of rings*. We normally write $+(x,y)$, $\cdot(x,y)$ and $-(x)$ as $x + y$, xy and $-x$ respectively, and we use standard mathematical notation such as $x \neq y$ for $\neg(x = y)$. The *theory of fields*, T_f, consists of the following sentences:

1. $\forall x \forall y \forall z\, (x + (y + z) = (x + y) + z)$

2. $\forall x \forall y\, (x + y = y + x)$

3. $\forall x\, (x + 0 = x)$

4. $\forall x\, (x + -x = 0)$

5. $\forall x \forall y \forall z\, (x(yz) = (xy)z)$

6. $\forall x \forall y\, (xy = yx)$

7. $\forall x\, (x \cdot 1 = x)$

8. $\forall x \forall y \forall z\, (x(y + z) = xy + xz)$

9. $0 \neq 1$

10. $\forall x \exists y\, (x \neq 0 \rightarrow xy = 1)$

We write 2 for $1 + 1$, 3 for $1 + 1 + 1$ and so on. A field is said to be *of characteristic 0* if it is also a model of the infinitely many axioms

11. $n \neq 0$

where n is any positive integer. We write x^2 for the term xx, x^3 for xxx and so on. Let $t_n(x, y_1, \ldots, y_n)$ be the term

$$x^n + y_1 x^{n-1} + y_2 x^{n-2} + \ldots + y_{n-2} x^2 + y_{n-1} x + y_n.$$

A field is said to be *algebraically closed* if it is a model of the infinitely many axioms

12. $\forall y_1\, \forall y_2 \ldots \forall y_n \exists x\, (t_n(x, y_1, \ldots, y_n) = 0)$

where n is any positive integer. The classes of fields, fields of characteristic 0 and algebraically closed fields were all well known before these axioms were written down as first-order sentences, and the first-order sentences say exactly the same as the earlier informal definitions of those classes.

In the light of our earlier definitions, several natural questions arise. For example:

Question One. Is there an algorithm to determine whether any given sentence ϕ is a consequence of T_{eq}?

Question Two. For which equivalence relations A is $\mathrm{Mod}(\mathrm{Th}(A))$ first-order definable?

Question Three. If A and B are two algebraically closed fields of characteristic 0, how can we tell whether they are elementarily equivalent?

Question Four. What is an example of a class **K** that is closed under elementary equivalence but not first-order axiomatisable?

We will return to these questions below.

The *infinite spectrum* of a class **K** is the class of infinite cardinals κ such that **K** contains a structure of cardinality κ. Questions about the possible infinite spectra of classes of the form $\mathrm{Mod}(T)$ were first raised by Leopold Löwenheim in 1915, and below we shall see some "Löwenheim-Skolem" theorems that describe these spectra.

DEFINING CLASSES OF ELEMENTS. The notions described above have analogues within a single structure. Suppose A is an L-structure. By an *n-tuple in A* we mean an ordered n-tuple $(a_1, \ldots, a_n)$ of elements of A. We write $\Phi(x_1, \ldots, x_n)$ for a set Φ of formulas of L of the form $\phi(x_1, \ldots, x_n)$ (the same integer n for each formula). We say that an n-tuple $(a_1, \ldots, a_n)$ in A *realises* Φ if

for all ϕ in Φ, $A \vDash \phi[a_1, \ldots, a_n]$.

We write $\Phi(A^n)$ for the set of all n-tuples in A that realise Φ. If Φ contains just one formula ϕ, we write $\Phi(A^n)$ as $\phi(A^n)$ and we say that this set of n-tuples is (*first-order*) *definable without parameters*. The sets $\Phi(A^n)$ are said to be *infinitarily definable without parameters*, or $\bigwedge$-*definable without parameters*.

For the analogous notions of definability *with parameters* we allow the formulas ϕ to contain constants (in an expanded signature) to name some elements of A. For example if we are talking about the rational numbers in a signature whose symbols are $<$ for the ordering and 0, 1 for the corresponding numbers, then the interval $(0,1)$ of rational numbers strictly between 0 and 1 will be definable without parameters, the interval $(3,4)$ will be definable with parameters, and the interval $(\sqrt{2}, \pi)$ will not be definable at all. When model theorists talk about definable sets, they sometimes mean with parameters and sometimes without; if in doubt you have to ask.

Let T be a theory in the first-order language L, and $\phi(x_1, \ldots, x_n)$ and $\psi(x_1, \ldots, x_n)$ formulas of L. We say that ϕ is *equivalent to* ψ *modulo* T if $\phi(A^n) = \psi(A^n)$ for every model A of T; this is equivalent to saying that the sentence

(2) $$\forall x_1 \ldots \forall x_n (\phi \leftrightarrow \psi)$$

is a consequence of T. Likewise we say that ϕ is *equivalent to* ψ *in the* L-structure A if $\phi(A^n) = \psi(A^n)$; this is equivalent to saying that (2) is true in A.

If $\Phi(x_1, \ldots, x_n)$ is a set of formulas of L, we can ask whether there is an L-structure A in which $\Phi(A^n)$ is not empty. If the answer is Yes, we say that Φ is an *n-type*, or more briefly a *type*, and we say that the structure A *realises* the type. There may be other structures B for which $\Phi(B^n)$ is empty; these structures are said to *omit* the type. We say that the type Φ is *complete* if for every formula $\phi(x_1, \ldots, x_n)$ of L, exactly one of $\Phi \cup \{\phi\}$ and $\Phi \cup \{\neg\phi\}$ is a type.

For example let $\mathbb{N}$ be the 'natural number' structure whose domain is the set of natural numbers $\underline{0}, \underline{1}, \underline{2}, \ldots$, with symbols to express 0, 1, addition, multiplication and 'less than' $<$. Consider the infinite set $\Phi(x)$ of formulas

$$0<x, \; 1<x, \; 2<x, \; \ldots$$

The set $\Phi(x)$ is in fact a type, but it is clear that $\mathbb{N}$ omits this type; there are no infinite natural numbers. A natural question is:

Question Five. Are there structures elementarily equivalent to $\mathbb{N}$ which realise this type?

The answers to Questions One to Five are not obvious. Many of the techniques of model theory were devised in order to answer just such questions. Historically the first three major techniques in this area were elimination of quantifiers, back-and-forth, and the Compactness Theorem. The next three sections discuss these.

ELIMINATION OF QUANTIFIERS

Thoralf Skolem, Charles Langford, and Alfred Tarski developed the method of elimination of quantifiers during the 1920s as a way of analyzing structures or classes of structures.

As the name indicates, the idea of elimination of quantifiers is to express as much as possible without using quantifiers. Let Φ be a set of formulas of a language L. Write Φ' for the smallest class of formulas of L such that (i) $\Phi \subseteq \Phi'$, (ii) if ϕ is in Φ' then $\neg\phi$ is in Φ', and (iii) if ϕ and ψ are in Φ' then $(\phi \wedge \psi)$ and $(\phi \vee \psi)$ are in Φ'. The formulas in Φ' are called the *boolean combinations* of formulas in Φ. There can be quantifiers in the formulas in Φ, but

when we form boolean combinations of them we add no more quantifiers.

Let L be a first-order language and **K** a class of L-structures. A successful elimination of quantifiers for **K** consists of the following items:

(i) a set T of sentences of L that are true in all structures in **K**;

(ii) a set Φ of formulas of L, called the *elimination set*;

(iii) a proof that if $\psi(x_1, \ldots, x_n)$ is any formula of L then ψ is equivalent modulo T to a boolean combination $\psi^*(x_1, \ldots, x_n)$ of formulas in the elimination set.

We carry out an elimination of quantifiers as follows. The class **K** of structures already determines the signature. We begin by choosing T to be—provisionally—a set of sentences that are clearly true in all structures in **K**; our exact choice could depend on aesthetic or pedagogic considerations. We launch (ii) by including all atomic formulas in the elimination set. From this point on, we aim to prove (iii) by induction on the number of occurrences of quantifiers in ψ, with a subinduction on the complexity. If $\psi^*(x_1, \ldots, x_n)$ and $\chi^*(x_1, \ldots, x_n)$ have been found, we can take $(\psi \wedge \chi)^*$ to be $\psi^* \wedge \chi^*$, and likewise for other truth-functional combinations. We can take $(\forall x_n \psi)^*$ to be $\neg \exists x_n \neg(\psi^*)$. This leaves the case $\exists x_n \psi$, and this is where we "eliminate the quantifier".

We first put ψ^* into disjunctive normal form, and then we use the logical equivalence

$$\exists x \, (\phi_1 \vee \phi_2) \equiv (\exists x \, \phi_1 \vee \exists x \, \phi_2)$$

to reduce to the case of a formula $\exists x_n \theta$ where θ is a conjunction of formulas in the elimination set and negations of formulas in the elimination set. The next step depends on **K** and perhaps on our mathematical skill. If we can find a boolean combination ϕ of formulas in the elimination set, and a proof that ϕ is equivalent to $\exists x_n \theta$ modulo T, then this case is taken care of. Otherwise we have two options. First if we can find a suitable formula ϕ that is certainly equivalent to $\exists x_n \theta$ in all structures in **K** but we can't prove this equivalence from T then we can add the equivalence statement to T. Second, as a last resort, we can add $\exists x_n \theta$ to the elimination set. We hope to reach a point where we can prove (iii) for all formulas. When this point is reached the quantifier elimination proper is complete. If heaven favors us (and this is not guaranteed) by this stage we will also know which boolean combinations of sentences in the elimination set are true in all structures in **K**. Adding these to T gives a theory T' equivalent to Th(**K**). With more good luck we may find that the reductions in (iii) allow us to construct an algorithm to determine whether any given sentence of L is a consequence of T', so that we have a decision procedure for Th(**K**).

Example 1 continued: Equivalence relations. For T we take the theory T_{eq} defining the class of equivalence relations. As a first attempt at the elimination set Φ we take all atomic formulas of L. There are two kinds of atomic formula, namely $(x = y)$ and Exy. Trial and error shows that for every positive integer n the formula $\chi_n(x)$ expressing "There are at least n elements that are in the same equivalence class as x" is not reducible to a boolean combination of atomic formulas; so we put χ_n in the set Φ too. Similarly we add to Φ all the sentences $\sigma_{m,n}$ expressing 'There are at least m equivalence classes containing at least n members each', where m and n are any positive integers, and the sentences $\theta_{m,n}$ expressing "There are at least m equivalence classes of size exactly n". It turns out that this is enough for an elimination set. There is an algorithm reducing each sentence to a boolean combination of sentences in Φ, and there is an algorithm determining which boolean combinations of sentences in Φ are consequences of T. Thus T is a decidable theory and we have an answer to Question One.

Example 3: The field $\mathbb{R}$ of real numbers. We take the signature to be the expansion of the signature of rings got by adding a binary relation symbol < for the ordering of the reals. (Without this added symbol we would need to put $\exists y \, (x = y^2)$ into the elimination set; with < this formula is equivalent to $(x = 0 \vee 0 < x)$.) Tarski showed that a set of axioms for Th($\mathbb{R}$) is given by the theory T_f of Example 2 together with an axiom saying that for every element r, either r or $-r$ is a square, an axiom saying that r <s if and only if $r \neq s$ and $s - r$ has a square root, axioms saying that -1 is not a sum of squares, and the axioms 12 for odd positive integers n. It then came to light that these axioms define the class of real-closed fields. Tarski also gave a decision procedure for the set of consequences of this theory. The elimination set is interesting: it consists exactly of the atomic formulas. As a corollary, the subsets of $\mathbb{R}$ that are first-order definable with parameters consist of the finite unions of sets of the following kinds: singletons $\{a\}$, intervals $(a,b$ (the set of elements r with $a < r$ and $r < b$), intervals $(-\infty$ (the set of all elements $< b$) and intervals (a,∞) (the set of all elements $>a$).

A structure A whose elements are linearly ordered by an ordering relation $<_A$, and for which the sets first-order definable with parameters are exactly the finite unions of singletons and intervals as in Example 3, is said to be *o-minimal*. The knowledge that a structure is o-minimal gives powerful information about the structure. Beginning with Alex Wilkie's demonstration in 1991 that the expansion of the field of real numbers with an exponentiation function x^y is o-minimal, many other o-minimal expansions of $\mathbb{R}$ have been found, and there is promise of deep applications in real function theory.

From around 1950 more powerful and algebraic methods were found that gave largely the same information as the method of elimination of quantifiers. But it remains one of the best methods for discovering decision procedures when the theory is decidable.

BACK-AND-FORTH

Suppose A and B are σ-structures, where σ is a signature. By a *partial isomorphism* from A to B we mean a function e from a subset X of dom(A) to dom(B) such that if $\phi(x_1, \ldots, x_n)$ is an atomic formula of L and $a_1, \ldots, a_n$ are any elements in X then

$$A \vDash \phi[a_1, \ldots, a_n] \text{ if and only if } B \vDash \phi[e(a_1), \ldots, e(a_n)].$$

If e is a partial isomorphism from A to B and the domain X of e is the whole of dom(A), we say that e is an *embedding* of A into B. If e is an embedding of A into B and every element of B is of the form $e(a)$ for some element a of A then we say that e is an *isomorphism* from A to B. We say that A is *isomorphic* to B, in symbols $A \cong B$, if there is an isomorphism from A to B. The relation $\cong$ is an equivalence relation on the class of L-structures, and its equivalence classes are called *isomorphism types*.

If A and B are isomorphic σ-structures, then A and B must be elementarily equivalent, $A \equiv B$. The definition of "partial isomorphism", and hence also the definition of $\cong$, are easily rewritten in ways that refer to the signature σ but not to any formula of the language $L(\sigma)$. In the 1950s one aim of research was to find an "algebraic" description of elementary equivalence that doesn't mention formulas either. Roland Fraïssé gave essentially the following answer, which is known as the *back-and-forth* method.

A *back-and-forth system* from A to B is a set I of partial isomorphisms from A to B such that

(a) I is not empty.

(b) If i is in I and a is an element of A then there are an element b of B and a partial isomorphism j in I such that

$$i \cup \{\langle a, b \rangle\} \subseteq j;$$

(c) If i is in I and b is an element of B, then there are an element a of A and a partial isomorphism j in I such that

$$i \cup \{ \langle a,b \rangle \} \subseteq j.$$

By a *finite relational signature* we mean a signature with only finitely many symbols, none of which are function symbols. (Constants are allowed.)

Theorem 2 *If there is a back-and-forth system I from A to B then $A \equiv B$. If $A \equiv B$ then for every finite relational signature σ, there is a back-and-forth system from $A|\sigma$ to $B|\sigma$.*

Example 4: Dense linear orderings without endpoints. We adopt a signature σ with one binary relation symbol $<$, and we write $x < y$ for $<(x, y)$. A *dense linear ordering without endpoints* is a σ-structure that is a model of the following set of sentences:

1. $\forall x \, \neg (x < x)$ (irreflexive)
2. $\forall x \forall y \forall z \, (x < y \wedge y < z \rightarrow x < z)$ (transitive)
3. $\forall x \forall y \, (x < y \vee y < x \vee x = y)$ (linear)
4. $\forall x \forall y \exists z \, (x < y \rightarrow x < z \wedge z < y)$ (dense)
5. $\forall x \exists y \exists z \, (y < x \wedge x < z)$ (no endpoints)

We shall write this set of sentences as T_{dlo}.

Suppose A and B are dense linear orderings without endpoints. An *order-preserving partial map* from A to B is a function e from a finite set X of elements of A to the domain of B such that if the elements of X are $a_1, \ldots, a_n$ with

(3) $$a_1 <_A a_2 <_A \ldots <_A a_n$$

then

(4) $$e(a_1) <_B e(a_2) <_B \ldots <_B e(a_n).$$

Write $I(A,B)$ for the set of all order-preserving partial maps from A to B.

One can check from the definitions that every function in $I(A,B)$ is a partial isomorphism from A to B. Also $I(A,B)$ is a back-and-forth system from A to B. Suppose for example e is in I with domain $\{a_1, \ldots, a_n\}$ as in (3), and a is an element of A that is not in the domain of e. One possibility is that $a <_A a_1$. By sentence 5 of T_{dlo} there is an element b of B with $b <_B e(a_1)$; then $e \cup \{ \langle a,b \rangle \}$ is a function in I that extends e and has a in its domain. The other possibilities for a are similar, using sentences 4 and 5. The same argument, going from B to A, shows that if e is in I and b is an element of B then there is a function in I that extends e and takes some element of A to b.

By Theorem 2 it follows that $A \equiv B$; so any two dense linear orderings without endpoints are elementarily equivalent, and the theory T_{dlo} is complete.

We can say more. Suppose A and B both have countably many elements; list the elements of A as $a_0, a_1, \ldots$ and the elements of B as $b_0, b_1, \ldots$. Let e_0 be any function in $I(A,B)$. There is e_1 in $I(A,B)$ that extends e_0 and has a_0 in its domain and b_0 in its image. Then there is e_2 that extends e_1 and has a_1 in its domain and b_1 in its image; and so on through e_3, e_4, and so on. Finally define a function e by putting $e(a_i) = e_{i+1}(a_i)$ for each element a_i of A. By construction all elements of A are in the domain of e and all elements of B are in the image of e, and it follows that e is an isomorphism from A to B. We have proved a famous theorem of Cantor:

Theorem 3 *If A and B are countable dense linear orderings without endpoints, then A and B are isomorphic.*

There are many adaptations of Fraïssé's idea. One different presentation (though with the same content) uses the idea of a game between two players who take turns to choose elements from the structures A and B. The criteria for the second player to win can be set up so that this player has a winning strategy if and only if there is a back-and-forth system from A to B.

In another adaptation, we require that the domains of the functions in the back-and-forth system all have cardinality $\leq n$ for some positive integer n, dropping the requirements (b) and (c) when i has domain of size n. The existence of a back-and-forth system of this kind corresponds (as in Theorem 2) to the condition that A and B agree in all sentences with quantifier rank $\leq n$, in symbols $A \equiv_n B$. We omit the full definition of $\equiv_n$ here, but we note that any sentence with at most n occurrences of quantifiers in it has quantifier rank $\leq n$, and that in a finite relational signature there are only finitely many pairwise nonequivalent sentences of rank $\leq n$. It follows that a class **K** with finite relational signature is first-order definable if and only if it is closed under $\equiv_n$ for some n. This leads quickly to an answer to Question Two.

Theorem 4 *The equivalence relations A with $\mathrm{Mod}(\mathrm{Th}(A))$ first-order definable are precisely the finite ones.*

Back-and-forth methods are a model-theoretic generalisation of techniques developed in several areas of mathematics, notably in the study of linear orderings and abelian groups. They also adapt to some languages that are not first-order, and unlike much of first-order model theory, they work as well for finite structures as for infinite ones. This has made them useful tools of theoretical computer science, for example in database theory.

One shouldn't come away from this section with the impression that proving elementary equivalence is a matter of finding a clever model-theoretic technique. Model-theoretic ideas can help to bring to the surface the place where work has to be done, but most proofs of elementary equivalence involve substantial mathematics. For example a problem that Tarski posed in the 1950s, namely whether all free groups with more than one generator are elementarily equivalent, resisted decades of efforts. About half a century after Tarski put the problem, a positive solution was announced by Zlil Sela; besides quantifier elimination, it used a range of techniques from different parts of group theory.

THE COMPACTNESS THEOREM

Almost everything in first-order model theory depends on the Compactness Theorem.

Theorem 5 (Compactness Theorem) *Let L be a first-order language and T a theory in L such that every finite subset of T has a model. Then T has a model.*

We sketch a proof using Hintikka sets as in the entry "First Order Logic." The proof needs a little set theory in the form of infinite cardinals and ordinals. (For the special case in which L has finite or countable signature, one needs only finite numbers.) Suppose the number of formulas of L is κ. We expand the language L to a language L^+ by adding κ new constants, the *witnesses*. Each of the clauses (H1)–(H6) in the definition of a Hintikka set describes a set of requirements on a Hintikka set; for example (H4) describes, for each formula $\phi(x)$ of L^+ and each equation $(s = t)$ where s and t are closed terms of L^+, the requirement that if $\phi(s)$ and $(s = t)$ are in the Hintikka set then $\phi(t)$ is in the Hintikka set. We list all these requirements as $(r_i : i < \kappa)$, in a list of order-type κ, arranging that each requirement appears as r_i for κ-many ordinals i.

Now we define a sequence of theories $(T_i : i \leq \kappa)$, by induction on i, in such a way that three properties hold:

(i) If $i < j \leq \kappa$ then T_i is a subset of T_j.

(ii) Each theory T_i has the property that every finite subset of T_i has a model.

(iii) For each $i < \kappa$ the number of sentences that are in T_{i+1} but not in T_i is finite.

The intention is that T_κ will be a Hintikka set.

We start by putting $T_0 = T$; this ensures that (ii) holds for T_0. If i is a limit ordinal then we take T_i to be $\cup_{j < i} T_j$; since (assuming (i)) every finite subset of T_i is already a subset of some T_j with $j < i$, this ensures that (ii) holds for T_i provided it already holds for each T_j with $j < i$.

Now for each ordinal $i < \kappa$ we define T_{i+1}, assuming that T_i has been defined, in such a way that requirement r_i will be met if it applies. (When r_i doesn't apply, we put $T_{i+1} = T_i$.) The details depend on r_i. We consider some typical cases.

Suppose r_i is the requirement (from (H1)) that if $(\phi \wedge \psi)$ is in the Hintikka set then so are ϕ and ψ. If this requirement applies, that is, if $(\phi \wedge \psi)$ is in T_i, then we take T_{i+1} to be $T_i \cup \{\phi, \psi\}$. It has to be checked that every finite subset of T_{i+1} has a model. Suppose U is a finite subset of T_{i+1}. Put $V = (U \cap T_i) \cup \{(\phi \wedge \psi)\}$. Then V is a finite subset of T_i, so by induction hypothesis it has a model, say A. Since A is a model of $(\phi \wedge \psi)$, it is also a model of ϕ and ψ, and hence it must be a model of U.

Suppose r_i is the requirement (also from (H1)) that if $\neg(\phi \wedge \psi)$ is in the Hintikka set then so is at least one of $\neg \phi$ and $\neg \psi$. If $\neg(\phi \wedge \psi)$ is in T_i then r_i applies. Put $S_1 = T_i \cup \{\neg \phi\}$ and $S_2 = T_i \cup \{\neg \psi\}$. If every finite subset of S_1 has a model then we put $T_{i+1} = S_1$. If not then there is some finite subset U of T_i such that $U \cup \{\neg \phi\}$ has no model. We claim that in this case every finite subset V of S_2 has a model. For consider $U \cup (V \cap T_i) \cup \{\neg(\phi \wedge \psi)\}$, which is a finite subset of T_i and hence has a model, say B, by induction hypothesis. Then B is a model of U and hence a model of ϕ; but B is also a model of $\neg(\phi \wedge \psi)$, so it must be a model of $\neg \psi$ and hence of S_2, as claimed. Hence in this case we can put $T_{i+1} = S_2$.

Suppose r_i is the requirement (from (H5)) that if $\exists x\ \phi(x)$ is in a Hintikka set then so is $\phi(c)$ for some constant c. Suppose that this applies, that is, that $\exists x\ \phi(x)$ is in T_i. By (iii) the number of witnesses used in sentences in T_i is less than κ, and so there must be at least one witness c not used yet. Choose such a c and put $T_{i+1} = T_i \cup \{\phi(c)\}$. Let U be a finite subset of T_{i+1}. Then $(U \cap T_i) \cup \{\exists x\ \phi\}$ is a finite subset of T_i, and so by induction hypothesis it has a model, say C. Since C is a model of $\exists x\ \phi$, there is an element a of C such that $C \models \phi[a]$. Let D be the same structure as C, except that $c_D = a$. Then since c appears nowhere in sentences of T_i, D is also a model of $U \cap T_i$. But by choice of c_D it is a model of $\phi(c)$ too, so it is a model of U.

Now suppose we have completed the definition of T_κ as described. Suppose $(\phi \wedge \psi)$ is in T_κ. Then $(\phi \wedge \psi)$ is already in T_i for some $i < \kappa$. Since the requirement referring to $(\phi \wedge \psi)$ is r_j for κ distinct ordinals j, it is r_j for some

$j > i$. So the requirement will have been met when T_{j+1} was defined, and hence T_κ meets the requirement. A similar argument for each of the requirements (H1)–(H6) shows that T_κ meets all these conditions for a Hintikka set. Condition (H7) holds because every finite subset of T_κ has a model. So T_κ is a Hintikka set, and by Metatheorem 16 in the entry "First-Order Logic," it has a model, say A. Since T is a subset of T_κ, A is a model of T, proving the theorem.

Now we can answer Question Five. Let L^+ be the first-order language of the structure $\mathbb{N}$, but with one extra constant c. Let T be $\mathbb{N}$ together with the infinitely many sentences

$$\underline{0} < c, \underline{1} < c, \underline{2} < c, \dots$$

If U is any finite subset of T, then U includes at most finitely many of the sentences $\underline{n} < c$, and so we can choose a natural number m greater than any of the numbers n for which U mentions $\underline{n}$. Let $\mathbb{N}^+$ be the expansion of $\mathbb{N}$ got by putting

$$c_{\mathbb{N}}^+ = m.$$

Then $\mathbb{N}^+$ is a model of U. It follows that every finite subset of T has a model, and hence by the Compactness Theorem there is a model A of the whole of T. Let B be the reduct of A to the language of $\mathbb{N}$. Then $B \equiv \mathbb{N}$ since T contains $\mathrm{Th}(\mathbb{N})$. But also B contains the element c_A which realizes the type consisting of all the formulas $\underline{n} < x$.

This argument illustrates the model-theoretic idea behind nonstandard analysis.

We can also answer Question Four. In any signature σ, let $\mathbf{K}$ be the class of finite structures. If A is a structure in $\mathbf{K}$ and B is a σ-structure elementarily equivalent to A, then A and hence also B are models of a sentence expressing "There are exactly n elements", for some finite n. So B is also in $\mathbf{K}$. This shows that $\mathbf{K}$ is closed under elementary equivalence. But let τ be the expansion of σ got by adding infinitely many new constant symbols $c_0, c_1, \dots$ and let T' be the theory consisting of all the sentences $(c_i \neq c_j)$ where $i < j$. Since every finite subset of $\mathrm{Th}(\mathbf{K}) \cup T'$ has a model (expanding a structure in $\mathbf{K}$), the Compactness Theorem tells us that $\mathrm{Th}(\mathbf{K}) \cup T'$ has a model, and hence that $\mathrm{Th}(\mathbf{K})$ has an infinite model. Thus $\mathbf{K}$ is not first-order axiomatisable.

The general setting of our proof of the Compactness Theorem has many adaptations in model theory. A structure is built in a well-ordered sequence of steps, and we list in advance what feature of the structure has to be ensured at each step. Typical examples are the construction of models of a theory that omit certain types, the construction of "existentially closed" models of a theory, and the construction of "two-cardinal" models in which some definable parts are large but other definable parts are kept small.

SUBSTRUCTURES AND ELEMENTARY EMBEDDINGS

If X is a subset of Y then the *inclusion map* from X to Y is the function $i : X \to Y$ such that $i(x) = x$ for each element x of X. Let σ be a signature and A a σ-structure. We say that a σ-structure B is a *substructure* of A, and that A is an *extension* of B, in symbols $A \subseteq B$, if

- $\mathrm{dom}(B)$ is a subset of $\mathrm{dom}(A)$,
- the inclusion map from $\mathrm{dom}(A)$ to $\mathrm{dom}(B)$ is an embedding of A into B.

An embedding $e : A \to B$ between L-structures (for some first-order language L) is said to *preserve* a formula $\phi(x_1, \dots, x_n)$ of L if

$$A \vDash \phi[a_1, \dots, a_n] \Rightarrow B \vDash \phi[e(a_1), \dots, e(a_n)]$$

for all elements $a_1, \dots, a_n$ of A. We say that e is an *elementary embedding* if e preserves all formulas of L. If A is a substructure of B and the inclusion map is an elementary embedding, then we say that B is an *elementary extension* of A and that A is an *elementary substructure* of B, in symbols $A \preccurlyeq B$. Always $A \preccurlyeq A$. Also if $A \preccurlyeq B$ and $B \preccurlyeq C$ then $A \preccurlyeq C$. If $A \preccurlyeq B$ then $A \equiv B$.

Two important facts about elementary extension are:

Theorem 6 (*a*) *Let A be a substructure of the L-structure B such that*

> *for every formula $\phi(x_1, \dots, x_n)$ of L and all elements $a_1, \dots, a_{n-1}$ of A such that $B \vDash \exists x_n \phi[a_1, \dots, a_{n-1}]$ there is b in A such that $B \vDash \phi[a_1, \dots, a_{n-1}, b]$.*

Then $A \preccurlyeq B$.

(*b*) (**Union of elementary chains**) *Suppose α is an ordinal and for every ordinal $i < \alpha$ an L-structure A_i is given, so that $A_i \preccurlyeq A_j$ whenever $i < j < \alpha$. Then writing A_α for the union of all the structures A_i, we have $A_i \preccurlyeq A_\alpha$ for all $i < \alpha$.*

Part (a) of Theorem 6 can be used to prove the following important result.

Theorem 7 (Downward Löwenheim-Skolem Theorem) *Let L be a first-order language, A an L-structure, X a set of elements of A, and κ an infinite cardinal number which is (i) at least as great as the number of sentences of L, (ii) at least as great as the cardinality of X and (iii) no* *greater than the cardinality of A. Then A has an elementary substructure of cardinality κ whose domain contains all the elements of X.*

This is the result that creates the Skolem paradox. If the axioms of set theory have a model at all, then by this theorem they have a model of countable cardinality, although a sentence expressing "There are uncountably many real numbers" is true in the model!

Part (b) of Theorem 6 is useful for proving a similar result in the other direction. The argument after Theorem 5 adapts to show that every infinite structure has a proper elementary extension. By making repeated elementary extensions and using (b) to take unions at limit ordinals, we reach arbitrarily large elementary extensions.

Theorem 8 (Upward Löwenheim-Skolem Theorem) *Let L be a first-order language, A an infinite L-structure and κ a cardinal number which is at least as great as (i) the cardinality of A and (ii) the number of sentences of L. Then A has an elementary extension of cardinality κ.*

There is also a more algebraic construction that yields a proof of Theorem 8. It involves taking a cartesian product A^I of copies of the structure A and defining a homomorphic image in terms of an ultrafilter D on the set I indexing the copies. The resulting elementary extension A^I/D of A is called an *ultrapower* of A. Ultrapowers also yield a characterisation of ≡:

Theorem 9 *The following are equivalent, for any two L-structures A and B:*

(a) $A \equiv B$.

(b) There are a set I and an ultrafilter D on I such that A^I/D is isomorphic to B^I/D.

Many useful properties of ultrapowers spring from the fact that we can make them "highly saturated," that is to say, realizing many types. One can also use the Compactness Theorem and union of elementary chains to build highly saturated structures.

The upward and downward Löwenheim-Skolem Theorems led to a natural question about first-order theories: How far can a first-order theory restrict its models? Assuming that the theory T is in a countable language and has an infinite model, we know that it has a model in each infinite cardinality. So the tightest restriction possible is that in every infinite cardinality κ, T is κ-*categorical*, that is, it has a model of cardinality κ but all its models of cardinality κ are isomorphic to each other.

Michael Morley published the following theorem in 1965. Its main importance lies in its proof, which revolu-

tionised the techniques of model theory and began the developments reported in the final part of this article.

Theorem 10 (Morley's Theorem) *Let L be a countable first-order language with infinite models, and T a theory in L. If T is κ-categorical for at least one uncountable cardinal κ then T is λ-categorical for all uncountable cardinals λ.*

A theory that is κ-categorical for all uncountable κ is said to be *uncountably categorical*. One major effect of Morley's Theorem was to switch attention from theories to the detailed construction of their models, and a mark of this is that the models of an uncountably categorical theory are now also said to be *uncountably categorical*. A theory that is κ-categorical in all infinite cardinalities κ is said to be *totally categorical*, and so are its models.

By linear algebra, the theory of infinite dimensional vector spaces over a given finite field is totally categorical. A well-known theorem of Ernst Steinitz says that any two algebraically closed fields of the same characteristic and transcendence degree are isomorphic, and it follows that the theory of algebraically closed fields of a given characteristic is uncountably but not totally categorical. An answer to Question Three follows as well. Suppose A and B are any two algebraically closed fields of the same characteristic. Choose a cardinal κ greater than the cardinalities of both A and B. By Theorem 8, A and B have elementary extensions A' and B' of cardinality κ. Then $A' \cong B'$ by uncountable categoricity, and hence $A \equiv A' \equiv B' \equiv B$.

INTERPOLATION AND DEFINABILITY

Let L be a first-order language containing a relation symbol R. Suppose φ is a sentence of L. We say that R is *upwards monotone* in φ if the following holds:

> If A and B are two L-structures which are identical except that $R_A \subset R_B$, and $A \vDash \phi$, then $B \vDash \phi$.

Likewise we say that R is *downwards monotone* in φ if the following holds:

> If A and B are two L-structures which are identical except that $R_A \subset R_B$, and $B \vDash \phi$, then $A \vDash \phi$.

In the late middle ages a relation symbol (a 'term' in the medieval terminology) was described as *undistributed* in a sentence if it was upwards monotone in the sentence, and *distributed* if it was downwards monotone in the sentence. For example one can symbolise 'All swans are white' as $\forall x\,(S(x) \to W(x))$; in this sentence S is distributed and W is undistributed. ("All swans are white" entails both of the sentences "All Bewick swans are white" and "All swans are non-red". The medievals said that "swans" is distributed and "white" is undistributed in "All swans are white.")

There is a syntactic test for upwards and downwards monotonicity. We say that a formula ϕ is in *negation normal form* if $\rightarrow$ and $\leftrightarrow$ never occur in ϕ, and $\neg$ never occurs in ϕ except immediately in front of atomic formulas. Every formula is logically equivalent to one in negation normal form and with the same free variables. For example

(5) $$\forall x \, (S(x) \rightarrow W(x))$$

is logically equivalent to

(6) $$\forall x \, (\neg S(x) \vee W(x)).$$

When ϕ is in negation normal form, we say that an occurrence of a relation symbol R in ϕ is *negative* if it has $\neg$ immediately to the left of it, and *positive* otherwise. For example the occurrence of S in (6) is negative and the occurrence of W in (6) is positive. The next theorem is a straightforward consequence of the definition of satisfaction.

Theorem 11 *Let L be a first-order language, R a relation symbol of L and ϕ a sentence of L in negation normal form. If R has no negative occurrences in ϕ then R is upwards monotone in ϕ. If R has no positive occurrences in ϕ then R is downwards monotone in ϕ.*

Since upwards and downwards monotonicity clearly aren't affected when we pass between logically equivalent sentences, Theorem 11 confirms that S is downwards monotone and W is upwards monotone in (5).

Unlike Theorem 11, the next theorem is deep. It is known as *Lyndon's Interpolation Theorem*, after Roger Lyndon who published it in 1959.

Theorem 12 *Let L be a first-order language and ϕ, ψ sentences of L in negation normal form, such that ϕ entails ψ. Then there is a sentence θ of L in negation normal form such that*

- *ϕ entails θ and θ entails ψ,*
- *any relation symbol (apart from =) with a positive occurrence in θ has positive occurrences in both ϕ and ψ, and*
- *any relation symbol (apart from =) with a negative occurrence in θ has negative occurrences in both ϕ and ψ.*

The sentence θ in the theorem is called a *Lyndon interpolant*.

The following immediate consequence of Lyndon's Interpolation Theorem is called *Craig's Interpolation The-*

orem. It was proved by William Craig before Lyndon's theorem was known.

Theorem 13 *Let L be a first-order language and ϕ, ψ sentences of L such that ϕ entails ψ. Then there is a sentence θ of L such that*

- *ϕ entails θ and θ entails ψ,*
- *any relation symbol (apart from =) that occurs in θ occurs in both ϕ and ψ.*

The sentence θ here is called the *Craig interpolant*.

We give two applications of these interpolation theorems.

LAWS OF DISTRIBUTION. A *syllogistic sentence* is a sentence of one of the forms $\forall x \, (R(x) \rightarrow S(x)$, $\forall x \, (R(x) \rightarrow \neg S(x))$, $\exists x \, (R(x) \wedge S(x))$ and $\exists x (R(x) \wedge \neg S(x))$, where R and S are different relation symbols. For each syllogistic sentence and each relation symbol in it, Theorem 11 tells us that the relation symbol is distributed or that it is undistributed. A *syllogism* is a sequent of the form ϕ, $\psi \vDash \chi$ where each of ϕ, ψ and χ is a syllogistic sentence, three relation symbols are used, and each of them occurs in two sentences. For example one syllogism is

(7) $\forall x(P(x) \rightarrow Q(x))$, $\forall x(R(x) \rightarrow Q(x)) \vDash \exists x(P(x) \wedge R(x))$.

This syllogism happens to be invalid, but there are many examples of valid syllogisms.

Late medieval logicians looked for criteria to tell when a syllogism is valid. Two of their criteria were the following, known as the *laws of distribution*:

> If a relation symbol occurs in both premises, then it must be distributed in at least one of them. If a relation symbol occurs in a premise and the conclusion, and is undistributed in the premise, it must be undistributed in the conclusion.

Why do these criteria work? The answer is Lyndon's Interpolation Theorem. We illustrate with the invalid syllogism (7) above, which fails the first distribution law by having Q undistributed in both premises. The same recipe works for all cases.

Suppose for contradiction that (7) is valid. Then after a small rearrangement we have

$$\forall x(P(x) \rightarrow Q(x)) \vDash \forall x(R(x) \rightarrow Q(x)) \rightarrow \exists x(P(x) \wedge R(x)).$$

Convert the sentences to negation normal form, and let θ be a Lyndon interpolant for the resulting sequent. Since Q

occurs only positively on the left and only negatively on the right, it never occurs in θ. So we can introduce a new relation symbol Q', and we have a valid sequent

$$\forall x(P(x) \to Q'(x)) \vDash \theta.$$

Hence by combining the sequents again we infer that the sequent

$$\forall x(P(x) \to Q'(x)) \vDash \forall x(R(x) \to Q(x)) \to \exists x(P(x) \wedge R(x))$$

is valid, and hence so is

$$\forall x(P(x) \to Q'(x)), \forall x(R(x) \to Q(x)) \vDash \exists x(P(x) \wedge R(x)).$$

But it can't be because the two premises have no relation symbols in common and hence can't establish any non-trivial relationship between P and R.

The Port-Royal Logic of Arnauld and Nicole (1662) explains that (7) is invalid because Q "may be taken for two different parts of the same whole" (Rule I in their III.iii). This is vague and not properly justified, but one can see our argument above as a repair of the Port-Royal argument.

EXPLICIT AND IMPLICIT DEFINABILITY. Suppose L is a first-order language, one of whose symbols is a relation symbol R of arity n, and T is a theory in L. One can ask whether R is redundant in T, in the sense that in any model A of T the relation R_A is determined by the rest of A. Here are two different ways of making this notion of redundancy precise. (We write σ for the signature of the language L but with R removed.)

(a) T has a consequence of the form

$$(8) \qquad \forall x_1 \dots \forall x_n \, R(x_1, \dots, x_n) \leftrightarrow \phi(x_1, \dots, x_n))$$

where ϕ is a formula of $L(\sigma)$.

(b) Whenever A and B are two L-structures that are models of T, and $A|\sigma = B|\sigma$, we have $A = B$.

When (a) holds we say that R is *explicitly definable* in T, and the sentence (8) is called an *explicit definition* of R in T. When (b) holds we say that R is *implicitly definable* in T.

It turns out that explicit definability and implicit definability are equivalent. (This is for first-order logic; part (b) in the theorem below fails for many other logics.)

Theorem 14 *Let L be a first-order language, R a relation symbol of L and T be a theory in L.*

(a) *If R is explicitly definable in T then R is implicitly definable in T.*

(b) *If R is implicitly definable in T then R is explicitly definable in T.*

Part (a) of the theorem, or more strictly its contrapositive, is known as *Padoa's method*, after Alessandro Padoa who was a researcher in Giuseppe Peano's school around 1900. The proof is straightforward.

Part (b) is called *Beth's Theorem*. It was proved by Evert Beth in 1953, but the following derivation from Craig's Interpolation Theorem is due to Craig. Assume that R is implicitly definable in T. Let T' be T but written with a new relation symbol R' in place of R, and let L^+ be L with R' added. Then the statement that R is implicitly definable in T implies the following:

Suppose an L^+-structure A is a model of $T \cup T'$. Then $R_A \subseteq R'_A$.

We can rewrite this as a sequent:

$$(9) \, T \cup T' \vDash \forall x_1 \dots \forall x_n \, (R(x_1, \dots, x_n) \to R'(x_1, \dots, x_n)).$$

Add n new constants $c_1, \dots, c_n$ to the language L^+. By (9), using Metatheorem 10 of the entry "First-Order Logic",

$$(10) \qquad T \cup T' \vDash R(c_1, \dots, c_n) \to R'(c_1, \dots, c_n).$$

Now by the Compactness Theorem there are finite subsets U, U' of T, T' respectively, such that

$$(11) \qquad U \cup U' \vDash R(c_1, \dots, c_n) \to R'(c_1, \dots, c_n).$$

Adding sentences to U and U' if necessary, we can suppose that U' is the same as U except that R is replaced by R'. Write ψ for the conjunction of the sentences in U, and ψ' for ψ with R replaced by R'. Then after some rearrangement (11) gives

$$(12) \qquad \psi \wedge R(c_1, \dots, c_n) \vDash \psi' \to R'(c_1, \dots, c_n).$$

Now apply Craig's Interpolation Theorem to find an interpolant θ such that the following sequents are valid:

$$(13) \qquad \psi \wedge R(c_1, \dots, c_n) \vDash \theta,$$

$$(14) \qquad \theta \vDash \psi' \to R'(c_1, \dots, c_n).$$

Since R occurs only on the left of (12) and R' occurs only on the right, neither symbol occurs in θ. So by (14) we have the following valid sequent:

$$(15) \qquad \theta \vDash \psi \to R(c_1, \dots, c_n).$$

By (13) and (15),

$$\psi \vDash R(c_1, \dots, c_n) \leftrightarrow \theta.$$

Now let ϕ be θ but with each constant c_i replaced by the variable x_i. (If necessary we first change the bound variables of θ so that no quantifier in θ binds any of these variables x_i.) Then by Metatheorem 10 again, we have

(16) $T \vDash \forall x_1 \ldots \forall x_n (R(x_1, \ldots, x_n) \leftrightarrow \phi(x_1, \ldots, x_n))$

as claimed.

There are many model-theoretic results that are close relatives of the examples above, either in their statements or in their proofs. For example a *preservation theorem* is a theorem stating that some syntactic condition is necessary and sufficient for a formula to be preserved under some algebraic operation. Here follows a typical preservation theorem. We say that a formula φ is a ∀ formula if φ has the form $\forall y_1 \ldots \forall y_n \psi$ where ψ is quantifier-free.

Theorem 15 (Łoś-Tarski Theorem) *Let L be a first-order language,* $\phi(x_1, \ldots, x_n)$ *a formula of L and T a theory in L. Then the following are equivalent:*

(a) For every embedding $e : A \to B$ *between models of T and all elements* $a_1, \ldots, a_n$ *of A,*

$B \vDash \phi[e(a_1), \ldots, e(a_n)] \Rightarrow A \vDash \phi[a_1, \ldots, a_n].$

(b) φ is equivalent modulo T to a ∀ formula $\psi(x_1, \ldots, x_n)$.

EXTENSIONS OF FIRST-ORDER LOGIC

The structures that we defined above are sometimes called *first-order structures* because of their connection with first-order languages. There are other kinds of structure that have analogous connections with other kinds of formal language. Here are two important examples.

(a) Suppose L is a first-order language. Let I be a nonempty set carrying a binary relation R, and for each element of I let A_i be an L-structure. Then, given an element i of I and a sentence φ of L, we can ask whether $A_j \vDash \phi$ for all j such that Rij. We can introduce a sentence □φ which counts as true in A_i if and only if the answer is Yes. Indexed families of structures of this type appear in modal logic, temporal logic and some logics of action.

(b) We can consider structures with two domains, where the second domain is a set of subsets of the first domain. Structures of this kind appear in second-order logic, where we have first-order and second-order variables ranging respectively over the first domain and the second domain. They are also found in topological logics, where the second domain contains (for example) a base of open sets for a topology over the first domain.

Sortal structures and languages are a less drastic extension. A sortal signature lists a set of "sorts" and may put restrictions on the function symbols in terms of the sorts. Each sortal structure with this signature has a family of domains, one for each sort. The corresponding sortal language has separate variables for each sort. Sortal structures have some natural mathematical applications. For example a vector space involves a set of vectors and a set of scalars; we can multiply a vector by a scalar, but in general we can't multiply two vectors. So it is natural to work with one sort for vectors and another sort for scalars, and to restrict multiplication so that two vectors can't be multiplied.

If the only changes we make in passing from first-order to sortal are those just described, then the resulting languages behave very much as ordinary first-order languages, and the model theory of sortal structures and languages is hardly distinguishable from ordinary first-order model theory. If we put further restrictions the situation may change; for example if we require that the elements of one sort are exactly the sets of elements of some other sort, then we move into second-order logic.

But even for ordinary first-order structures we need not restrict ourselves to first-order languages. For example we can add to first-order logic

- quantifiers $Q_\kappa x$ that express 'There are at least κ elements x such that …';
- infinitary conjunctions of formulas $\bigwedge_{i<\kappa}\phi_i$ meaning 'ϕ_0 and ϕ_1 and …', and likewise infinitary disjunctions;
- transitive closure operators that express, given a formula φ(x,y), the property 'There is a finite sequence $a_1, \ldots, a_n$ such that $\phi(x,a_1)$ and $\phi(a_1,a_2)$ and $\phi(a_2,a_3)$ and … and $\phi(a_{n-1},a_n)$ and $\phi(a_n,y)$'.

For example the models of the infinitary disjunction

$$\bigvee_{i<\omega} \text{There are at most } i \text{ elements}$$

are exactly the finite structures. In section 5 we saw that there is no first-order sentence defining this class.

Some of these extensions of first-order logic, using first-order structures, have an elegant and well-developed model theory. But the general truth seems to be that none of them work as smoothly as first-order logic. In 1969 Per Lindström proved some theorems that capture this fact. He showed that if a logic $\mathscr{L}$ contains first-order logic and obeys some of the metatheorems that hold for first-order logic, then $\mathscr{L}$ must be equivalent to first-order logic, in the sense that for every sentence φ of $\mathscr{L}$ there is a first-order sentence with exactly the same models as φ. For example

Theorem 16 *Let $\mathscr{L}$ be a logic that contains first-order logic. Suppose that $\mathscr{L}$ has the properties:*

(a) Every sentence of $\mathscr{L}$ with infinite models has a model that is at most countable.

(b) If T is a set of sentences of $\mathscr{L}$ and every finite subset of T has a model then T has a model.

Then $\mathscr{L}$ is equivalent to first-order logic.

A fuller account would explain more precisely what is meant by a "logic that contains first-order logic".

STABILITY AND GEOMETRIC MODEL THEORY

Mathematical model theory has become a highly sophisticated branch of mathematics. The items below can be no more than pointers.

Morley's Theorem (Theorem 10) created a new paradigm for model theory. He made it possible to show that a purely model-theoretic condition—uncountable categoricity—on a theory T imposes some strong structural features on all the models of T. Each such model must contain a *strongly minimal set*, which is a set carrying a dependence relation that behaves like linear or algebraic dependence. In particular the strongly minimal set has a dimension in the same sense as a vector space, and the strongly minimal set is determined up to isomorphism by its dimension and T. (Steinitz' Theorem in section 6 is a special case of this fact, since every algebraically closed field is a strongly minimal set.) The rest of the model is very tightly constructed around the strongly minimal set. We can define a function assigning a "rank" to each set definable with parameters in the model; this *Morley rank* is a generalisation of Krull dimension and it allows a very detailed analysis of the model.

Much of the work following on from Morley's Theorem organised itself around one or other of two heuristic principles, known as *Shelah's dichotomy* and *Zilber's trichotomy*. Both of these principles rest on the fact that uncountably categorical theories are "good" in the sense that their classes of models are well-behaved. Both of them have been proved as theorems in certain cases.

For Saharon Shelah, "good" theories form one end of a scale from good to bad. There are several ways that a theory can be bad. One is that it has too many non-isomorphic models to allow any kind of cataloguing by invariants. Another is that it has models that are not isomorphic but are hard to tell apart. Shelah's policy is that at each point of the scale from good to bad, one should aim to maximise the difference between the theories on the "good" side and those on the "bad" side. On the "good" side one should aim to find as much good behaviour as possible, in terms of dependence relations, definability properties, rank functions, and so forth. On the "bad" side one should aim to construct intractable families of models, for example large families of models none of which is elementarily embeddable in any other. Though he applies this principle at all points of the scale, he also identified a *main gap* between the good side and the bad side, and when one speaks of "Shelah's dichotomy" one often has this particular gap in mind.

Shelah created a powerful body of techniques for handling models of theories towards the "good" end of the scale. Together with Morley's work it forms the bulk of *stability theory*. Shelah has also done a large amount of work towards eliminating the restriction to first-order theories. He has suggested several abstract frameworks, for example *excellent classes*, in which there is no counterpart of the Compactness Theorem but some techniques of stability theory still work.

Boris Zilber is more interested in exploiting the "goodness" of the good end of the scale. He is convinced that uncountably categorical structures should all be mathematically interesting, and in fact that they should all be equivalent, up to model-theoretic interpretation, to structures of interest in "classical" mathematics. So he set out to catalogue them, and in the early 1980s he pointed out a natural three-way division of uncountably categorical structures. The division rests on the dependence relation of the strongly minimal set. In the first place there are structures where this relation is "trivial". If it is not trivial, one looks at the lattice of closed sets under the dependence relation. The second class is where this lattice is modular, the third is where it is non-modular. So we have a division of uncountably categorical structures into trivial, modular, and non-modular. The trivial structures are now essentially all known. Modularity turns out to be a strong property, guaranteeing that the structure contains an infinite definable abelian group which exerts a controlling influence; broadly speaking, modular structures exhibit linear algebra.

Zilber conjectured that all non-modular uncountably categorical structures are (up to model-theoretic interpretation) algebraically closed fields. Several pieces of evidence pointed in this direction, notably (i) Angus Macintyre's observation in 1971 that an uncountably categorical field must be algebraically closed, and (ii) observations by Zilber himself and Greg Cherlin that uncountably categorical groups behave remarkably like algebraic groups over an algebraically closed field. *Zilber's trichotomy* is the division into trivial, modular and non-modular, together with the conjecture that the non-modular structures are algebraically closed fields (up to interpretation). Zilber's trichotomy has been proved to hold for *Zariski geometries*; these are uncountably categorical structures that obey an axiomatisation of the Zariski topology. Ehud Hrushovski saw how to use this fact to solve some major open problems of diophantine geometry, for example proving the Mordell-Lang conjecture for function fields in all characteristics. (His proof in characteristic 0 has since been simplified by replacing the Zariski geometries by differential jet spaces). In 1998 Ya'acov Peterzil and Sergei Starchenko showed that a version of Zilber's trichotomy is true for o-minimal fields.

In 1989 Hrushovski found counterexamples to Zilber's conjecture: uncountably categorical non-modular structures containing no infinite field. At first Hrushovski's examples were mysterious. But Zilber was sure that they must have classical interest, and after some years he discovered structures of Hrushovski's type arising in complex analysis. He also pointed out a close link between Hrushovski's construction and Schanuel's Conjecture in number theory. At the same time Zilber gave examples from complex analysis to illustrate Shelah's excellent classes, thus bringing together two separate lines of research in model theory.

Through the 1990s a body of results converged to show that tools of stability theory are useful in contexts far outside those of 'good' first-order theories. In fact the complete theory Th(*A*) of a structure *A* can be largely irrelevant to the application of these tools to *A*. The need to translate classical descriptions into first-order sentences had always been a practical obstacle to integrating model theory with classical mathematics, and this need seemed to be receding in part. In this context Ludwig Faddeev, after reading the relevant papers presented to the International Congress of Mathematicians in Beijing in 2002, said at the closing ceremony

> Take for instance the sections of logic, number theory and algebra. The general underlining mathematical structures as well as language, used by speakers, were essentially identical.

See also Arnauld, Antoine; Computability Theory; Craig's Theorem; First-Order Logic; Hintikka, Jaakko; Infinitesimals; Infinity in Mathematics and Logic; Logic, History of, overview article; Modal Logic; Montague, Richard; Nicole, Pierre; Peano, Giuseppe; Second-Order Logic; Semantics; Set Theory; Tarski, Alfred.

Bibliography

Arnauld, Antoine, and Pierre Nicole. *La logique ou l'art de penser*. Paris: Gallimard, 1992.

Barwise, Jon, and Solomon Feferman. *Model-Theoretic Logics*. New York: Springer, 1985.

Bell, John L., and Alan B. Slomson. *Models and Ultraproducts*. Amsterdam: North-Holland, 1969.

Börger, Egon, and Robert Stärk. *Abstract State Machines: A Method for High-level Design and Analysis*. Berlin: Springer, 2003.

Buechler, Steven. *Essential Stability Theory*. Berlin: Springer, 1996.

Chang, Chen-Chung, and H. Jerome Keisler. *Model Theory*. 3rd ed. Amsterdam: North-Holland, 1990.

Doets, Kees. *Basic Model Theory*. Stanford, CA: CSLI Publications, 1996.

Dries, Lou van den. *Tame Topology and O-minimal Structures*. Cambridge, U.K.: Cambridge University Press, 1998.

Ebbinghaus, Heinz-Dieter, and Jörg Flum. *Finite Model Theory*. 2nd ed. Berlin: Springer, 1999.

Ebbinghaus, Heinz-Dieter, Jörg Flum, and Wolfgang Thomas. *Mathematical Logic*. New York: Springer, 1984.

Haskell, Deirdre, Anand Pillay, and Charles Steinhorn, eds. *Model Theory, Algebra, and Geometry*. Cambridge, U.K.: Cambridge University Press, 2000.

Hodges, Wilfrid. *Model Theory*. Cambridge, U.K.: Cambridge University Press, 1993.

Manzano, Maria. *Model Theory*. Oxford: Oxford University Press, 1999.

Marcja, Annalisa, and Carlo Toffalori. *A Guide to Classical and Modern Model Theory*. Dordrecht: Kluwer, 2003.

Marker, David. *Model Theory: An Introduction*. New York: Springer, 2002.

Morgan, Mary S. , and Margaret Morrison. *Models as Mediators*. Cambridge, U.K.: Cambridge University Press, 1999.

Pillay, Anand. *Geometric Stability Theory*. Oxford: Clarendon Press, 1996.

Robinson, Abraham. "On the Application of Symbolic Logic to Algebra." In *Proceedings of International Congress of Mathematicians. Cambridge, MA. 1950*. Reprinted in *Selected Papers of Abraham Robinson*. Vol. 1, *Model Theory and Algebra*, edited by H. Jerome Keisler, 3–11. Amsterdam: North-Holland, 1979.

Rothmaler, Philipp. *Introduction to Model Theory*. Amsterdam: Gordon and Breach, 2000.

Tarski, Alfred. "Contributions to the Theory of Models, I." *Indagationes Mathematicae* 16 (1954): 572–581.

Tarski, Alfred, and Robert L. Vaught. "Arithmetical Extensions of Relational Systems." *Compositio Mathematica* 13 (1957): 81–102.

Tatsien, Li, ed. *Proceedings of the International Congress of Mathematicians, Beijing 2002*. Vols. I, II. Beijing: Higher Education Press, 2002. Available from http//:math.ucdavis.edu/ICM2002.

Wilfrid Hodges (2005)

MODERNISM

Modernism was a movement in Catholic religious thought, and particularly in biblical criticism, that developed in the late nineteenth century and spent itself, as a distinctive movement, before World War I. It aimed at bringing Catholic traditions into closer accord with modern views in philosophy and in historical and other scholarship and with recent social and political views. Modernism ran parallel to liberal Protestantism; both tended to reject authority and rigid forms and, in their more extreme versions at least, to aspire to a kind of Christianized rationalism.

The kind of Christology and biblical exegesis undertaken in Germany by D. F. Strauss and in France by Ernest Renan, aided and encouraged by such philosophical currents as positivism and evolutionism, culminated in the late-nineteenth-century attempt to reconcile science with religion and historical criticism with belief. Renan's rejection of the supernatural, combined with his vague evolutionary religiosity, anticipated much that was to be written during the fifteen years following his death in 1892.

Modernism was represented in England by George Tyrrell, Friedrich von Hügel (a friend of Alfred Loisy), and Maude Petre; in Italy by Antonio Fogazzaro, Romolo Murri, and Salvatore Minocchi; and in Germany by Franz Xavier Kraus and Hermann Schnell. However, most of the controversy centered in France, on account of the writings and influence of Loisy, Édouard Le Roy, and Lucien Laberthonnière, who brought to their approach to religion the spirit of contemporary science and philosophy. Loisy, like Renan, rejected the supernatural and explained religion in terms of an immanent rather than a transcendent principle. Le Roy circumvented the difficulties inherent in Catholic dogmas by treating them as pragmatically true. Laberthonnière edited the *Annales de philosophie chrétienne,* a journal that was committed, according to its program, to a rationalistic interpretation of religion, recognizing "the duty to submit to reflection what we believe no less than what we do and think." The review's general policy favored the view that religion is progressively revealed, primitive revelation being only potentially complete. The maneuverings necessitated by the desire to reconcile faith and reason led to some inconsistency and self-contradiction.

From its inception, modernism was in constant trouble with the ecclesiastical authorities, but orthodoxy did not become militant until the accession of Pope Pius X in 1903. In 1907 the papal decree *Lamentabili Sane Exitu,* a collection of sixty-five condemned propositions aimed chiefly at Loisy, and the more general and philosophically grounded encyclical *Pascendi Dominici Gregis,* condemned the modernists' views. The requirement in 1910 that all clerics take the antimodernist oath, known as *Sacrorum Antistitum,* marked the end of the movement as such, although its spirit persisted and prospered in less rebellious forms.

See also Hügel, Baron Friedrich von; Laberthonnière, Lucien; Le Roy, Édouard; Loisy, Alfred; Positivism; Rationalism; Renan, Joseph Ernest; Strauss, David Friedrich.

Bibliography

Riviere, J. *Le modernisme dans l'église.* Paris, 1929.

Vidler, A. R. *The Modernist Movement in the Roman Church.* Cambridge, U.K.: Cambridge University Press, 1934.

Colin Smith (1967)

MODERNISM AND POSTMODERNISM

Modern philosophy is construed as beginning sometime in the Renaissance. A philosophy that seeks new foundations for knowledge was offered as an alternative to that provided by the ancient philosophers. Modern philosophy was presented as starting afresh from new beginnings—turning to nature directly (Francis Bacon), turning to the mind directly (René Descartes), turning to experience directly (Thomas Hobbes). The "quarrel between the ancients and the moderns" resulted from this basic disagreement as to the sources of philosophical knowledge.

Modern philosophy turned away from the past and toward the future, toward the advancement of knowledge, toward human understanding, and toward progress through method or through experience. With the break between the Continental rationalists (Descartes, Nicolas Malebranche, Gottfried Wilhelm Leibniz, and Benedict de Spinoza) and the British empiricists (Hobbes, John Locke, and David Hume) at the end of the eighteenth-century Enlightenment, a new formulation in modern philosophy was called for. Immanuel Kant brought together in his "critical" philosophy the commitments to the analytic exercise of the mind, on the one hand, and the empirical reception through the senses on the other. With Kant, modern philosophy combined the "transcendental unity of apperception" with the "manifold of experience." Modern philosophy was no longer based on a theory of representation—representation to the mind through reason or representation to the mind through experience—but on the linking of transcendental subjectivity and empirical objectivity. This "doublet," as Michel Foucault came to name it, accounted for a whole new way of philosophizing.

Modernism is distinguished from modern philosophy in that it is linked to certain movements in art and literature that began sometime around the end of the nineteenth century. While drawing upon some similar characteristics of "modern philosophy," modernism in art, literature, and philosophy involved novelty, break with tradition, progress, continuous development, knowledge derived either from the position of the subject or from claims to objectivity, and concomitantly the crisis in knowledge produced by this very dichotomy. Hence in modernism, at the same time that certain theories based knowledge on a centered, transcendental, interpreting subjectivity, and others based knowledge on certain, atomistic, analytic, empirical objectivity, the crisis in knowledge created a sense of uncertainty, paradox, incompleteness, inadequacy, emptiness, and void. Modernism in art and literature involved a shift away from the dichotomies of romanticism and realism to the stream of consciousness, lived and internal time-consciousness, transcendental subjectivity, narrated remembrance and awareness, portrayed speed, mechanisms, objects, and abstractions. Latent content was allowed to penetrate through the surfaces of manifest content. Understanding would have to delve more deeply than surfaces and mere appearances. A phenomenology would be needed in order to inventory the contents of consciousness (Edmund Husserl) or a psychoanalysis to delve the depths of what the mind was really thinking (Sigmund Freud), or a logical positivism would take the alternative tack by excluding all knowledge that cannot be verified logically and empirically (Bertrand Russell, early Ludwig Wittgenstein, A. J. Ayer). Modernism in philosophy involved at each stage the Kantian combination of the empirical and the transcendental, the objective and the subjective, the material and the intellectual—but each time measuring the doublet with weight on one side or the other.

The disintegration of modernism in philosophy was internal. The radical claims of logical positivism excluded all that was of value: metaphysics, aesthetics, axiology, and so forth. The rigorous science of transcendental phenomenology excluded the very existence of what it was investigating. The dualism of creative evolutionism left

an irreparable dichotomy between lived experience and objective knowledge. The pragmatism of radical empiricism failed to provide a way to interpret the meanings of experience. The center of modernism in philosophy could not hold because its very foundations were in question. But attempts to retrieve it from itself by the turn to language—ordinary language, analytic philosophies of language, hermeneutics of language, semiologies of language—could not resolve the dilemmas of human existence. Modernism in philosophy faced the absurd, the ambiguous, and the dialectical. And it worked these theories to their limits.

In the mid-1960s philosophy came to look at its epistemological formations and to ask whether the humanisms and anthropologisms of modern philosophy had not circumscribed themselves. Maurice Merleau-Ponty's interrogations were reformulated in Foucault's archaeology of knowledge. The human sciences placed the optimisms and pessimisms of modern philosophy in question by circumventing the theory of "man." Knowledge formations were articulated in terms of multiple spaces of knowledge production and no longer according to a central source or position, or ego, or self, or subject, nor according to a multiplicity of sense-data, objective criteria, material evidence, or behaviors. Knowledge formations crossed disciplines and operated in multiple spaces where questions of structure, frame, margin, boundary, edge, limit, and so on would mark any discursive practice. In other words, knowledge was no longer produced from a center, foundation, ground, basis, identity, authority, or transcendental competency. Knowledge was dispersed, multiple, fragmented, and theoretically varied. Knowledge was no longer based on continuity, unity, totality, comprehensiveness, and consistency. Knowledge began to be understood in terms of discontinuity, difference, dissemination, and differends.

By the early 1970s postmodernism—a term that Daniel Bell used in connection with postindustrial society in the 1950s, that architects appealed to in the 1960s, and that art and literary historians invoked in the 1970s—had still not been invoked in connection with philosophy. Jacques Derrida's grammatology and theory of "difference" in 1967 (building upon Martin Heidegger's account of "the end of philosophy and the task of thinking") turned into a full-fledged deconstruction in the 1970s. Gilles Deleuze and Felix Guattari's notion of rhizomal thinking (as opposed to hierarchical, authorizing arborescent thinking) marked a move against psychoanalytic theories based on Oedipal authority and paternal insistence. Their idea of nomadism placed emphasis on knowledge, experience, and relations that were not organized around a central concept. J. Kristeva's account of the revolution in poetic language marked the distinction between the semiotic and the symbolic. Where symbolic—scientific, theoretical, phallic, paternal—thinking had pervaded philosophy and science, Kristeva invoked the semiotic as the poetic, fluid, receptacle-like, maternal thinking that has been hidden in modern thought. Yet postmodern was hardly the term that was invoked to describe this kind of philosophizing. Correspondingly, the more restricted study of phenomenology and existentialism in philosophy gave way to the more multiple and diverse theories implicit in Continental philosophy: deconstruction, archaeology of knowledge, semanalysis, schizoanalysis, feminist theory, and so forth. Yet, while poststructuralism (in connection with Foucault, Derrida, Deleuze, Kristeva, et al.) was hailed as the successor to structuralism (Claude Lévi-Strauss, Roland Barthes, Jacques Lacan, Louis Althusser), and existential phenomenology (Heidegger, Jean-Paul Sartre, Merleau-Ponty, Simone de Beauvoir), postmodernism was still not a relevant category in philosophy until well into the 1980s. As time passed, postmodernism and postmodern thought came to take precedence over poststructuralism as the prevalent theoretical formulation.

Postmodern thought means the appeal to differences—differences in theories, differences in formulations, differences in identities. Postmodern thought rejects hierarchies and genealogies, continuities and progress, resolutions and overcomings (*Überwindungen*). Postmodern thought, in fact, cannot operate outside of the modern, for it is itself what can be called an "indecidable." The postmodern signals the end of modernity, but it operates at the same time necessarily within the modern. To claim that the postmodern is outside the modern is to identify it as other than the modern, but that which is outside or other reinscribes the identity of the modern and therefore the postmodern inscription within it. Hence the postmodern both marks places of difference within the modern and calls for an alternative to the modern. The postmodern in any case does not call for the destruction of the modern, not does it seek to deny the modern, since it is necessarily part of the modern.

The postmodern involves the question of the end or limit or margin of what is in question. History, man, knowledge, painting, writing, the modern—each is posed in terms of its end. The end is not a matter of termination or conclusion any more than a matter of goal and aspiration. The postmodern involves, as G. Vattimo notes, a *Verwindung* of modernity—a getting over, a convales-

cence, a recovering from modernity. This means that modernity is itself placed in question and no longer taken as an unquestioned given. The cracks and fissures in modernity, the places where modernity cannot be fully aware of itself, the moments of unpresentability in the modern—these are the concerns of postmodern thought. As J.-F. Lyotard has noted in his famous *The Postmodern Condition* (1984), the postmodern involves the presentation of the unpresentable in presentation itself—that is, in modernity, the concern was to present something new, something unheard of, something unique, something shocking, something unpresentable. The postmodern involves the presentation of the unpresentable in presentation itself—the formulation of the moments of unpresentability as they mark what is presented. Lyotard calls attention to the role of the "differend" as the place of conflict between two alternative positions. The differend does not belong to either side. It belongs only to the place between, to the gap between the two presentations on either side. This is the postmodern moment—such moments or events with which the modern is distinctively scarred and animated.

See also Ayer, Alfred Jules; Bacon, Francis; Barthes, Roland; Beauvoir, Simone de; Continental Philosophy; Deconstruction; Deleuze, Gilles; Derrida, Jacques; Descartes, René; Existentialism; Foucault, Michel; Freud, Sigmund; Heidegger, Martin; Hobbes, Thomas; Hume, David; Husserl, Edmund; Kant, Immanuel; Kristeva, Julia; Lacan, Jacques; Language; Leibniz, Gottfried Wilhelm; Locke, John; Logical Positivism; Lyotard, François; Malebranche, Nicolas; Merleau-Ponty, Maurice; Phenomenology; Postmodernism; Realism; Renaissance; Romanticism; Russell, Bertrand Arthur William; Sartre, Jean-Paul; Self; Spinoza, Benedict (Baruch) de; Structuralism and Post-structuralism; Wittgenstein, Ludwig Josef Johann.

Bibliography

Derrida, J. *Margins of Philosophy.* Translated by A. Bass. Chicago: University of Chicago Press, 1982.

Foucault, M. *The Order of Things.* Translator anon. New York: Pantheon, 1970.

Kristeva, J. *Revolution in Poetic Language.* Translated by M. Waller. New York: Columbia University Press, 1984.

Lyotard, J.-F. *The Postmodern Condition.* Translated by G. Bennington and B. Massumi. Minneapolis: University of Minnesota Press, 1984.

Lyotard, J.-F. *Toward the Postmodern.* Translated by R. Harvey and M. Roberts. Atlantic Highlands, NJ: Humanities Press, 1993.

Natoli, J., and L. Hutcheon, eds. *A Postmodern Reader.* Albany: State University of New York Press, 1993.

Silverman, H. J., ed. *Postmodernism—Philosophy and the Arts.* New York: Routledge, 1990.

Silverman, H. J. *Textualities: Between Hermeneutics and Deconstruction.* New York: Routledge, 1994.

Vattimo, G. *The End of Modernity.* Translated by J. R. Snyder. Baltimore: Johns Hopkins University Press, 1988.

Hugh J. Silverman (1996)

MOIRA/TYCHĒ/ANANKĒ

All three Greek words denote causal powers that are beyond the reach of human control, and hence were often personified as goddesses.

The word "moira" means a share, part, or portion, and by derivation, the fate allotted to a person. In mythological contexts, it was personified either as a single goddess or, as in Hesiod's *Theogony* and in the myth of Plato's *Republic* X, as a group of three goddesses (Clotho, Lachesis, Atropos). Moira or the Moirai determine the fate of individuals by "spinning" the thread of one's life. The word "moira" sometimes euphemistically refers to death, as the fate of all humans. In other contexts it refers to one's rank or distinction or to the positive abilities allotted by the gods, such as poetic inspiration. In Stoic determinism, it is used in relation to universal fate (*heimarmenē*).

The noun "tychē" (fortune) is related to the verb "tynchano" (happen, befall). Tychē was taken to be the cause of chance events—events that one could not or did not calculate and that do not fit into a regular pattern. While moira determines one's course of life as a whole, tychē tends to be responsible for singular events of varying importance. The connotations of the word were originally more positive, but by Hellenistic times it regularly had the pejorative meaning of blind, impersonal, arbitrary chance. In philosophical contexts it is most often contrasted with rational choice and goal-driven action. Plato, in the *Laws* X, grouped tychē together with the mechanistic force of nature and opposed it to the rational, purposeful activity of a cosmic god. Aristotle, in the *Physics* II.5–7, classified tychē under spontaneity (*automaton*) and defined it as an accidental and indeterminable cause in the sphere of purposeful actions involving rational choice. In other words, tychē for Aristotle is the cause of events that might have been the outcome of rational human choice but in fact are not.

The word "anankē" originally referred to an external constraining force, and from this meaning it obtained the more abstract meaning of logical and physical necessity during the pre-Socratic period. It is often represented as the ultimate power with which even the gods must comply. In Parmenides' *Aletheia*, the personified Anankē guarantees that Being is unchangeable and immobile, and "holds [Being] in the bonds of a limit" (Diels and Kranz 1954, B8.30), while in the *Doxa* she keeps the starry heaven enchained (B11.6). In Empedocles' writings, Anankē's oracle sets the punishment of those who commit the ultimate sin of bloodshed (B115.1). In the myth of Plato's *Republic* X, Anankē is the mother of the three Moirai. Her function is primarily cosmological in that she holds a spindle whose movement stands for the celestial motions. In Plato's *Timaeus*, anankē is the regular but nonteleological causal force inherent in the physical realm. Insofar as the physical properties of the elements can be put into the service of the purposeful activity of reason, anankē becomes the auxiliary cause (*sunaition*) in teleological causation. Aristotle's distinction between simple and hypothetical necessity in the *Physics* II.9 shows clear traces of the conception of anankē in the *Timaeus*.

See also Aristotle; Being; Causation: Metaphysical Issues; Death; Empedocles; Parmenides of Elea; Plato; Pre-Socratic Philosophy.

Bibliography

Cornford, Francis Macdonald. *Plato's Cosmology.* London: Routledge and Kegan Paul, 1937.

Diels, Hermann, and Walther Kranz. *Die Fragmente der Vorsokratiker.* 7th, rev. ed. Berlin: Weidmann, 1954.

Dietrich, Bernard Clive. *Death, Fate, and the Gods: The Development of a Religious Idea in Greek Popular Belief and in Homer.* London: Athlone Press, 1965.

Schreckenberg, Heinz. *Ananke: Untersuchungen zur Geschichte des Wortgebrauchs.* Munich, Germany: C. H. Beck'sche Verlagsbuchhandlung, 1964.

Gábor Betegh (2005)

MOLESCHOTT, JACOB
(1822–1893)

Jacob Moleschott, a physiologist and philosopher often regarded as the founder of nineteenth-century materialism, was born in Holland. After studying at Heidelberg, Moleschott practiced medicine in Utrecht. He later became lecturer in physiology at Heidelberg. The controversial doctrines expressed in his book, *Der Kreislauf des Lebens* (The circuit of life; Mainz, 1852), and the materialistic tendencies of his teaching forced him to move to

Zürich. He later became professor of physiology at Rome, where his lectures were popular and his important research on diet earned him respect and many honors.

Materialism at that period was a philosophical trend with political, social, and scientific implications. The state-controlled German universities had produced an official philosophy (a watered-down Hegelianism) that was used as a defense against social reform and as a shield for religion or the spiritual life. Certain important scientists held conservative views about the role of science. The biologist Rudolf Virchow, for example, believed that all speculation about consciousness should be left to the church or even to the state. The German materialists, attempting to free scientific inquiry from such control, saw these conventional philosophical tendencies as obstructing intellectual and social progress.

PHILOSOPHIC MONISM

Moleschott's *Der Kreislauf des Lebens* went through many editions and helped to spur the materialist movement. The book was directed against Justus von Liebig's theologizing views as he had expressed them in his *Chemischen Briefen*. Liebig had especially objected to Moleschott's famous statement epitomizing materialist monism: "No thought without phosphorus." The German materialists of this period criticized dualists as being engaged in a system of philosophic double-entry bookkeeping.

Moleschott maintained, as did Ludwig Büchner, that force and matter were inseparable. Force cannot be viewed in an Aristotelian way, nor teleologically, nor as a vital force. It is not an entity separate from a material substratum, but is rather "one of its eternal indwelling properties." Matter cannot occur or be conceived without force, and vice versa; "A force unconnected with matter, hovering loose over matter, is an utterly empty conception."

Thus, any materialism attributing existence to matter independently of force was rejected. Moleschott maintained that to call his theory materialistic in this sense would be as wrong as to call it spiritualistic: "I myself was well aware that the whole conception might be converted, for since all matter is a bearer of force, endowed with force or penetrated with spirit, it would be just as correct to call it a spiritualistic conception." On the other hand, once the restriction of the term *material* to "dead matter" is given up, Moleschott appears materialistic indeed. He regarded the brain as the source of consciousness and emphasized physical conditions as the major determinants of human life. He was fascinated by circular processes, such as the miner digging lime phosphate from the earth, and the peasant later fertilizing his field with the same chemical. Life circulates through all parts of the world, and with life goes thought.

As was also typical of the materialists of the time, Moleschott emphasized the doctrine of the conservation of matter. This notion, he held, was discovered by the eighteenth-century encyclopedists. Recent science had confirmed it, and future science had to be built upon it. Chemistry is the basic science, and the solution to social questions depends on our discovering the proper way to distribute the matter with which thought and will are bound up. A rigid determinism was emphasized: "Natural law is the most stringent expression of necessity."

THEORY OF KNOWLEDGE

Moleschott inveighed against the Kantian thing-in-itself and emphasized the importance of what things could be known as rather than what they are alleged to be. All knowledge, he maintained, presupposes someone who knows and, thus, a relation between the object and the observer. The observer could be an insect or other creature; there is no restriction to man. All existence is by means of qualities; there is no quality that exists other than through a relation. In the case of a man's perceiving a tree, "it is just as necessary for the tree as for the man that it stands to him in a relation that manifests itself by the impression upon his eye."

Moleschott maintained a certain relativism, but also a certain objectivism: "Steel is hard as opposed to soft butter, ice is only cold to the warm hand, trees only green to a healthy eye." He argued that a vorticella with an eye having only a cornea must receive different representations of objects than a spider, which has a more complex eye with lenses. Yet, "Because an object is [exists] only through its relation to other objects, for instance, through its relation to the observer, because the knowledge of the object resolves itself into the knowledge of their relations, all my knowledge is an objective knowledge." Although there are difficulties in understanding Moleschott's doctrine here, it appears to have a strong family resemblance to recent objective relativism.

ETHICS

The German materialists were frequently criticized for promulgating doctrines subversive of received morality, especially theologically sanctioned morality. In general, they did protest against duty-centered, puritanical views of morality and adopted a kind of utilitarian hedonism. However, they did not advocate a continuing round of sensual pleasures. Moleschott argued that even a misguided hedonism was socially less dangerous than some other views of morality: "The erroneous theory of seeking after pleasure will scarcely find half as many disciples, as the rule of priests of all shades had claimed unfortunate victims."

As was true of other contemporary materialistic theories, many of Moleschott's doctrines that once aroused immense wrath seem relatively mild today. His insistence that scientific inquiry is relevant to the solutions of many problems is now commonplace, but it caused shudders in the nineteenth century. The materialists' struggle against giving theological answers to scientific questions seems to have been largely successful.

See also Büchner, Ludwig; Encyclopédie; Hedonism; Materialism; Natural Law.

Bibliography

ADDITIONAL WORKS BY MOLESCHOTT

Die Physiologie der Nahrungsmittel. Darmstadt: C.W. Leske, 1850.

Physiologie des Stoffwechsels in Pflanzen und Thieren. Erlangen: F. Enke, 1851.

Lehre der Nahrungsmittel. Erlangen: F. Enke, 1853. Translated by Edward Bronner as *The Chemistry of Food and Diet.* London: Houlston and Stoneman, 1856.

Eine physiologische Sendung. Giessen: E. Roth, 1864.

Für meine Freunde. Lebenserinnerungen von Jacob Moleschott. Giessen: E. Roth, 1894.

WORKS ON MOLESCHOTT

Lange, Frederick A. *Geschichte des Materialismus,* 2 vols. Iserlohn, Germany, 1866. Translated by E. C. Thomas as *The History of Materialism,* 3 vols. London: n.p., 1877–1892. Gives an account of Moleschott.

Merz, John T. *A History of European Thought in the Nineteenth Century.* Edinburgh: Blackwood, 1903. Discusses Moleschott briefly and contemporary issues in considerable detail.

Rollo Handy (1967)

MOLINA, LUIS DE

(1535–1600)

Luis de Molina, S.J., was a central figure in the sixteenth-century renaissance of scholasticism on the Iberian peninsula. He was born in Cuenca, Spain, in 1535. At eighteen he entered the Jesuit order. He studied and later taught at Coimbra and Évora in Portugal. In 1583, he left his academic post to devote himself to writing. He spent the next fifteen years in Cuenca, Lisbon, and Évora. He died on October 12, 1600, shortly after being called to take a chair in moral theology at the newly established Jesuit University in Madrid.

Molina's best known work, *Liberi arbitrii cum gratiae donis, divina praescientia, providentia, praedestinatione et reprobatione concordia* (The compatibility of free will with the gift of grace, divine foreknowledge, providence, predestination, and reprobation) was first published at Lisbon in 1588; a second, expanded edition was published at Antwerp in 1595. He also authored a three volume commentary on Part One of St. Thomas's *Summa Theologiae*, titled *Commentaria in primam divi Thomae partem*, published at Cuenca in 1592. Although these works, especially the *Commentaria*, range broadly over theological and philosophical topics, critical attention focused on Molina's theory of *middle knowledge (scientia media)*, which was formulated to reconcile God's comprehensive foreknowledge and providence with a strongly indeterministic conception of human free will.

According to the tradition shared by Molina and his rivals, at the moment of creation, God has perfect and infallible foreknowledge of everything that will happen in the created world. The tradition also maintains that God's knowledge is not like that of a passive observer. Rather, he specifically intends or knowingly permits everything that takes place, and he arranges created causes and exercises causal influence sufficient to bring about his creative plan to the last detail. God's foreknowledge, consequently, is to be explained in terms of his providence. He knows what will happen in the created world by his knowledge of his own decrees, together with his knowledge of what follows from those decrees, either directly or through the mediation of created causes. The fundamental difference between the positions of Molina and his adversaries lies in where they locate the main resources for God's providential foreknowledge. The Molinists emphasize the role of God's practical knowledge, his adversaries emphasize the role of his voluntary decrees.

The tradition distinguishes God's *prevolitional* knowledge, which he has independently of his will from his *postvolitional* knowledge, which depends on his free decrees. A majority of traditional philosophers and theologians maintain that God's knowledge of metaphysically necessary truths exhausts his prevolitional knowledge. On this view, God's knowledge of necessary truths (which Molina calls *natural knowledge*) is identified with his prevolitional knowledge, and his knowledge of contingent truths is identified with his postvolitional knowledge (which Molina calls *free knowledge*). Call this the standard view. It is also commonly held that propositions concerning what is metaphysically possible are themselves metaphysically necessary.

Consequently, God's knowledge of these propositions is part of his natural knowledge. According to the standard view, God is able to bring about any metaphysically possible state of affairs. God's creative activity can thus be described as (1) deciding which metaphysically possible states of affairs will be actual, and (2) making a causal contribution sufficient to actualize those states of affairs. It must be emphasized that, on the standard view, God's causal activity completely determines what is going to take place in the created world.

According to Molina, however, the *free* choices of a rational creature are not causally or logically necessitated either by God's causal activity or by the operation of created causes, including the beliefs, desires, character, and dispositions of the agent. For any free choice a rational creature makes in a fully specified set of circumstances, it is metaphysically possible that that creature makes a different choice in those very same circumstances. So, on Molina's view, God's natural knowledge of metaphysical possibilities, together with his knowledge of his own causal activity, cannot provide him with foreknowledge of the free choices that his creatures will make. Therefore he holds that an essential component of the theory of divine foreknowledge and providence is God's knowledge of a special class of propositions called *conditional future contingents*. These propositions concern what choices rational creatures *would* freely make in any of possible circumstances in which they may find themselves. Molina contends that God must have knowledge of these propositions *prior to* his creative decrees to exercise providence over the world, otherwise he would be unable to guarantee that his creation conforms to his providential design in all its detail.

Molina calls God's knowledge of conditional future contingents *middle knowledge*, because it stands between his natural knowledge of what is merely possible and his free knowledge of what is actually, though contingently, the case. Like his natural knowledge, but unlike his free knowledge, God's middle knowledge is prevolitional. Like his free knowledge, but unlike his natural knowledge, the objects of God's middle knowledge are contingent truths. According to Molina, then, God's providence and foreknowledge is a function of (1) his prevolitional natural knowledge of the possible arrangement of created causes, (2) his prevolitional middle knowledge of the contingent choices free creatures would make in each of these possible arrangements, and (3) his postvolitional free knowledge of the way in which he has decided to arrange created causes. This is how Molina reconciles God's providence and foreknowledge with his strongly indeterministic conception of freedom. In addition, Molina and his followers maintain that the theory of middle knowledge has fruitful applications in explaining a broad range of philosophical and theological issues such as the efficacy of grace, predestination and reprobation, petitionary prayer and prophecy.

Perhaps the weakest point in the Molinist theory is his explanation of *how* God can know what free creatures would do in various possible circumstances, given his strongly indeterministic conception of freedom. Critics maintain that there can be no basis for God's perfect and infallible knowledge of the choices that free creatures would make, given that these choices are not logically or causally determined by the activity of God or the operation of secondary causes. Unlike other defenders of middle knowledge (such as Suarez), Molina refuses to appeal to the determinate truth of conditional future contingents to explain God's knowledge of them. In fact, Molina follows Aristotle in maintaining that contingent propositions concerning the choice a free creature would make in specified circumstances do not have determinate truth prior to the creature making that choice in those circumstances.

Molina's explanation of God's knowledge of conditional future contingents involves what later came to be called *supercomprehension*. Given the indeterminacy of future contingent propositions, Molina believes that God's certain and infallible knowledge of them is due to the cognitive perfection of the knower. For Molina and his contemporaries, all of God's knowledge is ultimately grounded in his self-knowledge, either knowledge of his own essence or knowledge of his decrees. God's middle knowledge is grounded in his knowledge of his own essence, in which all possible creatures are eminently contained.

By perfectly comprehending his own essence, according to Molina, God is able to infallibly cognize the choices each possible creature would make in any possible circumstance in which they may find themselves, even though these choices are metaphysically indeterminate. Supercomprehension, on Molina's view, is a mode of cognition possible only for an infinite intellect with respect to finite creatures. Molina's readers, including those who defend middle knowledge (e.g., Suarez), are nearly unanimous in their rejection of the theory of supercomprehension. However, for Molina, the theory has the advantage over its competitors in explaining why God cannot have prevolitional knowledge of the choice he himself would make in various possible circumstances. Such knowledge, Molina believes, would destroy divine freedom.

The publication of Molina's *Concordia* aroused bitter controversy between the Molinists and the defenders of the standard view, primarily Domingo Bañez, Diego Alvarez, and other members of the influential Dominican order. The Dominicans accused the Molinists of undermining God's sovereignty over the created world by maintaining that God has no direct control over the choices of free creatures. The Molinists accused the Dominicans of destroying human freedom and making God morally responsible for sinful actions. The Vatican, anxious to avoid another divisive clash over the issues of grace and free will, called the factions to Rome to examine the matter. In 1597, Pope Clement VIII convened the *Congregatio de auxiliis*, and over the next ten years the Molinist position was scrutinized in eighty-five hearings and forty-seven debates. Initially things did not go well for the Molinists, and Molina died fearing that the censure of his views was imminent. However, the theory of middle knowledge ultimately escaped condemnation. In 1607, Pope Paul V closed the proceedings. He allowed both parties to continue teaching their doctrines and ordered the sides to refrain from accusing each other of contradicting the faith.

Though Molina's best known contributions are to speculative theology, he also authored a seven-volume treatise in moral and political philosophy entitled *De Justitia et jure* (published posthumously at Venice in 1614). This work discusses the source of legitimate political authority, the permissibility of slavery, and the justification of war, as well as economic issues such as taxation, free markets and monetary policy.

See also Báñez, Dominic; Foreknowledge and Freedom, Theological Problem of; Philosophy of Religion, History of; Scientia Media and Molinism; Suárez, Francisco; Thomas Aquinas, St.

Bibliography

WORKS BY MOLINA

Liberi Arbitrii cum Gratiae Donis, Divina Praescientia, Providentia, Praedestinatione et Reprobatione Concordia, edited by J. Rabeneck. Oña and Madrid: 1953.

On Divine Foreknowledge: Part IV of the Concordia. Translated by Alfred J. Freddoso. Ithaca, NY: Cornell, 1988.

Neue Molinaschriften, edited by Friedrich Stegmüller, in *Beiträge zur Geschichte der Philosophie und Theologie des Mittelalters*, Band 32. Münster, Germany: 1935.

WORKS ABOUT MOLINA

Adams, Robert M. "Middle Knowledge and the Problem of Evil." In *The Virtue of Faith and Other Essays in Philosophical Theology*, edited by Robert M. Adams. New York: Oxford University Press, 1987.

Bañez, Domingo, et al. *Apologia en defensa de la doctrina antigua y catholica por los maestros dominicos de la Provincia de España contra las afirmaciones contenidas en la Concordia de Luis de Molina sobre la gracia, praesciencia divina, providencia, predestinacion y reprobacion*. In *Domingo Bañez y las controversias sobre la gracia*, edited by Vincente Beltran de Heredia. Salamanca, Spain: 1968.

Flint, Thomas. "Two Accounts of Providence." In *Divine and Human Action*, edited by Thomas V. Morris. Ithaca, NY: Cornell University Press, 1988.

Freddoso, Alfred J. "Introduction." In *On Divine Foreknowledge: Part IV of the Concordia*, 1–81. Translated by Alfred J. Freddoso. Ithaca: Cornell University Press, 1988.

Opera Omnia, Tomus XI, edited by Carol Berton. Paris: Vivès, 1858.

Pegis, Anton. "Molina and Human Liberty." In *Jesuit Thinkers of the Renaissance*, edited by G. Smith. Milwaukee, WI: Marquette, 1939.

Michael V. Griffin (2005)

MOLINA GARMENDIA, ENRIQUE
(1871–1962)

Enrique Molina Garmendia, the Chilean spiritualist philosopher, was born at La Serena, Chile. After several years of practicing law and teaching on the faculty of the Liceo de Chillán, he became the first rector of the University of Concepción in 1919. He was one of the leading members of the generation of Latin American intellectuals who, under the influence of William James, Henri Bergson, and the French spiritualists, reacted against the positivism that had dominated the political and cultural life of Latin America for half a century.

Throughout the eleven books that he published between 1912 and 1952, Molina was basically concerned with philosophical anthropology and with offering "an interpretation of [the human spirit], acceptable even to the skeptics, formulating a consideration of the spiritual in human life where it is constructive and creative, and where it is involved with ethical exigencies" (*De lo espiritual en la vida humana*). This concern raised the problem of the nature of consciousness and its relation to being, as well as the problem of the origin and status of values in the natural order.

Rejecting both idealistic and materialistic ontologies, Molina maintained the priority of being over consciousness, although he noted that the emergence of the latter within natural processes indicates the potentiality for consciousness within being. Following the German philosopher Edmund Husserl, Molina declared that being and consciousness are integrally united within experience. The priority of being "is affirmed, because it is first *lived* by consciousness as a totality of which consciousness forms a part" (*De lo espiritual en la vida humana*). Molina restated René Descartes's basic premise as "I think, therefore I exist *and Being exists.*" An adequate conception of being must incorporate both the subjective and the objective poles of experience.

It is in man that spirit has become most fully actualized. Closely associated with consciousness, spirit is the locus of values and is characterized by the freedom that makes activity leading toward the realization of value possible. The realm of the spirit embraces all the realms that are the result of human creativity—morality, religion, the sciences, the arts, "all the work of enlightened intelligence." Spirit is that element within each of these realms which aspires to be, which strives to perfect itself and to go beyond itself. Reason is the highest structure of spirit. Through reason, the presence of being is recognized, mere automatic functioning of the organism is overcome, and the horizons of consciousness are opened to the possibilities for creative advance.

See also Bergson, Henri; Descartes, René; Husserl, Edmund; James, William; Latin American Philosophy; Philosophical Anthropology.

Bibliography

WORKS BY MOLINA

De lo espiritual en la vida humana (Concerning the spirit in human life). Concepción, 1936.

Confesión filosófica (Philosophical confession). Santiago: Nascimento, 1942.

Tragedia y realización del espíritu. Del sentido de la muerte y del sentido de la vida (Tragedy and realization of the spirit. The meaning of death and life). Santiago: Nascimento, 1952.

WORKS ON MOLINA

Enríquez Frodden, Edgardo. *Proyección del pensamiento y de la personalidad de Concepción* Chile: Universidad de Concepción, 1972.

Lipp, Solomon. *Three Chilean Thinkers.* Waterloo, ON: Wilfrid Laurier University Press, 1975.

Salvat Boloña, Pablo. *Visión del hombre y visión de América según Enrique Molina G.* Santiago, 1982.

Vidal Muñoz, Santiago. "Apuntes sobre la filosofía en Chile." *Cursos y conferencias* 48 (272) (1956): 39–60.

Fred Gillette Sturm (1967)
Bibliography updated by Michael Farmer and Vladimir Marchenkov (2005)

MONAD AND MONADOLOGY

The Greek term μονάς, from which the word *monad* is derived, means a "unit" or a "one." In Pythagorean writings it is the unity from which the entire number system, and therefore—as a consequence of the doctrine that "everything is number"—all things, are derived. Through Plato, who applied the Pythagorean term to the Ideas or Forms (*Philebus* V, 15B), it entered the tradition of Neoplatonism and Christian Platonism to mean a simple, irreducible, self-determining entity whose activity is the source of all composite beings. In this sense it was sometimes used to designate God as the simple source of all being and sometimes to signify the simplest irreducible entities in the created order out of whose harmonious action all existence is compounded.

A monadology is a metaphysical system that interprets the world as a harmonious unity encompassing a plurality of such self-determining simple entities. The term was first used in the early eighteenth century of the metaphysics of Gottfried Wilhelm Leibniz.

In its modern meaning since Leibniz, a monad is held to be (1) a simple, irreducible, and sometimes indestructible entity; and (2) the minimal unity into which the cosmos and all composite things in it can be resolved; yet (3) containing within itself, in contrast to material atoms, powers and relations of which it is itself the source. It is therefore conceived after the analogy of a mind or a *res cogitans* rather than a material substance. It is held to constitute, along with other monads, an all-inclusive unity or harmony of the cosmos as a whole.

A monadology may thus entail a theory of cosmic harmony, based upon a mathematical or scientific functionalism or upon a psychology of intersubjective relations, as well as a theory of relations, in which the relations constituting this cosmic harmony are brought into being through monadic action, although they do not affect the monads or organizations of monads that are the objects of the acts (Leibniz's perceptions and Alfred North Whitehead's prehensions are examples of such relations).

This intermonadic harmony may itself be regarded as a unity, or cosmic Monad, and this view may involve pantheism or a theistic theory of creation. The relation of the minimal monads to the supreme Monad is one of mirroring rather than being a part of; since the supreme Monad must itself be simple, each monad may be held to be a finite (unclear and indistinct) reflection of the attributes of the supreme Monad. (The metaphors of mirroring, of echoing, and of the infinite circle whose center is everywhere have commonly been used in monadologies.)

Monadologies may disagree in their fundamental categories. Monads are active substances and, therefore, also processes; Leibniz attempted, but with incomplete success, to unite a logical and a psychological analysis of the monad by applying the notions of intensionality and extensionality. The finite monads may be of a temporal nature; the cosmic order may be either eternal or temporal, or—as Whitehead and Charles Hartshorne held—both eternal and temporal. The finite monads themselves may be eternal changeless souls (John McTaggart). The cosmic harmony may be thought of as a divine Person or merely as the unitary society of monads.

In the history of modern monadologies, three conceptions have been operative: the Christian Platonist tradition of the soul as a simple substance possessing self-certainty in immediate unity (Augustine, *De Trinitate*, IX, 3; X, 9, 10); the Neoplatonic-Stoic conception of the One that is essentially represented in each of its parts; and a spiritualized form of atomism ultimately derived from this Neoplatonic-Stoic conception. The first tradition, mediated by Boethius, the Franciscans, and other medieval Platonists, became prominent in the seventeenth century in Francisco Suárez, René Descartes, and others. The second tradition emerged in the Renaissance in the concepts of the microcosm and macrocosm after a long history during which the Stoic doctrine of the Logos had been combined with the Neoplatonic theory of the One and the subordinate intelligences. This tradition involved the principle of plenitude, according to which the universe can achieve its maximal being only when God multiplies or reduplicates his nature in every created being. This principle was suggested by Meister Eckhart and explicated by Nicholas of Cusa in his doctrine of the coincidence of maximum and minimum in God. Giordano Bruno developed the principle of plenitude into a theory of material monads as spherical atoms that are spiritual reflections of the Divine Nature (*De triplice minimo et mensura … Libri quinque*, 1591; *De monade, numero, et figura Liber*, 1591).

Leibniz's concept of monad is variously ascribed to Bruno, Henry More, or Franciscus Mercurius van Helmont, all of whom had made use of the term. But the terms *Monas* and *monadica* appear in the early papers of Leibniz, written long before he had come to know any of these thinkers or had developed his mature metaphysics.

Leibniz's monadology involves a harmonious universe composed of an infinite number of monads, each of which was an infinite series of perceptive acts defined by a unique point of view or a unique law of series; each such law, in turn, was a particular finite combination of the perfections of God expressed in his creation. Leibniz presented a succinct but incomplete account of this system in his *Principles of Nature and of Grace* and the so-called *Monadology,* both written in 1714; he then devoted the last twenty years of his philosophical activity to a defense and amplification of his monadology through various papers and a vast correspondence. His system and that of Whitehead, who ascribed greater spontaneity and creativity to the monads and interpreted them as mind-like entities of limited duration, are the most detailed modern monadologies.

Trained in the Leibniz-Wolff tradition, Immanuel Kant wrote *Physical Monadology* in his precritical period (1756), in which the monads were treated as sources of motion in a Newtonian space. In the *Critique of Pure Reason* (1781), Kant called his second antinomy "the dialectic principle of monadology" (1st ed., p. 442). This antinomy is directed at the metaphysical claims for a monadology made by the Wolffian school. In their development of a realistic, spiritualistic metaphysics, Johann Friedrich Herbart, Hermann Lotze, and Gustav Theodor Fechner developed monadologies on a Kantian basis. In his third *Essai de critique générale* (Paris, 1859), and in *La nouvelle monadologie* (Paris, 1899), Charles Renouvier built a monadology upon his relativized interpretation of Kant, making the highest attainable harmony in "the best of all possible worlds" depend upon the freedom of human monads or persons. In contrast to this relativized monadism, Edmund Husserl, in his *Cartesian Meditations* (1929–1931), suggested a monadic completion of his transcendental phenomenology, describing a type of "indirect experience that possesses its own modes of verification" within one's own monadic experience and that also provides "the transcendental base" for an objective natural order; implied in this is a "sphere of monadological intersubjectivity." Other recent monadologies include Dietrich Mahnke's attempt to reconcile Leibniz's monadology with recent science and philosophy; H. Wildon Carr's *Theory of Monads* (London, 1922), influenced by the British personalistic tradition; and William Stern's hierarchical system of persons and things, inspired by Benedict de Spinoza, Fechner, and Lotze.

See also Augustine, St.; Boethius, Anicius Manlius Severinus; Bruno, Giordano; Descartes, René; Eckhart, Meister; Fechner, Gustav Theodor; Herbart, Johann Friedrich; Husserl, Edmund; Kant, Immanuel; Leibniz, Gottfried Wilhelm; Lotze, Rudolf Hermann; Macrocosm and Microcosm; McTaggart, John McTaggart Ellis; More, Henry; Neoplatonism; Nicholas of Cusa; Plato; Platonism and the Platonic Tradition; Renaissance; Renouvier, Charles Bernard; Spinoza, Benedict (Baruch) de; Stern, Louis William; Suárez, Francisco; Whitehead, Alfred North.

Bibliography

Discussions of monadologies are to be found in Heinz Heimsoeth, *Atom, Seele, Monade. Historische Ursprünge und Hintergründe von Kant's Antinomie der Teilung* (Wiesbaden, 1960). W. Cramer, in *Die Monade* (Stuttgart, 1954), begins with Kant's antinomy and treats him in terms of intermonadic relations. P. F. Strawson subjects a Leibnizian monadology to critical analysis in *Individuals: An Essay in Descriptive Metaphysics* (New York, 1963), pp. 114–133.

See also Dietrich Mahnke, *Eine Neue Monadologie* (*Kantstudien*, Erganzungsheft 39; Berlin: Reuther and Reichard, 1917) and *Unendliche Sphäre und Allmittelpunkt* (Halle: M. Niemeyer, 1937) by the same author; Edmund Husserl, *Cartesianische Meditationen und Pariser Vorträge*, edited by S. Strasser (The Hague, 1950), especially sections 55–56; William Stern, *Person und Sache*, 3 vols. (Leipzig: J. A. Barth, 1906–1924), Vol. I (Leipzig, 1906); and A. N. Whitehead, *Process and Reality* (New York: Macmillan, 1929).

L. E. Loemker (1967)

MONISM AND PLURALISM

How many things are there? Or how many kinds of thing? Monism is the doctrine that the answer to one or other of these questions is "Only one." Opposed to monism is the doctrine of pluralism, which is that there are many kinds of thing, or that there are many things. It will be apparent, on reflection, that this weaker form of pluralism, that there are many things, is quite consistent with the weaker form of monism, that there is only one *kind* of thing to which the many particular things belong. For instance, materialism, in the sense that everything existent is material, is a form of monism because it insists that all existent things are of a single *kind*, the material kind. Thus monism and pluralism, though opposed, do not always exclude each other.

A doctrine that might be regarded as a form of pluralism, possibly the most important form of it, is dualism, the belief that there are two things or two types of thing. In view of its importance, it will be treated below in a separate section.

MONISM

"Monism" is a name for a group of views in metaphysics that stress the oneness or unity of reality in some sense. It has been characteristic of monism, from the earliest times, to insist on the unity of things in time (their freedom from change) or in space (their indivisibility) or in quality (their undifferentedness). Such a view of the world is already found in a developed form in the pre-Socratic philosopher Parmenides and was nicknamed the "block universe" (by Thomas Davidson, a friend of William James), that is, the universe thought of as a single closed system of interlocking parts in which there is no genuine plurality and no room for alternative possibilities. Although this world view and similar ones are now classified as forms of monism, they may not have been seen as falling into a single category at all until the term *monism* had itself been invented. The term was coined by Christian Wolff (1679–1754), and he used it only in a narrow sense, applying it to the two opposite theories that everything is mental (idealism or mentalism) and that everything is material (materialism). The term was subsequently applied to a particular doctrine of the relation between mind and matter, namely, the theory of their absolute identity (the *Identitätsphilosophie* so often mentioned by William James). The main proponents of this doctrine were Friedrich Schelling and G. W. F. Hegel, although it actually originated with Benedict de Spinoza and is sometimes known as the double-aspect theory. It holds that mind and body are only modes of the same substance, and it is this substance to which they are both reducible, not one to the other. A more recent version of this theory is the "neutral monism" of William James, which Bertrand Russell at one time also adopted. On the other hand, it should be noted that the *Identitätsphilosophie* and neutral monism differ from the "identity theory," which is a form of materialism recently set forth by J. J. C. Smart, Herbert Feigl, and others. The identity theory holds that the mind is not some third thing, some "neutral stuff" like sensation, but is literally identical with the brain.

In the nineteenth century the word *monism* came to be given wider application and so to have a systematic ambiguity, that is, a consistent variation of meaning according to context. Since then any theory that tries to reduce all phenomena to a single principle, or to explain them by one principle, or to make statements about reality as a whole, has been labeled "monism." The ambiguity is not harmful, provided that theories about how many substances there are (substantival monism) are distinguished from theories about what *kinds* of substance exist (attributive monism). This distinction also needs to be observed in the case of pluralism (see below).

Substantival and attributive monism are logically independent views, and the various possible combinations of attitude to these questions are actually found in the doctrines of major philosophers. Thus if by "substantival monism" we mean the theory that the apparent multiplicity of substances is really a manifestation of only a single substance in different states or from different points of view, then Spinoza, with his God-or-Nature, and Francis Herbert Bradley, with his Absolute, are typical substantival monists. Indeed, Part I of Spinoza's *Ethics* is the classic exposition of substantival monism, offering a proof that there can be only one self-subsistent and independent thing. But Spinoza rejected attributive monism, which maintains that all the substances that there are, whether one or many, are ultimately of a single kind. He believed in an infinity of real attributes. An opposite case is that of Gottfried Wilhelm Leibniz, who rejected substantival monism but accepted a monism of attributes, for in his philosophy all the monads are of one kind, being souls.

A further possible doctrine, that might be called partial monism, is the belief that even if there is more than one realm of being, there is only one substance within some particular realm. For example, René Descartes, who is the classic dualist insofar as he divides the world into the two realms of mind and matter, accepted partial monism about matter, which he treated as a unitary substance, while he rejected partial monism about minds.

If monism in one or other of these various senses keeps on turning up in quite diverse philosophical systems, that is not really surprising. A striving for unity in a world description, perhaps for the sake of easier comprehensibility and greater economy of explanation, perhaps resulting from the direct appeal of simplicity, is a perennial urge in human thought. Even a substantival pluralist, Leibniz for instance, usually maintains that the plurality of substances in his world do form a systematic unity "ideally" or when looked at from the viewpoint of an omniscient being. To many minds, a monistic theory is always the most attractive option if the obstacles to holding it can be removed.

DUALISM

Dualism is the position of those thinkers who find some radical and irreducible difference in the world, an insuperable gulf between two realms of being. Any philosophical system that divides the world into two categories or types of thing, or uses two ultimate principles of expla-

nation, or insists that there are two substances or kinds of substance, is a form of dualism. (The same ambiguity is found here as with the other labels.) Even the presence of a cardinal though not all-embracing contrast in a philosophical system may justify calling it a dualism in a looser sense, as when we speak of the dualism of Plato, in whose works the world of flux presented to the senses is sharply contrasted with the world of Forms known by the intellect, or when we consider the corresponding dualism of phenomena and noumena in Immanuel Kant.

Although superficially dualism can be seen as a special case of pluralism, it should be clear from the foregoing that it has often been, so to speak, the expression of failed monism. Nor is it merely that monism has to many minds the attractiveness described earlier; the dualistic position is inherently unstable and puzzle-generating. Once we have divided the world into two—for example, into natural and supernatural, temporal and eternal, material and mental, particular and universal—we have on our hands the problem of the relation between the two resulting worlds. These bridging problems have bulked large in both ancient and modern philosophy. Even though dualism of mind and body, for instance, may be said to reflect the time-honored view of common sense and was adopted by philosophers at least as early as Anaxagoras, Descartes's version of it, with thinking substances operating mysteriously on bits of extended substance, set the problem for all subsequent philosophers until Gilbert Ryle, in *The Concept of Mind* (1949), dismissed it as a "category-mistake."

There may be thinkers for whom oppositions themselves have an attraction, just as triads certainly do for some others. If so, the series of opposites set up by the Pythagoreans may have had this motivation. Since, however, they reduced the two sets to two fundamental principles, the Limit and the Unlimited, they may have been forced by their mathematical discoveries to acknowledge a difference that blocked the way to monism. Whatever the correct interpretation in their case, it is plain that no philosopher would in advance adopt dualism as an ideal at which to *aim*, in creating his world picture.

What in fact drew attention to dualism as a type of theory was theology, where doctrines like Manichaeism, with its two ultimate principles of good and evil, or darkness and light, are found. Those who put forward such doctrines were labeled "dualists" by Thomas Hyde, writing in Latin about 1700. Later the term found its way into philosophy in various languages.

PLURALISM

If there is more than one kind of existent, why not any number instead of just two? The unsuccessful would-be monist may, through thinking in this way, lapse into pluralism. Others, like William James, may find they have a temperamental objection to monism, with its emphasis on the totality and its exclusion of individuality and quirkiness. Yet others may from the start see the world as having some kind of disconnectedness as an essential feature, without which motion, change, and free will, for example, would be impossible. The rejection of any form of monism of course entails adopting the corresponding pluralist viewpoint. There may, however, be different types of rejection. Pluralism may arise from the rejection of the metaphysical conception of the "block universe" or of the logical doctrine that all true statements are, in the last analysis, logically necessary. For if there are some truths of a merely contingent nature, the doctrine of internal relations, that all relations are grounded in the natures of the related terms, must be false, and this doctrine is fundamental to the idealist versions of monism. The case of Leibniz, who is often taken as a standard pluralist, does not illustrate this point, but an instance of this sort of conversion to pluralism is afforded by Russell, who writes of his early position, "I came to disbelieve Bradley's arguments against relations, and to distrust the logical bases of monism" (*The Philosophy of Bertrand Russell*, edited by P. A. Schilpp, Evanston, IL, 1944, pp. 11–12). Russell later adopted a full-blown pluralism associated with logic: For instance, "When I say that my logic is atomistic, I mean that I share the common-sense belief that there are many separate things" ("The Philosophy of Logical Atomism," 1918; reprinted in his *Logic and Knowledge*, New York, 1956, p. 178). Though this phase of Russell's philosophy is usually known as logical atomism, he also described it himself as "absolute pluralism." Even after abandoning logical atomism, Russell remained an enthusiastic pluralist; in 1931 he wrote of the proposition that the world is a unity, "the most fundamental of my intellectual beliefs is that this is rubbish. I think the universe is all spots and jumps, without unity, without continuity, without coherence or orderliness or any of the other properties that governesses love" (*The Scientific Outlook,* New York, 1931, p. 98).

See also Bradley, Francis Herbert; Categories; Descartes, René; Dualism in the Philosophy of Mind; Hegel, Georg Wilhelm Friedrich; James, William; Kant, Immanuel; Leibniz, Gottfried Wilhelm; Mani and Manichaeism; Mind-Body Problem; Parmenides of Elea; Plato; Pluralism; Russell, Bertrand Arthur William; Ryle, Gilbert; Schelling, Friedrich Wilhelm Joseph von; Smart, John Jamieson Carswell; Spinoza, Benedict (Baruch) de; Wolff, Christian.

Bibliography

Helpful general discussions of monism, dualism, and pluralism are rather few in number. The only good general account of all three is A. M. Quinton, "Pluralism and Monism," in the *Encyclopaedia Britannica.* The best sources, though more difficult to use, are the actual works of the philosophers mentioned as proponents of the various doctrines.

MONISM

On monism see the works of philosophers named in the text, such as Parmenides, Spinoza, and Bradley. A useful discussion is C. E. M. Joad, "Monism in the Light of Recent Developments in Philosophy," in *PAS* 17 (1916–1917): 95–116. Now somewhat antiquated is A. Worsley, *Concepts of Monism* (London, 1907). A typical short account from the heyday of monism in British philosophy is A. E. Taylor, *Elements of Metaphysics* (London: Methuen, 1903), Chs. 2–3. Compare J. A. Smith, "The Issue between Monism and Pluralism," in *PAS* 26 (1925–1926): 1–24. See also Marvin Farber, "Types of Unity and the Problem of Monism," in *Philosophy and Phenomenological Research* 4 (1943–1944): 37–58, and postscript, ibid., 6 (1945–1946): 547–583; Raphael Demos, "Types of Unity According to Plato and Aristotle," ibid., 534–545; Abraham Edel, "Monism and Pluralism," in *Journal of Philosophy* 31 (21) (October 1934): 561–571; and Jonathan Bennett, "A Note on Descartes and Spinoza," in *Philosophical Review* 74 (3) (July 1965): 379–380. Such nineteenth-century works as Ernst Haeckel, *Der Monismus als Band zwischen Religion und Wissenschaft* (Bonn: E. Strauss, 1893; translated by J. Gilchrist as *Monism as Connecting Religion and Science,* London: A. and C. Black, 1895), are not now of much philosophical interest, for they are not about monism in general but are presentations of an outdated type of materialism.

DUALISM

On dualism see the main works of Descartes. The difficulties of the dualist position in general are well brought out by John Passmore in his *Philosophical Reasoning* (London: Duckworth, 1961), Ch. 3. See also Simone Pétrement, *Le dualisme chez Platon, les gnostiques, et les manichéens* (Paris: Presses Universitaires de France, 1947).

PLURALISM

The most readable book on pluralism and other theories is William James's *A Pluralistic Universe* (London: Longman, 1909). For further reading, there is James Ward, *The Realm of Ends, or Pluralism and Theism* (Cambridge, U.K.: Cambridge University Press, 1911). A dry but clear account is to be found in C. D. Broad, *The Mind and Its Place in Nature* (London: Kegan Paul, 1925), introduction. More difficult and technical but classic is G. E. Moore, "External and Internal Relations," in *PAS* 20 (1919–1920): 40–62, reprinted in his *Philosophical Studies* (New York: Harcourt Brace, 1922). Compare Bertrand Russell, "The Nature of Truth," in *Mind* 15 (1906): 528–533, reprinted as "The Monistic Theory of Truth," in Russell's *Philosophical Essays*

(London: Allen and Unwin, 1910). See also J. H. Muirhead, F. C. S. Schiller, and A. E. Taylor, "Why Pluralism?," in *PAS* 9 (1908–1909): 183–225; and P. Laner, *Pluralismus oder Monismus* (1905).

Roland Hall (1967)

MONTAGUE, RICHARD
(1930–1971)

Richard M. Montague, a logician who taught in the Philosophy Department at the University of California at Los Angeles from 1955 until his premature death in 1971, is probably best known for his contributions to linguistic semantics, although he also made important contributions to mathematical logic and philosophy.

Montague was born in 1930. He attended the University of California at Berkeley both as an undergraduate and a graduate student, concentrating not only in mathematics and philosophy, but in Semitic languages. Working with Alfred Tarski, he completed a doctoral dissertation in 1957 entitled "Contributions to the foundations of axiomatic set theory." By that time he had published a large number of papers in various areas of mathematical logic.

Montague's interests in mathematical logic were general and included set theory, proof theory, model theory, and abstract recursion theory. One early theme in his work in mathematical logic concerned the consequences of semantic reflection for axiomatic versions of set theory and other mathematical theories. That work has been widely cited and is still important.

The work for which Montague is best known was carried out late in his life (beginning with the 1968 publication of "Pragmatics") and dealt with the development of logics intended to serve as vehicles for the interpretation of natural language and the formalization of philosophy. From Tarski, Montague inherited the view that semantic theories could and should be formulated with mathematical precision. However, his project of applying Tarski's techniques to natural language seems to derive more naturally from the work of Rudolf Carnap and Alonzo Church.

Both Carnap and Church worked with a framework for logical formalization, which, although it was developed in connection with the language of mathematical theories, was clearly more broadly applicable. Carnap was mainly interested in using formalization as a tool for clarifying philosophy. Church considered what he called the "logistic method"—that is, the method of logical formalization developed in the first half of the twentieth century—to be applicable in a more general linguistic setting.

Carnap and Church both addressed a major obstacle standing in the way of generalizing Tarskian semantic theories to natural language—the problem of intensionality (which had already been raised by Gottlob Frege). Carnap explored how what are now called possible worlds could be used to model intensionality, while Church sought to formalize Frege's theory of sense and denotation. Influences of both can be seen in Montague's logical framework for interpreting natural language. Like Carnap, Montague appealed to possible worlds, and, like Church, he used higher-order logic. Montague's insight that a logic combining possible worlds with higher-order logic provided a flexible and powerful tool for natural language semantics proved to be fundamentally important.

All of Montague's publications concerning "Montague Grammar" are collected together in *Formal Philosophy: Selected Papers of Richard Montague* (1974). These papers develop the logical framework of "intensional logic." This is a higher-order logic involving on a system of types based on three primitive domains: entities (type e), possible worlds, and the two truth values T and F (type t). If σ and τ are types, then $<\sigma,\tau>$ is also a type and corresponds to the set of functions from the domain of σ to the domain of τ. Thus, for instance, $<e,t>$ is the type of functions from entities to truth values. If σ is a type, then $<s,\sigma>$ is also a type and corresponds to the set of functions from possible worlds to the domain of σ: $<s, <e,t>>$, then, is the type of intensions of sets of entities. For a book-length, systematic treatment of intensional logic, see Daniel Gallin's *Intensional and Higher-Order Logic* (1975).

A Montague grammar for a fragment of a language consists of a syntactic account of that fragment, which defines a set of syntactic structures showing how complex phrases are decomposed into components, and a semantic component that shows how a semantic value can be assigned to the structure given an assignment of values to the lexical items occurring in the structure. These values belong to the domains of a model of intensional logic. Intensional logic can serve as an intermediary in the mapping of syntactic structures to values, and as a vehicle for formulating postulates about the meanings of lexical items. This mapping conforms to a correspondence between grammatical categories like "Sentence" and "Noun-Phrase" and the types of intensional logic.

To see how the idea might work, consider the sentence "John wants a car." The noun phrase 'a car' has type $<<e,t>,t>$; it denotes the set of sets containing at least one car. (The insight that noun phrases denote sets of sets goes back to Frege's 1884 work, *The Foundations of Arithmetic.*) The verb 'wants' corresponds to a function that inputs the intension of a Noun-Phrase denotation and returns a function from entities to truth values. Give this function the intension of 'a car' and it returns a function saying of each entity whether that entity wants a car. The type of 'wants' is therefore $<<s, <<e,t>,t>>, <e,t>>$. Barbara Partee and Herman L. W. Hendriks provide a useful extended survey of Montague's semantic framework and its subsequent influences in their 1996 essay "Montague Grammar."

Montague himself saw intensional logic and his theory of language as a basis of formalizing philosophy, but the most important direct influence of his work was on the development of linguistic semantics, where its impact was enormous. Montague's semantic techniques can be associated with any generative syntactic framework; his syntactic approach has been less influential, outside of subsequent work in the categorical grammar framework. (See Jacobson 1996, for example.)

Although few philosophers would agree that the goal of formalizing philosophy is enabled by Montague's work, foundational questions raised by his approach have preoccupied and shaped subsequent work in analytic metaphysics and philosophy of language. Much of this influence is indirect, occurring through the work of David Lewis, who attended Montague's courses at UCLA and was influenced by his ideas.

Because of Montague's uncompromising emphasis on the technical dimension, his papers are difficult reading. But even now, they repay careful study. The linguistic papers and other philosophically relevant work were compiled in 1974 in *Formal Philosophy: Selected Papers of Richard Montague.* Further biographical information concerning Montague can be found in Anita and Solomon Feferman's biography of Tarski, *Alfred Tarski: Life and Logic* (2004).

See also Artificial and Natural Languages; Carnap, Rudolf; Church, Alonzo; Computability Theory; Frege, Gottlob; Lewis, David; Logic, History of: Modern Logic; Mathematics, Foundations of; Modal Logic; Model Theory; Proof Theory; Semantics, History of; Set Theory; Tarski, Alfred; Type Theory.

Bibliography

Carnap, Rudolf. *Meaning and Necessity.* 2nd ed. Chicago: University of Chicago Press, 1956. The first edition was published in 1947.

Church, Alonzo. "The Need for Abstract Entities in Semantic Analysis." *Proceedings of the American Academy of Arts and Sciences* 80 (1951): 100–112.

Church, Alonzo. *Introduction to Mathematical Logic.* Vol. 1. Princeton, NJ: University of Princeton Press, 1959.

Church, Alonzo. "Outline of a Revised Formulation of the Logic of Sense and Denotation (Part I)." *Nous,* 7 (1973): 24–33.

Church, Alonzo. "Outline of a Revised Formulation of the Logic of Sense and Denotation (Part II)." *Nous,* 8 (1974): 135–156.

Feferman, Anita Burdman, and Solomon Feferman. *Alfred Tarski: Life and Logic.* Cambridge, U.K.: Cambridge University Press, 2004.

Frege, Gottlob. *The Foundations of Arithmetic.* 2nd ed. Translated by J. L. Austin. Oxford, U.K.: Oxford University Press, 1953. Originally published in 1884.

Furth, Montgomery, C. C. Chang, and Alonzo Church. "Obituary of Richard M. Montague." Unpublished manuscript. Los Angeles: University of California at Los Angeles Department of Philosophy, 1971.

Gallin, Daniel. *Intensional and Higher-Order Logic.* Amsterdam: North-Holland, 1975.

Jacobson, Paulene. "The Syntax/Semantics Interface in Categorical Grammar." In *The Handbook of Contemporary Semantic Theory,* edited by Shalom Lappin, 89–116. Oxford, U.K.: Blackwell Publishers, 1996.

Montague, Richard. *Formal Philosophy: Selected Papers of Richard Montague.* New Haven, CT: Yale University Press, 1974. Edited and with an introduction by Richmond H. Thomason.

Partee, Barbara H., with Herman L. W. Hendriks. "Montague Grammar." In *Handbook of Logic and Language,* edited by Johan van Benthem and Alice ter Meulen, 5–91. Amsterdam, Netherlands: Elsevier Science Publishers, 1996.

Richmond H. Thomason (2005)

MONTAGUE, WILLIAM PEPPERELL
(1873–1953)

William Pepperell Montague, an American realist philosopher, received his BA from Harvard in 1896, his MA the following year, and his PhD in 1898. He taught briefly at Radcliffe, Harvard, and the University of California. In 1903 he began teaching at Barnard and from 1907 to 1910 was an adjunct professor and a member of the Columbia University graduate faculty of philosophy. He became associate professor in 1910, professor in 1920, and was the Johnsonian professor of philosophy from 1920 to 1941. In 1928 he was Carnegie visiting professor in Japan, Czechoslovakia, and Italy. He served as chairman of several delegations to the International Congress of Philosophy (1920, 1934, 1937) and as president of the eastern division of the American Philosophical Association in 1923.

REALISM

Montague advocated a frankly Platonic "subsistential realism." He called it a right-wing realism, in contrast with left-wing realism, whose adherents included the behaviorists, objective relativists, and—to some extent—pragmatists. At the turn of the twentieth century, the idealist claim that the object of knowledge was dependent on the knower and thus was "ideal" had come increasingly under attack in England and America. Montague, in "Professor Royce's Refutation of Realism" (1902), was one of the first to attack idealism by means of the realist theory of independence. This theory—that the object of knowledge is not dependent for its reality on the knowing relation—became one of the cardinal tenets of the New Realist movement, of which Montague was a charter member. However, by itself it was not enough to establish that the known is independent of the knower. It also had to be shown how a conscious, knowing organism could be in such a unique kind of rapport with events whose loci and dates were different from its own. Thus the central issue in epistemology for Montague was to establish the independence and the immanence of the object of knowledge.

Montague proposed his "subsistential realism" as a resolution of this issue. Subsistence included everything that could be made an object of discourse. The objects of knowledge then are subsistently real, that is, propositions and terms rather than commonsense objects, and as such they are directly present to mind (immanent), though independent of it. Montague thus brought the things of the earth into the realm of ideas by interpreting existence as a subclass of subsistence, hence also as a set of propositions.

With his idea of subsistent and existential propositions, Montague could distinguish nonveridical and unreal objects from the veridical and real. Existential propositions are the objects of true or real knowledge, and the "merely subsistent" propositions are the objects of false or unreal knowledge. Thus there is a tendency in Montague's thinking to identify the true, real, and existent on the one hand, and the false, unreal, and nonexistent on the other.

What, then, is the cause of error? Truth and falsity attach to our judgments, Montague said, because of their content, not because they are stated or believed. Error is the result of the selective action of sense perception and conception. He attributed error to these factors of the "personal equation" (as realists called the subjective aspect of knowledge) because he had said existential subsistent propositions cause themselves to be known in a way the "merely subsistent" cannot. But how can a proposition cause itself to be known?

The answer apparently was in the difference between the "merely subsistent" propositions and the existential subsistent propositions. Montague identified existential propositions with facts, and he described a fact as "something done," a fait accompli. But this was as far as he went.

ANIMISTIC MATERIALISM

Epistemology was secondary, however, to Montague's preoccupation with the psychophysical problem of the nature of mind and its relation to the body. Naturalistic monism, strongly supported by science, could not, Montague claimed, adequately account for such characteristics of mind as purpose, privacy, duration, and integration. Traditional dualism could account for them, but it was scientifically sterile in its reliance on concepts of spirit. Montague's answer, which he called "animistic materialism," was the hypothesis of a physical soul possessing all of the traits of mind although still physically describable.

Throughout his career, Montague considered the soul to be the only answer to the psychophysical problem. After proposing the idea of a substantial soul in his first published writing, Montague soon rejected it in favor of considering the soul as a new kind of energy, purely private, and internally observable as sensation. This "potential" energy comes into existence when and where the kinetic energy of a stimulus ceases to be externally observable as motion. Sensations (or consciousness) and their externally observable causes are thus qualitatively identical. The potentiality of the physical is the actuality of the psychical, and vice versa. Just as when successive twists are imposed upon a coiled spring there is left unobservable potential energy, so too the potential energies of sensations leave traces superposed on one another. These traces constitute the memory system and modify the organism's responses to later stimuli.

Thus, within the organism there arises a field of potential energy that is externally unobservable yet is causally effective upon the visible cerebral matrix; this inner organism possesses all the characteristics of mind. In Montague's relational dualism, therefore, mind and body are in radical contrast as relations but not as substances. The truths of psychophysical dualism were thus saved without departing from material categories. Montague in general maintained this materialistic dualism, yet at one point (in "A Realistic Theory of Truth and Error," 1912) he admitted to what he called a qualified panpsychism: Matter had something psychical about it.

RELIGIOUS VIEWS

Montague's "Promethean challenge to religion" (as he called it in *Belief Unbound*) was a challenge to authoritarianism, supernaturalism, and asceticism in religion. Montague denied what he termed the "pseudo creativeness" that idealism and pragmatism attribute to humans. Man has no transcendent power to legislate for nature, or to support infinite space and time by his consciousness. Realism instead gives to man an even greater responsibility of membership in the independent order of nature. Realism also adds to existent things the "quiet and infinitely great immensities of the realm of subsistence" where mind gains access to new and imperishable sources of joy and peace. Philosophy's one certainty is that ideals are eternal things, and the life that incarnates them attains an absolute value that time alone could not create and that death is powerless to destroy.

Ideals are not dependent on God's will. God is neither finite nor infinite in all things. He is infinite and eternal like the universe that is his body, all-perfect in himself and in his will but limited in power by that totality of actual and possible things which is within him yet not himself. God is to be loved because he is good, not because he is powerful.

Montague had a genuinely speculative and daring mind that explored not only the fields of philosophy but also such areas as time perception, mathematics, relativity theory, and quantum mechanics. At the beginning of Montague's career, philosophy suffered from what he called "internalism," a subjectivism sometimes carried to the point of solipsism, which, if it perhaps contained a grain of truth, was sterile. By the end of his life Montague feared that philosophy had gone to the other extreme. In "The Modern Distemper of Philosophy" (1951), he expressed his concern that it now suffered from an "externalism," a "distemper" that was eliminating important philosophical problems from discussion because they were insufficiently empirical.

See also Epistemology, History of; Idealism; New Realism; Platonism and the Platonic Tradition; Propositions; Realism.

Bibliography

Works by Montague include the following: "A Plea for Soul-Substance," in *Psychological Review* 6 (5) (September 1899): 457–476; "Professor Royce's Refutation of Realism," in *Philosophical Review* 2 (January 1902): 43–55; "A Realistic Theory of Truth and Error," in E. B. Holt and others, *The New Realism* (New York: Macmillan, 1912), pp. 251–300; *The Ways of Knowing; or The Methods of Philosophy* (New York: Macmillan, 1925), a good example of Montague's desire to save the truths in all philosophies; *Belief Unbound; a Promethean Religion for the Modern World* (New Haven, CT: Yale University Press, 1930); "Confessions of an Animistic Materialist," in *Contemporary American Philosophy*, edited by W. P. Montague and G. P. Adams, Vol. II (New York: Macmillan, 1930), pp. 135–158; *The Ways of Things: A Philosophy of Knowledge, Nature and Value* (New York: Prentice-Hall, 1940), the best single source for an overall view of Montague's philosophy; "The Human Soul and the Cosmic Mind," in *Mind* 54 (213) (January 1945): 50–64; *Great Visions of Philosophy: Varieties of Speculative Thought in the West from the Greeks to Bergson* (La Salle, IL: Open Court, 1950), Montague's Carus Lectures; and "The Modern Distemper of Philosophy," in *Journal of Philosophy* 48 (14) (1951): 429–435.

See also Helen Huss Parkhurst et al., "The Philosophic Creed of William Pepperell Montague," in *Journal of Philosophy* 52 (21) (1954): 593–637, which consists of articles on Montague and tributes to him by former colleagues and students.

Thomas Robischon (1967)

MONTAIGNE, MICHEL EYQUEM DE
(1533–1592)

Michel Eyquem De Montaigne, French essayist and skeptical philosopher, was born near Bordeaux. His father was an important merchant, and his mother belonged to a wealthy Spanish-Portuguese Jewish family that had fled to Toulouse. Montaigne was raised a Catholic and was given special training by his father, who would not allow him to hear any language other than Latin until he was six. At this time he was sent to the Collège de Guyenne at Bordeaux, where he studied with some of the leading humanistic teachers of the time, among them the learned Latin poet George Buchanan (1505–1582), who would later be arrested and charged by the Portuguese Inquisition for "judaizing" and skepticism. Montaigne also apparently studied at the University of Toulouse, a leading center of humanism and unorthodox religious ideas. For thirteen years he was a member of the *parlement* of Bordeaux and made several trips to Paris and the court seeking a more important position. His closest friend at this time was the stoic humanist and poet Étienne de La

Boétie (1530–1563). Montaigne's first significant writing was a letter describing La Boétie's death, published at the end of the latter's *Oeuvres* in 1570.

In 1568 Montaigne published his French translation of *Theologia Naturalis sive Liber Creaturarum* ("Natural Theology or the Book of Creatures") by Raimond Sebond (Raymond of Sabunde, d. 1436), a fifteenth-century Spanish theologian who had taught at Toulouse. In Montaigne's translation he somewhat modified Sebond's rationalistic claims that unaided human reason could comprehend the universe and establish the existence and nature of God. Montaigne also published La Boétie's works before retiring from public life in 1571. The following year he began writing his most important work, the *Essays*, a series of rambling, erudite, witty discussions on a variety of topics, serving as a self-portrait. The longest of the essays, the "Apology for Raimond Sebond," was written about 1576 while Montaigne was studying the recently rediscovered treasury of Greek skepticism—the works of Sextus Empiricus—and undergoing a personal skeptical crisis. He had mottoes from Sextus carved into the rafter beams of his study and adopted as his own motto, "Que sais-je?" ("What do I know?"). In 1580 the first two books of the *Essays* were published. Besides writing, Montaigne tried in vain during the 1570s to mediate between the Catholics and the Protestant leader, Henri of Navarre (later Henri IV).

In 1580 Montaigne went to Paris to present a copy of his *Essays* to the king; he then set out on a trip to Germany, Switzerland, and Italy, which he describes in his *Travel Journal*. The following year he was called back from Italy to become mayor of Bordeaux, a post he held for four years. He then added material to his earlier *Essays* and wrote a third volume of them; the complete edition was first published in 1588 in Paris. Montaigne went to Paris and probably negotiated on behalf of Henri of Navarre concerning his succession to the throne, his conversion to Catholicism, and the temporary settlement of the religious wars, which was later incorporated into the Edict of Nantes. Illness apparently prevented Montaigne from joining Henri IV's court, but he continued to revise his *Essays*. The final version was published posthumously in 1595.

"APOLOGY FOR RAIMOND SEBOND"

Montaigne's most important philosophical work, the "Apology for Raimond Sebond," had an enormous influence on the subsequent history of thought. A superbly written presentation of skepticism, it formulated a challenge that affected Descartes, Pierre Gassendi, Bacon, and

many others and inspired monumental efforts to meet the challenge. The "Apology" gradually reveals a series of waves of doubt, continuously coupled with a new type of Christian fideism.

The essay begins with an account—probably not very accurate—of Montaigne's reasons for translating Sebond's *Theologia Naturalis*. Pierre Bunel, a Renaissance scholar, gave Montaigne's father a copy of the book, saying that it had saved him from Lutheranism. Long afterward, Montaigne's father asked his son to render it into French (from what Montaigne claimed was Spanish with Latin endings). After the translation appeared, Montaigne reported that some readers—mainly female—needed help in comprehending Sebond's contention that all the articles of the Christian faith could be established by reason. Two major objections to this thesis had been raised: the first held that Christianity should rest on faith rather than reason, and the second maintained that Sebond's reasons were not good ones. Montaigne purported to defend Sebond by showing that because all reasoning is unsound, Sebond's is no worse than anyone else's and, therefore, religion should rest on faith alone.

Montaigne held that people are vain, stupid, and immoral, and he pointed out that they and their achievements do not appear impressive when compared with animals and their abilities. The "noble savage" of the New World seemed to possess an admirable simplicity and ignorance that did not involve him in the intellectual, legal, political, and religious problems of the civilized European.

Montaigne suggested that our sole contact with the truth was due not to our intellect or reason, but rather to the grace of God; he agreed with St. Paul that ignorance is more useful than learning in acquiring truth. To show this, Montaigne examined the teachings of the ancient schools of philosophy and argued that those of the Pyrrhonists were the best and the most compatible with the Christian religion. All of the other philosophies were in conflict with one another, contained contradictions and absurdities, and relied on fallible human faculties and questionable premises to reach their conclusions. Only Pyrrhonists showed humans as naked and empty, portrayed their natural weaknesses, and by ridding them of their false or dubious opinions, left their minds a blank tablet, ready to receive whatever God might wish to write upon them. The modern Pyrrhonist would not be led into heresy, because he or she would accept no reasons or arguments that are open to question. In contrast to the Pyrrhonists, who suspended judgment on all matters, other philosophers offered their own opinions as genuine truths. They thought that they had discovered the real nature of things and had measured the universe in terms of their own systems; they were only deceiving themselves.

In the later portions of the "Apology," Montaigne presented the Pyrrhonistic evidence that everything is dubious and that genuine knowledge must be gained either by experience or by reasoning. We do not, however, know the essence of what we experience (for example, the real nature of heat), and we do not even know the nature of our own faculties. We are constantly changing as our physical and emotional conditions alter, and the judgments we make and accept at one time, we find doubtful at another. Not only does this seem to happen to each of us, but it also appears to be the fate of humans in general. Each alleged scientific discovery is superseded by another, and what is thought true at one time is regarded as false or silly at another.

The new sciences of Copernicus and Paracelsus claimed that the ancient sciences of Aristotle, Ptolemy, and others were false. How could we know, Montaigne asked, that some future scientist would not make similar claims, on equally firm grounds, about these new discoveries? These same variations and disagreements occur in every area of human concern.

Montaigne then presented the more theoretical objections that Sextus Empiricus had raised about the possibility of gaining knowledge. All of our alleged knowledge, he argued, appears to come from sense experience, but perhaps we do not possess the requisite number of senses for gaining knowledge. Even if we do possess all of them, the information we gain through them is deceptive and uncertain. Illusions lead us to wonder when our senses are accurate. Dreams are often so similar to sense experiences that we cannot tell if sense experience itself is not really a dream. Each of our experiences differs from that of animals, from that of other human beings, and even from our other experiences; we cannot, therefore, know when to accept an experience as accurate. Such conditions as illness or drunkenness distort what we perceive. Perhaps normal experience itself is a kind of distortion.

In order to determine the accuracy of our experiences, we require a criterion. But we need some way of testing that criterion, and this requires a second criterion to establish how to test it, and so on. If reason is to be the judge of our experiences, then we need reasons to justify our reason, and so on, to infinity. Thus, if our ideas come from our sense experiences, we are hardly in a position to use our ideas to judge the nature of objects. Our experiences and our ideas tell us only how things seem to be, but not necessarily how they are in themselves. Trying to know reality, Montaigne concluded, is like trying to clutch water. We can deal with the world only in terms of appearances, unless and until God decides to enlighten us. In our present state, we can only try to follow nature, living as best we can.

INTENTIONS AND INFLUENCE

Montaigne questioned and cast doubt upon almost all of humankind's beliefs in philosophy, theology, science, religion, and morality, and criticized almost every superstition and accepted view. He insisted that he was merely showing the human inability to find truth by means of natural capacities and the human need to rely on faith as the sole access to truth. Montaigne's own portrayal of the human predicament succeeded in intensifying the doubts already produced by the religious crisis of the Reformation, the humanistic crisis of the Renaissance, and the philosophical-scientific crisis of revived Pyrrhonism. The three currents were fused into a massive and forceful onslaught in this "Apology." Montaigne's formulation of skepticism and the more didactic one of his disciple, Pierre Charron, provided the issues for seventeenth-century thought. Some, such as François de La Mothe Le Vayer, were to follow out the more destructive and anti-intellectual tendencies of Montaigne's doubt. Others, such as Marin Mersenne and Gassendi, were to formulate a mitigated skepticism that could accept its doubts while seeking information about the world of appearances. Still others, such as Bacon, Herbert of Cherbury, and Descartes, were to seek new philosophical systems to provide for human knowledge a basis impervious to Montaigne's doubts.

Some have seen Montaigne as a skeptic, questioning religion with everything else, and as the founder of the critical spirit of the Enlightenment. They have taken his fideism as a mask for his actual views and have portrayed him as a genuine freethinker and free spirit. Others have interpreted his fideism as an expression of his own resolution of his doubts. Although Montaigne lacked the religious fervor of Pascal, who regarded him as a skeptical nonbeliever, many of his contemporaries and later admirers took his skepticism as part of the Counter-Reformation, because it opposed the reasons and arguments of the Reformers by undermining the validity of all reasoning.

Montaigne played a vital role in the development of both Christian skeptical fideism and of the so-called *libertinage*, a later movement of critical freethinking that preceded the Age of Reason. His views are compatible with both roles, in that his doubts neither imply nor contradict either a religious or an irreligious conclusion. He was probably mildly religious, accepting Catholicism in the light of the religious wars of his time. He apparently opposed fanaticism and wished for toleration of all sides, recognizing man as a fallible, limited creature struggling to live and comprehend with weak and uncertain capacities. Without God's assistance, man could only try to understand himself, guided by the past and the present. To understand himself and his situation would at least make him doubtful of radical proposals for solving everything, make him more tolerant, and—most important—make him capable of accepting himself and his fate. To philosophize, Montaigne said, was to learn to die.

See also Epistemology; Philosophy of Religion.

Bibliography

WORKS BY MONTAIGNE

The Essayes. Translated by John Florio. London, 1603. New York: Modern Library, 1933. The first English edition, probably known to Shakespeare and Francis Bacon.

The Essays. Translated by Jacob Zeitlin. 3 vols. New York: Knopf, 1934–1936. Good introduction and notes.

The Complete Essays of Montaigne. Translated by Donald M. Frame. Stanford, CA: Stanford University Press, 1958. The best modern translation, containing the essays, journals, and letters, plus an excellent introduction and annotated bibliography.

Œuvres complète. Paris: Gallimard, 1976.

Apologie de Raimond Sebond de la Theologia à la Théologie. Paris: Librairie Honoré Champion, 1990.

WORKS ABOUT MONTAIGNE

Allen, Don Cameron. *Doubt's Boundless Sea: Skepticism and Faith in the Renaissance.* Baltimore, MD: Johns Hopkins Press, 1964. Reasserts the irreligious interpretation of Montaigne. See chapter 3.

Boase, Alan M. *The Fortunes of Montaigne: A History of the Essays in France, 1580–1669.* London: Methuen, 1935. A study of Montaigne's impact.

Brahami, Frédéric. *Le scepticisme de Montaigne.* Paris: Presses universitaires de France, 1997.

Brunschwicg, Léon. *Descartes et Pascal, lecteurs de Montaigne.* New York: Brentano's, 1944. Shows the influence of Montaigne on both Descartes and Pascal.

Brush, Craig B. *Montaigne and Bayle: Variations on the Theme of Skepticism.* The Hague: Nijhoff, 1966. See chapter 3.

Busson, Henri. *Le Rationalisme dans la literature française de la renaissance (1533–1601).* Paris: J. Vrin, 1957. Interprets Montaigne as a freethinker and as part of an irreligious, rationalistic milieu.

Frame, Donald M. *Montaigne: A Biography.* New York: Harcourt, Brace, 1965.

Frame, Donald M. *Montaigne's Discovery of Man: The Humanization of a Humanist.* New York: Columbia University Press, 1955. A study of the development of Montaigne's thought.

Frame, Donald M. "What Next in Montaigne Studies?" *French Review* 36 (1963): 577–587. A survey of the state of scholarship on Montaigne and an evaluation of various interpretations.

Giocanti, Sylvia. *Penser l'irrésolution: Montaigne, Pascal, La Mothe Le Vayer, Trois itinéraires sceptiques.* Paris: Honoré Champion éditeur, 2001.

Laursen, John Christian. *The Politics of Skepticism in the Ancients, Montaigne, Hume, and Kant.* Leiden, Netherlands: Brill, 1992. See chapters 4 and 5.

Limbrick, Elaine. "Was Montaigne Really a Pyrrhonian?" *Bibliothèque d'Humanisme et Renaissance* 39 (1977): 67–80.

Malvezin, Théophile *Michel de Montaigne, son origine, sa famille.* Bordeaux: C. Lafebvre, 1875. Contains much data about Montaigne's background and environment.

Popkin, Richard H. *The History of Scepticism: From Savonarola to Bayle.* Rev. ed. Oxford, U.K.: Oxford University Press, 2003.

Popkin, Richard H. "Skepticism and the Counter-Reformation in France." *Archiv für Reformationsgeschichte* 51 (1960): 58–87. The role of Montaigne's skepticism in French Catholic theology of the time.

Strowski, Fortunat. *Montaigne.* 2nd ed. Paris: F. Alcan, 1931. The best-known scholarly modern French interpretation of Montaigne.

Villey, Pierre. *Les Sources et l'évolution des essays de Montaigne.* Paris: Hachette, 1908. Basic study of Montaigne's sources and the development of the *Essays.*

Villey, Pierre. *Montaigne devant la posterité.* Paris: Boivin, 1935. A study of how Montaigne has been interpreted.

Richard Popkin (1967, 2005)

MONTESQUIEU, BARON DE
(1689–1755)

The philosopher and political theorist Charles-Louis de Secondat, Baron de Montesquieu, afterward Baron de la Brède et de Montesquieu, was born at Labrède, near Bordeaux, in the year of the English revolutionary settlement that established the preeminence of Parliament. He was a follower of John Locke and the outstanding champion in France of the supposedly "English" notions of freedom, toleration, moderation, and constitutional government. He was also a pioneer in the philosophy of history and in the sociological approach to problems of politics and law. Honored in his own country, Montesquieu was even more revered in the English-speaking world. He described the constitution of England as "the mirror of liberty," and although his analysis of the English principles of government was generally considered defective by later historians, it was hailed as marvelously penetrating by English readers of his own time. Charles Yorke, the future lord chancellor, told Montesquieu, "You have understood us better than we understand ourselves." Moreover, the founders of several new political societies, notably that of the United States, were profoundly affected by Montesquieu's teaching. Especially influential was his theory that the freedom of the individual could best be guaranteed by the division of the powers of the state between three distinct organs that could balance and check one another—a separation of powers Montesquieu, rightly or wrongly, believed to be characteristic of the English system.

Montesquieu belonged to the *noblesse de robe*. Part of his design in recommending the separation of powers in France was to elevate the French aristocracy to a position comparable to that of the English, for whereas Rousseau believed that political liberty could be achieved only in a democracy and Voltaire believed it could best be achieved by a philosopher-king, Montesquieu held that liberty was most secure where there was a potent aristocracy to limit the despotic tendency of both the monarch and the common people. He believed that the way to preserve freedom was to set "power against power."

No one wrote with greater eloquence against despotism than did Montesquieu, yet he was far from sharing the conventional liberal outlook of the eighteenth-century *philosophes*. He had all the conservatism characteristic of the landowner and the lawyer. In many respects he was positively reactionary; for instance, he wished to strengthen rather than diminish hereditary privileges. But like Edmund Burke, whom he influenced considerably, Montesquieu was able to reconcile his reforming and reactionary sentiments by insisting that he sought to restore old freedoms, not promote new ones. He argued that the centralizing monarchistic policy of Louis XIV had robbed Frenchmen of their ancient liberties and privileges. The only kind of revolution Montesquieu advocated was one that would give back to the French Estates—and to the nobility and the *parlements* in particular—the rights they had enjoyed before the seventeenth century. The actual French Revolution, which sought to enfranchise the bourgeoisie and the common people and to bring about a variety of other innovations, was far from the sort of change that Montesquieu had favored, although he inadvertently did help to inspire the events of 1789 and after.

Montesquieu's parents were not well off. He inherited his title and much of his wealth from an uncle who at the same time bequeathed him the office of *président à mortier* of the *parlement* at Bordeaux. About the same

time his worldly position was further secured by a prudent marriage to a Protestant named Jeanne de Lartigue, who, although exceedingly plain in appearance, was heiress to a considerable fortune. Even so, Montesquieu remained an ambitious man, and, after twelve years as *président* in Bordeaux, he forsook his chateau and vineyards, to which he was deeply attached, and his wife, whom he loved perhaps rather less, to seek fame in Paris and to travel to other countries collecting material for his books. He was a success in the Paris salons, and although there seem to be no recorded examples of his wit in talking, he was celebrated as a conversationalist. He made friends with influential people and became the lover of the Marquise de Grave, among others. She inspired one of his early anonymous works, *Le temple de Gnide,* a mildly indecent erotic fantasy that was also a satire on the court of the infant Louis XV. After some difficulties Montesquieu was admitted to the French Academy in 1728.

He was on the whole a popular, but certainly not a generous, man. As a landowner he was most rigorous in the collection of even the smallest debts; at the same time he was slow to pay money he owed to others. In Paris he had a reputation for parsimony; more than one contemporary remarked that he "never ate at his own table." At his chateau, La Brède, English guests were struck by what they politely called the "plainness" of the fare, and Montesquieu even economized on the arrangements for the wedding of his daughter Denise. He once warned his grandson, "La fortune est un état et non pas un bien."

LES LETTRES PERSANES

Montesquieu made his name as a writer at the age of thirty-two with the publication of *Les lettres persanes* (1721). Presented in the guise of a series of letters sent from France by two Persian visitors, Usbek and Rica, and translated into French by Montesquieu, this book is a satirical attack on French values and institutions. It is written with great wit and skill. The Persian visitors begin by remarking on the strange customs of the French in such matters as cutting their hair and wearing wigs and reversing the Persian rule of giving trousers to women and skirts to men. They then proceed by degrees to express delicate amazement at the things the French choose to respect or hold sacred. They comment on the mixture of grossness and extravagance in the manners of Parisian society. Their sly digs at French politics are even more telling. They describe Louis XIV as a "magician" who "makes people kill one another even when they have no quarrel." The Persians also speak of "another conjuror who is called the Pope ... who makes people believe that three are only one, and that the bread one eats is not bread or that the wine one drinks is not wine, and a thousand other things of the same sort." The Spanish Inquisitors are described as a "cheerful species of dervishes who burnt to death people who disagreed with them on points of the utmost triviality." The revocation of the Edict of Nantes is likewise mocked, Louis XIV being said to have contrived "to increase the numbers of the faithful by diminishing the numbers of his subjects."

In the same book Montesquieu sought to establish two important principles of political theory—first, that all societies rest on the solidarity of interests and, second, that a free society can exist only on the basis of the general diffusion of civic virtue, as in the republics of antiquity.

Although Montesquieu attacked the manners of polite society in France, he did not fail to give *Les lettres persanes* a fashionable appeal. The two Persian travelers offer piquant descriptions of the pleasures of the harem and the sufferings of the women they have left behind them. Satire is nicely spiced with wit and the wit with impropriety, although this book is not quite so risqué as *Le temple de Gnide*. Montesquieu was said by Rutledge, one of his many admirers, to have "conquered his public like a lover; amusing it, flattering its taste, and proceeding thus step by step to the innermost sanctuary of its intelligence."

DE L'ESPRIT DES LOIS

Montesquieu's *Considérations sur les causes de la grandeur des Romains et de leur décadence* (1734), is a brilliantly written attempt to apply a scientific method to "historical understanding," to set forth—admittedly in a distinctly literary style—a sociological explanation of one phase of historical experience as a model for a new kind of positivistic history. This book is perhaps best read as a prolegomenon to Montesquieu's masterpiece, *De l'esprit des lois*, on which he worked for seventeen years.

De l'esprit des lois was first published in Geneva in 1748 against the advice of all the friends to whom Montesquieu had shown the manuscript. It was promptly placed on the Index, but it sold twenty-two editions in less than two years. It was a resounding success. Even so, it is a long, rambling, ill-arranged book that reflects the developments and changes in the author's point of view in the seventeen years he took to write it. But like *Les lettres persanes* and the *Considérations*, it is the work of an unmistakable master of French prose and of a man who knows how to entertain his readers as well as to instruct them.

By the *esprit des lois*, Montesquieu meant the raison d'être for laws, or the rational basis for their existence. Like Locke, he believed in natural law, but he was a much more thoroughgoing empiricist in his method than was Locke. Montesquieu believed that the way to learn about law was to look at the actual legal systems in operation in various states. Formal recognition of natural rights did not mean that men had positive rights. Mere a priori principles have little real value; it is important, he argued, to have the actual verifiable facts of the situations in which men find themselves.

Similarly, in his approach to the question of freedom, Montesquieu was less interested in abstract assertions of a general concept than in the concrete circumstances in which freedom had been or was being enjoyed. "Liberty," he wrote, "has its roots in the soil." He noted that freedom is more easily maintained in mountainous countries, such as Switzerland, than in fertile plains, and on islands, such as England, than on continents. Island and mountainous states find it easier to defend themselves from foreign invasion; in mountainous countries the very poverty of the soil encourages industry, frugality, and independence and so promotes individualism among the people. Another condition of freedom, he suggested, is that tranquility which comes from security. This can be enjoyed only where the constitution sets inviolable limits to the action of the state and where the law itself guarantees the rights of the individual.

Montesquieu always insisted that political liberty could never be absolute. "Freedom," he wrote, "is the right of doing whatever the laws permit." For example, he maintained that free trade did not mean that traders should do what they liked, for that would be to enslave the nation. Restrictions on traders were not necessarily restrictions on trade but might well be measures conducive to the liberty of all. Good laws were those that protected the common interest, and it was the mark of a free society that all the people be allowed to follow their own inclinations as long as they did not disobey the laws.

THE CONCEPT OF LAW

Montesquieu gives a rather bewildering definition of laws as "necessary relations," or "the relations which necessarily follow from the nature of things." Like most philosophers before David Hume, he failed to distinguish clearly between the normative laws of morals and the descriptive laws of science, but he was nevertheless conscious of having two tasks in seeking the raison d'être of laws. On the one hand, he was embarking on a sociological study of existing legal and political institutions, including the institutions of positive law. Here Montesquieu the empiricist came to the front. On the other hand, Montesquieu the rationalist and the votary of natural law was seeking beyond his inductive generalizations for some general principles of justice and conduct, which he believed to be founded on reason.

> I first of all examined men, and I came to the conclusion that in the infinite diversity of their laws and customs they were not guided solely by their whims. I formulated principles, and I saw particular cases naturally fitting these principles: and thus I saw the histories of all nations as the consequence of these principles, with every particular law bound to another law and dependent on a further more general law.

At the highest level of abstraction, Montesquieu saw a uniform law—"Men have always been subject to the same passions"—but in various societies this higher natural law is expressed in differing systems of positive law. The systems differ because the external conditions differ. Montesquieu made much of the differences of climate and attempted to describe how different climates promote different customs, habits, economic arrangements, and religions. Much of political wisdom consists in adapting general principles to local circumstances. Solon was right to give people "the best laws they could bear."

The measure of relativism in Montesquieu affronted his friends among the *philosophes,* who believed in a kind of abstract universal individualism, but Montesquieu's method proved the more acceptable to social theorists of later generations. Émile Durkheim said it was Montesquieu who gave modern sociology both its method and its field of study. Montesquieu was ahead of his time in regarding social facts as valid objects of science, subject to laws like the rest of nature; he was also ahead of his time in seeing social facts as related parts of a whole, always to be judged in their specific contexts.

VIEWS ON RELIGION

Montesquieu resisted the notion that a "scientific" approach to problems of human conduct entailed determinism. He believed that God existed and that God had given men free will. "Could anything be more absurd," he asked, "than to pretend that a blind fatality could ever produce intelligent beings?" Assuredly, God had laid down the laws that govern the physical world, and "man, as a physical being, is, like all other bodies, governed by immutable laws." On the other hand, precisely because he is a rational, intelligent being, man is capable of transgressing certain laws to which he is subject. Some of the laws he transgresses are his own laws, namely positive laws, but governing the conduct of men are other laws antecedent to positive laws, and these are the general "relations of justice" or, in a more conventional term, natural law.

Montesquieu's attitude toward religion was very like that of Locke. He did not believe in more than a few simple dogmas about the existence of God and God's benevolence, but to that minimal creed he clung with the utmost assurance. On the other hand, Montesquieu grew to be much more cautious than Locke in his criticisms of religious institutions. In *Les lettres persanes,* Montesquieu did not hesitate to mock the Roman Catholic Church and clergy, but in later years he took care to avoid provocative utterances on the subject. In his biography of Montesquieu, Robert Shackleton gives an example of the philosopher's increasing wariness as revealed in successive drafts of the *Esprit des lois.* In the first draft of the chapter on religion, Montesquieu wrote, "Under moderate governments, men are more attached to morals and less to religion; in despotic countries, they are more attached to religion and less to morals." In the second draft Montesquieu introduced at the beginning of that sentence, "One might perhaps say that ...." In the published version he cut out the remark altogether.

Much has been made of the fact that Montesquieu was reconciled to the Church of Rome on his deathbed. An Irish Jesuit named Bernard Routh got into the chateau at La Brède during Montesquieu's last illness, and in spite of the efforts of the Duchess d'Aiguillon to prevent him from "tormenting a dying man," the priest succeeded (or, at any rate, claimed to have succeeded) in leading the philosopher back to the path of devotion and repentance. The pope himself read Father Routh's account of Montesquieu's death "with the deepest reverence and ordered it to be circulated." Madame d'Aiguillon was able to rescue from the clutches of the Jesuits only one manuscript, that of the *Lettres persanes.* "I will sacrifice everything for the sake of reason and religion," Montesquieu had told the duchess, "but nothing to the Society of Jesus."

These dramatic scenes are perhaps less important to an understanding of Montesquieu's religious sentiments than is his behavior in less emotional times. He never asked his wife to give up her Protestantism, and he was always a fervent champion of religious toleration. At the same time, he remained on the best of terms with his several relations who were in holy orders in the Catholic Church. Besides, according to his "sociological" principle that every country had the religion its geographical and climatic conditions demanded, Montesquieu held that

Catholicism was the "right" religion for France, just as Anglicanism was the "right" religion for England. This is not to say that Montesquieu inwardly believed in more than a fraction of the teachings of the Catholic Church or that—until his deathbed repentance—the church regarded him as a true son. But he always detested atheism. To him the idea of a universe without God was *effroyable*. The concept of a loving creator played as prominent a part in his political theory as it did in that of Locke; indeed, whereas Locke had been content to see the church apart from the state, Montesquieu favored an alliance of organized religion with the government. In *Esprit des lois* he suggested that Christian principles, well engraved in the minds of the people, would be far more conducive to a good political order than either the monarchist notion of honor or the republican notion of civic virtue. Montesquieu was thus a deist in his heart and an Erastian in his politics.

See also Burke, Edmund; Durkheim, Émile; Locke, John; Philosophy of History; Political Philosophy, History of; Political Philosophy, Nature of; Rousseau, Jean-Jacques; Voltaire, François-Marie Arouet de.

Bibliography

WORKS BY MONTESQUIEU

Oeuvres de Montesquieu, 7 vols. Edited by E. Laboulaye. Paris, 1875–1879.

De l'esprit des lois, 2 vols. Edited by G. Truc. Paris, 1945.

Spirit of the Laws. Translated by Thomas Nugent. New York, 1949.

Oeuvres complètes, 3 vols. Edited by A. Masson. Paris, 1950–1955.

Considerations on the Causes of the Greatness of the Romans and their Decline. Translated by David Lowenthal. New York: Free Press, 1965.

WORKS ON MONTESQUIEU

Actes du congrès Montesquieu. Paris, 1956. Introduction by L. Desgraves.

André, Desiré. *Les écrits scientifiques de Montesquieu.* Paris, 1880.

Aron, Raymond. "Montesquieu." In *Main Currents in Sociological Thought,* Vol. I, translated by Richard Howard and Helen Weaver. New York: Basic, 1965.

Barrière, P. *Un grand provincial.* Bordeaux, 1946.

Berlin, Isaiah. "Montesquieu." In his *Against the Current: Essays in the History of Ideas,* edited by Henry Hardy. New York: Viking Press, 1980.

Cabeen, D. C. *Montesquieu: A Bibliography.* New York: New York Public Library, 1947.

Carrithers, David W., Michael A. Mosher, and Paul A. Rahe, eds. *Montesquieu's Science of Politics: Essays on "The Spirit of Laws."* Lanham, MD: Rowman & Littlefield, 2001.

Cotta, S. *Montesquieu e la scienza della societa.* Turin, 1953.

Dedieu, J. *Montesquieu, l'homme et l'oeuvre.* Paris, 1913.

Destutt de Tracy, Comte Antoine-Louise-Claude. *Commentary and Review of Montesquieu's Spirit of Laws.* Translated by Thomas Jefferson. Philadelphia: Burt Franklin, 1969.

Dodds, Muriel. *Les récits de voyages: Sources de l'Esprit des lois de Montesquieu.* Paris, 1929.

Durkheim, Émile. *Montesquieu et Rousseau.* Paris, 1953. Translated by Ralph Manheim as *Montesquieu and Rousseau.* Ann Arbor: University of Michigan Press, 1960.

Fletcher, F. T. H. *Montesquieu and English Politics.* London: Arnold, 1939.

Hulliung, Mark. *Montesquieu and the Old Regime.* Berkeley: University of California Press, 1976.

Manent, Pierre. *The City of Man.* Translated by Marc A. LePain. Princeton, NJ: Princeton University Press, 2000.

Pangle, Thomas L. *Montesquieu's Philosophy of Liberalism: A Commentary on the Spirit of the Laws.* Chicago: University of Chicago Press, 1973.

Richter, Melvin. *The Political Theory of Montesquieu.* Cambridge, U.K.: Cambridge University Press, 1977.

Shackleton, Robert. *Essays on Montesquieu and on the Enlightenment.* Edited by David Gilson and Martin Smith. Oxford: Voltaire Foundation at the Taylor Institution, 1988.

Shackleton, Robert. *Montesquieu: A Critical Biography.* London: Oxford University Press, 1961. The outstanding work on Montesquieu.

Shklar, Judith N. *Montesquieu.* Oxford: Oxford University Press, 1987.

Sorel, A. *Montesquieu.* Paris, 1887.

Maurice Cranston (1967)
Bibliography updated by Philip Reed (2005)

MONTGOMERY, EDMUND DUNCAN
(1835–1911)

Edmund Duncan Montgomery, a Scottish-American philosopher, anticipated in his "philosophy of vital organization" ideas of emergent evolution, the energetic nature of matter, and the pragmatic functioning of knowledge. Born in Edinburgh, he studied medicine in Germany in the 1850s, did research on cell pathology in London in the 1860s, and emigrated to America in 1870 with his sculptor wife, Elisabet Ney.

After a short-lived communitarian experiment at Thomasville, Georgia, the Montgomerys settled on Liendo Plantation, near Hempstead, Texas. There Montgomery wrote most of his philosophical articles and, in his later years, took an active role in community affairs. As chairman of the Waller County Democratic Party in the 1896 Bryan-McKinley campaign, he argued the dependence of political liberty upon economic reforms.

By 1867 Montgomery saw life as a power of certain compounds to reintegrate their chemical unity after damage, a power evolved by the inherent creativity of matter interacting in new combinations. He tested views of matter, mentality, selfhood, knowledge, and morality by this touchstone in over sixty articles in such journals as *Mind, Monist, Index, Open Court,* and the *International Journal of Ethics* and in five books. His major book was *Philosophical Problems in the Light of Vital Organization.*

Even inorganic compounds, Montgomery said, are inherently reactive, evolving in unpredictable ways by virtue of their peculiar composition and organization. Conservation of energy is thus wrongly viewed as requiring inertness of matter. Mentality is not dependent on a separate substance but is a capacity of certain complex organisms (chemical unities of a high order), heirs of evolution through foregone ages. Human knowledge and action are products of man's interplay with environment; they are instruments in preserving and enhancing well-being.

Some data of consciousness, such as kinesthetic and emotive states, seem to derive in each of us only from his own body, even though the body's activity thus perceived is in turn activated by outside stimuli. Others of our conscious states (such as visual data) are occasioned by features of either our own bodies or of external objects. Montgomery denied that this difference warrants the inference that there are two distinct kinds of substance, mental and material. All inferences from sensory data are conjectural. Data do not copy things but give "hieroglyphic signs" that permit discovery, prediction, and testing of natural relations among things.

Montgomery argued for a "naturalistic humanitarianism," a "religion of life," stressing ethical self-determination in a struggle against indifferent and hostile forces, to convey to the next generation a heritage nobler than the one received. Making common cause with those who wanted a religion and an ethic consistent with scientifically established knowledge, he added to classic criticisms of prevailing theologies and moral systems his own emphasis upon their failure to heed the full potentialities of men, the preeminent heirs of an evolution far from completed.

See also Consciousness.

Bibliography

WORKS BY MONTGOMERY

On the Formation of So-Called Cells in Animal Bodies. London, 1867.

Die Kant'sche Erkenntnislehre widerlegt vom Standpunkt der Empirie. Munich, 1871.

The Vitality and Organization of Protoplasm. Austin, TX: Gammel-Statesman, 1904.

Philosophical Problems in the Light of Vital Organization. New York and London: Putnam, 1907.

The Revelation of Present Experience. Boston: Sherman, French, 1910.

WORKS ON MONTGOMERY

A complete bibliography of writings by and about Montgomery before 1950 and an index of writings by and about him appear in Morris Keeton, *The Philosophy of Edmund Montgomery* (Dallas, TX: University Press in Dallas, 1950). The definitive biography is I. K. Stephens, *The Hermit Philosopher of Liendo* (Dallas, TX: Southern Methodist University Press, 1951).

Morris Keeton (1967)

MOORE, GEORGE EDWARD
(1873–1958)

George Edward Moore was born into moderately affluent circumstances in Upper Norwood (a suburb of London), the third son of D. Moore, M.D., and Henrietta Sturge Moore. The Sturges were prominent Quaker merchants and philanthropists. On his father's side there had been some tendency toward, and some prominence in, the practice of medicine.

Upon reaching eight, George Edward Moore commenced attendance at Dulwich College, a boarding and day school of excellent reputation located within walking distance of his home. In the ten years of his attendance there he acquired a thorough mastery of the classics. It was also at this time that he underwent a very painful experience. Having been converted around the age of twelve to "ultra-evangelism," he felt it his duty to preach the word of Jesus and to distribute religious tracts. He found these activities extremely repugnant and suffered much inward torment in carrying them out. This experience, which lasted two years or more, may account in some measure for his subsequent coolness to religious enthusiasms of any sort. Before leaving Dulwich College he was persuaded, through discussions with his eldest brother, the poet Thomas Sturge Moore, to adopt the view that was then known as "complete agnosticism." This seems to have been the view that there is no evidence in support of a belief in God's existence and almost as little in support of a belief in his nonexistence. So far as can be determined from his writings, Moore never departed from this view.

In 1892 Moore entered Trinity College, Cambridge, as a student in classics. At the beginning of his third year he changed his major concentration to philosophy and completed the moral science tripos in 1896. On the basis of a dissertation treating Immanuel Kant's ethics he was elected in 1898 a fellow for a term of six years. During the period 1898–1904 he carried on frequent and consequential discussions with Bertrand Russell, wrote *Principia Ethica,* presented several papers to the Aristotelian Society (to which he had been elected), and published a number of reviews and articles.

With the termination of his fellowship in 1904, Moore left Cambridge. Because of an inheritance he was still able to pursue his philosophical activities. He wrote articles, papers, and reviews, as well as the small volume *Ethics,* and gave a series of private lectures at Richmond. In 1911 he was invited to return to Cambridge as university lecturer. He lectured regularly at Cambridge from 1911 to 1925, first on philosophical psychology and later on metaphysics. In 1925 he succeeded James Ward as professor of mental philosophy and logic. His courses appear to have enjoyed a good deal of popularity among the more serious students of philosophy and had an immense influence upon the philosophizing going on in England at the time, as did his publications (notwithstanding that they consisted entirely of articles and papers).

In 1939, having reached the mandatory age of retirement, Moore gave up his professorship at Cambridge, though not his philosophical activities. These, with a few interruptions due to illness, he carried on to almost the very last years of his life, writing articles, editing his previous writings, working on problems, and holding discussions with friends and students. He died at Cambridge at eighty-five, survived by his wife, Dorothy Ely, whom he had married in 1916, and two sons, Nicholas, a poet, and Timothy.

Although Moore's life was extremely active in academic and philosophic spheres, it was almost without incident otherwise. Except for a brief sojourn in Germany in the summer of 1895, a somewhat longer stay in Scotland from around 1904 to 1908, and a couple of years spent during World War II lecturing in the United States, he resided entirely in England, mainly in or near Cambridge. His most noticeable personal trait appears to have been his intense and passionate absorption in philosophy. It is said, for example, that when discussing a question, whether with his professional peers or with a student, he gave himself wholly to the inquiry and viewed its progress with the constant fresh surprise of one considering a matter for the first time. Another trait that has been commented on was his lack of any intellectual pretensions (in spite of a formidable erudition) and an almost childlike naïveté concerning ordinary affairs.

Moore served as editor of the philosophical journal *Mind* from 1921 to 1947. The major honors that he received during his lifetime were the Litt.D. from Cambridge (1913), the honorary degree of LL.D. from the University of St. Andrews and election as a fellow of the British Academy (1918), and appointment to the Order of Merit (1951).

FORMATIVE PERIOD OF MOORE'S PHILOSOPHY

Moore's published philosophy falls into two distinct parts, divided by the year 1903. Although the writings published prior to 1903 are few and cover no more than five years, at least three different philosophical positions can be detected in them. In his first publication, a paper titled "In What Sense, if Any, Do Past and Future Time Exist?" (1897), Moore agreed wholly with F. H. Bradley. He argued that time does not exist, and he did so using Bradley's methods and premises, in particular the dogmas of internal relations and concrete universals and the principle that identifies reality with the absence of contradiction. When his conclusions, like the one that time does not exist, proved to outrage common sense, Moore was prepared to say that common sense is simply wrong, and he did so more than once.

One year later, in the essay "Freedom," Moore replaced Bradley with Kant as the philosopher with whom he was "in most agreement." What he agreed with most in Kant was the method of the transcendental exposition and the doctrine of synthetic necessary truths. He did not agree with the critical restrictions of Kant's philosophy or with what he took to be its psychological bias. He contended, for instance, that Kant was wrong in trying to conceive freedom in terms of the will (a psychological concept); freedom is rather to be understood and explained in terms of the idea of Transcendental Freedom, into which temporal relations do not enter. Thus, while accepting much of Kant's system and terminology, Moore continued to speculate in the critically unrestricted manner of the absolute idealists, maintaining that a reality transcending time and the senses is something that can be theoretically known and that must be theoretically known before the major problems of philosophy can be solved.

The next year, 1899, in the article "The Nature of Judgment," Moore adopted a third position. As part of his continuing attack upon psychologism in philosophy (an attack he shared at the time with Russell), he proposed the doctrine, adumbrated in Thomas Reid, that mental acts and their objects are entirely separate existences. Applying this doctrine to Bradley's analysis of judgment, Moore concluded that the entire world—everything we can either think of or perceive with our senses—consists in qualitative universals, or what he called "adjectival concepts." These universals compose propositions, material objects, minds, and all other "complex objects." Not only do some universals (for example, red) exist through time, but some propositions also exist through time and are even objects of perception (for instance, the proposition that this book is red). Such universals and propositions are designated "empirical universals and propositions," as opposed to those that do not exist through time, such as the concepts *two* and *attribute,* which are called "a priori." This bizarre metaphysics, which might be termed "absolute realism" because according to it universals not only exist but, in fact, comprise everything that does exist, obviously repudiates all the major philosophical tenets to which Moore subscribed in his first essay: the dogmas of the nonreality of time, internal relations, concrete universals, and the transcendent monism that springs from them. Just as obviously it cannot be harmonized with the two-story world of phenomena and noumena that is attributed to Kant or with Kant's critical conclusions. Moore did, however, attempt to show that his realistic principles were compatible with, and even substantiated, Kant's method of transcendental exposition and distinction between a priori and empirical propositions and the doctrine of synthetic necessity. This Moore did by attempting to show that the possibility of a priori and empirical propositions, along with synthetic necessary truths, can be accounted for in terms of the realistic distinction between temporally existing (empirical) universals and nontemporal (a priori) universals and by shaping some of the arguments supporting this demonstration along the lines of a transcendental exposition. On the whole, though, the argumentation of "The Nature of Judgment," as well as of the articles and reviews that immediately followed (1899–1902), proceeds in the legislative, dogmatic manner of Bradley.

With this unstable amalgam of Bradley, Kant, and absolute realism, the first period of Moore's philosophizing came to a close. Marked by abrupt changes of doctrine, by either derivativeness (as in the first two positions adopted) or bizarreness (as in the third), it is recognizably an effort to find, rather than to express, a philosophy. It is therefore with some justice that these writings have been generally ignored by succeeding generations of philosophers, as they were ignored by Moore himself in his sub-

sequent summations and compilations of his work. On the other hand, a complete understanding of Moore's later philosophy is difficult to arrive at without some familiarity with these earlier works. It will then be understood, for instance, that the charge sometimes leveled against Moore that he criticized the metaphysical theses of philosophers like Bradley piecemeal, without attempting to comprehend them fairly and in their entirety, is groundless. It will be understood, for instance, that in attacking items of Bradley's metaphysics Moore was attacking not only a system of thought with which he was thoroughly conversant but one to which he had himself once been most strongly attracted.

MOORE'S PHILOSOPHY PROPER

The system of philosophical thought and method that has come to be associated with Moore's name and that he was alone concerned to defend issued fully formed in the volume *Principia Ethica* and the essay "The Refutation of Idealism" in 1903. This is not to say that no alterations thenceforth took place in the body of Moore's philosophical doctrines and aims. They did. For example, with the passage of time Moore became increasingly concerned with eliminating from the world various entities, such as propositions, that his principles generate. The theory proposed in "The Refutation of Idealism," that we directly perceive material things, was replaced by a disjunction of theories respecting the relation between sense data and material things. And the note of philosophical optimism that expressed itself in *Principia Ethica* and "The Refutation of Idealism" in the view that solutions to the problems under discussion have either been completed in their pages or are on the brink of completion finally gave way to a note of philosophical pessimism and puzzlement. But in its main outlines what might be called Moore's philosophy proper was now permanently formed.

As will be seen in subsequent discussion, the tenets of this philosophy are largely based on the principle that sentences such as "I think of X" describe (*a*) mental acts and (*b*) objects related to but distinct from those acts. From 1903 until the late 1930s Moore almost invariably interpreted this principle realistically, and even after the late 1930s, when he was prepared to admit that the *esse* of sense data is *percipi*, this realist tendency continued to make itself felt in his philosophizing, especially with respect to universals. Moore's philosophy proper resembles, therefore, the absolute realism of "The Nature of Judgment." There exists, however, a fundamental metaphysical difference between the two positions. This difference lies in the fact that Moore's absolute realism of 1899 is reductionistic, being the view that everything can be resolved into qualitative universals, whereas the realism he enunciated in 1903 and afterward is, in intention at least, nonreductionistic. Thus, within the compass of things that are, Moore now included both particulars—for example, material things—and universals, and though he was not perfectly clear about just what a universal or a particular is, he wanted to maintain neither that universals can be resolved into particulars nor that particulars can be resolved into universals. His new view was that each sort of thing is what it is and nothing else (or, in the words of Bishop Butler, quoted on the frontispiece of *Principia Ethica,* "Everything is what it is, and not another thing").

The most striking and significant difference between Moore's philosophizing prior to 1903 and his philosophy proper lies not, however, in doctrine or even in the mechanics of method (though differences here are pronounced) but in the attitude and style of his philosophizing. These now project the familiar picture of Moore: the picture of a cautious and probing observer, attempting by the patient dissection and scrutiny of minute and hardly distinguishable objects to set straight the confused descriptions by philosophers of what is the case. This posture of Moore's lends to his philosophizing the appearance of a completely empirical inquiry whose conclusions represent only what is found or not found to be the case, as opposed to what is merely thought to be or not to be the case. It is in the solvent of this empiricist posture that Moore's initial philosophical optimism, as one might predict, evaporated into pessimism and puzzlement. For the principle from which it originated, that sentences such as "I perceive *X*" describe acts of mind and distinct objects, is itself something no amount of observation would seem to confirm or lend substance to.

In the first of the lectures that he delivered in 1910–1911, some forty years later published under the title *Some Main Problems of Philosophy,* Moore listed the main topics of philosophy as three. The first and primary aim of philosophy, he said, is to provide a metaphysical inventory of the universe, that is, "a general description of the *whole* of this universe, mentioning all the most important kinds of things which we *know* to be in it, considering how far it is likely that there are in it important kinds of things which we do not absolutely *know* to be in it." The second aim is epistemological: to classify the ways in which we can know things. The third topic of philosophy is ethics.

In "A Reply to My Critics," published in 1942, Moore again divided his philosophical discussion into three parts: ethics, theory of perception, and method. Although this alteration in the classification of topics indicates certain real alterations in Moore's interests and views, it will be convenient to treat his philosophy proper under the five heads mentioned: method, metaphysics, general epistemology, theory of perception, and ethics.

METHOD. By Moore's "method" will be understood the topics encompassed by the following: (1) The question: What did Moore believe he was doing in philosophizing, that is, what project did he think he was engaged in? (2) The question: How did he attempt to carry out this project? (3) Certain questions that are often raised in specific connection with Moore's method, such as: What is the role of common sense in his method? What is the role of analysis?

Moore's intentions. It has been suggested by some of his commentators that what Moore was trying to do was to analyze ordinary language, to defend common sense, or to recommend ways of speaking. As an answer to the question What was Moore *actually* doing? it is possible that one or all of these suggestions may be true. But it is clear that none of them describes what Moore believed he was doing.

Moore's conception of what he was doing originated in the following two principles, to which he consistently subscribed: the principle that sentences like "I think that *P*" and "I perceive *X*" designate acts of consciousness, on the one hand, and objects related to but distinct from those acts, on the other; and the principle that every object of consciousness is either a simple, in which case it is unanalyzable, or a complex, in which case it always possesses a definable essence in terms of which it is the sort of thing it is and not some other sort of thing. The first principle makes it appear as if there should be discoverable as the objects of consciousness a great many more kinds of entities and properties than persons ordinarily envisage, and these entities and properties should comprise, at least in part, what is objectively in the universe. When applied to these entities, the second principle makes it appear as if every complex object should be unequivocally reducible to simples. But this picture of things raises a question: If the constitution of the universe is both so determinate and so open to consciousness, why is it that there has been so much disagreement and confusion in the attempts of philosophers to describe it? And to this question the most obvious answer seems to be that past errors and confusion in philosophy have arisen either from inattention on the part of philosophers to the objects of their consciousness or from a lack of clarity and preciseness in their statements and questions.

In fact, the two major concerns of Moore through the period 1903–1911 directly correspond to the above outline of subject matter. Primarily, Moore wished to determine what sorts of entities or properties fall within the province of his particular inquiry, for example, ethics, theory of perception; to classify these entities (where deemed necessary) as simples or complexes; and to analyze the essences of the complexes. Second, and always as a project subordinate to the first, he wished either to direct the reader's attention to the objects of consciousness that pertain to the inquiry at hand or to lay bare the ambiguities and unclarities of the terms customarily used by philosophers in conjunction with the inquiry at hand, and to supply "precising" definitions of the terms that he intended to use.

After the lectures of 1910–1911 an increasing concern with terminological questions was detectable in Moore's writing. This concern is traceable to an apparently growing conviction on his part (as well as on the part of his contemporaries) that the terminological sources of philosophical error and confusion are much more subtle, deeply rooted, and pervasive than he had originally thought and much more intimately connected with the logical grammar of ordinary language. In the last connection it is worth recalling that certain of Moore's contemporaries eventually decided that the root and cure of all philosophical problems lay in terminological confusion and clarification.

Moore never went so far as to assent to the last conclusion. He did, however, relinquish his earlier view that the primary concern of philosophy is to observe and delineate the entities objectively making up the universe. By 1940, when he composed his "Reply to My Critics," he described himself as engaged, not in the analysis of facts, but in the analysis of concepts. Although he was unclear about what the relation is between concepts, the entities objectively making up the universe, and verbal expressions, he appears to have thought that concepts are not only distinct from and (at least from their side) independent of their verbal expressions but also distinct from the entities objectively making up the universe (for otherwise, in analyzing concepts, he would be resolving philosophical doubts and questions in a way that he agreed that one cannot do and that he was not doing). But just what, then, are concepts according to Moore? In "A Reply to My Critics" he did not say. It is not improbable, however, that Moore had come full circle, back to

something like Bradley's psychologically grounded view of concepts, which, ironically, served in "The Nature of Judgment" as the launching platform for Moore's philosophy of realism.

Moore's procedure. In much the same way that Moore's doctrine of mental acts and objects dictated his conception of what he was trying to do, it also dictated his conception of how to accomplish what he was trying to do. It is evident, for instance, that once sentences like "I think that *P*" and "I perceive *X*" are interpreted according to that doctrine, it must seem unjustified to argue in the legislative manner of Bradley, which Moore employed in "The Nature of Judgment" and the essays previous to it. If the objects of acts of judging, perceiving, and thinking are entities distinct from, and indeed independent of, those acts, then whatever we can learn about those objects must be by means of synthetic observations, not a priori thought. Moore throughout his philosophy proper adhered to this viewpoint. Where he conceived himself as primarily engaged in reporting, classifying, and analyzing the entities objectively constituting the universe, he assumed that he was basing his reports and analyses on observation. Where, as in "A Reply to My Critics," he conceived himself as engaged rather in analyzing concepts, it is evident that he thought of concepts as comprising some sort of object he was engaged in observing.

As was noted previously, this picture of philosophical inquiry suggests that philosophical questions have determinate and easy solutions that it might be expected all philosophers will agree on. Moore's explanation of this discrepancy between expectation and fact—that the disagreements and failures of philosophers stem either from a lack of attention to what is present to their consciousness or from terminological unclarities—suggests, in turn, that in order to be certain we are observing what we think we are we must make sure both that our attention is directed to the right objects and that we know the precise meanings of the terms we are employing in our thoughts.

It turns out, however, that even with this supplement observation fails to bring about the results that Moore anticipated or that his assumptions might have led him to anticipate. The answers to philosophical questions remain stubbornly shrouded in obscurity and disagreement. Moore was therefore compelled to add to his methods and procedures. In cases where he felt there was no conclusive answer to a question, he resorted to what might be termed the principle of weighted certainties. If, for instance, he felt that proposition *A* possessed more certainty than proposition *B*, or if he felt that he knew the truth of *A* with more certainty than that of *B,* he would refuse to deny the truth of *A* on account of some argument based on *B.* In short, a lesser certainty (according to this principle) cannot rationally overturn a greater certainty per se (though a number of lesser certainties, cohering together, may). Moore also employed, in the same connection, the scholastic method of citing all the plausible arguments that can be advanced for or against a thesis in order to indicate its degree of credibility. And finally, in order to discredit a thesis (usually a thesis of skepticism), he employed either a *reductio ad absurdum* argument or what might be called a paradigm argument. He pointed out, for example, that the skeptic who maintains that we cannot know there are other persons is already contradicting himself by supposition in referring to the plural, *we.* Or he argued that if such-and-such is not an instance of knowing, then no one has ever known anything and there cannot be such a thing as knowing.

When these norms for evaluating philosophical conclusions are arranged in order of their indefeasibility, it would seem that where observation unequivocally reveals just what a thesis represents to be the case, according to Moore the thesis is indefeasible. Thus, Moore maintained that when we look at an inkwell we directly perceive a sense datum and that this claim is indefeasible in that observation unequivocally presents us with a sense datum. Where a thesis can be shown to contain an evident contradiction, according to Moore it is conclusively disproved. Thus, one can affirm with certainty that the skeptic who maintains that *we* cannot know other persons exist is wrong. Where the principle of weighted certainties or the method of citing plausible arguments has to be invoked, Moore would generally grant that answers are not conclusive or indefeasible, although there may be more to be said in favor of one answer than another. In certain cases, however, it would appear that the certainties or feelings of certainty (Moore rarely distinguished between the two) attaching themselves to a thesis are so absolute or overpowering that no denial of the thesis is either psychologically or rationally (in view of the principle of weighted certainties) possible.

Common sense. It is tempting, but wrong, to suppose that because Moore defended common sense, common sense constitutes a court of last appeal in his philosophy. Indeed, the very fact that he described himself as defending common sense indicates that it cannot.

In his works Moore used the term *common sense* to refer to two different, but related, things. He sometimes meant by it, he said, simply those beliefs that men universally or almost universally subscribe to at some particular epoch. At other times he meant either those beliefs that we are naturally inclined to hold or the propensity that issues in such beliefs.

Although there may exist a very intimate causal connection between these two forms of common sense, they are not one and the same thing. As the "universal" belief of men at a particular epoch, common sense can change, and Moore in fact argued that it can. As a natural tendency to believe something, common sense would not seem susceptible of change. It must be remarked, however, that Moore never explicitly drew the above distinction or attempted to "analyze" the notion of common sense beyond saying that it consists in the universal belief of men at a particular time. In practice, however, he would seem to have maintained that although both forms of common sense possess a certain amount of presumptive credibility, it is essentially as a natural tendency that common sense provides a foundation for philosophical conclusions. It does this in two ways. When we try to deny the latter form of common sense we find it virtually impossible to do so because what we naturally tend to believe keeps slipping into our assertions. We thus find ourselves contradicting ourselves by supposition, like the skeptic who says that *we* cannot know persons exist. On the other hand, what we naturally tend to believe will have attached to it some degree of certainty. This degree varies, it seems, from an absolute quantity, which makes dissent really impossible, to a quantity that only inhibits dissent. For example, Moore said he was naturally disposed to think that what he always saw directly when viewing a material thing was the surface, or part of the surface, of the material thing, but he finally decided it would be nonsense to maintain that he did.

Moore, then, defended common sense by showing that certain beliefs that we are naturally inclined to hold, and consequently that most men do hold, are supported by the principle of weighted certainties or by showing that the traditional counterclaims of skeptics are self-contradictory. He did not argue conversely that because a certain belief is a belief of common sense it is ipso facto indisputably true or need not be subjected to assessment.

Analysis. When Moore described himself as "analyzing," he conceived of himself as picking out and naming the essential constituents of complex objects. In his earlier works he viewed himself, when analyzing, as picking out and naming the essential constituents of various objective entities and facts; in his later works, as picking out and naming essential constituents of various complex concepts. In his reply to C. H. Langford in "A Reply to My

Critics," he explicitly denied that he ever engaged in the analysis of verbal expressions.

This last denial may not be disingenuous, but it is misleading. Moore maintained that the only proper meaning of the term *analyzing verbal expressions* is merely counting the letters in a sentence, noting the order of the letters, and so on. If this is true, then obviously Moore never engaged in analyzing verbal expressions, and just as obviously his denial that he did is trivial.

It may therefore be more significant to ask whether Moore engaged in linguistic analysis, where "linguistic analysis" is used as a technical term designating the following practices or inquiries: the determination of the meaning of a word or expression (not excepting the determination of its dictionary meaning); the determination of the various senses of a word or expression; the determination of the ordinary use of a word or expression; and the determination of discrepancies between the philosophical and ordinary uses of a word or expression. In all these senses of the technical term *linguistic analysis*, Moore, it is clear, engaged frequently in linguistic analysis. However, as was pointed out previously, he engaged in linguistic analysis never as an end in itself but always as an inquiry subordinate to the ascertainment of facts or the determination of the essential constituents of things or concepts.

METAPHYSICS. By the term *metaphysical* Moore sometimes meant to refer to nonnatural objects or qualities, that is, objects or qualities that are constituents of the universe but not of temporal events (or nature); sometimes he meant to refer to the sort of philosophical inquiry that concerns itself with the overall constitution of the universe. It is in the latter sense that the term *metaphysics* is being used here.

Although not without expressing some doubts on the matter, Moore inclined to the view that the things to be *found* in the universe are broadly of two sorts: those things that exist and those that simply *are* but do not exist. A third class of things consists of those that neither exist nor are; they simply are not. As Moore conceived of these categories, the main ontological division is between the things that are and those that are not. For the former, whether they exist or simply are, comprise the objective constituents of the universe and have equal claim to philosophical investigation. The latter are merely "chimeras" or "imaginary objects."

Moore suggested at least three ways of distinguishing between things that are and things that are not. First, the former possess the property of being; the latter do not.

Second, borrowing from Russell's theory of descriptions, Moore claimed that whereas an object that *is* or possesses *being* can be the bearer of a name, imaginary objects can be described only by incomplete symbols. Thus, for example, "centaur" is not the name of anything (for there is nothing to bear the name), whereas "chair" is a name. Third, if a thing's *esse* is *percipi*, then it is an imaginary object and actually *is not*. There are only thoughts of centaurs, for example; there are not centaurs independent of our thoughts. Hence, centaurs are imaginary objects. Moore, however, discovered difficulties with the last description in that he thought it likely that the *esse* of acts of consciousness and sense data is *percipi*, and at the same time he did not want to say that acts of consciousness and sense data *are not*.

Where he did distinguish between mere being and existence (and in places he did not), Moore generally cited two grounds as the basis for the distinction. Sometimes he argued that whatever endures through parts of time exists; what does not endure through parts of time does not exist. He also sometimes argued that whatever can be an object of sensory perception exists. Although he never discussed the connection between these two criteria for existence, it seems from what he said on other matters that the temporal criterion states both a necessary and a sufficient condition for existence, whereas the sensory criterion states but a sufficient condition. For in Moore's system it is possible that material things are never the contents of sensory perception, but they are, par excellence, things that exist.

In addition to existence, being, and nonbeing, Moore treated at length and in detail the category of *reality*. Although painstakingly carried out, his thoughts on this subject possessed little overall coherence. In *Principia Ethica* he equated reality with existence; in the lectures of 1910–1911 he equated it simply with *being*. In the same lectures he referred to reality as a property; on the other hand, in *Philosophical Studies*, in the essay "The Conception of Reality" (1917), he denied that reality is a property. What he consistently maintained is expressed in his rejection of Bradley's view that reality possesses degrees and that the highest degree of reality is at an extreme remove from material things. Moore denied that reality possesses degrees. But if it does, he said, then he wanted to maintain, in opposition to Bradley, that material things possess the highest degree of it.

Within the category of *being* Moore distinguished between three kinds of objects: particulars, truths or facts, and universals. He generally, though not always, argued as if particulars may be divided into five sorts:

material things, sense data (for instance, *patches* of yellow), acts of consciousness, volumes of space, and intervals of time. He did not appear to think that the term *mind* refers to a particular substance in which acts of consciousness inhere. The theory he seemed to favor is that acts of consciousness are located in material bodies and are properties of material bodies and that the word *mind* stands for something like a logical construction from acts of consciousness. Truths or facts are the objects of true beliefs and comprise such things as mathematical equations—for example, 2 + 2 = 4—and the references of indicative sentences, such as "Tom stood to the left of Henry." Universals are again divisible into three sorts: relations, relational properties, and a third sort of universal that is neither a relation nor a relational property. Moore never provided an essential description of this third sort of universal, but he cited as clear-cut examples of it numbers and nonnatural qualities or objects, such as *good,* and as possible examples of it shades of color.

Of the three sorts of *being*—that is, particulars, facts, and universals—particulars alone exist; facts and universals merely *are*: This, at least, was Moore's view when he was prepared to grant that a significant distinction holds between existence and mere being. It was also his view that the only *substantial* things we are acquainted with are material bodies and acts of consciousness.

It should be remarked that the above inventory of the universe was not considered by Moore to be exhaustive. There may be things in the universe that we are in fact ignorant of or must even necessarily remain ignorant of. For example, Moore thought it is not impossible that God exists but found no evidence for maintaining that he does. Moore described himself as being certain, though, that all the things that have been mentioned as *being* or *existing* do constitute at least some of the constituents of the universe.

GENERAL EPISTEMOLOGY. Although a number of the topics that have been treated under the heading of Moore's methodology might as reasonably be considered under the heading of his general epistemology, and vice versa, under his methodology it was asked what Moore in his philosophizing was attempting to do and how he was attempting to achieve his aims, whereas under his epistemology these quite different questions are being asked: (1) What, according to Moore's philosophic account, does knowledge consist in? (2) Does knowledge, as so conceived, exist, and if it does, what is it knowledge of?

(1) What does knowledge consist in? Moore's basic metaphysical and methodological principles dictate that

in order to discover what knowledge is, it is necessary to distinguish between the different senses (if there are different senses) of the verb "to know" and then to pick out and analyze the particular objects denoted by these senses of "to know" and the relations (if any) that hold between them.

Throughout his earlier writings and the lectures of 1910–1911, Moore was convinced that careful observation of facts and careful differentiation of terms provide us with the following results. First, every instance of cognition ultimately consists in an act of consciousness and, distinct from the latter, in an object. Second, an act of consciousness can exist only as long as the corresponding instance of cognition exists. Thus, when I cease to see a sense datum, my *seeing* of it ceases to exist. The object of cognition, however, may or may not exist after the act of consciousness to which it is related ceases. This is a matter to be decided by empirical considerations. Third, it is conceivable that an act of consciousness and its related object—for example, a sense datum—exist in two different locations. "It seems to me conceivable," wrote Moore in *Some Main Problems of Philosophy,* "that this whitish colour is really on the surface of the material envelope.... My seeing of it is in another place—somewhere within my body."

Reflecting this analysis of cognition and its objects, Moore thought that he could pick out four different ways of knowing and, corresponding to them, four different senses of the verb "to know." First and basic to an understanding of any other sense of "to know" is the sense in which "to know" stands for cases in which the relation between the object cognized and its correspondent act of consciousness is similar to or identical with the relation that a patch of color has to the consciousness of a person seeing that patch of color. This is knowledge by direct apprehension or knowledge by acquaintance. A second sense of "to know" represents cases in which the relation between the object cognized and the correspondent act of consciousness is similar to or identical with the relation that, for example, a hat on a table has to the act of consciousness of a person who is remembering that his hat was on the table. Thus, he knows that his hat was on the table, but neither the hat and table nor any sense data that were connected with the hat and table are directly present to his consciousness. This is knowledge by indirect apprehension. At least until 1911, Moore described himself as uncertain whether knowledge by indirect apprehension always necessitates direct apprehension of a proposition, by means of which, following Russell's theory of knowledge by description, one is made aware of the object indirectly apprehended, but he was inclined to think it does. Third, there is a sense of "to know" that represents cases in which the following complex relation between acts of consciousness and objects holds: there is an act of consciousness; there is a proposition directly apprehended; this proposition is in fact true; we believe that it is true; and we believe that it is true because of some further relation or condition that it satisfies. What this further condition is Moore left undecided, though one might plausibly suppose that it had to do with conclusive evidence. In any event, Moore termed this way of knowing "knowledge proper." Last, and involving the previous senses of "to know," is that sense of "to know" in which we describe a person as knowing something, such as the multiplication table, even though he may not at the time be conscious of anything. We imply, in such cases, that the person in question has at some time known, in one of the other three senses of "to know," the multiplication table.

Moore also distinguished between what he termed "immediate knowledge" and "knowledge by direct apprehension." Immediate knowledge is a species of "knowledge proper." Thus, immediate knowledge is distinguished from knowledge by direct apprehension in that the latter does not require the presence of a proposition (for instance, I can directly apprehend sense data), whereas the former does. It is specifically the "kind of way in which you know a proposition to be true—really know it, not directly apprehend it—when you *do not* know any other proposition from which it follows" (*Some Main Problems of Philosophy*).

(2) Does knowledge exist? and of what things? Since Moore, purportedly on the basis of observation, resolved knowledge into a certain complex of objects, it is evident that knowledge, or "acts of knowing," exists in his view. The question of its existence becomes, indeed, a psychological or introspective question (it would seem) rather than an epistemological one.

In dealing with the question of what sorts of things are known, Moore generally, however, treated it as a de jure or epistemological, rather than a de facto or psychological, question. Thus, in defense of asserting that such-and-such a sort of thing can be known, he would sometimes appeal to the principle of weighted certainties (for example, he would ask, "Which is more certain—that I know that I am holding a pencil in my hand or that the principles of the skeptic are true?") and sometimes to paradigm arguments of the sort "If I do not know that P, then I can know nothing." In this connection, it is worth noting that Moore sometimes argued de jure that we know such-and-such a sort of thing exists although he was unable to discover by introspection the way in which we know it. For instance, he insisted that we know the existence of material things, such as the earth and our own body and other bodies like it, but he was unable to determine with any certainty in just what way we know their existence.

Moore claimed that in addition to the existence of material things, we know the existence of our own acts of consciousness and our own sense data, past events in our lives, the being of universals and nonnatural qualities or entities (such as good), the existence of other minds, synthetic necessary truths, and practically all matters of fact that are commonly thought to be known—for instance, that Caesar crossed the Rubicon, that Earth goes around the sun, and so on. Thus, in contrast to the skeptic, who traditionally maintains that the circumference of knowledge is much smaller than people ordinarily think, Moore appears to have maintained that it is much larger than people ordinarily think. For it is doubtful that people ordinarily think they know the existence of some things called sense data and acts of consciousness or the being of some things called nonnatural qualities or universals.

THEORY OF PERCEPTION. It is apparent that Moore's general epistemological principles and the premises that he operated with in his methodology enforce an empiricist approach to knowledge. They imply that all knowledge must finally be based on the observation of objects presented in experience. In three respects, however, Moore consistently parted company with traditional empiricists. He refused to limit the term *experience* to mean simply sensory experience. That is, he wanted to maintain that many sorts of objects other than those discovered by the senses are the objects of acts of consciousness—for example, timeless facts, relational universals, and nonnatural qualities. He also wanted to maintain (following Kant) that there are necessary synthetic truths and that we can apprehend these truths. And finally, he was never willing to reject what seemed to him a certain truth—for instance, that he was holding a pencil—because some less certainly true analyses or philosophical principles were incompatible with it. Thus, he consistently refused to acquiesce in the skeptical conclusions that traditional empiricism and indeed, it seems, his own empiricist principles tend to establish.

At the same time, these principles seem to have had two distinct effects on Moore's overall philosophizing. First, as time passed his interests converged on theory of perception and questions concerning our knowledge of an external, material world. Second, the skeptical conclusions that empiricism appears to foster produced a constantly widening cleavage in his philosophy between what he wanted to assert preanalytically to be certainly true and what his analyses permitted him to assert to be certainly true. This ever-growing cleavage is nowhere more apparent than in his theory of perception.

In his essay of 1903, "The Refutation of Idealism," Moore maintained that material things can be directly apprehended and therefore can be known to exist with as much certainty as one's own acts of consciousness. Soon afterward, however, Moore was led to change his mind on this crucial point, apparently by what has sometimes been referred to as the argument from synthetic incompatibility. This argument assumes that the looks of things are the objects a person directly perceives, and then, because the looks of things change when the thing itself is not presumed to be changing, the argument concludes that what a person directly perceives is not the material thing or a part of its surface but some other kind of object that possibly exists only when he is perceiving it. This "other kind of object" is called by Moore a sense datum.

Moore had trouble in deciding just what a sense datum is: whether it is a particular or a universal, whether it is something like a color (in the case of visual sense data) or some other sort of thing. His final position on this question would seem to be that a visual sense datum is a *patch* of some color: The patch, which is a particular, is related to the color, which is a universal of the third sort (that is, it is neither a relation nor a relational property) in the way something is related to that which, in part, is spread over it.

The main problem concerning Moore in his theory of perception was not this, however, but the question of the relation between sense data and the material things to which they "belong." Although Moore concerned himself with this question in a series of remarkably closely reasoned essays, commencing with "The Status of Sense-Data" (1914) and concluding with his last published article, "Visual Sense-Data" (1958), he was never able to arrive at a definite or even a very plausible answer. Throughout most of these essays he presented three alternative theories as possibly true: phenomenalism, or what he termed the Mill-Russell theory—that is, the view that a material thing is simply a "logical construction" of sense data; some form of representational theory (varying from the theory that the relation between sense data and material things is an unanalyzable relation of "appearing" to causal theories resembling John Locke's); and the theory that visual sense data are identical with parts of the surfaces of material things. With all these alternatives he found grave difficulties and, indeed, was led in the end to dismiss the last as constituting, at least in most cases of perception, nonsense. But if we do not directly perceive material things or their surfaces (and Moore was willing to grant that perhaps we never do), and if by "material things" is meant nothing so Pickwickian as a logical construction of sense data (and Moore would have tended to agree that nothing so Pickwickian is meant), how can we possibly know that material things exist? Moore, in one of his last lectures, "Four Forms of Scepticism," suggested none too plausibly that we know their existence by analogical or inductive arguments.

ETHICS. As in the other branches of his philosophy, Moore was confident in his earlier works on ethics of the correctness and finality of the results he set forth; this confidence diminished constantly in the solvent of his empiricist methods of inquiry and was replaced in his later works by no more than tentative agreement with his earlier views. Also, as in the other branches of his philosophy proper, Moore's viewpoint toward both the proper method of ethical inquiry and the nature of the findings to be anticipated stemmed directly from his originally realist presuppositions.

Ethics, as Moore conceived of the discipline, takes the form of a partly definitional, partly descriptive science, resting on observation and induction. His theory is not, however, naturalistic. The fundamental object of observation for ethics, goodness, is a nonnatural quality or entity, according to Moore, and thus is one that neither exists through parts of time nor presents itself through sensory experience. On the other hand, his theory is not "metaphysical": it does not purport to *define* this fundamental entity or quality of ethics in terms of some *other* nonnatural entity or quality. Indeed, a main point of Moore's theory is that the fundamental entity of ethics cannot be defined at all and that any attempt to define it must commit what he termed "the naturalistic fallacy." This is essentially the fallacy that results from construing the "is" of attribution as an "is" of identity, and thus supposing, for example, that because pleasure is (attributive "is") good, good is identical with pleasure.

The fundamental object of ethics is the simple quality or entity good; being simple, good is unanalyzable and indefinable. One can only say that good = good. This is the outcome of the first and most basic inquiry any science of ethics must engage in, the answer to the question What is good?, where this ambiguous question is understood to ask for a definition.

A second important inquiry that the science of ethics undertakes is to determine what are the preeminent goods obtainable by men. Since the term *good* is here being used substantively (and not adjectively) to refer to complex wholes to which the quality or entity *good* attaches, definitions or analyses of such goods are possible, in the sense that the parts making up the wholes in question can be set forth. On the other hand, because the quality "good" is indefinable, it is not possible to determine which things are and which are not good analytically. This can be determined only by perceiving which wholes possess good, and to what degree or amount. Since they do not rest on any external evidence, such perceptions were termed by Moore "intuitions," and it is for this reason that his theory of ethics is sometimes called "intuitionistic." A further character of these perceptions is that when we perceive that a certain whole possesses in itself a certain amount of good, we perceive at the same time that any similar whole must possess in itself an equal amount of good. Thus propositions of the sort "Such-and-such possesses in itself such-and-such amount of good" or "Such-and-such is intrinsically good" express truths that are both synthetic and necessary.

The determination of what things are preeminently good is complicated by two factors. First, substantive goods are organic unities or wholes; that is, the good of a whole is not simply equal to the sum of the goods of its parts. This makes it impossible to determine what things are good and in what amount merely by determining previously the amount of good attaching itself to basic units of experience and adding up these units. Second, it is in fact difficult to separate, in our perceptions or intuitions, organic wholes from their consequences; hence, in assessing goods-in-themselves we are likely to include the good accruing to causal consequences of those wholes. In order to avoid the last sort of error, Moore proposed that we isolate the organic unity we are concerned with by imagining it as alone existing in the universe and then asking whether it is better that it exists or does not.

Applying this method to the question What are the preeminent goods obtainable by men? Moore maintained that "it is obvious that personal affection and aesthetic enjoyments include by far the greatest goods with which we are acquainted."

The third major inquiry of ethical science encompasses the questions of traditional casuistry: What are our duties? What is their order of precedence? What actions as a rule are right?, and so forth. The answers to all these questions are predicated, in Moore's system, on the assumption that unlike the term *good*, the terms *right*,

duty, virtue, and so on are definable. They are all, in fact, definable in terms of good. When we say that a certain sort of action is right or our duty *we mean* that it is productive of the greatest amount of good in comparison with any possible alternative action. Thus, in determining duties and right actions we must not only determine what things are good in themselves but what causal effects actions will have, and this is an almost impossible task, except when conceived in rather short-term measures. As so conceived, Moore generally argued that the rights and duties enjoined and sanctioned in conventional morality are indeed just what the science of ethics shows to be our rights and duties.

CRITICISM OF MOORE'S PHILOSOPHY PROPER

Moore, in his last writings, confessed that he had not been a good answerer of questions, and if by a "good answerer to a philosophical question" is meant one who leaves the question settled or seemingly close to being settled, it is hard not to agree. In his ethics Moore provided simple, clear-cut answers to the problems and questions of traditional ethics, but their very simplicity (like saying the world is made of water) produces its own disbelief, and this disbelief is borne out by subsequent reflection. For example, if good is a simple objective quality of some sort, why should persons be concerned with maximizing it? In the other branch of inquiry with which he was primarily concerned, theory of perception, Moore failed even to provide clear-cut answers or decisions.

Again, if by "good philosophical answers" are meant answers that can be formed into a consistent system, it must be agreed that Moore is not a good answerer. In his philosophy there are a great many loose ends that he never tied together or attempted to tie together. For instance, he made no attempt to tie together his discussions of the two questions What is the relation of sense data (i.e., patches) to universals? and What is their relation to material things? In the same connection, Moore sometimes admitted that he was inclined to hold at one and the same time two incompatible views (as on the question whether the surfaces of material things are directly seen) and was unable to choose between them.

On the other hand, if a good philosophical answer is conceived as one that is closely reasoned and demands and instills close reasoning on the part of its auditor or reader, then Moore was a good answerer. Studying Moore, it can be fairly said, is like holding one's mind to a whetstone: A mind composed of good stuff is bound to be sharpened (and one of poor stuff to be dulled).

Further, if philosophy is conceived as an inquiry rather than a closed system, Moore was a good answerer. It is the essence of inquiry that every problem considered be freshly considered, that pat answers be abjured, that truth be placed ahead of remaining consistent or reaching conclusions, and that alternatives be given a hearing and their merits weighed. These are precisely the virtues of Moore's philosophizing.

A more serious objection that can be urged against Moore is that there are a certain number of philosophical prejudices that he adopted without question, but that he ought to have questioned. It is arguable, for instance, that he adopted without question the principle that there is something called an act of consciousness and something called an object of that act. Applied to the various topics of philosophy, this principle produces all sorts of obvious nonsense: a ridiculous proliferation of entities, and so on. Why, it may be asked, did Moore not seriously question this presupposition and remove it? And if he had, might he not have arrived at sound conclusions instead of the perplexity that he does in fact arrive at?

There is unquestionably a good deal of justice in this last objection. Yet, with some justice too, one may retort on Moore's behalf: "What other principle *seems* as certainly true as the above principle? Has some alternative assumption permitted philosophers to arrive at indisputably true conclusions? And if not, why should Moore not explore the resources of this principle, which seems true to him, just as other philosophers explore the resources of the principles they have accepted, which seem equally true to them?"

See also Being; Bradley, Francis Herbert; Common Sense; Consciousness; Definition Empiricism; Epistemology, History of; Error; Ethics, History of; Existence; Experience; Good, The; Idealism; Kant, Immanuel; Locke, John; Metaphysics; Paradigm-Case Argument; Pessimism and Optimism; Presupposing; Propositions, Judgments, Sentences, and Statements; Realism; Russell, Bertrand Arthur William; Sensa; Universals, A Historical Survey; Ward, James.

Bibliography

WORKS BY MOORE

Except in ethics, Moore's major published philosophical writings consist almost entirely of articles, papers (to be delivered), reviews, and compilations of articles and lectures. Exceptions would be his autobiography (a minor masterpiece in its genre) and "A Reply to My Critics," included in the collection of critical essays concerning Moore's philosophy titled *The Philosophy of G. E. Moore*. In this bibliography, the more important or influential articles of Moore's are noted in the compilations in which they occur.

Principia Ethica. London: Cambridge University Press, 1903.

Ethics. London: Williams and Norgate, 1912.

Philosophical Studies. London: Routledge, 1922. Collection of papers, including "The Refutation of Idealism" (1903), "The Status of Sense-Data" (1914), "The Conception of Reality" (1917), "Some Judgements of Perception" (1918), and "External and Internal Relations" (1919). It is in the last paper that the term *entailment* is first used and defined philosophically.

The Philosophy of G. E. Moore. Edited by P. A. Schilpp. Evanston, IL: Northwestern University Press, 1942; 2nd ed., New York, 1952. Contains "An Autobiography" and "A Reply to My Critics." In the second edition is the "Addendum to My 'Reply.'"

Some Main Problems of Philosophy. London: Allen and Unwin, 1953. Contains Moore's lectures of 1910 and 1911.

Philosophical Papers. London: Allen and Unwin, 1959. With an obituary notice by C. D. Broad. Includes "A Defense of Common Sense" (1923), "Is Existence a Predicate?" (1936), and "Proof of an External World" (1939).

The Commonplace Book, 1919–1953. Edited by Casimir Lewy. New York: Macmillan, 1962.

WORKS ON MOORE

Bridge, Ursula, ed. *W. B. Yeats and T. Sturge Moore, Their Correspondence, 1901–1937.* London, 1953. In this correspondence the two well-known poets (one of them Moore's brother) refer at some length to Moore's philosophy and some of Moore's comments on their interpretations of his philosophy. Although of little philosophical interest, their references provide an amusing picture of nonphilosophers trying desperately to understand Moore. Typical is Yeats's remark "I find your brother extraordinarily obscure."

Keynes, John Maynard. *Two Memoirs.* London: Hart-Davis, 1949. In the second memoir, "My Early Beliefs" (pp. 78–103), Keynes describes the members and discussions of the "Bloomsbury Club," c. 1903–1914. This is a fascinating, witty, and informative account of the tremendous influence Moore's *Principia Ethica* had on some of the finer and younger intellects of the early twentieth century in England; of their attempts, largely verbal, to put Moore's ethical theories into some sort of practice; and of Moore's role in the group, his method of verbal argument, and the "pure and passionate intensity" of his realistic "vision."

Malcolm, Norman. *Knowledge and Certainty.* Englewood Cliffs, NJ: Prentice Hall, 1963. "George Edward Moore," pp. 163ff. In the first part of this important essay Malcolm presents a penetrating and intimate description of Moore's character as a man and as a philosopher, based in large part on personal recollections and impressions. In the remaining parts he discusses the relationship of certain of Moore's "common-sense propositions" to the concept of common sense, to traditional philosophy, and to Wittgenstein's views on the proper role of philosophy with respect to ordinary language. Included is a philosophic evaluation of Moore's purported defense of common sense. This essay is notable not only for the light it sheds on some central aspects of Moore's philosophizing but for the original philosophizing that it contains on the topics of ordinary language, the concept of common sense, and traditional skepticism concerning perception.

Passmore, John. "Moore and Russell." In *A Hundred Years of Philosophy*. London: Duckworth, 1957. Passmore presents a very searching account of Moore's earlier philosophy (especially as set forth in the 1899 essay "The Nature of Judgment") and his later views on the "analysis of meaning." Passmore also discusses, in an interesting and illuminating way, Moore's theory of sense data and his essays "The Refutation of Idealism" and "Proof of an External World."

Schilpp, P. A., ed. *The Philosophy of G. E. Moore* (see above). Contains critical essays on Moore's ethics by C. D. Broad, Charles L. Stevenson, William K. Frankena, H. J. Paton, Abraham Edel, and A. Campbell Garnett; on his theory of perception by O. K. Bouwsma, C. J. Ducasse, Paul Marhenke, and C. A. Mace; on what might broadly be called his method by Arthur E. Murphy, C. H. Langford, Norman Malcolm, Morris Lazerowitz, Alice Ambrose, John Wisdom, Richard McKeon, and V. J. McGill; and on his influence by L. Susan Stebbing. A number of the essays referred to, such as Bouwsma's "Moore's Theory of Sense-Data," are in their own right important contributions to the topics under discussion. But even when not intrinsically important, these essays constitute a particularly valuable commentary on Moore's philosophy in that Moore, in his "Reply," entered into several detailed discussions of their contents in an attempt to clarify his views. See especially his replies to the essays by Broad, Stevenson, Frankena, Bouwsma, Ducasse, and Langford.

Urmson, J. O. *Philosophical Analysis, Its Development between the Two World Wars*. Oxford: Clarendon Press, 1956. A penetrating work on the "analytic movement" that helps one place Moore in his later philosophical setting. Although only fragmentary references are made to Moore's philosophy, many of the points of view and many of the topics that Moore was concerned with and that influenced his own philosophizing (from 1910 on) are brought into the open and clarified.

Warnock, G. J. "G. E. Moore." In *English Philosophy since 1900*. London, 1958. This thin commentary propagates the thesis that Moore's philosophy can best be understood and appreciated through an understanding and appreciation of his temperament and character. The claim is made that Moore was a "man with no metaphysical quirks of temperament."

White, A. R. *G. E. Moore, a Critical Exposition*. Oxford, 1958. This work—the only English work of book length devoted exclusively to commentary on the philosophy of Moore—collects and collates most of the things Moore had to say on method, theory of ethics, and theory of perception.

John O. Nelson (1967)

MOORE, GEORGE EDWARD [ADDENDUM]

G. E. Moore's ethical writings, especially *Principia Ethica* of 1903, have long been regarded as philosophically revo-lutionary. In fact, Moore shared his main ethical views—nonnaturalism in metaethics and ideal consequentialism in normative ethics—with such late-nineteenth-century writers as Henry Sidgwick and Hastings Rashdall. But Moore defended these views with unusual vigor and so had a disproportionate influence on later moral philosophy.

Moore's nonnaturalism comprised two main theses. One was the realist thesis that moral judgments are objectively true or false; the other was the autonomy-of-ethics thesis that moral judgments are sui generis, neither reducible to nor derivable from nonmoral judgments such as scientific or metaphysical ones. Our knowledge of them must therefore derive from intuitive judgments of self-evidence.

Moore did not argue extensively for realism. Like others of his era, he took it largely for granted. But his argument for the autonomy of ethics has come to be known as the "open-question argument." If goodness were identical to pleasure, the claim that pleasure is good would be equivalent to the empty statement that pleasure is pleasure, which it plainly is not. Rather, whether pleasure is good is always an open question. Since this argument generalizes to all nonmoral properties, goodness cannot be identical to any such property. Some later philosophers challenged this argument against the "naturalistic fallacy"; others took it to support antirealist conclusions quite different from Moore's. But it remains a central argument for the irreducibility of moral claims.

Though these main theses were familiar, Moore did introduce two innovations. One was his view that the central irreducible moral property is *good* rather than *ought* or *right*; the other was that the intrinsic goodness can depend only on its intrinsic properties, apart from any relations to other states. It follows that to judge whether a given state is good, we must imagine a world containing only that state and ask whether such a world is good.

Moore's ideal consequentialism likewise comprised two theses. One was that right acts always produce the most good. The other was that there is a plurality of goods, all ideal in the sense that their being good does not depend on people's attitudes to them. (Moore thought that the naturalistic fallacy led philosophers to identify goodness with some one natural property and so to miss this plurality.) In *Principia Ethica* he held that one intrinsic good is beauty apart from any consciousness of it; another is vicious people's deserved pain. But the chief goods in this work were the admiring contemplation of beauty and personal love, which for Moore involved the admiring contemplation of others' good qualities. In characterizing both goods, he used his "principle of organic unities," according to which the value of a whole need not equal the sum of the values of its parts. Beauty on its own has little value, and the contemplation of merely imagined beauty just moderate value, but the contemplation of real beauty has great value, more than the sum of the values of those components.

Principia Ethica was written with a self-confidence bordering on arrogance. Moore thought most previous moral philosophers had made crude conceptual errors, and that once those were exposed, the moral truth would be self-evident to all. This tone helped make his presentation of nonnaturalism the canonical one. As a result, twentieth-century metaethics can be seen as a sequence of reactions to his views. His substantive views about the good received less attention, but at the beginning of the twenty-first century, interest has revived in his claims about, for example, appropriate attitudes and organic unities. His moral philosophy is again alive as a whole.

See also Ethics, History of; Good, The; Intrinsic Value; Intuitionism, Ethical.

Bibliography

WORKS BY MOORE

Principia Ethica. Cambridge, U.K.: Cambridge University Press, 1903.

"The Conception of Intrinsic Value." In his *Philosophical Studies*. London: Routledge and Kegan Paul, 1912.

The Elements of Ethics, edited by Tom Regan. Philadelphia: Temple University Press, 1991.

WORKS ON MOORE

Baldwin, Thomas. *G. E. Moore*. London: Routledge, 1990. See especially chaps. 3–4.

Frankena, William K. "The Naturalistic Fallacy." *Mind* 48 (1939): 464–477.

Hurka, Thomas. "Moore in the Middle." *Ethics* 113 (2003): 599–628.

Hutchinson, Brian. *G. E. Moore's Ethical Theory: Resistance and Reconciliation*. Cambridge, U.K.: Cambridge University Press, 2001.

Regan, Donald H. "How to Be a Moorean." *Ethics* 113 (2003): 651–677.

Regan, Tom. *Bloomsbury's Prophet: G. E. Moore and the Development of His Moral Philosophy*. Philadelphia: Temple University Press, 1986.

Shaver, Robert. "*Principia* Then and Now." *Utilitas* 15 (2003): 261–278.

Thomas Hurka (2005)

MORAL ARGUMENTS FOR THE EXISTENCE OF GOD

From the time of Immanuel Kant to the present day, a great many attempts have been made to base arguments for God's existence not upon the mere fact that there is a world, nor on the general orderliness it manifests, but on a very special feature of that world—human moral experience. The popularity of moral arguments is not hard to understand. David Hume and Kant had produced powerful and apparently disabling criticisms of the traditional arguments of natural theology, criticisms that seemed decisive against any conceivable type of argument to God as the explanation of the world. Hume had no alternative theistic argument to offer and, insofar as theoretical reasoning is concerned, Kant had none either. The structure of Kant's ethical philosophy, however, accorded to "practical reason" privileges not shared by theoretical reason. If God was to retain any place in the Kantian system, the weight of apologetic had to be shifted from the theoretical to the practical, to exploring the implications of our moral situation. Between Kant's day and the middle of the twentieth century, skepticism about the theoretical arguments tended to deepen rather than to lighten; hence, there has been no lack of religious apologists following Kant's new "moral route" to God.

Another reason for the popularity of moral argument is religious rather than philosophical. Even if the argument to God as First Cause or "necessary being" were valid, these notions of deity can be more of an embarrassment than a help to the religious imagination. They present us with a divine object or superobject, whereas religion demands that God be primarily known as *person*. A moral argument offers hope of overcoming that external and thinglike character: It ensures that concepts of God will be, from the outset, personal concepts.

TYPICAL MORAL ARGUMENTS

Among the many varieties of moral argument, the following are both historically important and recurrent patterns. Several of them may be found in a single author.

First, if one understands moral rules as "commands," one may argue to the existence of a "commander." The commander cannot be the individual human moral agent, for what today I command myself to do, I can tomorrow command myself not to do. I can have absolute moral obligations only if a God exists to command them. Because I do have absolute moral obligations, it follows that God exists.

Second, a minor variant of this moral argument claims that if we recognize moral authority, we must ipso facto recognize the existence of God as alone able to confer that authority. We judge that the moral law retains its authoritativeness whether particular human wills are at any time actually accepting its rules and principles or not; therefore, the source of its authority must lie altogether outside those human wills.

Third, the notion of "moral law" itself is said to be incomplete without reference to God, for law implies "lawgiver," a divine legislator. Our very acknowledgment of a moral law, therefore, presupposes theism.

Fourth, it has been claimed that there is a remarkable degree of agreement among the moral judgments made by men in widely different cultures and historical periods. Many apparent disagreements can be attributed to differences in belief and thus held to be not fundamental. This impressive measure of agreement, it is argued, can be accounted for only on the supposition that God has written his law in the hearts of men.

Certain of the most interesting and influential moral arguments take as their premise some part of the content of the moral law itself. We are under moral obligation to perfect ourselves and to attain a "highest good" (summum bonum) that is manifestly unattainable in a life lived under the conditions we know here and now. We can, at best, make a start to a moral development that requires very different conditions for its completion. But since that complete development is demanded of us as duty, it must be attainable. God and immortality are thus presupposed in our actual moral experience.

ANALYSIS OF MORAL ARGUMENTS

Let us briefly consider each of the varieties of moral arguments again and attempt to estimate their strengths and weaknesses.

Of the moral commander argument we can pertinently ask: Is the notion of command basic to ethics? Certainly not in the sense of parade-ground commands, commands passively received and acted upon unreflectively. Such obedience is a long way from moral deliberation and judgment. An immature moral agent may see his duties as commands (parental, for example); but the mark of mature moral judgment is self-commitment to a policy on which one has deliberated. This policy may or may not be in harmony with someone's command; in any case, it does not owe its authenticity to its being commanded. "Here I stand," one may say; and this can express

a settled resolution, one not to be made one day and rescinded the next.

Even if it were established that a celestial being unvaryingly commanded a certain policy as obligatory in an absolute sense, the unvaryingness of his command could not itself furnish the ground for the absoluteness of the obligation. For it is at least logically possible that this celestial being ought not to command unvaryingly what he does so command. If he commands what is right and obligatory, that is cause for thankfulness; but one could scarcely be thankful over a truth of logic. "Unvaryingly" must not equal "stubbornly" or "with chronic moral blindness"; these are unthinkable possibilities for Christian theism. But this does not affect the point being made: that absoluteness is not analyzable in terms of unvaryingness of command. Moreover, the Christian wishes to make one all-important moral judgment that could not possibly have its absoluteness reduced to commandedness by God—the judgment, namely, that God is morally perfect. But if a human being can make this moral judgment uncommanded, why can he not make others also?

Analogous criticisms can be made of the argument from the authority or authoritativeness of the moral law to the need for a divine source of authority. To put the main objection boldly: It is of the very nature of a fundamental moral judgment that it should be made on no authority but that of the agent who makes it. Certainly there are occasions when I may believe that another person has a superior measure of insight into the situation in which I have to act; I may then properly accept his judgment in lieu of my own. Yet if this is not to be a culpable moral abdication, I must have good grounds for trusting my temporary "authority": I must judge him to be morally reliable. But this is itself a moral judgment—one that I can make on nobody's authority but my own; or if on someone's authority, then this new person must be judged reliable on my own authority, and so on. A legitimate appeal to authority presupposes that autonomous moral judgments have already been made. Our argument held that we must postulate God as the authorizer of all our moral judgments—otherwise they would carry no authority; but we find, contrariwise, that God can play the role of authority only if we are able to make certain moral judgments without appealing to any external authority whatsoever.

The third version alleged that the notion of "moral law" is incomplete unless God is postulated as lawgiver. *Law,* however, is a word with many strands to its meaning; and it is only by failing to distinguish certain of the strands that this can appear to be a plausible line of argument. It is perfectly intelligible to say that some person or group of persons has laid down positive laws, rules for a community, backed by penal sanctions. The existence of a developed body of such laws normally implies the existence of lawmakers or codifiers. It is quite another thing (and not really intelligible) to speak of anyone, human or divine, "laying down" the moral law itself. Laws, rules, and regulations are of the right logical type to be laid down in accordance with, or in conflict with, the moral law. But the moral law itself is not the sort of thing that needs to be, or that logically can be, laid down or promulgated by anyone. No conceivable story about men or gods could be taken, without absurdity, to describe the inauguration (or the annulling) of the moral law. Commands might be uttered, inscriptions miraculously appear; but it would never become a trivial or tautological question to ask of their content, "Is this in fact morally binding?" The distinctively moral authority of a rule or law does not lie in the prestige or power of its initiator, nor in the circumstances of its first recognition.

The argument from the convergence of moral codes is most often set forth in an objectivist ethical context. The existence of objective moral qualities "seen" to be there, or "intuited," by different moral agents in widely different places and times remains inexplicable unless we posit a God who creates and morally guides. It is less often noticed that the argument is perhaps stronger—certainly no weaker—if it is set forth in a subjectivist context instead. This was apparently noted by F. R. Tennant, who (in a conversation reported by R. B. Braithwaite) argued on the following lines. Failing the existence of any objective moral properties or moral relations, it is all the more remarkable that there should be such a measure of congruity among moral judgments or decisions: sufficiently remarkable to point the way, again, to divine activity. Yet this argument is not at all conclusive. The supernatural hypothesis that it puts forward is not the only hypothesis available to account for the data; and it has the disadvantage that it is not empirically confirmable or refutable. Powerful competitors would be arguments from the relative stability of basic human needs, desires, and aversions or from the pervasiveness of aggressive and social drives in the personality. These alone might well account for the actual agreements among moral judgments and would account for them without invoking the immensely problematic notion of divine causality.

PRESUPPOSITION OF THE HIGHEST GOOD

Our last group of arguments began its history in modern philosophy with a statement of Kant: "The idea of the highest good … cannot be realized by man himself … ; yet he discovers within himself the duty to work for this end. Hence he finds himself impelled to believe in the cooperation or management of a moral Ruler of the world, by means of which alone this goal can be reached (*Religion within the Limits of Reason Alone*).

Kant was not betraying the austerity or rigor of his moral philosophy; he was not offering religious inducements to moral behavior. He would have denied distinctively moral worth to someone whose "dutiful" actions were aimed at securing his own postmortem happiness. The emphasis in his argument is wholly on the intelligibility and rationality of the moral demand; it was inconceivable to him that the categorical imperative should be a mocking voice, laying obligations upon us and at the same time denying the environment in which alone the obligations could be fulfilled. (It has been claimed that Kant had abandoned these moral arguments by the time he wrote the *Opus Postumum,* but the contrary view has been argued more forcibly; see G. A. Schrader, "Kant's Presumed Repudiation … .")

The strength of Kant's moral argument is clearly dependent on the strength of his ethical theory as a whole. It is only because he saw moral judgment as the work of practical reason (not as a matter of emotive reactions or responses) that he was able to make plausible use of those judgments as a basis for theological demands. Any fundamental criticism of the Kantian ethic would ipso facto imperil the theology.

The argument is equally imperiled if we deny that we are under obligation to attain the highest good and our individual moral perfection, saying that we are obliged only to strive toward these unrealizable ends. We might indeed reverse Kant's argument as follows. From our observation of the world we conclude that the highest good and our moral perfection are unattainable; therefore, we can have no obligation to attain these but, at best, only an obligation to strive toward them. We can interpret them in Kant's own term, *regulatively,* as Kant himself sometimes did. (See John R. Silber, "Kant's Conception of the Highest Good … .")

The postulating of God and immortality is aimed at solving an antinomy—of making intelligible what, without the postulate, is inexplicable. But does the postulation of God in fact produce intelligibility, a lifting of mystery?

Or is there not so much mystery in the postulate itself that the final effect is a deepening, not a lightening, of perplexity? If independence, autonomy, and freedom are essential to a moral agent, that autonomy will presumably remain essential in a hereafter as well as in the here and now. But, if so, the postulation of God and immortality can by no means ensure that the ultimate moral goals will, in fact, be reached, even though it was precisely to ensure their attainment that the postulates were made.

Kant's theory of time as a "form of sensibility" makes it very dubious whether he could have spoken meaningfully of a continuing moral development and the attainment of the highest good in a hereafter. Granted that he disclaimed all theoretical insight into what such an existence would be like (this measure of agnosticism is part of the force of *postulate* as distinct from *demonstrate*), the notion of time still remains essential to Kant's moral argument. If we are unable to give meaning to it in that context, the argument cannot but suffer.

It is possible to reject some portions of Kant's detailed argumentation and yet to advance a moral argument of a definitely Kantian type. This was notably done in W. R. Sorley's *Moral Values and the Idea of God* and in A. E. Taylor's *The Faith of a Moralist*. Neither of these writers held the moral argument to be the sole and all-sufficient theistic proof, but they did believe that without it the case for theism is weak and dubious.

Sorley attempted first to show that "the moral order is an objectively valid order, that moral values belong to the nature of reality," and that "the history of the world-process is fitted to realise this order." If we were to assume that the goal of the world-process is the realizing of happiness, there would be the weightiest empirical evidence against us. With moral worth and goodness it is different. Conditions that work against happiness may work for, not against, the developing, trying, and testing of moral fiber. "The very imperfection of the world [is] an argument pointing to the theistic conclusion." There remains yet a gap between the claim that the universe works toward a moral purpose and the full claim that God exists: Sorley seeks to fill this gap by arguing that belief in God is presupposed by belief in an objective and "eternally valid" morality. If the moral law is eternally valid, and valid whether we recognize it or not, "how could this eternal validity stand alone, not embodied in matter and neither seen nor realized by finite minds, unless there were an eternal mind whose thought and will were therein expressed?"

One can readily agree that the world as we experience it is better adapted to be a vale of soul-making than a hedonistic holiday camp. Yet there are difficulties about even the soul-making view. Some human suffering (the unmerited suffering of young children, for instance) cannot always be treated plausibly as developing moral fiber, or as realizing any other moral value. The natural environment can figure as the destroyer of moral personality as well as its preserver and nourisher. Sorley's further argument, from the validity of the law to an eternal mind, surely contains a confusion of the logical and the psychological. Questions about validity and about truth are logically independent of questions about the propositions that are actually entertained in someone's mind. Whether or not there exists a person who says (or thinks) *p*, has no bearing on the truth of *p* or, if *p* is a moral principle, upon its bindingness or validity in the relevant sense.

A. E. Taylor saw the moral life not as a mere conforming to given static principles and rules but as directing the moral agent along certain paths of self-development. There is development within the moral ideal: "We discover tomorrow that today's ideal 'had more in it' than we had supposed." The goal transforms itself as we approach it. The further we pursue it, the less able we become to conceive the human good in purely this-world, secular terms. There is development also within our awareness of time. Purposeful, valuable activity produces an extension of our "conscious present"; it delivers us from the dullness of "one thing after another." The limiting case in this development would be well expressed by Boethius's account of eternity—"the complete and simultaneous fruition of a life without bounds."

"We may argue," Taylor then claimed, "from the existence of a function to the reality of an environment in which the function can find adequate exercise." But no view of the world, short of theism, can guarantee the completion of these directions of development that Taylor has described.

Whatever is decided about the validity of the argument as an argument, Taylor's *The Faith of a Moralist* is a lastingly impressive and eloquent account of a religiously oriented morality. On validity, however, some searching criticisms were made by C. D. Broad in his review of Taylor's work published in *Mind* (1931). Taylor had taken as his premises certain moral judgments and certain trends of development in our experience of value. He then had asked what these entailed; whatever they entailed was to be added to our true beliefs about the universe. Broad argued that, in order to avoid a vicious circle, we must be sure that our premises do not already covertly assume the theistic conclusion. We must know that we have these duties and aspirations without already presupposing God and immortality. Only in this way could the existence of God and immortality be the conclusion of our argument. It is hard to be sure that these value judgments and aspirations are not the *consequence* of a prior theism. And a further point must be added: Only such a previously held theism, or cryptotheism, could entitle us to argue, with Taylor, "from the existence of a function to the reality of an environment in which [it has] adequate exercise." (Or, if this is true by definition of *function,* only such a theism can justify calling those value pursuits "functions.") Once again it might be added that the directions of moral development, although unrealizable in toto, could still be taken as targets for ever-nearer approximation. That they can be taken in this way, however, tells against Taylor's argument, for he wished to deny that we can be morally serious about these unless complete realization is possible.

Moral theories dominant in the mid-twentieth century did not tend to lead naturally into moral arguments for God. In Britain and the United States, at any rate, they were characteristically this-worldly. But exceptions do occur. Austin Farrer offered, if not a moral argument, then certainly a moral "persuasion" toward theism in the first chapter of *Faith and Logic,* "A Starting-Point for the Philosophical Examination of Theological Belief." His argument is that we are incontestably under an obligation to love our neighbor—that is, to hold him in highest regard; and that this is not impossible if our neighbor is a lovable person. If our neighbor occasionally lapses from lovability and from goodness, we may still manage to love his "normal" self, although it is temporarily obscured. If, however, he lapses chronically and grossly, how are we to love him? To love what he might be is now to love a fiction only; but it is persons, not fictions, that we ought to love. Farrer claimed Christianity provides a uniquely helpful way in which we can see the unlovable neighbor, admit his deficiencies, and yet succeed in loving him. In praying for and about our neighbor, we bring our view of him into relation with God's action—his action in creating our neighbor and his constant and costly redemptive action on our neighbor's behalf. Farrer insisted that, if these reflections help to give plausibility and impressiveness to the Christian view itself, they are not to be taken as a refurbishing of strong Kantian claims to establish God's existence.

Farrer appears to have assessed the capacity of this type of argument far more realistically than those who used it before him. If we judge that certain attitudes or evaluations are supremely worth realizing—for example, that "people ought to be held in the utmost regard"—then it is reasonable, even mandatory, to take up whatever stance will best further our task of realizing them. In our present example, we are required to meditate upon those reflections that uniquely put our neighbor in a regard-furthering light. Of course, provisos must be added. There must, for instance, be no logical incoherence in the description of the stance or of the context that furthers our neighborly love; otherwise, what we called the light or the stance might be in fact only a fugitive, quasi-aesthetic movement of feeling. To provide a point of entry to traditional Christianity, the stance must be capable of being expressed in a set of meaningful affirmations about reality. Another obvious proviso is that our premises must be sound. We must in fact be under obligation to hold our neighbor in highest regard, and all non-Christian ways of seeing our neighbor must be less helpful than the Christian way. It is particularly upon the second of these premises that, in a fuller discussion, argument necessarily would concentrate.

See also Broad, Charlie Dunbar; Ethics, History of; Hume, David; Immortality; Kant, Immanuel; Popular Arguments for the Existence of God; Presupposition; Sorley, William Ritchie; Taylor, Alfred Edward.

Bibliography

The chief sources for moral arguments to God are the following works of Kant: *Kritik der praktischen Vernunft* (Riga: J. F. Hartknoch, 1788), translated by T. K. Abbott (London and Dublin, 1879) and by L. W. Beck (Chicago, 1949), and *Die Religion innerhalb der Grenzen der blossen Vernunft* (Königsberg: Bey Friedrich Nicolovius, 1794), translated by T. M. Greene and H. H. Hudson as *Religion within the Limits of Reason Alone,* 2nd ed. (New York: Harper, 1960).

Post-Kantian works in which moral arguments to God play an important part are Austin Farrer, "A Starting-Point for the Philosophical Examination of Theological Belief," in *Faith and Logic* edited by B. G. Mitchell (New York, 1957); John Henry Newman, *A Grammar of Assent* (London, 1901), especially pp. 109–110; Hastings Rashdall, *The Theory of Good and Evil,* 2 vols. (Oxford: Clarendon, 1907), and *God and Man* (Oxford, 1930); W. R. Sorley, *Moral Values and the Idea of God* (Cambridge, U.K.: Cambridge University Press, 1918); and A. E. Taylor, *The Faith of a Moralist* (London: Macmillan, 1930), reviewed by C. D. Broad in *Mind* 40 (1931): 364–375.

Among contemporary studies of the Kantian argument are the following: H. P. Owen, *The Moral Argument for Christian Theism* (London: Allen and Unwin, 1965); G. A. Schrader, "Kant's Presumed Repudiation of the 'Moral Argument' in the Opus Postumum," in *Philosophy* 26 (1951): 228–241; John R. Silber, "Kant's Conception of the Highest Good as Immanent and Transcendent," in *Philosophical Review* 68 (1959): 469ff.; and W. H. Walsh, "Kant's Moral Theology," in *Proceedings of the British Academy* 49 (1963): 263–289.

Ronald W. Hepburn (1967)

MORAL ARGUMENTS FOR THE EXISTENCE OF GOD [ADDENDUM]

The moral argument purports to show that evidence from our moral experience supports the existence of God. From the 1970s onward, various forms of the moral argument have been developed by many philosophers. While defenders argue with increased sophistication, they also tend to make more modest claims about the force of the moral argument.

MORAL ARGUMENTS AS ABDUCTIVE AND CUMULATIVE ARGUMENTS

If the moral argument is construed as a deductive argument that moves from, say, the objectivity of moral values to the existence of God, then to rebut the argument, the critic needs to show only that the objectivity of moral values and the nonexistence of God are logically compatible. This is a relatively easy task. However, developments in epistemology and philosophy of science since the 1960s lead many to think that it is more realistic to look, in most areas of inquiry, for an abductive argument, an inference to the best explanation. We can formulate the moral argument too as an abductive argument, that is, argue that among diverse worldviews, the theistic worldview is the best explanation of, say, the objectivity of morals, especially in contrast with naturalism.

Since abductive arguments are by nature cumulative arguments, the force of an abductive moral argument will depend not on any single feature of morality, but rather on how well it can explain the whole gamut of moral experience, both its form and its content. For example, Louis Pojman argues, "Given the assumption of standard contemporary secular moral philosophy: I. The notion of *moral obligation* becomes seriously problematic; II. The notion of the *supremacy of morality* either becomes problematically analytic or it vanishes; III. The problem of morality and self-interest becomes insoluble; IV. The idea that human beings have intrinsic value ceases to make sense." Hence, "most contemporary secular ethical systems offer no hope of guiding human conduct, and should be abandoned" (1992b, p. 4).

In contrast, ethical systems that proceed from transcendent assumptions can offer resources unavailable to secular ethical systems. For example, the Christian tradition can appeal to a perfectly good, omnipotent God who created humanity in his image. Each person is endowed with a specific telos, which the individual must seek to realize. Within this framework, all humans have equal intrinsic worth, free will, and eternal destiny (see also Pojman 1991, 1992a). Morality consists of obeying God's commands, which promote human flourishing and are backed by rewards and punishments. All these provide a solid foundation for the existence of moral obligation and responsibility.

ARE MORAL TRUTHS ANALYTIC?

Not all theistic philosophers accept the moral argument. For example, Richard Swinburne (1974) believes that fundamental moral truths are necessary truths and do not need to be explained. Defenders have several ways to respond. First, they may flatly deny Swinburne's claim by pointing out that moral nihilism and moral relativism at least appear to be logically coherent positions. Second, even if many moral principles are necessary truths, it does not follow that they cannot be explained by more basic necessary truths about God's essential moral nature and logically necessary existence. Charles Taliaferro even suggests a cosmological-ethical argument that utilizes "the resources of a theistic metaphysic in providing a singular, comprehensive explanatory account of moral truths as well as other essential truths," in addition to explaining the existence of the cosmos. In this way, theism may exhibit "a marked simplicity and force missing from its competitors" (1996, p. 290).

Third, the realm of necessary moral truths appears to be mysterious and odd from a naturalistic perspective. It is puzzling why we should be aware of these truths and why moral consciousness features so prominently in human existence. Necessary moral truths by themselves do not have any power to endow agents with morality, and a naturalistic universe cannot have any causal interaction with these abstract truths. Why, then, should we suppose that a morally blind world would endow us with correct moral intuitions? The case is different with sense experience, whose reliability is to some extent tied with our survival. It is not without reason that most naturalists prefer moral skepticism. As John Mackie admits, "There can be a secular morality, not indeed as a system of objective values or prescriptions, but rather as something to be made [that is, invented]" (1977, p. 227; see also Harman 1984).

THE ODDITY OF MORAL OBLIGATION

For Mackie, another reason why morality is so odd is that moral claims are authoritative and objectively prescriptive: "Any wrong (possible) course of action would have not-to-be-doneness somehow built into it" (1977, p. 40).

George Mavrodes (1986) points out that naturalistic evolution may well produce creatures with moral sentiments conducive to survival. However, the existence of *actual* moral obligations appears to be strange, especially because moral obligations often come into conflict with self-interest.

Some atheists (David Gauthier [1986], Gregory S. Kavka [1984]) try to reconcile moral obligations with self-interest, and claim that in the long run it is in the best interests of everyone for every individual to act morally. The viability of this kind of contractual project depends on whether it can satisfactorily answer questions like these: Should one still be moral when in fact not everyone else will act morally? What about the moral free-rider? Do extremely powerful people really need to act morally? Why should we sacrifice our own interests for the benefits of people who cannot reciprocate, such as future generations, extremely marginalized people in one's own society, and people in distant countries? Is it rational to sacrifice one's life for the sake of morality?

THE MORAL GAP

A broadly Kantian moral argument continues to find defenders. Ronald Green (1978) starts from the question "Why should I be moral?" John Hare (1996) focuses on the gap between the demand that one act morally and our capacities to meet this demand, according to most moral theories. Since "ought" implies "can," the description of the moral life in this moral gap is incoherent. To resolve this incoherence, secular moralists either exaggerate our moral capacity, reduce the moral demand, or try to find some substitute for God to help bridge the gap. Hare criticizes many of these options and argues that the Christian doctrines of atonement and incorporation in Christ can solve the problem. Debates surround whether Hare's criticisms of the secular options are cogent and whether the Christian faith can really offer something that other options cannot (see Zagzebski 1999).

THE *EUTHYPHRO* DILEMMA

Atheistic philosophers such as Kai Nielsen (1990) and Michael Martin (2002) have produced sustained replies to the moral argument. They think that the *Euthyphro* dilemma (are morally good acts commanded by God because they are morally good, or are they morally good because they are commanded by God?) shows that morality has to be independent of God. If morality depends on God's command, then morality will be arbitrary, because God might command cruelty for its own

sake. If one denies this possibility, one already commits to an independent standard of the good apart from God.

Some theists reply by saying that God's essential nature, from which the divine will flows, provides the ultimate standard of goodness, and this is neither independent of God nor arbitrary. Robert M. Adams has proposed a modified divine-command ethics that, as a postulate, equates being contrary to the commands of a *loving* God with the *essence* of being wrong (Adams 1987). This is not an analysis of the *meaning* of "right" and "wrong," because Adams grants that our moral practice gives us some basic understanding of morality apart from religion. However, it does not follow, he thinks, that, on the basis of this basic understanding, we can understand the *essence* of being wrong. (Someone who understands the meaning of "water," can further discover that the nature, or essence, of water is H_2O.) On Adams's view, the answer to the *Euthyphro* dilemma is that a *loving* God would not command cruelty for its own sake.

A CRITICAL DIALOGUE BETWEEN ETHICAL SYSTEMS

The success of the moral argument in the long run depends on the relative merits of the theistic and atheistic accounts of morality. (We should also include, say, Confucian ethics and Buddhist ethics among the contenders.) Adams (1999) has developed his theistic ethics into a comprehensive theory of the good and the right. Michael Moore (1996) and Michael Martin (2002) have used naturalistic moral realism (Brink 1989) to show that naturalistic ethics is superior and that theistic ethics is superfluous (see also Copan 2003, 2004). The moral argument does not appear to be conclusive. Its significance mainly lies in its contribution to a cumulative case for God's existence and its capacity to stimulate a lively debate on the implications of different worldviews on morality.

See also God, Concepts of; Mackie, John Leslie; Moral Skepticism.

Bibliography

Adams, Robert M. *Finite and Infinite Goods.* Oxford, U.K.: Oxford University Press, 1999.

Adams, Robert M. *"The Virtue of Faith" and Other Essays in Philosophical Theology.* Oxford, U.K.: Oxford University Press, 1987.

Brink, David O. *Moral Realism and the Foundations of Ethics.* Cambridge, U.K.: Cambridge University Press, 1989.

Copan, Paul. "The Moral Argument." In *The Rationality of Theism*, edited by Paul Copan and Paul K. Moser. London: Routledge, 2003.

Copan, Paul. "Morality and Meaning without God, Another Failed Attempt: A Review Essay on *Atheism, Morality, and Meaning*." *Philosophia Christi* 6 (2) (2004): 295–304.

Gauthier, David. *Morals by Agreement*. New York: Oxford University Press, 1986.

Green, Ronald. *Religious Reason: The Rational and Moral Basis of Religious Belief*. New York: Oxford University Press, 1978.

Hare, John. *The Moral Gap*. Oxford, U.K.: Oxford University Press, 1996.

Harman, Gilbert. "Is There a Single True Morality?" In *Morality, Reason, and Truth: New Essays on the Foundations of Ethics*, edited by David Copp and David Zimmerman. Totowa, NJ: Rowman and Allanheld, 1984.

Kavka, Gregory S. "The Reconciliation Project." In *Morality, Reason, and Truth: New Essays on the Foundations of Ethics*, edited by David Copp and David Zimmerman. Totowa, NJ: Rowman and Allanheld, 1984.

Mackie, John. *Ethics: Inventing Right and Wrong*. Harmondsworth, U.K.: Penguin Books, 1977.

Martin, Michael. *Atheism, Morality, and Meaning*. Amherst, NY: Prometheus, 2002.

Mavrodes, George I. "Religion and the Queerness of Morality." In *Rationality, Religious Belief, and Moral Commitment*, edited by Robert Audi and William J. Wainwright. Ithaca, NY: Cornell University Press, 1986.

Moore, Michael S. "Good without God." In *Natural Law, Liberalism, and Morality: Contemporary Essays*, edited by Robert P. George. Oxford, U.K.: Clarendon Press, 1996.

Nielsen, Kai. *Ethics without God*. Rev. ed. Amherst, NY: Prometheus, 1990.

Pojman, Louis P. "Are Human Rights Based on Equal Worth?" *Philosophy and Phenomenological Research* 52 (1992a): 605–622.

Pojman, Louis P. "A Critique of Contemporary Egalitarianism: A Christian Perspective." *Faith and Philosophy* 8 (1991): 481–504.

Pojman, Louis P. "Ethics: Religious and Secular." *Modern Schoolman* 70 (1992b): 1–30.

Swinburne, Richard. "Duty and the Will of God." *Canadian Journal of Philosophy* 4 (1974): 213–227.

Taliaferro, Charles. "God's Natural Laws." In *Natural Law, Liberalism, and Morality: Contemporary Essays*, edited by Robert P. George. Oxford, U.K.: Clarendon Press, 1996.

Zagzebski, Linda. "Review of *The Moral Gap*." *Philosophical Review* 108 (1999): 291–293.

Kai-man Kwan (2005)

MORAL DILEMMAS

The label *moral dilemma* is commonly applied to any difficult moral problem. Several introductory anthologies in ethics have been titled *Moral Dilemmas*, suggesting that all of the issues discussed therein are moral dilemmas, regardless of their structure, simply because they raise hard moral questions. Many people even talk about moral dilemmas when it is not clear whether or not morality is relevant at all.

Moral philosophers, in contrast, usually have in mind something more specific. Minimally, they count a situation as a moral dilemma only if one moral reason conflicts with another (moral or nonmoral) reason. Reasons conflict in a situation if the agent is not able in that situation to comply with all of the reasons. For example, if it is in Ann's interest to lie to a potential employer, then Ann's prudential reason to lie conflicts with Ann's moral reason not to lie. Similarly, moral reasons can conflict with religious reasons (as on one interpretation of the biblical story of Abraham being commanded by God to sacrifice his son, Isaac) or with aesthetic reasons (as on one understanding of Gauguin's decision to leave his family to pursue his art).

Moral philosophers normally restrict the class of moral dilemmas further to include only conflicts between one moral reason and another reason that is also moral in nature. In Plato's example, if Brad holds a weapon for a friend and promises to return it when that friend asks for it, then Brad has a moral reason to return it when the friend asks. But if Brad knows that this friend is going to use the weapon to commit a harmful crime, then Brad has a moral reason not to return the weapon to the friend (at least at that time).

Many philosophers would not classify this conflict as a moral dilemma because it is resolvable—the moral reasons against returning the weapon override the moral reasons in favor of returning the weapon, so overall Brad morally ought not to return the weapon, assuming that the harmful crime is serious enough. In contrast, even if moral dilemmas must be unresolvable, Carol is in a moral dilemma on this account if Carol has a moral reason to help the needy but can help only one of two equally needy people.

Some philosophers limit moral dilemmas even further to include only conflicts among certain kinds of moral reasons. A moral reason is a moral requirement just in case it would be morally wrong not to act on it without an adequate justification or excuse. Carol's moral reason to help a particular needy person, for example, is not a moral requirement if it would not be morally wrong for Carol to refuse to help this needy person (as long as Carol helps enough other needy people at other times). Then, if moral dilemmas are limited to unresolvable conflicts between moral requirements, Carol is not in a moral dilemma when she can help only one of two equally needy people. In contrast, if David can keep only one of two conflicting promises, assuming that David has a moral requirement to keep his promises, then David is in a moral dilemma, even if moral dilemmas are defined as unresolvable conflicts of moral requirements.

Other moral theorists define moral dilemmas in different terms, for instance, as situations where every alternative is morally wrong. The term *wrong*, however, is unclear in this context. If an act is called morally wrong when, and only when, it violates a non-overridden moral requirement, then this definition reduces to the previous one. In contrast, if an act is called morally wrong only when it violates an overriding moral requirement, then this definition makes moral dilemmas obviously impossible. That obviousness suggests that philosophers who claim that moral dilemmas are possible do not use this strong definition of moral dilemmas. Instead, they seem to identify moral dilemmas with unresolvable moral requirement conflicts.

To show that a situation fits that definition, it is not enough to cite nonmoral facts, such as that the agent cannot do both acts or even that each act is necessary to fulfill a promise. The situation is not a moral dilemma unless there are moral requirements for conflicting alternatives and neither moral requirement overrides the other. In support of the claim that there is a real moral requirement on each side, philosophers who see the situation as a moral dilemma cite the counterfactual that it would be morally wrong not to choose a particular alternative if there were no moral reason to choose the conflicting alternative. They also often argue that moral requirements on each side provide the best explanation of why remorse (or guilt, but not just regret), an apology, compensation, or some other moral residue is appropriate after either choice.

In support of the claim that neither moral requirement overrides the other, philosophers who assert the possibility of moral dilemmas can argue that some situations are so symmetrical that neither moral requirement could override the other. A common symmetrical example is Sophie's choice between her two children when a Nazi guard threatens to kill her and both of her children if she does not pick one child to be killed. In nonsymmetrical cases, some philosophers also argue that conflicting moral requirements can be incomparable, in which case neither moral requirement overrides the other (although they are also not exactly equal).

Opponents who deny the possibility of (even resolvable) conflicts between moral requirements sometimes object that if one conflicting moral requirement overrides the other, then the other is no longer a moral require-ment. This objection conflates overriding with cancellation. Like physical forces, moral requirements that are overridden by stronger moral requirements can still retain some moral force, as shown by their ability to justify remorse, apologies, compensation, and other forms of moral residue.

Another common objection to the possibility of moral dilemmas charges that, if neither moral requirement overrides the other, then the agent is morally permitted to choose either alternative and, hence, is not in a moral dilemma. However, if an act is not morally permitted only when it violates an overriding moral requirement, then the claim that both acts are morally permitted is compatible with the situation being a conflict between non-overridden moral requirements and, hence, a moral dilemma on the above definition. In contrast, if an act is not morally permitted when it violates a non-overridden moral requirement, then neither act is morally permitted in an irresolvable moral requirement conflict. Either way, the notion of permission does not rule out moral dilemmas.

Additional arguments against the possibility of moral dilemmas try to derive a contradiction from the definition of moral dilemmas. If the agent in a moral dilemma morally ought to adopt each alternative separately, then the agent morally ought to adopt both alternatives together, according to the agglomeration principle. If the agent morally ought to adopt both alternatives, then the agent must be able to adopt both alternatives, according to the principle that *ought* implies *can*. The agent cannot adopt both alternatives in a moral dilemma, by definition. Thus, the definition of moral dilemmas plus agglomeration and *ought* implies *can* imply a contradiction. Defenders of moral dilemmas respond by denying either agglomeration or *ought* implies *can*, or both.

Another formal argument applies a closure principle: An agent has a moral requirement not to do whatever prevents that agent from fulfilling a moral requirement. This closure principle implies that an agent in a moral dilemma has a moral requirement to adopt and also not to adopt each alternative. This is supposed to be absurd, because an agent cannot be required not to do what that agent is required to do. Defenders of moral dilemmas respond by denying either the closure principle or the claim that *required* implies *not required*, or both.

More arguments have been given against the possibility of moral dilemmas. Some philosophers claim that moral theories that yield moral dilemmas must be inconsistent or must fail to fulfill some purpose of moral theories, such as to prescribe particular decisions. Others argue that it would be unfair to blame or hold the agent responsible for failing to adopt one alternative when the agent adopted the other alternative in order to fulfill a non-overridden moral requirement. Defenders of moral dilemmas, of course, have responses to such arguments, but it remains controversial whether their responses are adequate.

See also Deontological Ethics; Duty; Moral Rules and Principles.

Bibliography

Gowans, Christopher W. *Innocence Lost: An Examination of Inescapable Wrongdoing.* New York; Oxford: Oxford University Press, 1994.

Gowans, Christopher W., ed. *Moral Dilemmas.* New York; Oxford: Oxford University Press, 1987.

Mason, G. E., ed. *Moral Dilemmas and Moral Theory.* New York: Oxford University Press, 1996.

Morton, Adam. *Disasters and Dilemmas: Strategies for Real-Life Decision Making.* Oxford; Cambridge, MA: Blackwell, 1991.

Sinnott-Armstrong, Walter. *Moral Dilemmas.* Oxford; New York: Blackwell, 1988.

Statman, Daniel. *Moral Dilemmas.* Amsterdam, Netherlands: Rodopi, 1995.

Zimmerman, Michael J. *The Concept of Moral Obligation.* New York: Cambridge University Press, 1996.

Walter Sinnott-Armstrong (2005)

MORAL EPISTEMOLOGY

It is easy to find examples of moral claims. People often say or write such things as: (a) Deliberate targeting of innocent civilians in war is wrong. (b) Women should get equal pay for equal work. I shall refer to the contents of moral claims as moral statements. I presuppose nothing controversial regarding the real nature of moral statements. The first two examples of moral statements are general, but many are particular, for example: (c) George Bush should not have invaded Iraq. (d) I ought to make a contribution to tsunami relief. Not all moral statements concern what is right or wrong, or what we should or should not do. Some concern our rights: (e) Everyone has a right to his or her own opinion. (f) The KKK has a right to adopt a highway just as any other group does. Other moral claims concern what is morally good or bad, what is virtuous or vicious, what is praiseworthy, when morally significant feelings such as guilt, remorse or gratitude, are appropriate, and so on. I hope this makes it sufficiently clear what I mean to count as moral statements.

Just as a person can be insincere in making a non-moral claim, such as an ordinary factual claim, so a person can make a moral claim insincerely. It is not hard to imagine someone expressing agreement with others about some moral statement just to avoid confrontation, argument, or ridicule. In addition, we all recognize that what we say or write about morality does not exhaust our moral views, just as our factual beliefs can be more extensive than what we choose to make public. Let us therefore distinguish between people's moral judgments—that is, what they really think—and the public moral claims they make. I take no controversial stand regarding the nature of moral judgments.

A NARROW AND A BROAD UNDERSTANDING OF MORAL EPISTEMOLOGY

According to one traditional understanding, epistemology is the theory of knowledge. It is concerned with analyzing knowledge or specifying the conditions that must be satisfied for something to count as knowledge, with determining what we know and accounting for how we know it. Accordingly, moral epistemology would be concerned with moral knowledge. It would seek to determine whether any of our moral judgments count as knowledge and to provide an account of whatever moral knowledge we do have. Unfortunately this traditional understanding puts moral epistemology at risk of being a field with which many ethical theorists can have no substantial engagement.

Although there is a great deal of debate regarding the proper analysis of knowledge, nearly everyone agrees that for a person to know a statement (or proposition), that statement must be true. There is almost as wide agreement that a person must believe something in order to know it. In spite of the consensus that knowledge requires true belief, epistemologists do not work much on accounts of either truth or belief. They instead focus on figuring out what knowledge requires in addition to true belief and at understanding the precise nature of whatever else is required. Epistemologists do not agree about exactly what more is required for knowledge, but nearly all would accept that for a true belief to be knowledge it must be *good* in some yet to be specified but particularly epistemic sense. Epistemologists are, therefore, primarily concerned with understanding something normative or, more broadly, evaluative. When they attempt to determine whether we know something or how we might know it, they are engaged in an evaluative enterprise, seeking to address such questions as whether we ought to hold the belief in question, whether we are justified or responsible or warranted in holding it, or simply whether the belief has some special positive epistemic status. Philosophically significant debates about skepticism regarding some type of belief rarely begin with the skeptics arguing that the beliefs are false. They typically charge that the beliefs are deficient in some other way—that they are unjustified or unwarranted—whereas nonskeptics try to show that the beliefs are legitimate or up to standard.

If we adopt the traditional knowledge-centered understanding of moral epistemology, many ethicists cannot take moral epistemology seriously; if they allow that there are any significant evaluative questions regarding moral judgments, they must take them to fall outside moral epistemology. One reason for this is that a great many ethical theorists accept some version of noncognitivism. This was the dominant metaethical position for a large part of the twentieth century, and it may still be the majority view. In spite of the apparent similarities between moral statements such as "Murder is wrong" and descriptive statements such as "The cat is black," noncognitivism holds that moral statements are not descriptive, that they do not state facts. Noncognitivists variously hold that moral statements instead do such things as vent emotions, state how one feels about certain actions and call upon others to feel the same way, make universal prescriptions, or express one's acceptance of norms.

Hence, according to noncognitivism, moral judgments blatantly fail to satisfy the most obvious necessary conditions for knowledge. No moral judgments are true for the simple reason that they are not the sort of thing that could possibly be true; like questions or commands, they are neither true nor false. We could put the point in other ways by saying that moral claims do not really make statements at all or that moral judgments do not have propositions—things that carry truth values—as their objects or contents. Hence, even when we sincerely make a moral claim, we are not really expressing a belief. If moral statements such as "Theft is wrong" are not descriptive but have some sort of noncognitive content— if they are, for example, ventings of emotion ("Theft: big time yucko!") or prescriptions ("Don't steal!")—then clearly their contents are not the sorts of things that one could possibly believe or, for that matter, disbelieve.

So noncognitivism entails the impossibility of moral knowledge. Regardless of how interesting the various versions of noncognitivism might be or how subtle and deep are the arguments that support them, no interesting normative epistemology is necessary to see this entailment. We need not get involved in any sort of epistemic evalua-

tion of moral judgments to reach the skeptical conclusion. One need not do anything like reconstruct the evidence we have for our moral judgments and evaluate it to see how strong it is. One need not investigate the cognitive processes that produce moral judgments and attempt to determine how reliable they are. Since moral judgments just are not, according to noncognitivism, the sorts of things that could possibly be knowledge, there is no reason to get involved in the distinctive kind of evaluation of belief or judgment that is the special business of epistemology. Indeed, it would seem that epistemic evaluation of moral judgments could not really make any sense for a noncognitivist. Moral epistemology as an area of serious inquiry is left open only to cognitivists.

But of course this is not the way things are. Most people, regardless of their metaethical views, evaluate moral judgments, and they evaluate them in ways that seem no different from straightforward epistemic evaluations of ordinary factual judgments. They take some moral judgments to be epistemically better and others worse. People are dubious, for example, of moral judgments made on the basis of incomplete information or made when someone is tired or emotionally distraught, just as one would doubt factual judgments made in such circumstances.

We think we can at least sometimes provide reasons or evidence for or against moral judgments and that the reasons or evidence can be evaluated. We sometimes seek reasons for moral judgments we have already made, and at other times we try to find reasons that would allow us to make a moral judgment when we are unsure. In certain cases we ask others about their reasons for moral judgments and look askance upon their judgments if they can provide no adequate reasons. We are perfectly comfortable applying terms of epistemic evaluation such as *reasonable* and *unreasonable*, *rational* and *irrational*, *warranted* and *unwarranted*, or *justified* and *unjustifed* to moral judgments. When we apply these terms to moral judgments, it seems that we use them in the same way as when we apply them to other kinds of judgments.

There are two hard lines that affirm the restrictive understanding of epistemology as concerned exclusively with knowledge and accept that the conjunction of this conception with noncognitivism entails that the epistemic evaluation of moral judgments makes no sense. The one hard line concludes that epistemic evaluation of moral judgments, that is, moral epistemology, makes no sense. The other accepts the epistemic evaluation of moral judgments and rejects noncognitivism. I expect the first hard line approach would be more popular than the second. But I prefer a third alternative. It maintains that epistemic evaluation of moral judgments makes perfectly good sense, as common practice suggests, and that most metaethical positions, including most versions of noncognitivism, can recognize this; it instead rejects the narrow understanding of epistemology. One advantage of this approach is that there are independent reasons for preferring a broader conception of epistemology.

We can extend the conception of epistemology, and specifically epistemic evaluation, in two ways. First, we should allow that epistemology is concerned with more than knowledge and its constituents. There are significant concepts of epistemic evaluation that do not figure in the analysis of knowledge. Some epistemologists account for knowledge in terms of reliable belief formation. Others disagree because a person's reliability may not be subjectively accessible to that person. They hold that knowing requires responsible belief, and that belief is irresponsible unless we have reason to think the belief is likely to be true. Others hold that to be known a belief must be properly based or grounded, while others hold that to be known a belief must be part of an extensive coherent system of beliefs. Yet others think a belief must be formed by a properly functioning cognitive mechanism. There are still more contenders: for example, those who analyze knowledge in terms of the exercise of intellectual virtues. Presumably at most one of these accounts provides a correct analysis of knowledge, but even those accounts that fail as analyses of knowledge may still succeed in identifying something that has epistemic value.

Whether reliable belief is necessary for knowledge, it is a good thing to be reliable in forming beliefs. The same holds for subjectively accessible reasons: It is clearly a good thing to have such reasons for a belief, regardless of whether they are necessary for knowledge—and so on for the various other evaluative characteristics of belief that have been put forward as necessary for knowledge. A strong case can be made that each is a real epistemic good. There are also concepts of epistemic evaluation that do not even seem to be required for knowledge. According to one account, rational beliefs are those that would stand up upon thorough reflection because they satisfy the believer's own deep epistemic standards. This is a highly subjective sense of rationality and therefore it is probably not required for knowledge. Nevertheless, it is epistemically good to have beliefs that satisfy one's own epistemic standards rather than beliefs that one would, upon careful consideration, regard as epistemically flawed. There are doubtless still more concepts of epistemic evaluation.

The second way to broaden epistemology is by abandoning the dominant monistic view of epistemic evaluation that regards truth as sole intrinsic epistemic good and all other epistemic goods as valuable because of some connection to truth such as being a means to true belief. There have been attempts to show that some features, such as coherence, make truth more likely, but these attempts have not met with much success. It has seemed obvious all along that other features, such as subjective rationality, do not make true belief objectively likely. We need not conclude that no such features are epistemically valuable. It is better to allow that some things we value epistemically do not make true belief likely. In the case of something like reliable belief, at least on some understandings, the connection with truth is obvious. But even here we should take a broader view, at least for moral judgments. As we have seen, noncognitivism entails that moral judgments have no truth values and hence cannot be reliable.

Nevertheless, it seems obvious that some moral judgments are more reliable than others. For example, moral judgments made by a person who is emotionally distraught or who has selfish interests at stake are less than reliable. Most noncognitivists can easily accept such seemingly obvious examples, since most draw some sort of distinction between correct and incorrect moral judgments. Hence a notion of reliability is available that is an extension of the familiar, truth-connected notion. It makes more sense to recognize judgments that are reliable in this extended sense as epistemically valuable than to think that we are making an epistemic evaluation when we criticize a factual belief because a person formed it, say, when in a rage, but some totally different kind of evaluation when we criticize a moral judgment for exactly the same reason.

EPISTEMIC EVALUATION OF MORAL JUDGMENTS

If the broad conception of moral epistemology is basically correct, we should not ask simply whether any moral judgments are known or justified. Recognizing that there are various significant concepts of epistemic evaluation, we should ask what, if any, positive epistemic statuses moral judgments might have and also whether moral judgments suffer from any epistemic flaws so severe that we should regard them with a robust skepticism—a skepticism that holds not merely that no moral statements are known, but that moral judgments are so flawed that it makes no sense to use them either in moral theorizing or as a guide to life and action.

Some moral judgments are bound to be epistemically flawed for straightforward reasons—for example, because they were formed by a person who was emotionally distraught or who stood to gain or lose depending upon the judgment, or because they were made on the basis of an incomplete or incorrect understanding of the facts of the case, or because the person judging feels unsure or has no stable opinion. We know that judgments like these run a significant risk of error, regardless of their content. Let us set aside such obviously flawed judgments and focus on those that are free of all such well recognized sources of error. Such moral judgments already have some positive epistemic status—they have managed to avoid some significant pitfalls. But this is not, perhaps, a very impressive status, so let us consider what more might be said on behalf of moral judgments.

Among the remaining moral judgments, we can distinguish between those formed or not formed on the basis of inference. We obviously cannot have formed all of our judgments by inferring them from other judgments. Some of our judgments must be noninferential. It might be that all moral judgments are inferred from nonmoral judgments, either immediately or by means of inferential chains that eventually terminate exclusively in nonmoral judgments. Certain ethicists have tried to ground moral judgments in something like this way, deriving them from theses regarding the meanings of moral terms in conjunction with purely empirical claims. But it seems highly unlikely that anything like this will work out, and near certain that the moral judgments of ordinary people are not grounded in this way. Ordinary people, and even philosophers when they are being ordinary, form many noninferential moral judgments, and when they do infer moral judgments, the inferences have moral premises that are, or eventually trace to, noninferential moral judgments. So let us focus on noninferential moral judgments.

Consider the widely shared judgment that it is wrong to cause animals suffering for no good reason. Those who share this general judgment will also make judgments regarding the wrongness of many particular cases of animal torture. It is certainly possible to reach the general judgment via inference or to infer the particular judgments from it. But it is also possible to make both judgments noninferentially. Even where the judgments are noninferential, it is quite obvious that they do not come from nowhere. We were taught to make such judgments as children. At some time or other when we were children, our parents or some other adult caught us, or perhaps a sibling or a friend tormenting some helpless small

animal and scolded us. Maybe one incident was enough; maybe similar incidents were repeated, but eventually the lesson stuck.

Perhaps, then, our noninferential moral judgments get their epistemic status in the same way as our beliefs in other things we were taught as children. I believe that my maternal grandfather was killed in World War II, before I was born. This belief is noninferential, but it does not just pop into my head from I know not where. I know full well that it arises from testimony and memory. When I was a child my mother told me this. I believed her. Although I never received any objective confirmation of the belief—for example, by reading a letter from the War Department—neither did I encounter any reason to doubt what I was told. And I still remember what I was told. This is sufficient for my belief to have some fairly impressive epistemic credentials. My belief is rational or reasonable. You could say that I am epistemically responsible in believing. The belief coheres with other things I believe, although I would have to admit that most of the relevant beliefs are also things I remember being told by my parents. My mother has usually been reliable, and I know this to be so because in many cases what she told me has been borne out by the future course of experience. And I know my memory is fairly reliable as well, at least about things like this.

As good as all this is, however, it is still possible that my belief is seriously flawed. Suppose my grandfather mysteriously disappeared around the start of the war, and, although my mother knew he was involved with organized crime, she deceived herself into believing he had gone off to the war. When he didn't return at the end of the war, she came to believe he had been killed in action. Under this scenario, given the fact that my mother's original belief about her father's fate had little positive epistemic status—indeed, was flawed—my belief would be seriously flawed. It is significant that in such cases a testimonial belief can have a higher epistemic status than the belief of the testifier. Nevertheless, the epistemic status attainable by beliefs that are (solely) grounded in testimony and memory is constrained by the epistemic status of the testifier's belief. The epistemic status of memorial beliefs is similarly constrained by the status of the original belief.

Of course, the adults who taught us about morality when we were children probably did not fabricate their own moral views in some strange way. They were taught about morality by their parents, who were taught by theirs, and so on. This suggests a somewhat different problem: In the case of beliefs that have their source in chains of testimony and memory involving a series of people, somewhere along the line someone must have formed the relevant beliefs in some other way. And if the beliefs that come later in the chain are to be free from significant epistemic defect, somewhere along the line some beliefs must have attained some fairly strong positive epistemic status in virtue of something other than testimony and memory.

In the case of historical beliefs, which presumably trace back to persons who witnessed the events in question, it might make sense to suppose that the original source beliefs had the requisite epistemic credentials. But in the case of moral judgments it is hard to credit such a view, unless one takes something like the biblical narrative of Moses quite literally and holds that all our moral judgments can be traced through a long chain of testimony and memory all the way back to Moses or some other prophet whose moral judgments came straight from God. My guess is that even many theists will find such a supposition incredible.

How, then, might noninferential moral judgments attain a significant positive epistemic status? Here is a possibility: We were also taught to make simple arithmetical judgments. I can well remember trying to memorize multiplication and division tables. But although testimony and memory are surely somehow involved in the arithmetical judgments we now make, these judgments do not get their epistemic status primarily from testimony and memory. Indeed, I doubt that our simple arithmetical judgments are even produced by memory and testimony any longer. Somewhere along the line, no doubt as a result of our training, we reached a point where we could simply see for ourselves that simple arithmetical propositions are true. Simple mathematical and logical propositions, and perhaps some few others, are special. Any person with the conceptual resources to really understand the propositions can simply see that they are true, or at least this is one venerable and still widely held view. Some ethicists have wanted to say that certain ethical statements are like this as well. So the first part of the current proposal is that although we were taught to make moral judgments when we were children, such judgments are no longer merely products of testimony and memory. Rather, when we understand and consider certain moral statements, they simply seem to us as though they are true, so we form the moral judgment. The second, explicitly epistemic part of the proposal is that such moral judgments have the same positive epistemic status as simple arithmetical judgments and come to have this status in the same way.

There are reasons for being suspicious that things are quite so simple. Before I explain why, here are a couple of terminological notes. Contemporary discussions of moral epistemology and methodology frequently are conducted in terms of considered moral judgments and moral intuitions. Considered moral judgments are typically characterized simply as noninferential moral judgments that are not subject to obvious sources of error. When we narrowed our focus to such judgments above, however, I did not refer to them as considered moral judgments because judgments formed through testimony are not inferential in their origin, and neither are memorial judgments. Nevertheless, moral judgments formed via testimony or memory are not considered moral judgments even if they have avoided the usual sources of error. In the first part of the proposal regarding moral judgments we have restricted our attention to judgments that are free of the usual sources of error and are not only noninferential but are also held simply because it seems to the believer that they are true. Such judgments are appropriately regarded as considered moral judgments.

The term *intuition* can be used in a stronger, epistemically loaded sense or a weaker, nonepistemic sense. In the weaker sense, intuitions are simply noninferential judgments that do not arise from any of the traditionally recognized sources of knowledge: Intuitions are not produced by sense perception, introspection, memory, or testimony. A person makes an intuitive judgment simply because the proposition seems true upon due consideration. Considered moral judgments are, therefore, a subset of moral intuitions, namely, those that have avoided obvious causes or error. Limiting ourselves to the first part of the current proposal regarding moral judgments, we could say these judgments are moral intuitions in the weak sense. There are various stronger concepts of intuition that add to the weak notion a claim to some positive epistemic status—often some strong status such as certainty or infallibility or incorrigibility. Critical discussions of intuitionism often assume a strong notion of intuition, most frequently one involving a very strong epistemic status. The second part of the current proposal takes moral judgments to be moral intuitions in a very strong sense.

I would like to consider two significant grounds for doubting that our considered moral judgments are epistemically similar to simple mathematical judgments. They also may seem to be grounds for doubting that considered moral judgments are intuitions in any strong sense and even that considered moral judgments could have a significant positive epistemic status. The first ground for doubt is based on the fact that our considered moral judgments seem to be revisable; the second is based on the fact that there is considerable disagreement regarding these judgments.

Most people who reflect on their moral views encounter conflicts among their considered moral judgments. Many of us find certain moral principles intuitively obvious, particularly midlevel principles such as "It is right to keep one's promises" and "It is wrong to lie." One need not reflect very long to come up with cases where application of an intuitive principle produces a judgment at odds with our considered moral judgment regarding the case. (This is just what one does when arguing by counterexample.) Conflicts can also emerge if we make different intuitive moral judgments about different particular cases and there is no difference between the cases that we judge sufficient to justify our different moral judgments. When we encounter conflicts among our considered moral judgments, moral reflection obviously does not halt. We decide what to revise and move on. But the existence, or more properly, the frequency of such conflicts does seem to count against the claim that our considered moral judgments are epistemically similar to simple mathematical beliefs.

The problem is not that our intuitive judgments about simple logical and mathematical propositions could never come into conflict and can never be revised. There are mathematical propositions that seem intuitively obvious but lead to paradox—that is, they come into conflict with other intuitive mathematical propositions. In such cases we are led to revise some intuitive judgments. But such occurrences are the rare exception in mathematics and logic, however, and vastly more common with moral judgments. Hence, although we might get away with claiming that simple mathematical propositions can be seen to be true by anyone who adequately understands them, even though we are forced to allow that those who adequately understand are sometimes mistaken when they think they see something to be true, the parallel claim regarding considered moral judgments seems much less plausible.

People seem to disagree a lot about morality. Some of the differences might not constitute conflicts—that is, cases where the judgments are inconsistent. Some of the differences might arise from misunderstanding on the part of one or both parties, and some might not involve considered moral judgments. But even setting aside such disagreements, there are many real conflicts between the considered moral judgments of mature adults who fully understand. Not only does the existence and extent of these conflicts render untenable the claim that considered moral judgments have the same epistemic status as simple mathematical judgments, but it also could be taken to block the claim that considered moral judgments have any significant positive epistemic status. One reason is that, in many cases of conflict, the parties to the different sides come from different societies or cultures, a circumstance that seems to support the idea that moral judgments are some sort of social or cultural construct. They might then be reliable guides to the taboos or mores of the judge's own culture but not to anything more substantial or objective. When conflicts among considered moral judgments within cultures are added to the mix, we seem to have ample reason to doubt whether they are reliable guides to anything at all.

Actually, the fact that a single person's considered moral judgments can conflict and require revision is not a bad thing. Indeed, it is a fundamental element of the most influential approach to the construction and justification of moral theories. According to the method of reflective equilibrium, we should strive to mold our considered moral judgments and a set of moral principles that account for them into a coherent system via a series of mutual adjustments to principles and judgments, with revisions guided only by what seems most likely to be true upon due consideration. If only considered moral judgments and moral principles are involved, a narrow reflective equilibrium emerges. Inquirers should next strive to bring their judgments into a wide equilibrium, which also includes background theories and judgments—for example, views regarding the nature of persons or the role of morality in society. Once again, in the search for a wide reflective equilibrium, no type of judgment has a privileged status. Coherence is attained by a series of mutual adjustments.

The method of reflective equilibrium is an idealization of the kind of moral inquiry carried on by many philosophers and presumably by at least some reflective nonspecialists. We might, then, shift away from the considered moral judgments of ordinary people and ask about the epistemic status of the moral judgments we would hold if we brought our moral judgments into wide reflective equilibrium. It might be all but impossible for us ever to attain such equilibrium, but perhaps we can approach it ever more closely. The moral judgments a person holds in reflective equilibrium would have a number of epistemically good features: they would have been formed after careful and thorough reflection, they would not conflict with either the person's other moral judgments or any of the person's other beliefs, and they would be part of a highly coherent system of beliefs and judgments. Moreover, we might hope that there would be fewer conflicts between the moral judgments of different people who had brought their beliefs into reflective equilibrium. One reason for this hope is that part of the method explicitly involves considering alternatives to one's own moral system.

Unfortunately, I fear we cannot expect that inquirers will converge upon a single system of moral judgments in wide reflective equilibrium. It is too easy to imagine people who begin with radically different moral perspectives being led to revise their judgments in different ways to overcome the conflicts internal to their own moral perspectives, and so at the end of their inquiries being led to accept very different, incompatible moral systems in reflective equilibrium. So questions about the reliability of moral judgments persist.

I will close by briefly describing one possible way of addressing such questions. Suppose that people differ in their capacities for making moral judgments. Suppose that this capacity needs to be developed through experience and possibly even training, but that it can also be corrupted. (For what it is worth, common sense strongly supports these suppositions.) Let's call a person with a well-developed capacity for moral judgment a competent moral judge. If two people with unequally developed capacities for moral judgment were to bring their moral judgments into reflective equilibrium, they would probably disagree to some extent. Such disagreement would not establish that the moral judgments of both inquirers were unreliable, however, for it might be that only one of the inquirers is a competent moral judge. Presumably the moral judgments the competent judge would make in reflective equilibrium would be quite reliable. Since the other person's moral judgments would also be in reflective equilibrium, it would not be possible to prove to that person that his or her judgments are unreliable or that the competent judge's moral judgments are reliable. But this would not change the fact that the competent judge's moral judgments would be reliable.

One might require that, in order for a person's moral judgments to have a significant positive epistemic status, a person must be able to prove that his or her moral judgments are reliable or that he or she is a competent moral judge. If this is right, then we will have to grant that even the moral judgments competent judges hold in reflective equilibrium have no significant positive epistemic status. We should note, however, that if similar requirements were imposed across the board, we would be forced to conclude that almost none of our beliefs or judgments

have a significant positive epistemic status. On the other hand, if actually being reliable is sufficient for having a significant positive epistemic status, at least in conjunction with all the other epistemic goods we have identified, then it seems that the moral judgments competent judges would make in reflective equilibrium will have such a status. One might doubt whether there are any competent judges, but I do not think we know that there are not. So there is reason to hope that moral judgments can attain a strong positive epistemic status.

See also Metaethics; Meaning; Moral Skepticism; Noncognitivism; Rationality.

Bibliography

Alston, William. "Epistemic Desiderata." *Philosophy and Phenomenological Research* 53 (1993): 527–551.

Alston, William. "Level Confusions in Epistemology." In *Studies in Epistemology.* Vol. 5 of *Midwest Studies in Philosophy*, edited by Peter A. French, Theodore E. Uehling Jr., and Howard K. Wettstein, 135–150. Minneapolis: University of Minnesota Press, 1980.

Audi, Robert. *Epistemology: A Contemporary Introduction to the Theory of Knoweldge.* London: Routledge, 1998.

Audi, Robert. *The Good in the Right: A Theory of Intuition and Intrinsic Value.* Princeton, NJ: Princeton University Press, 2004.

Ayer, A. J. *Language, Truth, and Logic.* London: V. Gollancz, 1938.

Blackburn, Simon. *Spreading the World.* Oxford: Clarendon Press, 1984.

BonJour, Lawrence. *The Structure of Empirical Knowledge.* Cambridge, MA: Harvard University Press, 1985.

Brandt, Richard. *A Theory of the Good and the Right.* Oxford: Clarendon Press, 1979.

Brink, David. *Moral Realism and the Foundations of Ethics.* Cambridge, U.K.: Cambridge University Press, 1989.

Darwall, Stephen, Allan Gibbard, and Peter Railton. "Toward fin de siècle Ethics: Some Trends." *The Philosophical Review* 101 (1992): 115–189.

Daniels, Norman. "Wide Reflective Equilibrium and Theory Acceptance in Ethics." *Journal of Philosophy* 76 (1979): 256–282.

DePaul, Michael R. *Balance and Refinement: Beyond Coherentism in Moral Inquiry.* London: Routledge, 1993.

DePaul, Michael R. "Value Monism in Epistemology." In *Knowledge, Truth, and Duty: Essays on Epistemic Justification, Responsibility, and Virtue,* edited by Matthias Steup. Oxford: Oxford University Press, 2001.

DePaul, Michael R., and William Ramsey. *Rethinking Intuition: The Psychology of Intuitions and Their Role in Philosophical Inquiry.* Lanham, MD: Rowman and Littlefield, 1998.

Foley, Richard. *The Theory of Epistemic Rationality.* Cambridge, MA: Harvard University Press, 1987.

Gibbard, Allan. *Wise Choices, Apt Feelings.* Cambridge, MA: Harvard University Press, 1990.

Goldman, Alvin. "What Is Justified Belief?" In *Justification and Knowledge*, edited by George Pappas. Dordrecht: D. Reidel, 1979.

Hare, R.M. *The Language of Moral*. Oxford: Clarendon Press, 1952.

Harman, Gilbert. *The Nature of Morality*. New York: Oxford University Press, 1977.

McDowell, John "Values and Secondary Qualities." In *Morality and Objectivity*, edited by Ted Honderich. London: Routledge & Kegan Paul, 1985.

Moore, G. E. *Principia Ethica*. Cambridge, U.K.: Cambridge University Press, 1903.

Nagel, Thomas. *The View from Nowhere*. New York: Oxford University Press, 1987.

Plantinga, Alvin. Warrant: *The Current Debate*. Oxford: Oxford University Press, 1993.

Prichard, H. A. "Does Moral Philosophy Rest on a Mistake?" *Mind* 21(1912): 21–37.

Rawls, John. "Outline of a Decision Procedure for Ethics." *The Philosophical Review* 60 (1951): 177–197.

Rawls, John. *A Theory of Justice*. Cambridge, MA: Harvard University Press, 1971.

Ross, W. D. *The Right and the Good*. Oxford: Oxford University Press, 1930.

Sinnott-Armstrong, Walter, and Mark Timmons, eds. *Moral Knowledge? New Readings in Moral Epistemology*. Oxford: Oxford University Press, 1996.

Smith, Michael. *The Moral Problem*. Oxford: Blackwell, 1994.

Sosa, Ernest. "Minimal Intuition." In *Rethinking Intuition: The Psychology of Intuitions and Their Role in Philosophical Inquiry*, edited by Michael DePaul and William Ramsey. Lanham, MD: Rowman and Littlefield, 1998.

Stevenson, Charles L. "The Emotive Meaning of Ethical Terms." *Mind* 46 (1937): 14–31.

Stich, Steven. *The Fragmentation of Reason*. Cambridge, MA: MIT Press, 1990.

Wiggins, David. *Needs, Values, Truth: Essays in the Philosophy of Value*. Oxford: Basil Blackwell, 1987.

Williams, Bernard. *Ethics and the Limits of Philosophy*. Cambridge, MA: Harvard University Press, 1985.

Zagzebski, Linda. "What Is Knowledge?" In *The Blackwell Guide to Epistemology*, edited by John Greco and Ernest Sosa. Oxford: Blackwell, 1999.

Michael R. DePaul (1996, 2005)

MORALITY

See *Ethics; Ethics and Morality*

MORAL LAW, THE

See *Kant, Immanuel*

MORAL MOTIVATION

See *Moral Psychology; Moral Sentiments; Virtue Ethics*

MORAL NATURALISM

See *Ethical Naturalism*

MORAL PHILOSOPHY

See *Ehtics, History of*

MORAL PRINCIPLES: THEIR JUSTIFICATION

The problem of how, if at all, we could set about justifying assertions about what we ought to do in various practical situations is one that has been the major concern of moral philosophers. Such basic questions are indeed endemic in most branches of philosophy. We ask not only if we can ever know what we ought to do but whether we can justify our claims to knowledge of an external world, how we can know the truth of statements about the past, or whether we can ever be sure of the existence of minds other than our own. But in ethics the problem seems more recalcitrant and, indeed, to many nonphilosophers at least, more real. For while skepticism about the existence of an external world or of other minds may seem difficult to refute, to most it is impossible to embrace, whereas skepticism about the possibility of claiming knowledge of any objective truths about what we ought to do is not so rare, either among men in general or those who would wish to characterize themselves as philosophers.

It is not, of course, surprising that this should be so. Ethical attitudes vary much more, from society to society and even between individuals, than do our beliefs about the external world or other people's feelings. The patent fact of ethical disagreement forces us to reexamine the bases of our moral beliefs. Furthermore, the disagreements we encounter concerning moral issues often seem to involve deep matters of principle that leave no common ground between the disputants. This is sometimes referred to as the problem of disagreement about ultimate moral principles. It is this problem—whether ultimate moral principles are susceptible of rational justification—that will be examined in this article.

Most philosophers would agree that the particular way in which a philosophical problem is formulated will make a great deal of difference to what solution is possible to it or, indeed, whether any solution is possible. It will be necessary therefore to set out in detail what is meant by a disagreement about ultimate moral principles and to defend this way of expressing the issue against certain objections before a possible solution is set out.

MORAL PRINCIPLES

A "man of principle" is sometimes thought of, with distaste, as a man who acts in accordance with a fixed set of rules, ignoring the complexities of the situation and failing to adapt his behavior to changing circumstances. The morality of principles and rules is sometimes contrasted with the morality of sensibility, which emphasizes such virtues as sympathy and integrity as against a rigid code of behavior. In either kind of morality, however, particular judgments will have to be made, based on a view of the situation in which the agent acts, and some factors in the situation will have to be regarded as reasons for acting in one way rather than another. There is, therefore, a more general sense of "moral principle," which can be regarded as common to both views, in which a moral principle indicates some factor that is generally relevant to what ought to be done.

Moral principles can then be regarded as statements picking out those factors of situations that can be appealed to as moral reasons. "Lying is wrong" suggests that the fact that a statement is known to be false is a reason for not making it to someone. "Adultery is wrong" suggests that the fact that someone is married is a reason for his refraining from sexual intercourse with any person who is not his spouse. And, again, "One ought to be kind" suggests that there are reasons for performing kind actions rather than unkind ones. Asserting a moral principle of this kind and denying the suggestion about reasons results in paradox. Thus, for example, if somebody says "Lying is wrong, but the fact that a statement constitutes a lie is no reason whatsoever for not making it," he seems to have taken back in the second half of his sentence what he asserted in the first.

If saying that someone ought to do something commits one to claiming that there is some fact in the situation that is a reason for doing the thing in question, then this reason must be subject to the requirement that reasons in general must satisfy: that anything that is a reason in any one case must be a reason in every case unless there are other special reasons for ignoring it. This applies to reasons generally, not just to moral reasons. For example,

if the fact that it is raining is a reason for saying Smith will get wet, it is a reason for saying anyone else will unless there are some relevant differences in their cases, such as being indoors or carrying an umbrella. It is this that leads to the claim that moral principles must be universal, at least to the degree that they pick out factors that are universally relevant to what we ought to do, although not necessarily universally determining what we ought to do in every particular case. Thus it would seem that the correctness of the universal moral principle involved—or, in other words, that what is appealed to as a reason should indeed be a reason—is a necessary although not a sufficient condition of the correctness of the particular judgment about what ought to be done.

JUSTIFICATION OF MORAL JUDGMENTS. If the correctness of universal moral principles is a condition of the correctness of particular moral judgments, then obviously the first question we must ask in investigating how our particular moral judgments can be justified is, How can we justify claiming that certain moral principles are correct? There are, however, some objections to this way of treating the problem that must be considered.

It may be pointed out that value judgments in other areas do not seem to require justification by reference to some universally relevant factors. And if we are willing to allow that in other realms of value there are judgments that do not require to be backed by universal principles, why not in morals? For example, there are very considerable difficulties in representing judgments about the value of a work of art as being backed by or dependent on principles at all. It may be impossible, when we say some work of art is good, to indicate any feature the possession of which is bound to make any other work of art good. (One might be tempted to say that beauty is such a feature. But this is unconvincing because one is using the term either narrowly, in which case there are plenty of good works of art that one would never describe as beautiful, or so widely that it means only "good in the way that a work of art is good.") Surely, however, it must be agreed that the goodness of anything, including a work of art, depends on what qualities it has, however difficult it may be to say in a given case precisely what qualities it has that make it good. And in order to begin to justify the judgment that something is good, one must refer to its qualities; one cannot draw anyone's attention to the goodness itself. If it is proper to refer to these qualities to back one's claim that the object is good, then it is at least to the point to ask why something else, which has the same qualities, is not good. If such a question is to the point, it shows that we accept that the possession of certain qualities is being put forward as a general reason for saying that the object is good.

Even if this is correct, however, it is clear that the features by virtue of which any given work of art is judged to be good tend to be many, complicated, and organically related. Although any feature pointed to in support of a judgment that a work of art is good must also be relevant to the criticism of other works of art, there may be in every other case many other relevant factors that alter the situation completely. The same thing might be claimed for moral cases. It may be said that every human situation is infinitely complicated, so that however many relevant features one may pick out in a particular case, there will always be a host of others that can be set against them. Such considerations would lead not so much to a denial of the universality of morally relevant features as to doubt about the utility of stating the problem in terms of principles. To this there are two answers.

First, it would be against common sense to claim, for example, that the wanton murder of children is not wrong. Even where other features that are regarded as morally relevant are also present—such as that one had promised one's old mother on her deathbed to try to exterminate the Jews—few would regard them as justifying child murder. So anyone who persists in claiming that it is always possible that such actions as child murder may be justified because of the complex character of every particular human situation is, at best, someone who has an unusual moral outlook, and this means that his very claim that every situation is so complicated that no general principles can be admitted is dependent on his having a different set of moral principles from most people's. So even to consider whether this objection is correct, we still have to ask which general principles are justifiable.

Second, we have already remarked that moral principles will be a necessary but not a sufficient condition of the correctness of our particular moral judgments. Although on their own they may never be sufficient to solving all moral problems, they will certainly be necessary to our having any moral problems at all. This may be illustrated in terms of a case mentioned by Jean-Paul Sartre. A young man has a dilemma. Should he join the French Resistance, or should he stay at home and look after his aging mother? Sartre points out that no rehearsal of general principles would ever serve to solve such a problem. This is no doubt true, but it does not show that the correctness of such principles is not relevant. For why is the young man worried about only those two possibilities? There are plenty of other things he could do. He could learn tightrope walking or set up as an ice-cream

vendor or enlarge his earlobes with brass rings. But these are obviously of no importance, whereas looking after the old mother and joining the resistance are important. Why is Sartre's case serious and dramatic and the other suggestions frivolous and silly? Why does it matter what the young man does, to himself or to anyone? There can surely be no problem at all unless such things as joining the resistance (defending one's country) or looking after the old mother (kindness to a dependent) are morally relevant features of the situation—unless they are things that it is reasonable to consider in deciding what to do. And if there are morally relevant features in the situation, there are corresponding moral principles. If these principles are not correct (and, indeed, there are those who would question patriotic principles), then there is no problem, or at least not the same problem.

A different kind of objection can be disposed of very briefly. It is that as a matter of experience, we do not think in terms of principles. Rather, on particular occasions we simply know instinctively what is right. Now this may very well be true or perhaps true for a number of people. However, the question at issue is not a psychological one about the kind of process that goes on before a moral judgment is made; it is a philosophical one about how we may justify making the moral judgments we do make, by whatever psychological process we make them. Whatever goes on in the heads of mathematicians, it is still Euclid's proofs alone that can justify Euclid's theorems.

ULTIMATE MORAL PRINCIPLES

Moral principles in the sense adumbrated above will be of varying degrees of generality, and some will be held to be more fundamental than others. For example, the principle that one ought not to commit adultery may be defended on the ground that adultery is inimical to the stability of the family. In terms of reasons for acting, this can be put as follows. The fact that someone is married is held to be a reason for his refraining from sexual intercourse with anyone other than his spouse. But why is this a reason? Because, it might be said, *in fact* sexual infidelity is apt to break up the unity of the family. Such an argument would, of course, presuppose that the fact that something is apt to disrupt the family is a reason for avoiding it or, in other words, that one ought not to disrupt the family. Thus the principle "One ought not to commit adultery" would be regarded as less fundamental than the principle "One ought not to disrupt the unity of the family." In the process of trying to justify particular moral judgments, we will usually find ourselves trying to show that certain necessary conditions of their correctness, our moral principles, have further necessary conditions in terms of more fundamental moral principles. The process will usually be much more complicated than I have represented it; in justifying a less fundamental moral principle, we will usually find a variety of more fundamental moral principles coming into play. But however complicated such a process may be, it is obvious that we cannot suppose it to go on forever. At some point we should reach some principles that we regard as the most fundamental. For example, we might want to say that we do not claim that one ought to be kind because this follows from some further principle; we ought to be kind because we ought, and that is an end to the matter. These we may call ultimate moral principles, and their correctness is a necessary condition of the correctness of all other moral judgments. Unless some such ultimate moral principles can be shown to be justifiable, no other moral judgments can be shown to be justifiable.

Some philosophers hold that this representation of the matter is utterly mistaken and, indeed, that it is precisely because of this "justificationist" view that so many philosophers despair of finding an answer and become ethical skeptics. If, it is argued, moral principles are regarded not as first premises from which a moral system is deduced but as conjectures that can be altered and amended by subsequent moral experience, we at least have a method of correcting our moral attitudes that will justify us in claiming that they are more or less rationally defensible. It will not be possible to do this view justice in a small space. It can only be said here that the major difficulty with this view is that the test of the moral principle is taken to be the particular judgments we are inclined to make, particular judgments that conflict with the supposed principle and thus refute it. But what is now the test of the correctness of the particular judgment? The suggested method would seem to be a way of finding out, by examining someone's particular judgments, what his moral principles are rather than a way of finding out which moral principles are correct. Furthermore, it has not been claimed in this article that moral principles are first premises from which whole moral systems can be deduced but only that moral principles are statements of relevant moral factors. Their correctness is a necessary, not a sufficient, condition of the correctness of moral judgments.

Nevertheless, the charge is certainly well founded that this way of setting out the problem is a most plausible invitation to ethical skepticism. For it would on the face of it appear that the very statement of the problem precludes its solution. If we look on more and more general moral principles as representing a regress of necessary conditions of the correctness of moral judgments, then either this regress is viciously infinite or there is a point at which it must stop. But any attempt to justify some principle as a stopping point would appear to start the whole process off again. To acquiesce in some stopping point would be to accept an ultimate principle and, it would seem, to accept that nothing further could be said in its justification. It looks then as if this way of putting the problem makes inevitable the conclusion that ultimate principles are unjustifiable.

AUTONOMY AND OBJECTIVITY OF MORAL PRINCIPLES

One way to put the problem is to regard it as a conflict between the autonomy and the objectivity of moral principles. The demand that ethics be regarded as autonomous originated with Immanuel Kant, in the view that an action is not moral unless it is determined by the agent's rational will rather than by something external to that will, such as a desire, or the will of another (a king, a friend, the state, God). Here the concern is with the determination of action, not directly with the determination or, rather, justification of moral judgment. The autonomy of moral principles, with which we are concerned, is not, however, entirely unconnected with Kant's sense of autonomy. It is the idea that a moral judgment can never depend for its correctness entirely on factors that are nonmoral; that is, that in the justification of any moral judgment one must have recourse to a moral principle, which must in turn be justified in terms of some more general moral principle and so on. In other words, a moral judgment or principle is never deducible from any set of premises that contain no moral judgment or principle.

The demand that morality be regarded as objective was also emphasized by Kant. A moral act for Kant was one that could be willed by an autonomous, rational will; its character as a moral act depended not on the particular nature or desires of the willing agent but on the nature of a rational will as such. For Kant a maxim is objective when it is valid for any rational being. Again, Kant's concern was with the determination of action rather than the justification of judgment. But once again our sense of objectivity is not unconnected with Kant's. When someone's judgment is stigmatized as subjective rather than objective, this means that some idiosyncratic factors such as the hopes and fears or special interests of the speaker have affected his judgment; an objective judgment, however, is one not affected by such idiosyncratic factors but one that any reasonable and unbiased person would form in the circumstances. Obviously, we can speak of objective matters only in respect of matters that are publicly determinable, where we can talk of what would be judged by any reasonable and careful observer rather than what appears to be the case to some individual because of some peculiarities of his own. Thus, we might say with Kant that objectively true judgments are those that are "valid for all rational beings" rather than what merely seems to be so to certain individuals. The demand of objectivity in ethics may then be put at its most minimal as the demand that the truth of any moral judgment shall not depend on the peculiarities of the person making it but, rather, that it shall be determinable by any rational observer who is apprised of the facts. Its truth will not depend on the fact that it is judged so by some one person rather than another but on objective considerations.

The conflict between the demands of objectivity and autonomy is now not difficult to see. For how can ultimate principles, which cannot be based on any further considerations, be based on objective considerations? How can we claim that they are matters that are publicly determinable when it would seem that, if they were autonomous, no considerations beyond themselves would make their truth determinable at all?

Henry Sidgwick, impressed by the utilitarian moral system but despairing of the kinds of argument put forward by earlier utilitarians such as Jeremy Bentham and John Stuart Mill to justify their ultimate principle, substituted instead the doctrine of intuition, a doctrine that was accepted by many other philosophers who were very far from being utilitarians. It was thought that the problem of justification in ethics was parallel to similar problems in other fields of knowledge and that in each case one would find oneself with incorrigible starting points, truths known directly, without inference or the necessity or possibility of further justification. Thus, in our knowledge of the world we might be thought to begin with direct awareness of our experience; in mathematics, with the direct perception of mathematical relationships. In ethics we begin simply with the perception of universal ethical relationships, between what is right or fitting and certain states of affairs. Whatever the difficulties in this general epistemological theory, in ethics there is the additional difficulty that the commonsense roots of the problem of justification—the inescapable fact of disagreement on fundamental ethical matters—are untouched by the doctrine of intuitionism. The appeal to intuition in the face of this disagreement leaves no way of rationally resolving it.

TRANSCENDENTAL ARGUMENTS

It is possible, however, that an account of the justification of ultimate principles can be given that avoids both an infinite regress of justifying principles and any arbitrary stopping point. Kant's demands for autonomy and objectivity amount to the requirement that a morally good action be rationally chosen in accord with a law that is valid for all rational beings universally and that is determined by nothing beyond itself. The difficulties in making the demands of autonomy and objectivity compatible, so that this requirement becomes a feasible one, seem capable of only one kind of solution, which was the one adopted by Kant. If moral principles cannot be justified by considerations outside themselves yet must be regarded as objectively justifiable, then it seems that certain moral principles must somehow be demanded by the formal character of morality itself; certain rules must be required by any morality that is to satisfy the two demands.

Kant's particular solution has not seemed very satisfactory, but if a solution is to be found at all, it must be in the same direction. To put the point in more contemporary language, the only kind of solution that seems possible is one that shows that certain moral principles must be regarded as correct if moral discourse is to be possible at all, at least as an autonomous and objective form of practical discourse. An argument to this effect may be called a transcendental argument. If such arguments can be constructed, it should be easy to see how they solve the problem we have been considering. For a principle can be shown to be objectively true, without appealing to factors outside itself, if it can be shown that the form of discourse of which the principle is an example is impossible without presupposing the principle. That is, by showing that no one can claim to be using a form of autonomous, practical, and objective discourse unless he at the same time accepts the principle in question.

Three arguments of this kind can be advanced to establish three ultimate principles, which we may call the principles of impartiality, rational benevolence, and liberty. It is important that throughout it should be borne in mind that these arguments are intended to establish ultimate principles—that is, factors of the most general moral relevance, which will be necessary, but by no means sufficient, to establishing any correct moral theories, rules, or particular judgments. Even given that these arguments establish the ultimate principles of impartiality, rational benevolence, and liberty, there will still remain the difficult problem of their application in practice.

IMPARTIALITY. As far as we are concerned with a form of discourse in which we objectively judge actions right or wrong, so that a correct practical judgment is one that could in principle be reached by anybody, such judgments must be made in terms of features that the actions or the situations in which they are done possess and not on any other factors arbitrarily introduced by the person making the judgment. Thus, any feature picked out as relevant must be one that is always relevant unless there is some special explanation, for a feature that is relevant in one case and not in another, where there is no further difference, is one that is not relevant at all in any ordinary sense and forms no guide to action. It follows that any action that it is right or wrong for one person to do is right or wrong for every person to do unless there are some special factors present in the other cases. And from this demand of universality it follows, insofar as morality is practical, that one ought to act in accordance with it: What anyone ought to do in any given set of circumstances is what anyone else ought to do, as long as his case is not relevantly different, and anything one ought to do on any given occasion is what one ought to do on every occasion unless again there are factors present that are relevantly different. That one ought to treat similar cases similarly is obviously a general case of the particular requirement of justice toward men, that any form of treatment that is thought to be right for one man must be right for all others, unless the others are significantly different.

RATIONAL BENEVOLENCE. The principle of rational benevolence is that stated by Sidgwick, that one ought in action to consider the interests of all beings in the universe. That this is a most impractical injunction is important, but not fatal, for how in practical situations we may apply any ultimate principle is another, though admittedly difficult, question.

The principle may be justified as follows. The demand of objectivity is that what is right or wrong should be determinable at least in principle by all rational beings. This requires that moral discourse should be a form of public discourse, in which the relevance and force of any consideration is dependent on its content and not on the will or status of whoever puts it forward. That is, the remark of any rational being may be relevant to the question whether some action is right or wrong. The ideal of this form of discourse therefore requires that it should be possible for any rational being to participate in it as an interlocutor; if any is excluded arbitrarily then all may be, and the form of discourse as a public institution would be impossible. This does not mean that other forms of discourse may not be constructed in which certain possible interlocutors are excluded by fiat, but this would not then be the fully rational, autonomous, and objective form of discourse we require. A parallel may be found in scientific discourse. As far as it is objective, considerations must be dealt with on their merits and not in terms of the will or status of whoever puts them forward. If any arbitrary exclusion of possible interlocutors is made, then we do not have public objective scientific discourse but a sort of game in which arbitrarily selected players alone are entitled to make certain moves and in which what is determined in the outcome is who has won rather than what is true.

If moral discourse is to be public and objective, then it must allow for the participation of any possible rational interlocutor. Now let us define an interest as that which any rational being should seek for himself insofar as he considers the effects of his actions on himself and not on others except insofar as what affects others also affects him (for example, if it is rational for anyone to avoid pain, then it is in my interest to seek those actions that avoid pain to myself but not necessarily those that avoid pain to others except insofar as the pain of others causes pain to me or prevents my achieving some other end that it would be rational for me to choose for myself). Now it is by definition necessary that every rational being should seek his own interests as far as possible. It would be irrational for any being to participate in a form of discourse the practical effect of which would be to deny his interests; hence, it would be irrational for anyone to adopt moral discourse without further justification if from the beginning his interests were to be ruled out. But this means that anyone who wishes to adopt moral discourse must allow that any possible interlocutor must not have his interests ruled out of consideration from the beginning, and any rational being is in principle a possible interlocutor. It follows that as far as public objective moral discourse is to be possible, it is presupposed that what is determined by such means will not neglect the interests of any rational being—that is, that in deciding what I ought to do, or what anyone ought to do, the interests of all rational beings whatsoever must be taken into account.

LIBERTY. The principle of liberty is that one ought not to interfere, without special justification, in the chosen course of any rational being or impose on any rational being conditions that will prevent him from pursuing his chosen courses of action. Moral discourse is a form of discourse in which we try to guide action rationally. We try to determine action on the basis of a rational consideration of the nature of the action and its context, not by some other means such as violence. Any interference with the chosen course of a rational being is a determination of his action by force or at least a limit imposed by force on the extent to which his actions may be rationally determined. Such interference must then be presupposed as absent in public objective practical discourse in which action is determined by reason, and hence in using such discourse, in participating in it as an institution, one is presupposing that one ought not to interfere by force, but only by rational persuasion, in the chosen course of any rational being.

The arguments given for these three principles are very much oversimplified, and it could not be claimed that they have the force of demonstrations. But enough has been said to show that the type of argument they represent is at least a possible one and hence that the apparent conflict between autonomy and objectivity is not a real one and that the problem of the justification of ultimate principles may not be insoluble.

COMPLETENESS AND APPLICATION OF PRINCIPLES. Two important problems remain. The first we may deal with briefly. It is one that was very important to Kant, with regard to both theoretical and practical principles. How can we be sure that we have achieved completeness in any list of principles? If ultimate principles can be established only by transcendental arguments, we have at least some clue to the answer to this problem; for the rest it might be argued that the problem is not so urgent as some have thought.

A transcendental argument is one that depends on an account of what is necessary to a given form of discourse; in ethics we are concerned with what is necessary to a form of discourse that is practical, universal, objective, and autonomous. We are, that is, dependent on a consideration of the formal characteristics of the form of discourse. This gives at least some negative criterion for deciding what principles may be justified as ultimate. Thus, it would be most implausible to suggest, for example, that "One ought not to drink alcoholic liquor on Sundays" could be justified as an ultimate moral principle. For it is reasonably obvious that no direct connection could be established between the purely formal characteristics of any form of discourse and such particular matters as are picked out by the concepts of the principle in question. Such a principle would have to be, if justifiable at all, one that would depend on matters beyond the purely formal characteristics of practical reason. It is always possible, however, though in this case surely a fan-

tastic suggestion, that someone with sufficient ingenuity might show that some apparently low-level principle is in fact justifiable as an ultimate one by a transcendental argument. And this may disturb us, for how can we be sure that we are not failing to take account of such principles all the time? We should not, however, be much disturbed, for two reasons. First, if a principle is a necessary condition of the possibility of moral discourse, one would expect to find it as a pervasive explicit or implicit principle of most moral codes (allowing for the resources of human confusion), and this is true for the three principles—justice, benevolence, and liberty—we have mentioned. Second, when it is suggested that there is a reason for acting in one way rather than another, the suggestion requires justification, in the absence of which the suggestion may be reasonably ignored. The onus of proof is on anyone who suggests that a certain principle is correct; until such proof is at least suggested, the fear that there may be quite unknown principles, which are not generally accepted but which could, with sufficient ingenuity, be justified transcendentally, is an idle one.

The second difficulty that we face at this point is of the utmost importance; indeed, one might fairly say that out of it all the really important and difficult questions of substance in ethics arise. It is the problem of the application of these principles to particular situations, both in themselves and in relation to one another. Unless it is possible to show that these principles can be rationally applied, then no amount of rational demonstration of the ultimate principles will enable us to show that the particular moral judgments we make can be rationally justified.

In this article it has been argued that any account of how particular judgments about what ought to be done can be justified will need to examine principles that are necessary but not sufficient to justify particular judgments. These principles will pick out factors of general moral relevance, and the principles in turn will require justification. This may then require reference to more general principles, but some principles that are incapable of further justification will be reached in this way, and these we have called ultimate principles. It would seem that ultimate principles could never be justified objectively, but it is suggested that arguments that show them to be necessary if objective practical discourse is to be possible would justify them and that such arguments are possible. It is, however, emphasized that since ultimate principles are necessary but not sufficient to the justification of particular judgments, we have not by this suggestion solved the whole problem of how ethical disagreement can be rationally resolved. We have only removed one ground for saying that they can never be rationally resolved.

See also Bentham, Jeremy; Ethical Objectivism; Impartiality; Intuition; Kant, Immanuel; Liberty; Mill, John Stuart; Moral Rules and Principles; Moral Sense; Rationality; Sartre, Jean-Paul; Sidgwick, Henry; Value and Valuation.

Bibliography

For an account of objectivity and autonomy, and an attempt to justify certain factors as ethically relevant from a consideration of the formal character of practical reason, see Immanuel Kant, *The Moral Law: Kant's Groundwork of the Metaphysic of Morals,* translated by H. J. Paton (London, 1964).

Attempts to justify ultimate principles are to be found in Jeremy Bentham's *Introduction to the Principles of Morals and Legislation* in *A Fragment on Government, and an Introduction to the Principles of Morals and Legislation,* edited by W. Harrison (Oxford, 1948); J. S. Mill's *Utilitarianism* in *Utilitarianism, Liberty, and Representative Government,* No. 482A in Everyman's Library; Henry Sidgwick's *Methods of Ethics* (London, 1907; reprinted 1962).

More recent attempts to justify some factors as of ultimate ethical relevance are to be found in Kurt Baier's *The Moral Point of View: A Rational Basis for Ethics* (Ithaca, NY: Cornell University Press, 1958), especially Chs. 7–8, and Baier's two articles in *Philosophical Studies,* 4 (1953)—"Good Reasons," 1–15, and "Proving a Moral Judgment," 33–44; J. N. Findlay's *Values and Intentions* (London: Allen and Unwin, 1961), his "Morality by Convention," in *Mind,* n.s., 53 (1944): 142–169, and his "Justification of Attitudes," in *Mind,* n.s., 63 (1954): 145–161; Philippa Foot's "Moral Arguments," in *Mind,* n.s., 67 (1958): 502–513, and her "Moral Beliefs," in *PAS,* n.s., 59 (1958–1959): 85–104; A. P. Griffiths's "Justifying Moral Principles," in *PAS,* n.s., 58 (1957–1958): 103–124; D. L. Pole's *The Conditions of Rational Inquiry* (London: University of London, Athlone Press, 1961), especially Ch. V; M. G. Singer's *Generalisation in Ethics* (London, 1963); S. E. Toulmin, *An Examination of the Place of Reason in Ethics* (Cambridge, U.K.: Cambridge University Press, 1950; reprinted 1958).

A. Phillips Griffiths (1967)

MORAL PSYCHOLOGY

Moral psychology is the area of scholarship that investigates the nature of psychological states that are associated with morality—states such as intentions, motives, the will, reason, moral emotions (such as guilt and shame), and moral beliefs and attitudes. The purview of moral psychology also includes associated concepts of virtue, character trait, and autonomy. It has generally been thought of as a descriptive enterprise rather than a normative one, though this is not always the case.

Traditionally we can see two different approaches to moral psychology. The first is the *a priori* approach to understanding moral psychology and the significance and function of psychological states. The second is the empirical approach that considers the evidence of their significance, function, and development. Both of these strands will take as their starting point common sense intuitions about how people think about morality, make moral decisions, and the circumstances under which they feel moral emotions. These intuitions may be based on a long history of observation of human behavior, or they may simply be the result of natural selection leading to similarity in thought which itself might be adaptive. Either way, common sense provides the baseline for research in moral psychology.

The *a priori* strand engages in conceptual analysis of the relevant psychological states and their connections. There is a debate, for example, about whether reason alone can motivate, or not. What *explains* our actions? Is it the case that when I give money to charity I do so simply because I believe it will help people who need help, or do I also need to desire to help them? This will engage us in a discussion of the distinction between belief and desire. A view, which can be traced back at least as far as David Hume, holds that beliefs are of matters of fact and can be true or false; desires, on the other hand, have no truth-value. And, it is desires that are essentially motivating.

Thus, whenever one wants to fully explain an action one needs to be able to identify the belief/desire combination that gives rise to it. But this seems to present a puzzle for moral action: often, morality requires us to act against our desires. I am required to keep my promises, even if I don't want to. But how can I keep my promises if I don't want to, when desire is necessary for action? So there is also a *normative* question that can be raised. Presumably I am giving money to charity because I think that it is a good thing to do. I accept the norms of giving. So, is it the case that if I think that giving to charity is good, it *necessarily* provides me a motivating reason for giving? Is there a necessary connection, or conceptual tie, between the normative reason (the recognition that giving is good) and my motivation to perform the action of giving? If I think there is, then I am an "internalist"; if, however, I do not believe that there is a necessary connection, then I am an "externalist." The acceptance of the norm, the recognition that giving to charity is a good thing, will then necessarily mean that I have at least a weak desire to act on the reason. This could, of course, be defeasible.

But there are those who disagree. Those who are externalists, such as David Brink, argue that amoralists can recognize moral reasons—for example, the amoralist can recognize that it is good to give to charity—yet utterly fail to be moved by this recognition. Indeed, that is what it is to be an amoralist. They are defective not because they fail to see moral reasons as moral, but precisely because they recognize them and yet fail to be moved by them at all. Internalists argue that amoralists, when they articulate a belief that "*x* is good" and then fail to be moved, do not *really* believe what they have articulated. They are trying to make moral judgments, but they are failing to actually do so. Michael Smith also allows that such agents may be practically irrational.

A related feature of Hume's view of moral psychology is its commitment to the view that desire is a given. That is, one cannot reason oneself into a *basic* desire. One can reason about non-basic desires—for example, perhaps I would like to eat ice cream today. Then someone points out that ice cream really isn't very healthy. Since I would rather eat healthy food, I now no longer desire to eat the ice cream. But the desire to eat the ice cream is not basic. Rather, I would like to feel good—and once someone points out to me that a habit of eating ice cream will make me less likely to keep feeling good in the long run, that desire to eat ice cream falls away. But I have not been reasoned out of the basic desire. Indeed, it is its conflict with this desire that makes me ready to jettison the other.

But other writers disagree with this Humean conception of desire, and the reason/desire dichotomy. They believe that we can rationally reflect on basic desires and come to change them through the force of this rational reflection alone. For example, one might argue that desires, even some fundamental ones, are based in part on beliefs that we have. If I desire, for example, to avoid treating persons as means, it may be that I have this desire because I think that being respectful toward others requires this, and I believe, with good reason, that respecting others is obligatory. This desire could be basic in that it cannot be reduced to another desire. If this case is plausible, then we have a basic desire supported by reason.

One way to view this case is as that of a commitment one has. The desire to avoid treating others disrespectfully is more than just a strong basic desire that I have, which happens to be stronger than the other desires I have that might conflict with it. It is a commitment, a normative commitment that I have, and I have it for rea-sons that are motivating reasons. These reasons carry the desire to be respectful of others with them. Further, there are reasons for this desire having to do with my beliefs about, perhaps, what it is to be a flourishing human being. Presumably I could be argued out of the desire, then. A Humean might try to respond to this, however, by pointing out that any "argument" one would give would in turn depend upon some stronger desire for its force. Desires are not themselves true or false, but they can loosely be considered irrational if based on false beliefs. Beliefs exposed as false would then presumably lead to an alteration of the desire one had based on that belief. In the example that I cited above, then, the Humean would probably say that my desire to be respectful of others is based on the belief that this is good and obligatory—so that simply shows that I have a more basic desire to live up to my obligations.

The field of moral psychology also has a more empir-ical side. Aristotle believed that the observation of human beings could reveal to us what, for human beings, was *eudaimonia*. Thomas Hobbes believed that an astute observer of human nature would find support for psychological egoism. Charles Darwin believed that natural selection could account for the sorts of emotions that human beings feel, including the moral emotions. Data that psychologists have gathered about human behavior have influenced the way some think about morality. For example, the work of psychologist Carol Gilligan raised the issue of gender differences in approaches to thinking about moral problems, which in turn influenced writers in feminist ethics.

More recently, empirical psychological research has been brought into moral theory to shed light on a host of issues, ranging from the issue of what, exactly, goes on in a person's brain when she thinks about moral issues, to the issue of the innateness of our moral cognition, to the seemingly basic commitment human beings have to moral objectivity. There is also the extremely interesting and important issue of how natural selection has shaped our sense of morality and moral practices, as well as our moral intuitions. For example, Jesse Prinz has done work in comparative psychology that offers evidence against moral nativism. He believes that the evidence best sup-ports the view that there is not even a minimal innate moral competence—instead it is culture that guides the formation of our moral capacities.

The work of Shaun Nichols draws on literature in developmental psychology to investigate the claim, widely argued in meta-ethics, that people are generally moral objectivists. That is, that people accept the view that there are some true moral judgments, and when a moral judgment is true, it is non-relativistically true. Nichols points out that experiments in developmental psychology, though not at this point in time conclusive, point to the view that for persons, generally, moral objectivism is the "default position" when it comes to commonsense, or lay, meta-ethics.

There is also a trend in moral philosophy of exploring the significance of emotion in moral judgment. This has a counterpart in the psychological research. Joshua Greene and Jonathan Haidt refer to this as the "affective revolution." The interest in this area of psychological research was sparked by Antonio Damasio's work showing that good reasoners needed affect. When portions of the brain that regulate affect are damaged, agents do not perform very well on follow-through in practical reasoning tasks. The classic case, discussed by Damasio, is Phineas Gage. Gage was a railway worker who suffered damage to his frontal lobe in an accident in 1848. This caused an apparently extreme personality change that involved inappropriate emotional responses and a disposition to impulsive behavior. He became unreliable and untrustworthy. He was able to reason in the abstract but was not able to carry through. Affect thus at least seems crucial to effective moral motivation. This conclusion was supported by studies involving more recent cases of frontal lobe damage.

Greene's own work explores brain activity when persons consider moral dilemmas. He and his colleagues discovered that when personal dilemmas were presented to subjects—that is, situations in which those being harmed are close to the subject—there is far more brain activity in the emotional areas of the brain, and those areas of the brain underlying social cognition, than when the problem cases were impersonal. We do seem moved to help in personal cases to a greater extent than impersonal cases. This research supports what charitable organizations have long realized. To promote giving there is a need to make the plight of the suffering personal to potential givers—through photographs and letters, for example. Of course, this leaves untouched the question of what people ought to do. While it is true that our emotions are engaged more in these personal situations, that has no implications for what our obligations are in these cases. This is where we need normative ethics.

Still, this line of research supports the descriptive view that when we behave morally, or at least think about moral issues, in a way that has more motivating force, there is considerable engagement of our affective capacities. Further, when those affective capacities are impaired,

we are left with agents whom we would describe as morally defective. Phineas Gage was widely considered to be a deadbeat after his accident. That is a moral judgment of his character, and the appropriateness of that judgment has something to do with the fact that he lacked the correct emotional responses, those appropriate for the circumstances in which he found himself.

Empirical psychological research has also influenced literature on virtue ethics. Virtue ethics is a type of normative ethical theory that bases moral evaluation on virtue concepts. The approach has been attacked for its failure to reflect psychological reality. For example, Gilbert Harman's work on virtues makes use of situationist literature in social psychology. He argues, citing situationist experiments, that there are no character traits. Rather, the best explanation for a person's behavior is his situation—so, if one would like a reliable way to predict behavior, one needs simply to look at the person's situation. Persons who are in a hurry will be less likely to help than persons who are not. Persons who smell fresh cookies baking are more likely to act benevolently than those who are not smelling the cookies, and so forth.

Thus, character traits need not be cited at all in reliable predictions or explanations. There is no reason to think they exist. Further, if there are no character traits, then there are no character traits that are virtues. It would follow then that virtue ethics is a non-viable normative ethical theory, since it assumes what does not in fact exist. There are no stable character traits, at least, no stable and robust moral character traits. John Doris has softened Harman's claim somewhat, also by bringing in evidence from empirical psychology. On Doris's view all that is warranted by the empirical data is the view that character traits are not "global"—that they are more narrowly prescribed and local than intuition would have it. Thus, there may not be a general robust trait of benevolence, but there may be a trait of "benevolence when one smells cookies" and "benevolence when one is not in a hurry," and so forth. Doris still views even this weaker position as a threat to virtue ethics since it cuts against the assumption that there are robust, global character traits. A virtue ethicist is free to respond that even if Doris is correct, virtue ethics may still offer a regulative ideal. After all, it is a theory of how we ought to be, not how we are.

Assuming, with common sense intuitions, that there are character traits that qualify as virtues, is there any particular psychology that characterizes moral virtue? Here we move away from use of evidence from experimental psychology and back to philosophical analysis of normative concepts that is, nevertheless, sensitive to our views of psychological reality. In my own work I argue there is no special psychology that characterizes moral virtue, and that what counts as a moral virtue is characterized by externalities such as the consequences that the traits systematically produce. Other writers, such as Rosalind Hursthouse, disagree. Taking Aristotle as her inspiration, she holds that virtue states require that the agent have certain psychological states, such as a kind of practical wisdom that is needed for deliberating well about what to do—presumably, one needs to deliberate well in order to be a good person. Another writer who has attacked this moral psychology of the virtues is Nomy Arpaly, who argues that all that is needed is that the agent be responsive to the right sorts of reasons.

It is true that one thing that we hold people responsible for is their failure to be responsive to the right sorts of reasons. If one observes an agent acting with a callous disregard for the well-being of others, this can give rise to feelings of outrage. Thus, these failures of appropriate responsiveness can generate moral emotions that are indicative of our moral commitments. For example, we have a commitment to a norm of honesty. This norm is important to regulating our social interactions. In a person of reasonably good character, a failure to be honest will lead to feelings of remorse. Also, in a person of reasonably good character, seeing another behave dishonestly will give rise to a reactive attitude of outrage or resentment. When such feelings are appropriately felt, this may serve as good evidence that there has been a moral failure.

Reactive attitudes, then, can figure into accounts of moral responsibility and moral accountability. R. Jay Wallace, for example, has developed an account of what it is to hold someone responsible, morally—it is an attitudinal stance toward someone, a third-person stance that crucially involves reactive attitudes. If one holds someone responsible for having done something bad, then it is appropriate to feel something like resentment toward that person. Note that this is not a descriptive claim. It is true that normal persons do feel resentment under these circumstances. It is also the case that this indignation or resentment is *appropriate* when one has been wronged. Thus, though there is some disagreement over this, the sphere of moral psychology does involve an investigation of some normative issues having to do with the normative status of some of the mental states and character traits central to moral evaluation.

See also Egoism and Altriusm; Human Nature; Moral Motivation; Moral Sentiments; Sympathy and Empathy; Virtue and Vice; Virtue Ethics

Bibliography

Arpaly, Nomy. *Unprincipled Virtue*. Oxford and New York: Oxford University Press, 2003.

Damasio, Antonio. *Descartes' Error*. New York: Putnam, 1994.

Darwin, Charles. *The Descent of Man* (1888). Amherst, NY: Prometheus, 1998.

Doris, John. *Lack of Character*. Cambridge and New York: Cambridge University Press, 2002.

Driver, Julia. *Uneasy Virtue*. Cambridge and New York: Cambridge University Press, 2001.

Gilligan, Carol. *In a Different Voice*. Cambridge, MA: Harvard University Press, 1982.

Greene, J. D., et. al. "An fMRI Investigation of Emotional Engagement in Moral Judgment." *Science* 293 (2001): 2105–2108.

Greene, Joshua, and Jonathan Haidt. "How (and Where) Does Moral Judgment Work?" *TRENDS in Cognitive Sciences* 6 (December 2002): 517–523.

Harman, Gilbert. "Moral Philosophy Meets Social Psychology: Virtue Ethics and the Fundamental Attribution Error." *Proceedings of the Aristotelian Society* 99 (1999): 315–331.

Hume, David. *A Treatise of Human Nature*, edited by L. A. Selby-Bigge (1896), revised by P. H. Nidditch. Oxford: Clarendon Press, 1978.

Hursthouse, Rosalind. *On Virtue Ethics*. Oxford and New York: Oxford University Press, 1999.

Nichols, Shaun. *Sentimental Rules*. Oxford and New York: Oxford University Press, 2004.

Prinz, Jesse. "Against Moral Nativism." Manuscript.

Smith, Michael. *The Moral Problem*. Oxford: Blackwell, 1994.

Wallace, R. Jay. *Responsibility and the Moral Sentiments*. Cambridge, MA: Harvard University Press, 1994.

Julia Driver (2005)

MORAL REALISM

Moral realism is a metaethical view committed to robust objectivity in ethics. No single description is likely to capture all realist views, but a reasonably accurate rule is to understand moral realism as the conjunction of three theses:

> The semantic thesis: The primary semantic role of moral predicates (such as "right" and "wrong") is to refer to moral properties (such as rightness and wrongness), so that moral statements (such as "honesty is good" and "slavery is unjust") purport to represent moral facts, and express propositions that are true or false (or approximately true, largely false, and so on).

> The alethic thesis: Some moral propositions are in fact true.

> The metaphysical thesis: Moral propositions are true when actions and other objects of moral assessment

have the relevant moral properties (so that the relevant moral facts obtain), where these facts and properties are robust: their metaphysical status, whatever it is, is not relevantly different from that of (certain types of) ordinary non-moral facts and properties.

To deny any one of these three theses is to embrace some form of moral irrealism. Many philosophers consider moral realism the default position because it appears best to capture many central features of ordinary moral thought: the assertoric surface character of ordinary moral discourse, the phenomenology of moral experience, our claim to have moral knowledge, and the possibility (and nature) of genuine moral error, progress, and disagreement even among sincere, open-minded, and well-informed people (Dancy 1986, Brink 1989, Shafer-Landau 2003).

The semantic thesis is (for better or worse) often associated with the related psychological thesis called cognitivism, according to which the primary role of moral judgments is to express beliefs. One form of irrealism, non-cognitivism, holds that their primary role is to express motivational "non-cognitive" states of mind, such as approving, prescribing, commending, or planning, but can assign moral predicates and judgments a secondary role of referring to (non-moral) properties and expressing (non-moral) beliefs (Copp 2001). How well realists can explain the reliable connection between moral judgment and moral motivation is a matter of some dispute (Smith 1994).

The alethic thesis says that some moral propositions are robustly true only if we combine it with the realist's metaphysical thesis. The irrealists' attitude to the alethic thesis depends on their conception of truth. Error theory accepts a robust reading of the semantic thesis but rejects the alethic thesis on this robust reading. It holds that ordinary moral thought presupposes the existence of robust moral facts and properties but is systematically in error: every moral judgment with existential import is mistaken because there are no robust moral facts to make any such judgment true (Mackie 1977). Non-cognitivist irrealists can accept a non-robust reading of the alethic thesis if they endorse minimalism about truth (but see Dreier 2004). This move may eventually earn them the right to speak of moral facts and truths, and to say all the same things that any morally decent person would say about what is right or wrong, good or bad, just or unjust, and so on, even though they reject the realist's metaphysical thesis (Blackburn 1993).

The metaphysical thesis is central to moral realism because realism is primarily a view about metaphysics,

not about truth or semantics. It holds that moral facts and properties are not metaphysically inferior in kind to many ordinary sorts of non-moral facts and properties. What is it for a fact or property to be metaphysically robust, though? One sense in which ordinary non-moral properties are robust is that they enter into explanations of real phenomena; water has its surface properties because it is H_2O, for example. In this sense, the realist's metaphysical thesis says that moral properties enter into explanations of phenomena that irrealists would explain by other means (Dreier 2004). An irrealist might take the fact that one believes that inequality is unjust to consist in some such fact as that one has decided to include the reduction of inequality among one's aims. A realist might instead say it consists in standing in a certain belief-like relation to the properties of inequality and injustice. Likewise, the realist might say, whether such a belief is correct or mistaken is just a matter of whether the two properties are related as the belief represents them as being related. The realist's explanation of the assertoric features of ordinary moral discourse, possession of moral knowledge, and nature of moral disagreement would be analogous.

Understanding the metaphysical thesis as above affords one (albeit not the only) way of capturing many realists' conviction that ethics concerns objective matters of fact whose existence and nature are independent of anyone's sentiments, opinions, evidence, or theories about what is right or wrong, obligatory, permissible, or impermissible, good or bad, and so on. So understood, the thesis also classifies as irrealist any view according to which explanations of moral phenomena involve no essential reference to moral facts or properties, but only to such factors as our individual tastes, cultural or social conventions and agreements, basic human sentiments, or the beliefs or plans we would have if we were fully informed and rational. Thus ethical subjectivism, ethical relativism, projectivism, and most forms of constructivism in ethics rightly count as irrealist even though they accept the realist's semantic and alethic theses.

Disputes within the realist camp concern primarily the nature of moral facts and properties. Non-naturalist realists hold that moral properties are robust properties that are distinct from but supervene (see below) on natural properties (Moore 1903, Shafer-Landau 2003). Naturalist realists hold that moral properties are robust natural properties. Reductive naturalists hold that moral properties are identical to natural properties that we can represent in austerely non-moral terms (Railton 1986). Non-reductive naturalists hold that moral properties are an irreducible subclass of the class of natural properties, which we may be unable to represent in austerely non-moral terms (Boyd 1988, Brink 1989).

Arguments for and against different forms of moral realism differ also depending on whether we take true statements of property identity to be analytic (true in virtue of the meanings of their constituent terms) or synthetic, and what we think qualifies a property as natural. If, for example, natural properties are just those that we can investigate empirically, then naturalism will hold that knowledge of any synthetic moral proposition is answerable to empirical evidence, whereas non-naturalism will hold that knowledge of some synthetic moral propositions is empirically indefeasible (Copp 2003, Shafer-Landau 2003). An issue for synthetic naturalists in particular is what determines the reference of moral predicates to the supposedly natural moral properties. Given their view of the matter, can they explain the intelligibility of such "open questions" as whether something that satisfies a given naturalistic non-moral predicate (such as "is pleasant") also satisfies a given moral predicate (such as "is good") (Moore 1903, Horgan and Timmons 1992)?

According to the supervenience argument against moral realism, we can distinguish between a weaker, true claim and a stronger, false claim about the supervenience of the moral on the natural. (*Supervenience* is a technical name for a relation of necessary covariance.) The alleged problem for the realist is that she cannot, but the irrealist can, explain why the weaker supervenience claim should be true, given that the stronger claim is false (Blackburn 1993). According to one clear version of the argument (Dreier 1992), the true claim is that it is analytically necessary that, for each moral property M that an object O has, there is a (possibly complex) natural property N that O has, and it is metaphysically necessary that M always accompanies N. The stronger, putatively false claim differs in saying that M always accompanies N as a matter of analytic necessity. (Variations of the argument concern predicates rather than properties and involve different types of necessity.) The objection is that if realists are committed to the thesis called "lack of entailment," according to which no set of non-moral naturalistic truths entails any particular moral truth, then they must admit (falsely) that it is possible for M sometimes not to accompany N.

Different forms of moral realism respond differently to the supervenience argument. Analytic naturalists may regard the argument as question-begging, for they deny that the stronger supervenience claim is false (Jackson 1998). Non-naturalists may accept a lack of analytical entailment but claim that duly specified sets of naturalis-

tic truths metaphysically entail particular moral truths because the facts which the former concern exhaustively constitute (in some sense to be explained) the facts which the latter concern (Shafer-Landau 2003). Some synthetic naturalists may say that their theory explains why the weaker supervenience claim is true (since moral properties are natural ones), but entails that no set of non-moral naturalistic truths analytically entails any particular moral truth (since any connection between non-moral and moral truths is synthetic). Others may express doubts as to whether the relevant supervenience claims are formulated so as to make them both interesting and acceptable to synthetic naturalists.

According to the explanatory argument against moral realism, properties of a certain kind are metaphysically robust only if they make a distinctive contribution to our overall explanatory picture of the world (the "explanatory requirement"), but moral properties make no such contribution; therefore, moral properties are not metaphysically robust. A prominent version of this argument claims that mentioning moral properties such as wrongness makes no distinctive contribution to causal explanations of such occurrences as a person's indignation or her judgment "that's wrong" upon seeing some hoodlums set a cat on fire, above and beyond the contribution of mentioning the person's prior beliefs, aversions, and moral principles (Harman 1977). If so, the causal version of the explanatory requirement gives us good reason to deny that there are robust moral facts.

One realist response is to argue that the causal requirement is dubious; for if it is, then it would be no objection to moral realism if moral properties violated that requirement (Shafer-Landau 2003). Moral properties could still play non-causal explanatory roles. A very different response is to accept the causal requirement, but argue that mentioning moral properties can make a distinctive contribution to causal explanations of both intentional occurrences, such as moral judgments, and non-intentional ones (Sturgeon 1988, Brink 1989). On the latter score, one may argue that a person's kindness can cause her to help others or that injustice or oppression can provoke resistance, and that these properties can play such causal-explanatory roles only if they are real, and indeed natural, properties. Here the intricate question arises whether moral properties are epiphenomenal, in that they play no causal-explanatory role over and above the causal-explanatory role of the non-moral properties on which they supervene, or by which they are realized (Miller 2003, Sturgeon 2005).

What unites these debates about moral realism is the concern whether, and how, robust moral facts and properties enter into accounts of various phenomena that irrealists would explain by other means. One general moral may be that arguments in metaethics often are arguments about the best explanation of the phenomena in question. Other important debates between realists and irrealists and within the realist camp concern the rational authority of morality, the extent to which moral realism affords a rational basis for resolving moral disagreements, the existence of an internal connection between moral judgment and moral motivation and whether such "motivational internalism" would make moral properties metaphysically strange, and questions about moral methodology and moral epistemology, such as the place of ethics in a naturalistic worldview and the parity or continuity of ethics with empirical inquiry and the sciences.

See also Ethical Naturalism; Internalism and Externalism in Ethics; Intuitionism, Ethical; Metaethics; Moral Epistemology; Noncognitivism; Objectivity in Ethics; Rationalism in Ethics (Practical Reason Approaches).

Bibliography

Blackburn, Simon. *Essays in Quasi-Realism.* Oxford: Oxford University Press, 1993.

Boyd, Richard. "How to Be a Moral Realist." In *Essays on Moral Realism,* edited by Geoffrey Sayre-McCord. Ithaca, NY: Cornell University Press, 1988.

Brink, David O. *Moral Realism and the Foundations of Ethics.* Cambridge, U.K.: Cambridge University Press, 1989.

Copp, David. "Realist-Expressivism: A Neglected Option for Moral Realism." In *Moral Knowledge,* edited by Ellen Frankel Paul, Fred D. Miller Jr., and Jeffrey Paul. Cambridge, U.K.: Cambridge University Press, 2001.

Copp, David. "Why Naturalism?" *Ethical Theory and Moral Practice* 6 (2003): 179–200.

Dancy, Jonathan. "Two Conceptions of Moral Realism." *Proceedings of the Aristotelian Society,* suppl. 60 (1986): 167–187.

Dreier, James. "The Supervenience Argument against Moral Realism." *Southern Journal of Philosophy* 30 (1992): 13–38.

Dreier, James. "Meta-ethics and the Problem of Creeping Minimalism." *Philosophical Perspectives* 18 (2004): 23–44.

Harman, Gilbert. *The Nature of Morality.* Oxford: Oxford University Press, 1977.

Horgan, Terence, and Mark Timmons. "Troubles for New Wave Moral Semantics: The 'Open Question Argument' Revived." *Philosophical Papers* 21 (1992): 153–175.

Jackson, Frank. *From Metaphysics to Ethics.* Oxford: Oxford University Press, 1998.

Mackie, J. L. *Ethics: Inventing Right and Wrong.* New York: Penguin, 1977.

Miller, Alexander. *An Introduction to Contemporary Metaethics.* Cambridge: Polity Press, 2003.

Moore, G. E. *Principia Ethica.* Cambridge, U.K.: Cambridge University Press, 1903.

Railton, Peter. "Moral Realism." *The Philosophical Review* 95 (1986): 163–207.

Shafer-Landau, Russ. *Moral Realism: A Defence.* Oxford: Oxford University Press, 2003.

Smith, Michael. *The Moral Problem.* Oxford: Blackwell, 1994.

Sturgeon, Nicholas L. "Moral Explanations." In *Essays on Moral Realism,* edited by Geoffrey Sayre-McCord. Ithaca, NY: Cornell University Press, 1988.

Sturgeon, Nicholas L. "Moral Explanations Defended." In *Contemporary Debates in Moral Philosophy,* edited by James Dreier. Oxford: Blackwell, 2005.

Sturgeon, Nicholas L. "What Difference Does It Make Whether Moral Realism Is True?" *Southern Journal of Philosophy,* suppl. 24 (1986): 115–142.

Wright, Crispin. "Realism, Antirealism, Irrealism, Quasi-Realism." *Midwest Studies in Philosophy* 12 (1988): 25–49.

Pekka Väyrynen (2005)

MORAL RESPONSIBILITY

See *Responsibility, Moral and Legal*

MORAL RULES AND PRINCIPLES

Normative rules and principles say what things are required or permitted or good or bad. In other words, normative rules and principles say what agents ought to do or what agents are allowed to do; or what deserves to be promoted, praised, or approved; or what deserves to be opposed, criticized, or disapproved. Moral rules or principles differ from normative ones of other kinds (such as rules or principles of law, etiquette, or clubs) in that moral rules or principles indicate what agents morally ought to do or are morally allowed to do, or what deserves moral praise and admiration.

Rules and principles are (to at least some extent) general—that is, they are about kinds of situations or about classes of cases, not about individual instances. So rules or principles are juxtaposed with judgments about a particular instance. The judgment that Martin Elginbrodde ought to feed his hamster at 8 a.m. on July 7, 2007, does not articulate a rule. Rather, it articulates a judgment about what a particular person should do on a particular occasion. Because rules and principles are about kinds of situations or classes of cases, rules or principles entail judgments about particular instances. The principle that people ought to feed their pets entails that Miguel ought to feed his cat, that Janet ought to feed her dog, that Rahul ought to feed his bird, that Jo ought to feed his ferret, and so on for as many pet owners as there are.

Many philosophers have held that moral rules and principles must apply universally. What it is right for one person to do must be right for anyone else to do unless there is some morally relevant difference between the cases. This thought is reflected in the Golden Rule and serves as a cornerstone of the moral philosophies of Immanuel Kant and Richard M. Hare. But one important difference between Kant and Hare concerns the degree of detail and complexity they allow into moral principles. Kant thought moral principles had to be quite simple; Hare thought they could be highly detailed and complex as long as they were formulated in completely universal terms.

How stringent are moral rules and principles? Most people must take moral rules and principles to be very important—in particular, to generate very strong reasons for action. Otherwise, the degree of social cooperation and solidarity that moral rules and principles are supposed to provide is unlikely to be achieved. Some philosophers—for example, Ronald Dworkin (1977)— have held that moral rules can be more specific and less stringent than moral principles. A moral rule might be: "Be especially kind to your parents." A more general and stringent principle might be: "Be especially kind to your benefactors." In a case where a parent has not been a benefactor, for example, a father who always ignores the plight of his offspring, the rule "Be especially kind to your parents" might fade to nothing.

Admittedly, even the rule "Be especially kind to your benefactors" can be overridden. To take an extreme example, being kind to benefactors might conflict in some situation with saving many innocent lives. Suppose that for some reason one can either go to thank benefactors or devote the time to saving innocent lives, but not both of these things. With respect to such a case, the principle "Be especially kind to benefactors" seems morally less important than the principle "Prevent harm to others." Many other moral rules or principles are likewise capable of being outweighed or overridden in certain cases by other moral rules or principles.

Are there any rules or principles that always outweigh any opposing moral considerations? Consider the principles "Do not do what is morally wrong" and "Do what you morally ought to do." Such principles concern compliance with all-things-considered moral verdicts.

These principles tell us to do whatever is, all things considered, morally required. They give us no indication which moral considerations win out over others to generate all-things-considered moral verdicts.

Are there any rules or principles that both provide information about what morality requires and always outweigh any opposing moral considerations? Two kinds of principles have been suggested. One of these kinds consists of moral principles outlawing evil purposes, such as "Do not, for its own sake, harm others" and "Do not, for its own sake, deceive others." The other kind consists of principles offered as the most general and basic principle of morality, such as Kant's "Act only on maxims that you can will to be universal laws" and the act-utilitarian's "Do whatever acts promote aggregate well-being."

There are other moral theories that put forward other foundational principles. For example, T. M. Scanlon's (1982) contractualist theory of morality claims that moral wrongness is determined by rules for the general regulation of behavior that no one could reasonably reject as the basis of informed, unforced, general agreement. Richard B. Brandt's (1967) rule-utilitarian theory holds that moral wrongness is determined by rules that have the highest expected impartial utility. Rosalind Hursthouse's (1999) virtue ethics holds that an act is wrong if it is one that would not be done by someone with a full set of the character traits that benefit others or the agent.

Some philosophers think that the theories just mentioned are mistaken to claim that morality is so unified. For example, pluralists such as William David Ross (1930) think that there is a plurality of basic moral principles that identify the features that count morally in favor of actions that have them (moral pros) and other features that count morally against the actions that have them (moral cons). These moral pros and cons are the appropriate inputs to moral assessment; a verdict about all-things-considered moral rightness or wrongness is the appropriate output. Rossian pluralists think that these moral principles (and thus the moral pros and cons that the principles identify) can conflict. For example, the fact that an act would benefit others counts in its favor, and the fact that an act would keep one's promise counts in its favor. Sometimes, however, keeping one's promise is not what would benefit others.

Rossian pluralists also think that the principles do not come in a strict hierarchy of importance that would resolve all the possible conflicts among them. This presents the question of what is the right thing to do when the Rossian principles conflict. Rossian pluralists hold that which principle wins when there is conflict among them cannot be captured in a correct, informative, general principle. For example, a general principle that benefiting others always trumps keeping promises is not correct. Neither is a general principle that keeping promises always trumps benefiting others. Instead, in some situations it is right to keep a promise though one could benefit others more if one broke the promise, but in other situations it is right to break a promise if this is necessary in order to benefit others. So Rossian pluralists admit that moral verdicts about right and wrong cannot be systematized in correct informative general principles. They maintain that, when basic principles conflict, the right thing to do is a matter of judgment rather than a further principle. Still, Rossian pluralists think that moral principles have an important place, namely, in identifying the moral pros and cons.

Some philosophers think even principles about what counts as a moral pro or a moral con are incorrect. These philosophers are called moral particularists. Particularists hold that, for any feature of an action or its consequence that is a moral pro in one situation, that same feature might be a moral con in another situation. Whereas Rossians think that the fact that an act would benefit someone is always a reason in favor of the act, particularists think that, in some situations, the fact that an act would benefit someone is morally positive but in other situations it is morally negative. Wiping sweat from a torturer's brow, for example, would benefit the torturer but would not count in favor of the action. More generally, particularists maintain that features of actions can switch moral "polarity," depending on the context. Most will agree that one should try to help the person being tortured rather than wiping the torturer's brow. The question is how to explain what the inputs to that verdict are. Particularists say that the fact that wiping the torturer's brow would benefit him is no reason to do it, but rather, a reason against doing it.

On this issue, antiparticularists divide into two groups. Antiparticularists in one group say that the potential benefit to the torturer is massively outweighed by the importance of trying to help the person being tortured. But antiparticularists in this group hold that the fact that wiping the torturer's brow would benefit him counts at least a little bit in favor of wiping his brow. Antiparticularists in the other group agree with particularists that the fact that wiping the torturer's brow would benefit him is no moral reason to wipe his brow. Antiparticularists in this second group thus agree with particularists that the example about wiping the torturer's brow

refutes the claim that benefiting someone is always a moral pro. But these antiparticularists oppose particularism by claiming there is some other feature that does always have the same moral polarity. For example, these antiparticularists might claim that any act with the feature of benefiting an innocent person has at least this in its moral favor. In other words, antiparticularists in this second group abandon the more general claim that benefiting a person is always a morally positive feature, but they insist on the somewhat less general claim that benefiting an innocent person is always a morally positive feature.

The debate over particularism is mostly about whether there are any correct informative general principles, either that specify all-things-considered moral rightness or that indicate which features always operate as moral pros or cons. Antiparticularists win the debate if they come up with correct informative general principles of one or both kinds. Particularists win if they show that every informative general principle put forward is incorrect.

The debate over particularism has other elements as well. On the one hand, particularists say that one can often see not only which features count in which way in a particular situation but also what is all-things-considered morally right in that situation. If particularists are right about that, the question is posed: What is the point of trying to formulate general principles if we can see which particular acts are right without them?

On the other hand, antiparticularists point out that we commonly take being unprincipled as a serious moral flaw. Why is being unprincipled such a moral flaw if acting on principles is not part of being moral? Furthermore, why does moral education start with learning rules and principles if these end up playing no role in determining moral rightness? And why does moral reasoning so often consist in comparing different cases if correct moral judgments are always about particular cases rather than about classes of cases or types of situations?

Particularists pose a challenge to the idea that principles play an essential role in morality. This challenge has forced other moral philosophers to be more specific about which principles they defend and about what roles they think principles must play. Rossian pluralists think correct informative principles are only about moral pros and cons. Many other philosophers—for example, utilitarians, Kantians, contractualists, and virtue ethicists—think that there is a correct informative general principle specifying a foundational principle of right and wrong, yet there is persisting disagreement among them over what this principle is.

See also Deontological Ethics; Divine Command Theories of Ethics; Duty; Golden Rule; Dworkin, Ronald; Hare, Richard M.; Kant, Immanuel; Moral Dilemmas; Moral Principles: Their Justification; Rights; Ross, William David; Utilitarianism.

Bibliography

Blackburn, Simon. *Ruling Passions: A Theory of Practical Reasoning*. Oxford: Oxford University Press, 1998. See especially p. 281.

Brandt, Richard B. "Some Merits of One Form of Rule-Utilitarianism." In *University of Colorado Studies in Philosophy*, 39–65. Boulder: University of Colorado Press, 1967. Reprinted in Richard B. Brant, *Morality, Utilitarianism, and Rights*, 111–136. Cambridge, U.K.: Cambridge University Press, 1992.

Dancy, Jonathan. *Ethics without Principles*. Oxford, U.K.: Oxford University Press, 2004.

Dancy, Jonathan. *Moral Reasons*. Oxford, U.K.: Blackwell, 1993.

Dworkin, Ronald. *Taking Rights Seriously*. London: Duckworth, 1977.

Hare, R. M. *Moral Thinking: Its Levels, Method, and Point*. Oxford: Oxford University Press, 1981.

Hare, R. M. "Objective Prescriptions." In *Naturalism and Normativity: Philosophical Issues*. Vol. 4., edited by E. Villanueva. Atascadero, CA: Ridgeview, 1993. Reprinted in R. M. Hare, *Objective Prescriptions and Other Essays*, 1–18. Oxford, U.K.: Oxford University Press, 1999.

Hooker, Brad, and Margaret Olivia Little, eds. *Moral Particularism*. Oxford, U.K.: Oxford University Press, 2000.

Hursthouse, Rosalind. *On Virtue Ethics*. Oxford, U.K.: Oxford University Press, 1999. See especially part 3, 198–228.

Mackie, J. L. *Ethics: Inventing Right and Wrong*. Harmondsworth, U.K.: Penguin, 1977. See especially chap. 4, 83–102.

Mackie, J. L. "The Three Stages of Universalization." In *Persons and Values: Collected Papers*. Vol. 2., edited by Joan Mackie and Penelope Mackie. Oxford, U.K.: Oxford University Press, 1985. See especially p. 178.

Kant, Immanuel. *Groundwork of the Metaphysics of Morals* [1785]. Translated by H. J. Paton. New York: Harper & Row, 1964.

Ross, W. D. *The Right and the Good*. Oxford, U.K.: Oxford University Press, 1930.

Scanlon, T. M. "Contractualism and Utilitarianism." In *Utilitarianism and Beyond*, edited by Amartya Sen and Bernard Williams. Cambridge, U.K.: Cambridge University Press, 1982.

Scanlon, T. M. *What We Owe to Each Other*. Cambridge, MA: Harvard University Press, 1998. See especially chap. 5, 189–247.

Sidgwick, Henry. *Methods of Ethics*. 7th ed. London: Macmillan, 1907.

Brad Hooker (2005)

MORAL SENSE

In the first half of the eighteenth century certain British philosophers argued that the "moral sense" is the faculty by which we distinguish between moral right and wrong. The deliverances of this faculty are feelings or sentiments; hence, it is counted as a sense. Our observation of an instance of virtuous action is the occasion for a feeling of pleasure or satisfaction, which enables us to distinguish that action as virtuous. Similarly, our observation of an instance of vicious action is the occasion for a feeling of pain or uneasiness, which enables us to distinguish that action as vicious. The moral sense is also an influencing motive in our pursuit of virtue and our avoidance of vicious behavior, and it plays a part in our bestowal of praise and blame.

HISTORICAL BACKGROUND

Arguments for and against the moral sense take their character from the larger social and intellectual context in which they were advanced. The late seventeenth century and early eighteenth century in Europe saw the culmination of certain lines of thought that had their origin in earlier times. The Protestant insistence on individual conviction in purely religious matters had an effect on other areas of thought as well. The rejection of external authority as the guarantor of religious truth and the consequent reliance of each believer on his own inner light led to a full-blown theory of knowledge in which the different ways a person can know different kinds of subject matter were definitively cataloged. The way of knowing a given subject was appealed to as the foundation or guarantee of truth. The first account of this theory of knowledge was John Locke's *Essay concerning Human Understanding* in the late seventeenth century. The most comprehensive statement of it was the *Treatise of Human Nature* by David Hume in the eighteenth century. These developments in theory of knowledge were closely related to a growing interest in feelings and their expression. The new theory of knowledge was also closely connected with changes in beliefs about God's relation to the world. Speculations about the will of God were no longer a necessary preliminary to doing physics. When the notion of a physics without God met in men's minds with a resistance to religious authority in all matters, including morals, the problem was posed of the possibility of accounting for morality without an appeal to a divine source. But if morality is not founded on God's will, where is the foundation laid? In line with the new theory of knowledge, the most promising direction for a search appeared to be in human nature itself.

The first Englishman to search for the foundation of morals in human nature, Thomas Hobbes, returned with a brilliantly stated but outrageous report. He found that *good* and *evil* are relative to the person who uses these words; and when people are joined together in a commonwealth, then good and evil are subject to the determinations of the commonwealth. As for our motives for pursuing good and avoiding evil, they may be summed up as self-interest. Were it to our own interest to pursue what others, or the commonwealth, have designated as evil, we certainly would; but, for the most part, our appreciation of the convenience that follows from everyone's following the same rules and, at the worst, our fear of punishment on being caught deter us from the practice of evil.

Hobbes's unflattering picture of human nature and his relativistic account of morals, which he presented in *Leviathan,* are the ominous and ever-present background of all discussions of moral philosophy for the next hundred years. They called forth their contradictory counterpart in the writings of the third earl of Shaftesbury. Shaftesbury argued that Hobbes had made a shortsighted survey of human nature. There is benevolence in human nature, as well as selfishness; and indeed, if men were not originally endowed with a disposition to be sociable, the formation of a commonwealth would be impossible. Shaftesbury was the first to attribute to a moral sense our ability to distinguish between good and evil, virtue and vice. This sense, along with our natural affection for virtue, accounts for the possibility of morality. Shaftesbury, however, did not make clear how the possession of a moral sense enables us to avoid relativism in moral judgments; and indeed the specter of relativism must inevitably haunt the proponents of the moral sense.

DEVELOPMENT OF THE DOCTRINE

The systematic development of the doctrine of a moral sense was left to Shaftesbury's successors: first Francis Hutcheson and later Hume. Their first move was to fit the moral sense into the mainstream of eighteenth-century philosophy by finding a place for it in Locke's theory of knowledge. Looking into the human mind, Locke found that all knowledge consists of perceptions, which must arrive in the mind by one of two routes, either sensation or reflection. Whatever can be known must be accounted for as a perception; and whatever cannot be accounted for in this way is not knowledge. The proponents of the moral sense accounted for our knowledge of moral right and wrong as Lockean reflexive perceptions. When someone observes a given action or considers a certain charac-

ter trait, these first perceptions are immediately followed by a secondary set of feelings of either pleasure or uneasiness, according to whether the action or character is virtuous or vicious. By consulting these secondary perceptions, we can make our moral judgments. The proponents of the moral sense were careful to point out that actions are not virtuous *because* they please. Rather we know them to be virtuous because we are pleased in a *certain manner.* Thus, moral pleasures and pains are distinctive feelings. Hume argued for the possibility of distinguishing different kinds of pleasure by pointing out, for example, that someone may be pleased both by a good musical composition and by a good bottle of wine, and their goodness is determined merely by the pleasure they give; but we do not say on that account that the wine is harmonious or the music of good flavor.

Besides accounting for our knowledge of right and wrong, the moral sense closes the gap between moral knowledge and moral behavior by providing a motive for moral behavior. Since moral knowledge consists of feelings of pleasure and uneasiness, the prospect of enjoying or avoiding these feelings is a sufficient motive for pursuing virtue and avoiding vice. If moral knowledge were not ultimately a matter of feelings, it would be possible for someone to know that a certain kind of action is virtuous but still have no motive for doing it. The moral sense also enables us to account for our approval and condemnation of actions and characters as following from our being pleased or pained by them.

CRITICISM

The moral sense was subjected to two sorts of criticism. The first sort was directed against supposed defects in the doctrine of the moral sense itself. The second sort of criticism advanced the claims of rival candidates for the title of moral faculty.

DEFECTS IN THE DOCTRINE. The bluntest form of the first sort of criticism was to interpret the proponents of the moral sense as talking about an extra organ of sense, "a moral nose" or "a moral ear." How acute they were to have discovered a new human organ which no one had noticed until they came along! Merely to mention the possibility was enough to show the nonexistence of such an organ and to render the doctrine of a moral sense laughable. Hutcheson was especially plagued with this kind of criticism. But he spoke of the moral sense as a determination of the mind, which left the way open for viewing the moral sense not as an organ but as a faculty that can be looked for only in the way memory or will can be looked for. Hume's defenses against this criticism were somewhat better. He boldly asserted the principle that our acquaintance with our senses or faculties can never be anything but an acquaintance with their characteristic perceptions. Hence, he was justified in confining himself to talk of moral feelings and sentiments; and indeed, he never actually used the phrase "moral sense" in any argument but relegated it to a section title.

The next most severe criticism was to point out that although all men are said to be endowed with a moral sense, there is no universal agreement about moral right and wrong. Hutcheson turned aside this criticism by arguing that the moral sense may be inoperative or defective, just as human eyes may be. Hume added that differences in moral judgments may be attributed to differences in experience and education and to a failure to pass judgment from a disinterested point of view; and he hoped that by additional experience or by a greater effort to achieve disinterestedness moral disputants might be able to reach agreement.

But the critics of the moral sense thought that by far the most serious fault in the doctrine was its apparent foundation of the distinction between moral right and wrong on human nature itself. This opened the door to Hobbesian relativism: Whatever action pleases is virtuous, and whatever displeases, vicious. Actually, Hutcheson based the distinction between virtue and vice on the will of God, one step removed from human nature. It just so happens, he held, that God determined us to be pleased by benevolent actions; and when nothing interferes with the moral sense, we count benevolence a virtue and malevolence a vice. But, his opponents argued, to base the distinction between moral good and evil on God's will is no less arbitrary than to base it on human nature itself. If, by divine fiat, we count benevolence a virtue, we might very well have done the opposite, had God so pleased. What is more, the distinction between good and evil cannot possibly rest on God's will, for if good and evil have not some real character in themselves, what is there to determine his will in the first place?

Hume based the distinction between moral right and wrong directly on human nature—that is, our power to be pleased and displeased by different ways of acting—without an appeal to any divine determination of this power. But if there is to be a stability in the distinction between moral right and wrong, then there must be a consistency in human nature. This is no easy thing to show, for the slightest inspection of human affairs appears to tell against it. Yet Hume argued that, on balance, man is more of a social being than not. Indeed, this contention had always been strongly supported by proponents of the moral sense; but Hume added the refinement that man's very inclination to be social leads him to be pleased by those actions and character traits which tend to make society possible and to be displeased by those which tend to disrupt society. Thus, while the distinction between virtue and vice does indeed rest on human nature, it is not an arbitrary distinction. We do have a good reason for preferring one sort of action to another, namely the action's tendency to maintain society. Should someone ask, "And why should I prefer the maintenance of society to its destruction?" Hume had no answer in the form of a logical argument. He certainly recognized the possibility of someone's preferring the destruction of society over its maintenance; but on such a fundamental issue, he held, there can be no arguments pro or con, but only an appeal to feelings. Society exists because, as a matter of fact, by far the greater number of people have the kind of feelings that make it possible.

RIVAL MORAL FACULTIES. Another set of objections to the moral sense was advanced by those who argued that the faculty by which we discern moral right and wrong must be reason, or the understanding. The most notable members of this school were Samuel Clarke, John Balguy, and Richard Price. Their most characteristic doctrine was that moral right and wrong are unchanging and unchangeable and, thus, independent of any human, or even divine, determination. This school accepted Locke's theory of knowledge with the modification that the understanding is capable of originating new simple ideas for itself by considering those it gets by way of the two great avenues of sensation and reflection. Thus, according to Clarke, the understanding can discern a certain eternal fitness that things and actions bear to one another in their natures. He likened these moral discoveries to mathematical reasoning in which one discovers the consistency of certain concepts. The implication is that the absolute and immutable character of moral distinctions is such that they can be known only by reason. Therefore, the moral faculty could not possibly be a sense.

Hume endeavored to answer these arguments by pointing out that, strictly considered, reason is capable only of comparing ideas. Since moral knowledge is a sentiment or feeling that arises on the observation of an action or character trait, it is not the result of comparing ideas, and thus it cannot be a conclusion of reason. What is more, since our moral sentiments about certain actions may excite us to perform or to avoid these actions, it is even more doubtful that our moral knowledge comes from reason, for, according to Hume, the conclusions of reason alone can never be an exciting motive to action. A person may know that a certain way of acting may have a certain result, but in order for him to act to achieve that result, he must first find it pleasing.

The moral sense and reason were not the only candidates for a moral faculty proposed at that time. Joseph Butler argued for conscience; and Adam Smith chose to argue for sympathy—which had also figured in Hume's moral philosophy—as the source of moral distinctions. Considering the arguments advanced on behalf of the different candidates for the moral faculty, one can see that the issue was never one that could be settled by empirical investigation. The search for a moral faculty had its origin in the general acceptance of a faculty psychology, supplemented with the Lockean assumption that the acts attributed to our mental faculties are to be accounted for as the occurrence of various sorts of perceptions. When one recognizes the ad hoc character of the conceptual framework in which the disputes over the nature of the moral faculty took place, one can see why there was no resolving them. When one no longer finds a need for a faculty psychology, the need to search for a moral faculty goes too.

The present-day moral philosopher no longer casts his study as an investigation of the deliverances of a moral faculty, but rather as a study of the logic of moral discourse. Despite their central preoccupation, the proponents of the moral sense have made a contribution to the development of modern moral philosophy. In particular, they contributed the points that morality assumes the value of society and is incomprehensible apart from this presupposition; that conduct must be judged by general rules; and that a general rule of definitive importance to morality is the injunction to act for the greatest good of the greatest number. But perhaps the most important contribution to moral philosophy by the proponents of the moral sense was their insistence that feeling has a place in morals and that to miss this fact is to omit a distinctive element in moral discourse.

See also Ethics, History of; Objectivity in Ethics.

Bibliography

For original statements of the moral sense doctrine, see Shaftesbury (Anthony Ashley Cooper), *An Inquiry concerning Virtue or Merit* (1699), to be found in *Characteristics of men, morals, opinions, times,* 3 vols. (London, 1711), Vol. II; Francis Hutcheson, *An Inquiry into the Original of our Ideas of Beauty and Virtue* (London, 1725) and *An Essay on the Nature and Conduct of the Passions and Affections with Illustrations upon the Moral Sense* (London, 1728); and David Hume, *A Treatise of Human Nature* (London, 1740), Book III.

For rival moral faculties, see, for reason, Samuel Clarke, *A Discourse concerning the Unchangeable Obligations of Natural Religion and the Truth and Certainty of the Christian Revelation* (London, 1706); John Balguy, *The Foundation of Moral Goodness* (London: John Pemberton, 1728); and Richard Price, *A Review of the Principal Questions and Difficulties in Morals* (London, 1758). For conscience, see Joseph Butler, *Fifteen Sermons upon Human Nature, or Man Considered as a Moral Agent* (London, 1726). For the rival moral faculty of sympathy, see Adam Smith, *Theory of Moral Sentiments* (London: Millar, 1759).

For modern studies, see James Bonar, *Moral Sense* (New York: Macmillan, 1930) and D. Daiches Raphael, *The Moral Sense* (London: Oxford University Press, 1947).

Elmer Sprague (1967)

MORAL SENTIMENTS

One's sentiments are the contents of one's sensed, or felt, experience—in contrast to the contents of simply one's thoughts. Whatever else they are, then, sentiments are affective phenomena. In common parlance, talk of sentiments refers alternatively to occurrent feelings, affective dispositions, and emotional attitudes taken toward people and objects. Moral sentiments, where the adjective *moral* is used in a descriptive sense, would then be some subset of these feelings, dispositions, and attitudes: those that are more or less intimately related to moral phenomena. Whether any of the moral sentiments thus understood are moral in a normative sense, that is, whether one morally may or should experience or express any of these sentiments in relevant circumstances, is a further question.

One problem that immediately confronts any philosophical account of moral sentiments is the question whether such affective phenomena in fact form a unified category. Affective responses vary widely with respect to their causes, phenomenology, duration, intentional objects (if any), and mode of expression, as well as their susceptibility to rational assessment and control. This variability is no less present in the case of that subset of affective phenomena related in some way to morals. Contrast, for example, rationally impervious and visceral disgust to resentment, a comparatively subdued attitude that arguably is a response fitting only to moral wrongs. Both disgust and resentment, however, are moral sentiments in the sense that people commonly experience these affective reactions in response to moral phenomena.

Just which phenomena one admits to the category of moral sentiments depends, of course, on the specific theory of the sentiments one accepts. Consideration of contemporary theories of the emotions is instructive here. Although such theories are quite varied, a common taxonomy distinguishes between cognitivist and noncognitivist theories of emotion. Cognitivist theories of emotion hold that emotions necessarily involve thoughts, beliefs, or judgments ascribing properties to their objects. Some cognitivists (Nussbaum 2001) identify emotions with evaluative judgments, for example, identifying fear with the evaluative judgment that the object of fear somehow threatens one's welfare or identifying one's resenting another's action with the judgment that the other wrongs one in so acting. Sentiments, understood as essentially affective phenomena, apparently play at best a peripheral role on some such theories of emotion.

Noncognitivist theories of emotion, in contrast, embrace a view of emotions as essentially felt experiences different in kind from thoughts beliefs or judgments. William James (1842-1910), famously identified emotions with the perception of bodily changes—or feelings—caused by external stimuli. Contemporary followers of James (Prinz 2004) have built on his emotional noncognitivism to avoid what they view as shortcomings of the cognitivist alternatives. Some noncognitivists object that emotions, unlike beliefs or judgments, are not properly subject to assessment in terms of truth or falsehood. Noncognitivists also object that cognitivist theories require that those subject to emotions possess a conceptual or propositional repertoire that obvious subjects of emotion—human infants and animals, for example—do not, in fact, possess. In response to such objections, some philosophers opt for mixed theories according to which emotions are some amalgam of cognition and affect (Oakley 1992).

Clarity about the correct theory of affective responses is a prerequisite for progress in the longstanding philosophical debate over the role of moral sentiments in moral agency. Philosophers have long debated the role of moral sentiments in, for example, (1) moral deliberation and judgment, (2) moral motivation, and (3) moral responsibility.

In examining the role of moral sentiments in moral deliberation and judgment, moral motivation, and moral responsibility, modern moral philosophers have been concerned especially with the role one should attribute to moral sensibility—generally understood as a capacity for experiencing, or disposition to experience, feelings, emotions, and attitudes that include guilt, resentment, respect, esteem, honor, pride, and shame—relative to the role of reason, understood as a cognitive capacity whose objects (e.g., thoughts or propositions) are amenable to

evaluation in terms of truth or falsehood. Moral philosophers committed to treating moral judgments as bona fide judgments, whether by taking them to refer to causally explanatory moral properties or by regarding them as subject to similarly robust standards of truth and falsehood as is descriptive discourse, are often known as metaethical cognitivists. Metaethical noncognitivists, in contrast, deny that moral evaluations identify irreducibly moral properties or report truth-evaluable beliefs. The distinction between cognitivism and noncognitivism in one's metaethical theory is independent of the distinction between cognitivism and noncognitivism about emotions. However, differences among philosophers concerning the relative role of sentiment and reason in the moral domain reflect philosophical differences in the specific theory of sentiment, or emotion, they accept.

HISTORICAL CONTEXT

Although contemporary moral philosophers might be inclined to trace the term *moral sentiments* to developments in eighteenth-century British moral philosophy, philosophical interest in the affective aspects of one's moral experience is not limited to any specific epoch. Already in ancient Hellenistic philosophy, one finds a concern with the place of feelings, emotions, and affective attitudes generally in the constitution and care of the psyche, or soul.

For Plato (c. 429–347 BCE) and Aristotle (384–322 BCE), for example, human excellence (for them the subject of ethics) required that one's soul be properly constituted in the relation of its rational, desiderative, and appetitive parts—the latter comprising the domain of sentiments or emotions. For Plato, the proper constitution of the soul was an achievement of an upbringing where one's appetites (e.g., natural urges for food and sex), desires (e.g., aspirations for the goods of honor and victory), and rational judgments were in harmony. Absent a proper upbringing, the desiderative and appetitive parts of the soul were bound to prove unruly and psychically divisive, thereby making a good life unattainable. On such a view, arguably, all affects of the soul have ethical import, whether or not they have ethical content.

Aristotle further developed an account of the education of the soul where the parts concerned with feeling pleasures and pains functioned, at least in persons properly reared, as important guides for choosing and acting well. Affective dispositions of the soul could play this role for Aristotle because he understood the feeling part of the soul according to a perceptual model on which it could provide one with knowledge of the objects it perceived through pleasure and pain, much as one's visual perceptions provide knowledge of the objects of sight. On this view, to possess virtues of character such as courage and justice consists in part in being disposed to experience the appropriate emotions in response to, respectively, fearful circumstances and the unfair distribution of goods.

The Stoic school of Hellenistic philosophers (of which Zeno of Citium [335–263 BCE] is an example) combined a rich cognitivist theory of the emotions as judgments concerning value with the prescription that the wise person, or sage, should ultimately expurgate himself of emotion altogether. The motivation for the prescription derived from the Stoic view that virtue is the only good. Other things of value (e.g., health, and wealth), while typically choice-worthy, are things about which the Stoic sage is properly indifferent. To the extent that emotions give importance to things other than virtue by judging them good, then, they implicate one in false judgments about the good. As such, emotions are antagonistic to reason, by whose power one should strive to eliminate them.

This antagonistic divide between sentiment and reason reappears in the early modern period, fueled by changes brought by the advance of Newtonian science, religious strife, and philosophy itself (e.g., John Locke's [1632–1704] philosophy of mind). It is in this, the early modern period, beset by changes that sustained doubt about the status of morality as a deliverance of revelation or of reason alone, that one first encounters the school of moral philosophers known as the *sentimentalists*: Anthony Ashley Cooper (the third Earl of Shaftesbury [1671–1713]) Frances Hutcheson (1694–1746), David Hume (1711–1776), and Adam Smith (1723–1790).

Shaftesbury is perhaps most often credited with having first used the phrase *moral sense*, defending it as a sense, quite literally, of moral right and wrong. According to Shaftesbury, the moral sense enables all persons to experience affections of approval or disapproval upon reflection on the first-order affections, or motives, of oneself and others. Judgments about what is morally right and morally wrong, as well as the motivations to action that they support, are on this view expressions of the reflective approval or disapproval that is fitting for one's and others' motives.

Hutcheson adapted Shaftesbury's theory of a moral sense that apprehended with approval virtuous motives, which Hutcheson understood as forms of benevolence, and responded with disapproval to the vicious. However, Hutcheson abandoned Shaftesbury's metaphysical views, among them the view that the immutable order of nature guarantees the fittingness of these moral affections for their objects. Hutcheson also viewed reason, as opposed to sentiment, as a purely theoretical and, so, motivationally inert faculty. These two features of Hutcheson's philosophy are echoed in the empiricist sentimentalism of Hume.

An admirer of Cicero (106–143 BCE) and Tacitus (c. 56–120 CE), Hume inverted the Stoic hierarchy of reason and sentiment when he announced that "Reason is, and ought only to be the slave of the passions" (Hume 1973, II. iii. 3, p. 415). To be sure, Hume's slogan conceals a more nuanced Humean view of moral evaluation and moral motivation. Humans are naturally constituted, on Hume's view, to feel certain passions, or sentiments, in response to certain causes. Reason, exclusively concerned as it is with matters of fact and relations of ideas, cannot oppose passion in the sense that reason cannot cause us to form moral beliefs or motivate us to act in the absence of some affective input. Hume nonetheless distinguishes between better and worse ways of forming evaluative beliefs and between better and worse motives. He does so by privileging moral assessments made from what he calls the common or general point of view, a point of view one succeeds in occupying when one evaluates motives or character traits in terms of their typical effects. Such evaluation proceeds not through the operations of a moral sense but through the influence of the general point of view on what Hume identifies as the mechanism of sympathy. For sympathetic creatures occupying the general point of view, moral evaluation consists in apprehending whether the motives or character traits being evaluated are immediately agreeable or useful to oneself or others. In this way, Hume concludes "Morality…is more properly felt than judg'd of " (Hume 1973, III. i. 2, p. 470).

Smith developed his brand of moral sentimentalism in his *The Theory of Moral Sentiments* (1759/1982). Smith's sentimentalism resembled Hume's in privileging sympathy as a psychological process by means of which one comes to take pleasure in virtue and be pained by vice. Significantly, however, the two differed in their conceptions of precisely how sympathy operates on the sentiments. Whereas Hume envisaged moral evaluation being made from an observer's point of view on the motives or character traits of others, Smith's sympathetic exercise required one to consider motives and character traits by projecting oneself into the point of view of the possessor or those affected by that point of view. By thus imagining oneself in another's situation, Smith maintained, one comes to share in the feelings that the other person experiences. Sympathy, understood as an imaginative capacity for fellow-feeling, in this way provides one a motive toward benevolence, according to Smith.

The antagonistic sentiment–reason divide that some early modern philosophers championed is transposed into a semantic key in the work of some twentieth-century Anglo-American philosophers. The work of metaethical noncognitivists such as Charles Stevenson (1908–1979) and Alfred Jules Ayer (1910–1989) especially influenced the development of contemporary philosophical debate over the respective roles of sentiment and reason in morals. Ayer notably argued for a distinction between cognitive meaning (possessed by descriptive statements and analytic statements) and emotive meaning (possessed by moral statements). On Ayer's view, moral utterances, appearances notwithstanding, serve not to assert facts but to express the emotions of the speaker. "In saying that a certain type of action is right or wrong," he wrote in *Language, Truth, and Logic* (1936/1952), "I am not making any factual statement, not even a statement about my own state of mind. I am merely expressing certain moral sentiments." Thus, on Ayer's view, ethical utterances are not candidates for assessment in terms of truth or falsity. Stevenson endorsed Ayer's so-called emotive view of moral language, though he was careful to stress the interconnections between descriptive and emotive meaning, as well as a meaning of *true* that might appropriately (albeit emotively) be applied to ethical statements. Caveats notwithstanding, Ayer's philosophy of language, combined with the view that the proper task of philosophy is analysis of cognitively meaningful language, issued in an era when the work of the moral philosopher was limited to that of metaethical reflection on moral language and phenomena.

CONTEMPORARY DEBATE

Although the days when Anglo-American moral philosophers limited their task to metaethical reflection have ended, the debate about the respective roles of sentiment and reason in moral deliberation and judgment, moral motivation, and moral responsibility lives on.

In the area of moral deliberation and judgment, the expressivists are the noncognitivist inheritors of emotivism. Like the emotivists, expressivists (e.g., Allan Gibbard and Simon Blackburn) distinguish between descriptive and evaluative discourse. Whereas emotivists such as Ayer hold that ethical utterances express the speaker's sentiments, however, the expressivists defend a more complicated account of the affective phenomena expressed in ethical utterance. They do so in an attempt to avoid now-familiar problems with emotivism; for, example, its difficulties accommodating ethical disagreement and explaining the behavior of ethical expressions in the embedded contexts and inferences common to moral deliberation.

More recently, a form of sentimentalism about ethical judgment has become popular that holds that ethical utterances that predicate some evaluative property *P* (such as, "murder is wrong") do not express emotion but, rather, express the speaker's endorsement of the having of certain emotions in response to property *P*. Following on the work of Gibbard, Daniel Jacobson and Justin D'Arms have begun to develop a form of *rational sentimentalism* that clarifies the kind of endorsement that is at issue in evaluative judgments generally. Making use of a generic relationship of *fittingness*, they offer an account of when one's moral sentiments are fitting to their objects, which distinguishes this question from other appraisals of the sentiments (such as prudential and moral appraisals of these responses). Correcting past philosophers' conflation of the claim that an emotion is fitting its object with the claim that it is morally appropriate to its object, their work promises to reinvigorate philosophical study of moral emotions that, while arguably fitting to their objects in certain circumstances, nonetheless have suffered neglect due to their perception as being somehow morally undesirable. Contempt and moralized disgust are examples.

Neosentimentalism about ethical judgment of the D'Arms/Jacobson variety is a form of emotional rationalism that bridges the metaethical noncognitivism/cognitivism divide. In some ways this neosentimentalism resembles the so-called sensibility theories of moral judgment espoused by metaethical cognitivists such as John McDowell. McDowell holds that moral sensibility functions much like perceptual ability: One's moral sensibility enables one to apprehend and form beliefs whose contents are irreducibly moral properties, much as one's visual perception allows one to apprehend color properties. Some contemporary moral philosophers rely on metaethical cognitivism, such as McDowell's, to urge a return to an Aristotelian view of moral sentiment that rejects an inherently antagonistic divide between reason and sentiment. On such an Aristotelian view, ethical deliberation and judgment primarily differ from deliberation and judgment about nonmoral phenomena, not in any metaphysical or epistemological peculiarities pertaining to their content but in the necessarily practical nature of their progeny.

In stressing the obviously practical nature of moral deliberation and judgment (that is, the way in which it engages with intention, action, and affect), however, the metaethical cognitivist risks unwittingly fueling the metaethical noncognitivist program. If one holds, with the metaethical noncognitivists, that propositional attitudes such as beliefs are motivationally impotent in themselves, then acknowledging the practical character of moral deliberation and judgment requires one to reject a view of moral deliberation and judgment as exclusively cognitive phenomena. The metaethical noncognitivist's rejection is complete in denying that they are even partly so, a rejection supported by the noncognitivist tendency to understand mental phenomena in terms exclusively of beliefs or desires.

One response to this denial proceeds from arguing that such a mental repertoire is impoverished in failing to admit that certain mental phenomena, emotions among them, may possess the representational character of beliefs while also possessing the motivational force of desires. In this way, a more nuanced moral psychology might advance contemporary debate.

Finally, it is worth noting that although the necessarily practical character of moral deliberation and judgment typically is raised as a challenge for the metaethical cognitivist, cognitivism in the theory of emotion—at least those versions that simply equate emotions with evaluative beliefs—also invites the question of how to account for the motivational potency of emotions.

As this brief taxonomy suggests, different theoretical commitments—whether in moral theory or the theory of emotions—support different conceptions of how sentiments figure in moral experience. These commitments also support different views concerning responsibility for one's moral emotions. If emotions are akin to urges and desires, to pleasures and pains, or to perceptions of some sort—with respect to which individuals arguably are passive—is it even intelligible to regard oneself and others as accountable for emotions? If, alternatively, emotions are judgments, are individuals thereby any closer to locating a form of control one exercises over them that would justify holding oneself and others accountable for them? Or should one challenge the assumption, as do some philosophers, that such control is necessary for justifying attributions of responsibility?

The philosopher P. F. Strawson famously argued that even should the metaphysical thesis of determinism hold true, individuals could not avoid holding themselves and others in general responsible for what he called the reactive attitudes (for example, gratitude, resentment, forgiveness, love, and hurt feelings). To be sure, he recognized, one often suspends these attitudes in special cases: the cases of children; the incapacitated. In the case of typical mature agents, however, susceptibility to the reactive attitudes is a condition of membership in a common humanity. On such a view, the theoretical question whether one possesses the freedom to control one's emotions is abandoned in favor of attending to the necessity of regarding oneself and others as responsible for emotions if one is to regard oneself and others as moral agents at all. The alternative, Strawson argued, is not a rational expurgation of such attitudes in deference to the determinist thesis but an objective stance toward oneself and others that amounts to viewing humans as perpetual patients, appropriate objects not of emotional engagement but of treatment. If Strawson is correct, philosophical interest in the moral sentiments is likely to continue to evade constraint to any single historical epoch, central as they are to moral personhood.

See also Aristotle; Ayer, Alfred Jules; Cicero, Marcus Tullius; Emotion; Emotive Theory of Ethics; Hellenistic Thought; Hume, David; Hutcheson, Francis; Locke, John; McDowell, John; Metaethics; Moral Sense; Newton, Isaac; Plato; Shaftesbury, Third Earl of (Anthony Ashley Cooper); Shame; Smith, Adam; Stevenson, Charles L.; Strawson, Peter Frederick; Virtue Ethics; Zeno of Citium.

Bibliography

Aristotle. *Nicomachean Ethics*. Translated by Christopher Rowe. New York: Oxford University Press, 2002.

Ayer, A. J. *Language, Truth, and Logic*. London: V. Gollancz, 1936. Reprinted, New York: Dover, 1952.

Blackburn, Simon. *Ruling Passions*. New York: Oxford University Press, 1998.

D'Arms, Justin, and Daniel Jacobson. "The Moralistic Fallacy: On the 'Appropriateness' of Emotion." *Philosophy and Phenomenological Research* 61 (2000): 65–90.

D'Arms, Justin, and Daniel Jacobson. "Sentiment and Value." *Ethics* 110 (4) (2000): 722–748.

Deigh, John. "Cognitivism in the Theory of Emotions." *Ethics* 104 (4) (1994): 824–854.

De Sousa, Ronald. *The Rationality of Emotion*. Cambridge, MA: MIT Press, 1987.

Gibbard, Allan. *Wise Choices, Apt Feelings*. Cambridge, MA: Harvard University Press, 1990.

Greenspan, Patricia. *Practical Guilt: Moral Dilemmas, Emotions, and Social Norms*. New York: Oxford University Press, 1995.

Griffiths, Paul E. *What Emotions Really Are*. Chicago: University of Chicago Press, 1997.

Hume, David. *A Treatise of Human Nature*, edited by L. A. Selby-Bigge and P. H. Nidditch. Oxford, U.K.: Calrendon Press, 1973.

Hursthouse, Rosalind. "Virtue and the Emotions." In *On Virtue Ethics*. New York: Oxford University Press, 1999.

Hutcheson, Frances. *An Essay on the Nature and Conduct of Passions and Affections, with Illustrations on the Moral Sense*. London 1728. Reprinted, Aaron Garrett, ed. Indianapolis: Liberty Fund, 2002.

James, William. "What Is an Emotion?" *Mind* 9 (34) (1884): 188–205.

Kenny, Anthony. *Action, Emotion, and Will*. New York: Routledge and Kegan Paul, 1963.

Mason, Michelle. "Contempt as a Moral Attitude." *Ethics* 113 (1) (2003): 234–272.

McDowell, John. "Values and Secondary Qualities." In *Mind, Value, and Reality*, 131–150. Cambridge, MA: Harvard University Press, 1998.

Nussbaum, Martha. *Upheavals of Thought*. New York: Cambridge University Press, 2001.

Oakley, Justin. *Morality and the Emotions*. New York: Routledge, 1992.

Pitcher, George. "Emotion." *Mind* 74 (295) (1965): 326–346.

Prinz, Jesse J. "Embodied Emotions." In *Thinking About Feeling*, edited by Robert C. Solomon, 44–60.

Shaftesbury. *Characteristics of Men, Manners, Opinions, Times*, edited by Lawrence E. Klein. New York: Cambridge University Press, 2000.

Smith, Adam. *A Theory of Moral Sentiments*, edited by D. D. Raphael and A. L. Macfie. Indianapolis: Liberty Fund, 1982.

Solomon, Robert C. *The Passions: Emotions and the Meaning of Life*. Indianapolis: Hackett, 1993.

Solomon, Robert C., Ed. *Thinking about Feeling*. New York; Oxford University Press, 2004.

Stocker, Michael, and Elizabeth Hegeman. *Valuing Emotions*. New York: Cambridge University Press, 1992.

Strawson, P. F. "Freedom and Resentment." Reprinted in *Free Will*, edited by Gary Watson, 59–80. New York: Oxford University Press, 1982.

Taylor, Gabriele. *Pride, Shame, and Guilt: Emotions of Self-Assessment*. Oxford: Clarendon Press, 1975.

Velleman, J. David. "Love as a Moral Emotion." *Ethics* 109 (2) (1999): 338–374.

Wallace, R. Jay. *Responsibility and the Moral Sentiments*. Cambridge, MA: Harvard University Press, 1996.

Williams, Bernard. "Morality and the Emotions." In *Problems of the Self: Philosophical Papers 1956–1972*, 207–229. New York: Cambridge University Press, 1973.

Williams, Bernard. *Shame and Necessity*. Berkeley: University of California Press, 1993.

Wollheim, Richard. *On the Emotions*. New Haven, CT: Yale University Press, 1999.

Michelle Mason (2005)

MORAL SKEPTICISM

The two main forms of skepticism about morality are skepticism about moral truths and skepticism about reasons to comply with moral considerations. These doctrines challenge the cognitive significance or rational authority of morality.

Skepticism about moral truths denies that there are—or that we can know that there are—true moral propositions (or facts) that entail that something has a moral attribute. This form of skepticism seems to imply that rational and informed agents would give moral claims no credence. It has been supported by a variety of arguments, including arguments about moral disagreement. One deep motivation for it is the difficulty of explaining the normativity or action-guiding nature of moral claims.

Noncognitivists attempt to explain the normativity of moral judgments by supposing that their function is to express states of the speaker and to affect behavior rather than to express propositions. Noncognitivists would agree that there are no true moral propositions, since they hold that moral claims do not express propositions. Yet they do not view moral claims as defective. According to noncognitivists, one who makes a claim, such as "Truthfulness is morally required." expresses a moral attitude or acceptance of a moral norm (Ayer, [1936] 1946; Gibbard, 1990; cf. Hume, [1739–1740] 1978).

Cognitivists object that our moral thinking cannot be understood except on the assumption that moral claims express propositions. To avoid skepticism, cognitivists must believe that there are moral properties that are sometimes exemplified. For if no moral property exists, or if none is exemplified, it follows that there are no moral requirements, no moral goods or bads, no moral virtues or vices. It may follow that there are no *honest* persons, for example, although there may be truthful persons.

A skeptic might hold that moral properties exist but that none is exemplified. This position seems implausible, however, for if there is the property of wrongness, it would be astonishing if nothing were ever wrong. Alternatively, a skeptic might argue that there are no moral properties. According to widely accepted views about propositions, however, the proposition that lying is wrong, for example, would attribute the property wrongness to acts of lying. The property would be a constituent of the proposition. Hence, if there are no moral properties, these views about propositions may lead to the conclusion that no proposition is expressed by sentences such as "Lying is wrong."

J. L. Mackie argued that there are no moral properties (1977). We conceive of moral properties as intrinsic; if an action is wrong, it is wrong "as it is in itself." But we also conceive of moral properties as intrinsically action guiding; we can be motivated to act in an appropriate way simply by coming to know that an action would be wrong, regardless of any antecedent motivations. Yet, Mackie thought, it is not intelligible that it be intrinsic to an action's having an intrinsic property that the mere recognition that the action has the property could motivate a person. The idea of a moral property is not intelligible; moral properties would be metaphysically "queer."

Gilbert Harman (1977) argued for an epistemic version of skepticism about moral truths. He argued that there seems to be no good reason to affirm any moral proposition, for moral hypotheses are never part of the best explanation of any observation. There is always a better nonmoral explanation. The belief that there are true moral propositions is therefore unwarranted.

Skepticism about moral truth appears to have a life of its own in secular cultures, independent of skeptical arguments. Some people believe that moral truths are grounded in God's commands. A secular culture would tend to think, however, that all substantive facts are empirical and "natural." And natural facts do not seem to be normative in the way moral facts are normative. It is therefore difficult to see how a natural fact could be a moral fact.

The second skeptical doctrine is the thesis that there need be no reason to comply with moral considerations. According to this thesis, rational agents would not give attention to moral considerations, as such, in deciding how to live their lives. To be sure, we may desire to live morally, and this desire may give us a reason to live morally. Or we may find ourselves in a context in which living morally is in our interest. Yet these possibilities do not show that there is necessarily a reason to comply with moral considerations (Nielsen, 1974); they do not distinguish moral considerations from considerations of etiquette, for example.

Skepticism about compliance is typically motivated by the idea that morality can require actions that are not to the agent's advantage. Assuming that there are reasons for one to do something just in case it would be to one's advantage, this idea implies that there may be no reason to comply with morality.

The two main skeptical doctrines are closely linked, on certain ways of thinking. First, it may seem, we cannot be guaranteed to have reasons to comply with moral considerations unless there are moral truths of which we have knowledge. Second, a kind of "internalist" theory holds that moral facts are "constituted" by reasons. On this view there are no moral facts unless there are reasons of a relevant kind.

Internalist antiskeptical theories attempt to defeat both skeptical doctrines at once. Immanuel Kant held, in effect, that if a moral imperative corresponds to a truth, it does so in virtue of the fact that it would be complied with by any fully rational agent (Kant, [1785] 1981). "Externalist" theories attempt to deal with skepticism about moral truths independently from skepticism about compliance (Sturgeon, 1985). Those who believe that moral truths are grounded in God's commands may suppose, for example, that God necessarily gives us reasons to comply.

Philosophers who accept one of the skeptical doctrines typically try to defuse it. Skeptics about rational compliance may argue that people with normal psychologies invariably have reasons to comply with morality. Skeptics about moral truth may argue that there nevertheless are reasons to engage in the practice of judging things morally.

See also Ayer, Alfred Jules; Harman, Gilbert; Hume, David; Kant, Immanuel; Mackie, John Leslie; Metaethics; Moral Realism; Skepticism, History of.

Bibliography

Ayer, A. J. *Language, Truth, and Logic* (1936). London: Gollancz, 1946.

Copp, D. "Moral Skepticism." *Philosophical Studies* 62 (1991): 203–233.

Gibbard, A. *Wise Choices, Apt Feelings: A Theory of Normative Judgment.* Cambridge, MA: Harvard University Press, 1990.

Harman, G. *The Nature of Morality: An Introduction to Ethics.* New York: Oxford University Press, 1977.

Hume, D. *A Treatise of Human Nature* (1739–1740). Edited by P. H. Nidditch. Oxford: Clarendon Press, 1978.

Kant, I. *Grounding for the Metaphysics of Morals* (1785). Translated by James W. Ellington. Indianapolis: Hackett, 1981.

Mackie, J. L. *Ethics: Inventing Right and Wrong.* Harmondsworth, U.K.: Penguin, 1977.

Nielsen, K. "Why Should I Be Moral?" In *Introductory Readings in Ethics,* edited by W. K. Frankena and J. T. Granrose. Englewood Cliffs, NJ: Prentice-Hall, 1974.

Nietzsche, F. *Basic Writings of Nietzsche.* Edited and translated by Walter Kaufmann. New York: Modern Library, 1968. See *The Genealogy of Morals* and *Beyond Good and Evil.*

Sturgeon, N. "Moral Explanations." In *Morality, Reason, and Truth,* edited by D. Copp and D. Zimmerman. Totowa, NJ: Rowman and Allanheld, 1985.

David Copp (1996)

MORE, HENRY
(1614–1687)

Henry More, the philosopher, poet, and Cambridge Platonist, was born at Grantham, Lincolnshire. His father, "a gentleman of fair estate and fortune," was a strict Calvinist but supported church and king against the Puritans. He introduced his son to Edmund Spenser's *Faerie Queene*, and Spenser's Platonism, allegorizing, and moral attitudes persist in More's own writings. At Eton, where More was educated, the religious atmosphere was latitudinarian; More abandoned the Calvinist doctrine of predestination without losing what he called "an inward sense of the divine presence." In December 1631 he entered Christ's College, Cambridge, where he was elected to a fellowship in 1639. He remained at Cambridge until his death, refusing preferments, except those he could pass on to such fellow Platonists as Edward Fowler and John Worthington. Unlike most of the Platonists he took no part in public affairs or in university administration. In *An Explanation of the Grand Mystery of Godliness* (1660) he defended what he called a "neutrality and cold indifference in public affairs."

When More entered Christ's College, it was split into three factions—the high church party, the Calvinistic Puritans, and the Medians, so called because they stood for a moderate church and had as their leader Joseph Mede, or Mead (1586–1638), author of *Clavis Apocalyptica* (1627), an allegorical interpretation of the Scriptures. More's tutor Robert Gell, whose *Remaines* were published in 1676, was a member of Mede's party; he emphasized even more strongly than Mede that salvation depended upon "good works," not on blind faith, and he shared Mede's fascination with demonology and Scriptural interpretation. More himself described Mede as an "incomparable interpreter of Prophecies," and in *The Grand Mystery of Godliness* defends his biblical interpretations against the criticisms of Hugo Grotius.

NEOPLATONISM

Developing a passion for philosophy, More read widely in Aristotle and the Scholastics. However, he became impatient with their failure, as he thought, to provide a satisfactory account of the relation between God and the individual self. He therefore turned to the Neoplatonists and to mystical writings, especially the *Theologia Germanica*, an anonymous fourteenth-century mystical handbook that Martin Luther republished in 1516. From the mystics and Neoplatonists More derived his belief that to acquire knowledge, one must first seek moral per-

fection and his definition of perfection as the process of becoming godlike by subduing egoism. More did not refer to Benjamin Whichcote, none of whose writings was published until just before More's death, but he told his biographer that 1637 was the date of his conversion to his "new way of thinking"; this was the year of Whichcote's appointment as Sunday lecturer at Trinity Church. More shared certain fundamental epistemological and metaphysical ideas with Ralph Cudworth. These were ultimately derived from Platonism, and how far Cudworth's formulation of them influenced More or vice versa is impossible to determine.

More's first philosophical writings were allegories in Spenser's manner, collected in 1647 as *Philosophical Poems*. They present a complicated world view in which the basic concepts of Neoplatonism are interpreted in Trinitarian terms. Christ is presented as a living demonstration that a human being can be wholly possessed by God, rather than as a Calvinistic redeemer. More's poems preach the lesson common to Cambridge Platonism that the life we live, not the creed we preach, is our path to salvation, but their obscure allegorical manner is quite remote from Whichcote's direct, epigrammatic style.

METAPHYSICS

In atmosphere the *Philosophical Poems* carry us back to the Renaissance. More saw Plato through the eyes of Plotinus and Plotinus through the eyes of Renaissance humanists such as Marsilio Ficino, who set out with the help of allegory to Christianize Neoplatonic metaphysics. Yet on December 11, 1648, More wrote the first of four Latin letters to René Descartes, in which he not only expressed the highest admiration for Descartes's work but added that Descartes's views "appear indeed to be my own—so entirely have my own thoughts run along the channels in which your fertile mind has anticipated me." Nor was this a merely transient enthusiasm. In the general preface to his *A Collection of Several Philosophical Writings* (1662), he still spoke with admiration of Descartes. Yet in the *Divine Dialogues* (1668) and even more severely in *Enchiridion Metaphysicum* (1671) More criticized "the superstitious admiration" for Descartes and alleged that his views led to atheism, a charge against which he had previously defended Descartes.

Not surprisingly, More's French critics accuse him of irresponsible fickleness. But if *Enchiridion Metaphysicum* is the first of More's writings to be officially an anti-Cartesian tract, the fact remains, as Descartes realized from the beginning but More only slowly, that More's leading ideas had always been in complete opposition to

Cartesianism. The central point in More's metaphysics as it is developed in *The Immortality of the Soul* (1659) and the metaphysical sections of *Divine Dialogues* and *Enchiridion Metaphysicum* is that extension is a characteristic of all substances and not, as Descartes had argued, a peculiarity of matter. Substances fall into two classes—spirits and material objects. Spirits are physically indivisible, can penetrate both other spirits and material objects, and can initiate motion; material objects are physically divisible, impenetrable, and capable of motion only when it has been communicated to them. But both spirits and material objects are extended. There are familiar objections to such an ontology; these concern, particularly, the compatibility of the two properties of being extended and being spiritual. In meeting these objections, More began by making two logical points. The first is that since we are never acquainted with essences but only with attributes, it is no objection to the extendedness of thinking beings that we "cannot see why" a being which thinks should also be extended. The second is that the intellectual separability of the properties of being extended and being spiritual is no proof of their incompatibility.

More's opponents have to show, he argued, that it is logically impossible for anything to be extended and yet to think. Most of the arguments that are supposed to establish this impossibility depend, according to More, upon the tacit identification of extension and materiality; the rest can be met by distinguishing between two forms of extension—metaphysical and physical. Metaphysical extension—pure space—is eternal, infinite, physically indivisible; physical extensions are finite, physically divisible, mutable. We can break up a particular cylinder, and we can easily imagine it not to exist, but we cannot take a piece out of space or imagine it not to exist. These properties it shares with God; indeed, space is an "obscure representation of the essence or essential presence of the divine being."

More came to see in Descartes the leader of what he calls the nullibists, who deny extension to spirits. And although Descartes had set out to defend God and immortality—this was one main reason why More approved of him—More finally concluded that nullibism is atheistic in tendency. For More the essential feature of the soul is that it initiates movement. To do this, however, it must be where body is. This is possible because unlike material objects spirits can penetrate both other spirits and material objects, contracting or expanding like Isaac Newton's "aether," as the occasion makes necessary. Thus, God, an individual mind, and a material object can all be present in the one place without losing their independ-

ence as substances. Spirit can be regarded, More argued, as a sort of fourth dimension; a body that contains a spirit has a certain "spissitude," or density of substances.

More's criticism of mechanical explanation is along the same general lines. At first, he had welcomed Descartes's mechanical explanations; by carrying ingenuity, so More thought, as far as it could be carried, they made it clear just what the limits of mechanical explanation were. But his conclusion is that mechanical explanation is never possible and that to suppose otherwise leads to atheism. (The emergence of Benedict de Spinoza from the Cartesian school encouraged More in this belief.)

A material object, he said, is nothing but a "congeries of physical monads"—that is, a collection of atomic particles. To explain how these particles are held together in solid objects, we have to introduce a nonmaterial, although spatial, spiritual agent. Equally, he argued, gravity is inexplicable in mechanical terms; mechanics—he meant, of course, Cartesian mechanics—cannot explain why a bullet once fired from a gun should ever return to Earth's surface. Even more obviously, the behavior of living organisms cannot be derived from a collection of particles.

Indeed, in order to explain any natural process, we have to refer to spirit as something additional to material particles; spirits are the true cause of all activity. This does not mean that all activity is the work of conscious rational beings. Spirit exists at various levels; "seminal forms," which are neither sensitive nor rational but are still capable of initiating motion, are responsible for actions at a level lower than animal feeling.

RELIGION AND ETHICS

More's metaphysical theories are not worked out in detail. His main interests, indeed, were religious rather than metaphysical: to defend Christianity against its three main enemies—namely, atheists, Roman Catholics, and "enthusiasts." *An Antidote against Atheism* (1653) reformulates the Ontological Argument but mainly relies upon anecdotes about animals to establish an Argument from Design and upon anecdotes about witches and apparitions to establish that spiritual forces are at work in the world. *Conjectura Cabbalistica* (1653), with the aid of the Jewish kabbalah, discerns Platonism and Cartesianism in Genesis; indeed, More expressed his regret that he had ever wasted his time on philosophy seeing that all fundamental truths are contained in the Bible. *A Brief Discourse of the Nature, Causes, Kinds and Cure of Enthusiasm* (1656) is directed against "enthusiasm," defined as "a full but false persuasion in a man that he is inspired."

More found the origin of enthusiasm in "melancholy"—that is, in a manic–depressive constitution. *The Grand Mystery of Godliness* defends the Cambridge Platonist concept of religion against Calvinists, atheists, and Roman Catholics alike; *An Antidote against Idolatry* (1674) attacks Roman Catholics. More had a special animosity against Quakers that increased in intensity when his disciple and admirer Anne Finch, Lady Conway, at whose home in Ragley, Warwickshire, he had been a frequent guest, became a convert to Quakerism.

More's *Enchiridion Ethicum* (1667), translated into English by Edward Southwell in 1690 with the appropriate title *An Account of Virtue*, was the most popular of More's writings in his own time but has since been neglected. It can be most succinctly described as a Christian version of Aristotle's *Nicomachean Ethics*, although the detail is influenced by Descartes's account of the passions and by mathematical ideals. (More set out a number of "moral axioms," which incorporate an ethical calculus.) Virtue, More argued, consists in pursuing what seems to be in accordance with right reason, but both our capacity to discover what actions accord with reason and our inclination toward those actions flow from a special "boniform" faculty. Reason itself cannot incite action; virtuous action can be instigated only by the passional side of our nature. The ultimate ground of all virtue is intellectual love. Thus, More hoped to weld the Christian doctrine of love and the Aristotelian doctrine of intellectual activity into a single ethical system.

INFLUENCE

More devoted the last seven years of his life to translating his English works into Latin in the hope of attracting wider interest on the Continent. They caught the attention of Gottfried Wilhelm Leibniz, but although he took an occasional phrase from More, he was interested in him mainly as a representative of the sort of view he particularly wished to avoid. In fact, More, the only one of the Cambridge Platonists to publish at all extensively, quite failed in what he conceived as his main task—to halt the advance of the mechanical worldview. More's metaphysics, however, had a considerable influence on Newton even if mathematicians, not metaphysicians, were Newton's principal masters. Newton did not refer explicitly to More—the Cambridge group almost never referred to one another—but the resemblances are conspicuous. Newton was taught mathematics at Grantham, More's birthplace, by a former pupil of More's; Newton's correspondence reveals that he and More stood close to one another.

See also Cambridge Platonists.

Bibliography

WORKS BY MORE

More's *Philosophical Poems* are reprinted in Alexander Balloch Grosart, *The Complete Poems of Henry More* (Blackburn, U.K, 1878). Geoffrey Bullough, *Philosophical Poems of Henry More* (Manchester, U.K.: University of Manchester, 1931), is a selection with a valuable introduction and notes. More's main philosophical writings are included in *A Collection of Several Philosophical Writings* (London, 1662) and his theological writings in *Theological Works* (London, 1708); the Latin version, *Opera Omnia* (London, 1675–1679), contains in addition a number of controversial pamphlets. Sections of the *Enchiridion Metaphysicum* were translated by Joseph Glanvill in his *Saducismus Triumphatus* (London, 1681) and are included in Flora Isabel MacKinnon, *Philosophical Writings of Henry More* (New York: Oxford University Press, 1925), with a useful bibliography and expository essays. Edward Southwell's translation of *Enchiridion Ethicum* has been reprinted by the Facsimile Text Society (New York, 1930). The correspondence with Descartes is partly translated by Leonora D. Cohen in *Annals of Science* 1 (1) (1936): 48–61, and is included in Geneviève (Rodis-)Lewis, *Correspondance avec Arnaud et Morus* (Paris, 1953).

WORKS ON MORE

For works on More see the bibliography under the "Cambridge Platonists" entry. See also Richard Ward, *The Life of Dr. H. More* (London, 1710); M. F. Howard has edited this life, but his introduction is not reliable (London, 1911). See also Marjorie Nicolson, ed., *The Conway Letters* (London: Oxford University Press, 1930), and Paul Russell Anderson, *Science in Defense of Liberal Religion* (New York and London: Putnam, 1933). For More's relation to Newton see Edwin Arthur Burtt, *The Metaphysical Foundations of Modern Physical Science* (London: Kegan Paul Trench and Trubner, 1925; rev. ed., 1950), and Alexandre Koyrè, *From the Closed World to the Infinite Universe* (Baltimore: Johns Hopkins Press, 1957). On the opposite side see Edward William Strong, *Procedures and Metaphysics* (Berkeley: University of California Press, 1936), and Stephen Edelston Toulmin, "Criticism in the History of Science: Newton on Absolute Space, Time and Motion," in *Philosophical Review* 68 (1) (1959): 1–30, and (2) (1959): 203–228.

Other Recommended Sources

Almond, Philip C. "The Journey of the Soul in Seventeenth-Century English Platonism." *History of European Ideas* 13 (6) (1991): 775–791.

Armstrong, Robert L. *Metaphysics and British Empiricism.* Lincoln: University of Nebraska Press, 1970.

Burnham, Frederic B. "The More-Vaughan Controversy: The Revolt against Philosophical Enthusiasm." *Journal of the History of Ideas* 35 (1974): 33–49.

Coudert, Allison. "A Cambridge Platonist's Kabbalist Nightmare." *Journal of the History of Ideas* 36 (1975): 633–652.

Daniel, Stephen. "Berkeley's Pantheistic Discourse."
  International Journal for Philosophy of Religion 49 (3) (2001):
  179–194.

Gabbey, Alan. "Philosophia Cartesiana Triumphata: Henry
  More." In *Problems of Cartesianism*, edited by Thomas M.
  Lennon, John M. Nicholas, and John W. Davis. Montreal:
  McGill Queens, 1982.

Hutton, Sarah. "Henry More and Anne Conway on
  Preexistence and Universal Salvation." In *Mind Senior to the
  World*, edited by Marialuisa Baldi. Milano: FrancoAngeli,
  1996.

Jacob, Alexander. "The Metaphysical Systems of Henry More
  and Isaac Newton." *Philosophia Naturalis* 29 (1) (1992):
  69–93.

Osler, Margaret J. "Triangulating Divine Will: Henry More,
  Robert Boyle, and Rene Descartes on God's Relationship to
  the Creation." In *Mind Senior to the World*, edited by
  Marialuisa Baldi. Milano: FrancoAngeli, 1996.

Patrides, C. A. *The Cambridge Platonists*. Cambridge, U.K.:
  Cambridge University Press, 1980.

Power, J. E. "Henry More and Isaac Newton on Absolute
  Space." *Journal of the History of Ideas* 31 (1970): 289–296.

Reid, Jasper. "Henry More on Material and Spiritual
  Extension." *Dialogue* 42 (3) (2003): 531–558.

Rogers, G. A. J. "Hobbes's Hidden Influence." In *Perspectives on
  Thomas Hobbes*, edited by G. A. J. Rogers and Alan Ryan.
  New York: Clarendon Oxford, 1988.

Sprague, Elmer. "Hume, Henry More and the Design
  Argument." *Hume Studies* 14 (1988): 305–327.

Staudenbaur, C. A. "Galileo, Ficino, And Henry More's
  Psychathanasia." *Journal of the History of Ideas* 29 (1968):
  565–578.

John Passmore (1967)
Bibliography updated by Tamra Frei (2005)

MORE, THOMAS
(1478–1535)

Sir Thomas More, later canonized St. Thomas More, was a lawyer and statesman rather than a philosopher. More was born the son of a London lawyer who later became a judge. He was educated at St. Anthony's School and was appointed a page in the household of Archbishop (later Cardinal) Morton, who sent him to Canterbury Hall, Oxford, in the early 1490s. More left without a degree to study at New Inn and Lincoln's Inn in London. His lectures dealt not only with law but also with St. Augustine's *City of God*. He early composed various English poems and Latin epigrams that were not printed for years. However, a Latin translation of four Greek dialogues of Lucian appeared in 1506, and an English translation of the Latin life of his model, Giovanni Pico della Mirandola, in 1510. Increasingly involved in public affairs, More became a member of Parliament in 1504, beginning the career that led to the well-known events of his chancellorship and his martyrdom. By the time of the *Utopia* (1516), he had long since mastered Greek and enjoyed the friendship of such humanists as Desiderius Erasmus, Thomas Linacre, William Grocyn, John Colet, Cuthbert Tunstall, and St. John Fisher.

PHILOSOPHICAL ORIENTATION

With respect to his philosophy, Thomas More belonged very much to the early or Erasmian period of the English Renaissance in his emotional and intellectual attitudes—toleration of eclecticism, search for simplicity, stress on ethics, return to Greek sources, and desire for reform: social, political, educational, religious, and philosophical. These traits appear not only in his highly imaginative and durably significant creation, *Utopia*, but also in his most pertinent pronouncements in real life. The latter may be divided into two philosophical periods, roughly separated by the year 1521, the year of publication of Henry VIII's *Defense of the Seven Sacraments* (*Assertio Septem Sacramentorum*), which More undertook to defend by his pseudonymous diatribe (1523) against Martin Luther's strictures.

During his first period, in his justly famous letters to Martin Dorp (1515), to the University of Oxford (1518), and to a monk (1519–1520), More opted for a simplified logic, the study of all Aristotle's works in Greek with their classical Greek commentaries, and the mastery of the Greek New Testament and Greek Fathers as well as the pagan classics in the original language. He praised the Aristotelian paraphrases of Jacques Lefèvre d'Étaples and, in a letter to Erasmus (May 26, 1520), expressed complete agreement with Juan Luis Vives's *False Dialecticians* (*Pseudodialectici*). His attack on contemporary Schoolmen centered on their preoccupation with logic, the universals, and a mere fragment of the Aristotelian corpus.

In his second, controversial period, More rose to the defense of Thomas Aquinas and the scholastic theologians, whose doctrine he showed to agree with that of the earlier church. However, since the interest of these works, even of *A Dialogue of Comfort against Tribulation* (1534), is almost entirely theological, there is no need to dwell on them, except to point out that he held the common scholastic views on the mutual relationship, harmony, and assistance between reason and revelation, with philosophy as the propaedeutic to theology and as the handmaid of theology. This synthesis appears in a fundamental form even on the island of Utopia, where ethical norms are bolstered by religious truths and where the true religion can prevail in an atmosphere of free and calm reasoning.

UTOPIA

Since *Utopia* is More's major, or at least most influential, writing, its philosophical elements will be discussed in detail.

BACKGROUND. Renaissance thinkers usually held that there were four great philosophical schools: Platonism, Aristotelianism, Stoicism, and Epicureanism, which differed mainly according to their opinions of the *summum bonum*. The Christianization of Aristotle was accomplished in the thirteenth and fourteenth centuries by the Schoolmen, and that of Plato in the fifteenth century by Marsilio Ficino and other humanists. Stoicism had found expression in almost boundless humanistic admiration for the writings of Seneca and especially Cicero before reaching definite formulation later in the Christian Stoicism of Justus Lipsius. It was therefore inevitable that humanistic attempts, if only rhetorical ones, should be made to Christianize Epicurus, too. The latter's rehabilitation had been much accelerated in the early fifteenth century by Ambrogio Traversari's Latin translation of his life by Diogenes Laërtius. Lorenzo Valla had set forth Epicurus's doctrine favorably in *De Voluptate ac de Vero Bono* (*Pleasure and the True Good*). Finally Erasmus undertook his thorough baptism in *De Contemptu Mundi* (*The Contempt of the World*, written c. 1490) and the colloquy *The Epicurean* (published 1533). In both these works, Erasmus manipulated the concept of pleasure and the principles of selection to establish a Christian Epicureanism.

EPICUREANISM IN *UTOPIA*. More's main sources for classical Epicureanism were undoubtedly the *Lives* of Diogenes Laërtius and the *De Finibus* of Cicero, with minor borrowings from Seneca, Quintilian, Lucian, and Aulus Gellius. The "Christian" modifications already introduced by such humanists as Lorenzo Valla and Erasmus should not be minimized. The preoccupation of Renaissance men with the problem of pleasure is evident from the many humanistic treatments of the subject, including that by Ficino. Consequently Epicurus and Epicureanism are here viewed not according to their historical reality but according to the light in which they appeared to Thomas More through his reading and conversation.

In spite of the great to-do in the *Utopia* about the philosophy of pleasure and in spite of the deliberate but superficial rejection of Stoicism, the emphasis on virtue and virtuous living is disproportionate, even extraordinary, and therefore suspicious. This respect for Stoicism also becomes explicit in the stress on the guidance of nature, the assumed existence of natural law, and the natural community of humankind.

There are several contacts between Utopian and Epicurean hedonism. The most evident, naturally, is the exaltation of pleasure as the *summum bonum*, to which all human activities, including the operations of the virtues, are directed and subordinated. But the term *pleasure* (*coluptas*) is so manipulated in the *Utopia* that it embraces everything from scratching an itch to enjoying eternal bliss with God. Like Epicurus, the Utopians hold to both kinds of pleasure: pleasure as a state and pleasure as motion. Hence health for them is a true pleasure. Like Epicurus, they belittle neither the joy arising from conferral of a benefit, nor the testimony of a good conscience as the reward for just deeds, nor the importance of mental pleasures. There is a common emphasis with Epicurus on the simple life, which in Utopia leads to the ridicule of false, unnatural delight in fine clothing, noble ancestry, glittering jewelry, gold and silver, gambling, and hunting. Perhaps the most important connection is the enunciation of the principles of selection; the single positive criterion is that a pleasure be natural—a criterion recognized as so obscure that it is delimited by three negative norms: that no pain follow the pleasure chosen, that no greater pleasure be lost, and that no social harm result.

DIVERGENCES FROM CLASSICAL EPICUREANISM. The departures from the postulates of classical Epicureanism are so radical that the Utopian philosophy in action can be labeled Epicurean, or even hedonistic, only in the broadest sense. For example, good Utopians must believe in the providence of God, the immortality of man's soul, and divine retribution in a future life. These Utopian principles are taken not from Epicurus but from More's great favorite, Plato, especially his *Laws*. Utopian ascetics, with their hope of reward in a future life, would be ridiculous to Epicurus. The Platonic origin of Utopian communism also is evident, for Epicurus thought that the holding of property in common by friends implied mutual mistrust. Minor points of divergence are the emphasis upon marriage (in contrast with its disapproval by Epicurus in spite of his traditional devotion to his parents), upon euthanasia (in comparison with Epicurus's denial of suicide even to the blind), and upon learning (Epicurus urged his disciples to fly from learning in the swiftest ship available). Utopians love their gardens, but for practical rather than philosophical purposes, so that, surprisingly, no reference is made in *Utopia* to the connection between Epicurus and gardens.

RAPHAEL HYTHLODAEUS. The unconscious pull of Platonism and Stoicism, not to mention Christianity, is too great to allow a full-fledged Epicureanism in Utopia. This is perfectly consistent, however, with the engrossing character of the main narrator, Raphael Hythlodaeus, who is a philosopher by nature and profession and interjects mild expressions of disapproval of Utopian hedonism. He is unattached: His only commitment is to freedom, truth, and justice. Negligent in dress, he has divested himself of the cares of riches by giving his patrimony to his relatives. He now lives as he pleases (according to Cicero's definition of freedom), and he must speak his mind openly. In spite of being accused of too great speculativeness and idealism by Thomas More, he travels and searches for something quite practical: the good state and the good citizen. In this emphasis on the useful, and in his return to the sources (especially the Greek), Hythlodaeus is at one with the early English, as well as the northern, Renaissance. In his chosen field of philosophy, he finds nothing of value in Latin except Seneca and Cicero. But he is far from being narrow. The great books in Greek that he carries with him include Plato and Plutarch, as well as Aristotle and Theophrastus, dramatists, poets, historians—and Lucian. Devotion to Lucian undoubtedly helped to mark More's philosophical character as his friends saw him—as "another laughing Democritus." More's emphasis upon the Greek sources in medicine (Galen and Hippocrates) and science (Aristotle's *Meteorology*) makes him, in a sense, an unwitting scientific reactionary.

PLATO'S INFLUENCE. Of all the Greek authors, Plato is cited most frequently in the *Utopia* proper and in its preliminary materials. This is hardly surprising, since its true title may be translated as *The Best Order of Society* (*De Optimo Reipublicae Statu*). More is indebted, however, as much to Plato's *Laws* as to his *Republic*. His obvious but modified borrowings from Plato are dialogic form, but with a monologue in Book II; communism, which he broadens to embrace a whole nation, not merely an elite class; preeminence of learning, with transformation of the philosopher-king into the scholar-governor; the almost complete equality of men and women; and the connections between goodness and religion. The differences are radical: Utopia is a casteless democracy, not an aristocracy; and the family, not a ruling class with common wives and children, is the basic social and political

unit. It is significant that More also briefly introduces the Aristotelian objections to communism of property.

PLEASURE AND THE BEST SOCIETY. It is a tribute to More's rhetoric (not philosophy) that the unwary reader is left under the impression that the Utopians espouse thoroughgoing hedonism. But this does not involve merely a humanistic *jeu d'esprit* or even a literary tour de force, for pleasure is related intimately to the main subject of the *Utopia*, the best society. The best society is one whose aim is the temporal well-being or happiness—or pleasure, as defined and described in Utopian terms—of all the citizens, not only of the rich or of the well-born. All are to share equally and equitably in all the good things—or pleasures—of this life and this world: food, clothes, houses, work, play, sleep, and education. More bridges the gap between Utopian philosophy and Utopian communism by the use of the basically Aristotelian phrase "the matter of pleasure" (*materia voluptatis*). Vital commodities (food, clothing, housing) constitute the pleasurable *matter*, which must be determined by a *form* (either private ownership or common possession). The Utopians have chosen communism, not private property, to bring the greatest pleasure to the whole nation. Only in this way will justice be introduced into an unjust society. In this at least theoretical espousal of communism, More agreed with Erasmus and many fellow humanists.

WEAKNESSES. On the debit side of the *Utopia* might be listed the deliberately static nature of this ideal society and the failure to recognize the individual person and his basic instincts, liberties, and even imperfections. The removal of all struggle and all insecurity would logically and psychologically lead to the prayer: "Give me something to desire."

INFLUENCE. The major influence of the *Utopia* lies not in its philosophic hedonism, with its concomitant communism, but in its establishment of a pattern for ideal commonwealths. Historically the type proliferated into a thousand different forms that can be found discussed in bibliographies and commentaries. In particular, the *Utopia* itself set an example for what might be termed the philosophical utopia that continued well into the eighteenth century. The most notable productions are Francis Bacon's *New Atlantis*, Tommaso Campanella's *City of the Sun*, and Samuel Johnson's *Rasselas*.

See also Aristotelianism; Aristotle; Augustine, St.; Bacon, Francis; Colet, John; Communism; Diogenes Laertius; Erasmus, Desiderius; Epicureanism and the Epicurean

School; Epicurus; Ficino, Marsilio; Galen; Hedonism; Hippocrates and the Hippocratic Corpus; Johnson, Samuel; Lipsius, Justus; Luther, Martin; Pico della Mirandola, Count Giovanni; Plato; Platonism and the Platonic Tradition; Pleasure; Plutarch of Chaeronea; Renaissance; Seneca, Lucius Annaeus; Stoicism; Theophrastus; Thomas Aquinas, St.; Universals, A Historical Survey; Utopias and Utopianism; Valla, Lorenzo; Vives, Juan Luis.

Bibliography

The best modern edition of More's Latin and English writings is the Yale edition: *The Complete Works of St. Thomas More*, R. S. Sylvester, executive ed. (New Haven, CT, 1963–1997), 21 volumes. Vol. IV, *Utopia* (New Haven, CT: Yale University Press, 1965), is edited by Edward Surtz and J. H. Hexter. Also see the Selected Works edition (New Haven: Yale University Press, 1961–), planned in seven volumes, of which two have appeared: *Selected Letters*, E. F. Rogers, ed. (1961), and *Utopia*, Edward Surtz, ed. (1964). E. F. Rogers had previously edited More's *Correspondence* (Princeton, NJ: Princeton University Press, 1947). Only the first two volumes of a contemplated seven-volume modern version of More's *English Works* (1557), edited by W. E. Campbell, were issued (London: Eyre and Spottiswoode, 1927–1931).

More's best biographers are the earliest: William Roper, *The Lyfe of Sir Thomas Moore*, edited by E. V. Hitchcock (London: Oxford University Press, H. Milford, 1935); and Nicholas Harpsfield, *The Life and Death of St. Thomas Moore*, edited by E. V. Hitchcock and R. W. Chambers (London: Oxford University Press, H. Milford, 1932). The best modern life is still R. W. Chambers, *Thomas More* (London, 1935), to be supplemented by E. E. Reynolds, *Saint Thomas More* (London: Burns and Oates, 1953).

Bibliographical data can be found in *St. Thomas More: A Preliminary Bibliography … to the Year 1750*, compiled by R. W. Gibson, with a bibliography of Utopiana compiled by R. W. Gibson and J. M. Patrick (New Haven, CT: Yale University Press, 1961). Also see F. and M. P. Sullivan, *Moreana, 1478–1945* (Kansas City, MO: Rockhurst College, 1945). In 1963, the international Amici Thomae Mori began publication of *Moreana: Bulletin Thomas More* (Angers).

Illuminating studies of the background can be found in W. E. Campbell, *Erasmus, Tyndale, and More* (London: Eyre and Spottiswoode, 1949); Fritz Caspari, *Humanism and the Social Order in Tudor England* (Chicago: University of Chicago Press, 1954); Pearl Hogrefe, *The Sir Thomas More Circle* (Urbana: University of Illinois Press, 1959); R. P. Adams, *The Better Part of Valor: More, Erasmus, Colet, and Vives on Humanism, War, and Peace* (Seattle: University of Washington Press, 1962); and especially G. Marc'hadour, *L'univers de Thomas More* (Paris: Vrin, 1963), corrected and supplemented currently in *Moreana*.

The principal interpretations of *Utopia* are those by Karl Kautsky, *Thomas More and His Utopia* (1888), translated by H. J. Stenning (reprinted, New York: Russell and Russell, 1959); H. W. Donner, *Introduction to Utopia* (London: Sidgwick and Jackson, 1945); Russell Ames, *Citizen Thomas More and His Utopia* (Princeton, NJ: Princeton University Press, 1949); J. H. Hexter. *More's "Utopia": The Biography of an Idea* (Princeton, NJ: Princeton University Press, 1952); Edward Surtz, *The Praise of Pleasure: Philosophy, Education, and Communism in More's "Utopia"* (Cambridge, MA: Harvard University Press, 1957); and Edward Surtz, *The Praise of Wisdom: A Commentary on the Religious and Moral Problems and Backgrounds of St. Thomas More's "Utopia"* (Chicago: Loyola University Press, 1957).

The fate of the utopia as a literary form can be followed in Richard Gerber, *Utopian Fantasy* (London: Routledge and Kegan Paul, 1955); J. O. Hertzler, *The History of Utopian Thought* (New York: Macmillan, 1923); and G. R. Negley and J. M. Patrick, eds., *The Quest for Utopia* (New York: Schuman, 1952).

See also Michael Jackson, "Imagined Republics: Machiavelli, Utopia, and *Utopia*," *Journal of Value Inquiry* (34[4] [2000]: 427–437; Anthony Kenny, *Thomas More* (Oxford: Oxford University Press, 1983).

Edward Surtz, S.J. (1967)
Bibliography updated by Tamra Frei (2005)

MORGAN, AUGUSTUS DE

See *De Morgan, Augustus*

MORGAN, C. LLOYD
(1852–1936)

C. Lloyd Morgan, an English biologist and philosopher, was born in London. His early education "was almost exclusively literary," but he later became attracted to scientific studies, attended the Royal School of Mines, and received a diploma in metallurgy. His deepest interest, however, was in the bearing of science on philosophical issues. This interest was given encouragement and direction by T. H. Huxley, under whom he studied biology. Henceforth, Morgan's vocation was to be that of an investigator of "borderland problems of life and mind" and the expositor of a philosophy of "emergent evolution." After teaching for five years at a small college near Cape Town, South Africa, he was appointed in 1884 to the chair of geology and zoology at University College, Bristol. When the college received a university charter in 1909, Morgan agreed to serve temporarily as its first vice-chancellor. At his own request, however, he resigned the next year and resumed his chair, now designated the chair of psychology and ethics. He retired in 1919. During his career at Bristol, Morgan devoted himself to the study of animal psychology and published such books as *Animal Life and Intelligence, Habit and Instinct, Animal Behavior,* and *Instinct and Experience.*

When he was elected a fellow of the Royal Society in 1899, he became the first person to be thus honored for scientific work in psychology. After his retirement he was invited to deliver the Gifford Lectures and used the occasion to expound his philosophical ideas, which subsequently appeared in *Emergent Evolution* and *Life, Mind, and Spirit*. Two other works, *Mind at the Crossways* and *The Emergence of Novelty*, contain elaborations of his position.

Morgan's psychological studies had a Darwinian background. Accepting the view that evolution is a continuous process, he sought to trace the development of mental characteristics in the world of living things. The focal point of his investigations was the behavior of those organisms that showed some capacity to learn from experience. He contended that the rudiments of intelligence are to be found wherever learning results from "the method of trial and error"—a phrase that he coined in 1894. Much of his experimental work was designed to show how this method is employed, even by relatively simple forms of life. Unlike his predecessors in animal psychology, Morgan was alert to the dangers of using casual reports of animal behavior, especially reports from untrained observers. He urged the importance of a methodological "law of parsimony," according to which we should never interpret what an animal does as the outcome of a higher psychical power if the action "can be interpreted as the outcome of the exercise of a power which stands lower in the psychological scale." Morgan's experiments usually were not strictly laboratory ones but involved artificially produced situations in the natural habitat of animals. His accurate and detailed observations of their behavior in these situations, however, gave comparative psychology a new scientific status.

The conceptual background of Morgan's work was neither mechanistic nor finalistic. He rejected the view that biological processes are to be understood in physico-chemical terms and that physiology can give an adequate account of animal behavior. Radical behaviorism was likewise unacceptable to him. On the other hand, he rejected the view that teleology is operative throughout the living world and that even reflex action and instinctive responses must be explained teleologically.

In *Instinct and Experience* Morgan criticized Henri Bergson's teleological speculations. Morgan's own position, which he described as "naturalism," was that in all behavior there occurs an "unrestricted concomitance" of physical and psychical events. Hence, each behavior episode is susceptible of interpretation in both physiological and psychological terms. There are two stories to be told, each throwing light on the other, "but neither story as such *makes* the other what it is."

Philosophically, Morgan adopted the hypothesis that the twofold story was really about *one* natural order of events. Moreover, that one order of events has a progressive natural history designated by the word *evolution*. An adequate description of this process requires us to recognize that evolution has not been uniformly continuous, as Charles Darwin believed, but has involved from time to time major discontinuities or "critical turning points." These turning points are marked by the abrupt appearance of certain phenomena that Morgan called *emergents*, a term used by G. H. Lewes in 1874. An emergent (1) supervenes upon what already exists, (2) arises out of what already exists, (3) is something genuinely new in the history of the universe, (4) occurs in a manner that is unpredictable in principle since it conforms to no general laws, and (5) cannot be naturalistically explained but must be accepted "with natural piety." The successive emergents in the panorama of evolution mark stages of progress from lower to higher. Hence, Morgan followed Samuel Alexander in picturing the totality of nature as "a pyramidal scheme."

The full significance of emergent evolution cannot be grasped, however, as long as one remains at the level of "a philosophy based on the procedure sanctioned by the progress of scientific thought." It was essential, Morgan thought, to construct a metaphysical system within which the naturalistic version of evolution could be set. This system would formulate certain fundamental concepts and presuppositions by whose aid an "ultimate explanation" of the evolutionary process could be given. Nothing affirmed in this constructive scheme was to be at variance with science, but it would "complete the otherwise incomplete delivery of strictly scientific thought."

A necessary basic presupposition of the system Morgan proposed was the existence of a physical world that "is nowise dependent on being perceived or thought of by any human or sub-human mind." Since no conclusive proof of this contention had ever been given, it was simply "accepted under acknowledgment." Morgan then elaborated a psychophysiologically oriented theory of how organisms perceive the external world. Physical events exert an "advenient influence" on the sense receptors of organisms. By virtue of their psychical power, the organisms respond by referring the signs arising within the psychophysical system to regions of physical space in a process Morgan called "projicient reference." The result is an emergent object correlated with the external event in such a way as to be biologically useful to the organism.

Morgan's second presupposition was that the pyramid of emergent evolution is a hierarchy of kinds of relatedness. Four basic concepts are needed to unfold its consequences—stuff, substance, quality, and property. The ultimate stuff consists of psychophysical events, and the mode of their relatedness in a given system is that system's substance. Each system has intrinsic qualities grounded in its substance and extrinsic properties grounded in its relation to other systems. Besides the emergents there are *resultants,* or phenomena that are repetitive, predictable, and the source of quantitative continuity. Emergence generates progress in continuity, but through resultants there is continuity in progress.

The third presupposition that Morgan acknowledged was the universal correlation of physical and psychical events. He recognized a similarity between his system and that of Benedict de Spinoza in this respect, yet Morgan's view that "mind" is "a quality emergent at a high level of evolutionary advance" would have been quite unacceptable, or possibly unintelligible, to Spinoza. Even that from which mind in this sense emerges—the pervasive psychical correlate—is scarcely to be compared with a Spinozistic attribute.

The last presupposition introduced by Morgan affirmed that a directing activity, otherwise called "spirit" or "God," is manifested everywhere. Thus, "the whole course of events subsumed under evolution is the expression of God's purpose," which embraces all that has been and all that will be brought about in the course of evolutionary advance. This postulate can be neither proved nor disproved but only adopted to satisfy the need for an ultimate explanation of things.

Morgan's philosophy of evolution gave wide currency to the idea of emergence. Yet when compared with later discussions, his treatment of the idea lacks precision. He was not a close reasoner, and his speculative scheme was much less carefully worked out than that of Alexander, to whom he was indebted. A hostile critic might well question Morgan's policy of "acknowledging," rather than arguing for, important principles in his system. And, although he opposed Darwinism by insisting that evolution is "jumpy" and not continuous, each jump is, in Morgan's view of evolution, a mystery, unexplained and inexplicable except, perhaps, to God.

See also Alexander, Samuel; Animal Mind; Bergson, Henri; Darwinism; Emergence; Emergent Evolutionism; Huxley, Thomas Henry; Lewes, George Henry; Spinoza, Benedict (Baruch) de; Teleology.

Bibliography

WORKS BY MORGAN

Animal Life and Intelligence. London: Arnold, 1890.
An Introduction to Comparative Psychology. London: W. Scott, 1894.
Habit and Instinct. London and New York: Arnold, 1896.
Animal Behaviour. London: Arnold, 1900.
Instinct and Experience. New York: Macmillan, 1912.
Emergent Evolution. London: Williams and Norgate, 1923.
Life, Mind, and Spirit. London, 1926.
Mind at the Crossways. London: Williams and Norgate, 1929.
The Animal Mind. London: Arnold, 1930.
The Emergence of Novelty. London: Williams and Norgate, 1933.

WORKS ON MORGAN

McDougall, William. *Modern Materialism and Emergent Evolution.* New York: Van Nostrand, 1929.
MacKinnon, Flora I. "The Meaning of 'Emergent' in Lloyd Morgan's 'Emergent Evolution.'" *Mind* 33 (1924): 311–315.

T. A. Goudge (1967)

MORGAN, LEWIS HENRY
(1818–1881)

Lewis Henry Morgan was an American anthropologist and social philosopher. After graduating from Union College in 1840, he practiced law in Rochester, New York, from 1844 to 1864, but he devoted much of his time to anthropological research, which eventually became his exclusive interest. One of the most celebrated American scholars of his time, Morgan was elected a member of the National Academy of Sciences in 1875 and president of the American Association for the Advancement of Science in 1879. The results of his investigations into the life of various Indian tribes appeared in his *League of the Ho-dé-no-sau-nee or Iroquois* (Rochester, NY, 1851) and his later work, *Systems of Consanguinity and Affinity* (Washington, DC, 1871); these two books were hailed as pioneering achievements of the first order in the study of kinship systems by even the most outspoken of his critics.

Morgan's aim was not merely to describe how different civilizations had evolved; he wished to elicit from their history a general pattern of institutional progress. In his most ambitious work, *Ancient Society* (New York, 1877), Morgan sought to establish that human history falls into three main stages—savagery, barbarism, and civilization—and that each stage reflects a close correlation between economic and cultural achievements. Savagery was the period before pottery; barbarism was the ceramic era; civilization began with writing and the phonetic alphabet. The first two periods are further subdivided, and each subperiod is defined in terms of its characteristic technological innovations. The discovery of fire and the beginning of fishing, for example, are characteristic of the second subperiod of savagery, the invention of the bow and arrow of its third subperiod.

Although Morgan shared the view of his Swiss contemporary and fellow anthropologist Johann Jakob Bachofen that society had emerged from a state of primitive communism, and also accepted the Bachofen hypothesis of matrilineal descent, he had little interest in ancient myths and religions. His principal attention was focused on technological factors, kinship systems, and property systems, and their relations to social and political institutions. In spite of gaps and distortions, Morgan's account of the growth of civilization has been considered by so severe a critic of his ethnological theories as Robert H. Lowie to be a comprehensive scheme of cultural wholes far beyond anything attempted up to that time. Lowie has written, "Morgan's *Ancient Society* was a synthesis of sociological material that for the first time brought together material on Australian and American natives, on ancient Greece and Rome; and all this in an orderly arrangement prescribed by an evolutionary doctrine" (*The History of Ethnological Theory,* London, 1937, p. 56).

Moreover, *Ancient Society* speaks for a distinct social philosophy and philosophy of history. The collation and comparison of human institutions, inventions, and discoveries convinced Morgan of humankind's unity of origin, of the similarity of human wants in different societies at comparable stages of advancement, and of the uniformity in the operations of the human mind in similar conditions of society. He formed the view that the human race was "one in source, one in experience and one in progress" (*Ancient Society,* p. vi). The problem that preoccupied Morgan in his historical researches was the existence of social and economic inequality. He could not conceive that "a mere property career" was the final destiny of humankind. Man's obsession with private property, he felt, was only a transient stage of human civilization. For if it was not, it was bound to lead to society's self-destruction. If progress was to be the law of the future as it had been of the past, property would have to be diffused and if necessary controlled, so that "democracy in government, brotherhood in society, equality in rights and privileges, and universal education" would foreshadow the next higher plane of society, "to which experience, intelligence and knowledge are steadily tending" (*Ancient Society,* p. 552).

Morgan recognized that civilization could be aggressive as well as progressive. But his theory of social evolution has nothing in common with such imperialist notions as Rudyard Kipling's concept of the white man's burden. Progress, Morgan insisted, echoing Herder, is inherent in all cultures, civilized or not, and each has to advance along its own lines. Culture is a process, not an administrative imposition.

Although Morgan's theories were invoked by Karl Marx and by Friedrich Engels (notably in his *Origin of the Family, Private Property and the State*) in support of their interpretation of history, Morgan's social message bears only superficial similarities with Marxist doctrines. Nonetheless, the optimistic flavor of his evolutionism had a powerful appeal to social reformers. At the same time this very quality made it suspect to the uncommitted social scientist.

See also Bachofen, Johann Jakob; Culture and Civilization; Engels, Friedrich; Herder, Johann Gottfried; Marx, Karl; Philosophy of Social Sciences.

Bibliography

ADDITIONAL WORKS BY MORGAN

Diffusion against Centralization. Rochester, NY, 1852.

The American Beaver and His Works. Philadelphia: Lippincott, 1868.

Houses and House Life of the American Aborigines. Washington, DC: Government Printing Office, 1881.

Pioneers in American Anthropology: The Bandelier-Morgan Letters. Edited by Leslie A. White. Albuquerque: University of New Mexico Press, 1940.

WORKS ON MORGAN

Childe, V. Gordon. *Social Evolution.* New York: Schuman, 1951.

Colson, Elizabeth. *Tradition and Contract: The Problem of Order.* Chicago: Aldine, 1974.

Fortes, Meyer. *Kinship and the Social Order: The Legacy of Lewis Henry Morgan.* Chicago: Aldine, 1970.

Lowie, Robert H. "Evolution in Cultural Anthropology." *American Anthropologist* 48 (1946): 223–233.

Lowie, Robert H. *The History of Ethnological Theory.* New York: Farrar and Rinehart, 1937.

Resek, Carl. *Lewis Henry Morgan, American Scholar,* Chicago: University of Chicago Press, 1960. Contains a full bibliography.

Stern, Bernhard J. *Lewis Henry Morgan, Social Evolutionist.* Chicago: University of Chicago Press, 1931.

White, Leslie A. "Evolutionism in Cultural Anthropology." *American Anthropologist* 53 (1951): 11–18.

White, Leslie A. "Morgan's Attitude toward Religion and Science." *American Anthropologist* 46 (1944): 218–230.

Frederick M. Barnard (1967)
Bibliography updated by Philip Reed (2005)

MORGAN, THOMAS
(d. 1743)

Thomas Morgan, the Welsh deist, dissenting minister, doctor of medicine, freethinker, and religious controversialist, was born of a poor family but received a free education from the Reverend John Moore, a dissenter. Morgan was ordained in 1714 and became minister of Burton two years later and subsequently of Marlborough; in 1720 he was dismissed from this last post for his growing unorthodoxy. He then took up the study of medicine and produced several books on that subject—*Philosophical Principles of Medicine* (1725), *The Mechanical Practice of Physic* (1735), *Letter to Dr. Cheyne in defence of the "Mechanical Practice"* (1738).

Morgan is chiefly remembered, however, for his deistical tracts, or "Christian deistical," as he preferred to call them, in which he described himself as "M.D. and Moral Philosopher." *The Moral Philosopher, in a Dialogue between Philalethes, a Christian Deist, and Theophanes, a Christian Jew* (1737) is his major work. Controversy produced two further works under the same title, the second of 1739, subtitled "Being a farther Vindication of Moral Truth and Reason," and the third of 1740, subtitled "Superstition inconsistent with Theocracy." In 1741 he published *A Vindication of the Moral Philosopher; Against the False Accusations, Insults, and Personal Abuses, of Samuel Chandler, Late Bookseller and Minister of the Gospel.*

In general, Morgan was a rationalist espousing the five Common Notions of Lord Herbert of Cherbury. He was also one of the pioneers of historical criticism of the Bible, particularly of the Pentateuch, and was considerably influenced by John Toland and to some extent by Thomas Chubb. The latter's advocacy of free will, however, he strongly attacked in 1727 in *A Letter to Mr. Thomas Chubb, occasioned by his "Vindication of Human Nature"* and in 1728 in *A Defence of Natural and Revealed Religion.*

Morgan believed in the corruption of human nature and defended suicide for the "weary or satiated with living." His criticism of the Scriptures centered on the fact that so many different interpretations are possible and are accepted by so many different and sincere believers. Traditional religion, therefore, is not infallible but only probable, as is all history. Priestcraft, which instituted superstition, enthusiasm, and finally persecution, is the culprit for the erroneous notion of the infallibility of a catholic church. Reason and tolerance are the only cures.

See also Deism.

Bibliography
Additional works by Morgan include *A Collection of Tracts … occasioned by the late Trinitarian Controversy* (1725); *A Philosophical Dissertation upon Death. Composed for the Consolation of the Unhappy* (1732); *The History of Joseph Considered … by Philalethes* (1744). See also Sir Leslie Stephen's *History of English Thought in the Eighteenth Century* (London: Putnam, 1876; the paperback edition, 2 vols., New York: Harcourt Brace, 1963, follows the revised edition of 1902), and the general bibliography under the Deism entry.

Ernest Campbell Mossner (1967)

MORITZ, KARL PHILIPP
(1756–1793)

Karl Philipp Moritz, German novelist, man of letters, and aesthetician, was born to poor and radically Quietist (Protestant) parents. Moritz started his career as an apprentice hatmaker at the age of twelve and ended up as an intimate of Johann von Goethe, Friederich Schiller, and Johann Georg Herder, and as professor of archaeology and aesthetics at the Berlin academy of art as well as a member of the Prussian Academy of Sciences. A prolific writer, his works include the psychological novel *Anton Reiser* (1785–1790), a fictionalized account of his own passage from his narrow religious origins to the center of the German Enlightenment; the satirical novel *Andreas Hartknopf* (1786); a widely read account of *The Travels of a German in England in 1782* (1783); an *Essay toward a Practical Logic for Children* (1786); an English grammar for Germans (1784); as well as a work on German prosody (1786) and much more; and he edited the *Magazine for Empirical Psychology* from 1783 to 1793 as well as the *Monthly of the Academy of Arts and Sciences* in 1789 and 1790. But among philosophers, he is best known for the brief "Essay on the Unification of all Fine Arts and Sciences under the Concept of *That Which Is Perfect in Itself*" (1785) and the longer essay *On the Imaginative [bildende] Imitation of the Beautiful* (1788).

The first of these essays offers an early defense of the idea of *art for art's sake*. Moritz argues that an object is beautiful neither because it gratifies us nor because it is useful to us but because it possesses an entirely internal purposiveness that is so perfect that contemplation of it causes us to leave all our ordinary concerns behind: In such a moment of contemplation, "we sacrifice all of our individually limited existence to a kind of higher existence" (Moritz 1989, p. 11; Moritz 1993, vol. 2, p. 545). This position leads Moritz to the extreme conclusion that when one feels bad at seeing a play performed before an empty house, one shares the disappointment not of the playwright, actors, and producers but of the work of art itself.

Moritz's longer essay on the imitation of the beautiful is less radical and more deeply entrenched in long-standing traditions in aesthetics: Here the influence of neo-Platonism, Leibnizo-Wolffian aestheticians such as Alexander Gottlieb Baumgarten and Moses Mendelssohn (in spite of his criticism of Mendelssohn in the essay on the perfection of art), and Herder all become clear. Moritz argues that in properly imitating a beautiful work of art, one does not ape its outward appearance but, rather, strives to exercise one's own active powers in a way analogous to the exercise of the artist's powers that produced the object. At the same time, however, one seeks contemplation and repose in the experience of such an object. The apparent contradiction between these claims is resolved in Moritz's view that in contemplating the beauty of an object as a self-contained whole, one both experiences an intimation of the perfection of the cosmos as a whole and is also led to strive to transcend the limits of individuality and thereby to make one's own contribution to the perfection of that whole. Both passive and active relation to a beautiful work of art is thus a mirror of both passive and active relations to the perfection of the cosmos as a whole.

Although Moritz's name was not much mentioned by leading philosophers, his influence is clear. Kant surely knew Moritz's 1785 essay (it appeared in a number of the *Berlin Monthly* in which Kant also published an article), and his own concept of the *subjective purposiveness* of the experience of beauty may well have been intended as a corrective to Moritz's conception of the internal perfection of the work of art itself. There is no direct evidence that Kant knew Moritz's 1788 essay, but Kant's own distinction between being moved by the originality of a work of genius and merely aping its outward manner could certainly have come from Moritz. Moritz's analysis of one's both passive and active relation to beauty surely influenced Schiller's analysis of one's diverse drives with regard to beauty in his *Letters on the Aesthetic Education of Mankind*. And Moritz's idea that the contemplation of beauty allows one to transcend the limits of one's own individuality also anticipates a central theme of Schopenhauer's aesthetics. Moritz thus represents an important transition between the aesthetics of the mid-eighteenth century and classical German aesthetics.

See also Aesthetics, History of; Goethe, Johann Wolfgang Von; Herder, Johann Gottfried; Kant, Immanuel; Schopenhauer, Arthur.

Bibliography

WORKS BY MORITZ

Schriften zur Ästhetik und Poetik: Kritische Ausgabe, edited by Hans Joachim Schrimpf. Tübingen: Neimeyer, 1962.

Beiträge zur Ästhetik, edited by Hans Joachim Schrimpf and Hans Adler. Mainz: Dieterich, 1989.

Werke, edited by Horst Gunter. 3 vols. 2nd ed. Frankfurt am Main: 1993.

Anton Reiser: A Psychological Novel. Translated by Ritchie Robertson. New York: Penguin Books, 1997.

WORKS ON MORITZ

Boulby, Mark. *Karl Philipp Moritz: At the Fringe of Genius*. Toronto: University of Toronto Press, 1979.

Saine, Thomas P. *Die ästhetische Theodizee: Karl Philipp Moritz und die Ästhetik des 18. Jahrhunderts*. Munich: Finck, 1971.

Schrimpf, Hans Joachim. *Karl Philipp Moritz*. Stuttgart: Metzler, 1980.

Woodmansee, Martha. *The Author, Art, and the Market: Rereading the History of Aesthetics*. New York: Columbia University Press, 1994.

Paul Guyer (2005)

MOSCA, GAETANO
(1858–1941)

Gaetano Mosca, an Italian legal and political theorist and statesman, was born in Palermo. He was one of several social theorists, including Vilfredo Pareto and Robert Michels, who gave currency to the conception of ruling elites and their circulation as being the basic characteristic of politically organized societies. Mosca outlined his conception in *Sulla teorica dei governi e sul governo parlamentare* and elaborated it in his major work, *Elementi di scienza politica*, first published in 1895 and considerably expanded in the third edition, which appeared in 1923 (translated as *The Ruling Class*).

The *Elementi* ranges over a large number of problems in the philosophy of history and in the analysis of political organization and development. Mosca speculated about the stages of political and social development, the types of political and social systems, the role of moral forces and religions in political organization and change, the function of international and civil wars, the causes and types of revolutions, race and nationality, and the causal significance of economic factors. However, the notion of the "political class," or "ruling class," is central to the *Elementi*.

Mosca asserted that every politically organized society of any degree of complexity is characterized by the existence of an organized minority that rules and a majority that is ruled. He rejected the Marxist position that the ruling class always derives from the organization of the economy. He held that in different types of societies, different qualities and functions characterize the members of the ruling class. In certain societies, warriors occupy a central role within the ruling class; in others, economic functions are important in determining membership; and still other societies have been characterized by a hereditary ruling class. In modern societies an important section of the ruling class is always the bureaucracy, the body of salaried officials professionally entrusted with the administration of the machinery of political, economic, and social life. (Mosca was particularly interested in the emergence of modern bureaucratic states and treated bureaucratic societies as one of the chief social types.)

It appears that Mosca loosely identified the ruling class with those who occupy the controlling or governing positions within the political organization of society. At times, however, he spoke as if the ruling class were a multiplicity of political, social, and economic elites, as when he wrote, for example, that "below the highest stratum of the ruling class there is, even in autocratic systems, another that is much more numerous and comprises all the capacities for leadership in the country." Without a ruling class, Mosca claimed, all forms of social organization would be impossible. He added that the democratic tendency—the tendency to replenish ruling classes from below—"is constantly at work with greater or less intensity in all human societies." Mosca, unlike Karl Marx, did not think of classes as necessarily conflicting social forces; nor did he think of the ruling class as always imposing its will on, and maintaining its distinctive class interests against, the rest of society.

He said that every organized political society has its "political formula," a doctrine or body of belief that legitimizes the political structure and the authority of the ruling class; there are, for example, the doctrines of divine right, and of democracy. It may often be the case that the power of the ruling class requires the use of force or violence; but Mosca thought that in stable, progressive, and flourishing societies the position of the ruling class may be founded on its intellectual and moral preeminence as well as on its care for the collective interests of the nation; the political formula that legitimizes the authority of the ruling class may be accepted by all members of the society.

In fact, in arguing that all developed societies are governed by a ruling class (and that the idea of democracy in the literal sense of government by the majority is an illusion) Mosca did not wish to imply that all societies are authoritarian or autocratic. Throughout the *Elementi* he argued strongly in support of a society marked by a high measure of what he called "juridical defence"—a society in which members of the ruling class are limited in their exercise of authority and power by moral codes that protect individual rights and liberties; a society that is pluralistic, or "open," in the sense that power is widely diffused throughout the community, and hence many different interests or social forces are able to express themselves within the political framework. Mosca was critical of parliamentary government in his early work, but later, especially in the material added to the 1923 edition of the *Elementi*, he spoke strongly of its merits; he saw it as the one form of organization able "to utilise almost all human values in the political and administrative departments of government, … [in which] the door has been left open to all elements in the governed classes to make their way into the ruling classes" (*The Ruling Class*, p. 389). Thus, although Mosca thought that recognition of the inevitable existence of the ruling class in any society was sufficient to destroy the illusions of democratic ideologies, his conclusions are not easy to distinguish from the standard doctrines of liberal-democratic political philosophy.

See also Marx, Karl; Michels, Robert; Pareto, Vilfredo; Philosophy of History; Social and Political Philosophy.

Bibliography

WORKS BY MOSCA

Sulla teorica dei governi e sul governo parlamentare. Turin: Loescher, 1884; 2nd ed., Rome, 1925.

Le costituzioni moderne. Palermo: Amenta, 1887.

Elementi di scienza politica. Rome, 1895; 2nd ed., Rome, 1896; 3rd ed., Turin, 1923; 4th ed., with preface by Benedetto Croce, Bari, 1947. There is a translation by Hannah D. Kahn of the third edition, edited and revised and with introduction by Arthur Livingstone, titled *The Ruling Class*. New York: McGraw-Hill, 1939.

Lezioni di storia delle istituzioni e delle dottrine politiche. Rome: Castellani, 1933. A revised, corrected, and retitled edition appeared in 1937 as *Storia delle dottrine politiche* (Bari, Italy: Laterza).

WORKS ON MOSCA

Bobbio, Norberto, "Liberalism Old and New," *Confluence* 5 (1956): 239–251.

Bottomore, T. B. *Elites and Society.* London, 1964.

Meisel, James H. *The Myth of the Ruling Class: Gaetano Mosca and the Elite.* Ann Arbor: University of Michigan, 1958.

Piane, Mario delle. *Gaetano Mosca: Classe politica e liberalismo.* Naples, 1952.

Piras, Quintino. *Battaglie liberali: Profili e discorsi di Benedetto Croce, Gaetano Mosca, Francesco Ruffini.* Novara, Italy, 1926.

P. H. Partridge (1967)

MOTION

The nature of motion and the philosophical problems surrounding it have been perennial issues in Western philosophy. Motion is a special case of change, and much discussion relevant to motion extends naturally to change in general (see Mortensen 2002).

Notable among the problems of motion are those provided by Zeno's paradoxes. Perhaps the hardest of these is the Arrow paradox. Consider an object in motion. At any instant of that motion, since it is an instant, the object makes no advance on its journey. But if it makes no advance in any instant of its journey, how can it make advance in all of them? The sum of a collection of nothings—even an infinite collection—is nothing. It would seem that it cannot move at all.

MOTION AND THE CALCULUS

Substantial progress concerning the topic of motion was made with the development of the calculus by Isaac Newton and Gottfried Wilhelm Leibniz in the seventeenth century. The velocity of an object at time t, $v(t)$ (with respect to a frame of reference), is given by the derivative of its spatial location, $x(t)$, with respect to time. That is, $v(t_0)$ is $dx(t)/dt$, evaluated at t_0. An object is in motion at an instant if its velocity at that instant is nonzero; it is at rest if its velocity is zero.

The understanding of motion thus provided is, of course, parasitic on an understanding of the calculus itself and specifically on the notion of a derivative. In the eighteenth and early nineteenth centuries this depended on the notion of an infinitesimal; and infinitesimals behaved in a notoriously inconsistent fashion. Specifically, they were assumed to be nonzero (sometimes) and zero (sometimes).

HEGEL ON MOTION

Georg Wilhelm Friedrich Hegel, writing at the start of the nineteenth century, put the contradictory properties of the infinitesimal to the service of his dialectic. The continuous and the discrete are contradictory notions. There is, therefore, something that is their synthesis. This is a variable point: the infinitesimal. It has the property of being a point, so having zero extension, and being extended, so having nonzero extension.

This understanding allows him a particular view of the account of motion provided by the calculus. To be in motion at an instant is precisely to move an infinitesimal amount. Thus,

> [when a body is moving] there are three different places: the present place, the place about to be occupied and the place which has just been vacated; the vanishing of the dimension of time is paralyzed. But at the same time there is only *one* place, a universal of these places, which remains unchanged throughout all the changes [i.e., the variable point]; it is duration existing immediately in accordance with its notion, and as such it is motion. (Hegel 1970, p. 43)

That is, "Something moves not because at one moment of time it is here and at another there, but because at one and the same moment it is here and not here, because in this 'here' it at once is and is not" (Hegel 1969, p. 440). This provides Hegel with a simple solution to the Arrow paradox. The object advances on its journey because it does advance at each instant: It moves a tiny amount at each instant.

RUSSELL ON MOTION

Within fifty years Hegel's analysis of motion was rendered obsolete by new mathematical developments. Toward the end of the nineteenth century the notion of an infinitesimal disappeared from standard mathematics. This was because, through the work of Baron Augustin-Louis Cauchy, and particularly Karl Weierstrass, a different understanding of the derivative was developed. A derivative came to be understood simply as the limit of a certain ratio as some variable approaches a value. In particular, the velocity $v(t_0)$, that is, $dx(t)/dt$ as evaluated at t_0, came to be understood as the limit of $(x(t_0+\epsilon)-x(t_0))/\epsilon$ as ϵ approaches 0.

Therefore, the new interpretation of the calculus provided a different understanding of motion. This was spelled out by Bertrand Russell in *The Principles of Mathematics* as follows:

> [I]n consequence of the denial of the infinitesimal, and in consequence of the allied purely technical view of the derivative of a function, we must entirely reject the notion of a *state* of

motion. Motion consists *merely* in the occupation of different places at different times.... There is no transition from place to place ... no such thing as velocity except in the sense of a real number which is the limit of a certain set of quotients. (1938, p. 473)

The paradox of the Arrow can then be dismissed:

In the case of motion, [Zeno's Arrow paradox] denies that there is such a thing as the *state* of motion. In the general case of a continuous variable, it may be taken as denying actual infinitesimals. For infinitesimals are an attempt to extend to the *values* of a variable the variability which belongs to it alone.... [The modern account of the variable has clarified this confusion, but] its absence in Zeno's day led him to suppose that continuous change was impossible without a state of change, which involves infinitesimals and the contradiction of a body's being where it is not. (Russell 1938, pp. 350–351)

PROBLEMS WITH THE ORTHODOX ACCOUNT

The view concerning motion expressed by Russell became the orthodox view of motion in the twentieth century. It is not without its problems, however. As Russell makes clear, according to this account there is no such thing as an intrinsic state of motion. That is, the instantaneous states of two objects, one in motion and one at rest at that instant, but at the same place, would be identical. Whether the object is in motion or at rest at that instant depends entirely on its states at neighboring instants. This is highly counterintuitive: Motion turns out to be a sequence (albeit a continuous one) of states that are indistinguishable from rest-states. There is no genuine flux. Motion occurs in much the same way as it appears to when successive stills in a cinema film are shown so fast that something seems to move. Indeed, one might call this the cinematic view of change. One way to bring home its oddity is as follows. Suppose that there is a particle that behaves as follows: At any time it exists simply at some place, but at any time it may disappear and reappear at some other place. Suppose that, by an accidental string of occurrences, the positions of the particle over a short period just happen to be a continuous function of time with a nonzero derivative. One would not, on this account, be inclined to say that the particle is in motion at each instant.

The cinematic account of change is not just counterintuitive. It has a number of other untoward consequences, as Russell himself notes (1938, p. 482). It is natural to take laws of nature to state causal relations between various quantities, such as velocity and its derivative, acceleration. Indeed, one normally takes it that the states of these quantities at a time are causal determinants of later states. If, in nature, there are no such things as these quantities, all this must be foregone—including the possibility of Laplacean determinism: the view that the intrinsic state of a system at any time determines its future states.

Further problems arise when one considers discontinuities of various kinds. Thus, suppose that an object is at rest before time t, and then starts to move with velocity 1. That is, $x(t) = 0$ if $t<0$ and $x(t) = t$ if $t\geq0$. The object has no velocity at $t = 0$ (since $x(t)$ has no derivative there), and a fortiori no acceleration. Still, it would seem that it ought to, if the motion is the result of an impulse applied to the object at $t = 0$. Worse: suppose that the object moves instantaneously at $t = 0$ to some other position where it is at rest; so $x(t) = 0$ if $t<0$ and $x(t) = 1$ if $t\geq 0$. If $t \neq 0$, the velocity of the particle is 0; and if $t = 0$, the velocity is undefined. Hence, the particle has changed places at $t = 0$, yet it has never been in motion!

Finally, and Russell's protestations to the contrary notwithstanding, it would appear that he has not so much solved the Arrow paradox as ignored it. He accepts that no progress is made on the journey in an instant, but simply insists that, nonetheless, progress is made in the whole journey. This is not a solution, it is what must be explained.

TOOLEY'S ACCOUNT

These and other objections were leveled against the Russellean account by Graham Priest (1985, 1987) and Michael Tooley (1988), each of whom offers an account of motion according to which velocity (relative to a frame of reference) is an instantaneous property of an object.

According to Tooley velocity is a theoretical (i.e., unobservable) property of an object that is causally efficacious in determining its behavior. Specifically, it is a quantity, $v(t)$, satisfying the equations:

$$x(t_1) = x(t_0) + {_0}\!\int^1 v(t)dt$$

$$m(t_1).v(t_1) = m(t_0).v(t_0) + {_0}\!\int^1 F(t)dt$$

where $m(t)$ is the inertial mass of the object at t and $F(t)$ is the force acting on it at that time. These, note, are the two key laws in (relativistic) kinematics involving velocity. The first relates velocity to position; the second to the forces acting. The crucial point is that, on Tooley's view, these equations should be interpreted as stating relations between (instantaneous) physical quantities.

PRIEST'S ACCOUNT

Priest's account draws on Hegel. It does not resurrect Hegel's account of the categories; nor does it rehabilitate the notion of the infinitesimal. What it does do is take seriously the possibility that, at an instant, the position of a moving object may be spread out over a short (but non-infinitesimal) region. Because the object is in motion it may be impossible to localize it to any one position. This is called the spread hypothesis.

More specifically, let $x(t)$ be the locus of motion of an object, as it occurs in the laws of motion cited in the previous section. One can write r_t for the value of this function at t. For Russell, the state of the object at time t is characterized by the set of statements $S_t = \{$'The object is at r_t'$\} \cup \{$'The object is not at r'; where $r \neq r_t\}$. Given the spread hypothesis, one must suppose that there is an interval of times containing t, θ_t, such that the object is equally at $x(t')$ for all $t' \epsilon \theta_t$. The state of the object at t is therefore characterized by the set of all those statements in S_t' for $t' \epsilon \theta_t$. (What, exactly, θ_t is, is a matter to be determined by other consideration; possibly by nature itself. But it is not unnatural to suppose that the width of θ_t is proportional to $dx(t)/dt$ if this is defined.)

If $x(t')$ is constant for $t' \epsilon \theta_t$ (and, in particular, if θ_t contains just t), the state-description is identical to the Russellean state-description; in particular, it is consistent. But if $x(t')$ takes different values, r_1 and r_2, for $t' \epsilon \theta_t$, then it will be inconsistent: it will contain the statements that the object both is and is not at r_1 (and r_2).

To be in motion at an instant, then, according to this account, is to have an inconsistent state description at that instant. Objects in motion are at one place at one time, and another at another. But this is not sufficient. This would be equally true of an object at rest at each of these places. To be in motion at a time, an object must both be and not be at a place at that time.

THE ARROW AGAIN

If one is to have a theory according to which motion is an intrinsic property of an object, then the accounts of Tooley and Priest may not be the only ones; but they are the only two presently on offer. Therefore, it is natural to compare their relative merits.

One feature of Tooley's account, unlike Priest's, is that it is consistent. Priest's account (and Hegel's) presupposes that one can make sense of the possibility that the truth about a situation can be contradictory (dialetheism). It requires the use of a logic that is such that contradictions do not imply everything. One may take this to be a strong mark in Tooley's favor. Other objections against Priest can be found by consulting Tooley (1988). It appears that there are perfectly natural replies to these objections, but this is not the place to go into the matter.

On the other side, it is clear that Priest's account solves the Arrow paradox essentially as does Hegel's. The object, by occupying more than one point at an instant, does make progress during each instant, and so in the whole comprising them. Tooley's account would not appear to solve the paradox. It still leaves one with the fact that the object makes no progress during an instant of its journey. Russell, whether rightly or wrongly, took the problem to be solved by rejecting instantaneous states of motion. Even this step is not open to Tooley.

Doubtless, there is more to be said on these matters. Regardless, one thing is clear: Even after the development of the calculus, the theory of the limit, the understanding that it is possible to postulate unobservables in science, and even of paraconsistency, Zeno's paradox of the Arrow still haunts us.

See also Hegel, Georg Wilhelm Friedrich; Motion, A Historical Survey; Russell, Bertrand Arthur William; Zeno of Elea.

Bibliography

Boyer, Charles B. *The History of the Calculus and Its Conceptual Development*. New York: Dover, 1959.

Cajori, Florian. *A History of Mathematics*. 5th ed. New York: Chelsea, 1991.

Hegel, Georg W. F. *Hegel's Philosophy of Nature: Being Part Two of the Encyclopaedia of the Philosophical Sciences*. Translated by A. V. Miller. Oxford, U.K.: Clarendon Press, 1970. Originally published as *Encyclopädie der Philosophischen Wissenschaften im Grundrisse* (Heidelberg, Germany: Druk und Verlag von August Owald, 1827).

Hegel, Georg W. F. *Hegel's Science of Logic*. Translated by A. V. Miller. London: Allen and Unwin, 1969. Originally published as *Wissenschaft der Logik* (Nuremberg: Johann Leonhard Schrag, 1812–1816).

Mortensen, Chris. "Change." In *Stanford Encyclopedia of Philosophy*, edited by Edward N. Zalta. Stanford, CA: Metaphysics Research Lab, Center for the Study of Language and Information, Stanford University, 2002. Available at http://plato.stanford.edu/entries/change/.

Priest, Graham. *In Contradiction: A Study of the Transconsistent*. Dordrecht, Netherlands: Nijhoff, 1987.

Priest, Graham. "Inconsistencies in Motion." *American Philosophical Quarterly* 22 (1985): 339–346.

Russell, Bertrand. *The Principles of Mathematics*. New York: Norton, 1938.

Salmon, Wesley C., ed. *Zeno's Paradoxes*. Indianapolis, IN: Bobbs-Merrill, 1970.

Tooley, Michael. "In Defence of the Existence of States of Motion." *Philosophical Topics* 16 (1988): 225–250.

Graham Priest (2005)

MOTION, A HISTORICAL SURVEY

"Motion," or "movement," in its modern meaning, is change—or more precisely, change of the relative positions of bodies. The concept of motion thus involves the ideas of space and time. Kinematics, in the nineteenth century usually called "kinetics" or "phoronomics," is the science that deals exclusively with the geometrical and chronometrical aspects of motion, in contrast to dynamics, which considers force and mass in relation to motion. In medieval terminology, following Aristotelian tradition, "motion" (*motus* or *kinesis*) had a much wider significance, denoting any continuous change in quality, quantity, or place.

EARLY CONCEPTS OF MOTION

Ever since the beginning of philosophical speculation and scientific analysis, the concept of motion has played a predominant role in Western thought. Anaximander of Miletus (sixth century BCE) saw in motion an eternal agent of the cosmos. For Heraclitus motion was a cosmological principle underlying all physical reality (*panta rhei*, "everything is in perpetual flow"). Yet in spite of their insistence on the universality of motion, neither Anaximander nor Heraclitus seems to have inquired into the nature of motion itself. The Eleatics were probably the first to do so, when they discovered the contradiction inherent in the idea of motion and consequently denied the reality of motion, relegating its appearance to the realm of illusions and deceptions. A body, they argued, can move neither where it is nor where it is not; hence, reality is motionless and unchanging. Zeno's famous antinomies (Aristotle, *Physics* 239), such as the "Arrow" and "Achilles," seem to have been aimed, at least in part, at a refutation of the possibility of motion. On the other hand, for the atomists, such as Democritus and Leucippus, motion was a fundamental property of the atoms. All changes in nature were reduced to the movements of atoms in the void, and with the eternity and uncreatedness of the atoms their motion was eternal and uncreated; this motion itself, in the atomists' view, was not further analyzable. It remained a primary concept until Epicurus searched for a causal explanation. This (according to Lucretius) he thought to have found in weight, the cause of the downward movements of atoms, and in their little "swerves," by which he explained the otherwise incomprehensible collisions and redistributions of atoms without which physical processes could not be accounted for.

ARISTOTLE. In Aristotle's natural philosophy the concept of motion played a decisive role, since for him nature was the principle of movement or change: "We must understand what motion is; for, if we do not know this, neither do we understand what nature is" (*Physics* 200b12), a statement recurrent in Peripatetic philosophy under the motto *Ignato motu, ignatur natura* ("To be ignorant of motion is to be ignorant of nature"). For Aristotle, in contrast to his predecessors, motion raised a profound problem—not merely from the logical point of view. Expressing the deeply rooted metaphysical conviction of Western thought that motion is neither logically nor ontologically self-sufficient but requires an explanation, Aristotle contended that motion is neither in the causal, or genetic, nor in the ontological sense a primary concept. Causally, every motion originates in another motion; only animate organisms possess an inherent power to move. Hence his famous dictum *Omne quod movetur ab aliquo movetur* ("All things that move are moved by something else"). To avoid infinite regression and to find a satisfactory explanation of the existence of motion, Aristotle reduced the ultimate origin of all movements to an eternal mover who is himself unmoved. (*Physics* 258b). Ontologically, Aristotle derived motion from the basic notions of his metaphysics of substance and form by defining it as "the progress of the realizing of a potentiality *qua* potentiality" (*Physics* 201a10). Motion as the actualization of that which exists in potentiality may produce a substantial form (*generatio*), may change qualities (*alteratio*) and quantities (*augmentatio* or *diminutio*), or, finally, may be a change of place (*motus localis*). Although Aristotle did not reduce qualitative differences to quantitative relations of size and position, as did the atomists, his physics is essentially a physics of qualities. He did regard local motion as of a more fundamental character than the other kinds of motion (*Physics* 208a31); it is "the primary and most general case of passage and prior to all other categories of change" (*Physics* 260b22). Yet in spite of this preferential status, local motion for Aristotle is only a necessary concomitant of change, not, as the mechanistic physicists of the post-Newtonian era maintained, the essential and exclusive constituent of change.

In kinematics Aristotle distinguished between circular and rectilinear motion (*De Caelo* 268b17), the former, the more perfect, being the motion of the celestial bodies (*De Generatione et Corruptione* 338a18). Dynamically, motion is either natural or violate. Natural motion is circular for celestial and rectilinear for terrestrial objects; violate motion is the removal of a body from its natural place (*locus naturalis*) through the action of an external force.

ANCIENT AND MEDIEVAL CONCEPTS. Aristotle's kinematics, like his physics in general, was a qualitative science, incapable of providing a precise definition of such notions as velocity and acceleration. In fact, Greek mathematics, with its insistence on the illegitimacy of proportions or ratios between heterogeneous quantities, did not provide even the formal means of defining velocity as the ratio between distance and time; only topological, not metrical, determinations of motion could be formulated. Thus, Aristotle said that a body is quicker than another if it traverses equal spaces in less time or greater spaces in equal time (*Physics* 215a26). As related by Simplicius, Strato of Lampsacus, in a lost treatise "On Motion" (*De Motu*), was apparently the first to analyze in great detail these kinematic notions, in particular the concept of acceleration, although without trespassing the boundaries imposed by the Aristotelian conceptual scheme. The kinematics of uniform motion could be fully developed and rigorously formulated at least *in abstracto*, as exemplified by the treatise "The Motion of the Sphere" (300 BCE), written by the astronomer Autolycus of Pitane. Nevertheless, as far as is known, the earliest kinematicist to associate concrete numerical designations with velocities was Gerard of Brussels, in the thirteenth century (*Liber de Motu*).

The formulations of the basic concepts in the science of motion did not, however, evolve out of practical necessities, the study of simple machines, or other scientific or technical considerations; they were, rather, the outcome of a curious development that originated in connection with a purely philosophical, ontological, and even theological problem. The point of departure was the much discussed problem of the increase and decrease of qualities (*intensio et remissio formarum*), the question of how such qualities as warmness or blackness could vary in their intensities. Aristotle explicitly admitted (*Categories* 10b26) such alterations, but he also described such qualities as numbers (*Metaphysics* 1044a9) as immutable and unchangeable. One of the solutions, as listed by Simplicius, is that of Archytas, who suggested that every quality possesses a certain range of indeterminacy, or margin of variability (*platos*).

In Peter Lombard's "Books on the Sentences" (*Libri Quatuor Sententiarum*, c. 1150 CE) the same problem reappears in the realm of theology when it is asked, with reference to Scripture, how an intensification or diminution of the Holy Spirit or of the *caritas* is possible in man. Until well into the thirteenth century the Christian concept of *caritas* was par excellence the subject of discussions on the intension and remission of qualities and served as the standard example for intricate analyses of the notions of change and motion. One solution, advanced by Henry of Ghent in one of his *Quodlibeta*, referred in this connection explicitly to Archytas's previously mentioned conception of margin of variability, now termed the "latitude" (*latitudo*) of quality or change, a notion that was destined to play an important role in the foundation of classical kinematics.

GROWTH OF THE SCIENCE OF KINEMATICS

In order to understand the subsequent development of the concept of motion another problem that engaged the thirteenth century to a great extent must be mentioned, the question of what category change, or motion, belongs to. Aristotle was usually interpreted as having advocated an identification of *motus* with *terminus motus*—that is, viewing motion as an evolving process in the same category as the terminal, or the perfection, of this process. According to this view motion is a *forma fluens,* to use the terminology of Albert the Great, whereas the opposing view, which relates motion and its terminus to different categories, is the *fluxus formae* conception of motion. In the special case of local motion the *forma fluens* interpretation regards the process of motion as merely the continuous and gradual acquisition of the final *terminus motus,* just as the qualitative change of *nigrescere* (to become black) is merely the gradual acquisition of the *nigredo* (blackness). The concept of motion obtained its final and most radical formulation along these lines in the nominalistic statement of William of Ockham that motion is merely a name for the set of successive positions occupied by the mobile.

The nominalistic interpretation, often epitomized as *motus est mobile quod movetur,* met with considerable opposition, curiously enough among the Parisian terministic philosophers, such as Jean Buridan. One of the arguments for its rejection was undoubtedly its logical inapplicability to the motion of the outermost sphere, which, not further surrounded by any object, possessed neither place nor space, according to the Aristotelian-scholastic theory of space; thus its motion clearly could not be interpreted as a set of successive positions. No wonder, then, that the *fluxus formae* interpretation of motion, which distinguished between the process, on the one hand, and the terminus or position (*locus*), on the other, and regarded motion as a specific quality inherent in the mobile, became predominant. Buridan, for example, defined motion, or *moveri*, as an inherent property in the mobile—*intrinsice aliter et aliter se habere*—and Blasius of Parma characterized local motion as a quality that is capable of gradual intensification or remission and is inherent in the moving object (*motus localis est qualitas gradualis intensibilis et remissibilis, mobili inhaerens subjective*).

Meanwhile the notorious *calculatores* of Merton College at Oxford, including Thomas Bradwardine, Richard Swineshead, and William Heytesbury, established their famous formalism of subjecting qualities of all kinds, but primarily the quality of *caritas,* to mathematical analysis and quantification. It was there, at Merton College, that the different trends converged. For motion, itself a quality according to the *fluxus formae* conception, soon became the favorite subject of mathematical description and took the place of *caritas* in these discussions. Employing the notion of latitude, the calculators analyzed the various possibilities of changes of motion and illustrated their theorems by graphical representations. Thus, through the conflux of various conceptual trends the foundations of modern kinematics were laid at Oxford: The concept of velocity was clarified by the introduction of the notion of instantaneous velocity, uniformly accelerated motion was unambiguously defined, the distance traversed by a body in uniformly accelerated motion was calculated, and, finally, a clear distinction between kinematics and dynamics was drawn. The results thus obtained seem, however, never to have been applied to any motions encountered in nature; they were, rather, a theory for the classification of possible motions.

The new knowledge soon spread to France, Germany, and Italy. Only Galileo Galilei, and possibly Dominic de Soto, applied these results to the study of specific natural phenomena, such as free fall. Since kinematic investigations formed the point of departure for the subsequent development of mechanics and physics in general, the analysis and clarification of the concept of motion may rightfully be regarded as of primary importance for the rise of modern science as a whole. With the establishment of a scientific kinematics the notion of motion also became purified from certain connotations

that it carried from ancient times. Thus, according to the Aristotelian theory of motion the movement of any object presupposes the existence of an immobile body. Themistius, Averroes, and other commentators interpreted this statement as a proof of the immobility of Earth. In fact, for Averroes the immobility of the center was a necessary prerequisite not only for the motion of the spheres but also for the very spatiality of the outermost sphere (*caelum est in loco per centrum*). Not only was Earth unique as being the abode of man; its distinction was due also to the fact that it served as the basis for the localizability of the celestial spheres.

However, as soon as the *fluxus formae* conception characterized motion as a property inherent solely in the mobile, the Aristotelian presupposition of an immobile correlate lost its logical legitimacy. Celestial motions no longer needed to be conceived of as dependent on the immobility of Earth, and a severe obstacle to the Copernican doctrine could easily be removed.

RELATIVITY OF MOTION

It is a curious fact that the modern conception of motion, though historically and conceptually connected most intimately with the Copernican revolution, led to a partial reinstatement of the Aristotelian presupposition. Not the immobility but the existence of a correlate is the indispensable requirement for any physical significance of the concept of motion. For the relativization of the notion demands a body of reference. The question whether absolute motion, motion without reference to a physical object extraneous to the mobile, is a scientifically or philosophically meaningful conception or whether motion is only relative—that is, whether the statement "*A* moves" makes sense only if it means "*A* moves relative to *B*"—is the problem of the relativity of motion and has a long history of its own.

Aristotle's distinction between ordinary motion and motion *per accidens* may be regarded as the first implicit differentiation between absolute and relative rest, an idea further developed by Sextus Empiricus (*Adversus Mathematicos* 2, 55). The dynamical equivalence, under certain conditions, between relative rest and absolute rest was essential to the acceptance of the Copernican theory and, in fact, was explicitly stated by Nicolas Copernicus himself: *Inter motu ad eadem, non percipitur motus* (*De Revolutionibus Orbium Coelestium*, Nuremberg, 1583, Bk. 1, Ch. 3). It was further elaborated by Galileo (*Dialogo sopra i due massimi sistemi del monde,* second day) into what is now called the Galilean principle of relativity. René Descartes, fully aware of the implications of the relativity of motion for the Copernican controversy, adopted a compromise position by distinguishing between "the common and vulgar conception of motion" as the passing of a body from one place to another and the "true or scientific conception" of motion as the transfer of matter from the vicinity of those bodies with which it was in immediate contact into the vicinity of other bodies (*Principia Philosophiae,* Part 2, Section 24). He thereby associated the relativity of true, or scientific, motion with the Aristotelian contiguity as the determinant of localization. Descartes is often credited with having been the first to enunciate explicitly the relativity of motion, and Gottfried Wilhelm Leibniz is cited as one of its most enthusiastic proponents.

For Isaac Newton and his doctrine of absolute space the notion of absolute motion was, of course, of physical significance, being "the translation of a body from one absolute place into another" (*Principles*). He defined relative motion, corresponding to the concept of relative space, as "the translation from one relative place into another." In spite of his professed adherence to Galileo's principle of relativity, Newton maintained the possibility of distinguishing absolute from relative motion by their "properties, causes and effects." His belief in the reality of absolute motion was based on his thesis that real forces create real motion. The reality of absolute motion, he argued, is manifested by the effects that such motions produce, for example, the appearance of centrifugal forces or effects. For Newton forces are metaphysical entities, and the motions they produce are therefore more than merely geometricotemporal or kinematic phenomena. Thus, rotation is an absolute motion, as he thought to have proved by an analysis of his famous pail experiment.

Apart from Christian Huygens, who from 1688 maintained the relativity of circular motion on physical grounds, and Leibniz, who rejected the Newtonian conception on philosophical grounds, it was primarily George Berkeley who treated the epistemological aspects of the problem (*Treatise concerning the Principles of Human Knowledge; De Motu*). He concluded:

> It does not appear to me, that there can be any motion other than *relative*: so that to conceive motion, there must be at least conceived two bodies, whereof the distance or position in regard to each other is varied. Hence if there was one only body in being, it could not possibly be moved. This seems evident, in that the idea I have of motion doth necessarily include relation.

However, in the eighteenth and early nineteenth centuries, primarily as a result of Leonhard Euler's justification of absolute motion on the basis of the principle of inertia (*Mechanica; Theoria Motus,* Secs. 84, 99) and Immanuel Kant's argumentations in his "Metaphysical Foundations of Natural Science" (*Metaphysische Anfangsgründe der Naturwissenschaft,* 1786), absolute motion was regarded by the majority of philosophers as a meaningful concept, not only in physics but also in philosophy. Toward the middle of the nineteenth century the situation changed. At first it was admitted that rotational motion is absolute but translational motion is relative (James Clerk Maxwell, P. G. Tait, H. Streinitz, L. Lange), and later all motion was regarded as relative. One of the most ardent proponents of the universal relativity of motion was Ernst Mach (*Die Mechanik in ihrer Entwicklung,* Leipzig, 1883); he refuted Newton's argument concerning the rise of centrifugal forces as evidence of the absolute nature of motion and explained it as an induction effect produced by the motion relative to the fixed stars. Whether Mach's conjecture can be corroborated rigorously is still a problem that engages modern research, especially in the theory of general relativity.

The question of the relativity of motion, initiated, as we have seen, by Descartes, gained increased importance, owing to the fact that the concept of motion became the basic element of physical explanation. In fact, it was Descartes's insistence on the exclusive admissibility of local motion that was decisive in this development. As is suggested in the *Principles of Philosophy* (Pt. 2, Sec. 23) and expounded in a letter to Marin Mersenne (1643), Descartes refused to attribute any reality to the so-called qualities of substances. The conception of such qualities, he contended, complicates and confuses rather than simplifies the explanation of physical phenomena in natural philosophy. In concluding such deliberations, Descartes declared local motion to be the only admissible element for physical explication. Descartes's rejection of the Aristotelian physics of qualities had a great appeal to philosophers (see, for example, Thomas Hobbes, *Elementorum Philosophiae Sectio Prima,* 1655; *De Corpore,* Sec. 8, Ch. 9) and was instrumental in the development of the mechanistic orientation of modern classical physics, which tried to reduce all natural phenomena to motions of masses in space.

Characteristic of this conception of classical physics is a statement by Maxwell: "When a physical phenomenon can be completely described as a change in the configuration and motion of a material system, the dynamical explanation of that phenomenon is said to be complete" (*Scientific Papers*, Cambridge, U.K., 1890, Vol. 2, p. 418). The predominant role of the concept of motion in physical science poses a problem of great importance to philosophy. Why is it that all processes, laws, and formulas of physics—and modern physics is no exception—ultimately refer to motion, and why is it that even problems in statics, the science of equilibrium and absence of motion, are solved in terms of fictitious motions and virtual velocities? Is the answer to be found only in the historical circumstances, namely that kinematic investigations were the earliest successful approach to the establishment of a physical theory and that consequently forces were regarded as manifesting themselves only through motions? The answer probably lies in a vestige of ancient Eleatic philosophy that seems still to motivate our mode of thinking: A physical explanation of a natural phenomenon becomes more satisfactory the nearer it approaches the statement that nothing has happened. Motion, as Wilhelm Wundt pointed out, is the only conceivable process in which an object, so to speak, both changes and remains the same: It changes by assuming a different position relative to other objects; it remains the same by preserving its complete identity.

See also Albert the Great; Anaximander; Aristotle; Averroes; Berkeley, George; Bradwardine, Thomas; Buridan, John; Change; Copernicus, Nicolas; Descartes, René; Epicurus; Galileo Galilei; Henry of Ghent; Heraclitus of Ephesus; Heytesbury, William; Hobbes, Thomas; Kant, Immanuel; Leibniz, Gottfried Wilhelm; Leucippus and Democritus; Lucretius; Mach, Ernst; Maxwell, James Clerk; Mersenne, Marin; Motion; Newton, Isaac; Peripatetics; Peter Lombard; Philosophy of Physics; Relativity Theory; Sextus Empiricus; Soto, Dominic de; Space; Swineshead, Richard; Themistius; Time; Wundt, Wilhelm; Zeno of Elea.

Bibliography

PRIMARY SOURCES

Aristotle. *Works.* Edited by J. A. Smith and W. D. Ross. Oxford, 1908–1952. See especially the *Physics.*

Berkeley, George. *The Works of George Berkeley, Bishop of Cloyne,* Edited by A. A. Luce and T. E. Jessop, 9 vols. London, 1948–1957. See especially the *Treatise … of Human Knowledge* (1710), *De Motu* (1721), and *Siris* (1744).

Copernicus, Nicolas. *De Revolutionibus.* In *Opera Complete.* Warsaw: Officina Publica Libris Scientificis Edendis, 1873. Translated by C. G. Wallis in *Great Books of the Western World,* Vol. XVI. Chicago, 1952.

Descartes, René. *Philosophical Works.* Translated by E. S. Haldane and G. T. R. Ross, 2 vols. Cambridge, U.K.: Cambridge University Press, 1911–1912; 2nd ed., 1934. See especially the *Principia Philosophiae.*

Euler, Leonhard. *Opera Omnia,* 3 series. Leipzig: Teubner, 1911–1942; Lausanne, 1942–. See especially *Opera Mechanica et Astronomica.*

Galileo Galilei. *Dialogue concerning the Two Chief World Systems.* Translated by S. Drake. Berkeley: University of California Press, 1953.

Kant, Immanuel. *Sämtliche Werke.* Edited by the Preussiche Akademie der Wissenschaften, 22 vols. Berlin, 1902–1955.

Mach, Ernst. *Science of Mechanics.* Translated by T. C. McCormack. Chicago: Open Court, 1902.

Newton, Isaac. *Sir Isaac Newton's Mathematical Principles of Natural Philosophy and His System of the World.* Edited by Florian Cajori. Berkeley, CA, 1947.

Sextus Empiricus. *Philosophical Works,* 4 vols. Loeb Classical Library. Cambridge, MA, 1939–1957. See nos. 273, 291, 311, 382.

SECONDARY SOURCES

Lange, L. *Die geschichtliche Entwicklung des Bewegungsbegriffs.* Leipzig, 1886.

Wundt, Wilhelm. *Die physikalischen Axiome und ihre Beziehung zum Causalprincip.* Erlangen: F. Enke, 1886.

M. Jammer (1967)

MO TZU

See *Mozi*

MOUNIER, EMMANUEL
(1905–1950)

Emmanuel Mounier, the French personalist philosopher, was born in Grenoble. He studied philosophy from 1924 to 1927 in Grenoble and in Paris, where he was successful in the *agrégation* examination of 1928. After teaching philosophy in schools during 1931 and 1932, he collaborated with others in bringing out a work on the thought of Charles Péguy, whom Mounier as a Roman Catholic greatly admired. This collaboration was extended to plans for a review to carry on Péguy's work, and *Esprit* was launched in October 1932. Mounier continued to edit the review in the face of difficulties, not least of which was the feeling of some Catholics that his position was virtually Marxist. He taught at the French *lycée* in Brussels from 1933 to 1939. He was called up for military service on the outbreak of war and was demobilized shortly after the fall of France in 1940. Mounier contrived to continue the production of *Esprit* until August 1941, when the Vichy government banned it.

Suspected of subversive connections, he spent some months in prison in 1942, but was eventually acquitted and settled with his family, incognito, near Montélimar.

Mounier returned to Paris in 1945, and until his death he continued to produce books and a resuscitated *Esprit*, inspired by the times and his personalist response to them.

Mounier is the chief representative of the movement known as personalism. It is closely related, in the ideas it propounds, to existentialism. Personalism, however, is distinctively Christian and sees the personal "vocation" as seeking communication between unique persons, whereas existentialism is often divorced from religious belief, rejects the possibility of shared values, and is often strongly pessimistic concerning human relationships.

Mounier held that the person is entirely distinct from the political individual, who is "an abstract, legal, self-seeking entity, asserting his rights and presenting a mere caricature of the person." The person is "a spiritual being … subsisting by his adherence to a hierarchy of values freely adopted, assimilated, and lived through, thanks to a responsible commitment and a constant process of conversion."

The "unique vocation" of the person has little more specifiable content than Jean-Paul Sartre's "original project." Mounier, however, insisted on the distinctive character of legitimate commitment, which is both personalist and *communautaire*, or directed toward a fellowship of other persons. Man's chief task, Mounier wrote in *Qu'est-ce que le personnalisme?*, is not to master nature but increasingly to bring about communication leading to universal understanding.

Personalism is a natural product of the kind of French philosophy that has, since Maine de Biran, stressed the notion of a self that in some measure owes its being to an external reality which it apprehends or upon which it acts. Such thinking led Mounier to say that "as the philosopher who first shuts himself up within thought will never find a door leading to being, so he who first shuts himself up in the self will never find a path to others." Mounier criticized René Descartes, despite his modernity, for first adumbrating the solipsism that has since hung over modern man. In the economic field, bourgeois values "exalt the isolated individual and strengthen that economic and spiritual individualism" that still bedevils us. Mounier pointed the way from spiritually sterile self-absorption to the apprehension of reality in the form of not-self, particularly in the form of the other person with whom we communicate. The primitive experience of the person is the experience of the second person. The thou, including the we, precedes the I, or at least accompanies it. Mounier's objection to egoism was not only to economic individualism but also to its subtler

forms, such as a fastidious withdrawal from modern vulgarity into the purity of the self. All true living is a transaction with the reality of the world and others in a process of mutual enrichment. There is no true inwardness that is not nourished by its interaction with an outer reality. "We must find our way out of our inwardness in order to sustain that inwardness."

See also Descartes, René; Egoism and Altruism; Existentialism; Maine de Biran; Marxist Philosophy; Personalism; Sartre, Jean-Paul.

Bibliography

WORKS BY MOUNIER

La pensée de Charles Péguy. Paris: Plon, 1931.

Révolution personnaliste et communautaire. Paris, 1935.

De la propriété capitaliste à la propriété humaine. Paris: Desclée de Brouwer, 1936.

Manifeste au service du personnalisme. Paris, 1936.

L'affrontement chrétien. Neuchâtel, 1944.

Introduction aux existentialismes. Paris, 1946.

Liberté sous condition. Paris, 1946.

Traité du caractère. Paris: Éditions du seuil, 1946.

Qu'est-ce que le personnalisme? Paris, 1947.

L'eveil de l'Afrique noire. Paris, 1948.

Le personnalisme. Paris, 1949.

Carnets de route. 3 vols. Paris, 1950–1953.

Oeuvres. 4 vols. Paris: Editions du Seuil, 1961–63.

TRANSLATIONS

A Personalist Manifesto. London, New York: Longmans, Green, 1938.

Be Not Afraid: Studies in Personalist Sociology. London: Rockliff, 1951.

Personalism. Notre Dame: University of Notre Dame Press, 1952.

The Spoil of the Violent. West Nyack, NY: Cross Currents, 1955.

The Character of Man. London: Rockliff, 1956.

WORKS ON MOUNIER

Amato, Joseph Anthony. *Mounier and Maritain: A French Catholic Understanding of the Modern World*. Tuscaloosa: University of Alabama Press, 1975.

Cantin, Eileen. *Mounier: A Personalist View of History*. New York: Paulist Press, 1973.

Copleston, Frederick. *Contemporary Philosophy*, 109–115. London: Burns and Oates, 1956.

Guissard, Lucien. *Mounier*. Paris, 1962.

Hellman, J. *Emmanuel Mounier and the New Catholic Left, 1930–1950*. Toronto: University of Toronto Press, 1981.

Lurol, G. *Mounier*. Paris: Édition universitaires, 1990.

Moix, Candide. *La pensée d'Emmanuel Mounier*. Paris: Éditions du Seuil, 1960.

Colin Smith (1967)
Bibliography updated by Thomas Nenon (2005)

MOZI

(c. 470–c. 391 BCE)

Mozi, also called Mo Di, was the founder of one of the classical systems of Chinese philosophy, Mohism, as well as of a religious community. After serving for a brief period as a civil servant, Mozi spent a number of years as a traveling counselor to feudal lords and princes, and, having never been given the opportunity to put his teachings into practice or the world in order, he had eventually to be contented with conducting a school and preparing his disciples for public office. He left a work consisting of seventy-one chapters, known as *The Mozi*. It is said that Mozi was at first a follower of Confucianism but later renounced it to found a system of thought of his own. He was critical of Confucianism for its emphasis on the codes of rituals and social elegance, which were to him burdensome and wasteful.

The rigoristic temperament of Mozi made him also a man who practiced what he preached. A chief concern for Mozi, for instance, was to reduce the recurrent military conflicts among the feudal states. There are records of his taking distant journeys to prevent the outbreak of impending wars. On one of his journeys, according to the record, he had to walk ten days and ten nights and tear off pieces of cloth from his garments to wrap up his sore feet.

A distinctive characteristic of Mozi's thought was his stress on methodology. He declared: "Some standard of judgment must be established. To make a proposition without regard for standard is similar to determining the directions of sunrise and sunset on a revolving potter's wheel." He attached great importance to the threefold test and the fourfold standard. The threefold test refers to the basis, the verifiability, and the applicability of a proposition. Explained in present-day language, this test is employed to examine a proposition for its compatibility with the best of the established conceptions, its consistency with experience, and its conduciveness to desirable ends when put into operation. The benefits resulting from the application of a proposition, the last part of the threefold test, are conceived in terms of the fourfold standard, namely, enrichment of the poor, increase of the population, removal of danger, and regulation of disorder. Mozi evidently would employ these tests and standards on all propositions without exception, and contemporary scholars have sometimes called him a pragmatist, and sometimes a utilitarian. There is a section of six chapters in *The Mozi* that has come to be spoken of as the section on Mohist logic. Most of the material contained therein has little utilitarian application, but it must have been written in Mozi's tradition, if not by his hand. This logical development is an outgrowth of Mozi's insistence on "standard of judgment" but is generally regarded as constituting a neo-Mohist movement.

A common problem that confronted all the thinkers of the classical age was how to bring order out of chaos. The system of feudalistic hierarchy instituted at the beginning of the Zhou dynasty had crumbled, the Period of Warring States (403–222 BCE) was setting in, and the people were living in suffering and bewilderment. By Mozi's diagnosis, the chaotic condition was brought about by selfishness and partiality. And the cure? "Partiality should be replaced by universality." Universal love is the keystone of Mozi's teaching. Mozi was dissatisfied with Confucianism for its gradation in benevolence, and he exhorted everyone to regard the welfare of others as he regarded his own. He was convinced that the practice of universal love would bring peace to the world and happiness to man, and he took pains to demonstrate that the principle of universal love was grounded simultaneously in its practicability on earth and its divine sanction from Heaven. Universal love for Mozi was at once the way of man and the way of God.

In contrast to most Chinese philosophers, Mozi spoke of Heaven with feeling and conviction; his conception of it was similar to the Western conception of God. The will of Heaven was to be obeyed by man and was to be the standard of human thought and action. Heaven loved all men, and it was the will of Heaven that men should love one another. Soon after Mozi's death the teacher's system became embodied in an organized church with a succession of elder masters and a considerable following.

As a religious congregation Mohism did not last long, but as a system of thought and teaching Mohism ranked with Confucianism for some two centuries as one of "the eminent schools of the day." Mohism was pushed into the background if not into complete oblivion by the ascendancy of Confucianism for the next two thousand years and was rediscovered only in the mid-twentieth century.

See also Chinese Philosophy; Heaven and Hell, Doctrines of; Logic, History of; Peace, War, and Philosophy; Scientific Method.

Bibliography

For the secondary literature on Mozi, see the bibliography in *Journal of Chinese Philosophy* 28 no. 1 & 2 (2001).

Fraser, Chris. "Mohism", *The Stanford Encyclopedia of Philosophy* (Winter 2002 Edition), Edward N. Zalta (ed.), URL: http://plato.stanford.edu/archives/win2002/entries/mohism/.

Lowe, Scott. *Mo Tzu's Religious Blueprint for a Chinese Utopia.* Lewiston, NY: Edwin Mellen, 1992.

Mei, Yi-pao, tr. *The Ethical and Political Works of Motse.* London: Probsthain, 1929; Westport, CT: Hyperion Press, 1973. Complete translation.

Mei, Yi-pao. *Mo-tse, the Neglected Rival of Confucius.* London: Probsthain, 1934; Westport, CT: Hyperion Press, 1973.

Tseu, Augustine. *The Moral Philosophy of Mozi.* Taibei: China Printing Limited, 1965.

Watson, Burton, tr. *Mo Tzu: Basic Writings.* New York: Columbia University Press, 1963. Selected translation.

Y. P. Mei (1967)
Bibliography updated by Huichieh Loy (2005)

MUKAMMAṢ, DAVID BEN MERWAN AL-

See *Muqammiṣ, David ben Merwan al-*

MULLĀ ṢADRĀ
(1571/1572–1640)

Mullā Ṣadrā is the name usually given to Muḥammad ibn Ibrāhīm Ṣadr al-Dīn Shīrāzī, the most outstanding of the later Muslim philosophers. (*Mulla* means teacher.) He is also known by the honorific title *Sadr al-muta'allihin,* "the foremost among the theosophers." Born in Shiraz into an aristocratic family, he received his early education in that city and his advanced training in Ispahan, the Safavid capital, where he studied with Mīr Dāmād and Bahā' al-Dīn 'Amilī. After completing his formal education he retired to a village near Qum, where he spent ten years in asceticism and self-purification. Then, upon the demand of the Persian king, he returned to Shiraz as a professor in the school of Allāhwirdī Khān, where he taught and wrote for the rest of his life. He died in Basra on the return journey from his seventh pilgrimage to Mecca.

Mullā Ṣadrā wrote over fifty books, most of them after leaving his spiritual retreat. All his books are in Arabic except his "spiritual defense," the *Sih aṣl* (Three principles) and a few poems and letters, which are in Persian. His works can be classified into those dealing primarily with religion, such as his commentaries on the Qur'an and the *Uṣūl al-Kāfī* (Principles of Kāfī) of Kulainī, and those which deal mostly with philosophy and theosophy.

In the latter category the most important is *Al-Ḥikmat al-muta'āliyah fi'l-asfār al-arba'ah* (The exalted wisdom concerning the four journeys of the spirit), or simply *Asfār* (The journeys), a work of monumental proportions and the most advanced work on Islamic philosophy. Mullā Ṣadrā also wrote a large number of shorter treatises, such as *Al-Mashā ir* (The book of metaphysical penetrations), *Al-Shawāhid al-rubūbīyah* (Divine witnesses), and *Al-Ḥikmat al-'arshīyah* (The book of theophany inspired by the throne), which treat specific metaphysical and philosophical questions.

In Mullā Ṣadrā's work Muslim Peripatetic philosophy, especially that of Avicenna, the illuminationist theosophy of Shihāb al-Dīn Yahyā Suhrawardī, the gnostic doctrines of Muhyī al-Dīn ibn al-'Arabī and certain themes of Muslim theology (*Kalām*) became unified in the background of Shī'ism and the teachings of the Shī'ite imams. The philosophy of Mullā Ṣadrā, however, is synthetic rather than eclectic, because out of these various threads he created a new intellectual perspective in which reason, revelation, and mystic vision are harmonized into a total, unified view of things.

Mullā Ṣadrā brought to fruition the attempt of Muslim thinkers from the beginning of the Middle Ages to harmonize religion and philosophy. In his thought the tenets of revelation, the dicta of reason, and the verities of gnosis discovered through illumination are all considered possible sources of knowledge and are blended together. His writings bridge discursive and intuitive knowledge by making the discoveries of reason the necessary background of spiritual knowledge, which is above reason without being irrational. Mullā Ṣadrā also revised many of the tenets of Peripatetic and illuminationist philosophy and established philosophy upon a set of principles, many of which were derived from Sufism, that had not been demonstrated as such and had not existed in philosophy before.

These principles include the unity, gradation, and principality of being, by which is meant that it is being rather than the quiddity or essence of things that is ultimately real. Moreover, being is inwardly unified as a single reality that possesses states and gradations. It is upon this principle that Mullā Ṣadrā built his "metaphysics of being." Another principle of his philosophy is the unity of the intellect, or intelligence, and the intelligible, of the knower and the known. At the moment of intellection the intellect becomes identified with the intelligible form of the object perceived. Thus, knowledge is intimately connected with being and affects the ontological state of the knower.

Mullā Ṣadrā also posited the principle of substantial motion. According to the previous Muslim philosophers and going back to Aristotle, motion is possibly only in the accidents of things, not in their substance. Mullā Ṣadrā thought that, on the contrary, motion implies an inner becoming within the substance of things and therefore a continuous development toward higher states of being (without in any way implying the modern theory of evolution).

Another important principle asserted by Mullā Ṣadrā is the catharsis and independence of the imaginative faculty from the body. There is an intermediate "imaginal world" (*mundus imaginalis*) not to be confused with the "imagination" of current usage. The human imagination is a microcosmic aspect of this cosmic imagination and it is precisely in this domain possessing a reality of its own that eschatological problems whose solution escaped earlier philosophers take place and can be understood. These and many other principles, some of whose roots are to be found in the writings of the earlier Sufis and philosophers, Mullā Ṣadrā systematized and developed to their full conclusion.

Mullā Ṣadrā had many students, of whom the most famous are Mullā Muhsin Faiḍ Kāshānī and ʿAbd al-Razzāq Lāhījī, who were among the leading Shīʿite thinkers. His disciples propagated his works and teachings in both Persia and India, and in fact he founded a school that has dominated the intellectual life of Persia for the past four centuries. It is, however, against his worldview that the founder of the Shaikhī movement, Shaikh Aḥmad Ahsāʾī, wrote his criticisms. The Bāb, the founder of Babism, also belongs to the current against Mullā Ṣadrā and should by no means be considered as a product of his school. The school of Mullā Ṣadrā is still alive in Iran today and is the most important traditional school of philosophy and theosophy there.

See also Aristotle; Avicenna; Ibn al-ʿArabī, Islamic Philosophy; Logic, History of; Peripatetics; Sufism; Suhrawardī, Shihāb al-Dīn Yaḥyā.

Bibliography

WORKS BY MULLĀ ṢADRĀ

Kitāb al-Ḥikmat al-ʿarshīyah (The book of theosophy inspired by the throne). Teheran, 1278 AH/1861 CE.

Al-Ḥikmat al-mutaʿālīyah fiʾl-asfār al-arbaʿah (The exalted wisdom concerning the four journeys of the spirit). Teheran, 1282 AH/1865 CE; new ed., edited by M. H. Ṭabāṭabāʾī, Teheran, 1378 AH–/1958 CE–.

Al-Shawāhid al-rubūbīyah (The divine witnesses). Teheran, 1286 AH/1869 CE.

Rasāʾil (Treatises). Teheran, 1302 AH/1884 CE.

Taʿlīqāt ʿalā ilāhīyāt Kitāb al-Shifā (Glosses upon the metaphysics of the book of the remedy of Ibn Sīnā). Teheran, 1303 AH/1885 CE.

Sharh al-hidāyat al-athīriyah (Commentary upon the guide of Athīr al-Dīn Abharī). Teheran, 1313 AH/1895 CE.

Kitāb al-mabdaʾ waʾl-maʿād (The book of origin and return). Teheran, 1314 AH/1896 CE.

Taʿlīqāt ʿalā Kitāb Ḥikmat al-ishrāq (Glosses upon the theosophy of the orient of light [of Suhrawardi]). Teheran, 1315 AH/1897 CE.

Asrār al-āyāt (Secret of Quranic verses). Teheran, 1319 AH/1901 CE.

Sih aṣl (The three principles). Edited by S. H. Nasr. Teheran, 1380 AH/1960 CE.

Kitāb al-mashāʿir. Edited and translated by Henry Corbin as *Le livre des pénétrations métaphysiques*. Teheran and Paris, 1964. Contains Arabic text, Persian version, and French translation.

Mafātīḥ al-ghaib (Keys to the hidden world). Teheran, n.d.

Sharḥ al-uṣūl min al-Kāfī (Commentary upon the principles of Kāfī). Teheran, n.d.

WORKS ON MULLĀ ṢADRĀ

Āshtiyānī, S. J. *Sharḥ-i ḥāl wa ārāy-i falsafi-i Mullā Ṣadrā* (The biography and philosophical views of Mullā Ṣadrā). Meshed, 1382 AH/1962 CE. In Persian.

Corbin, Henry. "La place de Mollā Ṣadrā Shīrāzī dans la philosophie iranienne." *Studia Islamica* 18 (1963).

Corbin, Henry. *Terre céleste et corps de resurrection: De l'Iran mazdéen à l'Iran shīʿite.* Paris: Buchet/Chastel, 1960.

Horten, Max. *Das philosophische System con Schirazi (1640) übersetz und erläutert.* Strassburg, 1913.

Langarūdī, Muḥammad Jaʿfar. *Sharḥ al-mashāʿir* (Commentary upon the book of metaphysical penetrations). Edited by S. J. Āshtiyānī. Meshed, 1384 AH/1964 CE.

Nasr, S. H. *Islamic Studies.* Beirut: Librairie du Liban, 1967.

Nasr, S. H., ed. *Mulla Ṣadra Commemoration Volume.* Teheran, 1380 AH/1960 CE.

Nasr, S. H. "Ṣadr al-Dīn Shīrāzī." In *A History of Islamic Philosophy*, Vol. II, edited by M. M. Sharif. Wiesbaden, 1966.

Sajjādī, S. J. *Muṣṭalaḥat-i falsafi-yi Ṣadr al-Dīn Shīrāzī mashbūr bi Mullā Ṣadrā* (The philosophical vocabulary of Ṣadr al-Dīn Shīrāzī). Teheran, 1380 AH/1960 CE. In Persian.

Seyyed Hossein Nasr (1967)

MULLĀ ṢADRĀ [ADDENDUM]

In developing his concept of existence Mullā Ṣadrā works against the backdrop of Shihāb al-Dīn Yaḥyā Suhrawardī's essentialist metaphysics on the one hand, and Avicenna's rather incomplete and occasionally imprecise remarks on being on the other. Suhrawardī had defended essence (*māhiyya*) as the sole reality and as the proper subject matter of metaphysics. For him, existence (*wujūd*) is a common term and a secondary intelligible, shared by a multitude of objects without corresponding to any particular being. Suhrawardī proposed two objections against the primacy of existence. First, if existence is to be the real attribute of an essence in the extramental world, then this essence will have to have an existence of its own before receiving existence as an attribute. In this case existence will be the attribute of something that already exists. Second, if existence is to be the basis of reality, then it will have to exist before being such a basis. In this case this second existence will have to exist before serving as a basis for the first existence, and so on ad infinitum. Therefore, existence is a secondary intelligible posited by the mind, adding nothing to the concrete existence of quiddities.

Ṣadrā's response to this is based on a position he calls the primacy of existence (*aṣālat al-wujūd*). Instead of defining existence as a generic term and attribute, which things take on *a posteriori*, Ṣadrā construes it as that by which things are what they are. According to Ṣadrā one cannot say "existence exists" just as one cannot logically say "whiteness is white." When one talks about beings that exist, what one means is that things exist or simply are rather than they have existence. This means that the existence of something is its reality. According to Ṣadrā Suhrawardī's essentialism results from his failure to make a distinction between the concept and reality of existence. While existence as a concept is a secondary intelligible applicable to a multitude of objects, the reality of existence is such that it leaves no distance between the existence of something and its reality. Furthermore, Ṣadrā posits existence as the principle of both unity and difference. On the one hand, existence is that which makes things exist and, on the other, it is that which makes them what they are as a specific quiddity. Existence becomes delimited and multiplied by itself alone, displaying various modes of intensification and diminution. Ṣadrā explains this process with his central concept of the gradation of existence (*tashkīk al-wujūd*). In this gradational ontology essences are nothing but mental constructions produced by the human mind to denote the different particularizations of existence, which ultimately remain one and the same.

Ṣadrā's insistence on existence as the sole reality has far-reaching consequences for his epistemology. He defines knowledge as a mode of existence and relegates all cognition to the immediate perception of existence. In this view, to know something is to know its intelligible form. But since Ṣadrā takes intelligible forms to be various manifestations and self-delimitations of existence, one's epistemic access to things ought to be through the existence of what one knows. Furthermore, Ṣadrā's realist ontology considers intelligible forms ontologically more real and epistemologically more reliable than their material existence. The climax that one reaches through the unification of the intellect, the intelligible and the intellected is thus a mode of existential intensification and not a simple process of conceptual augmentation. These considerations lead Ṣadrā to develop a mystical theory of knowledge without totally jettisoning the traditional peripatetic noetics.

See also Avicenna; Essence and Existence; Mysticism, Nature and Assessment of; Peripatetics; Suhrawardī, Shihāb al-Dīn Yaḥyā.

Bibliography

WORKS BY ṢADRĀ

The Metaphysics of Mulla Ṣadrā. Translated by Parviz Morewedge. New York: Society for the Study of Islamic Philosophy and Science, 1992. Originally published under the title *Kitab al-Mashaʿir*.

Tafsir al-qurʾan al-karim. Qum: Bidar Press, 1366–1369/1987–1990. 7 vols. edited by Muhammad Khwajawi. Ṣadrā's incomplete commentary on the Qurʾan written from a philosophical and mystical point of view.

Maʿani al-alfaz al-mufradah min al-qurʾan (The meanings of Qurʾanic terms). A short exposition of certain Qurʾanic terms and expressions.

Mutashabihat al-qurʾan (Allegorical verses of the Qurʾan). Ṣadrā's explanation of the Qurʾanic verses that are called allegorical or metaphorical (*mutashabih*) by the Qurʾan (Al-i ʿImran, 3:7) such as 'God's hand.' Published in Sayyid Jalal al-Din Ashtiyani, *Sih Risalah* (Mashhad: Mashhad University Press, 1352 (A. H. Lunar)).

Sharh usul al-kafi (Commentary on the *Usul al-kafi*). A commentary on the famous Shiʿite book of Hadith compiled by Abu Jaʾfar Muhammad ibn Yaʾqub Kulayni (d. 329/940). Edited by Muhammad Khwajawi in 3 Vols. (Tehran: Muʾassasa-yi Mutalaʿat wa Tahqiqat-i Farhanghi, 1366 (A. H. Solar)).

Risalat al-Hashr (The treatise of resurrection). Muhammad Khwajawi has published a critical edition with Persian translation under the title *Risalat al-hashr ya kitab-i rastakhiz-i jahan* (Tehran: Intisharat-i Mawla, 1377 (A. H. Lunar; second edition)).

Huduth al-ʾalam (Temporal origination of the world). Ṣadrā's most important work on the temporal origination of the world. Printed in the *Rasaʾil* (Qom: Maktab al-Mustafawi, 1302 (A. H. Lunar)) (first treatise).

Iksir al-ʾarifin fi maʾrifat tariq al-haqq waʾl-yaqin (The elixir of the gnostics for knowing the path of the truth and certainty). One of Ṣadrā's mystical works; Translated by William C. Chittick as *The Elixir of the Gnostics: A Parallel English-Arabic Text*. Provo, UT: Brigham Young University Press, 2003.

Kasr al-asnam al-jahiliyyah fi dhamm al-mutasawwifin (The demolition of the idols of ignorance in blaming those who pretend to be Sufis). Ṣadrā's attack on those who pretended to be Sufis and held excessive views during the Safawid period; edited by M. T. Danechepazuh (Tehran: 1340 (A. H. Solar)).

Kitab al-Masha'ir. Translated by P. Morewedge as *The Metaphysics of Mulla Ṣadrā*. Texas: Global Publications Associations, 1992. A summary of some key issues of Sadrean metaphysics.

Al-Mazahir al-ilahiyyah fi asrar al-'ulum al-kamaliyyah (Divine manifestations concerning the secrets of the sciences of perfection). One of Ṣadrā's major theological works synthesizing philosophical arguments with quotations from the Qur'an; edited with an introduction by Sayyid Muhammad Khamanei. Tehran: Bunyad-i Hikmat-i Islami-yi Ṣadrā, 1378.

Zad al-musafir (Provisions of the traveler) also known as *Zad al-salik* and *Ma'ad al-jismani*. A short treatise summarizing Ṣadrā's views on eschatology. Edited by S. J. Ashtiyani. Tehran: Mu'assa-yi Intisharat-i Amir Kabir, 1379 (A. H. Lunar).

Majmu'a-yi rasa'il-i falsafi-yi Sadr al-Muta'allihin, edited by Hamid Naji Isfahani. Tehran: Intisharat-i Hikmat, 1375 (A. H. Lunar). Contains a number of Ṣadrā's short treatises.

WORKS ABOUT ṢADRĀ

Açikgenç, Alparslan. *Being and Existence in Sadrā and Heidegger: A Comparative Ontology*. Kuala Lumpur: International Institute of Islamic Thought and Civilization, 1993.

Alawi, Hadi. *Nazariyyat al-Harakat al-Jawhariyyah 'ind al-Shirazi*. Beirut: Dar al-Tali'ah, 1983.

Horten, Max. *Die Gottesbeweise bei Shirazi*. Bonn, 1912.

Jambet, Christian. *Se rendre immortel: Traité de la résurrection*. Paris: Fata Morgana, 2000.

Kalin, Ibrahim. "An Annotated Bibliography of the Works of Mulla Sadra with a Brief Account of His Life." *Islamic Studies* 42 (1) (2003): 21–62.

Kalin, Ibrahim. "Between Physics and Metaphysics: Mulla Sadra on Nature and Motion." *Islam and Science* Vol. I, 2003, pp. 65–93.

Khajawi, Muhammad. *Du Sadraddin*. Tehran: Mawla, 1999.

Khajawi, Muhammad. *Lawami' al-'Arifin fi Ahwal Sadr al-Muta'allihin*. Tehran: Mawla, 1987.

Khurram-dashti, Nahid Baqiri, and Fatimah 'Asghari *Kitab shinasi-yi jami'-yi Mulla Sadra*. Tehran: Bunyad-i Hikmat-i Islami-yi Sadra, 1378/1999.

Morris, James Winston. *The Wisdom of the Throne: An Introduction to the Philosophy of Mulla Sadra*. Princeton, NJ: Princeton University Press, 1981.

Morris, Zaylan. *Revelation, Intellectual Intuition, and Reason in the Philosophy of Mulla Sadra: An Analysis of the al-Hikmat al-'Arshiyyah*. London: Routledge Curzon, 2003.

Musawi, Musa al-. *al-Jadid fi Falsafat Sadr al-Din al-Shirazi*. Baghdad: al-Dar al-'Arabiyyah li't-Tiba'ah, 1978.

Nasr, Seyyed Hossein. *Sadr al-Dīn al-Shīrāzī and His Transcendent Theosophy*. 2nd ed. Tehran: Institute for Humanities and Cultural Studies, 1997.

Peerwani, L. "Qur'anic Hermeneutics: The Views of Sadr al-Din Shirazi" in British Society for Middle East Studies Proceedings (1991), pp. 468–477.

Rahman, Fazlur. *The Philosophy of Mullā Sadrā*. Albany: SUNY Press, 1975.

Sajjadi, Ja'far. *Mustalahat-i Falsafi-yi sadr al-Din Shirazi*. Tehran: Danishgada-yi 'Ulum-u Ma'qul wa Manqul, 1961.

Ibrahim Kalin (2005)

MULTICULTURALISM

In many academic fields in the United States after 1970, multiculturalism has meant that members of historically disadvantaged nonwhite or minority racial and ethnic groups have distinctive knowledge and ways of knowing that ought to be incorporated into curricula and recognized in research. This idea has led to area studies programs and departments that concentrate on cultures from specific geographical locations, such as Africana or African American studies, Latino/a studies, Asian American studies, Native American studies, and more generally, American studies and ethnic studies. As well, new texts and different cultural perspectives have been incorporated into traditional fields in the humanities and social sciences.

Multiculturalists have advocated greater diversity and representation in the academic community, by increasing members of historically disadvantaged groups among faculty, staff, and students, and recognizing and addressing their distinctive intellectual and socially relevant interests. Multiculturalism has often been associated with identity politics, or advocacy of the interests of minority groups, by their members, in both national and local politics and representations of ideas and persons in specific institutional contexts. Multiculturalism has been opposed in academia, because it is believed to weaken traditional subject matter by minimizing the established canon and neglecting universal knowledge. This opposition has been largely from conservative white intellectuals, but not exclusively so. For example, sociologist Yehudi Webster has argued that multiculturalism deprives students of the opportunity to develop critical thinking skills, and philosopher Jason Hill has argued that in emphasizing the value of racial and ethnic identities, multiculturalism stifles individual creativity and shared cosmopolitanism.

MULTICULTURALISM IN THE U.S. PROFESSION OF PHILOSOPHY

The practice of academic philosophy in the United States has tended to be restricted to the work of English, French, German, and ancient Greek philosophers, with varied recognition of American philosophy or pragmatism. Advocates of multicultural inclusion have argued that philosophical inquiry has not been limited to the United States, Europe, and ancient Greece, but exists in intellectual traditions in China, India, Africa, and South America, as well as in the cultures of groups worldwide. Multicultural advocates therefore conclude that the canon of American academic philosophy ought to reflect more geographical diversity. Also, when Western European philosophy has presented itself as universal, the incorporation of multicultural philosophical perspectives would seem to imply that Western European philosophy itself is as local as philosophies from other parts of the world.

Such intellectual multiculturalism has been undertaken by a number of American philosophers since the end of the twentieth century; James Sterba (2002) has argued that there is a Western bias in ethics that can be corrected. In *Native Pragmatism* (2002), Scott Pratt identifies Native American perspectives in nineteenth and early twentieth century American philosophy, and tracks their transmission. Also, introductory anthologies have become more inclusive of African, Asian, and East Indian traditions—Max Hallman's (2003) collection, *Traversing Philosophical Boundaries*, is one example.

American philosophers have also addressed demographic multiculturalism, which aims to increase the racial and ethnic diversity of philosophers and resembles the kinds of multiculturalism in other fields that has been associated with identity politics. In 2003 the American Philosophical Association's (APA) Committee on Inclusiveness proposed that the APA Board consider, for possible approval by all APA members, the following statement on inclusiveness:

> The American Philosophical Association is committed to expanding and enhancing the inclusiveness of the profession by: (A) Increasing the numbers and respected presence of persons from groups that have historically been subjected to invidious discrimination. These groups include, but are not limited to, disabled persons; persons of African descent; American Indians; Asians and Asian Americans; Hispanics and Latinos/as; Jews; persons of Middle Eastern descent; multiracial persons; lesbian, gay, bisexual, and transgendered persons; women. (B) Recognizing and supporting the development of scholarly philosophical research, teaching, service, and professional activity pertaining to the concerns of these groups.

The APA Board and the profession of U.S. academic philosophers are likely to approve the statement on inclusiveness, although as the profession develops over the twenty-first century, both intellectual and demographic multiculturalism, and external political and social changes will probably result in its augmentation and revision. Still, many traditional philosophers have opposed multiculturalism, on the grounds that its distinctive knowledge and epistemologies are not contributions to the field of academic philosophy, but rather applications of philosophical methods to new subjects, or else simply not philosophical at all. There are also concerns about time constraints on courses resulting in superficial instruction of a variety of traditions, in place of more thorough investigation of one or two.

Nonetheless, the APA, which is the primary professional organization of U.S. academic philosophers, publishes biannual newsletters on: American Indians in philosophy; Asian and Asian American philosophers and philosophies; the black experience; and Hispanic/Latino issues in philosophy. Also, the APA Committee on Inclusiveness is a standing committee that includes APA special committees on: American Indians, Asian and Asian American philosophers and philosophies, blacks in philosophy, and Hispanics. All of these committees were formed to address the relatively small numbers of nonwhite philosophers, and the absence of strong professional support of multicultural writing and teaching in the field. In 2002, the number of nonwhite academic philosophers was lower than the 10 percent of nonwhites in the U.S. professoriate overall, a figure that had not changed since 1989, and the percentage of African American philosophers was less than the national 4.4 percent of the U.S. professoriate, half of whom were employed in traditional black colleges (see Wilson [2002] for the national figures).

As of 2005, multicultural scholarly work in philosophy has mainly focused on African American concerns, although in the late 1990s, Asian American, Native American, and Hispanic concerns began to appear in philosophy courses and publications. In addition, since the late 1970s, feminist philosophers have attempted to address issues raised by nonwhite women, partly in response to criticism by bell hooks, Elizabeth Spelman, and others, that academic feminists were overly preoccupied with the problems of white middle class women.

This growing body of multicultural philosophical work is to some extent independent of the intellectual multiculturalism already mentioned, because it tends to be motivated by concerns about demographic inclusiveness and past oppression. It should be noted that the adjective *multicultural* does not always appear in multicultural scholarly work by philosophers, who are instead likely to use the terms *race* or *racial*, *black*, *African American*, *Asian American*, *Hispanic or Latino/a*, or *Native American* in their titles and within their work.

Still, the multicultural work of philosophers has often been multidisciplinary, with forays into anthropology, literature, sociology, law, the history of ideas, economics, and social theory. At the same time, multicultural philosophy has made use of traditionally analytic, continental (phenomenological and existentialist), and postmodern philosophical methodologies, sometimes combining different methodologies in the same texts. Much of the multicultural philosophical work is about race in U.S. society, and much of it is centered on social and individual problems or questions: Can affirmative action be morally justified? What is racism and how can it be remedied? What is racial identity? Are reparations for past oppression, such as slavery and the appropriation of indigenist lands, morally imperative? Does biology support ideas of human racial divisions in society?

Writings of historical figures have also been reexamined, for instance: David Hume and Immanuel Kant for their belief in the existence of hierarchies of human races; W. E. B. DuBois and Alain Locke for their ideas about racial identity; Frederick Douglass and Julia Ann Cooper for their contributions to theories of liberation; Frantz Fanon and Jean-Paul Sartre for ideas on individual freedom and authenticity and group emancipation. Overall, the subject of race in U.S. multicultural philosophy unifies into a set of logically connected concepts and subjects that scholars analyze from diverse starting premises, with considerable disagreement, albeit a common goal of increasing social justice for disadvantaged groups. At least three of these subjects merit closer examination in this context of multiculturalism in philosophy: the existence of biological race, racism, and affirmative action.

THE EXISTENCE OF BIOLOGICAL RACE

Whether or not human races exist as biological divisions of humankind has philosophical implications: If races are biologically real, then the social problems concerning race are matters of race relations; if races are not biologi-

cally real, then many social problems as well as much of the discourse about race must be understood by philosophers in terms of false beliefs that participants hold. That is, if biological races exist, then the philosophical discussion about race is in part a direct discussion about the world, whereas if biological races are fictional, then the philosophical discussion becomes a second-order discourse about what people believe. David Hume, Immanuel Kant, and other Enlightenment thinkers thought that the existence of human races was self-evident. During the time they wrote, the new sciences of biology and anthropology had begun to produce systems of classification that appeared to explain those physical differences among human groups, which were apparent in common sense.

By the mid-nineteenth century, human races were believed to be biological groups with common inherited physical, cultural, and psychic traits. American anthropologists were prominent proponents of natural human hierarchies, based on race and ultimately caused by racial essences, believed to be inherited in the blood. However, during the early twentieth century, anthropologist Franz Boas and his students Claude Lévi-Strauss, Margaret Meade, and Melville J. Herskovits established that history and culture were the causes of nonphysical racial differences. Subsequently, biological anthropologists came to agree that there were no general physical essences or even stable sets of particular traits shared by every member of any race. Blood types do not correspond to social racial groups. Mitochondrial DNA, used to track existing populations to ancestral groups in Asia, Africa, and Europe, has no relation to genes that determine inherited traits considered racial in society. And there is greater variation within races of those inherited racial traits than between any two races. In short, while biology confirms the existence of inherited physical traits that are considered to be racial in society, biology, according to some scholars, offers no support for a taxonomy of human races.

In the early 1990s, Kwame Anthony Appiah was the first U.S. philosopher to examine the lack of a scientific biological foundation for human races and he then argued that racial identities ought to be reconsidered. His work was taken up through controversial justifications for mixed race identity and more extensive philosophy of science analyses of how ideas of race are precluded by the findings and methodologies of biological anthropology, Mendelian heredity, and population genetics as of the late twentieth-century (Zack 1993 and 2002).

Yet, by 2005, most Americans continued to believe that human races are real physical divisions and that the social taxonomy of three (or four or five) races can be verified within the biological sciences. Multicultural scholars in all fields and philosophers who begin their inquiries on the basis of common sense or received opinion, tend to concur with the public, although often for avowedly political motivations. Thus, Lucius Outlaw, writing in the tradition of W. E. B. Dubois and Alain Locke, advocates a conservation of ordinary ideas of race, with their biological connotations, for the sake of continued self-esteem and social justice for African Americans. Amy Gutman claims that retention of ideas of race is essential for identifying those groups who have been oppressed or discriminated against on the basis of their purported race, so that their members may be assisted toward equality of opportunity for success in society.

Furthermore, scholars of Latino philosophy such as Linda Alcoff, Jorge Gracia, Eduardo Mendieta, and Ophelia Schutte have included discussions of racism in their analyses of Hispanic and Latino ethnicity. This suggests that members of dominant white Northern European groups have sometimes viewed Hispanics and Latinos as a distinct race and that addressing discrimination associated with that view could include the construction of positive distinctive racial identities for Hispanics and Latinos. And even in a purely conceptual analysis, Michael O. Hardimon (2003) dismisses disputes about the scientific standing of race and their relation to the ordinary concept of race. Hardimon then asserts, "The ordinary concept of race is our concept. It is part of our discourses, our practices, our conceptual repertoire" (Hardimon 2003, p.438).

Similarly, in an Op-Ed piece in the *New York Times* on March 14, 2005, Armand Mare Leroi, an evolutionary developmental biologist, called upon scientists to resurrect notions of biological race in light of its cultural significance, citing the importance of the preservation of the Negritos, an ancient tribe on the Andaman Islands in the Indian Ocean. It is a paradox that while philosophical multiculturalism enables analysis of the biological foundations for race, multiculturalist beliefs about how to attain social justice are held to be incompatible with the results of such conceptual analyses, even though everything of social value that used to be called race can be captured by ideas of family heredity and culture.

RACISM

The term *racism* came into broad usage in the United States during the late 1960s and there has since been both implied and explicit disagreement about what racism is. The concept of racism is broader than its predecessors, bigotry, discrimination, intolerance, and prejudice, because it can refer to social conditions as well as intentions and attitudes of individuals. By the late twentieth century, there was a consensus in business, academia, politics, and public life generally that racism in individuals is morally wrong and that the practice of racism by representatives of institutions and organizations is unjust, as well as in violation of Title VII of the Civil Rights Act of 1964, which prohibits employment discrimination based on race, sex, national origin, or religion. (Title VI prohibits public access discrimination, which was relevant to the implementation of school desegregation and Title VIII was the first federal fair housing law).

Moral philosophers have traditionally posited justice as a cardinal social and individual virtue. Given the premise that racism is a kind of injustice against human beings based on their racial identities, the main philosophical argument has focused on whether the causes of racism and remedies for it are confined to individuals or can be understood as institutional. Because racism, as a wrong, requires remedies where it exists, the individual view focuses on psychological and educational remedies, whereas the institutional view supports progressive legal action and public policy. Both views are motivated by concepts of responsibility in the sense that both individuals and societies are believed to be accountable and subject to blame for wrongs they commit.

Some proponents of individual views of racism have worked within a Kantian moral tradition. J. L. A. Garcia (1997) has argued that racism is a kind of ill will or contempt in the hearts and minds of individuals, a lack of benevolence for which they are morally responsible. Racism in this sense may be present when others are not harmed by it and it may not be present when others are harmed in ways associated with their race.

Philosophers who study racism with a multidisciplinary approach are inclined to define racism institutionally, because historians, sociologists, and political scientists have provided many extended examples of behavior, traditions, and laws that explicitly or implicitly disadvantage members of nonwhite groups in comparison to whites. Slavery, segregation, and the status of African Americans according to many measures of demographic well-being are one set of examples; the failure of the U.S. government to honor its treaty obligations to Native Americans is a second; restrictions on nonwhite immigration are a third.

For all minority groups, evidence of institutional racism against them includes disproportionately higher rates of incarceration, poverty, and unemployment, and disproportionately lower rates of income, family assets, advanced educational degrees, and presence in the political leadership class. Whereas most scholars in philosophy and other fields focus on institutional racism as a modern and postmodern phenomenon, several have drawn wider connections. Berel Lang (1997) claims that racism is historically prior to modern ideas of race and that metaphysical racism is a set of ideas and practices that can be attached to varied specific notions of race; Charles Mills (1997) argues that modern Western history has developed on the basis of a racial contract that places Europeans and Americans at the top of a hierarchy in which indigenist Americans, Africans, and Asians are oppressed and exploited.

In the context of American history, critical race theorists such as Derek Bell and Patricia Williams have argued that the American legal system is structurally racist, from the acceptance of slavery in the U.S. Constitution to the neglect of race-based disadvantage in laws presumed to be color blind. Finally, there is disagreement among philosophers about who the most disadvantaged or paradigm victims of racism are: Lewis Gordon (1995) has claimed that antiblack racism is more extreme than other forms, because of the historical association of darkness with sin in the Christian tradition; Native American philosophers refer to European conquest as a holocaust; Asian Americans claim group histories of exclusion in immigration law and exploitation as cheap labor.

There are also issues of whether nonwhites can be racist against whites and whether racism can be practiced by some members of the same race against others. Nonwhites can be individually racist against whites, although not institutionally because they do not have sufficient influence within major social institutions. Preferences for lighter skin color within nonwhite groups, as well as self-hatred on the grounds of nonwhite race would be examples of same-race racism.

AFFIRMATIVE ACTION

In 1965, according to U.S. Executive Order 11246, President Lyndon Johnson required that government officials take affirmative action (AA) to address the ongoing disproportionately low numbers of minorities directly and indirectly employed by the federal government. At that time, the concept of institutional racism was not widely accepted, but it was assumed that AA would override individual racism that could not otherwise be proved in hiring decisions. Arguments in favor of AA have been based on the value of minority role models, the justice of compensation and reparations for past wrongs, and the

presumption that U.S. society has not ceased to disadvantage minorities on the grounds of race. Arguments against AA often proceed from the premise that minorities have gained formal and legal equality in the United States, to the claim that AA is unnecessary, and unjust because it penalizes otherwise deserving and innocent whites who are not responsible for past injustice.

In 2003 the U.S. Supreme Court's rulings in two University of Michigan cases offered a practical resolution of these disputes. In both *Grutter v. Bollinger* and *Gratz v. Bollinger*, the Court recognized the value of a diverse student body but used strict scrutiny in its rulings, determining whether two different forms of AA constituted a compelling government interest and were narrowly tailored to advance that interest. In *Grutter v. Bollinger*, the Court ruled in favor of the University of Michigan Law School's policy of considering the race of applicants holistically, as one factor among many; in *Gratz v. Bollinger*, the Court ruled against the University of Michigan's undergraduate admissions policy of uniformly giving the same number of points for minority racial identities. In its rulings in these and previous cases, the Court declared as unconstitutional, role model and compensation/reparation justifications for AA. However, in *Grutter v. Bollinger* the Court upheld the value of a critical mass of minority students, as opposed to tokenism. The Court's main justification for AA was the value of a racially integrated leadership class, which would in time make AA unnecessary.

Philosophers of race and racism are unlikely to accept judicial decisions on AA as the last word, because courts may revise or overturn previous rulings and legal reasoning has distinctive constraints, one of which is to assume that existing laws are effective. In the Michigan cases, the Supreme Court appeared to assume that formal legal equality guarantees equal opportunity. It therefore seemed to view AA as a strategy for achieving diversity, on the assumption of unequal ability, rather than a strategy for social justice. That is, the Court seemed to accept the fairness of admissions criteria that nonwhites disproportionately fail to meet and did not address the possibility of racism in the face of official race neutrality.

FURTHER ASPECTS OF MULTICULTURAL PHILOSOPHY

Whether multicultural academic philosophy will remain a distinct range of specializations or become part of the core curriculum is an open question. Africana Philosophy, which includes studies of race and racism, did become a recognized philosophical subfield by the 1990s.

Native American philosophers Anne Waters (2000) and V.P. Cordova (2000) have argued that Western philosophy has Christian religious foundations that are inimical to indigenist world views, a perspective that undermines beliefs in the universalism of traditional philosophy. Hispanic and Latin American philosophy has never been part of the recognized philosophical canon, although by 2000 it was clearly part of multicultural philosophy. Although Asian or Eastern philosophy has a long history as a distinctive body of knowledge, often addressed within comparative philosophy, the status and concerns of Asian Americans would be a new subject.

By 2005, the existence of philosophical multicultural research, published by academic book presses and journals, constituted a tradition capable of supporting graduate research and further professional scholarship, as well as the curricula of multicultural courses. Where studies of race have been limited to U.S. society, further work is likely to include international and world perspectives. Multidisciplinary approaches are likely to continue, drawing on studies in law, political science, sociology, public policy, and economics. Philosophy of science analyses of ideas of race in biological anthropology and population genetics could expand into ideas of race in the social sciences (for example, psychologist Roy Freedle [2003] has presented statistical data on standardized test scores, which indicate that minority students score higher than traditional white students on difficult questions). Feminist interest in racial differences among women adds a multicultural dimension to existing feminist philosophy. And finally, analyses of racism and its remedies are relevant to established work in the philosophy of education, as well as moral theory, ethics, and applied ethics.

In considering future directions for both intellectual and demographic multiculturalism in philosophy, and assessing progress at any given time, the subject itself suggests cross-national comparisons. In general, the extent of multiculturalism in philosophy seems to be more sensitive to external political, social, and demographic factors, than to purely intellectual interests in inclusion or exclusion. For example, as university subjects in the Soviet Union, *philosophy* referred to the work of Karl Marx and Vladimir Lenin, whereas Western philosophy, which was what Western Europeans and Americans called *philosophy*, was taught as a distinct and subsidiary subfield.

There have been two models of political and social pluralism that are relevant to multicultural philosophy, considered as an international subject. The assimilationist model encourages subordinate groups to achieve inclusion through their contributions to the common culture of dominant groups. The autonomous or diversity model advocates that subordinate groups participate in a shared but diverse common culture. American academic philosophy is becoming multicultural according to the diversity model.

In contrast, the trend in Great Britain has been to assimilate white women and minorities within the existing academic field of philosophy. Julian Baggini, editor of *The Philosophers' Magazine*, who interviewed sixteen leading British philosophers about their profession, observed in 2003 that participants in the main British philosophy conference were often all white, with a very small minority of women. Since the 1970s, Canada has had a strong multicultural political movement that has been reflected in its intellectual life. James Tully (1995) has examined how constitutionalism can coexist with diversity in *Strange Multiplicity*. And in *Multicultural Citizenship* (1995), Will Kymlicka argues that immigrant and indigenous groups in a multicultural society have disparate needs.

Developing parts of the world have perhaps been more interested in examining and constructing their own national and cultural intellectual perspectives, in a postcolonial era. Their work may be included in multicultural studies for Northern and Western audiences—for example, V. Y. Mudimbe's *Nations, Identities, Cultures*. But, multiculturalism for postcolonial critics is more likely to be a matter of deconstruction than inclusion. For example, in *Dislocating Cultures* (1997), Uma Narayan examines how British representations are an integral part of what is accepted as Indian culture and its products. Nevertheless, it is increasingly difficult to generalize about scholarly trends in multiculturalism. Chinese academics have launched *The Journal of Multicultural Discourses*, a forum for multicultural approaches to language, communities of discourse, cultural and literary criticism, and comparative studies, which will aim to be multidisciplinary across the social sciences and humanities, including philosophy.

See also Affirmative Action; Business Ethics; Enlightenment; Feminist Philosophy; Hume, David; Kant, Immanuel; Lenin, Vladimir Il'ich; Marx, Karl; Pluralism; Racism; Sartre, Jean-Paul; Toleration.

Bibliography

Alcoff, Linda, and Eduardo Mendieta. *Identities: Race, Class, Gender, and Nationality.* Malden, MA: Blackwell, 2003.

Appiah, K. Anthony. "'But Would That Still Be Me?': Notes on Gender, Race, Ethnicity as Sources of Identity." *The Journal of Philosophy* 77 (10) (1990): 493–499.

Appiah, K. Anthony, and Amy Gutman. *Color Conscious: The Political Morality of Race.* Princeton, NJ: Princeton University Press, 1993.

Baggini, Julian. "Two Philosophies, Separated by a Common Language." *The Chronicle of Higher Education* (2003).

Blackburn, Daniel G. "Why Race Is Not a Biological Concept." In *Race and Racism in Theory and Practice*, edited by Berel Lang. Lanham, MD: Rowman and Littlefield, 2000.

Boxill, Bernard. "The Morality of Reparation." *Social Theory and Practice* 2 (1) (1972): 113–122.

Cavalli-Sforza, Luigi Luca, and Francesco Cavalli-Sforza. *The Great Human Diaspora.* MA: Addison-Wesley, 1995.

The Civil Rights Project. *Reaffirming Diversity: A Legal Analysis of the University of Michigan Affirmative Action Cases: A Joint Statement of Constitutional Law Scholars.* Cambridge, MA: The Civil Rights Project at Harvard University, 2003. Available from http://www.civilrightsproject.harvard.edu.

Cohen, Carl, and James P. Sterba. *Affirmative Action and Racial Preferences: A Debate.* Oxford: Oxford University Press, 2003.

Cordova, V. P. "Exploring the Sources of Western Thought." In *Women of Color and Philosophy*, edited by Naomi Zack. Camden, MA: Blackwell Publishers, 2000.

Dubinin, N. P. "Race and Contemporary Genetics." In *Race, Science, and Society*, edited by L. Kuper. New York: Columbia University Press, 1965.

Eze, Emmanuel Chukwudi, ed. *Race and the Enlightenment: A Reader.* Cambridge, MA: Blackwell, 1997.

Freedle, Roy O. "Correcting the SAT's Ethic and Social-Class Bias: A Method for Reestimating SAT Scores." *Harvard Educational Review* 73 (1) (2003): 1–43.

Garcia, J. L. A. "Racism as a Model for Understanding Sexism." In *Race/Sex: Their Sameness, Difference, and Interplay*, edited by Naomi Zack. New York: Routledge, 1997.

Gordon, Lewis. *Bad Faith and Antiblack Racism.* Atlantic Highlands, NJ: Humanities Press, 1995.

Gracia, Jorge. *Hispanic/Latino Identity: A Philosophical Perspective.* Oxford: Blackwell, 2000.

Hallman, Max O., ed. *Traversing Philosophical Boundaries.* Belmont, CA: Wadsworth/Thompson Learning, 2003.

Hardimon, Michael O. "The Ordinary Concept of Race." *The Journal of Philosophy* 9 (2003): 437–455.

Hill, Jason. *On Becoming a Cosmopolitan: What It Means to Be a Human Being in the New Millennium.* Lanham, MD: Rowman and Littlefield, 2000.

Kymlicka, Will. *Multicultural Citizenship: A Liberal Theory of Minority Rights.* New York; Oxford: Clarendon and Oxford University Press, 1995.

Lang, Berel. "Metaphysical Racism." In *Race/Sex: Their Sameness, Difference, and Interplay*, edited by Naomi Zack. New York: Routledge, 1997.

Leroi, Armand Marie. "A Family Tree in Every Gene." *New York Times*, March 12, 2004, p. A23.

Mills, Charles. *The Racial Contract.* Ithaca, NY: Cornell University Press, 1997.

Mudimbe, V. Y. *Nations, Identities, Cultures.* Durham, NC: Duke University Press, 1995.

Narayan, Uma. *Dislocating Cultures: Identities, Traditions, and Third-World Feminism (Thinking Gender).* New York: Routledge, 1997.

Outlaw, Lucius, Jr. *On Race and Philosophy.* New York: Routledge, 1996.

Outlaw, Lucius, Jr. "2002–2003 Report of the American Philosophical Association Committee on Inclusiveness." Available from http://www.apa.udel.edu/apa/governance/committees/Inclusiveness/report2003.html.

Schutte, Ophelia. *Cultural Identity and Social Liberation in Latin American Thought.* Albany: State University of New York Press, 1993.

Spelman, Elizabeth V. *Inessential Woman: Problems of Exclusion in Feminist Thought.* Boston: Beacon Press, 1988.

Spratt, Scott. *Native Pragmatism: Rethinking the Roots of American Philosophy.* Bloomington: Indiana University Press, 2002.

Sterba, James P. *Three Challenges to Ethics: Environmentalism, Feminism, and Multiculturalism.* New York, Oxford: Oxford University Press, 2002.

Tully, James. *Strange Multiplicity.* New York; Cambridge, U.K.: Cambridge University Press, 1995.

Waters, Anne Schullherr. "That Alchemical Bering Strait Theory! or Introducing America's Indigenous Sovereign Nations Wolrdviews to Informal Logic Courses." In *Women of Color and Philosophy*, edited by Naomi Zack. Malden, MA: Blackwell, 2000.

Waters, Anne Schulherr, ed. *American Indian Thought: Philosophical Essays.* Malden, MA: Blackwell, 2003.

Webster, Yehudi. *Against the Multicultural Agenda: A Critical Thinking Alternative.* Westport, CT: Praeger, 1997.

Wilson, Robin. "A Kinder, Less Ambitious Professoriate." *The Chronicle of Higher Education* (2002): 10–11.

Young, Iris Marion. *Justice and the Politics of Difference.* Princeton, NJ: Princeton University Press, 1990.

Zack, Naomi. "American Mixed Race: Theoretical and Legal Issues." *Harvard Blackletter Law Journal* 17 (2001):33–46.

Zack, Naomi. *Philosophy of Science and Race.* New York: Routledge, 2002.

Zack, Naomi. *Race and Mixed Race.* Philadelphia: Temple University Press, 1993.

Zack, Naomi. "Race and Racial Discrimination." In *Oxford Handbook of Practical Ethics*, edited by Hugh Lafolette. Oxford: Oxford University Press, 2002.

Zack, Naomi. *Thinking About Race.* 2nd ed. Belmont, CA: Thompson Wadsworth, 2005.

Naomi Zack (2005)

MULTIPLE REALIZABILITY

Multiple realizability is a key issue in debates over the nature of mind and reduction in the sciences. The subject consists of two parts: multiplicity and realizability. "Multiplicity" designates variability in the mechanism and materials from which a particular type of thing can be made. "Realizability" designates a specific relation that exists when there is the stated variability.

REALIZABILITY

Apart from the broad folk notion of realization meaning that a thing is made real, philosophers apply several technical notions of realization to paradigm cases such as computational states realized by engineering states, minds realized by brains, and persons realized by their bodies. The technical notions fall into three broad traditions: mathematical, logico-semantic, and metaphysical.

The mathematical tradition equates realization with a form of mapping between objects. Generally speaking, x (mathematically) realizes y because elements of y map onto elements of x. The notion is useful for many purposes, for example, when constructing a formal model of a particular domain. However, since mapping extends to models as well as reality, it fails to distinguish between simulated versus genuine realizations. Heavenly stars can be mapped onto grains of sand, but grains of sand do not realize heavenly stars in any genuine sense. Similarly, the mental states described by a cognitive program can be mapped onto unthinking groups of things, but unthinking groups of things do not realize mental states in any genuine sense (Block 1978). Hence, to capture what is essential to genuine realization, William Lycan (1987) adds ideas about evolutionary function, while David Chalmers (1994) emphasizes facts about the causal structure of a system. To present Chalmers's idea and cast in terms of a computational model that informs the literature cited, a set of mental properties that constitute the cognitive program of a system is realized by a set of engineering properties possessed by that system if and only if (a) there is a one-to-one mapping between instances of the two sets of properties, and (b) the engineering involved has the causal structure to satisfy the computational state transitions required by the program.

The logico-semantic tradition translates realization into an interpretation of symbolic objects. Generally speaking, x (semantically) realizes y because x can be interpreted to meet the conditions for satisfying the term "y." Thus, logicians say that a set of objects is the realization of a formal language when the objects satisfy the predicates of that language (Tarski 1936/1956). Being a matter of semantic interpretation, might appear irrelevant to paradigm cases of realization whereby one thing (engineering or brains) generates or produces another thing (computation or minds). Yet Daniel Dennett (1978) addresses such cases by employing a method of agent interpretation, in effect turning the interpretation of symbols into an interpretation of rational symbol systems. Roughly, a set of mental properties that constitutes a system's cognitive program is realized by a set of engi-

neering properties possessed by that system if and only if (a) the system's behavior supports an interpretation according to which instances of the computational properties are internal symbols involved in the operations of the system, and (b) it is rational for the system to possess those symbols and operations under the stated interpretation.

Finally, the metaphysical tradition views realization as a species of determination between objects. Generally speaking, x (metaphysically) realizes y because the properties of x determine the properties of y. Unlike other forms of determination, philosophers see a very close connection in paradigm cases of metaphysical realization. Regarding the particulars, some philosophers add that instances of realized and realizing properties occur at the same time, with the former composed out of the latter (Tye 1995). Regarding the properties, Stephen Yablo (1992) applies the notion of determinables and determinates by maintaining that a realized property stands to a realizing property as the determinable color red stands to its more determinate color scarlet. So human neurophysiology is a way of being a mind, like scarlet is a way of being red. In a different vein, Sydney Shoemaker (2001) employs metaphysical and set-theoretic notions by viewing the causal powers of a realized property as a subset of the causal powers of its realizing property. So mental abilities are a mere portion of the causal capacities of the appropriate engineering systems.

Many philosophers explain realization in terms of functionalism, the leading doctrine in the philosophy of mind. On this view, mental processes are understood by the functions they perform and not by the materials that realize the processes. On one popular version, each mental property is a higher-order property whose nature is defined as the possession of a lower-order physical property that plays an associated functional role. To present this idea in computational format, a set of mental properties that constitutes a system's cognitive program is realized by a set of engineering properties possessed by that system if and only if (a) the mental properties are higher-order properties that require lower-order physical properties to play their associated functional roles, and (b) the physical engineering properties of the system play the required functional roles.

MULTIPLE REALIZABILITY

Multiple realizability is a kind of variability in materials that philosophers call "property variability" or "compositional plasticity." Functionalists have this variability in mind when they observe that different physical properties can play the same functional role in different individuals. Indeed, this observation is commonplace in computer science. Thus Alan Turing judged that the specific physical properties of an engineering system are unimportant for a theory of computation because the same computational function can be performed by systems with different engineering:

> Importance is often attached to the fact that modern digital computers are electrical, and that the nervous system is also electrical. Since Babbage's machine was not electrical, and since all digital computers are in a sense equivalent, we see that this use of electricity cannot be of theoretical importance. ... If we wish to find [computational] similarities we should look rather for mathematical analogies of function. (Turing 1950, p. 439)

That is, while an instance of a given physical property may be sufficient to realize a computational property, as when the human brain computes addition, nevertheless that same physical property is not necessary. Other systems with quite different physical properties can compute addition: someone with a different neurophysiology, an artificial machine with a microprocessor, and so on. So the key to property variability is that sufficient conditions for the realization of higher-level properties are not necessary conditions.

More formally, property G is lawfully sufficient for property F if, as a matter of physical law, F is realized when G is realized. But G is not a necessary condition for F if F can be realized without G. For example, G is sufficient but not necessary for F if F is a computational function that can be realized on some occasion without the property G of having a human neural assembly but with the property H having an artificial microprocessor. To incorporate this idea into a formal definition in which A is a set of realized properties and B its realizing base:

> Property F in set A has variability with respect to set B if and only if there exist properties G and H in B such that
>
> > (i) it is possible that G and F but not H are realized, and, as a matter of physical law, if G is realized then so is F;
> >
> > (ii) it is possible that H and F but not G are realized, and, as a matter of physical law, if H is realized then so is F; and
> >
> > (iii) there is no property K in set B such that, as a matter of physical law, F is realized if and only if K is realized. (Endicott 1994)

Clauses (i) and (ii) jointly express a minimal form of property variability, while the addition of clause (iii) expresses a form of deep property variability by guaranteeing that the variability of F with respect to G and H is not a superficial fact that masks an underlying common property, that is, ruling out any property in B that is lawfully coextensive with F.

Property variability also comes in degrees. Being a planet has many physico-chemical realizations (all possible minerals constituting large dense bodies in orbit), while being jade has only two such realizations (jadeite and nephrite). Accordingly, there is the project of explaining how variability arises and why. Dennett (1991) appeals to the forces of evolution, claiming that the brain developed variability in how it realizes cognitive functions to enhance the organism's ability to adapt to a changing environment. Robert Batterman (2000) offers a more general explanation based upon the notion of universality in physics, which concerns the procedure of finding similarities in behavior among physically diverse systems.

But however property variability is explained, it appears widespread. Neural plasticity is well documented (Johnson 1993). In particular, the brain is capable of compensatory plasticity, in which areas in the brain formerly dedicated to one cognitive task can, after injury or disease, become dedicated to another cognitive task (Rauschecker 1995). The brain is also capable of experience-dependent plasticity, in which the basic wiring of the brain is refined by an individual's sensory experience, creating individual differences in how the brain realizes mental functions (King 1999). At a more abstract level, functional properties are variable with respect to different physical properties, shapes can be shared by different kinds of matter, and the same spatial patterns can be discerned among physically distinct structures.

SUBSEQUENT DEBATE OVER IDENTITY AND REDUCTION

Hilary Putnam (1967/1975) and Jerry Fodor (1974/1981) developed an argument concerning special sciences such as psychology that was then extended by David Hull (1974) to the biological sciences. As a result of this argument, it became the dominant opinion among philosophers in the late-twentieth century that property variability supplies adequate evidence against type identity and physical reduction. Type identity is the theory that mental properties are identical with physical properties. And physical reductionism is the doctrine that all scientific theories reduce to basic physical theories. Below is an outline of Putnam's and Fodor's multiple-realizability argument:

(1) If a mental property F is identical with or reducible to a physical property G, then, as a matter of physical law, F is realized if and only if G is realized (they must be lawfully coextensive).

Yet (2) this requirement that identical properties be lawfully coextensive is not met in cases where property variability applies, because F can be realized without G.

So (3) mental property F is not identical with or reducible to physical property G.

Yet the issue is not settled. There are several responses, which divide into three main areas of discussion: variability, the notion of a property, and reduction versus identity.

VARIABILITY REEXAMINED. Jaegwon Kim (1972) challenges premise (2) by observing that physical differences between individuals who share the same psychology does not imply that no physical property is realized when and only when a given mental property is realized. In other words, the minimal form of property variability expressed by clauses (i) and (ii) does not imply the deep property variability captured by clause (iii) that rules out mental-physical identities. Moreover, Kim believes that the world reveals interlevel identities along with minimal property variability. For example, temperature is identical with mean kinetic energy in ideal gases, yet two aggregates of molecules with the same temperature will differ physically by having constituent molecules with different positions and directions. Accordingly, reductionists are optimistic that neuroscience will discover mental-physical identities, like the specialized Hubel-Wiesel cells, which detect edges in a visual field, or the identification of visual awareness with 40–70 Hz oscillations in the cortical system (Crick and Koch 1990/1997). Indeed, Patricia Churchland (1986) foresees that portions of psychology and neuroscience will coevolve to a point where they reductively converge because their methodologies are interdependent, as when neuroscientists employ psychofunctional criteria to identify brain structures, thereby establishing mental-physical correlations.

Antireductionists counter that, while mere physical differences do not guarantee that each mental property is not coextensive with some physical property, deep variability remains extremely plausible, given the functional nature of mental phenomenon and the actual record of how cognitive systems are built in a physically variable way. Consider again the case of computation. Having devised computational mechanisms that exhibit quite different engineering properties—from electrical charges passing through silicon pathways to light signals flashing across optical channels—scientists cannot point to a single necessary and sufficient physical condition for any computational function. So it seems unlikely that computation is like temperature in ideal gases, whose necessary and sufficient physical condition is mean kinetic energy. Moreover, antireductionists claim that neuroscientific discoveries only establish mental-physical correlations, not the coextensions that support property identity. Thus, various systems of computer vision carry out algorithms for edge detection, which shows that the activity of Hubel-Wiesel cells is sufficient but not necessary for that function. Furthermore, even if artificial systems are discounted and psychological theory is restricted to biological systems such as mammals, and even if neuroscience employs psychofunctional criteria to identify mammalian brain structures, those identifications must be compatible with compensatory and experience-dependent plasticity as well as any other physical variations that arise from evolution (Rosenberg 2001). This makes the identification of particular types of mental functioning with coextensive physical functioning unlikely.

RECONCEPTUALIZED PROPERTIES. Many reductionists challenge premise (2) in Putnam's and Fodor's argument by reconceptualizing the pertinent properties. On the side of the mental, David Lewis (1969) suggests that mental properties are lawfully coextensive with physical properties when the former are narrowly conceived species-specific properties. Thus, unlike pain per se, which might be realized in physically different ways across various species, pain *in human beings* may be lawfully coextensive with a human neurophysical property (see also Kim 1972, 1992/1993). On the side of the physical, Kim (1998) suggests that mental properties are lawfully coextensive with physical properties when the latter are broadly conceived disjunctive properties. Thus, the property of having pain is lawfully coextensive with the disjunctive property of having a particular human neural assembly *or* a particular extraterrestrial neural assembly *or*, and so on. Here the disjunctive property includes every possible realization of pain.

Yet, regarding species-specific mental properties, antireductionists counter that psychological theory also requires more general properties to explain cross-species generalizations. Moreover, they argue that even if theories are restricted to species-specific properties, there remains the fact that variability occurs within a species and even the same individual over time (Horgan 2001). As for disjunctive physical properties, some critics deny that they exist, because they do not guarantee meaningful statements of similarity among objects or plausible statements about the causal powers of objects (Teller 1983). Others argue that disjunctive predicates do not always express natural kinds, yet projectible natural-kind predicates are needed for scientific prediction and explanation (Block 1997).

REDUCTION VERSUS IDENTITY. Finally, rather than cast doubt upon premise (2) in Putnam's and Fodor's argument, some philosophers promote views of reduction that do not require the identities at issue in premise (1). Granted, on the traditional account of scientific reduction associated with Ernest Nagel, one theory reduces to a more basic theory when the former can be deduced from the latter by means of connecting principles that express property identities. But there are other accounts that advertise no requirement concerning lawful coextensions which support intertheoretic property identities, including variations on approximate reduction (Paul Churchland 1979, Bickle 1998) and physicalist interpretations of functionalism (Kim 1998).

Critics counter that, among other problems, traditional connecting principles resurface within these alternatives (Endicott 1998, Marras 2002). Critics also add that, to the extent that any account avoids property identities, it is best understood as a model of scientific replacement, not reduction. In the end, philosophers have proposed many notions of reduction. But the fundamental metaphysical question remains: whether the properties of special sciences and physical sciences are identical or whether, because of multiple realizability, they fail to be identical.

See also Computationalism; Dennett, Daniel C.; Fodor, Jerry A.; Functionalism; Mind-Body Problem; Nagel, Ernest; Physicalism; Putnam, Hilary; Reduction; Reductionism in the Philosophy of Mind; Turing, Alan M.

Bibliography

REALIZABILITY

Block, Ned. "Troubles with Functionalism." In *Readings in Philosophy of Psychology*, edited by Ned Block. Vol. 1, 268–305. Cambridge, MA: Harvard University Press, 1978.

Chalmers, David. "On Implementing a Computation." *Minds and Machines* 4 (1994): 391–402.

Dennett, Daniel. Introduction. In his *Brainstorms: Philosophical Essays on Mind and Psychology*, xi–xxii. Cambridge, MA: MIT Press, 1978.

Lycan, William. *Consciousness*. Cambridge, MA: MIT Press, 1987.

Polger, Thomas. *Natural Minds*. Cambridge, MA: MIT Press, 2004.

Shoemaker, Sydney. "Realization and Mental Causation." In *Physicalism and Its Discontents*, edited by Carl Gillet and Barry Loewer, 74–98. Cambridge, U.K.: Cambridge University Press, 2001.

Tarski, Alfred. "On the Concept of Logical Consequence" (1936). In his *Logic, Semantics, Metamathematics: Papers from 1923 to 1938*, 409–420. Oxford: Clarendon Press, 1956.

Tye, Michael. *Ten Problems of Consciousness: A Representational Theory of the Phenomenal Mind*. Cambridge, MA: MIT Press, 1995.

Yablo, Stephen. "Mental Causation." *Philosophical Review* 101 (1992): 245–280.

MULTIPLE REALIZABILITY

Batterman, Robert. "Multiple Realizability and Universality." *British Journal for the Philosophy of Science* 51 (2000): 115–145.

Dennett, Daniel. *Consciousness Explained*. Boston: Little, Brown, and Co., 1991.

Endicott, Ronald. "Constructival Plasticity." *Philosophical Studies* 74 (1994): 51–75.

Heil, John. "Multiple Realizability." *American Philosophical Quarterly* 36 (1999): 189–208.

Johnson, Mark. *Brain Development and Cognition: A Reader*. Oxford: Oxford University Press, 1993.

King, Andrew. "Sensory Experience and the Formation of a Computational Map of Auditory Space in the Brain." *BioEssays* 21 (1999): 900–911.

Rauschecker, Josef. "Compensatory Plasticity and Sensory Substitution in the Cerebral Cortex." *Trends in Neurosciences* 18 (1995): 36–43.

Turing, Alan. "Computing Machinery and Intelligence." *Mind* 59 (1950): 433–460.

SUBSEQUENT DEBATE OVER IDENTITY AND REDUCTION

Bechtel, William, and Jennifer Mundale. "Multiple Realizability Revisited: Linking Cognitive and Neural States." *Philosophy of Science* 66 (1999): 175–207.

Bickle, John. *Psychoneural Reduction: The New Wave*. Cambridge, MA: MIT Press, 1998.

Block, Ned. "Anti-reductionism Slaps Back." *Philosophical Perspectives* 11 (1997): 107–132.

Churchland, Patricia. *Neurophilosophy: Toward a Unified Science of the Mind/Brain*. Cambridge, MA: MIT Press, 1986.

Churchland, Paul. *Scientific Realism and the Plasticity of Mind*. New York: Cambridge University Press, 1979.

Crick, Francis, and Christopher Koch. "Towards a Neurobiological Theory of Consciousness" (1990). In *The Nature of Consciousness*, edited by Ned Block, Owen Flanagan, and Guven Guzeldere, 277–292. Cambridge MA: MIT Press, 1997.

Endicott, Ronald. "Collapse of the New Wave." *Journal of Philosophy* 95 (1998): 53–72.

Endicott, Ronald. "Species-Specific Properties and More Narrow Reductive Strategies." *Erkenntnis* 38 (1993): 303–321.

Fodor, Jerry. "Special Sciences: Still Autonomous After All These Years," *Philosophical Perspectives* 11 (1997): 149–163.

Fodor, Jerry. "Special Sciences" (1974). In his *Representations: Philosophical Essays on the Foundations of Cognitive Science*, 127–145. Cambridge, MA: MIT Press, 1981.

Horgan, Terence. "Multiple Reference, Multiple Realization, and the Reduction of Mind." In *Reality and Humean Supervenience: Essays on the Philosophy of David Lewis*, edited by Gerhard Preyer and Frank Siebelt, 205–221. Landham, MD: Rowman and Littlefield, 2001.

Horgan, Terence. "Nonreductive Materialism and the Explanatory Autonomy of Psychology." In *Naturalism: A Critical Appraisal*, edited by Steven Wagner and Richard Warner, 295–320. Notre Dame, IN: University of Notre Dame Press, 1993.

Hull, David. *Philosophy of Biological Science*. Englewood Cliffs, NJ: Prentice-Hall, 1974.

Kim, Jaegwon. *Mind in a Physical World: An Essay on the Mind-Body Problem and Mental Causation*. Cambridge, MA: MIT Press, 1998.

Kim, Jaegwon. "Multiple Realization and the Metaphysics of Reduction" (1992). In his *Supervenience and Mind: Selected Philosophical Essays*, 309–335. London: Cambridge University Press, 1993.

Kim, Jaegwon. "Phenomenal Properties, Psychophysical Laws, and the Identity Theory." *Monist* 56 (1972): 177–192.

Lewis, David. Review of *Art, Mind, and Religion*. *Journal of Philosophy* 66 (1969): 23–35.

Marras, Ausonio. "Kim on Reduction." *Erkenntnis* 57 (2002): 231–257.

Pereboom, Derk, and Hilary Kornblith. "The Metaphysics of Irreducibility." *Philosophical Studies* 63 (1991): 125–145.

Putnam, Hilary. "The Nature of Mental States" (1967). In *Mind, Language, and Reality*. Vol. 2 of *Philosophical Papers*, 429–440. New York: Cambridge University Press, 1975.

Rosenberg, Alex. "On Multiple Realization and the Special Sciences." *Journal of Philosophy* 98 (2001): 365–373.

Sober, Elliot. "The Multiple Realizability Argument against Reductionism." *Philosophy of Science* 66 (1999): 542–564.

Teller, Paul. "Comments on Kim's Paper." *Southern Journal of Philosophy* 22, suppl. (1983): 57–61.

Ronald Endicott (1996, 2005)

MUQAMMIȘ, DAVID BEN MERWAN AL-

David ben Merwan al-Muqammiș was one of the first medieval Jews to respond to the philosophical challenge of Muslim rationalism. Nothing about his life is known with any certainty, but he probably flourished in the early years of the tenth century. According to the account given by the tenth-century Karaite historian Kirkisani, David al-Muqammiș was a native of Raqqa, in Mesopotamia.

Born into the Jewish faith, Kirkisani stated, al-Muqammiș became a Christian and then studied philosophy and theology at the well-known school of Nisibis, in Syria. Later, as reported by Kirkisani, he returned to Judaism but is supposed to have made good use of his Christian learning in his commentaries on Genesis and Ecclesiastes, which have been lost. In the latter part of the nineteenth century some quoted fragments of al-Muqammiș's philosophical work were discovered in Judah ben Barzilai's Hebrew "Commentary on the *Sefer Yezirah*" (early twelfth century). In addition, a substantial section of al-Muqammiș's major work, ʿ*Ishrūn maqālāt* (Twenty Chapters), in the original Arabic, was found by Abraham Harkavy in 1898 in the Russian Imperial Library at St. Petersburg, but it was never published.

This fragmentary and incomplete knowledge enables us to assert that al-Muqammiș's thought was deeply rationalistic, influenced in this direction by the Muʿtazilites (Arab theologians). His philosophy was, like theirs, generally cast in an Aristotelian mold, modified by some Neoplatonic elements. He shared with all Muslim philosophers a rigorous view of the divine unity; possibly it was the crystallization of this conviction that led to his rejection of Christianity and his return to Judaism. His discussion of the nature of the concept of unity as applied to God led him to distinguish between several ways of speaking about unity in ordinary language and to realize that none of these ways suggests what we mean in speaking of the unity of God, which is unique. More generally, al-Muqammiș argued, whenever we use the language of description we imply comparison and classification; however, God is incomparable and unclassifiable. Strictly, then, whether we speak of God in the language of the Bible or in that of philosophy, our language cannot be understood in any ordinary sense. If God is One, then each expression we use in speaking of him must be synonymous with every other expression. To use a variety of different expressions adds nothing, therefore, to our description of God. Al-Muqammiș suggested, however—anticipating Moses Maimonides in this suggestion—that although the different attributions add nothing positive, they do have the value of denying their antonyms.

In al-Muqammiș, then, we have the first suggestion in medieval Jewish philosophy of the theory of negative attributes. On other matters, such as the doctrine of rewards and punishments, al-Muqammiș seems to have had no difficulty in blending the traditional thought of the rabbis into his rational system.

See also Aristotelianism; Islamic Philosophy; Jewish Philosophy; Maimonides; Neoplatonism; Rationalism.

Bibliography

WORKS BY AL-MUQAMMIS

'Ishrūn maqālāt (Twenty Chapters), edited and translated by Sarah Stroumsa as Dawud ibn Marwan al-Muqammis's Twenty Chapters. Leiden: Brill, 1989.

WORKS ON AL-MUQAMMIS

Ben-Shammai, Haggai. "Kalam in Medieval Jewish Philosophy." In History of Jewish Philosophy, edited by D. Frank and O. Leaman. London: Routledge, 1997.

Blau, Joseph L. The Story of Jewish Philosophy. New York: Random House, 1962.

Husik, Isaac. History of Mediaeval Jewish Philosophy. New York: Macmillan, 1916.

"Muqammis." In Jewish Philosophy Reader, edited by D. Frank, O. Leaman, and C. Manekin. London: Routledge, 2000.

Stroumsa, Sarah. "Saadya and Jewish Kalam." In Cambridge Companion to Medieval Jewish Philosophy, edited by D. Frank and O. Leaman. Cambridge, U.K.: Cambridge University Press, 2003.

Vajda, Georges. Introduction à la pensée juive du moyen âge. Paris: Vrin, 1947.

Vajda, Georges. "Le probleme de l'unité de Dieu d'après Dawud ibn Marwan al-Muqammis." In Jewish Medieval and Renaissance Studies, edited by A. Altmann. Cambridge, MA: Harvard University Press, 1967.

J. L. Blau (1967)
Bibliography updated by Oliver Leaman (2005)

MURDOCH, IRIS
(1919–1999)

Iris Murdoch is best known to the world as a novelist—she wrote twenty-six—but she was a tutor in philosophy at Oxford University from 1948 until 1963 and wrote several influential essays on moral philosophy in the 1950s and 1960s. Her collection of three such essays, The Sovereignty of Good (1970), remains her most influential work. Her most sustained philosophical work is Metaphysics as a Guide to Morals (1993), a sprawling work ranging over an extraordinary range of topics and also a difficult work not enjoying the impact on philosophy of her earlier work. Murdoch also wrote on literature, religion, and art. Her thought is a unique appropriation of Platonic, Freudian, and existentialist themes.

Murdoch's thought emerged from, and against, British moral philosophy of the 1950s and 1960s (which she calls "linguistic philosophy"), perhaps best represented by Richard Hare's Language of Morals (though Murdoch does not mention Hare by name). This school of thought held that the techniques of linguistic analysis could illuminate moral concepts while remaining neutral regarding substantive moral views.

In "Sovereignty of Good over Other Concepts," Murdoch rejects this distinction. "Moral philosophy can not avoid taking sides and would-be neutral philosophers merely take sides surreptitiously" (Murdoch 1970, p. 78). British philosophy, Murdoch says, suggests that the moral life does not present us with moral concerns of great depth or urgency. Its behaviorist proclivity, implying that morality resides only in outer behavior, does away with the substantial inner life of the mind and, by implication, any notion of moral vision.

Murdoch was initially attracted to Jean-Paul Sartre's existentialism (she had met Sartre briefly in 1945) as a philosophy that one could actually live by and also as a philosophy that subjects individual consciousness to philosophical scrutiny. (In 1953 she published the critical but appreciative study Sartre: Romantic Rationalist.) Yet she came to feel that Sartre's moral philosophy was quite similar to linguistic philosophy in its faulty conception of moral agency and the moral life, despite the enormous differences in aspiration and mood in the two schools of philosophy. The "existentialist/behaviorist" view, as she frequently refers to the two views, sees the self as a solitary will and sees the core of moral agency as lying in the exertion of the will at the moment of choice. This solitary moral agency operates in a shared world of evaluatively neutral facts, with freedom as a central value, and confers value through choices.

Murdoch regards this conception of moral agency as entirely faulty. The moral agent perceives the world as saturated with value, and one's choosings arise almost automatically from how one antecedently perceives situations. Moral activity is not confined to outward behavior; seeing other persons in a just and accurate manner is moral activity, even if one never performs actions affecting such persons. Therefore, moral life does not sporadically occur only at moments of choice, but is pervades throughout the agent's existence, shaping the perceptions that issue in action. We erect structures of value around us, generally without recognizing that we are doing so.

Murdoch also chastises British moral philosophy for failing to focus centrally on how agents can morally improve—a task that she understood primarily as gaining a clear grasp of the moral reality outside themselves. To characterize the psychic process by which this is accomplished, Murdoch appropriates the term "attention" from Simone Weil, a French philosopher of the 1930s and 1940s who exerted a strong influence on her. By attending to the outer world, the moral agent becomes open and receptive to a reality other than oneself in a way uncontaminated by personal needs, fantasies, illusions, and the like. Murdoch sometimes speaks of attention as a kind of love and is critical of contemporary moral philosophy for leaving no room for love as a central moral notion.

Murdoch's conception of moral reality takes two somewhat distinct directions. The first is Platonic. (Plato is the philosopher Murdoch embraces most unambivalently.) On her Platonic conception, the ultimate moral reality is a transcendent Good, as she says in "On 'God' and 'Good',' a "single perfect transcendent non-representable and necessarily real object of attention"—a description that Murdoch draws partly from religion, though she explicitly rejects traditional theism (Murdoch 1970, p. 55). Murdoch thinks of the Good as something that can be contemplated, that exerts a kind of magnetic pull, and from which moral agents can draw a moral energy to overcome selfishness. She faults linguistic philosophy for discrediting metaphysics, which she sees as required for rendering the idea of the Good intelligible, an idea she develops further in *Metaphysics as a Guide to Morals*.

The second strand in Murdoch's conception of moral reality is particular other persons, especially those emotionally close to us, Murdoch's favored context for moral attention in her novels as well as her philosophy. "The fat, relentless ego" revealed by Freud, with its self-serving fantasies and illusions, presents daunting obstacles to apprehending moral reality. Murdoch is also pessimistic that by turning one's attention inward, one can identify and perhaps dispel one's particular psychic obstacles. Self-knowledge, she thinks, is largely a delusion.

Murdoch offers no systematic account of how to attain a state of attention, how to know the morally real, but she offers a few examples of things that can take us out of ourselves toward a reality external to us: art, natural beauty, prayer, a foreign language with its own logic, which cannot be distorted by personal wishes or fantasies. Her central example is art, especially literature. Good literature portrays human situations and human truth in an accessible form that provides readers a way to get outside themselves to a moral reality. Indeed, Murdoch sees the production of literature too as a moral task, a task in which authors must keep their own fantasies and illusions from distorting the creation of their characters. Murdoch's philosophy of art, inseparable from her moral philosophy, is developed in *The Fire and the Sun: Why Plato Banished the Artists* and in several essays.

Murdoch contributed to moral philosophy's greater attention to moral psychology (especially moral perception) since the 1970s, and she occasionally speaks of virtue. On the whole, however, Murdoch's work does not readily fit within any of the familiar schools of contemporary moral thought, and her insights and perspective remain a largely untapped resource and a formidable challenge to moral philosophy.

See also Moral Psychology; Sartre, Jean-Paul; Weil, Simone.

Bibliography

WORKS BY MURDOCH

Sartre: Romantic Rationalist. New Haven, CT: Yale University Press, 1953.

The Sovereignty of Good. London: Routledge and Kegan Paul, 1970.

The Fire and the Sun: Why Plato Banished the Artists. Oxford, U.K.: Clarendon Press, 1977.

Metaphysics as a Guide to Morals. New York: Penguin Books, 1993.

Existentialists and Mystics: Writings on Philosophy and Literature. New York: Penguin Books, 1998. A collection of all of Murdoch's nonfiction writings, including *The Sovereignty of Good*, but excluding *Metaphysics as a Guide to Morals* and *Sartre*.

WORKS ON MURDOCH

Antonaccio, Maria. *Picturing the Human: The Moral Thought of Iris Murdoch*. New York: Oxford University Press, 2000.

Antonaccio, Maria, and Schweiker, William, eds. *Iris Murdoch and the Search for Human Goodness*. Chicago: University of Chicago, 1996.

Blum, Lawrence. *Moral Perception and Particularity*. New York: Cambridge University Press, 1994. Several essays related to Murdoch's moral philosophy.

Broackes, Justin, ed. *Iris Murdoch, Philosopher*. New York: Oxford University Press, 2006.

Holland, Margaret. "Touching the Weights: Moral Perception and Attention." *International Philosophical Quarterly* 38 (3) (1998): 299–312.

Lawrence Blum (2005)

MURO KYŪSŌ
(1658–1734)

Muro Kyūsō was a Japanese Confucianist who was instrumental in defending the Zhu Xi school of Neo-Confucianism as the official learning of the Tokugawa government. Born in Edo (Tokyo), he was a pupil of Kinoshita Junan (1621–1698) in Kyoto. In 1711 he became, through the recommendation of the scholar-statesman Arai Hakuseki (1657–1725), the official scholar of the Tokugawa government. He was commissioned to compile the *Rikuyu engi-tai* (Outline of principles of Confucianism) that in 1724 became the standard textbook on Zhu Xi's doctrine for all official schools. Muro in his early years was not a follower of the Zhu Xi school; as he tells us in his *Shundai zatsuwa* (Conversations at Surugadai), it was only at the age of forty, after a long period of doubt, that he embraced Zhu Xi's thought. The doctrine was then under heavy attack by such of the "ancient learning" scholars as Yamaga Sokō, Itō Jinsai, and Ogyū Sorai. Muro believed he had been chosen to defend the teaching of Zhu Xi, and to this task he dedicated the rest of his life with unsparing zeal.

Muro's ideas are not strikingly original, but they have the power of sincerity and conviction. Typical are his denunciations of hypocrisy, a trait not so uncommon among formalist Confucians, and his insistence upon virtue as springing from the inner self; two of his favorite maxims were "Be true to the self" and "The root of evil lies in the innermost recesses of the mind." His ideas on the Godhead bear a similarity to the Christian conception of the attributes of God. The deity (or deities) is omnipresent and omniscient. He stressed self-vigilance and the realization of heavenly reason in human life. The heavenly order was to be reflected in the social one, thus consolidating the immutability of Tokugawa society. His sense of the indebtedness (*gi*) and the gratitude (*on*) man owes to Heaven, the earthly lord, the parent, and the teacher was bound to foster obedience rather than self-assertiveness. Muro opposed the scholars of the "ancient learning" school, who, with others, supported the emperor; Muro stood solidly for the Tokugawa government. He was also critical of Buddhism and Shinto. But the tide was against him; especially in vain was his effort to preserve the ancient spirit of the samurai who more and more assimilated into the merchant class.

See also Chinese Philosophy; Itō Jinsai; Japanese Philosophy; Ogyū Sorai; Virtue and Vice; Yamaga Sokō; Zhu Xi (Chu Hsi).

Bibliography

Muro's *Rikuyu engi-tai* (Outline of principles of Confucianism) was published in Kyoto in 1722. His *Shundai zatsuwa* (Conversations at Surugadai) is available in *Nihon rinri ihen* (Library on Japanese ethics; Tokyo, 1903), edited by Inoue Tetsujirō, Vol. VII, pp. 81–122; it has been translated by G. W. Knox as "A Japanese Philosopher," in *Transactions of the Asiatic Society of Japan* 20, Part I (1893): 28–133. See also W. T. de Bary, Ryusaku Tsunoda, and Donald Keene, eds., *Sources of Japanese Tradition* (New York: Columbia University Press, 1958), pp. 433–442.

Gino K. Piovesana, S.J. (1967)

MURPHY, ARTHUR EDWARD
(1901–1962)

Arthur Edward Murphy, an American philosopher, was the creator of the phrase "objective relativism." Murphy was born in Ithaca, New York, and received his training in philosophy at the University of California (A.B. in 1923, Ph.D. in 1926). He taught successively at California, Chicago, Brown, Illinois, Cornell, Washington, and Texas; at the last four he was department chairman.

Murphy attracted attention at an early age with his article "Objective Relativism in Dewey and Whitehead" (1927). He argued that the writings of these two influential philosophers exhibited a convergence on a common doctrine, which reversed a tradition of treating "objects as primary, as substantives, and events as characters of objects." In contrast, for John Dewey and Alfred North Whitehead "the event is substantive and objects are characters of events. Thus relatedness, in all its complexity and interconnections, is made basic for the objective world." Murphy, himself, supported this doctrine, which had a vogue for a time.

In 1930, however, Murphy attacked Whitehead's *Process and Reality* in his article "The Development of Whitehead's Philosophy." In later writings he repeatedly charged both Dewey and Whitehead, among other metaphysicians, with attempting to prove by speculative metaphysics what would better be offered as sheer speculation, to be tested in appropriate contexts. Commenting on Dewey, he wrote: "What Mr. Dewey says about cognition is true of it as he defines it and false of it as more ordinarily understood" ("Dewey's Epistemology and Metaphysics," in *The Philosophy of John Dewey*, edited by P. A. Schilpp, p. 210, Evanston and Chicago, 1939).

Throughout his career Murphy maintained an acquaintance with philosophers of varied opinions. As a graduate student on a traveling fellowship, he explored the philosophical currents of Europe in 1924–1925, when realism was at its height. During the 1930s his work as book editor of the *Journal of Philosophy* gave him occasion to examine and to pass judgment on the purpose and achievements of his generation and the previous one.

Murphy spent the year 1937–1938 in England, and from his remarks it is apparent that he was directly influenced by Ludwig Wittgenstein through reading the *Blue Book*, as well as indirectly through Wittgenstein's colleagues in England. He grew increasingly dissatisfied with speculative metaphysics, as may be seen in his contributions to the Dewey, G. E. Moore, and Whitehead volumes of the Library of Living Philosophers. His disillusionment with his own creation, objective relativism, is reported in "What Happened to Objective Relativism." Yet, to the end, it was his opinion that the speculative philosophers had opened roads to "a better understanding of the values that are basic to human life" than had most of the so-called analytic philosophers.

Murphy's strong convictions on the importance of philosophy in a liberal education led him to expend a great deal of time on the work of the Commission on Philosophy in American Education of the American Philosophical Association. His opinions on this subject are to be found in the chapters that he contributed to *Philosophy in American Education* (1945) and in his own essays.

Much of his work illustrates his expressed intent "to write philosophy … with explicit reference to contemporary issues" (*The Uses of Reason,* p. 5). His early concern with epistemology and metaphysics changed to a dominating preoccupation with the uses of reason in ethical and social enterprises. His last twenty years were directed toward the working out of a systematic account of ethics. Sketches of this attempt appear in the chapter, "The Context of Moral Judgment," in *The Uses of Reason,* and in his essays. Murphy made good use of his powers of assimilation and criticism in examining the great moralists with a view to extracting and identifying points that must be taken account of in any subsequently defensible ethical theory. At his death, he left a long manuscript, *The Theory of Practical Reason,* which elaborates his Carus Lectures of 1955, originally known as "An Enquiry concerning Moral Understanding."

See also Dewey, John; Epistemology; Ethics, History of; Metaphysics; Moore, George Edward; Philosophy of Education, History of; Realism; Whitehead, Alfred North; Wittgenstein, Ludwig Josef Johann.

Bibliography

Murphy's *The Uses of Reason* was published by Macmillan in New York in 1943. He contributed Chs. 2, 3, and 10 to *Philosophy in American Education* (New York: Harper, 1945). *Reason and the Common Good. Selected Essays of Arthur E. Murphy,* edited by W. H. Hay and M. G. Singer (Englewood Cliffs, NJ: Prentice Hall, 1963), includes a bibliography and the papers on objective relativism and Whitehead mentioned in this article. See also *The Theory of Practical Reason,* edited by A. I. Melden (La Salle, IL: Open Court, 1965).

William H. Hay (1967)

MUSIC, PHILOSOPHY OF

Since the veritable renaissance of aesthetics and philosophy of art in the 1960s, there has been a clear tendency to deal with the individual arts as presenting philosophical problems peculiar to themselves. This is not to say that philosophy of art in general has not also been pursued. Ambitious theories of art, attempting to encompass all of the fine arts in synoptic definitions, have occupied some of the best philosophical minds of the period, and brought much needed clarity and rigor to the discipline. But alongside of this more traditional, Socratic project there has flourished a busy community of philosophers exercising their analytic skills on the individual problems of arts such as literature, painting, dance, photography, cinema, drama, architecture, and, of course, music, the topic here.

MUSIC AND THE EMOTIONS

The oldest and most persistently scrutinized philosophical question with regard to music is the question of its emotive character. Plato expressed the view that music has the power to engender emotive states in the listener. Aristotle made the intriguing, though puzzling, suggestion that music "imitates" or represents the emotions. But we know little, if anything, about what their music sounded like. And without that knowledge we are at a loss to know what these philosophers were talking about, and consequently what they were really saying about it.

Modern speculation on this matter began at the beginning of the seventeenth century, when the inventors of opera began to speculate about music as the source of emotive expression in the newly minted dramatic form. But the problem did not take on the form in which contemporary aesthetics deals with it until, in the late eighteenth century, instrumental music emerged as a major musical genre and *the* major genre in the philosophy of music.

In the past seventy years, the question has taken a schematic form: What are we saying when we say "The music is *sad*"? Some answers have been that the music makes us sad; that the music expresses the composer's sadness; that the music somehow symbolizes or represents sadness; that the music possesses sadness as a perceptual quality, just as an apple possesses redness; some combination of the above; and finally, that the music just is *not* sad and it is nonsense to say that it is. The majority view, at the turn of the century, is that the emotive properties of music are perceived properties of it, although opinion is divided about whether it also *arouses* the emotions it is expressive of. Those who argue against arousal (Peter Kivy, for example), argue that emotions are aroused in ordinary life by beliefs formed about states of affairs, which the appropriate emotions then take as intentional objects, and that music cannot provide the necessary conditions for such arousal, nor is there evidence that listeners are so aroused. In contrast, those who argue for arousal (Stephen Davies and Jerrold Levinson) maintain that because the emotions aroused by music are not full-blooded emotions, but close enough to be taken for them, music does indeed have the power to arouse emotions, though these emotions do not give rise to the normal behavioral responses of real-life emotions.

FORMALISM

While the topic of music and the emotions has perhaps been the most talked about in music aesthetics since time out of mind, it is arguable that the vital center of philosophy of music has been, since the end of the eighteenth century, the debate over musical formalism. Immanuel Kant seemed to entertain no doubt that pure instrumental music, "absolute music," as it came to be called, was a purely formal art (although he acknowledged its emotive aspect), and because it lacked ideational content, he was reluctant to consider it one of the fine arts at all.

Arthur Schopenhauer pretty much settled the issue in favor of absolute music as a fine art. He did so by considering music a *representational* art form, and thus an art form conforming to the eighteenth-century dogma of *mimesis* (imitation). But the cost was heavy, for the cumbersome metaphysical underpinnings of his theory would hardly be countenanced by philosophers with modern philosophical sensibilities.

The first full-blown formalist account of absolute music, that of Eduard Hanslick (1825–1904), followed not too long after. In musical aesthetics, formalism, as Hanslick construed it and as it continued to be construed until the 1980s, is the doctrine that absolute music, as an art object, must be considered a purely formal structure in sound, with no emotive significance at all. But when some writers came to see that the emotive properties of music could themselves be construed as perceptual properties of music, they saw that a formalism with emotive properties as part of the formal structure is, in spirit, a formalism as well. This view has come to be called "enhanced formalism."

As things stand at the beginning of the twenty-first century, there are those, particularly in historical musicology, who find even enhanced formalism too pallid, and views of absolute music as a "narrative without words" are surfacing in great profusion. What had seemed to many to be an issue firmly settled in favor of formalism has now become an issue very much in doubt.

MUSICAL UNDERSTANDING

Closely related to the concept of musical form is that of musical understanding. Whether or not one is a formalist, one has to assume that understanding the pure musical fabric is a prerequisite for understanding anything beyond the pure fabric—narrative content, for example. In other words, one must hear what one is listening to as *music* before one can hear it as a story *in* music.

It is generally agreed that understanding music is a matter of hearing it as a *connected* series of events that makes musical sense to the listener. How this basic musical understanding is to be recognized and construed are contentious questions. Furthermore, there is substantial disagreement about whether or not musical understanding requires knowing and attending to the large structural elements of musical compositions and the musical techniques that may govern the connections between events. This disagreement extends to whether or not knowledge of what is known in the trade as music theory has any relevance to the appreciation and enjoyment of absolute music. In the 1990s these questions were hotly disputed. In *Music in the Moment*, Jerrold Levinson maintained that normal listening requires attention merely to the connections between short segments of musical texture present to immediate perception, in what he calls "quasi-hearing." In the opposite camp, Peter Kivy, in *Music Alone* and elsewhere, has argued that music-theoretical knowledge, though not essential to minimal musical understanding, enlarges the intentional object of musical understanding, thus increasing by orders of magnitude the satisfaction of the musical experience.

REPRESENTATION

The question of whether instrumental music is capable of anything like pictorial representation is not high on the list of questions that philosophers of music at the beginning of the twenty-first century concern themselves with, although in the heyday of nineteenth-century Romanticism it was much discussed as a matter of "practical" music aesthetics and was closely associated with the issue of absolute versus program music. There are those who claim that music in principle cannot pictorially represent but can only imitate sounds, which is obviously a very different matter. Others maintain that there are instances of pictorial representation in music, although of a very minimal kind. Those committed to more or less elaborate narrative interpretations of the canon of absolute music are committed, at least implicitly, to some more liberal view of music's representational capacities, although little philosophical light on the issue has been forthcoming from that quarter.

WORDS AND MUSIC

As questions in musical practice, how words are set to music and what role words and music play in this give-and-take enterprise have been argued vigorously, sometimes acrimoniously, since the last half of the sixteenth century, with opera as the major motivating force. Whether these are philosophical questions is debatable. Nonetheless, in the literature after 1990 those who *do* think of themselves as philosophers have shown an increase in interest in opera as an art form worthy of separate scrutiny. Among the issues raised have been whether opera is basically a musical form or a literary form with music, how we are rationally to understand a drama with characters who sing rather than speak, how drama can accommodate itself to musical form, how we are to understand, on rational grounds, the ubiquitous orchestral presence in the sung drama, and what capacity the music in opera has of "saying" things, beyond the capacity of the libretto to do so. These debates have blurred, in an intellectually healthy way, the boundaries between philosophy and various musical disciplines. At the same time, those outside both the philosophical and musical academic communities have made substantial contributions to the philosophical discourse.

Perhaps the central philosophical issue in the words-music debate is best revealed by the title that Joseph Kerman, a musicologist by trade, gave to his groundbreaking, widely admired book *Opera as Drama*. On Kerman's view, opera is to be viewed, at its best, as principally a form of drama, *dramma per musica*, in the venerable Latin phrase. Taking the opposite view, Peter Kivy, in *Osmin's Rage*, has put the emphasis, not on opera as *drama*, but rather on opera as *music*, drama-made-music, as he terms it.

THE WORK

Whatever one may think about the philosophical credentials of some of the questions that philosophers of music interest themselves in, the question of the ontological status of the musical work seems unequivocally philosophical. Who *else* but a philosopher, it might well be asked, would raise such a question, or be interested in the answer?

Musical ontology emerged in the 1960s in the form of two opposing answers to the question, What is a musical work? The term "art object" clearly suggests the kind of artwork that can, at least on first reflection, be identified with a physical object, locatable in space and time. But if the "object" in question is a musical work, it seems clear that it is not located anywhere. The *Mona Lisa* is in the Louvre. Where is Beethoven's *Fifth Symphony*?

Nevertheless, there are physical objects, broadly speaking, associated with musical works, namely their performances. One direction in which musical ontology went was the Platonic direction, taking musical works as universals or types, performances as their instances or tokens. The other direction, eschewing the specter of timeless, nonphysical Platonic entities, identified the musical work with the class of its performances. Both directions have problems, but the Platonic model, somewhat surprisingly, has been the one most exploited.

The major problem of musical Platonism has been the apparent conflict between two basic intuitions. Platonic entities are timeless, and hence cannot have come into being, whereas musical works do indeed come into being, are created, through the labor and inspiration of their composers. Platonists of the more doctrinaire kind have tried to argue that we can preserve our notion of composers as inspired, "creative" artists, in some sense or other, while biting the Platonic bullet and affirming that musical works are discovered rather than brought into being. Other, more moderate Platonists have opted for a kind of universal or type that comes into being in the composer's creative act but, in other respects, preserves the character of a Platonic universal or type so as to make the universal/particular or type/token distinction suitable for what they want to say about the relation between works and their performances. The latter approach seems to be more popular at the beginning of the twenty-first century, while the attempt to identify works with classes of their performances seems just about dead in the water.

THE PERFORMANCE

Since the most popular analyses of the musical work construe it as some kind of universal, with performances as the particulars, one would expect a substantial literature on musical performance. But until the late 1990s, this had not been so, it being assumed that performers and performances are philosophically transparent, presenting no conceptual puzzles. Then in the 1990s a movement in the *practical* world of performer and performance, the movement for so-called "historically authentic performances," began to generate considerable interest among philosophers in the relation between performance and work, performer and composer. The historicist project in musicology, so long directed at establishing musical texts that are historically authentic, became, in the 1990s, directed as well at the historical authenticity of the musical performance of that authenticated text, the practical result being that more and more performances of music composed prior to the nineteenth century are attempts to reproduce, both physically and in interpretation, the kind of performance that the composer himself had in mind when he composed it.

After the turn of the century, philosophers began to cast an analytic eye on the concept of the historically authentic performance and on the aesthetic imperative that supposedly drives it. What is a historically authentic performance? One that reproduces a physical object or an intentional one? Does the integrity of the musical text require a historically authentic performance, or does the text survive an unabashedly modern one? Is the performer an artist in his own right, as tradition would have it, or is he the composer's machine? Is there an ideal performance of a work, and is it the historically authentic one? These questions have begun to generate articles and books of interest not only to the philosophical community but also to the musical community as well. Moreover, what the musical community has written about performance is now undergoing philosophical scrutiny. The results are not yet in.

THE REWARDS OF LISTENING

Finally, what contribution of value does the art of absolute music make to the human experience. What kind of satisfaction does it provide? Schopenhauer argued that since absolute music satisfies in the same manner as the other fine arts, which are unquestionably representational arts, absolute music too must be a representational art. He then cast about for an object that absolute music might represent, fixing on the metaphysical will—a result that few today would find plausible. Be that as it may, those who interpret the absolute-music canon in narrative terms are implicitly committed to Schopenhauer's general argument, if not to his conclusion about music's relation to the will. For the quest for stories in symphonies assumes that the satisfaction provided by such music requires an account, and since the satisfaction of temporal art forms lies in their story-telling capacity, the same must be true for the temporal art of absolute music. (Schopenhauer himself, however, does not carry his argument to this extreme.)

Formalists, of course, must find other sources for the value and satisfaction of absolute music. One answer, distinctly in the spirit of Schopenhauer, is that absolute music provides a kind of escape, a liberation from the world, from this veil of tears, into a world of pure sonic forms. The narrative and representational arts, anchored in this world as they are, cannot provide this liberation. Another answer simply rejects the question. There is no mystery about the satisfactions of absolute music. They lie simply in all the components of absolute music that music critics, analysts, and theorists talk about. It is obvious why these components please us. No further answer, it is claimed, is either needed or available.

Is the satisfaction of absolute music a mystery or a pseudomystery? Whatever the answer, absolute music, since the mid-1950s, has become a topic of intense interest in the philosophy of art, and the philosophy of music has become a recognized subdiscipline of the field. The interest shows no signs of abating.

See also Aesthetics, History of; Art, Definitions of; Art, Expression in; Art, Formalism in; Art, Ontology of; Art, Representation in; Art, Style and Genre in.

Bibliography

MUSIC AND THE EMOTIONS

Aristotle. *Politics*. In *The Complete Works of Aristotle: The Revised Oxford Translation*, edited by Jonathan Barnes. Princeton, NJ: Princeton University Press, 1984. Book 8, chapter 5.

Davies, Stephen. *Musical Meaning and Expression*. Ithaca, NY: Cornell University Press, 1994. Chapters 4–6.

Hanslick, Eduard. *On the Musically Beautiful*. Translated by Geoffrey Payzant. Indianapolis, IN: Hackett, 1986. Chapters 1, 2, and 4.

Kivy, Peter. *The Corded Shell: Reflections on Musical Expression*. Princeton, NJ: Princeton University Press, 1980.

Langer, Susanne K. *Philosophy in a New Key*. New York: Mentor Books, 1959. Chapter 8.

Levinson, Jerrold. *Music, Art, and Metaphysics*. Ithaca, NY: Cornell University Press, 1990. Chapter 13.

Levinson, Jerrold. *The Pleasures of Aesthetics*. Ithaca, NY: Cornell University Press, 1996. Chapter 6.

Plato. *Republic*. In *The Collected Dialogues of Plato*. Princeton, NJ: Princeton University Press, 1963. Books 3 and 10.

Pratt, Carroll C. *The Meaning of Music*. New York: McGraw-Hill, 1932.

Strunk, Oliver, ed. *Source Readings in Music History: From Classical Antiquity through the Romantic Era*. New York: Norton, 1950. Section 8.

FORMALISM

Gurney, Edmund. *The Power of Sound*. London: Smith, Elder, 1880.

Hanslick, Eduard. *On the Musically Beautiful*. Translated by Geoffrey Payzant. Indianapolis, IN: Hackett, 1986. Chapter 3.

Kivy, Peter. *The Fine Art of Repetition*. Cambridge, U.K.: Cambridge University Press, 1993. Chapters 18 and 19.

Kivy, Peter. *Music Alone: Philosophical Reflections on the Purely Musical Experience*. Ithaca, NY: Cornell University Press, 1990.

McClary, Susan. *Feminine Endings: Music, Gender, and Sexuality*. Minneapolis: University of Minnesota Press, 1991. Chapter 3.

Meyer, Leonard. *Emotion and Meaning in Music*. Chicago: University of Chicago Press, 1956.

Newcomb, Anthony. "Once More 'Between Absolute and Program Music': Schumann's Second Symphony." *Nineteenth-Century Music* 7 (1984): 233–250.

MUSICAL UNDERSTANDING

Kivy, Peter. *Music Alone: Philosophical Reflections on the Purely Musical Experience*. Ithaca, NY: Cornell University Press, 1990. Chapter 6.

Levinson, Jerrold. *Music in the Moment*. Ithaca, NY: Cornell University Press, 1997.

Tanner, Michael. "Understanding Music." *Proceedings of the Aristotelian Society*, supp. vol. 59.

REPRESENTATION

Kivy, Peter. *Sound and Semblance: Reflections on Musical Representation*. Princeton, NJ: Princeton University Press, 1984.

Robinson, Jenefer. "Music as a Representational Art." In *What Is Music?* edited by Philip Alperson. University Park: Pennsylvania State University Press, 1994. Chapter 6.

Scruton, Roger. "Representation in Music." *Philosophy* 51 (1976).

WORDS AND MUSIC

Kerman, Joseph. *Opera as Drama*. New York: Vintage Books, 1956.

Kivy, Peter. *Osmin's Rage: Philosophical Reflections on Opera, Drama, and Text*. Princeton, NJ: Princeton University Press, 1988.

Levinson, Jerrold. *The Pleasures of Aesthetics*. Ithaca, NY: Cornell University Press, 1996. Chapter 4.

Robinson, Paul. *Opera and Ideas from Mozart to Strauss*. New York: Harper and Row, 1985.

THE WORK

Goodman, Nelson. *Languages of Art: An Approach to a Theory of Symbols*. Indianapolis, IN: Bobbs-Merrill, 1968. Chapters 4 and 5.

Ingarden, Roman. *The Work of Music and the Problem of Its Identity*. Translated by Adam Czerniawski. Berkeley: University of California Press, 1986.

Kivy, Peter. *The Fine Art of Repetition*. Cambridge, U.K.: Cambridge University Press, 1993. Chapters 2–4.

Levinson, Jerrold. *Music, Art, and Metaphysics*. Ithaca, NY: Cornell University Press, 1990. Chapters 4 and 10.

Wollheim, Richard. *Art and Its Objects: An Introduction to Aesthetics*. New York: Harper and Row, 1968. Sections 1–39.

Wolterstorff, Nicholas. *Works and Worlds of Art*. Oxford: Clarendon Press, 1980. Part 2.

THE PERFORMANCE

Davies, Stephen. *Musical Works and Performances: A Philosophical Exploration*. Oxford: Clarendon Press, 2001.

Dipert, Randall R. "The Composer's Intentions: An Evaluation of Their Relevance for Performance." *Musical Quarterly* 66 (1980).

Godlovitch, Stan. *Musical Performance: A Philosophical Study*. London: Routledge, 1998.

Kivy, Peter. *Authenticities: Philosophical Reflections on Musical Performance*. Ithaca: Cornell University Press, 1995.

THE REWARDS OF LISTENING

Budd, Malcolm. *Values of Art: Pictures, Poetry, and Music*. London: Penguin Books, 1995.

Kivy, Peter. *Philosophies of Arts: An Essay in Differences*. Cambridge, U.K.: Cambridge University Press, 1997. Chapter 7.

Peter Kivy (2005)

MUSLIM PHILOSOPHY

See *Islamic Philosophy*

MUSONIUS RUFUS
(30–100 CE?)

Musonius Rufus belongs to a group of Roman Stoic thinkers that also includes Seneca and Marcus Aurelius. He was Epictetus's teacher. Only fragmentary accounts of his views, recorded by others, have survived (English translation in the edition by Cora Lutz).

Like other Stoics, Musonius rejects the distinction between theoretical and practical wisdom: philosophy is nothing else but to practice and put in good deeds what Stoic doctrine prescribes. All human beings have the potential to strive towards virtue. This view is anchored in a radically embedded concept of human nature: a human is a composite of soul and body and a member of the universe's community of gods and men, the so-called cosmopolis. Musonius reinforces this ontological embeddedness by emphasizing social responsibility in general, in existing communities of human beings.

Musonius is perhaps best known for his positive views on women (fragments 3 and 4): Both men and women have the same intellectual and moral capacities, and hence women should be educated in philosophy just as men are. But it is equally important that this stance has a social corollary in Musonius's highly positive assessment of marriage as a symmetrical and fully reciprocal relationship among equals that entails a union of soul as well as of body (fragments 12, 13 A and B, 14). Thus

Musonius represents a Stoicism that upgrades traditional relationships such as marriage to the level of philosophically inspired friendship between men.

The importance of social responsibility is also evident in Musonius's views on suicide. As fragment 29 states, "One who by living is of use to many has not the right to choose to die unless by dying he may be of use to more" (tr. Lutz). Hence the concern for others ought to be central in one's decision-making process.

Other themes in the preserved fragments reflect on the need for a king to be a philosopher, on the duties of parenthood, on curtailing one's bodily and material wants, and on patience with and forgiveness of people who have wronged one. Rudolf Hirzel (1895, 2: 239) dubbed Musonius "the Roman Socrates."

See also Epictetus; Stoicism.

Bibliography

Geytenbeek, A. C. van. *Musonius Rufus and Greek Diatribe.* Translated by B. L. Hijmans Jr. Assen, Netherlands: van Gorcum, 1963.

Hirzel, Rudolf. *Der Dialog, ein literarhistorischer Versuch.* 2 vols. Leipzig: S. Hirzel, 1895.

Lutz, Cora Elizabeth. *Musonius Rufus, "The Roman Socrates."* New Haven, CT: Yale University Press, 1947.

Nussbaum, Martha C. "The Incomplete Feminism of Musonius Rufus, Platonist, Stoic, and Roman." In *The Sleep of Reason. Erotic Experience and Sexual Ethics in Ancient Greece and Rome,* edited by Martha C. Nussbaum and Juha Sihvola. Chicago: University of Chicago Press, 2002. 283–326.

Reydams-Schils, Gretchen J. *The Roman Stoics: Self. Responsibility, and Affection.* Chicago: University of Chicago Press, 2005.

Gretchen J. Reydams-Schils (2005)

MYSTICISM, HISTORY OF

Mystical experience is a major form of religious experience, but it is hard to delineate by a simple definition for two main reasons. First, mystics often describe their experiences partly in terms of doctrines presupposed to be true, and there is no one set of doctrines invariably associated with mysticism. Some of the definitions of mysticism advanced by Western writers are quoted by W. R. Inge in his *Mysticism in Religion* (p. 25): "Mysticism is the immediate feeling of the unity of the self with God" (Otto Pfleiderer); "Mysticism is that attitude of mind in which all relations are swallowed up in the relation of the soul to God" (Edward Caird); "True mysticism is the conscious-

ness that everything that we experience is an element and only an element in fact, i.e. that in being what it is, it is symbolic of something else" (Richard Nettleship). Quite clearly, such definitions import a religious and philosophical interpretation to the phenomenon of mysticism that would not be shared by all contemplatives. For instance, the Buddhist mystic, not believing in a personal God, would reject the first two of these definitions; and he might well be skeptical about the third—in what sense is the experience of nirvāṇa symbolic of something else?

Second, there is quite a difference between mystical experience and prophetic and, more generally, numinous experience, but it is not easy to bring out this phenomenological fact in a short definition. (A numinous experience is an experience of a dynamic external presence—described classically in Rudolf Otto's *The Idea of the Holy* as that of a *mysterium tremendum et fascinans,* an awe-inspiring and fascinating mystery.) Sidney Spencer says, for instance, "What is characteristic of the mystics is the claim which they make to an immediate contact with the Transcendent" (*Mysticism in World Religion,* p. 9). Such a definition includes under mysticism the experiences of the Old Testament prophets, those of Muḥammad, and the theophany described in the *Bhagavad-Gītā.* However, these differ so markedly from the interior illumination of such figures as Meister Eckhart, Teresa of Ávila, Śankara, and the Buddha that it is misleading to bracket the two kinds of experience. This article will explicitly exclude the prophetic and numinous experience, save where it becomes relevant to the experiences and doctrines of those properly called mystics. It is thus best to indicate what is meant by "mysticism" by referring to examples, such as Eckhart and the others cited above, and by sketching some of the important features of the type of experience in question without interpreting it doctrinally.

Generally, mystics as typified by Eckhart, Teresa of Ávila, Śankara, and the Buddha feel that their experience is somehow timeless, that it involves an apprehension of the transcendent (of some thing, state, or person lying beyond the realm of things), that it gives them bliss or serenity, and that it normally accrues upon a course of self-mastery and contemplation. These are certainly features of what has been called introvertive mysticism by W. T. Stace (*Mysticism and Philosophy,* p. 60). There are other experiences, however; those of extrovertive mysticism, where, according to R. C. Zaehner, one gains a kind of rapport with the world, or "panenhenic" feeling (*Mysticism Sacred and Profane,* Ch. 1). These neither coincide with prophetic experiences nor strictly with those of introvertive mysticism, but since they sometimes occur in conjunction with the latter, it is convenient to treat them as mystical. Various abnormal mental states, such as those induced by mescaline, lysergic acid, and alcohol are sometimes considered mystical, but they are far enough removed from mainstream mysticism for it to be reasonable to neglect them here.

In the light of all this, we can distinguish various aspects of mysticism: The experiences themselves, the paths or systems of contemplative techniques often associated with them, and the doctrines that arise from mysticism or are affected by it. Also, such paranormal phenomena as levitation are sometimes ascribed to mystics, although they usually regard these as of secondary significance.

There is no single history of mysticism because some of the major religious traditions have been largely independent of one another. Further, there is no way of knowing the real origins of mysticism, since for such an intimate type of experience we must rely chiefly on written records and thus have no access to prehistoric mysticism. Studies of contemporary nonliterate cultures—in Africa, for instance—do not reveal the presence of much or any mysticism proper; for example, the religious experiences of the Nuer in the Sudan are more akin to those of Old Testament prophecy. It is thus convenient to confine attention to the main literate religious traditions: Indian religions (Hinduism, Buddhism, Jainism, Sikhism); Chinese and Japanese religions; and the Semitic faiths (Judaism, Christianity, and Islam). It may be noted that early Christian mysticism was influenced by Greek, notably Platonist, ideas.

THE INDIAN TRADITION

The mainstream of Indian mysticism centers on the practice of yoga, which in its general sense involves techniques of pacifying the mind and of attaining interior insight. Evidence from the pre-Aryan Indus Valley civilization indicates that it may have been practiced in the second millennium BCE or earlier. By contrast, the religion of the Aryans who settled in north India centered on sacrifice set in a polytheistic framework. As this ritual religion became more complex, questions arose concerning the inner meaning of the sacrificial rites. The *Upaniṣads* (the chief of which date from about 800 BCE to about 500 BCE) were in part concerned with extending and deepening sacrificial ideas in the quest for *vidyā*, or knowledge of sacred reality. Quasi-magical ideas surrounded this notion—for instance, that knowledge gives power over the thing known and that one can become identified with

the thing known. At the same time, mystical ideas began to permeate religious thinking, notably the idea that through austerity and self-control one could attain a realization of one's eternal self. A confluence of these streams of religious thought resulted in the famous central identification expressed in the *Upaniṣads,* "That art thou"; the sacred reality embracing and sustaining the cosmos ("That") and the eternal self ("thou") are one. In brief, inner mystical knowledge brings a union with the Divine.

This union is described in various ways: "Just as a man embraced by his dear wife knows nothing at all, outside or inside, so does the eternal life-monad [*puruṣa*], embraced by the supreme spiritual Self, know nothing at all, outside or inside" (*Bṛhadāraṇyaka Upaniṣad*, IV. 3.21); "As rivers flow to their rest in the ocean and there leave behind them name and form, so the knower, liberated from name and form, reaches that divine Person beyond the beyond" (*Chāndogya Upaniṣad,* 6). Sometimes the lack of duality between the divine Being and the soul is stressed: "Where there is a duality, as it were, one sees another, tastes another, speaks to another.... But when everything has become one's own self then whom and how would one see? ... The Self is not this, not that" (*Bṛhadāraṇyaka Upaniṣad*, IV. 5.15). Mystical consciousness is also said to be like a state beyond dreamless sleep. These passages hint at what is virtually universal throughout Indian yoga, the fact that the contemplative state in its highest form involves going beyond ordinary perceptions, mental images, and thoughts. It is thus not describable by the ordinary expressions for mental states. It is no doubt partly for this reason that the distinction between perceiver and perceived is not regarded as applicable, and so the contemplative who conceives himself as "seeing" *Brahman* (the divine Being) thinks of this as a kind of union with *Brahman*. By contrast, in atheistic systems of Indian religion, where there is nothing for the self to be identified *with,* the contemplative state is conceived in a rather different way.

Although identification between the self and *Brahman* is a central theme in Upaniṣadic religion, some of the writings, notably the *Kaṭha* and the *Śvetāśvatara Upaniṣads,* are more theistic in spirit and less inclined to speak in terms of identification. These differences of emphasis are partly the reason for the divergences in interpretation found in different types of Vedānta in the medieval period.

JAINISM AND YOGA. Jainism, Buddhism, and the tradition later formulated as classical yoga involved an atheistic or agnostic interpretation of mystical experience.

Jainism and classical yoga (the long-extinct Ājīvika school) were monadistic: They believed in an infinity of eternal life monads or souls, and the aim of the ascetic was to bring about the isolation of the soul from its material environment. Such an isolation would involve the cessation of reincarnation and thus final deliverance from suffering. Jainism, because it held that karma, the force determining people's situations as a result of their previous deeds, is a subtle form of matter, considered extreme *tapas* (austerity), which had the effect of annihilating this material force, the central means of liberation. Nevertheless, it seems that the Jain teacher Vardhamāna (known also as Mahāvīra), a contemporary of the Buddha, and his disciples claimed to attain a certain kind of higher state analogous to the experience of nirvāṇa in Buddhism. Thus, in Jain doctrine the life monad in its emancipated state gains omniscience, a concept reflecting the intense sense of insight accruing upon the contemplative experience.

BUDDHISM. The accounts of the Buddha's enlightenment—a crucial event in the history of Indian religion and likewise centrally important in the history of Indian mysticism—are elaborate and circumstantial. During the first night, the Buddha, seated under the bo tree, remembered the series of his former births; during the second, he acquired the "heavenly eye," which enabled him to view the entire world and the whole cyclical process of rebirth; during the third, he saw how the latter depended upon grasping and ignorance—if living beings were liberated from these, they would escape rebirth; and in the fourth, he attained supreme insight after going through the various stages of meditation (Sanskrit, *dhyāna*; Pāli, *jhāna*). In all this he gained supreme peace. No doubt the scriptural records are a formalized account, hardly based on the Buddha's autobiographical report, but they certainly point to the type of inner experience early Buddhism prized. Something can be learned from the *Theragāthā* and *Therīgāthā*, verses composed by monks and nuns and expressing the flavor of early Buddhist contemplative experience. These poems often show the sensitivity of the recluse to the beauty of nature:

The peacocks shriek. Ah, the lovely crests
   and tails
And the sweet sound of the blue-throated
   peacocks.
The great grassy plain with water now
Beneath the thunder-clouded sky.
   Your body is fresh; you are vigorous now and fit
To test the teaching. Reach now for that
   saintly rapture,

So bright, so pure, so hard to fathom,
The highest, the eternal place.

(*THERAGĀTHĀ* CLXVI)

The eternal place is, of course, nirvāṇa.

The achievement of inner peace and insight, as opposed to the use of complex psychological categories in explaining human nature, was given comparatively little doctrinal elaboration in early Buddhism because the Buddha apparently felt that the concepts of the transcendent state (nirvāṇa) and the cessation of rebirth through the perception or attainment of nirvāṇa were sufficient means of interpreting mystical experience. Certainly, he did not give the more elaborate type of interpretation found in the *Upaniṣads* and in theistic mysticism. It is clear, however, that the experience or experiences involved both the attainment of a marvelous serenity and a kind of knowledge or insight (something regarded as knowledge, given the presuppositions of the Buddhist mystical quest). Grasping and ignorance are dispelled by this peace and knowledge.

Buddhism rejected the doctrine of a plurality of eternal souls, but in a sense it can be seen as a transcendence of monadism, with the concept of the eternal soul replaced by that of the capacity to attain release. Thus early Indian mysticism is typically monadistic, except in the *Upaniṣads*, where the interior experience is related to the *Brahman* and where, therefore, the *Brahman-ātman* (self) equation is formulated. Only because the eternal self of the mystic is identified with the presupposedly single divine Being is the plurality of souls denied. The numinous religion of Brahmanism overlays that of the contemplative mysticism of yoga, and the mystical experience is interpreted in terms of union with the unitary divine Principle.

Mahāyāna Buddhism, from the first century BCE on, moved toward a more elaborate interpretation of the contemplative path. Nirvāṇa was identified with the Absolute, variously named Suchness (*tathatā*) and the void (*śūnya*). These terms served to bring out the ineffability and undifferentiated nature of ultimate reality, which in turn corresponded to the undifferentiated and "void" nature of the contemplative experience itself. The Absolute was also identified, from the standpoint of the ordinary worshipers, with the Truth Body of the Buddhas—the transcendent and essential aspect of buddhahood—and thus the mystical path involved being a bodhisattva (buddha-to-be). The distinctionless, nondual experience of ultimate reality, the goal of the path, was the achievement of identity with the Absolute, which was equated with buddhahood. This is why the Mahāyāna path of contemplation was thought of as the path of bodhisattvahood, so that on his enlightenment the mystic would himself become a buddha.

As a preliminary, the aspirant practices individual worship (*pūjā*) of the celestial buddhas and bodhisattvas and can gain assurance from a living buddha that his aspiration to buddhahood will be fulfilled. He practices the perfections of the path, culminating in supreme wisdom or insight (*prajñā*).

There are three chief differences between Mahāyāna and Hīnayāna, now represented by the Theravāda (in Myanmar, Sri Lanka, and parts of Southeast Asia). First, the Mahāyāna stresses self-giving more strongly, so that the aspirant continually looks to the welfare of others; second, it is a path accessible to laymen as well as to monks; third, contemplation is supplemented by the use of sacramental and ritual practices, at least in certain phases of the Mahāyāna. Some of these practices, known as tantra, became well developed in the middle of the first millennium CE in both Hinduism and Buddhism and deeply affected the Buddhism of Tibet. It sometimes involved the ritual breaking of taboos (against meat-eating and against sexual intercourse outside marriage): Such a breaking of taboos was regarded as a means of testing and developing detachment. Coordinate with this type of Buddhism was a highly ritualistic use of sacred texts and recitations. The most outstanding figure of Tibetan mysticism was the poet and yogi Milarepa (1040–1123).

HINDUISM. The theistic religion implicit in some of the *Upaniṣads,* reinforced by popular cults and by an emphasis on *bhakti,* or loving adoration of God, led to a different valuation of mysticism in the *Bhagavad-Gītā.* The poem speaks of three paths to salvation: the way of knowledge (primarily contemplative knowledge), the way of works, and the way of devotion (*bhakti*). The three paths are stressed in different parts of the *Gītā,* but two significant lessons emerge. First, the pursuit of works (religious and moral duties) need not bind one to the world if they are performed in a spirit of self-surrender to God; the way of works should be seen in the light of the way of devotion. Second, the yogi who pursues knowledge (*jnana*) can become *Brahman* (VI.27). Elsewhere, however, *Brahman* is spoken of as part of God; the personal aspect of God is more important than his impersonal aspect. Thus the yogi, in pursuing a strictly contemplative path, can only unite himself with the lower, rather than the more important, aspect of the

Lord's nature. This doctrine represented a higher evaluation of *bhakti* than of contemplative yoga. (It must be pointed out that traditional Indian commentators are divided on the question of what is the correct interpretation of the *Gītā.* However, there is little doubt that extraneous theological and philosophical presuppositions have played a large part in determining interpretations.)

The continued growth of devotional or *bhakti* religion led to a similar interpretation of mysticism during the medieval period. Thus, in the twelfth century Rāmānuja reversed the doctrinal priorities of Śankara (ninth century). Śankara's monism represented the most radical interpretation of the Upaniṣadic identity texts, asserting a numerical identity between the soul and the divine Being. While for Śankara the personal Lord was a lower manifestation of the Absolute, so that worship and devotion could be transcended when one had attained the apprehension of identity with Brahman, Rāmānuja, although recognizing identity as one religious goal, conceived it as an inferior form of release. The higher form was the vision of the personal God, in which the soul was in a state of loving dependence on the Lord. Both Madhva (thirteenth century) and the theistic Śaivite schools of Indian philosophy interpreted mystical experience in terms of union with God, but not a union involving the numerical identity of the soul and God. Thus, mystical experience was interpreted by reference to the duality of the soul and God implicit in the religion of *bhakti*: The worshiper has a strong sense of the majesty and glory of God, and thus of the difference between himself and the object of worship. Various analogies were used, including that of the marriage of the soul and God, since sexual love symbolizes the intimate union between the lover and the beloved while presupposing the difference between the two. This analogy tied in with the cult of Krishna: The legend of Krishna's amorous dalliance with the milkmaids was seen as an allegory of the relation between God and men's souls.

The interiorization of religion involved in both devotionalism and contemplation influenced Nānak (1469–1538), founder of the Sikh religion, who preached doctrines combining the anti-idolatrous monotheism of Islam and such characteristic Hindu ideas as reincarnation and karma.

There have been a number of outstanding contemplatives in modern Hinduism. Chief among them was Ramakrishna Paramahamsa (1834–1886), whose disciple Vivekananda (1862–1902) did much to popularize his teachings in both the East and the West; Vivekananda's organizing ability was chiefly responsible for the flourishing state of the Ramakrishna movement, in which the contemplative life is geared to social service and also provides a pattern of living that can, according to the teachings of the movement, transcend the differences between the great living faiths. A twentieth-century mystic who tried to adapt traditional teachings to modern thought was Aurobindo. Contemplation and yoga, through the activities of numerous recluses, holy men, and gurus, continue to play a prominent role in Indian religion.

CHINA AND JAPAN

Chinese mysticism has two main sources, Daoism and Buddhism. A product of their interaction was Ch'ān, better known under its Japanese name, Zen. The teachings of Confucius were not much concerned with the contemplative quest for inner illumination, although certain mystical ideas were expressed in the *Book of Mencius* of the Confucian tradition. On the whole, however, early Confucianism was indifferent to the contemplative ideal.

DAOISM. The chief early mystical writing in China was the *Dao-de-jing,* traditionally ascribed to Laozi, who is thought to have been an older contemporary of Confucius. It is likely, however, not only that the book was later but also that it was the work of several men. The anthology expresses a roughly consistent viewpoint, one that, on the most natural account of it, has its roots in contemplation (although some commentators give it a nonmystical interpretation).

The Way, or Dao, referred to in the *Dao-de-jing* is both a principle underlying natural processes and a mode of life whereby the sage can gain identity or harmony with nature. Since nature acts spontaneously and effortlessly, the book claims that the sage likewise can be effective through inaction (*wu-wei*) and effortlessness. Thus, the pattern of life suggested is one of withdrawal and passivity. In these themes the *Dao-de-jing* reflects some of those found elsewhere in mystical literature: The sense of identification with the Principle (*li*) underlying the world and the need for an unworldly mode of existence. Because the attainment of harmony with Dao was seen as living in accord with nature, the Daoists reacted against what they considered the artificialities of social life and etiquette as practiced by the Confucians, and from the doctrine of *wu-wei* they derived political views not far from anarchism.

In practice the effortlessness of the Daoist contemplative was modified by the use of techniques of meditation, such as controlled breathing, analogous to those employed in Indian yoga. The Daoist aim of an immediate, intuitive, inner illumination was sufficiently close to the aim of Buddhist meditation for it to be natural that the two streams of religion should influence each other in the period after Buddhism's arrival in China, in the first century CE. In particular, it was during the sixth and following centuries that this interplay was most marked.

NEO-CONFUCIANISM. The success of Buddhism, which in part resulted, at least among intellectuals, from the subtlety of its metaphysical doctrines, was a factor in stimulating the so-called neo-Confucian revival, in which a metaphysics was elaborated to underpin the Confucian ethic.

One main phase of this revival was the growth of philosophical idealism, which owed something to mystical ideas. Thus, Lu Xiangshan (1139–1193) argued that there is a single underlying principle, *li,* that explains all things and is spiritual. Thus, he claimed, his mind and the universe were one. It followed that one can discover the truth by introspection.

Such an idealism was further developed by Wang Yangming (1472–1529), about whom a significant story is told. He and a friend were concerned about the method by which one should purify the mind, for Zhu Xi (1130–1200) had said that one should investigate the nature of things. Wang and his friend decided to contemplate a bamboo in the front courtyard but gave up after several days. It is notable that this attempt corresponds to one of the preliminary methods of Buddhist contemplation. Although unconvinced by such "external" contemplation, Wang nevertheless considered the interior quest—the purification of consciousness—important. He believed that through looking inward at one's own nature one could gain an intuitive knowledge of the whole of reality. It is said that while in banishment and living under poor and menial conditions, Wang had a mystical experience in which he realized this doctrine existentially. However, Wang was far from abandoning the traditional Confucian emphasis on ethical behavior; he did not advocate quietism and passivity but saw in mysticism a way of enhancing moral goodness. Inner illumination would shine through in active concern for others. However, in such neo-Confucianism the influence of Ch'ān Buddhism can be detected.

BUDDHISM. Ch'ān, or Zen, Buddhism embodies the most distinctive feature of both Chinese and Japanese mysticism, since it incorporated Daoist ideas into Buddhist mysticism. Other schools of Far Eastern Buddhism in varying ways carried on and developed the Buddhist tradition and therefore incorporated Buddhist contemplative ideals. A powerful aspect of Far Eastern Buddhism was the success of the Pure Land school, which centered its teachings on the faith and devotion whereby the ordinary person could receive supernatural aid from the Buddha Amitābha and gain rebirth in the paradise of the Pure Land. With its stress on devotion and the efficacy of the Buddha's grace, this school tended to bypass contemplative mysticism and to focus religion upon worship.

JUDAISM

Although the Hebrew Bible contains virtually no expression of contemplative religion, mysticism developed within Judaism by the first century BCE. It centered mainly on the imagery of the *merkabah* (chariot), described in Ezekiel as a complex vision of the manifestation of divine power in the shape of supernatural beings riding on a mysterious four-wheeled chariot (Ezekiel 1). The Talmud indicates that some of the early rabbis practiced asceticism and self-purification as a preparation for a mystical "ascent into heaven." Philo Judaeus (fl. 20 BCE–40 CE) mentioned a community of Therapeutae near Alexandria who practiced a form of contemplative monasticism, and likewise mysticism may have been part of the Essene way of life. Philo himself was the greatest figure in these early phases of contemplative Judaism, although he was so deeply affected by Greek ideas that he is outside the mainstream of Jewish thought and piety. According to Philo, man, through his intellect, has an affinity with God; and through the contemplative life he can in principle attain a state where he can see God's essence. In accordance with Platonist and mystical ideas, Philo expounded a negative theology: God eludes the affirmations we try to make about him. Consequently, Philo's interpretation of Scripture was not at all literalistic, and he made lavish use of the allegorical method. He attempted, moreover, to show that the experiences of the prophets were mystical.

The most important period of Jewish mysticism was the Middle Ages. Beginning in the twelfth century there developed Hasidism, which made a lasting imprint on central European Judaism, and Kabbalism, mainly in Spain and southern France. The former takes its name from the term *Hasidim* ("devout ones"), a name originally applied to a movement of the second century BCE that was a forerunner of Pharisaism. Medieval Hasidism concentrated on the cultivation of the sense of divine presence. Modern Hasidism, dating from the eighteenth century, is more directly contemplative and is indebted to Kabbalism.

KABBALISM. Kabbalism centered on the esoteric teachings known as the Kabbalah, which found their chief expression in the *Zohar* ("splendor"), a work traditionally ascribed to the second century but actually dating from the thirteenth century or a little earlier, that conceives of God as the En-Sof, the "Endless" or "Infinite." In itself the En-Sof is qualityless, but there are ten ideal qualities, known as the *Sefirot*, that emanate from the Infinite—wisdom and power, for instance. These are used to explain the creation of the world. The cosmos that man inhabits, however, is the lowest sphere in which the *Sefirot* operate—a doctrine that expresses the way in which the perfect Infinite is far removed from the imperfect world we inhabit. The hierarchy of stages between God and the material world is reminiscent of Gnosticism. Nevertheless, the En-Sof, being infinite, does in some sense embrace lower forms of existence; and every entity in the universe reflects and interpenetrates everything else.

How is all this related to traditional Jewish teachings? According to the Kabbalah, the doctrine of interpenetration implies that lower events will stimulate corresponding activity from on high. The fall of Adam brought about a rupture in the cosmos; the Shekinah, or Divine Presence, became exiled from the En-Sof. No longer does the Presence pervade the whole world; it appears intermittently here and there—for instance, in ancient Israel—and has continued to be especially associated with the Jewish people. The aim of the pious should be to bring about a reunion of the En-Sof with the Shekinah. Since the human soul contains some of the *Sefirot*, the individual experience of such a reunion will have its cosmic effects and help to restore universal harmony. Consequently, the mystical life was given a dramatic and central place in the operations of the universe.

It will be apparent that some of these ideas, such as the ineffability of the En-Sof and the rather impersonal description of God, echo similar notions in Neoplatonism and other forms of mystical theology. Despite the unorthodoxy of much of their speculation, the Kabbalists continued the detailed observance of Jewish law, ascribing to it a mystical significance.

Isaac Luria. An important figure in the development of Kabbalism was Isaac Luria (1534–1572), of a Spanish Jewish family living in Palestine. He believed in reincarnation, which would give men ever fresh chances of living the pure life and would provide a framework for the punishment of those who had transgressed. Luria conceived of Adam as a universal being who before the Fall embraced the universe, then in an ideal state. With his fall, the material world was created, and the light of his divine nature was fragmented into the sparks that illuminate the myriads of living souls. In the final consummation, all will be reunited. Asceticism and the practice of *kavannah*—concentrated devotion in all one's acts—were the means of purifying the soul. Social conditions may have helped the growth of such doctrines, for the emphasis on meekness, love, and a quiet interior life were well adapted to the unhappy outer circumstances of the Jewish people, and the Kabbalistic reinterpretation of the Messianic hope gave the contemplative a cosmic role.

MODERN HASIDISM. The founder of modern Hasidism was Israel Baal Shem-Tov (c. 1700–1760), who lived in Carpathia in eastern Europe. He gathered round him disciples who were devoted to the mystical life. His successor, Baer of Meseritz (1710–1772), was an energetic organizer and missionary who spread the movement among Jews throughout eastern Europe and the Ukraine. Stress was laid on the concept of the zaddik, or perfectly righteous man, through whom the favor of God is channeled. Only he can attain union with the divine Being; less perfect folk must find their spiritual development through his guidance. This doctrine is reminiscent of Hindu ideas about the guru as conveyor of illumination. In any event, Hasidism implied that the zaddik, rather than the rabbi or learned person, was the immediate source of authority. This gave Hasidic mysticism a popular following and organization, and the essential simplicity of its message—that salvation can be attained through prayer and pious acts—made it adaptable to the experience of people of no great sophistication or learning.

As elsewhere in the history of mysticism, antinomian tendencies made their appearance. Thus Sabbatianism, named after Sabbatai Zevi (1626–1676), a self-styled Messiah who preached apostasy from Judaism, made use of Kabbalistic ideas in order to justify the concept of the God-man who is "beyond good and evil," as in the teachings of Jacob Frank (c. 1726–1791).

Although the Hasidim often attacked official rabbinical teaching, the revival of Jewish learning in the nineteenth century paved the way for a reconciliation between orthodoxy and Hasidic piety, so that the latter still remains a force within the fabric of Jewish religion.

CHRISTIANITY

ORIGINS. As has been mentioned, there was little mysticism in the traditions of Judaism until the time of Christ, and there also seems to have been little in the experience of the earliest church. It is true that Paul underwent a powerful experience of being "caught up to the third heaven," which could have had a mystical character, although it is also reminiscent of certain prophetic experiences, such as those of Muḥammad. The origins of Christian mysticism can more plausibly be sought elsewhere, in the rise of monasticism and the influence of Neoplatonism. Some stimulus to such a development may also have been given by the existence of Gnostic sects both within and outside Christianity, from the end of the first century CE.

Gnosticism. Gnosticism—a term derived from the word *gnosis,* meaning knowledge, particularly the immediate inner knowledge of the divine Being—tended to be ascetic and esoteric. Its asceticism was expressed by the doctrine that matter is evil, so that liberation of the soul is achieved through withdrawal from the world. Because of the evil nature of the world, Gnostics frequently postulated a hierarchy of beings below God and concerned with the creation of the world. Thus God himself was not contaminated, so to speak, by direct contract with matter. Such a doctrine was heretical, for it did not square with the Christian doctrine of creation or with Christian attitudes to the world, but it was one factor in stimulating an orthodox asceticism and mysticism within Christianity.

Monasticism. Monasticism grew out of eremitic practices, mainly in Egypt. Famous among early hermits was Anthony the Great, whose asceticism became almost legendary. Early in the fourth century monasticism proper was established in Egypt, the key figure being Pachomius. Thereafter the movement spread rapidly in Egypt and the Eastern church. It was further organized by Basil the Great (c. 330–379), whose rule formed the basis of Orthodox monasticism. John Cassian (c. 360–c. 434) brought Egyptian-style monasticism to the West, founding two monasteries in the south of France. His rule underlay that of St. Benedict, who lived in the following century. The connection of monasticism with mysticism was a straightforward one, for a main rationale of monasticism was the cultivation of the spiritual life, whereby a foretaste of the beatitude of the blessed in heaven could be gained. Thus the ultimate destiny of man was seen in contemplative terms, and it was thought possible to anticipate this destiny by a regulated life withdrawn from the world.

Neoplatonism. Neoplatonism, which expressed a view of the world in part stemming from, and in part providing a rationale for, mystical experience, made a lasting imprint upon Christian contemplation. A sign of this was the composition of the Pseudo-Dionysian writings, which were ascribed to Dionysius the Areopagite, a convert of St. Paul, but really date from approximately the beginning of the sixth century. These writings had a wide impact upon medieval mysticism. The negative theology expounded in them was not merely the result of logical difficulties involved in the ascription of ordinary predicates to God but, more importantly, was geared to the expression of the contemplative's inner experience of a "darkness clearer than light." Thus the mystical experience, being different from, and not expressible in terms of, perceptual and related forms of experience, seemed to imply that its object was likewise indescribable and therefore better conveyed by negations than by positive affirmations.

Neoplatonism also, of course, deeply influenced St. Augustine, and he has been a principal source of the notion, enshrined in monastic practice, that introvertive contemplation can give a foretaste of the heavenly life. Thus the highest state of Christian blessedness was increasingly identified with contemplation, and mysticism became the pattern after which eternal life was conceived.

EASTERN ORTHODOX MYSTICISM. The Pseudo-Dionysian writings also formed an important part of the fabric of Eastern Orthodox mysticism, for there were also features of the general theology of Orthodoxy that favored the contemplative ideal. John of Damascus, who in the eighth century summed up the work of the Cappadocian Fathers (fourth century), expressed in his writings a doctrine of deification that was both typical of and formative of Eastern Orthodox theology. Man was considered the connecting link between the visible and invisible worlds. He was created perfect but through the Fall lost his immortal, incorruptible, and passionless nature. A certain scope for free will remained, however. The image of God, although defaced, was not entirely lost. The restoration of man to the true end for which he was made—the contemplation of God—was effected through Christ's incarnation. Christ, by uniting the Godhead to human nature, restored that nature to its perfection; and by sharing in his perfect humanity, men also can be raised up and deified. In terms of Dionysian mysticism, this deification takes place through the illumination of the soul; its divinization, through the divine Light. Virtually throughout Eastern mysticism this imagery of light was to play a central part, and thus St. Simeon (949–1022), perhaps the most important of Eastern Orthodox mystics, identified the inner light with the glory emanating from God.

Hesychasm. Simeon was also a forerunner of the significant contemplative movement known as Hesychasm (from the Greek word *hesychos,* "quiet"), whose methods of training had some analogy to those found in Indian yoga.

The Hesychasts (eleventh–fourteenth centuries) held that their methods were conducive to the inner vision of the uncreated Light, identified with that which suffused Christ at the Transfiguration on Mount Tabor. This Light was conceived as emanating from God and was not to be identified with his essence, which is unknowable (this was a means of retaining orthodox teaching, by safeguarding mysticism from a full doctrine of union with, or knowledge of, God). Among the training methods used were breathing exercises and the continued repetition of the Jesus Prayer—"O Lord Jesus, Son of God, have mercy on me, a sinner." In a mysterious manner, the very repetition of the sacred name of Jesus was supposed to contain the divine power.

Gregorius Palamas (c. 1296–1359), the most noted and controversial exponent of Hesychasm, considered the Jesus Prayer as the central act of piety; and although the use of breathing techniques, which persisted until the eighteenth century, has been discontinued, the Jesus Prayer has survived as a characteristic part of Orthodox religion. Palamas and the Hesychasts were not, however, unopposed. Some opponents thought that the doctrine of the uncreated Light made a division within the Godhead—Palamas had even spoken of "divinities." Thus the attempt to soften the idea of mystical union by regarding it as identification not with the divine essence but with the divine illuminative energy, was criticized on the ground that it transferred the difficulty to another locus by introducing something like polytheism. Nevertheless, Hesychastic teaching came to be recognized officially, and the movement was the mainspring of medieval Orthodox contemplation.

ROMAN CATHOLICISM. The mystical life served to counterbalance the worldly tendencies that had permeated the early medieval church in the West. Pope Gregory the Great (c. 540–604) discovered in his own experience something that could be expressed in terms of the irradiation of the divine Light; and Gregory VII, elected pope in 1073, undertook extensive ecclesiastical and monastic reforms that were partly inspired by the intense cultivation of the personal and contemplative life he had discovered in the Cluniac movement—a monasticism whose rules and ideals emanated from the monastic center at Cluny in Burgundy.

The most important figure in monastic reform was Bernard of Clairvaux (1090–1153). Although he was influenced by Augustine, his concerns were not primarily expressed in metaphysical language. He believed that in the mystical experience the soul is emptied and wholly lost in God, but he did not conceive this as an actual union with the Godhead. The soul and God remain distinct in substance, although they are joined by the "glue of love." Through man's love flowing up to God and through the downward movement of God's grace, the two become united. Bernard combined this intense mysticism with great powers of leadership and played a large part in the forward movement of the Cistercian order.

Other important mystics were Hugh and Richard of St. Victor, an Augustinian abbey in Paris in the twelfth century, and St. Bonaventure (c. 1217–1274) in the following century. St. Bonaventure evolved a theory of mysticism that set forth the three ways of the spiritual life: purgative, illuminative, and unitive. In the first stage, the individual purifies himself through meditation; in the second, he is illuminated by the divine mercy; in the third, he gains a continuing union with God through love. This love is nourished by concentrating upon God, to the exclusion of mutable things. Thus, Bonaventure's path typically followed that of introversion, while his theological doctrines leaned upon Augustine and Pseudo-Dionysius.

There were ways, however, in which mystical teachings, especially where they strongly emphasized the negative theology of Pseudo-Dionysius, could seem unorthodox. The work of Thomas Aquinas (1224?–1274), in excogitating a novel synthesis between Christian theology and Aristotelianism, accentuated differences of emphasis between some of the mystics and orthodox doctrine. Thus Meister Eckhart (c. 1260–1327/1328), a Dominican and therefore versed in Thomism, fell under condemnation.

The greatest of the German contemplatives, Eckhart spoke in ways that suggested not merely that there is an ontological distinction between the Godhead, which is beyond description, and the Trinity of describable Persons but also that it is possible for the contemplative to go "beyond God" in achieving identity with the Godhead. Despite his unorthodox language, Eckhart inspired a strong following, and the mysticism of Johannes Tauler (c. 1300–1361), Heinrich Suso (1295/1300–1366), Jan van Ruysbroeck (1293–1381), and the partly lay group known as the Friends of God in Germany, the Low Countries, and Switzerland owed much to him.

It was out of the Friends of God that the anonymous but famous mystical treatise, the *Theologia Germanica*, originated, stressing the abandonment of the soul to God.

The corruption of the church and the disillusioning events of the Great Western Schism were motives for the Friends of God to attempt to revitalize faith through the inner life, and this sometimes involved a highly critical attitude toward ecclesiastical authority. It is worth noting, however, that the rather sudden flowering of mysticism in Germany during the fourteenth century owed much to the fact that in 1267 the Dominican friars had been charged by Pope Clement IV with the spiritual direction of the nuns in the numerous convents in the Rhineland. Hitherto they had frequently been without proper religious supervision.

Mysticism could lead in directions that seemed to be the reverse of Christian piety. The sect known as the Brethren of the Free Spirit, which dated from the early thirteenth century, believed that men are of the same substance as God: Every man is capable of becoming divine. It followed that when this divinization was achieved, a person could no longer sin, for God is sinless. Thus, whatever one did, it would not be a sin. Commandments and conventional tests of morality could no longer apply, and mysticism was therefore interpreted as justifying antinomianism. (Thus, it was not surprising that some of Eckhart's language, although not intended in this sense, could be regarded as dangerous—as when he said that God is beyond good.) Despite the efforts of the Inquisition, the Brethren of the Free Spirit spread, partly because they were able to organize themselves into a secret society.

The asceticism often associated with mystical religion may also be seen in another heretical movement of the twelfth and thirteenth centuries—the Albigensians or Cathari, found in southern France, northern Italy, and parts of Spain, who held doctrines close to those of Manichaeism.

The fourteenth century also saw a marked development of mysticism in England, as exemplified by the writings of Richard Rolle de Hampole (c. 1290–1349), who led the life of a hermit; the anonymous author of the famous *Cloud of Unknowing*, which was influenced by Pseudo-Dionysius; Julian of Norwich (c. 1340–1415); Walter Hilton (d. 1396), and others. On the whole, the temper of their mysticism was nonspeculative, and they emphasized the practical means of developing the inner life.

A movement closely related to the Friends of God was that of the Brethren of the Common Life, which was deeply influenced by Ruysbroeck. Its best-known fruit was the widely read *Imitation of Christ*, attributed to Thomas à Kempis. With its stress on practical love, it was well adapted to the needs of those who did not necessarily feel the call to the cloister and was a means of giving mysticism a wider social impact. Similarly, Catherine of Siena (1347–1380) exhibited a dynamic concern for social and ecclesiastical service. She ministered to victims of the Black Death and played a part in the attempt to strengthen the ailing papacy, persuading Gregory XI to return from Avignon to Rome.

Catherine of Siena spoke vividly of mystical experience in terms of spiritual marriage, paralleling the symbolism whereby the church was looked on as the bride of Christ. Another woman mystic, Teresa of Ávila (1515–1582), gave further expression to this imagery. Her accounts of her own experiences in pursuing the contemplative life, in such works as *The Interior Castle* and in her autobiography, are valuable and sensitive sources for understanding the inner phenomena of mysticism.

Another important mystic who used the imagery of marriage was a younger contemporary of St. Teresa, John of the Cross (1542–1591). He gave detailed expression to the experience of the "dark night of the soul," an experience also recorded by Ruysbroeck and others. The mystic has, according to St. John, periods of despair in which he feels deserted by God. This he interprets as a means of purgation sent by God. The experience probably reflects the contrast between the bliss of union and the condition of striving for that bliss. It is not much written about in nontheistic mysticism, although Buddhist meditation involves the attempt to repress the feeling of bliss accruing on the attainment of higher states of consciousness, in order to obviate the depression liable to occur upon their cessation.

PROTESTANTISM. In one way, Protestantism provided a favorable milieu for mysticism, but in another and ultimately more important way, it provided an unfavorable one. The Protestant emphasis on personal experience of God could easily link up with the ideals of the contemplative life. Thus, the writings of the most famous Protestant mystic, Jakob Boehme (1575–1624), were widely diffused. Groups of followers known as the Behmenists flourished in England and were later absorbed in the Quaker movement, whose doctrine of the "inner light" was characteristically mystical. However, the type of experience that figured so centrally in early Protestantism and that has continued to be stressed in evangelical Christianity was that which gives the individual certitude of salvation. Such a "conversion" experience differs from the imageless rapture that is at the center of mystical religion. Moreover, Protestantism was organizationally unfavorable to the contemplative life, since this had flourished

principally in monasteries and indeed had provided a main rationale for their existence. Protestantism could be puritanical, but it did not favor withdrawal from the world.

The antinomian tendencies exhibited by the Brethren of the Free Spirit in the thirteenth and fourteenth centuries were reproduced in various offshoots of Protestant mysticism, as in the movement known as the Ranters, who were strong in seventeenth-century England. Their doctrines were held by opponents to be pantheistic, but more correctly they believed in the essential divinity of all human beings. Since God cannot sin, neither can divinized men, however wrong their actions may look from the standpoint of conventional morality. This was another instance in the history of religion where mystical teachings, normally nurtured in the context of asceticism and unworldliness, were interpreted to justify the opposite. Other important mystics in the Protestant tradition were George Fox (1624–1691), the founder of Quakerism; William Law (1686–1761); and the eccentric poet William Blake (1757–1827).

Although contemplative writings have been less prominent in more recent times, there have been a number of striking mystics since 1850, among them the pseudonymous Lucie-Christine (1844–1908), whose experiences are recorded in her *Spiritual Journal*; the converted French army officer Charles de Foucauld (1858–1916), and the Indian Christian Sadhu Sundar Singh (1889–1929).

Moreover, there has been a renewed scholarly interest in mysticism, as seen in the writings of William James, Evelyn Underhill (1875–1941), and William Inge (1860–1954). Further stimulus to the study of mysticism has been provided by the increased interaction between Eastern religions and Christianity.

ISLAM

Early Islam was not especially conducive to mysticism, since its main spirit was that of the prophetic dynamism of Muḥammad's numinous experiences. Nevertheless, by the eighth century mysticism was developing within Islam. Greek philosophy had already made its impact on the Arabs and thus had opened the way to speculation about God that was partly contemplative. More important, the ex-Christians who had been absorbed into the faith in many Middle Eastern areas carried with them a respect for the ascetic life. Further, the culture of the Arabian desert had encountered the rich and sophisticated standard of living of the conquered, and this confrontation had induced tensions within Islam. Those who held to the older tradition were moved to accentuate the puritanism of early Islam, and such asceticism accorded with the practice of contemplation. Moreover, it was possible for Muslims to interpret Muḥammad's prophetic experience in a mystical sense.

Muslim mysticism is generally known as Sufism. The word Ṣūfī is probably derived from the term Ṣūf, "undyed wool," which was the material of a garment worn as a sign of simplicity and austerity. Although complete world denial was scarcely in accord with Muḥammad's teachings, the world acceptance expressed in the struggle for power among his successors brought conformity with mere orthodoxy into disrepute among the pious. This represented an opportunity for the growth of an ascetic otherworldliness. Those who adopted the contemplative life could withdraw from politics and could harness self-mortification to the task of concentrating solely upon Allah.

The general structure of Islamic faith was adapted to the service of the inner life. The repetition of prayers enjoined by Islam could be extended from that normally required of the faithful until every moment could be spent in remembrance of God and adoration of him. Almsgiving, one of the seven "pillars of Islam," could be interpreted in terms of thoroughgoing self-denial. The whole of life could be seen as a pilgrimage to a spiritual Mecca. Although the earliest teachings of Islam had laid duties on the individual as a member of the community—conceived as a brotherhood—tendencies later developed that made religion essentially a matter for the individual alone.

The new asceticism was regarded primarily as a means toward inner illumination. Fear and obedience of God melted into a burning interior love of him that carried with it the hope that union with him might be gained through negation of the self. This interior knowledge was described in terms of light, and an important passage in the Qur'an (Koran), the so-called Light Verse, was quoted as a backing for mysticism: "God is the light of the heavens and of the earth; His light is like a niche wherein there is a lamp, a lamp encased in glass, the glass as it were a glistening star." Also, the Sufis came to use the imagery of love as some Christian mystics did. An early example of this is to be found in the life and teachings of Dhū'l-Nūn (d. 861), an Egyptian influenced by Greek speculation.

HERETICAL ASPECTS. The knowledge prized by the Sufis was not the rational knowledge developed by the scholastic theologians (in Islam this meant mainly those who had come into contact with Greek philosophy); rather, it was the direct knowledge of Allah, or ma'rifa.

This ma'rifa or gnosis was the crown of the Sufi path. However, the idea of direct acquaintance with God could have consequences that were scandalous to the orthodox.

Thus, Abū Yazīd of Bistam (d. 875) was so convinced of his identity with God in the experience of ma'rifa that he could say "Glory to me—how great is my majesty." This seemed like claiming divinity, which was blasphemous and strictly contrary to the orthodox opposition to any doctrine of incarnation. Abū Yazīd also put forth an idea destined to play a large part in subsequent Islamic mysticism—that of fanā', the passing away and extinction of the empirical self, which follows self-control through asceticism and contemplative techniques. The "passing away" involved the loss of the consciousness of one's own individuality and helps to explain why the Sufis sometimes spoke in terms that suggested that they became merged or identified with God. As has been seen, similar ideas were expressed on occasion by Christian mystics such as Eckhart and are found in Hindu and Buddhist mysticism.

The most notable example of this trend was the experience of al-Hallāj (854–922) of Baghdad, who spoke as though he were an incarnation of the divine Being through mystical experience and consciously and overtly modeled himself upon Jesus. Such ideas were intolerable to the orthodox and he was (appropriately) crucified.

Although at first the Sufis operated individually, they later associated in loose groups. The elaboration of contemplative techniques and the trend toward celibacy (scarcely in accord with the spirit of the revealed law contained in the Qur'an) brought about the creation of orders of Sufis who could work, and often live, together. It was common for such a group to be under the spiritual direction of a shaykh or pīr, and very often his residence would turn into a monastic community. The prestige of such holy men became great, and miraculous powers were ascribed to them. This prestige, combined with concepts clustering around ma'rifa, brought the ideal of the divine human and the cult of saints into Islam.

Persecution, as in the case of al-Hallāj, was no lasting answer to threats to orthodoxy; what was required was a synthesis between the new ideas and traditional theology that could harness Sufi piety to Qur'anic ends. Al-Ghazālī (1058–1111) provided the most acceptable and influential solution to the problem. In his The Revival of the Religious Sciences he dealt with the question of how fanā' could most properly be interpreted. He held that the mystic, in experiencing the vision of God, is so overwhelmed that he imagines he is united with him. However, this is a sort of illusion, analogous to the belief of a person who sees wine in a transparent glass and thinks that wine and glass are a single object. When the contemplative returns from the state of ecstasy ("drunkenness," as Ghazālī called it—metaphors of drinking were common in Sufi writings), he recognizes that there is a distinction between the soul and God. In such ways, Ghazālī tried to do justice both to the actual experience of the contemplative and to a religion's requirements of worship, which presupposes a dualism between the worshiper and the object of worship. Ghazālī stressed the way in which self-purification, as part of the Sufi path, follows penitence, which in turn depends on the recognition of the awe-inspiring majesty and holiness of Allah. Thus he tried to show that contemplation and orthodox religion go hand in hand. Hence, he also did not believe in a mysticism that involved withdrawal from the world. The mystic returns to ordinary life, revitalized by the dazzling vision of the divine Reality. Ghazālī's synthesis meant that henceforth Sufism had an accepted place within orthodox Islam, but contemplative and philosophical thought were not restricted.

PANTHEIST TENDENCIES. Notable among those who expressed a poetical and metaphysical Sufism was Ibn al-'Arabī (1165–1240) of Spain. He influenced Dante Alighieri, who adopted the outline of Ibn al-'Arabī's description of the ascent into heaven (combining astronomical theory and the story of Muḥammad's journey to heaven). His doctrines were pantheistic, and he considered human beings as offshoots of the divine essence that exist because of God's desire to be known; and in the realization of the divine Being, the contemplative reflects in his own person the structure of the universe. He also made use of the logos idea: The logos as the creative principle in the universe was identified with the spirit of Muḥammad. However, there are hints in Ibn al-'Arabī's work that he considered himself superior to Muḥammad, having realized identity not with the logos but with the Godhead.

His voluminous writings, although regarded with distaste by the orthodox, were influential, especially in Persia, among such mystical poets as Jalāl ad-Din Rūmī (1207–1273) and Mawlana Nur ad-Din Jāmī (1414–1492). Rūmī, who founded one of the *darwīsh* orders (*darwīsh* literally means "mendicant," and is commonly transliterated *dervish*), also wrote poetry expressing the longing of the soul for its return to God. However, he was also keenly appreciative of the beauties of nature, and he saw in the ritual of the Mevlevi order, which he founded, with its solemn swirling dance to the sound of drum and pipe, a reflection of the movements of the planets and of nature in general.

It may be noted that some of the orders experimented with various external means of inducing ecstatic experiences, and the dance was one. (The term *dervish* should properly apply to all mendicant orders, and not just to the Mevlevi "dancing dervishes.")

Certain features of Sufi teaching are reminiscent of Indian mysticism, and it has been argued, although not conclusively, that there were borrowings from India. (See R. C. Zaehner, *Hindu and Muslim Mysticism*, on this question.) For instance, Abū Yazīd's language is similar to that of the *Upaniṣads*; and Ibn al-'Arabī argued, with a logic like that of Śankara, that it is inappropriate to speak of *becoming* God through mystical experience, since one is already essentially identical with God—mystical realization involves no change of ontological status. Again, like nearly all Hindu theologians, Ibn al-'Arabī treated hell as a purgatory, rather than as a place of everlasting punishment. Various similarities of this kind can probably best be explained not so much as borrowings but rather as reflections of similar patterns of experience and speculation.

MODERN SUFISM. In the modern period, Sufism has undergone a considerable decline, and the revitalization of Islam has come about through other forces—the puritanism of the Wahhābi, Pan-Arabism, and political advance. Sir Muhammad Iqbal (1877–1938), however, an important figure in Muslim modernism, was influenced by Sufi thought. Since he wished to distinguish sharply between religion and science—the former having to do with personal life—he found the interior quest of Sufism attractive.

See also Absolute, The; al-Ghazālī, Muhammad; Asceticism; Augustine, St.; Bernard of Clairvaux, St.; Blake, William; Boehme, Jakob; Bonaventure, St.; Buddhism; Buddhism—Schools: Chan and Zen; Caird, Edward; Chinese Philosophy; Confucius; Dante Alighieri; Eckhart, Meister; Gnosticism; Hinduism; Ibn al-'Arabī; Illumination; Inge, William Ralph; Iqbal, Muhammad; Jainism; James, William; John of Damascus; John of the Cross, St.; Kabbalah; Laozi; Law, William; Lu Xiangshan; Mani and Manichaeism; Mysticism, Nature and Assessment of; Mysticism: The Indian Tradition; Neoplatonism; Nirvāṇa; Otto, Rudolf; Philo Judaeus; Pseudo-Dionysius; Rāmānuja; Ruysbroeck, Jan van; Śankara; Stace, Walter Terence; Sufism; Suso, Heinrich; Tauler, Johannes; Teresa of Ávila, St.; Thomas à Kempis; Thomas Aquinas, St.; Thomism; Wang Yangming; Yoga; Zhu Xi (Chu Hsi).

Bibliography

A good introduction to mysticism is Sidney Spencer, *Mysticism in World Religion* (Baltimore: Penguin, 1963). Evelyn Underhill's *Mysticism*, 6th ed. (London: Methuen, 1916), is a classic, although dated in some respects and confined largely to theistic mysticism. The same is true of William James, *Varieties of Religious Experience* (New York: Longmans Green, 1902). See also W. R. Inge, *Mysticism in Religion* (London, 1907); R. C. Zaehner, *Mysticism Sacred and Profane* (Oxford: Clarendon Press, 1957); W. T. Stace, *Mysticism and Philosophy* (Philadelphia: Lippincott, 1960); Steven Katz, ed., *Mysticism and Religious Traditions* (New York: Oxford University Press, 1983); Bernard McGinn, *The Presence of God,* 3 vols (New York: Crossroad, 1991–1998); Barry Windeatt, *English Mystics of the Middle Ages* (Cambridge, U.K.: Cambridge University Press, 1994); Geoffrey Parrinder, *Mysticism in the World's Religions* (New York: Oneworld, 1995); and Steven Katz, ed., *Mysticism and Sacred Scripture* (New York: Oxford University Press, 2000).

On Indian mysticism, see Edward Conze, *Buddhist Meditation* (New York: Dover, 2003); S. N. Dasgupta, *Hindu Mysticism* (London, 1927); D. T. Suzuki, *Mysticism: Christian and Buddhist* (London: Allen and Unwin, 1957); Rudolf Otto's classical *Mysticism East and West,* translated by B. L. Bracey and R. C. Payne (New York and London, 1957, in paperback); Ninian Smart, *Doctrine and Argument in Indian Philosophy* (London: Allen and Unwin, 1964), Ch. 10; Krishna Sivaraman, ed., *Hindu Spirituality: Vedas through Vedanta,* World Spirituality Series vol. 6 (New York: Crossroad, 1989); K.R. Sundararajan and Bithika Mukerji, eds., *Hindu Spirituality II: Postclassical and Modern,* World Spirituality Series vol. 7 (New York: Crossroad, 1997).

On Chinese and Japanese mysticism, see K. L. Reichelt, *Meditation and Piety in the Far East* (London: Lutterworth Press, 1953) and *Religion in Chinese Garment* (London: Lutterworth Press, 1951); Henri Maspero, *Le Taoisme* (Paris, 1950); Fung Yu-lan, *A History of Chinese Philosophy,* 2 vols. (Princeton, NJ: Princeton University Press, 1952–1953); and Julia Ching, *Mysticism and Kingship in China: The Heart of Chinese Wisdom* (Cambridge, U.K.: Cambridge University Press, 1997); Livia Kohn, *Early Chinese Mysticism: Philosophy and Soteriology in the Taoist Tradition* (Princeton, NJ: Princeton University Press, 1992). The *Dao-de-jing* has numerous English translations, ranging from that of Lionel Giles (London, 1911) to that of D. C. Lau (Baltimore: Penguin, 1963).

For mysticism in Judaism, see G. G. Scholem, *Major Trends in Jewish Mysticism* (London: Thames and Hudson, 1955); E. Müller, *History of Jewish Mysticism* (London, 1956); Martin Buber, *The Legend of the Baal-Shem,* translated by Maurice Freedman (London: Horowitz, 1956); Ira Chernus, *Mysticism in Rabbinic Judaism: Studies in the History of Midrash* (Berlin: Walter de Gruyter, 1982); and Arthur Green, *Keter: The Crown of God in Early Jewish Mysticism* (Princeton: Princeton University Press, 1997).

On Christian mysticism, see R. M. Grant, *Gnosticism and Early Christianity* (London: Oxford University Press, 1959); W. R. Inge, *The Philosophy of Plotinus,* 2 vols. (London: Longmans Green, 1918); A. J. Festugière, *Personal Religion among the Greeks* (Berkeley: University of California Press, 1954); Cuthbert Butler, *Western Mysticism,* 2nd ed. (London: Constable, 1922); Evelyn Underhill, *The Mystics of the Church* (London: James Clarke, 1925); Vladimir Losskii, *The Theology of The Eastern Church,* translated by the members of the Fellowship of St. Alban and St. Sergius (London: James Clarke, 1957); Jon Gregerson, *The Transfigured Cosmos* (New York: Ungar, 1960); Margaret Smith, *Studies in Early Mysticism in the Near and Middle East* (London: Sheldon Press, 1931); R. M. Jones, *Studies in Mystical Religion,* 3rd ed. (London: Macmillan, 1909); E. A. Peers, *Studies of the Spanish Mystics,* 3 vols. (London: Sheldon Press, 1927–1960); and Louis Bouyer, et al., *A History of Christian Spirituality,* 3 vols (New York: Seabury, 1969).

On mysticism in Islam, see A. J. Arberry, *Sufism—An Account of the Mystics of Islam,* 2nd impression (London, 1956); Alexander Knysh, *Islamic Mysticism: A Short History* (Leiden: Brill, 2000); R. A. Nicholson, *Studies in Islamic Mysticism* (Cambridge, U.K.: Cambridge University Press, 1921, reissued 1979); Annemarie Schimmel, *Mystical Dimensions of Islam* (Chapel Hill: University of North Carolina Press, 1975); A. J. Wensinck, *La pensée de Ghazzali* (Paris: Adrien-Maisonneuve, 1940); and R. C. Zaehner, *Hindu and Muslim Mysticism* (London: University of London, Athlone Press, 1960).

Ninian Smart (1967)
Bibliography updated by Christian B. Miller (2005)

MYSTICISM, NATURE AND ASSESSMENT OF

Attempts to define mystical experience have been as diversified and as conflicting as attempts to interpret and assess its significance. This is not surprising, for the language used to express and describe mystical experience is richly paradoxical, figurative, and poetical. Even if at times a mystic chooses what look like austere and precise metaphysical terms, this may be only an apparent concession to logic, for he will employ these terms in senses far from normal. Mystics have called the Godhead a sheer "Nothing" and yet the ground of all. They have affirmed simultaneously that the world is identical with God and that the world is not identical with God.

Some discriminations are possible, even if exact definition is not. Mystical experience is religious experience, in a broad but meaningful sense of "religious." It is sensed as revealing something about the totality of things, something of immense human importance at all times and places, and something upon which one's ultimate well-being or salvation wholly depends. More specifically, a mystical experience is not the act of acquiring religious or theological information but is often taken to be a confrontation or encounter with the divine source of the world's being and man's salvation. An experience is not held to be mystical if the divine power is apprehended as simply "over-against" one—wholly distinct and "other."

There must be a unifying vision, a sense that somehow all things are one and share a holy, divine, and single life, or that one's individual being merges into a "Universal Self," to be identified with God or the mystical One. Mystical experience then typically involves the intense and joyous realization of oneness with, or in, the divine, the sense that this divine One is comprehensive, all-embracing, in its being. Yet a mystical experience may be given much less theological interpretation than this description suggests. A mystic may have no belief whatever in a divine being and still experience a sense of overwhelming beatitude, of salvation, or of lost or transcended individuality.

Some mystical experiences occur only at the end of a lengthy, arduous religious discipline, an ascetic path; others occur spontaneously (like much nature-mystical experience); others are induced by drugs such as mescaline or take place during the course of mental illness.

An important distinction can be made between the extrovertive (outward-looking) and introvertive (inward-looking) types of mystical experience. In the first of these, the subject looks out upon the multiplicity of objects in the world and sees them transfigured into a living, numinous unity, their distinctness somehow obliterated. In nature mysticism, a form of extrovertive experience, the items of nature are not lost to consciousness; rather they are seen with unusual vividness and all as "workings of one mind, the features/Of the same face, blossoms upon one tree" (William Wordsworth, *The Prelude*, Book 6). In the introvertive type, the mystic becomes progressively less aware of his environment and of himself as a separate individual. He speaks of being merged in, identified with, dissolved into, the One. The subject-object distinction vanishes altogether. Some of the best-known mystics testify to experiences of both types, but the introvertive, being at the furthest remove from ordinary experience, is usually held to be the more developed of the two.

Although we can call mystical experience a kind of religious experience, we do not discover agreement among mystics about the nature and status of the mystical goal. Christian and Islamic mysticism, for example, interpret the experience theistically, although not with complete consistency; the Upanishads and Theravāda Buddhism are not theistic. Pantheist, monist, and agnostic interpretations have been offered, all with some prima facie plausibility.

ALTERNATIVE RELIGIOUS INTERPRETATIONS

The pantheist argues that mystical experience compels us to strip away anthropomorphic conceptions of deity and that although theism begins this work of refining, it stops long before it should. The theistic notion of God remains that of an infinite, supernatural individual. But apart from being intellectually unsatisfactory (infinity and individuality go awkwardly together), this picture contradicts the mystic's own experience, which is one not of an external face-to-face meeting with a deity but rather of merging with, and realizing one's own basic identity with, the mystical One. The theist has to set a great gulf between himself and his God; the mystic's experience testifies both to the existence of this gulf and, paradoxically, to its elimination. Brahman is both far and near.

Why have so many of the greatest Christian mystics used theistic language to describe their obviously intense mystical experiences? The pantheist will say that either they have simple-mindedly used the only religious terms they had been taught—despite their unsuitability—or else that the desire to conform to orthodox Christian dogma about God's transcendence has led them to muffle those parts of their individual experience that were opposed to it.

A pantheist interpretation claims that it alone does full justice to God's infinity and that its theology eliminates the last primitive remnants of deism. Since a mystical experience is a discovery, a realization, of what is eternally true, there need be no perplexing doctrines about special divine self-revelations and self-communications nor any interference with natural law. Accordingly, a mystical experience induced by drug or disease does not have to be judged illusory or demonic. In the determination of whether it is authentic or not, its causal circumstances are simply beside the point.

The theist, however, is not without a reply. He will reject the pantheist's conception of religious development. There has not been any general historical trend toward pantheism or monism in religion; and although early theisms were crudely anthropomorphic, this does not by itself entail that all personal language about God is equally false and crude. The doctrine of the Incarnation should teach the contrary—at least within Christendom.

Pantheism and monism, argues the theist, map only the lower slopes of the mystic's ascent. They are concerned with the preliminary purging of the senses and intellect; their raptures do not testify to an achieved union with God but only to what is perhaps an unusually fresh, innocent, and aesthetically intense awareness of the created world and its beauty. The mescaline-user and the temporarily psychotic, who make extravagant claims for their own identity with the mystical One, ought to—often do—think more humbly of their experiences once normality returns. To the theist, the *unio mystica* is an objective that cannot be taken by assault; in the end, it is only the initiative, the grace, of God that bestows it. Causation does matter in this interpretation, and the inner, felt nature of the mystical experience cannot alone determine its authenticity.

PARADOXES OF RELIGIOUS INTERPRETATIONS

Short decisive arguments can hardly be invoked to settle the dispute between these interpretations of mystical experience. The experiences themselves seem able to bear either interpretation; the choice between pantheism and theism is a choice between two massive conceptual systems. Neither account can claim the merit of being free from internal difficulties both conceptual and religious. Theism has somehow to combine the notions that God is immeasurably "other" to man and, yet, that mystical union is possible. Pantheism identifies world and God while maintaining their distinctness; it denies that "God" is simply another way of saying "world."

Still more perplexingly, some mystics of great eminence speak the languages of both pantheism and theism. Meister Eckhart's writings give full-blooded examples of each, as do those of the Indian mystic Śankara. Even in the Upanishads, although Brahman is said to be beyond relation, featureless, unthinkable, it (or he) is acknowledged to have personal aspects.

No precise or determinate idea, no particularized image, is allowed to be adequate to the mystical One. Although the ontological status of God seems at times to be that of a numinous individual being, at other times all hints of such a status are repudiated. "Simple people," said Eckhart, "imagine that they should see God, as if He stood there and they here. That is not so." The Divine is a "desert," a "void," an "abyss," a "wheel rolling out of itself," a "stream flowing into itself."

Mystics will not always allow one even to say unequivocally that God exists. The pseudo-Dionysius, for example, denied that either the category of existence or of nonexistence applied to the Divine. These tensions and this indeterminateness—God is, or is not, a particular being, he is, or is not, an existent—can also be found in nonmystical theologies, but mysticism can enormously magnify them. Even Theravāda Buddhism contains deep-running paradox, despite its comparative reluctance to speculate at all. Attaining nirvāṇa, for instance, is like the extinguishing of a flame, yet nirvāṇa is not sheer simple extinction.

What attitude is it reasonable to adopt toward this display of tensions and antinomies? Four possibilities are worthy of serious discussion. (1) The paradoxes cannot be eliminated; they are to be taken literally and at their face value. Without paradox, we cannot speak of the mystic's experiences or of his God, but this is no argument against the truth of the mystic's claims. (2) The paradoxes are necessary in the same way that distortions of grammar and syntax are necessary to a poet attempting to say something that cannot be encompassed by ordinary language. They are not to be taken literally but are to be construed as analogies, hyperboles, metaphors, or oxymorons. (3) Since no logically coherent account of mystical vision seems attainable, it is more sensible to admit this fact and to believe the mystic's claim that his experience is ineffable and that all language falsifies it. We would now have a mysticism without a theology. A very high value could still be set upon mystical experience, but we should be reverently agnostic on all questions of interpretation. (4) The appearance of paradox in a piece of discourse is very often taken by philosophers as a reductio ad absurdum of its claims. (Compare the logician's story of the barber who shaves only those who do not shave themselves. When paradox arises over the question "Does the barber shave himself?," it is reasonable to infer that there logically cannot be a barber, so described.) Because the mystic says so many contradictory things about God, this demonstrates the logical impossibility of God's existence, so described. Criticisms charging illogicality can be supported by attempts to explain in naturalistic terms the mystical experiences themselves.

EVALUATION OF RESPONSES TO PARADOXES

Whether or not the paradoxes are finally to be judged literal and irreducible, we must clearly reject some of the speculations that are aimed at reducing their offense. For example, how God can be, but not by being an individual entity, is profoundly obscure. The mystery is not removed if we say that God is Being Itself or Being as such. Even if our ontology allowed such universals as "courage itself" or "blueness itself," we still could not meaningfully include Being Itself among their number; there is no characteristic named "being" that is common to all actual entities and that should figure in their complete description. "Being Itself" cannot logically refer to anything either particular or universal, divine or nondivine.

Similarly, if we are offended by the claim that God neither exists nor does not exist, we might try a familiar palliative and say that he is above being. Our concepts fail to grasp him precisely for that reason. "Above being" carries echoes of "above the turmoil," "above suspicion," "above praise," with "above" indicating distance from and superiority to something. But in order to be "above," one must first of all be—and continue to be. "God is above being" really fails to satisfy the conditions under which any "above" sentence of this kind can have meaning. It can, of course, be given a sense if "being" here means finite and dependent being. But if God is superior to this sort of being, if he is infinite and independent, then that is a superiority of his nature, and to learn this about him gives us no help with the original paradox.

LITERAL VERSUS FIGURATIVE LANGUAGE. The paradoxes and enigmas may have to stand, but why not take them as poetical, metaphorical, or symbolic language? Against that suggestion, it may be argued that if the paradoxes are metaphors, it should be possible to translate them—at least roughly—into direct, nonmetaphorical language. The only language available to the mystic, however, seems to be a language of irreducible paradox.

This argument is not very powerful. There are nonmystical topics about which it is impossible to speak without metaphor, such as important topics within the philosophy of mind. The history of conceptions of the mind is, in many of its facets, the history of changing metaphors, myths, and analogies. To defend a parallel account of mystical discourse would be less of a scandal to reason and logic than to insist on the literal view.

The literalist will reply that there is, in fact, no scandal to reason. The laws of logic work admirably for every situation where multiplicity is present. In the mystic's unique case, all multiplicity has vanished and with it, therefore, the applicability of those laws. The mystic's discourse is about the One that has no other; it lies beyond the province of logic.

This leaves us with a discomforting worry. If logic is inapplicable to the mystic's discourse, does that not come very close to saying that discriminations cannot be made in this field between sense and nonsense, the sound and the unsound?

The literal approach must be, for a philosopher, a desperate measure, a last resort only. To treat it as anything else would be methodologically perverse. Apart from the difficulties of discrimination, where logic is inoperative, the approach demands an unshakable prior conviction that the mystic's paradoxes are to be taken at their face value as reports of veridical insights. Here there is much that can be challenged.

We refused to dismiss the figurative account for not being able to translate its metaphors, or to give literal equivalents for its symbols and analogies. Yet that inability is nonetheless an embarrassment to it. When the mystic says, "God is a desert"; "God is a blinding light"; "God is, and is not, identical with the world"; or "The mystical enlightenment is an absolute emptiness which is absolute fullness"; we are compelled to accept these metaphors and paradoxes on the faith—if we accept them at all—that they can be true in some inscrutable way of one and the same deity. This cannot be shown, although the mystic *feels* intensely that it is so. The skeptic complains that he cannot begin to see how such wildly incompatible predicates can refer to any one being, whereas he can understand with relative ease how they might, in fact, be the expression of some ecstatic inner experience of a quite noncognitive kind. He does not deny that some apparently incompatible predicates may be revealed as ultimately compatible. A psychoanalytic story can reveal how love and hate, desire and fear, can be harbored simultaneously by a person for a single object; the same can be true with conflicting analogies and metaphors. The last word of the mystic, however, is "ineffable"; he does not profess to have a reconciling story.

An objector might now suggest that it is easy enough to see how we could choose senses for the words *abyss, desert, light,* that would give us at least a glimmer of insight into their metaphorical reference to the same divine being. The words are rich enough in their connotations and implications, both near and remote. This is true, but it cannot be a key to all the paradoxes. Certain ones (like that of identity and difference between God and world) offer no scope at all for such imaginative siftings and surmisings—unless we paraphrase the mystic's claim so freely that he will disown our translation. "The world is, and is not, identical with God" does not mean to the pantheistic mystic that the world is godlike in some respects and not in others.

If a city were referred to as a desert, a trap, or a furnace, the selection of appropriate meanings for these words in their metaphorical use would be possible because of the knowledge of the given fixed point of reference: a city. However, the concept of city is ontologically stable and intelligible in a way that the concept of God is not. The mystic's paradoxical discourse is related ultimately to his basic assertions about God's metaphysical status; this makes his semantic situation enormously more complex and precarious. Once again, these reflections do not attempt to disprove the mystic's statements or even to show that they cannot be figurative as well as semantically sound. If the mystic had independent grounds for believing in God, then one could readily accept the claim that he could speak about this God only in oblique language. Some mystics would say that they do have such independent grounds, but for others the mystical experiences themselves, reported in the language of paradox, furnish the grounds of belief. Here the risk of delusion is higher.

MYSTICAL EXPERIENCE AND AGNOSTICISM. "According to our scale of values," Rudolf Otto wrote, we shall consider the mystic's intuition "either a strange fantasy or a glimpse into the eternal relationships of things" (*Mysticism East and West*, p. 42). Need these be the only options? Might it not be possible to reject all the traditional interpretations of mystical experience but yet accord it very high intrinsic value? If the mystic cannot interpret his experience theologically without talking nonsense, it is then better for him not to attempt theology or metaphysics at all, lest he bring his experience itself into needless disrepute.

An approach of this kind would have strong sympathy with the agnostic elements of early Buddhism. Buddha taught the path to nirvāṇa but turned away any question about deities or the nature of a life hereafter. His emphasis was upon the moral quality of a life and upon attitudes toward life, death, suffering, and release from suffering. Mystical experience was attained in the course of a personal, practical discipline. It was understood as the culmination of such a discipline and given only the minimal theoretical interpretation. The lack of speculation did not, however, make the mystical experience unavailable to one who followed the Buddha's prescription for attaining it.

To insist that mysticism is possible without interpretation has the merit of avoiding unnecessary intellectual offense; it also allows us to admit as mystical the experiences of people outside both the theistic and monistic traditions but whose testimony, at the phenomenological level, shows great affinities with the mysticism of both traditions. Nevertheless, the mystical experiences of an agnostic are surely bound to differ in important respects from those of a Christian, a Buddhist, or a Muslim. The concepts used in interpretation help to determine the mystic's expectations of future experiences and to determine his map of the mystical path and the plotting of his position upon it. They shape the actual quality of his experience itself in a most intimate way. This does not imply that, but for the interpretative concepts, no experience could occur.

It may be feared that the theologically uninterpreted experience would tend to become a mere psychological curiosity, a luxury or consolation, isolated from all other parts of the subject's life. This can happen, but need not. Mystical experience basically involves a powerful urge toward the reconciliation, unification, and harmony of all with all, a feature that can readily be integrated with a moral outlook in which primacy is given to love. "Integrated," in fact, is really too weak a term; that moral ideal may receive its fullest and most splendid development in the mystical vision, and the moral agent gains a source of energy for the pursuit of the moral life.

These reflections may show, at least, that we cannot fairly assess the importance of mystical experience solely in terms of the interpretations that may be offered of it, whether speculatively pretentious or modest. An equally relevant question is what the mystic does with his experience, that is, what place he gives it in his total personal and moral existence. Evaluations based on this issue may often be at variance with those based upon a comparison of theories. A mystic may interpret elaborately and use his mystical experience as a mere refuge from responsibility, or he may be quite at a loss for interpretation, while recognizing in his experience the center and spring of a morally dedicated life.

OTHER PHILOSOPHICAL CRITICISMS

Our fourth type of response to the phenomena of mysticism was that offered by the radical philosophical critic, determined to call nonsense by its name, who takes the mystic's antinomies as a reductio ad absurdum of his claims. To those logical objections philosophers have added various epistemological and psychological difficulties.

THE PROBLEM OF OBJECTIVITY. The mystic (and we are no longer thinking of the agnostic mystic) normally claims that his experience is not only a way of being inwardly, subjectively moved, but also that it discloses the nature of reality, that it is a cognitive, objective experience. To support this he may appeal to the impressive convergences of testimony on fundamentals among mystics of different periods and parts of the world. The critic may contest this. In reports upon perceptual illusions, for instance, even unanimity does not remove their illusoriness.

That the experiences are disclosures about the entire universe in its ultimate nature may be an almost irresistible conclusion for the mystic. Nonetheless, it must involve interpretation of a demonstrably fallible kind. To feel that the experience is revelatory is one thing; to judge confidently that it is so is quite another. A dream under nitrous oxide may strike the dreamer with the force of a satanic revelation, but on awakening and correlating the nightmare with the shock of tooth extraction, he may have little temptation to judge the experience as a genuine disclosure. The feeling of revealedness can attach itself with equal intensity to incompatible contents.

W. T. Stace has argued that mystical experience is neither objective nor subjective but that it transcends this distinction and is best classified as transsubjective. To be objective, an experience must be orderly and law governed; the criteria of subjective experience are disorderliness and incoherence. Mystical experience fits neither category. It is an experience of unity, untouched by plurality; and without plurality there can be neither order nor disorder.

This is an ingenious treatment, but it seems open to criticism at least on two points. First, the criterion of objectivity may be questioned. We may be quite properly convinced that certain phenomena are objective before we have assured ourselves of their orderliness, and they may indeed remain anomalous. The subjective events of dreams and fantasies are not disorderly, although the laws governing dreams are very different from those governing events in the public world. Second, we may wish to deny that mystical experience is, in fact, experience of a totally undifferentiated unity. There is, no doubt, a stage in which the mystic not only apprehends the world of plurality as issuing from a single divine source but sees that source and the world as a unity. Mystical experiences, however, cannot usefully be restricted to this one type. Perception of multiplicity does play a role, even if it is a subordinate one, in many other types. This is obviously so with extrovertive mystical experience in general, which is an experience not simply of oneness but of oneness in multiplicity. It is also apparent in the statement from Sri Aurobindo that "those who have … possessed the calm within can perceive always welling out from its silence the perennial supply of the energies which work in the universe" (*The Life Divine*, 1949, p. 28). The most favorable verdict we can pass upon claims to objectivity is "not proven."

EPISTEMOLOGICAL PROBLEMS. When we ask more particularly what sort of apprehension, what modes of knowing are involved in mysticism, the answers swell our fund of paradoxes. If one mystic claims to perceive the cosmic energies welling forth from the One, another denies that anything like perception takes place. St. John

of the Cross speaks of a "supernatural knowledge and light" that is so completely "detached and removed from all intelligible forms, which are objects of the understanding, that it is neither perceived nor observed" (*The Ascent of Mount Carmel*, Vol. I, p. 123). Nor is mystical insight a purely intellectual act, for "the higher and more sublime the Divine light, the darker is it to our understanding." Union with God "transcends all knowledge." The difficulty is increased by the doctrine that in mystical experience the subject-object distinction breaks down, and with it, naturally enough, go all our thought models for cognitive activities. Faced with the risk of a complete failure in communication, the mystic usually resorts to a characteristic complex use of language. This works in part by negations ("not ordinary perception," "not simply emotion") and in part by descriptions of his religious situation as he interprets it in metaphysical and theological terms, enhanced with poetical imagery; God now dwells in him, or has "absorbed" him "in the embrace and abyss of His sweetness." It is easy to see why the mystic resorts to these forms of discourse and also why they offer little comfort to the epistemologist. For the interpretations assume precisely what is at issue: that mystical experiences are objective and reliably cognitive in nature.

Some critics maintain that the mystic's claim to "know" must at least be suspected of being spurious. When such expressions as "objectivity," "discovery," and "vision" are used in senses so radically far from normal and applied with obscure and idiosyncratic criteria, it is legitimate to ask whether some quite different (and noncognitive) thought model might give a more intelligible clue to what is being described.

For example, it is sometimes suggested that the mystic's language might be best understood not as a description of reality but as the expression of a state of mind. Certainly, some of the mystic's language is clearly emotive, and even when it seems to describe his "situation," as we have been using the word, this may still be an indirect expression of his state of mind. Instead of saying, "I have an oppressive, worried feeling," one may say, "I feel as if there were something terribly wrong." Instead of "I feel uneasy, insecure," he may say, "There is no sure footing; everything and everybody is working against me." Instead of "I have a feeling of unreality," he may say, "I am not real anymore." The use of such examples does not imply that the mystic is psychotic. Some psychotic experiences are mystical experiences, but it hardly follows that all mysticism is psychosis. The critic could confine himself to pointing out this disturbing parallel in the use of language: Both mystics and psychotics use situation-descriptive language for what, in the latter case at any rate, is a serious misperception of one's situation, a projection of inner disturbances upon the outer world. Furthermore, the projection occurs, partly at least, because the disturbances are not understood for what they are, and there is a failure of insight.

In the mystic's defense, it must be pointed out that to analyze his experience as a state of mind is not necessarily to discredit it. States of mind can be—and normally are—elicited by objective states of affairs, properly interpreted. People do, on occasion, fall victim to real persecution; their fears and anxieties can be very well founded.

But decisiveness, either in criticism or defense, is once more not to be had. Of course one's fears can be well-founded, but a person who says he does not really exist any more *must* be deluded. Significantly, as soon as such remarks verge on the paradoxical, we cease to take them at their face value and treat them as certain signs of disorder.

CONTENT AND QUALITY OF MYSTICAL EXPERIENCE. We have been considering some epistemological and linguistic problems set by mysticism and some ways in which a philosophical critic can assault, although probably not overthrow, the mystic's claims. Of the central mystical experience, characterized by loss of individuality and dissolution in a limitless divine totality, little or nothing has been said from a philosophical or psychological viewpoint. How far could a naturalistic account of mystical experience cope with these central features? Or could justice be done to them only in a thoroughgoing mystical philosophy, reared upon the paradoxes themselves? Here a suggestion or two must suffice.

In the first place, the mystical experience is a vision of the world that is free, to a very unusual extent, from the interposition of concepts. Normal perception is closely linked to practical projects; we see the world in terms of our needs and desires and our intentions to manipulate it in various ways. Aesthetic experience provides a sharp contrast. One may succeed briefly in contemplating a pastoral landscape not in terms of land utilization or of the practical problems of traveling across it, but simply as colors, shapes, or volumes. Seen in this way, the landscape can be excitingly and startlingly different from its everyday utilitarian appearance. Mystical experience is even more disturbingly strange because it suspends the application of still more basic concepts and categories. "As long as a man has time and place and number and quantity and multiplicity, he is on the wrong track and God is far from him" (Meister Eckhart, *Sermons,* p. 202).

When concepts are withdrawn and fundamental distinctions obliterated, it is understandable that our ordinary sense of the limits and boundaries between thing and thing, person and person, should also temporarily disappear. In this we may have an important clue to the mystic's claims about the overcoming of finite individuality, the cessation of the subject-object relation, and mergings and meltings into the infinite. Because our normal sense of our powers and their limits is fostered by the utilitarian and practical view of the world, when that view is suppressed, there can come the sense of exhilarating expansion or liberation that is often described in the mystical literature.

Similarly, if the practical orientation is suspended and, with it, the related conceptual framework of normal experience, we may lose awareness of the passage of time. We are not demarcating event from event in the normal time-articulating manner. In introvertive mystical experience the awareness of space is also obliterated, for there is a still more thoroughgoing withdrawal from perception and even from sensation. The intensity and strangeness of mystical experience reinforce the effect of timelessness; the experience is dramatically discontinuous with the flow of events before and after and hence is felt as not belonging to it.

The mystic himself can afford to be sympathetic to many such naturalistic explanations. He can refuse to admit that they discredit his experience. They are simply (he will say "necessarily") incomplete, for they cannot account for the qualitatively unique tone of mystical feeling, and they do not disprove his claim that the object of mystical vision itself must elude the categories of naturalistic philosophy.

Mysticism can be upgraded or downgraded with bewildering ease through the choice of a metaphor or a simile; its paradoxes are unutterable truths or blatant contradictions; its clearest affinities are with trustworthy modes of knowing or with psychotic, delusory states of mind; of all human experience it is the most valuable or it is a psychological curiosity, fashioned by the unconscious from infantile materials. The excesses of these opposite poles are avoided in our remarks about an "agnostic" or "noninterpreting" mysticism, although this is perhaps more of a practical compromise than the germ of a full-fledged theory. It tries at least to stress the potential human importance of mystical experience—when yoked to moral vision—and it expresses the wishful thought that the paradoxes of mystical interpretation should not be altogether allowed to mask that importance.

See also Agnosticism; Aurobindo Ghose; Being; Buddhism; Eckhart, Meister; Islamic Philosophy; John of the Cross, St.; Logical Paradoxes; Mysticism, History of; Mysticism: The Indian Tradition; Nirvāṇa; Otto, Rudolf; Pantheism; Pseudo-Dionysius; Religious Experience, Argument for the Existence of God; Religious Language; Śankara; Stace, Walter Terence.

Bibliography

PRIMARY SOURCES

Boehme, Jakob. *Works,* 4 vols. London, 1764–1781. An English translation.

Eckhart, Meister. *Selected Treatises and Sermons.* Translated by J. M. Clark and J. V. Skinner. London: Faber and Faber, 1958.

John of the Cross, St. *The Ascent of Mount Carmel.* London, 1943.

Progoff, Ira, ed. *The Cloud of Unknowing.* New York: Julian Press, 1957. An anonymous fourteenth-century treatise on contemplative prayer.

Ruysbroeck, Jan van. *The Chastising of God's Children. ...* Edited by J. Bazire and E. Colledge. Oxford, 1957.

Underhill, Evelyn, ed. *The Cloud of Unknowing.* London, 1912. Contains introduction.

GENERAL STUDIES

Butler, C. *Western Mysticism.* London: Constable, 1922.

Hügel, F. von. *Eternal Life.* Edinburgh: Clark, 1912.

Hügel, F. von. *The Mystical Element of Religion.* London: Dent, 1908.

Inge, W. R. *Christian Mysticism.* London: Methuen, 1899.

Inge, W. R. *The Philosophy of Plotinus,* 2 vols. London: Longman, 1918.

Otto, R. *Das Heilige.* Breslau: Trewendt and Granier, 1917. Translated by J. W. Harvey as *The Idea of the Holy.* London: Oxford University Press, 1923.

Otto, R. *Mysticism East and West.* Translated by B. L. Bracey and R. C. Payne. New York: Macmillan, 1932.

Underhill, Evelyn. *Mysticism.* London: Methuen, 1911. Contains a substantial bibliography.

PSYCHOLOGY OF MYSTICISM

James, William. *The Varieties of Religious Experience.* London: Longman, 1902. Lectures XVI–XVII.

Leuba, J. H. *The Psychology of Religious Mysticism.* London: K. Paul, Trench, Trubner, 1925.

ACCOUNTS OF MYSTICISM

Smart, Ninian. *Reasons and Faiths.* London: Routledge and Paul, 1958. Particularly valuable for its discussions of various non-Christian as well as Christian forms of mystical and numinous religion.

Stace, W. T. *Mysticism and Philosophy.* Philadelphia: Lippincott, 1960.

Zaehner, R. C. *Mysticism Sacred and Profane.* Oxford: Clarendon Press, 1957.

PHILOSOPHICAL DISCUSSIONS

Glasgow, W. D. "Knowledge of God." *Philosophy* 32 (1957): 229ff.

Horsburgh, H. J. N. "The Claims of Religious Experience." *Australasian Journal of Philosophy* 35 (1957): 186ff.

Kennick, W. E. Review of Stace's *Mysticism and Philosophy. Philosophical Review* 71 (1962): 387–390.

Martin, C. B. *Religious Belief.* Ithaca, NY: Cornell University Press, 1959.

Ronald W. Hepburn (1967)

MYSTICISM, NATURE AND ASSESSMENT OF [ADDENDUM]

Since the 1960s, philosophical controversies concerning the nature of mysticism mainly surround the relationship between mysticism and language, and the typology of mysticism. Moreover, as standard empiricist epistemologies no longer dominate the scene, new types of epistemology, which grant mystical experiences much more evidential force, have been formulated.

MYSTICISM AND LANGUAGE

Concerning the relationship between mysticism and language, some believe that mysticism transcends language, as reflected in the claim that mysticism is essentially ineffable. Taken literally, this claim generates many paradoxes, and Keith Yandell (1993, chaps. 3–5) has made sharp criticisms of various versions of the ineffability thesis (Alston 1992, Matilal 1992).

At the other end of the spectrum, Steven Katz claims that mystical experiences are largely constructed out of the language provided by the mystics's conceptual framework and practice. His work has been largely responsible for the contextualist turn in the study of mysticism in the 1980s (Katz 1978, 1983). This kind of mystical constructivism has been fiercely contested, especially by Robert Forman (1990, 1998, 1999). He argues for the universality of the "Pure Consciousness Event," which is a purely nonconceptual state of consciousness without any intentional object, and that mystical constructivism cannot adequately explain mysticism's unpredicted and novel nature. Jess Hollenback (1996) provides cases of paranormal mystical experiences that "shatter the recipient's previous expectations" (p. 15). William Wainwright (1981) contends that while mystical experiences are shaped to some extent by the mystics's traditions, it does not follow that those experiences are entirely determined or created by those traditions.

It seems hazardous to make universal statements about the relationship between mysticism and language.

Perhaps it is more advisable to reflect on the meaning of ineffability claims made by mystics within their contexts, and the complex ways of interaction between mystical experiences and mystical traditions (Katz 1992).

THE DEBATE OVER THEISTIC MYSTICISM

How we should classify different types of mysticism continues to be controversial. Some scholars do not regard theistic mysticism as a separate type. They argue that all mystical experiences have basically the same phenomenological content—the pure consciousness. Theistic mysticism is just the imposition of theistic interpretation on this core mystical experience.

However, R. C. Zaehner, William Wainwright, Stephen Payne, and Nelson Pike vigorously defend the distinctiveness of theistic mysticism. They appeal to the phenomenological data of Christian mysticism: God and the soul are said to be close, or in mutual embrace. The "language is radically dualistic" (Pike 1992, p. 108). Furthermore, the same mystic sometimes offers a theistic description and sometimes a monistic description. They seem to reflect differences in the content of the experiences. Moreover, the phenomenon of "spiritual sensations" can hardly be explained as the imposition of the Christian tradition.

Pike also argues that even if the theistic mystic may experience a monistic interval, the meaning of this experience should be determined with respect to the phenomenological context, which is a series of dualistic experiences of God. So it is legitimate to think that during a "monistic" interval, the spirit is simply "deluded by love into not noticing the difference between itself and God" (p. 156).

DRUG-INDUCED MYSTICISM

Mysticism can be induced by drugs. This kind of chemical mysticism has been made popular by Aldous Huxley, and confirmed by some empirical studies (Tisdale 1980, chap. 15). However, its philosophical significance is unclear. Some regard the drug-induced alternative states of consciousness as gateways to extra-mundane reality. Others think that chemical mysticism demonstrates that reductive explanations of mysticism are available. Both interpretations can be resisted. On the one hand, the skeptics argue that we cannot distinguish alternative states of consciousness from hallucinations.

On the other hand, some scholars contend that it has not been really established that drugs are sufficient to produce genuine mystical experiences. The experimental evidence only suggests that it can raise the likelihood and enhance the intensity of the experiences (Davis 1989, p. 220; Heaney 1973, p. 116; Vergote 1997, pp. 197ff). Even if drugs are causally sufficient to produce mystical experiences, it does not follow that they are unveridical. God may have laid down some psychophysical laws to the effect that whenever certain brain states are produced, a certain perception of the divine would be produced. There is no reason why those brain states cannot be caused by taking drugs. It has been argued that as long as the whole process is set up and upheld by God, such perception of God should be counted as veridical.

In any case, even if drug-induced mystical experiences are unveridical, it does not follow that non-drug-induced mystical experiences are also unveridical. What is shown is that on the experiential level, mystical experience can be faked. This is neither surprising nor uniquely true of mystical experience. Sense experiences can also be faked.

NEURAL SCIENCES AND MYSTICISM

Eugene d'Aquili, Andrew Newberg, and Vince Rause (2001) have proposed a neurophysiological theory of mysticism. They explain mystical states as the effect of "deafferentation"—the cutting off of neural input into various structures of the nervous system. As a result, an experience of "absolute unitary being" occurs. In similar ways, the theory proposes explanations of a continuum of mystical experiences, both theistic and non-theistic.

The theory of d'Aquili and Newberg is by no means proven at this stage. Moreover, they point out that " tracing spiritual experience to neurological behavior does not disprove its realness … both spiritual experiences and experiences of a more ordinary material nature are made real to the mind in the very same way—through the processing powers of the brain and the cognitive functions of the mind" (Newberg, d'Aquili, and Rause 2001, p. 37).

They also ask, " Why should the human brain, which evolved for the very pragmatic purpose of helping us survive, possess such an apparently impractical talent?" (Newberg, d'Aquili, and Rause 2001, p. 123). They in fact tend to think their biology of transcendence is congenial to religion. The neurophysiological theory by itself does not disprove the mystical experiences, just as psychophysical laws governing sense experiences would not disprove those experiences (Jerome Gellman 2001, p. 99). Of course, there are deep questions about naturalistic explanations of mysticism that deserve further exploration (Wainwright 1973; Yandell 1993, chaps. 6–7).

THE ASSESSMENT OF MYSTICISM AND THE DEMISE OF FOUNDATIONALISM

Since the 1980s, there is a revival of the argument from mystical experience. Richard Swinburne (1979) defends the "Principle of Credulity," which says we should trust our experiences unless there are special considerations to the contrary. William Alston has defended the rationality of mystical perception by propounding his "doxastic practice" approach. By "doxastic practice" Alston means a system of belief-forming mechanisms. His *Perceiving God*(1991) is an impressive work which argues that it is practically rational to regard all socially established doxastic practices as prima facie reliable. It is important to note that Alston requires those doxastic practices to have a significant degree of self-support, and an internal overrider system.

Alston's sophisticated argument has attracted a lot of criticisms (Fales 2004). Space does not permit detailed discussions of the debate. It is important to appreciate the significance of Alston's work (together with Swinburne, Yandell, and Gellman) as a new research project in epistemology. They are not only reviving natural theology, but also proposing a new approach that navigates between strong foundationalism and postmodern relativism. They admit our epistemic base is fallible but they advocate an attitude of prima facie trust to replace Cartesian doubt. While "trust without infallible proof" was formerly treated as irrational, they suggest that the spirit of rationality should instead be construed as "trust until shown otherwise by criticisms."

They maintain the emphasis on experience but try to break loose of the straightjacket of traditional empiricism by broadening the evidential base of experience. The basic rationale is that in the end we need to adopt an attitude of *basic trust* (i.e., a trust that cannot be non-circularly justified) toward our perceptual experiences. It would be unfair to grant this kind of basic trust to sense experiences alone while adopting skepticism toward other kinds of perceptual experiences. In the end, the epistemic assessment of mysticism will probably depend on the ability of this radically new epistemology to withstand objections. The controversy is still raging.

See also Religious Experience.

Bibliography

Alston, William. "Literal and Nonliteral in Reports of Mystical Experience." In *Mysticism and Language*, edited by Steven T. Katz. New York: Oxford University Press, 1992.

Alston, William. *Perceiving God: The Epistemology of Religious Experience*. Ithaca, NY, and London: Cornell University Press, 1991.

Davis, Caroline. *The Evidential Force of Religious Experience*. Oxford: Clarendon Press, 1989.

Fales, Evan. "Do Mystics See God?" In *Contemporary Debates in Philosophy of Religion*, edited by Michael L. Peterson and Raymond J. VanArragon. Oxford: Blackwell, 2004.

Forman, Robert K. C., ed. *The Innate Capacity: Mysticism, Psychology and Philosophy*. New York: Oxford University Press, 1998.

Forman, Robert K. C. *Mysticism, Mind, Consciousness*. Albany: State University of New York Press, 1999.

Forman, Robert K. C., ed. *The Problem of Pure Consciousness: Mysticism and Philosophy*. New York: Oxford University Press, 1990.

Gellman, Jerome. *Mystical Experience of God: A Philosophical Inquiry*. Aldershot, U.K.: Ashgate, 2001.

Heaney, John J., ed. *Psyche and Spirit*. New York: Paulist Press, 1973.

Hollenback, Jess Byron. *Mysticism: Experience, Response, and Empowerment*. University Park: The Pennsylvania State University Press, 1996.

Huxley, Aldous. *The Doors of Perception and Heaven and Hell*. London: Flamingo, 1994.

Katz, Steven T., ed. *Mysticism and Language*. New York: Oxford University Press, 1992.

Katz, Steven T., ed. *Mysticism and Philosophical Analysis*. New York: Oxford University Press, 1978.

Katz, Steven T., ed. *Mysticism and Religious Traditions*. New York: Oxford University Press, 1983.

Matilal, Bimal Krishna. "Mysticism and Ineffability: Some Issues of Logic and Language." In *Mysticism and Language*, edited by Steven T. Katz. New York: Oxford University Press, 1992.

Newberg, Andrew, Eugene D'Aquili, and Vince Rause. *Why God Won't Go Away: Brain Science and the Biology of Belief*. New York: Ballantine Books, 2001.

Payne, Stephen. *John of the Cross and the Cognitive Value of Mysticism: An Analysis of Sanjuanist Teaching and its Philosophical Implications for Contemporary Discussions of Mystical Experience*. Dordrecht, Netherlands: Kluwer, 1990.

Pike, Nelson. *Mystic Union: An Essay in the Phenomenology of Mysticism*. Ithaca, NY: Cornell University Press, 1992.

Swinburne, Richard. *The Existence of God*. Oxford: Clarendon Press, 1979.

Tisdale, John R., ed. *Growing Edges in the Psychology of Religion*. Chicago: Nelson-Hall, 1980.

Vergote, Antoine. *Religion, Belief and Unbelief: A Psychological Study*. Amsterdam: Rodopi, 1997.

Wainwright, William. *Mysticism*. Brighton: The Harvester Press, 1981.

Wainwright, William. "Natural Explanations and Religious Experience." *Ratio* 15 (1973): 98–101.

Yandell, Keith E. *The Epistemology of Religious Experience*. Cambridge, U.K.: Cambridge University Press, 1993.

Kai-man Kwan (2005)

MYTH

The relation between philosophy and mythology can be usefully set out under three main headings. There is first the period in Greek philosophy when philosophers wanted to discard and to criticize mythological modes of thought but when they were still so close to those modes of thought that mythology recurred in philosophical contexts. Then in modern thought there is the period from Giambattista Vico to Auguste Comte, when mythology was taken seriously as a clue to the primitive history of thought, and from the nineteenth century on, when there was a variety of systematic attempts at a science of mythology. Finally, there is the role of myth in modern irrationalisms.

To this scheme three objections may be made. The first is that in discussing the Greeks what is said will inevitably be conditioned by the writer's beliefs about what modern scientific approaches to mythology have yielded. Thus, the second section should precede the first. To this objection everything can be conceded except the conclusion, for it would be equally difficult to discuss the growth of the science of mythology before anything had been said about mythology itself.

A second objection might be that no initial definition of mythology has been offered. But here the danger is that by delineating the field of mythology too sharply, one biases one's account in favor of one sort of theory. And any definition broad enough to escape this charge would be either vague or a mere catalog.

The third objection would be that the Christian era until the time of Vico appears to be neglected by this schematism. For this there is good reason, however. In that era mythologies were predominantly treated as false theological accounts, rivals to the one true theological account, the Christian.

GREEK PHILOSOPHY

Greek myths, like those of other Mediterranean and Near Eastern cultures, include cosmogonies and accounts of great discoveries and inventions, such as that of fire; of the founding of cities; and of the ancestry of kings, in which relationships between gods and men are codified. In different stages of the mythology, such as in the distinction between the Olympian gods and the dark, chthonic deities, one can distinguish different social origins. From the time of Émile Durkheim and Jane Harrison anthropologists have stressed the function of myths as explanations of rituals that express the social consciousness of a group. In Greek society the public ritual continued to express the life of the community long after belief in gods had become questionable.

Greek philosophy only gradually separated itself from mythology. Personification, for example, was common in pre-Socratic philosophy, but at the same time rationalist criticism of mythology originated with writers like Xenophanes, who attacked anthropomorphic representation of the gods, and Euhemerus, who argued that myths were to be explained as stories about men who had been deified. Heraclitus attacked Homer and Hesiod for their dependence on myth.

PLATO. Plato used myths and allegories for a variety of purposes. Perceval Frutiger draws a distinction between myths properly so called and allegories, which, for example, lack the element of story; among allegories he would include the account of the Cave in the *Republic* or the noble lie about precious and base metals in the souls of different types of men. He divides myths in the full sense into those that function as allegories, those that function as genetic explanations, and those that function as other types of parascientific explanations. An example of allegorical myth is Diotima's account of the birth of Eros in the *Symposium*; among genetic explanations is the account of the creation in the *Timaeus*; and typical examples of what Frutiger calls parascientific are the accounts of a future life and of rewards and punishments for virtue and vice given in the *Republic, Gorgias, Phaedo,* and *Phaedrus*. Frutiger sees three features of Platonic myth as outstanding: the use of symbols, the freedom exhibited in the handling of the narrative, and what he pleasantly calls a prudent imprecision. The last is important. Plato uses myth where he wishes the precise extent of his own intellectual commitment to remain unclear. Thus, Plato's use of myth helps us to understand how the break with mythological thought forms involves the raising of sharp questions about truth and falsity which the mythological forms themselves are able to evade. This throws light on certain characteristics of mythology.

The subject matter of mythological narratives is no different from that of later philosophy and science; what differentiates myth from these is not merely its narrative form or its use of personification. It is, rather, that a myth is living or dead, not true or false. You cannot refute a myth because as soon as you treat it as refutable, you do not treat it as a myth but as a hypothesis or history. Myths that could not easily coexist if they were hypotheses or histories, as, for example, rival accounts of creation, can comfortably belong to the same body of mythology. There are often gradual processes of reconciliation and of integration into a single narrative, but the discrepancies that give so much pleasure to the anthropologist are not discrepancies at all from the standpoint of the narrator.

Thus Plato, by falling back into myth, may be deliberately avoiding too direct an encounter not only with certain philosophical difficulties but also with rival religious traditions. For myth is not theology any more than it is hypothesis or history. Indeed, the dominance of theology in later religious thought and the insistence in the mystery religions and in Christianity on treating myth as theology are as responsible for the death of mythology as is any philosophical rationalism bred by the pre-Socratics and Plato. Of course, it was not only Greek mythology that was treated by Christianity in this way. Both Norse and Celtic mythology met the same fate, although they both survived in medieval literature as beliefs and not just as a source for tale telling.

MODERN THOUGHT

The first serious modern treatment of mythology occurs in Vico's *Scienza nuova*. In Vico's theory of history each period has its own unity and character, and periods succeed one another in a determinate order. The beginnings of civilization occur in "the age of the gods," when men live in families and center their lives around religion, marriage, and the burial of the dead; this period is followed by the "age of heroes," in which aristocratic states arise. Only then comes the "age of men," the age of democratic republics. By the third stage rational inquiry is established, but in the early stages poetry and myth express the vulgar wisdom of a people. Only from mythology can we discover the religion, morals, law, and social life of early society. Myths are not false narratives, nor are they allegories. They express the collective mentality of a given age.

Vico's treatment of myth is far closer to that of modern anthropology than is that of his immediate successors. The Enlightenment's belief in progress and attack on superstition produced an unsympathetic climate for such interests. Even Johann Gottfried Herder, whose sympathy was awakened by seeing in primitive poetry and song the spirit of the folk, was inclined to treat myths as pardonably false beliefs. In the nineteenth century this assumption underlay the first systematic attempts at a science of mythology, but there was also a new consciousness of the widespread prevalence of mythology and a wish to apply comparative methods.

In 1856 F. Max Müller published his *Comparative Mythology*, in which he tried to interpret mythologies by means of principles derived from philology. All Aryan languages are derived from Sanskrit, in which originally there were certain words named sun, sky, clouds, rain, and dawn. But language became diseased, the original meanings were lost, the words became treated as the names of divine beings, and what had been accounts of the sun ushering in the dawn and ending the reign of night were transformed into myths about battles between gods, heroic quests for gold, and the like. To understand a myth, asserted Müller, discover the etymology of the names.

Andrew Lang pointed out that rival philologists would give different etymological explanations of the same myth with apparently equal plausibility. Lang himself regarded myths as survivals of earlier social norms. The classical Greeks recount myths in which cannibalism and human sacrifice occur, although they practiced neither; however, among Polynesian and African peoples, of whom Lang's contemporaries were newly aware, just such customs and accompanying myths are found. In classical Greece the custom had vanished, but the myth remained. Or a nature myth may be found with its meaning plain in its Maori form today, whereas in its Greek version the story has been so changed that the original meaning has been lost. The anthropology Lang and his school used was that of E. B. Tylor, who himself criticized Müller's theorizing by showing how convincingly the nursery rhyme "Sing a Song of Sixpence" could be explained as a solar myth in Müller's terms.

RECURRENT THEMES AND COMPARATIVE METHODS. Lang took it for granted that the "same" myth could turn up both in Greece and in New Zealand. The modern collection of mythologies has emphasized nothing so much as the strikingly similar themes and stories that recur in widely different places and times. Myths of the creation of the world are widespread; myths of the creation of humankind occur everywhere. But even in detail myths resemble one another. Clyde Kluckhohn has written that he knows of no culture lacking myths of witchcraft in which were-animals move about at night; poisons can be magically introduced into the victim, causing illness and death; and there is some connection between incest and witchcraft. Rank has discussed the common myth pattern of a hero, born of noble parents, against whose birth an oracle warns his father, so that the child is left to die of exposure; the child is saved by shepherds or animals, grows up to return, perform great deeds, avenge himself, and finally be recognized. In the Far East, among the Navajo, and in Greece, as well as in many other places, we find this pattern. What is the explanation of its recurrence? We can distinguish three main types of explanation.

The first is psychoanalytic. Otto Rank, a Freudian, explains the hero as the ego of the child who rebels against his parents. His father, on whom the child's hate is projected, is pictured as exposing the child in a box on water. The box symbolizes the womb; the water, birth. The order of the story follows a sequence analogous to that of dreams in which natural events and symbols are combined in a single fantasy. The myth is the expression of all paranoid characters who hate the father who ousted them from the maternal love and care. Because such a character is widespread, the myth that expresses it is widespread, too; in general, it is the common biological, and, consequently, psychological, inheritance of humankind that underlies the common stock of mythology.

By contrast, the Jungian approach to mythology rests upon belief in a common human access to the collective unconscious. The individual continually finds himself giving expression to an archetypal symbolism that dominates not only the mythology but also much of the sophisticated literature of the world. The same myths recur in different times and places because all mythology has a common source. Modern man, who has overdeveloped the rational side of his nature, encounters in his dreams the same figures that appear in ancient and primitive mythology.

The difficulties in the Jungian account of mythology are difficulties that confront all Jungian theory. If the existence of the collective unconscious is a hypothesis designed to explain the recurrence of certain themes and symbols in myths and dreams, then it must be formulable in a way that is testable. But if such a hypothesis is to be testable, we must be able to deduce from it predictable consequences over and above the data it was originally formulated to explain. Yet no such consequences seem to follow from the hypothesis of the collective unconscious. It seems to be untestable; it certainly remains untested. As an explanation of the recurrence of mythological themes and symbols, it is also unnecessary, for there are simpler and less incoherent explanations.

Joseph Campbell has used the Jungian theory of archetypes to interpret the story The Frog King, one of the myths collected by the brothers Grimm. He sees the frog as a small-scale dragon whose outward ugliness conceals the depths of the unconscious, in which unrecognized and unknown treasure is to be found. The frog king summons the child to attain maturity and self-knowledge by exploration of the unconscious. Fortunately, we also have

a Freudian interpretation of The Frog King by Ernest Jones according to which the frog is a symbol for the penis and the myth represents the child's overcoming disgust in approaching the sexual act. Müller had, of course, long before interpreted The Frog King as one more solar myth.

In the face of these rival interpretations the need for a criterion of correct interpretation is clearly urgent, and with this need goes the need for a criterion for deciding when two myths are and are not versions of the "same" myth. The first step toward providing such criteria is the collection and tentative classification of as many bodies of mythology as possible. The most interesting work here has been done by Kluckhohn, who has systematically established not only the recurrence of plots and characters but also the existence of constant tendencies within this recurrence. For example, we can discover cases where a myth is reinterpreted to fit a new cultural or social situation. Clearly, where we can distinguish the original from the reinterpreted version, we are in a stronger position to compare a myth with similar myths for other cultures. We can study and compare not merely one version of a myth with another but the development of one myth through a series of versions with the development of another; from this it is clear that even if we wish to stress certain psychological functions of myth (Kluckhohn has thrown light on Navajo mythmaking by showing how it exemplifies mechanisms of ego defense), it is only when we put myth into a social context that we are likely to understand what the nature of mythmaking and recounting is.

ANTHROPOLOGY. The work of Claude Lévi-Strauss is important not only because its treatment of myth does not abstract myths from the social and economic relationships of those who tell and hear them but also because by invoking a wider context he has been able to pick out hitherto unnoticed features of mythology. In Totemism, for example, Lévi-Strauss shows how a myth of the North American Ojibwa and a myth from Polynesian Tikopia both express relationships between nature and culture, between the species that provide food and the kinship system. In each case the myth helps to express both continuity and discontinuity in these relationships; both myths also stress that no direct and simple connection between the one type of relationship and the other is possible. The myths, as it were, warn anthropologists not to oversimplify.

If one did not notice the connection of these myths with foodstuffs and with kinship but simply abstracted the "story," one would certainly not necessarily conclude that the Ojibwa myth and the Tikopia myth were the same myth. The resemblances between them appear fully only because Lévi-Strauss poses certain questions about the myths. These questions are formulated in the light of his general theory of kinship systems and invoke the notion of relationships that are specified in purely formal terms. Lévi-Strauss elsewhere has analyzed other myths with a view to showing that in their structure formal properties are both exhibited and implicitly commented upon. Perhaps not surprisingly, these formal properties parallel the formal properties exhibited by kinship systems and also parallel to some extent, much more surprisingly, the formal properties of certain linguistic structures.

What emerges from these studies is the thesis that myths incorporate and exhibit binary oppositions that are present in the structure of the society in which the myth was born. In the myth these oppositions are reconciled and overcome. The function of the myth is to render intellectually and socially tolerable what would otherwise be experienced as incoherence. The myth is a form in which society both understands and misunderstands its own structure. Thus, Lévi-Strauss gives a precise meaning to Vico's contention that "The fables of the gods are true histories of customs."

This judgment is perhaps inverted in the work of Lévi-Strauss's most important rival, Mircea Eliade. The customs of men, in Eliade's view, often turn out to be the expression of their beliefs about the gods. Thus, the behavior of shamans, who in a state of trance imitate animal sounds (birds' song, for example, among many peoples) is a reenactment and an attempt to restore man's primitive, paradisal, unfallen state in which he not only did not die or have to work but also communicated with the animals and lived in peace with them. Hence, Eliade concludes both that shamanism is part of the central religious tradition of humankind, stretching from primitive African myths to Christian theology, and that it is therefore not, as it first appears to be, an irrational phenomenon. Eliade distinguishes sharply between the particular cultural and social trappings that may surround a myth and what he calls the ideology behind the trappings that is exhibited in the myth itself. Thus, where Lévi-Strauss analyzes the content of a myth in terms of what is local and particular to a given society, Eliade wishes to relate the content to general human religious interests and as far as possible divorce it from the local and particular.

IRRATIONALISM. "Myths must be judged as a means of acting upon the present," said Georges Sorel in 1908.

Sorel distinguishes those beliefs that it is appropriate to characterize in terms of truth and falsity and those it is appropriate to characterize in terms of effectiveness and ineffectiveness. A myth is essentially a belief about the future that embodies the deepest inclinations of some particular social group. The myth that Sorel himself wanted to propagate was the syndicalist project of a general strike. Other socialists treated their beliefs about the future as predictions; Sorel regards this as for the most part irrelevant. The only predicates in which he is interested are self-fulfilling ones.

Yet to regard beliefs about the future in this way is paradoxical. For example, when I try to propagate a myth, I am inviting people to believe. But insofar as I do this, I invite them to treat it as true rather than false and as susceptible to truth or falsity. It is difficult to resist the conclusion that anyone who holds a view like Sorel's will fall into a form of doublethink, treating the myth as true or false in certain situations but retreating into the assertion that questions of its truth or falsity are inappropriate in other situations. Certainly, just this kind of doublethink characterizes modern irrationalist mythmakers after Sorel. They wish to avoid hard questions that philosophers or social scientists might raise about their myths, but they also wish to claim some kind of truth for their utterances. Thus, we also get a concomitant doctrine of special kinds of truth or special criteria for truth—for example, in works as different as Alfred Rosenberg's *Myth of the Twentieth Century* and D. H. Lawrence's *The Plumed Serpent*. Rosenberg's version of Houston Stewart Chamberlain's amalgam of anti-Semitism, racism, and authoritarian German nationalism is, of course, utterly different in content and implications from Lawrence's appeal to "the dark gods" and his attempt to restore an imagination violated by the wrong kind of arid rationalism. However, the difficulty with all irrationalism is that the abandonment of the criteria of rationality leaves us defenseless before the most morally outrageous appeals to emotion. In such appeals the revival of myth has a key place.

See also Chamberlain, Houston Stewart; Comte, Auguste; Durkheim, Émile; Freud, Sigmund; Functionalism in Sociology; Heraclitus of Ephesus; Herder, Johann Gottfried; Homer; Irrationalism; Jung, Carl Gustav; Philosophical Anthropology; Plato; Pre-Socratic Philosophy; Sorel, Georges; Vico, Giambattista; Xenophanes of Colophon.

Bibliography

Eliade, Mircea. *Aspects du mythe*. Paris: Gallimard, 1963.

Frutiger, Perceval. *Les mythes de Platon: Étude philosophique et littéraire*. Paris: F. Alcan, 1930.

Hooke, S. H., ed. *Myth, Ritual, and Kingship*. Oxford: Clarendon Press, 1958.

Jones, Ernest. *Essays in Applied Psychoanalysis, Vol. II, Essays in Folklore, Anthropology and Religion*. London, 1951.

Jung, C. G., and Carl Kerényi. *Essays on a Science of Mythology*. Translated by R. F. C. Hull. New York: Pantheon, 1949.

Lang, Andrew. *Custom and Myth*. London, 1901.

Lévi-Strauss, Claude. *Structural Anthropology*. Translated by Claire Jacobson and Brooke Grundfest. New York: Basic, 1963.

Lévi-Strauss, Claude. *Totemism*. Translated by R. Needham. Boston: Beacon Press, 1963.

Müller, F. Max. *Chips from a German Workshop*. New York: Scribners, 1871.

Murray, Henry A., ed. *Myth and Mythmaking*. New York: G. Braziller, 1960.

Rank, Otto. *The Myth of the Birth of the Hero*. Translated by F. Robbins and S. E. Jellife. New York: R. Brunner, 1952.

Sebeok, Thomas A., ed. *Myth: A Symposium*. Bloomington: Indiana University Press, 1955.

Stewart, J. A. *The Myths of Plato*. London: Macmillan, 1905.

Vico, Giambattista. *The New Science*. Translated by T. G. Bergin and M. H. Fisch. New York, 1948; paperback ed., 1961.

Alasdair MacIntyre (1967)

MYTH [ADDENDUM]

As Alasdair MacIntyre says, some philosophers have treated myth, disparagingly, as the opposite of logos, as a nonrational form of understanding the world that either has been or should be displaced by science and reason. Others have agreed that myth is the opposite of logos but have consequently valorized it as a fruit of the primordial mind, a product of an archaic form of experience or mystical consciousness that the modern scientific mind, to its detriment, has lost. There is then a range of philosophical views of the relative value of myth, but philosophers have largely agreed with Ernst Cassirer in seeing myth as a quintessential product of pretheoretical consciousness and therefore as a foil for the scientific mentality of modern European civilization. Since 1967, however, this assumption has been problematized. The concept of myth has been deconstructed, and this deconstruction represents a double obstacle for any philosopher who wants to see in myths truths about the human condition.

The first obstacle arises as scholars realize the extent to which mythical accounts of the origins of the cosmos, of the gods, or of a people have been intimately tied to the social and historical context in which they are told. Far from being the ahistorical products of the unconscious or whimsical flights of speculation—"the wonderful song of the soul's high adventure," to quote Joseph Campbell—myths have typically served to legitimate a particular social order. A clear example is the story of Purusha in the Rig Veda, a story that inscribes the divisions of the caste system as a cosmic reality rather than as a human and hence contingent arrangement. Myths are therefore partisan, not apolitical. In Bruce Lincoln's (1999) slogan myths are "ideology in narrative form." A culture will typically have more than one cosmogony, some mythical accounts of origins will seek to justify the status quo, and rival accounts will seek to undermine it. In short myths typically have a legitimating function, and this fact is concealed by traditional philosophical approaches that ignore the myths' social and historical roots.

The second obstacle arises as scholars realize the extent to which the category of myth reflects the interests of those who employ it. To identify a particular story as a myth—identifying it as the product, for example, of pretheoretical consciousness—has operated to illustrate the superiority of certain ways of thinking over other ways of thinking and, sometimes explicitly, the superiority of certain cultures over other cultures. Thus, one can see that the category of myth is ideological. From this perspective the traditional account of the emergence of *mythos* and its struggle with and eventual defeat by *logos* is itself a myth, that is, a partisan, legitimating story that modern European philosophers tell of their own origins. *Myth* is in this sense therefore a construction of the scholar: myths are not discovered, they are invented, and philosophers who claim to find in myths *la pensée sauvage* tell us more about their own worldviews than they tell us about *les sauvages*.

A few Continental philosophers, such as Cassirer and Hans Blumenberg, explored the idea that myths play a role in the development of consciousness, but Anglophone philosophers were not especially interested. Modern philosophers of religion (who one might think would have a natural interest in myths) have tended to focus on religious "beliefs" deracinated from the oral and literary contexts from which they were drawn. They have also tended to avoid the study of any religion that is not monotheistic. When deconstructive arguments like those mentioned earlier are added to this aversion to the concrete, the result has been that myths have been left for social scientists to study. At the beginning of the twenty-first century there is almost no philosophical work being done on myth.

A FUTURE FOR THE PHILOSOPHICAL STUDY OF MYTHS

But this result is not inevitable. Two observations may point to a future for the philosophical study of myths. In the first place, even when it is not a philosopher studying the myth, philosophy is still present, because answers to philosophical questions are always already embedded in the theories of myth. Social scientific approaches to myths are not philosophically neutral. They inevitably embody a particular set of normative assumptions about what is real and not real, knowable and not knowable, and good and not good, and in this way theories of myth carry certain metaphysical, epistemological, and axiological presuppositions. That the study of myths is unavoidably "philosophy-laden" is perhaps seen most easily when one looks at how the theorist answers questions about rationality, for every theory of myth assumes a judgment regarding what is and is not rational to say. For example, when the Victorian anthropologist Edward Tylor proposed that myths were rational insofar as they originated in observations about natural phenomena, his empiricism was showing.

In the second place, that some scholars pursue questions about the social or political dimensions of myths does not preclude others from asking philosophical questions about the existential, phenomenological, metaphysical, or ethical dimensions of those same narratives. That a story serves ideological ends does not rule out the possibility that it might also house truths about the human condition. To argue otherwise is to collapse the questions of provenance with those of truth, the genetic fallacy. And granting that philosophers' use of the term *myth* has itself been ideological, the solution is not simply to switch the focus of reflection away from the narratives and onto the way that philosophers construct categories, but to practice philosophy self-consciously, self-reflexively, and without naïveté. Philosophers who work on culture should therefore become comfortable with working with historians, anthropologists, and others who deal with the contexts in which the myths have their sense, but they need not abandon the idea that philosophy has its own contribution to make.

In short, then, a philosophical contribution to the study of myths, though now moribund, waits on an appreciation, first, of the ways in which philosophical issues are woven into the theories at work in the social sciences and, second, of the ways in which philosophers of religion or of culture might broaden their studies to include narratives. The fact is that communities often tell stories that explain how the different forms of existence were established; stories that sanction a particular interpretation of history; stories that identify paradigmatic forms of proper behavior. Such stories can provide models of the lived world and of how best to operate within it, and philosophers can analyze and evaluate the truth and the rationality of these models. It can be expected that such stories will typically have an ideological function, but coming to terms with the interpretive and explanatory work of social scientists should strengthen and not eliminate a philosophy of myths.

See also Cassirer, Ernest; Hermeticism; Logos; MacIntyre, Alasdair.

Bibliography

Barbour, Ian G. *Myths, Models, and Paradigms: A Comparative Study in Science and Religion*. New York: Harper and Row, 1974.

Blumenberg, Hans. *Work on Myth*. Translated by Robert M. Wallace. Cambridge, MA: MIT Press, 1985.

Cassirer, Ernst. *The Philosophy of Symbolic Forms. Vol. 2: Mythical Thinking*. Translated by Ralph Manheim. New Haven, CT: Yale University Press, 1955.

Lincoln, Bruce. *Theorizing Myth: Narrative, Ideology, and Scholarship*. Chicago: University of Chicago Press, 1999.

Schilbrack, Kevin, ed. *Thinking through Myths: Philosophical Perspectives*. London: Routledge, 2002.

Kevin Schilbrack (2005)

NĀGĀRJUNA

(c. 150–250 CE)

Nāgārjuna is the first and most important philosopher of the Mahāyāna Buddhist tradition. His work is fundamental to all Mahāyāna philosophy and is widely discussed in the subsequent Buddhist literature of India, Tibet, and East Asia. His work has also attracted considerable attention in Europe and North America.

LIFE AND CONTEXT

Canonical hagiographies of Nāgārjuna report that he was born a Brahman in South India, became a Buddhist monk, and later adviser to a king of the Sātavāhana dynasty. He is credited with retrieving the *Prajñāpāramitā sūtras* from the undersea world of the *nāgās* to whom, according to legend, the Buddha had entrusted them for safekeeping. Given that Nāgārjuna probably lived at about the time that some of these texts were composed, it is possible that he was associated with their composition or dissemination. Nāgārjuna's philosophical work is grounded in the views articulated in these sūtras, and he develops a thorough exposition and defense of the central doctrine they articulate—that all phenomena are empty of essence. While Nāgārjuna's philosophical program,

including his interpretation of emptiness and his doctrine of the two truths, is in many respects highly original, it is also in other respects continuous with early Buddhist accounts of the impermanence, interdependence, and selflessness of the person and of phenomena (Vélez 2005).

While there is disagreement regarding Nāgārjuna's dates and regarding the area of India in which he lived, a confluence of evidence, including Kumārajīva's biography and Joseph Walser's [(2004)] (2005) analysis of the context of the composition of *Ratnāvalī* (Jeweled Garland of Advice to the King)indicates that Nāgārjuna probably lived in the late second and early third centuries in the lower Krishna River Valley. If this is correct, Nāgārjuna was writing at a time when the Mahāyāna was a nascent movement, and his texts provide both the philosophical foundations for that movement and polemical defense of its doctrinal probity.

MAJOR WORKS

A large number of works are attributed to Nāgārjuna, including not only the philosophical works noted here, but also hymns, devotional poetry, and letters to royal patrons, as well as tantric and alchemical texts. It is likely that these latter were composed by another figure of the same name, and that at least some of the devotional material ascribed to Nāgārjuna was not composed by the author of the philosophical texts that constitute the core of his corpus. The core texts, which are almost certainly composed by the same author, are *Mūlamadhyamakakārikā* (*Fundamental Verses on the Middle Way*), *Íunyatāsaptati* (*Seventy Verses on Emptiness*), *Yukti∑a∑†ika* (*Sixty Verses of Reasoning*), *Vigrahavyāvartanī* (*Replies to Objections*), *Ratnāvalī* (*Jeweled Garland of Advice to the King*), and *Vaidalyasūtra* (*Devastating Discourse*).

Of these, *Mūlamadhyamakakārikā* is the most important. The text comprises four hundred forty verses organized by Candrakīrti (c. 600–650 CE), in his commentary *Prasannapadā* (*Lucid Exposition*) into twenty-seven chapters. Nāgārjuna addresses a wide range of fundamental Buddhist categories and phenomena, arguing that each of them lacks essence. The text is terse and is difficult to interpret without a commentary, often considering opposing positions from non-Mahāyāna Buddhist schools and refuting them. Nāgārjuna relies almost exclusively on reductio ad absurdum arguments, arguing that any account of the essence of a phenomenon, or any account according to which something exists permanently, substantially, or independently, collapses into absurdity. As a consequence, he argues, all phenomena exist only interdependently, impermanently, and conventionally. Most importantly, the text identifies two truths: an ultimate truth—the emptiness of phenomena of any essence or substance; and a conventional truth—the empirical reality and interdependence of things, and argues that these two truths are mutually implicative.

Vigrahavyāvartanī is a reply to objections to *Mūlamadhyamakakārikā*, principally those of Nyāya philosophers. The first half of the text develops a series of objections, each to the effect that the doctrine that all phenomena are empty is self-refuting, on epistemological, logical or metaphysical grounds. In the second half, Nāgārjuna confronts each of these objections, demonstrating that each rests on a misunderstanding of emptiness—taking emptiness to be not essencelessness, but nonexistence. When emptiness is understood as interdependence, he argues, not only are none of these objections sound, but the alternative each proposes collapses into absurdity. This text is accompanied by a detailed and closely argued autocommentary.

Íunyatāsaptati and *Yukti∑a∑†ika* are each detailed verse explorations of specific themes raised in *Mūlamadhyamakakārikā*. *Íunyatāsaptati* addresses the relationship between the ultimate emptiness of phenomena and their conventional existence, arguing that the emptiness of phenomena does not undermine, but instead underwrites, their empirical reality. *Yukti∑a∑†ika* explores the sense in which Nāgārjuna's position constitutes a middle path, and characterizes the extremes between which it is a midpoint. One extreme is that of reification—the view that anything that exists does so in virtue of having some essence, that things remain in existence over time, and that anything that exists can in principle exist independently; the other is the extreme of nihilism—the view that because there is no essence, because all phenomena are impermanent and independent, nothing really exists at all. These extremes, Nāgārjuna argues, share the erroneous view that to exist is to exist substantially, independently and continuously, and that once this view is rejected the moderate view that things exist conventionally, dependently and impermanently is the only coherent metaphysical position. *Vaidalyasūtra* is a refutation of the foundationalist Nyāya epistemology, arguing that none of the kinds of foundations that school proposes for knowledge is in fact appropriately self-justifying and that none of their ontological categories is in fact basic.

Each of these texts is written in a technical vocabulary, in an academic style and involves arguments intended to be read by scholars. Each focuses on issues in metaphysics and epistemology. *Ratnāvalī*, while a closely argued philosophical text, is different. It is aimed at a lay audience, and is addressed to a royal patron. While it surveys Madhyamaka metaphysics, it also addresses topics in ethics, political philosophy and statecraft. Indeed, it is probably the first scholarly text on Mahāyāna ethics and the only Mahāyāna text on political philosophy. In *Ratnāvalī* Nāgārjuna explicitly grounds the Mahāyāna ethic that takes compassion as its foundation in the doctrine of emptiness, and defends a theory of statecraft according to which the ruler's obligations include a wide range of social welfare programs. The text is also sectarian, arguing in favor of the legitimacy of the Mahāyāna at a time when this movement and its texts would have been marginal and controversial, and appealing to the king for support for the monasteries.

PHILOSOPHICAL CONTRIBUTIONS

Nāgārjuna extends certain fundamental Buddhist doctrines to develop the metaphysics and epistemology distinctive of Madhyamaka. Five ideas deserve special attention: (1) the doctrine that all phenomena, including emptiness, are empty; (2) the doctrine of the two truths and the account of their relation to one another; (3) the deployment of both positive and negative tetralemmas;

(4) the claim that madhyamaka is not a philosophical position on a par with others, in that it is not an account of the nature of reality, but a refusal of all such accounts; and (5) the attack on epistemological foundationalism.

Nāgārjuna argues that all phenomena are empty of essence, of independence, of substance, in virtue of the fact that essence, independent existence and substance are incoherent. He argues that emptiness is not another essence, but rather is the complete absence of anything that could be an essence. Emptiness itself is just as empty, in just the same sense, as anything else. The emptiness of phenomena is, for Nāgārjuna, the ultimate truth about things—the truth found when the analysis of a thing is complete; this amounts to the fact that things are impermanent, interdependent, and have merely conventional, nominal identity conditions, but no basic nature. The conventional truth about things is the truth about them delivered by our ordinary faculties when used appropriately. But this is just the fact that things are impermanent, interdependent, and have conventional identity conditions. Hence the two truths, according to Nāgārjuna, are, from an ontological point of view, identical. Ultimate truth is therefore not a separate reality; conventional truth is not a veil of illusion. Rather, they are two aspects of one reality.

Nāgārjuna makes extensive use of the Buddhist tetralemma—the partition of logical space into affirmation, negation, both affirmation and negation and neither affirmation nor negation. His deployment is distinctive in that he presents both positive and negative forms of the tetralemma. From the perspective of conventional truth he argues, on the one hand, that we can say that there is a self (conventionally); that there is no self (ultimately); that there both is (conventionally) and is not (ultimately) a self; and that there neither is (ultimately) nor is not (conventionally) a self. On the other hand, from the ultimate point of view none of these can be asserted, as from that point of view there is only emptiness, which cannot be grasped discursively as it is, because discursive thought always involves reification and the mediation by universals. Hence, from the ultimate view there is neither a self, nor not a self, nor both nor neither.

Nāgārjuna asserts that he rejects all views, and that Madhyamaka is not a view. This assertion is variously interpreted by subsequent commentators. Candrakīrti's reading is the most straightforward: Many metaphysical positions are views about the fundamental nature of reality. Metaphysical disagreements are predicated on the view that there is a fundamental nature of reality, and reflect divergent views of what that nature is. Madhya-maka, Nāgārjuna argues, is the rejection of the coherence of the idea of a fundamental nature of reality. Hence it is not a metaphysical view in the sense that its rivals are.

According to many Indian philosophers, there are foundations of knowledge. Some argue that these are objects of knowledge; others that they are our means of gaining knowledge, such as perception or inference. Nāgārjuna argues that neither of these positions can be maintained: that objects of knowledge are only known in virtue of the employment of warranted means of obtaining knowledge, and that in turn these warranted means are only validated by the objects they deliver. Knowledge, such as the reality toward which it is directed, is hence groundless, interdependent, and conventionally constituted.

CANONICAL COMMENTARIES

Mūlamadhyamakakārikā is the subject of many commentaries in India, China and Tibet. The earliest is the *Akutobhayā*, whose authorship is not known. Some traditions regard it as Nāgārjuna's autocommentary, but because it cites the work of his immediate disciple óryadeva casts doubt on this attribution. Pingala's commentary (c. fourth century) exists only in a Chinese translation. Buddhapālita (fifth to sixth centuries) composed an important commentary, the *Buddhapālita*. Bhāvaviveka (sixth century) composed an extensive commentary *Prajñāpradipa* (*Lamp of Wisdom*) and subcommentary *Tarkajvāla* (*Blaze of Argument*). Bhāvaviveka offers extensive reconstructions of Nāgārjuna's arguments in line with the developments in Nyāya and Buddhist logic and takes issue with Buddhapālita's interpretation of the role of reductio argument in Madhyamaka methodology. Candrakīrtii (seventh century) in *Prasannapadā* defends Buddhapālita's reading against Bhāvaviveka's critique. His distinction between their respective understandings of Nāgārjuna's methodology and his account of the metaphysical implications of those understandings form the basis for the Tibetan distinction between the *svātantrika* (Tib: *rang rgyud pa*) and *prāsaṅgika* (Tib: *thal 'gyur ba*) schools of Indian *madhyamaka* that has come subsequently to systematize much understanding of the diverse developments of Nāgārjuna's philosophy in India and Tibet. Candrakīrti also composed an extensive commentary on *Yukti∑a∑†ika*. Many commentaries on *Mūlamadhyamakakārikā* were composed in Tibet. The most extensive and influential is Tsong khapa's *rTsa she tik chen rigs p'ai rgya mtsho* (*Ocean of Reasoning: An Extensive Commentary on Mūlamadhyamakakārikā*) which compares the Indian commentaries, defending Candrakīrti's reading.

TWENTIETH-CENTURY SCHOLARSHIP

The diversity of Western readings of Nāgārjuna's philosophical program is even greater than the diversity of Asian readings. Andrew Tuck (1994) notes that readings of Nāgārjuna in the West often follow fashions in Western philosophy and religious studies. He has been read as a mystic (Streng 1967), as a nihilist (Wood 1994), as a pragmatist (Kalupahana 1986), as an antirealist (Siderits 1988) and as a skeptic (Garfield 1995). There is also considerable debate concerning the degree to which Nāgārjuna argues cogently, and regarding whether his logic should be understood as akin to a European bivalent classical logic or as akin to a four-valued or paraconsistent logic (Robinson 1957, Hayes 1994, Garfield and Priest 2003).

See also Buddhism; Buddhism Schools: Madhyamika.

Bibliography

Battacharya, K., trans. *The Dialectical Method of Nāgārjuna*, edited by E. H. Johnston and A. Kunst. Delhi: Motilal Banarsidass, 1978.

Dunne, J., and S. McClintock. *The Precious Garland: An Epistle to a King—A Translation of Nagarjuna's Text from Sanskrit and Tibetan.* Boston: Wisdom Publications, 1997.

Garfield, J. *Fundamental Wisdom of the Middle Way: Nāgārjuna's Mūlamadhyamakakārikā.* New York: Oxford University Press, 1995.

Garfield, J., and G. Priest. "Nagarjuna and the Limits of Thought." *Philosophy East and West* 53 (2003): 1–21.

Hayes, R. "Nāgārjuna's Appeal." *Journal of Indian Philosophy* 22 (1994): 299–378.

Inada, K. *Nāgārjuna: A Translation of his Mūlamadhyamakakārikā with an Introductory Essay.* Tokyo: Hokuseido Press, 1993.

Kalupahana, D. *Nāgārjuna: The Philosophy of the Middle Way.* Albany: State University of New York Press, 1986.

Lindtner, C. *Master of Wisdom: Writings of the Buddhist Master Nāgārjuna.* Oakland, CA: Dharma Press, 1986.

Robinson, R. "Some Logical Aspects of Nāgārjuna's System." *Philosophy East and West* 6 (1957): 291–308.

Ruegg, D. S. *The Literature of the Madhyamaka School of Philosophy in India.* Wiesbaden, Germany: Harrassowitz, 1981.

Siderits, M. "Nāgārjuna as an Anti-Realist." *Journal of Indian Philosophy* 16 (1988): 311–325.

Sprung, M., and T. R. V. Murti. *Lucid Exposition of the Middle Way.* Boulder: Prajña Press, 1979.

Streng, F. *Emptiness: A Study in Religious Meaning.* Nashville: Abingdon Press, 1967.

Tsong khapa. *Ocean of Reasoning: A Great Commentary on Nagarjuna's Mūlamadhyamakakārikā.* Translated by G. N.

Samten and J. L. Garfield. New York: Oxford University Press, [2005] 2006.

Tuck, A. *Comparative Philosophy and the Philosophy of Scholarship: On the Western Interpretation of Nāgārjuna.* New York: Oxford University Press, 1990.

Veléz, A. "Emptiness in the Pali Suttas and the Question of Nāgārjuna's Orthdoxy." *Philosophy East and West* 55 (4) (2005).

Walser, J. *Nāgārjuna in Context: Mahāyāna Buddhism and Early Indian Culture.* New York: Columbia University Press, 2005.

Wood, T. *Nāgārjunian Disputations: A Philosophical Journey Through an Indian Looking-Glass.* Honolulu: University of Hawaii Press, 1994.

Jay L Garfield (2005)

NAGEL, ERNEST
(1901–1985)

Ernest Nagel, the American philosopher of science, was born at Nove Mesto, Czechoslavakia and came to the United States at the age of ten, becoming naturalized in 1919. He was graduated from City College in 1923 and received an MA in mathematics from Columbia in 1925 and a PhD in philosophy in 1930. He served as the John Dewey professor of philosophy at Columbia University from 1955 to 1966, then took the position of university professor there until 1970, becoming emeritus in 1970. He expressed indebtedness to the teachings of Morris R. Cohen, John Dewey, and Frederick J. E. Woodbridge and to the writings of Charles S. Peirce, Bertrand Russell, and George Santayana.

PHILOSOPHY OF SCIENCE

Nagel belonged to the naturalist and logical empiricist movements, and he is primarily noted for his contributions to the philosophy of science. In 1934 he published, with Morris R. Cohen, *An Introduction to Logic and Scientific Method.* This noted text has been praised for its high level of rigor and for its enrichment of the traditional dry fare of logic with illustrations of the functions of logical principles in scientific method, in the natural and social sciences, and in law and history.

Nagel's book *The Structure of Science* is a unified and comprehensive distillation of many years of teaching and of his many publications on special aspects of scientific thought. It is the most complete exposition of Nagel's analysis of the nature of explanation, the logic of scientific inquiry, and the logical structure of the organization of scientific knowledge, and it illuminates the cardinal issues concerning the formation and the assessment of explanation in physics and in the biological and social sciences.

Two other contributions by Nagel to logic and the philosophy of science are *Principles of the Theory of Probability* (1939) and *Gödel's Proof* (1958), written in collaboration with James R. Newman. These studies range over many issues, from the logic of probable inference to the basic conditions of the structure of formal systems.

GENERAL PHILOSOPHY

Two philosophical essays of a general scope by Nagel have been widely acclaimed. In "Logic without Ontology" Nagel defended a naturalistic interpretation of logic. He argued that logico-mathematical principles must be understood according to their functions in specific contexts, namely, in inquiries, and he criticized attempts to adduce an ontological ground or transcendent authority for the meaning, warrant, and necessary character of logical laws. Nagel had already repudiated his early view that logical principles "are inherently applicable because they are concerned with ontological traits of utmost generality" (*An Introduction to Logic and Scientific Method*, p. v). In "Logic without Ontology" he showed that the view that logic is ontologically determined or entails ontological commitments arises primarily from a failure to heed certain contextual and operational qualifications of the sense in which logical principles are supposed to possess "necessary truth."

In "Sovereign Reason" Nagel presented a penetrating critique, focused on the doctrine of internal relations, of Brand Blanshard's rational idealism. This critique exemplifies one of Nagel's strongest philosophical convictions and a main theme of "Logic without Ontology": Logical principles (and even pure Reason), just because they are analytic, are necessary but not sufficient instruments for acquiring knowledge or discovering truths about reality. The task of logic, according to Nagel, is to disclose the assumptions and clarify the methods on which responsible claims to knowledge are based and by which they are critically assessed. All claims to knowledge, even those most impressively supported by evidence and experiment, are subject to revision or rejection in the light of new advances in knowledge. This empiricist tenet led Nagel to accept contingency as a real trait of nature and fallibility as an inescapable feature of human inquiry.

SCIENCE AND SOCIETY

Nagel's technical interest in the logic and history of scientific knowledge did not prevent him from appreciating the social consequences and problems of science and technology in a democratic society. Much of his critical activity as a speaker, reviewer, and essayist was devoted to imparting a clearer understanding of the nature of science and to dispelling philosophical vagaries and bizarre notions concerning such matters as causality and indeterminism in physics; the alleged paradoxical character of abstract science or its utter disparity with common sense; the frequent claims that science is value-free, or metaphysically inspired, or mere codified sense data; and the revulsion or despair and the impassioned remedies that science has occasioned in some literary and theological circles.

MATERIALISM, DETERMINISM, AND ATHEISM

Nagel's philosophical naturalism led him to take a decisive stand on certain broad philosophical issues, notably materialism, determinism, and atheism. It has been charged that naturalists, being materialists, are unable to account for mental phenomena. Nagel replied, fully aware of the many senses of the word *materialism*, that naturalists are not materialists if materialism is taken to mean that such psychological predicates as "fear" or "feeling of beauty" logically entail or are reducible to physical terms such as *weight, length,* or *molecule*. Although he repudiated reductive materialism, Nagel held that mental events are aspects of and contingent on the organization of human bodies. Events, qualities, and processes are dependent on the organization of spatially and temporally located bodies. In this sense, naturalism is committed to materialism: Organized matter has a causal primacy in the order of nature. It follows that there can be no occult forces or disembodied spirits directing natural events and no personal immortality when bodily organizations disintegrate.

To assess the role of determinism in history and in ethical theory, Nagel formulated the meaning of *determinism* in natural science. A scientific theory is deterministic with respect to a set of properties when, given a specification of the set at any initial time, a unique set of the properties for any other time can be deduced by means of the theory. The theory might be a mechanical theory, and the sets of properties mechanical states. This theory might conceivably be of use in calculating the mechanical states of a human organism, but only its mechanical states. Whether other properties of the organism and its history were deterministic would remain an open empirical question. Nor would determinism in human history, if it were established, automatically empty moral endeavor and responsibility of significance. Which modes of human experience and behavior, if any, are subject to deterministic theory remains an empirical question; and the sense in which these conditions might be characterized as "deterministic" remains an issue of analysis.

In several places, including his influential paper "The Causal Character of Modern Physical Theory," Nagel concerned himself with the philosophical implications of quantum theory. Like Albert Einstein and Max Planck, but unlike the majority of writers on the subject, Nagel denied that quantum theory has indeterministic consequences. He also showed in some detail how intellectual confusion thrives when distinctions of context and the relevance of theoretical language to specific contexts are ignored; for example, when "particle" in the context of Newtonian theory is transported into discussions of the uncertainty principle in modern physics. In another well-known essay, "Russell's Philosophy of Science," Nagel argued that the physical and physiological facts of perception do not require the abandonment of common sense in favor of the strange conclusions held by Russell and Arthur Stanley Eddington.

Nagel was one of the few naturalists to present a forthright statement of the naturalist critique of theism. His formulation of atheism is not couched as a sheer negation of theism but proceeds from a positive moral position according to which, while it is granted that there are inevitable tragic aspects of life, knowledge of life and nature is to be preferred to illusions. On matters of such supreme moment, the truth rather than fiction is the more fitting ideal of rational men.

Nagel did not, however, deny the value and authenticity of other than purely cognitive pursuits. He never argued that aesthetic qualities, ideals, suffering, and enjoyments are not genuine aspects of experience. On the contrary, he urged that naturalism, although obliged to render a competent account of scientific knowledge, also include in its scope a place for imagination, liberal values, and human wisdom.

See also Atheism; Determinism, A Historical Survey; Materialism; Philosophy of Science, History of.

Bibliography

WORKS BY NAGEL

On the Logic Measurement. New York, 1930.

An Introduction to Logic and Scientific Method. New York: Harcourt Brace, 1934. Written with Morris R. Cohen.

Principles of the Theory of Probability. Chicago: University of Chicago Press, 1939. Vol. I, No. 6, of *The International Encyclopedia of Unified Science*.

"Russell's Philosophy of Science." In *The Philosophy of Bertrand Russell*, edited by P. A. Schilpp. Evanston, IL: Open Court, 1944. Reprinted in *Sovereign Reason*.

"Logic without Ontology." In *Naturalism and the Human Spirit*, edited by Y. H. Krikorian. New York: Columbia University Press, 1944. Reprinted in *Logic without Metaphysics* (see below).

"Are Naturalists Materialists?" *Journal of Philosophy* 42 (1945): 515–530. Reprinted in *Logic without Metaphysics*.

"Sovereign Reason." In *Freedom and Experience. Essays Presented to Horace M. Kallen*, edited by Sidney Hook and Milton R. Konvitz. Ithaca, NY: Cornell University Press, 1947. Reprinted in *Sovereign Reason*.

"The Causal Character of Modern Physical Theory." In *Freedom and Reason*, edited by S. W. Baron, Ernest Nagel, and K. S. Pinson. Glencoe, IL: Free Press, 1951. Reprinted with revisions as part of Ch. 10 in *The Structure of Science*.

Sovereign Reason. Glencoe, IL: Free Press, 1954.

Logic without Metaphysics. Glencoe, IL: Free Press, 1956.

Gödel's Proof. New York: New York University Press, 1958. Written with James R. Newman.

"A Defense of Atheism." In *Basic Beliefs*, edited by J. E. Fairchild. New York: Sheridan House, 1959.

The Structure of Science. New York: Harcourt Brace, 1961.

Philosophy, Science, and Method: Essays in Honor of Ernest Nagel, edited by Sidney Morgenbesser, Patrick Suppes, and Morton Gabriel White. New York: St. Martin's, 1969.

With Sylvain Bromberger and Adolf Grünbaum, Adolf. *Observation and Theory in Science*. Baltimore, MD: Johns Hopkins, 1971.

Teleology Revisited and Other Essays in the Philosophy and History of Science. New York: Columbia University Press, 1979.

H. S. Thayer (1967)
Bibliography updated by Michael J. Farmer (2005)

NAGEL, THOMAS
(1937–)

Thomas Nagel has contributed to a wide spectrum of philosophical topics in ethical theory, moral psychology, applied ethics, and political theory, as well as to metaphysics and epistemology. His work is distinguished by its breadth, clarity, and acumen.

While there is not a single, narrowly defined theme running through all his work, Nagel has persistently engaged the problem of reconciling an objective view of reality with one's subjective, individual experience as a person. In his magisterial work, *The View from Nowhere*, Nagel writes: "This book is about a single problem: how to combine the perspective of a particular person inside the world with an objective view of that same world, the person and his viewpoint included. It is a problem that faces every creature with the impulse and the capacity to transcend its particular point of view and to conceive of the world as a whole" (1986, p. 3). Nagel's defense of the legitimacy of both one's subjective perspective and an objective, nonindividual point of view, has been part of Nagel's resistance to philosophies that do away with either. So, in several books and many articles, Nagel has authored an influential critique of forms of physicalism that eliminate or do not take seriously the reality of subjective experience, and he has also been highly critical of philosophies that give way to skepticism because they grant excessive authority to subjectivity.

The Possibility of Altruism, his first book, argues that in an individual's recognition of goods and ills for him- or herself over time, there is an implicit recognition of the goods and ills that face other individuals. "In accepting goals or reasons myself I attach objective value to certain circumstances, not just value for myself" (1970, p. 85). In later work, Nagel refines the conviction that ethical and political theory needs to be comprehensively impartial and only comprised of agent-neutral reasons; these reasons are comprised of "what everyone ought to value, independently of its relation to himself" (1991, p. 40). Nagel allows that there is some tension between such an agent–neutral perspective and some of the values that have their place in specific, personal contexts. Nagel advocates an egalitarian social ideal (1991), while also recognizing that some goods are private and should be concealed from public surveillance and control (2002). Nagel's concern for the integrity of the individual pits him against overriding social engineering.

In philosophy of mind, Nagel is widely known for his essay "What Is It Like to Be a Bat?" (first published in *Philosophical Review* 1974, pp. 435–450, reprinted in *Mortal Questions* and widely anthologized). In this essay, Nagel identifies subjective, phenomenal experience as the central problem facing contemporary physicalism. He contends that a fully developed neurobiological, functional, materialist account of the human body would still leave out subjective experience (what it is like experientially to be conscious and undergo experiences), just as a fully developed neurobiological, functional, materialist account of a bat would still leave out what it is like to be a bat. In *What Does It All Mean?* Nagel employs the thought experiment of an inverted spectrum and other inverted sensations to exhibit the apparent contingency of the relationship between conscious, experiential states and functionalist, materialist ones. These are cases when the physicalist account of seeing some color or experienc-

ing some taste is inverted, so that while the physicalist would conclude that one is having some taste, when it turns out one is having a quite different one. In *The View from Nowhere, Other Minds*, and elsewhere, Nagel opposes all philosophies of mind that fail to recognize the reality of subjective, lived experience.

Although Nagel's defense of the reality of phenomenal experiences and the apparent contingency of the mental-physical relation has seemed to some to lend credence to at least a modified form of dualism, Nagel himself holds that dualism can be avoided by developing a conceptual revision of one's current concept of the physical world and subjective experience. While philosophers do not yet possess this new world view, Nagel urges that future philosophical work be focused on conceiving of a single natural world that incorporates what one now sees as objective physical states and one's internal, mental subjectivity.

In his short book, *The Last Word*, Nagel offers an impassioned defense of reason as a reliable mode of inquiry, not subject to the objections of relativists, postmodernists, or contemporary pragmatists like Richard Rorty:

> Reason … can serve as a court of appeal not only against the received opinions and habits of our community but also against the peculiarities of our personal perspective. It is something each individual can find within himself, but at the same time it has universal authority. Reason provides, mysteriously, a way of distancing oneself from common opinion and received practices. … Whoever appeals to reason purports to discover a source of authority within himself that is not merely personal, or societal, but universal—and that should also persuade others who are willing to listen to it.
>
> (1997, PP. 2–3)

Nagel acknowledges the many ways in which one's reasoning may be impaired, but he nonetheless maintains the necessity of making recourse to reason in order to correct, however gradually, such impairments.

Nagel received a BA from Cornell University in 1958, a PhB from Oxford in 1960, and his PhD from Harvard in 1963. He has held academic appointments at the University of California at Berkeley, Princeton University, and New York University where he was appointed as University Professor in 2002. In addition to his specialized philosophical writing, Nagel has written on practical political and moral problems. For example, he has argued for a highly restricted account of when and how a just war may be engaged.

See also Applied Ethics; Consciousness; Metaethics; Moral Psychology; Physicalism.

Bibliography

WORKS BY THOMAS NAGEL

The Possibility of Altruism. New York: Oxford University Press, 1970.

Mortal Questions. Cambridge, U.K.: Cambridge University Press, 1979.

The View from Nowhere. New York: Oxford University Press, 1986.

What Does It All Mean? New York: Oxford University Press. 1987.

Other Minds. New York: Oxford University Press, 1995.

The Last Word. New York: Oxford University Press, 1997.

Concealment and Exposure. New York: Oxford University Press, 2002.

The Myth of Ownership: Taxes and Justice. With Liam Murphy. New York: Oxford University Press, 2002.

WORKS ABOUT THOMAS NAGEL

Darwell, S. "The View from Nowhere." *Ethics* 98 (1987): 137–157.

McGinn, C. "The View from Nowhere." *Mind* 96 (1987): 263–272.

Charles Taliaferro (2005)

NAIGEON, JACQUES-ANDRÉ
(1738–1810)

Jacques-André Naigeon, a French writer, was an associate of Denis Diderot. Naigeon was not an original thinker; he became an editor, compiler, and commentator after having tried painting and sculpture, but he considered himself a philosopher and was proud of his classical erudition. A bibliophile, too, he accumulated one of the great collections of Greek and Latin classics of his time. Having been accepted into the group of Encyclopedists surrounding Baron d'Holbach, he became an aggressive atheist. He attached himself to Diderot as a disciple and tried to imitate his tone, his manner, and his ideas. Diderot in turn enjoyed Naigeon's wit and tolerated his bad temper, stiffness, and pedantry; Naigeon helped Diderot with the *salons* and the *Encyclopédie.* Naigeon later persuaded Diderot to make him his literary executor. He preserved and edited many of Diderot's manuscripts but did not publish others. He put out an incomplete edition of Diderot's works in 1798 and wrote a valuable but unfinished commentary on his life and writings, *Mémoires historiques et philosophiques sur la vie et les ouvrages de Diderot* (Paris, 1821). He also arranged the clandestine printing of several of Holbach's works in the Netherlands, and in 1770 published *Mélange de pièces sur la religion et la morale,* which contained some minor pieces by Holbach and other writers.

Naigeon edited the works of Seneca, completing the translation begun by N. La Grange and adding notes; he published it with Diderot's defense of Seneca, *Essai sur les régnes de Claude et de Néron* (Paris, 1778). A one-act musical comedy, *Les Chinois* (1756), is sometimes attributed to him, perhaps in collaboration with Charles-Nicolas Favart. His only "original" work was *Le militaire philosophe, ou Difficultés sur la religion, proposées au P. Mallebranche* (London and Amsterdam, 1768), which is based on an earlier anonymous manuscript and has a final chapter by Holbach. This dull work is of minor value as an example of dogmatic atheism and materialism, but it merely repeats the same ideas and arguments that had run throughout the radical writings of the entire century. Naigeon supports hatred of priests and the church with the doctrine of materialism and a naturalistic utilitarian morality. He denounces Christian ethics (asceticism, humility, etc.), demanding fulfillment of legitimate natural demands and a moral code based on social well-being. He points out contradictions in Christian ethics and doctrine, stressing its cruelty and its failure. He argues that Christian ethics leads to an inversion of the natural order of values, hence to intolerance, inhumanity, and crimes. Earth would be peaceful and happy if the idea of God were eliminated.

Naigeon continued this attack in his contributions to C. J. Panckoucke's *Encyclopédie méthodique.* This work consisted of separate dictionaries, and Naigeon edited the *Dictionnaire de la philosophie ancienne et moderne* (3 vols., Paris, 1791–1793), which was largely a compilation. In *Adresse à l'Assemblée nationale sur la liberté des opinions* (1790) he demanded absolute freedom of the press and again gave vent to his hatred of priests.

There are no studies on Naigeon, except in relation to his publication of Diderot's manuscripts, nor is any needed.

See also Diderot, Denis; Encyclopédie; Holbach, Paul-Henri Thiry, Baron d'; Seneca, Lucius Annaeus.

L. G. Crocker (1967)

NAIVE REALISM

See *Realism*

NAKAE TŌJU
(1608–1648)

Nakae Tōju, "the sage of Ōmi" (his native town in Shiga prefecture), the most respected Confucianist in the Tokugawa era, was an advocate of the Wang Yangming school. The ideas of Wang Yangming (in Japanese, Ōyōmei) were made known in Japan by the Zhu Xi scholar Fujiwara Seika (1561–1619), but only with Nakae did the Wang Yangming doctrine become a school of thought. The importance of this school lies in its impact on Japanese thinking and the nonconformists it produced. Its stress on *ryōchi* (literally, "good conscience"; more exactly, the innate knowledge that every man has from Heaven) favored the formation of strong individualists guided by the inner light of conscience without the formalistic restraints of Zhu Xi Confucianism. The cultivation of the mind combined with a stress on deeds rather than formal learning was another aspect of Nakae's teaching. His upright character showed in practice what it meant to be a Confucian sage, that is, almost a saint.

Nakae's intuitive and practical morality centering on filial piety had a great attraction for his pupils as well as for many later followers who for different reasons claimed him as their master. His outstanding followers were Kumazawa Banzan (1619–1691) and such men prominent in the nineteenth-century movement to restore the emperor as Ōshio Heihachirō, Yoshida Shōin, and Saigō Takamori. Kumazawa tried to persuade his master to leave the obscure village of Ogawa and enter the service of the lord of Okayama, but the humble Nakae shunned the proposal. In addition, Nakae's inclinations were ethico-religious rather than politico-economic, the characteristic of many of his followers. Nor was he a radical, although some of his admirers were.

Nakae strove for a middle way, mildly criticizing other points of view. He spoke of *ri*, the "principle," and *ki*, Zhu Xi's material force (which Nakae interpreted as matter-life), as two aspects of the "supreme ultimate." Nakae's terminology recalls the ancient Chinese sages and suggests Christian influence; *Jōtei*, the "Supreme Lord Above," he called "the absolute truth and the absolute spirit," and he ascribed almost personal attributes to this Being. Nakae also had pantheistic leanings, however, and he used anthropomorphic expressions to ally his *Jōtei*

with Shinto deities. His moral ideas, though, are much more important than his cosmological views. Filial piety (*kō*) is the pivotal virtue, for him both the universe's moral power and its reason for being. Everyone, from the emperor to the most despised woman—Nakae being quite an equalitarian—was affected by filial piety, the creative force descending by degrees from Heaven. This virtue became in his late followers patriotism toward the emperor. Still, for Nakae, it was a cosmic and religious force not limited to one family or nation.

See also Japanese Philosophy; Kumazawa Banzan; Pantheism; Wang Yangming; Zhu Xi (Chu Hsi).

Bibliography

See *Tōju sensei zenshū* (The complete works of Nakae Tōju), 5 vols. (Tokyo: Iwanami Shoten, Shōwa, 1940). A secondary source in Japanese is Bitō Masahide, *Nihon hōken shisōshi kenkyū* (Studies on the history of feudal thought in Japan; Tokyo, 1961), pp. 136–216. See also G. M. Fisher, "The Life and Teaching of Nakae Toju," in *Transactions of the Asiatic Society of Japan* 36, Part 1 (1908): 24–94; W. T. de Bary, Ryusaku Tsunoda, and Donald Keene, eds., *Sources of Japanese Tradition* (New York: Columbia University Press, 1958), pp. 378–384, which offers selections, with an introduction.

Gino K. Piovesana, S.J. (1967)

NAMES, PROPER

See *Proper Names and Descriptions*

NAṢĪR AL-DĪN AL-ṬŪSĪ
(1201–1274)

Naṣīr al-Dīn al-Ṭūsī (1201–1274) is a Shiʿa Iranian author of some two hundred treatises in a number of disciplines, including philosophy, mathematics, astronomy, mysticism, and theology.

LIFE AND TIMES

Naṣīr al-Dīn was born in the city of Tus in the province of Khurasan in northwestern Iran, the first area to be devastated by the Mongolian invasion of the Middle East by Helagu Khan (1217–1265), grandson of Genghis Khan (1167?–1227). After completing his formal studies, al-Ṭūsī carried out research and publications under the patronage of various Ismaili rulers from 1227 until 1256, when he assisted the Ismaili ruler to surrender to Helegu

Khan, who employed al-Ṭūsī as his adviser until Helagu's death and then joined Abaq (1265–1282) until his own death. Al-Ṭūsī accompanied Helagu Khan in the Monogol attack on the last Sunni caliph in Baghdad, after which he built an observatory at Maragha in Azarbayijan in northwest Iran. There he spent the rest of his life in supervising innovations in astronomy and mathematics; in addition, he attracted the patronage of the Mongol ruler toward scientists, Shiʿa theologians, and writers on mysticism.

COSMOGONY AND ITS ETHICS

In formulating his views on the existence of God, al-Ṭūsī appeals to the Avicennan doctrine that God has no (external) cause; because entities are known by their causes, there cannot be any affirmative scientific type of knowledge (ʿilm) of God. In this light, one needs to note the Qurʾanic indication that the divine expresses creation in the language of command (amr) and in the logos of be/make (kun), which express the good intention of the creator as the paradigm of action. Here al-Ṭūsī proffers an Ismaʿili doctrine that the Imam is a physical incarnation, or an earthly instantiation of the divine goodwill. As a self-caused entity God must be a unity; and as a unity he can only create one entity, namely the Necessary Existent (al-wajib al-wujud), which has been equated with the First Intelligence (nous), from which the rest of the universe emanates in a series that has been represented by Neoplatonists as follows: After the Universal Soul emanates, the Individual Souls come forth and finally matter. Whereas Ibn Sīnā does not equate his Necessary Existent with the God of Islam, the major Ismaʿili theologian prior to al-Ṭūsī, Naṣir Khosrow, explicitly states that God creates the Necessary Existent, from whom the rest of the universe then emanates. A Zoroastrian and a Nietzschian type of ethics is implied in al-Ṭūsī's cosmogony, where the good is associated with the good intention of the agent in the context of imitating the Imam.

THE THEODICY OF SOFT DETERMINISM

Al-Ṭūsī held that free will, determinism, and indeterminism are metalinguistic terms for explaining actions. A system is determined if the future can be predicted from a knowledge of all events and laws. When people are unaware of causes of behavior, free will is attributed to an agent, whose will corresponds with necessity—for example, a pregnant mother who wills the birth of her child. Having free will does not imply that the will is free and

indeterminism is true. Total freedom is an intentional state of an agent that is achieved through knowledge of causes of events and one's "love"-receptivity to accept one's fate-role in the best of all possible worlds, as is exemplified by parents who graciously accept the facts of aging and welcome their children's well-deserved authority. In this tenor, al-Ṭūsī's system resembles Gottfried Leibniz's view of the best of all possible worlds. H. A. Wolfson notes that such a resemblance is due to Leibniz's copying Spinoza's theodicy, which in turn can be traced to the influence of Avicennan thought on Maimonides. Following Tolstoy's view that "free will is the essence of life, but it is an illusion," al-Ṭūsī holds that free will is an intentional concept. "Will per se," he states, "cannot be cause of any action in a mind-independent world" (pm: see Metaphysics of Tusi, p. 39–40). Al-Ṭūsī holds that to God, who is a unity, neither free will nor determinism applies, because an agent is free, if his or her will agrees with necessity (which implies a duality in the agent).

REFUTATION OF MATTER

Through a number of proofs al-Ṭūsī points out the incompatibility of the notion of the ultimate indivisible material substance of early Sunni theologians. Consider, for example, the following 4 by 4 arrangement of material substances:

$$A \ 0 \ 0 \ 0 \ 0 \ B$$

$$0 \ 0 \ 0 \ 0$$

$$0 \ 0 \ 0 \ 0$$

$$C \ 0 \ 0 \ 0 \ 0 \ D$$

Imagine a triangle, where hypotenuse is BC, the base is CD, and a side is BD. According to the atomic theory of homogeneous indivisible matters with no space between them, the base CD would equal the hypotenuse, which is BC. But this conclusion contradicts the Euclidean rule that a hypotenuse (BC) is longer then the base CD. Upholding the absoluteness of the Euclidean geometry, al-Ṭūsī uses this and seven other proofs to refute the material theory of substance.

THE APPLICATION OF PHILOSOPHICAL ANALYSIS TO DIFFERENT SENSES OF INFINITY

Al-Ṭūsī faces the following dilemma: As a philosopher he has to agree with Aristotle and Ibn Sīnā in holding that the "actual infinite" is not a legitimate notion, yet as a mathematician he needs to employ "infinity" in the theory of numbers. Moreover, as a phenomenologist he had to use a continuum to explain perception and a continuum is often expressed by real numbers. In a clever manner that resembles R. Carnap's celebrated method of reconstructionalism and fits into the tradition of philosophical analysis, al-Ṭūsī proffers the following solution. He begins by distinguishing different senses of infinity in their application to various domains such as the "syntactical" realm, the actual world, the phenomenology of experiences such as perception, and the like.

INTENTIONAL MYSTICAL VIRTUES

Al-Ṭūsī wrote several texts on intentional analyses of the moral psychology of mystical experience. A number of investigators, such as Wilfred Madelung, hold that al-Ṭūsī's main purpose was to propose a practical experiential praxis of mysticism of the Shiʿa kind that was an alternative to the Sunni school of Ibn ʿArabi that had been advocated by Al-Qunawi.

See also Aristotle; Avicenna; Carnap, Rudolf; Determinism and Freedom; Ibn al-ʿArabī; Islamic Philosophy; Leibniz, Gottfried Wilhelm; Logos; Maimonides; Neoplatonism; Spinoza, Benedict (Baruch) de; Tolstoy, Lev (Leo) Nikolaevich.

Bibliography

Dabashi, H. "Khwajah Nasir al-Din al-Tusi: The Philosopher/Vizier and the Intellectual Climate of His Times." In *History of Islamic Philosophy*, edited by Sayyed H. Nasr and Oliver Leaman, 527–584. London: Routledge,1998.

Metaphysics of Tusi. Translated by Parviz Morewedge. New York: Institute of Global Cultural Studies, 1992.

Morewedge, P. "The Analysis of 'Substance' in Tusi's Logic and in the Ibn Sinian Tradition." In *Essays on Islamic Philosophy and Science*, edited by G. Hourani. Albany, NY: Suny Press, 1975.

Naṣīr al-Dīn al-Ṭūsī. *Contemplation and Action: The Spiritual Autobiography of a Muslim Scholar*, edited and translated by S. J. Badakhsahni. London: I. B. Tauris, 1998.

The Nasirean Ethics by Nasir al-Din Tusi. Translated by G. M. Wickens. London: George, Allen and Unwin, 1964.

Parviz Morewedge (2005)

NASR, SEYYED HOSSEIN
(1933–)

Seyyed Hossein Nasr is a Persian Islamic scholar and traditionalist philosopher. After receiving his primary school education in Iran, he was sent to the United States at the age of twelve and graduated from the Peddie School in New Jersey in 1950. He studied physics and mathematics at Massachusetts Institute of Technology (MIT) and received his doctorate from Harvard University in 1958 with specialization in Islamic cosmology and science. From 1958 until 1979, Nasr was professor of the history of science and philosophy at Tehran University where he became dean of the Faculty of Letters for some years. He also served as president of Aryamehr University in Iran. It was during these years in Iran that Nasr studied with such traditional philosophers as S. M. Kazim ʿAssar and S. M. Hossein Tabatabaʾi.

After the Iranian Revolution of 1979, Nasr migrated to the United States and taught at Temple University before joining the George Washington University in 1984. In 1981, Nasr gave the Gifford Lectures at the University of Edinburgh, which was published the same year as *Knowledge and the Sacred*. In 1999 he was chosen to be the first Muslim scholar to receive the Templeton Religion and Science Course Award. Most recently, a volume in the *Library of Living Philosophers Series* has been dedicated to him and his work.

As a prolific scholar and philosopher, Nasr has written extensively on topics as diverse as metaphysics and cosmology, tradition and modernity, Islamic science, comparative mysticism, Islamic art, interfaith dialogue, Sufism, and the environmental crisis. He is a prominent member of the traditionalist school of thought that includes such names as René Guénon, Ananda Coomoraswamy, and Frithjof Schuon. Nasr has played a key role in formulating and disseminating the ideas of the traditionalists on traditional metaphysics, sacred view of nature, and the critique of modern science. His *Knowledge and the Sacred*, his magnum opus in the field of philosophy and comparative religion, attempts to reconstruct traditional philosophy as an alternative to the modern worldview that Nasr describes as metaphysically blind and reductionist. Like the other traditionalists, Nasr places religion—or what Schuon calls *religio perennis*—at the heart of human history. A closely related term that permeates his work is perennial philosophy, which again points to the universality of tradition. In this view, tradition does not mean customs but signifies that primordial truth of divine origin that lies at the center of all cultures and religious traditions. Tradition is thus closely related to revelation and its articulation in philosophy, theology, mysticism, and sacred art.

Nasr's concept of traditional metaphysics is centered around a holistic and hierarchic view of reality. Saturated with traditional theocentrism, Nasr's view of metaphysics posits God or the One as the source, center, and end of all there is. This principle takes on many different forms and formulations in different traditions but remains essentially the same. In keeping with the spirit of premodern philosophy, the spiritual has a higher ontological status over the material because the former is taken to reveal the divine and the latter to conceal it. The imagery of the great chain of being defines a good part of Nasr's metaphysical works. Nasr also attempts to create a holistic view of reality by showing the interrelatedness of the various levels and states of being.

Because every level of reality has its own meaning and place in the total economy of divine creation, none of them can be reduced to a lower order of reality nor the whole to one single element. According to Nasr, it is this teleological and hierarchic view of the universe that has prevented the premodern sciences of nature from slipping into reductionism and materialism. In addition to *Knowledge and the Sacred*, Nasr has provided a detailed analysis of these issues in his other works including *The Need for a Sacred Science* (1993) and *An Introduction to Islamic Cosmological Doctrines* (1964). In his major works on traditional metaphysics and cosmology, Nasr's main concern has been to revive *scientia sacra* (sacred science) by showing the underlying unity and interrelatedness of the transmitted, intellectual, and physical sciences under the umbrella of metaphysics.

Nasr sees all cultures and civilizations emanating from an essentially religious vision of the universe. This has led him to author a number of works on what he calls the "sacred view of the universe." From an ethical point of view, nature is seen as a sacred trust from God and from a metaphysical and theological point of view as *vestigia Dei* (signs of God; *ayāt Allah* in Arabic). This suggests that the order of nature has an essential telos, which makes it teleological, sacred, and intrinsically intelligible all at once. Nasr's lifelong interest in traditional and modern science can thus be seen as an extension of his view of metaphysics. In a number of works on *Islamic science*, a term Nasr has introduced to the field, he discussed the meaning of science within the context of the Islamic religious worldview and analyzed the achievements of Islamic scientific tradition in such fields as medicine, astronomy, mathematics, algebra, chemistry, physics, geography, and natural history.

Nasr's works on the relationship between religion, science, and the environmental crisis have had a long-standing impact in both the Islamic and European intellectual circles. His early work *The Encounter of Man and Nature: The Spiritual Crisis of Modern Man*, first appeared in 1968 and was one of the first books to predict the envi-

ronmental crisis. The book is a philosophical critique of the modern conception of nature as inert matter. This is also the first book in which Nasr takes up the challenge of modern science and its secular outlook. The second important book to appear in this line of writings is *Religion and the Order of Nature* (1996) in which he gives an account of the rise of modern science, criticizes the secular and reductionist philosophies of nature, and presents the traditional religious view of cosmos and the human body as a viable alternative to modern scientism and reductionism.

An overall concern of Nasr's thought has been to define the fault lines of tradition and modernity. As a traditionalist philosopher, Nasr defines modernity as a distinct worldview based on the denial of the transcendent, and rejects it. He considers the environmental crisis, the modern culture of nihilism and skepticism, and the rise of scientific positivism and materialism a direct result of the various forms of modernism. Against the proponents of modernism in both the European and the Islamic world, Nasr calls for a revival of the Islamic intellectual tradition in particular and traditional thought in general to address the challenges of the modern world. His work on Islamic philosophy and Sufism has been instrumental in showing the relevance of this tradition for questions of immediate concern to the contemporary Muslim world.

See also Cosmology; Islamic Philosophy; Metaphysics; Nature, Philosophical Ideas of; Sufism.

Bibliography

WORKS BY NASR IN ENGLISH

An Introduction to Islamic Cosmological Doctrines. Cambridge, MA: Harvard University Press, 1964.

Three Muslim Sages. Cambridge, MA: Harvard University Press, 1964.

The Encounter of Man and Nature: The Spiritual Crisis of Modern Man. London: Allen and Unwin, 1968.

Science and Civilization in Islam. Cambridge, MA: Harvard University Press, 1968.

Sufi Essays. London: Allen and Unwin, 1971.

Islamic Spirituality. 2 vols. New York: Crossroads Publications, 1987–1992.

Knowledge and the Sacred. New York: Crossroad, 1981.

The Need for a Sacred Science. Albany: State University of New York Press, 1993.

The Islamic Intellectual Tradition in Persia. Edited by M. Aminrazavi. London: Curzon Press, 1994.

History of Islamic Philosophy, edited, with Oliver Leaman. London: Routledge, 1996.

Religion and the Order of Nature. Oxford: Oxford University Press, 1996.

The Philosophy of Seyyed Hossein Nasr, edited by L. Hahn, L. Stone, and R. Auxier. Chicago and La Salle, IL: Open Court, 2000.

Ibrahim Kalin (2005)

NATIONALISM

In defining the word *nationalism,* at least five senses can be identified: (1) a sentiment of loyalty to a nation (a variety of patriotism); (2) a propensity, as applied to policies, to consider exclusively the interests of one's own nation, especially in cases where these compete with the interests of other nations; (3) an attitude that attaches high importance to the distinctive characteristics of a nation and, therefore, (4) a doctrine that maintains that national culture should be preserved; and (5) a political and an anthropological theory that asserts that humankind is naturally divided into nations, that there are determinate criteria for identifying a nation and for recognizing its members, that each nation is entitled to an independent government of its own, that states are legitimate only if constituted in accordance with this principle, and that the world would be rightly organized, politically speaking, only if every nation formed a single state and every state consisted exclusively of the whole of one nation.

NATURE AND CRITERIA OF NATIONALITY

Nationalist doctrines and theories of the kinds referred to in (4) and (5) date from the end of the eighteenth century. Attachment to one's nation and the belief that, for instance, all Englishmen constitute an English nation are, no doubt, much older. Men have always had this kind of attachment to an in-group—whether tribe, city, or nation—and a corresponding awareness of (and perhaps hostility toward) nonmembers as foreigners. But what characterizes nations, distinguishing them from groups of other kinds?

THE NATION DEFINED BY THE STATE. A nation, wrote the French revolutionary ideologist the Abbé Sieyès in 1789, is "a union of individuals governed by *one* law, and represented by the same law-giving assembly." Thus conceived, a nation's unity and identity derive from political organization, and the state would thus be logically prior to the nation. This view was consistent with the individualist or atomistic interpretation of group phenomena of which John Locke was a typical exponent and

which was characteristic of much of the social theorizing of the eighteenth-century Enlightenment. Writers like Denis Diderot and Marquis de Condorcet considered that individuals must be taken to concur in the setting up of a political order because (or insofar as) it is in their interests, several and collective. A public interest, thus created, is the ground of a duty to preserve and defend the order, and the state, as the subject of this interest, becomes a proper object of loyalty. Those sharing in such a common interest would constitute one people, or nation. This view of nationality is supported by the way in which, in ordinary speech, citizenship and nationality are interchangeable in many contexts. (This was once true of legal usage, too; however, many states now distinguish the rights and duties of a citizen from those of a national.) If, however, we do distinguish nationality from citizenship in ordinary speech, it is principally by narrowing citizenship to matters of political and legal status, whereas to determine nationality we take into account criteria like place of birth, parentage, language, and cultural tradition.

THE NATION DEFINED BY LANGUAGE AND CULTURE. The conception of nationality as language and culture became articulate, as an element in nationalist ideology, at the end of the eighteenth century, mainly through the work of German writers such as Johann Gottfried Herder, Novalis, Friedrich Schleiermacher, and Johann Gottlieb Fichte. Whereas for the French revolutionaries a nation was a group of individuals subject to a single political order, for the Germans nations were distinguished from one another by God and nature. Each had its peculiar character closely related to its common language. Since language is the vehicle of a tradition, preserving and transmitting sentiments, symbols, emotional associations, and myths, to share a native language is to share a common culture. "Every language," wrote Schleiermacher, "is a particular mode of thought, and what is cogitated in one language can never be repeated in the same way in another." This concept of nationality tended to be associated with a metaphysical doctrine that saw every nation as the expression of a spirit or idea, which in turn expressed a particular aspect of the divine image. The diversity of nations was a reflection of the diversity of reality, and each nation made its necessary contribution to the progress of humankind. Its members therefore had a moral duty to preserve and foster it. Thus, in reacting against the Francophile cosmopolitanism of the *Aufklärung* (German Enlightenment), the German cultural nationalist nevertheless continued to see the nations against the backcloth of humanity, each with a role to play in what, in the end, was a drama of humankind.

As these writers saw it, a nation's existence did not depend on its members' choice or recognition; or, rather, because it formed their consciousness, they could hardly choose not to be members. If the German nation was a natural fact, it was because men reared in a German tradition would be essentially different from Englishmen or Frenchmen. Thus, a German who tried to ape the French inhibited the expression of his own nature and made do with what for him were artificial second bests.

THE NATION DEFINED BY COMMON HERITAGE. The conception of nationality as language and culture was challenged by Ernest Renan in the famous lecture *Qu'est-ce qu'une nation?* of 1882. It is a mistake, says Renan, to confuse nations with ethnographic and linguistic groups. Common racial origin, language, or religion, common economic interests, or the facts of geography are not sufficient to constitute a nation. There are nations like the Swiss, who do not share such characteristics, and there are linguistic groups like the English-speaking peoples, who do but who do not form a single nation. According to Renan, what constitutes a nation is the possession, first, of a common history, particularly of sufferings—of a store, that is, of common memories that are a source of common sympathy and pride. But it is important that some things be forgotten, too, for until old wounds have healed, the sense of sharing a common heroic tradition will be lacking. Thus, the second condition of nationality is a will to live together and to keep the common heritage alive. "To have done great things together, and the will to do more, these are the essential conditions for a people. ... The existence of a nation is ... a daily plebiscite."

Granted the importance of personal identification with a common tradition in the life of a nation, the metaphor of common memories does little, perhaps, to elucidate what gives a national tradition its unity and continuity. In the sense in which memory is important for individual self-knowledge and identity, individuals cannot remember what happened before they were born. Nor need their heroic ancestors stand in any generative relation to them. It is only in a figurative sense that a Frenchman could claim Joan of Arc for an ancestor. It is only because he is already a participant in a national tradition that he knows whom to call ancestor. Different situations call out different loyalties, and the ancestors a man acknowledges may differ accordingly. An American Jew of German descent might identify himself now with Thomas Jefferson, now with Judas Maccabaeus, now with Frederick the Great. Again, although men may share memories simply by having been present at the same event, to share a common history is not just to know the same historical facts; it is to identify with the same historic symbols, feel vicarious pride in the same achievements, and feel indignation at the same affronts. A Frenchman may *know* as much about Frederick as about Joan; it is because Joan is *his* and Frederick *theirs* that he is a Frenchman. A nation exists, then, where there is a group of individuals, attached in this way to a common body of symbols, who recognize one another as fellow members sharing similar attitudes to these symbols and who, because of this, feel a loyalty and concern for one another that they would not extend to outsiders. Linguistic, religious, or physiognomic features may have a part in determining who is so recognized, and the importance of any one of them may be different in different situations.

THE NATION DEFINED BY TERRITORY. A characteristic of nationality distinguishing it from most other kinds of group attachment is its relation to territory. For a group to have no special territorial affinity would not prevent one from calling it a sect, a family, or a social class. The idea of a homeland, however, seems essential to the idea of a nation. The true cosmopolitan has no place where he belongs. This illumines the close conceptual relation between nation and state, for a state is also territorially based and will admit nonmembers only on its own terms.

Where an area has a history of conflict among religious, linguistic, or racial groups each concentrated in a particular territory, the members of each will be conscious of themselves as a separate group with a history of supremacy or suffering associated with that territory; the characteristics that significantly differentiate the group from those around it will come to be thought of as those of people who belong to that territory, even when they are also found outside it. Any such group excluded from political power may be expected to aspire to independence and to want to settle in its own territory the terms on which power and prestige are enjoyed. There is, then, a wide range of features by which a national group might identify itself and its members. Which of them becomes the focus of nationality in any given case will depend on how the group has come to self-consciousness; that feature will very often correspond to the criterion by which it has been singled out as an object of oppression. Its homeland will be the territory in which the group so defined now predominates or predominated in some earlier period to which its common recollections go back.

THE NATION DEFINED BY COMMON AIM. However, because nationalism is so often a form of protest, the concept of the nation to which it is tied may depend as much on the definition of the out-group against which it is aimed as on the positive delineation of the in-group. In the twentieth century African and Asian nationalisms, for instance, relied heavily on the repudiation of white colonialism and on an aspiration to count as the white man's equal. However, on its own this cannot be enough to constitute a nation, for though the same sentiments are found throughout Black Africa, only a few Africans see themselves as a single nation aspiring to unity in a single state. Nationalism, in fact, can exist before the nation, as the aspiration of a European-trained elite aiming at native independence in a territory defined by an imperial power for administrative convenience, not by any native tradition or symbolic attachment. Having transformed a colony into a state, nationalists in countries such as Ghana must then create a nation. That states can be as important in making nations as nations can be in making states is borne out by the success of the United States. The failure of the Austro-Hungarian Empire to create a nation was the cause of its disintegration.

NATURE SELF-DETERMINITION

The twin sources of modern nationalist doctrine are the French conception of popular sovereignty and German romantic anthropological nationalism. In eighteenth-century political theory the attribution of sovereignty to the people instead of the monarch gave the people the right to determine its own mode of government. This implied no threat to the existing order of states and gave rise to no irredentisms in France and England, where the territorial boundaries of the self-conscious nation corresponded more or less with the established frontiers of the state and where the state itself was already a national symbol. In Germany and Italy, however, nationality spilled across frontiers. If the people, being sovereign, might choose the political order it wished and if "the people" was defined by nationality irrespective of existing states, then a national will to unity and independence was self-justifying even though it dismembered existing states, upset dynastic legitimacy, and sanctioned the invasion of one sovereign state by another in the interest of national liberation. The Italian nationalist Giuseppe Mazzini put the case in extreme terms, professing the belief that the political unity and independence of every nation within its natural boundaries was ordained by God. A characteristically more moderate view was stated by J. S. Mill in *Representative Government* (1861):

Where the sentiment of nationality exists in any force, there is a *prima facie* case for uniting all the members of the nationality under the same government, and a government to themselves apart. This is merely saying that the question of government ought to be decided by the governed. One hardly knows what any division of the human race would be free to do if not to determine with which of the various collective bodies of human beings they would choose to associate themselves.

There are very great difficulties, however, in the notion of a right to self-determination, whether individual or collective. The idea of a state as an organization exercising authority over everyone within its boundaries is not compatible with the idea of conceding to each man a right to choose whether to give it his allegiance. Of course, everyone may have a right to some influence on how and by whom he will be governed. But this amounts to a right to participate in certain constitutional decision procedures that take the political framework for granted, not to a right to take or leave it as one likes. Nor is a collective right any easier. On the practical level no amount of fragmentation or partition could put every individual in an area like the Balkans into the right state.

A more fundamental problem, however, is to decide what constitutes a national group for the purpose of self-determination. In the name of national unity Ghanaian nationalists deny self-determination to the Ashanti as the Congolese denied it to Katanga. If Germans claim that all German-speaking people, as members of the German nation, ought to be included in Germany, would the principle of national self-determination leave so-called Germans abroad any choice in the matter? And if they demurred, would it be as Germans or as non-Germans? If as Germans, would this be compatible with the self-determination of the whole German people? Clearly, if nationality is to be judged by objective criteria like language, the principle of national self-determination would support irredentist expansion policies irrespective of the wishes of the subgroup concerned since the nation's will would presumably be more authoritatively expressed by the greater part than by the lesser. But if nationality is judged by subjective criteria, like a will to live under one government, repudiation by the subgroup would appear to be ground enough for saying that it was not part of the same nation after all. But a dissentient minority within that subgroup could then equally well claim a separate national identity and so on. If one accepts subjective criteria for group self-determination, there is no reason for stopping short of individual self-determination.

The objective criteria, though often difficult to apply in actual cases, do provide clear principles for the proper constitution of states. However, they can claim no support from the individualist doctrine that political obligation must rest on consent. This principle has played its part in the history of nationalist doctrine. Immanuel Kant maintained that the principle of moral freedom and autonomy implied that men, as self-legislating members of the kingdom of ends, must impose political obligation upon themselves and that authority must derive from and be subject to the general will as expressed in law. Nationalists like the German political economist Adam Müller transformed the argument, however, by identifying the individual with the nation, insisting that the individual's permanent will was more truly expressed in the *Volksgeist,* or national spirit, than in any particular individual preference. Thus, the general will, which for Jean-Jacques Rousseau and Kant reconciled individual moral autonomy with political authority and obligation, became a way of denying the relevance of personal choice when it ran counter to the national spirit.

Early nineteenth-century nationalism was nevertheless liberal and humane in intention. Fichte and Mazzini would have argued that unless a nation was united in an independent sovereign state, its members, unable to command the respect of others as equals, would be lacking in dignity and self-respect. Much of the persuasive charm of nationalism in Africa and Asia has a similar source. Men of color repudiating white superiority feel that for their own self-respect they must be ruled by men of their own color and kind with whom they can identify and who will be received on equal footing by the leaders of other sovereign states.

However, the moral uncertainty out of which nationalism is born and which is perhaps its main justification, readily turns, once unity and independence has been won, into an aggressive assertiveness and national egoism, akin to what in France Charles Maurras called "integral nationalism," "the exclusive pursuit of national policies, the absolute maintenance of national integrity, and the steady increase of national power." The nation-state is no longer set in the context of a larger humanity; it is its own sufficient justification. Nationalism in this key is frankly irrationalist, delighting in the symbolic rhetoric of "blood and soil." Enormously important as it is for the historian and sociologist, it would be absurd to treat it as if it invited serious rational criticism.

See also Condorcet, Marquis de; Diderot, Denis; Enlightenment; Fichte, Johann Gottlieb; Herder, Johann Gottfried; Jefferson, Thomas; Kant, Immanuel; Loyalty; Mill, John Stuart; Novalis; Patriotism; Philosophical Anthropology; Racism; Renan, Joseph Ernest; Rousseau, Jean-Jacques; Schleiermacher, Friedrich Daniel Ernst; Self-Interest; Social and Political Philosophy; Sovereignty; State.

Bibliography

HISTORICAL STUDIES

Hayes, Carlton J. H. *Historical Evolution of Modern Nationalism.* Chicago, 1948.

Kohn, Hans. *The Idea of Nationalism.* New York: Macmillan, 1945. History of nationality and nationalism before 1789.

Kohn, Hans. *Nationalism: Its Meaning and History.* Princeton, NJ: Van Nostrand, 1955. Introductory study with readings and selected bibliography.

GENERAL STUDIES

Hertz, Frederick. *Nationality in History and Politics.* London: K. Paul, Trench, Trubner, 1944. Sociological and historical study of nationalist ideology.

Shafer, Boyd C. *Nationalism—Myth and Reality.* London: V. Gollancz, 1955. Has twenty-page bibliography.

Snyder, Louis L. *The Meaning of Nationalism.* New Brunswick, NJ: Rutgers University Press, 1954.

CLASSIC EXPOSITIONS

Fichte, J. G. *Reden an die deutsche Nation.* Berlin, 1808. Translated by R. F. Jones and G. H. Turnbull as *Addresses to the German Nation.* Chicago: Open Court, 1922.

Maurras, Charles. *Enquête sur la monarchie.* Paris: A. Fayard, 1924. Originally published in 1900.

Mazzini, Giuseppe. *Doveri dell'uomo.* London, 1860. Translated by Ella Noyes as "The Duties of Man," in *The Duties of Man and Other Essays, by Joseph Mazzini,* edited by Ernest Rhys. London and New York, 1907.

Reiss, H. S., ed. *The Political Thought of the German Romantics, 1793–1815.* Oxford: Blackwell, 1955. Contains readings from Fichte, Novalis, Adam Müller, Schleiermacher, and Friedrich Karl von Savigny; also has selected bibliographies.

Renan, Ernest. *Qu'est-ce qu'une Nation?* In *Oeuvres complètes de Ernest Renan,* Vol. I, edited by Henriette Psichari. Paris, 1947. Originally published in 1882.

CRITICAL STUDIES

Acton, John Emerich Edward. "Nationality." In *Essays on Freedom and Power by Lord Acton,* edited by Gertrude Himmelfarb. Glencoe, IL: Free Press, 1948. For criticism of Mazzini.

Cobban, Alfred. *National Self-Determination.* Chicago: University of Chicago Press, 1948.

Kedourie, Elie. *Nationalism.* London: Hutchinson, 1960; 2nd rev. ed., London and New York, 1961. Has notes for further reading; examines metaphysical foundations of nationalism and its influence on Europe and the Middle East.

Kohn, Hans. *Prophets and Peoples.* New York, 1957. Studies of J. S. Mill, Jules Michelet, Mazzini, Heinrich von Treitschke, Fëdor Dostoevsky.

                                        Stanley I. Benn (1967)

NATIONALISM [ADDENDUM]

However it is characterized, nationalism is a phenomenon of central importance in the modern world because it reflects the special moral significance that most people in fact attach to their ties as members of a particular nation. All forms of nationalism share the view that it is right and good for some particular people, or all peoples, to promote a common national identity through appropriate institutions. Contemporary philosophers are increasingly concerned to evaluate the claims of nationalism. Are ties of nationality desirable? Do they generate special obligations among conationals that do not extend to others? Is national identity compatible with the rights of national minorities in a larger nation-state, and duties of global justice that are owed to distant peoples? Is nationalism compatible with standard liberal assumptions concerning the equal worth of all persons, and the impartiality required for justice? If liberalism, nationalism, and global justice come into conflict, which should give way to better accommodate the prior claims of the other? What separates a morality of nationalism from a politics of tribalism?

Such issues have come to the fore in the work of contemporary liberals, communitarians, multiculturalists, and cosmopolitans. They advance rival normative models of nationalism and justice within and without borders. Many liberals are drawn to a thin civic paradigm of nationality. Communitarians favor a thicker cultural paradigm closer to the historical experience of shared nationality. On the civic paradigm, the demands of impartial justice within and between nation-states are most secure when ties of nationality consist in nothing more than individuals' relations as equal citizens of one and the same political society. This paradigm grows out of republican traditions of thought that identify the nation or people, the sole legitimate source of sovereignty, with members of the state—individuals born and living within its political borders. The civic paradigm is exemplified by Rawls's seminal reinvention of contractarian liberalism in *A Theory of Justice* (1971). In this framework, political society is a system of social cooperation for mutual advantage, which can be ordered entirely on the basis of principles of justice and political ideals of freedom, equality, and fairness. Political society is just when it conforms to principles that free and equal persons would agree to under conditions that are impartial. Rawls's principles (equal civil and political liberties, equality of opportunity, and economic arrangements that either ensure material equality or use inequality to raise the material well-being of all) are embodied in his model of a just liberal-democratic welfare state.

Rawls argues that this model provides a stable, well-ordered nation-state on its own terms. It sustains the very sense of justice and mutual respect among persons as citizens that are necessary and sufficient to motivate them to support their political obligations, independently of any thicker ties of history, culture, religion, ethnicity, family, class, gender, and so on. For Rawls, justice is the primary virtue of human life in society. To this end, the civic paradigm of nationality constructs ties of nationality as the relations of equal citizens who recognize one another in a common allegiance to their shared political ideals and institutions. These ties are precisely what justice requires and all that justice requires by way of community. Of course the civic paradigm leaves ample room for the many cultural, ethnic, or religious attachments people may embrace. But for the Rawlsian liberal, the requirements of justice do not derive from any of these more particular ties. Furthermore, the requirements of social justice operate as background constraints on the permissible structure of all such ties, conforming them to persons' equal rights and duties as citizens. A civic nationalism justifies the politics of building just institutions and peoples bound together as citizens by their allegiance to shared political ideals.

COSMOPOLITAN LIBERALS

For cosmopolitan liberals such as C. R. Beitz, Thomas W. Pogge, and Brian M. Barry, John Rawls's contractarianism and the civic paradigm have a great advantage in that they lay the basis for impartial and egalitarian principles of global justice. On their cosmopolitan argument, ignoring particular ties of nationality, as well as other contingencies such as race or gender, is a natural extension of Rawlsian liberalism. It justifies a choice of principles of global justice that do for the poorest persons in the world what Rawls's principles are supposed to do for the worst off in any particular nation-state. The civic paradigm of nationality as political citizenship seems well suited to allow each person to be a citizen of a just world because it rests on political ideals that are supposed to be universal and impartial in scope. Cosmopolitan justice redistributes the wealth and resources of the world and reconstructs international arrangements with the aim of gaining rough equality in all persons' individual liberties, standards of living, and political rights. These arrangements provide a background justice, which constrains the conduct of nation-states and reconciles individuals' rights and duties as citizens of a particular nation with their rights and duties as cosmopolitan citizens of the world. Whether or not cosmopolitan liberalism leaves room for any recognizable ties of nationality comes into question by communitarian nationalists.

COMMUNITARIANS

Communitarians such as Michael Sandel, Michael Walzer, Will Kymlicka, David Miller, and Charles Taylor provide the bases for an alternative cultural paradigm of nationality and nationalism. Communitarians argue that the civic paradigm is too thin to capture the bonds between persons that are both necessary and desirable for the robust experience of nationality. The ties of nationality are and ought to be the rich bonds of membership in a historic community marked by a shared societal culture and way of life. Such a culture involves a common language, time-honored customs, shared traditions, inherited institutions, agreed-on social meanings and values, and the exercise or aspirations of political autonomy in a certain geographic area. Nationalism is the process through which a societal culture of this sort is built up, enters into the identity of its members, and finds expression in political acts through which its members seek to create and preserve it as an independent entity. As such, national identity is not reducible to political ties of citizenship, or shared political ideals. Rather, a shared societal culture actively preserved by its members constitutes a people or nationality and this is precisely what a political society ought to recognize and protect. For communitarians, the existence of a nation in this rich culture and historical sense justifies rights of national self-determination, whether it is the right of a people to independent statehood (Walzer 1977) or more limited rights of self-determination within a multinational confederated state (Kymlicka 1989). The violation of these rights is taken to ground just war theory (Walzer 1977) and the right of a national minority to secede and form its own sovereign state (Buchanan 1991).

This paradigm of nationality as shared historical culture may be justified, and by implication challenged, in various ways. Some communitarians defend it on the basis of a philosophical conception of the self that holds that the self always gains its identity, purposes, and obligations from the particular community(ies) in which it is embedded (Sandel 1982). Aspects of this conception motivate the nationalist argument that the very rights and duties of citizenship, stressed by the civic paradigm, depend on the fact that citizens are already bound together by a common nationality and thick cultural ties to their compatriots (Kymlicka 1989, Miller 1995). Others argue that any knowledge of justice and framework of moral deliberation always depend on the intersubjective meanings and values shared by a particular political community (Walzer 1977). The cultural framework provided by national identity can be justified by the argument that such a framework is necessary to provide persons with their meaningful options in life. Without such options, people lack any genuine individual freedom and liberal equality (Kymlicka 1989). A shared national identity is also defended on the grounds that it provides the only appropriate basis of reciprocal recognition among peoples, encompassing both a respect for cultural difference and human commonality (Taylor 1994). The ties of national culture are defended as intrinsically valuable because of the special human virtues and goods they make possible, such as loyalty, courage, love of country among compatriots (Miller 1995). National identities provide persons with rich cultural self-images that probably cannot, and should not, be replaced by a bare image of oneself as part of humanity, a citizen of the world, or a disembodied impartial deliberator; so the communitarian argument goes.

The import of the cultural paradigm of nationality, and communitarian nationalism, critically depends on what kinds of national community one has in mind. In modern history, nationalism in its cultural communitarian form has often implied tribalism, and a virulent hostility, intolerance, or indifference to other peoples (Arendt 1948). More generally, what of illiberal or oppressive national communities that violate the rights or stigmatize the identities of some of their own members, or of nonmembers, outsiders, foreign peoples (Doppelt 1998, 1999, 2002)? In liberal theory, the moral right of national self-determination universally applies to all peoples and implies duties of every people to respect or even defend the rights of other peoples. In practice, what sort of national cultures and nationalism are compatible with the rights of all individuals and peoples? These concerns inspire recent debates among communitarian nationalists and liberals concerning the possibility of a liberal nationalism based on a cultural paradigm of national identity.

LIBERAL NATIONALISTS

Liberal nationalists seek to harness the special value of national belonging to liberal ideals so that each informs and constrains the other. For Kymlicka, one central problem for liberal nationalism arises because most nation-states contain several nationalities, involving majority and minority cultures. His multicultural liberalism employs the culture paradigm of nationality to justify group rights for national minorities in a larger nation-state, as a requirement of domestic justice. Such group rights to a limited measure of self-government, territorial sovereignty, and cultural autonomy empowers a national minority (French Canadians in Quebec; Native American bands on their tribal homelands) to preserve its historical community and national identity from assimilation to the dominant culture. The liberal nation-state should foster multinational cultures and institutions, as Canada, the United States, and other states in fact do. This multinationalism is supposed to be a liberal nationalism for two reasons. First, group rights are justified as necessary means to the fulfillment of liberal individualist ideals of freedom and equality for members of national minorities. Secondly, group rights to cultural autonomy are supposed to be fully compatible with the individual rights people possess as citizens of a liberal state. By this route, multiculturalism reconciles the cultural paradigm of nationality with the civic paradigm, and thus nationalism with liberalism. The citizen of a multinational state is supposed to combine a nationalist attachment to his or her own cultural community with a political attachment to the general rights and duties of citizenship.

NATIONALISM VS. LIBERALISM IN THE MULTICULTURAL MODEL

Tensions arise between nationalism and liberalism in the multicultural model if group rights protect minority cultures with some illiberal or oppressive practices, or these group rights are embraced by minorities to shield them from oppression by an illiberal majority culture. The societal cultures protected by group rights are not supposed to define national identities in essentialist terms that exclude people or discriminate against them, on the basis of alleged racial characteristics, blood, descent, and the like (Kymlicka 1989). The model may also be unstable to the extent that multiple national identities in one and the same nation-state may fail to sustain sufficient unify for domestic liberal justice (Doppelt 1998, 1999, 2001). Such instability can motivate the descent of multiculturalism into either secession, assimilation, or domination. Miller's model of liberal nationalism suggests that

a weak or fragmented nation-state can be countered by providing unifying ties of national identity among all groups of citizens. It can do so by building a pluralistic national culture and identity, which is continually reshaped to include groups that have been oppressed, excluded, or marginalized. From this standpoint, the best liberal response to the existence of diverse ethnic and national minorities is not necessarily either group rights or cultural assimilation. To some extent, a liberal nationalism may require a democratic expansion of national culture and identity such that all groups can express and recognize themselves in it. All states engage in the construction of nationality through their activities in the spheres of law and public policy, immigration practices, public schooling, military service, political rhetoric, public ceremonies, and holidays, and so on. Criteria of liberal nation-building should be based on the extent to which a nation employs means that are consistent with democratic rights, and achieves results that embody an inclusive nationality (Kymlicka 1989).

FURTHER APPROACHES TO LIBERAL NATIONALISM

Rawls's turn in his later work to political liberalism and the law of peoples provides yet another approach to liberal nationalism. He develops a conception of political society with communitarian components that moves his liberalism from a civic to a more cultural paradigm of the nation, though not as thick as other communitarian nationalists. Rawls now grounds the liberal ideals underlying contractarian justice in our particular historical tradition of legal and political institutions and ideas. Our political tradition is expressed in canonical texts such as the Declaration of Independence, the U.S. Constitution, the Bill of Rights, and landmark legislation. It lives in all the ways their basic principles enter into our democratic institutions and political practices. Rawls's political liberalism responds to the perennial worry of liberal nations that agreement on the fundamentals of justice is blocked by the divergent comprehensive views of life held by people of different religions, ethical outlooks, national or ethnic identities, and so on. Yet by public reflection on the meaning of our shared political culture, people with divergent views of life can attain an overlapping consensus on the most basic ideals of American democratic citizenship, and thus on political justice. With this focus on building democratic institutions and a national political identity, Rawls appropriates the cultural paradigm of nationality to vindicate his account of domestic justice and civic nationalism. This challenges the liberal nationalists who require much thicker cultural ties of nationality to explain why the conception of free and equal persons built into democratic culture is not sufficient for national identity.

CHALLENGES TO LIBERAL NATIONALISM

The sharpest challenge to liberal nationalism is posed by cosmopolitan liberals who apply Rawls's principles of justice to generate the global egalitarian justice described above (Beitz 1983, Pogge 1994, and Barry 1999). Strong ties of nationality of the sort stressed by communitarians (liberal or not) support special obligations and affinities among conationals that either directly contradict their duties of cosmopolitan justice or weaken their motivation to comply with them. For example, the right of a people to national self-determination defended by communitarian nationalists is typically taken to include a right to control the national resources, wealth, and capital possessed by that people. But from the cosmopolitan standpoint, the distribution of wealth among nations may reflect a legacy of injustice or bad luck, and is, in any case, incompatible with the demands of global egalitarian justice. Nations have little or no independent moral standing except in the degree that their internal and external relations conform to the (Rawlsian) principles of justice that every person in the world could reasonably accept.

Liberal nationalists respond to this challenge by arguing either against the cosmopolitan conception of global justice or in favor of its compatibility with liberal nationalism. Walzer and Miller reject egalitarian cosmopolitanism because it fails to make sense of the ways persons' obligations to one another are typically rooted in a particular nation-state and not understood to extend to all humanity. Some philosophers underscore the ways common sense morality supports the dependence of persons' duties on the special associative ties of family, friendship, membership in a particular nationality, and the like (Scheffler 2001). Indeed, Rawls's turn to a conception of justice grounded in a people's own political traditions supports a nation-based account of international justice (his law of peoples) at odds with egalitarian cosmopolitanism. This tradition-based view of domestic justice allows that other peoples or nations with different, indeed illiberal political traditions can be just and decent; provided that they are well-ordered societies that respect the most basic rights of their own members (e.g., to physical security, the material means of life, etc.) and the rights of other just or decent peoples to self-

determination. Liberal and illiberal but decent nations can reasonably agree to principles of international justice that imply some mutual rights and duties among peoples. These include duties of material assistance to burdened nations that need it to become well-ordered, decent, and just, but not duties of egalitarian global redistribution.

From this standpoint, cosmopolitan justice is unreasonable because it ignores that peoples with different cultural traditions, exercising their rights of national self-determination, can be expected to have different levels of economic development, standards of living, and criteria of domestic justice. As such, nations bear some responsibility for their standards of living and thus differences between them do not in themselves imply global injustice. So while both Miller and Rawls support duties of distributive global justice and the rights of all persons to the basic means of life, health, and subsistence, both argue that cosmopolitan egalitarian principles come at the price of people's national identities, responsibilities, and rights of self-determination. By this route, liberal nationalism is reconciled with a much less demanding account of global justice, and one more in tune with the communitarian view of the independent moral standing of nations.

Other liberal nationalists such as Kok-Chor Tan defend cosmopolitan egalitarianism and argue that properly understood, it is compatible with a limited form of nationalism. The debate between nationalists and cosmopolitans often lump together different claims concerning what is supposed to make them incompatible: conflicting institutional requirements, nation-state versus global state; conflicting identities or attachments, national identity versus citizen of the world; conflicting moralities, nationalist partiality versus liberal impartiality; and conflicting views of justice, special duties of justice among conationals versus duties to all humanity in cosmopolitan justice. Liberal nationalists who defend egalitarian cosmopolitanism take the issue of justice to be the one that is fundamental to their reconciliation. The basic strategy is to limit or circumscribe the special rights and duties individuals have as conationals, the right of nations to self-determination, and the imperatives of domestic justice, so that they conform to the morally prior requirements of global egalitarian justice. The thought is that even so, the rigorous constraints imposed by cosmopolitan justice leave some room for associative ties of nationality and special duties arising from them. Cosmopolitan justice constrains domestic justice, and how nations may exercise rights of national self-determination, but does not destroy the important space they occupy. Such a vision of liberal justice is in principle neutral concerning institutional, cultural, and identity issues that are used to drive a wedge between nationalism and cosmopolitanism (Tan 2004). For example, cosmopolitan equality does not necessarily require one global government in place of national political institutions. Nor does people's acceptance of duties to support egalitarian global arrangements imply the abandonment of any national identity or partiality to one's compatriots in some respects.

For these reasons, a liberal nationalism may be compatible with cosmopolitan justice, at least in principle. In practice the dynamics of human motivation might raise anew the tensions between nationalism and cosmopolitanism, as conflicting attachments and identities. In any case, these debates enrich political philosophy by bringing issues of political culture, national identity, nationalism, and global justice into the heart of contemporary liberalism.

See also Civil Disobedience; Cosmopolitanism; Multiculturalism; Postcolonialism; Republicanism; Social and Political Philosophy.

Bibliography

Arendt, Hannah. *The Origins of Totalitarianism*. London: Harvest, 1976. First published in 1948.

Barry, Brian. *Culture and Equality: An Egalitarian Critique of Multiculturalism*. Cambridge, U.K.: Polity Press, 2001.

Barry, Brian. "International Society from a Cosmopolitan Perspective." In *International Society: Diverse Ethical Perspectives*, edited by D. Mapel and T. Nardin. Princeton, NJ: Princeton University Press, 1998.

Barry, Brian. "Statism and Nationalism: A Cosmopolitan Critique." In *Global Justice*, edited by I. Shapiro and L. Brilmayer. New York: New York University Press, 1999.

Beitz, Charles R. "Cosmopolitan Ideal and National Sentiment." *Journal of Philosophy* 80 (10) (1983): 591–600.

Beitz, Charles R. *Political Theory and International Relations*. Princeton, NJ: Princeton University Press, 1979.

Buchanan, Allen E. *Secession*. Boulder, CO: Westview Press, 1991.

Doppelt, Gerald D. "Illiberal Cultures and Group Rights: A Critique of Multiculturalism in Kymlicka, Taylor, and Nussbaum." *Journal of Contemporary Legal Issues* 12 (2): (2002): 661–692.

Doppelt, Gerald D. "Is There a Multicultural Liberalism?" *Inquiry* 41 (1998): 223–238.

Doppelt, Gerald D. "Liberalism, Multiculturalism, and the Politics of Identity." In *Applied Ethics: Proceedings of the 21st International Wittgenstein Symposium Vienna*, edited by P. Kampits, K. Kokay, and A. Weiberg. Vienna: Verlag Holder-Pichler-Tempsky, 1999.

Habermas, J. "Citizenship and National Identity." *Praxis International* 12 (1992): 1–19.

Hurka, T. "The Justification of National Partiality." In *The Morality of Nationalism*, edited by R. McKim and J. McMahan. Oxford, U.K.: Oxford University Press, 1997.

Kymlicka, Will. *Liberalism, Community and Culture*. New York: Oxford University Press, 1989.

Kymlicka, Will. *Multicultural Citizenship: A Liberal Theory of Minority Rights*. Oxford, U.K.: Oxford University Press, 1995.

Kymlicka, Will. *Politics in the Vernacular: Nationalism, Multiculturalism and Citizenship*. Oxford, U.K.: Oxford University Press, 2001a.

Kymlicka, Will. "Territorial Boundaries: A Liberal Egalitarian Perspective." In *Boundaries and Justice*, edited by D. Miller and S. Hashmi. Princeton, NJ: Princeton University Press, 2001b.

Margalit, A., and J. Raz. "National Self-Determination." *Journal of Philosophy* 87 (1990): 439–461.

Miller, David. *Citizenship and National Identity*. Cambridge, U.K.: Polity Press, 2000.

Miller, David. "The Ethical Significance of Nationality." *Ethics* 98 (4) (1988): 647–662.

Miller, David. "The Limits of Cosmopolitan Justice." In *International Society*, edited by D. Mapel and T. Nardin. Princeton, NJ: Princeton University Press, 1998.

Miller, David. *On Nationality*. Oxford, U.K.: Oxford University Press, 1995.

Moellendorf, D. *Cosmopolitan Justice*. Boulder, CO: Westview Press, 2002.

Pogge, Thomas W. "An Egalitarian Law of Peoples." *Philosophy and Public Affairs* 23 (3) (1994): 195–224.

Pogge, Thomas W. *Realizing Rawls*. Ithaca, NY: Cornell University Press, 1989.

Rawls, John. *The Law of Peoples: With, "The Idea of Public Reason Revisited."* Cambridge, MA: Harvard University Press, 1999.

Rawls, John. *Political Liberalism*. Paperback ed. New York: Columbia University Press, 1996. First published in 1993.

Rawls, John. *A Theory of Justice*. Cambridge, MA: Harvard University Press, 1971.

Sandel, Michael. *Liberalism and the Limits of Justice*. Cambridge, U.K.: Cambridge University Press, 1982.

Scheffler, Samuel. *Boundaries and Allegiances*. New York: Oxford University Press, 2001.

Tan, Kok-Chor. *Justice without Borders: Cosmopolitanism, Nationalism, and Patriotism*. Cambridge, U.K.: Cambridge University Press, 2004.

Taylor, Charles. "The Politics of Recognition." In *Multiculturalism: Examining the Politics of Recognition*, edited by Amy Gutmann, 52–56, and 58–60. Princeton, NJ: Princeton University Press, 1994.

Walzer, Michael. *Just and Unjust Wars*. New York: Basic Books, 1977.

Gerald Doppelt (2005)

NATIVISM, INNATISM

See *Innate Ideas; Innate Ideas, Nativism*

NATORP, PAUL

(1854–1924)

Paul Natorp was born in Düsseldorf and died in Marburg. Along with Hermann Cohen, he is known as one of the founders of the Marburg School of Neo-Kantianism. He studied history, philology, mathematics, and philosophy in Berlin, Bonn, and Strassburg. After completing his doctorate in history at the University of Strassburg in 1876, he went to Marburg where Cohen was working on the restoration of Kant's critical philosophy. In 1881 Natorp obtained his postdoctoral qualification with a thesis on the prehistory of criticism titled *Descartes' Erkenntnistheorie* (Descartes's theory of knowledge). He became an associate professor at the University of Marburg in 1885 and eventually a full professor of philosophy and pedagogy. In spite of being offered several chairs at other universities, Natorp remained in Marburg throughout his lifetime.

Despite their close relationship, Natorp cannot be seen as a genuine follower of Cohen, especially because of the explicitly historical foundation of his philosophy. Beside his interests in epistemology and the theory of science, both orientated on Cohen's logic, Natorp worked on problems in ethics, the philosophy of religion, philosophical psychology, and the philosophical foundations of pedagogy.

Three main periods of Natorp's philosophical work can be distinguished. During the earliest period, Natorp developed a methodical idealism that takes Kant and Cohen as its point of departure and is presented in *Die logischen Grundlagen der exakten Wissenschaften* (The logical foundations of the exact sciences, 1910) as well as in *Die Philosophie. Ihr Problem und ihre Probleme* (Philosophy. Its problem and its problems, 1911). Both books focus on the problem of definition in the natural sciences from an epistemological perspective. They take the mathematical approach as a paradigm for the object-creating function of consciousness. Natorp reduces the transcendental-logical analysis of the constitution of objects to the categories of scientific definition. Science, in this context, stands for the transcendental subject. This is the main characteristic of Natorp's philosophy: The sciences as *facts of reason* are taken as the only legitimate starting points of the *transcendental method* so that epistemology is understood as a theory of science.

Natorp attempted to find a basis for his methodical idealism not only through systematic thought but also through studies in the history of philosophy. His studies of Plato, as recorded in an extensive work on *Platons*

Ideenlehre (Plato's theory of ideas, 1903), are a good example of his historically orientated method. The book is still discussed as an example of a strictly systematic view on the history of philosophy.

The second period in Natorp's work is introduced by the *Allgemeine Psychologie nach kritischer Methode* (General psychology according to a critical method, 1912). In this book, Natorp proposes philosophical psychology as a discipline that should be able to examine the transcendental constitution of objects through reference to the subject's concrete nexus of experiences. Natorp hereby added a genetic aspect to epistemology, which was adopted by several philosophers of his time and had a significant influence on Edmund Husserl's foundation of phenomenology. At the same time Natorp abandons the restriction of the transcendental analysis to the *fact of science* by enlarging the *factum* to a *fieri*, the *what is* to the *what is to be*, so that cognition is no longer taken as a mere fact but rather as a process within the subject.

The psychological method is *reconstructive* insofar as the psychologist analyses the cognitive *process* and goes back to the very origin of cognition in a step-by-step analysis. The subject's experience is taken as the original source of cognition, but it is not intuitively given (as the phenomenologist would put it). According to Natorp the experience of the subject can only be reconstructed in a genetically oriented epistemological process. Concrete experience inevitably has to be transformed into an abstract definition of experience. The correlative of the object—the subject—is *reconstructed* post hoc. However, the reconstruction itself is a cognitive act and, as such, bound to definition and the interruption of cognition in process. Reconstruction, like any other cognitive process, is an approximative approach to and a concretization of the object, except that it does not lead back to the natural object but to its correlate, namely, the subject. The individual subject is correlated to an individual object, and every individual *case* of definition corresponds to an individual *case* of cognition. Natorp's concept of subject here is still a very restrictive one.

In his later philosophy Natorp connected logic and psychology by transforming his understanding of cognition as a concretization of being into a *general logic* concerning the relation of objects that is integrated into an extensive metaphysical conception. In his *Vorlesungen über praktische Philosophie* (Lectures on practical philosophy, edited in 1925) as well as in the *Philosophische Systematik* (Philosophical systematics, edited in 1958). Natorp attempted to preserve the guiding themes from of his early thought in a transformed way that now incorporates an ontological perspective. Instead of analyzing the object in terms of a theory of knowledge or pursuing a psychological analysis of the subject, Natorp turns his attention to the correlation between subject and object. The unity of the object depends on the basic condition that there *is* something ("it is"—*estin*—whereby the "it" remains undefined). On the other hand the specific unity of the individual subject is the correlate of the defined object's unity (the specific "this one"—*tode ti*). Both parts of the correlation are connected by the process of categorical–ontological definition. This dialectic approach is elucidated in detail in Natorp's *Philosophische Systematik* and extended to a theory of categories, which is only faintly reminiscent of Kant. In contrast to the older type of logic (á la Cohen) in Neo-Kantianism, Natorp outlines the *it is* as the epitome of being, which is prior to any logical definition. In the end, Natorp argued for an ontological interpretation of the *origin* in transcendental philosophy.

Overall, Natorp's impact on the history of philosophy has been primarily indirect. His ideas were carried on above all by the youngest representative of the Marburg School, Ernst Cassirer. The logical motif of Natorp's earliest period had a great influence on Cassirer's philosophy of culture, which did influence the broader philosophical discussion. The early phenomenologists also referred to Natorp, even if these references were primarily critical, as when Husserl and Martin Heidegger, for example, tried to avoid Natorp's one-sided emphasis on transcendental logic. At present the general philosophical audience is becoming increasingly aware of the close relationship between Natorp's later thought and Heidegger's thinking of being. In some ways Natorp's philosophical development even illustrates the general development of transcendentalism during the twentieth century, which starts with a logic of pure cognition and ends with the problem of thinking, which is already and inevitably related to being.

See also Being; Cassirer, Ernst; Cohen, Hermann; Epistemology; Ethics; Heidegger, Martin; Husserl, Edmund; Neo-Kantianism; Phenomenology; Philosophy of Religion; Plato; Thinking.

Bibliography

WORKS BY NATORP

Please note: No English translations of these texts are available.

Forschungen zur Geschichte des Erkenntnisproblems im Altertum (Studies in the history of the problem of knowledge in antiquity). Berlin: Hertz, 1884 (later edition published by Hildesheim: Olms, 1965).

Einleitung in die Psychologie nach kritischer Methode (Introduction to psychology according to a critical method). Freiburg: Mohr, 1888.

Religion innerhalb der Grenzen der Humanität (Religion within the bounds of humanity). Tübingen: Mohr, 1894 (later edition published in 1908).

Sozialpädagogik. Theorie der Willensbildung auf der Grundlage der Gemeinschaft (Social pedagogy. A theory of the cultivation of the will on the basis of community). Stuttgart: Frommann, 1899 (later editions published in 1904, 1909, 1920, 1922).

Platons Ideenlehre (Plato's theory of ideas). Leipzig: Dürr, 1903 (later edition published in 1921 with a metacritical appendix and by Darmstadt: Wiss. Buchges, 1975).

Philosophie und Pädagogik. Untersuchungen auf ihrem Grenzgebiet (Philosophy and pedagogy. Studies in the area of their frontiers). Marburg: Elwert, 1909.

Die logischen Grundlagen der exakten Wissenschaften (The logical foundations of the exact sciences). Leipzig/Berlin: Teubner, 1910 (later editions published in 1921, 1923).

Philosophie. Ihr Problem und ihre Probleme (Philosophy. Its problem and its problems). Göttingen: Vandenhoeck & Ruprecht, 1911 (later editions published in 1918, 1921).

Allgemeine Psychologie nach kritischer Methode. First (and single) book: *Objekt und Methode der Psychologie* (General psychology according to a critical method). Tübingen: Mohr, 1912.

Deutscher Weltberuf. Geschichtsphilosophische Richtlinien (German calling for the world. Outlines of a philosophy of history). Jena: Diederichs, 1918.

Der Idealismus Pestalozzis (Pestalozzi's idealism). Leipzig: Verlag Felix Meiner, 1919.

Sozialidealismus. Neue Richtlinien sozialer Erziehung (Social idealism. New outlines for social education). Berlin: L. Springer, 1920 (later edition published in1922).

Individuum und Gemeinschaft (Individual and society). Jena: Diederichs, 1921.

Natorp, H., ed.*Vorlesungen über praktische Philosophie* (Lecture on practical philosophy). Erlangen: Verlag der philosophischen Akademie, 1925.

Natorp, H., ed. *Philosophische Systematik* (Philosophical systematics). Hamburg: Meiner, 1958.

SECONDARY LITERATURE

Holzhey, Helmut. *Cohen und Natorp.* 2 vols. Basel: Schwabe, 1986.

Jegelka, Norbert. *Paul Natorp: Philosophie, Pädagogik, Politik.* Würzburg: Königshausen & Neumann, 1992.

Lembeck, Karl-Heinz. *Platon in Marburg.* Würzburg: Königshausen & Neumann, 1994.

Sieg, Ulrich. *Aufstieg und Niedergang des Marburger Neukantianismus.* Würzburg: Königshausen & Neumann, 1994.

Karl-Heinz Lembeck (2005)

NATURALISM

Put most succinctly, metaphysical naturalism affirms that the natural world is the only real one, and that the human race is not separate from it, but belongs to it as a part. The term *naturalism* refers also to an aesthetic style in literature, drama, and painting, and in ethics, to the theory that the full meaning of value concepts such as good and evil can be spelled out using only terms from a natural, or factual vocabulary. These are not of concern here. What follows is a discussion of naturalism in metaphysics and epistemology.

Everyone has a rough working notion of what can happen in the course of nature, and is familiar with the idea that perhaps a transcendent or supernatural realm lies beyond nature, another world that may occasionally make contact with the everyday world by, for example, miraculous interventions. Yet the distinction between what is natural and what is not needs to be made with some care. As St. Thomas Aquinas pointed out, everything that happens is in some way natural. Thus, according to classical philosophical theology, God must always, of necessity, act in accordance with his own nature. So from the divine point of view, special miraculous intervention, or general providential guidance, lies entirely within the realm of what happens according to nature.

What is needed is the conception of a world all of whose normal workings count as natural, while whatever lies outside this limit does not. The space-time world, with its material constituents working according to the laws of cause and effect, seems a good place to start. The natural world is the world of space, time, matter, energy, and causality, and naturalism affirms that this natural world is the only one there is. Yet even here care is needed: In some modern interpretations of quantum theory, the so-called Many Worlds interpretations, this particular space-time world is not by any means the only one. What lies beyond this world are other spatio-temporal realms, inaccessible from this one, perhaps evolving under different laws, but equally a part of nature in its entirety. So naturalists must allow that nature comprises this spatio-temporal world together with all other realms required by the best scientific explanations of this one.

NATURALISM AS METHOD AND AS ONTOLOGY

Because specifying what nature is brings in reference to scientific explanation in this way, naturalism is sometimes regarded as a rule of method rather than a metaphysical doctrine. There is a natural method of inquiry, which consists in setting out to explain and understand the world by finding the natural causal processes by which natural objects come into being, produce their effects, and pass away. All genuine knowledge is of this natural, experimental kind; human beings, themselves part of the natural order, have no special insight or intuition that could provide a more direct path to knowledge. And the methods of the natural sciences, which are so successful, are these natural methods refined and made more systematic.

If naturalism is in this way a matter of method in inquiry, the natural world is the world revealed by the methods of the natural sciences. This does not, in itself, place many constraints on what sort of world that might be: One cannot tell in advance what the scientific method might reveal. Maybe it will uncover not just familiar items—ships and shoes and sealing wax, for instance—but fire-breathing dragons, the Fountain of Youth, or the Philosopher's Stone. Naturalism regarded as a method maintains that ontology should be developed a posteriori—whatever is vindicated by the sciences is acceptable, whatever is not, is not.

The attempts made during the twentieth century to establish the existence of the paranormal phenomena (telepathy, precognition, and telekinesis) illustrate this approach. The methods adopted were naturalistic methods, which in themselves set no limits to what can exist.

A more affirmative naturalism goes rather further: It claims not only that the scientific method provides the only sound basis for knowledge of reality, but also that it has already established that all nature has a physical basis. The fundamental causal network consists in chains of physical cause and physical effect, produced by the operation of physical forces. All realities have at least a physical nature of this kind, whatever else may prove to be true of them. This leaning toward a physical basis for everything has been encouraged by the development of more and more sophisticated instruments for probing the observable, tangible, and manipulable world of matter, and of increasingly successful physical theories to account for what is discovered.

Yet this tendency to regard physics and chemistry as the basic and comprehensive sciences does not in itself require a materialistic ontology. Physicalism is a particularly stringent version of naturalism. A physical basis for everything does not rule out other characteristics. It is possible to affirm naturalism while insisting that the higher faculties in humans and other animals cannot be given a physicalistic reduction, and nonmaterialistic naturalism avoids the difficulties that materialism has, for example, in accounting for the intensional characteristics, such as linguistic meaning and psychological understanding.

THE CASE FOR NATURALISM

Bertrand Russell was once charged, as Hamlet had charged Horatio, that there are more things in heaven and earth than were dreamt of in his philosophy. He retorted that he preferred it to be that way, rather than the other way around. He thus expressed the naturalist attitude, which is imbued with the spirit of Ockham's Razor: Extravagance in ontology is to be avoided. We must recognize the reality of what most plainly exists, the familiar natural world in which we live and move, and have our being. Beyond that, one should be cautious. There is no compelling evidence, of any kind, that there is more to reality than the nature revealed by scientific investigation. So the rational position to adopt is the economical, minimalist one that there are no further realms.

THE ELEATIC ARGUMENT. The Eleatic Stranger in Plato's *Sophist* proposes that "Power is the mark of Being"—that the true test of reality is to be efficacious. That which is real makes a difference, changes things, has effects. The outcome of a serious and sustained inquiry into what actually passes this test, is naturalism. For whatever operates in such a way as to alter the course of nature belongs by that very fact to the causal network of the natural world. And whatever has no such impact has no claim to reality.

The Eleatic argument is perhaps even more powerful as a methodological one: The only way in which anything can call attention to itself, and so stake a claim to reality, is by having an effect, either directly, in perception, or indirectly, through the traces it leaves in instruments. Without any such impact, there can be no reason to suppose that the thing in question exists. And that which there is no reason to think exists, should have no place in any ontology.

This argument needs to be elaborated to cover purely theoretical reasons for admitting other realms—parallel universes, for example, or sets to underpin mathematics. It is then not so straightforward to exclude higher realms, with unmoved movers, divine providences, or guardian angels. Here the argument must be that, unlike the extra worlds of quantum theory, these other worlds have no essential link to the natural explanation of what occurs in this one.

THE SELF-CORRECTING VINDICATION. Naturalism should be adopted as the proper stance in philosophy, just because it is open to development. Wherever the current conception of the world of nature is inadequate, this deficiency is likely, sooner or later, to be revealed, for there will be unaccountable phenomena that need to be accounted for. Current explanatory resources having proved inadequate, they must be expanded. New entities, properties, or forces must be recognized. The ontology of naturalism will grow to whatever extent the facts require, no more, but no less. So naturalism will always be the best philosophical stance. To maintain this position, a naturalist must show that explanatory reasoning does not advance in this way from the natural to the supernatural.

These three lines of support for naturalism all rest on a negative base: the claim that there is no valid method of discovery beyond those used in the natural sciences. So a thorough naturalism must explore, and reject, a priori reasoning in natural theology, and the claims of religious experience to provide knowledge of a transcendent divinity. It must also argue that the hermeneutic method of some social sciences, and the empathy by which humans reach a commonsense understanding of one another, does not involve entities or processes beyond those revealed by naturalistic methods.

THE IMPLICATIONS OF NATURALISM

In general, naturalism and religion are at odds with one another. Most religions posit powerful and purposeful supernatural forces, responsible for creating the natural world, for shaping its progress, and for determining the destinies of its inhabitants. These beliefs are not compatible with the naturalistic outlook. This does not, however, preclude a religious attitude accompanying naturalism, involving feelings of awe and wonder toward the natural realm, and impulses to value and care for it. Nor does it rule out a pantheism such as Benedict de Spinoza's. Spinoza identified God with Nature, insisting, as naturalists do, that there is nothing beyond this law-governed world. The atheistic varieties of Buddhism, in which this world is the only one, and where law governs the world's unfolding, would also be naturalistic religions if they were to accord independent reality to the material realm.

Naturalism requires that religious experience, and in particular mystical experience, be given a reductionist interpretation. Such experiences are regarded as unusual states of mind that have their own causes and consequences within the natural world, but do not provide any contact with, or insight into, a supernatural realm.

METAPHYSICAL IDEALISM. Naturalism takes its cue from the natural sciences, and with the exception of some more fanciful interpretations of the measurement paradoxes in quantum theory, the sciences are resolutely realist about the material world. Realism maintains that the world of nature is as it is, irrespective of any human opinions about it. The natural world is not dependent on, or brought into being by human mind, will, or experience. As this is the working philosophy of the natural sciences, it is difficult to combine naturalism with metaphysical idealism, which implies that matter is in some way a function or aspect of mind.

A thorough-going phenomenalism, such as an atheistic version of George Berkeley's philosophy, might be thought to count as an idealistic naturalism in which every object of experience does indeed belong to a law-governed spatio-temporal world, but where to be spatio-temporal is to have a derivative status, with perceptual experiences as the basic elements out of which it is constructed.

However, such a view places the experiencing mind outside the world of nature, and this puts it in conflict with one of the most profound aspects of naturalism, the view that the human species enjoys no specially privileged position in the scheme of things. Naturalism implies that human beings share with all other beings a common status, as contingent, temporary configurations in the law-governed natural world. The human world is a part of the natural realm, not a distinct cultural sphere to be contrasted with it.

Realist naturalism takes the Earth and its living inhabitants as genuine independent realities, and by locating the human race within the natural world, can make progress toward explaining how it came into being, and how humans came to have the epistemic and cognitive capacities that they do. Not even the more objective post-Hegelian metaphysical idealisms can provide any basis for an explanation of how humans came to be as they are.

THE PROBLEM OF UNIVERSALS. Realists about universals—properties and relations—divide into the Platonists, who allow the real existence of properties even where there is nothing in this world that instantiates them, and Aristotelians, who admit the reality of instantiated universals only. Plato's heaven, a higher realm containing perfect patterns for the properties imperfectly realized here below, is clearly incompatible with naturalism, and it seems probable that unless they can be vindicated as being required for explanations of what happens in this world, no system that admits uninstantiated universals can be naturalistic. Nominalist accounts of properties do not face any problem so far as naturalism is concerned.

DETERMINISM. Although naturalism stresses that it is by natural processes, involving natural causes only, that anything at all occurs, it is not committed to an absolute determinism. If there are causes at work, they are natural ones, but there may not be a cause in every case. There has to be at least enough general order in the world for it to provide an environment suitable for life and consciousness, but that admits of exceptions, here and there, to every rule. Quantum theory is not fully deterministic, as its causal relations are probabilistic. Naturalism requires there to be at least as much causality and law in the world as the development of natural sciences calls for, but it does not require any more than that.

MATHEMATICS AND LOGIC. Naturalism is almost bound to take a reductionist view of the so-called abstract objects of mathematics and logic—their numbers, functions, and relations. For the number twenty-seven, or the square root of negative one, or the relation of contrariety seem to fail both the spatio-temporal location test, and the Eleatic causal power test for natural reality. W.V.O. Quine, who was very much of a naturalistic bent, found himself forced to accept the reality of sets as a foundation for mathematics, something essential for physics, which provides the best description of the world. So sets, although not themselves naturalistic beings, have a place in the best ontology. This is a departure from pure naturalism. Hartry Field (1980), among others, has attempted to develop a philosophy of mathematics that dispenses with numbers or other mathematical objects.

The situation with the objects of geometry seems less problematic. If space-time is taken realistically (not, as with G.W. Leibniz, as a mere system of relations among physical objects), then the objects of geometry (points, lines, shapes, and geometrical solids) can be given a naturalistic home as aspects or parts of space-time.

MODALITY

The natural world comprises not only objects and the properties they actually possess. It includes what might be, yet is not (natural possibility), and what not only is but must, in the course of nature, come to pass (natural necessity). To meet this situation, the properties that things now actually possess (categorical properties) must be distinguished from those that provide the basis on which things will change and develop (dispositional properties or powers). Aristotle and the medieval Aristotelians such as Thomas Aquinas introduced potentiality (in contrast with *act*) to specify what an object is capable of—its range of possibilities. The modern version of this is the specification of an object's powers. The power to become *F* is a different property from being *F*, but it is itself a real categorical property, perhaps some feature of the underlying fine structure of the object that possesses it.

The powers that there are in the world determine and explain what is naturally possible, should they be exercised. And where they are exercised, the powers are bound to act as they do and produce their effects. This situation is therefore one of natural necessity.

Beyond natural possibility and necessity, however, lie that which is logically possible, even though ruled out by the laws of nature (such as a ball thrown into the air and just remaining there), and that which is, not just naturally, but logically necessary or impossible. Some philosophers treat possibility and necessity by introducing possible worlds, worlds in some way additional to the one actual world. This at least seems to be a departure from naturalism because additional, merely possible worlds do not belong in the same causal network with this world, and thus fail the Eleatic test on which naturalism insists.

Naturalism therefore seems to be committed to providing an account of the logical modalities that does not involve any special ontological commitments. The proposal that logical necessity is a reflection of language, of meaning and use, was an attempt to provide such an account. The linguistic theory has fallen out of favor; more recent accounts attempt to construct possible worlds from appropriately selected sets—sets of descriptions, or unactualized recombinations of elements from the actual world. These are accounts in terms of ersatz possible worlds. Provided a naturalistic account of sets can be given, such proposals would be naturalistic theories of necessity.

OBJECTIVE MORALITY

Morality is another problematic area for naturalism. The standard naturalistic characteristics are the contingent factual actualities, and these do not include in any straightforward way the values that objects or situations may have. The size and shape of an object enters into the natural causal nexus, but its goodness does not seem to. A naturalistic account of morality must find a place for good and evil, but not in the inherent structure of the world, as a fully objective moral realism does. Nor can naturalism ground moral law in the commands of a deity.

It must explain right and wrong, good and evil, as arising in the nature, preferences, or reactions of people, and in the structure of the societies within which people live out their lives. Whether an account of morality along these lines can satisfactorily explain the authority and impersonal binding force that moral imperatives seem to possess, is perhaps the most difficult issue for naturalist theories of morality.

See also Aristotelianism; Berkeley, George; Determinism, A Historical Survey; Ethical Naturalism; Evil; Field, Hartry; Leibniz, Gottfried Wilhelm; Many Worlds/Many Minds Interpretation of Quantum Mechanics; Ontology, History of; Platonism and the Platonic Tradition; Quine, Willard Van Orman; Realism and Naturalism, Mathematical; Russell, Bertrand Arthur William; Spinoza, Benedict (Baruch) de; Thomas Aquinas, St.; Universals, A Historical Survey.

Bibliography

Armstrong, D. "Naturalism, Materialism, and First Philosophy." *Philosophia* 8 (1978): 261–276.

Craig, William Lane, and J. P. Moreland. *Naturalism, A Critical Analysis.* London: Routledge, 2000.

De Caro, M., and D. Macarthur, eds. *Naturalism in Question.* Cambridge, MA: Harvard University Press, 2004.

Field, Hartry. *Science Without Numbers.* Oxford: Blackwell, 1980.

French, Peter A, Theodore E. Uehling, and Howard K. Wettstein, eds. *Philosophical Naturalism.* Notre Dame, IN: University of Notre Dame Press, 1995.

Maxwell, Nicholas. *The Human World in The Physical Universe; Consciousness, Free Will, and Evolution.* Lanham, MD: Rowman & Littlefield, 2001.

Nielsen, Kai. *Naturalism and Religion.* Amherst, NY: Prometheus Books, 2001.

Papineau, D. *Philosophical Naturalism.* Oxford: Blackwell, 1993.

Quine, W. V. O. "Naturalism; Or, Living within One's Means." *Dialectica* 49 (1995): 251–261.

Quine, W. V. O. *Word and Object.* Cambridge, MA: MIT Press, 1960.

Rea, Michael. *World without Design: The Ontological Consequences of Naturalism.* Oxford: Oxford University Press, 2002.

Shook, John R., ed. *Pragmatic Naturalism and Realism.* Amherst, NY: Prometheus Books, 2003.

Villanueva, E., ed. *Naturalism and Normativity.* Atascadero, CA: Ridgeview, 1993.

Keith Campbell (2005)

NATURALISM IN ETHICS

See *Ethical Naturalism*

NATURALISTIC RECONSTRUCTIONS OF RELIGION

See *Religion, Naturalistic Reconstructions of*

NATURALIZED EPISTEMOLOGY

Naturalized epistemology is the proposal that the theory of knowledge bears a close relation to empirical studies of cognition. The proposal was first made by W. V. O. Quine in his influential article, "Epistemology Naturalized" (1969). Quine is usually interpreted as subscribing to *replacement naturalism*: epistemology is to be replaced with empirical psychology. But his proposal may well fall short of full replacement.

In his article, Quine distinguishes conceptual studies, which seek to clarify concepts by defining some of them in terms of others, from doctrinal studies, which attempt to establish laws by proving them. The conceptual studies, were they successful, would facilitate the doctrinal ones because clarifying concepts increases the chance that truths that would otherwise go unrecognized will come to be obvious or come to be perceived as "derivable from obvious truths" (p. 70). Quine allows that progress was made in conceptual studies when Jeremy Bentham suggested paraphrasing sentences about bodies in terms of sentences about sensory experience.

Unfortunately, the project of reducing talk of bodies to talk of sensory experience together with set theory, pursued by Rudolf Carnap in *The Logical Structure of the World* (1928/1967), did not come to fruition. Carnap's later attempts at a rational reconstruction of science abandoned the aim of providing equivalences that would enable us to eliminate the terms of science in favor of sensory terms, and so they did not legitimate science. Carnap's reduction failed, according to Quine, because scientific theories do not have observational consequences except in the presence of collateral scientific theories. In view of the failure of the reduction, Quine proposes that conceptual studies seeking to clarify terms be replaced by an empirical psychology that describes how science is related to experience: "If all we hope for is a reconstruction that links science to experience in explicit ways short of translation, then it would seem more sensible to settle for psychology" (p. 78). This is the first part of Quine's proposal that empirical psychology is

to enter into epistemology: Empirical studies of the cognitive development of science are to succeed the earlier reductive conceptual studies.

Regarding the doctrinal studies, Quine notes that it has been clear since Hume's treatment of induction (1739/1978) that we cannot derive scientific theories from sensory observations. Moreover, Quine claims that scientific theories have consequences for sensory experience only in the presence of collateral science (the Duhem-Quine Thesis). So scientific theories are not supported by observation alone. Since support for any scientific theory depends in this sense on further science, there is no reason to persist in the Cartesian stricture that any reliance on empirical science to understand how science is related to observation is circular. And so, for Quine, there is no point in excluding empirical psychology from such an understanding. This is the second part of Quine's proposal that empirical psychology is to enter into epistemology.

But Quine's reasoning here can be challenged on two grounds. He infers from the permissibility of relying on collateral scientific theories to support a given scientific theory that it is permissible to rely on a specific scientific theory, psychology, to understand how the given scientific theory is related to observation. But psychology is generally not the collateral scientific theory on which, according to the Duhem-Quine Thesis, we are allowed to rely for support of a given scientific theory; and the argument from the permissibility of relying on a collateral theory to *support* a given scientific theory to the permissibility of relying on psychology to *understand* how the theory is related to observation is not clearly valid. The latter challenge raises the worry that, in moving from the issue of the support of the theory by observation to the issue of understanding how the theory is related to observation, Quine makes room for psychology, but only by changing the subject from the support of the theory to understanding the relation between theory and observation. This challenge does not, however, undermine Quine's argument if he does not propose a full replacement thesis but rather the idea that empirical psychology is to figure in the project of supporting scientific theory.

The naturalized epistemology that results from Quine's proposals thus has two parts. The conceptual studies that attempted to clarify concepts by reduction are to be replaced by a psychology that understands how science is related to observations. The doctrinal studies are also to be altered. Regarding the latter, most commentators have assumed that Quine intends that we replace normative epistemology with a descriptive psychology of the cognitive development of theories. Quine's summary, however, leaves room for a normative as well as a descriptive enterprise:

> Epistemology, or something like it, simply falls into place as a chapter of psychology and hence of natural science. It studies a natural phenomenon, viz., a physical human subject. This human subject is accorded a certain experimentally controlled input—certain patterns of irradiation in assorted frequencies, for instance—and in the fullness of time the subject delivers as output a description of the three-dimensional external world and its history. The relation between the meager input and the torrential output is a relation that we are prompted to study for somewhat the same reasons that always prompted epistemology; namely, in order to see how evidence relates to theory, and in what ways one's theory of nature transcends any available evidence. (p. 83)

This passage could be taken to propose the replacement of epistemology with psychology: "evidence" could have the descriptive meaning of observation rather than a normative meaning, and seeing how theory transcends evidence might be a descriptive enterprise.

But there are other interpretations that make better sense of Quine's argument in "Epistemology Naturalized." He might mean that we are to use psychology to judge the amount of support the observations provide for given scientific theories, but only in light of an assumed epistemology (that is, an account of what support amounts to) distinct from psychology. On this interpretation, the epistemology tells us how far beyond the observations a scientific theory may go before the observations no longer support the theory; the psychology measures how far beyond our observations the theory actually goes; and the epistemology and psychology combine to tell us whether the theory enjoys support. Alternatively, Quine might mean that we are to use psychology to judge how any suggested epistemology fares in light of whether our actual achievement meets its demands. On this alternative interpretation, the results of psychology constrain epistemology. The psychology measures how far beyond our observations our scientific theories go; and a suggested epistemology is rejected if the measured distance between our scientific theories and our observations exceeds the distance the epistemology sets as the threshold for support.

This second interpretation makes the best sense of the text. Psychology contributes to an account not merely

of the causal but also of the support relation between observation and theory. Thus, there is continuity between the old task of supporting science by observations and the new task of accounting for the support relation between observation and theory. The interpretation responds to the charge that Quine's argument from the Duhem-Quine Thesis to the permissibility of relying on psychology changes the subject. And the interpretation is suggested by the fact that Quine assumes that the failure of the conceptual reduction of science to observations, or of the doctrinal derivation of science from observations, does not count decisively against a positive epistemic status for science. Without this assumption, Quine would have no reason to propose that epistemology should abandon reduction and derivation for psychology, rather than that we should terminate epistemology with the judgment that science lacks support because reductions and derivations fail despite being necessary for support. On the preferred interpretation, psychology enters after the failed conceptual reductions and doctrinal derivations, but the use of psychology is warranted only by the separate epistemological claim that the success of science is jeopardized by overshooting the observations, though the jeopardy is not so rigid that the failure of reduction and derivation entails skepticism.

Quine's "Epistemology Naturalized" led many philosophers to take seriously the relevance of psychology to epistemology. Although almost all interpreters read Quine as proposing to replace epistemology with psychology, few epistemologists follow Quine in embracing replacement. Many endorse instead a *conceptual naturalism*: our everyday epistemic concepts of knowledge, justified belief, or rational belief can be defined or clarified in naturalistic terms, where naturalistic terms are usually taken to be the terms of some respectable science, notably psychology. (On a more liberal view, naturalistic terms are simply those not patently normative.)

Most proponents of conceptual naturalism hold that our epistemic concepts are both normative and naturalistic. The motivations for conceptual naturalism are not often articulated, but they presumably include these: the concepts employed by our respectable sciences are our best-understood concepts and thus the best candidates for definitions in terms we can understand and also the best candidates for clarifying definitions; these are concepts with which we cannot now dispense in our intellectual lives, so for now these concepts are clearly available to provide definitions; and these are the concepts we have the best reason to believe succeed in referring to properties that are actually exemplified, so that knowledge defined in terms of them does not turn out inadvertently to fail to obtain.

Perhaps the most popular version of conceptual naturalism has been *reliabilism*, according to which knowledge is true belief that results from a reliable belief-forming process—a process that tends to yield true beliefs (and similarly, justified belief is belief that results from a reliable process). Whether reliabilism is fully naturalistic depends on whether the notion of truth is naturalistic. Reliabilism has been most extensively developed by Alvin Goldman. In *Epistemology and Cognition* (1986), Goldman divides his epistemology into two parts. The first part is an analysis of epistemic concepts. Both knowledge and justified belief are defined in terms of reliability. Justified beliefs are (roughly) beliefs permitted by some right J-rule system. J-rules license certain cognitive processes, and "A J-rule system R is right if and only if R permits certain (basic) psychological processes, and the instantiation of these processes would result in a truth ratio of beliefs that meets some specified high threshold (greater than .50)" (p. 106).

This analysis is supported by intuitions in narrow reflective equilibrium. The second part of Goldman's enterprise is an attempt to discover which sorts of beliefs are justified given his analysis of justified belief. This would ideally lead to discovering a right system of J-rules, but Goldman regards such an effort as premature, since "Cognitive science is still groping its way toward the identification of basic processes" (p. 181). Instead, Goldman considers candidates for basic processes individually and attempts to discern their reliability or contribution to a high truth ratio. He examines perception, memory, deduction, probability judgments, judgments under uncertainty, and belief revision in light of the findings of cognitive science. It is fair to say that his review of the reliability of cognitive processes is the most detailed and comprehensive yet undertaken. This second part of Goldman's enterprise exemplifies *methodological naturalism*: that a significant part of epistemology is an inquiry into whether conditions of epistemic status are satisfied in light of empirical cognitive science. Quine, on the interpretation of his views suggested above, is a methodological naturalist in this sense.

Reliabilism is not the only proposed version of conceptual naturalism. Alvin Plantinga (1993) offers a *proper function theory* of knowledge that is conditionally naturalistic. According to the theory, knowledge is belief that results from the proper functioning of our cognitive faculties. This theory is naturalistic if proper functioning is naturalistic, although Plantinga denies that it is. More

than one writer has noted, however, that most analyses of knowledge and justified belief that eschew the label "naturalism" nevertheless meet the requirements of conceptual naturalism just as well as reliabilism does (Foley 1994, Goldman 1994). For example, some coherence theories define justified belief in nonnormative and even naturalistic terms, such as consistency, mutual entailment, and the like. Despite this, versions of reliabilism differ from coherence theories in usually resulting from an inquiry motivated by the desire to define knowledge and justified belief in natural terms. Coherence theories do not usually result from a naturalistically motivated inquiry.

A view consistent with conceptual naturalism is *property naturalism*: the property of knowledge or justified belief is *identical* with certain natural properties—properties to which respectable science refers. Ruth Millikan (1984) offers a proper function account of knowledge along these lines, for which the relevant science is evolutionary biology. A view entailed by both conceptual and property naturalism is *supervenience naturalism*: epistemic properties *supervene* on natural properties. However, it has been noted (Foley 1994) that few epistemologists have wished to deny supervenience naturalism: Roderick Chisholm (1989) allows that justified belief supervenes on nonnormative properties, despite defining it in normative terms. Keith Lehrer (1997) is rare among epistemologists in denying that justified belief supervenes on nonnormative properties.

Within the category of conceptual and property naturalism, certain views are versions of what Goldman (1994) calls *substantive naturalism*, according to which the defining terms refer to natural processes or to relations between the subject's belief and the environment. Reliabilism would fit this label. But so would John Pollock's (1989) internalist version of naturalism based on classical artificial intelligence, and Paul Thagard's (1992) coherence theory, which understands the acceptability of a scientific theory as involving a connectionist mechanism. In an influential article, Philip Kitcher (1992) emphasizes a version of *psychologism* as central to naturalism: knowledge turns on the character of psychological belief-forming processes, as opposed to logical or statistical relations between evidence and belief.

Accounts of knowledge as involving or constituted by psychological processes like intuition and demonstration, and of justified belief as involving causal inference, were common in early modern philosophy. Louis Loeb (2002) argues that, in *A Treatise of Human Nature* (1739/1978), David Hume held a stability theory of justification: justified belief is the result of a belief-forming operation that tends to produce stable beliefs. C. S. Peirce is also commonly regarded as holding a stability theory in "The Fixation of Belief" (Schmitt 2002). But this psychologism was rejected in the late nineteenth and early twentieth centuries in tandem with the rejection of psychologism in semantical theory by Gottlob Frege. Recent naturalism, such as reliabilism and proper function theory, has brought psychological processes back to the fore in accounts of knowledge and justified belief. The chief ground for giving psychological processes a role in justification has been an attack on the "arguments on paper" thesis, which sees justification as turning merely on an evidential relation between the proposition believed and the evidence possessed by the subject (Goldman 1986, Kaplan 1994).

Related to the role of psychological processes is naturalist opposition to idealized epistemology, which derives norms or standards of justification from logic, probability theory, utility theory, or statistics, without attention to human limitations. For example, epistemologists have endorsed norms of rational belief-revision such as the following: we are to avoid contradictory beliefs, and we are to believe the proposition favored by the total evidence available to us. Hilary Kornblith (2002) cites reasons for doubting that we are generally able to guarantee that our beliefs are consistent. Goldman (1986) criticizes the claim that there must be a failure of rationality if one's belief fails to conform to the total available evidence; the fault may lie in one's access to memory rather than in one's reasoning, which is the focus of the evaluation of rationality.

Of course, the norm of avoiding contradiction or of conforming to the total available evidence could be understood as the qualified requirement that we are to avoid contradiction or conform to the total available evidence when we are able to do so. But if it turns out that we are rarely if ever able to satisfy to these norms, there is little plausibility to the view that rational belief-revision requires satisfying, or even being guided by, such norms. Again, the norm of avoiding contradiction could be understood as the requirement that we are to approximate as nearly as feasible (or as cost-effective) to avoiding contradiction. But if it turns out that we are far short of being able to approximate the goal, then it seems there is no such norm. The question concerns the content of epistemic norms and an associated issue of the methodology of identifying norms: Can we formulate norms in ignorance of contingent facts about our cognitive powers, protecting the norm from empirical disconfirmation by

making it merely a requirement to approximate a goal, or must we craft norms under assumptions about human limitations that would best be empirically informed (Schmitt 2004)? The naturalistic methodology finds support in the theoretical point that the approximate idealizing view has no means of suppressing epistemic ideals that are intuitively plausible but so demanding that no norm should require approximating them to any degree.

A final issue within naturalism is methodological. Should we conduct epistemology by defining knowledge so as to explain the functions (biological, social, or cognitive) served by our *concept* of knowledge and *practices* of epistemic evaluation? Or should we instead identify knowledge with the real properties involved in states we label "knowledge," studying knowledge on the model of a natural kind like aluminum or frog, opening the possibility that knowledge diverges from the properties represented in our concept, and that it serves primary functions quite different from any suggested by the functions of our use of the concept?

An account of the first sort is offered by Edward Craig (1990), who defines knowledge so as to explain the functions served by our applications of the concept. He proposes that our concept has its content in virtue of serving the social-cognitive function of picking out good informants. Craig rests his conditions of knowledge on everyday observations of the function of our concept, but it would be possible to rely on scientific sociology in such a study. An account of the second sort is offered by Hilary Kornblith (2002). He argues, by appeal to studies of animal cognition, that animals possess knowledge, and he defends the view that human knowledge is no different in kind from animal knowledge. In effect he proposes that we infer the conditions of knowledge from the biological functions of the states we label "knowledge." As it happens, Craig's conditions of knowledge roughly coincide with Kornblith's: both are versions of reliabilism about knowledge. But Craig's methodology is incompatible with Kornblith's. For conditions of knowledge inferred from the social-cognitive functions of applying the concept of knowledge need not be coextensive with conditions inferred from the biological functions of knowledge itself. Nothing guarantees that the properties that humans ascribe in order to pick out good informants must be the properties that enable animals to survive in their habitats.

It is a further question whether, given Kornblith's approach and findings, knowledge turns out to be a natural kind—for example, in the sense of a homeostatic property cluster or a cluster of self-maintaining properties. If instances of knowledge are to be instances of a natural kind and knowledge is to be reliable belief, then every instance of knowledge must be a state of a cognitive system in which a variety of reliable processes (perhaps perceptual, memorial, and inferential processes) routinely support one another in producing knowledge. This would seem to be the weakest sense in which the properties essential to an instance of knowledge could be said to be self-maintaining. If so, the claim that knowledge is a natural kind entails two key assertions: that knowledge requires not merely a reliable process yielding the given belief but also that instances of knowledge are embedded in a nexus of reliable processes. We may wonder, however, whether there is any informative condition of embedding in such a nexus that holds for all instances of knowledge across species; if not, there is no general natural kind of knowledge.

See also Carnap, Rudolf; Chisholm, Roderick; Cognitive Science; Epistemology; Frege, Gottlob; Goldman, Alvin; Hume, David; Lehrer, Keith; Memory; Millikan, Ruth; Peirce, Charles Sanders; Perception; Plantinga, Alvin; Psychologism; Quine, Willard Van Orman; Reliabilism; Underdetermination Thesis, Duhem-Quine Thesis.

Bibliography

Carnap, Rudolf. *The Logical Structure of the World.* Translated by R. George. Berkeley and Los Angeles: University of California Press, 1967. First published in 1928.

Chisholm, Roderick. *Theory of Knowledge.* 3rd ed. Englewood Cliffs, N. J.: Prentice Hall, 1989.

Craig, Edward. *Knowledge and the State of Nature.* Oxford: Oxford University Press, 1990.

Dretske, Fred. *Knowledge and the Flow of Information.* Cambridge, MA: MIT Press, 1981.

Feldman, Richard. "Methodological Naturalism in Epistemology." In *The Blackwell Guide to Epistemology*, edited by John Greco and Ernest Sosa. Oxford: Basil Blackwell, 1999.

Foley, Richard. "Quine and Naturalized Epistemology." In *Midwest Studies in Philosophy.* Vol. 19, *Philosophical Naturalism*, edited by Peter A. French, Theodore E. Uehling, Jr., and Howard K. Wettstein. South Bend, IN: University of Notre Dame Press, 1994.

Goldman, Alvin I. *Epistemology and Cognition.* Harvard University Press, 1986.

Goldman, Alvin I. "Naturalistic Epistemology and Reliabilism." In *Midwest Studies in Philosophy.* Vol. 19, *Philosophical Naturalism*, edited by Peter A. French, Theodore E. Uehling, Jr., and Howard K. Wettstein. South Bend, IN: University of Notre Dame Press, 1994.

Hume, David. *A Treatise of Human Nature.* 2nd ed, edited by P. H. Nidditch. Oxford: Oxford University Press, 1978. First published in 1739.

Kaplan, Mark. "Epistemology Denatured." In *Midwest Studies in Philosophy.* Vol. 19, *Philosophical Naturalism*, edited by Peter A. French, Theodore E. Uehling, Jr., and Howard K. Wettstein. South Bend, IN: University of Notre Dame Press, 1994.

Kitcher, Philip. "The Naturalists Return." *Philosophical Review* 101 (1992): 53–114.

Kornblith, Hilary. *Inductive Inference and Its Natural Ground.* Cambridge, Mass.: MIT Press, 1993.

Kornblith, Hilary. *Knowledge and Its Place in Nature.* Oxford: Oxford University Press, 2002.

Lehrer, Keith. *Self-Trust: A Study of Reason, Knowledge, and Autonomy.* Oxford: Oxford University Press, 1997.

Loeb, Louis. *Stability and Justification in Hume's Treatise.* Oxford: Oxford University Press, 2002.

Millikan, Ruth Garrett. "Naturalist Reflections on Knowledge." *Pacific Philosophical Quarterly* 65 (1984): 315–334.

Peirce, C. S. "The Fixation of Belief." In *The Essential Peirce: Selected Philosophical Writings.* Vol. 1 (1867–1893), edited by Nathan Houser and Christian Kloesel. Bloomington, IN: Indiana University Press, 1992.

Plantinga, Alvin. *Warrant and Proper Function.* Oxford: Oxford University Press, 1993.

Pollock, John. *How to Build a Person: A Prolegomenon.* Cambridge, MA: MIT Press, 1989.

Quine, W. V. "Epistemology Naturalized." In *Ontological Relativity and Other Essays.* New York: Columbia University Press, 1969.

Quine, W. V. "The Nature of Natural Knowledge." In *Mind and Language*, edited by Samuel L. Guttenplan. Oxford: Oxford University Press, 1975.

Schmitt, Frederick F. "Justification and Consensus: The Peircean Approach," *Protosociology: An International Journal of Interdisciplinary Research* 16 (2002): 241–286.

Schmitt, Frederick F. "Epistemology and Cognitive Science." In *Handbook of Epistemology*, edited by Ilkka Niiniluoto, Matti Sintonen, and Jan Woleński. Dordrecht: Kluwer, 2004.

Shatz, David. "Skepticism and Naturalized Epistemology." In *Naturalism: A Critical Appraisal.* South Bend, IN: University of Notre Dame Press, 1993.

Thagard, Paul. *Conceptual Revolutions.* Princeton: Princeton University Press, 1992.

Frederick F. Schmitt (2005)

NATURALIZED PHILOSOPHY OF SCIENCE

Naturalization in the philosophy of science is related to projects for naturalization in other areas of philosophy, including ethics, the philosophy of language and mind, and, especially, epistemology. So there are some general features of naturalism shared by these different philosophical projects. Still, in each of these areas the impulse to naturalization has had different motivations and a distinctive history. Projects for naturalizing the philosophy of science were advanced independently within the Vienna Circle by Otto Neurath and in the United States by John Dewey from roughly 1925 to 1945. A decade later a philosopher of science, Ernest Nagel, familiar with both Neurath and Dewey, defended a general philosophical naturalism in his presidential address to the American Philosophical Association. And in 1969 Willard Van Orman Quine published his influential article "Epistemology Naturalized." Nevertheless, interest in naturalization in the philosophy of science dates only from the 1980s. Three influences stand out. First, a growing dissatisfaction with logical empiricism and, more generally, with any philosophy of science conceived of as the logical or conceptual analysis of scientific and methodological concepts. Second, this dissatisfaction was in part sparked by a growing interest in the history of science, particularly as employed in Thomas S. Kuhn's 1962 book *The Structure of Scientific Revolutions*. Finally, beginning in the 1970s there was a challenge from a newly militant sociology of science claiming to provide the whole story of how science works.

In thinking about science, it is usual to distinguish between the process of doing science, scientific practice, and the product of that process, usually understood as scientific knowledge. The project of naturalization applies to both processes and products. The naturalist project for examining knowledge in various special fields rejects claims to special forms of logical and philosophical analysis, preferring to employ fundamentally the same tools used by the relevant scientists themselves. But philosophers may ask different questions than those that typically concern working scientists. For example, a philosopher of science may ask how the concept of causality in quantum mechanics differs from that in classical mechanics, or how the theories and methods of classical genetics differ from those of molecular genetics. The answers will be framed in terms that can be understood by both scientists and educated laypersons. No peculiarly philosophical concepts are required. This entry will focus on the naturalizing project for understanding the process of science, including methods for certifying particular knowledge claims.

BASIC FEATURES OF NATURALIZED PHILOSOPHY OF SCIENCE

In advancing a naturalized philosophy of science, one immediately rules out any philosophy of science invoking supernatural factors, which, however, occurs only in limited contexts. More generally, a naturalized philosophy of science rules out appeal to a priori principles, including the results of logical or conceptual analysis. Positively, a naturalized philosophy of science restricts its resources to those provided by the sciences themselves. So a naturalized philosophy of science becomes a kind of theoretical science of science. Even this minimal general characterization of naturalized philosophy of science raises several problems.

First, how could one justify ruling out the imposition of a priori principles, or even appeals to the supernatural, in the philosophy of science? This would seem itself to require an a priori argument, thus violating naturalism's own prohibition against the use of a priori principles. Second, given that the content of the sciences is continually changing, how can one specify just what counts as a resource for a naturalized philosophy of science? More simply, what counts as natural in either the philosophy of science or in the sciences themselves?

Both of these problems presume that naturalism is a thesis, indeed, a metaphysical thesis. Both problems vanish if, rather, naturalism is taken primarily as a methodological stance, a determination to employ only well-established scientific findings and methods, whatever they might be. Methodological naturalism, unlike metaphysical naturalism, can be defended simply in terms of past successes, first in physics and chemistry, but also especially in biology. Evolutionary theory and modern molecular genetics have pretty much demystified the phenomena of life. This provides a scientific reason for expecting that mental phenomena and even consciousness will some day be similarly demystified. Of course, this appeal to past scientific success to justify methodological naturalism strikes most nonnaturalistic philosophers of science as circular or regressive.

NATURALISM AND NORMATIVITY

The most common objection to the whole project of naturalized philosophy of science is that, based only on scientific findings, it can at most describe actual scientific practice; it cannot provide a normative basis for distinguishing good science from pseudoscience. Naturalism, it is often argued, leads straight to relativism. Naturalists point out that this objection assumes that there exists an extrascientific criterion for demarcating good science from pseudoscience. They argue, naturalistically, that the failure to find an agreed on criterion is good evidence that no such criterion exists. Still, it is a fact that scientists and others claim to distinguish good science from pretenders to that status. Naturalists need an account of the bases for such judgments.

The usual naturalist account is that the norms operative in science are all conditional norms of the general form: If the goal is G, use method M. The justification for such norms is itself empirical, consisting of evidence that employing M is a relatively reliable means of obtaining G. This reply itself raises several problems. One is the specification of the goal, or goals, of scientific inquiry. A second problem is the threatened regress of methods, since taking the determination of whether M is a reliable means to G as itself a goal of inquiry seems to require another method of inquiry whose reliability itself must be investigated.

REALISM VERSUS EMPIRICISM

Both naturalists and nonnaturalists argue that there is a single overarching goal to scientific inquiry throughout the history of modern science. Some make similar claims for scientific method. Proposed general goals include knowledge and truth, while proposed methods include "making use of evidence." These goals and methods are, however, so general as to be nearly vacuous. Surely one must ask: Knowledge (or truths) about what? What kind of evidence? How is evidence to be used?

Historians of science and historically oriented philosophers of science have identified at least two divergent general goals that have been pursued, often explicitly, by scientists since the seventeenth century. One is broadly empiricist while the other is broadly realist. Isaac Newton's professed refusal to "feign hypotheses" and injunctions only to make inductions from the phenomena are identified with empiricism. The nineteenth-century invocation of an aether to support electromagnetic radiation was an example of scientific realism. The later nineteenth-century debate between supporters of thermodynamics and supporters of statistical mechanics is seen as a dispute between empiricists and realists regarding the existence of atoms. In the twentieth century the weirdness of quantum physics (relative to classical physics) invited empiricist responses while molecular biology seemed uninhibitedly realist. Although most naturalists tended to argue for either an exclusively empiricist or realist understanding of science, the proper naturalist response seemed to reject the demand for a single goal for all of science as objectionably essentialist and to accept the historical diversity of goals as a natural part of science as a whole. Both empiricists and realists can be said to be seeking knowledge of the natural world rather than, say, spiritual enlightenment.

Returning to the threatened regress of methods, one question is whether or not avoiding an unacceptable relativism requires a method that can be justified a priori. Naturalists again argue that the failure of philosophers of science to agree on any such method is good evidence that no such method exists. More positively, it can be argued that the general pattern of inductive reasoning is fundamentally the same for higher-level claims about the effectiveness of various methods to deliver correct judgments at the object level as it is for object-level empirical claims themselves. There need be no regress of fundamentally different methods.

Nevertheless, naturalists tend to agree that, whatever the details of various methods for certifying scientific claims, there are no methods that can be employed without assuming that some empirical conditions obtain. There are no foundational methods any more than there are foundational empirical truths that can be known with certainty. To the extent that naturalists think this stance requires philosophical justification, that justification is usually sought in an appeal to some form of pragmatism.

NATURALISM AND PRAGMATISM

It is no accident that prominent naturalists of earlier generations embraced pragmatism. Naturalism needs a philosophical orientation that makes sense of its rejection of a priori metaphysical and epistemological principles. Pragmatism provides that orientation. The relevant pragmatist doctrine begins with the rejection of any view of knowledge that requires either deduction from a priori truths or induction from incorrigible sense experience. The positive doctrine is that one always begins from the current state of what is taken to be known. From that point, anything can be questioned and subjected to experimental tests, provided that there is some basis for doubt. But not everything can be questioned at once. Universal Cartesian doubt is ruled out. Thus, in place of a foundationist picture of knowledge of either rationalist or empiricist persuasion, one has claims to knowledge regulated by a method of motivated doubt and empirical investigation. It is this general method, not any particular claims, that matters for science.

A pragmatist orientation also fits well with a typical naturalist appeal to the evolutionary history of humans as providing an understanding of the origins of human knowledge. Evolutionary survival requires early humans to have had a serviceable understanding of the world around them, including other humans. Survival did not require having beliefs that one would now regard as true. Rather, it only required beliefs that made it possible to perform appropriate actions at appropriate times. Later, humans could develop methods for questioning and improving earlier beliefs apart from their immediate application to particular courses of action.

Some naturalist philosophers of science argue that the development of modern science itself follows an evolutionary pattern and maybe even involves evolutionary-like mechanisms. Others disagree. This dispute takes place within a naturalistic framework and the answer does follow from that framework alone. It remains an empirical question within a naturalistic approach to the philosophy of science.

RESOURCES FOR A NATURALISTIC PHILOSOPHY OF SCIENCE

The purest statement of the logical empiricist approach to the philosophy of science was that the philosophy of science is the study of the logic of the language of science. This stance automatically put the focus of the philosophical study of science on the products of scientific activity rather than on the process of doing science. The naturalist project for the philosophy of science places greater emphasis on the practice of science. A programmatic formulation would be that a naturalized philosophy of science focuses on scientists as embodied agents practicing in a particular scientific culture. The question is what broadly scientific resources are to be employed in this study. Here, there is a diversity of opinion among those pursuing a naturalist program.

Following Kuhn and others, many philosophers of science study the activity of science using primarily historical concepts and methods. Sociologists of science, including historical sociologists partly inspired by Kuhn, invoke primarily historical and sociological categories, but differ among themselves as to which historical and sociological categories to employ. They mostly agree, however, on the desirability of there being a single unified sociological account. Some philosophers of science and cognitive scientists pursue the study of scientific practice as primarily a cognitive activity, borrowing concepts and methods from the cognitive sciences. A few philosophers and economists employ concepts from economics in their studies of science practice. Finally, feminist philosophers of science, for whom the idea of scientists as embodied and socially embedded is central, introduce concepts from feminist theory into the naturalized study of science.

Here again, the proper naturalistic response to this plurality of approaches would seem not to insist on a single unified approach, but to embrace a diversity of complementary approaches as appropriate for understanding a complex phenomenon such as science.

See also Confirmation Theory; Ethics, History of; Moore, George Edward; Naturalized Epistemology.

Bibliography

Boyd, Richard. "Scientific Realism and Naturalistic Epistemology." In *PSA 1980*. Vol. 2, edited by Peter D. Asquith and Ronald N. Giere. East Lansing, MI: Philosophy of Science Association, 1981.

Giere, Ronald N. "Philosophy of Science Naturalized." *Philosophy of Science* 52 (3) (1985): 331–356.

Godfrey-Smith, Peter. "Dewey on Naturalism, Realism, and Science." *Philosophy of Science* 69 (3) (2002): S25–S35.

Hankinson-Nelson, Lynn. "A Feminist Naturalized Philosophy of Science." *Synthese* 104 (3) (1995): 399–421.

Hooker, Clifford A. "Evolutionary Naturalist Realism: Circa 1985." In *A Realistic Theory of Science*, edited by Clifford A. Hooker. Albany: SUNY Press, 1987.

Hull, David L. *Science as a Process: An Evolutionary Account of the Social and Conceptual Development of Science*. Chicago: University of Chicago Press, 1988.

Kitcher, Philip. "The Naturalists Return." *Philosophical Review* 101 (1) (1992): 53–114.

Kuhn, Thomas S. *The Structure of Scientific Revolutions*. Chicago: University of Chicago Press, 1962.

Laudan, Larry. "Progress or Rationality? The Prospects for Normative Naturalism." *American Philosophical Quarterly* 24 (1) (1987): 19–33.

Nagel, Ernest. "Naturalism Reconsidered." In *Logic without Metaphysics and Other Essays in the Philosophy of Science*, edited by Ernest Nagel. Glencoe, IL: Free Press, 1957.

Nersessian, Nancy. "The Cognitive Basis of Model-Based Reasoning in Science." In *The Cognitive Basis of Science*, edited by Peter Carruthers, Stephen Stich, and Michael Siegal. New York: Cambridge University Press, 2002.

Quine, W. V. O. "Epistemology Naturalized." In *Ontological Relativity and Other Essays*, edited by W. V. O. Quine. New York: Columbia University Press, 1969.

Rosenberg, Alex. "A Field Guide to Recent Species of Naturalism." *British Journal for the Philosophy of Science* 47 (1) (1996): 1–30.

Solomon, Miriam. *Social Empiricism*. Cambridge, MA: MIT Press, 2001.

Thagard, Paul. *Conceptual Revolutions*. Princeton, NJ: Princeton University Press, 1992.

Uebel, Thomas E. "Neurath's Programme for Naturalistic Epistemology." *Studies in History and Philosophy of Science* 22 (4) (1991): 626–646.

Ronald N. Giere (2005)

NATURAL KINDS

Whether engaged in high-level scientific activity or in the ordinary business of living, we spend a great deal of our time sorting the objects we come across into kinds. Philosophers are concerned with the *kinds of kinds* into which we sort these objects, and with the principles that distinguish one kind of kinds from another. One kind of kinds that has loomed large in recent philosophical discussions is that of so-called *natural* kinds. And one conception of natural kinds has dominated discussion in the contemporary philosophies of science, language, and mind, and this conception will concern us here. But first, some background.

Historical discussions of natural kinds (Ayers 1981) usually start with Aristotle and his conception of the *individuals* that are members of a kind of *substance* in virtue of the fact that they share a certain property (an *essence*) with all and only the other members of that kind. This essence can be specified in a *real definition* in terms of two of the five *predicables*: genus, species, difference, properties, and accidents. To give the most famous example, the *species* human being is part of the *genus* animal, and is distinguished from other animals by the *difference* rational; thus the essence of human beings is that they are rational animals. This essence determines the *properties* human beings possess (language, for example), although some members of the kind will also possess further properties that are not so determined, and these are the *accidents* (high intelligence, say, or lustrous skin).

In reaction against this Aristotelian vision, John Locke offered the distinction between real and nominal essences. Locke distinguished between the real essence ("the being of anything whereby it is what it is") and the nominal essence ("the abstract idea which the general, or sortal … name stands for") (1975 [1689]). He argued that when we use general terms, we refer to kinds whose definition can be given entirely in terms of their nominal essence. He maintained, first, that the members of a kind share a real essence in virtue of sharing some property concerning their microstructure, and, second, that because we lack "microscopical eyes," we can never know if an entity has this property or not. He then claimed that the features constitutive of the nominal essence of an entity are nonproblematically open to our view, and that as a result only these features are capable of ensuring that our use of a term refers to the kind in question.

This view rests upon some questionable assumptions. First, it is not obvious that our reference to an entity must be secured by features that are unproblematically open to our view. Second, it is not obvious that we cannot know that an entity possesses some microstructural feature simply because that feature is not observable. The modern view of natural kinds rejects both of these assumptions.

This modern view was inspired by the writings of Saul Kripke (1980) and Hilary Putnam (1975). The numerous advances in natural-scientific knowledge since Locke's time have greatly increased our sense that we are able to know about the microstructures of things, and these advances helped lead Kripke and Putnam to reject the second of Locke's epistemological assumptions. Far more radical, however, was their rejection of his first assumption. They insisted that the reference of a natural-kind term is secured by the real essence of the kind, even if no one has any idea what this essence is. A connection with the mental lives of those who use the relevant natural-kind term remains, but is secured instead by the requirement that they use the term with the *intention* of referring to entities of the relevant kind. More specifically, when people learn the meaning of a natural-kind term, they are presented with a sample of the kind, and their competent use of the term is then (partly) a matter of their using it with the intention of referring to anything whose nature is the same as the relevant sample. This idea of a nature has clear Aristotelian resonances, and like Aristotle, Kripke and Putnam took the nature of an entity to be identical to its real essence.

Putnam analyzed the meaning of a natural-kind term into the following four components: a *syntactic marker* (the part of speech to which it belongs, obviously "noun"), a *semantic marker* (in the case of "water," this would be "liquid"), a *stereotype* (in effect, the nominal essence, the range of observable features commonly associated with the term; in this case, "colorless, tasteless liquid," for instance), and an *extension* (the things in the world determined by the real essence of the kind, whatever that may be). In the Kripke and Putnam picture, the stereotype provides guidelines for the use of the term, but it does not fix the reference of the term in a sentence containing it. Nonetheless, use of a term that is guided by the stereotype is still genuine use—partly in virtue of the intention to refer, and partly in virtue of what Putnam called "the division of linguistic labor" (the idea that a competent user of the term would defer to relevant experts on the matter of whether something actually is a member of the relevant kind).

This account of natural-kind terms has numerous advantages. It seems to provide an easy solution to the apparent problem of incommensurability, for example. Formulations of this problem start from an assumption characteristic of logical-empiricist accounts of scientific terms, namely, that the reference of a natural-kind term is fixed by the theoretically informed general beliefs of those who use that term. Consequently, when those beliefs change to a certain degree, so does the reference of the term. In the light of Thomas Kuhn's idea that science undergoes massive revolutions in the theoretical beliefs of scientists, it seems, once this assumption is granted, that past scientists who used the term "electrons" were not speaking about the same things that present-day scientists speak about when they use this term. By insisting that reference is fixed by the real nature of kinds and not the transitory beliefs of scientists, the theory of Kripke and Putnam allows scientific terms to refer to the same entities over time even though the relevant beliefs of scientists change massively.

In more recent years, some philosophers have started to become suspicious of attempts to extend this account to all natural-kind terms (Dupré 1993). It is questionable how far the theory is capable of handling the kinds that biologists appear to speak of, for instance. Terms of ordinary language such as "frog," "toad," "rabbit," "hare," "onion," "garlic"—terms that one might assume are both natural kind terms and of relevance to biologists—are deployed by the latter in ways that radically diverge from how they are deployed by ordinary speakers. When ordinary speakers use these terms, it seems that their intention is not to refer to the putative real essence of, say, "garlic," but rather to something that serves a certain *function* ("garlic" refers to that which serves a certain culinary purpose, for instance). One obvious response at this point is to say that these terms refer not to natural kinds but to functional kinds (Wiggins 2001), and that their reference is fixed by some description available to the users of the term. This possibility of diverging intentions suggests that one kind term might be a natural-kind term among a group of scientists (given how they use it) and a functional-kind term among a group of lay persons (given how they use it).

There are interesting questions as to whether this account of natural-kind terms contravenes or accords with a Fregean view of meaning (Evans 1973). There are also questions about the exact role that an appeal to natural-kind terms should play in arguments for an externalist account of mental content (that the content of a mental state is determined by suitably 'external' features). In addition, if the arguments for externalism that rely on the Kripke and Putnam account of natural-kind terms are sound and if a term such as "garlic" denotes a natural kind on the lips of a scientist but a functional kind on the lips of a layperson, and if the reference of functional kind terms is fixed by a description, then we seem to be saddled with the idea that scientists have a greater number of broad, externally determined mental states than laypersons.

See also Aristotle; Essence and Existence; Kripke, Saul; Kuhn, Thomas; Laws of Nature; Locke, John; Meaning; Natural Law; Proper Names and Descriptions; Properties; Putnam, Hilary.

Bibliography

Ayers, Michael R. "Locke versus Aristotle on Natural Kinds." *Journal of Philosophy* 78 (1981): 247–272.

Dupré, John. *The Disorder of Things: Metaphysical Foundations of the Disunity of Science*. Cambridge, MA: Harvard University Press, 1993.

Evans, Gareth. "The Causal Theory of Names." *Proceedings of the Aristotelian Society*, supp. vol. 47 (1973): 187–208.

Kripke, Saul. *Naming and Necessity*. Cambridge, MA: Harvard University Press, 1980.

Locke, John. *An Essay concerning Human Understanding*, edited by P. H. Nidditch. Oxford: Oxford University Press, 1975 (1689): bk. III, ch. 3, sec. 15, p. 417.

Putnam, Hilary. "The Meaning of 'Meaning.'" In his *Mind, Language, and Reality*. Vol. 2 of *Philosophical Papers*, 215–271. New York: Cambridge University Press, 1975.

Wiggins, David. *Sameness and Substance Renewed*. Cambridge, U.K.: Cambridge University Press, 2001.

Adrian Haddock (2005)
John Dupré (2005)

NATURAL LAW

Natural Law is a long-standing and widely influential theory in ethics and legal philosophy. Because of its long and varied history, and the diversity of definitions of the term "natural," it is somewhat difficult to summarize exactly what makes a position or methodology one of natural law—at least in such a way as to neatly include all the positions and methodologies that have gone by that name. In attempting to establish a broad set of characteristics such a theory would have to possess in order to be considered natural law, it is useful then to look at the historical development of paradigmatic theories, paying attention to David Hume's advice that when trying to understand a discourse that employs the concept of "nature," we must consider what the concept is contextually being opposed to, and "the opposition will always discover the sense, in which it is taken" (Hume 2000, p. 305, n.).

In general, we can say that the traditional notion of natural law has held to the following four propositions: (1) morality is ultimately real and objective and is not relative in its primary truths to culture, subjective taste, or social agreement; (2) morality is somehow grounded in human nature, which is a specific part of the general order of nature, and is crucial for human happiness and flourishing; (3) the normative force and obligatoriness of morality is somehow the result of this grounding and may be understood using the terminology associated with a legal code; (4) the application of reason in examining human nature, and to some extent general nature, provides evidence for the specific content of our moral obligations.

Some theories, especially contemporary ones, may not clearly fit the pattern of this list. However, this speaks to a criticism that some recent "natural law" theories are not really natural law theories at all. It is in reference to the sort of positions specified above that such criticisms are made. There is also a problem in producing such a list as to whether reference should be made to God as a divine legislator of natural law. While the original and most traditional theories of natural law do rely on a theological foundation, it is characteristic of modern and contemporary versions that they do not, and therefore theism has not been listed as a basic proposition.

ANCIENT SOURCES

It is generally held that the first complete formulation of a natural law theory was a product of Stoic philosophers. It is also generally held, however, that classical Greek philosophers made significant conceptual contributions to what became natural law. Plato suggests the first, moral realist, tenet of traditional natural law theory in proposing his division of the Forms and appearances. In taking such a strong realist position, Plato provides material for the claim that goodness, or at least good order, is fundamentally real and our knowledge of it can be directly produced through reason. In dialogues such as *Gorgias*, *Protagoras*, and *Phaedrus*, Socrates defends a notion of objective truth and knowledge over the relativistic claims of sophists, which fits the natural law emphasis on moral realism. In the *Republic*, he analogizes the virtuous person to a healthy body and state, which fits the second proposition that morality is self-rewarding, tends toward happiness, and is the proper state of being. In the *Laws*, Plato touches upon the fourth proposition by referring to a law of nature forbidding homosexual sex as unnatural, appealing to animal behavior as evidence (836c–e).

Aristotle has an even stronger claim on influencing natural law, though his contribution is contested. One writer considers natural law his "principal legacy to Christian thought" (Hastings 2000, p. 465), whereas another believes that he "figures as a natural law thinker only ambiguously and not very helpfully" (Haakonssen 1992, p. 890). Howard P. Kainz (2004) points out that the

passages in Aristotle commonly used to indicate support of natural law—"Universal law is the law of nature. For there really is, as every one to some extent divines, a natural justice and injustice that is binding on all men, even on those who have no association or covenant with each other" (pp. 6–8)—come from the *Rhetoric* (1373b5–1373b15), and are embedded in a section giving advice to lawyers on how to argue cases. Aristotle suggests using the rhetoric of natural law when "the written law tells against our case" but suggests that when "the written law supports our case" it is better to argue that "trying to be cleverer than the law is just what is forbidden by those codes of law that are accounted best" (Rhetoric, 1375a25–1375b25). But though Aristotle may not be as clearly a natural lawyer as some have thought, he does bequeath three important ideas that get taken up by natural law later on. First, in the *Physics*, Aristotle speaks at length concerning teleology—the notion that all natural objects have an end they are internally driven to fulfill (their telos) and that to understand a thing we must understand the end toward which it aims (194b15–199b30). Second, in the *Nicomachean Ethics*, Aristotle applies this principle to discover the end of human beings, arguing that humans, as natural, aim at some specific highest good for humans, which he defines as happiness—virtuous, rational, satisfactory activity (1097a15–1098a15). The teleology of natural objects and a complex virtuous happiness as the end of human beings will figure prominently in later natural law formulations, particularly those of Aquinas. Third, in the *Politics*, Aristotle argues that living in a political organization is entirely natural for humans. In fact, nature implants in us a social instinct and we can tell by the fact that humans are not individually self-sufficient that the purpose of the state is to produce well-being (1253a25–1253a35). States that work for this common well-being are genuine; states that do not are "perversions" (1279a25–1279b10).

It is commonly considered, however, that the first full-fledged description of natural law arises in Stoic philosophy. In general, Stoic philosophers were drawn to the idea that the universe is controlled by a perfectly rational and fateful principle called the logos, a concept prominent in Heraclitus's thought. The logos, as a rational principle that is creative, pervades all nature, and is reflected in human beings' ability to consciously reason and express logical relations in language, unites the metaphysical, the epistemological, and the ethical. As A. A. Long (1986) writes: "[I]t is clear that logos is something which can be heard, which serves to explain things, which is common to all" (p. 145). This unity is important for a view of reason as a law that connects nature, thought, and morality. In ethics, Zeno of Citium and other Stoics advise us to accept the logos-determined activity of the universe as right and unchangeable. It is our moral obligation to live in accordance with nature and our nature includes the instinct for self-preservation and the possession of reason (Diogenes Laertius 1925, pp. 193–197). The mostly widely cited statement of Stoic natural law, however, comes from Cicero, who wrote:

> True law is right reason in agreement with nature; it is of universal application, unchanging and everlasting; it summons to duty by its commands, and averts from wrongdoing by its prohibitions. … It is a sin to try to alter this law, nor is it allowable to attempt to repeal any part of it, and it is impossible to abolish it entirely. We cannot be freed from its obligations by senate or people, and we need not look outside ourselves for an expounder or interpreter of it. And there will not be different laws at Rome and at Athens, or different laws now and in the future, but one eternal and unchangeable law will be valid for all nations and all times, and there will be one master and ruler, that is, God, over us all, for he is the author of this law, its promulgator, and its enforcing judge. Whoever is disobedient is fleeing from himself and denying his human nature, and by reason of this very fact he will suffer the worst penalties. (1928, p. 211)

In this passage, many of the traditional characteristics of natural law theory are asserted—the appeal to reason, natural ends, and universality, the lawlike features of obligation, commandment and punishment, the connection to human nature, our internal ability to determine natural law obligations through intuition, conscience, or acknowledgement of impulses, and the reliance on God as legislator. These aspects of natural law were subject to refinements and modifications at the hands of later thinkers including Roman jurists, such as Gaius, who focused on understanding natural law as the rational underpinning of positive law; Ulpian, who applied the natural law to all animals; and Gratian, who focused on natural law being spelled out as biblical commands (Kainz 2004).

MEDIEVAL SOURCES

With St. Thomas Aquinas (1225–1274), natural law reached a summary moment and was systematized and incorporated into the dominant Christian theological tradition of the West. Aquinas is so influential on the natural law tradition that his position is often seen as paradigmatic—a response that both limits the tradition and over-theologizes it.

Aquinas begins his discussion of the nature of law in the *Summa Theologiae* by defining law in general as "a rule and measure of acts, whereby man is induced to act or is restrained from acting" (Summa, Part 2, Part 1, Question 90, Answer 1), which is immediately "nothing else but a dictate of practical reason emanating from the ruler who governs a perfect community" (2.1.91.1). Proper laws always aim toward the general good and, following Aristotle, the goal of human life and thus the common good, is happiness (2.1.90.2). Aquinas then distinguishes between four types of law. Eternal law is the very idea of how things should be and has been intended in God's mind. This idea of how things should be according to God has "the nature of a law" (2.1.91.1). The natural law is essentially the way in which human beings, as rational beings, are positioned within this divinely designed order of things, directed toward fulfilling their nature in that order. Aquinas says:

> Wherefore, since all things subject to Divine providence are ruled and measured by the eternal law … it is evident that all things partake somewhat of the eternal law, in so far as, namely, from its being imprinted on them, they derive their respective inclinations to their proper acts and ends. Now, among all others, the rational creature is subject to Divine providence in the most excellent way.… Wherefore it has a share of the Eternal Reason, whereby it has a natural inclination to its proper act and end: and this participation of the eternal law in the rational creature is called the natural law.… It is therefore evident that the natural law is nothing else than the rational creature's participation of the eternal law. (2.1.91.2)

Aquinas adds the categories of human law (specific determinations of practical regulations) and divine law (scriptural revelations of certain specifics). It is the relationship between natural law and eternal law that is most important here, however. As Aquinas sees it, the natural law is the way in which humans participate in the eternal law, by fulfilling our natural ends in the created order which is itself the expression of the eternal idea of God. The natural law is "imprinted" on us so that we have certain inclinations toward our ends but we also have reason, which allows us to perceive and choose to follow the imprinted inclinations in the proper way. In this sense, Aquinas frames natural law as objective, grounded in human nature, dependent ultimately on God as the creator of its content, understood through reason and through observation of our own innate tendencies and capacities.

When it comes to laying out the actual rules that the natural law prescribes, the first general principle is "good is to be done and pursued, and evil is to be avoided" which is coupled with the principle that "good has the nature of an end, and evil, the nature of a contrary, hence it is that all those things to which man has a natural inclination, are naturally apprehended by reason as being good, and … their contraries as evil" (2.1.94.2). Aquinas then develops from these two principles other precepts, including the duty of self-preservation, procreation and education of offspring, seeking knowledge of God, living in society, and avoiding offending others. It is here that Aquinas begins a popular tradition among natural law theorists of laying out a set of necessary and basic human goods.

Aquinas goes on elsewhere to develop more specific rules dictated by the natural law, for example, famously outlawing masturbation, noncoital sex, and homosexual intercourse as "contrary to the natural order of the venereal act as becoming to the human race" (2.2.154.11). It is also largely on the basis of natural law reasoning that the teaching of the Roman Catholic Church rules out contraception as ever morally permissible (Hastings 2000, Catechism of the Catholic Church 1994).

It is important to realize, however that there is no simplistic equation of the natural with the moral in Aquinas. In addressing the question of whether the natural law can be changed, he distinguishes between adding to and subtracting from the requirements of the natural law and also between primary and secondary principles of the natural law. Adding to what the natural law requires is not by itself any problem "since many things for the benefit of human life have been added over and above the natural law, both by Divine law and by human laws" (2.1.94.5). Subtracting from what the natural law requires, however, depends on what level of principle we are considering. The primary principles, such as the first precept of pursuing good and avoiding evil and the immediately derivative precepts of self-preservation, and so on, cannot be changed at all. The secondary principles, however, which are "certain detailed proximate conclusions drawn from the first principles" may be changed "in some particular cases of rare occurrence, through some special cause hindering the observance of such precepts" (2.1.94.5).

With this added layer of complexity, it is incumbent upon people to use their reason and to attend to circumstances in order to determine what is and is not permissible according to the secondary principles. For example, in the pursuit of procreation, it might seem eminently natural for men to have multiple wives, yet the tradition of the church is for monogamy. How to decide this question? Aquinas argues that marriage has a primary end of producing and raising children, but also a secondary end of a social function within a community:

> Accordingly plurality of wives neither wholly destroys nor in any way hinders the first end of marriage, since one man is sufficient to get children of several wives. … But though it does not destroy the second end, it hinders it considerably for there cannot be peace in a family where several wives are joined to one husband, since one husband cannot suffice to satisfy the requisitions of several wives.… (3.suppl.65.1)

Thus according to a Thomistic reading of natural law, noncoital sex to the point of climax may never be permitted but a plurality of wives might be permitted if the material resources of the husband and culture made it workable.

Finally, for understanding the immense influence of Thomistic natural law, it is important to note that human law relies on natural law for its justification and authority. While human law may add various requirements in specifics (tax codes, civil regulations, etc.) it may not subtract from primary principles. Therefore, human laws are subject to a comparative test for their justification and authority. If they conflict with the natural law, they are not just, and not true law. Aquinas says:

> Now in human affairs a thing is said to be just, from being right, according to the rule of reason. But the first rule of reason is the law of nature, as is clear from what has been stated above. … Consequently every human law has just so much of the nature of law, as it is derived from the law of nature. But if in any point it deflects from the law of nature, it is no longer a law but a perversion of law (2.1.95.2).

As with Cicero years before, this idea makes it possible to judge human laws as unjust and nonobligatory, and opens the way for the possibility of just revolutions against unjust states and human laws.

Aquinas's analysis of natural law set the stage for an ongoing debate over the nature of the relationship between morality, God's will, and God's intellect. For Aquinas, the eternal law, which was expressed in material creation, was found in God's intellect, God's perfect reason. As such, natural law was not simply an edict of God's will, as divine command theorists would argue, but rather was the automatic rational relationship between a created, purposeful order and the rational beings within that order. Presumably, if God had created a different type of purposeful world than he did, there would still automatically be a derived natural law that applied to that world as a function of reason, though its specific content would be different than the existing world. In this sense, God is bound by reason, and the natural law is the immediate rational product of created order. As Aquinas writes: "the natural law is something appointed by reason, just as a proposition is a work of reason" (Summa, Part 2, Part 1, Question 94, Answer 1).

One position, credited to Gregory of Rimini, took from this view that the natural law simply illuminated which actions and goals were intrinsically good and which were intrinsically evil. As such, the natural law "demonstrates" but is not literally a law in the sense of being legislated. As Francisco Suárez (1548–1617) encapsulates it in his influential *De legibus*, Gregory's position is "that the natural law is not a preceptive law … since it is not the indication of the will of some superior; but that, on the contrary, it is a law indicating what should be done, and what should be avoided, what of its own nature is intrinsically good and necessary, and what is intrinsically evil" (1944, p. 189). Another group of theologians called voluntarists, including to various degrees Bonaventure, Duns Scotus, and most prominently, William of Ockham, were defenders of the notion that the natural law was the product of God's will, not his intellect. As such, God could make the natural law, and thus morality, be anything he wished. Suárez writes: "This is the view one ascribes to William of Occam … inasmuch as he says that no act is wicked save in so far as it is forbidden by God and that there is no act incapable of becoming a good act if commanded by God" (p. 190).

Suárez himself, however, takes a middle course between the "intellectualist" and "voluntarist" positions, which he sees as being consistent with Aquinas. Suárez claims that the natural law not only demonstrates what is intrinsically good and evil but also "contains its own prohibition of evil and command of good" (p. 191). As indicating intrinsic good and evil, the natural law cannot be said to be simply willed by God. However, this does not mean that there is no divine command to follow the natural law on top of whatever rational obligation we might have to follow it. In fact, "it is revealed by the light of natural understanding, that God is offended by sins committed in contravention of the natural law, and that the

judgments and the punishment of those sins pertain to Him" (p. 207). What this means is that although right reason can show us the intrinsic moral status of actions, and somehow produces some binding moral force, it is natural law's necessary connection to (but not identity with) the divine law that provides commanding obligation. Suárez writes:

> The binding force of the natural law constitutes a true obligation; and that obligation is a good in its own way, existing in point of fact; therefore, this same obligation must proceed from the divine will, which decrees that men shall be bound to obey that which right reason dictates. … Therefore, although the additional obligation imposed by the natural law is derived from the divine will, in so far as it is properly a preceptive obligation, nevertheless … that will presupposes a judgment as to the evil of falsehood, for example, or similar judgments (pp. 196-197; 199).

Suárez thus describes a natural law that is both morally independent of God's Will but always joined by willed legislation to follow it.

The concerns over the actual obligations implied by natural law made their way into important political and cultural disputes, including the formal debate between the theologians Juan Ginés de Sepúlveda (1494–1573) and Bartolomé de Las Casas (1474–1566) over the treatment of Native Americans by the Spanish kings. Sepúlveda, appealing to Aristotle (who claimed slavery was justified by nature in his Politics), Aquinas, and Augustine, argued that the Native Americans were "barbaric … ignorant, unreasoning … sunk in vice … cruel, and are of such character that, as nature teaches, they are to be governed by the will of others" concluding "that the Indians are obliged by the natural law to obey those who are outstanding in virtue … This is the natural order, which the eternal and divine law commands to be observed … " (Las Casas 1992, p. 11-12). Las Casas, defender of the natives, relies partially on natural law ideals by arguing that the leaders of a community are obligated to seek the common good and waging war does not seek that end, and also that the Indians are not unreasoning but instead have rational, though still incorrect, defenses of their barbaric practices. For the most part, however, he gives consequentialist arguments as to why war should not be waged, arguing that war will produce much more harm than good.

MODERN SOURCES

Hugo Grotius (1583–1645) is variously credited with being the "father of modern natural law," the "father of natural rights," and the "father of international law." While Grotius spends most of his writing analyzing the nature of international war and its adjudication, his appeal to natural law leads in several influential directions. First, Grotius rejects the skeptical view (typified by classical Greek opponent of natural law, Carneades [c. 214–129 BCE]) that humans and all animals are simply driven by self-interest and that therefore all laws have their source in individual expediency, which may change as conditions do. Instead, Grotius argues in his *Prolegomena to the Law of War and Peace*, humans have "an impelling desire for society, that is, for the social life—not of any and every sort, but peaceful, and organized … this social trend the Stoics called 'sociableness'" (*Prolegomena* 6). Grotius indicates that this innate sympathy and desire for peace is central: "This maintenance of the social order, which we have roughly sketched, and which is consonant with human intelligence, is the source of law properly so called. To this sphere of law belong the abstaining from that which is another's, the restoration to another of anything of his which we may have … the obligation to fulfill promises" (*Prolegomena*, pp. 8-9). In addition to sociableness, humans also have the rational power to discriminate between alternative actions and can choose what will actually "follow the direction of a well-tempered judgment, being neither led astray by fear or the allurement of immediate pleasure, nor carried away by rash impulse. Whatever is clearly at variance with such judgment is understood to be contrary also to the law of nature, that is, to the nature of man" (*Prolegomena*, p. 10).

Second, and largely because of this innate sociality and intelligence, Grotius claims that "what we have been saying would have a degree of validity even if we should conceded that which cannot be conceded without the utmost wickedness, that there is no God, or that the affairs of men are of no concern to him." (*Prolegomena*, p. 10). While Grotius was not the first to conceptually detach the natural law from God, his arguments lead to a significant shift in natural law language, making it easier to talk about natural law as intrinsically part of being human rather than something that reflects a divine idea. In fact, Grotius's later clarification on the importance of God's will—"the law of nature … proceeding as it does from the essential traits implanted in man, can nevertheless be rightly attributed to God because of his having willed that such traits exist in us"—ends up showcasing more the belief that human nature immediately provides the law, whatever the ultimate source of human nature (*Prolegomena*, p. 11). This move will permit the disconnection of God and natural morality, while making the source of obligation to follow the law a significant problem.

Third, the shift away from specifically religious natural law is made even more rhetorically available because of Grotius's development of the concept of natural rights. In *The Rights of War and Peace*, he first describes the term "right" as signifying what is just or at least not unjust, but then he goes on to say that "there is another signification of the word RIGHT … which relates directly to the person. In which sense, RIGHT is a moral quality annexed to the person, justly entitling him to possess some particular privilege, or to perform some particular act" (1901, p. 19). While the idea that individuals can possess moral qualities that produce privileges and impose duties on others has many conceptual problems, the upshot is that it allows for a discourse of human rights that steers clear of theological connections.

The emphasis on the social nature of human beings becomes central at this point, informing as it does both the content and general character of natural law. Some will agree with Grotius that humans have a natural sociability; some will argue that humans are naturally individualistic self-maximizers who are sociable only for practicality's sake. But the philosophical import of this talk is that even though modern philosophers will generally agree that there is a more or less fixed human nature and will continue to use the phrase "natural law," they may mean significantly different things by it.

For example, Thomas Hobbes (1588–1679) argues that nature has provided humans with certain set traits, including rough physical and intellectual equality. Out of this equality come roughly equal hopes of attaining the objects of desire and thus competition over goods, resources, and honor. With no limitations on such competition, violence ensues and a "war of every man against every man" arises. In analyzing a way out of this situation, Hobbes discusses "rights of nature," "laws of nature," and other phrases associated with the natural law tradition. Yet, when we read what Hobbes says about the character of natural laws, something seems to have changed. Hobbes says that

> a law of nature, (*lex naturalis*) is a precept, or general rule, found out by reason, by which a man is forbidden to do, that, which is destructive of his life. … and consequently it is a precept, or general rule of reason, that every man ought to endeavor peace … and when he cannot

obtain it ... seek and use all helps and advantages of war. ... From this fundamental law of nature ... is derived a second law; that a man be willing, when others are so too ... to lay down this right to all things. (1988, pp. 86–87)

What appears to be happening here, in spite of some of the language used, is not that humans have a natural law moral obligation to seek peace, in the way Grotius might have envisioned, but rather that reason teaches us that our self-interest cannot be satisfied unless we agree with each other to give up some of our liberties and make social contracts. This means that the "law of nature" is not an objective moral obligation, but rather a pure practical realization of what we have to do in order to achieve our goals. Although it is tricky to try to use contemporary language here, it seems as if Hobbes's natural law is more about factual psychological principles and pragmatic planning. He agrees with traditional natural law theorists that we have a human nature and self-preservation is the first trait of that nature, but he sees the implications of that fact to have more to do with the satisfaction of desire than moral obligation.

This seems even clearer when Hobbes reductively defines human rights of nature as liberties to act and then defines liberties as merely "the absence of external impediments" (p. 86) and then later says that "where no covenant hath preceded, there hath no right been transferred, and every man has right to every thing; and consequently, no action can be unjust" (p. 95). Contrasting sharply with the traditional natural law claim that theft, for example, is immoral, Hobbes argues that theft only has meaning, and only becomes wrong, after social covenants are set up describing it as so. So here we see a case where the language of natural law is used but the substance is one of self-interested prudence. It is not surprising here that Hobbes's phrase, "state of nature," describes a dangerous environment that reason must be used to change. Our natural state is one of horror; our happy and peaceful state is one of artifice produced by reason.

Samuel Pufendorf (1632–1694) takes an approach both similar and somewhat more traditional. He agrees that humans are naturally self-interested and likely to engage in warlike activity to acquire the things they want. However, humans also seem to go beyond nature in excessive pursuit of the basics nature has provided them—lusting more than is necessary for procreation, seeking clothes more for show than for necessity, desiring tasty food far beyond what we need for nutrition (1991, p. 34). In a vein similar to Hobbes, Pufendorf writes:

Man, then, is an animal with an intense concern for his own preservation ... incapable of protection without the help of his fellows.... Equally, however, he is at the same time malicious, aggressive, easily provoked, and as willing as he is able to inflict harm on others. The conclusion is: in order to be safe, it is necessary for him to be sociable.... The laws of this sociality ... are called natural laws. On this basis it is evident that the fundamental natural law is: every man ought to do as much as he can to cultivate and preserve sociality. (p. 35)

Here, though the term "natural law" and "ought" are used, they seem to be used prudentially, not as objective moral terms. However, Pufendorf recognizes, as did Suárez, this divide between self-preserving practicality and moral obligation and brings God back in to secure obligation. "Though these precepts have a clear utility, they get the force of law only upon the presuppositions that God exists and rules all things by His providence, and that He has enjoined the human race to observe as laws those dictates of reason which He has Himself promulgated by the force of the innate light. For otherwise though they might be observed for their utility, like the prescriptions doctors give to regulate health, they would not be laws" (p. 36). Thus, Pufendorf reverts to a modified form of divine command theory in order to fasten down the lawfulness of natural law.

John Locke (1632–1704), the most important social contract theorist after Hobbes, forms yet another subtle synthesis that ends up making natural law a moral constraint on the sorts of social contracts we can legitimately produce. As in that of Hobbes, in Locke's state of nature humans have the ability to do whatever they want but unlike Hobbes, they do not have the right to do whatever they want. Locke writes:

Yet he has not liberty to destroy himself, or so much as any creature in his possession, but where some nobler use, than its bare preservation call for it. The state of nature has a law of nature to govern it, which obliges every one: And reason, which is that law, teaches all mankind, who will but consult it, that being all equal and independent, no one ought to harm another in his life, health, liberty or possessions. For men being all the workmanship of one omnipotent and infinitely wise Maker ... they are his property ... made to last during his, not another's pleasure. (Locke 1960, p. 271)

So we see here that even in the state of nature there is a natural law that provides a minimum moral code, namely, not to interfere with another's body, freedom, or property, and as Locke later lays out, the natural law also provides each person the authority to enforce and punish violations of this natural law (the abuse of which leads to the need to develop an unbiased state through social contract).

What is a bit uncertain here is the role of reason and God. In one sense, Locke says that reason is the natural law, which suggests a kind of prudential characterization, but he also says that it is the fact of our being the property of God that obliges us not to harm each other, which suggest a divine origin of obligation. However, it may be that reason teaches us first the moral principle that property is sacrosanct and that this principle is what informs us that as God's property we do not have the right to harm others. Locke also says that what makes a criminal is that he chooses to live by some other rule than reason, but then states that reason "is that measure God has set to the actions of men, for their mutual security" (Locke 1960, p. 272). In his constant appeal to reason for determining the specific obligations the natural law requires of us, however, Locke seems to work with the idea that reason both teaches us the content of moral truth instrumentally (we consult it), and is the natural law itself in some way.

With these sort of modifications, revisions, and perhaps even reversals, it is not surprising that natural law as a general ethical theory began to wane and by the eighteenth and nineteenth centuries, concerns about ethical theory shifted to debates among social contract theorists, skeptics, moral sense theorists, Kantians, and utilitarians. While the early social contract theorists still used the language of natural law, other philosophers clearly challenged the language and theory explicitly.

David Hume (1711–1776) famously maintained that it is a simple logical mistake to think you can "derive" a moral obligation from a biological or psychological fact (the is/ought distinction) and argued that because of the divergent definitions of the term "natural" that "nothing can be more unphilosophical than those systems which assert, that virtue is the same with what is natural, and vice with what is unnatural" (2000, pp. 302, 305).

Immanuel Kant (1724–1804) sought moral obligation in the realm of pure reason and repudiated any connection of actual contingent human psychology with moral truth. He argued in *Groundwork of the Metaphysics of Morals* that

everyone must grant that a law, if it is to hold morally, that is, as a ground of an obligation, must carry with it absolute necessity; that, for example, the command 'thou shalt not lie' does not only hold for human beings, as if other rational beings did not have to heed it … ; that, therefore, the ground of obligation here must not be sought in the nature of the human being or in the circumstances of the world in which he is placed, but a priori in concepts of pure reason. (1997, pp. 2–3)

It is worth noting, however, that one of Kant's formulations of the categorical imperative is "Act as if the maxim of your action were to become by your will a universal law of nature" (p. 31). In spite of this phrasing, this is not natural law theory. What Kant is talking about is the understanding of a law of nature as a Newtonian universal regularity and is asking us to consider whether we could logically will our maxims to have such a universal character. He writes: "The universality of law in accordance with which effects take place constitutes what is properly called nature in the most general sense … that is, the existence of things insofar as it is determined in accordance with universal laws." (p. 31) and later comments that "We must be able to will that a maxim of our action become a universal law. … Some actions are so constituted that their maxim cannot even be thought without contradiction as a universal law of nature" (p. 33).

John Stuart Mill (1806–1873) criticized the entire project of trying to couple morality with nature, arguing that virtually all of our actions alter nature in some way and that an attempt to imitate nature would have us follow a guide of cruelty (1969, pp. 373–402). Of course, Mill here is arguing against the claim that we should look to nature in the large sense as a guide to behavior rather than specifically paying attention to the narrower concept of human nature (something he did pay attention to), which indicates how the concept of "nature" as a more narrow moral guide was being used by the 1800s.

Finally, John Austin (1790–1859), the founder of modern legal positivism, argued that law

may be said to be a rule laid down for the guidance of an intelligent being by an intelligent being having power over him. … in the largest meaning which it has … the term law embraces the following objects:—Laws set by God to his human creatures, and laws set by men to men. The whole or a portion of the laws set by God to men is frequently styled the law of nature, or natural law: being, in truth, the only natural law of which it is possible to speak without a metaphor. … But, rejecting the appellation law of nature as ambiguous and misleading, I name those laws or rules … the Divine law, or the law of God. (2004, p. 24)

This command theory of law undermined the position that an obligation to act followed from anything other than sheer power and thus reduced natural law to nothing more than a confusing way of referring to divine command.

CONTEMPORARY SOURCES

In the twentieth century there was a revival of interest in natural law, as seen in the works of Jacques Maritain, Elizabeth Anscombe, Yves Simon, Ralph McInerny, Russell Hittinger, Robert George, Peter Geach, Anthony Kenny, and Alisdair McIntyre. In large part, the new attention to natural law was spurred by the Catholic Church's teachings on social and moral issues, including Pope Paul VI's encyclical letter *Humanae Vitae* (1968), which drew on Aquinas's moral theories to condemn artificial birth control. Prominent among the theological and philosophical defenders of the church's natural law teaching on contraception, abortion, homosexuality, and healthcare (though not necessarily following in the Thomistic tradition) were Germain Grisez and John Finnis. Grisez published an influential commentary on Aquinas's natural law system in 1965, which inspired John Finnis's work, culminating in *Natural Law and Natural Rights* (1980).

The heart of that book is Finnis's list of basic human goods, including life, knowledge, play, aesthetic experience, sociability (friendship), practical reasonableness (intelligently choosing and affecting one's own life), and religion (concern with transcendence) (1980, pp. 85–90). These are not moral goods, but more basically goods-for-us. It is our fundamental and self-evident awareness of these basic goods that creates moral choices for us—what are we to do? How are we to use our practical reasonableness to decide what to do? Finnis then attempts to use a "natural law method" of ethics, while still only using modern (presumably not natural law) terminology, to show purely through logic and other self-evident truths what we ought to do (p. 103). He argues for a set of basic requirements of practical reasonableness, which include a coherent, rational plan for our lives, no arbitrary preferences among either the basic goods or among persons, detachment and commitment, choosing efficient methods to achieve good, a limited attention to preference satisfaction (excluding such things as theft and murder), seeking the common good, following conscience, and

perhaps the most controversial principle, "one should not choose to do any act which of itself does nothing but damage or impede a realization or participation of any one or more of the basic forms of human good." (p. 118).

It is this latter principle that Finnis believes rules out any consequentialist reasoning. Consequentialist ethics, he argues, is irrational because goods cannot possibly be measured, and therefore the ends never justify the means where the means includes damaging a basic good. Once he rules out consequentialism, the principle that a basic good cannot be impeded is "self-evident" and the moral rule can be summarized as "Do not choose directly against a basic value" (pp. 119, 123). This formulation of natural law begins with empirical claims about what things it is in our nature to value and then logically tries to come to our obligations. However, with no legislator to provide the traditional source of obligation (such as Suárez's and Pufendorf's God) there remains the question of whether this theory is actually a natural law theory. Finnis himself tells us that, like scientific laws, which are actually only metaphorically laws, "'Natural law'—the set of principles of practical reasonableness in ordering human life and human community—is only analogically law" (p. 280).

Finnis seems to think that reason by itself provides obligation, but it is not clear how this is supposed to occur. Reason can help us discover what desired ends we find in our psychological constitutions and can help us determine instrumentally how to achieve those ends, but how does reason create an *obligation* to pursue any end?

This question of whether their theory is properly called natural law theory also follows the most prominent twentieth century legal theorists. Lon Fuller (1964) describes a set of eight requirements that civil law must meet in order to be considered genuine law—requirements such as generality, noncontradictoriness, and nonretroactivity. In this, he is appealing to a set of objective conditions that one may subject civil laws to as a test for true lawfulness, but he emphasizes that this test is procedural rather than substantive (Bix 1996). Ronald Dworkin (1967, 1986) argues that principles of values always govern how we produce and interpret civil laws, and so there is no fundamental separation of the realms of law and morality, but this could be essentially a descriptive claim and does not imply that there is a self-evident objective moral order to which civil laws must adhere in order to provide obligations. It is perhaps primarily in the sense of providing opposition to legal positivism that these theories are classified as natural law theories.

CONNECTIONS TO OTHER ETHICAL THEORIES

While natural law is its own set of theories, the differences between it and other ethical theories are often exaggerated and oversimplified. There are significant connections and shared assumptions. For example, although Kant explicitly rejects appealing to empirical facts about human nature to determine the moral law, he begins his moral philosophy with a teleological principle widely held by natural law theorists, stating in *Groundwork* that "in the natural constitution of an organized being ... we assume as a principle that there will be found in it no instrument for some end other than what is also most appropriate to that end and best adapted to it" (p. 8). Unlike natural lawyers, however, he concludes from this that the job of reason cannot be to produce happiness, because instinct would best accomplish that. Instead, reason's purpose is to produce a good will. Kant does connect nature and law through teleology though by claiming in *Idea for a Universal History from a Cosmopolitan Point of View* that "If we gave up this fundamental principle, we no longer have a lawful but an aimless course of nature" (1963, p. 13), and concluding that "The greatest problem for the human race, to the solution of which Nature drives man, Is the achievement of a universal civic society which administers law among men" (p. 16). In view of these commitments, it might be said that Kant shares with the Stoics a view of the metaphysical and epistemological aspects of the natural law, but not the essential moral aspects.

Mill, for all his criticisms of the use of the term "natural" in moral theory (Nature), is as quick as a natural law theorist to point to empirical facts about human psychology:

> The only proof capable of being given that an object is visible, is that people actually see it ... the sole evidence it is possible to produce that anything is desirable, is that people do actually desire it ... No reason can be given why the general happiness is desirable, except that each person, so far as he believes it to be attainable, desires his own happiness. (1998, p. 168)

He is quick also to appeal to our consciences as guides: "The internal sanction of duty ... is one and the same—a feeling in our mind; a pain, more or less intense, attendant on violation of duty. ... This feeling, when disinterested ... is the essence of Conscience" (p. 161).

And of course, given the natural law emphasis on the pursuit of happiness, the importance of developing character traits which lend themselves to happiness and flourishing, the fundamental desire for self-preservation, the practical need to interact with others, and the ability to apprehend our obligations through internal self-observation, we see strong shared assumptions with virtue theory, social contract theory, and intuitionism.

PROBLEMS FOR NATURAL LAW

As seen through its historical development, the primary arguments for natural law have been that it is warranted theologically, that nature or human nature somehow imply that we should act in certain ways, that reason itself simply shows us the self-evident truth of natural law, and that it is necessarily practical that we act in certain ways given our nature. Criticisms have been leveled against these arguments and other aspects of natural law theory.

First, concerns about religion: If natural law theory relies on the existence of God, then proof of God must be forthcoming before we can move on to moral metaphysics—a complicated task. However, this point would only obviously apply to those versions of natural law which require God for moral obligation and some versions of natural law do not make this assumption. Problems do arise, though for relating natural law to divine command theory. For example, if, as Grotius argues, innate human traits have been directly willed in to us by God, then God's will is the source of moral obligation and thus natural law may be only a thin technical layer between human obligation and divine command theory. If, as Aquinas seems to think, some sort of natural law would proceed automatically from whatever world God created, irrespective of God's will, then this sort of moral relationship seems to be at least as fundamental and necessary as God—a point about which voluntarists are concerned.

Philip Quinn (2000), for example, actually emphasizes the divine command elements of Aquinas's thought, arguing that the *Summa*'s exoneration of Abraham in the sacrifice of Isaac story (Summa, Part 2, Part 1, Question 100, Answer 8, Reply 3) shows that Aquinas believed "the slaying of Isaac by Abraham, which would be wrong in the absence of the divine command, will not be wrong in its presence if Abraham obeys it" (p. 62). The issue is fundamentally about whether natural moral obligations are products of pure reason, and whether this implies there is some truth or reality that does not depend entirely on God.

Second, concerns about relativism: Just as voluntarist divine command theory is often seen as a type of moral relativism because God could (in some views at least) have made anything a moral obligation, the apparent natural law assumption that morality depends on the actual contingent facts of biology and psychology seems to make morality relative to species (rather than culture or the individual, as traditional relativisms argue). This is not a practical problem for determining obligations when there is only one sapient species to consider, but for ethicists such as Kant, morality could only be said to be truly objective if it was necessary for all possible rational beings.

Third, concerns about is and ought: Hume pointed out that many attempts at moral philosophy make a near-imperceptible shift from the way things are to the way things should be—a move that logically requires connecting premises often not given (Hume 2000, p. 302). This criticism has been analyzed at great length (Hudson 1969). Natural law may be an attempt to breach the is/ought divide, but historically it often either does nothing to supply the connection, or supplies it arbitrarily, or tries to supply the connection simply by appealing to reason. It is unclear, however, how reason is supposed to produce moral obligation. It may be true, for example, that choosing a short-term pleasure over a long-term basic good interferes with comprehensive happiness, and thus may in one sense be called unreasonable or irrational. But this sense of "unreasonable" is more a matter of acknowledging empirical constraints on what will actually satisfy our desires, health, or continued existence rather than serving as any sort of logical proof of a moral obligation.

Instrumentally, reason can help us to satisfy the desires and inclinations we do in fact naturally have, but it is not clear how reason is supposed to indicate that we should try to satisfy them. There is nothing formally illogical about not satisfying desires we have or securing our own health and happiness. For versions of natural law that retain God as a moral lawmaker, this problem seems to be avoided because obligation can been seen in a positivist sense as legislated—but then this Ockamist or Austinian approach returns us to the problem of whether natural law simply reduces to divine command theory.

Fourth, concerns about the goodness of nature: There is the assumption in natural law that human nature is fundamentally good (even though flawed), which legitimates our appeal to it. This is an inheritance of Christian theology, even for those versions of natural law that argue for no dependence on God. Other explanations, less committed to design and eternal law formulations of the world's development, see aspects of human nature as more adventitious and thus less morally authoritative. Human traits are not necessarily here because they are supposed to be but because they survived. As a result, many inherent traits may be prone to producing what we think of as evil acts and ends. As Mill writes in "Nature":

> With regard to this particular hypothesis, that all natural impulses, all propensities sufficiently universal and sufficiently spontaneous to be capable of passing for instincts, must exist for good ends … this is of course true of the majority of them, for the species could not have continued to exist unless most of its inclinations had been directed to things needful or useful for its preservation. But unless the instincts can be reduced to a very small number indeed, it must be allowed that we have also bad instincts which it should be the aim of education not simply to regulate, but to extirpate. … among them one which they call destructiveness: an instinct to destroy for destruction's sake. I can conceive no good reason for preserving this. (p. 398)

Fifth, and related to the fourth, concerns about best explanation: One of the key purposes of natural law ethics, particularly in its modern versions, is to oppose the idea that there is no human nature, or that human nature is so widely divergent that no cultural or moral norms can be said to be better or worse than any other. In this sense, natural law is opposed to cultural moral relativism, behaviorist environmental determinism, and postmodern social constructivism. However, natural law is not the only theory that holds there is a human nature, that can produce a list of basic human goods, pays attention to biology and psychology, and opposes relativism. To some extent Rawlsian contractarianism does this, but in a way even more related to natural law, evolutionary ethics does as well.

Evolutionary ethics can take seriously the claim that the moral law is "written on our hearts" and that we only need our conscience to apprehend it. As Grotius defended the existence of the natural law by pointing to widespread regularities in moral beliefs (1957, pp. 25–26), evolutionary theorists defend the existence of an evolved moral sense, which explains cross-cultural similarity in moral emotions such as guilt and shame, and cross-culturally widespread moral restrictions on murder, betrayal, and sexual infidelity. But there is a difference.

Just as evolutionary theory covered much of the same territory as the argument from Design for the existence of God, but could explain both complexity and the existence of "imperfections" such as vestigial organs (having given up a perfect designer and therefore eliminating any expectation of perfect design), evolutionary ethics can explain both the widespread facts of human cooperation and widespread selfish violations of moral norms (having given up a perfect moral inculcator and therefore eliminating any expectation of perfect moral inculcation).

Even for nonreligious versions of the natural law, there remains the idea that our consciences and innate natures are essentially good and trustworthy and thus have some difficulty explaining why warmongering, murder, lying, addiction, and rape are both so self-evidently bad and so persistent. It seems to some then that evolutionary ethics does a better job of explaining human moral nature and human immoral nature. Of course, evolutionary ethics is at heart descriptive, arguing that moral attitudes are simply what have been successful at replication over time and not that they represent any objective moral truth (anymore than our bodies reflect imperfectly some infallible objective body). This is indeed a disadvantage if one is in search of moral prescriptions, but evolutionary ethicists can attempt moral prescription as well, having at first glance no lesser or greater obstacle to overcome in moving from facts to obligations than natural law theorists (Rachels 2000).

CONTEMPORARY STANDING

Natural law theory is still active as an applied ethics (forming as it does the foundation of the Catholic Church's moral philosophy). It is also still active in some academic investigations, generating numerous titles each year in ethics and legal philosophy. It is safe to say, however, that it is a minority position in mainstream academic ethics, at least in its traditional form, and typically appeals mostly to ethicists of particular religious bents. However, the descendants (or perhaps distant cousins?) of natural law theory thrive in the form of natural rights or human rights theory, which form the backbone of much of the world's international moral discourse—particularly when criticizing a particular state's or culture's practices. Practically speaking, though, much of the rhetoric concerning natural law in its more explicit and narrow sense (in appeals to naturalness and unnaturalness) is spent on ethical issues of sexuality and reproduction, leading some critics to claim that debates over sexual morality are actually the last stand for popular traditional natural law appeals (Mohr 2005, pp. 122–123).

See also Anscombe, Gertrude Elizabeth Margaret; Aristotle; Augustine, St.; Austin, John; Bonaventure, St.; Carneades; Cicero, Marcus Tullius; Consequentialism; Duns Scotus, John; Dworkin, Ronald; Gregory of Rimini; Grotius, Hugo; Heraclitus of Ephesus; Hobbes, Thomas; Hume, David; Kant, Immanuel; Laws of Nature; Legal Positivism; Locke, John; Logos; Maritain, Jacques; Medieval Philosophy; Mill, John Stuart; Moral Realism; Peace, War, and Philosophy; Philosophy of Law, History of; Philosophy of Law, Problems of; Plato; Pufendorf, Samuel von; Rawls, John; Rights; Social Contract; Socrates; Sophists; Stoicism; Suárez, Francisco; Thomas Aquinas, St.; Thomism; William of Ockham; Zeno of Citium.

Bibliography

Aristotle. *Nichomachean Ethics*. Translated by W. D. Ross, revised by J. O. Urmson. In Barnes, *The Complete Works of Aristotle*, Vol. 2.

Aristotle. *Physics*. Translated by R. P. Hardie and R. K. Gaye. In Barnes, *The Complete Works of Aristotle*, Vol. 2.

Aristotle. *Politics*. Translated by B. Jowett. In Barnes, *The Complete Works of Aristotle*, Vol. 2.

Aristotle. *Rhetoric*. Translated by W. Rhys Roberts. In Barnes, *The Complete Works of Aristotle*, Vol. 2.

Austin, John. "A Positivist Conception of Law" In *Philosophy of Law*. 7th ed., edited by Joel Feinberg and Jules Coleman. Belmont, CA: Wadsworth/Thomson Learning, 2004.

Barnes, Jonathan, ed. *The Complete Works of Aristotle: The Revised Oxford Translation*. 2 vols. Princeton, NJ: Princeton University Press, 1984. A sixth printing with corrections published in 1995.

Bix, Brian. "Natural Law Theory." In *A Companion to Philosophy of Law and Legal Theory*, edited by Dennis Patterson. Oxford, U.K.: Blackwell, 1996.

Catechism of the Catholic Church. New York: Doubleday, 1994.

Cicero. *The Republic*. Translated by Clinton Walker Keyes. Loeb Classical Library. Cambridge, MA: Harvard University Press, 1928.

Copleston, Frederick. *A History of Philosophy*. Vol. 3, *Late Medieval and Renaissance Philosophy: Ockham, Francis Bacon, and the Beginning of the Modern World*. New York: Doubleday, 1993.

Diogenes Laertius. *Lives of Eminent Philosophers*. Translated by R. D. Hicks. Loeb Classical Library. Cambridge, MA: Harvard University Press, 1925.

Dworkin, Ronald. *Law's Empire*. Cambridge, MA: Belknap Press of Harvard University Press, 1986.

Dworkin, Ronald. "The Model of Rules," *University of Chicago Law Review* 35 (14) (1967). Reprinted in *Philosophy of Law*. 7th ed., edited by Joel Feinberg and Jules Coleman. Belmont, CA: Wadsworth/Thomson Learning, 2004.

Finnis, John. *Natural Law and Natural Rights*. Oxford, U.K.: Clarendon Press, 1980.

Fuller, Lon. "Eight Ways to Fail to Make Law." In *Philosophy of Law*. 7th ed., edited by Joel Feinberg and Jules Coleman. Belmont, CA: Wadsworth/Thomson Learning, 2004.

Fuller, Lon. *The Morality of Law*. New Haven, CT: Yale University Press, 1964.

Grisez, Germain. *Christian Moral Principles: The Way of the Lord Jesus*. Chicago: Franciscan Herald Press, 1983.

Grisez, Germain. "The First Principle of Practical Reason: A Commentary on the Summa Theologiae 1–2, Question 94, Article 2." *Natural Law Forum* 10 (1965): 168–196.

Grotius, Hugo. *Prolegomena to the Law of War and Peace.* Translated by Francis W. Kelsey. Indianapolis: Bobbs-Merrill, 1957.

Grotius, Hugo. *The Rights of War and Peace, Including the Law of Nature and of Nations.* New York: M. Walter Dunne, 1901.

Haakonssen, Knud. "Natural Law." In *Encyclopedia of Ethics.* Vol. 2, edited by Lawrence C. Becker and Charlotte B. Becker. New York: Garland, 1992.

Hastings, Adrian. "Natural Law." In *The Oxford Companion to Christian Thought*, edited by Adrian Hastings, Alistair Mason, and Hugh Pyper. Oxford, U.K.: Oxford University Press, 2000.

Hobbes, Thomas. *Leviathan.* Oxford, U.K.: Oxford University Press, 1988.

Hudson, W. D. *The Is-Ought Question: A Collection of Papers on the Central Problems in Moral Philosophy.* London: Macmillan, 1969.

Hume, David. *A Treatise of Human Nature.* Oxford Philosophical Texts Edition, edited by David Fate Norton and Mary J. Norton. Oxford, U.K.: Oxford University Press, 2000.

Kainz, Howard P. *Natural Law: An Introduction and Re-examination.* Chicago: Open Court, 2004.

Kant, Immanuel. *Groundwork of the Metaphysics of Morals.* Translated by Mary Gregor. Cambridge, MA: Cambridge University Press, 1997.

Kant, Immanuel. "Idea for a Universal History from a Cosmopolitan Point of View." In *On History*, edited by Lewis White Beck. New York: Macmillan, 1963.

Las Casas, Bartolomé de. *In Defense of the Indians.* Translated by Stafford Poole. Dekalb: Northern Illinois University Press, 1992.

Locke, John. *Two Treatises of Government.* Cambridge, MA: Cambridge University Press, 1960.

Long, A. A. *Hellenistic Philosophy: Stoics, Epicureans, Sceptics.* 2nd ed. Berkeley: University of California Press, 1986.

Mill, John Stuart. "Nature." In *Essays on Ethics, Religion and Society.* Collected Works of John Stuart Mill, edited by J. M. Robson. Toronto: University of Toronto Press, 1969.

Mill, John Stuart. "Utilitarianism." In *On Liberty and Other Essays*, edited by John Gray. Oxford, U.K.: Oxford University Press, 1998.

Mohr, Richard. *The Long Arc of Justice: Lesbian and Gay Marriage, Equality, and Rights.* New York: Columbia University Press, 2005.

Paul VI, Pope. *Humanae Vitae.* Papal Encyclical. Available from http://www.vatican.va/holy_father/paul_vi/encyclicals/docu ments/hf_p-vi_enc_25071968_humanae-vitae_en.html. 1968.

Plato. *Complete Works*, edited by John M. Cooper. Indianapolis: Hackett, 1997.

Pufendorf, Samuel. *On the Duty of Man and Citizen According to the Natural Law.* Cambridge, MA: Cambridge University Press, 1991.

Quinn, Philip L. "Divine Command Theory." In *The Blackwell Guide to Ethical Theory*, edited by Hugh LaFollette. Oxford, U.K.: Blackwell, 2000.

Rachels, James. "Naturalism." In *The Blackwell Guide to Ethical Theory*, edited by Hugh LaFollette. Oxford, U.K.: Blackwell Publishing, 2000.

Suárez, Francisco. *Selections from Three Works.* Translated by Gwladys L. Williams, Ammi Brown, John Waldron, and Henry Davis. Oxford, U.K.: Clarendon Press, 1944.

Thomas Aquinas, St. *Summa Theologica.* 2nd, rev. ed. Translated by the Fathers of the English Dominican Province, 1920. Available from http://www.newadvent.org/summa/. Online edition copyright 2003 by Kevin Knight (15 February 2005).

Patrick D. Hopkins (2005)

NATURAL SELECTION

See *Evolutionary Theory*

NATURE, PHILOSOPHICAL IDEAS OF

In its widest sense "nature" can mean "the totality of things," all that would have to appear in an inventory of the universe. It can also refer to the laws and principles of structure by which the behavior of things may be explained. These two senses cannot be kept independent of each other at any sophisticated level of inquiry, for to state in any of the sciences what an entity is involves describing what it does, its patterns of activity or behavior, and the activity of its constituent elements, as far as they can be known and subsumed under laws.

In a particular philosophical context the sense in which nature is being used can be brought out most clearly by insisting upon the question "What is nature (or the natural) being contrasted with in this context?" In one group of cases the natural is contrasted with the artificial or conventional. This contrast requires some conception of how the object or organism would behave by reason of its immanent causality alone, the causal factors that are peculiar to that type of thing and make it whatever it is— a stone, a fish, or a man. The artificial and conventional are seen as interferences, modifying by an alien causality the characteristic patterns of behavior. In the sphere of human nature this distinction is at the center of an ancient and continuing controversy, for it is by no means easy—if, indeed, possible—to delineate a human nature free of interferences, left to itself. Organism and environment, individual and cultural climate, are in ceaseless interplay. An activity (like moral evaluation or social organization) that seems to some theorists on the "convention side" of the boundary may be represented by others, with no less reason, as a development of natural potentialities. The controversy is further complicated by the intrusion of evaluative nuances in the distinction itself, so that the natural, for instance, may come to be more highly esteemed than the artificial and conventional, as the spontaneous or the basic is contrasted with the labored and derivative. The preference may be reversed, however; the natural can be taken as the mere raw material, the unfinished and preparatory, requiring artifice to complete and crown it.

In some contexts man is contrasted with nature; in others he is taken as part of nature. The difference is not trivially linguistic. To set man against nature is to emphasize his distinctiveness—his rationality, creativity, and freedom. But it may also support an unwarranted and distorting anthropocentricity. To count man as part and parcel of nature emphasizes the continuity of the human, animal, organic, and inorganic worlds and suggests that human behavior may be amenable to the same kinds of investigation that are effective in studying other domains of nature. Similarities as well as differences can be exaggerated, however, and overfacile generalizations can be made from the behavior, say, of rats to human behavior. Human distinctiveness and complexity may be overlooked in a tempting reductive analysis like that of behaviorism.

In still other contexts the natural world, man included, is contrasted with the supernatural. In part at least, the idea of the supernatural has tended to be constructed from allegedly miraculous events, events that, it is claimed, the power and laws of nature could not bring about. (There can be also an a priori element in the grounding of belief in the supernatural. Belief in a transcendent creator-God, who may be himself the subject of a priori proofs, implies the belief that nature's laws and processes can be overruled.)

It is anything but easy, however, to elaborate coherently the nature-supernature distinction. Crucial to it is the claim that we can distinguish what lies within the capacities of nature from what lies beyond them. Our knowledge of nature's powers and laws is itself derived from our experience and observation of events. What we judge to be possible depends upon what we have reason to believe actually occurs or has occurred. When we assemble the experiences out of which we are to construct these judgments about the possible, what shall we do with the happenings that, eventually, we wish to label miraculous? To exclude them would be to imply that we *already* know what nature's powers are, that there are criteria

prior to experience by which we interpret our observations. But to include them makes it impossible for us to treat them later as miraculous exceptions to natural laws.

Certainly, it is not legitimate to move from saying, "This event is inexplicable in terms of our scientific knowledge of nature," to saying, "This event must be a supernatural intervention." The scientist is by no means committed to claiming that he has at any particular moment the concepts and theories adequate for every explanatory task. He is constantly revising and adding to these. We are not, therefore, forced to conclude that an event has a supernatural source on the grounds that it is inexplicable or anomalous in terms of present-day science. Indeed, it is only with the help of an independently established set of beliefs about God that one could plausibly interpret an event as supernatural. (See P. H. Nowell-Smith, "Miracles," in A. G. N. Flew and A. MacIntyre, eds., *New Essays in Philosophical Theology*, New York, 1955; and A. G. N. Flew, *Hume's Philosophy of Belief*, London, 1961.)

Although it has been implied above that God must be conceived in contradistinction to nature, this is true only if God is transcendent, not immanent (or, if immanent, then transcendent as well). In a pantheistic view if nature may be distinguished from God, it is only as different views or aspects of one and the same reality.

HISTORICAL TRANSFORMATIONS

The history of philosophical ideas of nature almost coincides with the history of philosophy itself. Where a philosophy is at all systematic, even if it is avowedly antimetaphysical, it cannot avoid stating or implying some interpretation of nature. This makes it impossible to compress the history of these interpretations into one entry. The comments that follow are thus no more than indications that the philosophers named made significant contributions to the development of the idea.

When the Ionian pre-Socratic philosophers asked, "What is nature?" they assumed that the question demanded an answer in terms of a primitive substance or substances out of which the world is constructed. One of the more reasonable answers was that of Anaximander, who claimed that the ultimate world stuff must be indeterminate and indefinite (apeiron) and could not be identified with familiar stuffs like water, air, and so on. But although plausible, Anaximander's answer was also unhelpful precisely because the apeiron lacked all determinateness and explanatory power. Far more fruitful was the Pythagorean concern not primarily with the question "What is nature made from?" but with "What is its structure?" where "structure" means geometrical form. We need to know only that the constituents of the world are able to receive mathematically describable form, and the way is opened for investigating how natural objects are related, in detail, to their underlying geometrical structure.

To Plato the possibility of knowledge of nature (or of the natures of things) rests on the intelligibility of the Forms that things imitate (or in which they participate). The creation story in the *Timaeus* (which came to have enormous influence) represents God and the Forms as distinct from each other, the spatiotemporal world—mutable nature—being created after the model of the eternally unchanging Forms. It is a world necessarily deficient in important respects; the very existence of time makes it unstable and incomplete. On the other hand, it is the product of a *divine* creativity. God in his goodness does not withhold being from anything that might exist, and thus nature displays his fecundity. Here is the initial statement of the vision of nature as a great chain, or ladder, of being.

Aristotle's Unmoved Mover stands to nature as its final or teleological cause, inspiring nature to imitate the divine activity as far as its various constituents are able. Particular things, therefore, are seen as striving to realize their appropriate forms, and in so doing, they realize their own natures. Underlying this view of nature is a clear analogy with biological growth.

To Christian thinkers the primary distinction has, of course, been between the underivative creativity of God and the derivativeness and dependence of nature. Augustine, for instance, contrasts the divine "first cause that causes all and is not caused itself" with "the other causes" (the world of nature) that "both cause and are caused" (created spirits) or are primarily passive effects, corporeal causes (*City of God* V, 9). This does not preclude a wider use in which mutable spatiotemporal nature is contrasted with divine nature, "the Nature which is immutable is called Creator" (*Epistolae*, 18, Sec. 2). In Thomas Aquinas, too, God can be called *natura naturans* and the contrast made with *natura naturata*, the creating contrasted with the created nature (*Summa Theologiae* IIa–IIae, 85, 6).

It was the Pythagorean-Platonic strand in philosophy of nature that furthered and came to dominate the rise of modern science. In Johannes Kepler, for example, nature appears as the realm of the quantitative, a realm amenable to mathematical study and, indeed, to more precise study than ancient philosophy ever demonstrated. Such a view of nature could coexist with a religious inter-

pretation of things, for the mathematical structure could be taken as supplied and sustained by the mind of God.

Although in one way the growth of a mathematical science promised most impressively to unify nature by bringing widely diversified phenomena under laws, in another way it produced new problems about the relation of man to his world, problems that led to various dualisms—bifurcations of nature—such as René Descartes's. Those aspects of our experience that were not amenable to exact measurement were no longer to be identified with objectively real, accurately cognized features of the world. The measurable qualities were primary, the rest secondary, qualities—colors, sounds, tastes, and the like. Although materialist metaphysics boldly attempted (and still attempts) to reunite nature and man by describing the full range of his perceptual, moral, and imaginative life in terms of matter and motion, in a writer like Thomas Hobbes, for example, such explanations were only promissory notes. A great deal of development in physiology had to occur before the details of the mechanisms involved could be conjectured with any real plausibility.

Descartes gave the world of mind distinct ontological status alongside corporeal nature. Although this dualism saved mind from loss of reality or reduction to the nonmental, it introduced the problem, unsolvable in Cartesian terms, of how this bifurcated nature can yet be one, how the processes of mind and of matter can impinge on each other. The philosophies of nature in Benedict de Spinoza and Gottfried Wilhelm Leibniz both try strenuously to deal with this problem. Spinoza affirms a monistic and pantheistic position (*Deus sive natura*), but the dualism breaks out again in the inexplicable relation between extension and thought—a dualism not of substances but of attributes. In Leibniz's pluralist world the relation between material and mental aspects of monads is no more intelligible.

George Berkeley's account of nature involves a radical criticism and rejection of the notion of material substance. Our experience could, he argued, be explained simply in terms of minds and their ideas, including, crucially, the divine mind, in which the totality of sensible things exists.

In the philosophy of Immanuel Kant the burden of creativity further shifts to the human percipient. If we ask Kant why nature presents to us the persistent basic structure that it does present (such as the ubiquity of cause-effect relations and the spatiotemporal nature of all experience), his answer is that we are here dealing with the inescapable conditions for any experience of nature at all because "the understanding is itself the source of the laws of nature" (*Critique of Pure Reason*, A 127). The natural world, in the sense of the totality of things, is not in Kant's view a given whole, not an object of knowledge; for instance, whether we try to show that the world is finite or infinite, our thought runs into an impasse.

In G. W. F. Hegel the dominant language is of development, nisus, toward the realization of Absolute Spirit, the end for which nature exists. Necessary transitions, logical rather than temporal, are made from level to level, from nature as inert matter with its externality to life, consciousness, the inwardness of spirit. Subsequent philosophies of nature, however, like those of Henri Bergson, Samuel Alexander, and A. N. Whitehead, were avowedly evolutionary, understandably so in an age that saw rapid development of the biological sciences, particularly biological evolutionary theory, and that had a new historical consciousness of human existence. Alexander saw the evolutionary process as the continuing "emergence" of the qualitatively new: God was to be conceived not as the initial creator or sustainer of nature but as the extrapolation of the evolutionary process to an ideal limit.

Theories involving a life force or other speculative, teleological accounts of nature have been strenuously opposed by various forms of materialism and antimetaphysical positivism.

USE OF ANALOGIES. Successive conceptions of nature (like conceptions of the state) can be seen as a procession of images or controlling analogies. Dominant in Greek cosmology, for instance, was the image of nature as suffused with life and intelligence, like a living and growing organism. At the opposite pole, as in some seventeenth- and eighteenth-century cosmologies, nature is pure machine, directed from without by the divine intelligence. Or, again, nature is neither permeated by mind nor is it a mechanism in the hand of its Mechanic; it is a self-transforming system, essentially temporal, whose development is best understood through the analogies of biological evolution or human history. To make explicit the guiding analogy is an important step in appraising an account of nature. For example, it is a standing temptation for a philosopher who is working out such an account to overextend an explanatory principle that is proving dramatically fruitful in some limited area of investigation to make it seem to cover nature as the totality of things and processes.

NATURE AS NORM

Corresponding to different philosophies of nature are markedly different answers to questions about the relation of nature to value: Can values be in any way derived from descriptions of nature? does nature set any norms for man? can appeals to nature and the natural properly settle moral or aesthetic perplexities? Various answers to these questions have been suggested in naturalistic ethical theories and in discussion of the naturalistic fallacy.

If, on the one hand, nature is seen as irreducibly complex, the theater not of a simple cosmic process but of countless and diverse processes, and if these processes have produced mind but are not themselves guided by intelligence, then there will be little plausibility in arguing directly from "natural" to "good" or "obligatory."

On the other hand, where nature is taken as created by a wholly good, wise, and omnipotent deity, to be natural is prima facie, to be *worthy* of being created by such a deity. But the existence of evil, however accounted for, makes the inference, even in this context, unreliable. The natural man may now be contrasted with the regenerate man, and "natural" thus come to have a depreciatory sense. Alternatively, the sinful can be held as unnatural—that is, as perverting the divinely appointed course of nature. The question "What *is* natural?" cannot now, however, be answered from a simple inspection of what actually happens in the world.

HISTORICAL EXAMPLES. The demand that we should follow nature occurs in a wide variety of ethical theories, not only in Christianity. It was against an ethic of following nature that J. S. Mill eloquently argued in his "Essay on Nature" (in *Three Essays*). To Mill nature means either (1) "the sum of all phenomena, together with the causes which produce them" or (2) those phenomena that take place "without the agency ... of man." Which of these senses can be intended when someone is enjoined to follow nature or when some act is condemned as unnatural? In the first sense *every* action is natural; no ground is given for discrimination between alternative courses. But is the second sense more helpful? "For while human action cannot help conforming to Nature in the one meaning of the term, the very aim and object of action is to alter and improve Nature in the other meaning." Behind the injunction to follow nature lies a dim belief that "the general scheme of nature is a model for us to imitate." Look at nature in some detail, however. Its processes are quite indifferent to value and desert. "Nearly all the things which men are hanged or imprisoned for doing to one another, are nature's every day performances." Even if it were true that some good ends were ultimately and obscurely served and realized by nature's processes, that would give no license to men to follow nature as a moral exemplar (to "torture because nature tortures," for example).

In any case, Mill argues, the presence of evil and indifference to value in nature cannot be reconciled with theistic claims about the omnipotence and perfect goodness of God. It is nonsense to argue that such a God has to bend to stubborn necessities since he "himself makes the necessity which he bends to."

With regard to *human* nature, as with nature at large, Mill's imperative is "not to follow but to amend it." Morality cannot be founded on instinct but on a strenuously achieved victory *over* instinct, as courage is a victory over fear. Similar views are found in T. H. Huxley and even, with important qualifications, in the later Sigmund Freud.

Philosophical views of nature can be relevant to problems of evaluation in much more complex ways than we have thus far noted. One's conception of how man is related to the rest of the natural world may help to determine—in conjunction with many other factors—one's sense of the importance or unimportance of human life, the roles judged reasonable and unreasonable for men to adopt. Here are some historical examples.

Did a geocentric astronomy give a uniquely privileged place to Earth and to humanity? The symbolism was ambiguous; to be in the center was certainly to be the focus of the cosmic drama of fall and redemption. "Man is but earth," said John Donne. "'Tis true; but earth is the centre" ("Sermon Preached at St. Paul's, Christmas Day, 1627"). Yet the center, the sublunary region, was nevertheless the humblest position, the realm of mutability, in contrast to the unchanging heavens. The shift to a heliocentric view was not, therefore, a catastrophic and disorienting demotion. It could be seen as an equally effective symbolic expression of creatureliness, Earth being placed in a proper subordination to the sun (for example, see Nicolas Copernicus and Kepler). "The sun, seated on his royal throne, [does] guide his family of planets" (Kepler, *De Revolutionibus,* Book I, Ch. 10).

A far more radical shift in sixteenth- and seventeenth-century cosmology was the move toward acceptance of the universe as infinite and with that the obliterating of a locatable center or circumference. But this view, which, in fact, had no effective *scientific* backing, was largely a late development of the metaphysical Platonic idea of God's infinite fecundity, a view that also guaranteed humanity a position of dignity in the ladder of being (see A. O. Lovejoy, *The Great Chain of Being,* Ch. 4). This well shows how (at least in a period of metaphysical confidence) the importance or unimportance of man has not been a matter of attempted inference from observations of nature alone.

The same point can also be illustrated from sixteenth- and seventeenth-century arguments about the alleged "cosmic fall." If nature is inclement and hostile, this is because nature participated in the effects of man's fall into sin. It follows that the proper, God-intended destiny of man cannot be found in this fallen nature; it must be discovered in the revealed word of God.

More generally, reference to man's place in nature, for instance to his physical minuteness, could be used to depreciate the quest for "worldly" glory as a preparation for spiritual discipline. "Who can be great," asked Drummond of Hawthornden, "on so small a Round as is this Earth?" And Blaise Pascal asked: "Qu'est ce qu'un homme dans l'infini?" ("What is a man in face of the infinite?"). The vastness of nature could equally well be taken as evidence of man's importance in God's eyes; for on independent theological grounds the whole of nature could be seen as primarily a dwelling place for man. As Pierre de la Primaudaye expressed it, "I cannot marvell enough at the excellencie of Man, for whom all these things were created and are maintained." Most of these arguments, with their ingredients capable of endless variation, assume that "in order to form a correct estimate of ourselves we must consider the results of the investigations … into the dimensions and distances of the spheres and stars" (Maimonides)—*mutatis mutandis* for later cosmologies.

In sharp contrast, at a time when there is little or no metaphysical and theological confidence and when deriving value judgments from statements of fact is deemed logically impossible, it is tempting to deny that accounts of nature can have any bearing on problems of value. F. P. Ramsey wrote: "My picture of the world is drawn in perspective, and not like a model to scale. The foreground is occupied by human beings, and the stars are all as small as threepenny bits" (*Foundations of Mathematics*). It is possible to make one's judgments about the value of human life independently of cosmic reflections and then to adopt an imaginative picture of the natural world that harmonizes rather than conflicts with that evaluation. There can be no logical or philosophical objections to that as long as one realizes exactly what is being done. Such an imaginative exercise, however, must be distinguished from a thoroughgoing anthropocentric philosophy of nature, and Ramsey himself has been criticized for falling into exactly that (see J. J. C. Smart, *Philosophy and Scientific Realism,* New York, 1963, p. 25). For Ramsey went on to say: "I don't really believe in astronomy, except as a complicated description of human … and possibly animal sensation."

It is worth noting, finally, that arguments about aesthetic judgments have also relied on the vocabulary of *nature* and *natural* and relied on it in many differing and conflicting ways. Presenting or being true to nature has sometimes meant the faithful mirroring of the empirical world *or* the pursuit of the ideal type *or* the pursuit of the average type or a concern with whatever has not been modified by man (see A. O. Lovejoy, *Essays in the History of Ideas,* "Nature as Aesthetic Norm"). Works of art have been commended as sharing the characteristics of nature through being regularly patterned (compare to nature's mathematical intelligibility), through being rich in content, or through being austerely simple. To be natural can be to show spontaneity, to be unfettered by artificial rules, to reach toward the unspoiled and primitive. Where there is such extraordinary conflict of senses, only a scrutiny of the context can determine what criteria are being applied in any particular case, and a writer who is aware of this web of ambiguities in "natural" and "nature" may well decide to choose—wherever possible—words of greater precision and stability of meaning.

See also Aesthetic Judgment; Alexander, Samuel; Anaximander; Augustine, St.; Bergson, Henri; Berkeley, George; Copernicus, Nicolas; Cosmology; Descartes, René; Hegel, Georg Wilhelm Friedrich; Hobbes, Thomas; Kant, Immanuel; Kepler, Johannes; Laws of Nature; Leibniz, Gottfried Wilhelm; Lovejoy, Arthur Oncken; Maimonides; Mill, John Stuart; Natural Law; Pascal, Blaise; Plato; Ramsey, Frank Plumpton; Smart, John Jamieson Carswell; Spinoza, Benedict (Baruch) de; Thomas Aquinas, St.; Whitehead, Alfred North.

Bibliography

Because of the almost unlimited scope of the topic, references are for the most part confined to works mentioned in the text of the article or to which the article is in some general way indebted.

BACKGROUND TO GREEK PHILOSOPHIES OF NATURE

Aristotle. *Metaphysics.* Edited by W. D. Ross. rev. ed., 2 vols. Oxford, 1924. Δ (V), 4.

Bumet, John. *Greek Philosophy: Thales to Plato.* London, 1914; paperback ed., 1962.

Crombie, I. M. *An Examination of Plato's Doctrines.* 2 vols. New York: Humanities Press, 1962–1963. Vol. II, Ch. 2.

Guthrie, W. K. C. *A History of Greek Philosophy,* Vol. I. Cambridge, U.K.: Cambridge University Press, 1962.

Heinemann, F. *Nomos und Physis.* Basel: F. Reinhardt, 1945.

Kirk, G. S., and J. E. Raven. *The Presocratic Philosophers.* Cambridge, U.K.: Cambridge University Press, 1957.

Pohlenz, M. "Nomos und Physis." *Hermes* 81 (1953): 418–438.

Popper, Karl. *The Open Society and Its Enemies.* 2 vols. London: Routledge, 1945. Vol. I, especially Ch. 5, on nature and convention.

Ross, W. D. *Aristotle.* London, 1923; 2nd ed., 1930. Ch. 3.

WIDE-RANGING HISTORICAL INTERPRETATIONS

Burtt, E. A. *The Metaphysical Foundations of Modern Physical Science.* London: K. Paul, Trench, Trubner, 1925.

Collingwood, R. G. *The Idea of Nature.* Oxford: Clarendon Press, 1945.

Lovejoy, A. O. *Essays in the History of Ideas.* Baltimore: Johns Hopkins University Press, 1948. See "Nature as Aesthetic Norm."

Lovejoy, A. O. *The Great Chain of Being.* Cambridge, MA: Harvard University Press, 1936.

Lovejoy, A. O. and George Boas, eds. *Primitivism and Related Ideas in Antiquity.* Baltimore: Johns Hopkins University Press, 1935. See "Some Meanings of 'Nature.'"

OTHER STUDIES

Dewey, John. *Experience and Nature.* La Salle, IL: Open Court, 1925; paperback ed., New York, 1958.

Maritain, Jacques. *La philosophie de la nature.* Paris: Téqui, 1935.

Mill, John Stuart. *Three Essays on Religion.* London, 1874; reprinted, 1904.

Ramsey, F. P. *The Foundations of Mathematics.* London: K. Paul, Trench, Trubner, 1931; paperback ed., Paterson, NJ, 1960. See epilogue.

Russell, Bertrand. *Mysticism and Logic.* London: Allen and Unwin, 1917. See especially Ch. 3, "A Free Man's Worship."

Russell, Bertrand. *Why I Am Not a Christian, and Other Essays,* edited by Paul Edwards. New York: Simon and Schuster, 1957.

Sherrington, Charles. *Man on His Nature.* Cambridge, U.K.: Cambridge University Press, 1940.

Weizsäcker, C. F. von. *Die Geschichte der Natur.* Göttingen, 1948. Translated by F. D. Wieck as *The History of Nature.* London: Routledge, 1951.

Whitehead, Alfred North. *The Concept of Nature.* Cambridge, U.K.: Cambridge University Press, 1920.

Whitehead, Alfred North. *Nature and Life.* Cambridge, U.K.: Cambridge University Press, 1934.

Ronald W. Hepburn (1967)

NEGATION

Negation, or denial, is the opposite of affirmation. It may be something that somebody does ("I deny what you have said") or the answer "No" to a question, but its full expression is generally a sentence. One sentence or statement may be the negation or denial of another, or we may call a statement simply a negation, or a negative statement, as opposed to an affirmative one, or affirmation. A negation in the last sense will contain some sign of negation, such as the "not" in "Grass is not pink" or "Not all leaves are green," the "no" in "No Christians are communists," or the phrase "it is not the case that" in "It is not the case that grass is pink." The negation of a sentence may simply be the same sentence with "it is not the case that" prefixed to it, or it may be some simpler form equivalent to this. For example, it might be said that "It is not the case that grass is pink" is negated or denied not only by "It is not the case that it is not the case that grass is pink" but also by the plain "Grass is pink" and that "If he has shut the door, it must have been open" is negated or denied by "He could have shut it even though it was already shut."

Contradictory negation, or contradiction, is the relation between statements that are exact opposites, in the sense that they can be neither true together nor false together—for example, "Some grass is brown" and "No grass is brown." Contrary negation, or contrariety, is the relation between extreme opposites (which may very well both be false)—for example, "No grass is brown" and "All grass is brown." Incompatibility is the relation between statements that cannot both be true, whether or not they stand at opposite ends of a scale ("This is black all over" is incompatible with "This is green all over" as well as with "This is white all over"). Incompatibles imply one another's denials (what is black all over is not green all over or white all over).

Some of these technical expressions apply to terms as well as to statements. The terms *black, green,* and *white,* for example, are incompatible; nothing can be more than one of these at once, at least not at the same time, at the same point, from the same angle, and so on. There are also "negative terms," usually formed by prefixing "non" or "not" to the corresponding positive term—for instance, *nonred, not-red.*

The concept of negation is closely related to that of falsehood, but they are not the same. Sometimes it is the negation that is true and the corresponding affirmation that is false. But in denying a statement, we implicitly or explicitly assert that the statement in question is false, though, of course, the assertion that something is false may itself be true.

There is also a connection between the concept of negation, especially as applied to terms, and that of otherness or diversity. What is not red is other than anything that is red, and what is other than anything that is red is not red. The class of things that are other than all the things included in a given class—that is, whatever exists besides the members of that class—constitutes the remainder or complement of the given class.

INTERNAL AND EXTERNAL NEGATION

When a proposition is complex, it is often important to distinguish the negation of the proposition as a whole ("external" negation) from propositions resulting from the negation of some component or components of it ("internal" negation). The Stoics noted, for example, that the contradictory denial of an implication "If p, then q" should not be formulated as "If p, then not-q" but as "Not (if p, then q)"—"That p does not imply that q." "If p, then q" and "If p, then not-q" are not even incompatible, although when they are both true, it follows that the component p (since it has contradictory consequences) must be false. Again "Not (p and q)," which is true as long as p and q are not true together, is not to be confused with "Not-p and not-q," which is true only if p and q are both false and is equivalent to "Neither p nor q"—that is, "Not (p or q)." "Either not-p or not-q" is similarly equivalent to "Not (p and q)." These relations between the internal and external negations of "and" and "or" statements are called De Morgan's laws, although they were well known to the medieval Scholastics long before the birth of the nineteenth-century logician Augustus De Morgan.

Some of the distinctions made in the preceding section are now commonly treated as special cases of external and internal negation. For instance, propositions with negative terms are thought of as involving the negation, not perhaps of internal propositions strictly so called, but of internal "propositional functions" ("open sentences")—for example, "Every non-A is a non-B" may be paraphrased as "For any x, if it is not the case that x is an A, then it is not the case that x is a B"; the difference between "No A is a B," the contrary opposite of "Every A is a B," and the contradictory opposite of the latter, "Some A is a B" or "Not every A is a B," is perhaps simply that between the internally negated form "For every x, if x is an A, then not (x is a B)" and the external negation "Not (for every x, if x is an A, then x is a B)." It is obviously possible to place a sign of negation either inside or outside a variety of other qualifying phrases; for example, we may distinguish "It will be the case that (it is not the case that p)" from "It is not the case that (it will be the case that p)" and "It is thought that (it is not the case that p)" from "It is not the case that (it is thought that p)."

By the use of open sentences all the varieties of negation are reduced to the placing of "not" or "it is not the case that" before some proposition or proposition like expression, the whole being either contained or not contained within some wider propositional context. This reduction assumes that with the basic singular form "*x* is an *A*" or "*x* ϕ's" there is no real distinction between the internal negation "*x* is not an *A*" (or "*x* is a non-*A*") or "*x* does not ϕ" and the external negation "Not (*x* is an *A*)" or "Not (*x* ϕ's)." When the subject "*x*" is a bare "this," such an assumption is plausible, but when it is a singular description like "The present king of France," we must distinguish the internal negation "The present king of France is not bald" (which suggests that there is such a person) from the external negation "It is not the case that the present king of France is bald" (which would be true if there were no such person). The thesis that all forms of negation are reducible to a suitably placed "it is not the case that" can be maintained only if the last two cases have an implicit complexity and may be, respectively, paraphrased as "For some *x*, *x* is the sole present king of France, and it is not the case that *x* is bald" and "It is not the case that (for some *x*, *x* is the sole present king of France and is bald)."

POSITIVE PRESUPPOSITIONS

It is sometimes held that no negation can be bare or mere negation and that whenever anything is denied, some positive ground of denial is assumed, and something positive is even an intended part of what is asserted. It is trivially true that even in denials, such as that grass is pink, something is made out to be the case—namely, that it is not the case that grass is pink. But something more than this is usually intended by the contention.

One thing that could be meant is that every denial must concern something which, whatever else it is not, is itself and, indeed, simply is (exists). We have seen that some types of denial—"This is not a man" and "The man next door does not smoke" (also "Some men do not lie")—do assert or presuppose the existence of a subject of the denial. But this does not seem to be the case with all forms; for example, no existing subject seems to be involved when we say that there are no fairies. Or if this is taken to mean that among existing things no fairies are to be found (thus presupposing a body of "existing things"—of values for the bound variable *x* in "For no *x* is it the case that *x* is a fairy"), even this positive presupposition seems absent from "There could not be round squares."

It is also sometimes said that in denying that something is red, we at least assume that it is some other color (counting white, black, and gray as colors); in denying that something is square, we assume that it is some other shape. In general (to use the terminology of W. E. John-

son), in denying that something has a "determinate" form of some "determinable" quality, we assume that it has some other determinate form of it. Sometimes a distinction is made at this point between the predication of a negative term and the simple denial of a predication; for example, it is argued that in saying that a thing is nonblue, we do assume that it is some other color but we do not assume this in simply saying that it is not blue. Others contend that we assume that a thing is some other color even in simply denying that it is blue. All denial, it is said, is implicitly restricted to some universe of discourse; if we deny that something is blue or classify it as nonblue, it is assumed that we are considering only colored things.

Against the weaker form of the theory that the predication of a negative term has positive implications which the denial of a predication does not have, it may be objected that there is no more than a verbal difference between "*x* is a non-*B*" and "Not (*x* is a *B*)." Against the stronger form the objection is that it is perfectly proper to say that virtue is not blue simply on the ground that it is not the kind of thing that could have any color at all. We must always distinguish between what we say and our reasons for saying it (otherwise, there could be no inference at all, as premises and conclusion would coalesce), and there may be diverse reasons for saying exactly the same thing of different subjects—Jones's favorite flower is not blue because it is pink, and virtue is not blue because being an abstraction, it is not colored at all. But it is perfectly true of each of these subjects, and true in the same sense, that it is not blue.

It may be answered that "This flower is blue" and "Virtue is blue" fail to be true in profoundly different ways—the former because it is false, and the latter because it is meaningless, as meaningless as, for example, "Virtue is but" would be—and, further, whereas the denial of a false statement is true, the denial of a meaningless form of words (that is, the result of attaching a negation sign to it) is itself a meaningless form of words. To this, one possible reply (made by J. M. Shorter in "Meaning and Grammar") would be to deny that the negation of a meaningless form of words is meaningless; even "Virtue is not but" might be defended as true precisely because it is not only false, but also meaningless, to say that virtue is but. Less desperately, it could be argued that "Virtue is (is not) blue" is not on a par with "Virtue is (is not) but" since the former is at least a grammatically correct sentence while the latter does not even construe. Perhaps, however, the conception of grammar that suggests this distinction is a rather superficial one. Grammar concerns what words go with what; it is not a set of commands directly fallen from heaven but reflects at least partly the feeling we already have for what does and what does not make sense. Perhaps we need only let this feeling lead us to slightly finer distinctions than the crude one between an adjective and a conjunction to see that "is (is not) blue" no more goes with "virtue" than "is (is not) but" goes with anything.

What is important is the line between falsehood (the negation of which is true) and nonsense (the negation of which is generally agreed to be only further nonsense), wherever this line be drawn. It is also important that what looks like true or false sense may on closer inspection turn out to be nonsense.

NEGATIVE FACTS

Many philosophers who have found negation a metaphysically embarrassing concept have expressed this embarrassment by denying that there are any negative facts. There are obviously negative as well as affirmative statements, but according to these philosophers, it is incredible that the nonlinguistic facts that make our statements true or false should include negative ones. (The linguistic fact that there are negative statements is, of course, not itself a negative, but a positive, fact.)

This question should not be confused with the question of whether there are objective falsehoods—that is, whether the universe contains such objects as the falsehood that Charles I died in his bed even if no one has ever believed or asserted this falsehood (whether there are falsehoods which are, as it were, waiting around to be asserted or believed, or even denied or disbelieved, just as there are facts waiting to be discovered and stated). For such objective falsehoods, if there were any, would not be facts—a fact is what is the case, not what is not the case. The present question is, rather, whether there are special facts that verify true negative statements, whether, for example, there is any such fact as the fact that Charles I did not die in his bed. There is nevertheless some connection between the two questions. For if there is any such language-independent and thought-independent fact as the fact that it is not the case that Charles 1 died in his bed, then, that Charles I died in his bed, which in itself is not a fact but a falsehood, would nevertheless seem to have some kind of existence "out there" as a constituent of this more complex object that is a fact.

In both cases, moreover, what deters the philosophers is partly the multiplicity of the objects involved. They cannot believe that there should be not only the fact that Charles I died on the scaffold but also, over and above that fact, the additional facts that he did not die in his bed, that he was not immortal, that he did not die by drowning, and, furthermore, the facts that he did not die in his bed of appendicitis, that he did not die in his bed of consumption, that he did not die by drowning in six minutes, that he did not die by drowning in six and a half minutes, and so on. This causes an embarrassment of the same sort as the idea that, over and above the fact that he died on the scaffold, there are "out there" the falsehoods that he died in his bed, that he was immortal, that he was drowned in six and a half minutes, and so on.

The most obvious way to reduce this excessive metaphysical population, and the one taken by Raphael Demos (one of the main opponents of negative facts), is to hold that what makes it false to say that Charles I died in his bed and true to say that he did not, false to say that he died by drowning and true to say that he did not, and similarly with all the other alternatives is simply the one positive fact that he died on the scaffold. Against this, however, it may be said that what is asserted by any true statement would seem to be some fact, and the true statement that Charles I did not die in his bed does not assert that he died on the scaffold (even if this is also true). It may be suggested that what the true statement asserts is that Charles died in some positive way that was incompatible with his dying in his bed. This suggestion has the disadvantage (a) that it only exchanges negative facts for facts that are vague and general in the way that assertions about something or other (but nothing in particular) are always vague and general and that philosophers who are uneasy about the former (because whatever is real must be particular and positive) are likely to be equally uneasy about the latter. The suggestion also presupposes (b) that there are facts of incompatibility—for example, the fact that Charles I's dying on the scaffold is incompatible with his dying in his bed and that these would seem, like straightforwardly negative facts, to contain objective falsehoods as constituents and would have the same dismaying multiplicity as negative facts or objective falsehoods do.

One way of answering objection (b) is to argue that the facts of incompatibility which explain the truth of negative statements never concern incompatibilities between propositions but always concern incompatibilities between qualities, like the incompatibility between red and blue or between one way of dying and another. This is to make a certain sort of internal negation the fundamental form in terms of which all other types of negation are to be defined. This eliminates the horde of positive falsehoods that are incompatible with the actual positive facts in favor of a possibly smaller and anyway more acceptable horde of incompatible qualities, each capable in itself of qualifying a real object but unable to do so at the same time as the others. But although there is some plausibility in accounting for simple singular negations in this way (that is, in taking the simple "x is not A" to be true, when it is true, because x is something incompatible with being A), it is hard to deal similarly with the negations of more complex forms—for example, "Not everything is A" or "It is not the case that if x is A, then y is B."

Difficulties in dealing with more complex negations also arise with the suggestion that the facts that verify negative statements are facts not so much about incompatibility as about otherness. It is important to note that the otherness account cannot take quite the same form as the incompatibility one; although the fact that x is something incompatible with being red will suffice to verify "x is not red," "x is something other than red" will not, for x may be something other than red (for instance, round) and be red as well. The otherness account would have to claim that what verifies "x is not A" is the fact that x is other than everything that is A. This account, like the preceding one, seems to be applicable only to simple singular negation. However, if the complexities that can arise are capable of being listed, it might be possible to give a separate account of the negation of each kind of complexity. Thus, having said what the simple "x is not A" means, we may say that in forms like "Not (not-p)," "Not (p and q)," "Not (p or q)," "Not (everything ϕ's)," and "Not (something ϕ's)" (that is, "Not anything ϕ's"), the apparently external "not" is to be defined in terms of a comparatively internal "not" as follows:

Not (not-p) = p,
Not (p or q) = (Not-p) and (not-q),
Not (p and q) = (Not-p) or (not-q),
Not (for every x, x ϕ's) = For some x, not (x ϕ's),
Not (for some x, x ϕ's) = For every x, not (x ϕ's).

In any given complex formed in these ways the innermost negations—the only ones that remain when all the reductions have been performed—will be simple singular negations explainable as above in terms of otherness or incompatibility.

NEGATION, FACTS, AND FALSEHOOD

Another way of eliminating negative facts might be by defining negation in terms of disbelief or falsehood. Affirmative statements, we might say, express beliefs whereas negative ones express disbeliefs. Disbelief, however, is not just the absence of belief, and like belief it must have an object—it must be disbelief in something or disbelief of something—and it must be justified or unjustified; if justified, whatever justifies it must be either a negative fact or whatever we replace negative facts with when using some other and more objective method of dissolving them.

In terms of falsehood we might say that the contradictory negation of a statement is the statement that is true if the given one is false and false if the given one is true. This amounts to defining negation by means of its truth table, a course advocated by Ludwig Wittgenstein in the *Tractatus*. To this it may be objected that talk of the statement which is true when a given statement is false and false when it is true is legitimate only if we know that there is one and only one statement which meets these conditions, and this seems unlikely; for example, since "Oxford is the capital of Scotland" is false in any case, "Either Oxford is the capital of Scotland or grass is not green" is true if "Grass is green" is false and false if it is true, but what is stated by this complex does not seem to be simply the negation of "Grass is green." It may also be objected that statements are not simply true and false in themselves, as if truth and falsehood were simple properties requiring no further explanation. By the usual definition "Grass is green" is true if grass is green and false if it is not, but to say this is to define falsehood in terms of negation rather than vice versa.

Perhaps the whole problem about negative facts—and the problem about the objective falsehoods that would be parts of such facts if there were any—arise from thinking of facts (and falsehoods) too literally as objects or entities. It is not merely that there are no negative facts but, rather, that there are no facts. That is, expressions of the form "The fact that p" do not name objects, whether or not our "p" is negative in form. The word *fact* has meaning only as part of the phrase "it is a fact that" (that is, "it is the case that"), and "It is a fact that grass is (or is not) green" is just another way of saying the simple "Grass is (or is not) green." "There are negative facts" is true and, indeed, makes sense only if it means "For some p, it is not the case that p." But in this sense it is true and metaphysically harmless; it does not mean that there are objects called "That p" which go through a performance called "not being the case," and still less does it mean that there are objects called "The not-being-the-case of that p."

Even with this caution, however, one can sensibly inquire whether signs of negation are really indispensable—whether what we say when we use them cannot also be said, and more directly, without them—and whether signs of negation are not just convenient abbreviations for complex forms into which no such signs enter. Putting the question in this way, modern logic has evolved other devices for eliminating negation besides the ones thus far mentioned, devices which are worth examining, even though they are a little technical, and which require some preliminary account of negation as the logician sees it.

LAWS OF NEGATION. Negation figures in formal logic primarily as the subject of certain laws, of which the best known are those of contradiction and excluded middle. The law of contradiction asserts that a statement and its direct denial cannot be true together ("Not both p and not-p") or, as applied to terms, that nothing can both be and not be the same thing at the same time ("Nothing is at once A and not-A"). The law of excluded middle asserts that a statement and its negation exhaust the possibilities—it is either the case that p or not the case that p—or, as applied to terms, that everything either is or is not some given thing—say, A. Each of these laws may be put in the form of an implication, or "if" statement; the law of contradiction then appears as "If p, then not not-p," and the law of excluded middle as "If not not-p, then p." Sometimes the combination of these two, "p if and only if not not-p," is called the law of double negation.

Each of these laws involves a number of derived or related laws. From the law of contradiction it follows that what has contradictory consequences is false; if p implies q and also implies not-q (and so implies "q and not-q"), then not-p. From the law of excluded middle it follows that what is implied by both members of a contradictory pair is true; if p implies q and not-p equally implies q, then q. Again, because of the law of contradiction whatever implies its own denial is false, for if p implies not-p, it implies both p and not-p (since it certainly implies p) and thus cannot be true. This is the principle of *reductio ad absurdum*. To take an ancient example, if everything is true, then it is true (among other things) that not everything is true; hence, it cannot be the case that everything is true. Perhaps we can also argue that if it is a fact that there are no negative facts, then that is itself a negative fact; thus, it cannot be that there are no negative facts. Correspondingly, from the law of excluded middle it follows that whatever is implied by its own denial (that is, what we are compelled to affirm even when we try to deny it) is true. (The later Schoolmen called this the *consequentia mirabilis*.)

Another important law involving negation is the law of contraposition, or transposition, that if p implies q, then the denial of q implies the denial of p or, for terms,

if every A is a B, then every non-B is a non-A. If this is combined with the first law of double negation ("If p, then not not-p"), we obtain "If p implies not-q, then q implies not-p"; if it is combined with the second law of double negation ("If not not-p, then p"), we obtain "If not-p implies q, then not-q implies p," and with both we obtain "If not-p implies not-q, then q implies p."

Many logicians have questioned the law of excluded middle and the laws associated with it. In particular, the intuitionist logic of L. E. J. Brouwer and Arend Heyting contains none of the laws "Either p or not-p," "If not not-p, then p," "If p implies q and not-p also implies q, then q," "If not-p implies p, then p," "If not-p implies q (not-q), then not-q (q) implies p."

FORMAL DEFINITIONS OF NEGATION. The laws just discussed and many others figure in modern symbolic calculi as theorems derived by stated rules of inference from given axioms. Some of them, indeed, may themselves appear as axioms, different formulas being taken as axiomatic in different symbolic presentations. The symbols used, moreover, will be divisible into "primitive" symbols that are introduced without explanation and other symbols that are introduced by definition as abridgments of complexes involving other symbols. Which symbols are taken as primitive and which are defined will vary with the particular systematic presentation adopted.

Gottlob Frege, for example, took symbols corresponding to "if" and "not" as undefined and introduced the form "p or q" as a way of writing "If not-p, then q" ("Either I planted peas, or I planted beans" = "If I did not plant peas, I planted beans"). Bertrand Russell at one stage did the same, but he later took "not" and "or" as his primitives, defining "If p, then q" as "Either not-p or q" ("If you smoke, you'll get a cough" = "Either you won't smoke, or you'll get a cough") and "p and q" as "Not either not-p or not-q." Other writers have defined all the other symbols in terms of "not" and "and." For example, they have defined "If p, then q" as "Not (p without q)"—that is, "Not (p and not-q)" and "p or q" as "Not both not-p and not-q."

In all these examples the negation sign appears as one of the primitive or undefined symbols, but there are also systems in which this is not the case and in which "not" is defined in terms of something else. For example, Jean Nicod uses a single undefined stroke in such a way that "$p \mid q$" amounts to "Not both p and q" and "Not-p" is defined as "$p \mid p$" (Not both p and p). Russell sometimes attempts to avoid even the appearance of complexity in his verbal rendering of Nicod's stroke by reading "$p \mid q$" as "p is incompatible with q," but this would ordinarily be understood as a little stronger than what is intended. We would not normally say that "London is the capital of England" was incompatible with "Berlin is the capital of France," but it is correct to say "London is the capital of England | Berlin is the capital of France," since the two components are not both true.

An earlier and more interesting device was that of C. S. Peirce, who defined negation as the implication of something false. This is not quite a definition of negation in terms of falsehood. Formally, what is meant is that we arbitrarily choose some false proposition—say, "The ancient Romans spoke Polish"—and introduce "Not-p" as an abbreviation for "If p, then the ancient Romans spoke Polish." It is also possible to take as our standard false proposition for this purpose a formula which itself has some logical significance. In his later years Peirce himself liked to use the proposition "For all p, p," which is, roughly, "Everything is true" (which was shown to be false in the previous section of this entry). In common speech we come close to defining "Not-q" as "If q, then for all p, p" when we say of something we wish to deny, "If you believe that, you would believe anything." A similar definition of "Not-p," used by Russell in his early writings, is "For all q, if p, then q." Starting in this way, it is possible to define all the symbols of logic in terms of "if" and the quantifier "for all x." Certain further technical devices make it possible to define both "if" and "for all x" in terms of a single operator that can be read as "For all x, if …, then …" or "If ever …, then …" (Russell's "formal implication," perhaps better called "universalized implication").

Given definitions of this type, the characteristic laws of negation fall into place as special cases of the characteristic laws of implication or of universality (or both). For instance, the law of transposition, "If (if p, then q), then (if not-q, then not-p)," expands to "If (if p, then q) then if (if q; then anything-at-all), then (if p, then anything-at-all)," which is just a special case of the law of syllogism, "If (if p, then q), then if (if q, then r), then (if p, then r)." Moreover, the peculiarities of the intuitionistic negation of Brouwer and Heyting turn out simply to reflect those of intuitionistic implication.

Intuitionistic logic, for example, contains the law "If p implies q, then if p also implies that q implies r, p implies r"; therefore, it contains the special case "If p implies q, then if p also implies that q implies the falsehood, then p implies the falsehood"—that is, "If p implies q, then if p also implies not-q, then not-p." But it does not contain the law "If p implies r, then if p's implying q also implies r, then r" (this law, being verified by the usual truth-tables for "if" and "not," does appear in nonintuitionistic or classical implicational logic) and therefore does not contain the law "If p implies r, then if p's implying the falsehood also implies r, then r" ("If p implies r, then if not-p also implies r, then r").

It is also possible in both intuitionistic and classical logic to separate those laws of negation which are (or may be represented as) merely special cases of laws of implication (as in the above examples) and those that reflect the special features of what a proposition is being said to imply when we negate it. For example, both versions of logic contain the law (1) "If p, then if also not-p, then anything-at-all." But neither logic contains as a law the implicational formula of which this would be (if they had it) a special case, "If p, then if p implies r, then anything-at-all." However, they do both have, quite naturally, (2) "If p, then if p implies that everything is true, then anything-at-all." To get (1), in other words, it is important not only that we should see "Not-p" as something of the form "If p, then r" but also as this particular thing, "If p, then everything is true." If we drop from intuitionistic logic those laws of negation which require attention to this more special point, we obtain the "minimal" calculus of I. Johannson ("Der Minimalkalkül," *Compositio Mathematica*, Vol. 4, 119–136).

TECHNICAL ELIMINATIONS OF NEGATION

Do the developments just sketched mean that we can dispense with negative facts by saying that the facts stated by true negative statements are ones that do not involve any special concept of negation but only (in one version) Nicod's stroke or (in the other) implication and universality? The suggestion, especially in its Peircean form, has its attractions. Peirce's definition would at least explain why negation is a proper subject of study for pure logicians. Logic studies universal rules of implication; even the purest logic must study whatever is involved in the very notions of implication and universality; and what Peirce means by negation is thus involved. Facts as to what is not the case are in this view only an instance of a more general type of complex fact without which logic would be impossible—namely, facts as to what leads to what.

Against this suggestion one might adduce the extreme artificiality and arbitrariness of these symbolic devices. Consider the fact that it is equally possible in a symbolic system to define "and" in terms of "or" and "not" and "or" in terms of "and" and "not." Whatever this fact signifies, it cannot signify that "Not (not-*p* or not-*q*)" is the real meaning of "*p* and *q*" and that the very form "*p* or *q*" that is used in this explanation has for its real meaning "Not (not-*p* and not-*q*)." This procedure would obviously be circular, and for this reason we cannot, even symbolically, have both definitions in the same system. It is obvious that the form "or" cannot be both simple and unanalyzable and a complex built up out of "and" and "not"; at least, it can only be this by being used ambiguously and, similarly, *mutatis mutandis,* with "and." The systems with the different definitions are equivalent in the sense that, given suitably chosen axioms, the same formulas will appear in them as theorems, and the undefined "and" (or "or") and the defined one are equivalent in the sense of having the same truth tables. But if there is an intuitively simple meaning of the form "*p* and *q*," "and" in this sense simply does not appear (is not symbolized) in a system which has only "or" and "not" as its undefined symbols and introduces "*p* and *q*" as short for "Not (not-*p* or not-*q*)." Primitiveness in a convenient calculus is one thing; intuitive or conceptual simplicity, another. No one symbolic system, we may surmise, can express everything, and in any given system we can take whatever we please as undefined, even if its intuitive meaning is complex.

Turning now to the calculi in which "not" is defined, it is notoriously difficult to explain the meaning of Nicod's stroke except by saying that "*p* | *q*" means "Not both *p* and *q*" or that it means "Either not-*p* or not-*q*"; furthermore, the "not" that is introduced by defining "Not-*p*" as "*p* | *p*" cannot be the "not" which is used in this explanation, though for purposes of logical calculation it may serve just as well. It could similarly be said that the "if" which Peirce uses in his definition of "not" cannot be understood without a more primeval "not" being presupposed. For Peirce did not use "If *p*, then *q*" in the familiar sense in which it means that *q* would be a logical consequence of *p*; it is not true that whenever *p* happens not to be the case, it would logically follow from it that everything whatever is true. Even the colloquial "If you believe that, you would believe anything" is not said of anything we wish to deny but only of particularly outrageous items (things that not only are not, but also could not, be the case). What Peirce meant by "If *p*, then *q*," it might be said, can be explained only by saying that it means "Not at once *p* and not-*q*," and this explanation uses a "not" that cannot be derived from his definition because the definition presupposes that "not."

Additionally, it might be argued that our intuitions as to what is a construction from simpler conceptions and what is itself simple are not very reliable and that if a definition introduces new economies into a calculus and, still more, if it brings a new unity to a whole subject, this may well be a symptom that it also reveals what is conceptually fundamental. The treatment of "not being the case" as an extreme case of implication—as "implying too much," so to speak—does at least reflect something important about the relation between the two concepts. A proposition's implying something, having consequences, is like its taking a risk, and its not being the case is its having too strong consequences.

See also Brouwer, Luitzen Egbertus Jan; Correspondence Theory of Truth; De Morgan, Augustus; Frege, Gottlob; Logic, Traditional; Nothing; Peirce, Charles Sanders; Presupposition; Propositions, Judgments, Sentences, and Statements; Russell, Bertrand Arthur William; Stoicism.

Bibliography

For clear summaries of the stock problems see J. N. Keynes, *Formal Logic,* 4th ed. (London, 1906), Part I, Ch. 4; Part II, Ch. 3; and Appendix B. See also W. E. Johnson, *Logic* (Cambridge, U.K.: Cambridge University Press, 1921), Part I, Chs. 5 and 14.

For the special insights of certain major writers see C. S. Peirce, *Collected Papers,* edited by Charles Hartshorne, Paul Weiss, and Arthur W. Burks, 8 vols. (Cambridge, MA: Harvard University Press, 1931–1958), II.356, 378–380, 550, 593–600; III.381–384, 407–414. See also Peirce's article "Syllogism," in *Century Dictionary* (New York: Century, 1889–1901); Gottlob Frege, "Negation," in *Translations from the Philosophical Writings of Gottlob Frege,* edited by P. T. Geach and Max Black (Oxford: Blackwell, 1952); and Bertrand Russell, *Introduction to Mathematical Philosophy* (London: Allen and Unwin, 1919), Ch. 14; "The Philosophy of Logical Atomism," Lectures I–II, in *Logic and Knowledge* (London: Allen and Unwin, 1956); *An Inquiry into Meaning and Truth* (New York: Norton, 1940), Ch. 4; and *Human Knowledge, Its Scope and Limits* (New York: Simon and Schuster, 1948), Ch. 9.

See also Ludwig Wittgenstein, *Tractatus Logico-Philosophicus,* translated by D. F. Pears and B. F. McGuinness (London: Routledge and Paul, 1961), 1.12, 2.06, 4.06–4.1, 4.25–4.463, 5.254, 5.43–5.44, 5.451, 5.512, 5.5151, 6.1201–6.1203.

On Wittgenstein (and Russell and Frege) see also G. E. M. Anscombe, *An Introduction to Wittgenstein's Tractatus* (London: Hutchinson University Library, 1959), Chs. 1–4.

On falsehood and meaninglessness see J. M. Shorter's classic piece, "Meaning and Grammar," in *Australasian Journal of Philosophy* 34 (1956): 73–91.

Various philosophical problems concerning the nature of negation are discussed in the following works: F. H. Bradley, *Principles of Logic* (London: K. Paul, Trench, 1883; 2nd ed., London: Oxford University Press, 1922), Vol. I, Book 1, Ch. 3, and Terminal Essay 6; Bernard Bosanquet, *Logic or the Morphology of Knowledge*, 2 vols. (London: Clarendon Press, 1888), Vol. I, Ch. 7, Secs. 1–3, 5; Raphael Demos, "A Discussion of a Certain Type of Negative Proposition," *Mind* 24 (1917): 188ff; Ralph M. Eaton, *Symbolism and Truth* (Cambridge, MA: Harvard University Press, 1925); J. Cook Wilson, *Statement and Inference*, 2 vols. (Oxford: Clarendon Press, 1926), Vol. I, Ch. 12; J. D. Mabbott, Gilbert Ryle, and H. H. Price, symposium, "Negation," *PAS*, Supp., 9 (1929); F. P. Ramsey, "Facts and Propositions" (1927), in his *Foundations of Mathematics* (London: K. Paul, Trench, Trubner, 1931), pp. 138–155; A. J. Ayer, "Negation," *Journal of Philosophy* 49 (1952): 797–815, reprinted in his *Philosophical Essays* (London: Macmillan, 1954); Morris Lazerowitz, "Negative Terms," *Analysis* 12 (1951–1952): 51–66, reprinted in *Philosophy and Analysis,* edited by Margaret MacDonald (Oxford, 1954); R. L. Cartwright, "Negative Existentials," *Journal of Philosophy* 57 (1960): 629–639, reprinted in *Philosophy and Ordinary Language,* edited by Charles E. Caton (Urbana: University of Illinois Press, 1963); and Gerd Buchdahl, "The Problem of Negation," *Philosophy and Phenomenological Research* 22 (1961): 163–178.

A. N. Prior (1967)

NEGATION IN INDIAN PHILOSOPHY

From the early centuries CE onward, the philosophical traditions of ancient India produced theories of negation in a broad variety of contexts, dealing with such diverse issues as negative existentials, the referentiality of empty terms, and the laws of the excluded middle and double negation. Highly technical expositions of logical principles pertaining to negation can be found in particular, though not exclusively, in the literature of the so-called New Nyāya (*Navya-Nyāya*) as of approximately the tenth century (Ingalls 1951, Matilal 1968). Earlier theories are noteworthy especially for their reflections on the nature of absence and its knowledge, in other words, for addressing the issue of negative facts and negative knowledge. These theories developed on the background of an overarching discourse about instruments of knowledge (*pramāṇa*) that shaped philosophical debate from the first centuries CE onward throughout the first millennium and is one of the most distinctive traits of classical Indian philosophizing.

Modern research on Indian theories of negation is still at a preliminary stage, and source materials in some important areas are transmitted only in fragments. On the basis of what is currently known, the Vaiśeṣika, the Nyāya, and the Mīmāṃsā traditions of Indian philosophy, as well as the logico-epistemological branch of Buddhism, deserve to be highlighted for their theories of negative knowledge. The Vaiśeṣika, an early philosophy of nature that emerged during the first two centuries CE, is mainly concerned with comprehensive enumeration and identification of the constituents of the world. The Nyāya, which originated in an old debate tradition and is primarily interested in the method of proof, integrated the Vaiśeṣika's ontological foundations into its own set of logical and epistemological principles (Franco and Preisendanz 1998). The Mīmāṃsā, originally devoted mainly to the exegesis of the Veda, likewise took over Vaiśeṣika ontology, but with much more creative adaptation. Within the Mīmāṃsā, the views of Kumārila (early seventh century CE) about absence and its knowledge differ from those of Prabhākara, who may have been Kumārila's contemporary. The logico-epistemological branch of Buddhism has as its two main representatives Dignāga (late fifth/early sixth century) and Dharmakīrti (early seventh century), of whom the latter developed a succinct theory of negative knowledge, perhaps in critical response to Kumārila.

FORMS OF ABSENCE AND THEIR KNOWLEDGE IN VAIŚEṢIKA LITERATURE

In the *Vaiśeṣikasūtra* (*VS*), a compilation of often elliptic mnemonic sentences that gradually grew as of the first two centuries CE, we find disparate identifications of specific forms of absences and brief statements of how some of them are known. As interpreted by the earliest available commentary by Candrānanda (active between the sixth and tenth centuries), *VS* 9,1–5 present four varieties of absence: the prior absence of an effect in its cause (*prāgabhāva*), the posterior absence of a cause after its destruction (*pradhvaṃsābhāva*), the mutual absence (*anyonyābhāva*) as the mutual difference between two things like a cow and a horse, and the absolute absence (*atyantābhāva*) of, for example, a hare's horn. Further forms of absences, added in *VS* 9,8–11, were most likely inserted into the text at a later stage. *VS* 9,6–7 describe, again according to Candrānanda, how prior and posterior absence are known, but without specifying an instrument of knowledge.

According to the *Praśastapādabhāṣya* by Praśastapāda (early sixth century), which comes to represent classical Vaiśeṣika thought, absence is cognized through inference, but not through a separate instrument of knowledge, for just as an arisen effect is an inferential sign for the occurrence of its sufficient causes, so is the nonarisen effect an inferential sign for the nonoccurrence of its sufficient causes. Candramati, whose *Daśapadārthaśāstra* was most probably composed between 450 and 550 and is only preserved in Chinese translation and presents an idiosyncratic version of Vaiśeṣika, lists absence as a separate ontological category. Divided into five forms, it is the object of inference. In *Śrīdhara's Nyāyakandalī* (late tenth century), and in *Udayana's Kiraṇāvalī* (early eleventh century), absence is likewise accorded the status of a separate ontological category.

THE KNOWLEDGE OF ABSENCE IN *NYĀYASŪTRA, -BHĀṢYA,* AND *-VĀRTTIKA*

In the *Nyāyasūtra* (*NS*), the foundational text of the Nyāya tradition that was formed between the second and fifth centuries, the knowability of further forms of absences, over and above prior and posterior absence—mutual and absolute absence are not dealt with—is emphatically defended, on the basis of an example that Vātsyāyana's commentary *Nyāyabhāṣya* (late fifth century) explains as follows: With regards to a pile of marked and unmarked clothes, someone is told "get the unmarked clothes!" and then cognizes the absence of marks in some clothes (commentary on *NS* 2,2,8; Kellner 1997; for a different interpretation of this section from *NS*, compare Matilal 1968). Whereas these remarks can be read as an attempt to expand the scope of knowable absence, the beginning portion of the *Nyāyabhāṣya* addresses the knowability of absence from a general viewpoint. For Nyāya, knowing reality, that is, the "being such [of the sixteen cardinal principles of Nyāya]" (*tattva*), is required for attaining liberation from the cycle of rebirth. Reality is the existence of what exists and the nonexistence of what does not exist. Knowledge that something does not exist arises when, through a certain instrument of knowledge, something else is known to exist, based on the thought process "if this [absentee] existed here, it would have to be cognized just like this [actually existing thing]; because its cognition is absent, it does not exist." The instrument of knowledge that illuminates something existent also illuminates something nonexistent. In keeping with this line of thought, the subcommentator Uddyotakara (c. 550–610) specifies absence as an object of

sensory perception in his *Nyāyavārttika*; this becomes the orthodox Nyāya position.

THE MĪMĀṂSAKA KUMĀRILA: A SEPARATE INSTRUMENT OF KNOWLEDGE FOR KNOWING ABSENCE

Both the Buddhist epistemologist Dharmakīrti and the Mīmāṃsaka Kumārila developed comprehensive and detailed theories about the knowledge of absences. But whereas Dharmakīrti appears to have found his way of formulating and addressing the knowledge of absence as a philosophical problem only gradually, in the course of his works *Pramāṇavārttika, Pramāṇaviniścaya,* and *Hetubindu* (Kellner 2003), Kumārila's conception of absence and its knowledge in his *Ślokavārttika* is already part and parcel of a general philosophical approach that John Taber (2001) dubs a theory of the unitary nature of substance. All features of a substance, while different from each other, are identical with the substance itself and indirectly with each other. Nonexistence is an integral building block of reality in that every real entity is existent as itself and nonexistent as everything else (Kellner 1996, 1997). Accordingly, nonexistence has the function of accounting for the unmixed character of real entities. Kumārila distinguishes the four types of absence that are later enumerated by Candrānanda while commenting on *Vaiśeṣikasūtra* 9,1–5. In keeping with the claim that an entity is nonexistent as something else, Kumārila describes all four types with the help of relational statements—a hare's head, for instance, is nonexistent as a horn-bearer, or a cow is nonexistent as a horse.

Though a part of every real entity, nonexistence is nevertheless separate from existence and requires an instrument of knowledge of its own. The five instruments of knowledge—perception, inference, verbal knowledge, analogy, and implication—are limited to grasping existence, whereas nonexistence is apprehended by the sixth instrument of knowledge called absence, an idea that in general must have been voiced already before Praśastapāda, as he rejected it. According to his commentators, Kumārila took it over from an earlier commentator on the *Mīmāṃsāsūtras* cited in the *Śabarabhāṣya* (early sixth century), but Kumārila's interpretation of this commentator's statements are heavily contested by the Prābhākara-Mīmāṃsakas.

As an instrument of knowledge, Kumārila's *absence* is the nonarising of the other five instruments. It can manifest itself either as the soul's (*ātman*) not being transformed into the knower of the absentee as existent, or as the knowledge of nonexistence as a part of a real entity (on the latter alternative whose interpretation is problematic, see Kellner 1996, Taber 2001). Whether an entity is known as itself, or as not another, depends on the cognizing subject's intention; the respectively uncognized part always acts as a supporting factor. Kumārila strongly disagrees with the Nyāya view that absence is grasped by sensory perception; his main counterargument is that the five external senses are incapable of coming into contact (sannikarṣa) with absence, and Nyāya, after all, requires such contact for any sense perception. Among others, it is this argument that led later Nyāya philosophers like Jayanta (late ninth century) and Bhāsarvajña (tenth century) to revisit the role of contact in the definition of perception (for Jayanta, see Gillon 1997). In addition, Kumārila also argues against the theory that the absence of an object is known through an inference from the nonarising of the five other instruments of knowledge, mainly because this nonarising cannot have an established inferential connection with the absence of the object that any inference requires for being sound, and because the nonarising itself cannot be known—as the absence of arising, it would itself have to be inferred from a further nonarising of instruments of knowledge, and so forth.

In the *Ślokavārttika* and in his *Tantravārttika*, Kumārila applies this instrument of knowledge in arguments that reject entities that opponents assume to exist (Kellner 1996). After demonstrating that these cannot be known by any of the five other instruments, Kumārila concludes that they can only be known through absence, as a result of which they are nonexistent. Such types of arguments are aimed at, for instance, the emptiness (*śūnyatā*) of external reality of Buddhist idealism, a human author of the Vedas as propagated by Buddhists, and an omniscient human being that is, again, assumed by Buddhists. On the whole, Kumārila's theory of nonexistence and its knowledge seems to be geared to accounting for the nature of reality and to establishing philosophical and religious truths. Empirical knowledge of negative states of affairs in everyday life are at best a secondary concern.

DHARMAKĪIRTI'S THEORY OF NEGATIVE ASCERTAINMENT THROUGH INFERENCE

Like other Buddhist philosophers before him, Dharmakīirti believed that absence cannot be an object of perception because perception arises from its particular object as a cause, bearing the object's shape; an absence, however, is devoid of any causal capacity. This belief also informs Dharmakīirti's rejection of absence as a separate instrument of knowledge, condensely articulated in *Pramāṇaviniścaya*, chapter 3, prose after verse 48, for any such instrument would have to be directly or indirectly caused by its object, and *absence* as an object lacks such a capacity.

Because for Dharmakīirti there is no further instrument of knowledge besides perception and inference, negative knowledge is for him the result of inference. While perception has direct and unmediated access to real particulars in a nonconceptual fashion, inference operates with properties and concepts that are superimposed on particulars in accordance with the practical function that these jointly fulfill, and in accordance with linguistic conventions. As a result, inferences that establish negative states of affairs, based on a special type of evidence called nonperception (*anupalabdhi*) that is exclusively reserved for this purpose, ultimately prove that something is suitable for being ascertained as, and in a second step verbally referred to or physically treated as absent. They do not in any way prove a real absence that might be given independently of being cognized.

Furthermore, such inferences are limited to ascertaining the absence of particular objects that, if they existed under given circumstances, would inevitably be perceived. For entities where such a necessary perceivedness cannot be ensured, either because they are intrinsically beyond the realm of perception or because the specific environmental conditions for their perception are incomplete, not perceiving them only establishes that we do not know that they exist, not that we know that they do not exist. A proper inference on the basis of the nonperception of a perceptible object is accordingly exemplified as "in this spot on the ground, a jar does not exist because, as an object that would necessarily be perceived if it existed here, it is not perceived." From this basic inferential structure, a variety of patterns are derived with the help of further relationships such as causality, extensional relations between genus and species, and factual incompatibility, as well as contrariety and contradiction between concepts.

In his further explication of the nonperception of perceptibles, Dharmakīirti works with the notion of an implicative negation (*paryudāsa*) developed in Sanskrit grammatical literature (Cardona 1967). When understood as expressing implicative negation, a negative nominal compound formed with the prefix *a(n)*-—here: *an-upalabdhi*—affirms a state of affairs other than the negated one. Nonperception is thus explicated as another perception, that is, as the perception of a specific object other than the absentee—not perceiving an entity like a jar is nothing other than perceiving an empty spot on the ground.

In Dharmakīrti's earliest work, the *Pramāṇavārttika*, this claim is adopted because the alternative consideration of nonperception as the mere absence of a perception would result in specific antinomies, such as an infinite justificational regress. As an absence of a perception, nonperception itself would have to be established with the help of a further instance of nonperception, and so forth. Once nonperception is assumed to be the perception of another object, it can be established through the intrinsic self-awareness of that perception. In its most developed form in the *Hetubindu*, the absence of the absentee is likewise explained away as the presence of the perceived object, and the argumentation acquires a more reductive ontological flavor. In addition, the otherness of the absentee and the object perceived in its stead is narrowed down to one where, if both objects existed, they would have to mix within one perception. Prabhākara, the Mīmāṃsā philosopher who rejects Kumārila's separate instrument of knowledge, is credited with a similar view that identifies the nonperception of one object with the perception of another that lacks the absentee. However, as his statements in the *Bṛhatī* are highly elliptic, further details of his theory and its historical and theoretical relationship to Dharmakīrti's remain obscure.

Dharmakīrti's commentators contrast his account with that of his teacher, Īśvarasena (late sixth/early seventh century), whose works are lost. Īśvarasena is said to have understood nonperception as the simple absence of the absentee's perception, based on the notion of a simple negation (*prasajyapratiṣedha*), which, like that of implicative negation (*paryudāsa*), was developed in grammatical literature. As a counterpart to implicative negation, simple negation involves only the denial of an action—here: perception—and does not further imply the affirmation of a different state of affairs. It is not known whether Īśvarasena developed his theory of nonperception, which he is said to have assumed as a third instrument of knowledge besides perception and inference, merely to solve specific problems of the theory of inference, or whether he intended it as a general theory of negative knowledge.

See also Atomic Theory in Indian Philosophy; Brahman; Causation in Indian Philosophy; Knowledge in Indian Philosophy; Liberation in Indian Philosophy; Meditation in Indian Philosophy; Philosophy of Language in India; Self in Indian Philosophy; Truth and Falsity in Indian Philosophy; Universal Properties in Indian Philosophy.

Bibliography

Cardona, George. "Negation in Pāṇinian Rules." *Language* 43 (1) (1967): 34–56.

Chakrabarti, Arindam. *Denying Existence: The Logic, Epistemology, and Pragmatics of Negative Existentials and Fictional Discourse*. Dordrecht, Netherlands: Kluwer Academic, 1997.

Cox, Collett. "On the Possibility of a Nonexistent Object of Consciousness: Sarvāstivādin and Dārṣṭāntika Theories." *Journal of the International Association of Buddhist Studies* 11 (1) (1988): 31–87.

Franco, Eli, and Karin Preisendanz. "Nyāya-Vaiśeṣika." In *Routledge Encyclopedia of Philosophy*, edited by Edward Craig. London: Routledge, 1998.

Gillon, Brendan. "Negative Facts and Knowledge of Negative Facts." In *Relativism, Suffering, and Beyond*, edited by Purushottama Bilimoria and Jitendra Mohanty, 129–149. Delhi, India: Oxford University Press, 1997.

Gillon, Brendan. "Two Forms of Negation in Sanskrit." *Lokaprajñā* 1 (1) (1987): 81–89.

Ingalls, Daniel H. H. *Materials for the Study of Navya-Nyāya Logic*. Cambridge, MA: Harvard University Press, 1951.

Kellner, Birgit. "Integrating Negative Knowledge into *Pramāṇa* Theory: The Development of the *dṛśyānupalabdhi* in Dharmakīrti's Earlier Works." *Journal of Indian Philosophy* 31 (1–2) (2003): 121–159.

Kellner, Birgit. *Nichts bleibt nichts. Die buddhistische Zurückweisung von Kumārilas abhāvapramāṇa. Übersetzung und Interpretation von Śāntarakṣitas Tattvasaṅgraha vv. 1 647–1 690 mit Kamalaśīas Tattvasa:grahapañjikā sowie Ansätze und Arbeitshypothesen zur Geschichte negativer Erkenntnis in der indischen Philosophie*. Vienna, Austria: Arbeitskreis für Tibetische und Buddhistische Studien, Universität Wien, 1997. The second part of this German-language publication contains the relevant textual materials mentioned in this entry, with German translation and analysis.

Kellner, Birgit. "There Are No Pots in the Ślokavārttika: SV *abhāvapariccheda* 11 and Patterns of Negative Cognition in Indian Philosophy." *Journal of the Oriental Institute* (Baroda) 46 (3–4) (1996): 143–167. Though marked with a publication date of 1996, this article was written in 1999 and supersedes parts of Kellner 1997.

Matilal, Bimal Krishna. *The Navya-Nyāya Doctrine of Negation*. Cambridge, MA: Harvard University Press, 1968.

Matilal, Bimal Krisha. "Reference and Existence in Nyāya and Buddhist Logic." *Journal of Indian Philosophy* 1 (1970): 83–110.

Shaw, J. L. "The Nyāya on Cognition and Negation." *Journal of Indian Philosophy* 8 (1980): 279–302.

Staal, J. F. "Negation and the Law of Contradiction in Indian Thought: A Comparative Study." *Bulletin of the School of Oriental and African Studies* 25 (1) (1962): 52–71.

Taber, John. "Much Ado about Nothing: Kumārila, Śāntarakṣita, and Dharmakīrti on the Cognition of Non-being." *Journal of the American Oriental Society* 121 (1) (2001): 72–88. A review article of Kellner 1997.

Birgit Kellner (2005)

NELSON, LEONARD

(1882–1927)

Leonard Nelson, a German critical philosopher and the founder of the Neo-Friesian school, was born in Berlin. After studying mathematics and philosophy he qualified for teaching as a *Privatdozent* in the natural science division of the philosophical faculty at Göttingen in 1909. In 1919 he was appointed extraordinary professor.

THE CRITICAL SCHOOL

Nelson's philosophical work was concerned mainly with two problems: the establishment of a scientific foundation for philosophy by means of a critical method and the systematic development of philosophical ethics and philosophy of right and their consequences for education and politics.

Nelson's search for a strictly scientific foundation and development of philosophy soon led him to critical philosophy. Nelson took the *Critique of Pure Reason* to be a treatise on method and regarded the critical examination of the capacities of reason as its decisive achievement. Through this critique alone could philosophical concepts be clarified and philosophical judgments traced back to their sources in cognition. Therefore, Nelson undertook a close examination of the thought of Jakob Friedrich Fries (1773–1843), the one post-Kantian philosopher who had concentrated on Immanuel Kant's critical method, carried it further, and tried to clarify its vaguenesses and contradictions.

While Nelson was still a student, he began to collect Fries's writings. These were not easily available, for Fries was hardly known at that time; when he was mentioned at all in philosophical treatises, it was as the representative of an outmoded psychologism. In his own first works Nelson attempted to defend Fries against this reproach. Together with a few friends whom he had interested in Fries's philosophy, he began to publish a *neue Folge* (new series) of *Abhandlungen der Fries'schen Schule* in 1904—the same year in which he wrote his doctoral dissertation on Fries. A few years later he founded, together with these same friends, the Jakob-Friedrich-Fries-Gesellschaft to promote the methodical development of critical philosophy.

CRITICAL METHOD AND CRITIQUE OF REASON

In his own writings devoted to the critical method, Nelson distinguished between the critique of reason and two misinterpretations of it, transcendentalism and psychologism. The critique of reason was to prepare the grounds for a philosophical system and to give this system an assured scientific basis by means of a critical investigation of the faculty of cognition. Posing the problem in this way seems to require the critique of reason and the system of philosophy to be adapted to each other in such a way that either the critique of reason must be developed a priori as a philosophical discipline, because of the rational character of philosophy, or philosophy must be conceived as a branch of psychology, since the investigation of knowledge by means of the critique of reason belongs to psychology. Transcendentalism sacrifices the main methodical thesis of the critique of reason, that the highest abstractions of philosophy cannot be dogmatically postulated but must be derived from concrete investigation of the steps leading to knowledge. Psychologism fails to recognize the character of philosophical questions and answers, which is independent of psychological concepts.

Kant did not unequivocally answer the question whether the critique of reason should be developed as a science from inner experience of one's own knowledge or as a philosophical theory from a priori principles. His subjective approach, according to which philosophical abstractions should be introduced by a critique of the faculty of cognition, indicates the first interpretation, but in carrying out his investigations—and in the asserted parallelism between general and transcendental logic as well as in the demand for a transcendental proof of metaphysical principles—Kant tacitly assumed the second interpretation and interpreted the theorems of the critique as a priori judgments. Fries, who was mainly concerned with countering the contemporary tendency to develop Kant's teaching in the direction of transcendentalism, took the subjective approach and developed it consistently from inner experience, without, however, transforming philosophical questions and answers into psychological ones. The boundary between Fries's work and psychologism is not so clear, and for this reason most of his critics misunderstood his philosophy as a psychologistic system, albeit not a consistent one.

Nelson solved the problem that philosophy based on the critique of reason seemed necessarily to lead either to transcendentalism or to psychologism by proving that both tacitly assume that a basis of knowledge must consist of proving philosophical principles from theorems of the critique of reason. If the theorems of the critique and the foundations of the philosophical system were in fact related to each other in the same way that the premises and conclusions of logical problems are related, then indeed the critique of reason and philosophy would have to be identical—that is, they would both have to be either empirical and psychological or rational and a priori. By investigating the problem of the critique of reason Nelson showed that and why this premise is mistaken: The critique serves to clarify one's understanding of the origin of philosophical notions and of their function in the human cognition of facts. Cognition is an activity of the self, motivated by sensual stimulation; data acquired by sensual stimulation are related to one another by cognition of the surrounding world. The function of the critique of reason is to demonstrate the connecting ideas in this process and the assumed criteria by which these ideas are applied by analyzing the concrete steps in cognition and to follow these connecting ideas back to their origin in the cognitive faculty by means of psychological theory; it is not its function to prove the objective validity of the principles in which these criteria are expressed. These principles themselves are of a philosophical rather than a psychological nature. They cannot be derived from the statements of the critique; indeed, since they are the basic assumptions of all perception, they cannot be derived from any judgments more valid than they are.

CRITIQUE OF REASON AND PHILOSOPHY. The connection between the critique of reason and the system of philosophy, according to this theory, is not one of logical proof; it is derived, rather, from "reason's faith in itself," as Fries put it, from the fact that all striving for knowledge assumes faith in the possibility of cognition. This faith is faith in reason, inasmuch as reason is the faculty of cognition instructed by the stimulation of the senses. This faith is maintained by the agreement of cognitions, but it cannot be further checked or justified by a comparison of cognitions with the object cognized. This sets an unsurpassable limit to the provability of cognitions. Nelson expressed this in his paper on the impossibility of the theory of knowledge, in which he understood the theory to be an attempt to investigate scientifically the objective validity of cognition. In contrast, the critique of reason should limit itself to investigating the direction in which faith in cognition is in fact turned.

In carrying out this investigation Fries and Nelson distinguished between indirect cognition, supported by some other claim to truth, and direct cognition, which simply claims the faith of reason and which therefore neither needs nor has any justification, even when it is obscure and enters consciousness only in its application as a criterion for the unity of sensually perceivable isolated cognition. Fries and Nelson, in agreement with Kant, considered the criteria which belong solely to rea-

son to include the pure intuition of space and time and their metaphysical combinations according to the categories of substance, causality, and reciprocal action.

NATURAL PHILOSOPHY. Nelson's interpretation of cognition led him to the problem of a mathematical natural philosophy that had been sketched by Kant and further developed by Fries; this philosophy established a priori an "armament of hypotheses" for the empirical-inductive investigation of natural laws. It coincided in fact with the basic principles of classical mechanics and thereby came into conflict with modern physics. Nelson neither minimized this conflict nor confused it with problems of the principles of critical natural philosophy. He saw physics as being in the process of a radical changeover to modern theories, which had by no means yet been ordered into a conflict-free system comparable to that of classical physics. He was sure that every physical theory must go beyond the data provided by observation and experiment in developing concepts and making assertions. And he was convinced that the positivistic, antimetaphysical tendencies of contemporary physicists promoted a tacit and therefore uncritical metaphysics. Without himself being able to solve the conflict that had arisen within critical philosophy, he was convinced the progressive clarification of modern theories would lead back to a physics based on classical mechanics.

CRITICAL ETHICS

BASIC PRINCIPLES. Nelson systematically applied the critical method in his studies in practical philosophy—ethics in the broadest sense of the word, including philosophy of right and philosophically based educational and political theory. He added his own critique of practical reason to those of his predecessors. He developed his own processes, both for what he called abstraction (analysis of the assumptions underlying practical ethical value judgments) and for determining, by an empirical study of value judgments, "the interests of pure practical reason," that is, ethical demands put to the human will by reason itself. It is these interests that make value judgments possible. Nelson derived two basic ethical principles from these interests: the law of the balanced consideration of all interests affected by one's own deeds and the ideal of forming one's own life independently, according to the ideas of the true, the beautiful, and the good. These two principles were linked by the fact that, on the one hand, the law of balanced consideration, as a categorical imperative, determines the necessary limiting condition for the ideal value of human behavior; on the other hand, the ideal of rational self-determination leads to the doctrine of the true interests of man and finds in these interests the standard for a balanced consideration of conflicting interests.

NELSON'S SYSTEM. From these two principles alone Nelson developed his system of philosophical ethics; he limited himself to such consequences as could be derived from these principles purely philosophically—without the addition of experience—but he attempted to grasp them completely and systematically. In this he was influenced, first, by his interest in systematically and strictly justifying the assumptions used in every single step and the logical connections of the concepts appearing in the principles and, second, by his interest in applying this practical science. The principles demonstrated are formal and permit determination of concrete ethical demands only through their application to given circumstances as justified by experience. But it is precisely this application of the principles to the world of experience that requires preparatory philosophical investigation if the application is to be guarded against hasty generalization of single results, in which changing circumstances are not taken into account, and against opportunistic adaptation to circumstances without regard for the practical consequences of ethical principles. In the system as a whole, ethics and philosophy of right appear side by side. Nelson distinguished between them according to different ways of applying the law of balanced consideration. As a categorical imperative, this law demands of the human will the balanced consideration of other persons' interests affected by its actions. By its content it determines the duties of the individual by the rights others have with regard to him; in this respect it is related to communal life and thereby provides a criterion for the value of a social order. Nelson defined this criterion as the concept of the state of right, by which he meant the condition of a society in which the interests of all members are protected against wrongful violation. Ethics, by this definition, is concerned with the duties of the individual; philosophy of right is concerned with the state of right. To each of these disciplines Nelson added another concerned with the conditions of realizing the values studied by them: philosophical pedagogics, as the theory of the education of man to the ethical good, and philosophical politics, as the theory of the realization of the state of right.

VALIDITY OF ETHICAL PRINCIPLES. The logically transparent construction of the entire system reveals clearly that the principles behind all further developments are strictly valid in all cases but can be applied only through full consideration of the concrete circumstances in each individual case; since they are objectively valid, they are not subject to arbitrary decisions and are valid even in cases where human insight and will fail to understand them; but they are justified only by reference to reason, which makes possible for each individual the autonomic recognition of these standards and the critical examination of their applications. Thus, the demands of equality for all before the law and of equality of rights are compatible with the demand to differentiate according to given circumstances; and the demands of force against injustice remain linked to those of freedom of criticism and of public justification for the legal necessity of certain coercive measures. Such coercive measures are particularly necessary when the freedom of man to form himself rationally within the framework of his own life is threatened; this freedom can be threatened because man's true need for it is at first obscure and can therefore be mistaken and suppressed.

Nature and chance. One conclusion appears again and again, determining the structure of the whole system. In each case it is a question of fighting with chance, to which the realization of the good is subject in nature. What happens in nature is, according to the laws of nature, dependent on the given circumstances and on the forces working through them, which are indifferent to ethical values: Under the laws of nature it is a matter of chance whether what should happen is in fact what happens or whether ethical demands are ignored. But what ethics demands should not be subject to chance but assured by the human will. Following this line of thought, Nelson derived the law of character in ethics, which demands from man the establishment of a basic willingness to fulfill his duty, by which he makes himself independent of given concrete circumstances; his inclinations and the influences on his will may or may not be in agreement with the commands of duty.

In the philosophy of right Nelson correspondingly finds certain postulates. These determine the forms of reciprocal action in society which alone assure just relations between individuals; among them are public justice, prosecutability, the law of contract, and the law of property. The transitions from ethics to pedagogy and from philosophy of right to politics are made in the same spirit. Education, among the many influences on man, should strengthen or create those elements that develop his capacity for good and oppose those that could weaken this capacity. Politics is concerned with the realization and securing of the state of right determined by the postulates of philosophy of right. This problem leads to the postulation of a state seeking the rule of law and having the power to maintain itself against forces in society opposing the rule of law. A sufficiently powerful federation of states is necessary to regulate the legal relationships between states.

The same conclusion is reached in the last section of Nelson's *System der philosophischen Rechtslehre und Politik.* Here again, in a state of nature it is a matter of chance to what degree states realize the rule of law or violate its demands, unless men having insight into justice and moral will work to transform the existing state into a just state. These men must interfere in the struggle between social groups and parties and must themselves band together into a party. In this case, therefore, the ideal of a just state leads to that of a party working to achieve it.

FREEDOM AND NECESSITY. The conflict between natural necessity and man's freedom and responsibility impelled Nelson's thinking. Ethical standards are valid for human action in nature and are therefore directly relevant to two apparently mutually exclusive forms of legality: The theoretical form, according to which everything that happens in nature (including human behavior) is determined by natural laws working through the existing powers, and the practical one, which presents the human will with duties that can either be violated and ignored or become man's purpose.

Thus on the one hand Nelson insisted that demonstrated ethical standards be maintained without compromise and rejected the skeptical assumption that man, as a limited creature of nature, was incapable of maintaining them; this assumption he considered a sacrifice of known ethical truth, a mere excuse for those who were able but not willing. On the other hand, he expected the human will to act according to the strongest motivation of the moment, without any guarantee from nature that this motivation would direct man toward what is ethically required. For this reason he rejected any speculation that in a state of nature the good would pave its own way.

Within the framework of the critique, Nelson thoroughly examined the question of how man's freedom could be reconciled with this natural law. He sought the answer in the doctrine of transcendental idealism that human knowledge is limited to the understanding of relationships in the sphere of experience but cannot achieve absolute perception of reality itself. In the consciousness of his freedom, which is indissolubly bound to the knowledge of his responsibility, man relates himself by faith to the world of that which is real in itself and superior to the limitations of nature. Nelson unified the two points of view by connecting two results of his investigations of the critique of reason: the principle of the existence of pure practical reason, which as a direct moral interest makes moral insight and moral motivation possible, and the principle of the original obscurity of this interest, according to which it does not determine judgment and will by its very existence but rather requires enlightenment and is dependent on stimulation.

EDUCATION AND POLITICS. Concern with the realization of ethical requirements led Nelson beyond his philosophical work to practical undertakings, in which he gave primary emphasis to politics, particularly to political education.

Toward the end of World War I Nelson collected a circle of pupils and coworkers who were willing to undergo intensive education and discipline in preparation for the political duties imposed by ethics and philosophy of right. Together with these pupils he founded the Internationaler Jugendbund and in January 1926 developed his own political organization, the Internationaler Sozialistischer Kampf-Bund. In 1924 he opened a "country educational institution," Landerziehungsheim Walkemühle, directed by his coworker Minna Specht. Here youths and children were trained in a closely knit educational and working community for activity in the workers' movement, until the school was closed and appropriated by the National Socialists in 1933.

As a teacher and educator Nelson had a strong effect on his pupils. He led them by masterly Socratic discussions to a clarification and critical examination of their own convictions, and he required them to carry out what they had recognized as just and good in their actions with the same consistency that he demanded of himself. "Ethics is there in order to be applied."

See also Epistemology; Epistemology, History of; Ethics; Fries, Jakob Friedrich; Kant, Immanuel; Neo-Kantianism; Psychologism.

Bibliography

WORKS BY NELSON

"Die kritische Methode und das Verhältnis der Psychologic zur Philosophic." *Abhandlungen der Fries'schen Schule,* n.f., 1 (1) (1904): 1–88.

"Jakob Friedrich Fries und seine jungsten Kritiker." *Abhandlungen der Fries'schen Schule,* n.f., 1 (2) (1905): 233–319.

"Bermerkungen über die nicht-Euklidische Geometric und den Ursprung der mathematischen Gewissheit."

Abhandlungen der Fries'schen Schule, n.f., 1 (2) (1905): 373–392; 1 (3) (1906): 393–430.

"Inhalt und Gegenstand, Grund und Begründung. Zur Kontroverse über die kritische Methode." *Abhandlungen der Fries'schen Schule,* n.f., 2 (1) (1907): 33–73.

"Ist metaphysikfreie Naturwissenschaft möglich?" *Abhandlungen der Fries'schen Schule,* n.f., 2 (3) (1908): 241–299.

"Über das sogenannte Erkenntnisproblem." *Abhandlungen der Fries'schen Schule,* n.f., 2 (4) (1908): 413–850.

"Bemerkungen zu den Paradoxien von Russell und Burali-Forti." *Abhandlungen der Fries'schen Schule,* n.f., 2 (3) (1908): 301–334. Written with Kurt Grelling.

"Untersuchungen über die Entwicklungsgeschichte der Kantischen Erkenntnistheorie." *Abhandlungen der Fries'schen Schule,* n.f., 3 (1) (1909): 33–96.

"Die Unmöglichkeit der Erkenntnistheorie." *Abhandlungen der Fries'schen Schule,* n.f., 3 (4) (1912): 583–617.

"Die Theorie des wahren Interesses und ihre rechtliche und politische Bedeutung." *Abhandlungen der Fries'schen Schule,* n.f., 4 (2) (1913): 395–423.

"Die kritische Ethik bei Kant, Schiller und Fries." *Abhandlungen der Fries'schen Schule,* n.f., 4 (3) (1914): 483–691.

Die Rechtswissenschaft ohne Recht. Kritische Betrachtungen über die Grundlagen des Staats- und Völkerrechts, insbesondere über die Lehre von der Souveränität. Leipzig: Veit, 1917.

Die Reformation der Gesinnung durch Erziehung zum Selbst-vertrauen. Gesammelte Aufsätze. Leipzig, 1917; 2nd enlarged ed., Leipzig, 1922.

Vorlesungen über die Grundlagen der Ethik. 3 vols. Leipzig: Veit, 1917–1932. Vol. II translated by Norbert Guterman as *System of Ethics.* New Haven, CT: Yale University Press, 1956.

Die Reformation der Philosophie durch die Kritik der Vernunft. Gesammelte Aufsätze. Leipzig, 1918.

Demokratie und Führerschaft. Leipzig, 1920.

Spuk, Einweihung in das Geheimnis der Wahrsagerkunst Oswald Spenglers. Leipzig: P. Reinhold, 1921.

"Kritische Philosophic und mathematische Axiomatik." *Unterrichtsblätter für Mathematik und Naturwissenschaft,* 34th year, (4 and 5) (1927): 108–115 and 136–142.

"Sittliche und religiöse Weltansicht." *XXVI Aasaner Studenten-Konferenz,* 7–25. Leipzig, 1922.

"Die Sokratische Methode." *Abhandlungen der Fries'schen Schule,* n.f., 5 (1) (1929): 21–78. Translated by Thomas K. Brown in *Socratic Method and Critical Philosophy.* New Haven, CT: Yale University Press, 1949. Selected essays.

Fortschritte und Rückschritte der Philosophie; von Hume und Kant bis Hegel und Fries. Frankfurt: Öffentliches Leben, 1962.

WORKS ON NELSON

Specht, Minna, and Willi Eichler, eds. *Leonard Nelson zum Gedächtnis.* Frankfurt, 1953. Contains essays.

Grete Henry-Hermann (1967)
Translated by Tessa Byck

NEMESIUS OF EMESA
(fl. c. 390)

Nemesius of Emesa was the author of a treatise, *De Natura Hominis* (On the nature of man), which is the earliest extant handbook of theological or philosophical "anthropology." All that is known of his life is that he was probably bishop of Emesa in Syria.

As a Christian, Nemesius viewed the Bible as his primary authority, but he derived the content of his work chiefly from Galen's *On the Use of the Parts of the Body,* which is superior to Nemesius's treatise both in thoroughness and originality; from Origen's *Commentary on Genesis*; and from some commentators on Aristotle, a few works by the Neoplatonist Porphyry, and doxographical materials. His subjects and sources can be outlined as follows: Ch. 1, man in the creation (Galen, Origen); Chs. 2–3, the soul and the body (doxographical, Porphyry, Galen); Chs. 4–5, the body and the elements (Galen); Chs. 6–14, the faculties of the soul, including human development, the senses, thought and memory, reason and speech (Galen, Porphyry); Chs. 15–28, the parts of the soul, the passions, and such matters as the nutritive and generative faculties and respiration (mostly Galen); Chs. 29–41, freedom, possibility, and fate (commentaries on Aristotle, Neoplatonists); Chs. 42–44, providence (in part ultimately from Posidonius, in part from Christian theologians).

In the last part of his book (Chs. 35ff.), Nemesius turns from minimizing the function of free will in human affairs (deliberation concerns only indifferent possibilities) to an elaborate attack upon the Stoic doctrine of fate and teaching about destiny. Utilizing Aristotle's distinction between voluntary and involuntary acts, he insists that men actually have free will, that its extent can be discovered (interrelated with the action of providence), and that it was given to mutable men so that they might become immutable. The work ends abruptly and seems to lack a conclusion.

Nemesius argued that the soul is an incorporeal being and is therefore immortal (in his opinion the latter point is also proved by the Bible). The problem of how it is united with the body is solved (Chs. 20–21) by following the Neoplatonist Ammonius. "Intelligibles" are capable of union with things adapted to receive them, but in such a union they remain confused and imperishable. The soul is "in a body" not locally but "in habitual relation of presence." From this analysis Nemesius turns in Ch. 22 to discuss the union of the divine Word with his manhood—as William Telfer points out, thus reversing the usual patristic argument. Nemesius claims that the union in Christ is therefore not by "divine favor" but is "grounded in nature."

See also Aristotle; Galen; Neoplatonism; Origen; Philosophical Anthropology; Porphyry.

Bibliography

The Greek text, with Latin translation, of *De Natura Hominis* is in *Patrologia Graeca,* edited by J. P. Migne (Paris, 1857–1866), Vol. XL, Cols. 508–818. There is an English translation by William Telfer in *Cyril of Jerusalem and Nemesius of Emesa,* Vol. IV of the Library of Christian Classics (Philadelphia: Westminster Press, 1955).

For works on Nemesius, see Werner Jaeger, *Nemesios von Emesa* (Berlin: Weidmann, 1914); H. A. Koch, *Quellenuntersuchungen zu Nemesius von Emesa* (Berlin, 1921); Johannes Quasten, *Patrology* (Westminster, MD: Newman Press, 1960), Vol. III, pp. 351–355, which includes a full bibliography. See also the articles by E. Skard, "Nemesiosstudien," in *Symbolae Osloenses* 15–16 (1936): 23–43; 17 (1937): 9–25; 18 (1938): 31–41; 19 (1939): 46–56; 22 (1942): 40–48; and Skard's article "Nemesios," in *Realencyclopädie der classischen Altertumswissenschaft,* Supp., VII (Stuttgart, 1940): Cols. 562–566.

Robert M. Grant (1967)

NEO-KANTIANISM

"Neo-Kantianism" is a term used to designate a group of somewhat similar movements that prevailed in Germany between 1870 and 1920 but had little in common beyond a strong reaction against irrationalism and speculative naturalism and a conviction that philosophy could be a "science" only if it returned to the method and spirit of Immanuel Kant. These movements were the fulfillment of Kant's prophecy that in a hundred years his philosophy would come into its own.

Because of the complexity and internal tensions in Kant's philosophy, not all the Neo-Kantians brought the same message from the Sage of Königsberg, and the diversity of their teachings was as great as their quarrels were notorious. At the end of the nineteenth century the Neo-Kantians were as widely separated as the first-generation Kantians had been at its beginning, and the various Neo-Kantian movements developed in directions further characterized by such terms as Neo-Hegelian and Neo-Fichtean. But whereas G. W. F. Hegel, Friedrich Schelling, Johann Gottlieb Fichte, and others had used the words of Kant while being alien to their spirit, the Neo-Kantians were, on the whole, faithful to the spirit while being revisionists with respect to the letter.

Attempting to legitimize their revisions by the *ipsissima verba* of Kant, they established the craft of "Kant-philology" and began an analysis of Kant's texts that had not been equaled in microscopic punctiliousness except in the exegesis of the Bible and of a few classical authors. Hans Vaihinger's immense commentary on the first seventy pages of the *Critique of Pure Reason* (*Commentar zu Kants "Kritik der reinen Vernunft,"* 2 vols., Berlin and Leipzig, 1881–1893) is an exemplar of this craft and industry.

Neo-Kantianism grew out of the peculiar social-cultural situation of German science and philosophy, and in turn it constituted a new academic situation with many characteristics of a long intellectual fad. Most of the groups of Neo-Kantians had their own journals—the *Philosophische Arbeiten* at Marburg, *Logos* at Heidelberg, the *Annalen der Philosophie und philosophischer Kritik* of Vaihinger, and the *Philosophische Abhandlungen* at Göttingen. (*Kant-Studien,* like the Kant *Gesellschaft,* was open to all.) Doctrines were known by the names of the universities where they originated; men entered and left the movement as if it were a church or political party; members of one school blocked the appointments and promotions of members of the others; eminent Kant scholars and philosophers who did not found their own schools or accommodate themselves to one of the established schools tended to be neglected as outsiders and contemned as amateurs. As many as seven distinct schools have been described by historians, but they do not agree on the programs, heresies, and bona fide membership of each school.

THE BEGINNINGS

So far as an intellectual movement can be said to have a beginning at a specific moment of time, Neo-Kantianism began with the publication at Stuttgart in 1865 of Otto Liebmann's *Kant und die Epigonen,* whose motto—"Back to Kant!"—has become famous. German philosophy was generally weak toward the middle of the nineteenth century; there was less interest in it, and less ability among its practitioners, than at perhaps any other time in modern German history. Earlier in the century, when Kant's philosophy had been submerged first in the great idealistic systems and then in those of nature-philosophy, there had been modest calls for a return to Kant (for instance, by I. H. Fichte, the son of J. G. Fichte, and by Ernst Reinhold, the son of K. L. Reinhold) as a means of escape from the kinds of philosophy that Kant would have held to be impossible and that seemed more and more to offer nothing of value to German cultural life as a counterbalance to the materialism attendant upon the flourishing of natural science, technology, and national economy. However, in the decade preceding Liebmann's book there had been signs of change.

ZELLER AND FISCHER. Eduard Zeller (1814–1908), in his Heidelberg lecture, *Ueber Bedeutung und Aufgabe der Erkenntnistheorie* (published Heidelberg, 1862), called for a return to epistemology; and this, he spelled out explicitly, meant a return to Kant. Kuno Fischer (1824–1907), the greatest historian of philosophy at that time and the teacher of Liebmann, Johannes Volkelt, and Wilhelm Windelband, in 1860 published a monumental book on Kant (*Kants Leben und die Grundlagen seiner Lehre*, Mannheim and Heidelberg) that presented, in a form still useful although outmoded in details, a picture of Kant that could not but excite interest in and study of Kant. In 1865 Fischer initiated a great controversy with Adolf Trendelenburg on the proper interpretation of Kant's theory of space; this controversy mobilized most of the philosophical public in Germany on one side or the other, including Trendelenburg's pupil Hermann Cohen, who had hitherto concentrated mostly on Plato.

HELMHOLTZ AND LANGE. Two other men, Hermann von Helmholtz and F. A. Lange, almost simultaneously with Liebmann made their spiritual pilgrimage to Königsberg.

Helmholtz. Hermann von Helmholtz (1821–1894), then Germany's greatest scientist, had been arguing for years for a view whose origin he found in Kant. The doctrine of specific energies of sensory nerves had led him to a theory of the subjectivity of sensory qualities, which he regarded as signs of unknown objects interacting with our sense organs; he then extended this commonly held view to the conclusion that space itself is dependent upon our bodily constitution. This theory made it possible for Helmholtz to argue that there could be alternative spaces and geometries, each appropriate to a particular kind of nervous apparatus and necessary to the being so constituted, but none of them picturing the real structure of the world. Thus, while Helmholtz gave up Kant's theory of the unique status of Euclidean geometry, he held that his own theory of space was in keeping both with Kant's theory and with the most modern work in mathematics, physics, and physiology. Moreover, in his theory of unconscious inferences he accepted the Kantian theory that perception involves judgment. The guiding principle in such unconscious inference is the a priori principle of causation, which extends our knowledge no further than possible experience, but gives us the right to posit

unknown causes of our sensations. Helmholtz vigorously rejected metaphysics but extolled philosophy as an ancilla to science. Both the strengths and the obvious weaknesses of Helmholtz's Kantianism were effective in making a return to Kant seem fruitful to science, for it meant that the greatest of German thinkers could be used on the side of science, against metaphysics.

Lange. The year 1866 saw the publication of Friedrich Albert Lange's *Geschichte des Materialismus* (Iserlohn and Leipzig; translated by E. C. Thomas as *History of Materialism*, 3 vols., London, 1877–1879). Lange, who was born in 1828 and died, while professor of philosophy at Marburg, in 1875, wrote his massive but readable book to point out the metaphysical mysteries and pretensions of materialism, which traditionally claimed to be only a courageous but unspeculative extension of the results of science into regions previously occupied only by theology and superstition. Like Helmholtz, Lange held that the sensible world is a product of the interaction between the human organism and an unknown reality. The world of experience is determined by this interaction, but the organism itself is only an object of experience, and it is to be understood by psychology and physiology. Causality, needed in all such sciences, is a mode of thought necessary to a mind constituted like ours; processes and principles of thought have physiological bases. Thus, materialism (although a phenomenal materialism, since matter itself is only a phenomenon) is the most likely truth about reality so far as it can be known. But what of Kant's intelligible world? Lange completely rejected Kant's teaching of the rational necessity of the structure of an intelligible but unknowable world; he held that our views of it are only products of poetic fancy (*Dichtung*). While Lange defended materialism as a doctrine of reality (phenomena) that serves as a bulwark against theology and metaphysics, he held that because knowledge is not man's whole goal, *Dichtung* is also important. "Man needs to supplement reality [about which materialism is the best truth we know] with an ideal world of his own creation," and this is a world of value "against which neither logic nor touch of hand nor sight of eye can prevail" (*History of Materialism*, Vol. III, pp. 342 and 347).

Two things stand out in the works of these precursors—if not direct progenitors—of Neo-Kantianism. Their Kantianism was exclusively theoretical, oriented entirely around the *Critique of Pure Reason* and neglectful or disdainful of Kant's practical philosophy. This puts them in the line of development of German positivism, a line that goes from them through Alois Riehl and the fictionalist Hans Vaihinger to Ernst Mach and Moritz Schlick. Their Kantianism was also psychological and even physiological—the a priori elements they acknowledged were dependent upon the human constitution; the transcendental and logical aspects of Kant's work were neglected or rejected. In this respect they were followed by Hans Cornelius (1863–1947) and by Richard Hönigswald (1875–1947), a pupil of Riehl.

METAPHYSICAL NEO-KANTIANISM

Theoretical and physiological Kantianism was in the air when the twenty-five-year-old Liebmann published his manifesto. *Kant und die Epigonen* argued that Kant made one great mistake: believing in the existence of the thing-in-itself. This belief, however, was not an essential part of Kant's doctrine, but only a dogmatic residue that could be removed without damage to the rest of the system. However, Fichte, Schelling, Hegel, Jakob Friedrich Fries, Johann Friedrich Herbart, and Arthur Schopenhauer either did not recognize the belief that there is a thing-in-itself as an error (for instance, Schopenhauer) or, while recognizing it as an error, made analogous errors in their efforts to correct it (Fichte's transcendental ego is as unknowable and unthinkable as the thing-in-itself). The weaknesses thus introduced into their systems were fatal, since they depended upon a concept that Kant had only inadvertently admitted. Hence, none of them could be followed; one had to return to their common source, remove its error, and apply this improved Kantianism to present problems.

While Liebmann's first book showed remnants of a psychological interpretation of Kant, his next book, *Zur Analysis der Wirklichkeit* (Strasbourg, 1876) argued for a strictly transcendental "logic of facts" whose inspiration was as much Spinozistic as Kantian. In this book Liebmann stood close to the Marburg school, at least in his conclusions. However, in his later *Gedanken und Tatsachen* (2 vols., Strasbourg, 1882–1901) he admitted the need and argued for the possibility of a "critical metaphysics" as a "rigorous consideration of human views and hypotheses about the essence of things," growing out of "deep-rooted, ineradicable spiritual needs and intellectual duty" (ibid., 2nd ed., Vol. II, p. 113). His critical metaphysics makes hypotheses about the transcendent and the unknowable, but leaves open a field for value decisions that do not depend on claims to valid knowledge, but only on our wills as they are nurtured by culture. In this line of thought Liebmann seemed to draw closer to the Heidelberg school, but even in his earlier work there were anticipations of Windelband's famous

analysis of the differences between historical and scientific knowledge.

RIEHL. Less openly metaphysical than Liebmann's was the realistic Neo-Kantianism of Alois Riehl (1844–1924). In contrast to Liebmann, Riehl insisted that Kant held to the real existence of things-in-themselves and that this concept is essential to Kant's—and to any sound—theory of knowledge. He asserted that Kant proved only that things-in-themselves cannot be known by pure reason, not that they are not known mediately in sense perception. Phenomena are simply their modes of appearance; they are not in a different ontological realm, but are merely actualizations of their Aristotelian potentialities in the context of a mind. The laws of the organization of phenomena are transcendentally (not psychologically) based on the activity of self-consciousness; their specific characteristics depend on the reality of that of which they are appearances. All knowledge is or can become scientific; philosophy is nothing but a theory of science; metaphysics is "an opiate of the mind."

Nevertheless, Riehl believed it both unavoidable and legitimate to reason hypothetically from phenomena to reality, for metaphysical hypotheses cannot be entirely excluded from science itself. He argued, for instance, for a double-aspect psychophysical theory of the relationship between mind and the world, for a partial duplication of phenomenal laws in the real world, and for complete determinism. The tone of his philosophy, however, was somewhat positivistic; he said he acknowledged "the metaphysical" but not "metaphysics." With *wissenschaftliche* (scientific) philosophy he contrasted *unwissenschaftliche* philosophy, or classical speculative metaphysics, which he rejected; and with both he contrasted *nichtwissenschaftliche* philosophy as a practical discipline for the realization of humanly created values (*Wertbegung* and *Geistesführung*). In his later life he was most concerned with the latter.

OTHER METAPHYSICAL INTERPRETATIONS. Another realistic metaphysical interpretation of Kant was given by the Kant philologist Erich Adickes (1866–1928) in his *Kants Lehre von der doppelten Affektion unseres Ich* (Tübingen, 1929).

Other attempts at "critical metaphysics" on a Kantian basis were made by Johannes Volkelt (1848–1930) and by Friedrich Paulsen (1846–1908). The former's *Kants Erkenntnistheorie* (Leipzig, 1879) and the latter's *Entwicklungsgeschichte der Kantischen Erkenntnistheorie* (Leipzig, 1875) tried to show that Kant himself was an idealistic metaphysician *malgré lui.* Later works designed to bring out the metaphysics in Kant were by Max Wundt (*Kant als Metaphysiker,* Stuttgart, 1924), Heinz Heimsoeth (articles collected in *Studien zur Philosophie Immanuel Kants,* Cologne, 1956), and Gottfried Martin (*Kant, Ontologie und Wissenschaftslehre,* Cologne, 1951; translated by P. G. Lucas as *Kant's Metaphysics and Theory of Science,* Manchester, U.K., and New York, 1955). Martin Heidegger's *Kant und das Problem der Metaphysik* (Bonn, 1929; translated by J. S. Churchill as *Kant and the Problem of Metaphysics,* Bloomington, IN, 1962) presented an extreme form of this view but falls outside the scope of Neo-Kantian intentions.

MARBURG NEO-KANTIANISM

By the standards of recent philosophy Marburg Neo-Kantianism, or panlogistic transcendental philosophy, was no less metaphysical, but by the standards of the time its orientation around the "fact of science" seemed to make it at least antispeculative. In launching the journal of the Marburg school, Hermann Cohen and Paul Natorp wrote: "Whoever is bound to us stands with us on the foundation of the transcendental method.... Philosophy, to us, is bound to the fact of science, as this elaborates itself. Philosophy, therefore, to us is the theory of the principles of science and therewith of all culture" (*Philosophische Arbeiten,* Vol. I, No. 1, 1906).

HERMANN COHEN. Hermann Cohen (1842–1918), a younger colleague of Lange's at Marburg, rejected the naturalism he believed to be inherent in the Kantianism of Helmholtz, Lange, and Liebmann. They were wrong in thinking philosophy should begin with an analysis of consciousness and should show how conscious human beings apply concepts to the data of sensation in order to produce phenomenalistic world pictures that are distinguished from things as they are. The fact to be understood is not this highly dubious psychological process; the fact is science itself and, in ethics, it is not human motives and aspirations and feelings of duty but the fact of civil society under law as constructed in the science of jurisprudence. Kant himself had tried to understand "the fact of science and culture," but he failed to separate this fact from dubious psychological and phenomenological facts he seemed to be dealing with.

Logic for Cohen is not at all psychologistic; it is not even formal. The very notion of formal logic presupposes something not formal: data drawn from some other source, be it pure intuition or perception. Logic, as Cohen saw it, is the logic of knowledge, not the logic of empty thought; it is the logic of truth, in which any assertion gains its status as true solely by virtue of its systematic position in a body of universal laws that, in turn, require each other on methodological grounds. Thought, Cohen taught, accepts nothing as given and is not true of anything independent of it—certainly not of intuitional data, as Kant believed. Thought generates content as well as form, and the content of self-contained thought is reality itself as object and goal of knowledge. This extravagant panlogism was based on Cohen's ingenious interpretation of the history of the differential calculus, which he saw as the logic of mathematical physics. Not number and not observed motion, as Kant believed, are given as raw data to science; rather, the mathematical differential, which is not given at all but is created by thought, is the necessary device for the creation of nature as object of possible experience: "This mathematical generation of motion [by integration of the derivative] and thereby nature itself is the triumph of pure thinking" (*Logik der reinen Erkenntnis,* Berlin, 1902, p. 20). Through an interpretation of Kant's teachings concerning intensive magnitudes of sensations, Cohen saw in the method of the calculus a paradigm of the category of origin (*Ursprung*) and the logical process of production (*Erzeugung*) to which every fact owes its reality; that is, its position in a logically necessary scheme.

Through the work of thought on its own materials, Cohen believed he could dispense with all independent givens in knowledge. Nothing is given (*gegeben*); all is problematic (*aufgegeben*). Fact is that which is completely determined by thought. The thing-in-itself is not a thing at all. It does not exist, but is only a thought of a limit (*Grenzbegriff*) to our approach to a complete determination of things as they are; that is, as they would fully satisfy systematic thought.

Cohen's pupil Ernst Cassirer spoke of him as "one of the most resolute Platonists that has ever appeared in the history of philosophy." When Cohen said, for example, "Thinking itself produces what is to be held to be" (ibid., p. 67; cf. p. 402), he was not speaking of thought as a process in an individual. "Thought" is not the name of a process, but refers only to the corpus of the unending history of science. To be, then, is to be thought, but not to be thought in somebody's consciousness; to be thought means to be asserted under valid and immanent a priori principles that inescapably determine the unique structure of mathematical physics. Cohen was as much of a dogmatist as Kant himself with regard to the structure of science.

The original stages of Cohen's teachings are found in his three commentaries on Kant (*Kants Theorie der Erfahrung,* Berlin, 1871; *Kants Begrundung der Ethik,* Berlin, 1877; *Kants Begrundung der Aesthetik,* Berlin, 1889), one on each *Critique.* They are continuous criticisms of all of Kant's "givens"; for example, experience, intuition, categories, duty, things-in-themselves. The final stages are contained in his three systematic works (*Logik der reinen Erkenntnis,* Berlin, 1902; *Ethik des reinen Willens,* Berlin, 1904; *Aesthetik des reinen Gefühls,* 2 vols., Berlin, 1912), which parallel the three *Critiques.* At its midpoint Cohen's thought was close to the contemporary rejections of psychologism by Alexius Meinong and Edmund Husserl; at its end it would have taken only the "bathos of experience," to use Kant's words, to change it, in principle, into a kind of positivism or even historicism.

NATORP. The principal thinker among the second generation of Marburg Neo-Kantians was Paul Natorp (1854–1924). It fell to him to deal with the new developments in science (especially the theory of relativity, in his *Die logischen Grundlagen der exakten Wissenschaften,* Leipzig, 1910) by penetrating to a deeper level of methodology than Cohen could reach in his own work, which was largely restricted to classical mathematics and physics.

More important, it was Natorp's task to introduce the whole field of psychology into the body of knowledge considered and understood in Cohen's way, and thereby to fill the lacuna Cohen left between *Bewusstsein überhaupt* (consciousness in general, the "fact" of science) and the limited individual human consciousness. Natorp's *Einleitung in die Psychologie* (Freiburg, 1888) and his *Allgemeine Psychologie nach kritischer Methode* (Tübingen, 1912) attempted, first, to apply Cohen's transcendental method to psychology instead of leaving it exposed to the naturalistic methods of Cohen's and Natorp's rivals, such as Riehl. In this attempt Natorp came close to results like those of Wilhelm Dilthey without, he thought, having to draw his relativistic, skeptical, and historicistic conclusions. And, second, these books attempted to bridge the gap between the objective world of phenomena and the nonphenomenal, nonnatural self that possessed the knowledge of the phenomenal world. Cohen had moved so far from Kant toward Hegel that it was for him an almost insignificant accident that individual men and women know anything; *Bewusstheit* (known-ness), not *Bewusstsein* (consciousness), was important for him. Natorp had to undertake another almost Copernican revolution against objective panlogism without at the same time naturalizing the knowing subject, which would have led to relativism and skepticism.

He performed the first part of his task by the classical Kantian move of seeing empirical ego and empirical object as standing in a necessary correlation with each other, not as independent phenomena; the latter part he accomplished by insisting that the pure ego cannot be an object—it is as much a *Grenzbegriff* as the thing-in-itself. For Natorp the objective and the subjective were not two realms, either opposed to each other or one including the other. Rather, they were two directions of knowledge, objectification and subjectification, each starting from the same phenomenon and each employing the transcendental method of categorial constitution, resolution into *Ursprung* and *Erzeugung.* Just as Cohen's antipsychologistic panlogism had brought him close to Husserl's *Logische Untersuchungen,* Natorp's linking of psychology and panlogism brought him close to Husserl's *Ideen*; and it is easy to see how Nicolai Hartmann, Natorp's pupil, could move over into the phenomenological camp (J. Klein, "Hartmann und die Marburger Schule," in *Nicolai Hartmann, der Denker und sein Werk,* by Heinz Heimsoeth and Robert Heiss, Göttingen, 1952).

CASSIRER. The last great representative of Marburg Neo-Kantianism was Ernst Cassirer (1874–1945), whose works on the philosophy of science continued the line of argument initiated by Natorp and show some close resemblances to positivism. Cassirer's most important contribution, however, was to extend the Marburg conception of *Erzeugung* to the whole range of human culture (language, myth, art, religion, statecraft), ending not in panlogism but in "pansymbolism."

Other important Marburg Neo-Kantians were Rudolf Stammler (1856–1938) in the philosophy of law; Karl Vorländer (1860–1928), the historian of philosophy and the leading Kantian socialist (*Kant und der Sozialismus,* Berlin, 1900; *Kant und Marx,* Tübingen, 1911); Artur Buchenau (1879–1946), Albert Görland (1869–1952), and Arthur Liebert (1878–1946). A moderate form of Marburg Neo-Kantianism is represented in America by W. H. Werkmeister (*The Basis and Structure of Knowledge,* New York, 1948).

GÖTTINGEN NEO-KANTIANISM

In strong reaction against Marburg there arose, at the beginning of the twentieth century, the Neo-Friesian school in Göttingen, under the leadership of Leonard Nelson (1882–1927). Jakob Friedrich Fries (1773–1843) had interpreted Kant psychologically, not transcendentally; in this he was followed by Jürgen Bona Meyer (1829–1897) in his *Kants Psychologie* (Berlin, 1870). Lange and Helmholtz were psychologistic in their Kantianism, taking the results of experimental psychology as having a bearing on the a priori. Nelson, on the contrary, professed to avoid psychologism and its attendant skepticism by using psychological introspection to discover the principles of experience in the spontaneity of reason; these principles could then be deduced (in the Kantian sense) from the analysis of experience into its necessary conditions. In this, Nelson developed the views of Fries, whom he defended against the accusation of psychologism, and opposed the psychological or physiological interpretations of the experimental and empirical psychologists.

Kant's transcendental deduction was regarded by Nelson as circular if it was meant as a proof; it began with the experience (science, mathematics, morality) it was meant to justify. The circle might have been broken by Kant's subjective deduction, but this was jettisoned in the second edition of the *Critique*. Nelson proposed to reestablish it, or rather to put his own deduction into its place. Upon introspection, we find principles we know immediately to be true and that we hold by a Cartesian-like "principle of the self-confidence of reason." The discovery of these self-evident principles is a psychological process; the principles, however, are not psychological but metaphysical in Kant's sense; that is, as a priori synthetic truths based on concepts, not on intuition. They are shown to be the same as those uncovered by a transcendental analysis of science and ordinary experience. (In ethics Nelson followed an analogous procedure.) In this way Nelson thought he could use psychology without falling prey to either naturalism or skepticism. A good example of his method is to be found in the well-known *Das Heilige* (Gotha, 1917; translated by J. W. Harvey as *The Idea of the Holy*, New York, 1958) by Nelson's colleague Rudolf Otto. Nelson never had the influence in Germany that was enjoyed by many other Neo-Kantians, although he was revered by many disciples in fields related to philosophy. There has recently been an increased interest in his work, and several English translations have appeared.

HEIDELBERG NEO-KANTIANISM

The Heidelberg school of Neo-Kantianism, led by Windelband and Heinrich Rickert, was not restricted to the University of Heidelberg, and is sometimes known as the Baden school or the Southwest German school of Neo-Kantianism. Wilhelm Windelband (1848–1915) was the most eminent historian of philosophy of his time, with the possible exception of Dilthey. Like Dilthey, he did not succeed in working out a complete system of philosophy, but certain of his ideas were decisive for the more systematic work of his followers in Heidelberg. His most characteristic doctrine was that the epistemological problem is really a problem in axiology; a judgment is known to be true not by comparison with an object (thing-in-itself) but by its conformity to an immediately experienced obligation to believe it. The teaching for which Windelband is chiefly remembered, however, was his distinction between natural and historical sciences as nomothetic and ideographic (law-giving and picturing the unique individual), respectively. The elaboration of these two points led to the systematic priority of axiological criteria to epistemological criteria, to the theory of the parallelism of norms and cultural consciousness, and to efforts to develop a Kantian categorization of historical and cultural experience.

RICKERT. The great system builder of the Heidelberg school was Heinrich Rickert (1863–1936), professor in Freiburg and then Windelband's successor in Heidelberg. Rickert, like Windelband, regarded judging as a form of valuing, truth being the value intended by this act. There are two realms of objects that may be judged; that is, that are objects of knowledge—the sensible world of science (about which Rickert accepted most of Kant's views) and an intelligible world of nonsensuous objects of experience that we know not by perception but by understanding (*Verstehen*). These latter are cultural objects (history, art, morality, institutions). Although not reducible to sense and thus not under the categories of nature, they are not metaphysical but are within experience and correspond, roughly, to Hegel's objective spirit. Both cultural objects and nature, as objects, require (in the Kantian manner) a correlative subject that cannot be objectified. This is "the third realm of being," which Rickert calls "pro-physical"; it is Kant's transcendental ego and Hegel's subjective spirit. There is a fourth realm of being, the metaphysical proper, which is only an object of faith (in the Kantian sense) and which we refer to in religion and in the transition from scientific philosophy to *Weltanschauung*.

By keeping the ethical "this side" of the division between the experiential and the metaphysical, Rickert was able to bring about a closer liaison between the theoretical and the practical than Kant had established. The primacy of practical reason does not, for Rickert, mark the supremacy of valuing over knowing, but signifies the valuational dimension of knowing itself. Autonomy is thus the basis not only of ethics but also of thought even in science. Rickert criticized the Kantian conception of experience as too thin; not only nature, but also history, must be categorized out of the heterogeneous continuum of data, and from these categorizations arise the nomothetic and ideographic disciplines. In all these points Rickert was under the influence of both Fichte and Hegel, but his conceptual framework remained Kantian: a transcendental nonobjectifiable basis (realm 3) for experience (realms 1 and 2) and an unknown realm of objects of faith (realm 4).

OTHERS. Other important Heidelberg Neo-Kantians were Hugo Münsterberg (1863–1916), Jonas Cohn (1869–1947), Bruno Bauch (1877–1942; *Wahrheit, Wert und Wirklichkeit,* Leipzig, 1923), and Richard Kroner (*Von Kant bis Hegel,* 2 vols., Tübingen, 1921–1924). Kroner's *Kant's Weltanschauung* (Tübingen, 1914, translated by J. E. Smith, Chicago and Cambridge, U.K., 1956) is the only presentation in English of the characteristic Heidelberg interpretation of the historical Kant.

SOCIOLOGICAL NEO-KANTIANISM

Several philosophers close to *Lebensphilosophie* and concerned with the methodology of the *Geisteswissenschaften* were influenced by Kant's doctrine that we categorially construct the world of experience and that speculative metaphysics is impossible as science, but instead of having theories concerning the transcendental origin of the structural factors, they found the origin of the world of experience in the social situation. The most important of these philosophers were Wilhelm Dilthey (1833–1912), who is not usually characterized as a Neo-Kantian although Kantian elements are present in his thought, and Georg Simmel (1858–1918).

At various times Simmel took different attitudes toward, or at least emphasized different aspects of, Kantianism—the psychologistic and pragmatic, the transcendental, and the sociohistorical. He held that categories develop in the course of history, and that the structures of Hegel's objective spirit are historical products that cannot be taken ready-made for analysis in the Marburg manner. "[Even] the kind of science humanity has at any given moment depends upon the kind of humanity it is at that moment" (*Hauptprobleme der Philosophie,* Leipzig, 1910, Ch. 1). Because forms cannot be discerned except in the specific contents in which they appear, no categorial system is capable of structuring all experience. Different types of individuals have different styles for this structuring, and cultures are identified by their production of

specific a priori forms for knowledge, the experience of values, and images of the world as a whole (systems of metaphysics).

Between the Heidelberg tradition and the Dilthey-Simmel position there were Max Weber (1864–1921) and Eduard Spranger. Neo-Kantian elements in the sociology of knowledge are especially clear in the works of Max Adler (*Das Soziologische in Kants Erkenntniskritik,* Vienna, 1924) and Karl Mannheim (1893–1947).

Windelband said, "To understand Kant means to go beyond Kant." Most of the philosophers dealt with here did go beyond Kant, and their later works contained little that was specifically Kantian. Even the movements as a whole were more explicitly Kantian in their early periods than in their later ones. All this was to be expected of active and creative minds and groups. By the end of World War I, Neo-Kantianism as an institution ceased to be a dominant force in German intellectual life, partly through the death of most of its leaders and partly through defection. Rapid changes in logic and natural science favored the more pragmatic systems of positivism in Berlin, Prague, and Vienna; the greater experiential resources of phenomenology favored the rival school in Freiburg, Munich, and Cologne; the German cultural crisis called for *Lebensphilosophie* and speculative metaphysics. None of these movements, however, was free of Kantian elements, which might not have been passed on to them but for the Neo-Kantians' rediscovery of Kant. Their Neo-Kantian heritage has given repeated confirmation of an aphorism attributed to Liebmann: "You can philosophize with Kant, or you can philosophize against Kant, but you cannot philosophize without Kant."

See also Cassirer, Ernst; Causation: Philosophy of Science; Cohen, Hermann; Dilthey, Wilhelm; Fichte, Johann Gottlieb; Fischer, Kuno; Fries, Jakob Friedrich; Hegel, Georg Wilhelm Friedrich; Heidegger, Martin; Helmholtz, Hermann Ludwig von; Herbart, Johann Friedrich; Hönigswald, Richard; Husserl, Edmund; Irrationalism; Kant, Immanuel; Kantian Ethics; Lange, Friedrich Albert; Liebert, Arthur; Liebmann, Otto; Logical Knowledge; Mach, Ernst; Mannheim, Karl; Materialism; Meinong, Alexius; Natorp, Paul; Nelson, Leonard; Otto, Rudolf; Paulsen, Friedrich; Positivism; Psychologism; Rationalism in Ethics; Reinhold, Karl Leonhard; Rickert, Heinrich; Riehl, Alois; Schelling, Friedrich Wilhelm Joseph von; Schlick, Moritz; Schopenhauer, Arthur; Simmel, Georg; Spranger, (Franz Ernst) Eduard; Vaihinger, Hans; Weber, Max; Windelband, Wilhelm.

Bibliography

Studies of and works by individual Neo-Kantians are listed in the respective articles. There is very little material in English on Neo-Kantianism, but see Ernst Cassirer, "Neo-Kantianism," in *Encyclopaedia Britannica,* 14th ed. (1930), Vol. XVI, pp. 215–216; and R. B. Perry, *Philosophy of the Recent Past* (New York: Scribners, 1926), pp. 145–160. A complete history is being written by Mariano Campo; Vol. I of his *Schizzo storico della esegesi e critica kantiana* (Varese, 1959) covers the period up to about 1900. The most complete study, with excellent bibliographies, is K. Oesterreich in *Friedrich Überwegs Grundriss der Geschichte der Philosophie,* 12th ed. (Berlin, 1923), Vol. IV, pp. 410–483.

G. Lehmann reports the beginnings of the movement in "Kant im Spätidealismus und die Anfänge der neukantischen Bewegung," in *Zeitschrift für philosophische Forschung* 17 (1963): 438–457; see also his "Voraussetzungen und Grenzen der systematischen Kantinterpretation," in *Kant-Studien* 49 (1957): 364–388.

Good comparative studies of Neo-Kantianism are included in Wolfgang Ritzel, *Studien zum Wandeln der Kantauffassung* (Meisenheim, 1952) and H. Levy, *Die Hegel-Renaissance in der deutschen Philosophie* (Charlottenburg, Germany: R. Heise, 1927). Johannes Hessen, *Die Religionsphilosophie des Neukantianismus* (Freiburg: Herder, 1924) gives a Catholic criticism.

Authoritative presentations of two school programs are Paul Natorp, *Kant und die Marburger Schule* (Berlin, 1912; also in *Kant-Studien* 17 [1912]: 193–221) and Heinrich Rickert, *Die Heidelberger Tradition und Kants Kritizismus* (Berlin, 1934). The posthumously published (and incomplete) work by H. Dussort, *L'école de Marburg* (Paris, 1963) is excellent on the movement up through Cohen.

OTHER RECOMMENDED SOURCES

Adair Toteff, Christopher. "Neo-Kantianism: The German Idealism Movement." In *The Cambridge History of Philosophy 1870–1945,* edited by Thomas Baldwin. Cambridge, U.K.: Cambridge University Press, 2003.

Brandist, Craig. "Two Routes 'To Concreteness' in the Work of the Bakhtin Circle." *Journal of the History of Ideas* 63(3) (2002): 521–537.

Hallberg, Fred W. "Neo-Kantian Constraints on Legitimate Religious Beliefs." *American Journal of Theology and Philosophy* 16(3) (1995): 279–298.

Kröhnke, Klaus C. *The Rise of Neo-Kantianism: German Academic Philosophy Between Idealism and Positivism,* translated by R. J. Hollingdale. New York: Cambridge University Press, 1991.

Luthe, Rudolf. "The Development of the Concept of Concrete Subjectivity from Kant to Neo-Kantianism." *Journal of the British Society for Phenomenology* 13 (1982): 154–167.

Lewis White Beck (1967)

NEO-MANICHAEISM

See *Mani and Manichaeism*

NEOPLATONISM

GENERAL CHARACTERIZATION

Neoplatonism was the dominant philosophical current in late antiquity, and it had a lasting influence in the Middle Ages when it was adopted by Christian and Muslim thinkers. The term Neoplatonism was coined in the late eighteenth century and was used (in a rather pejorative sense) to distinguish authentic Platonism (as found in Plato's dialogues) from the later systematization and transformation(s) it underwent in the third through fifth centuries, starting with Plotinus.

By using the term Neoplatonism, historians of philosophy wanted to dissociate themselves from the perspective that for centuries had determined, if not distorted, the interpretation of Plato. Yet Plotinus would have been surprised if he had known he would once be called a Neoplatonist. He never intended to be anything other than a faithful interpreter of Plato's doctrines, coming, as he saw it, after centuries of neglect and distortion during which Stoicism and Aristotelianism had set the philosophical agenda, and true, that is, dogmatic, Platonism had, as it were, gone underground in order to survive. This is also how Augustine presents the history of the Platonic Academy in his *Against the Academics*: "Once the clouds of errors had been dispelled, Plato's face, which is the most pure and bright in philosophy, shone forth, above all in Plotinus. This Platonic philosopher is considered to be so similar to Plato that one could believe that they had lived together; but as there is so much time between them, one should think that Plato revived in him." (XVIII 41). One and a half centuries later, Proclus, in his *Platonic Theology* hails Plotinus and his followers Porphyry, Iamblichus, and all others following him, until his master Syrianus (d. 437CE), for having restored Platonism in its original splendor.

PLOTINUS'S RENEWAL OF PLATONISM. What then was so innovative in Plotinus's interpretation of Platonism to praise him so lavishly and to consider him as the founder of Neoplatonism? Plotinus came after two centuries of Platonic revival (in handbooks since Karl Praechter (1858–1933), this period is commonly called Middle Platonism). This does not mean that Plato had ever been neglected during the Hellenistic period. His dialogues, however, seem to discuss problems without arriving at a definite solution, they use dramatic scenery and mythological stories, and do not always provide concordant views. It may have seemed impossible to find in the works of Plato a systematic philosophy that could compete with that of the Stoics. This could explain why a skeptic, nondogmatic interpretation of the dialogues prevailed for a long time. In the schools of the early Roman Empire, however, Plato was rediscovered as a dogmatic author, and Platonists attempted to systematize his views in handbooks and explain them in commentaries. Many innovations attributed to Plotinus are already present in the Platonists of the first centuries (such as Atticus, Alcinous, and Numenius of Apamea). Recent research has questioned the distinction between Middle and Neoplatonism and stressed once again the continuity of the Platonic tradition. In fact, the debate over the right interpretation of Plato's philosophy had already started in the Old Academy. Neoplatonism is in many respects a development of tendencies already present in the early school and even in the later dialogues of Plato himself as well as in his *unwritten doctrines*, in particular, in the speculations about the derivation of all beings from first principles. This continuity should not, however, make us underestimate the innovative character of Plotinus's philosophy.

The later tradition has always seen the doctrine of the three hypostases—Soul, Intellect, the One (or the Good)—as the most characteristic feature of Neoplatonism and has credited Plotinus with the first clear statement of this theory. Yet most elements of the doctrine are to be found in previous philosophers, as Plotinus himself admits, and, of course, in Plato's own work. With all Platonists, Plotinus strictly distinguishes the sensible from the intelligible realm. The sensible world is not a *hypostasis*, that is, it is not an independently subsisting reality, but depends for its being entirely on incorporeal principles that derive ultimately from the ideal Forms. Only what is incorporeal and intelligible can have hypostatic reality. Within this realm we have to distinguish between Soul, Intellect, and the One, which constitute an ascending series. This theory could strike one as a needless complication of reality and not as its explanation. From a Neoplatonic view, however, these three hypostases are essential steps in the ultimate explanation of all that exits.

Neoplatonism is, in fact, the most radical answer to the question that motivates Greek philosophy since Thales: What are the first principles of all things? To explain a complex reality such as this cosmos means to reduce it to the more simple elements from which it originates. To explain the multiple, Plotinus argues, is to reduce it to its ultimate principle of unity (*anagôgê eis hen*). Whatever exists, exists thanks to its unity. For without unity a thing has no essence, no being, falls apart: A house would no longer be a house but a mere heap of stones; a living being not an organism but flesh and bones; the soul not a soul but a bundle of emotions, memories, thoughts, and so on. Unity, then, is much more fundamental than *essence* or *form*. For being depends on being one. As Plotinus puts it, *being is a trace of the One*. Neoplatonism does not primarily offer a theory of being, an ontology as can be found in the Aristotelian metaphysics, but a doctrine of what is one and what ultimately explains unity and is therefore rather a henology. Proclus's *Elements of Theology* start with the proposition that "every multiplicity in some way participates in unity". It is not itself, however, the One, but a unified manifold, having unity as an attribute, and is therefore posterior to the One upon which it depends. For that reason no being can ultimately be explained by a principle of unity that is intrinsic to it. Unity that is participated in depends upon a transcendent principle of unity. Thus the living organism is one thanks to the soul giving life and unity to the body. The One must be identified with the Good, since it is the proper function of the One to hold together all things and maintain them in existence, which is also the function of the Good. For to hold a thing together and make it one is to give it its perfection and well-being whereas dispersion is the cause of its destruction and evil. Therefore, all things pursue unity as the good because they all strive to continue to exist and shun division as evil. Therefore, the One is to be identified with the Good, and the origin of the procession (*proodos*) of all things is also the end of their return (*epistrophê*).

In our search for an ultimate explanation, we will find always higher levels of unity until we arrive at the One itself. The whole sensible cosmos is one complex living organism wherein all things are connected in a chain of causes and linked by mutual sympathy, as the Stoics said. But what explains the unity and coherence of this world cannot itself be a material principle, such as the Stoic active principle, but has to be an incorporeal world soul. As Plato argued in the *Timaeus*, the soul is an intermediate between the sensible and the intelligible, the temporal and the eternal. But because it is incorporeal, the soul, at least the rational soul, is never entirely cut off from the intelligible world, not even when it is incarnated in a body. The soul, however, is not itself the origin of the specific forms and of the organic structure incorporated in this world. Whatever the soul (as *demiurge* or creative cause) conveys to this world derives from the ideal Forms contemplated by it. In fact, all production results from contemplation. If one subtracts from this sensible world matter, mass, spatial differences and time, coming to be, corruption and death and only understands what is essential and eternal in it, one finds a wonderful organism, an articulated system of specific forms, eternal objects of thought. This is the intelligible world, true reality and divine Intellect, as one perfect science that comprehends in itself all being known in its essential structures. Although comprehending all forms eternally and at once, this self-thinking Intellect or Intelligible Being cannot be the ultimate explanation of the universe, as Aristotle thought. For it is characterized by the multiplicity of the Forms and by the duality of thinker and object of thought. This leads Plotinus to a provocative conclusion that seems to go against the grain of philosophy itself: "For thinking itself does not come first either in reality or in value, but is second and is what has come into being when the Good [already] existed." (V 6, 5, 5–6). This Good is, as Plato famously said, *beyond* (*epekeina*) thinking and being. It desires nothing, needs nothing. It is just One. Because it is nothing, it can be the origin of all things, not because it creates or produces them, but because they all come forth from its overflowing simplicity. Characteristic of Neoplatonism is this double transcendence: that of the Intelligible with respect to the sensible and that of the Good with respect to the Intelligible.

A SPIRITUAL EXPERIENCE. The amazing success of Neoplatonic philosophy, also beyond the limited circle of pagan philosophers, cannot be explained solely by elements of the doctrine. What made it so attractive was that it not only offered a theoretical understanding of reality, but also promised a way to ascend to the first principle of all, bringing the soul back to its own origin. Philosophy begins with the Delphic maxim *know thyself*, which is understood as an exhortation to return into thyself. "Go back into yourself and look," says Plotinus (I 6, 9, 7). This *epistrophê*, or return, of the soul upon itself is also the beginning of the return to the intellect and the One from which the soul proceeded. For within itself the soul does not only discover its own essence but also has access to the intelligible world to which it belongs essentially. Plotinus tells us of his personal experience: "Often I have woken up out of the body to my self and have entered into myself, going out from all other things. I have seen a beauty wonderfully great and felt assurance that then most of all I belonged to the better part; I have actually lived the best life and come to identity with the divine" (IV 8, 1, 1ff.). The truly wise person therefore "has already finished reasoning and turned to himself: all is within him" (VI 5, 12 17–18). The three hypostases, Soul, Intellect, the One do not solely exist *in nature*: We find them in ourselves, at least if we first discover that we are a *self*.

Through a moral life we have to gather our self from the fragmentation of the daily needs of the body, which distract our attention toward the outside. We are more than souls taking care of our body. We belong to the intelligible world, or rather, each of us is the intelligible world, and in our deepest self, we are one, one with one another, one with the One cause of everything.

The different hypostases of reality are not just three levels of reality; they are different levels of spiritual existence, or different modes of being *self*. Neoplatonic philosophy is not just a theory about unity, for such a theory could never succeed on its own. It is an exhortation to find the one by becoming one and simple, eventually giving up reasoning and explanation, just being one, or even going beyond being, by reaching an *ecstatic experience*. This unification with the One is not an alien supplement, not a denial of philosophy, but a realization and radicalization of what always was the intention of philosophy: to reach the first principle; to overcome the distinction of knower and object known.

NEOPLATONISM: THE FULFILLMENT OF HELLENIC CULTURE. Neoplatonism is not just an effort to offer a comprehensive understanding of the Platonic doctrines scattered all over the dialogues. It also integrates within this Platonic perspective the whole philosophical tradition starting with Pythagoras. Aristotle himself is seen as essentially a Platonic thinker, at least if purified of the distortions of some later Peripatetics. Without a full knowledge of the Aristotelian logical writings and his treatise *On the Soul* it is not possible to understand the subtle Neoplatonic theory of knowledge. Aristotle's analyses of substance, matter and form, potency and act, quality and quantity, the different forms of causality provide the conceptual framework in which Plato's arguments are construed. To the Neoplatonists we owe the great commentaries on Aristotle, which made possible the reception of his philosophy by the medieval thinkers. When Neoplatonism took over the intellectual hegemony, after five centuries of being dominated by Stoicism, it also adopted many Stoics doctrines, in particular (part of) their ethics, and their views on providence and fate. Thus, they secured it an influence beyond antiquity. In short, Neoplatonism not only comes at the end of ancient philosophy, it integrates, in a way, the whole philosophical tradition in all its richness and diversity, making a synthesis of what had been for a very long time opposing schools.

In contrast to Plotinus, the later Neoplatonists became increasingly interested in the wisdom transmitted through the ancient religious traditions, not only the Hellenic religion (as it was known through Homer and Hesiod (c. 700 BCE) between the Orphic revelations), but also the arcane doctrines and rituals of the barbarians, in particular, the Egyptians and Chaldaeans. Of particular interest for the later development of the school were the so-called *Chaldaean Oracles*. These oracles offer, in epic hexameters, a mythical theogony and cosmogony of Platonic inspiration. They are supposed to have been revealed by the gods to a certain Julian the Chaldaean and his son, the *theurgist* (c. 160–80 BCE). The term *the-urgy* (divine work) indicates certain ritual actions, which connect those who practice them with the gods. From Iamblichus onward, the *Chaldaean Oracles* gained a considerable authority comparable only to that of the sacred texts of Jews and Christians. This positive attitude toward the diverse religious traditions did not, however, include Christianity. Porphyry and Iamblichus wrote polemical treatises against the Christians and, following them, the emperor Julian, called the Apostate (331–363), even started persecuting them. They considered Christianity as a threat for the whole of Hellenic culture with its tradition of education, literature, religious practices, and philosophy. The intolerant attitude of the Christians made it impossible to integrate their views together with the other religious traditions in one comprehensive *Platonic theology*. The growing opposition against Christianity may explain why Neoplatonic philosophy itself, from Iamblichus onward, became increasingly *theological* in its project. The Christian authors liked to point to the contradictions within the pagan philosophical tradition. They perceived all schools to have divergent opinions, which would almost naturally lead to skepticism. In response to this the Neoplatonists made an attempt to systematize and reconcile the most diverse doctrines from an overall Platonic perspective, integrating in it all that was valuable in the mythological and religious traditions. Just like the Christians they had their own sacred books (which were wonderfully in agreement with Plato's wisdom), and their theurgical practices could be seen as a rival to the sacramental practices of the Christians aiming for the salvation of the soul.

At the end of antiquity, in particularly in the Athenian school, Neoplatonism had thus become the ideological justification of the old pagan culture wherein all the wisdom of the Hellenic tradition was integrated: the theology of Homer, Hesiod and Orpheus, Pythagoras, Parmenides, Plato himself, and also Aristotle and the Stoics.

HISTORICAL SURVEY

THE LEGACY OF PLOTINUS. Plotinus undoubtedly set off the Neoplatonic movement, though it is difficult to call him the founder of a school. His philosophy was in a way too *original*, too much linked to his own spiritual experience. Plotinus is provocative and daring in his expression, as he himself admits, as when he says that the soul is never fully distanced from the intellect. From a scholarly point of view, much in what he says remains unclear: How can the One be beyond all things and still be the *power of all things*; how can the One bring forth a multiplicity; what exactly is the role of the soul in the production of the World; and so on. Particularly challenging was Plotinus's philosophical appropriation of religion. The philosopher is the true priest who can ascend within himself to the divine principle of all. He has no need to go to temples, the gods "will come to him" (*Vita Plotini*, 10). Enough questions to stimulate further debate in the later school for over two centuries.

It would wrong, indeed, to see Neoplatonism as a unified movement: There was considerable divergence within the school, with conflicting interpretations of Plato; different views on essential points of the doctrine, such as the status of the One and the explanation of the procession of all things; the relation between the Intellect and the intelligible and the status of the Ideas; the role of the demiurge in the creation of the sensible world; the function of demons and other intermediary beings; the nature of the soul and its relation to the intelligible world; and above all, the role of theurgy. Nevertheless, all shared a common doctrine, the three hypostases: the transcendence of the One, the distinction between the sensible and the intelligible, the return upon the self as the origin and the end of philosophy.

The following survey shall sketch the main lines of the historical and institutional development of Neoplatonism, referring to the relevant entries in this Encyclopedia for more in-depth studies of major figures.

THE FIRST GENERATION AFTER PLOTINUS. After his arrival in Rome, Plotinus soon attracted to his lectures students and devotees who often belonged to the high Roman society. We are well informed about the intellectual climate in this close circle—about the texts that were read and the topics they discussed, about the interaction in the group—thanks to the *Life of Plotinus* written by his close disciple Porphyry as an introduction to his edition of the works of his master. As Porphyry tells us, Plotinus for a long time refused to write down his lectures. Only at the age of forty-nine, at the insistence of his students, did he start scribbling down his arguments. It took Porphyry a great effort and a long time to make the texts ready for publication. The *Enneads*, as they were called (they consist of six groups of nine essays), were published about thirty years after the death of the master. This edition made the reputation of Plotinus and gave his thought a wide circulation beyond the circle of his immediate disciples. Soon a Latin adaptation of the work was made (probably a selection), which attracted enthusiastic readers among young intellectuals in Milan, as the example of Augustine shows. Porphyry also wrote a systematic introduction to Neoplatonic philosophy, the "Pathways to the Intelligible," making abundant use of material from Plotinus. Without the effort of Porphyry, the philosophy of Plotinus, this original individual, would never have had such an immense influence on the development of late antique and medieval thought. Porphyry defended *the harmony of Plato and Aristotle* (this is the title of one of his lost works) and contributed to the reception of Aristotle's works in the Neoplatonic curriculum as an introduction to the study of Plato. He wrote two commentaries on Aristotle's *Categories* and a short *Introduction* (*Eisagôgê*) to the study of categories, which soon gained the authority of an Aristotelian treatise.

In a famous treatise (the concluding part of which is known as Ennead II 9 [33]), Plotinus attacked some Gnostic Christians and defended the beauty of the Cosmos against their dualistic views. Porphyry in his *Against Christians* launches a direct attack against the Christians. This anti-Christian outlook would also be that of the later school. Despite his anti-Christian polemics, Porphyry has a great interest in the diverse religious traditions as a source of wisdom. He is the first philosopher to pay attention to the *Chaldaean Oracles* and is fascinated by the theurgical rituals as a means to achieve the *salvation of the soul* (that is, the return of the soul to God). But, maybe under the influence of Plotinus, he adopted a more intellectual interpretation of religion, which led him to question theurgy and other aspects of the Egyptian religion (for which he would be criticized by Iamblichus). Hence, Porphyry limits the efficacy of theurgical practices to the lower degrees of salvation (those concerned with the purification of the pneumatic body and the lower soul) while demanding strictly philosophical means for achieving the union with the One.

THE SYRIAN SCHOOL OF IAMBLICHUS. The Syrian Iamblichus stayed for some time as a student with Porphyry in Rome. He had, however, diverging views on many issues and did not hesitate to attack Porphyry in writing. Having returned to his native Syria at the end of the third century, he set up his own school at Apamea. While Porphyry's influence remained mostly limited to the Western part of the Empire (including the Latin tradition), Iamblichus left a definitive stamp on the development of Neoplatonism in the Greek world, both through his metaphysical speculations on the first principles and his passionate defense of theurgical practices. Whereas Porphyry, interpreting Plotinus, intended to see the One as the summit of the Intellect, Iamblichus emphasizes even more the transcendence of the first principle, putting the Ineffable even beyond the One. Within the intelligible realm, he further distinguishes the purely intelligible from the intellectual level. And whereas Porphyry, following Plotinus, identified the supreme part of the soul with the intellect, Iamblichus insists that the soul is a separate ontological entity, intermediate between the intelligible and the sensible and therefore lower than intellect. Situated between the soul and the intellectual gods, the classes of demons, angels, and heroes have an important mediating function. All this announces a tendency that will become dominant in the later development of the school: the introduction of ever more intermediaries in the procession from the One to the multiple to make the transition from one level to another less abrupt. It is also Iamblichus who introduces the distinction between a non-participated and a participated status of a principle (such as soul or intellect). He also develops the triadic schema of remaining, procession, and reversion and applied this and other structures to different ontological levels. Iamblichus seems to have developed all important principles that support the architecture of Neoplatonic metaphysics. He also deserves credit for having established the educational canon of Plato's dialogues as well as their reading order and for having developed the exegetical principles for the interpretation of Plato, the most important of which being the determination of the right scope or intention of a dialogue. Iamblichus also initiates the Pythagoreanizing trend in Neoplatonism. He considers Pythagoras as the real founder of the philosophical tradition in all of its branches and as the model of the philosophical life. Plato himself, so Iamblichus believes, was the most eminent exponent of that tradition. Iamblichus's Pythagorean leanings also explain the heavy emphasis on mathematics as the most universal science, having applications in all possible branches of philosophy, not only in physics, and astronomy, but also in ethics and theology. For his attempt to fuse Pythagoras and Plato into one mathematical–metaphysical system, Iamblichus could find inspiration in Neopythagorean authors of the first centuries CE, such as Nicomachus of Gerasa (c. 60–120 CE).

Even more important for the future development of the school is Iamblichus's novel attitude to religious rites. He could not agree with Porphyry's reserved rationalistic attitude toward religious practices and theurgy in particular, as is evident from his anonymous reply to the latter's *Letter to Anebo* (an Egyptian priest). Iamblichus's reply, since the Renaissance known under the title *On the Mysteries of the Egyptians*, is a comprehensive defense of religious practices, magic, and sacrifices:

> It is not thought that links the theurgists to the gods: for otherwise what should prevent the theoretical philosopher from enjoying a theurgic union with the gods? But this is not the case; theurgic union is attained only by the perfective operation of ineffable acts worthily performed, which are beyond all understanding, and by power of the unutterable symbols, which are intelligible only to the gods.

By thus insisting on the necessity of the practice of theurgic rites to accomplish the union with the gods, Iamblichus rejects, as E. R. Dodds notes, "the whole basis of the Plotinian intellectual mysticism" and "opens the door to all those superstitions of the lower culture which Plotinus had condemned in that noble apology for Hellenism, the treatise *Against the Gnostics*." (Dodds 1963, p. XX with quotation of *De myst.* II 11).

Some of Iamblichus's students devoted a lot of attention to the philosophical justification of magical and esoteric practices. They set up a school in Pergamum that seems to have gained some reputation when one of its students, Julian, became emperor. Julian drew upon Neoplatonic philosophy in his attempt to restore pagan rituals and traditions against the increasing influence of the Christians. Sallustius (fl. fourth century CE), who published a small introductory manual of Neoplatonic theology *On the Gods*, was probably a member of the same school.

THE ATHENIAN SCHOOL. The philosopher Plutarch of Athens (d. 432) gave a new inspiration to the Platonic Academy in Athens, which from then on adopted the philosophical style of Iamblichus. Although they no longer taught in the original building of the Academy, the successive heads of the school in Athens proudly considered themselves to be the "*diadochoi*," successors of Plato. Of Plutarch we have only indirect and fragmentary evidence. Proclus attributes to him an important role in the search for the right interpretation of the Parmenides. As a young student, he read with him Aristotle's treatise On the Soul and Plato's Phaedo. One would like to know how

Plutarch attempted to reconcile the opposing views of Plato and Aristotle on the nature of the soul and its immortality, and on the origin of knowledge (anamnesis vs. abstraction).

After Plutarch's death in 432, Syrianus, a native from Alexandria, became the new head of the school. Of Syrianus we have only a commentary on some books of the *Metaphysics* in which he is often very critical of Aristotle. He recognizes Aristotle's great contribution in logic, ethics, and natural philosophy, even in theology. But, as he says, Aristotle's attack on the doctrine of the first principles of Pythagoras and Plato (an in particular, the doctrine of the Forms) is so unfair and shows so much misunderstanding that he felt compelled to defend the truth by showing Aristotle's arguments to be invalid (*In Metaph*. 80, 4-81, 14.)

When Syrianus died (c. 437), he was succeeded by Proclus who was born from a Lycean family still faithful to the old religion and had come from Alexandria to study philosophy in Athens. After a short term with Plutarch, Proclus continued his philosophical education under the guidance of Syrianus: "In less than two years Proclus read with him all of Aristotle's treatises on logic, ethics, politics, physics, and the theological science which surpasses them all. When Proclus was suitably educated through those studies which, so to speak, are a kind of preparatory initiation, or lesser mysteries, Syrianus led Proclus to Plato's mystagogy." (Marinus, *Life of Proclus*, §13).

Because of the loss of most of Syrianus's, work, it will never be possible to determine which ideas and doctrines Proclus inherited from his master and which ones he contributed himself. But it is evident that Syrianus had a profound influence on Proclus, as the latter gratefully acknowledges: "It is he who has granted us the privilege of partaking in the philosophy of Plato as a whole and who has communicated to us what he had received in secret from those senior to himself, and, above all, who joined us with himself as co-celebrants of the mystical truth of the divine principles." (*Theol. Plat*. I 1, p. 6.16-7.8 ed. Saffrey-Westerink, transl. J. Dillon). As is clear from this text, Proclus understands his Platonic education not just as a transmission of a philosophical doctrine but as a revelation of a mystical truth coming from the gods through Plato, and even as an initiation in a mystery cult and a participation in a ritual practice of life.

As we know from his biographer (and successor) Marinus (c. 440–c. 500), Proclus's whole life was devoted to teaching and writing. He wrote commentaries on the Platonic dialogues that were part of the Neoplatonic-school curriculum. The course started with the reading of the *Alcibiades I*, a dialogue about self-knowledge, which was regarded as an introduction to philosophy. The curriculum culminated in the explanation of the two major dialogues of the Platonic corpus, which were considered to incorporate the whole of Plato's philosophy, namely the *Timaeus* (about the generation of the physical world), and the *Parmenides* (about the procession of all beings from the One). The commentaries of Proclus are masterpieces in their genre, as they not only offer a systematic interpretation of the text but also provide a wealth of information about the discussions within the Platonic tradition. In addition to his commentaries, Proclus owes his reputation to his two great syntheses of Neoplatonic philosophy, the *Elements of Theology* and the *Platonic Theology*.

In the *Elements of Theology*, Proclus demonstrates *in a geometrical way* the most fundamental theorems of the theological or metaphysical science as he understands it. The first part examines the fundamental principles that govern the structure of all reality, such as the relation between the One and the many; cause and effect; whole and parts; transcendence and participation; procession and reversion; continuity and discontinuity. In the second part he expounds the procession of the divine principles (henads, intellects, souls). The *Elements of Theology* is without doubt his most original work, not so much because of its content (which offers the standard doctrine of the Athenian school) but because of its extraordinary attempt to develop the entire Neoplatonic metaphysics from a set of axioms. It also had a tremendous influence, in particular through the Arabic adaptation that was made in the ninth century in the circle of Al-Kindi (805–873). In the middle of the twelfth century, this Arabic treatise was translated into Latin. The *Liber de Causis*, as it was named, circulated as the work of Aristotle and thus obtained a great authority in medieval scholasticism. The systematic character of the *Elements* and its rigorous method make it the best introduction for the student not only to Proclus's own thought but also to Neoplatonism in general.

Proclus was convinced that the truth about the gods had been revealed in many different ways—in obscure oracles, myths, and symbols. It was his ambition to prove the harmony between Plato and the other sources of divinely inspired wisdom, in particular, the *Chaldaean Oracles* and the Orphic poems. In his view only a genuinely philosophical approach could offer the conceptual framework for such a comprehensive interpretation. One finds such a framework in the *Parmenides* if one adopts

the theological interpretation of this dialogue developed first by Syrianus. The *Platonic Theology*, written at the end of Proclus's life, is the perfect realization of this theological project—a pagan Summa of theology.

It is difficult to evaluate the originality of a thinker who, in most of his works, proclaims to be nothing but a faithful follower of his master Syrianus. But it is Proclus who put his mark on the subsequent development of Neoplatonism in Byzantine, Arabic, and Latin medieval thought. His huge influence—much greater than that of Plotinus—could extend itself mainly through two important indirect channels of transmission: the Arabic adaptation of the *Elements* in the *Liber de Causis*, and the Christianization of his Platonic theology by Dionysius the Areopagite. The latter author pretends to be, and was for centuries believed to have been, the Dionysius mentioned in the Acts of the Apostles who became Christian after the preaching of Saint Paul on the Areopagus (Acts 17:34). This *authorship* gave this work an almost apostolic authority both in Byzantium and in Latin Europe. Although the real identity of this author still remains unknown, he probably was a Syrian Christian who followed classes in Athens at the end of the fifth century (he may even have been a direct disciple of Proclus). In his works, and in particular in his treatise *On the Divine Names*, he expounded the Christian doctrine of the transcendent God, of the Trinity, and of creation and incarnation in terms of Proclus, eliminating references to the pagan religion and substituting the Christian sacred writing for the *Chaldaean Oracles*.

Among Proclus's fellow students under Syrianus were Hermias, who would return to his hometown Alexandria and start teaching there, and Domninus of Larissa (c. 420–480), who had a predominantly mathematical interest and was criticized by Proclus for his unorthodox interpretation of Plato.

On the further history of the Platonic school in Athens at the turn of the fifth century, inside information is provided by Damascius, the last head of the school, in his *Life of Isidore* (Isidore [fifth century] was his predecessor). Thanks to his energetic reforms and inspiring teaching, the Academy would revive one last time. Damascius is known, among other things, for his commentaries on the *Philebus* and the *Parmenides*, but above all things, for his treatise *On the First Principles* (*De principiis*). This work concludes a period of a thousand years of philosophical speculation on the first causes. Damascius has no ambition to develop a system that would surpass that of his predecessors. His own thought is primarily aporetic: He raises critical questions in the margin of the doctrine of the principles as it had been developed in the Neoplatonic tradition and confronts it with all sorts of difficulties. When he risks a solution—and on many issues he can be very original (for instance, his doctrine on time)—he again calls it into question by raising new aporias. The most fundamental aporia is discussed at the beginning. Is the first principle itself a part of the whole of which it is the principle? The first, it seems, is neither principle nor cause nor does it fit in any other category used to explain relations between beings: It is an ineffable *nothing* we have to postulate beyond the one whole. This ineffable is even beyond the One, which is the first principle of all things. More than any other Platonic philosopher, Damascius is aware of the precarious nature of all rational discourse when dealing with questions that go beyond the limits of what can be experienced. About the first principles we can only speak by making use of analogies and *indications*. His sharp critical mind does not, however, lead him to skepticism. If a philosophical explanation remains tentative and fragile, there is also the mythological tradition and religious practice, to which Damascius remains very devoted. In many ways his work is a wonderful swan song of pagan Hellenism.

The renaissance of the Academy under Damascius may have been one of the reasons for its closing by a decree of the emperor Justinian (c. 482–565) in 529. The decree is one of the multiple measures of the emperor against pagans: They were formally excluded from all official positions, including teaching. According to the historian Agathias (536–582), Damascius, together with Simplicius, Priscianus the Lydian, and other philosophers went into exile at the court of King Chosroes (?–579) in Persia. After two years Chosroes concluded a peace treaty with Justinian, which contained a clause about the exiled philosophers: "They were free to return to their country and live quietly by themselves without being compelled to accept any belief against their conviction or to renounce the creed of their fathers" (Agathias, II, 28–32 ed. Keydell, transl. Westerink). Whether they returned to Athens or Alexandria or stayed in other places remains uncertain.

ALEXANDRIAN SCHOOL. Alexandria had always been a city with a dynamic intellectual life, and it remained so in late antiquity though Christian theological debates now dominated the scene and church authorities set restrictions to the teaching of pagan philosophy. A notorious case, symbolic of the changing times, is the lynching of Hypatia in 415 by a Christian mob. Educated by her father Theon (335–405), Hypatia had become an outstanding mathematician. What her philosophical inter-

ests were are unknown, but among her admiring disciples was Synesius (c. 370–414), author of *On Dreams* of Neoplatonic inspiration, who also shows an interest in the *Chaldaean Oracles* even after he had become a Christian bishop.

The first to introduce Neoplatonic philosophy in Alexandria was Hierocles (c.400–460 CE), who studied in Athens with Plutarch. He is the author of a commentary on the *Golden Verses* of Pythagoras and a treatise *On Providence*. In the introduction of the latter work, he criticizes "all those who try to break up the unanimity of Plato and Aristotle". Thanks to his master Plutarch, he was educated in a tradition that harmonizes the thought of both great philosophers and goes back to Ammonius (c. 175–243 CE), who was teacher of Plotinus in Alexandria: "This man, Hierocles says, was the first to bring the teachings of Plato and Aristotle into one and the same view and to transmit a philosophy without factions to all his students." This hermeneutical approach—different from the more polemical attitude to Aristotle of Syrianus and Proclus—would be continued in Alexandria by the following generations of philosophers and find its magnificent expression in the great commentaries on Aristotle of Simplicius.

The leading Neoplatonic philosopher in Alexandria was another Ammonius (c. 440–526) who had come from Athens with his father Hermias. In his youth Ammonius followed courses with Proclus, and he would adopt the basic principles of the latter's Neoplatonic synthesis. Of Ammonius, however, we possess only commentaries on Aristotle, one of which he wrote himself (on *De Interpretatione*), others of which were published in the form of lecture notes by his students. Since most of his teaching was devoted to the explanation of Aristotle's logic and (meta-)physics, the typical Neoplatonic doctrines (the three hypostases; the procession of all things from the One; the structure of the intelligible world; the ascent and mystical union of the Soul) are rarely discussed and explained. Had we also had Ammonius's commentaries on Plato, the picture might have been somewhat different. But it may also be the case that Ammonius intentionally avoided controversial subjects as he noticed the growing number of Christian students in his audience. The Alexandrian School was a much more open system of education than the Athenian Academy, which had in its last phase become somewhat of an esoteric group. However, from the extant texts, it emerges that Ammonius had more interest in explaining the structure of the physical world than in elucidating the architecture of the intelligible world.

Scholars have often said that the Alexandrian School represents a different kind of Platonism from that of Athens:

> In Athens the speculative, mystical, theurgic, and religious elements predominated; and that school remained to the end a stronghold of paganism. In Alexandria scholarly interests and a noncommittal exegesis of texts prevailed. The Platonism that the Alexandrian School professed was in some respects closer than that of the Athenian School to the pre-Plotinian version; thus, the doctrine of the ineffable One and the mystic union with it had no prominent place.... Thus, the "baptizing" of Greek philosophy—including the stress on those parts of the Aristotelian philosophy that were metaphysically neutral—so often considered characteristic of the medieval period, was to a certain extent anticipated in Alexandria; after the Arab conquest it was perhaps replaced by 'Islamizing.'"

Thus writes Ph. Merlan in the first edition of this Encyclopedia, following the views of Praechter. Recent studies (in particular, by Ilsetraut Hadot), however, tend to minimize the differences between the two schools. There were indeed very close relations, even family relations, between the members of both schools, and there was a lively intellectual exchange. All members were educated in the same tradition. The fact that some doctrines are less prominent in the extant works of the Alexandrians can be explained by the fact that only their work on Aristotle have come down to us. A close reading of the works of the Alexandrian philosophers shows that they had fundamentally the same views on the most important metaphysical issues (such as the distinction between the demiurge and the absolute One) as their colleagues in Athens. And yet it cannot be denied that there are important differences between the two schools and that the view of Praechter and Merlan contains some truth. First, as noticed, there is the harmonizing, not polemical, approach to Aristotle. One may even go so far to say that the Alexandrians were primarily interested in presenting a Platonized Aristotle. Second, though Hadot may be right in denying that the Alexandrian thinkers return to a pre-Plotinian form of Platonism, they tend to simplify considerably the highly complicated Proclean system. Third, the philosophy of the school of Ammonius is less connected with openly pagan beliefs. The project of a comprehensive Platonic theology seems to be alien to them. According to Damascius (who speaks about it with contempt), Ammonius had concluded a pact with the patriarch Athanasius. We do not know what concessions he made to preserve the freedom of teaching in the school. Maybe he promised not to discuss certain doctrines contrary to Christian faith, such as the eternity of the world or the preexistence and reincarnation of the soul.

Two of the most famous students of Ammonius deserve special mention: John Philoponus and Simplicius. The latter is rightly famous for his voluminous commentaries on the *Physics*, the *De Caelo*, and the *Categories* (the commentary *On the Soul* is not his work but probably of his colleague Priscianus), which still are of great use to any interpreter of Aristotle. Simplicius attended Ammonius's courses on Aristotle, but he mentions also Damascius as his teacher. This double education situates him somehow halfway between Alexandria and Athens. He is well acquainted with Damascius's metaphysical speculations (on the procession of all things, on time and place), but never forgets the first intention of his work, which is to offer a faithful elucidation of the views of Aristotle in a Neoplatonic perspective. His commentaries also contain rich historical and doxographical information on the Presocratics (of whom he preserves many fragments), on Stoic philosophy, and on the later developments of the Peripatetic and Platonic school. He also quotes long sections from Plato's *Dialogues* and misses no opportunity to demonstrate that there is no contradiction between Plato and Aristotle in doctrinal matters. When Aristotle does seem to attack his master, so Simplicius argues, his critique only concerns the manner in which Plato expresses his views. For Plato often uses a narrative form and a metaphorical language, which, if taken literally, may lead the reader to erroneous views. To defend the harmony of Plato and Aristotle was for Simplicius also of great strategic importance in his controversy with the Christian Philoponus. The latter liked to exploit the oppositions within the philosophical tradition in order to undermine it.

Philoponus was one of the brightest students of Ammonius. He published several of his lecture courses and continued to comment on Aristotle in the manner of his master. What sets Philoponus apart from the other members of the school, however, is the publication of a treatise against Proclus in which he attacked, from an overtly Christian point of view, the doctrine of the eternity of the world. Philoponus attempts to prove that the world had a temporal origin and that this was also the authentic doctrine of Plato in the *Timaeus*. In the later versions of his commentaries on Aristotle, he adopts the same polemical attitude whenever he finds Aristotle in contradiction with the Christian understanding of creation.

The publication of *Against Proclus* in 517 must have provoked quite a scandal in the school, where Philoponus was one of the leading figures. Scholars have advanced many solutions to explain his sudden change from a Neoplatonic to a Christian philosophy. The fact that the publication of the polemical treatise coincides with the closing of the Academy in Athens and with other hostile measures that were taken against pagan philosophers may provide a useful clue. By publishing his book against Proclus, Philoponus probably wanted to distance himself from the allegedly pagan elements in Neoplatonic philosophy. In his later work he is only engaged in theological discussions.

Simplicius says he never met Philoponus and speaks of this *newcomer*, not really a *philosopher*, with utter disdain. In his commentary on the *De Caelo*, he came to the defense of Aristotle and of the old Hellenic pagan view of the cosmos as an everlasting, wonderful expression of the intelligible world.

The successor of Ammonius as head of the school was Olympiodorus (c. 500–565). We also have some of his commentaries on Plato, which show that he did not consider himself to be a Christian. For he continued to defend, though with caution and without offending his audience, some views that belonged to the pagan tradition. He upheld polytheism by explaining the lower gods as powers of the first God rather than as many gods.

Olympiodorus's two pupils, Elias and David, who lectured on Aristotle's *Organon*, certainly were Christians though their belief does not really have an impact on their teaching. The last teacher in the school was Stephanus, who became professor at the newly founded academy in Constantinople (in 610). The transfer of the school (and its library) to Constantinople may explain why so many works of pagan Neoplatonists have survived.

LATIN NEOPLATONISM. In the western part of the empire, too, we find authors who were influenced by Neoplatonic ideas. Since they all wrote in Latin, they would have a determinative influence on the formation of Medieval Platonism. There are, of course, Christian thinkers, such as Ambrose (c. 339–397), Marius Victorinus (c. 280–365), and above all Augustine, who all considered Plato closer to Christian faith than any other philosopher. Yet besides them there also was a small group of authors who continued to practice philosophy in the old tradition. Even if they were Christians, their beliefs had almost no effect on their arguments (contrary to what we see happen in Augustine). A good example is Calcidius (late fourth century), who translated and commented the *Timaeus* and followed Porphyry in many of his interpretations. His work had an immense success in the early Middle Ages. The same is true for the *Commentary on the "Dream of Scipio"* by Macrobius (c. 400), who quotes also from Plotinus and Porphyry. Also Martianus Capella (early fifth century), author of the much read *On the Marriage of Philology and Mercury* that offers an allegorical introduction to the seven liberal arts and makes them part of the philosophical wisdom, shows a thorough acquaintance with the Platonism of late antiquity. Last but not the least is Boethius who is undoubtedly a Christian (as his theological work shows). Yet in his practice of philosophy, he does not allow Christian arguments to interfere directly. He is author of the celebrated *Consolation of Philosophy*, which is profoundly Neoplatonic in its argument, but he also wrote translations and commentaries on Aristotle. It was his ambition to translate and comment on all of Plato's and Aristotle's works and to demonstrate that they are in agreement on fundamental questions. This program situates him in the tradition of Alexandria, with which he was well acquainted. He shows also to be familiar with the works of Porphyry and Plotinus.

EPILOGUE: CHRISTIAN NEOPLATONISM

As we have seen Neoplatonic philosophy from the beginning took a very polemical attitude toward Christianity. Plotinus attacked some Gnostic Christians in his entourage; Porphyry wrote a vehement attack against the Christians, as did Iamblichus and Julian. The latter even used the Neoplatonic philosophy in his policy of restoration of paganism. In the Athenian School Neoplatonism became the ideology of pagan religion in its multiple guises. When Christianity became the dominant religion, philosophers had to be more cautious and could only make indirect criticism. Proclus and Damascius just ignored Christian thought and looked down with contempt upon the Christian establishment. The Christian authors, of course, attacked paganism, but were, on the other hand, surprisingly positive toward Neoplatonism, which they considered to be the philosophy that came closest to the Christian Weltanschauung. This is the case for Augustine in the west and for Gregory of Nyssa and Gregory of Nazianzus in the East. The reasons for this fascination are manifold: the other-worldness of Neoplatonism; the emphasis on the transcendence of God; the nondualistic doctrine of creation (procession); the spiritual antimaterialistic interpretation of the world; the immortality of the soul; the access to the divine through the soul's return upon itself. The differences were no less evident, in particular, the doctrine of incarnation, personal providence, and the belief in resurrection. Whereas Christian thinkers were often deeply influenced by Neoplatonic thought, the pagan philosophers, on the contrary, showed no influence from Christianity: They absolutely ignored it. There was no interaction between Neoplatonism and Christianity, only a strong influence in one direction.

The integration of Neoplatonic arguments in the explanation of the Christian wisdom give rise to original speculations about creation, the world, the place of humankind, and the relation of soul-body. Some scholars may argue that this Christian appropriation of Neoplatonism is a betrayal of the original spirit of philosophy. But this transformation is in itself a wonderful testimony to the creativity of Neoplatonic thinking. Take the concept of the *self*, which in Neoplatonism gained a much greater richness than ever before in Greek philosophy. Augustine took over the notion of self-reflexivity but gave it an incredible concrete existential richness, making it a leitmotif of his autobiography (*Confessions*). Another example is eschatology. According to the Neoplatonic view, the procession and return are constitutive movements of each being in relation to its cause. Christian thinkers historicized this process: At the beginning of time, all things proceeded from God and will return to Him at the end of time. This interpretation made it possible to give a meaning to history and even to the contingent events of human life.

Thanks to this creative modification, Neoplatonism had a continuing and expanding influence after the death of the pagan intellectual culture. Already prior to Justinian's decision to close the school of Athens, the pagan philosophical tradition had become a rather marginal phenomenon in late antique civilization. Its practitioners were an esoteric group of intellectuals, nostalgic for the past glories of Hellenic culture, practicing magical rituals, and praying to old gods. Pagan Neoplatonism had become an ideology at the service of a disappearing civilization. Once this philosophy became integrated in the Christian culture, and later in the Muslim world, it gained a new importance, which Plotinus could never have foreseen.

See also Alcinous; Aristotle; Augustine, St.; Boethius, Anicius Manlius Severinus; Damascius; Gregory of Nazianzus; Gregory of Nyssa; Hellenistic Thought; Homer; Iamblichus; Liber de Causis; Medieval Philosophy; Metaphysics; Numenius of Apamea; Parmenides of Elea; Peripatetics; Philoponus, John; Plato; Plotinus; Porphyry; Proclus; Pseudo-Dionysius; Pythagoras and Pythagoreanism; Simplicius; Stoicism; Thales of Miletus.

Bibliography

For a bibliographical survey of recent studies, see Steel, Carlos, and Christoph Helmig. "Neue Forschungen zum Neuplatonismus (1995–2003)." *Allgemeine Zeitschrift für Philosophie* 29 (2004): 145–162; 225–247.

GENERAL

Armstrong, Arthur H., ed. *The Cambridge History of Later Greek and Early Medieval Philosophy*. Cambridge, U.K.: Cambridge University Press, 1967.

Beierwaltes, Werner. *Platonismus in Christentum*. 2nd ed. Frankfurt am Mainz: Klostermann, 2002.

Cleary, John, ed. *The Perennial Tradition of Neoplatonism*. Leuven: Leuven University Press, 1997.

Dillon, John. *The Golden Chain: Studies in the Development of Platonism and Christianity*. Aldershot, U.K.: Variorum, 1990.

Dillon, John. *The Great Tradition: further Studies in the Development of Platonism and Early Christianity*. Aldershot, U.K.: Variorum, 1997.

Dillon, John, and Lloyd P. Gerson, eds. *Neoplatonic Philosophy. Introductory Readings*. Indianapolis, IN: Hackett, 2004.

Dörrie, Heinrich, ed. *Karl Praechter. Kleine Schriften*. New York: Georg Olms, 1973.

Dörrie, Heinrich, and Mathias Baltes, eds. *Der Platonismus in der Antike*. 6 vols. Stuttgart: Frommann-Holzboog, 1987–2002.

Gersh, Stephen. *Middle Platonism and Neoplatonism. The Latin Tradition*. 2 vols. Notre Dame, IN: University of Notre Dame Press, 1986.

Haase, Wolfgang, ed. *Aufstieg und Niedergang der römischen Welt*. Vol. II/ 36/1–2 and II/36/7. Berlin: de Gruyter, 1987–1994.

Lloyd, A. C. *The Anatomy of Neoplatonism*. Oxford: Clarendon Press, 1990.

O'Meara, Dominic. *Pythagoras Revived, Mathematics and Philosophy in Late Antiquity*. Oxford: Clarendon, 1989.

Merlan, Philip. "Alexandrian School." In *Encyclopedia of Philosophy*. 1st edition. New York: Macmillan, 1967.

Saffrey, Henri Dominique. *Le néoplatonisme après Plotin*. Paris: Vrin, 1992.

Saffrey, Henri Dominique. *Recherches sur le néoplatonisme après Plotin*. Paris: Vrin, 1990.

Smith, Andrew. *Philosophy in Late Antiquity*. London: Routledge, 2004.

Sorabji, Richard, ed. *Aristotle Transformed*. London: Duckworth, 1990.

Sorabji, Richard, ed. *The Philosophy of the Commentators, 200–600 AD: A Sourcebook in Three Volumes*. London: Duckworth, 2004.

Wallis, R.T. *Neoplatonism*. London: Duckworth, 1972.

SPECIAL

On individual authors, see the more than fifty volumes in the series *Ancient Commentators on Aristotle*, edited by R. Sorabji). London: Duckworth. Excellent biographical notes in Goulet, Richard, ed. *Dictionnaire des philosophes antiques*, 4 vols. Paris: Editions du Centre national de la recherche scientifique, 1994– 2003.

Athanassiadi, Polymnia, ed. *Damascius. The Philosophical History*. Athens: Apameia 1993 (on the Athenian school after Proclus).

Armstrong, Arthur H. *Plotin. Enneads*. VII vol. Harvard University Press 1966–1988.

Dodds, E. R. *Proclus. The Elements of Theology*. 2nd ed. Oxford: Clarendon Press, 1963.

Hadot, Ilsetraut. *Le problème du néoplatonisme Alexandrin. Hiéroclès et Simplicius*. Paris: Etudes augustiniennes, 1978.

Hadot, Ilsetraut, ed. *Simplicius, sa vie, son oeuvre, sa survie*. Berlin: de Gruyter, 1987.

Saffrey, Henri Dominique, and Alain-Philippe Segonds, eds. *Marinus. Proclus ou sur le bonheur*. Paris: Les belles lettres, 2001. On the life of Proclus and the school of Athens.

Schibli, Hermann, ed. *Hierocles of Alexandria*. Oxford: Oxford University Press, 2002.

Steel, Carlos. *The Changing Self. A Study on the Soul in later Neoplatonism: Iamblichus, Damascius and Priscianus*. Brussels: Academie, 1978.

Thiel, R. *Simplikios und das Ende der neuplatonischen Schule in Athen*. Stuttgart: Steiner, 1999.

Carlos Steel (2005)

NEOPLATONISM [ADDENDUM]

When Islam took over the Middle East it came into contact with a flourishing local culture heavily influenced by Greek thought. As far as philosophy was concerned, neoplatonism was the leading approach. For example, many of the most important neoplatonists such as Plotinus, Porphyry, and Proclus had studied in Alexandria, a city conquered by the Muslims in 642. A number of key texts became important when translated into Arabic. These were the *Theology of Aristotle*, in fact mainly parts of Plotinus's *Enneads* and the *Liber de causis*, based on Proclus's *Elements of Theology*. Also popular among philosophers were the extensive commentaries on Aristotle by Alexander of Aphrodisias, Themistius, and others—commentators imbued with the values of neoplatonism to some extent. One significant aspect of neoplatonism was the idea that Plato and Aristotle did not differ much on important issues, together with the doctrine of emanation and a cosmology that has the world being produced out of one being or principle. The translation project that transmitted Greek manuscripts into Arabic introduced a good many of these ideas and doctrines into the Islamic world, and so philosophy in the sense of *falsafa* or Peripatetic philosophy became identified in the first few centuries with neoplatonic philosophy.

THE MAIN DOCTRINES

The emphasis on the unity of the creator may well have found a welcoming reception by Muslim thinkers, and it is certainly there strongly in Islamic neoplatonism. One of the central issues is how there came to be many things in existence when really there exists only one absolute being or principle. An explanation is that the One thinks and through thinking brings other things into existence, because once it thinks it realises that it is a thinking thing, and this brings about a mental bifurcation in its unity, a bifurcation that leads to the production of a range of beings that exist either closer or more distantly from it. The more perfect and abstract they are, the closer they are, the less perfect and the more material are more distant.

Another issue was how God related to the world. If God is identified with the One, then the usual account is that he creates the world by emanation, not production. God thinks about himself and through a variety of stages other things are brought into existence, but it would be an interference with God's perfection were he to know about any of these lesser things. The only thing he should think about is himself, and so the world comes about as an indirect effect of this form of thought. An implication of this is that the world is eternal, because God has always existed, and so has always thought about himself. He did not suddenly start thinking, since it is part of his essence to think. Because God is eternal, his thinking must be eternal, and whatever stems from it eternal also. As can be seen, these are all doctrines that do not fit neatly within the framework of a religion such as Islam. The Qur'an suggests, although does not explicitly state, that God created the world at a particular time, when he wanted to, and it states that he knows everything that goes on in the world. The indirect account of creation as emanation in neoplatonism seems different from the understanding of creation in the Qur'an.

THE MAIN PHILOSOPHERS

The first Islamic philosopher to construct a thoroughly neoplatonic philosophy was al-Fārābī, and he led the way to Ibn Sīnā (Avicenna), who produced the most developed such theory. They both described emanation as consisting of ten intellects that link the Necessary Being or One with our world, where the active intellect (often identified with the moon) is the highest level of thought that we can attain. The political implications of the theory are important too. Those who can attain the active intellect are the appropriate rulers, and prophets are those who are able to think at the level of the active intellect, or come into contact with it at least occasionally. This enables them to understand the organization of the world because the active intellect is the most abstract form of thought that human beings can attain, and once it is combined with the facts we observe in the world the prophet can easily predict what is going to happen. For one thing, the organization of the world, according to Ibn Sīnā, is in terms of necessity, so the pattern of existence is something that may be understood rationally by an advanced thinker.

ATTACKS ON NEOPLATONISM

Neoplatonism came under attack by Muḥammad al-Ghazālī, who criticized it in his "Refutation of Philosophy" both for being heretical and also for being invalid philosophically. He picked out in particular the theses that God cannot know individual things, that the world is eternal and that bodily resurrection is inconceivable. The latter follows from neoplatonism due to its prioritization of the soul over the body, and the principle that the material aspects of human beings are not important enough to survive death. The account of immortality in the Qur'an is clearly material, and the idea that only souls survive death does not seem to fit it. God would not know individual things because he has no sense machinery and he is separated from the everyday activities of this world. Yet as al-Ghazālī argues, how can he punish and reward us on the day of judgement if he has no idea what we do in this world? He rightly points to a range of ideas that really give God little to do, whereas the God of the Qur'an is directly involved in our everyday affairs.

But these are theological points, and al-Ghazālī also uses the arguments of his opponents to refute them. He tries to disprove the whole neoplatonic apparatus, importing God's will to keep nature in operation as a unified system instead of necessity. He argues in particular that causal necessity is only an idea we have and we could easily think of different connections, or no connections at all, between familiar causes and effects. This really does threaten the whole neoplatonic system, because this involves necessary connections between events, so that when one thing occurs, something else has to occur also. Al-Ghazālī makes a lot of use of imagination here, using thought experiments to try to show that the putative necessary connections are not necessary at all. When Ibn

Rushd (Averroes) responded to his attack in his "Refutation of the Refutation" he was fighting with one hand tied behind his back, because Ibn Rushd disapproved of many of the neoplatonic principles as incompatible with the thought of Aristotle, where his main allegiance lay. Ibn Rushd was able to discern many of the divergences between Aristotle and neoplatonism, but in order to defend philosophy as such he was obliged to defend neoplatonism, because this was the main form of philosophy in the Islamic world at that time. Islamic neoplatonism also had a considerable effect on Isma'ili thought, and on ishrāqī (illuminationist) thought. The esoteric Brethren of Purity (Ikhwān al-Safa') were thoroughly imbued with neoplatonic ideas, although often not very orthodox ones.

DECLINE OF ISLAMIC NEOPLATONISM

Neoplatonism also came under attack by the mystics in Islam who saw its limited access to God as a significant problem. The highest we can come to God is to come into contact with the active intellect, a range of abstract thinking that is really a long way from God. Mystics tend to advocate a much closer connection to God and criticized neoplatonists for their view on this. However, they could use aspects of the theory to explain different levels of reality and their interconnections, although these had to be suitably reinterpreted of course along Sufi lines. Similarly some ishrāqī thinkers replaced the language of the levels of intelligences and worlds with levels of illumination, while at the same time arguing against neoplatonism itself. Neoplatonic philosophy went into a serious decline in the Arab world after the twelfth century, but interest in it continued up to now in the Persian cultural sphere, because its contribution to ishrāqī and Sufi thought was acknowledged and respected.

See also Alexander of Aphrodisias; al-Fārābī; al-Ghazālī, Muhammad; Aristotle; Averroes; Avicenna; Islamic Philosophy; Mysticism, History of; Plato; Plotinus; Porphyry; Proclus; Sufism; Themistius.

Bibliography

Fakhry, Majid. *Al-Fārābī: Founder of Islamic Neoplatonism; His Life, Works and Influence.* Oxford: OneWorld, 2002.

Leaman, Oliver. *Brief Introduction to Islamic Philosophy.* Oxford: Polity, 1999.

Leaman, Oliver. *Introduction to Classical Islamic Philosophy.* Cambridge, U.K.: Cambridge University Press, 2003.

Nanji, Azim. "Isma'ili Philosophy." In *History of Islamic Philosophy*, edited by S. H. Nasr and O. Leaman. London: Routledge, 1996.

Netton, Ian. *Allāh Transcendent: Studies in the Structure and Semiotics of Islamic Philosophy Theology and Cosmology.* London: Routledge, 1989.

Oliver Leaman (2005)

NEO-PYTHAGOREANSIM

See *Pythagoras and Pythagoreanism*

NEO-SCHOLASTICISM

See *Scotism; Thomism*

NEO-THOMISM

See *Thomism*

NEUMANN, JOHN VON
(1903–1957)

American mathematician, physicist, and economist John von Neumann was born in Budapest, Hungary. He showed an early precocity in mathematics and was privately tutored in the subject; his first paper was written before he was eighteen. He studied at the universities of Berlin, Zürich, and Budapest and received his doctorate in mathematics from Budapest in 1926, almost simultaneously with an undergraduate degree in chemistry from Zürich. After serving as *Privatdozent* at Berlin, he accepted a visiting professorship at Princeton in 1930. Following three years there, he became a professor of mathematics at the Institute for Advanced Study, a position that he held for the rest of his life. In 1955 he was appointed one of the commissioners of the U.S. Atomic Energy Commission, on which he served brilliantly until his death.

Von Neumann made fundamental contributions to mathematics, physics, and economics. Furthermore, these contributions were not disjointed and separate but arise from a common point of view regarding these fields.

Mathematics was always closest to his heart, and it is the field to which he contributed the most. His earliest significant work was in mathematical logic and set theory, topics that occupied him from 1925 to 1929. His accomplishments were of two sorts; they concerned the axiomatics of set theory and David Hilbert's proof theory.

In both of these subjects he obtained results of extraordinary importance. He became the first to set up an axiomatic system of set theory that satisfied the two conditions of allowing the development of the theory of the whole series of cardinal numbers and employing axioms that are finite in number and are expressible in the lower calculus of functions. This work contained a full classification of the significance of the axioms with regard to the elimination of the paradoxes. With regard to Hilbert's proof theory, von Neumann clarified the concept of a formal system considerably.

His work on the theory of Hilbert space and operators on that space was probably stimulated by what he had done on rigorous foundations for quantum theory. Essentially, von Neumann demonstrated that the ideas originally introduced by Hilbert are capable of constituting an adequate basis for the physical consideration of quantum theory and that there is no need for the introduction of new mathematical schemes for these physical theories. Von Neumann's papers on these subjects constitute about one-third of his printed work and have stimulated extensive research by other mathematicians.

Von Neumann was one of the founders of the theory of games; since the publication of von Neumann's first paper in 1928 it has become an important combinational theory, applied and developed with continuing vigor. Von Neumann's first paper contains rigorous definitions of the concepts of pure strategy (a complete plan, formulated prior to the contest, that makes all necessary decisions in advance) and of mixed strategy (the use of a chance device to pick the strategy for each contest). The central theorem in this theory, the minimax theorem, was not only enunciated and proved by von Neumann but in his hands became a powerful tool for obtaining new methods for combinatorial problems.

A decade after this fundamental paper was written, von Neumann began a collaboration with Oskar Morgenstern that led to *The Theory of Games and Economic Behavior*, a book that has decisively affected the entire subject of operations research.

Von Neumann's principal interest in his later years was in the possibilities and theory of the computing machine. He not only conceived the concept of the so-called stored program computer in 1944 but he made three other signal contributions. First, he recognized the importance of computing machines for mathematics, physics, economics, and industrial and military problems; second, he translated this insight into active sponsorship of a machine (it was called Johniac by his collaborators) that served as a model for several important computers; third, he was one of the authors of a series of papers that provided a theoretical basis for the logical organization and functioning of computers. These papers set out the complete notion of the flow diagram and contained the genesis of many programming techniques.

See also Computing Machines; Decision Theory; Game Theory; Hilbert, David; Mathematics, Foundations of; Proof Theory; Quantum Mechanics; Set Theory.

Bibliography

Much of von Neumann's work, with the exception of certain still-classified reports or papers that are essentially duplicates of other works, is published in *John von Neumann, Collected Works,* 6 vols. (New York: Macmillan, 1961–1963). Other important books by von Neumann are *Continuous Geometry,* 2 vols. (Princeton, NJ: Institute for Advance Study, 1936–1937); *Mathematical Foundations of Quantum Mechanics* (Princeton, NJ: Princeton University Press, 1955); *The Computer and the Brain* (New Haven, CT: Yale University Press, 1958). For a survey of von Neumann's life and work, see the memorial volume *John von Neumann, 1903–1957, Bulletin of the American Mathematical Society* 64 (3:2) (May 1958).

Herman H. Goldstine (1967)

NEURATH, OTTO
(1882–1945)

Otto Neurath, an Austrian sociologist and philosopher, was one of the originators of logical empiricism and an independent Marxist socialist. A man of great vitality, intelligence, and good humor, Neurath was a polymath and an energetic organizer of academic, educational, and economic affairs. His major work was in sociology, economic and social planning, scientific method, and visual education, this last especially by means of an international language of simplified pictures ("isotypes"), but he was also interested in the history of science, political and moral theory, economic history, and statistical theory and was engaged in recurrent efforts to create a new encyclopedism.

ECONOMIC AND COMPARATIVE HISTORY

Neurath's first article, published in 1904, was "Geldzins im Altertum" (Commercial interest in antiquity), and in 1909 he published a popular history of the economic systems of classical Greece and Rome, *Antike Wirtschaftsgeschichte* (Leipzig, 1909), which he supplemented by shorter studies of ancient economic thought. His historical interests then turned to physical science. A little-known paper of 1915, "Prinzipielles zur Geschichte der Optik," compared the ideas on optics of Isaac Newton, René Descartes, Nicolas Malebranche, Francesco Maria Grimaldi, Christian Huygens, Thomas Young, Augustin-Jean Fresnel, Jean-Baptiste Biot, and Étienne-Louis Malus with respect to their conceptual images of periodicity, polarization interference, and Huygens's principle of continuity of centers of force.

Neurath generalized the logic of this analysis to compare systems of hypotheses by a procedure that selects basic notions to be calculated and then enumerates all theories that may be constructed from permutations of these notions. The simple view that theories of light may be divided into wave theories and corpuscular theories is replaced by a more accurate, complex, and systematically clear historical development. To Neurath this use of basic explanatory notions, which are sometimes images and sometimes abstractions, illustrated the value of philosophical understanding for the historian of natural and social science. Neurath's own philosophical understanding anticipated later reliance on alternative sets of epistemologically basic sentences in the structural elucidation of scientific theories.

In 1916, Neurath wrote a general paper on classification, "Zur Klassifikation von Hypothesensystemen," and elaborated on this topic in his monographs *Empirische Soziologie* (1931) and *Foundations of the Social Sciences* (1944). Classification by hypotheses seemed to Neurath to be a principal method for comparative studies of theories and explanations and a crucial tool for rational understanding of cross-cultural phenomena.

ECONOMIC PLANNING, WAR, AND SOCIALISM

During 1919, Neurath served in the Central Planning Office of the Social Democratic government of Bavaria and of its successor, the short-lived Bavarian Soviet Republic. Although he was a civil servant and not a party man, he was imprisoned when the Communist regime was overthrown; upon his release in 1920 he went to Vienna. He there took up again an earlier career as a publicist for socialist economics by efforts on behalf of a socialist conception of civic education, moral and religious reform, and individual responsibility. With Josef Popper-Lynkeus, Neurath was one of the first socialists to call for a centrally planned, rational economy based on Marxist concepts but deriving its policy recommendations from welfare goals and a statistical analysis of the production and distribution of goods and of standards of living.

Less clear to Neurath than equitable distribution of wealth was how a community spirit could be developed while the workers themselves were still overwhelmed by the established culture and the habits of the competitive capitalist order. Nevertheless, he fused his hypotheses about social-economic planning with a moral optimism about the acceptance by the workers of enlightened and rational attitudes toward all life's problems. Neurath's *Lebensgestaltung und Klassenkampf* poignantly tried to teach the reader about a transformed way of life in which he could realistically experience something of the peaceful and cooperative future at least in his private life, and at the same time come to sober realization of the obstacles placed by exploitative society in the way of a rich inner life and good personal relations as well as in the way of the transformation of society by rational socioeconomic planning.

EMPIRICAL SOCIOLOGY

In the 1930s and early 1940s, between the publication of the two monographs on sociology (the *Empirische Soziologie* and the *Foundations*), Neurath published several smaller papers on sociological topics. The most important were "Soziologie im Physikalismus," a physicalist restatement of sociological theories and problems, "Soziologische Prognosen," on social-historical predictions, and "Inventory of the Standard of Living," on the problem of making a rational calculation of the standard of living.

To make sociology scientific, Neurath urged the use of a physicalist language in which all the possible empirical statements would be descriptive of space-time things and properties; this was, roughly, a demand for behaviorism in social theory. He believed that this social behaviorism carried out Karl Marx's claim that historical materialism was empirical, starting from the factual situation of real men in objective circumstances and basing theories upon hypotheses which are free of wishful or evaluative assumptions. Human beings, streets, religious books, prisons, gestures can be so described, and they may be grouped in accord with physicalist theoretical systems. Happiness and suffering, too, may be described empirically, even in a manner similar to a mechanical description of space-time entities. But man, in some situations, dominates the lawlike mechanism of the natural environment. In Neurath's typical formulation: Formerly when there was a swamp and man, man disappeared; nowadays the swamp disappears.

But the language of mechanism is laden with myth and metaphysical presuppositions, and Neurath tried to eliminate all impure or careless terminology. Just as he would ban metaphysics as a misuse of unverifiable but grammatically correct word-signs, so he wished to forbid social theorists to use words that carry multiple meanings and assumptions; he himself never used the word *capital*. Sociological descriptions demand arguments over the entire range of environmental and causal science; biological, geological, ethnological, and chemical statements must join social, psychological, economic, legal, and other statements of purely human reference. Hence it would be useful to invent an empirical language suited to all the sciences, one that avoids descriptive distinctions that are the result of mere linguistic convention. Neurath hoped that empirical sociology might be formulated with clear and univocal physicalist predicates. However, we start with inexact "clots," with indistinct and unanalyzed evidence, and we must tolerate and even carefully devise a correspondingly rich vocabulary which is also amenable to analysis of regularities and at times to the creation of a calculus.

Neurath often wrote of an essential uncertainty in all scientific description and predication, of the probabilistic nature of learning from experience. Historians should explain the present from knowledge of portions of the past, but to predict the future with precision is beyond us. There are too many variables; at least some of these are unknown, and the greater the anticipated change, the less our scientific assurance about its realization. We may, in Neurath's view, strive to construct a future state of affairs, but whether we feel hesitant or confident, we have in sociological lawlike historical statements no rational ground for predictions that are certain. Moreover, some predictive statements, notably self-fulfilling or hortatory prophecies, are codeterminant; they carry causal weight which disturbs their subject matter. Other predictions seem impossible on their face. How should a nation that could not invent the wheel predict the invention of the wheel? Others are too complex. Will painters in misty regions paint misty pictures or, just because of the mistiness, sunny ones? Neurath carried out this analysis of pseudorational certainty throughout his work, using it with a moral force. Decisions cannot be replaced by calculation or by reasoning—not in practical life, and not in scientific work.

SCIENTIFIC METHOD

Physicalism was developed mainly by Neurath and Rudolf Carnap. It may be seen as Neurath's attempt to express, in epistemological terms, the materialist (objective) foundation of knowledge, since the persistent recognition he gave to the natural fact of socially intersubjective agreement was a principal source of his antiphenomenalist role within the Vienna circle. Despite Neurath's insistence on a sharp distinction between scientific and metaphysical expressions by means of criteria for empirical meaning, it was his view that intersubjective agreement provides approximate unanimity about the grounds for judgments, not for meanings. By use of a physicalist language, skeptical inquirers display and share a common standard for confirmation. Physicalism had the further merit for Neurath that it was a linguistic doctrine which overcame any systematic mutual incomprehension of special disciplines not by reduction to the special discipline of physics but by a doctrine of reference to the generalized physics of public space-time states (in the human macroscale).

Neurath freely admitted that this doctrine was a hypothesis; the world was assumed to be unified, a causal network whose multiplicity of descriptions should tend toward a unified language that includes the social, biological, and physical sciences. Moreover, as an analysis of the process of scientific knowledge, physicalism programmatically explicated (for any special science) the relations among the physiology and social psychology of sensuous perception, the physics of experimental and measurement technology, and the known scientific or commonsense entities. Neurath saw physicalism as the further hypothesis that the world is knowable in principle everywhere and throughout. Finally, in "Protokollsätze" (1932) Neurath represented physicalism as providing a sophisticated revision of the doctrine of atomic bits of knowledge, conveyed by individual reports, or "basic sentences," also known at the time as "protocol sentences," by demanding that they, too, be intersubjective and, however psychologically certain, logically tentative and empirically testable. Indeed, the truth of protocol sentences was attributable to their cohering role in a theory (or system of theories) to which empirical evidence gave confirmatory evidence, and consequently the possibility existed that a conflict between a particular protocol statement and a theoretical statement of more complex form and function might, by choice and for convenience, be resolved by discarding the protocol. Neurath found his early analysis of alternative hypothesis systems and their fact-fitting auxiliary statements borne out within this empirical conventionalist interpretation of the physicalist basis.

VISUAL EDUCATION

Both the union of scholars and ordinary workers and the overcoming of national and linguistic divisions were in Neurath's mind when he began to develop his "Vienna method" of visual education. In rudiment, he used an invariant and self-explanatory pictorial sign for a given thing, so as to give quick information, unencumbered by irrelevancies and easily remembered. Neurath's maxims were simple: He who knows what best to omit is the best teacher; to remember simplified pictures is better than to forget accurate figures.

UNITY OF SCIENCE AND ENCYCLOPEDISM

Neurath was the principal organizer of several related philosophical enterprises. By 1929 the regular but informal Thursday meetings of philosophers and scientists who met for discussion with Moritz Schlick in Vienna had gathered sufficient force to produce a noted manifesto of a scientific world conception, signed by Neurath, Hans Hahn, and Carnap although it was largely Neurath's work. This led in the same year to the first of a series of international congresses for scientific philosophy. Neurath's stress upon the unification of the sciences by means of a unifying language, unity of method, and interdisciplinary dialogue led him to plan the *International Encyclopedia of Unified Science*, edited by himself, Carnap, and Charles Morris as the principal effort of the new Institute for the Unity of Science (founded in the Hague in 1936 and later removed to Boston, Massachusetts), directed chiefly by Philipp Frank. The first two introductory volumes appeared in parts, but even these were still incomplete nearly two decades after Neurath's death. Only the Institute for Visual Education (Isotype) continued with vigor after 1945, directed by Neurath's colleague and third wife, Marie Reidemeister Neurath.

See also Basic Statements; Behaviorism; Carnap, Rudolf; Descartes, René; Historical Materialism; Logical Positivism; Malebranche, Nicolas; Marx, Karl; Marxist Philosophy; Newton, Isaac; Physicalism; Popper-Lynkeus, Josef; Schlick, Moritz.

Bibliography

WORKS BY NEURATH

"Geldzins im Altertum." *Plutus* 29 (1904): 569–573.

"Prinzipielles zur Geschichte der Optik." *Archiv für die Geschichte der Naturwissenschaft und die Technik* 5 (1915): 371–389.

"Zur Klassifikation von Hypothesensystemen." *Jahrbuch des Philosophischen Gesellschafts an der Universität Wien*, 27ff. Liepzig, 1916.

Durch die Kriegswirtschaft zur Naturalwirtschaft. Munich: Callwey, 1919.

Lebensgestaltung und Klassenkampf. Berlin: Laub, 1928.

Wissenschaftliche Weltauffassung: Der Wiener Kreis. Vienna: Arthur Wolf, 1929. Written jointly by Neurath, Carnap, and Hans Hahn.

"Wege der wissenschaftlichen Weltauffassung." *Erkenntnis 1* (1930): 106–125.

Empirische Soziologie: Der wissenschaftliche Gehalt der Geschichte und Nationalökonomie. Vienna: J. Springer, 1931.

"Soziologie im Physikalismus." *Erkenntnis 2* (1931): 393–431.

"Protokollsätze." *Erkenntnis 3* (1932): 204–214. Translated into English by Frederick Schick (who is credited as "George") in *Logical Positivism*, edited by A. J. Ayer. Glencoe, IL: Free Press, 1959.

"Soziologische Prognosen." *Erkenntnis 6* (5/6) (1936): 398–405.

"Inventory of the Standard of Living." *Zeitschrift für Sozialforschung 6* (1937): 140–151.

Foundations of the Social Sciences. Chicago: University of Chicago Press, 1944. This is Vol. 2, No. 1, of the *International Encyclopedia of Unified Science.*

Philosophical Papers, 1913–1946. Edited by Marie Neurath and R. S. Cohen. Dordrecht, Holland, and Boston: D. Riedel, 1983. With a bibliography.

OTHER RECOMMENDED WORKS

Cartwright, Nancy. *Otto Neurath: Philosophy between Science and Politics.* New York:; Cambridge University Press, 1996.

Hofmann-Grüneberg, Frank. *Radikal-empiristische Wahrheitstheorie: Eine Studie über Otto Neurath, den Wiener Kreis und das Wahrheitsproblem.* Wien: Hölder-Pichler-Tempsky, 1988.

International Encyclopedia of Unified Science Vol. II, no. 1. Chicago, University of Chicago, 1970.

Koppelberg, Dirk. *Die Aufhebung der analytischen Philosophie: Quine als Synthese von Carnap und Neurath.* Frankfurt am Main: Suhrkamp, 1987.

Logical Empiricism at Its Peak: Schlick, Carnap, and Neurath. Edited by Sahotra Sarkar. New York: Garland, 1996.

Morris, Charles W. *Otto Neurath and the Unity of Science Movement: A Collection of Material Commemorating Otto Neurath's Place in the Unity of Science Movement.* Jerusalem, 1966.

Nemeth, Elisabeth. *Otto Neurath und der Wiener Kreis: Revolutionäre Wissenschaftlichkeit als politischer Anspruch.* Frankfurt am Main; New York: Campus, 1981.

Nemeth, Elisabeth, and Friedrich Stadler. *Encyclopedia and Utopia: The Life and Work of Otto Neurath (1882–1945).* Dordrecht; Boston: Kluwer, 1996.

Neurath, Otto. *Empiricism and Sociology.* Edited by Marie Neurath and R. S. Cohen. Boston: Reidel, 1973.

Neurath, Otto. *Gesammelte philosophische und methodologische Schriften.* Wien: Hölder-Pichler-Tempsky, 1981.

Neurath, Otto. *Philosophical Papers, 1913–1946.* Edited by Marie Neurath and R. S. Cohen. Dordrecht, Holland; Boston: D. Riedel; Hingham, MA: Kluwer, 1983.

Neurath, Otto, ed. *Unified Science: The Vienna Circle Monograph Series Originally Edited by Otto Neurath, Now in an English Edition.* Edited by Brian McGuinness. Dordrecht, Holland; Boston: D. Reidel; Norwell, MA: Kluwer Academic, 1987.

Neurath, Paul, and Elisabeth Nemeth. *Otto Neurath, oder, Die Einheit von Wissenschaft und Gesellschaft.* Wien: Böhlau, 1994.

Neurath, Gramsci, Williams: Theorien der Arbeiterkultur und ihre Wirkung. Hamburg: Argument-Verlag, 1993.

Schlick und Neurath—Ein Symposion. Wien, Amsterdam: Rodopi, 1982.

Uebel, Thomas E. *Overcoming Logical Positivism from Within: The Emergence of Neurath's Naturalism in the Vienna Circle's Protocol Sentence Debate.* Amsterdam; Atlanta: Rodopi, 1992.

Uebel, Thomas E., ed. *Rediscovering the Forgotten Vienna Circle: Austrian Studies on Otto Neurath and the Vienna Circle.* Dordrecht; Boston: Kluwer, 1991.

Uebel, Thomas E. *Vernunftkritik und Wissenschaft: Otto Neurath und der ersten Wiener Kreis.* Wien: Springer, 2000

Zolo, Danilo. *Reflexive Epistemology: The Philosophical Legacy of Otto Neurath.* Dordrecht; Boston: Kluwer, 1989.

Michael J. Farmer (2005)
Robert S. Cohen (1967)

NEUROSCIENCE

Neuroscience is the scientific study of nervous tissue, activity, organization, systems, and interactions. It is paradigmatically interdisciplinary, currently including biophysics, organic and biochemistry, molecular through evolutionary biology, anatomy and physiology, ethology, neuropsychology, and the cognitive and information sciences. Investigators include basic scientists and clinicians. During the late twentieth century, neuroscience underwent enormous growth. Quantitative information available on the Society for Neuroscience's Web site speaks to this. Beginning in 1970 with 500 members, at last count (summer 2004) the Society boasts more than 34,000 members worldwide. More than 30,000 registrants attended the 2004 annual meeting, where more than 14,000 posters and oral presentations were delivered. There are now more than 300 graduate training programs worldwide in neuroscience. With its increasing academic influence and its obvious connection with philosophy's perennial mind-body problem, it was inevitable that philosophers would begin taking serious interest.

Academic philosophy's systematic interest might be dated to 1986, the year that Patricia Churchland's *Neurophilosophy* appeared. She boldly proclaimed that "nothing is more obvious than that philosophers of mind could profit from knowing at least something of what there is to know about how the brain works" (p. 4). Her book presented what was then textbook neuroscience, contextualized by developments in postlogical empiricist philosophy of science. It set the stage for much neurophilosophy and philosophy of neuroscience that followed, especially the branch of neuroscience that philosophers attended to (cognitive neuroscience). This entry will present some neuroscientific techniques and results that have attracted philosophers' attention. In the interest of pedagogy, the emphasis will be on the scientific details. It will close with a section describing another field of contemporary neuroscience that unfortunately has captured less philosophical attention, followed by a more detailed discussion of implications for mind-brain reductionism. Space limitations preclude a comprehensive survey and the bibliography is limited, both in number of entries and primarily to textbook sources and review articles (all containing extensive references to the primary scientific literature, however). This is befitting an encyclopedia entry, but philosophers who are interested in acquiring a serious understanding of actual neuroscience are urged not to stop with these sources. There is no shortcut around delving into the primary literature. Superficial neuroscience still serves too often in straw arguments in the philosophy of mind.

Ideally this entry would also include work on pain processing, especially on the two types of pain circuits (rapidly conducting Ad and slowly conducting C fibers) and the different pain qualities carried by each; the neural mechanisms of dream sleep, especially endogenously produced activity in sensory regions; the discovery of mirror neurons in primate brains that are active when the subject performs a specific motor task and when the subject observes a cohort performing that task; the sea change in computational neuroscience during the 1990s, away from abstract network modeling (inspired by early successes of "connectionist" artificial intelligence) and toward compartmental modeling, where the patch of neural membrane and its ion-specific conductance capacities become the basic units of analysis; and the neurobiology and behavioral genetics of schizophrenia (as elaborated in numerous publications by Kenneth Schaffner). Philosophers have argued for implications from each. But choices were necessary.

FUNCTIONAL NEUROIMAGING

Functional neuroimaging provides a window into the active, healthy brain. Results from two imaging techniques have dominated philosophers' attention: positron emission tomography (PET) and functional magnetic resonance imaging (fMRI). PET is based on radioactive decay of positrons (positively charged electrons). Subjects are injected with water (or sugars) labeled with a radioactive, positron-emitting isotope (such as oxygen-15, whose nuclei are manufactured to contain the normal eight protons but only seven neutrons). During the minute following injection, radioactive water accumulates in biological tissues in amounts directly proportional to local blood flow. Positrons leave the nuclei of the unstable, radioactive atoms and travel only a short distance through biological tissue (at most a few millimeters).

After losing their kinetic energy positrons are attracted to negatively charged electrons. This collision annihilates both and the resulting energy manifests in two photons traveling 180o away from the annihilation site. These photons exit the tissue being imaged and are detected by radiation detectors arranged in coincidence circuits (the "PET camera"). Photons arriving simultaneously at opposing detectors are counted and these counts are converted into an image that reflects the relative number of annihilation collisions localized to a given region. A single ring of coincident detectors can only image a single "slice" through the tissue; but modern PET cameras contain multiple rings and so can image multiple parallel "slices" simultaneously. Powerful algorithms and computer graphics can reconstruct the functional images in any desired orientation. Color codes are typically used to denote intensity of activity.

By subtracting images generated during a carefully selected control task from those generated during an experimental task, PET generates a picture of the location and intensity of activity specific to performing the experimental task. These are the colorful images published in PET studies. But what PET measures directly is localized blood flow to a small region of biological tissue. The activity interpretation exploits the known (and independently verified) positive correlation between increased local blood flow and increased cellular activity in that region.

fMRI—more precisely, Blood Oxygenation Level Dependent (BOLD-) fMRI—also exploits the established correlation between localized blood flow changes and cellular activity in tiny neural regions. But to measure these changes, it takes advantage of the different properties of oxygen-bearing and deoxygenated hemoglobin in a strong magnetic field. Oxygenated hemoglobin is more prevalent in the bloodstream in regions of high cellular activity. The metabolic demands of highly active neurons and glial cells generate signals to blood vessels to increase blood flow to the region (the "hemodynamic response"). The resulting supply exceeds the cells' capacity to remove oxygen from hemoglobin. As of 2004, these different magnetic properties can be measured and localized in fMRI scanners approved for human use to less than one millimeter. Stronger magnetic fields generate more precise measurements and localizations. Algorithms and graphics capabilities comparable to PET technology reconstruct "slices" through the imaged tissue at any desired orientation. By normalizing and contrasting BOLD signals across experimental and carefully selected control tasks, experimenters can image activity location and intensity specific to the experimental task. A variety of postprocessing techniques are employed to account for the potentially variable hemodynamic delays between neural activity generated by task performance and increased blood flow.

A handful of functional neuroimaging studies (mostly older ones from the early days of PET!) recur in philosophical discussions. (All of the studies discussed below are also discussed and referenced in Michael Posner and Marcus Raichle's popular book, *Images of Mind*, 1997.) One still sees reference to Per Roland and his colleagues' regional cerebral blood flow studies from the mid-1980s. Their subjects performed a number of cognitive tasks, including verbalizations, arithmetical calculations, and a complicated memory imagery task involving walking familiar streets and making a system of turns while reporting landmarks visualized along the way. The memory imaging task produced increased blood flow bilaterally to regions in the parietal and temporal lobes—regions that lesion data from human neurological patients had previously revealed to be involved in mental imagery. Stephen Kosslyn's work on mental imagery using neuroimaging techniques, especially work reported in his *Image and Brain* (1994), is also discussed often by philosophers in debates about the structure of cognitive representations. Much of Kosslyn's work demonstrates that the same neural regions are activated when subjects form a visual mental image and when they visually perceive a similar stimulus. He has demonstrated these effects as far back in the visual processing pathways as primary visual cortex (V1). They hold for locations containing neurons known to specialize for the size of perceived stimuli and for stimuli viewed from typical or atypical perspectives.

Much philosophical attention on functional neuroimaging focuses on its implications for localization hypotheses of cognitive functions. Steve Petersen and his colleagues' studies on language processing and use from the late 1980s are still cited and discussed. They employed PET and a hierarchical experimental design that enabled them to separate activations generated by passively viewing words, passively listening to words, speaking words viewed or heard, and generating semantically related words to those viewed or heard. Different tasks in this hierarchy produced PET activation increases in different neural regions, suggesting to some the localization of different tasks involved in language processing, including word perception, speech production, and semantic access. Localization arguments and their scientific grounding in functional neuroimaging studies have been challenged, notably by William Uttal in *The New Phrenology* (2001).

A handful of functional neuroimaging studies on attention rose to philosophical prominence with growing interest in consciousness. A popular example uses the Stroop task to induce conflict. Color words are presented visually in either compatible or incompatible print colors (e.g., compatible: "red" printed in red; incompatible: "red" printed in green). Subjects are asked to name the color of the print. Behaviorally, as measured by errors and response time, subjects find incompatible conditions much harder. Some psychologists have argued that incompatible conditions require conscious effort to inhibit saying the color word. José Pardo and his colleagues in the early 1990s found strong activation effects specific to the (forebrain) anterior cingulate gyrus when compatible PET activation results were subtracted from incompatible ones. These results are consistent with behavioral data from patients with anterior cingulate lesions and lend empirical support to earlier speculations about the neural components of an executive atttentional control network.

CLINICAL NEUROPSYCHOLOGY AND NEUROLOGY

Philosophers have long taken interest in the behavioral effects of brain damage and disease. (Bryan Kolb and Ian Whishaw's *Fundamentals of Human Neuropsychology*, 2003, is an excellent textbook that includes discussions of topics covered in this section and extensive references to the primary scientific literature.) Commissurotomy ("split brain" surgery) is one contemporary example. To treat otherwise intractable epilepsy, neurosurgeons in the early 1960s revived a surgical technique of cutting a patient's corpus callosum. The corpus callosum is a huge bundle of axon fibers that connect homologous regions of the left and right cortical hemispheres.

The procedure was clinically successful with a minimum of apparent behavioral effects, until Roger Sperry and his collaborators (Michael Gazzaniga, Joseph Bogen) applied more sophisticated tests. They discovered that these patients had lost the capacity of their two cerebral hemispheres to communicate directly with each other. Owing to the segregation and crossing of axon projections from sensory receptor organs to relay neurons in the thalamus and sensory cortex, experimenters could direct, for example, different visual stimuli to the left and right cortical hemispheres. If one then asked the subject to pick up an object related to the visual display with his or her left hand, the subject would pick up an object related to the visual display in his or her right hemisphere. (As with sensation, the motor system also crosses over: Right motor cortex controls left side movement and vice versa.) If one then asked that subject to explain verbally why he or she was holding that object (and the subject was among the roughly 85 percent of humans with speech localized to the left hemisphere), the subject indicated no awareness in his or her verbal response of the display presented to the right visual hemisphere and instead confabulated a verbal account that related the chosen object to the left hemisphere's visual display. The variety and number of similar results led to speculations about two seats of conscious awareness and control in a single human brain, and subsequent philosophical reflections about the unity of self (or lack thereof).

Blindsight refers to preserved visual capacities following damage to visual cortex. Such damage produces a scotoma (a "blind spot") at circumscribed locations in the patient's visual field. Despite no conscious awareness of visual stimuli presented there, these patients nevertheless display some impressive visual abilities when prompted to guess about stimuli presented in their scotoma, including pointing accurately to visual stimulus location, detecting movement, and discriminating shapes (and in a few cases, colors). Their performances far exceed chance. As reviewed in Lawrence Weiskrantz's *Consciousness Lost and Found* (1998), experimental work over the past three decades has mostly confirmed early results and has introduced controls to address methodological criticisms of the early studies. Blindsight has figured into philosophical discussions of the nature of visual consciousness and the location of its neurobiological mechanisms, as well as epistemological discussions about accurate perceptual judgments and the purported necessity of awareness.

Denial symptoms are the opposite of blindsight. Blindness denial (Anton's syndrome) can result from cortically induced blindness and renders patients functionally blind by all objective tests and measures; yet these patients vehemently claim that they can see. Paralysis denial can result from damage to motor cortex and ren-

ders patients functionally paralyzed on the side of their bodies opposite the damage; yet these patients vehemently deny that they are paralyzed. Many patients generate spontaneous confabulations (e.g., "it is dark in this room," "I have bad arthritis in my left shoulder—it hurts to move my left arm") to explain their failures on simple behavioral measures. Numerous controls are standard in neurological assessment to rule out cases of confusion or persistent stubbornness to accept or admit the deficit. Some philosophers and neurologists have argued from these clinical details toward revisions of our commonsense conceptions of awareness, conscious control, and the initiation of behavior. Vilayanur Ramachandran and Susan Blakeslee's popular book, *Phantoms of the Brain* (1998), is a good example, with elaborate discussions of clinical cases and a good bibliography to primary sources.

Contralateral neglect ("hemineglect") is a condition whereby patients ignore the side of their body and the world opposite the side of damage to parietal cortex. (Typically the damage is to right hemisphere, producing left side neglect.) The neglect invades all sensory modalities, is sometimes accompanied by denial and confabulation (to the point of patients denying that their neglected limbs even belong to them), and even invades memories and images. A famous study from the late 1970s by neurologist Edoardo Bisiach and his colleagues asked recent stroke patients demonstrating neglect symptoms to remember a famous square in Milan from one vantage point and to describe all objects they remembered. They were then asked to visualize the square from the opposite vantage point and describe the objects remembered. In both cases, they described objects only on their nonneglected sides—meaning that they described a different set of objects from the separate vantage points. Hemineglect appears to be an awareness deficit. If the only available objects for patients to attend are on the neglected side, they can attend to them. But when objects are present on the nonneglected side, they seem to lose all awareness of the opposite space. Philosophers working on consciousness, awareness, their brain mechanisms, and on body awareness and body-in-space representations have appealed to neglect data.

THE BINDING PROBLEM

Conscious experiences are present to us as unified wholes. Visual object perception provides rich examples. In ordinary circumstances I see a football zooming toward me, not separately brown color, oblong shape, in motion (speed, trajectory) toward me. Yet each of these visual qualities is extracted by neuronal activity in spatially separated areas. Separate neural pathways respond to qualities that characterize a perceived object's identity (the ventral or "what" stream through inferior temporal cortex) and its location, motion, and my actions toward it (the dorsal or "where/how" stream through posterior parietal cortex). Neurons specialized for specific aspects of the visual stimulus are at distinct locations within each pathway. Seeing an object requires neuronal activity in spatially separated regions and there is no evidence for "grandmother" neurons further downstream onto which all of these active neurons project. This is the "binding problem." How is activity in these spatially separated regions bound together to become active as a unit and so produce a unified visual percept? And given that an object seen is often also heard, felt, or smelled simultaneously, and that these multimodal perceptual experiences are also unified in conscious experience, we actually confront a set of binding problems. (Neuropsychologist Ann Treisman's 1996 review article is an excellent introduction.)

Throughout the 1990s a variety of "temporal synchronicity" solutions were popular. These held that binding results from induced synchronous activity in specific neurons in the separate pathways and processing areas. The discovery of a robust "40 Hz oscillation pattern" across the mammalian cortex during wakeful attention and rapid eye movement (REM, "dreaming") sleep inspired this approach. Feedforward and reciprocal feedback anatomical projections between sensory modality-specific and nonspecific neuron clusters ("nuclei") in the thalamus and sensory cortex provided a biologically plausible hypothesis for how temporal synchronicity might be induced.

However, problems quickly surfaced. It is notoriously difficult to determine the "binding window," the time interval during which the spatially separated processing must occur. Are mechanisms sensitive to temporally coherent discharges tied to the full length of activated neuronal discharges, making the binding window up to several hundred milliseconds? If so, then because distinct and changing stimuli clutter the visual field continuously over this long an interval, how do we successfully bind together the right combination of features? Is activity onset or rise time of discharge the relevant temporal feature? If so, this leads to difficulties when we consider the variable latencies of activity in different areas of modality-specific sensory pathways. Latency differences exist all the way back to activity in sensory receptor cells: Hair cells at different locations on the cochlea and photoreceptors at different locations on the retina respond at slightly different times to a single auditory or visual stimulus. Moving up both auditory and visual processing streams, the temporal differences at which information about different aspects of a single stimulus reaches later points can be tens of milliseconds. Somehow, a temporal synchronicity binding mechanism must compute these processing time differences. (The problem of latency differences is exacerbated when we consider multimodal—for example, visual-auditory binding mechanisms.)

These biological details suggest the need for neural regions where temporal information converges (to carry out the latency computations); but now temporal synchronicity solutions confront a similar problem to the one that sunk purely spatial solutions—no solid evidence for such convergence sites. Temporal synchronicity solutions are less popular now. But the binding problem continues to attract philosophers' attention due to its obvious connections with consciousness and brain mechanisms. Rodolfo Llinás and Patricia Churchland's *The Mind-Brain Continuum* (1996) is a good edited volume that was published at the time that these debates about binding and temporal synchronicity were raging.

MOLECULAR AND CELLULAR COGNITION

The reader might have noticed that most examples of neuroscientific work that has attracted philosophers' attention are dated. This is not necessarily a bad thing. Philosophical reflection on scientific results depends on their scientific credibility and that takes time to establish. However, this limitation risks missing important new developments and changing foundational assumptions in a rapidly developing science. The lessons philosophers draw might then be dated as well. There is evidence that "foundational" change has occurred recently in neuroscience, having to do with the increasing impact of molecular biology.

More than a decade ago neurobiologists Eric Kandel, James Schwartz, and Thomas Jessell, in the third edition of their textbook, *Principles of Neural Science* (1991), wrote that "the goal of neural science is to understand the mind: how we perceive, move, think, and remember. In the previous editions of this book, we stressed that important aspects of behavior could be explained at the level of individual nerve cells. ... Now it is possible to address these questions directly on the molecular level" (p. xii). With the publication of the text's fourth edition (2000), and after another decade of cellular and molecular investigations, these same authors announce mind-to-molecules "linkages" as accomplished scientific results:

This book ... describes how neural science is attempting to link molecules to mind—how proteins responsible for the activities of individual nerve cells are related to the complexity of neural processes. Today it is possible to link the molecular dynamics of individual nerve cells to representations of perceptual and motor acts in the brain and to relate these internal mechanisms to observable behavior. (p. 3–4)

These are heady claims, backed up by more than 1,400 pages of textbook evidence drawn from a huge scientific literature. Yet to read much philosophical discussion of neuroscience, one would not even know that this work and attitude exists—much less that it constitutes the current mainstream of the discipline. (This mountain of supporting evidence also refutes the pitying lament so often uttered by philosophers and cognitive scientists: "If we only knew more about how the brain works ..." We do.)

Much of this research is congealing around a field dubbed "molecular and cellular cognition." According to the Molecular and Cellular Cognition Society's Web site, the field's stated goal is to discover "explanations of cognitive processes that integrate molecular, cellular, and behavioral mechanisms, literally bridging genes and cognition." The field emerged in the early 1990s, after gene engineering techniques were introduced into mammalian neurobiology to generate knockout and transgenic rodents for behavioral studies. Memory has been a principal research focus, with an emphasis on consolidation (the transformation of labile, easily disrupted short-term memories into stable, enduring long-term forms) and on hippocampus-based memories that neuropsychologists call "declarative" or "explicit." This field's methodology is ruthlessly reductive. Its basic experimental strategy is to intervene into cellular or intracellular molecular pathways and then track their effects in the behaving animal using standard tests borrowed from experimental psychology for the phenomenon under investigation. (So despite the new molecular-genetic techniques for intervening directly at increasingly lower levels of biological processes, the basic experimental logic remains interestingly similar to that of classical lesioning and pharmacological studies.)

At last count, more than sixty molecules have been implicated in the molecular mechanisms of mammalian long-term potentiation (LTP), an activity-dependent form of synaptic plasticity with memorylike features. However, a few figure prominently and have been targets of bioengineered mutations and subsequent behavioral study in declarative memory consolidation tasks. Cyclic adenosine monophosphate (cAMP) is a product of adenosine triphosphate (ATP) conversion into energy to drive cellular metabolism and activity. cAMP is the classic "second messenger" of molecular biology, functioning as an intracellular signal for effects elsewhere in the cell. When available in high quantities in active neurons it binds to the regulatory subunits of protein kinase A (PKA) molecules, freeing the catalytic PKA subunits. In high enough quantities, the latter translocate back to the neuron's nucleus, where they phosphorylate cAMP response element binding proteins (CREB), a family of gene transcriptional enhancers and repressions that turn on or inhibit new gene expression and protein synthesis.

Specific targets of phosphorylated CREB transcriptional enhancers include genes coding for regulatory proteins that keep PKA molecules in their active state and effector proteins that resculpt the structure of active synapses, keeping those synapses potentiated to presynaptic activity for days to weeks. Numerous features of LTP have made it an attractive theoretical mechanism for memory consolidation for years; results from molecular and cellular cognition have finally lent experimental backing to this decades-old speculation.

Alcino Silva's group has used mice with a targeted mutation of the CREB gene on a variety of short- and long-term memory tasks, including the Morris water maze task, a combined environment-conditioned stimulus fear conditioning task, and a social recognition memory task. These mice do not synthesize the CREB molecules required for long-lasting "late" LTP (L-LTP), although they have all the molecules necessary for shorter-lasting "early" LTP (E-LTP). Eric Kandel's group has developed PKA regulatory subunit transgenic mice that overexpress those molecules in specific neural regions. When activity-driven cAMP molecules release PKA catalytic subunits, an abundance of regulatory subunits are available to block PKA catalytic subunit translocation to the neuron's nucleus (in the regions of the brain where the transgene is expressed). This effect halts the gene expression and protein synthesis necessary for L-LTP. If the molecular mechanisms of L-LTP are those of memory consolidation, then Silva's CREB enhancer mutants and Kandel's PKA regulatory transgenics should be intact in short-term memory tasks but impaired in their long-term form. These are exactly their published experimental results. Kandel's results are especially compelling because the transgenic mice acquire long-term memories on tasks that involve activity in brain regions where the transgene is not expressed—tasks they learn simultaneously with the long-term memory tasks on which they fail. This suggests that the deficit is not sensory, motor, or attentional, but instead is specific to memory consolidation.

New results from molecular and cellular cognition are reported in virtually every issue of journals such as *Cell, Neuron, Journal of Neuroscience, Journal of Neurophysiology*, and *Nature Neuroscience*. However, they have yet to creep into philosophical awareness. This is unfortunate for at least two reasons. First, this is mainstream neuroscience at the turn of the twenty-first century, employing techniques common to the bulk of the discipline's practitioners (especially compared to the number of cognitive neuroscientists). Second, this work is reductionistic, especially compared to higher-level neuroscience. Philosophers who limit their attention to the latter not only come away with a mistaken impression of what constitutes state-of-the-art neuroscience; they also miss the reductionist attitude that informs the mainstream. This carries problems especially for philosophy of mind. These implications are serious enough to motivate fuller discussion in the final section.

PHILOSOPHICAL IMPLICATIONS: REDUCTION REVISITED

When presenting important neuroscientific findings above, some philosophical implications were mentioned. In this final section, implications for reductionism will be discussed in more detail. Philosophical attention to neuroscience began with this concern. Reduction occupied an entire chapter in Patricia Churchland's ground breaking *Neurophilosophy* (1986). Other concerns emerged as philosophers engaged neuroscience, but reduction remains central to neurophilosophy—as witnessed by its prominent treatment in the first single-authored, introductory neurophilosophy textbook (Churchland 2002). Unfortunately, the term "reduction" is less univocal than it once was, and its philosophical treatments and discussions remain frustratingly abstract and distant from actual scientific practice. These features cast suspicion on assessments of psychoneural reductionism's philosophical potential. Might closer attention to mainstream (cellular and molecular) neuroscience rectify this?

Philosophical discussions of reduction were clearest and most fruitful when *intertheoretic reduction* was their explicit concern. This treatment goes back most prominently to Ernest Nagel's classic *The Structure of Science* (1961, ch. 11). According to Nagel, reduction is deduction—of the reduced theory, characterized syntactically as a set of propositions, with the reducing theory serving as premises. In interesting scientific reductions, the reduced theory contains descriptive terms that don't occur in the reducing, so the premises of the derivation must also contain bridging principles or correspondence rules. Typically these principles were treated as material biconditionals (although Nagel explicitly permitted material conditionals) containing terms from the two theoretical vocabularies. In interesting scientific cases, the reducing theory also often corrects the reduced. On Nagel's account, this feature is handled by introducing premises expressing counterfactual limiting assumptions and boundary conditions on the application of the reducing theory.

Both of these features came under serious philosophical criticism, many of which resulted from attempts by philosophers to apply Nagel's account to increasingly better described cases from the history of science (including classical equilibrium thermodynamics to statistical mechanics and the kinetic theory of gases, Nagel's own detailed example). Led by Thomas Kuhn, Paul Feyerabend, Kenneth Schaffner, Lawrence Sklar, Robert Causey, and Clifford Hooker, philosophers of science proposed alternatives to Nagel's conditions. Patrick Suppes even proposed scraping the entire syntactical view of theories and replacing it with a semantic view—theories as sets of models sharing set-theoretic or category-theoretic features. Intertheoretic reduction then turns into a mapping of these sets into one another in light of a variety of constraints and conditions.

One problem with applying these detailed accounts from the philosophy of science to philosophy of mind is that neither neuroscience nor psychology seems to provide robust enough theories. Most theories of intertheoretic reduction require a complete account of lower level phenomena in terms of laws, generalizations, or their model-theoretic counterparts. But even in the best cellular and molecular neuroscience, as in cell and molecular biology in general, few (if any) explanations are framed in terms of laws or generalizations. Many interactions are known to occur with predictable regularity and have both theoretical and experimental justification; but biochemistry hasn't even provided molecular biology with a general (and hence generalization-governed) account of how proteins assume their tertiary configurations. Molecular biologists know much about how specific molecules interact in specific contexts, but few explanatory generalizations are found in experimental reports, review articles, or textbooks; and the few that are found do not by themselves yield extensive predictions or explanations of lower level interactions. Finally, real molecular neuroscience does not provide what some law-based accounts of scientific theory structure require. Its explanations do not specify how molecular biological entities interact in all possible circumstances. In light of these mismatches, intertheoretic reduction looks like a naive account of actual scientific practice.

Furthermore, its philosophical successor, *functional reductive explanation*, fares no better. According to this view, whose prominent advocates include Jaegwon Kim, David Chalmers, and Joseph Levine, a reductive explanation of a higher-level phenomenon is a two-step process. Step 1 requires a functional characterization of the phenomenon, in terms of its principal causes and effects. Step 2 involves the empirical, scientific search for the lower level processes, events, or mechanisms that realize this functional characterization. The reductive explanation of water by aggregates of H_2O molecules is a commonly cited example. Scientists characterize the causal roles of water and its basic properties, like its boiling point at sea level; and empirical research reveals that aggregates of H_2O molecules, with their physical and chemical properties and dynamics, provide the underlying mechanisms for those causes and effects. (This account of reductive explanation is often employed by critics of mind-brain reductionism. Many philosophical champions of the qualitative features of consciousness insist that no reductive explanation of them should be expected, because any attempt to functionalize these features will fail to capture their qualitative essence. Hence Step 1 of their potential reductive explanation cannot be achieved.)

It is not illuminating—quite the reverse, in fact—to force the actual details of state-of-the-art "molecular and cellular cognition" into this format. No procedures that typically occur in these experiments are serious candidates for Step 1 functionalization. And the empirical searches for mechanisms typically focus on finding specific *divergences* from control group behavior in experimental protocols that are commonly used to study the cognitive phenomenon whose neurobiological reduction is at issue. The key step in these experiments is the intervention step, where techniques of cell and molecular biology are used to manipulate increasingly lower levels of biological organization in living, behaving organisms. Animals receiving the intervention—be it cellular, pharmacological, or a bioengineered mutation—are compared to control animals on a variety of behavioral tests to find specific, narrow behavioral deficits.

These experiments are designed to leave most behaviors intact. For only then do experimenters claim to have found a "reduction," an "explanation," or a "mechanism" of cognition. To force this experimental practice into the common philosophical model of functional reductive explanation occludes the subtlety of choosing which cellular or molecular pathways to intervene into, the exquisiteness of the invention techniques employed, and the specificity of the measured behavioral effects when these experiments are successful. Good philosophical accounts of a scientific practice should illuminate, not obscure, these types of features-in-practice. Any consequences drawn about "psychoneural reduction" from an account that obscures them should be treated with suspicion.

This problem is beginning to look like one of imposing borrowed philosophical ideals onto actual scientific practice. Based on prior epistemological or metaphysical commitments, many philosophers approach the neuroscientific literature with preconceptions about "what reduction has to be." When they fail to find their relation obtaining, they either deny that psychoneural reduction is on offer or redescribe actual cases so that these at least approximate it. Both responses are objectionable. The first drives philosophy of mind continuously farther away from mainstream neuroscience, which grew increasingly reductionistic in the last two decades of the twentieth century. The second keeps borrowed philosophical ideals alive when their actual value grows increasingly questionable, and engenders criticisms of "reductionism" based on "better knowledge of the actual scientific details." A better approach within the philosophy of neuroscience might be to articulate the actual practices of reductionistic neuroscientists—the ones whose work contributes to the "mind-to-molecular-pathways-linkages" expressed in the quote cited above by Kandel, Schwartz, and Jessell. The result will be an account of real reduction in real reductionist neuroscience. One could then ask the different question of whether these practices and their results serve the philosophical purposes that reductionism claimed to serve.

It is still too early in this metascientific investigation to know the answer to the last question. But careful examination of the experimental work described toward the end of the previous section above shows that the dominant reductionistic methodology involves *intervening* into cellular or molecular processes and then *tracking* the behavioral effects in the living animal using standard tests drawn from experimental psychology. Often much *in vitro* experimental work must be done first to discover where these interventions are best placed and which intervention techniques are best suited for the task. Cellular physiology still contributes intervention techniques such as cortical microstimulation; pharmacology still contributes a variety of drugs and delivery systems. During the last decade of the twentieth century, transcranial magnetic stimulation developed more precise techniques for delivering a circumscribed magnetic field to increasingly precise neuronal targets. And molecular biology and biotechnology provided powerful techniques for gene manipulations, enabling experimenters to develop targeted gene knockouts and to insert transgenes to inhibit or exacerbate specific protein synthesis. Attached to appropriate promoter regions (base pair sequences in the genetic material that control the onset of gene expression), transgenic expression and subsequent protein synthesis can be limited to increasingly localized neuron populations.

Armed with these cellular and molecular intervention techniques, and coupled with detailed neuroanatomical knowledge about cell circuits leading ultimately to motor neurons and the muscle fibers they innervate, neuroscientists can make increasingly accurate predictions of behavioral effects on a variety of experimental tasks. Successful experimental results yield the conclusion that the specific cognitive phenomenon, "operationalized" using the behavioral tests employed, reduces to the cellular or molecular processes intervened into, within the neurons comprising the circuits leading ultimately to the musculature. Appeals to "higher level" neuroscientific concepts and resources no longer appear in the resulting explanations. One reads in this scientific literature about contributions to "a molecular biology of cognition, to "bridges linking genes and behavior," and to explanations "of cognitive processes that integrate molecular, cellular and behavioral mechanisms." Within "molecular and cellular cognition," resources from cognitive neuroscience play essential heuristic roles. But once they have served their purposes to yield new "intervene molecularly and track behaviorally" results, they fall away from the discipline's best available account of cognition's neural mechanisms. Philosophers (and many cognitive scientists) might not recognize these scientific practices and results, but that reaction reflects nothing more than their lack of familiarity with ongoing neuroscientific practice. This methodology is central to mainstream reductionistic neuroscience at the turn of the twentieth century. If one wishes to rail against "psychoneural reductionism," one should at least rail against the actual practices and results of real reductionistic neuroscience—not against preconceived assumptions about what those practices and results "have to be."

This final point raises the intriguing question of whether neuroscience as a whole is univocal about the nature of reduction. More than likely it is not. Midway through the first decade of the twenty-first century, neuroscience is a remarkable interdisciplinary melding of different experimental techniques, methodological hunches, and interpretive assumptions. Molecular biology revolutionized the discipline in the late twentieth century, but so did new tools for functional brain imaging. Dynamical systems mathematics, applied initially to analyze artificial neural networks, provided fruitful new formal resources. Neuroscience's traditional core disciplines, neuroanatomy and electrophysiology, have enjoyed continual refinement. Rigorous neurological and neuropsychological assessment continue to develop. With so many questions being pursued—and philosophers would do well to compare attendance at their annual professional meetings with the more than 30,000 registrants at the 2004 Society for Neuroscience annual meeting—and so many techniques pitched at so many different levels of brain organization, it would be astonishing if "reduction"s meant the same thing across this discipline. Perhaps disagreements within philosophy about the neuroscientific plausibility of "psychoneural reduction" result more from philosophers latching onto different uses of this notion across neuroscience, rather than from ignorance or mistaken analysis. Sorting through these notions and discovering which neuroscientific practices employ each is one way that philosophers could contribute to ongoing neuroscientific development, instead of serving as mere sideline spectators or "science journalists."

See also Kim, Jaegwon; Kuhn, Thomas; Memory; Mind-Body Problem; Nagel, Ernest; Philosophy of Biology; Philosophy of Mind; Reductionism in the Philosophy of Mind.

Bibliography

Churchland, Patricia. *Brain-Wise: Studies in Neurophilosophy.* Cambridge, MA: MIT Press, 2002.

Churchland, Patricia. *Neurophilosophy: Toward a Unified Science of the Mind-Brain.* Cambridge, MA: MIT Press, 1986.

Kandel, Eric R., James S. Schwartz, and Thomas J. Jessell, eds. *Principles of Neural Science.* 3rd ed. New York: McGraw-Hill, 1991.

Kandel, Eric R., James S. Schwartz, and Thomas J. Jessell, eds. *Principles of Neural Science.* 4th ed. New York: McGraw-Hill, 2000.

Kolb, Bryan, and Ian Q. Whishaw. *Fundamentals of Human Neuropsychology.* 5th ed. New York: Bedford, Freeman, Worth, 2003.

Kosslyn, Stephen M. *Image and Brain: The Resolution of the Imagery Debate.* Cambridge, MA: MIT Press, 1994.

Llinás. Rodolfo, and Patricia Churchland, eds. *The Mind-Brain Continuum: Sensory Processes.* Cambridge, MA: MIT Press, 1996.

Molecular and Cellular Cognition Society. Available from http://www.silvalab.com/approachesf0.htm.

Nagel, Ernest. *The Structure of Science: Problems in the Logic of Scientific Explanation.* New York: Harcourt, Brace and World, 1961.

Posner, Michael I., and Marcus E. Raichle. *Images of Mind.* New York: Scientific American Library, 1997.

Ramachandran, Vilayanur S., Susan Blakeslee. *Phantoms in the Brain: Probing the Mysteries of the Human Mind.* New York: William Morrow, 1998.

Society for Neuroscience. Available from http://apu.sfn.org/.

Treisman, Ann. "The Binding Problem." *Current Opinion in Neurobiology* 6 (1996): 171–178.

Uttal, William R. *The New Phrenology: The Limits of Localizing Cognitive Processes in the Brain.* Cambridge, MA: MIT Press, 2001.

Weiskrantz, Lawrence. *Consciousness Lost and Found: A Neuropsychological Exploration.* New York: Oxford University Press, 1998.

John Bickle (2005)

NEWCOMB'S PROBLEM

See *Decision Theory*

NEW ENGLAND TRANSCENDENTALISM

The New England transcendentalists were an influential but decidedly heterogeneous group of young writers, critics, philosophers, theologians, and social reformers whose activities centered in and around Concord, Massachusetts, from about 1836 to 1860. Insofar as they can be considered to have subscribed to a common body of doctrine, their leader and spokesman was Ralph Waldo Emerson (1803–1882). Apart from Platonism and Unitarian Christianity, the chief formative intellectual influence on the group was German idealism. It was not, however, the dense and difficult epistemological works of Immanuel Kant, Johann Gottlieb Fichte, Friedrich Schelling, and G. W. F. Hegel that primarily attracted the transcendentalists; although nearly all had made some attempt to read the German philosophers, very few had persevered to the point of mastering them. Rather, it was the more personalized and poetic expressions of Johann Wolfgang von Goethe, Novalis, William Wordsworth, Samuel Taylor Coleridge, and Thomas Carlyle, together with the belletristic expositions of Mme. de Staël's *De l'Allemagne* (New York, 1814) and Victor Cousin's *Introduction à l'histoire de la philosophie* (English translation, Boston, 1832) that provided Emerson and his disciples with whatever philosophical nourishment they possessed. Thus, far from being in any strict sense a primarily philosophical movement, New England transcendentalism was first and foremost a literary phenomenon. It was a passionate outcry on the part of a number of brilliant and highly articulate young Americans who had become so intoxicated with the spirit of European romanticism that they could no longer tolerate the narrow rationalism, pietism, and conservatism of their fathers.

After Emerson and Henry David Thoreau (1817–1862), the more important early transcendentalists were William Ellery Channing (1780–1842)—"Dr. Channing," as Emerson called him—distinguished clergyman and social reformer, leader of the Unitarian revolt against Calvinism; Amos Bronson Alcott (1799–1888), mystic, educationalist, and reformer; George Ripley (1802–1880), Germanist, disciple of François Marie Charles Fourier, and one of the founders of the Brook Farm community and of the *Dial* (the chief transcendentalist periodical); Orestes Augustus Brownson (1803–1876), journalist and clergyman whose lifelong attempt to reconcile religious conviction with radical views about social reform led him to embrace, in turn, nearly every available variety of Christianity from Presbyterianism to Catholicism; Frederic Henry Hedge (1805–1890), scholar, authority on German philosophy, founder in 1836 of the informal Transcendental Club for "exchange of thought among those interested in the new views in philosophy, theology and literature"; Margaret Fuller (1810–1850), literary critic, political radical, feminist, author of *Woman in the Nineteenth Century* (1845), and first editor of the *Dial* (1840–1844); Theodore Parker (1810–1860), dissenting Unitarian preacher and abolitionist whose ordination discourse, "The Transient and Permanent in Christianity" (delivered in Boston in 1841), denied the necessity of believing in biblical inspiration and in miracles and led Emerson to nickname him the Savonarola of transcendentalism; Jones Very (1813–1880), poet and eccentric; James Freeman Clarke (1810–1888), Unitarian minister and religious pamphleteer; and Christopher Pearse Cranch (1813–1892), minister, painter, critic, and poet. Among the later transcendentalists were John Weis (1818–1879), Samuel Longfellow (1819–1892), J. E. Cabot (1821–1903), O. B. Frothingham (1822–1895), and Moncure D. Conway (1832–1907). It is debatable whether Nathaniel Hawthorne should be counted as a transcendentalist, but it is certain that, with other major imaginative writers like James Russell Lowell, John Greenleaf Whittier, Henry Wadsworth Longfellow, and Walt Whitman, Hawthorne owed much to his contact with transcendentalist modes of thought and feeling.

THE NATURE OF TRANSCENDENTALISM

"What is popularly called Transcendentalism among us," Emerson explained to a Boston audience in 1842, "is Idealism; Idealism as it appears in 1842" ("The Transcendentalist"). Yet we must add that it was a form of idealism that included and frequently confused the technical or epistemological idealism of the post-Kantian philosophers and the more vaguely understood "idealism"—in the sense of romantic aspirationism—of Wordsworth's "Intimations" ode and Novalis's *Fragmente*. The term *transcendental* was derived, Emerson claimed, from the use made of it by Kant, who had demonstrated that there was "a very important class of ideas, or imperative forms, which did not come by experience, but through which experience was acquired; that these were intuitions [*sic*] of the mind itself"; and that Kant had called them "Transcendental forms." This somewhat subjective exposition (contrast, for example, *Critique of Pure Reason*, B 25, A 11–12) led Emerson to conclude that consequently "whatever belongs to the class of intuitive thought, is popularly called at the present day *Transcendental*." Here, of course, the word *intuitive* is being employed in its most general sense, quite dissociated from any philosophical use, so that Emerson could immediately go on lamely to characterize the "Transcendentalist" as one who displays a predominant "tendency to respect [his] intuitions."

The failure on the part of the movement's leader to give any really informative definition of transcendentalism is nevertheless instructive. Because of their intellectual eclecticism and avowed individualism, their subjective fads and eccentricities, and, above all, their wide range of activities, which embraced almost every aspect of American cultural life in the mid-nineteenth century, any attempt to express the outlook of the New England transcendentalists in a single formula is bound to fail. O. B. Frothingham was certainly right when he admitted that transcendentalism was not a systematic theory of life but something more like a state of mind, "an enthusiasm, a wave of sentiment, a breath of mind that caught up such as were prepared to receive it, elated them, transported them, and passed on—no man knowing whither it went."

In a clear sense, however, the transcendentalists were the inheritors of certain forms of sensibility already well developed within the European romantic movement: a vague yet exalting conception of the godlike nature of the human spirit and an insistence on the authority of individual conscience; a related respect for the significance and autonomy of every facet of human experience within the organic totality of life; a consequent eschewal of all forms of metaphysical dualism, reductivism, and positivism; nature conceived not as a vast machine demanding impersonal manipulation but as an organism, a symbol and analogue of mind, and a moral educator for the poet who can read her hieroglyphics; a sophisticated understanding of the uses of history in self-culture; in general, the placing of imagination over reason, creativity above theory, action higher than contemplation, and a marked tendency to see the spontaneous activity of the creative artist as the ultimate achievement of civilization—these were the more pervasive principles shared by all thinkers of the New England school. Yet if "idealism," or, better still, "romanticism," serves roughly to denote the genus of transcendentalism, it is important to determine the specific characteristics of the American version.

AMERICAN CHARACTERISTICS

American transcendentalism differed from its European counterparts in at least two important ways. First, unlike most forms of European idealism in the nineteenth century, transcendentalism was not simply closely allied with contemporary theological speculation and debate but arose directly out of it. The majority of its original adherents, including Channing, Emerson, Parker, Ripley, and Cranch, were, or had been, Unitarian clergymen, and from the point of view of cultural history the advent of transcendentalism must be seen as the final liberation of the American religious consciousness from the narrow Calvinism that Unitarianism had already done much to ameliorate. This is not, however, to imply that transcendentalism was primarily a movement within the Christian church. For its outcome, as the works of Emerson and Thoreau, for example, amply testify, was essentially secular and humanist in the widest sense.

Second, the later inception of romantic idealism in the United States led its exponents to less fluctuating and at the same time less radical programs of social reform. If the typical German or English romantic began with an enthusiasm for the ideals of the French Revolution, became disillusioned by the Terror, and ended his career a conservative, Emerson's disciples felt the outcome of the Revolution as something more distant and, in any case,

European. Their social philosophy was the natural out-come of their reactions to the very different American scene. The majority of transcendentalists never wavered in their active opposition to slavery, imperialism, bureau-cratization, and cultural philistinism; yet, partly because the United States had already achieved a democracy and partly because Western expansion kept economic condi-tions relatively good, the transcendentalists were not incited to the more extreme forms of political protest characteristic of such European inheritors of idealism as Karl Marx and Pierre-Joseph Proudhon.

See also Brownson, Orestes Augustus; Carlyle, Thomas; Channing, William Ellery; Coleridge, Samuel Taylor; Cousin, Victor; Emerson, Ralph Waldo; Fichte, Johann Gottlieb; Fourier, François Marie Charles; Goethe, Johann Wolfgang von; Hegel, Georg Wilhelm Friedrich; Idealism; Kant, Immanuel; Marx, Karl; Neo-Kantianism; Novalis; Parker, Theodore; Platonism and the Platonic Tradition; Proudhon, Pierre-Joseph; Schelling, Friedrich Wilhelm Joseph von; Staël-Hol-stein, Anne Louise Germaine Necker, Baronne de; Thoreau, Henry David.

Bibliography

Perry Miller's two collections, *The Transcendentalists: An Anthology* (Cambridge, MA: Harvard University Press, 1950) and *The American Transcendentalists: Their Prose and Poetry* (Garden City, NY: Doubleday, 1957), provide excellent selections of transcendentalist writings; they also contain bibliographies. O. B. Frothingham, *Transcendentalism in New England: A History* (New York: Putnam, 1876), is still the best intellectual history of the movement.

Michael Moran (1967)

NEW ENGLAND TRANSCENDENTALISM [ADDENDUM]

The transcendentalist departure from Unitarianism was bolstered by the Biblical criticism of Johann Gottfried von Herder, who suggested in *The Spirit of Hebrew Poetry* (1782/1833) both that the Bible is a human poetic con-struction, and that works just as authoritative can still be written. This was precisely Emerson's standpoint at the opening of *Nature* (1836), where he asked, "Why should not we have a poetry and philosophy of insight and not of tradition, and a religion by revelation to us, and not the history of theirs?" (1971–, 1:7). In his controversial

"Divinity School Address" (1838), Emerson urged Har-vard graduates to find redemption in the "Soul," not in an "eastern monarchy of a Christianity" that proceeded "as if God were dead" (1971–, 1: 82, 84).

In "Experience" (1844), Emerson developed most fully and creatively the Kantian idea that there are forms through which we acquire experience. Stating that the universe "inevitably wear[s] our color," Emerson devel-oped a categoreal scheme that he called "the Lords of Life"—including "Temperament," "Surface," "Succes-sion," "Surprise," and "Illusion." Against this background he set out an epistemology of moods, according to which moods are like beads strung on the iron wire of tempera-ment, each showing "only what lies in its focus" (1971–, 3: 30). Emerson stated in "Circles" that "our moods do not believe in each other" (1971–, 2: 182)—a statement show-ing that moods contain beliefs and at the same time indi-cating their radically inconsistent outlooks.

Emerson's ethical thought centered on "self-reliance," which is both a positive search for the best in oneself—our "unattained but attainable self," as he put it in "History" (1971–, 2: 5)—and, in its negative moment, an "aversion" to "conformity." Emerson characterized society as "in conspiracy against the manhood of every one of its members" (1971–, 2: 29)—a conspiracy all too effective in producing individuals who "skulk" and "sneak" through their lives, or gather together like "bugs" and "spawn." Emerson's critique was thus directed not so much at specific actions as at a manner of living. He gave an existentialist twist to a passage from René Descartes's *Meditations* when he wrote, "Man is timid and apologetic; he is no longer upright; he dares not say 'I think,' 'I am,' but quotes some saint or sage" (1971–, 2: 38). For Emer-son, as for his contemporary Søren Kierkegaard, thinking and existing are not just given; they are risky ventures. Emerson's heroes manifest a sense of command and over-flowing worth, as well as a tendency toward spontaneity and whim. Friendships of such heroes are alliances of "large formidable natures, mutually beheld, mutually feared" (1971–, 2: 123).

Henry David Thoreau, in *Walden* (1854/1989), pro-duced a work of ethical and political philosophy that, like Plato's *Republic*, considers the necessities of life. On the basis of his "experiment" of living at Walden Pond for two and a half years, Thoreau concluded that he can survive for a year on six weeks of labor. This left him time to "own" the landscape by sitting in it, sound the depths of the pond, watch the spring come in, talk with the occa-sional visitor, and, more generally, "improve the nick of time." Guided by the Greek and Roman philosophy he read as an undergraduate at Harvard College and by his readings in Indian and Chinese thought, Thoreau understood philosophy as the search for "a life of simplicity, independence, magnanimity, and trust." In this sense, he observed, "there are nowadays professors of philosophy, but not philosophers" (p. 14).

In the "Economy" chapter of *Walden*, Thoreau considered human life as a precious commodity: "The cost of a thing is the amount of what I will call life which is required to be exchanged for it, immediately, or in the long run." He concluded that people pay a high cost for the lives they lead, that their lives are modes of strange "penance," and that a "stereotyped but unconscious despair is concealed even under what are called the games and amusements of mankind" (p. 8).

Although he portrayed himself variously as growing beans, peering through the ice of the pond, walking and sitting and "suddenly finding himself neighbor to the birds," the main outcome of Thoreau's time at Walden Pond was the book in which he recorded his life there, a book that, in the chapter "Reading," offered a theory of itself. Thoreau contrasted with the "classics" of every great culture a popular series of books called "Little Reading": books, as he put it, that "we have to stand on tiptoe to read and devote our most alert and wakeful hours to." After he finished *Walden*, Thoreau began to think of his immense journal as just such a book, perhaps even closer to nature, with "each page … written in its own season & out of doors" (1993, p. 67).

Thoreau's "Resistance to Civil Government" (1849) was a response to his night in jail for not paying the poll tax, and served as a source for the nonviolent resistance practiced by Mahatma Gandhi and Martin Luther King Jr. Thoreau argued that the citizen has no duty to align his conscience with the state, and a responsibility to oppose its immoral actions. He wrote, "I cannot for an instant recognize that political organization as my government which is the slave's government also" (1973, p. 67). The country could rid itself of slavery, he argued, if large numbers of people refused to pay their taxes and were willing to go to jail. Later, as Thoreau and Emerson became more agitated about slavery, Thoreau supported violence to end it. In "A Plea for Captain John Brown" (1859), he stated, "A man has a perfect right to interfere by force with the slaveholder, in order to rescue the slave" (1973, p. 132).

Margaret Fuller's death in a shipwreck in 1849 deprived the transcendentalists of a powerful journalist and feminist writer. In *Woman in the Nineteenth Century* (1845), a revision of her essay "The Great Lawsuit" (1843), she maintained that masculinity and femininity are intertwined, that there is "no wholly masculine man, no purely feminine woman." Women's free self-development, she argued, is necessary for the renovation of society, including marriage. "Union," she wrote, "is only possible to those who are units" (Myerson 2000, pp. 418, 419).

INFLUENCES ON PHILOSOPHY

Friedrich Nietzsche read Emerson at three critical points in his life, transcribed passages from Emerson's essays in his journals, and wrote, "*Emerson.*—Never have I felt so much at home in a book, and in *my* home" (Goodman 1997, p. 160). Emerson's ideas about nobility, history, friendship, overcoming self-inertia, and self-reliance presage Nietzsche's *Untimely Meditations* and *Thus Spoke Zarathustra*. A sentence from Emerson's "History" is the epigraph to the first edition of Nietzsche's *Gay Science*: "To the poet, to the philosopher, to the saint, all things are friendly and sacred, all events profitable, all days holy, all men divine" (Emerson 1971–, 2: 8).

In the United States, Emerson's stress on action and the future, his humanistic or Kantian portrayal of the role of the self in forming the world, and his focus on the individual chimed with central emphases of William James's pragmatism. John Dewey considered Emerson "the one philosopher of the New World fit to have his name uttered in the same breath with that of Plato," and found in his writings an anticipation of his view that ideals are present in our "immediate experience." Emerson and Thoreau are central to Stanley Cavell's investigations of "reading," "aversive thinking," and "moral perfectionism," and to his related discussions of Martin Heidegger, Friedrich Nietzsche, and Ludwig Wittgenstein in *The Senses of Walden* (1981), *Emerson's Transcendental Etudes* (2003), and other works.

See also Cavell, Stanley; Conscience; Descartes, René; Dewey, John; Emerson, Ralph Waldo; Emotion; Heidegger, Martin; Herder, Johann Gottfried; James, William; Kierkegaard, Søren Aabye; King, Martin Luther; Neo-Kantianism; Nietzsche, Friedrich; Plato; Pragmatism; Thoreau, Henry David; Wittgenstein, Ludwig Josef Johann.

Bibliography

PRIMARY SOURCES

Emerson, Ralph Waldo. *The Collected Works of Ralph Waldo Emerson*, edited by Robert B. Spiller, et al. Cambridge, MA: Harvard University Press, 1971–.

Emerson, Ralph Waldo. *Emerson's Antislavery Writings*, edited by Joel Myerson and Len Gougeon. New Haven, CT: Yale University Press, 1995.

Emerson, Ralph Waldo. *The Journals and Miscellaneous Notebooks of Ralph Waldo Emerson*, edited by William H. Gilman, et al. Cambridge, MA: Harvard University Press, 1960–.

Fuller, Margaret. *Margaret Fuller, Critic: Writings from the New-York Tribune, 1844–1846*, edited by Judith Mattson Bean and Joel Myerson. New York: Columbia University Press, 2000.

Fuller, Margaret. *"These Sad but Glorious Days": Dispatches from Europe, 1846–1850*, edited by Larry J. Reynolds and Susan Belasco Smith. New Haven, CT: Yale University Press, 1991.

Myerson, Joel, ed. *Transcendentalism: A Reader*. New York: Oxford University Press, 2000.

Thoreau, Henry David. *Journal*, edited by John C. Broderick, Elizabeth Hall Witherell, et al. Princeton, NJ: Princeton University Press, 1984–.

Thoreau, Henry David. *Reform Papers*, edited by Wendell Glick. Princeton, NJ: Princeton University Press, 1973.

Thoreau, Henry David. *Walden* (1854). Princeton, NJ: Princeton University Press, 1989.

Thoreau, Henry David. *A Year in Thoreau's Journal: 1851*, edited by H. Daniel Peck. New York: Penguin Classics, 1993.

SECONDARY SOURCES

Baumgarten, Eduard. "Mitteilungen und Bermerkungen über den Einfluss Emersons auf Nietzsche." *Jahrbuch für Amerikastudien* 1 (1956): 93–152.

Cameron, Sharon. *Writing Nature*. New York: Oxford University Press, 1985.

Cavell, Stanley. *Emerson's Transcendental Etudes*. Stanford, CA: Stanford University Press, 2003.

Cavell, Stanley. *The Senses of Walden*. Exp. ed. San Francisco: North Point Press, 1981.

Conant, James. "Nietzsche's Perfectionism: A Reading of Schopenhauer as Educator." In *Nietzsche's Postmoralism*, edited by Richard Schacht. Cambridge, U.K.: Cambridge University Press, 2000.

Goodman, Russell B. *American Philosophy and the Romantic Tradition*. Cambridge, U.K.: Cambridge University Press, 1990.

Goodman, Russell B. "The Colors of the Spirit: Emerson and Thoreau on Nature and the Self." In *Nature in American Philosophy*, edited by Jean De Groot, 1–18. Washington, DC: Catholic University of America Press, 2004.

Goodman, Russell B. "Moral Perfectionism and Democracy in Emerson and Nietzsche." *ESQ: A Journal of the American Renaissance* 43 (1997): 159–180.

Packer, B. L. "The Transcendentalists." In *The Cambridge History of American Literature*, edited by Sacvan Bercovitch, 2: 329–604. Cambridge, U.K.: Cambridge University Press, 1995.

Richardson, Robert D., Jr. *Emerson: The Mind on Fire*. Berkeley: University of California Press, 1995.

Versluis, Arthur. *American Transcendentalism and Asian Religions*. New York: Oxford University Press, 1993.

Von Frank, Albert J. *The Trials of Anthony Burns: Freedom and Slavery in Emerson's Boston*. Cambridge, MA: Harvard University Press, 1998.

Russell B. Goodman (2005)

NEWMAN, JOHN HENRY
(1801–1890)

John Henry Newman, an English philosopher of religion and cardinal of the Roman Catholic Church, was born in London, the son of a banker (later a brewer) who gave his children a love of music and literature. The young Newman was thoroughly familiar with the writings of both the romantic poets and the English deists. Raised as an Anglican, he underwent a deep religious experience when he was fifteen, and thenceforth he was strongly convinced of God's interior presence and providence. The mottoes chosen by Newman at this time foreshadowed his religious quest and interest in development: "Holiness rather than peace," and "Growth the only evidence of life."

He matriculated in 1816 at Trinity College, Oxford, where he read strenuously in the classics and mathematics. A fellowship at Oriel College at Oxford won him entrance to its common room, which proverbially "stank of logic." In 1824 Newman took holy orders.

The Oriel noetics, led by Richard Whately, gave Newman a taste for cool logical analysis of religious problems. His greatest influence at Oxford was exerted in company with Richard Froude, John Keble, and Edward B. Pusey. The Oxford movement sought to revive a living, full sense of the church and tradition through a series of incisive *Tracts for the Times* (1833–1841), culminating in Newman's *Tract 90*, which earned him an official censure. Newman's historical research in the Church Fathers and his theory of development in Christian doctrine eventually convinced him that the ideal of an Anglican *via media* was illusory. In 1845 he was received into the Roman Catholic Church, in 1847 he was ordained, and in 1848 he established the Birmingham Oratory as a center for those who shared his aspirations.

Newman struggled futilely during the years 1851–1858 to succeed as rector of the new Catholic University of Ireland, but political forces were too strong for him. Out of this defeat, however, came his main educational work, *The Idea of a University* (1852, 1859), which looked forward to a new synthesis of scientific, humanistic, and theological studies. Newman's strongly felt defense of his religious integrity and conversion expressed in his *Apologia Pro Vita Sua* (1864) restored his rapport with educated readers in England. It also cleared the path for the presentation of his basic philosophical views on knowledge and his defense of the reasonable character of the act of religious faith. Newman regarded his *Essay in Aid of a Grammar of Assent* (1870) as his way of discharging an intellectual debt to his generation and to religious seekers of every age. In recognition of his distinguished service to the church, Pope Leo XIII created him a cardinal in 1879. Even in his last years, Newman kept up an active interest in questions of science, biblical criticism, and religious beliefs.

Newman belongs in the tradition of British churchmen who have contributed to philosophical thought. This he did in the course of dealing with certain problems of a religious and theological nature. He was well read in such Enlightenment sources as David Hume, Voltaire, and Thomas Paine and had an early awareness of the modern philosophical difficulties propounded against Christianity. Under pressure from such critics, Newman felt obliged to sift the grounds for his own adherence to theism and the Christian faith. He made a close study of the rationalistic apologetic used by William Paley and by Whately in defense of the existence of God and the basic articles of the Christian creed. Although Newman appreciated their search for rigor, he remained unconvinced by their particular way of achieving it. Their formalism remained completely impersonal and abstract, leaving out of account the process whereby the individual mind comes to see the import of an argument and gives its assent to the statements under discussion. Newman found a much more realistic account of mental operations in the analyses of inquiry made by three sources: Aristotle (especially in the *Nicomachean Ethics*), the Greek Fathers, and Joseph Butler. These sources all stressed the importance of probable reasoning and analogy, especially in cases involving contingent realities and moral questions. Somewhat to his surprise, Newman also discovered a similar stress in Francis Bacon, Isaac Newton, and the Newtonians as soon as they faced the problem of relating their formal structures to concrete nature.

FORMAL AND INFORMAL REASONING

Groping during his Oxford years for a way of stating the difference between the sequence of logical steps and the path of the mind in discovery, Newman came to the distinction between formal and informal reasoning. In mathematics and formal logic, the regulative principle is furnished by the formal relations among the elements of the argument and the internal consequence of steps. The relations can be stated in a general way without taking into account the difficulties that individual minds may have in following the formal entailments. From the logicomathematical standpoint, questions about our way of grasping the proof are either deemed irrelevant or assigned to the psychological order. Newman accepted this position insofar as it was meant to preserve the integrity of the standpoint of formal reasoning and the rigor of its deductive method. But he was unable to accept Whately's rationalistic conclusion that nothing more is ever required for establishing a doctrine than to exhibit its conformity with a pattern of formal reasoning. If a statement asserts something about existent things and if we are invited to accept this assertion, then something more is involved than the application of a general pattern of formal argument. The particular ways of backing the argument must be considered, and they must be considered by individual minds called upon to weigh their agreement with the world we experience.

When Newman himself tried to set down in the *Apologia Pro Vita Sua* the stages in his religious journey toward Catholicism, he found further evidence of his contention that the grounds and stages of argument in concrete matters cannot be fully formalized. He did not regard religious inquiry as being peculiar in this respect, but rather as agreeing with the common human condition of informal reasoning. The religious inquirer uses his mind in much the same way as does the jurist, the historian, and the biologist: All share in a common pattern of inquiry that demands a distinctive and responsible use of intelligence moving in a region somewhere between formalism and psychologism. A prominent task of Newman's main philosophical book, *An Essay in Aid of a Grammar of Assent,* was to explore the middle ground of inference that eludes complete formalization and yet achieves results capable of surviving the formal tests. In a general way, he described this region as a concrete personal mode of reasoning, which he customarily divided into natural and informal inference.

"CONCRETE" REASONING

The reasoning is called "concrete" as an indication of its ultimate terms of reference and control. Newman was strongly convinced that ours is a world of individual unit things, each of which has its unique nature and history. There is sufficient likeness among individuals to permit comparison and general statements, but there is no real identity and hence no completely general way of following the logical rules to establish our statements about them. In the study of individual entities, a gap eventually opens between general rules and concrete matters of fact.

It cannot be closed by carrying on some further manipulation of the formal procedures in logic, and one is forced to bring into play the personal discernment of the living mind working upon what it experiences. Man's reasoning becomes concrete in response to this situation.

When he inquires about concrete existents, each man assumes personal responsibility for the conduct of his own understanding. Although he cannot violate the logical system or the pattern of the language, he must determine issues that cannot be settled solely in their formal terms. In the ordinary course of life, one does not stop to reflect upon the methodological issues involved but plunges directly into the particular matters at hand. Newman refers to this unreflective and implicit sort of concrete thinking as a natural mode of inference, one that is not burdened by any second-level questioning about the kind of use being made of the mind. Every person is faced with practical decisions and moral choices that require a personal assessment of the circumstances and particular means and end in view. There is a point at which even a great military leader cannot rely solely upon the rules of strategy and his formal conception of warfare; he must place all these aids at the service of his personal estimate of a particular military situation in order to make a responsible decision. He is directly engaged in concrete reasoning in the natural mode of inference.

Yet Newman did not restrict concrete reasoning to conditions of great practical stress, where reflection on one's method is a luxury that cannot be indulged. He recognized the pattern of concrete intelligence in the judgments made by the historian, the art critic, the jurist, and the scientist. Here there is often an opportunity for attending to the problem of method. In the degree that individuals who make these judgments reflect upon their procedures and make an explicit theme of them, they are involved in what Newman calls concrete reasoning in the informal mode of inference. The concrete uses of intelligence are now thematized and critically controlled. The reasoning is informal insofar as it deals with questions that cannot be settled by appealing simply to the formal logical rules, but still it is a quite deliberate and reflective way of reasoning. Informal reasoning is required by our world of particulars, but this world does not prevent us from reflecting upon the way in which we explore and interpret it.

THE ILLATIVE SENSE

Newman proposed the theory of the illative sense to account for the certitude that may be attached to informal judgments. Here he was not trying to burden the mind with a new and esoteric faculty but sought instead to account for a definite feature of our intellectual activity. Hence he remarked that illative sense is only a grand name for designating a very ordinary way of using the mind.

A distinction is needed between certainty and certitude. Newman regarded certainty as a formally determinable quality of propositions and assigned its study to the logician. Newman's own interest centers upon certitude as a quality of the mind when it is engaged in concrete reasoning of both the natural and the informal sort. Concrete reasoning yields certitude when it enables us to recognize and affirm the truth of some proposition. Certitude is not achieved, as the rationalists maintain, through an impersonal coercion of the mind by the force of the formal elements contained in it. In all reasoning, but especially in concrete inference, certitude consists in an active response of the mind to the weight and tenor of the argument, a living recognition of the meaning and the truth of the proposition that states some findings. Furthermore, this certitudinal apprehension of the truth of the proposition is an inalienably individual act. I come to grasp the import of an argument; I see the bearing of the evidence; I give my assent to the proposition as true.

For my warrant in accepting the proposition, I cannot fall back exclusively upon the general canons of logic and the common structure of the language. Although Newman recognized their indispensable contribution by way of opposition to sentimentalism in thought, he believed that in the final analysis these elements cannot settle issues about the concretely existent. The illative sense refers to the type of operation of the human mind as it engages in concrete reasoning, reaches a conclusion of inference, and determines whether to give its certitudinal assent to the inferred proposition about a concrete reality:

> The sole and final judgment on the validity of an inference in concrete matter is committed to the personal action of the ratiocinative faculty, the perfection or virtue of which I have called the Illative Sense. … It is the mind that reasons, and that controls its own reasonings, not any technical apparatus of words and propositions. This power of judging and concluding, when in its perfection, I call the Illative Sense. (*Grammar*, Ch. 9)

Thus when Newman claimed to be developing a theory of the mind more empirical than John Locke's, he instanced this functional analysis of the illative sense.

The illative use of the mind is observable not only in the concluding act of an inference in concrete issues but also at the outset and along the way of the reasoning. Newman pointed out the need for a personal use of intelligence—especially in creative work as done, for example, by Newton or Edward Gibbon—in order to suggest the governing hypothesis, to gauge the strength of some particular stage in the inquiry, and to discern the bearing of many outlying investigations upon the main problem. We seek to conduct ourselves responsibly in all these operations, and the term *illative sense* refers to the intellectual mastery or perfection that an individual develops for inquiries in some concrete field. It comes close to the Aristotelian habit of prudence or practical wisdom, except that it can reach into the speculative order and attain certitude there. Newman added that despite a similar pattern of concrete logic for different fields, the personal mastery cannot simply be transferred from one area to another. A man may give us good grounds for trusting his judgment in military affairs or biological questions, whereas he may be utterly lacking in sagacity in respect to political legislation.

Newman did not isolate religious inquiry from other concrete uses of intelligence but required it to conform to the common requirements of concrete inquiry. The religious person is not concerned solely with abstract and general issues but seeks the truth about the reality of God, the person of Christ, the complex life of the church, and the individual soul's response to them all. These matters belong in the region of concrete existence and thus impose their own requirements upon the searcher's mind. The interested individual cannot do justice to the issues if he confines himself to what can be ascertained exclusively from the use of formal reasoning. Such a restriction is bound to lead to a noncommittal attitude, not because of the religious issues as such but because of the failure to make use of the concrete reasoning required by the situation.

PROBABILITY AND ASSENT

At this juncture, however, Newman was confronted with a strong objection propounded by William Froude (brother of Richard Froude) and other members of the Victorian scientific community. They noted Newman's statement in the *Apologia* about his agreement with Joseph Butler that probability is the guide of our life. In addition they noted the function assigned by Newman to the illative sense of discerning the convergence of probabilities among several strands of argument. To Froude, it seemed that the unavoidable result is that Newman's way

of concrete reasoning can yield nothing higher than a probable conclusion, which is essentially open to constant revision. This falls considerably short of the certitude claimed by Newman for the act of religious faith.

Newman's treatment of this difficulty constitutes another major topic in the *Grammar of Assent*. Indeed, the book's title derives from his wrestling with this issue, as recorded in the following entry in his journal. "At last, when I was up at Glion over the Lake of Geneva, it struck me 'You are wrong in beginning with certitude—certitude is only a kind of assent—you should begin with contrasting assent and inference.' On that hint I spoke, finding it a key to my own ideas" (*Journal*, August 11, 1865). In fixing upon assent as something different from inference, Newman was able to clarify his position with respect to Froude's objection. His terminology was geared to the earlier, Lockean era in British empiricism, but the thrust of his argument concerns the relationship between religious faith and what Charles Peirce was already calling the ideal of scientific fallibilism.

Newman felt that at least one difficulty rested upon a linguistic confusion. His critics treated probability as a trait belonging to propositions and arguments, in which respect they contrasted it with the certainty of propositions. But just as he considered certitude a quality of the mind, so Newman viewed probability as a relationship involving the mind in an existential situation, rather than as a relationship among propositions in an argument. In Newman's conception, reasoning is probable to the extent that it is nonformal. Whenever inference is carried on in a context other than that of formal logic and mathematics, it is probable in the sense of not being governed by the intention of yielding a logicomathematical sort of proof. So understood, the probable is not contrasted with the demonstrative and the certain as such, but rather with the formal kind of demonstration and the abstract kind of certitude. Whenever the mind is inquiring about a concrete matter of fact, it is engaged in probable reasoning. This means that we are adapting our investigation to the conditions of particular existents, not that we are seeking only a weaker form of evidence and consequence in our reasoning. Thus probability, as understood by Newman, does not exclude certitude of assent but permits it to be achieved in matters pertaining to the concrete world and its connections in being.

Historically, Newman had to face Locke's restriction of probability to those inevident relations among ideas that permit neither intuitive nor demonstrative knowledge. Locke also held that belief is an act of assent that cannot rise above the probability of the inference leading to it and hence cannot enjoy the certainty of intuition or demonstration. Newman had two grounds of disagreement with this teaching. First, there is no general rule necessarily subsuming religious assent under Lockean probability. Whether there is certitude in an act of religious faith cannot be settled by general stipulation about the meaning of probability and the judgment of belief. There must be a direct examination of the particular case and its grounds for claiming something about the order of concrete fact. Second, the act of assent is no mere shadow or reduplication of the conclusion of the inferential process. Using J. S. Mill's canons of induction, Newman sought to show the distinctive nature of assent as an act of the mind that remains irreducible to either the formal conclusion of an inference or to its psychological correlate in the act of concluding. We always conclude in a referential and conditional way, in view of what the premises state. But assent is made directly to the proposition as true; hence assent intends the certitudinal acceptance of the proposition in itself as being a true one. Newman made an extensive analysis of such expressions as "half assent, "conditional assent," and "hesitating assent." These describe circumstances surrounding the assent or features of the content to which assent is given rather than the act of assent itself.

The drift of Newman's reply to Locke and Froude is fairly clear. The sort of probability that he accepts as a guide and about which the illative sense must make an appraisal consists in a relation of the human mind to concrete modes of being. We follow the way of probability when we adapt our analysis to the concrete particulars and make a personal appraisal of the particular evidence. Our concrete personal thinking does not always attain certitude, but there is no a priori reason drawn from the definition of assent and probability that prevents us in principle from attaining it. Furthermore, there remains a difference in structure and intention between the inferential process and the act of assent. The revisability attaching to the former, especially in scientific inquiries, does not prevent the achievement of assent with certitude in some concrete instances. Newman's defense of the certitude in the act of religious faith depends upon keeping inference and assent distinct, as well as upon interpreting probability in terms of his theory of concrete reasoning.

NOTIONAL AND REAL ASSENT

Within the order of assent itself, Newman distinguished between notional and real assent. His view cannot be understood if it is taken as implying an opposition in principle between these modes of assent, or as assigning all the intellectual worth to real assent. The distinction is a functional one, arising from Newman's study of the interpretative operations of the mind. In assenting to a proposition, we can intend to accept the statement itself as true or to accept the real thing intended by the statement. A notional assent is one made to the truth of the proposition itself, whereas a real assent is one made to the reality itself intended by the proposition. Thus one may give a notional assent to God in terms of some abstract divine attributes and also give a real assent to God considered as a personal being who cares for one as an individual person. This is a matter of interpretation on the part of the mind that is considering the statement. In the case of purely ideal inquiries, a notional assent is sufficient. But we live in a translinguistic world, and our questions reach out to the community of real existents, especially to other persons. Here, the mind's notional assent must be integrated with, and further perfected by, a real assent to the very realities under investigation.

For Newman, the fully appropriate intellectual response to our human situation is unavoidably a complex one, involving both notional and real assents. Taken by itself, the way of real assent is intense but unclarified. We need to engage in both formal and informal inference, weighing the evidence carefully and arriving at a careful act of notional assent. Inference and notional assent are indispensable elements in human cognition; otherwise we could not weigh the pertinent evidence on an issue, do justice to the difficulties, or formulate the theoretical findings with cool precision of statement. Thus Newman assigned a large role to the modes of formal and informal inference and to notional assent in the total composition of human knowledge.

But he also insisted upon the need for directly relating the mind to individual existents. The act of real assent achieves our intellectual orientation toward the domain of concrete existents and their values. It does so by furnishing a concrete image of the individual being under consideration and by establishing the relevance of that imaged reality to the inquirer's own personal life. Real assent does not necessarily ensure action, but it does furnish a necessary condition for our practical responses by directing our mind toward the real existent, grasped in an image that can appeal to our passions and will.

There is a strongly theistic motive behind Newman's insistence upon blending inference, notional assent, and real assent. Humankind's relationship to God is not yet one of direct vision; hence we must engage in inference. Since theistic inquiry concerns a real existent, it is not enough to employ formal inference, even though its resources must be used to analyze and test our arguments. A concrete personal mode of reasoning is also required in order to proportion our inquiry as fully as possible to the situation of man's search after the truth about God. Our aim must be the complex one of attaining some definite and well-grounded propositions to which we can legitimately give our notional assent, and also of forming a concrete image of the personal, morally good, and providential God to whose reality we can then give our real assent and practical attachment.

CONSCIENCE AND THE MORAL LIFE

Newman's final philosophical problem in the *Grammar* was to describe the area where he personally could realize this synthesis of intellectual acts bearing on the being of God. He readily admitted that there are many ways to God and that many natural informants lead us to him: the way of causality and purpose, the meaning of human existence and history, and the import of our moral life. As a reader of Hume and a contemporary of Charles Darwin, however, Newman refused to grant independent value to the design argument, which he regarded as a supplementary way of looking at nature on the part of those who already accept God on other grounds. To reach the transcendent, personal God, Newman examined the witness of our moral life, for this is a personal region where relations with other persons are best established. It is here that we have the experience of conscience, of being under command to do and not to do, of being responsible to a just and caring person who transcends our human reality but does so in a way that keeps him personally concerned about our conduct. Conscience as a commanding act discloses the full human situation of our responsibility toward the good God.

Three features of the living command of conscience recommend it to Newman as the best way of achieving real as well as notional assent to God: its intentional character, its personal significance, and its practical ordination. The dictate of conscience by its very structure refers the conscientious man beyond himself, pointing him toward the reality of the supreme lawgiver and judge of his moral actions. This is not a purely abstract orienting of our mind but involves a concrete image of God as our concerned father. Another advantage of the way of conscience is that the moral relationship in which it consists is personal in both poles of reference. Conscience engages me precisely as a personal self; hence it enables me to give a real assent to God as a morally concerned person. Finally, the acts of conscience relate us to the personal God in a concrete way that leads to moral and religious actions. Hence the approach to God from conscience encourages us to assent to the truth about God not only notionally but really, not only in respect to our propositions but also in respect to the personal, provident reality of God himself as the practical goal of our knowledge and love.

As a reader of Hume and Mill, Newman was very sensitive to the naturalistic criticism based upon physical and moral evil in our world. He suggested that the moral problem of theism be treated within a moral context. One cannot pose an objection to theism on moral grounds and then rule out the conditions that would permit theism to present its moral type of interpretation. Real assent to God as the lord of conscience furnishes a frame of reference for wrestling with evil and discerning his providential presence. A mind that is carefully formed upon the theistic implications of conscience "interprets what it sees around it by this previous inward teaching, as the true key of that maze of vast complicated disorder; and thus it gains a more and more consistent and luminous vision of God from the most unpromising materials. Thus conscience is a connecting principle between the creature and his Creator" (*Grammar*, Ch. 5). Whereas the naturalistic critic appeals to the vast disorder as an antecedent reason for withholding our assent from God, Newman asks us to secure first of all the inward principle of interpretation provided by the personal and moral relation of men to the lord of conscience. The work of this principle is not to soften or gloss over the power of evil, but to bring in the other considerations concerning God and moral man that will enable us to understand and work with hope against physical and moral evil in our world.

HISTORICAL DEVELOPMENT AND SOCIAL PRINCIPLES

Like other nineteenth-century thinkers, Newman was dissatisfied with the older empiricism's emphasis on the solitary and static individual perceiver. Hence he widened his horizon to include the social, developmental, and historical aspects of human experience. His *Essay on the Development of Christian Doctrine* (1845) opens with a chapter on the general nature and kinds of development among ideas. Here Newman explores the logic of those social ideals that grip the minds of men and account for developments in their beliefs and institutions.

For Newman, two questions are of prime importance in understanding the social growth of ideas and institutions: Why do certain ideas display themselves only through historical development? What pattern is common to diverse sorts of developing social principles? As an answer to the first question, Newman points to the interpretative activity of many minds as they are engaged in judging, relating, evaluating, and dealing practically with our complex world. There are some meanings that can be worked out only in this gradual social way. Historically important ideas are those that contain many facets and require the interpretative activity of many minds, testing and developing them over many years. "Ordinarily an idea is not brought home to the intellect as objective except through this variety; like bodily substances, which are not apprehended except under the clothing of their properties and results, and which admit of being walked around, and surveyed on opposite sides, and in different perspectives, and in contrary lights, in evidence of their reality" (*Development*, Ch. 1). We can grasp the intentional structure of basic human meanings only through studying their various perspectives, forcing them to enter the battlefield of critical discussion, and sometimes embodying them in visible, powerful social institutions.

Newman also suggested that there is a common pattern of development that has certain traits distinguishing a healthy growth from a sickly one. His seven criteria for genuine development are preservation of the type of principle that is socially influential, continuity of these principles, their capacity for assimilation of new data, their logical sequence in organizing a complex social process, their anticipation of their own future, conservation of their past achievements, and their chronic vigor. He deliberately illustrated these criteria by showing their development in kingdoms, economic policies, religious convictions, scientific hypotheses, and philosophical theories. Although the entire analysis is applied ultimately to the theological question of development among Christian doctrines, Newman's comparative use of empirical materials indicates the wider significance of his study of the dynamics of human thought and institutional forms. He himself, in fact, makes an explicit application of this theory of development to the ideas of civilization, the political constitution, and the university.

THE UNIVERSITY

Newman's effort at interpreting the Western ideal of the university in the context of his theory of development is revealed in *The Idea of a University*. He was more keenly aware than most of his contemporaries that the crucial decisions affecting the course of cultural development were being made within the university. It was replacing the episcopal palace, the banking house, and the parlia-

mentary floor as the real center for determining the long-range direction of human history. Newman looked for a fresh synthesis of tradition and originality in the university community. The task of such a community is to educate men for the world by gradually introducing them to the full complexity of our humanistic, scientific, and religious interpretations. This it should try to do by cultivating an understanding of the various methods and ways of knowing, along with an awareness of their differences, limitations, and possibilities for unification.

As a Catholic churchman, Newman devoted the bulk of his writings to problems raised by the Christian faith and its practical institutions, especially as they are brought into close relation with modern humanistic and scientific ideas. His contributions to these issues might be considered as a sustained effort at education that draws its strength from both Christianity and the other components in the university ideal.

See also Aristotle; Bacon, Francis; Butler, Joseph; Darwin, Charles Robert; Enlightenment; Hume, David; Locke, John; Mill, John Stuart; Newton, Isaac; Paine, Thomas; Paley, William; Peirce, Charles Sanders; Propositions, Judgments, Sentences, and Statements; Religion; Religion and Morality; Voltaire, François-Marie Arouet de; Whately, Richard.

Bibliography

WORKS BY NEWMAN

The following are modern editions of Newman's works: *Two Essays on Biblical and on Ecclesiastical Miracles* (New York, 1924); *An Essay in Aid of a Grammar of Assent*, edited by C. F. Harrold (New York: Longmans, Green, 1947); *The Idea of a University*, edited by C. F. Harrold (New York: Longmans, Green, 1947); *Essays and Sketches*, 3 vols., edited by C. F. Harrold (New York: Longmans, Green, 1948); *Apologia Pro Vita Sua*, edited by C. F. Harrold (New York: Longmans, Green, 1947); *An Essay on the Development of Christian Doctrine*, edited by C. F. Harrold (New York: Longmans, Green, 1949); *Sermons and Discourses*, 2 vols., edited by C. F. Harrold (New York: Longmans, Green, 1949); and *The Letters and Diaries of John Henry Newman*, edited by C. S. Dessain (New York: T. Nelson, 1961–; to be published in 30 vols.).

WORKS ON NEWMAN

Benard, E. D. *A Preface to Newman's Theology*. St. Louis: B. Herder, 1945.

Boekraad, A. J. *The Argument from Conscience to the Existence of God according to J. H. Newman*. Louvain: Nauwelaerts, 1961.

Boekraad, A. J. *The Personal Conquest of Truth according to J. H. Newman*. Louvain: Nauwelaerts, 1955.

Bouyer, Louis. *Newman: His Life and Spirituality*. New York: P.J. Kenedy, 1958.

Collins, James. *Philosophical Readings in Cardinal Newman.* Chicago: Regnery, 1961. A presentation of Newman's philosophical views in terms of his theory of personal knowledge, his concrete inference to God, his notion of social development, and his account of the relationship between faith and reason.

Culler, A. D. *The Imperial Intellect: A Study of Newman's Educational Ideal.* New Haven, CT: Yale University Press, 1955. An interpretation of the liberal and traditional strains in Newman's mind and educational outlook.

Walgrave, J.-H. *Newman the Theologian.* New York: Sheed and Ward, 1960. An advanced analysis of the theory of development and the psychological aspect of Newman's approach.

Ward, Wilfrid. *The Life of John Henry Cardinal Newman.* 2 vols. New York: Longmans, Green, 1912. A reliable, standard life, with many letters and documents.

James Collins (1967)

NEWMAN, JOHN HENRY [ADDENDUM]

Since 1967, the publication of new primary source material has generated an expanding resource pool for secondary scholarship on Newman, particularly with the appearance of 24 new volumes to complete the thirty-one volume collection of Newman's *Letters and Diaries.* In addition, two volumes of Newman's *Theological Notebook* (1970), two volumes of his *Theological Papers* (on Faith and Certainty [1976], and on Biblical Inspiration and Infallibility [1979]), and an annotated bibliography of his Tract and Pamphlet Collection (1984) have been published. A new critical edition of the *Grammar of Assent* was produced by Ian Ker in 1985, and new editions of several of Newman's works appeared: *Oxford University Sermons* (1970), *Apologia Pro Vita Sua* (1993), and *Arians* (2001). The celebration in 1990 of the centenary of Newman's death was the occasion for two new biographies by Ian Ker (1989) and Sheridan Gilley (1990). Moreover, the journal *International Cardinal Newman-Studien* (known until 1987 as *Newman-Studien*) continues to appear annually. The result of these increased resources has been a wide variety of secondary literature documenting Newman's contributions to classical themes, as well as the opening up of some new directions in scholarship.

Of particular relevance to philosophy is the continuing discussion of Newman's understanding of the relation between faith and reason and the relation between faith and doubt. Debates that locate Newman in the history of responses to skepticism (including Wittgensteinian responses) continue about the plausibility of Newman's claims that there are no degrees of assent, that assent (including the reflex assent of certitude) is an act of the will, that indubitability (the absence of "reasonable" doubt) can be achieved through convergent, nondemonstrative reasoning, and that certitude is indefectible. In particular, the period from 1969 to 1980 saw increased attention to a debate about whether Newman was a "volitionalist" (aligned with people like René Descartes and Søren Kierkegaard)—that is, whether assent was an act of the will distinguished from and following on the reasoning process, according to a "logic of decision." While there continue to be advocates of Newman's volitionalism, this debate opened up a new direction for research—namely, the theme of Newman and rhetoric. In addition to three book-length studies of Newman as a rhetorician, in the sense of classical rhetoric, three new studies of his preaching appeared. A collection of essays on romanticism and rhetoric in Newman's thought was complemented by the beginning of significant discussion of the role of imagination in Newman's proposals concerning concrete reasoning and the illative sense.

Theological interest in Newman's thought has resulted in works on his ecclesiology, and the topics of liturgy and revelation. Another interesting new direction in Newman studies has been an increased emphasis on spirituality. Although there were earlier works on Newman's spirituality, such as Hilda Graef's *The Spirituality of John Henry Newman* (1968), the late 1980s and early 1990s saw the publication of three additional works on Newman's spirituality, his "spiritual theology" and Newman's teaching on "Christian holiness." Perhaps this increased interest in spirituality is related to the initiation of the process of beatification and canonization of Newman begun by the Roman Catholic Church in 1980; in 1991 the first official step in that process was taken when Pope John Paul II declared Newman "Venerable."

While there has been no notable book-length feminist study of Newman's thought, there has been some interest in Newman's relation to women (Joyce Sugg, *Ever Yours Affly: John Henry Newman and His Female Circle,* 1996), as well as the influence of Mariology (Philip Boyce, *Mary: The Virgin Mary in the Life and Writings of John Henry Newman,* 2001).

Finally, in addition to publications in church history, in which Newman is related to the Oxford Movement and to Modernism, the centenary celebration of Newman's death brought about a number of retrospectives in the form of edited volumes of essays by specialists, for example, Ian Ker and Alan Hill's 1990 *Newman After a Hundred Years.* There followed a decade of increased interest in Newman, including two collections of interdisciplinary studies in which scholars consider Newman from the perspectives of literature, history, and education (edited by Magill, 1993 and 1994).

See also Descartes, René; Doubt; Faith; Kierkegaard, Søren Aabye; Modernism; Reason; Skepticism; Volition; Wittgenstein, Ludwig Josef Johann.

Bibliography

Biemer, Günter, and Heinrich Fries. *Christliche Heiligkeit Als Lehre Und Praxis Nach John Henry Newman—Newman's Teaching on Christian Holiness.* Sigmaringendorf, Germany: Regio Verlag Glock und Lutz, 1988.

Blehl, Vincent Ferrer. *The White Stone: The Spiritual Theology of John Henry Newman.* Petersham, MA: St. Bede's, 1994.

Boyce, Philip, ed. *Mary: The Virgin Mary in the Life and Writings of John Henry Newman.* Grand Rapids, MI: Eerdmans, 2001.

Britt, John. *John Henry Newman's Rhetoric: Becoming a Discriminating Reader.* New York: Peter Lang, 1989.

Coulson, John. *Religion and Imagination: "In Aid of a Grammar of Assent."* Oxford: Clarendon Press, 1981.

Ferreira, M. Jamie. *Doubt and Religious Commitment: The Role of the Will in Newman's Thought.* Oxford: Clarendon Press, 1980.

Gilley, Sheridan. *Newman and His Age.* London: Darton Longman and Todd, 1990.

Graef, Hilda. *God and Myself: The Spirituality of John Henry Newman.* New York: Hawthorn, 1968.

Jost, Walter. *Rhetorical Thought in John Henry Newman.* Columbia: University of South Carolina Press, 1989.

Ker, Ian. *The Achievement of John Henry Newman.* Notre Dame, IN: University of Notre Dame Press, 1990.

Ker, Ian. *Healing the Wound of Humanity: The Spirituality of John Henry Newman.* London: Darton, 1993.

Ker, Ian, and Alan Hill, eds. *Newman after a Hundred Years.* Oxford: Oxford University Press, 1990.

Kerr, Fergus, and David Nicholls. *John Henry Newman: Reason, Rhetoric and Romanticism.* Carbondale: Southern Illinois University Press, 1991.

Magill, Gerard. *Discourse and Context: An Interdisciplinary Study of John Henry Newman.* Carbondale: Southern Illinois University Press, 1993.

Magill, Gerard. *Personality and Belief: Interdisciplinary Essays on John Henry Newman.* Lanham, MD: University Press of America, 1994.

Pailin, David A. *The Way to Faith: An Examination of Newman's "Grammar of Assent" as a Response to the Search for Certainty in Faith.* London: Epworth Press, 1969.

Sugg, Joyce. *Ever Yours Affly: John Henry Newman and His Female Circle.* Leominster, U.K.: Gracewing, 1996.

Tolhurst, James. *The Church—A Communion in the Preaching and Thought of John Henry Newman.* Leominster: Fowler Wright, 1988.

Whalen, David M. *The Consolation of Rhetoric: John Henry Newman and the Realism of Personalist Thought.* San Francisco: International Scholars Publications, 1994.

Willi, Peter. *Sünde Und Bekehrung in Den Predigten Und Tagebüchern John Henry Newmans.* St Ottilien: Eos, 1992.

M. Jamie Ferreira (2005)

NEW REALISM

"New Realism" arose at the turn of the twentieth century in opposition to the Idealist doctrines that the known or perceived object is dependent for its existence on the act of knowing and that the immediately perceived object is a state of the perceiving mind. The Austrian philosophers Franz Brentano and Alexius Meinong first enunciated the cardinal tenet of this new realism: that what the mind knows or perceives exists independently of the acts of knowing and perceiving. Developing mainly as a polemic against Idealism, this new realism was represented prior to 1900 in England in the works of such men as John Cook Wilson, Thomas Case, H. W. B. Joseph, and H. A. Prichard. Similar realist polemics were taking place in Sweden and Italy.

In America the movement known as New Realism dates from the critical writings of William P. Montague and Ralph Barton Perry in 1901 and 1902. Their immediate aim was to refute Josiah Royce's "refutation" of realism, which he had based on the claim that the knower and the known could not be independent of each other and still be related. The movement took definite form when Montague and Perry were joined by four others in a statement of a New Realist program ("The Program and First Platform of Six Realists") in 1910.

In England, New Realism took explicit form in the works of T. P. Nunn, Bertrand Russell, and G. E. Moore. In both America and England, New Realists asserted the independence of consciousness and its object, but serious differences soon appeared between the two groups and between individuals within each group. The differences were particularly noticeable in their statements about the nature of consciousness and of its object, and of the relation between them. Moore claimed that the act of consciousness included both a nonmental, independent object and a transparent, or "diaphanous," mental act of consciousness. He agreed with Brentano and Meinong that consciousness involved awareness in the form of an act of intending something other than itself. To have an idea, to perceive or be aware at all, is already to be beyond consciousness and to be confronted by an independent object. American New Realists, on the other hand, took their view of consciousness from William James. While he, too, described consciousness as a relation, James denied that there was anything uniquely mental or psychic about it at all, and associated consciousness rather with the behavioral responses or functions of the organism.

But there were also differences between Moore, Nunn, and Russell. Nunn argued that both primary and secondary qualities not only exist as they are perceived, but also are really *in* their objects, whether perceived or not. He even argued that pain is something independent of mind, with which mind may come into various relations. In this he was closer to the American New Realism of Perry and E. B. Holt. Russell was influenced by Nunn's view, but his New Realism took a frankly Platonic turn that brought it closer to the New Realism of Montague. Russell's Realism, however, was soon significantly altered. Another variant of English New Realism, perhaps more a development from it than a version of it, was Samuel Alexander's. It, too, resembled American New Realism.

AMERICAN NEW REALISM

Although American, English, and, to a lesser extent, European New Realists influenced one another, it was among the Americans that New Realism flourished, particularly as a movement. Their aim was to produce an account of how a real object could be present in consciousness and knowledge and still be independent of that relation, and they sought to do this without a dualistic separation of knower and known. "The independence of the immanent" was their manifesto. Their first platform statement consisted of six lists of doctrines that had been discussed at length, revised, and agreed to by all, and that all thought were consistent. The lists were signed by Holt and Perry at Harvard, Walter T. Marvin at Rutgers, Montague and Walter B. Pitkin at Columbia, and Edward C. Spaulding at Princeton.

At a Philosophical Association meeting in 1909, five of these six had found themselves in agreement against a common foe that still spoke with authority and was listened to with deference: Idealism. Pitkin and Montague are credited with the idea of translating their agreement into an articulate statement, and papers soon began circulating. F. J. E. Woodbridge at Columbia gave encouragement, although he declined an invitation to join. Montague, in "Confessions of an Animistic Materialist," described E. B. McGilvary, Morris R. Cohen, J. E. Boodin, J. Lowenberg, and Douglas C. Macintosh as "unofficial" New Realists. Believing that philosophic disagreements were the result chiefly of a lack of precision and uniformity in the use of words, plus a lack of planned cooperation in research, the original six banded together in the hope of revealing the genuine philosophic disagreements that were more than mere differences of personal opinion. They hoped thereby to open the way to the solution of genuine philosophic disputes. They called for a new alliance between philosophy and science and formulated a statement of principles and doctrines, a program of constructive work with a method based on these, and an agreed-upon system of axioms, methods, hypotheses, and facts.

In 1912 they published their cooperative volume, *The New Realism; Cooperative Studies in Philosophy*. Although they were still preoccupied with polemics, the six authors hoped to go beyond criticism to produce a complete philosophy that would play a major part in human thought. They saw themselves as proponents of a doctrine concerning the relation between the knowing process and the thing known. They described their most urgent problem (one that had not been resolved by naive realism, dualism, or subjectivism) as how to give an adequate account of "the facts of relativity" in the knowing process from a Realist point of view; how, in other words, to reconcile the apparently hopeless disagreement of the world presented in immediate experience with the true or corrected system of objects in whose independent reality they believed. While New Realism succeeded in showing the fatal weaknesses in dualistic answers to this problem, it nonetheless failed to provide an adequate answer of its own.

THE "FACTS OF RELATIVITY." New Realism faced the above problem not just because Idealism had failed to resolve it but also because Idealism had made it impossible to ignore these "facts of relativity." Thus, any attempt by New Realists to return to the naïveté of earlier doctrines of realism, to a primitive notion that nothing intervenes between subject and object (particularly nothing attributable to the subject), was out of the question. Equally closed to them was any recourse to a Lockean or Cartesian dualism that, they thought, never escaped the subject's own mental states. The third traditional answer to the problem, subjectivism, was also impossible. Of the three approaches, subjectivism was most often the object of criticism by New Realists, and they identified it as the fatal doctrine of Idealism. They saw it as an illicit argument from the "egocentric predicament," an argument based on the difficulty of conceiving known things to exist independently of their being known. New Realists refuted Idealism by refuting this argument; but then it became their turn to reconcile the facts of relativity, of which the predicament was one, with their theory of the independent existence, or reality, of objects of consciousness and knowledge.

New Realist writings thus were largely devoted to such facts of relativity as illusion, error, secondary qualities, and—later—choosing, valuing, meaning or intending, and purposing. The New Realists also thought that Idealism had gone too far in its view of the subject's role. However, if Idealism went too far in that direction, New Realism went too far in the opposite direction; its polemical theory of independence could not be reconciled with the facts of relativity. This in turn provoked such reactions as Critical Realism, Perspective Realism, and Objective Relativism.

Chief among the positive aspects of the doctrines of the New Realists was what they called the "emancipation of metaphysics from epistemology," the result of their theory of independence. Contrary to the Idealist claim that knowing was the universal condition of being and hence constitutive of it, the New Realists argued that knowing and being were independent. This, Perry showed, did not mean they were therefore unrelated, as Royce had argued, but simply that there was not the particular relation of dependence between them. Dependence is a special type of relation in which the dependent element contains, implies, or is exclusively caused or implied by that on which it is dependent. Between knowing and being, therefore, it was possible for there to be relations both of independence (external relations) and of dependence (internal relations). In holding out this possibility against the Idealist claim that all relations are internal, New Realism became identified with a theory of external relations.

In "immediate and intimate connection" with this theory was the doctrine that the content of knowledge is numerically identical with the thing known; things, when consciousness is had of them, become contents of consciousness, thus figuring both in the external world and in "the manifold which introspection reveals." This view was very close to James's Neutral Monism, but only Holt worked out its fullest implications. The theory of numerical identity soon became the target of critics of New Realism, and it was difficult to determine whether, and to what extent, any New Realist other than Holt maintained it. Yet for a time, at least, it was said to be fundamental to New Realism. If there was a numerical identity between consciousness and its contents, then the "things" of thought would have to be given full ontological status along with the "things" of sense. This the New Realists claimed to do in their volume. They said they were Platonic Realists in granting this status to subsistents as well

as existents. Here, again, a belief held by all in the beginning became in the end the belief of but a few, notably Montague and Spaulding.

THE EGOCENTRIC PREDICAMENT. The facts of relativity haunted New Realism throughout the life of the movement. That the New Realists ultimately failed in their professed aim of doing justice to these facts was in part the result of their constant polemical concern with asserting their doctrine of independence against Idealism and in part the result of their failure to recognize some possibly constitutive elements within the knowing relation. One such fact was the egocentric predicament, described by Perry as the fact that the "extent to which knowledge conditions any situation in which it is present cannot be discovered by the simple and conclusive method of direct elimination" ("The Ego-Centric Predicament"). Perry thought this was merely a methodological difficulty, one faced by all philosophers. Idealism had used it to argue that since it was impossible to discover anything that is, when discovered, undiscovered by someone, therefore it is impossible to discover anything that is not thought. The argument, Perry contended, rested on a confusion between "everything which is known, is *known*," and "everything which *is*, is known."

Perry concluded that the predicament could not be used to support either Idealism or Realism. Idealists could not use it as an argument for dependence, or internal relations, and New Realists could not use it as an argument for independence, or external relations. But while exposing its illicit use, New Realists did not offer a convincing way out of the predicament. As a test for the dependence or independence of any element in consciousness, Perry proposed that insofar as the element was deducible from anything other than consciousness, it was independent. To be dependent, or subjective, the element would have to be exclusively determined by consciousness. However, it was pointed out, the predicament would prevent us, by the very test Perry proposed, from reaching an object that we could be sure was independent of consciousness, for we would be using consciousness (deduction) in order to get to it.

Spaulding maintained that New Realism had provided a solution to the predicament and that this solution was its most important doctrine. He argued that any sort of analysis purporting to discover—and not merely create—what is *there* would be impossible if it did not presuppose a Realist position; that is, presuppose relatedness with independence. Even a theory that argued against the Realist position would have to take that position toward the very state of affairs it described, assuming that it was a genuine state of affairs, not one created, altered, or modified by virtue of the knowing relation. Every philosopher, knowingly or not, solves the predicament by the Realist attitude he assumes toward his subject. But the question remained: What warrant do we have for such an assumption?

Pitkin attempted to support the doctrine of external relations by refuting the assertion that biology provided evidence for the internalist view. On the contrary, he argued, biology supports the externalist view through the discovery that organic parts do not depend upon the whole in which they naturally occur; and an organic whole does not depend upon its individual parts for its total specific organic character.

Beyond this, and apart from showing that independence did not rule out relatedness, the New Realists did not demonstrate how the knowing relation was external and independent, nor did they show how the facts of relativity were to be reconciled with externality and independence. In their cooperative volume they had refused to recognize ultimate immediacies, or any nonrelational or indefinable entities other than the simples in which they claimed analysis terminates. Their view that the knowing relation was external required such simples, or "neutral entities," that would maintain their identity no matter what relations they entered into. But it was never clear why analysis had to stop where the New Realists said it did—usually with the simples of mathematics and logic. Nor was it clear whether these simples were the product of their analysis or a genuine discovery by it.

EPISTEMOLOGY AND ONTOLOGY. In its constructive phase, New Realism proposed an epistemological monism and an ontological pluralism. James had argued that consciousness was not a substantive entity, and Moore similarly argued that it was diaphanous and transparent. In both cases, consciousness of something was viewed as a direct, unmediated, immanent affair. All content of consciousness, with the exception of Moore's psychical, diaphanous element, was thus objective in the sense that it consisted of objects in the real, external world. This was New Realism's epistemological monism: Thought and its object are numerically the same.

Its ontology was pluralistic, however: Some elements of the object would not be found in the consciousness of that object. Any elements in consciousness not found in the object would give consciousness a constitutive role beyond mere selection or grouping. The problem was to account for all of the "facts of relativity" through the selective and grouping function of consciousness without jeopardizing the New Realist theory of immanence that asserted that it was the "real" objects of the external world that were present in consciousness.

There were two principal positions taken on this matter among New Realists. Montague called them the left and right wings of New Realism. One was Neutral Monism, developed by Holt and, to a lesser extent, by Perry, but eventually abandoned by both. The other was a Platonic Realism developed by Montague into what he called Subsistential Realism.

Holt and Perry. Neutral Monism derived from James's idea of "pure experience." Pure experience was pure because it was uncontaminated by such distinctions as "object," "content," "subject," or "knower and known." It was "neutral" in terms of these distinctions; such distinctions could only be made later in terms of the relations between portions of pure experience. A "thing" could be said to be one portion of pure experience that was represented by another portion. A "thought" could be said to be one portion of pure experience that represented another portion. The dualisms of "inner" and "outer," mind and body, thus were undercut. All such distinctions were a matter of relations between bits of pure experience, but these relations had to be external. Hence, "mental," "nonmental," "real," "external," and "physical," are accidental features. New Realists thus were driven back to a realm of indefinable simples that come into and go out of various relations but never change their original identities. Where could such a realm be found? And what could these simples be?

Where James thought they were bits of pure experience (and may have been working toward an identification of experience with nature), Holt and Perry, influenced by developments in mathematics and symbolic logic, found these entities in a mathematical-logical realm of "being." It was a realm of entities having no definition or identity: neutral entities. These entities were similar to the simples that the New Realists had said analysis ultimately discloses. What we call consciousness is a grouping of these entities resulting from the selective (although not constitutive) response of the nervous system. This explanation enabled Holt and Perry to maintain the New Realist claim that consciousness and its objects were identical: Error and illusory experiences were no less objective or real than veridical experience. However, it failed to give an account of the difference between objects grouped and objects not grouped by consciousness. And it was still no easier to give an account of the organism's response to objects that were spatially or temporally distant.

Although he espoused Neutral Monism in his early years, Perry never went as far as Holt. He admitted that error and other nonveridical experiences were cases of "mis-taking" entities for something other than what they are. In a later development he identified this mis-taking as an anticipation or expectation of an event that does not, when acted on or verified, occur as expected. By this time, however, Perry had departed from the New Realist theories of independence and immanence.

Spaulding and Montague. Spaulding also identified error as a mis-taking, but he described it as a case of taking something to be existential that was only "subsistential." This mis-taking was the only subjective feature in consciousness. Therefore, he concluded, illusory objects and errors are objective and real because both the existential and subsistential are objective and real. It is the taking of a thing to be what it is not that is the psychic or subjective element in consciousness, and the problem of error—why error occurs—is one for psychologists and not for philosophers. Along with Pitkin, Spaulding also took a behaviorist view of consciousness, describing its objects as nonspatial projections or dimensions of spatial objects resulting from the interaction of organism and environment.

The second major attempt to formulate a New Realist epistemology and ontology consistent with the doctrines of independence and immanence was developed furthest by W. P. Montague, the only one of the New Realists who argued for uniquely mental, subjective elements in knowledge and experience. While admitting this was dualism, he insisted it was not the psychophysical dualism rejected by New Realism. He invoked a realm of subsistents, identifying them as propositions of which existential propositions, and hence existence, were a part. Error was a case of mis-taking the "merely" subsistential to be an existent as well.

CRITIQUES OF NEW REALISM. All of these attempted solutions raised the question of whether New Realism's epistemology, based on an independently real object immanent in experience, could coexist with its view that the real object was part of the commonsense world. When the independence of the object of knowledge was emphasized, the facts of relativity were slighted, but the object could more easily be identified with commonsense objects. On the other hand, when immanence of the object was emphasized, it tended to lose its commonsense quality, becoming instead a neutral entity, or subsistent,

or simple, supposedly disclosed by a rather sophisticated analysis. At the same time, however, the facts of relativity could more easily be taken into account. The former emphasis moved in the direction of dualism; the latter in the direction of monism.

Criticisms of New Realism in the second decade of the twentieth century were concerned mainly with showing that the organism intervenes in a considerably less naive way than the New Realists had thought and that their theories of external relations, independence, and immanence did not adequately account for what was given in knowledge and experience. Describing New Realism as the first phase of the "revolt against dualism," A. O. Lovejoy said its constructive program argued that since nothing "mental" could be admitted without leading to subjectivism and skepticism, therefore no content could be held to be psychically generated or dependent upon percipient functions. New Realism was left with things in a purely external relation to consciousness, or at best a bare and sterile awareness of them. In rejecting all mediated knowledge, he argued, New Realism could only hold the position that all content of experience must be identical with reality; everything before or "to" mind or consciousness was "objective." When this claim collided with the manifestly disparate content of nonveridical experience, an objective but "subsistent" content was said to be directly present or immanent; or, alternatively, this content was said to be no less objective than veridical content because it was at bottom ("neutrally") the same as it. But, Lovejoy concluded, this was little more than what the earlier naive, or commonsense, realism had said.

Although the New Realists hoped to produce other collections of studies, and although their discussions continued through 1914, according to Perry disagreements that had been subordinated and only imperfectly concealed, divergence of interests, and the ambition of each to write his own book soon divided them. As a movement, New Realism was soon displaced by the second major realist movement of the twentieth century, Critical Realism, which also developed and published a platform and joint program.

See also Alexander, Samuel; Brentano, Franz; Cohen, Morris Raphael; Critical Realism; Holt, Edwin Bissell; Idealism; James, William; Lovejoy, Arthur Oncken; McGilvary, Evander Bradley; Meinong, Alexius; Montague, William Pepperell; Moore, George Edward; Perry, Ralph Barton; Realism; Royce, Josiah; Russell, Bertrand Arthur William; Woodbridge, Frederick James Eugene.

Bibliography

WORKS BY NEW REALISTS

Holt, Edwin B. et al. "The Program and First Platform of Six Realists." *Journal of Philosophy* 7 (July 21, 1910): 393–401. Reprinted in their cooperative volume *The New Realism; Cooperative Studies in Philosophy*. New York: Macmillan, 1912.

Montague, William P. "Confessions of an Animistic Materialist." In *Contemporary American Philosophy*, edited by W. P. Montague and G. P. Adams. New York: Macmillan, 1930. Vol. II, 135–158. Pieces by other New Realists, "official" and otherwise, will be found in both volumes of this work.

Montague, William P. "Professor Royce's Refutation of Realism." *Philosophical Review* 11 (January 1902): 43–55.

Moore, G. E. "The Refutation of Idealism." *Mind*, n.s. 12 (1903): 442–453. Reprinted in Moore's *Philosophical Studies*. London: Routledge, 1922.

Perry, Ralph B. "The Ego-Centric Predicament." *Journal of Philosophy* 7 (1) (1910): 5–14. Reprinted in *The Development of American Philosophy*, edited by W. G. Mueder and L. Sears. Boston: Houghton Mifflin, 1940; 2nd ed., 1960.

Perry, Ralph B. "Professor Royce's Refutation of Realism and Pluralism." *Monist* 12 (1901–1902): 446–458.

Perry, Ralph B. "William Pepperell Montague and the New Realists." In "William Pepperell Montague." *Journal of Philosophy* 51 (21) (October 14, 1954): 593–637.

Spaulding, Edward G. *The New Rationalism*. New York: Holt, 1918.

WORKS ON NEW REALISM

Bowman, Lars. *Criticism and Construction in the Philosophy of the American New Realism*. Stockholm, 1955. One of the two extant studies devoted entirely to American New Realism, this work is mainly expository, using the tools of modem philosophical analysis in order to determine the central doctrines of New Realism. It includes one of the better short bibliographies.

Chisholm, Roderick M. *Realism and the Background of Phenomenology*. Glencoe, IL: Free Press, 1960. A collection of readings, with probably the best bibliography of the works of all major Realists and their critics.

Harlow, Victor. *A Bibliography and Genetic Study of American Realism*. Oklahoma City: Harlow, 1931. One of the best separate bibliographies of American Realism.

Hasan, Syed Zafarul. *Realism: An Attempt to Trace Its Origins and Development in Its Chief Representations*. Cambridge, U.K., 1928. An extensive treatment of New Realism (particularly of E. B. Holt) that includes a useful bibliography.

Hill, Thomas E. *Contemporary Theories of Knowledge*. New York: Ronald Press, 1961. Although limited to theories of knowledge, this work includes an extensive critical treatment of American New Realists, centering on Perry ("polemical"), Holt ("radical"), and Montague ("conservative").

James, William. "Does Consciousness Exist?" *Journal of Philosophy* 1 (18) (September 1, 1904). Reprinted in James's *Essays in Radical Empiricism*. New York: Longmans Green, 1938.

Kremer, René. *Le néo-réalisme américain*. Paris: Alcan, 1920. Devoted exclusively to New Realism.

Lapan, Arthur. "The Significance of James' Essay." PhD diss., Columbia University, New York, 1936.

Lovejoy, Arthur O. *The Revolt against Dualism: An Inquiry concerning the Existence of Ideas*. La Salle IL: Open Court, 1930. Lovejoy was probably the most persistent and incisive critic of New Realism.

Morris, Charles W. *Six Theories of Mind*. Chicago: University of Chicago Press, 1932. A discussion of the relationships of the various realisms, Pragmatism, and Objective Relativism.

Passmore, John. *A Hundred Years of Philosophy*. London: Duckworth, 1957. The chapter on New Realism is mainly concerned with English New Realism, most particularly Alexander's. Selected bibliography.

Piller, Christian. "The New Realism in Ethics." In *The Cambridge History of Philosophy 1870–1945*, edited by Thomas Baldwin. Cambridge, U.K.: Cambridge University Press, 2003.

Royce, Josiah. *The World and the Individual*. New York, 1912.

Schneider, Herbert W. *Sources of Contemporary Philosophical Realism in America*. Indianapolis: Bobbs-Merrill, 1964.

Werkmeister, W. H. *A History of Philosophical Ideas in America*. New York: Ronald Press, 1949. A good survey of the development of New Realism, including a detailed account of the polemical exchanges beginning with early New Realist statements in 1907.

OTHER RECOMMENDED TITLES

Almeder, Robert. *Blind Realism*. Lanham, MD: Rowman & Littlefield, 1992.

Alston, William. *A Realist Conception of Truth*. Ithaca, NY: Cornell University Press, 1996.

Baldwin, Thomas. "Ethical Non-Naturalism" In *Exercises in Analysis*, edited by Ian Hacking. Cambridge, U.K.: Cambridge University Press, 1985.

Devitt, Michael. *Realism and Truth*. Oxford: Blackwell, 1984.

Moser, Paul K. "Beyond Realism and Idealism." *Philosophia* 23 (1994): 271–288.

O'Connor, David. *The Metaphysics of G. E. Moore*. Boston: Reidel, 1982.

O'Leary-Hawthorne, John. "Anti-Realism, Before and After Moore." *History of Philosophy Quarterly* 12 (1995): 443–467.

Putnam, Hilary. *The Many Faces of Realism*. La Salle, IL: Open Court, 1987.

Skolimowski, Henryk. *Polish Analytical Philosophy: A Survey and Comparison with British Analytical Philosophy*. New York: Humanities Press, 1967.

Soames, Scott. *Philosophical Analysis in the Twentieth Century*. Vol. 1: *The Dawn of Analysis*. Princeton, NJ: Princeton University Press, 2003.

Stroud, Barry. *The Significance of Philosophical Skepticism*. Oxford: Clarendon Press, 1984.

Thomas Robischon (1967)
Bibliography updated by Benjamin Fiedor (2005)

NEWTON, ISAAC
(1642–1727)

Isaac Newton formulated the theory of universal gravity, was an inventor of the calculus, and made major discoveries in optics. He has long been regarded as, perhaps, the greatest scientist and as one of the greatest mathematicians ever to have lived. More recently, philosophers have begun to appreciate the extent to which Newton's remarks on scientific method illuminate the seminal contribution he made, especially in his *Principia*, to the transformation of natural philosophy into the physical sciences as we know them today. We now know, also, that Newton put at least as much effort into alchemy and theology as he did into his celebrated contributions to mathematics and science.

LIFE

Newton entered Trinity College Cambridge in 1661. In what has come to be called his *annus mirabilis*, he spent much of 1665 and 1666 at his family home in Woolsthorp while the university was closed because of the plague. This time at home was part of an extraordinarily productive period of intense effort concentrated on mathematics and natural philosophy. The binomial theorem and the fundamentals of the calculus are among the important new results in mathematics he obtained during this period. In natural philosophy he developed mechanics, including an analysis of circular motion. During this period he, also, conducted optical experiments that led to his account of white light and colors. In 1667 Newton became a fellow of Trinity College at Cambridge University.

In 1669 he became Lucasian Professor of Mathematics, presumably through the recommendation of Isaac Barrow (1630–1677), the first Lucasian Professor. It was Barrow who, in late 1671, delivered the reflecting telescope Newton had designed and built to the Royal Society of London. This led to Newton's being offered a fellowship in the Royal Society and to the publication in the Society's *Philosophical Transactions* of his account of white light and colors in 1672. This paper occasioned considerable debate. In that debate Newton began to articulate what he called his "experimental philosophy," which sharply distinguishes experimentally established results from conjectured hypotheses. By the late 1670s Newton withdrew from correspondence in natural philosophy.

In late 1679 Robert Hooke (1635–1703), who had recently become secretary of the Royal Society, wrote to encourage Newton to resume his public participation in natural philosophy. In this letter he invited Newton to use his mathematical methods to determine the trajectory a body would follow under a combination of inertial motion and an inverse-square force directed toward a center. In August 1684 a visit by Edmund Halley (1656–1742), who later became the Astronomer Royal, convinced Newton of the importance of the relation he had established between elliptical orbits and inverse square centripetal forces. By November Newton had sent Halley a small but revolutionary treatise, *De Motu*. An extraordinarily intense effort by Newton transformed this small treatise into his masterpiece, the *Principia*. It was published in 1687. Halley, who appreciated the importance of what Newton had achieved, oversaw the printing and paid for it out of his own pocket.

In 1689 and again in 1701, Newton was elected to represent Cambridge University in Parliament. He was made warden of the mint for England in 1696. By 1698 he had successfully carried out a major recoinage for the English economy. In 1699 he became master of the mint. In 1699 Newton also became an associate member of the French Academy of Sciences. He resigned his professorship at Cambridge in 1701. In 1703 he became president of the Royal Society of London, a post that, along with that of master of the mint, he held until his death. He was knighted in 1705.

In 1704 Newton published the first edition of his *Opticks*. It included two earlier mathematical papers as supplements, one of which was his first publication on the calculus. Newton's long delay in publishing his work led to his priority dispute with Gottfried Wilhelm Leibniz (1646-1716) over the invention of the calculus. This dispute extended from the mid-1690s until after Leibniz's death and came to focus on differences over natural philosophy as well as the calculus priority claims.

The second edition of *Principia* was published in 1713, after four years of effort under the able guidance of its editor Roger Cotes (1682–1716). The third edition was published in 1726. Conspicuous ways in which these two differ from the first edition appear to be responses to objections by Christian Huygens (1629–1695), Leibniz, and others. Some claims that had been called *Hypotheses* at the beginning of Book 3 in the first edition became, with changes and additions, *Regulae Philosophandi*, and others, such as Kepler's area and 3/2 power rules, became *Phaenomena*. The famous General Scholium clarifying what Newton took to be the proper practice of natural philosophy was added at the end.

The Latin editions of the *Optics* in 1706 and 1717 included queries that shed further light on his "experimental philosophy," as does his attack on Leibniz in his "Account of the Book Entitled *Commercium Epistolicum*" published anonymously in 1715. It ends as follows: "And must Experimental Philosophy be exploded as *miraculous* and *absurd*, because it asserts nothing more than can be proved by experiments, and we cannot yet prove by Experiments that all the Phaenomena in Nature can be solved by meer Mechanical Causes?" (1715, p. 224).

THE EXPERIMENTAL PHILOSOPHY IN THE LIGHT AND COLORS DEBATE

Newton's response to Hooke in the debate over his light and colors paper is a good illustration of his experimental philosophy. In that paper Newton claimed that his experiments conclusively established that the phenomenon of the oblong shape of the image of sunlight shined through a round hole and refracted through a prism is caused by sunlight's being made up of rays that are refracted different amounts by the prism. (Newton's reflecting telescope was designed to avoid problems caused by such differential refraction by using mirrors instead of lenses.)

Hooke interpreted Newton as claiming that the experiments established a corpuscular theory of light and argued that his own wave hypothesis could account for the results equally well. Newton responded by pointing out that the hypothesis that light is a body was put forward only as a conjecture suggested by the experiments, and not as part of what he claimed to have been established by them.

> But I knew, that the *Properties*, which I declar'd of *Light*, were in some measure capable of being explicated not only by that, but by many other Mechanical *Hypotheses*. And therefore I chose to decline them all, and to speak of *Light* in *general* terms, considering it abstractly, as something or other propagated in every way in streight lines from luminous bodies, without determining, what that thing is (1958, pp. 118–119).

Newton went on to outline how Hooke's wave hypothesis, as well as several other mechanical hypotheses, could explain the properties of differential refraction of different kinds of light he had concluded from the experiments.

In other contributions to the debate, Newton outlined how, according to his experimental philosophy, diligently establishing properties of things by experiment is to take precedence over framing hypotheses to explain them. He also made clear that the propositions he regarded as conclusively established by experiment were, nevertheless, subject to correction based on detailed criticism of the experimental reasoning establishing them or on further experimental results challenging them.

MATHEMATICS

Newton's mathematical papers include substantial discoveries in algebra, pure and analytic geometry, as well as his extensive work on the calculus and infinite series. His results on converging series allowed mathematicians to treat such infinite series as legitimate alternative forms of the functions they represented. These results also provided the basis for his approach to the calculus. In 1669 Newton first allowed one of his manuscripts on the calculus to circulate.

The basic mathematics of the *Principia* is not the calculus but a new form of synthetic geometry incorporating limits. Newton's lemmas on first and last ratios, which open Book 1, show that this alternative geometrical approach can recover many of the basic elementary results of the calculus. The need to rely on geometrical figures, however, makes this approach less able to facilitate more complex calculations made accessible by algebraic manipulation in the symbolic calculus.

STUDIES IN ALCHEMY, THEOLOGY, AND CHRONOLOGY

Newton's alchemical work may well have contributed to a corpuscular theory of matter that may have informed his scientific thinking; however, like his conjectured corpuscular account of light, such a theory of matter was not something Newton claimed to have established.

His extensive notes on his alchemical work indicate a number of elaborate chemical experiments carried out from the mid-1670s until 1693. These display Newton's great discipline as an experimenter. The reported results, however, appear to include nothing that would have altered the course of chemistry had they become public at the time.

Newton first became preoccupied with theology in the early 1670s, probably in response to the requirement that he accept ordination to retain his Trinity fellowship. (He was granted a dispensation in 1675.) By 1673 he had rejected the doctrine of the Trinity and concluded that Christianity had become a false religion through a corruption of the scriptures in the fourth and fifth centuries. He returned to these studies and to work on chronology and prophecies in subsequent decades, especially in the last years of his life. During his lifetime he conveyed his radical views to only a few. But, two such manuscripts were published within a few years of his death.

Recent investigations of the alchemical and theological writings suggest that Newton's natural philosophy was to be part of a larger investigation that would look through nature to see God. This may have helped him to free himself from the restraints of the mechanical philosophy. Newton's intense religious faith was no impediment, and may well have aided, his extraordinarily successful applications of his experimental philosophy in pursuit of empirically establishing scientific knowledge. Moreover, Newton's efforts at scientific understanding of nature did not prevent his efforts to inform his faith by the study of scripture.

SPACE, TIME, AND THE LAWS OF MOTION

Newton's distinction between absolute (or true) and relative (or apparent) motion are based on his laws of motion, which he described as "accepted by mathematicians and confirmed by experiments of many kinds" ([1687] 1999, p. 424). His distinctions between absolute and relative space and time, which have been such salient targets of criticism by philosophers, are mostly designed to accommodate this primary distinction between true and merely relative motions. Newton was aware of the empirical difficulties raised by such distinctions: "It is certainly very difficult to find out the true motions of individual bodies and actually to differentiate them from apparent motions, because the parts of that immovable space in which bodies move make no impression on the senses" (p. 414).

The *Principia*'s title, *Mathematical Principles of Natural Philosophy*, refers to the propositions of Books 1 and 2 that Newton demonstrated from his laws of motion. These provide his resources for addressing this difficulty: "But in what follows, a fuller explanation will be given of how to determine true motions from their causes, effects, and apparent differences, and conversely, of how to determine from motions whether true or apparent, their causes and effects. For this was the purpose for which I composed the following treatise" (p. 415). In Book 3 Newton shows how the calculation of centripetal forces and masses of central bodies from orbital motions around them can determine the center of mass of the planetary system. This calculation picks out the sun-centered Keplerian system as approximately true and the

corresponding earth-centered Tychonic system as wildly inconsistent with the measured masses.

Such inconsistencies among the measured forces and masses indicate a failure to be dealing with true motions. For Newton, the adequacy of his appeal to absolute space, time, and motion was an empirical issue to be decided by the long term development and application of a science of motion.

INFERENCES FROM PHENOMENA AND RULES OF NATURAL PHILOSOPHY

The propositions of Books 1 and 2 are powerful resources for establishing conclusions about forces from phenomena of motion. For example, propositions 1 and 2 together establish that Kepler's area rule holds if and only if the force acting on the moving body is centripetal. A corollary adds that the rate at which areas are swept out be radii from the center increases just in case the net force is off-center in the direction of motion, and decreases just in case it is off-center in the opposite direction. These systematic dependencies make the constancy of the areal rate measure the centripetal direction of the force. Similar systematic dependencies are involved in the inferences to the inverse-square variation of orbital centripetal forces from Kepler's 3/2 power rule and from the absence of orbital precession.

Newton was not the first to exploit such theoretical dependencies to draw inferences from phenomena. Huygens had used his laws of pendulums to measure the acceleration of gravity from the lengths and periods of pendulums. But, Newton turned the technique into a general way of using theory mediated measurements to do empirical science.

The rules of reasoning strengthen the inferences that can be drawn from measurements by phenomena.(See Scientific Method) The first two rules, for example, endorse the inference identifying the force holding the moon in orbit with terrestrial gravity on the basis of the moon-test, which shows that the length of a seconds pendulum at the surface of the earth and the centripetal acceleration of the moon's orbit can count as agreeing measurements of a single earth centered inverse-square acceleration field.

The third rule supports the inference that all bodies gravitate toward each planet with weights proportional to their masses. Newton argues that terrestrial pendulum experiments and the moon-test show this for gravitation toward the earth. Similarly, the harmonic laws for orbits about them show this for gravitation toward Saturn, Jupiter, and the sun. In addition, the agreement between the accelerations of Jupiter and its satellites toward the sun, as well as between those of Saturn and its satellites and those of the earth and its moon toward the sun also show this for weight toward the sun. All these count as phenomena giving agreeing measurements of the equality of the ratios of weight to mass for all bodies at any equal distances from the sun or any planet.

The fourth rule authorizes the practice of treating propositions appropriately supported by reasoning from phenomena as either "exactly or very nearly true notwithstanding any contrary hypotheses, until yet other phenomena make such propositions either more exact or liable to exceptions" (p. 796). It was added in the third edition to justify treating universal gravity as an established scientific fact, notwithstanding complaints that it was unintelligible in the absence of an explanation of how it results from mechanical action by contact. This rule and the related discussion of hypotheses in the General Scholium most distinguish Newton's experimental philosophy from the mechanical philosophy of his critics.

GRAVITY AS A UNIVERSAL FORCE OF INTERACTION

The systematic dependencies via which the basic inverse-square forces are measured by Keplerian phenomena are one-body idealizations. Universal gravity entails interactions among bodies, producing perturbations that require corrections to the Keplerian phenomena. Such corrections can count as higher-order phenomena that carry information that can be exploited to develop successively more accurate approximations.

The *Principia* includes a successful treatment of two-body interactions and some limited results on three-body interactions including Newton's account of the variational inequality in the lunar orbit. Applications of calculus facilitated by the use of Leibniz's notation by such figures as Leonard Euler (1707–1783), Jean Le Rond d'Alembert (1717–1783), and Alexis-Claude Clairaut (1713–1765) led to successful Newtonian treatments of more complex interactions. By the mid-1700s such successes in the treatments of the shape of the earth, the precession of the equinoxes, the lunar precession and motions of comets had led to the virtual abandonment of vortex theories as serious rivals. By the end of that century, the monumental treatise on celestial mechanics by Pierre Simon de Laplace (1749–1835), with his successful treatment of the long recalcitrant great inequality in

Jupiter-Saturn motions as a periodic perturbation, led to general acceptance of a Newtonian metaphysics of bodies interacting under deterministic laws.

Newtonian treatments of perturbations do more than provide the required corrections to Keplerian phenomena. They also show that Newton's original measurements of inverse-square centripetal forces continue to hold to high approximation in the presence of perturbations. Interactions with other bodies account for the precessions of all the planets except Mercury. The zero residuals in these precessions are agreeing measurements of the inverse-square variation of gravity toward the sun.

Even in the case of Mercury the famous forty-three seconds of arc per century residual in its precession yields -2.00000016 as the measure of the exponent, instead of the exact -2 measured for the other planets. That such a small discrepancy came to be a problem at all testifies to the extraordinary high level to which Newton's theory of gravity had realized a standard of empirical success. On this standard of empirical success, a theory succeeds by having its parameters be accurately measured by the phenomena it purports to explain.

In 1915, Einstein discovered that his theory of general relativity explains the missing forty-three seconds. The success of this explanation depends on the capacity of general relativity to also account for the additional precession of about 530 seconds per century explained by Newtonian perturbations of Mercury's orbit. This requires that Newton's theory count as an appropriate approximation for explaining that part of the phenomenon of Mercury's orbital precession.

Einstein's great excitement over this discovery is appropriate because it showed that his theory of general relativity did better than Newton's theory of universal gravitation by Newton's own standard of empirical success. There was and is no need to appeal to additional or different standards to count general relativity as better supported. The subsequent development of testing frameworks for general relativity continues to be guided by the same standard. Newton's methodology of successive approximations supported by the empirical success of theory mediated measurement accommodates, even, the radical conceptual transformation from Newton's metaphysics of bodies under forces of interaction to Einstein's conception of gravity as given by the geodesic structure of curved space-time.

See also Classical Mechanics, Philosophy of; Space.

Bibliography

WORKS BY NEWTON

"An Account of the Book Entituled *Comerciumm Epistolicum.*" *Philosophical Transactions* 29 (342) (1715): 173–224.

Observations upon the Prophecies of Daniel, and the Apocalypse of St. John. In *Sir Isaac Newton's Daniel and the Apocalypse: With an Introductory Study … of Unbelief, of Miracles and Prophecy*, by William Whitla. London: J. Murray, 1922. Reprinted in *Sir Isaac Newton's Daniel and the Apocalypse with an Introductory Study of Unbelief of Miracles and Prophecy*, London, 1733.

Opticks, or, A Treatise of the Reflections, Refractions, Inflections & Colours of Light. Based on the 4th. ed., 1730. New York: Dover, 1952.

Isaac Newton's Papers and Letters on Natural Philosophy and Related Documents, edited by I. B. Cohen and assisted by R. E. Schofield. Cambridge, MA: Harvard University Press, 1958. 2nd, rev. ed., 1978. Contains the publications in the dispute on light and colors as they appeared in the *Philosophical Transactions* of the Royal Society.

The Correspondence of Isaac Newton, edited by H. W. Turnbull, A. Scott, A. R. Hall, and L. Tilling. 7 vols. Cambridge, U.K.: Cambridge University Press, 1969–1977.

Unpublished Scientific Papers of Isaac Newton: A Selection from the Portsmouth Collection in the University Library, Cambridge, edited by A. R. Hall and M. B. Hall. Cambridge, U.K.: Cambridge University Press, 1962. Reprint, 1978.

The Background to Newton's Principia:. A Study of Newton's Dynamical Researches in the Years 1664–84, edited by J. W. Herivel. Oxford, U.K.: Clarendon Press, 1965.

The Mathematical Papers of Isaac Newton, edited by D. T. Whiteside. 8 vols. Cambridge, U.K.: Cambridge University Press, 1967–1981.

Isaac Newton's Philosophiae Naturalis Principia Mathematica. 3rd ed., 1726, edited by A. Koyré and I. B. Cohen. 2 vols. Cambridge, MA: Harvard University Press, 1972. Contains variant readings.

Certain Philosophical Questions: Newton's Trinity Notebook, edited by J. E. McGuire and M. Tamny. Cambridge, U.K.: Cambridge University Press, 1983. Reprint, 1985.

The Optical Papers of Isaac Newton. Vol. 1, edited by A. E. Shapiro. Cambridge, U.K.: Cambridge University Press, 1984.

Isaac Newton's Mathematical Principles of Natural Philosophy. Translated by I. B. Cohen, and A. Whitman. Los Angeles: University of California Press, 1999.

WORKS ABOUT NEWTON

General

Cohen, I. B. "Isaac Newton." In *Dictionary of Scientific Biography*, vol. 10, 42–103. New York: Scribners, 1974.

Cohen, I. B. *The Newtonian Revolution.* Cambridge, U.K.: Cambridge University Press, 1980. 2nd rev. ed., 1995.

Cohen, I. B., and G. E. Smith G.E. *The Cambridge Companion to Newton.* Cambridge, U.K.: Cambridge University Press, 2002.

Gjertsen, D. *The Newton Handbook.* London: Routledge & Kegan Paul, 1986. Contains a complete listing of Newton's work and an extensive bibliography of secondary sources.

Whiteside, D. T. "The Prehistory of the *Principia* from 1664–1686." In *Notes and Records of The Royal Society of London*, vol. 45, 11–61. London: Royal Society of London, 1991.

Wilson, C. "The Newtonian Achievement in Astronomy." In *Planetary Astronomy from the Renaissance to the Rise of Astrophysics*, edited by R. Taton and C. Wilson. Cambridge, U.K.: Cambridge University Press, 1989.

Life

Gleick, J. *Isaac Newton.* New York: Pantheon Books, 2003.

Hall, A. R. *Isaac Newton: Adventurer in Thought.* Oxford, U.K.: Oxford University Press, 1992.

Westfall, R. S. *Never at Rest: A Biography of Isaac Newton.* Cambridge, U.K.: Cambridge University Press, 1980. An abridged version, *The Life of Isaac Newton*, was published in 1993.

Further References

Bricker, P., and R. I. G. Hughes, eds. *Philosophical Perspectives on Newtonian Science.* Cambridge, MA: MIT Press, 1990. Among the many excellent collections inspired by the three-hundredth anniversary of the first edition of *Principia*, this one is especially focused on philosophy.

Earman, J. *World Enough and Space-Time Absolute verses Relational Theories of Space and Time.* Cambridge, MA: MIT Press, 1989.

Harper, W. L. "Howard Stein on Isaac Newton: Beyond Hypotheses?" In *Reading Natural Philosophy: Essays in the History and Philosophy of Science and Mathematics*, edited by David Malament, Chicago: Open Court, 2002.

Koyré, A. *Newtonian Studies.* Chicago: University of Chicago Press, 1968.

Palter, R., ed. *The Annus Mirabilis of Sir Isaac Newton, 1666–1966.* Cambridge, MA: MIT Press, 1971. This classic collection contains papers still relevant to most topics.

Smith G. " From the Phenomenon of the Ellipse to an Inverse-Square Force: Why Not?" In *Reading Natural Philosophy: Essays in the History and Philosophy of Science and Mathematics*, edited by David Malament, Chicago: Open Court, 2002.

Stein, H. "From the Phenomena of Motions to the Forces of Nature: Hypothesis or Deduction?" *PSA 90* 2 (1991): 209–222.

Theerman, Paul, and Adele F. Seeff, eds. *Action and Reaction: Proceedings of a Symposium to Commemorate the Tercentenary of Netwton's Principia.* Newark: University of Delaware Press, 1993.

William L. Harper (2005)

NICHOLAS OF CUSA
(1401–1464)

The theologian, philosopher, and mathematician Nicholas of Cusa, also known as Nicholas Kryfts or Krebs, was born at Kues on the Moselle River between Trier and Koblenz. After attending the school of the Brothers of the Common Life in Deventer, Holland, he studied philosophy at Heidelberg (1416), canon law at Padua (1417–1423), and theology at Cologne (1425). Nicholas received a doctorate in canon law in 1423. About 1426 he gave legal assistance to Cardinal Orsini, papal legate to Germany. At about the same time began his lifelong interest in collecting classical and medieval manuscripts. Among his notable discoveries were twelve lost comedies of Plautus. He took an active part in the Council of Basel, first as a lawyer of Count von Manderscheid and later as a member of the deputation *De Fide*. Nicholas's *De Concordantia Catholica*, a vast program for reform of the church and the empire, supported the conciliar theory of the supremacy of the council over the pope. Later, disillusioned by the council's failure to reform the church, he abandoned the conciliar theory and supported the papal cause.

Nicholas carried out several missions for the pope in an effort to unify and reform the church. He was a member of the commission sent to Constantinople to negotiate with the Eastern church for reunion with Rome, which was temporarily effected at the Council of Florence (1439). In 1450 Nicholas was sent to Germany as a legate to carry out church reforms. He was created a cardinal in 1448 and appointed bishop of Brixen (Bressanone) in 1450. He died in Todi, Umbria.

KNOWLEDGE

According to Nicholas, a man is wise only if he is aware of the limits of the mind in knowing the truth. Knowledge is learned ignorance (*docta ignorantia*). Endowed with a natural desire for truth, humans seek it through rational inquiry, which is a movement of the reason from something presupposed as certain to a conclusion that is still in doubt. Reasoning involves a relating or comparing of conclusion with premises. The greater the distance between them, the more difficult and uncertain is the conclusion. If the distance is infinite, the mind never reaches its goal, for there is no relation or proportion between the finite and infinite. Hence, the mind cannot know the infinite. The infinite is an absolute, and the absolute cannot be known by means of relations or comparisons.

Accordingly, the mind cannot comprehend the infinite God. By rational investigation we can draw ever nearer to him but cannot reach him. The case is the same with any truth, for every truth is an absolute, not admitting of degrees. Since reason proceeds by steps, relating conclusion to premises, it is relational and hence never arrives at absolute truth. According to Nicholas, "our

intellect, which is not the truth, never grasps the truth with such precision that it could not be comprehended with infinitely greater precision" (*De Docta Ignorantia* I, 3). As a polygon inscribed in a circle increases in number of sides but never becomes a circle, so the mind approximates to truth but never coincides with it.

Thus, knowledge at best is conjecture (*coniectura*). This is no mere guess or supposition that may or may not be true; it is an assertion that is true as far as it goes, although it does not completely measure up to its object. Reason is like an eye that looks at a face from different and even from opposite positions. Each view of the face is true, but it is partial and relative. No one view, nor all taken together, coincides with the face. Similarly, human reason knows a simple and indivisible truth piecemeal and through opposing views, with the result that it never adequately measures up to it.

The weakness of human reason was evident to Nicholas because its primary rule is the principle of noncontradiction, which states that contradictories cannot be simultaneously true of the same object. He insisted that there is a "coincidence of opposites" (*coincidentia oppositorum*) in reality, especially in the infinite God. He criticized the Aristotelians for insisting on the principle of noncontradiction and stubbornly refusing to admit the compatibility of contradictories in reality. It takes almost a miracle, he complained, to get them to admit this; and yet without this admission the ascent of mystical theology is impossible.

Nicholas preferred the Neoplatonists to the Aristotelian philosophers because they recognized in humans a power of knowing superior to reason which they called intellect (*intellectus*). This was a faculty of intuition or intelligence by which we rise above the principle of noncontradiction and see the unity and coincidence of opposites in reality. He found this faculty best described and most fruitfully cultivated by the Christian Neoplatonists, especially St. Augustine, Boethius, Pseudo-Dionysius, St. Anselm, the School of Chartres, St. Bonaventure, and Meister Eckhart. Following their tradition, he constantly strove to see unity and simplicity where the Aristotelians could see only plurality and contradiction. He frequently expressed his views in symbols and analogies, often mathematical in character, because the rational language of demonstration is appropriate to the processes of reason but not to the simple views of the intellect.

GOD

Nicholas was most concerned with showing the coincidence of opposites in God. God is the absolute maximum or infinite being, in the sense that he has the fullness of perfection. There is nothing outside him to oppose him or to limit him. He is the all. He is also the maximum, but not in the sense of the supreme degree in a series. As infinite being he does not enter into relation or proportion with finite beings. As the absolute, he excludes all degrees. If we say he is the maximum, we can also say he is the minimum. He is at once all extremes, the absolute maximum as well as the absolute minimum. In short, in God, the infinite being, all opposition is reconciled in perfect unity.

The coincidence of the maximum and minimum in infinity is illustrated by mathematical figures. For example, imagine a circle with a finite diameter. As the size of the circle is increased, the curvature of the circumference decreases. When the diameter is infinite, the circumference is an absolutely straight line. Thus, in infinity the maximum of straightness is identical with the minimum of curvature. Or, to put it another way, an infinite circle is identical with a straight line.

Nicholas offered several a priori proofs for the existence of the absolute maximum, or God. The first argued that the finite is inconceivable without the infinite. What is finite and limited has a beginning and an end, so that there must be a being to which it owes its existence and in which it will have its end. This being is either finite or infinite. If it is finite, then it has its beginning and end in another being. This leads either to an infinite series of actually existing finite beings, which is impossible, or to an infinite being which is the beginning and end of all finite beings. Consequently, it is absolutely necessary that there be an infinite being, or absolute maximum.

The second proof argued that the absolute truth about the absolute maximum can be stated in three propositions: It either is or is not. It is and it is not. It neither is nor is not. These exhaust all the possibilities, so that one of them must be the absolute truth. Hence there is an absolute truth, and this is what is meant by the absolute maximum.

As the absolute maximum, God contains all things; he is their "enfolding" (complicatio). He is also their "unfolding" (explicatio) because they come forth from him. Creatures add nothing to the divine reality; they are simply limited and partial appearances of it. As a face reproduces itself more or less perfectly in a number of mirrors, so God reflects himself in various ways in his creatures. In this case, however, there are no mirrors.

God transcends the universe but is also immanent in it, as a face is present in its mirrored images. Each crea-ture is also present in every other, as each image exists in every other. Thus, as Anaxagoras said, everything is in everything else. Gottfried Wilhelm Leibniz recalled this doctrine of Nicholas's in his *Monadology* when showing that each monad mirrors every other.

Like all medieval Platonists, Nicholas upheld the reality of universal forms. According to him, the most universal of all created forms is the form of the universe, called the Soul of the World. This form embraces in its unity all lower forms, such as those of genera and species. These lower forms are "contractions" of the form of the universe; they are the universe existing in a limited way. They exist in the universe, and it in turn exists in a limited way in them. Individuals are further contractions of universal forms—for example, Socrates is a contraction of the form of humanity. The universe as a whole is a contraction of the infinite God. Thus, all things exist in a unified manner in the universe, and the universe in turn exists in the unity of God. Oppositions and contradictions that appear on the level of individuals and lower universal forms are reconciled in the unity of the universe and ultimately in the unity of God.

COSMOLOGY

Since the universe mirrors God, it too must be a maximum—not the absolute maximum, to be sure, but the relative maximum, for it contains everything that exists except God. Nicholas denied that the universe is positively infinite; only God, in his view, could be described in these terms. But he asserted that the universe has no circumference and consequently that it is boundless or undetermined—a revolutionary notion in cosmology. (See Alexandre Koyré, *From the Closed World to the Infinite Universe*, Baltimore, 1957.) Just as the universe has no circumference, said Nicholas, so it has no fixed center. The earth is not at the center of the universe, nor is it absolutely at rest. Like everything else it moves in space with a motion that is not absolute but is relative to the observer.

Nicholas of Cusa's cosmology in some respects broke with the Ptolemaic and Aristotelian cosmological views of the Middle Ages and anticipated those of modern times. He was above all concerned with denying the absolute oppositions in the world of Ptolemy and Aristotle. In Nicholas's world there was no center opposed to its circumference, no maximum movement of the spheres opposed to the fixity of Earth, no movement of bodies in absolutely opposed directions, such as up and down. Nicholas also denied that the heavenly bodies are composed of a substance different from that of sublunar bodies.

Nicholas extended his principle of the coincidence of opposites to religion. In his irenical work *On the Peace of Faith*, while maintaining the superiority of Christianity over other religions, he tried to reconcile their differences. Beneath their oppositions and contradictions he believed there is a fundamental unity and harmony, which, when it is recognized by all, will be the basis of universal peace.

In a century of social, political, and religious unrest, Nicholas revitalized Neoplatonism as the most effective answer to the needs of his time. His thought was firmly rooted in the philosophy of Proclus and Christian medieval Neoplatonism and was opposed to the Aristotelianism that had prevailed in western Europe since the thirteenth century. It was also highly original and expressed in a language abounding in symbolism and paradox. Nicholas of Cusa had many of the traits of the Renaissance person: love of classical antiquity, all-encompassing curiosity, optimism, cultivation of literary style, critical spirit, preoccupation with the individual, and love of mathematics and science. His works were widely read for several centuries, and they influenced the philosophy of the Renaissance and of early modern times.

See also Anaxagoras of Clazomenae; Anselm, St.; Aristotelianism; Aristotle; Augustine, St.; Boethius, Anicius Manlius Severinus; Bonaventure, St.; Chartres, School of; Eckhart, Meister; Infinity in Theology and Metaphysics; Leibniz, Gottfried Wilhelm; Medieval Philosophy; Neoplatonism; Platonism and the Platonic Tradition; Proclus; Pseudo-Dionysius; Renaissance; Socrates; Universals, A Historical Survey.

Bibliography

Nicholas's religious-political works are *De Concordantia Catholica* (1433–1434); *De Pace Fidei* (1453); and *Cribratio Alchorani* (1461).

His theological-philosophical works are *De Docta Ignorantia* and *De Coniecturis* (1440); *De Deo Abscondito* (1444); *De Quaerendo Deum* (1445); *De Genesi* (1447); *Apologia Doctae Ignorantiae* (1449); *Idiotae Libri* (containing *De Sapientia*, *De Mente*, and *De Staticis Experimentis*; 1450); *De Visione Dei* (1453); *De Beryllo* (1458); *De Possest* (1460); *Tetralogus de Non Aliud* (1462); *De Venatione Sapientiae* (1463); *De Ludo Globi* (1463); and *De Apice Theoriae* (1463).

His mathematical-scientific works are *De Staticis Experimentis* (1450); *De Transmutationibus Geometricis* (1450); *De Mathematicis Complementis* (1453); and *De Mathematica Perfectione* (1458).

Editions of Nicholas's works are *Opera* (Basel, 1565); *Opera*, 3 vols. (Paris, 1514; reprinted Frankfurt am Main, 1962); *Nicolaus von Cues, Texte seiner philosophischen Schriften*, edited by A. Petzelt, Vol. 1 (Stuttgart: Kohlhammer, 1949); *Opera Omnia*, 14 vols. (Leipzig and Hamburg, 1932–1959); and *De Pace Fidei*, edited by R. Klibansky and H. Bascour (London: Warburg Institute, 1956).

Translations include *The Vision of God*, translated by E. G. Salter (New York: Dutton, 1928); *The Idiot*, translated by W. R. Dennes (San Francisco, 1940); *Of Learned Ignorance*, translated by G. Heron (London: Routledge and K. Paul, 1954); and *Unity and Reform; Selected Writings of Nicholas de Cusa*, edited by J. P. Dolan (Notre Dame, IN: University of Notre Dame Press, 1962).

Literature on Nicholas includes P. Duhem, "Nicholas de Cues et Léonard de Vinci." in *Études sur Léonard de Vinci*, Vol. II (Paris: Hermann, 1909); E. Vansteenberghe, *Le Cardinal Nicolas de Cues* (Paris: Champion, 1920); P. Rotta, *Il cardinale Nicolò di Cusa, la vita ed il pensiero* (Milan: Società editrice, "Vita e pensiero," 1928); and *Nicolò Cusano* (Milan: Bocca, 1942); A. Posch, *Die "Concordantia Catholica" des Nikolaus von Cusa* (Paderborn, 1930); H. Bett, *Nicholas of Cusa* (London: Methuen, 1932); M. de Gandillac, *La philosophie de Nicolas de Cues* (Paris: Aubier, Éditions Montaigne, 1941); J. Koch, *Nikolaus von Cues und seine Umwelt* (Heidelberg: Carl Winter, 1948); P. Mennicken, *Nikolaus von Kues* (Trier: Cusanus-Verl, 1950); Étienne Gilson, *Les métamorphoses de la cité de Dieu* (Paris: J. Vrin, 1952); K. H. Volkmann-Schluck, *Nicolaus Cusanus* (Frankfurt am Main: Klostermann, 1957); E. Meuthen, *Die letzten Jahre des Nikolaus von Kues* (Cologne: Westdeutscher, 1958); G. Santinello, *Il pensiero di Nicolò Cusano nella sua prospettiva estetica* (Padua: Liviana, 1958); G. Heinz-Mohr, *Unitas Christiana* (Trier, 1958); E. Zellinger, *Cusanus-Konkordanz* (Munich: Hueber, 1960); P. E. Sigmund, *Nicholas of Cusa and Medieval Political Thought* (Cambridge, MA: Harvard University Press, 1963); and Ernst Cassirer, *Individuum und Kosmos in der Philosophie der Renaissance* (Leipzig: Teubner, 1927), translated by Mario Domandi as *The Individual and the Cosmos in Renaissance Philosophy* (Oxford: Blackwell, 1963).

See also Louis Dupre and Nancy Hudson, "Nicholas of Cusa," in *A Companion to Philosophy in the Middle Ages*, edited by Jorge J. E. Gracia (Malden, MA: Blackwell, 2003); Jasper Hopkins, "Nicholas of Cusa (1401–1464): First Modern Philosopher?" *Midwest Studies in Philosophy* (26[2002]: 13–29; John Longeway, "Nicolas of Cusa and Man's Knowledge of God," *Philosophy Research Archives* (13[1987–1988]: 289–313.

Armand A. Maurer (1967)
Bibliography updated by Tamra Frei (2005)

NICHOLAS OF ORESME

See *Oresme, Nicholas*

NICOLAI, CHRISTIAN FRIEDRICH

(1733–1811)

Christian Friedrich Nicolai, a German publisher, editor, and author, was born in Berlin and studied there and at a Pietist institution in Halle, but he never attended a university. Nicolai spent three years as a business apprentice in Frankfurt an der Oder. Upon his father's death in 1752, he took over the family bookstore, managing it—except for a short period—until his death and expanding it into a very successful and lucrative publishing house. He became a close friend of G. E. Lessing and of Moses Mendelssohn, and was active in Berlin intellectual life. He edited the *Bibliothek der schönen Wissenschaften und freien Künste* (Library of aesthetics and fine arts) from 1757 to 1758, the *Literaturbriefe* (Letters on literature) from 1759 to 1765, and the *Allgemeine deutsche Bibliothek* (Universal German library) from 1765 on. The last-mentioned journal became the most famous German literary review of its time and was widely influential in theology as well.

Nicolai's own works, like those of many Enlightenment figures, were largely higher journalism consisting mainly in forceful and lively attacks on contemporary intellectual and literary personalities and trends. His *Briefe, den jetzigen Zustand der Schönen Wissenschaften betreffend* (Letters on the state of the arts; Berlin, 1755) were directed against the influential literary critic J. C. Gottsched. His philosophical novel *Sebaldus Nothanker* (3 vols., Berlin, 1773–1776) was an attack on certain reactionary circles in Halle. In various articles in his journals he attacked J. G. Hamann, Johann Caspar Lavater, Christian Garve, and others. He quarreled with J. G. Herder and F. H. Jacobi. The novels *Daniel Säuberlich* (Berlin, 1777–1778) and *Die Freunden des jungen Werthers* (Berlin, 1775) were parodies of Johann Wolfgang von Goethe, Johann Gottfried Herder, G. A. Bürger (author of the ballad *Lenore*), and the *Sturm und Drang*. He attacked Catholicism as a source of superstition and Jesuitism; and, although he was himself a member of the Order of the Enlightened (*Illuminaten*) and of the Freemasons, he accused both of being secret instruments of the Jesuits (which resulted in his forced resignation). In the philosophical novels *Geschichte eines dicken Mannes* (The story of a fat man; 2 vols., Berlin, 1794) and *Sempronius Gundibert* (Berlin, 1798) and in other works, he accused Immanuel Kant and his school and Johann Gottlieb Fichte of being crypto-Catholics. His *Vertraute Briefe von Adelheid B. an ihre Freundin Julie S.* (Confidential letters from Adelaide B. to her friend Julie S.; Berlin, 1799) was directed against Friedrich Schleiermacher.

Nicolai wrote many other works, notably a large work devoted to the economic, cultural, social, and religious life in Germany and Switzerland, *Beschreibung einer Reise durch Deutschland und die Schweiz im Jahre 1781* (Description of a journey through Germany and Switzerland in 1781; 12 vols., Berlin, 1783–1796). Although Nicolai was awarded an honorary doctorate by the Helmstedt Theological Seminary in 1799 and was made a corresponding member of the Academy of St. Petersburg in 1804, his hostility toward the most influential persons of his time and his lack of understanding of the new critical philosophy and of romanticism led to a negative evaluation of his work by his leading contemporaries and by the following generation.

Nevertheless, Nicolai was one of the most typical representatives of "popular philosophy." Basing his theories on common sense, he avoided abstract thought and complex speculation and favored useful and easy knowledge. He opposed orthodoxy, intolerance, enthusiasm, mysticism, and secret machinations. He attacked the scholastic Wolffian philosophy; the newer critical and idealistic philosophies; Protestantism, both orthodox and mystical, and Catholicism; secret societies; Gottsched's classicism in literature as well as the glorification of the peasant by J. H. Voss and Bürger; *Sturm und Drang*; and early romanticism. He considered them all to be reactionary and pernicious, and his writings were full of misunderstandings, misrepresentations, and exaggerations.

His religious views incorporated his rejection of intellectualism, dogmatism, and mysticism. He held that religion and science should not be confused. Orthodox religion corrupted morality and tended toward an obnoxious hierarchical system. He denied original sin and eternal damnation and accepted the doctrines of free will and of the immortality of the soul. Religion should be based on the individual conscience and not on revelation—on common sense and not on enthusiasm.

According to Nicolai, religion and morality are not the same. Morality is based on social sense and experience; religion is a feeling for God's goodness and providence as mirrored in the goodness and beauty of the Creation. Although Nicolai was a deist himself, he did not believe that a purely natural religion would suffice for the common people, and therefore he refused to reject publicly the Christian tradition.

Nicolai was influenced in aesthetics by the classicists Nicolas Boileau and Jean Baptiste Dubos and by the Swiss critics J. J. Bodmer, J. J. Breitinger, and J. G. Sulzer. He tried to find a middle ground between the classical doctrine of the imitation of nature and the newer stress on the imagination. He opposed the classical ideal of literature as deduced from a set of rules, the sentimental school of literature, and the *Sturm und Drang* emphasis on intuitive genius. He held that poetry should be simple and reasonable and designed chiefly for moral improvement.

See also Aesthetics, History of; Boileau, Nicolas; Common Sense; DuBos, Abbe Jean Baptiste; Enlightenment; Fichte, Johann Gottlieb; Garve, Christian; Goethe, Johann Wolfgang von; Gottsched, Johann Christoph; Hamann, Johann Georg; Herder, Johann Gottfried; Jacobi, Friedrich Heinrich; Kant, Immanuel; Lavater, Johann Kaspar; Lessing, Gotthold Ephraim; Mendelssohn, Moses; Religion and Morality; Schleiermacher, Friedrich Daniel Ernst; Sulzer, Johann Georg.

Bibliography

ADDITIONAL WORKS BY NICOLAI
Ueber meine gelehrte Bildung. Berlin, 1799.
Philosophische Abhandlungen. Berlin, 1808.

WORKS ON NICOLAI
Aner, K. *Der Aufklärer Friedrich Nicolai.* Giessen: A. Töpelmann, 1912.
Fichte, J. G. *Fr. Nicolais Leben und sonderbare Meinungen.* Tübingen, 1801.
Meyer, Friedrich. *Friedrich Nicolai.* Leipzig: Bücherstube, 1938.
Ost, G. *Fr. Nicolais Allgemeine Deutsche Bibliothek.* Berlin, 1928.
Philips, F. C. A. *Nicolais literarische Bestrebungen.* The Hague, 1926.
Sommerfeld, M. *Nicolai und der Sturm und Drang.* Halle, 1921.
Strauss, Walter. *Nicolai und die kritische Philosophie.* Stuttgart, 1927.

Giorgio Tonelli (1967)

NICOLAS OF AUTRECOURT
(c. 1300–after 1350)

Nicolas of Autrecourt, also called Nicolaus de Ultracuria, was a leading anti-Aristotelian philosopher of the fourteenth century. The condemnation of extreme Aristotelianism at Paris in 1277 was probably responsible for the critical tendencies in many fourteenth-century philosophers and theologians. An extreme form of this critical tendency is to be found in the writings and lectures of Nicolas of Autrecourt. He was at the Sorbonne as

early as 1328, lectured on the *Sentences* at Paris, and in 1340 was summoned by the Roman Curia to answer charges of heresy and error. His trial was interrupted when Pope Benedict XII died, and was resumed under Pope Clement VI by Cardinal Curty. In 1346 the trial was concluded, Nicolas was forced to recant many of his published statements, his works were publicly burned, and he was declared unworthy of advancement and unworthy to continue teaching. We last hear of him as a deacon at the cathedral of Metz in 1350.

His literary remains consist of (1) two complete letters to the Franciscan Bernard of Arezzo, a reply to a certain Giles (whose letter to Nicolas is also extant), and the fragments of seven other letters to Bernard of Arezzo; (2) a theological discussion concerning the increase of cognitive powers; and (3) the "universal tractate of Master Nicolas of Autrecourt for seeing whether the statements of the Peripatetics are demonstrative" (usually called *Exigit Ordo Executionis* from its *incipit*), which survives in a single manuscript that breaks off toward the end.

The continuing research on fourteenth-century thought will probably show that many other Schoolmen of the period expressed doctrines similar to those of Nicolas. In fact, similar doctrines have already been found in Robert Holkot and John of Mirecourt on epistemological issues, and in Henry of Harclay, Gerard Odo, and some others on atomism and the constitution of the continuum. Nevertheless, there is some reason to attribute to Nicolas a considerable measure of originality and of persistent thought. For one thing, his contemporary John of Mirecourt attributes to Nicolas the proof that causal connections cannot be demonstrated. This may mean merely that Mirecourt was making an acknowledgement to a colleague and was unaware that similar doctrines were taught at Oxford. But there must be some significance in the fact that Nicolas was singled out for attack by the decrees of the Paris faculty in 1339 and 1340 and was one of those summoned to the Curia in 1340.

The main historical origin of Nicolas's skeptical and critical views about the extent of natural knowledge was undoubtedly the prominence given to the article of the Creed "I believe in one God, Father Omnipotent, Maker of heaven and earth, …" after the condemnation of 1277. As the theologians of the fourteenth century interpreted this article, it meant that God can accomplish anything the doing of which involves no logical contradiction. Now, the miracles of the Old Testament and New Testament are incompatible with the doctrines of Aristotle and his strict interpreters, especially Averroes, in ways that touch directly on the point. Whereas Aristotle denies the possibility of accidents without substrata, the Eucharist involves the supernatural existence of the accidents of bread and wine after the substance no longer exists (that is, after the substance of bread and wine has been converted into the body and blood of Christ when the priest consecrates the Host). Again, whereas Aristotle had held that effects inevitably arise from their causes unless there is some natural impediment, the episode of the three Israelites who were not consumed in the fiery furnace involves the miraculous interruption of the natural effects of causes where there is no impediment. Consideration of these and like cases led theologians to the following result: The common course of nature can, without logical absurdity, be interrupted by divine power. Hence, the relation of causes and effects or of substances and their accidents is not logically necessitated.

CERTITUDE, SUBSTANCE, AND CAUSE

Nicolas of Autrecourt must have begun his reflections from the consideration of the theological doctrine just mentioned. He maintained that, excepting the certitude of faith, there is but one kind of certitude and this certitude depends on the principle of contradiction: Contradictories cannot be simultaneously true. Nothing is prior to this principle and it is the ultimate basis of all certitude. This certitude is absolute and no power can alter it. It has no degrees and all certitude is reducible to it. Thus, all reasoning by syllogism depends on the principle of contradiction. In every implication (*consequentia*) that is reducible to the principle of contradiction either immediately or by a number of intermediate steps, the consequent of the implication and the antecedent (or a part of the antecedent) are really identical. Otherwise it would not be evident that the antecedent is inconsistent with the denial of the consequent. From all this Nicolas derives the following result: From the fact that one thing is known to exist it cannot be inferred with an evidence reducible to that of the principle of contradiction that another thing exists. Neither the existence nor the nonexistence of one thing can be evidently inferred from the existence or nonexistence of any other thing.

The consequences of this discovery, Nicolas thought, were enough to destroy the whole intellectual enterprise of the Schools. Not only is it impossible that the existence of effects entails the existence of causes, but there is no way to have any evident knowledge of any substance other than one's own soul starting from the objects of sensation or of inner experience. Things apparent to the senses are not substances, and therefore substance cannot be evidently inferred from sensibly appearing objects.

Hence the existence of material substances or of other spiritual creatures cannot be inferred with certitude from the evidence of the senses. But this is not all. In one sense of "probable," there is not even a probability that there are any substances. For, in the sense in which the probable is what happens frequently, we can say, for example: When I in the past put my hand toward a fire, it was warmed; it is now probable that if I put my hand toward a fire, it will be warmed. But since there has never been (and could never be) a conjunction in my experience between any appearance and a substance, there is no appearance that renders the existence of a substance so much as *probable* in this sense of the word.

Some of Nicolas's critics urged that substance is deducible from appearances and that causes are deducible from their effects. But he replied that all such deductions depend upon descriptions of appearances and effects that, implicitly or explicitly, contain reference to substances or causes. The deductions from such descriptions are perfectly valid, but nothing in experience or in our stock of self-evident propositions provides the slightest evidence that anything corresponds to such descriptions. In a word, every attempt to prove the existence of substances or causes from appearances or effects begs the question. This point was made in other philosophical writings both before and after Nicolas. The Muslim theologian Mohammad al-Ghazālī, in his *Tahāfut al-Falāsifah* (Incoherence of the Philosophers; see *Averroes' Tahafut al-Tahafut,* edited and translated by Simon van den Bergh, London, 1954, pp. 329–333), pointed out that logically guaranteed inferences concerning causes depend on the description and definitions of terms and so, in a sense, are mainly verbal arguments. Nicolas could not have had access to this work because the relevant sections were not translated until sometime later. David Hume's negative critique of belief in causation and belief in substance parallels that of Nicolas very closely, but Hume had no possible access to the writings of Nicolas because these were not discovered until the nineteenth and twentieth centuries in the Bibliothèque Nationale and the Bodleian Library.

CRITIQUE OF ARISTOTLE

The purpose of Nicolas's critique of Aristotle and his followers is set forth in the prologue to his *Exigit Ordo Executionis.* He tells us that he read the works of Aristotle and his commentator Averroes and discovered that the demonstrations of their doctrines were defective, that arguments for the opposite of these doctrines can be found that are more plausible than arguments for them.

(The word *plausible* here is intended to translate the Latin word *probabilis* because, in this usage, it does not mean "frequent" but "plausible.") Moreover, men have spent their entire lives studying Aristotle to no avail while neglecting the good of the community. Men would live better lives and contribute to the common good, in matters religious and moral, if only they knew that very little certitude about things can be learned from natural appearances and that what little can be learned can be obtained in a short while, provided men attend to things rather than the treatises of Aristotle and Averroes. In a word, the intellectual culture of Nicolas's age is condemned as largely vain; and the purpose of his criticism is simply to show this in detail. This is not to say that Nicolas is opposed to empirical investigation, but it would be a mistake to see in his attack on Aristotle an interest in empirical investigation such as we find in the promoters of natural science in the sixteenth and seventeenth centuries.

The criticism of Aristotle as set forth in the *Exigit* has an aspect not indicated in his controversy with Bernard of Arezzo. In the letters to Bernard he declared that nothing that is said about infrasensible reality is even probable. In another sense of probability, introduced in the *Exigit* (but one of the accepted senses of the term in the Middle Ages and derived, in fact, from Aristotle), a proposition or opinion is probable if there are arguments in its favor that, although inconclusive, would be approved by an impartial judge. In this sense, a proposition or opinion has a probability that varies as our information increases. Accordingly, Nicolas begins with a conception that is accepted by his adversaries: The principle that the Good exists in our minds as a kind of measure for evaluating things. According to this, we may assume that the things in the universe are so arranged that whatever is good exists and whatever is bad does not exist. Since there is no way of demonstrating that things exist in a certain arrangement, we are obliged to depend on the principle of the Good in order to determine what is probably the case. Following this principle we can suppose that (1) all things in the universe are mutually connected so that one thing exists for the sake of another (like Aristotle's view that all things are ordered to one ultimate end, that is, God; cf. Aristotle, *Metaphysics* 1075a15ff.); (2) there is systematic subordination of all things to a single end so that nothing exists that does not somehow contribute to the good of the entire universe; (3) the universe, so conceived, must be at all times equally perfect.

ATOMISM

From the above, Nicolas concludes that any particular thing that now exists has always existed and will always exist. For whatever now exists, exists for the good of the whole, and because this whole is always and everywhere equally perfect, all its parts must always exist. Hence, on the principle of the Good, every ultimate entity in the universe is eternal.

The eternity of things is obviously incompatible with Aristotle's thought, in which the generation and corruption of substances and their accidents is an essential feature. Here Nicolas is content to show that all the Aristotelian arguments to prove the occurrence of generation, corruption, or other kinds of change are inconclusive. For example, we cannot prove conclusively that sensible qualities cease to exist. The only method of proving this is to argue that a quality ceases to exist because it no longer appears to us, and this is obviously inconclusive. Hence, Nicolas argues, the atomic theory in its most radical form is more plausible than Aristotle's nonatomistic theory of change. The *appearance* of change can be accounted for in terms of the aggregation and separation of atomic particles.

There is much of interest in the finer details of Nicolas's atomism, particularly in his defense of indivisible minima as the ultimate constituents of the continuum, his defense of the vacuum, and his theory of motion. But here he is by no means original. His theory of the nature of motion, for example, is taken over from William of Ockham, and his views about indivisibles owe much to other fourteenth-century Scholastics. Moreover, there are radical deficiencies in his views on these subjects. Nicolas also adopted the radical Ockhamist thesis that relations are reducible to their terms, so that there are no extracognitive referents to our relational concepts. The denial of extracognitive relations is mistaken, and this part of Nicolas's speculations suffers from this error.

The *Exigit* also develops a theory of knowledge in terms of which whatever appears to be the case is the case, that is, that the objects of cognition are all in some way real. Nicolas also develops a positive theory of causation, and there is a related theory of eternal recurrence. Whether he derived this from Stoic sources is not clear.

INFLUENCE AND IMPORTANCE

The skeptical and critical views, as well as Nicolas's probabilistic defense of atomism, produced some responses among his contemporaries and successors. Albert of Saxony, Jean Buridan, and others replied to his critical views on causation and substance, and Thomas of Strasbourg discussed his atomism. Many references to his views on the nature of propositions occur in later fourteenth-century theologians. Moreover, although Nicolas's views were formally condemned by the Curia in 1346, at the end of the century Cardinal Pierre d'Ailly not only adopted many of these views but also wrote that "many things were condemned against [Nicolas] because of envy which were later publicly stated in the schools."

The importance of Nicolas of Autrecourt in the history of thought can best be summarized as follows: He was a radical representative of an increasing tendency in fourteenth-century thought to reject the idea that any of the principles of natural theology admit of demonstration, and he thus contributed to the decline of the authority of Aristotle. Although some of his reflections are both important and valid, they seem not to have had any direct effect on the development of philosophy in early modern times. From one point of view, he and some of his contemporaries achieved a clarity about the nature of beliefs in causation and substance that was neither equaled nor surpassed until the eighteenth century in the writings of Hume.

See also Ailly, Pierre d'; Albert of Saxony; al-Ghazālī, Muhammad; Aristotelianism; Aristotle; Atomism; Averroes; Buridan, John; Henry of Harclay; Holkot, Robert; Hume, David; John of Mirecourt; Medieval Philosophy; William of Ockham.

Bibliography

Editions of Nicolas of Autrecourt's writings are found in J. Lappe's "Nicolaus von Autrecourt," in *Beiträge zur Geschichte der Philosophie des Mittelalters* 6 (2) (Münster, 1908), and J. Reginald O'Donnell's "Nicholas of Autrecourt," in *Medieval Studies* 1 (1939): 179–280, which contains an edition of the *Exigit.*

A study of Nicolas's work is found in Lappe's article. Other studies have been made by P. Vignaux, "Nicolas d'Autrecourt," in *Dictionnaire de théologie catholique,* Vol. XI (Paris, 1931); J. Reginald O'Donnell, "The Philosophy of Nicholas of Autrecourt and His Appraisal of Aristotle," in *Medieval Studies* 4 (1942): 97–125; J. R. Weinberg, *Nicolaus of Autrecourt* (Princeton, NJ: Princeton University Press for University of Cincinnati, 1948); Mario del Pra, *Nicola di Autrecourt* (Milan: Fratelli Bocca, 1951); and V. Zoubov, "Nicolas iz Otrekura i Drevnegrecheskie Atomisti," in *Trudi Instituta Istorii Estestvoznaniia i Tekhniki* (SSSR Akademiia Nauk) 10 (1956): 338–383.

Julius R. Weinberg (1967)

NICOLAS OF AUTRECOURT [ADDENDUM]

Documentation about Autrecourt's life is scarce. His date of birth is now placed sometime between 1295–1298. He came from the diocese of Verdun and attended the arts faculty at Paris. He also held a degree in civil law, which he must have obtained outside of Paris. His membership in the Collège de Sorbonne places Autrecourt back in Paris in the 1330s as a student in theology. He died in 1369, either on July 16 or 17.

Over the last two decades, it has become apparent that the study of Autrecourt's thought has been wrongly placed in the larger context of putatively skeptical tendencies in scholastic thought and the battle against Ockhamism at the University of Paris in the years 1339–1347. In his *Universal Treatise (Exigit ordo),* which originated at the arts faculty during the years 1333–1335, he defends the Aristotelian thesis that our sensory experiences are reliable—that what appears really is, and that what appears to be true really is true (*Metaphysics* IV, 5). He finds this view more plausible than its opposite, namely that the intellect is incapable of certitude.

In his *Letters,* Autrecourt attacks the "Academics" or ancient Skeptics. Yet, at the same time, he challenges the prevailing Aristotelian tradition, in particular of substance-accident structure of reality and the principle of causality. This view is the result of his stance that all *evident* knowledge (with the exception of the certitude of faith) must be reducible to the principle of noncontradiction (*primum principium*). This outlook was developed in his correspondence with a Master Giles (of Feno?) and his two extant letters to the Franciscan theologian Bernard of Arezzo, which must have been written sometime between October 1335 and June 1336. These exchanges hark to a previous discussion between Autrecourt and Bernard of Arezzo at their inaugural lectures (*Principia*) on the *Sentences* about the validity of Aristotle's principle of noncontradiction.

Bibliography

TRANSLATIONS OF AUTRECOURT'S WRITINGS

Nicolas d'Autrecourt, Correspondance, articles condamnés; texte latin établi par L.M. de Rijk; introduction, traduction et notes par Christophe Grellard. Paris: Vrin, 2001

Nicholas of Autrecourt: His Correspondence with Master Giles and Bernard of Arezzo: English translation by L. M. de Rijk. Leiden: E. J. Brill, 1994.

Nicholas of Autrecourt: The Universal Treatise. English translation by Leonard A. Kennedy, Richard E. Arnold, and

Arthur E. Millward; introduction by Leonard A. Kennedy. Milwaukee: Marquette University Press, 1971.

Nicolaus von Autrecourt: Briefe. German translation by R. Imbach and D. Perler. Hamburg: Meiner, 1988.

WORKS ON AUTRECOURT

Dutton, B. D. "Nicholas of Autrecourt and William of Ockham on Atomism, Nominalism, and the Ontology of Motion." *Medieval Philosophy and Theology* 5 (1996): 63–85.

Kaluza, Z. "Éternité du monde et incorruptibilité des choses dans l'Exigit ordo de Nicolas d'Autrecourt." In *Tempus, aevum, aeternitas. La concettualizzazione del tempo nel pensiero tardomedievale,* edited by G. Alliney and L. Cova, 207–240. Florence: L.S. Olschki, 2000.

Kaluza, Z. *Histoire littéraire de la France.* Vol. 42, *Nicolas d'Autrecourt. Ami de la vérité.* Paris: Histoire littéraire de la France, 1995.

Kaluza, Z. "Les catégories dans l'*Exigit ordo.* Étude de l'ontologie formelle de Nicolas d'Autrecourt." *Studie Mediewistyczne* XXXIII (1998): 97–124.

Scott, T. K., "Nicholas of Autrecourt, Buridan, and Ockhamism." *Journal of the History of Philosophy* 9 (1971): 15–41.

Tachau, K. H. *Vision and Certitude in the Age of Ockham: Optics, Epistemology, and the Foundations of Semantics, 1250–1345.* Leiden: Brill Publishers, 1988.

Thijssen, J. M. M. H. *Censure and Heresy at the University of Paris, 1200–1400.* Philadelphia: University of Pennsylvania Press, 1998.

Thijssen, J. M. M. H. "John Buridan and Nicholas of Autrecourt on Causality and Induction." *Traditio* 43 (1987): 237–255.

Thijssen, J. M. M. H. "The Quest for Certain Knowledge in the Fourteenth Century: Nicholas of Autrecourt against the Academics." In *Ancient Scepticism and the Sceptical Tradition,* edited by J. Sihvola, 199–223. Helsinki: Societas Philosophica Fennica, 2000.

Thijssen, J. M. M. H. "The 'Semantic Articles' of Autrecourt's Condemnation." *Archives d'histoire doctrinale et littéraire du moyen âge* 65 (1990): 155–175.

Zupko, J., "Buridan and Skepticism." *Journal of the History of Philosophy* 31 (1993): 191–221.

Johannes M. M. H. Thijssen (2005)

NICOLE, PIERRE
(1625–1695)

Nicole Pierre was born in Chartres, the son of Jean Nicole, a member of the Parlement de Paris. In 1642 he began his studies in philosophy in Paris, where he received his Master of Arts in 1644. Subsequently, he studied theology with Alphonse Le Moine and Jacques Sainte-Beauve, and under the direction of the latter he started an intensive consideration of the theological writings of St. Augustine. During this time Nicole became involved in the activities of the reformist convent of Port-Royal des Champs through his aunt, Marie des Anges Suireau, who was for a short time the abbess there. Nicole taught in the *petite écoles* attached to Port-Royal, where one of his students was Jean Racine, the future poet. After receiving his Bachelor of Arts degree in 1649, he withdrew to Port-Royal, becoming one of the solitaires associated with the convent.

During the 1650s Nicole went against the French theological and political establishment in defending the theological orthodoxy of the *Augustinus* of Cornelius Jansenius, the late theologian and bishop. He joined his fellow solitaire Antoine Arnauld and other Port-Royalists in protesting the papal bulls in the 1650s that attributed to this work four heretical propositions and one false proposition concerning sin, free will, and grace. The controversy that derived from this protest was such that when he returned to Paris in 1654, Nicole was forced to take the assumed name of M. de Rosny.

In 1658, during a tour in the German territories, he translated the *Provinciales* (1656–1657) into Latin, using the pseudonym Guillaume Wendrock. This work, written by the brilliant Port-Royalist Blaise Pascal, was a popular satirical critique of Jesuit moral theology. Nicole also defended both the *Augustinus* and Port-Royal throughout the 1660s, when Louis XIV exerted considerable pressure on the members of the convent to bring them into conformity with official church policy. During this time, in 1662, he published with Arnauld, under the pseudonym of Sieur le Bon, the first of what was to be six editions of the *Logique ou l'art de penser.* This work reflects the teaching at the petite écoles at Port-Royal before their disbandment by Louis XIV in 1660. This work combines an Augustinian distinction between a theology grounded in trust of authority and a philosophy grounded in trust of natural reason with René Descartes's rejection of radical Pyrrhonian skepticism and his metaphysical conclusion that mind as a thinking thing is a substance really distinct from body as an extended thing. Nonetheless, Nicole was never as enthusiastic about the new Cartesian philosophy as his coauthor, Arnauld, was. In several letters published in his four-volume *Essais de morale* (vol. 2, 1679) Nicole emphasized the weakness of human reason and the inability of the Cartesians to offer more than probable conclusions. This sort of emphasis was in line with the skepticism concerning the new philosophy reflected in the views of Port-Royal solitaires such as Le Maistre de Sacy and Louis-Paul du Vaucel. Such skepticism belies the claim of the Calvinist Pierre Jurieu that "the theologians of Port-Royal are as attached to Cartesianism as they are to Christianity" (*La politique du clergé de France* [Cologne, 1681], 107).

The Peace of the Church that Pope Clement IX established in 1669 with the help of Louis XIV brought about a decade-long cessation of hostilities against the Jansenists. During this period Arnauld and Nicole devoted themselves to their three-volume *La perpétuité de la foy*, in which they defended the Catholic doctrine that Christ is "physically present" in the Eucharist against the view of the Calvinist minister JeanClaude that Christ has a merely "spiritual presence" in this sacrament. Nicole and Arnauld also condemned the attempt of the French Benedictine Robert Desgabets to defend the view in Descartes's unpublished correspondence that the physical presence of Christ involves merely the union of His soul with the matter of the Eucharistic elements. The anonymous publication of this defense in the *Conisdérations sur l'état present* (1671) was one of the triggers of the official campaign against Cartesianism in France during the 1670s.

The Peace of the Church officially ended with Louis XIV's banishment of Nicole and Arnauld, along with other Port-Royalist sympathizers, to the Spanish Netherlands (now Belgium) in 1679. In contrast to Arnauld and the other Port-Royalists, however, Nicole was eager to reconcile himself with the French authorities, and negotiations with the bishop of Paris, François de Harlay de Champvallon, allowed him to return to Paris in 1683. After this return, he further revised his *Essais de morale* and attacked in print the views of the Calvinists. Nicole also attempted (unsuccessfully) to moderate the tone of the increasing bitter philosophical and theological debate during the 1680s and early 1690s that pitted Arnauld against the French Cartesian Nicolas Malebranche.

In the 1690s Nicole also became embroiled in his own dispute with Arnauld over Nicole's view that God grants us a "general grace" that involves at least an implicit knowledge of moral truth. Appealing to the Cartesian doctrine of the transparency of the mind, Arnauld objected to any knowledge of moral truth that does not involve explicit awareness. The response to this line of objection in Nicole and his defenders, including the Louvain theologian Gommaire Huygens and the French Benedictine François Lamy, invoked the purported implication in Augustine that we see truths in God by means of divine illumination that we do not grasp completely. The case of this dispute serves to further illustrate the complexities of the relations between Augustinianism and Cartesianism during the seventeenth century.

During the 1690s, Nicole also found himself opposed to Lamy over the "quietist" doctrine of the French Cardinal François de Fénelon that we are to have a "pure love" of God that involves no concern for the self. Whereas Lamy defended Fénelon, Nicole joined the French Bishop Jacques-Bénigne Bossuet in arguing for the conclusion, which Rome later endorsed, that quietism is heretical. Soon after this dispute, Nicole suffered a stroke, and he died in Paris on November 16, 1695, a little over a year after Arnauld's death.

See also Arnauld, Antoine.

Bibliography

Arnauld, Antoine, and Pierre Nicole. *Logic, or, The Art of Thinking*, edited by Jill Vance Buroker. New York: Cambridge University Press, 1996.

WORKS BY NICOLE

De l'éducation d'un prince [later, vol. 2 of *Essais de morale*]. Paris: Savreaux, 1670.

Die Philosophie des 17.Jahrhunderts. Band 2, Frankreich und Niederlande. Basil: Schwabe, 1993.

Essais de morale, contenus en divers traitez sur plusieurs devoirs importans. 4 vols. Paris: Savreux (vol. 1) 1671, and Desprez (vol. 2) 1679; (vol. 3) 1675; (vol. 4) 1678.

Traité de la grâce générale. 2 vols. N.p.: n.p., 1715.

Oeuvres. 25 vols. Paris: n.p., 1765–1782.

WORKS ON NICOLE

James, Edward D. *Pierre Nicole, Jansenist and Humanist: A Study of His Thought*. The Hague: Nijhoff, 1972.

[Rodis-] Lewis, Geneviève. "Augustinianisme et cartésianisme à Port-Royal." In *Descartes et le cartésianisme hollandaise*, edited by E. J. Dijksterhuis et al., 131–182. Paris: Presses Universitaires de France, 1950.

Solère, Jean-Luc. "Arnauld versus Nicole: A Medieval Dispute." In *Interpreting Arnauld*, edited by Elmar J. Kremer, 127–146. Toronto: University of Toronto Press, 1996.

Tad M. Schmaltz (2005)

NIEBUHR, REINHOLD
(1892–1971)

Reinhold Niebuhr was eminent in two fields. One was social action and analysis of current social problems; the other was the interpretation of the Christian faith. This entry will concentrate on his religious and ethical thinking.

Niebuhr was born in Wright City, Missouri. His father was Gustave Niebuhr, a minister in the Evangelical Synod of the Lutheran Church, who came to the United States when he was seventeen years old. His mother was the daughter of the Reverend Edward Jacob Hosto, a second-generation German American of the same religious sect. Niebuhr studied at Elmhurst College, Eden Theological Seminary, and Yale University. He was ordained in 1915 and was pastor at the Bethel Evangelical Church of Detroit until 1928. He was then appointed professor at the Union Theological Seminary in New York, where he taught until 1960, when he became professor emeritus.

RELIGIOUS VIEWS

The central theme of Niebuhr's religious teaching can be stated as follows: A divine, forgiving, and timeless love "beyond history" gives meaning to human life. Nothing actually operating in human history can ever be sufficiently dominant over sinful pride and sensuality to deliver men from despair, although men attempt to conceal reality with optimistic illusions. But if we look beyond the temporal process to transcendent being, we find, through faith, a forgiving and perfect love that gives to human life a grandeur beyond the reach of despair and a zeal beyond the reach of apathy. This love from beyond history has been revealed to us in Jesus Christ. We know it is from beyond history because in history this kind of love, called agape, is ineffective before the powers that rule this world. It is futile and meaningless except when, as in the Christian faith, it reveals the ultimate purpose of our existence by an evaluation that transcends history.

SIN AND ANXIETY.
Sin arises from anxiety, although anxiety is not sinful in itself. Man is rendered anxious by criticizing himself and his world, by recognizing his own limitations and the contingencies of his existence, and by imagining a life infinitely better than what actually is.

Anxiety would not lead to sin if we brought it under control by trusting ourselves to God's forgiving love and ultimate power. But instead of this, we seek to bring anxiety under control by pretending to have power or knowledge or virtue or special favors from God, which we do not have. This pretense leads to pride, cruelty, and injustice. Or we seek to escape anxiety by dulling the awareness of it with sensuality. All this is sin because it is a turning away from God to a self-centered existence. Sin thus induced is not inevitable, but it is universal. Also Niebuhr obscurely suggested that sin was in the world before men became sinners, this prehuman sin being symbolized by Satan.

In this predicament we have two alternatives. We may trust ourselves along with the whole of human history to God's forgiving love. The other alternative is twofold: to sink into annihilating despair or to conceal our predicament with illusions that render our condition even more desperate in the end. If we take the first alternative, we live not only for whatever love can be attained in history but also and primarily for the divine love beyond history. In this way the whole of history takes on meaning. Otherwise we have only glimpses of meaning in developments occurring here and there but no meaning for the whole of history.

TRANSCENDENCE.
Themes continuously recurrent throughout Niebuhr's writing are transcendence, freedom, reason, and love. Niebuhr's language often suggests that by "transcendence" he means the timeless ideal of perfect love. But for Niebuhr this love is not merely an ideal. It is a God who loves, yet is beyond time, cause, and world.

Self-transcendence is a central theme in Niebuhr's thought. If this merely meant that the self can change into a better self, the meaning would be obvious. But Niebuhr seems to mean that the self, while never escaping finitude in one dimension, does somehow, in another dimension, transcend time and causation and self. It does this by surveying past and future and by self-criticism. But to survey past and future is to be aware of one's involvement in time; and in self-criticism the self in retrospect is criticized by the present self; and this criticizing self may in turn be criticized by the self at a later time. Niebuhr would seem to be wrong, therefore, in claiming that in self-criticism the self can transcend time and causation.

FREEDOM AND REASON.
Niebuhr affirmed human freedom by paradox: Man is both bound and free, both limited and limitless; he is, and yet is not, involved in the flux of nature and time. As spirit he "stands outside" time, nature, world, and self, yet is involved in them. Freed of paradox, these affirmations assert that humankind is free in the dimension of spirit but not in the dimension of natural existence. The human spirit transcends the self, time, and nature because the individual can know himself as an object, can judge himself to be a sinner, can survey past and future. "The ultimate proof that the human spirit is free is its recognition that its will is not free" (*Nature and Destiny of Man,* Vol. I, p. 258).

Niebuhr would seem to be making contradictory statements. The self is not free if only the "spirit" transcending the self is free. The critical comment made above on his concept of transcendence would apply here also.

Reason is an instrument, says Niebuhr, which can be used for either good or evil. One evil use of reason is to impose rational coherence upon reality and to reject as unreal what cannot be fitted into that coherence. But Niebuhr is mistaken in thinking that one who insists on subjecting every affirmed belief to the tests of reason is thereby claiming that reason comprehends all reality. To the contrary, such a person fully admits that unknown reality extends beyond his knowledge; but he refuses to conceal his ignorance by superimposing religious beliefs where knowledge cannot reach. Niebuhr defended such beliefs because they relieve anxiety by providing courage and hope.

Another sinful use of reason, says Niebuhr, is to make it the basis of a false security, thus turning away from the one sure ground of security, which is a belief beyond the tests of reason, namely, that God in forgiving love will overrule all evil "at the end of history." Here again the question arises: Is true security to be found in beliefs exempt from the tests of reason or is it to be found by rejecting such beliefs and recognizing the unknown without concealing it beneath beliefs that cannot be rationally defended?

On the other hand, Niebuhr used to the full his own magnificent powers of rational intelligence in dealing with problems arising in the temporal process of human existence. He completely accepts the powers of reason in dealing with such problems. For him reason has the further use of demonstrating its own incapacity for dealing with those religious beliefs that Niebuhr affirms while admitting that they cannot be rationally defended.

In June Bingham's book *Courage to Change* (p. 224) she reports that Niebuhr wrote to a friend that he (Niebuhr) adhered to the religious pragmatism of William James. He validates Christian belief, when it cannot be rationally defended, by the courage, hope, peace, zeal, love, sense of being forgiven, and other psychological effects resulting when these beliefs are affirmed. Niebuhr identified these psychological effects as the grace bestowed upon us by God when we affirm these beliefs with the total self. Thus are we assured that we are loved and forgiven by God while we are yet sinners. Niebuhr also affirmed that beyond all the incoherence of our existence and beyond all our rational powers to know there is an all-comprehending and perfect coherence that somehow overcomes and absorbs all the manifest incoherences that we experience.

LOVE. Niebuhr distinguished three kinds of love: heedless love (agape), which seeks nothing in return; mutual love; and calculating love. Heedless love is God's way of loving; and human beings by God's grace may have it to some degree. Since it seeks nothing in return, it cannot have the intention of awakening responsive love, although this may be its unintended result. Suffering endured with intention to awaken responsive love would be calculating love. Hence God's suffering love in Christ is not to awaken responsive love, although this may be its unintended result; but the intention is to protect God's righteousness in forgiving sin because forgiveness without atonement would be condoning sin.

POLITICAL VIEWS

In making political judgments, the individual is inevitably biased by the social position and historical process in which he finds his security and personal identity. No one can be entirely free of this bias, but its distortions are reduced by a faith that finds its ultimate security not in any social position or historical process but in the God of love and mercy who rules supreme over the whole course of history, determining its final outcome as no plan or purpose of man can ever do. Such a faith in God's power and forgiveness enables one to practice "Christian realism," whereby one is able to see the evil in the self and in the historical process with which the self is identified, as well as the depth of evil in all of human life. Political judgment can then be more free of the illusions generated by false pride, on the one hand, and by despair, on the other.

Justice requires the coercions of government to support moral demands; and the power of opposing parties must be equalized if one is not to be subordinated unjustly to the interests of the other. Also, to have justice, freedom to criticize is required. Justice serves love by providing the social conditions required for the practice of love. Love is the final norm but cannot by itself guide political action, because every project set forth in the name of love amid the contests for political power is infected with self-interest whereby the needs of others are falsely identified with those of self.

With his highly developed rational powers and critical intelligence, Niebuhr sharply distinguished between problems subject to rational treatment and religious beliefs that cannot be rationally defended. This gives us what at times seems to be two Niebuhrs: One, the naturalist struggling with the problems of our existence with all the tools of human reason; the other, the mystic upholding a superstructure of religious belief beyond the tests of reason. Whether one of these, or both, will prevail in the course of history, only time can tell. However, the impact of Niebuhr's thought and action on our civilization will continue in one form or another for a long time.

See also Determinism in History; James, William; Love; Philosophy of History; Philosophy of Religion, History of.

Bibliography

WORKS BY NIEBUHR

Does Civilization Need Religion? A Study of the Social Resources and Limitations of Modern Life. New York: Macmillan, 1928.

Leaves from the Notebook of a Tamed Cynic. Chicago: Willett, Clark and Colby, 1929; new edition, Hamden, CT: Shoe String Press, 1955. A diary of experiences when pastor in Detroit.

Moral Man and Immoral Society: A Study in Ethics and Politics. New York: Scribners, 1932.

Reflections on the End of an Era. New York: Scribners, 1934.

An Interpretation of Christian Ethics. New York: Harper, 1935.

Do the State and Nation Belong to God or the Devil? London: Student Christian Movement Press, 1937.

Beyond Tragedy, Essays on the Christian Interpretation of History. New York: Scribners, 1937. Sermons.

Europe's Catastrophe and the Christian Faith. London: Nisbet, 1940.

Christianity and Power Politics. New York: Scribners, 1940.

The Nature and Destiny of Man: A Christian Interpretation. 2 vols. New York: Scribners, 1941–1943. The most complete statement of his thought.

The Children of Light and the Children of Darkness: A Vindication of Democracy and a Critique of Its Traditional Defense. New York: Scribners, 1944.

Discerning the Signs of the Times, Sermons for Today and Tomorrow. New York: Scribners, 1946. Sermons.

Faith and History: A Comparison of Christian and Modern Views of History. New York: Scribners, 1949.

The Illusion of World Government. Whitestone, NY: Graphics Group, 1949.

Christian Realism and Political Problems, Essays on Political, Social, Ethical, and Theological Themes. New York: Scribners, 1953.

The Self and the Dramas of History. New York: Scribners, 1955.

Pious and Secular America. New York: Scribners, 1958.

The Structure of Nations & Empires. New York: Scribners, 1959.

WORKS ON NIEBUHR

Bingham, June. *Courage to Change.* New York: Scribners, 1961.

Fox, Richard. *Reinhold Niebuhr: A Biography.* New York: Pantheon, 1985.

Gilkey, Langdon. *On Niebuhr: A Theological Study.* Chicago: University of Chicago Press, 2001.

Kegley, Charles, and Robert Bretall, eds. *Reinhold Niebuhr: His Religious, Social and Political Thought.* New York: Macmillan, 1956.

Lovin, Robin. *Reinhold Niebuhr and Christian Realism.* Cambridge, U.K.: Cambridge University Press, 1995.

Lovin, Robin. "Reinhold Niebuhr in Contemporary Scholarship: A Review Essay." *Journal of Religious Ethics* 31 (2003): 489–505.

Richards, Priscilla. *Annotated Bibliography of Reinhold Niebuhr's Works.* Madison, WI: American Theological Library Association, 1984.

Scott, Nathan, ed. *Legacy of Reinhold Niebuhr.* Chicago: University of Chicago Press, 1975.

Warren, Heather. *Theologians of a New World Order: Reinhold Niebuhr and the Christian Realists.* New York: Oxford University Press, 1997.

Henry Nelson Wieman (1967)
Bibliography updated by Christian B. Miller (2005)

NIETZSCHE, FRIEDRICH
(1844–1900)

Although trained as a philologist, Friedrich Nietzsche has been among the philosophers most influential upon European and North American culture and philosophy during the twentieth century. While he has always had an audience among writers, artists, and Germanists, through the first half of the twentieth century—and especially among philosophers—Nietzsche was read and discussed primarily by German philosophers, including Martin Heidegger, Karl Jaspers, and Karl Löwith. His criticisms of traditional philosophical positions, along with his often metaphorical and hyperbolic writing style, led to his being taken much less seriously by English-language philosophers. And Nietzsche's political views and the posthumous appropriation—many would argue misappropriation—of some of his ideas by thinkers associated with fascism and National Socialism (Nazism) led initially to a hostile response to his works among many British and French readers.

By the early 1960s, however, Nietzsche's fortunes had begun to change considerably. Anointed along with Marx and Freud as one of the three "masters of suspicion," Nietzsche's philosophical works found enthusiastic readers among those coming of age philosophically in the 1960s, and this—along with a new critical edition of his works and several generations of scholarly explication and analysis—resulted in Nietzsche being among the most widely read and known of Western philosophers by the end of the twentieth century.

BIOGRAPHY

Nietzsche was born October 15, 1844, in Röcken, a small village in Prussian Saxony, on the birthday of King Friedrich Wilhelm IV of Prussia, after whom he was named by his father Karl Ludwig, 31, and his mother Franziska (née Oehler), 18. His father, as well as both of his grandfathers, were Lutheran ministers. In 1846, Nietzsche's sister Elisabeth was born, and two years later, his brother Joseph was born. The following years were difficult ones: in 1848, Nietzsche's father became seriously ill; he died on July 30, 1849, of what was diagnosed as "softening of the brain" (a frequent diagnostic notation for tertiary syphilis). The following year, Nietzsche's younger brother died; and in April 1850, Nietzsche's mother moved the household—which now included her two young children, as well as Nietzsche's paternal grandmother and her two sisters—to Naumberg, a much larger town of 15,000 people.

In 1858, Nietzsche was offered free admission to Pforta, the most prestigious high school in Germany, located only a few miles from Naumberg. He was an excellent student and graduated in 1864 with a thesis in Latin on the Greek poet Theognis. After graduation, he registered at the University of Bonn as a theology student, but quickly changed his focus to philology, as Bonn's department had a distinguished reputation grounded on the work of two professors: Otto Jahn (1813–1869) and Friedrich Wilhelm Ritschl (1806–1876). There were, however, deep personal and professional disagreements between the two and when Ritschl decided to leave for the University at Leipzig, Nietzsche followed him there in 1865 and registered as a student of classical philology. Nietzsche soon became Ritschl's star pupil, and he was invited by Ritschl to publish an essay on Theognis in *Das Rheinische Museum für Philologie*, which Ritschl edited. In addition to his work in philology, writing essays on Diogenes Laertius and Democritus, among others, three other events took place in Leipzig that would profoundly influence the rest of Nietzsche's life: his discovery of Schopenhauer's *Die Welt als Wille und Vorstellung* (*The World as Will and Representation*) in 1865, of F. A. Lange's *Geschichte des Materialismus* (*History of Materialism*) in 1866, and in 1868, his meeting Richard Wagner, with whom he shared a love of music, of Schopenhauer, and a hope for the revitalization of European culture.

When a position at the University of Basel appeared in 1869, Ritschl gave an extraordinary recommendation for Nietzsche, who had not yet written a doctoral thesis, and Nietzsche was appointed to the Chair of Classical Philology at Basel in 1869 at the age of twenty-four. The University of Leipzig proceeded to confer the doctorate without either thesis or examination, and Nietzsche moved to Basel in April 1869. Basel offered him not only a university appointment but also easy access to the Wag-

ner residence at Tribschen, which allowed Nietzsche to develop a close relationship with both Wagner and his wife Cosima, the daughter of Franz Liszt. While at Basel, Nietzsche lectured on Homer, Hesiod, Plato, Aristotle, the pre-Socratics, Diogenes Laertius, and classical rhetoric. He was becoming increasingly disengaged from philology, however, and spent much of his time working on the texts of ancient Greek and Roman philosophy and thinking about broad cultural issues. These two features can be seen in his first book, *The Birth of Tragedy* (1872), which merged philosophical reflection with philological interpretation as it sought to frame Wagnerian opera as a way to recuperate what European culture had lost since the demise of ancient Greek tragedy. While Nietzsche thought his work would revolutionize the discipline of philology, it was poorly received and all but destroyed his professional standing as an academic philologist.

During the 1870s in Basel, Nietzsche became increasingly uncomfortable with Wagner and the Wagner circle at Tribschen and Bayreuth. While there is no question that *The Birth of Tragedy* proclaims Wagner's world-historical importance as a cultural phenomenon, *Richard Wagner in Bayreuth*, the fourth of his *Untimely Meditations*, is much more ambivalent. By 1878, Nietzsche had had enough of Wagner and among the reasons he offers subsequently to explain his break with Wagner are Wagner's turn to Christianity in *Parsifal* and his support for and association with political anti-Semitism. In 1879, Nietzsche resigned his chair at Basel because of the increasing severity of his health problems, and over the next ten years, he lived in several places in Europe, including Sils Maria, Switzerland, and Genoa and Turin, Italy. During these ten years, Nietzsche wrote ten books, living off a modest pension from the university, and he was plagued by constant and severe health problems. He suffered a total mental breakdown in Turin in January 1889, and after a brief stay at the psychiatric clinic run by Dr. Otto Binswanger in Jena, he spent the remaining years of his life under the care of his mother and then his sister until his death in Weimar on August 25, 1900.

No account of Nietzsche's life can avoid his health and his madness. Beginning in childhood, his health was poor. He was plagued by headaches that, as young as nine, kept him from school, and by age twelve, his eyes began to cause him serious problems. Throughout his life, his work habits were affected by the migraines that forced him to remain in darkened rooms, gastrointestinal problems, and limited eyesight that made reading at times painful and at times impossible. Not surprisingly, the themes of sickness, convalescence, and health, both metaphorically and literally, hold a central place in his philosophical reflections.

The question of his madness has been a focus of attention and speculation almost from its outbreak. What is clear is that on the morning of January 3, 1889, Nietzsche saw a horse being beaten by its coachman on a street in Turin, embraced the animal, and then collapsed. In the few days preceding and following this event, he sent letters to Jacob Burckhardt, Peter Gast, George Brandes, Cosima Wagner, and August Strindberg, among others, that, while at moments lucid and beautiful, are also clearly not the writings of a sane individual. While there has been much speculation as to the cause of Nietzsche's insanity, there is no conclusive evidence to support either of the two most common hypotheses: that he inherited syphilitic dementia from his father or he caught syphilis from prostitutes in a Leipzig brothel during his time as a student there. Recently, new research carried out by Dr. Leonard Sax, director of the Montgomery Center for Research in Child Development in Maryland and published in the *Journal of Medical Biography*, suggests that Nietzsche's symptomatology is consistent with cancer of the brain and in fact is not consistent with syphilis (based on the number of years Nietzsche remained alive following his breakdown). The syphilis story, it appears, can be traced to a book written by psychiatrist Wilhelm Lange-Eichbaum in 1946, *Nietzsche: Krankheit und Wirkung*, that sought to discredit Nietzsche, and this story was then adopted as fact by intellectuals who shared Lange-Eichbaum's politically motivated desire to destroy Nietzsche's reputation.

WRITINGS

During the sixteen years of Nietzsche's productive life, he wrote eighteen books in addition to leaving an extensive correspondence and several thousand pages of unpublished writings. While there are some minor differences in the way his works are periodized by scholars, his writings tend to be divided into three periods: his early more scholarly, philological work written while teaching in Basel from 1872–76; his aphoristic texts, written between 1878–1882; and his mature works, which begin with *Thus Spoke Zarathustra* in 1883 and continue until his last works in 1888.

THE BASEL WRITINGS. Nietzsche's early works, written while a professor of classical philology at the University of Basel, include *The Birth of Tragedy out of the Spirit of Music*, and the four *Untimely Meditations: Richard Strauss, Confessor and Writer; On the Use and Disadvan-*tage of History for Life; Schopenhauer as Educator; and Richard Wagner in Bayreuth. In addition to these published works, there are several unpublished works from this period that have attracted scholarly attention, the most important of which are the essays "On Truth and Lies in an Extra-moral Sense," "Homer's Contest," and "Philosophy in the Tragic Age of the Greeks."

First published in 1872, *The Birth of Tragedy* offers a theory of tragedy, a theory of art, and a proposal for cultural renewal. A second edition, published in 1886 with a new preface titled "Attempt at a Self-Criticism," and a new subtitle, "Hellenism or Pessimism," takes note of Nietzsche's move away from the Schopenhauerian sensibilities that marked this text by highlighting the opposition between Greek cheerfulness and Schopenhauerian pessimism. *The Birth* opens with Nietzsche's distinction between the Apollonian and Dionysian, which designates both forces of nature and basic artistic impulses. As forces of nature, the Apollonian names the principle of individuation that gives form to the chaos by isolating and distinguishing between things, whereas the Dionysian names the primal unity of all things in an endless play of forces of becoming. As artistic impulses, the Apollonian marks the world of beautiful illusions, whereas the Dionysian marks the sensual world of rapturous frenzy. Sculpture is the purest Apollonian art as a transfiguration of the real into a beautiful, illusory image, whereas music is the purest Dionysian art insofar as music is the process of change itself, with nothing that endures but the whole that survives each individual note's destroying what has come before it.

Nietzsche argues concerning Greek culture that when faced with the absurdity and horrible and terrifying aspects of existence, the Apollonian and Dionysian denote two opposing tendencies of human nature: to cover existence with beautiful illusions or to plunge into the absurdity and horror of existence and affirm it, as such, as a world of continual creation and destruction. From this comes his thesis about tragedy: Attic Tragedy— Sophocles and Aeschylus; Oedipus and Prometheus— manifests the pinnacle of Greek art as the perfect union of Dionysian joy and Apollonian illusion: It reflects both the Greek tragic wisdom that by accepting destruction as part of the great world-game, the tragic hero masters the cruelty of fate, and reveals the tragic Dionysian wisdom that the human spirit will not be broken by the pains and hardships of existence. This is the "metaphysical comfort" that tragedy leaves one with: "that life, despite all the changes in appearances, is at bottom indestructibly powerful and pleasurable" (§ 7). This tragic insight, which gave birth to Attic Tragedy, was, according to Nietzsche, destroyed by Socrates and his tragedian spokesman Euripides, for whom in order to be beautiful, everything had to be intelligible. Much of Nietzsche's *Birth* is spent analyzing the death of tragedy at the hands of Socrates and Euripides, and the anticipation of its rebirth in Wagnerian opera.

Nietzsche's four *Untimely Meditations* were published between 1873 and 1876. Originally planned as a series of thirteen volumes of cultural criticism, Nietzsche only published four (though he completed a substantial amount of work on a fifth volume on academic philology, "Wir Philologen"). In *David Strauss, the Confessor and Writer* (1873), Nietzsche criticizes Strauss, a Hegelian and author of *The Life of Jesus* (1835) and the then (1870s) popular work *The Old and New Faith*, for his smugness and the ease with which he dispenses with Christian doctrine. Strauss is also treated as representative of German popular culture, pleased with itself and its cultural "superiority" following Prussia's victory in the Franco-Prussian war, and Nietzsche spends much of the text challenging the *Bildungsphilister* or "cultural philistines" who mistake their "popular" culture for "genuine" culture. Because of Strauss's popularity, this was one of Nietzsche's most popular works, which although often critically reviewed was widely read.

On the Use and Disadvantage of History for Life (1873) has been the most widely discussed of the four meditations, although it was the least successful in its day. Taking as his critical foil Eduard von Hartmann's *Philosophy of the Unconscious* (1869), Nietzsche challenges the neo-Hegelian historicist tendency to valorize the present as the goal toward which history had been teleologically directed. While attacking the high value placed upon history in contemporary German culture and education, Nietzsche offers his tripartite account of historical scholarship—antiquarian, monumental, and critical—and offers an early version of what later became his genealogical method of examining the past in order to better understand the present.

Schopenhauer as Educator (1874), which Nietzsche later came to realize should have been called "Nietzsche as Educator," offers an early account of the exemplary individual engaged in a project of self-perfection. One finds relatively little comment in this text about Schopenhauer's philosophical views, about which Nietzsche had, by the time of its writing, come to question. Instead, one finds Nietzsche discussing Schopenhauer as an exemplary philosopher who willingly suffers in pursuit of the truth. It is, then, not Schopenhauer's philosophy but the

Schopenhauerian image of man that educates, and Nietzsche's third meditation is one of his most personal books in providing several comments that describe the exemplary individual that Nietzsche himself wanted to become.

That *Richard Wagner in Bayreuth* (1876) came to be published at all is due largely to Nietzsche's friend Heinrich Köselitz ("Peter Gast," 1854–1918). Begun in 1874, Nietzsche's adoration of Wagner began to fade in 1874–75 and he abandoned the project in 1875. Gast read the unfinished manuscript early in 1876 and persuaded Nietzsche first to complete the manuscript as a gift to Wagner for his birthday (May 22), and Nietzsche subsequently decided to publish the volume as the fourth *Untimely Meditation*, presenting it to Wagner in August during the first festival at Bayreuth. Although on the surface an homage to Wagner, with its liberal quotation and paraphrase from Wagner's own writings, the text also suggests that Wagner and his circle may themselves be "cultural philistines" who are failing to live up to the cultural and aesthetic ideals that Wagner's writings proposed. While important in terms of understanding Nietzsche's ambivalence toward Wagner during this period, and offering several insightful comments on art, culture, language, and science, this volume stands as perhaps Nietzsche's least popular and least read work.

In addition to these five published works, Nietzsche also left a number of unpublished essays and fragments from this period. Of these, three are of particular significance: "On Truth and Lies in an Extra-Moral Sense" (1873), in which he offers a tropological account of the origins of knowledge as grounded in the fundamental human drive toward the formation of metaphors; "Homer's Contest" (1872), in which he discusses the role of the *agon* or competition in Greek culture and democracy; and "Philosophy in the Tragic Age of the Greeks" (1873), in which he offers some of his most sustained commentary on the major pre-Socratic philosophers, including Heraclitus, Parmenides, Anaximander, and Anaxagoras.

APHORISTIC TEXTS. Between 1878 and 1882, Nietzsche wrote five works that, on the back cover of the final one, he noted as having a common goal: "to erect a new image and ideal of the free spirit." Motivated in part by his dissatisfaction with Wagner, he turned in these works against art, but more importantly, these works display a sympathy toward science as a legitimate source of truth and knowledge that has led some to refer to the works of this middle period as Nietzsche's "positivistic" works.

These works also shared a common style, that of the aphorism, which Nietzsche adopts in part as a way to mark his antipathy to the German philosophical tradition (Kant, Hegel) and his sympathy to French moral psychologists such as La Rochefoucauld, Montaigne, and Chamfort, whose aphoristic works he was then reading with his new friend Paul Rée (1849–1901).

In each of his aphoristic works, although themselves divided into chapters or parts, Nietzsche numbers his paragraphs sequentially from beginning to end. Some of these paragraphs are several pages long, and others are as short as a single sentence. The first of these works was *Human, All Too Human* (1878). Dedicated to Voltaire on the centenary of his death and subtitled "A Book for Free Spirits," it surveys a full range of philosophical topics, including metaphysics, epistemology, morality, religion, science, art and literature, culture, society, the family, and the state. In addition to being a public announcement of his break with Wagner, this volume also marked a break with the style of his earlier writings, and the multiplicity of authorial voices that speak through the 638 aphorisms are the first published expression of Nietzsche's perspectivist approach. *Human, All Too Human* was followed by two sequels, *Mixed Opinions and Maxims* (1879) and *The Wanderer and His Shadow* (1880), which each offer a collection of aphorisms on a variety of topics that have no apparent organizational structure, and were subsequently published together in 1886 as Volume Two of *Human, All Too Human*.

Unlike his earlier aphoristic works, *Daybreak: Thoughts on the Prejudices of Morality* (1881) remains relatively focused on the single topic of morality and the various themes that moral theorists typically address: moral judgment, moral psychology, moral values, the emotions, the virtues, and so on. It is an important text because it offers an early version of his critique of morality that anticipates many of the ideas that will receive extensive discussion in Nietzsche's later works, especially as concerns the origins of morality in general and some of the Western philosophical and religious traditions' privileged moral values in particular. In *Human, All Too Human*, one glimpses Nietzsche's first explorations into a naturalistic approach to ethics; in *Daybreak*, one finds Nietzsche much more committed to the idea that our moral values have their genesis in our biological and psychological needs.

The Gay Science (1882, 1887) is clearly the most significant work of this middle period, both in bringing to completion the series devoted to the free spirit and in being the text in which Nietzsche first formulates two of his most famous themes: the death of God (§125, "The Madman") and the eternal recurrence (§341: "The Greatest Weight"). While sharing the aphoristic style with the other works of this period, *The Gay Science* stands out in terms of its consistency with the themes that will be expressed in his subsequent writings. It stands out as well in terms of the internal coherence between aphorisms: Where the organization among the various aphorisms in his preceding four books often seems unclear if not nonexistent, there is often in *The Gay Science* a development from the topic of one aphorism to the next that rewards a careful attention to their sequence.

A case in point is the last three sections of Part Four—the last three sections of the first edition—in which Nietzsche moves from "The Dying Socrates" (§340), where Socrates, on his deathbed, discloses his true belief that existence is a disease; to "The Greatest Weight" (§341), in which Nietzsche first introduces the eternal recurrence through the voice of a demon, echoing Socrates's *daimon*, and suggests that contrary to Socrates's judgment, life might be affirmed; to *Incipit Tragoedia* (§342; "The Tragedy Begins"), which is identical to the first section of the Prologue of Nietzsche's next book, *Thus Spoke Zarathustra*, thus introducing Zarathustra as a teacher with an alternative to the moral teachings of Socrates, Kant, and Christianity. In 1887, Nietzsche published a second edition of *The Gay Science*, now with a new preface, an appendix of "Songs of Prince Vogelfrei," and a fifth book that offers some of Nietzsche's most sophisticated reflections on questions of language, consciousness, science, morality, religion, and art. Although appended to this earlier work, the fifth book really belongs to Nietzsche's "mature" period, in which he has fully committed to the perspectivist and constructivist accounts of knowledge.

MATURE PERIOD: TRANSVALUATION OF ALL VALUES. The texts of Nietzsche's mature period, written from 1883 to 1888, include those for which Nietzsche as a philosopher is best known: *Thus Spoke Zarathustra*, *Beyond Good and Evil*, and *On the Genealogy of Morals*. In addition to these works, he also wrote five books in 1888: two books on Wagner—*The Case of Wagner* and *Nietzsche contra Wagner*—*Twilight of the Idols*, *The Antichrist*, and *Ecce Homo*, an autobiography and appraisal of his works, which was published posthumously in 1908.

In *Thus Spoke Zarathustra*, Nietzsche offers the fictional narrative of Zarathustra, his image of the yes-saying spirit, who offers an alternative to the messages of the New Testament. Intentionally parodying the Gospels and, to some extent, the life of Jesus, Zarathustra opens by taking note of the death of God and subsequently offers his alternative teachings concerning the transvaluation of all values in which the values of this world, the body, self-overcoming, and creativity are all affirmed. Within the beautiful prose of this work, one can find all of Nietzsche's major themes discussed and, in particular, three of Nietzsche's most well-known themes find their primary expressions among his published works here: the *Übermensch* or overhuman (man is something to be overcome), the eternal recurrence (standing at the gateway of the *moment*—the present—two paths confront human beings, one forward in time, one backward, each infinite. And then each person must ask him- or herself: Must not all things that *can* happen *have already* happened and will they not continue to happen? Is not everyone entangled in a complex causal network that cannot be changed and that recurs eternally, in the identical form?), and the will to power (the metaphysical principle that animates all life).

While *Thus Spoke Zarathustra* was the work that first attracted attention to Nietzsche as a philosopher, and it had a profound influence on the existentialist interpretation of Nietzsche's philosophy, it is on the basis of his next two books, *Beyond Good and Evil* and *On the Genealogy of Morals*, that Nietzsche's reputation as a major philosopher resides. In the nine chapters of *Beyond Good and Evil*, Nietzsche offers his clearest criticisms of many central themes in the history of philosophy (free will, the Cartesian ego, the representational model of knowledge, idealism, realism, reason vs. instinct, Kant's transcendental philosophy). He also offers some of his most striking criticisms of religion, of morality (§260 first introduces the distinction between master morality and slave morality), of nationalism, and provides his clearest expression of a philosophy of power (§13: "A living thing seeks above all to discharge its strength.").

Beyond Good and Evil also offers Nietzsche's most sustained defense of perspectivism and his most serious questioning of the value of truth. The text opens with a preface that places truth, aligned with Plato, Christianity ("Platonism for the people"), and dogmatism, in contrast to perspective, and from there moves in Part One—"On the Prejudices of Philosophers"—to question the value of truth as well as the value of many of the central ideas, presumed to be true, of past philosophers, including Plato's Forms, Kant's thing-in-itself, Descartes's ego, and Schopenhauer's will. Throughout his analysis, Nietzsche suggests that the question that should be asked, when considering these philosophical articles of faith is not "Are they true?" but "Why is belief in their truth necessary?"

On the Genealogy of Morals offers Nietzsche's most sustained and powerful account of the origin and value of morality. The work itself unfolds in three carefully constructed essays. In the first, Nietzsche distinguishes between two moral frameworks: the noble morality that is based on distinguishing "good and bad," and the slave morality that makes judgments of "good and evil." The central idea of this first essay, Nietzsche writes, is his discovery of the birth of Christianity out of the slave's spirit of *ressentiment*. The second essay traces the moral concept guilt (*Schuld*) back to its origins in the economic relation of creditor and debtor, and offers an interpretation of the psychology of conscience, not as the voice of God in man, but as the instinct of cruelty that turns back on itself after it can no longer discharge itself externally.

In the third essay, Nietzsche inquires into the meaning of the ascetic ideal and, following an examination of the appearances of the ascetic ideal in philosophy, religion, art, morality, and science, discovers that the ascetic ideal is the harmful ideal par excellence. But the third essay also argues that the ascetic ideal has performed an essential, preservative function in that even though what the ascetic ideal has willed, throughout its long history, has in fact been imaginary (i.e., it has willed "nothing"), through its willing of nothingness, the will itself—that is, the ability to will—was saved. Nietzsche's genealogy of the ascetic will reveals that this will to nothingness, in the form of willing God or willing truth, while an aversion and hostility to life, was still a will that has preserved itself and has driven the deployment of *reactive* forces that is the history of the ascetic ideal. He offers, however, only tantalizing suggestions of a counter-will, a will to power that would no longer be a will to truth but would allow for the deployment of *active* forces that would make possible the overcoming of nihilism that has resulted from two thousand years of ascetic willing.

In 1888, the last year of his productive life, Nietzsche composed five short books. The first, *The Case of Wagner*, is Nietzsche's most sustained criticism of Wagner, and offers as well several insightful comments on art. Nietzsche describes *Twilight of the Idols* in letters on September 12 and 14, 1888, to his friends Peter Gast, Paul Deussen (1845–1919), and Franz Overbeck (1837–1905) as a "summary of my essential philosophical heterodoxies" (*Nietzsche Briefwechsel*), and this short text does indeed offer something of a survey of his basic themes while displaying his stylistic mastery, evidenced well in the title's play on Wagner's 1876 opera *Göttendämmerung*

ENCYCLOPEDIA OF PHILOSOPHY
2nd edition

(Nietzsche's *Götzen-Dämmerung* spoofing Wagner's "Twilight of the Gods"). Among the most interesting sections are his discussions of Socrates ("The Problem of Socrates") Kantian rationalism ("'Reason' in Philosophy"), philosophy ("Four Great Errors"), the influence of religion on morality ("Morality as anti-Nature"), and his highly condensed, six sentence history of Western philosophy and religion ("How the 'Real World' at last Became a Myth: History of an Error"), in which he moves from Plato to Christianity to Kant to positivism to the death of God and Nietzsche's own contributions of the free spirit and Zarathustra.

The Antichrist, which when published Nietzsche conceived, as he noted in the preface to *Twilight*, as the first volume of a longer work to be titled *Transvaluation of All Values*, is Nietzsche's most aggressive critique of Pauline Christianity. *Ecce Homo*, while completed in 1888, was withheld from publication by his sister Elizabeth until 1908. In it, Nietzsche offers a hyperbolic autobiographical and literary self-appraisal that only recently, with the increased attention to Nietzsche's writing style, has attracted the serious philosophical attention it deserves. Nietzsche's final published work, *Nietzsche Contra Wagner*, was dated Christmas 1888, less than two weeks before his collapse. Nietzsche's shortest work, he here reproduces with some minor emendations a selection of his earlier criticisms concerning Richard Wagner, thus making clear that the prosecution of Wagner in *The Case of Wagner* was not a late motif that Nietzsche arrived at only following Wagner's death.

No discussion of Nietzsche's work can fail to take account of his unpublished *Nachlass* of 1883 to 1888, in part because his sister published *The Will to Power*—a relatively small (slightly more than ten percent) and highly edited selection of these notes, first as approximately 400 sections in 1901, and in a second, expanded edition of 1067 sections in 1906—as if it had been a text written by Nietzsche himself. There is no doubt that for several years Nietzsche considered publishing a major work with this title, but there is equally no doubt that he definitively abandoned this project well before his collapse. As a consequence, claims made by Elisabeth and others as to this work being Nietzsche's *magnum opus* clearly cannot be sustained.

Heidegger's claim that *The Will to Power*, by which Heidegger meant the entire 1883 to 1888 *Nachlass* and not just Elisabeth's edition, contained the essence of Nietzsche's philosophizing is a more difficult claim to refute, especially as it relates as much to Heidegger's own desire to situate Nietzsche as the culminating figure in the his-

tory of metaphysics. What is clear is that many of Nietzsche's comments on his so-called major themes—most importantly, the eternal recurrence, will to power, and the *Übermensch*—are found primarily in these unpublished notes and, were one to discount the unpublished notes as well as Nietzsche's fictionalized account in *Thus Spoke Zarathustra*, it would be difficult to justify any of these three themes as being a significant part of Nietzsche's published prose works. That said, there is much of interest in these published notes for the philosopher as well as the Nietzsche scholar. While some passages are rough, or simply notes to himself for future work, or ideas and thought-experiments that he played with and chose, quite consciously, not to publish, others may well be ideas that he was still actively working on when his productive life ended.

Of particular note in this regard are his comments on scientists and scientific texts, especially biological texts, that he was reading in the mid- to late-1880s. Nietzsche was during this period reading as much if not more in scientific texts than philosophical texts, and while his biologistic account of life makes its way into some passages in *Beyond Good and Evil* and elsewhere, the best evidence of his thinking on these issues remains to be read in the unpublished notes of the *Nachlass*.

INFLUENCE

Walter Kaufmann opened and closed his article on Nietzsche in the first edition of the *Encyclopedia of Philosophy* with allusions to Nietzsche's influence upon modern philosophy and literature. Yet Kaufmann could scarcely have imagined the explosion of interest in Nietzsche's works, particularly in philosophical circles, that began in the mid-sixties and still continues. Kaufmann's bibliography, a perspectival review to be sure, lists only two secondary works on Nietzsche written in English—his own *Nietzsche: Philosopher, Psychologist, Antichrist* (1950) and George A. Morgan's *What Nietzsche Means* (1941). But since 1967, almost two thousand volumes focused primarily on Nietzsche—more than half of them in English—have appeared in English, French, and German, and perhaps ten times that number of essays, articles, or book chapters have been published.

Charting the expanding horizons of Nietzsche's influence quickly becomes a sociological study of the dominant motifs of late twentieth-century culture, and surveying the influence within the narrower field of philosophical inquiry is equally complex. There may in fact be no philosopher whose works admit less happily to a canonical or consensus interpretation, a claim supported by the staggering diversity of interpretations of Nietzsche's philosophy that have appeared since 1967. Nevertheless, some general observations can be made concerning the range of these new interpretations.

One can locate at least three primary factors in the increased philosophical attention to Nietzsche over the past forty years. First is the tremendous influence of Martin Heidegger's reading of Nietzsche. Published in Germany in 1960, translated into French in 1962 and into English between 1979 and 1987, Heidegger's overarching interpretation of Nietzsche as the culminating figure in the history of metaphysics inspired an enormous range of exegetical and critical response while leading several generations of philosophers and philosophy students back to read or re-read Nietzsche's texts.

A second reason for the increased attention by philosophers to Nietzsche can be located in the discovery of a "new Nietzsche" that emerged in conjunction with the rise of recent French philosophy. While most widely associated with Jacques Derrida and the deconstructionist attention to questions of textuality and the styles of philosophical discourse, Nietzsche's inclusion, along with Marx and Freud, as one of the three "masters of suspicion," and his importance in the philosophical works of Michel Foucault and Gilles Deleuze, have shown him to be an intellectual influence on much of what is called poststructuralist thought. And, as in the case of Heidegger, the popularity of poststructuralist French thought brought with it a renewed interest—among literary critics and theorists, historians, political theorists, and philosophers—in Nietzsche's thinking.

The third reason for the increased attention to Nietzsche concerns the transformation of philosophy within the anglo-American tradition. In the 1960s, Kaufmann's text, along with Arthur Danto's *Nietzsche as Philosopher* (1965), had first to justify Nietzsche as a philosopher whose ideas warranted serious philosophical consideration. As the scope of English-language philosophy has broadened, a distinctly anglo-American tradition of Nietzsche interpretation has appeared which is informed by the questions of ethics, metaphysics, and epistemology that occupy analytically trained philosophers.

This entry concludes with a brief survey of some of the main issues that have emerged in recent Nietzsche scholarship. To be sure, there is still much work offering interpretations of the classical Nietzschean themes: will to power, eternal recurrence, *Übermensch*, nihilism, perspectivism, and so on. But other issues have appeared as well. For example, an attention to questions of texts and textuality has played a role in much of the recent litera-

ture. It has become increasingly common to distinguish between Nietzsche's published texts and his unpublished notes, especially as concerns themes whose primary expression is to be found in the "book" constructed by his literary executors after his death and titled *The Will to Power*. One also finds an increasing tendency to read Nietzsche's texts *as* texts, following their internal development as opposed to simply viewing these texts as collections of remarks from which one can pick and choose the comments relevant to one's own argument. A third theme emerging from the recent interest in textuality is an attention to the various styles of Nietzsche's philosophical prose, in other words, an attention to his use of metaphor, to the literary character of much of his writing (in particular, *Thus Spoke Zarathustra*), to the different genre of writing (aphorism, essay, polemic, poem, etc.), and to other issues characterized collectively as the "question of style."

A second range of topics within the recent Nietzsche literature addresses some of the classic questions of philosophy: Does Nietzsche have a "theory of truth"? Does he have a "theory of knowledge"? An "ontology"? Is Nietzsche a metaphysician in the way that Heidegger defines metaphysics? Is Nietzsche an ethical naturalist? Within these questions, a topic that continues to draw attention is the issue of self-reference; in other words, when Nietzsche makes claims (about truth, reality, being, subjectivity, etc.), do these claims refer or apply to or hold true for his own philosophical conclusions? The most obvious case where the question of self-reference arises concerns the question of truth and interpretation: if Nietzsche claims that "there is no Truth," or that "everything is an interpretation," are these claims put forward as "true"? If they are, then they appear to contradict themselves; but if they are not true, then why should we be interested in them? The issue has been extended beyond the confines of epistemology, however, and one finds discussions of the eternal recurrence or the *Übermensch* or the ascetic ideal in terms of the question of self-reference.

A third and final set of issues that warrants noting is the extension of Nietzschean themes into new areas not discussed, or only hinted at, in the earlier Nietzsche scholarship. Among the most important topics producing much recent scholarship are Nietzsche's influence on postmodernism, his position on "woman" and his relevance for feminism, and his political philosophy and impact on twentieth-century political and social movements.

"Some are born posthumously," Nietzsche wrote in 1888. "One day my name will be associated with the memory of something tremendous," he claimed in *Ecce Homo*, at the beginning of a chapter titled "Why I am a Destiny?" One hundred years later, these remarks appear prophetic, and at the beginning of the twenty-first century, it would be difficult to find a philosopher whose influence on matters philosophical and cultural exceeds that of Nietzsche.

See also Anaxagoras of Clazomenae; Anaximander; Aristotle; Burckhardt, Jakob; Danto, Arthur; Deleuze, Gilles; Derrida, Jacques; Descartes, René; Diogenes Laertius; Existentialism; Foucault, Michel; Freud, Sigmund; Hartmann, Eduard von; Heidegger, Martin; Heraclitus of Ephesus; Homer; Jaspers, Karl; Kant, Immanuel; La Rochefoucauld, Duc François de; Leucippus and Democritus; Marx, Karl; Montaigne, Michel Eyquem de; Parmenides of Elea; Plato; Pre-Socratic Philosophy; Schopenhauer, Arthur; Voltaire, François-Marie Arouet de.

Bibliography

NIETZSCHE'S PUBLISHED WORKS AND SELECTED ENGLISH TRANSLATIONS

The definitive editions of Nietzsche's works as well as his letters and biography are the following:

Nietzsche Werke. Kritische Gesamtausgabe, edited by Giorgio Colli and Mazzino Montinari. Berlin: Walter de Gruyter, 1967ff. An English translation of the slightly abridged German critical edition *Kritische Studienausgabe* (Berlin: Walter de Gruyter, 1980) was begun under the General Editorship of Ernst Behler for Stanford University Press. The General Editorship was subsequently taken over by Bernd Magnus, and now is under the control of Alan D. Schrift and Daniel W. Conway.

Nietzsche Briefwechsel: Kritische Gesamtausgabe, edited by Giorgio Colli and Mazzino Montinari. Berlin: Walter de Gruyter, 1975ff.

Janz, Curt Paul. *Friedrich Nietzsche: Biographie*, 3 vols. Munich: C. Hanser Verlag, 1978–1979.

There are many translations available of Nietzsche's works. What follows are the full German titles, with year of publication, and the best available English translations:

Die Geburt der Tragödie aus dem Geiste der Musik (1872)

The Birth of Tragedy. Translated by Walter Kaufmann. New York: Random House, 1967.

The Birth of Tragedy and Other Writings, edited by Raymond Geuss and Ronald Speirs. Translated by Ronald Speirs. Cambridge, U.K.: Cambridge University Press, 1999.

The Birth of Tragedy. Translated by Douglas Smith. Oxford: Oxford University Press, 2000.

Unzeitgemässe Betrachtungen: I. *David Strauss, der Bekenner und Schriftsteller* (1873); II. *Vom Nutzen und Nachteil der Historie für das Leben* (1873); III. *Schopenhauer als Erzieher* (1874); IV. *Richard Wagner in Bayreuth* (1876)

Untimely Meditations. Translated by R. J. Hollingdale. Cambridge, U.K.: Cambridge University Press, 1983.

Unmodern Observations, edited by William Arrowsmith. Translated by Herbert Golder, Gary Brown, and William Arrowsmith. New Haven, CT: Yale University Press, 1990. (Includes a translation of *Wir Philologen* [We classicists]).

Unfashionable Observations. Translated by Richard T. Gray. Stanford, CA: Stanford University Press, 1995.

Menschliches, Allzumenschliches: Ein Buch für freie Geister (1878); *Menschliches, Allzumenschliches* Vol. II; *Vermischte Meinungen und Spruche* (1879); *Der Wanderer und sein Schatten* (1880)

Human, All Too Human: A Book For Free Spirits. Translated by R. J. Hollingdale. Cambridge, U.K.: Cambridge University Press, 1986. 2nd edition, 1996.

Human, All Too Human. Vol. One. Translated by Gary Handwerk. Stanford, CA: Stanford University Press, 1997.

Morgenröte: Gedanken über die moralischen Vorurtheile (1881)

Daybreak: Thoughts on the Prejudices of Morality. Translated by R. J. Hollingdale. Cambridge, U.K.: Cambridge University Press, 1982. 2nd edition, edited by Maudemarie Clark and Brian Leiter, 1997.

Die fröhliche Wissenschaft ("la gaya scienza") (1882, 1887)

The Gay Science. Translated by Walter Kaufman. New York: Vintage, 1974.

The Gay Science. Translated by Josefine Nauckhoff. Cambridge, U.K.: Cambridge University Press, 2001.

Also sprach Zarathustra: Eine Buch für Alle und Keinen (1883–1885)

Thus Spoke Zarathustra. Translated by Walter Kaufmann. New York: Viking Press, 1954.

Thus Spoke Zarathustra. Translated by R. J. Hollingdale. Harmondsworth, U.K.: Penguin, 1961.

Jenseits von Gut und Böse: Vorspiel einer Philosophie der Zukunft (1886)

Beyond Good and Evil: Prelude to a Philosophy of the Future. Translated by Walter Kaufmann. New York: Random House, 1966.

Beyond Good and Evil. Translated by Marion Faber and Robert C. Holub. Oxford: Oxford University Press, 1998.

Beyond Good and Evil. Translated by Judith Norman. Cambridge, U.K.: Cambridge University Press, 2002.

Zur Genealogie der Moral: Eine Streitschrift (1887)

On the Genealogy of Morals. Translated by Walter Kaufmann and R. J. Hollingdale. New York: Random House, 1967.

On the Genealogy of Morality and Other Writings, edited by Keith Ansell-Pearson and Carol Diethe. Translated by Carol Diethe. Cambridge, U.K.: Cambridge University Press, 1994.

On the Genealogy of Morals. Translated by Douglas Smith. Oxford: Oxford University Press, 1996.

On the Genealogy of Morality: A Polemic. Translated by Maudemarie Clark and Alan J. Swensen. Indianapolis: Hackett, 1998.

Götzendämmerung: Oder wie man mit dem Hammer philosophiert (1888)

Twilight of the Idols. Translated by Walter Kaufmann. In *The Portable Nietzsche*. New York: Viking Press, 1954.

Twilight of the Idols. Translated by R. J. Hollingdale. Harmondsworth, U.K.: Penguin, 1968.

Twilight of the Idols: or How to Philosophize with a Hammer. Translated by Duncan Large. Oxford: Oxford University Press, 1998.

Der Antichrist (1888)

The Antichrist. Translated by Walter Kaufmann. In *The Portable Nietzsche.* New York: Viking Press, 1954.

The Anti-Christ. Translated by R. J. Hollingdale. Harmondsworth, U.K.: Penguin, 1968.

Nietzsche contra Wagner (1888)

Nietzsche Contra Wagner. Translated by Walter Kaufmann. In *The Portable Nietzsche.* New York: Viking Press, 1954.

Der Fall Wagner (1888)

The Case of Wagner. Translated by Walter Kaufmann. New York: Random House, 1967.

Ecce Homo: Wie man wird, was man ist (1888)

Ecce Homo. Translated by Walter Kaufmann. New York: Random House, 1967.

Ecce Homo: How One Becomes What One Is. Translated by Duncan Large. Oxford: Oxford University Press, 2004.

Der Wille zur Macht (1883–1888)

The Will to Power. Translated by Walter Kaufmann and R. J. Hollingdale. New York: Random House, 1967.

SECONDARY WORKS

Abel, Gunter. *Nietzsche: Die Dynamik der Willen zur Macht und die ewige Wiederkehr.* Berlin: Walter de Gruyter, 1984.

Allison, David, ed. *The New Nietzsche.* New York: Dell, 1979.

Allison, David. *Reading the New Nietzsche.* Lanham, MD: Rowman and Littlefield, 2001.

Ansell-Pearson, Keith. *An Introduction to Nietzsche as Political Thinker: The Perfect Nihilist.* Cambridge, U.K.: Cambridge University Press, 1994.

Ansell-Pearson, Keith. *Nietzsche Contra Rousseau: A Study of Nietzsche's Moral and Political Thought.* Cambridge, U.K.: Cambridge University Press, 1991.

Babich, Babette E. *Nietzsche's Philosophy of Science: Reflecting Science on the Ground of Art and Life.* Albany: State University of New York Press, 1994.

Bataille, Georges. *Sur Nietzsche.* Paris: Gallimard, 1945. Translated by Bruce Boone as *On Nietzsche.* New York: Paragon House, 1992.

Blondel, Eric. *Nietzsche, le corps et la culture: La Philosophie comme généalogie.* Paris: Presses universitaires de France, 1986. Translated by Sean Hand as *Nietzsche, the Body and Culture.* Stanford, CA: Stanford University Press, 1991.

Breazeale, Daniel, ed. *Philosophy and Truth: Selections from Nietzsche's Notebooks of the Early 1870's.* Translated by Daniel Breazeale. Atlantic Highlands, NJ: Humanities Press, 1979.

Clark, Maudemarie. *Nietzsche on Truth and Philosophy.* Cambridge, U.K.: Cambridge University Press, 1990.

Conway, Daniel W. *Nietzsche's Dangerous Game: Philosophy in the Twilight of the Idols.* Cambridge, U.K.: Cambridge University Press, 1997.

Cox, Christoph. *Nietzsche: Naturalism and Interpretation.* Berkeley: University of California Press, 2000

Danto, Arthur C. *Nietzsche as Philosopher.* New York: Macmillan, 1965.

Deleuze, Gilles. *Nietzsche et la philosophie.* Paris: Presses universitaires de France, 1962. Translated by Hugh

Tomlinson as *Nietzsche and Philosophy.* New York: Columbia University Press, 1983.

Derrida, Jacques. *Eperons: Les Styles de Nietzsche.* Paris: Flammarion, 1977. Translated by Barbara Harlow as *Spurs: Nietzsche's Styles.* Chicago: University of Chicago Press, 1978.

Fink, Eugen. *Nietzsches Philosophie.* Stuttgart, Germany: Kohlhammer, 1968. Translated by Goetz Richter as *Nietzsche's Philosophy.* London: Continuum, 2003.

Gooding-Williams, Robert. *Zarathustra's Dionysian Modernism.* Stanford, CA: Stanford University Press, 2001.

Granier, Jean. *Le problème de la vérité dans la philosophie de Nietzsche.* Paris: Éditions du Seuil, 1966.

Hatab, Lawrence J. *A Nietzschean Defense of Democracy: An Experiment in Postmodern Politics.* Chicago: Open Court, 1995.

Hayman, Ronald. *Nietzsche: A Critical Life.* Oxford: Oxford University Press, 1980.

Heidegger, Martin. *Nietzsche. Band I-II.* Pfullingen, Germany: Neske, 1961. *Vol I: The Will to Power as Art.* Translated by David Farrell Krell. New York: Harper & Row, 1979. *Vol II: The Eternal Recurrence of the Same.* Translated by David Farrell Krell. San Francisco: Harper & Row, 1984. *Vol. III: The Will to Power as Knowledge and as Metaphysics.* Translated by Joan Stambaugh, David Farrell Krell, and Frank A. Capuzzi. San Francisco: Harper & Row, 1987. *Vol. IV: Nihilism.* Translated by Frank A. Capuzzi. New York: Harper & Row, 1982.

Hollingdale, R. J. *Nietzsche: The Man and His Philosophy.* London: Routledge and Kegan Paul, 1965.

Jaspers, Karl. *Nietzsche: Einführung in das Verständnis seines Philosophierens.* Berlin: Walter de Gruyter, 1936. Translated by Charles F. Wallraff and Frederick J. Schmidtz as *Nietzsche: An Introduction to the Understanding of his Philosophical Activity.* Tucson: University of Arizona Press, 1965.

Kaufmann, Walter. *Nietzsche: Philosopher, Psychologist, Antichrist.* Princeton, NJ: Princeton University Press, 1950.

Klossowski, Pierre. *Nietzsche et la cercle vicieux.* Paris: Mercure de France, 1969. Translated by Daniel W. Smith as *Nietzsche and the Vicious Circle.* Chicago: University of Chicago Press, 1997.

Kofman, Sarah. *Nietzsche et la métaphore.* Paris: Payot, 1972. Translated by Duncan Large as *Nietzsche and Metaphor.* Stanford, CA: Stanford University Press, 1993.

Lampert, Laurence. *Nietzsche's Teaching: An Interpretation of Thus Spoke Zarathustra.* New Haven, CT: Yale University Press, 1986.

Lampert, Laurence. *Nietzsche's Task: An Interpretation of Beyond Good and Evil.* New Haven, CT: Yale University Press, 2001.

Löwith, Karl. *Nietzsches Philosophie der ewigen Wiederkehr des Gleichen.* Hamburg: Meiner, 1978. Translated by J. Harvey Lomax as *Nietzsche's Philosophy of the Eternal Recurrence of the Same.* Berkeley, CA: University of California Press, 1997.

Magnus, Bernd. *Nietzsche's Existential Imperative.* Bloomington: Indiana University Press, 1978.

Magnus, Bernd, et al. *Nietzsche's Case: Philosophy And/As Literature.* New York: Routledge, 1993.

Magnus, Bernd, and Kathleen M. Higgins, eds. *The Cambridge Companion to Nietzsche.* Cambridge, U.K.: Cambridge University Press, 1996.

Müller-Lauter, Wolfgang *Nietzsche: Seine Philosophie der Gegensätze und die Gegensätze seiner Philosophie*. Berlin: Walter de Gruyter, 1971. Translated by David J. Parent as *Nietzsche: His Philosophy of Contradictions and the Contradictions of His Philosophy*. Urbana: University of Illinois Press, 1999.

Nehamas, Alexander. *Nietzsche: Life as Literature*. Cambridge, MA: Harvard University Press, 1985.

Oliver, Kelly, and Marilyn Pearsall, eds. *Feminist Interpretations of Friedrich Nietzsche*. University Park: Pennsylvania State University Press, 1998.

Parkes, Graham. *Composing the Soul: Reaches of Nietzsche's Psychology*. Chicago: University of Chicago Press, 1994.

Richardson, John. *Nietzsche's New Darwinism*. Oxford: Oxford University Press, 2004.

Richardson, John. *Nietzsche's System*. Oxford: Oxford University Press, 1996.

Roberts, Tyler T. *Contesting Spirit: Nietzsche, Affirmation, Religion*. Princeton, NJ: Princeton University Press, 1998.

Schaberg, William H. *The Nietzsche Canon: A Publication History and Bibliography*. Chicago: University of Chicago Press, 1995.

Schacht, Richard. *Making Sense of Nietzsche: Reflections Timely and Untimely*. Urbana: University of Illinois Press, 1995.

Schacht, Richard. *Nietzsche*. London: Routledge and Kegan Paul, 1983.

Schacht, Richard, ed. *Nietzsche, Genealogy, Morality: Essays on Nietzsche's Genealogy of Morals*. Berkeley: University of California Press, 1994.

Schrift, Alan D. *Nietzsche and the Question of Interpretation: Between Hermeneutics and Deconstruction*. New York: Routledge, 1990.

Schrift, Alan D. *Nietzsche's French Legacy: A Genealogy of Poststructuralism*. New York: Routledge, 1995.

Schrift, Alan D., ed. *Why Nietzsche Still? Reflections on Drama, Culture, and Politics*. Berkeley: University of California Press, 2000.

Schutte, Ofelia. *Beyond Nihilism: Nietzsche Without Masks*. Chicago: University of Chicago Press, 1984.

Sedgwick, Peter R., ed. *Nietzsche: A Critical Reader*. Oxford: Blackwell, 1995.

Shapiro, Gary. *Alcyone: Nietzsche on Gifts, Noise and Women*. Albany: State University of New York Press, 1991.

Shapiro, Gary. *Nietzschean Narratives*. Bloomington: Indiana University Press, 1989.

Small, Robin. *Nietzsche in Context*. Aldershot, England: Ashgate, 2001.

Solomon, Robert C., and Kathleen M. Higgins. *Reading Nietzsche*. New York: Oxford University Press, 1988.

Staten, Henry. *Nietzsche's Voice*. Ithaca, NY: Cornell University Press, 1990.

Strong, Tracy B. *Friedrich Nietzsche and the Politics of Transfiguration*. Berkeley: University of California Press, 1975. Rev. ed. Urbana: University of Illinois Press, 2000.

Thiele, Leslie Paul. *Friedrich Nietzsche and the Politics of the Soul: A Study of Heroic Individualism*. Princeton, NJ: Princeton University Press, 1990.

Tongeren, Paul van. *Reinterpreting Modern Culture: An Introduction to Friedrich Nietzsche's Philosophy*. West Lafayette, IN: Purdue University Press, 2000.

Warren, Mark. *Nietzsche and Political Thought*. Cambridge, MA: MIT Press, 1988.

Alan D. Schrift (2005)

NIHILISM

The term *nihilism* appears to have been coined in Russia sometime in the second quarter of the nineteenth century. It was not, however, widely used until after the appearance of Ivan Turgenev's highly successful novel *Fathers and Sons* in the early 1860s. The central character, Bazarov, a young man under the influence of the "most advanced ideas" of his time, bore proudly what most other people of the same period called the bitter name of nihilist. Unlike such real-life counterparts as Dmitri Pisarev, Nikolai Dobrolyubov, and Nikolai Chernyshevskii, who also bore the label, Bazarov's interests were largely apolitical; however, he shared with these historical personalities disdain for tradition and authority, great faith in reason, commitment to a materialist philosophy like that of Ludwig Büchner, and an ardent desire to see radical changes in contemporary society.

An extreme statement by Pisarev of the nihilist position as it developed in the late 1850s and 1860s in Russia is frequently quoted: "Here is the ultimatum of our camp: what can be smashed should be smashed; what will stand the blow is good; what will fly into smithereens is rubbish; at any rate, hit out right and left—there will and can be no harm from it" (quoted in Avrahm Yarmolinsky, *Road to Revolution*, p. 120). Bazarov echoes this idea, though a bit feebly, when he accepts a description of nihilism as a matter of "just cursing."

Use of the term spread rapidly throughout Europe and the Americas. As it did, the term lost most of its anarchistic and revolutionary flavor, ceasing to evoke the image of a political program or even an intellectual movement. It did not, however, gain in precision or clarity. On the one hand, the term is widely used to denote the doctrine that moral norms or standards cannot be justified by rational argument. On the other hand, it is widely used to denote a mood of despair over the emptiness or triviality of human existence. This double meaning appears to derive from the fact that the term was often employed in the nineteenth century by the religiously oriented as a club against atheists, atheists being regarded as ipso facto nihilists in both senses. The atheist, it was held, would not feel bound by moral norms; consequently, he would tend to be callous or selfish, even criminal. At the same time he would lose the sense that life has meaning and therefore tend toward despair and suicide.

ATHEISM

There are many literary prototypes of the atheist-nihilist. The most famous are Ivan in Fëdor Dostoevsky's *Brothers Karamazov* and Kirilov in Dostoevsky's *The Possessed.* It was into Ivan's mouth that Dostoevsky put the words, "If God does not exist, everything is permitted." And Dostoevsky made it clear that it was Ivan's atheism that led him to acquiesce to his father's murder. Kirilov was made to argue that if God does not exist, the most meaningful reality in life is individual freedom and that the supreme expression of individual freedom is suicide.

Friedrich Nietzsche was the first great philosopher—and still the only one—to make extensive use of the term *nihilism.* He was also one of the first atheists to dispute the existence of a necessary link between atheism and nihilism. He recognized, however, that as a matter of historical fact, atheism was ushering in an age of nihilism. "One interpretation of existence has been overthrown," Nietzsche said, "but since it was held to be *the* interpretation, it seems as though there were no meaning in existence at all, as though everything were in vain" (*Complete Works,* Edinburgh and London, 1901–1911, Vol. XIV, p. 480). Albert Camus later dealt with this historical fact at some length in *The Rebel* (1951).

The tendency to associate nihilism with atheism continues to the present. It is to be found, for instance, in a work by Helmut Thielicke titled *Nihilism,* which first appeared in 1950. During the course of the twentieth century, however, the image of the nihilist changed, with a corresponding change in the analysis of nihilism's causes and consequences. Professor Hermann Wein of the University of Göttingen wrote, for instance, that the members of the younger generation of his time tended to think of the nihilist not as a cynical or despairing atheist but as a robotlike conformist. For them nihilism is caused not so much by atheism as by industrialization and social pressures, and its typical consequences are not selfishness or suicide but indifference, ironical detachment, or sheer bafflement. The literary prototypes are not the romantic heroes of Dostoevsky but the more prosaic and impersonal heroes of Robert Musil's *Man without Qualities* (first volumes published 1931–1933) or Franz Kafka's *The Trial* (1925).

MORAL SKEPTICISM

If by nihilism one means a disbelief in the possibility of justifying moral judgments in some rational way and if

philosophers reflect the intellectual climate of the times in which they live, then our age is truly nihilistic. At no period in Western history, with the possible exception of the Hellenistic age, have so many philosophers regarded moral statements as somehow arbitrary. For many Continental philosophers, especially the atheistic existentialists, moral values are products of free choice—that is, of uncaused, unmotivated, and nonrational decisions. The most notable statement of this view is in *Being and Nothingness* (1943) by Jean-Paul Sartre. In England and America, most philosophers tend to the view known as emotivism, according to which moral statements are ultimately and essentially products of pure social conditioning or brute feeling. The most noted, though not the most extreme, representatives of this position are A. J. Ayer and Charles Stevenson.

It is impossible to state here with reasonable detail and accuracy the positions so summarily described in the last paragraph, much less to discuss their logical merits. For an understanding of nihilism, however, it is important to note how these positions relate to the ideas of those to whom nihilism of this kind is anathema. As already indicated, the most vociferous antinihilists were originally theologians, like Dostoevsky, who feared that disbelief in God would lead to selfishness and crime. If, they argued, there is no divine lawgiver, each man will tend to become a law unto himself. If God does not exist to choose for the individual, the individual will assume the former prerogative of God and choose for himself. For these antinihilists the principal enemy would have been Sartre. The later antinihilists, however, tend to save their fire for the emotivists, whom they accuse of sanctioning moral indifference and mindless conformity. If all moral codes are essentially matters of feeling and social pressure, then no one would be better or worse than another. The wise man, like the Sophists of Plato's day, would simply adjust as best he could to the code of the society in which he happened to be living. John Dewey's fervid insistence upon critical individual intelligence as the prime agent of social and moral reconstruction places him squarely in the second group of antinihilists.

Whether belief in atheistic existentialism or emotivism does in fact have the kinds of consequences suggested above is not at issue here. The point is simply that antinihilists of the older variety do not regard conventional morality, especially in its other-regarding aspects, as adequately justified unless it has a cosmic or divine sanction, whereas more contemporary antinihilists do not regard any moral code as adequately justified unless there is some standard or touchstone more universal than pure feeling or social pressure to which it may be shown to conform. The pertinent question here is whether the antinihilists have a good case for these views.

It would appear that the demand for justification of conventional moral rules by appeal to a divine or cosmic power cannot be logically admitted without abandoning widespread and deeply felt notions about the nature of moral justification. If the higher power that presumably legitimizes our moral code is by definition good and just, an appeal to that power would involve us in a vicious circle. How would we know that that power was good and just unless there were some purely human ideas about the good and the just to which we felt entitled independently of that power's sanction? If, on the other hand, the presumed higher power is not by definition good or just, if, for instance, it were defined merely as a creator and sustainer of life, by what right could we appeal to it to legitimize our moral views? Might or power, even the power to create and sustain life, is not to be confused with right or legitimacy.

The demand that moral codes be justified by more universal standards than pure feeling or social dictate is, on the contrary, much more consonant with widespread, intuitive notions about the nature of moral justification. If social pressure is taken as the touchstone of morality, we once again court a confusion between might and right; if feeling is taken as the touchstone, we must apparently abandon not only the notion of a universal morality, feelings being notoriously fluctuating and individual, but also the notion that one of the functions of morality is to refine, direct, and control individual feelings. It may, of course, be the case that there is no universal morality and that whatever power morality possesses must derive from individual feeling and social conditioning alone. It would be surprising, however, if even the emotivists did not experience a certain chagrin that the truth in ethical theory should be so contrary to human hopes.

MEANINGLESS OF LIFE

Passing to the second meaning of the term *nihilism*, we find that the pertinent questions are less logical or technically philosophical than psychological or sociological. There are two questions here, corresponding to the two forms of antinihilism. Is it true that a loss of faith in God or cosmic purposes produces a sense of despair over the emptiness and triviality of life, consequently stimulating selfishness and callousness? Is it true that industrialization and conformist social pressures have trivialized life in a similar way, causing us to adopt an attitude of ironic detachment? A negative answer to these questions would appear to fly in the face of most contemporary social criticism and analysis as well as the testimony of most contemporary literature.

It is doubtful, however, whether a simple yes would be a proper response to the first question. When it is assumed that humankind needs a sense of divine or cosmic purpose in order to lead a rich and morally wholesome life, one is generalizing far beyond the evidence. The most that the evidence can be made to support is that relatively large numbers of people in certain societies at certain times have felt this need. No one who has read, for instance, Lev Tolstoy's account of his religious crisis in middle age could doubt the depth of his despair or the reality of his need for a vital relationship to an eternal being. One can reasonably doubt, however, whether that need and despair spring from universal and firmly rooted human aspirations. Some psychologists regard Tolstoy's conversion crisis as a symptom of involutional melancholia, and there are many who believe it to be a consequence of Tolstoy's social position as a member of Russia's decaying aristocracy.

Bertrand Russell went through a similar crisis earlier in life. He not only survived that crisis without reverting to faith in God or cosmic purpose; he also survived it, as his essay "A Free Man's Worship" (1902) attests, by deliberately espousing a world outlook that emphasizes the finitude and cosmic isolation of humankind. And no one who is familiar with the facts of his life would dare to suggest that the later Russell was less morally earnest than the young believer or less wholeheartedly and happily engaged in the process of living.

Those who attribute the nihilistic malaise of our time to industrialization and conformity are less vulnerable to the charge of overgeneralization. This is not because they limit their analysis to a given historical epoch, for they, too, are making an implicit generalization about universal human needs. Their point is that all people need, if they are to be whole and healthy, the sense that they can by a unique and personal effort contribute to the social process and that society will appreciate and reward this individual effort. This generalization is less vulnerable than the first simply because there is more evidence for it. Novels and biographies, ethnographic reports and individual clinical histories, not to mention commonsense attitudes of most men in all societies at all historical periods, tend to support it. And the issue raised by nihilism in this sense of the term is one of the great unresolved political and social problems of the twentieth and twenty-first centuries. Whether philosophers in their professional capacity are competent to contribute to its solution is a question we shall not attempt to answer here.

See also Atheism; Ayer, Alfred Jules; Camus, Albert; Chernyshevskii, Nikolai Gavrilovich; Dewey, John; Dostoevsky, Fyodor Mikhailovich; Kafka, Franz; Life, Meaning and Value of; Moral Skepticism; Nietzsche, Friedrich; Pessimism and Optimism; Pisarev, Dmitri Ivanovich; Russell, Bertrand Arthur William; Russian Philosophy; Sartre, Jean-Paul; Stevenson, Charles L.

Bibliography

On Russian nihilism of the 1850s and 1860s, see Avrahm Yarmolinsky, *Road to Revolution* (New York: Macmillan, 1959), and Ivan Turgenev, *Fathers and Sons* (New York, 1958).

For interpretations of nihilism reflecting a theological or religious point of view, see Helmut Thielicke, *Nihilism* (New York: Harper, 1961); Ernst Benz, *Westlicher und östlicher Nihilismus* (Stuttgart: Evangelisches, 1948); Nikolai Berdyaev, *Sinn und Shicksal des russischen Kommunismus* (1937); and Lester G. Crocker, *An Age of Crisis* (Baltimore: Johns Hopkins Press, 1959).

For emotivism see A. J. Ayer, *Language, Truth and Logic*, 2nd rev. ed. (New York: Dover, 1952); Charles Stevenson, *Ethics and Language* (New Haven, CT: Yale University Press, 1944); and Ingemar Hedenius, "On Law and Morals," in *Journal of Philosophy* 56 (1959): 117–125.

For existentialist nihilism see Jean-Paul Sartre, *Being and Nothingness* (New York: Philosophical Library, 1956).

See also Friedrich Nietzsche, *Will to Power,* in *Complete Works,* edited by Oscar Levy (New York: Russell and Russell, 1964); Albert Camus, *The Rebel* (New York: Knopf, 1954); Hermann Wein, "Discussion on Nihilism," in *Universitas* 6 (2): 173–182; C. F. von Weizsäcker, *The History of Nature* (Chicago: University of Chicago Press, 1949), pp. 71ff.; Bertrand Russell, "A Free Man's Worship," in his *Mysticism and Logic* (London: Allen and Unwin, 1917), and "What I Believe," in his *Why I Am Not a Christian* (New York: Simon and Schuster, 1957), Ch. 3; Lev Tolstoy, "My Confession" and "What Is to Be Done," in *Complete Works* (New York, 1898), Vol. VII; and Hermann Rauschning, *The Revolution of Nihilism* (London, 1939).

Robert G. Olson (1967)

NIRVĀṆA

Nirvāṇa is the ultimate goal of Buddhist practice, although there has been disagreement among Buddhists concerning its nature and the means of attaining it. The word derives from a Sanskrit verbal root meaning "to blow" and a prefix meaning "out." The underlying meaning of the word is traditionally explained as expressing one of two metaphors. The first is that the term means the act of blowing out or extinguishing, as of a flame. The second is that it means the act of being cooled down, as by a breeze. The two metaphors have in common the notion of fire or heat as a source of pain that is alleviated by a breeze. So the principal characteristic of nirvāṇa is relief from pain and the prevention of future pain through the eradication of its root causes. It is, in other words, the permanent release from the conditions that make pain possible, both physical pain and forms of psychological suffering such as sadness, grief, despondency, melancholy, frustration, and anxiety. Traditionally nirvāṇa is said to occur in two stages: the extinction of the causes of rebirth and the end of rebirth itself. For ease of exposition, the latter will be discussed first.

NIRVĀṆA AS THE END OF REBIRTH

The Buddhist doctrine of nirvāṇa arose in the context of a view of the world that was common throughout India at the time when Buddhism was founded, in the sixth century BCE. According to that view, the world is both beginningless and endless and constantly changing. Among the many kinds of change in this world are the various stages undergone by a living being, or, more properly, an individual continuum of conscious. Such a being is born, matures, decays and eventually dies. When a living being dies, it does not cease to exist; rather it is transformed into another living being that also undergoes birth, maturity, decay and death. The cycle of rebirths that any given being undergoes is beginningless. The doctrine of Buddhism, and of many other systems of thought in ancient India, asserts that the cycle can, however, come to an end, provided that the conditions that keep the cycle going are eliminated. The name that is given to the end of the cycle of rebirths for any given continuum of consciousness is final nirvāṇa. It is described in Buddhist texts as the cessation of the process of being reborn into any kind of existence in any realm in the cosmos. Since all kinds of existence are at least potentially painful, the only way of eliminating the very possibility of experiencing physical or psychological pain is to stop existing altogether.

NIRVĀṆA AS THE EXTINCTION OF THE CAUSES OF REBIRTH

According to Buddhist doctrine, the ultimate cause of rebirth is simply the desire to continue existing. When a deity or human being or animal dies wishing that life could continue, life does continue. The consciousness of the dying person then finds itself associated with a different body, which may or may not belong to the same biological species as the body that has just died. The type of body with which the continuing consciousness finds itself associated is determined by the overall mentality of the consciousness continuum at the time of the death of the previous body. What all rebirth has in common is the desire to continue existing, and this is the consequence of delusion, a fundamental misunderstanding about the real nature of existence. The real nature of existence is that every existing thing is characterized by impermanence. Because of this impermanence, nothing that anyone experiences endures, and therefore nothing, however pleasant it may be, can be a source of enduring satisfaction. Because every satisfactory experience comes to an end, it is ultimately disappointing and unsatisfactory.

These two characteristics of existence, impermanence and disappointment, give rise to a third feature of existence, namely, that no existing thing is part of an abiding self, and nothing can ever be owned. The delusions that fuel the desire to continue existing, therefore, are the erroneous beliefs that anything can be permanent, satisfactory, and either part of oneself or a potential piece of property that one can own. Nirvāṇa, then, is the elimination of those delusions by understanding existence as it really is. This correct understanding is called awakening or enlightenment. All of Buddhist doctrine and practice, then, can be seen as a process of working toward the state of enlightenment that makes final nirvāṇa possible. Enlightenment is therefore described as a name that is given to the absence of specific delusions, in the same way that final nirvāṇa is a name given to the absence of further rebirth.

STAGES LEADING TO NIRVĀṆA

According to most schools of Buddhism, the path to enlightenment is incremental. One does not rid oneself of all delusion at once, because delusion itself is part of a complex mentality that consists of various vices that are caused by and that in turn reinforce the habit of having a naive and superficial perspective on one's experience. Although the specific manifestations of superficiality and its attendant vices differ for every individual, there is said to be a general pattern of how progress to enlightenment is made.

To understand the stages along the way to nirvāṇa, it is helpful to know that Buddhist tradition enumerates ten mental habits that obstruct peace of mind. They are

(1) the opinion that complex objects are real,

(2) suspicion or intense doubt,

(3) abiding by rules and vows for the sole purpose of gaining merit for oneself,

(4) desire for sensual pleasure,

(5) malevolence,

(6) passion for material things and for material forms of existence,

(7) passion for spiritual or nonmaterial things, such as meditative states, and for nonmaterial forms of existence,

(8) conceit, which is explained as the habit of constantly comparing and measuring oneself against others,

(9) agitation or excitement,

(10) misconception or ignorance, which includes any kind of failure to see things as they really are.

The first stage on the path to nirvāṇa is reached when the first three of these obstacles have been eliminated, and it is claimed that all three of these first three are eliminated at the same time, since the second and third are effects of the first. This first stage is also said to be reached more easily when one keeps good company, that is, the company of others who have reached at least the first stage. For this reason, much of Buddhist practice centers on maintaining a community of men and women who are helping one another strive for nirvāṇa. Although much of that struggle requires personal effort and a thorough knowledge of one's own mentality, the individual's efforts are said to be nearly impossible without the support of a community of like-minded people.

The second and third stages of the path to nirvāṇa are reached when one reduces and then eliminates the fourth and fifth obstacles. The final goal, nirvāṇa itself, is reached when one has eliminated all ten obstacles, and especially the passions for both material and spiritual states of being. A person who has attained nirvāṇa is called an *arhant* (feminine *arhatī*), which literally means "a person worthy of admiration." The *arhant* is someone who has all the characteristics of a buddha and differs from a buddha only in having required instruction to achieve nirvāṇa, whereas a buddha achieves nirvāṇa without ever having been taught how to attain it. All people who have reached any of these four stages that culminates in arhanthood are collectively known as nobles (*ārya*), and the path to nirvāṇa is known as the noble path or the path of the nobles.

KNOWLEDGE OF NIRVĀṆA

According to a formula often repeated in canonical sources, when a person attains nirvāṇa, then he or she knows "what needed to be done has been done, and I shall never again be reborn in any realm in any form." This raises the difficult question of how one can know an absence and especially a future absence. Obviously, one cannot directly experience an absence, nor can one directly experience anything that takes place, or fails to take place, in the future. The knowledge of the absence of one's future rebirths, then, must be an inference of some kind. Even the knowledge that in the present life there will never again arise the ten obstacles enumerated above must be an inference of some kind. Just how such an inference might work and what kind of inference is involved occupied the attention of Buddhist scholastics from the time of Dharmakīrti on.

THE SPECIAL ONTOLOGICAL STATUS OF NIRVĀṆA

According to Buddhist teachings, all conditioned things are impermanent, because the conditions upon which something depends can disappear, and when they disappear, so does anything that depends on them. nirvāṇa, however, is said to be a permanent achievement. If it is permanent, then it cannot be conditioned. From these considerations one of two possibilities follow. Either all things are conditioned, in which case nirvāṇa cannot be a thing at all, or nirvāṇa is an exception to the otherwise universal rule that all things are conditioned. Both of these possibilities have had their advocates among Buddhist scholastics. Those who regarded nirvāṇa as an unconditioned thing came to characterize nirvāṇa as a permanent entity that is constantly lucid and blissful, or as a state of being aware of a permanently lucid and blissful and essentially transcendent reality.

LATER DOCTRINAL DEVELOPMENTS: NONABIDING NIRVĀṆA AND HAPPY REALMS

Several centuries after the founding of the Buddhist community, a movement arose that placed an emphasis on a kind of virtuoso known as a bodhisattva. The term itself originally referred to a person who was dedicated to becoming a buddha and thus referred to the Buddha Gautama (the founder of Buddhism) in his previous lives. In an extension of that original meaning, the term *bodhisattva* came to be applied to anyone who had come to realize that suffering is present in all realms of the universe, that the vast majority of sentient beings lack the capacity to achieve nirvāṇa on their own strengths, and that they therefore require the help of someone dedicated to helping others attain nirvāṇa. A bodhisattva is a person who not only realizes all that but also vows not to attain final nirvāṇa until all other sentient beings have also attained it. Texts dealing with the bodhisattva ideal say that a bodhisattva may either postpone his or her own attainment of nirvāṇa until others have attained it or, preferably, may attain nirvāṇa and then renounce it in order to remain among sentient beings in need of help. Attaining nirvāṇa and then renouncing it is said to be preferable because the bodhisattva who does this already knows the way and can therefore better show others. This nirvāṇa that the bodhisattva attains and then renounces is called nonabiding nirvāṇa.

Another doctrine that began with the realization that most beings are incapable of attaining nirvāṇa through their own discipline alone was the myth that some buddhas have attained final nirvāṇa only after establishing special realms in which there are no environmental obstacles to tranquility. In such a realm, known as a happy land (*sukhavatī bhūmi*) or, following Chinese translations of the Sanskrit term, a pure land, all who abide there are surrounded by inspirational teachings. Even the babbling of brooks and the chirping of birds are discourses on virtue. In the absence of a painful external environment and in the presence of incessant sermons, the residents of the happy lands quickly attain final nirvāṇa. Two mythological buddhas who are said to have established happy lands are Amitābha and Akshobhya, the former of whom became the focus of an extensive cult in China and East Asia.

See also Buddhism; Mysticism, History of; Reincarnation.

Bibliography

Collins, Steven. *Nirvāṇa and Other Buddhist Felicities.* Cambridge, U.K.: Cambridge University Press, 1998.

Harvey, Peter. *An Introduction to Buddhism.* Cambridge, U.K.: Cambridge University Press, 1990.

Harvey, Peter. *The Selfless Mind: Personality, Consciousness and Nirvāṇa in Early Buddhism.* Surry, U.K.: Curzon Press, 1995.

Williams, Paul. *Mahāyāna Buddhism: The Doctrinal Foundations.* London and New York: Routledge, 1989.

Richard P. Hayes (2005)

NISHI AMANE
(1829–1897)

Nishi Amane, the pioneer in bringing Western philosophy to Japan, was born in Tsuwano, Shimane prefecture.

After the usual Confucian training he went to Edo (Tokyo) for further studies and was attached to Bansho Torishirabe-sho (Center for the Investigation of Western Books). In 1862 he was sent with other promising Japanese to Holland to study Western law and military science. In Holland his interest in philosophy was reawakened, and with his friend Tsuda Masamichi he became acquainted with the positivism of Auguste Comte, the utilitarianism of J. S. Mill, and Immanuel Kant's *On Eternal Peace*. He returned to Japan in 1865 and was appointed to the Kaisei School in Edo, where the government of the shogun requested him to translate books on law. After the Meiji restoration, Nishi was put in charge of educational matters for the Ministry of Military Affairs. At this time he also wrote most of his philosophical books. He became a member of the *Meirokusha*, the group of leading intellectuals of the time, who advocated Western culture and mores. Nishi was several times president of the Tokyo Academy. He was made a baron and was appointed to the upper chamber of the legislature, the House of Peers, in 1890.

Nishi's importance as the "father" of Western philosophy in Japan lies in the new terminology he created—from his Japanese term for philosophy, *tetsugaku*, to his various translations—and in the original works that established a new tradition of speculative thinking. His positivist bent is revealed in *Reikon ichigenron* (Monism of the soul), one of his earlier works. More famous are his panoramic treatments of Western learning and philosophy in *Hyakugaku renkon* (Encyclopedia; written in 1874), a kind of philosophical or cultural dictionary, and *Haykuichi shinron* (A new theory on the many doctrines; written in 1874). In these Nishi prefers Mill's inductive method to Comte's positivism. In 1874 Nishi also wrote *Chichi keimō* (Logic, an introduction), the first of its genre in Japan. His utilitarian ethics is clearly manifested in "Jinsei sampō-setsu" (The three treasures theory of man's life), which appeared in the *Meiroku Journal* in 1875. He replaced Confucian ethics with a quest for the three treasures: health, wealth, and knowledge.

As a translator Nishi has to his credit Mill's *Utilitarianism* and a work titled *Mental Philosophy* by Joseph Haven, an American philosopher influenced by Scottish realism.

In later life Nishi became more conservative in his view of Western ideas, an attitude consonant with the country's post-1886 reaction against ultra-Westernization. As a director of a teacher's college, Shihan Gakkō, he proposed a combination of East and West in ethics; but in the last analysis he remains an expositor of Western philosophy who never really tried to combine East and West in his thought and writing.

See also Comte, Auguste; Japanese Philosophy; Kant, Immanuel; Mill, John Stuart; Mill's Methods of Induction; Positivism; Utilitarianism.

Bibliography

Nishi's collected works are available in two editions. One is *Nishi Amane zenshū* (The complete works of Nishi Amane), 3 vols., edited by Okube Toshiaki (Tokyo, 1960–). Vol. I contains Nishi's philosophical works. The other edition is *Nishi tetsugaku chosakushū* (Collected philosophical works of Nishi Amane), edited by Asō Yoshiteru (Tokyo, 1933).

Studies of Nishi can be found in *Japanese Thought in the Meiji Era,* edited by M. Kōsaka, translated into English by D. Abosch (Tokyo: Pan-Pacific Press, 1958), pp. 99–113; Gino K. Piovesana, *Recent Japanese Philosophical Thought, 1862–1962* (Tokyo: Enderle Bookstore, 1963), pp. 5–18; and R. F. Hackett, "Nishi Amane, A Tokugawa-Meiji Bureaucrat," in *Journal of Asian Studies* 18 (2) (1959): 213–225.

Gino K. Piovesana, S.J. (1967)

NISHIDA, KITARŌ
(1870–1945)

One of modern Japan's most prominent philosophers, Nishida was born in the village of Unoke, located on the Japanese Sea near Kanazawa, which was the capital of the Ishikawa prefecture. He attended the Prefecture Gymnasium in Kanazawa, where he began a lifelong friendship with Teitaro (Daisetz) Suzuki. He then enrolled at the University of Tokyo, choosing philosophy over mathematics, in which he was quite gifted, and studied Western philosophy there from 1891 until 1894. After completing his studies with a thesis on David Hume, Nishida returned to his home, married, and devoted himself intensely for about ten years after 1897 to the practice of Zen.

In 1899 he was appointed as a teacher at the Forth Senior High School (previously the Prefecture Gymnasium) in Kanazawa, where he taught logic, ethics, psychology, and German until 1909. During this period, which Nishida would later characterize as the best of his life, he laid the solid and fertile groundwork for his subsequent philosophical work, a groundwork based on the unusual combination of Western philosophy and Zen. Each day he faithfully practiced Zen meditation and sitting exercises (*Zazen*), but he also worked through the main texts of Western philosophy from Plato and Aristotle through to Henri-Louis Bergson, William James,

Heinrich Rickert, and Alexius Meinong. His own philosophy was to emerge out of the seemingly impossible combination of these two parallel directions.

In 1910 he received an appointment as assistant professor for ethics at the University of Kyoto. The following year his first work titled *An Inquiry into the Good* appeared, in which a philosophy of pure experience is developed. It is the first monumental philosophical work in Japan according to the full sense of the word *philosophy* as it was imported into Japan from the West. In 1913 he was named full professor for the philosophy of religion and then in 1914 full professor in philosophy. This was the beginning of what has come to be known as the Nishida period in the philosophy department at the University of Kyoto, during which a philosophical community arose around him with both high scholarly standards and close personal attachments. Hajime Tanabe, later Nishida's successor, and Tetsurō Watuji were recruited by him. Similarly successful students arose under his tutelage, including Kiyoshi Miki and Keiji Nishitani. The philosophical department flourished during this period and became a significant factor in the intellectual and academic life of modern Japan. This circle of scholars came to be known as the Kyoto School. He retired from the university in 1928.

His family life during this time, however, was difficult and painful, as he recalled on the occasion of his retirement: "For ten years, I have pursued my scholarly work while faced with continually unbearable, unfortunate circumstances in my family, which has been very difficult for me." In 1920 he lost his beloved first son, in 1925 he lost his wife, who had been bedridden at home for six years as the result of a serious stroke. One of his daughters suffered with tuberculosis for several years. Two others were hospitalized for acute typhoid fever, one of whom never completely recovered. Earlier, during the Kanazawa period, he had already lost his brother and two young daughters. In several philosophical essays, Nishida wrote, "What impels one towards philosophy is the sorrow and pain of human life." Not wonder that there is something rather than nothing, not methodical doubt as a means to achieve certainty, but rather the fate of human life as a whole on earth motivated Nishida to pursue philosophy. Nishida's basic question is, "What is the structure of the actual world into which we are born, in which we labor, and in which we die? What is our self in this actual world?"

Nishida's concern is not only the life-world, not only the historical world, but also the world of life and death. Nishida is not concerning solely with the self that lives in the world, but rather the whole self that is born, lives, and dies. Sorrowful, painful events in human life tear open the world. This tear or rift opens up a window and gives access to the profundity of the world. Nishida says that "Grasping the common everydayness of our lives most profoundly leads to the most profound philosophizing." This profundity is nothing other than the profundity of everyday life. Nishida speaks of eschatological everydayness.

In the middle of the painful sorrows of his life, Nishida could say: "The ground of my heart, infinitely deep, will not be reached by all of the waves of joy and cares." For Nishida profundity or depth was experienced profundity. In his calligraphic work, for which he also counts as an artist, Nishida expresses a beautiful power rising out of this profundity. In spite of the difficult circumstances he faced in his life, he worked continuously every day. Even in the year in which he retired, he published five essays, including *Predicative Logic, The Place Wherein One Sees Oneself and the Place of Consciousness*, and *The Intelligible World*. His creative powers were sustained up to the end of his life, whereby the pathway for his thinking did not get any easier.

After his retirement Nishida spent half of each year in Kyoto and half in Kamakura at the seashore. He said, "I love the sea. There is something infinite that is suspended and moves in the sea." One student characterized Nishida's philosophy as a philosophy of the sea. His boyhood friend Suzuki also lived in Kamakura after he had returned from the United States so there the two of them often met for conversations in the space between Zen and philosophy, and Nishida attributed much in his philosophy to the influence of Suzuki. After his second marriage in 1931, Nishida's family situation was much better, but his concerns over Japan's worsening internal political situation and its external policies became increasingly grave. In 1939 the Second World War began and in 1941 the Pacific War with the United States began, which plummeted Japan on the war to its catastrophic defeat in August of 1945.

In May of 1945, Nishida wrote to Suzuki regarding the impending defeat: "Things are happening as we always feared they would. A state that is based on military power will perish by military power." As he was intensely searching for the possibility of a world culture that could unite humanity in the newly unified world that was to come after the world war, Nishida died on June 7, 1945, on account of an acute kidney infection. On his desk lay the unfinished manuscript of an essay *Concerning My Logic*. Nishida worked up until the last day of his life.

During the year before he died, he wrote articles titled *Concerning A Philosophy of Religion Governed by the Pre-established Harmony, Life, Philosophical Foundations of Mathematics*, and *The Logic of Place and the Religious World View*.

HIS WORK

In 1926 the essay *Place* (*Basho*) appeared. Concerning that article, Nishida wrote, "It seems to me that I attained my final standpoint with the notion of 'place.'" Nishida's philosophy can in a real sense be characterized as a philosophy of place. The basic idea behind the notion of place is: Everything that is, is located in a place. *Being* means *being in*. The proposition "S is P" means in truth that "S is in P." Nishida states one time simply and concretely, "Place is where we are located." *Place* for Nishida, then, corresponds to what Martin Heidegger called *world* as a component of being in the world. For Nishida, place consists both of the place of being and the place of the absolute nothing in the sense that the place of being is surrounded by the place of absolute nothing. The place of being as the place of limited disclosedness is located within the place of nothing as the unlimited disclosedness, infinite openness. *Place* thereby has a twofold disclosedness for us. Those of us who find ourselves in a place find ourselves not only in a world, but also in the unlimited openness that surrounds the world, a view that is different from Heidegger's. Nishida explicitly discusses the *we* as something that is located in a place in his essay *I and Thou* (1932).

According to Nishida, *I and thou* means that I am what I am in that I am nothingness in the unlimited openness, and conversely, *I and thou* means that you are what you are in that you are in the nothingness of unlimited openness. Nishida views the relationship differently than Martin Buber in that the I-thou is an aspect, the face-to-face aspect of the full reality of what is located in a place, a reality that consists in the fact that this one single individual and this other single individual are both in contradiction and in unity based on the abyss of the absolute nothingness where there is neither *I* nor *thou*. The basic traits of the notion of place according to Nishida can only be understood in correspondence to an originary pure experience because the notion of place is developed out of this experience.

Nishida's philosophy of pure experience arose through an original and radical encounter between West and East. There is a qualitative divide between the thinking of Western philosophy and the nonthinking in Zen. This rift inside Nishida himself, where both philosophy and Zen coexisted, threatened to rip him apart, but instead it came to serve as a magnetic field in which philosophy and Zen actually touched and permeated each other. This is where Nishida's philosophy was born, a philosophy of another beginning. For a philosophy of pure experience, it is crucial to explain everything through the fact that the only real reality is pure experience. In attempting to explain everything within a single context, Nishida orients himself on Western philosophy; his pure experience, however, comes from Zen.

Pure experience is not a monadic substance-like foundational entity, but rather an original occurrence of experiencing, an event like the following: "In the moment of seeing, of hearing, still without reflections such as 'I see flowers' and without judgments like 'These flowers are red,' in this moment of momentary seeing or hearing, there is neither subject nor object." This immediately experiencing experience occurs as the ground of the truly real reality because in immediate seeing and hearing the undifferentiatedness that obtains before splitting into difference is at work. Here, a direct connection between the empirical and the metaphysical is revealed in a unique way. For Nishida, the metaphysical does not disclose itself beyond experience but rather within experience, that is, within the immediately experiencing experience. Nishida sees the origin of the true self in pure experience because in it shackles of the ego are shattered. The empirical, the metaphysical, and the existential are integrated here prior to their differentiation.

Human experience, which is usually encountered as constrained or shackled inside the subject/object framework, breaks through this framework into the unlimited openness through the originary event of pure experience as immediate seeing and hearing. Pure experience is then articulated within the subject-object framework, but now not as a constraining frame, but rather as a projective ladder into openness. The place for the self-articulation of experience is now in the subject-object framework within the infinite openness. This is then the equivalent to the place of being within the place of the absolute nothingness. From this perspective, pure experience articulates itself as the originary unified whole, sometimes from the subjective side, but not as a subject, and sometimes from the objective side, but not as an object. Illustrating the differentiation of pure experience in dynamic relationships is what we mean by explaining everything.

Nishida actually does present these explanations. Explanation, however, is work that takes place at the level of reflection. How are pure experience and explanation related? To answer this question, the standpoint of pure experience turns into the standpoint of self-consciousness/self-awareness, which unites intuition and reflection within itself. Here, once again, the question of the place of self-consciousness is fundamental. This kind of awareness is more than self-consciousness because the limited place in the unlimited place of openness, this duality of place, is mirrored in the limited place that arises as the focal point of self-consciousness that is transparent to itself for the unlimited openness. Self-consciousness/self-awareness says, "I am I, in not being I" instead of simply "I am I."

The dynamic connection of "pure experience, self-consciousness or self-awareness, and place" (Basho) serves as the basis for further philosophical deliberations that Nishida carried out in the areas of art, history, society, the state, practical philosophy, the study of experience, mathematics, physics, and others areas in which he showed over and again how they are all permeated by this fundamental constellation. In the course of thinking that does not always proceed smoothly, Nishida tried out some unique categories such as active intuition, historical body, absolutely contradictory self-identity, and converse parallel to name just a few.

Nishida's thinking proceeds from a new beginning. Its basic category is place instead of substance, God, or the modern notion of an absolute (transcendental) subject. Logic as the logic of a contradictory self-identity, or rather the self-identity of the self-contradictory (the logic of place) instead of a logic of identity; the unity of the contradictory subject-object on the basis of something-before-the-split instead of a subject-object schema; reason as something that is active in intuition or rather acts as intuition instead of one side of a regional, qualitative distinction between sense and reason—all of these things arise out of pure experience. If global philosophy is going to take into account non-Western cultural traditions, Nishida's philosophy needs to be discussed within the horizon of that philosophy.

See also Buddhism; Phenomenology.

Bibliography

PRIMARY WORKS

Fundamental Problems of Philosophy: The World of Action and the Dialectical World. Translated by D. A. Dilworth. Tokyo: Sophia University Press, 1970.

Art and Morality. Translated by D.H. Dilworth and V. H. Viglielmo. Honolulu: University of Hawaii Press, 1973.

Intelligibility and the Philosophy of Nothingness. Translated by R. Schinzinger. Westport: Greenwood Press, 1973.

"The Logic of Topos and the Religious World View." Translated by M. Yusa. *The Eastern Buddhist* 19 (1986) and 20 (1987).

Intuition and Reflection in Self-Consciousness. Translated by V.H. Viglielmo with Y. Tekeuchi and J. S. O'Leary. Albany: SUNY Press, 1987.

Xenshu (Collected Works). 19 vols. 4th ed. Tokyo: Iwanami, 1987–1989.

An Inquiry into the Good. Translated by M. Abe and C. Ives. New Haven, CT: Yale University Press, 1990.

SECONDARY WORKS

Heisig, James W. *Philosophy of Nothingness: An Essay on the Kyoto School*. Honolulu: University of Hawaii Press, 2001.

Nishitani, Keiji. *Nishida Kitaro*. Translated by S. Yananoto and J.W. Heisig. Berkeley: University of California Press, 1991.

Wargo, Robert J. J. *The Logic of Nothingness: A Study of Nishida Kitaro*. Honolulu: University of Hawaii Press, 2005.

Yusa, Michiko. *Zen and Philosophy: An Intellectual Biography of Nishida Kitaro*. Honolulu: University of Hawaii Press, 2002.

Ueda Shizuteru (2005)

NJEGOŠ

See *Petrović-Njegoš, Petar*

NOMINALISM

See *Goodman, Nelson; Hobbes, Thomas; Quine, Willard Van Orman; Roscelin; Universals, A Historical Survey*

NOMINALISM, MODERN

In its main contemporary sense, nominalism is the thesis that abstract entities do not exist. Equivalently, it is the thesis that everything that does exist is a concrete object. Since there is no generally accepted account of the abstract-concrete distinction, and since it remains genuinely unclear how certain (putative) entities are to be classified, the content of modern nominalism is to some degree unsettled. Certain consequences of the view are, however, tolerably clear. For example, it is widely agreed that the objects of pure mathematics—numbers, sets, functions, abstract geometrical spaces, and so on—are to be classified as abstract. It is also widely agreed that certain objects of metaphysics and semantics—propositions, meanings, properties and relations, and so on—must be abstract if they exist at all. Modern nominalists thus commit themselves to rejecting these paradigmatic abstract entities and hence to rejecting any scientific, mathematical, or philosophical theory according to which such things exist. In this sense nominalism is standardly opposed to platonism (or, less commonly, antinominalism).

EARLY HISTORY

The first significant philosophical system in the modern period to insist on the existence of abstract objects is due to Gottlob Frege. Frege (1980) held that the truths of pure mathematics concern a domain of mind-independent abstract entities. Frege (1984) further held that any adequate account of thought and language must allow that meaningful linguistic expressions are associated, not simply with concrete worldly items, but also with senses (*Sinne*), and that for various reasons these linguistic senses must exist in a "third realm," distinct both from the realm of subjective mental items and the realm of sensible, concrete things. Frege's vigorous defense of platonism in semantics and the philosophy of mathematics forms the background for the emergence of modern nominalism in the 1920s.

The Warsaw school of logicians centered around Stanisław Leśniewski and Tadeusz Kotarbiński set itself the task of reconstructing modern logic and mathematics along nominalistic lines. Kotarbiński's reism, for example, was a methodological position according to which, wherever possible, statements that apparently concern abstract entities (e.g., "Bonds of brotherhood unite Orsetes and Electra") are to be replaced by statements that concern only concrete entities and parts thereof (e.g., "Orestes is Electra's brother") (Kotarbiński 1955). The principal motivation for the program was to prevent scientific work in these areas from becoming embroiled in ancient metaphysical and epistemological controversies. The nominalistic project was introduced into Anglophone philosophy by W. V. Quine, who first encountered it in conversations with Leśniewski and Alfred Tarski in 1933. Quine's main positive contribution to the program was the seminal 1947 manifesto "Steps Toward a Constructive Nominalism," coauthored with Nelson Goodman. Quine soon abandoned nominalism in favor of a moderate and distinctive form of platonism. It may nonetheless be said that all subsequent discussion of modern nominalism in the Anglophone tradition derives directly from this paper.

MOTIVATIONS FOR NOMINALISM

In "Steps Toward a Constructive Nominalism" Goodman and Quine defend their rejection of abstract entities by invoking "a philosophical intuition that cannot be justified by appeal to anything more ultimate" (1947: 97). In subsequent years philosophers have sought to provide a more explicit motivation for the view.

OCCAM'S RAZOR. According to a slogan associated with the tradition of medieval nominalism, "entities are not to be multiplied beyond necessity." Some modern nominalists appeal to this principle in motivating their position. These writers typically concede that existing scientific and mathematical theories entail the existence of abstract entities and are therefore nominalistically unacceptable. They maintain, however, that it is possible to produce nominalistically adequate versions of, or surrogates for, these theories, and so to "dispense" with abstract objects. Occam's razor is then invoked to argue that when such parsimonious surrogates are available, it is rational to reject the standard platonistic theories and to embrace the surrogates instead.

Much of the constructive work in the nominalist tradition consists in providing nominalistic surrogates for existing theories. Roughly speaking, a nominalistic surrogate T_N for a platonistic theory T_P is a theory whose quantifiers range only over concrete objects, but which is nonetheless fit to do much of the same theoretical or explanatory work as the original. For example, standard formalizations of physical theories involve quantifiers that range over both concrete physical entities (particles, fields, points, and regions of space-time, etc.) and mathematical entities (real numbers, vectors, functions, etc.) A nominalistic alternative to (say) classical electrodynamics would be a theory whose quantifiers range only over concrete objects, but whose predictive and explanatory power exactly matched that of the standard platonistic formulations.

Nominalistic surrogates for standard theories have been developed in a number of domains (Field 1980, Hodes 1984, Chihara 1990, Balaguer 1998). However, the significance of these reconstructive programs is open to doubt for several reasons. For example, while the nominalistic surrogates do indeed typically posit fewer entities than the platonistic originals, they are typically inferior to the originals in other respects. In some cases they require a substantial extension of the extensional first-order logic that suffices for platonistically formulated science. In most cases the nominalistic theory is significantly less perspicuous and flexible than its platonistic counterpart.

One may therefore concede that other things being equal, nominalistic theories are to be preferred on grounds of parsimony, while insisting that since other things are not equal, Occam's razor has no clear application. A more profound challenge is directed at the razor itself. Contemporary philosophers who cite ontological parsimony as a basis for theory choice often suppose that the principle derives its authority from its role in the sciences. But as critics have pointed out (Burgess and Rosen 1997), there is scant evidence that scientists accept the principle in its most general form. Scientists may be concerned to minimize the number of physical mechanisms or fundamental laws in the theories they accept. But working scientists and mathematicians have shown no interest in reducing the number of abstract entities posited by the mathematical theories they invoke. To the contrary, in mathematics and mathematical physics there is some concern to maximize the range of mathematical objects and structures (Maddy 1997). If this is correct, then proponents of the Occamist case for nominalism must maintain that the impulse to ontological parsimony to which they appeal is not a principle of scientific methodology, but an independently compelling philosophical principle.

THE ACCESS PROBLEM. The most widely cited ground for nominalism derives from Paul Benacerraf (1973). Benacerraf notes that since abstract mathematical objects are causally inert and therefore incapable of affecting our senses, even indirectly, there is a question as to how one might come to know that they exist. Benacerraf invokes the *causal theory of knowledge*, originally proposed by Alvin Goldman (1967) for other purposes, according to which, roughly, a person S knows that p only if S stands in some suitable causal relation to the objects with which p is concerned. This principle entails that true claims about abstract objects cannot be known to be true, even if they are true. And while this does not entail that there are no abstract entities, it does entail that platonism is unstable in the following sense: Proponents of a Platonistic theory must concede that they cannot know whether the theory they accept is true. However, as critics were quick to point out the causal theory of knowledge on which Benacerraf relies is objectionable on other grounds (Steiner 1975). In the subsequent debate nominalists rarely invoke this or any other detailed theory of knowledge. Instead, they maintain that the causal inefficacy of the abstract leaves our access to the abstract domain an utter mystery. Since it is clearly desirable to avoid such mysteries, this provides a motivation for pursuing, and perhaps also for accepting, nominalistic alternatives to standard theories.

THE DISPENSABILITY ARGUMENT. Hartry H. Field (1980, 1989) provides a number of motivations for nominalism that do not depend on the causal theory of knowledge. Field begins with a question for the platonist: What reason might one have for believing the claims of standard mathematics? If one has reason to believe the axioms, then one might acquire reason to believe the theorems by constructing proofs. So the question becomes: What reason might one have for believing the axioms of standard mathematics? Since the axioms involve substantial existential claims, it is hard to see how they could be known *a priori* (but see Wright 1983, Hale 1988). And since these claims concern causally inert abstract entities, it seems clear that they cannot be verified directly by observation or experiment. Field thus concludes that the only reason one can have for believing the axioms is that they play an indispensable role in one or another well-confirmed scientific theory. Earlier writers (Quine 1960, Putnam 1971) defended platonism in this way. For example, Hilary Putnam (1971) notes that since the laws of physics are standardly formulated in mathematical terms, someone who denies the existence of (say) real numbers is not in a position to formulate, much less to employ, even the most elementary laws of physics. Quine and Putnam thus offer the following indispensability argument for platonism:

> (1) One is justified in believing that abstract objects exist if, but only if, theories that entail the existence of such objects are indispensable for scientific purposes.

> (2) Standard mathematics entails the existence of abstract objects.

> (3) Standard mathematics is indispensable for scientific purposes.

> (4) Therefore, one is justified in believing that abstract objects exist.

Field rejects premise (3), thereby turning the argument on its head. He argues that in certain cases it is possible to produce reasonably attractive nominalistic versions of standard platonistic theories: versions in which the only objects posited are material bodies and space-time regions. Field maintains that to the extent that such nominalistic surrogates are available, they establish that abstract objects are dispensable for scientific purposes. The construction of such surrogates thus undercuts the only reason one might have had for believing in abstract objects, and so provides a roundabout motivation for nominalism.

Field concedes that the nominalistic alternatives he constructs are in certain respects inferior to the standard platonistic theories on which they are based. They are typically unwieldy and imperspicuous: Derivations are typically longer and harder to follow. Field concedes that it would be unreasonable for working scientists to use these nominalistic theories for most purposes and hence that platonistic theories are indispensable in practice. His central claim is that they are nonetheless dispensable in principle and that for the purposes of the Quine-Putnam challenge dispensability in principle is what matters.

One distinctive ingredient in Field's view is a demonstration that scientists who accept only the nominalistic physics that Field constructs are nonetheless entitled to use platonistic mathematics in the course of their work. This claim is supported by a formal result. Let T_P be a standard platonistic theory, and let T_N be a nominalistic surrogate for T_P constructed according to Field's method. It may then be shown (with certain important qualifications) that for any nominalistic statement S—that is, any statement whose quantifiers are restricted to concrete entities—S is a theorem of T_P if and only if S is a theorem of T_N. This conservative extension theorem supports the claim that a theorist who accepts T_N may legitimately employ the full mathematical resources of T_P for the purpose of deriving nominalistic claims about the concrete world (for a discussion on this, see Shapiro 1983, Burgess and Rosen 1997). Such theorists may then legitimately regard the mathematical apparatus of T_P as a useful fiction in which they indulge for various practical purposes. Field's version of nominalism is thus a form of fictionalism about mathematical objects.

Field's work has provoked an intense critical response (Irvine 1990). Field himself notes that his procedures for nominalizing platonistic theories are inapplicable to an important class of theories, including Albert Einstein's general theory of relativity and quantum mechanics, and hence that it remains an open question whether platonistic theories are dispensable even in principle for the purposes of contemporary physics (compare Balaguer 1996). Others wonder why Platonistic theories that are indispensable in practice should not provide one with adequate grounds for believing in the abstract objects they posit. Perhaps the most fundamental philosophical response to Field's approach calls into question premise (1) of the indispensability argument, which is also a crucial premise in Field's positive defense of nominalism. In effect, the premise asserts that abstract objects have the status of theoretical entities, in the sense that one acquires reason for believing in them only when the assumption of their existence is required for some urgent scientific purpose.

Against this, critics maintain that some propositions about abstract objects—for example, the claim that there is a number between 3 and 5, or the claim that Jane Austen wrote six novels—are perfectly ordinary claims. Anyone who has learned basic arithmetic can supply a reason for believing that there is a number between 3 and 5 (Parson 1986), and anyone who knows how to use the library can verify that Austen wrote six novels. It is a presupposition of the debate between Field and proponents of the indispensability argument that these relatively nontheoretical justifications for platonistic claims are inadequate. But this claim may be challenged. If one's ordinary reasons for believing platonistic claims are good enough, then the fact that such claims are dispensable for certain theoretical purposes has no immediate bearing on the debate over nominalism.

REVOLUTIONARY VERSUS HERMENEUTIC NOMINALISM

In the nominalist tradition that runs from Goodman and Quine (1947) to Field (1980), it is generally conceded that since standard mathematics entails the existence of abstract objects, the nominalist must supply an alternative to standard mathematics, both pure and applied. This alternative might take the form of a genuinely novel formulation, as with Field's nominalistic version of Newtonian gravitational theory. But it may also take the form of a reinterpretation of existing theories. On this approach the nominalist proceeds by supplying a revisionary account of the meanings of mathematical statements. For example, the nominalist may maintain that while existential arithmetical statements like "There is a number between 3 and 5" in fact affirm the existence of abstract entities, they should be reinterpreted as claims about (say) concrete numeral inscriptions. In either case the nominalist must argue for a revision in accepted science and mathematics. Nominalist programs of this sort have thus been labeled *revolutionary* (Burgess 1983).

Revolutionary nominalism is contrasted with hermeneutic nominalism. Hermeneutic nominalists maintain that it is a mistake to interpret ordinary mathematics as involving claims about abstract objects in the first place. They might maintain, for example, that as they are ordinarily understood, existential claims like "There is a number between 3 and 5" are in fact claims about concrete numeral inscriptions and hence that such claims might be true even if there were no abstract entities. On this sort of account nominalism requires no revision in settled doctrine.

The most straightforward version of hermeneutic nominalism would maintain that abstract singular terms like *3* and *the cosine function* denote particular concrete objects. Claims of this sort are rarely plausible, however, and so proposals in this domain are typically more complex. For example, Geoffrey Hellman (1989) proposes that a statement S in the language of arithmetic is true if and only if a certain modal condition holds: (a) there might have been an infinite sequence of objects satisfying the axioms of arithmetic, and (b), if there had been such a sequence, a certain structural condition derived from S would have been true of it. Hellman then argues that since this sort of modal claim might be true even if there are in fact no abstract objects, the original mathematical claim is nominalistically acceptable, appearances to the contrary notwithstanding.

There are two main objections to hermeneutic proposals of this sort. The first notes that since such claims are ultimately claims in empirical linguistics—they are claims about the meanings of ordinary mathematical statements—they require empirical support and that in the relevant cases no such support has been forthcoming (Burgess 1983). The second notes that even if hermeneutic nominalists' semantic claims were tenable, it is not clear that they would serve their purpose. Unlike their revolutionary counterparts, hermeneutic nominalists do not deny the claims of standard mathematics. But these claims include *existence theorems*: assertions of the form "There exists a number n such that …" Hermeneutic nominalists must therefore allow that these ordinary existence claims are true and hence that by their own lights, numbers and the like exist. On the face of it, however, this claim is incompatible with their nominalism (Alston 1958, Burgess and Rosen 1997; see also Stanley 2001).

CONTEMPORARY FICTIONALISM

As they are usually understood, the programs of revolutionary and hermeneutic nominalism both require detailed constructive work. Theorists proceed by constructing an autonomous, independently intelligible nominalistic theory T_N, which is then used either to replace or to interpret the original (apparently) platonistic theory, T_P. The development of a suitable theory T_N is typically a nontrivial task, which in many cases requires a profound analysis of the original.

However, some nominalists maintain that detailed constructions of this sort are unnecessary. Easy fictionalism, as the approach is sometimes called, holds that even in the absence of an autonomous nominalistic alternative, nominalists may make free use of standard mathematics and of other platonistic theories without thereby committing themselves to the existence of abstract objects.

Consider for example the claim (S): (S) the mass (in grams) of A = 3.6. On its face (S) asserts that the object A stands in a certain relation to a number. The claim is literally true only if two conditions are satisfied: on the concrete side, the object A must have a certain intrinsic property—a property for which one may have no standard name that does not invoke a relation to numbers; and on the abstract side, the number 3.6 must exist. To maintain the literal truth of (S) is thus to maintain that abstract objects exist. But consider the claim that things are, in all concrete respects, as if (S) were true. The suggestion is that this claim says just what (S) says about the intrinsic configuration of the concrete world, while making no claim whatsoever about the existence of abstract entities.

Easy fictionalists propose that as a matter of convenience one routinely pretends that abstract objects of various sorts exist and that one conveys information about the concrete world by endorsing theories that purport to affirm relations between concrete things and abstract things. Their suggestion is that in "endorsing" these theories, one commits oneself only to the nominalistically acceptable claim that things are, in all concrete respects, as if one's theories are true.

Easy fictionalism comes in a number of varieties. It may be put forward as a hermeneutic proposal, describing the attitude that scientists and mathematicians normally adopt toward their own claims about abstract entities (Yablo 2001). More commonly, it is put forward as a revolutionary proposal. Here, the suggestion is that in light of the arguments in favor of nominalism, it would be rational (or at least, rationally permissible) to adopt a fictionalist attitude toward discourse about abstract objects (Balaguer 1998, Rosen 2001). The main challenge for easy fictionalism is to provide a clear account of the central idiom, "Things are, in all concrete respects, as if S were true," or perhaps, "According to the fiction of mathematical objects, S." The most natural account involves a counterfactual conditional. To say that things are in all concrete respects as if S were true is to say that if there were abstract objects (and the concrete world were just as it is in all intrinsic respects), then S would be true. But counterfactuals of this sort are problematic. It is widely held that the existence of abstract objects could not possibly be a contingent matter (Hale and Wright 1992; compare Field 1993). And if this is right, then by nominalists' own lights, such conditionals involve a necessarily false antecedent. A second challenge for the approach is to provide an account of pure mathematics, where the aim of the discourse is not simply to provide information about the configuration of the concrete world.

See also Realism and Naturalism, Mathematical.

Bibliography

Alston, William. "Ontological Commitments." *Philosophical Studies* 9 (1958): 8–17.

Balaguer, Mark. *Platonism and Anti-Platonism in Mathematics.* New York: Oxford University Press, 1998.

Balaguer, Mark. "Towards a Nominalization of Quantum Mechanics." *Mind* 105 (1996): 209–226.

Benacerraf, Paul. "Mathematical Truth." *Journal of Philosophy* 70 (1973): 661–680.

Burgess, John P. "Epistemology and Nominalism." In *Physicalism in Mathematics*, edited by Andrew D. Irvine, 1–15. Dordrecht, Netherlands: Kluwer Academic, 1990.

Burgess, John P. "Why I Am Not a Nominalist." *Notre Dame Journal of Formal Logic* 24 (1983): 93–105

Burgess, John P., and Gideon Rosen. *A Subject with No Object: Strategies for Nominalistic Interpretation of Mathematics.* New York: Oxford University Press, 1997.

Chihara, Charles S. *Constructibility and Mathematical Existence.* New York: Oxford University Press, 1990.

Field, Hartry H. "The Conceptual Contingency of Mathematical Objects." *Mind* 102 (1993): 285–299.

Field, Hartry H. *Realism, Mathematics, and Modality.* New York: Blackwell, 1989.

Field, Hartry H. *Science without Numbers: A Defence of Nominalism.* Princeton, NJ: Princeton University Press, 1980.

Frege, Gottlob. *The Foundations of Arithmetic: A Logico-mathematical Enquiry into the Concept of Number.* 2nd ed. Translated by J. L. Austin. Evanston, IL: Northwestern University Press, 1980. This was originally published in German under the title *Der Grundlagen der Arithmetik* in 1884.

Frege, Gottlob. "Thoughts." In *Collected Papers on Mathematics, Logic, and Philosophy*, translated by Max Black and edited by Brian McGuiness. New York: Blackwell, 1984. This essay was originally published in German under the title "Der Gedanke" in 1918.

Goldman, Alvin. "A Causal Theory of Knowing." *Journal of Philosophy* 64 (1967): 357–372.

Goodman, Nelson, and W. V. Quine. "Steps toward a Constructive Nominalism." *Journal of Symbolic Logic* 12 (1947): 105–122.

Hale, Bob. *Abstract Objects.* New York: Blackwell, 1988.

Hale, Bob, and Crispin Wright. "Nominalism and the Contingency of Abstract Objects." *Journal of Philosophy* 89 (1992): 111–135.

Hellman, Geoffrey. *Mathematics without Numbers: Towards a Modal-Structural Interpretation.* New York: Oxford University Press, 1989.

Hodes, Harold. "Logicism and the Ontological Commitments of Arithmetic." *Journal of Philosophy* 81 (3) (March 1984): 123–149.

Irvine, Andrew D., ed. *Physicalism in Mathematics.* Dordrecht, Netherlands: Kluwer Academic, 1990.

Kotarbiński, Tadeusz. "The Fundamental Ideas of Pansomatism." *Mind* 64 (1955): 488–500. Originally published in Polish in 1935.

Maddy, Penelope. *Naturalism in Mathematics.* New York: Oxford University Press, 1997.

Parson, Charles. "Quine on the Philosophy of Mathematics." In *The Philosophy of W. V. Quine*, edited by Lewis Edwin Hahn and Paul Arthur Schilpp. La Salle, IL: Open Court Press, 1986.

Putnam, Hilary. *Philosophy of Logic.* New York: Harper and Row, 1971.

Quine, W. V. *Word and Object.* Cambridge, MA: Cambridge Technology Press of the Massachusetts Institute of Technology, 1960.

Rosen, Gideon. "Nominalism, Naturalism, Epistemic Relativism." *Philosophical Perspectives* 15 (2001): 69–91.

Shapiro, Stewart. "Conservativeness and Incompleteness." *Journal of Philosophy* 80 (1983): 521–531.

Stanley, Jason. "Hermeneutic Fictionalism." In *Midwest Studies in Philosophy. No. 25: Figurative Language*, edited by H. Wettstein and P. French, 36–71. New York: Blackwell, 2001.

Steiner, Mark. *Mathematical Knowledge.* Ithaca, NY: Cornell University Press, 1975.

Wright, Crispin. *Frege's Conception of Numbers as Objects.* Aberdeen, Scotland: Aberdeen University Press, 1983.

Yablo, Stephen. "Go Figure: A Path through Fictionalism." In *Midwest Studies in Philosophy. No. 25: Figurative Language*, edited by H. Wettstein and P. French, 77–102. New York: Blackwell, 2001.

Gideon Rosen (2005)

NOMOS AND PHUSIS

Phusis is the ancient Greek word for "nature," cognate with the verb "to grow" (*phuein*); as in English, it can be used both for the natural world as a whole and for the "nature" (i.e., the essential or intrinsic characteristics) of any particular thing, which it has "by nature" (*phusei*). *Nomos* encompasses both law and unwritten, traditional social convention. The contrast between the two concepts is central to ancient sophistic thought, with roots in the pre-Socratic inquiry into the underlying natures of things.

For the Sophists, nomos and phusis are polar terms, roughly equivalent (respectively) to the socially constructed and the universally, objectively given. The contrast was most strikingly applied in relation to justice. Antiphon's *On Truth* argues that justice is a matter of nomos, and nomos and phusis conflict; one should observe the requirements of justice when there are witnesses, but follow the dictates of nature otherwise. By "nature," Antiphon seems to understand what is physiologically given to all humans (Greeks and barbarians alike). By following it one gains what is advantageous to one's existence: life, pleasure, and freedom. In Plato's *Gorgias*, Callicles argues, with an appeal to animal behavior, that it is a matter of "justice according to nature," as opposed to convention, for the strong to prey upon the weak.

However, the same conceptual framework, including the assumption that nature represents an authoritative norm, could be used to support the opposite stance. The *Anonymous Iamblichi* argues that law and justice should be obeyed as having "kingly rule" among human beings—a rule established by human nature itself. So the nomos-phusis contrast was a framework for discussion rather than a theory in itself. It allowed for fruitful debate as to where the testimony of nature might be observed, what guidance it could provide, and how the norms of law and morality might relate to it.

Far from being restricted to justice, nomos-phusis is best understood as a catch phrase for the general sophistic inquiry into the institutions of human society. Thus various Sophists seem to have applied the concepts to slavery, gender roles, language, and religion. For instance, the *Sisyphus* fragment (by either Critias or Euripides) argues that religion was invented by ancient sages as a device for social control, implying that the gods exist only by convention. The contrast could even be extended to questions of general epistemology. Democritus (usually classed as a pre-Socratic, but associated by sources with Protagoras) summed up his atomism by claiming that sensory properties, such as colors and tastes, are merely conventional; in reality there are only atoms and the void. Here, conventional seems to be tantamount to mind-dependent, or merely apparent.

The adoption of nature as a normative standard is the most powerful legacy of sophistic thought. Plato and Aristotle both constructed their ethics and politics around their understanding of human nature, and took this to be in harmony with the nature of the cosmos and the divine. Later, Epicureans and Stoics both argued that the good life is one lived in accordance with nature (*kata phusin*), which they explicated by invoking animal behavior in the "cradle argument." But these philosophers differed widely in their treatment of nomos, and the nomos-phusis polarity as such faded from prominence after the Sophists.

See also Antiphon; Protagoras of Abdera; Sophists.

Bibliography

Guthrie, W. K. C. *A History of Greek Philosophy*. Vol. 3. Cambridge, U.K.: Cambridge University Press, 1969.

Heinimann, F. *Nomos und Physis*. Basel: F. Reinhardt, 1945.

Kahn, Charles. "The Origins of Social Contract Theory in the Fifth Century B.C." In *The Sophists and their Legacy*, edited by G. B. Kerferd. Wiesbaden: Steiner, 1981.

Kerferd, G. B. *The Sophistic Movement*. Cambridge, U.K.: Cambridge University Press, 1981.

Rachel Barney (2005)

NONCOGNITIVISM

Noncognitivists (or nondescriptivists) hold that the function of normative judgments is not, or not primarily, to describe or state facts and that because of this, these judgments lack a truth-value. A strong form of ethical nondescriptivism says that moral judgments have no descriptive function, but weaker forms say only that their nondescriptive function is primary or dominant.

Differing accounts of the nondescriptive function of moral language generate a variety of nondescriptivisms. Moral judgments have been said to express emotions, feelings, attitudes, or stances; and they have been characterized as tools for performing other nondescriptive tasks such as commanding, requesting, endorsing, or commending. A. J. Ayer, whose position is called emotivism, said that "ethical terms" express emotions or feelings and that they "are calculated also to arouse feelings, and so to stimulate action" (1952, p. 108). C. L. Stevenson, whose metaethical theory is called noncognitivism, argued that the major use of "ethical statements" is dynamic rather than fact stating. They are not, he said, primarily used to describe interests or attitudes but rather to change or intensify attitudes and to influence behavior. What Stevenson called the emotive meaning of ethical terms makes this dynamic use possible and also explains why ethical judgments, unlike factual ones, are capable of moving us to action.

From the thought that moral judgments are exclamations and disguised commands Ayer concluded that they "have no objective validity whatever" and that "it is impossible to dispute about questions of value" (1952, p. 110). Stevenson tried to show that there is a place for ethical arguments, but he did not go beyond the claim that a reason is "relevant" when it is likely to influence some attitude. This means, at least to the critics of Stevenson, that the relation between the premises and the conclusion of an ethical argument is psychological rather than logical and that there is no clear distinction between ethical argument and propaganda.

Both Ayer and Stevenson were in the positivist tradition, but by the 1950s an interest in ordinary language also led increasing numbers of analytic philosophers to nondescriptivism. These thinkers acknowledged that moral language can be used descriptively, but they insisted that its "primary" (basic, fundamental) use is to perform any of a number of nondescriptive speech acts. R. M. Hare argued that the primary function of the word *good* is to commend and that when we commend anything "it is always in order, at least indirectly, to guide choices, our own or other people's, now or in the future" (1952, p. 127). Words such as *right* and *ought* are used for giving advice or, as he said, for prescribing. According to Hare, the claim that something is good has both descriptive and prescriptive meaning. The descriptive meaning of the word *good* changes as it is applied to different things, but the prescriptive meaning remains constant because *good* is invariably used to commend. This is why the prescriptive meaning is primary.

Hare described his own position as nondescriptivism, but he was more positive than Ayer and Stevenson about the role and value of logic in ethical arguments. Moral judgments, he said, are a subclass of "prescriptive" rather than "descriptive" language—they are "universalizable prescriptions." Unlike attempts to persuade or to influence attitudes, a judgment that something is good or right is a prescription that is complete in itself, even if no change is brought about in the hearer's attitudes or behavior. Hare believed that there could be logical relations among prescriptive judgments, even commands; and he developed a logic of prescriptive discourse to account for those relations. In the end he concluded that while we can argue logically about what to do, a complete justification of a moral decision will always require the adoption, without justification, of some basic principle or principles as a part of a freely chosen "way of life."

P. H. Nowell-Smith offered a form of nondescriptivism he called multifunctionalism. He said that evaluative language is used "to express tastes and preferences, to express decisions and choices, to criticize, grade, and evaluate, to advise, admonish, warn, persuade and dissuade, to praise, encourage, and reprove, to promulgate and draw attention to rules; and doubtless for other purposes also" (1954, p. 98). Though his position is more complex than Hare's, he does agree that "the central activities for which moral language is used are choosing and advising others to choose" (p. 11).

After the contributions of Ayer, Stevenson, Hare, Nowell-Smith, and others, nondescriptivism was neglected as interest in applied ethics flourished and as those who did think about metaethics developed naturalistic forms of descriptivism. The new naturalists conceded that normative language has nondescriptive functions, but they then pointed out how those functions are compatible with simultaneous descriptive intent and therefore with the possibility of evaluating normative pronouncements in terms of truth and falsity. In the 1980s interest in metaethics was stimulated by new forms of nondescriptivism developed by Simon Blackburn and Allan Gibbard. The dominant issue at that time, however, was the dispute between moral (or ethical) realists and antirealists. Nondescriptivists are more likely to be antirealists, and descriptivists are more likely to be realists, but there are complications.

Formerly, both intuitionists and naturalists were descriptivists. Intuitionists identified moral facts with nonnatural facts, and naturalists identified moral facts with natural facts. If one who believes that moral facts are natural facts can be said to be a moral realist, then both naturalists and intuitionists were moral realists and were in a position to say that moral judgments are true when they correctly describe some natural or nonnatural reality. But there is a way to combine descriptivism with antirealism and another way to combine nondescriptivism with at least the practices of the realist. J. L. Mackie develops a descriptivist account of much normative language, but he argues that judgments of moral obligation, which are thought to be both objective and prescriptive, and judgments of "intrinsic" value are always false. One who says that something is "good in itself" is always speaking falsely because nothing is good in itself.

Both Blackburn and Mackie begin with a Humean projectivism according to which the normativity we think we discover in nature is projected onto a value-free world by us. When we see and are moved by cruelty to the bull, we objectify our negative attitude, and promote it too, by saying that bullfighting is wrong. Projectivists are antirealists. Mackie combines his antirealism with descriptivism and takes this to result in an error theory. Blackburn begins with antirealism, adds his version of nondescriptivism or "expressivism," and emerges with what he calls quasi realism, the idea that the linguistic practices of the realist—saying that bullfighting is really wrong, for example—are perfectly in order and that no error is made. One of his main concerns is to defend this quasi realism by showing how we "earn the right" to "practice, think, worry, assert, and argue" as though moral commitments are true in some straightforward way (1984, p. 257).

Blackburn's view is that we do not describe reality correctly or incorrectly when we make moral claims—we express "stances." He characterizes a stance as a "conative state or pressure on choice and action" but admits that we could also call this an attitude. But whatever we call it, "its function is to mediate the move from features of a situation to a reaction, which in the appropriate circumstances will mean choice" (1993, p. 168).

Gibbard also defends a nondescriptivist or "expressivist" account of normative judgments. Normative judgments, he says, take the form of saying that some act, belief, or feeling is "rational," or "makes sense." The point of making such a judgment is not to describe something, not to attribute a property to it, but "to express one's acceptance of norms that permit it" (1990, p. 7). A norm, according to Gibbard, is "a linguistically encoded precept," and the capacity to be motivated by norms "evolved because of the advantages of coordination and planning through language" (p. 57). There are norms of many kinds, but when we say that what someone did was morally wrong, we are expressing and endorsing norms that govern feelings of guilt by the agent and of anger by others.

Three arguments are traditionally deployed against nondescriptivists. According to the grammatical argument, since moral judgments are phrased in ordinary indicative sentences, there is a prima facie reason to treat them as statements and to treat those who make them as attempting to make statements. Nondescriptivists will reply that here the grammar is misleading, but they can then be asked to explain why this should be so. There is also a logical argument against nondescriptivism. If moral judgments lack a truth-value, then it is impossible for them to play a role in truth-functional constructions (implication, conjunction, and negation, for example) and in arguments. It is also difficult to know how they are to be interpreted when they occur embedded in complex constructions such as statements of belief and doubt. According to what has been called the phenomenological argument, not only do moral claims look and behave like descriptive utterances, they "feel" like them too. When we claim that something is good or right, we do not seem, even to ourselves, to be merely expressing ourselves or ordering others to do things. Nondescriptivists will try to explain why these judgments have this distinctive feel, but descriptivists will insist that the feeling is important data that cannot easily be explained away.

Starting with Ayer, each nondescriptivist has been forced to develop some reply to these, as well as to other, difficulties. Blackburn, for example, responds to the logical argument by developing an expressivist account of truth. He wants to show how it makes sense to claim moral truth even if there are no moral facts and even if our moral claims are no more than expressions of stances or attitudes. Gibbard sketches a solution to the embedding problem that exploits the idea that when we make a normative statement we are expressing a state of mind that consists in "ruling out various combinations of normative systems with factual possibilities." He develops a formalism that allows him to use this idea to account for "the logical relations that hold among normative statements" (1990, p. 99).

Owing to the work of Blackburn and Gibbard, nondescriptivism is alive and well, but its prospects are uncertain because it is truly difficult to develop convincing and definitive answers to the objections from grammar, logic, and phenomenology. Furthermore, nondescriptivism needs a fact/value distinction, and this is something about which philosophers have become increasingly nervous. The early descriptivists tried to reduce values to facts, or they accepted the fact/value distinction and then relegated values to a philosophically insignificant pragmatic limbo. Since then there has been a tendency to argue that many statements that appear to be safely descriptive must be understood to have nondescriptive elements. Nondescriptivists now point out that even if the line between facts and values is blurred or moved, we can still draw an important distinction between assertions and expressions. This claim, however, will continue to be challenged by those who are impressed by the descriptive nature of norms or the normative nature of descriptions.

See also Applied Ethics; Ayer, Alfred Jules; Hare, Richard M.; Mackie, John Leslie; Metaethics; Moral Realism; Projectivism; Stevenson, Charles L.

Bibliography

Ayer, A. J. *Language, Truth, and Logic.* New York: Dover, 1952.

Blackburn, S. "How to Be an Ethical Anti-realist." In *Essays in Quasi-Realism.* New York: Oxford University Press, 1993.

Blackburn, S. *Spreading the Word: Groundings in the Philosophy of Language.* Oxford: Clarendon Press, 1984.

Blackburn, S. "Wise Feelings, Apt Reading." *Ethics* 102 (1992): 342–356.

Darwall, S., A. Gibbard, and P. Railton. "Toward *Fin de Siècle* Ethics: Some Trends." *Philosophical Review* 101 (1992): 115–189.

Gibbard, A. *Wise Choices, Apt Feelings: A Theory of Normative Judgment.* Cambridge, MA: Harvard University Press, 1990.

Hare, R. M. *Freedom and Reason.* Oxford: Clarendon Press, 1963.

Hare, R. M. *The Language of Morals.* Oxford: Clarendon Press, 1952.

Mackie, J. L. *Ethics: Inventing Right and Wrong.* Harmondsworth, U.K.: Penguin, 1977.

Nowell-Smith, P. *Ethics.* London: Penguin, 1954.

Stevenson, C. L. "The Emotive Meaning of Ethical Terms." In *Facts and Values.* New Haven, CT: Yale University Press, 1963.

Stevenson, C. L. *Ethics and Language.* New Haven, CT: Yale University Press, 1944.

Urmson, J. O. *The Emotive Theory of Ethics.* London: Hutchinson, 1968.

Richard Garner (1996)

NONDESCRIPTIVISM

See *Noncognitivism*

NONEXISTENT OBJECT, NONBEING

We think and talk about things that do not exist—or so it seems. We say that Santa Claus lives on the North Pole and that unicorns are white. We admire Sherlock Holmes or judge him to be more clever than J. Edgar Hoover. People search for the Northwest Passage and the Fountain of Youth. They dream about lottery winnings and fear disasters that do not materialize. A childless couple hopes for a daughter. So, according to Alexius Meinong and others, there are things that do not exist. Even to deny that Santa Claus or the Fountain of Youth exists, we must be able, it seems, to identify what it is whose existence we are denying.

Bertrand Russell's rejection of this line of thought is well known. Sentences containing expressions that appear to denote nonexistents are to be paraphrased, in accordance with his theory of descriptions, with ones that do not. Russell shifted the emphasis from thoughts and other intentional attitudes that appear to have nonexistents as objects to the language in which those thoughts and attitudes are expressed. Many later analytic philosophers shared with Russell a distaste for what they saw as Meinong's bloated universe. Even those who rejected his theory of descriptions often assumed that apparent references to nonexistents can somehow be paraphrased away. But there have been few serious attempts since Russell's to

show how this can be done, and the task has proven to be much more difficult than it once seemed. Since 1970 several very different sophisticated realist theories were developed, some of which claim not that there are nonexistent objects, but that the entities in question exist (Woods, Van Inwagen, Parsons, Routley, Wolterstorff, Thomasson). These have been countered by a new generation of antirealist theories, many of them based on notions of pretense or make-believe (Evans, Walton, Yablo, Kroon; also see Currie).

Many discussions after 1970 have focused especially or primarily on one variety of purported nonexistents: characters and other objects in fiction and mythology. Posits of failed scientific theories (Vulcan, ether, phlogiston), sought after marvels and wished-for children, the golden mountain, the round square, and the present King of France are often treated along the way, although the issues they involve are not entirely analogous to those concerning fictions. Fictions are in some ways especially compelling, and also especially puzzling. We speak easily and elaborately about fictional characters as though they were ordinary people, describing Sherlock Holmes as a detective who lives on Baker Street, speculating about Hamlet's motivations, and recounting the amorous adventures of the various Don Juans. Yet when pressed in certain ways, we readily deny that there are such things as fictions. Parents assure their frightened children that there really are not any goblins or monsters or ghosts like the ones in storybooks, and they confess to having lied about Santa Claus.

LITERALISM

What sorts of things are nonexistents, if there are such? Some take descriptions of Sherlock Holmes as a man and a detective at face value, understanding characters to be people, to possess the same kinds of ordinary properties that real people do, and to differ only in lacking existence. The golden mountain is, literally, golden and a mountain, according to Meinong, and the wished-for child is a child. Such *literalists*, as Kit Fine (1982) calls them, usually accept that, unlike existing objects, most nonexistents are *incomplete* (Holmes neither has a mole on his back nor lacks one) and some are impossible (fictional time travelers, the round square).

Literalism threatens to get out of hand, at least as far as fictions are concerned. Not only do we readily describe Holmes as a person and a detective, we are also prepared to say, in much the same spirit (that is, speaking within the story), that he and other characters exist. Macbeth's dagger may be a mere figment of his imagination, but

Macbeth himself is real; he exists. (We do not, in a comparable spirit, describe the childless couple's wished-for child or the golden mountain as existing.) In general, we are prepared to assert what we take to be true in a story, or *fictional*. It is fictional both that Holmes is a person and that he exists. If Holmes is literally a person, it is awkward to deny that he literally exists. But fictional statements that do not involve fictitious particulars—statements such as "There are ghosts" and "Julius Caesar was warned of the ides of March" understood literally and straightforwardly, obviously may fail to be true. Why should "Holmes is a person," not to mention "Holmes exists," be different?

The most obvious alternative to literalism, in the case of fictions anyway, is to treat statements like "Holmes is a person and a detective" as elliptical, as short for "It is fictional (true in the story) that Holmes is a person and a detective." Of course, we still seem to have an entity on our hands—Holmes. He (or it) is not literally a person or a detective, but he is such that it is fictional that he possesses these attributes. And it is fictional that he exists, which does not have to mean that he literally exists. Holmes may possess other kinds of properties as well, ones that do not consist in something being fictional of him: He is a fictional character, and (on some accounts) was created by Conan Doyle, and is admired by millions of readers. Abandoning literalism in this way removes the embarrassment of an incomplete Holmes, and we need not worry about running into inconsistent fictional objects. Holmes is not such that fictionally he has a mole on his back, nor is he such that fictionally he does not have a mole on his back, even though, it is fictional that he either does or does not have one there. A character may, be such that it is fictional both that she is both *P* and that she is not *P*, but that does not mean that the character *really* does possess incompatible properties.

In an alternative to this strategy, developed by Edward Zalta (1988), Holmes is not a person in the sense that J. Edgar Hoover is; he does not *exemplify* personhood. Unlike Hoover, Holmes exemplifies properties such that of being a fictional character. Holmes bears a different relation, which Zalta calls *encoding*, to personhood, to being a detective, and to the other properties attributed to him in the Sherlock Holmes stories. J. Edgar Hoover, by contrast, is not the kind of thing that encodes properties.

ABSTRACT OBJECT THEORIES

If Holmes is not a person, what is he? What sort of thing is fictionally a person (or encodes personhood)? Realists who are not literalists usually understand fictions to be abstract entities of one sort or another, and to have whatever ontological standing the abstract entities in question do. Some take properties like being a person and a detective to *constitute* (rather than characterize) fictions, and so identify Holmes with the class of properties or conjunction of properties attributed to him in the stories. Some construe fictions as abstractions of other sorts: "theoretical entities of literary discourse" (Van Inwagen 1977), "kinds" (Wolterstorff), or "abstract artifacts" (Thomasson 1999). Zalta (1988) has fictions exemplifying abstractness. Different abstract-object theories give different answers to a battery of tricky questions about the identity and individuation of fictions and other nonexistents or nonactuals. Are they Platonic entities that *are* (some even say "exist") necessarily and eternally (Parsons 1980), or are they created when, for example, the relevant story is written or when they are thought about (Van Inwagen 1977, Thomasson 1999)? Do they cease to be if the story is destroyed and forgotten? If characters in different unrelated stories happen to have exactly the same characteristics attributed to them, are they identical? Are undifferentiated characters in a single fiction distinct from one another (the individual sheep in a fictional flock, for instance if nothing is said about any of them apart from the others)? Can the same character appear in more than one story if the characteristics attributed to it in each of them are not exactly the same? If so, by virtue of what are the characters identical?

The apparent fact that readers admire Holmes, or care about characters in stories, poses an awkward challenge for abstract-object theories. Do readers admire and care about abstract entities, be they properties or classes or theoretical entities or abstract artifacts? This is certainly not how readers themselves think of their experiences. It hardly helps to claim that Holmes is a person in the sense that he "encodes" personhood. He belongs to an ontological category fundamentally different from that of the usual objects of admiration—Mahatma Ghandi, Abraham Lincoln—which *exemplify* personhood and do not encode any properties at all.

The antiliteralist might deny that people do, literally, admire or care about Holmes or Willy Loman or Desdemona, just as he denies that it is literally true that they are persons (or that they exemplify personhood). But then what *is* the reader's relation to them? Does the reader *imagine* admiring or caring about these abstractions, or is it true in an extended fiction that he admires them? Does the reader imagine of an abstract object that it is a person, one that he admires and cares about? That would be quite an imaginative feat!

Similar worries arise simply with the notion of fictionality and infect purported nonexistents of other kinds, as well as fictions. Fictional propositions are commonly characterized as propositions that appreciators or readers are to imagine, or ones that works of fiction invite them to imagine. If it is fictional that Holmes is a person, readers are to imagine of this abstract object that it is a person (or to imagine of something that encodes personhood that it exemplifies personhood instead). To imagine this would be to imagine a blatant impossibility. If a wished-for daughter is not actually a daughter or a person but an abstract entity, does the childless couple wish, futilely, of this abstraction, that it is a daughter and a person?

PRETENSE THEORIES

Pretense or make-believe theories return to a more intuitive understanding of statements like "Holmes is a detective," without embracing literalism. The speaker pretends to refer to an ordinary existing person and to attribute to him, in the ordinary way, the ordinary property of being a detective. *Within the scope of the pretense,* everything is normal. Yet nothing is actually referred to, and what is said, understood literally, is not true. This is pretense, yet with a serious purpose. The speaker does actually assert something by engaging in the pretense, very likely something about the Sherlock Holmes stories. Pretense theorists need to give some account of what is asserted, though it may be asking too much to expect an exact literal paraphrase. Part of the point of speaking in pretense to make a serious assertion may be to express something that is difficult or impossible to express literally (Yablo 1998).

Some philosophers find pretense accounts of "Holmes is a detective," "Hamlet hesitated," and the like plausible, but draw a sharp line between these statements and statements such as "Holmes is a fictional character" and "Holmes is smarter than any real detective." In the Sherlock Holmes stories it is presumably fictional that Holmes is a detective; readers are to imagine that this is so. In saying "Holmes is a detective," speakers are playing along with the fiction, pretending to assert of a person they refer to as "Holmes" that he is a detective. But it is not fictional in the stories that Holmes is a fictional character. So, it is claimed, to say "Holmes is a fictional character" is not to play along with the fiction; the speaker must really be referring to something by means of "Holmes," not just pretending to, and attributing to the thing referred to the property of being a fictional character.

This line is not a sharp one, however, and in any case, it is not to be drawn in the place indicated. People often speak with tongue more or less evidently in cheek when what they are expressing is not fictional in an established work of fiction, not what a recognized work of fiction prescribes or invites them to imagine. We play along with established fictions in special or unusual or unauthorized ways, altering or extending them in various directions, in order to make serious points by engaging in pretense. Sometimes we improvise new fictions. The commentator who remarks that the Hardy Boys, still living at home and attending Bayport High, have turned 75, and that their publisher now equips them with cell phones, is speaking in pretense, although what he pretends to assert is not fictional in any of the stories or the series as a whole. He is, in effect, observing that the Hardy Boys stories have been published for 75 years, and that it is fictional in some of them that the brothers use cell phones. In explaining the tenets of a discredited scientific theory, we may convert it into a fiction, speaking as though we accept it as true. An example: "Vulcan is a planet in our solar system between Uranus and Neptune."

Pretense theorists propose to understand other kinds of apparent references to fictional objects and nonexistents as merely pretended, or at least as less than straightforwardly literal. Evaluating such proposals is not easy. Apparent references to wished-for children, failed scientific posits, and claims of existence and nonexistence often lack any apparent tongue-in-cheek flavor. But pretending, like other psychological states and processes, need not be explicit, conscious, or open to introspection. That people are engaging in pretense may be the conclusion of inferences to the best explanation. Moreover, there is room for adjusting or refining the notion of pretense, or replacing it with something weaker. Some pretense theorists prefer to characterize speakers as merely *making as if* referring to something.

In the end, what matters is the success of one or another variant of the pretense theory as a whole and how it compares to its competitors.

See also Existence; Fictionalism; Meinong, Alexius; Realism; Russell, Bertrand Arthur William.

Bibliography

Azzouni, Jody. *Deflating Existential Consequence: A Case for Nominalism.* Oxford, U.K.: Oxford University Press, 2004.

Currie, Gregory. *The Nature of Fiction.* Cambridge, U.K.: Cambridge University Press, 1990.

Donnellan, Keith. "Speaking of Nothing." *Philosophical Review* 83 (1974): 3–31.

Evans, Gareth. *The Varieties of Reference*. Oxford, U.K.: Oxford University Press, 1982.

Everett, Anthony, and Hofweber, Thomas, eds. *Empty Names, Fiction, and the Puzzles of Non-existence*. Stanford, CA: CSLI Publications, 2000.

Fine, Kit. "The Problem of Non-existence. I: Internalism." *Topoi* 1 (1982): 97–140.

Howell, Robert. "Fictional Objects: How They Are and How They Aren't." *Poetics* 8 (1979): 129–177.

Ingarden, Roman. *The Literary Work of Art: An Investigation on the Borderlines of Ontology, Logic, and Theory of Literature*. Translated by George G. Grabowicz. Evanston, IL: Northwestern University Press, 1973.

Kroon, Fred. "Belief about Nothing in Particular." In *Fictionalist Approaches to Metaphysics*, edited by Mark E. Kalderon. Oxford, U.K.: Oxford University Press, 2005.

Meinong, Alexius. "The Theory of Objects." In *Realism and the Background of Phenomenology*, edited by Roderick Chisholm. New York: Free Press, 1960.

Parsons, Terrance. *Non-existent Objects*. New Haven, CT: Yale University Press, 1980.

Quine, W. V. O. "On What There Is." In his *From a Logical Point of View*. New York: Harper, 1953.

Récanati, François. *Oratio Obliqua, Oratio Recta: An Essay on Metarepresentation*. Cambridge, MA: MIT Press, 2000.

Routley, Richard. *Exploring Meinong's Jungle and Beyond: An Investigation of Noneism and the Theory of Items*. Canberra, Australia: Research School of Social Sciences, Australian National University, 1980.

Russell, Bertrand. "On Denoting." *Mind*, n.s. 14 (1905): 479–493.

Thomasson, Amie L. *Fiction and Metaphysics*. Cambridge, U.K.: Cambridge University Press, 1999.

Van Inwagen, Peter. "Creatures of Fiction." *American Philosophical Quarterly* 14 (1977): 299–308.

Voltolini, Alberto, ed. *Do Ficta Follow Fiction?* Special issue, *Dialectica* 57 (2003).

Walton, Kendall. *Mimesis as Make-Believe: On the Foundations of the Representational Arts*. Cambridge, MA: Harvard University Press, 1990.

Wolterstorff, Nicholas. *Works and Worlds of Art*. Oxford, U.K.: Clarendon Press, 1980.

Woods John. *The Logic of Fiction: A Philosophical Sounding of Deviant Logic*. The Hague: Mouton, 1974.

Yablo, Stephen. "Does Ontology Rest on a Mistake?" *Proceedings of the Aristotelian Society*, supp. vol. 72 (1998): 229–263.

Zalta, Edward N. *Intensional Logic and the Metaphysics of Intentionality*. Cambridge, MA: MIT Press, 1988.

Kendall L. Walton (1996, 2005)

NON-LOCALITY

LOCAL PHYSICAL MAGNITUDES

Non-locality, as the term suggests, is best approached via the notion of locality. As it will be seen, the notion of locality as it appears in physics has several components, but the foundational component is that of a local state in space-time. If one conceives of space-time as a four-dimensional (or eleven- or twenty-six-dimensional) manifold, one can think of covering the manifold with overlapping open neighborhoods, such that every point is contained within at least one neighborhood. One can also imagine indefinitely shrinking the size of the neighborhoods and indefinitely increasing their number. For any particular neighborhood, the intuitive notion of a neighborhood-local state is a physical state that depends only on what is inside the neighborhood. To get a more formal handle on this, a necessary condition for a neighborhood-local state is that the values of quantities for such a state put no constraints on the values of neighborhood-local states for any nonoverlapping neighborhoods. By this criterion, familiar physical properties, like the locations and velocities of particles or the values of electric fields, are neighborhood-local, while global physical properties, like the total charge of the universe, are not. (It is tempting to try to take this notion to the limit, where the neighborhoods become punctate, but this leads to many technical problems that are unrelated to the basic notion.)

Classical physics has many neighborhood-local quantities: for example, mass and charge densities, field strengths, velocities and accelerations, and the relativistic space-time metric. Anything represented by a tensor in a classical theory will be, by this account, neighborhood-local. Indeed, in classical physics it appears that all non-neighborhood-local quantities, such as the total charge of the universe, are functions of the neighborhood-local ones in the following sense: Cover the space-time manifold with open neighborhoods in any way one likes and specify the neighborhood-local quantities in each neighborhood and the neighborhood-local quantities in all intersections of neighborhoods, and one will thereby fix the value of the global quantities. Given the charge in every little patch, and in the intersections of all the little patches, the total charge of the universe follows.

Physics textbooks do not typically present the notion of neighborhood-locality in this way: They rather get at it via an account of coordinatizing the manifold. Rather than demanding a single, global coordinate system that completely covers a manifold (which in many cases will not exist), one is rather required only to break up the manifold into overlapping neighborhoods (each of which is topologically simple) and to coordinatize each neighborhood. The coordinatization of each neighborhood is called a chart, and a collection of charts for neighborhoods that cover the manifold is called an atlas. In addition, one is required to specify how the coordinates assigned to a point in one chart are related to the coordinates assigned by any other chart in which the point occurs. That is, one is required to specify how the different coordinate systems relate to one another where they overlap. The assumption that all the physics is ultimately neighborhood-local is then essentially the supposition that physical states can be assigned to each charted neighborhood such that the total physical state of the universe is determined by the information in the atlas. One can say that in such a case the total physics is neighborhood-local.

The neighborhood-locality of physics accepts the physical reality of many global properties, such as the total charge. It also accepts the physical reality of more subtle global properties. Consider, for example, a cylinder and a Möbius strip. In a certain sense, a cylinder and a Möbius strip can be made to match locally: each can be divided into overlapping neighborhoods such that every neighborhood of the Möbius strip is exactly like the corresponding neighborhood of the cylinder. In this sense, the twist in the Möbius strip is not located anywhere in particular: it is a global rather than local feature of the space. Nonetheless, one could tell from an atlas whether one was dealing with a cylinder or a Möbius strip. Begin, for example, by drawing an F on one chart. The chart contains enough information to determine how the F could move rigidly in the neighborhood covered by the chart. So one could move it into a region that overlaps another chart, and the functions relating the chart would show how the F shows up in the new region. Continuing in this way, one could determine from the information in the atlas what the result of any rigid motion of the F would be. On a Möbius strip, some such motion will bring the F back to the original neighborhood mirror-reflected, while on a cylinder this can never happen.

The notion of neighborhood-locality is therefore quite broad: all of classical physics and relativity theory (both special and general) count as neighborhood-local in this way. One's commonsense picture of the world is also neighborhood-local. Albert Einstein powerfully expressed the notion of neighborhood-locality this way:

> It is … characteristic of … physical objects that they are thought of as arranged in a space-time continuum. An essential aspect of this arrangement of things in physics is that they lay claim, at a certain time, to an existence independent of one another, provided these objects "are situated in different parts of space." Unless one makes

this kind of assumption about the existence (the "being-thus") of objects which are far apart from one another in space—which stems in the first place from everyday thinking—physical thinking in the familiar sense would not be possible. … This principle has been carried to extremes in the field theory by localizing the elementary objects on which it is based and which exist independently of each other, as well as the elementary laws which have been postulated for it, in the infinitely small (four-dimensional) elements of space.

(IN BORN 1971, P. 170)

If one reads "situated in different parts of space" as "situated in nonoverlapping neighborhoods," and understands the "existence (the being-thus)" as the demand that the physical state defined on one neighborhood puts no constraint on the physical state in a nonoverlapping neighborhood, one sees that Einstein is expressing the same idea.

Suppose that physics is neighborhood-local in the sense that the physical information provided in any atlas is complete (determines all the physical properties of the universe). This appears to be a mild constraint, seeing as it takes in all of classical physics and relativity. It is hard to see, in fact, how the postulate of neighborhood locality puts any real empirical constraint on a theory: Could not any set of phenomena be accounted for by a neighborhood-local physics? As it will be seen, this is correct: To get an empirical constraint one will have to add on to neighborhood-locality in this sense. However, the postulate of neighborhood-locality does do something: It implies that, for any region in space-time, there is something that counts as the physical state of that region. Recall the twin requirements: The physical state in any neighborhood should not put any constraints on the physical state in a nonoverlapping neighborhood and the totality of physical states in an atlas (including appropriate information about overlapping charts) should determine the total physical state of the universe. Meeting these requirements demands that many well-defined quantities cannot count as local. For example, although the center of mass of the solar system is, one may suppose, always located at some particular point in space, it does not count as a part of the local physical state of that space. For taking a small neighborhood that contains that point, one cannot specify that the center of mass of the solar system occupies that point without thereby constraining the physical state of the nonoverlapping neighborhoods that contain the sun and planets.

If the requirement of neighborhood-locality is so mild, why was Einstein concerned with it? Because, taken at face value, the quantum theory rejects neighborhood-locality. Consider a pair of particles in the singlet state

$$1/\sqrt{2}|x\text{–up}\rangle_R|x\text{–down}\rangle_L - 1/\sqrt{2}|x\text{–down}\rangle_R|x\text{–up}\rangle_L$$

where the particle on the right and the particle on the left are far apart, in different regions of space. Then one's atlas could contain a neighborhood that includes particle R but not particle L, and a nonoverlapping neighborhood that contains L but not R. And the requirement of neighborhood-locality would then demand the existence of some physical state that can be assigned to (the neighborhood containing) R that puts no constraint on the state of L, and a state that can be assigned to L that puts no constraint on the state of R, such that from these two local states the singlet state for the pair can be recovered.

The singlet state itself cannot be used for this purpose: It makes reference to both particles and requires for its existence the existence of both particles. There is a well-defined state that quantum mechanics associates with particle R alone: It is called the reduced state for R from the singlet state. The reduced state supplies enough information to make quantum-mechanical (probabilistic) predictions for the result of any experiment carried out on R alone. There is a similar reduced state for L. These states are, mathematically speaking, mixed quantum mechanical states.

Why, then, can one not take the reduced state for R to be its neighborhood-local state, and the reduced state for L to be its neighborhood-local state, and do the physics using these? The reason is because different joint quantum mechanical states for the pair of particles give rise to exactly the same pair of reduced states for R and L, and these different joint states make different predictions for some measurements that involve both particles. For example, the singlet state is mathematically distinct from the m = 0 triplet state

$$1/\sqrt{2}|x\text{–up}\rangle_R|x\text{–up}\rangle_L + 1/\sqrt{2}|x\text{–down}\rangle_R|x\text{–down}\rangle_L.$$

Furthermore, the m = 0 triplet state makes different predictions for the pair: If one measures the spin of both particles in the x-direction, the singlet state predicts that the outcomes on the two sides will be different, while the m = 0 triplet state predicts they will come out the same. Even so, the reduced states for R and L that can be derived from these are identical (they both predict a 50 percent chance for the measurement of x-spin to be up). So one cannot use the joint state as a neighborhood-local state,

and one cannot use the reduced states as neighborhood-local states (and recover the full physical state of the pair from the atlas), and quantum mechanics provides no other states one can use.

What Einstein saw was that quantum mechanics is not neighborhood-local on account of the entanglement of states for spatially separated systems. And since Einstein thought that physics must be neighborhood-local, he thought quantum mechanics must not be giving one a complete account of the physical states of things.

NON-LOCALITY AND EXPERIMENT

So far, all one has is a remark about the formalism of quantum mechanics, not about the empirical predictions of quantum mechanics. However, Einstein saw that the peculiar entanglement of quantum-mechanical states forced another kind of non-locality on the standard quantum mechanical accounts of experiments.

Consider a pair of separated particles in the singlet state. Given only that state, the quantum formalism permits no definite predictions about the outcome of an x-spin measurement on either side: For each individual particle, quantum mechanics assigns a 50 percent probability for each possible outcome. If the quantum description is complete and leaves no physical facts about the particle out of account, then these probabilities must reflect objective indeterminacy in nature: Nothing in the universe determines which outcome will occur. Nonetheless, as Einstein saw, quantum theory does make a perfectly definite prediction: Whatever the outcome of the experiments on the two particles, the results for the pair will be opposite—one will yield x-spin up and the other x-spin down (in the m = 0 triplet state, the results are instead guaranteed to be the same). So the question is: If nothing in the whole universe determines what the result of measuring the particle on the right will be, and if the particle on the left can be arbitrarily far away, what could possibly ensure that the outcome on the left will be the opposite of that on the right?

In the standard quantum formalism, this correlation between the outcomes is secured by the collapse of the wave function: when the particle on the right displays, for example, x-spin up, then the overall quantum state for the pair suddenly changes from $1/\sqrt{2}|x\text{–up}\rangle_R|x\text{–down}\rangle_L - 1/\sqrt{2}|x\text{–down}\rangle_R|x\text{–up}\rangle_L$ to $|x\text{–up}\rangle_R|x\text{–down}\rangle_L$. Because of the non-locality of the wave function, this change is a change not only in the physical state of particle R but a change in the state of particle L as well. When particle R displays x-spin up, particle L changes from a state of indefinite *x*-spin to a state of definite *x*-spin down. It is by this "spooky action-at-a-distance" that the standard quantum interpretation manages to secure the correlation in spins between distant particles, neither of which is initially in a definite spin state.

There are several ways in which the wave collapse is "spooky." One is that is it unmediated: The measurement on the right influences the state on the left without the aid of any particles or waves traveling between the two sides. However, more important, the collapse is instantaneous: Even if there were mediating particles or waves, they would have to travel faster than light. This last property seems to contradict the theory of relativity. Einstein rejected the quantum theory because of this feature. He saw that, in this particular case, the spooky action-at-a-distance is not required by the empirical phenomena: The perfect correlations can be easily explained in a neighborhood-local physics without resorting to any direct causal connection between the two sides. One need only suppose (as the quantum theory does not) that the results of the spin measurements are predetermined by the local state of each electron and that the electrons are created in states in which they are disposed to give the opposite outcomes to all spin measurements.

Putting Einstein's two requirements together, one can now specify what it is for a theory to be simply local: First, all the fundamental physical properties of the theory should be neighborhood-local, and second, no physical influences in the theory should be allowed to propagate faster than light. (One could also add that causal connections between events should be mediated by continuous processes, but that is not needed for the sequel.) Einstein's argument against quantum theory as complete is that taking it to be complete requires that one treat the physics as non-local, even though the phenomena do not force non-locality on the theory. Einstein thought it perverse to insist that the theory is complete instead of trying to supersede it by a local theory that recovered all the same empirical predictions.

A local theory can be either deterministic or indeterministic. In a deterministic theory, every event is determined by the physical state that precedes it, and in a local deterministic theory, those determining factors cannot be so far away that it would require a superluminal influence for them to have their effect. Putting these together, it follows that in a local deterministic theory, every event is determined by the neighborhood-local state on its past light cone.

In an indeterministic local theory, an event need not be determined by the physical state of its past light cone, but the probability for the event will be. Furthermore, nothing outside the past light cone can have any influence on the event. That is, conditionalizing an event on the state of its past light cone should yield a probability that is screened off from any further information about events at space-like separation. (The probability will not be screened off from events in the future light cone, which can be effects of the event in question.) So positing that a theory is local is not the same as positing that it is deterministic, but it puts definite mathematical constraints on the nature of any local theory, whether deterministic or indeterministic. What Einstein had argued, in the 1935 Einstein, Boris Podolsky, and Nathan Rosen (EPR) paper, was that quantum mechanics is an indeterministic, non-local theory, but the sorts of correlations he discussed admit a deterministic, local explanation. And despite Einstein's oft-cited remarks about God's gambling habits, it was the spooky action-at-a-distance, the non-locality, that was the focus of his criticism in the EPR paper. As it turns out, if one is to recover the perfect EPR correlations with a local theory, it must also be a local deterministic theory (otherwise the correlations will not be perfect), but recovering determinism is not the main issue.

BELL'S THEOREM AND LOCALITY

What Einstein did not realize is that although the perfect correlations he discussed can be recovered by a local theory, the full range of quantum mechanical predictions cannot be recovered by any local theory. This was proven in 1964 by John Bell. Bell demonstrated that the predictions of any local theory, deterministic or indeterministic, must satisfy a certain statistical constraint called Bell's inequality. Furthermore, the predictions of the quantum theory violate that inequality, and the violations have been experimentally confirmed in the laboratory. So the non-locality of quantum theory is not just an artifact of the quantum formalism: It is a physical aspect of nature.

Although in principle a neighborhood-local theory could predict violations of Bell's inequality (by use of neighborhood-local items that travel faster than light), the only presently existing accounts of physical non-locality employ the quantum wave function, which is not a neighborhood-local object. The role of the wave function differs from interpretation to interpretation, but in every case it is the wave function that secures the violation of locality and the superluminal physical connection between the distant particles.

It is a first-order technical problem to reconcile the non-locality of quantum theory with the space-time structure postulated by the theory of relativity. The simplest way to construct a non-local theory is to add a pre-ferred foliation of space-time to the relativistic picture, thereby violating the spirit of relativistic physics. Such a foliation also allows for a straightforward causal account of the phenomena: Intraction with one of the particles is the cause of a change of behavior in the other. It is, how-ever, feasible (although quite tricky) to construct theories that achieve non-locality but employ only the relativistic space-time structure. In these cases, it appears that stan-dard causal locutions cannot the recovered: there is a real physical connection between space-like separated events, but one cannot identify one of the events particularly as a cause and the other as an effect.

See also Bell, John, and Bell's Theorem; Einstein, Albert; Philosophy of Physics; Quantum Mechanics; Relativity Theory; Space; Time.

Bibliography

Born, M. *The Born-Einstein Letters.* Translated by I. Born. New York: Walker, 1971.

The Collected Papers of Albert Einstein. Vols. 1–6, 8. Translated by Anna Beck. Princeton, NJ: Princeton University Press, 1987–1998.

Einstein, Albert, Boris Podolsky, and Nathan Rosen. "Can Quantum-Mechanical Description of Physical Reality Be Considered Complete?" *Physical Review* 47 (1935): 777–780.

Maudlin, Tim *Quantum Non-locality and Relativity: Metaphysical Intimations of Modern Physics.* Oxford, U.K.: Basil Blackwell, 1994.

Tim Maudlin (2005)

NON-MONOTONIC LOGIC

Modern symbolic logic was developed beginning in the latter part of the nineteenth century for the purpose of formalizing mathematical reasoning, in particular that process by which mathematicians arrive at conclusions on the basis of a small number of distinct basic princi-ples. This kind of reasoning is characterized by a particu-lar type of cogency: The conclusions are not merely *probable* or *plausible* on the basis of whatever evidential support the basic principles might provide, but *certain* and *indubitable*. In particular mathematical reasoning enjoys a property referred to as *monotonicity* by modern logicians: if a conclusion follows from given premises *A*, *B*, *C*, … then it also follows from any larger set of prem-ises, as long as the original premises *A*, *B*, *C*, …are included.

By contrast in many instances of ordinary or every-day reasoning, people arrive at conclusions only tenta-tively, based on partial or incomplete information, reserving the right to retract those conclusions should they learn new facts. Such reasoning is often called defea-sible or non-monotonic, precisely because the set of accepted conclusions can become smaller when the set of premises is expanded.

Taxonomies provide a rich source of examples of defeasible reasoning (but they are not by any means the only source). Suppose for instance that you are told that Stellaluna is a mammal. It is then natural to infer that Stellaluna does not fly, because mammals by and large are not capable of flight. But upon learning that Stellaluna is a bat, such a conclusion is retracted in favor of its oppo-site. In turn even the new conclusion can be retracted upon learning that Stellaluna is a baby bat and so on, in complex retraction patterns that seem to cry out for sys-tematization.

The aim of non-monotonic logic is precisely that of providing such a systematization. There is, in fact, no one thing which is called "non-monotonic logic," but rather a family of different formalisms, with different mathemat-ical properties and degrees of material adequacy, that aim to capture and represent such patterns of defeasible rea-soning.

A broad class of non-monotonic formalisms can be characterized as "consistency-based" approaches. The name is derived from the fact that while all non-monotonic formalisms deal with conflicts between new facts and tentative conclusions in the same way (the facts win and the conclusions are retracted), some of these for-malisms also allow for potential conflicts between the tentative conclusions themselves (and then they might differ as to the way this second kind of conflicts are han-dled).

Non-monotonic inheritance networks provide a consistency-based formalism developed for the purpose of representing taxonomies. A non-monotonic inheri-tance network is a collection of nodes (each associated with a particular taxonomic category) and directed links between nodes, representing the subsumption relation between categories. Suppose for instance that you are told by a reliable (but fallible) source that Nixon is both a Quaker and a Republican, and that while Quakers by and large are pacifists, Republicans are not. The network cor-responding to this situation is given below:

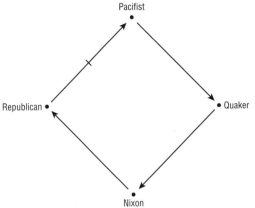

Obviously here we have a conflict between the two potential conclusions that Nixon both is and is not a pacifist. Steps need to be taken to maintain consistency. We will not go into detail here, but in general one can take a *credulous* approach and endorse one or the other conclusion, or one can take a *skeptical approach* and in the presence of conflict refrain from endorsing either conclusion.

Sometimes, special considerations such as *specificity* can be brought to bear on the resolution of conflicts in other inheritance networks. In the Stellaluna example above for instance one wants to conclude that bats fly (because information about bats is more specific than information about mammals) but that Stellaluna does not (because information about baby bats is more specific than information about bats). A network representing the situation is given below:

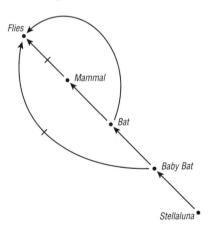

Inheritance networks are not well suited to deal with complex information (e.g., disjunctive or conjunctive statements). For this reason a more expressive formalism, *default logic* was developed. The basic representation formalism of default logic is the *default inference rule*, a rule of the form $A : B / C$, whose intended interpretation is that if A is known, and we have no reason to reject B (i.e., B is *consistent* with our knowledge base), then we can conclude C. Default logic provides a way for the consistency condition to be satisfied both *before* and *after* the default rule is applied.

Among the approaches to non-monotonic logic that are not consistency based, one needs to mention *circumscription*, which is based on the idea that many instances of defeasible reasoning have to do with the *minimization* of certain predicates, particularly those representing the set of *exceptions* to a given generalization. Circumscription uses the expressive power of second-order logic to ensure that any generalization has as few exceptions as possible. So, for instance, in the absence of information to the effect that bats are exceptional mammals, one would conclude that they do not fly, but when that information is adjoined to our knowledge base, circumscription immediately accounts for the exception.

See also Computationalism; Logic, History of: Modern Logic; Mathematics, Foundations of.

Bibliography

Antonelli, Aldo. " Non-monotonic Logic." In *The Stanford Encyclopedia of Philosophy*, edited by Edward N. Zalta. Available from http://plato.stanford.edu/archives/sum2003/entries/logic-nonmonotonic/.

Antonelli, Aldo. " Logic." In *The Blackwell Guide to the Philosophy of Computing and Information*, 263–275. Blackwell, 2004.

Gabbay, Dov, Christopher Hogger, and John Alan Robinson, eds. *Handbook of Logic in Artificial Intelligence and Logic Programming*. Vol. 3. New York: Oxford University Press, 1994.

Ginsberg, Matthew, ed. *Readings in Nonmonotonic Reasoning*. Los Altos, CA: Morgan Kauffman, 1987.

G. Aldo Antonelli (2005)

NONNATURALISM

See *Ethics, History of; Ethics, Problems of; Moore, George Edward*

NONREDUCTIVE PHYSICALISM

Beginning the 1960s Hilary Putnam, Jerry Fodor, and Richard Boyd, among others, developed a type of materialism that denies reductionist claims. In this view, explanations, natural kinds, and properties in psychology do not reduce to counterparts in more basic sciences, such as neurophysiology or physics (Putnam 1967, 1974; Fodor 1974; Boyd 1980a). Nevertheless, all token psychological entities—states, processes, and faculties—are either identical with (Fodor 1974) or just wholly constituted of (Boyd 1980a) physical entities, ultimately out of token entities over which microphysics quantifies. This view was soon widely endorsed and since then has persisted as an attractive alternative to reductionist and eliminativist forms of materialism. Reductionists, notably Jaegwon Kim, have raised a series of serious objections to this position, to which nonreductivists have responded, thereby developing the view more thoroughly.

IRREDUCIBILITY, MULTIPLE REALIZABILITY, AND EXPLANATION

In his early argument for nonreductive materialism, Putnam adduces the phenomenon of multiple realizability as its main justification (Putnam 1967). Kinds or types of mental states can be realized by many kinds of neurophysiological states, and perhaps by many kinds of non-neurophysiological states, and for this reason they do not reduce to kinds of neurophysiological states. Multiple realizability also has a key role in Fodor's more general argument against reductionism in the special sciences (Fodor 1974). Consider a law in some special science:

$$S_1 x \text{ causes } S_2 x$$

where S_1 and S_2 are natural kind-predicates in that science. A standard model for reduction requires that every kind featured in this law be identified with a kind in the reducing science, by way of bridge principles. Bridge principles might translate kind-predicates in one science into those of a more basic one, or they might specify a metaphysical relation, such as *being identical with* or *being a necessary and sufficient condition for*, between the kinds of one science and those of the reducing science. But in some cases, Fodor contends, the sort of bridge principle required for reducibility will not be available. If kinds in psychology, for instance, are multiply realizable in an indefinite variety of ways at the neurophysiological level, purported bridge principles for relating psychological to neurophysiological kinds will involve open-ended disjunctions. These purported bridge principles will be of the form:

$$P_1 = N_1 \text{ v } N_2 \text{ v } N_3 \dots$$

which states that a certain psychological state, P_1, is identical with an open-ended disjunction of neurophysiological states, N_1 v N_2 v $N_3 \dots$, or

$$P_1 \leftrightarrow N_1 \text{ v } N_2 \text{ v } N_3 \dots$$

which states that a certain psychological state is necessary and sufficient for an open-ended disjunction of neurophysiological states. Fodor argues that because open-ended disjunctions of kinds in neurophysiology are not natural neurophysiological kinds, psychological kinds cannot be reduced to neurophysiological kinds. Fodor's reason for denying that such disjunctions are not natural kinds is that they cannot appear in laws, and they cannot appear in laws because "laws" involving such disjunctions are not explanatory. Such "laws" are not explanatory because they do not satisfy our interests in explanation. Fodor's argument for irreducibility, then, appeals to the fact that purported explanations for psychological phenomena are unsatisfying when couched in terms of open-ended disjunctions.

One reductionist reply is that these open-ended disjunctions nevertheless constitute genuine laws and explanations, even if they fail to meet certain subjective requirements. If only we were capable of taking in more information at once, we wouldn't have any trouble regarding open-ended disjunctive "laws" as genuine laws (Jaworski 2002). That people fail to find laws satisfying when they contain open-ended disjunctions may simply show a failing on our part, rather than a failing of the putative laws. This standard argument for nonreductive materialism appears to rely on a certain formal prescription for laws and explanations—that they cannot contain disjunctive properties, or at least not wildly disjunctive properties.

But even if the formal argument fails, multiple realizability can still sustain an important component of nonreductive materialism. In general, whether or not a property is multiply realizable can indicate the level at which it should be classified. Is the kind *corkscrew* a kind of steel thing? No, for it also has a possible aluminum realization. Is the kind *believing that cats are nearby* a neural kind of thing? If mental states are also realizable in silicon, then no. Multiple realizability might then provide the key to precluding classification of mental states as essentially neural, or as essentially classified at some lower level yet.

Kim argues that multiple realizability might fail to undermine reductionism for a different reason. He contends that a higher-level property is precisely as projectible as the disjunction that expresses its multiply realizable character at a more basic level, and thus a generalization involving such disjunctive properties is just as lawlike as the higher-level generalization that it was meant to reduce (Kim 1992). The reason is that a higher-level property is nomically equivalent to such a disjunctive property. Nomic equivalence might be defined in this way: properties F and G are nomically equivalent if they are coextensive in all possible worlds compatible with the laws of nature. If Kim is right, then Fodor's formal argument does not appear to be sound, for it relies on the possibility that generalizations involving a higher-level property be lawlike whereas those involving the corresponding disjunctive property are not. But furthermore, Kim contends that wildly disjunctive properties are not projectible, and hence higher-level properties that are nomically equivalent to such properties are not projectible either. As a result, such higher-level properties cannot figure into laws, and they are not genuinely scientific kinds.

The example of a disjunctive property Kim adduces to make his point is *being jade*. "Jade" is a category that comprises two mineralogical kinds, *jadeite* and *nephrite*, and hence *being jade* is the same property as *being either jadeite or nephrite*. As a result, *being jade* will not be projectible. But in reply, *being jade* might turn out to be projectible despite its underlying complexity. Ned Block points out that all samples of jade share certain appearance properties, similarities that give rise to a certain degree of projectibility (Block 1997). More generally, properties that are multiply realizable can yet be projectible with respect to properties of selection, learning, and design. Because there are typically only a few ways in which entities of a particular higher-level type can be designed and produced, one can expect relatively broad similarities among these things that would render corresponding higher-level properties significantly projectible (Antony and Levine 1997).

Thus the heterogeneity of the possible realizations of a property is compatible with their having significant features in common, features that will sustain the projectibility of the property to some degree or other. This point is consistent with Kim's claim that a higher-level property is precisely as projectible as the disjunctive property that comprises all of its possible realizations. One should not conclude from the heterogeneity of the possible realizations of a higher-level property that there is no feature that can undergird its projectibility—in fact, of both the higher-level property and of the disjunctive property that comprises all of its possible realizations. Indeed, the projectibility-sustaining feature of a kind could be a characteristic that is significantly homogeneous across its heterogeneous realizations, one that

might instantiate a unitary causal power at the level of description of the kind (Pereboom 2002).

FUNCTIONALISM AND MENTAL CAUSATION

By way of objecting to Kim's reductionism, Block asks: "What is common to the pains of dogs and people (and all other species) in virtue of which they are pains?" (Block 1980, pp. 178–179). In reply to this concern, Kim points out that nonreductive materialists typically argue from a functionalist perspective, and that functionalists characterize mental states solely in terms of purely relational features of those states. Functionalism identifies mental state types with type-level dispositions to cause mental states and behavioral outputs given perceptual inputs and mental states—with the understanding that these dispositions are purely relational: that they are to be analyzed in terms of causal relations to perceptual inputs, behavioral outputs, and other mental states, and no intrinsic mental components. Functionalists claim that what all pains would have in common, by virtue of which they are all pains, is a pattern of such relations described by some functional specification. Kim then argues that in providing an answer to Block's question, the local reductionist—the one who opts for species- or structure-specific reductionism—is no worse off than the functionalist. Both are committed to the claim that there is no nonrelational or intrinsic property of pain that all pains have in common, and both can specify only shared relational properties (Kim 1992).

Kim implies that a functional specification does not provide a genuinely satisfactory answer to Block's question (Kim 1999). On the nonreductive view, if M is a mental property and B is its neural or microphysical base, then realizers for M can be found in B (at the level of B). This position allows that nondisjunctive realizing properties might be found in B for individual species- or structure-types—as long as there is no well-behaved (not wildly disjunctive) property in B that realizes every possible instance of M. The nonreductive materialist claims that none of this entails a genuine reduction of M to properties in B. As Kim assumes, the standard strategy for preserving M as meeting these specifications is to envision M as a functional mental property. But in Kim's view, the problem with the functionalist picture is that the causal powers of any instance of M will be causal powers in the physical base—they will not, at the token level, be irreducibly mental causal powers (Kim 1992, Block 1990). Hence functionalism cannot preserve the view that there exist causal powers that are in the last analysis irreducibly mental, and it is thus incompatible with a genuinely robust nonreductive materialism about the mental. Furthermore, Kim points out that given the genuine multiple realizability of the property M, the causal powers of the realizers of M in B will exhibit significant causal and nomological diversity, and for this reason the causal powers of M will exhibit such diversity. Thus, in his estimation, M will be unfit to figure in laws, and is thereby disqualified as a useful scientific property. He concludes that the functionalist model cannot protect m as a property with a role in scientific laws and explanations.

However, there is available a nonfunctionalist account of these higher-level powers that nevertheless remains nonreductive (Pereboom 1991, 2002). Functionalists typically maintain that the causal powers that have a role in explaining the dispositional features of mental states are nondispositional properties of their realization bases. For example, many suppose that nondispositional neural properties, which instantiate neural causal powers, would serve to explain why being pinched causes wincing behavior. But if these causal powers are all nonmental, a robust sort of nonreductive materialist account of the mental is precluded, for then none of the causal powers would be essentially mental themselves. By contrast, the nonreductivist might endorse intrinsic mental properties that instantiate specifically mental causal powers (Pereboom 1991, 2002; Van Gulick 1993). Such a view would be incompatible with functionalism. It need not deny that there exist functional mental properties, or, more generally, relational properties of mental states, but it would endorse nonfunctional mental properties that, by virtue of the causal powers they instantiate, play an important part in explaining dispositional features of mental state types.

Consider the example of a ball piston engine, the most recent version of the rotary internal combustion engine, which has a specific internal structural configuration. Characteristic of this engine is its having parts with particular shapes and rigidities, and these parts must be arranged in a particular way. These features are manifestly not functional relations that such an engine stands in; rather, they constitute intrinsic characteristics of this type of engine. At the same time, these characteristics are multiply realizable. The parts of the engine can be made of material of different sorts—as long as the material can yield, for example, the required shapes and rigidities. The ball piston engine, then, has nonfunctionalist intrinsic structural properties that instantiate its causal powers, but nevertheless admit distinct realizations.

Similarly, it might be that the heterogeneous physical realizations of the dog's and the human's belief *that cats are nearby* exhibit a structure of a single type that is intrinsic to this kind of mental state, a structure that instantiates the causal powers of this belief. This structure may be more abstract than any specific sort of neural structure, given that it can be realized in distinct sorts of neural systems (Boyd 1999). Perhaps this same structure can be realized in a silicon-based electronic system, and such a system could then also have the belief. Imagine a silicon system that replicates the capacities of and interconnections among neurons in a human brain as closely as possible, and suppose this system is excited to mimic as nearly as possible what happens when a human being has this belief about cats. It is possible that this silicon state would realize the same belief, and have a structure that, conceived at a certain level of abstraction, is similar enough to the structure of the ordinary neural system for both to count as examples of the same type of structure. In this case and more generally, one does not seem forced to retreat to mere functional resemblance prior to investigating whether the relevant similarities extend to intrinsic properties.

EXPLANATORY EXCLUSION

According to nonreductive materialism, an event such as Jerry's feeding the cat (M2) will have a psychological explanation in terms of a complex of mental states—beliefs and desires he has (M1). Each of M1 and M2 will be wholly constituted of microphysical events (P1 and P2 respectively), and there will be a microphysical explanation of P2 in terms of P1. The explanation of M2 by M1 will not reduce to the explanation of P2 by P1. Underlying the irreducibility of this explanation is that M1 is not type-identical with P1, and that M2 is not type-identical with P2.

This picture gives rise to a pressing question: What is the relationship between the microphysical and psychological explanations for M2? In particular, given that both sorts of explanation refer to causal powers, what is the relationship between the causal powers to which the microphysical explanation appeals and those to which the psychological explanation appeals? Here is where Kim's challenge from causal or explanatory exclusion enters in (Kim 1987, 1998). If a microphysical account yields a causal explanation of the microphysical constitution of M2, then it will also provide a causal explanation of M2 itself. How might there also be a distinct psychological causal explanation of this action? Kim argues that it is implausible that the psychological explanation appeals to causal powers sufficient for the event to occur, and at the same time the microphysical explanation appeals to distinct causal powers also sufficient for the event to occur, as a result of which the event is overdetermined. It is also implausible that each of these distinct sets of causal powers yields a partial cause of the event, and that each by itself would be insufficient for the event to occur.

By the solution to this problem that Kim develops, real causal powers exist at the microphysical level, and so the microphysical explanations refer to real microphysical causal powers. Only if psychological explanations in some sense reduce to microphysical explanations does it turn out that the psychological explanations also appeal to real causal powers—these causal powers will then ultimately be microphysical. Psychological explanations that do not reduce to microphysical explanations will fail to refer to causal powers, and thus will have some diminished status—such explanations might express regularities without at the same time referring to causal powers. This strategy solves the exclusion problem because if the causal powers to which the psychological explanation appeals are identical with those to which the microphysical explanation appeals, then there will be no genuine competition between explanations, and if the psychological explanations do not refer to causal powers at all, there will be no competition either. However, this solution, which Kim believes is the only possible solution to the problem he raises, would rule out any nonreductive view about mental causal powers.

Various proposals have been advanced in the name of nonreductive materialism according to which mental properties are causally relevant or causally explanatory, without being causally efficacious as mental properties. Such views, like Kim's, claim that all causal efficacy is nonmental (for example, Jackson and Pettit 1990). As Kim points out, these proposals do not amount to a robust sort of nonreductive materialism, which would preserve the claim that mental properties, as mental properties, are causally efficacious (Kim 1998).

What sort of response might the advocate of the robust view provide? First, in Kim's conception, any token causal powers of a higher-level property at a time will be identical with some token (micro)physical causal powers. There would be no token causal powers distinct from token microphysical causal powers, and this would preclude any robust nonreductive materialism. Higher-level kinds and explanations would at best group token microphysical causal powers in a way that does not correspond to the classifications of microphysics itself (Kim 1998, Horgan 1997). Such a classification might be of value for

prediction, but there would remain no sense in which there exist causal powers that are not microphysical.

However, is token mental state M identical with P, its actual token microphysical realization base? Suppose that M is realized by a complex neural state N. It is possible for M to be realized differently only in that a few neural pathways are used that are token-distinct from those actually engaged. One need not rule at this point on whether the actual neural realization N is token-identical with this alternative—it might well be. But it is evident that this alternative neural realization is itself realized by a microphysical state P* that is token-distinct from P. It is therefore possible for M to be realized by a microphysical state not identical with P, and thus M is not identical with P. But furthermore, this reflection would also undermine a token-identity claim for mental causal powers—should they exist—and their underlying microphysical causal powers. For supposing that the token microphysical realization of M had been different, its token microphysical causal powers would also have been different. Consequently, there is good reason to suppose that any token mental causal powers of M would not be identical with the token microphysical causal powers of its realization (Boyd 1980a, Pereboom and Kornblith 1991, Pereboom 2002).

On this conception, a token mental state would have the mental causal powers it does ultimately by virtue of the token microphysical states of which it is constituted (setting aside any fundamentally relational causal powers). For this reason it makes sense to say that token mental causal powers are wholly constituted by token microphysical causal powers. More generally, the causal powers of a token of kind F are constituted of the causal powers of a token of kind G just in case the token of kind F has the causal powers it does by virtue of its being constituted of a token of kind G.

And now, just as no competition between explanations arises in the case of reduction and identity, competition also does not arise in the case of mere constitution. For if the token of a higher-level causal power is currently wholly constituted by a complex of microphysical causal powers, there are two sets of causal powers at play that are constituted from precisely the same material (supposing that the most basic microphysical entities are constituted of themselves), and in this sense we might say that these powers *coincide constitutionally*. That they now coincide in this way might give rise to the thought that these causal powers are token-identical, but, as has been shown, there is a substantial argument that they are not. And because it is possible for there to be wholly constitutionally coinciding causal powers that are not even token-identical, it is possible that there be two causal explanations for one event that do not exclude each other and at the same time do not reduce to a single explanation (Pereboom 2002).

If identity and not just constitutional coincidence were necessary for explanatory noncompetition, then there would be features required for noncompetition that identity has and current constitutional coincidence does not. The candidate features would be constitutional coincidence at all other times, and constitutional coincidence at all other possible worlds, even now. But it is difficult to see how the token causal powers' constitutional noncoincidence at some past time, or at some future time, or their merely possible constitutional noncoincidence even now would result in explanatory competition, whereas actual current constitutional coincidence in absence of any features of this sort (i.e., identity) would guarantee noncompetition.

Imagine that a person's current token mental state M actually constitutionally coincides with token microphysical state P. Now assume with Kim that if M were identical with P, and if their causal powers were identical, there would be no explanatory competition. Then if mere constitutional coincidence without identity resulted in explanatory competition, that would have to be because at some time in the past or in the future, or at some other possible world even now, M and P and their causal powers are constitutionally noncoincident. Suppose that M would still exist even if a few neural pathways in its neural realization were token-distinct from what they actually are. These neural changes would render M's microphysical realization base distinct from P, and thus M and P would be constitutionally noncoincident in some other possible world, and, similarly, *mutatis mutandis* (that is, the necessary changes having been made) for their causal powers. How could a possibility of this sort introduce explanatory competition? It would appear that actual current constitutional coincidence alone is relevant to securing noncompetition, and thus for this purpose constitutional coincidence without identity would serve as well as identity. Consequently, it would appear that available to the nonreductivist is a solution to the exclusion problem no less adequate than Kim's own.

THE THREAT OF EMERGENTISM

Kim contends that nonreductive materialism is committed to emergentism (sometimes called *strong* emergentism, which he thinks is a radical and implausible view. In his analysis, emergentism claims a distinction between two sorts of higher-level properties, *resultant* and *emergent*, that arise from the basal conditions of physical systems (Kim 1999). The basal conditions of a physical system comprise (i) the basic particles that constitute the physical system, (ii) all the intrinsic properties of these particles, and (iii) the relations that configure these particles into a structure. The higher-level properties that are merely resultant are simply and straightforwardly calculated and theoretically predictable from the facts about its basal conditions—which presumably include the laws that govern the basal conditions—whereas those that are emergent cannot be calculated and predicted. Theoretical predictability contrasts with inductive predictability. Having regularly witnessed that an emergent property is realized by particular basal conditions, we would be able to predict this relationship, but this sort of inductive predictability is not at issue. Rather, according to emergentism, knowledge of the basal conditions alone, no matter how complete, does not suffice to yield a prediction of an emergent property.

Emergentism also endorses downward causation; it claims that higher-level states can have lower-level effects. Emergentism about the mental asserts that mental events can cause microphysical events. Plausibly, nonreductive materialism also countenances downward causation of this sort—M1 causes M2, but because M2 is wholly constituted of P2, M1 also causes P2. Kim thinks that by virtue of endorsing this sort of downward causation, nonreductive materialism is committed to emergentism.

However, the nonreductive view's allowing for downward causation is not by itself sufficient to render it emergentist. Endorsement of downward causation would indeed be radical if it also specified that mental properties could effect changes in the laws that govern the microphysical level independently of any emergent properties (call them the *ordinary* microphysical laws). Supposing that M1 were such an emergent mental property, M1 could cause P2 in such a way that P2 is no longer governed by the ordinary microphysical laws, but instead by laws that take into account the special characteristics of the emergent properties, or no laws at all. But nothing essential to nonreductive materialism entails this radical variety of downward causation (Pereboom 2002).

We might suppose that the capacity for altering the ordinary microphysical laws is what provides emergent properties with their distinctive nature. And this potentially explains why such properties would not be predictable from the microphysical base together with these ordinary laws. Information about the ordinary laws and the microphysical base might be insufficient to predict the law-altering behavior of the higher-level property. But there is no feature of the nonreductive model per se that renders higher-level properties any less theoretically predictable than they would be on a reductive model. In each model, holding relational conditions fixed, a particular set of basal conditions will necessitate the same unique higher-level properties. The nonreductivist is no more committed to some factor that threatens theoretical predictability, such as the capacity of higher-level properties to alter the ordinary microphysical laws, than is the reductionist.

Arguably, therefore, nonreductive materialism can respond effectively to the most serious arguments made against it over the last forty years, and as a result, it remains a viable position about the nature of the mental.

See also Functionalism; Mind-Body Problem; Multiple Realizability; Physicalism.

Bibliography

Antony, L., and J. Levine. "Reduction with Autonomy." In *Philosophical Perspectives*. Vol. 11, *Mind, Causation, and World*, 83–105. Oxford: Blackwell, 1997.

Block, N. "Anti-Reductionism Slaps Back." In *Philosophical Perspectives*. Vol. 11, *Mind, Causation, and World*, 107–132. Oxford: Blackwell, 1997.

Block, N. "Can the Mind Change the World?" In *Meaning and Method: Essays in Honor of Hilary Putnam*, edited by George Boolos, 137–170. Cambridge, U.K.: Cambridge University Press, 1990.

Block, N. "Introduction: What is Functionalism?" In *Readings in the Philosophy of Psychology*, vol. 1, edited by Block, 178–179. Cambridge, MA: Harvard University Press, 1980.

Boyd, R. "Kinds, Complexity, and Multiple Realization." *Philosophical Studies* 95 (1999): 67–98.

Boyd, R. "Materialism Without Reductionism." In *Readings in the Philosophy of Psychology*. Vol. 1, edited by N. Block, 67–106. Cambridge, MA: Harvard University Press, 1980a.

Boyd, R. "Scientific Realism and Naturalistic Epistemology." In *Proceedings of the Philosophy of Science Association*. Vol. 2. East Lansing, MI: Philosophy of Science Association, 1980b.

Clapp. L. "Disjunctive Properties: Multiple Realizations." *Journal of Philosophy* 98 (2001): 111–136.

Fodor, J. "Special Sciences: Still Autonomous After All These Years." In *Philosophical Perspectives*. Vol. 11, *Mind, Causation, and World*, 149–163. Oxford: Blackwell, 1997.

Fodor, J. "Special Sciences (or: The Disunity of Science as a Working Hypothesis)." *Synthese* 28 (1974): 97–115.

Heil, J. "Multiple Realizability." *American Philosophical Quarterly* 36 (1999): 189–208.

Horgan, T. "Kim on Mental Causation and Causal Exclusion." In *Philosophical Perspectives*. Vol. 11, *Mind, Causation, and World*, 165–184. Oxford: Blackwell, 1997.

Jackson, F., and P. Pettit. "Program Explanation: A General Perspective." *Analysis* 50 (1990): 107–117.

Jaworski, W. "Multiple Realizability, Explanation, and the Disjunctive Move." *Philosophical Studies* 108: (2002): 298–308.

Kim, J. "Making Sense of Emergence." *Philosophical Studies* 95 (1999): 3–36.

Kim, J. *Mind in a Physical World: An Essay on the Mind-Body Problem and Mental Causation.* Cambridge, MA: MIT Press, 1998.

Kim, J. "Multiple Realizability and the Metaphysics of Reduction." *Philosophy and Phenomenological Research* 52 (1992): 1–26.

Kim, J. "The Myth of Nonreductive Materialism." *Proceedings and Addresses of the American Philosophical Association* 63 (1989): 31–47.

Kim, J. "Phenomenal Properties, Psychophysical Laws, and the Identity Theory." *Monist* 56: (1972): 177–192.

Kitcher, P. S. "1953 and All That: A Tale of Two Sciences." *Philosophical Review* 93 (1984): 335–373.

Pereboom, D., and H. Kornblith. "The Metaphysics of Irreducibility." *Philosophical Studies* 63 (1991): 125–145.

Pereboom, D. "Robust Nonreductive Materialism." *Journal of Philosophy* 99 (2002): 499–531.

Pereboom, D. "Why a Scientific Realist Cannot Be a Functionalist." *Synthese* 88 (1991): 341–358.

Putnam, H. "Language and Reality." In his *Philosophical Papers*, vol. 2, 272–290. Cambridge, MA: Harvard University Press, 1975. This paper was delivered as a Machette Lecture at Princeton University, May 22, 1974.

Putnam, H. "The Nature of Mental States." In his *Philosophical Papers*. vol. 2, 429–440. Cambridge, MA: Harvard University Press, 1975. First published as "Psychological Predicates," in *Art, Mind, and Religion*, edited by W. H. Capitan and D. D. Merill, 37–48 (Pittsburgh: Pittsburgh University Press, 1967).

Shapiro, L. "Multiple Realizations." *Journal of Philosophy* 97 (2000): 635–654.

Sober, E. "The Multiple Realizability Argument Against Reductionism." *Philosophy of Science* 66 (1999): 542–564.

Van Gulick, R. "Who's in Charge Here? And Who's Doing All the Work?" In *Mental Causation*, edited by J. Heil and A. Mele, 233–256. Oxford: Oxford University Press, 1993.

Yablo, S. "Mental Causation." *Philosophical Review* 101 (1992): 245–280.

Derk Pereboom (2005)

NON-TRUTH-CONDITIONAL MEANING

There are two dominant approaches to semantics. One sees the task of semantics as to provide a systematic account of the truth conditions of (actual and potential) sentence uses. The other assumes that a use of a sentence expresses a statement (proposition, thought—terminology varies here), a statement being the sort of thing that can be asserted and believed, and also the sort of thing that, as a representation of how the world is, can be assessed as true or false. The task of semantics, on this view, is systematically to spell out how sentence uses are associated with statements.

While the aims of the two types of theories are different, they are related. A use of a sentence to make a statement is, after all, presumably true (or false) in virtue of the truth (or falsity) of the statement made. Hence, to assign statements to sentence uses is to assign those uses truth conditions. Thus both approaches give pride of place in semantics to an account of how sentence uses come to be true or false.

No one thinks that giving an account of truth conditions or of what statements say, for a language, says all there is to say about conventional meanings of expressions in the language, though exactly what more there might be is a matter of controversy. Here are the main candidates for what might be left out of such accounts.

MOOD AND FORCE

The theories just discussed aim to illuminate what is going on when one uses the sentences of a language to make assertions, to commit to the truth of a claim. But, of course, we can do much more than make assertions with our sentences, and some aspects of conventional meaning are obviously keyed to doing things other than asserting. Examples are grammatical and phonological forms associated with questioning, ordering, and exclaiming. It is a fact about conventional meaning if anything is, that subject/auxiliary inversion is used to question in French, German, and English, that prefixing a declarative sentence in English with "if only" signals a wish, that sentences such as "Yuck!" and "Damn it!" express attitudes that are not to be evaluated as true or false. One task not discharged by truth-conditional or statement semantics, then, is detailing when and how linguistic forms have as part of their conventional meaning the task of signaling that a particular sort of speech act (asserting, questioning, promising, warning, expressing disgust, etc.) is being performed.

One might question the extent to which this is more than just an appendicle to truth-conditional or statement semantics. One might say that interjections like "Grody!" and "Awesome!" are elliptical for truth bearers ("That is grotesque!" "That's awesome!") uttered with a particular force. Whether or not this is so, the interjections do not combine with connectives and the range of sentences in the language to produce complex sentences; their meanings, if different from that of declaratives, would thus seem to be walled off from other aspects of meaning. There seems to be a rather small catalog of devices, like

auxiliary inversion and the subjunctive, to indicate force; such devices, furthermore, do not seem to be iterable, as constructions that contribute to truth conditions are. While one can disjoin a negation, then enclose the result inside the consequent of a conditional, etc., force indicators *seem* by and large to exclude one another (one cannot, for example, turn the optative "would that he were gone" into a question). Furthermore, it is not clear that any particularly novel sort of meaning is required in an account of the meanings of, for example, orders and questions. One might suspect that in some sense the content of the declarative "You will sit" and of the imperative "Sit!" are the same, the difference lying only in the force of their utterance. Perhaps questions have a slightly novel meaning. For example, it is often suggested that the meaning of "Who will sit?" is something like the set of (contextually relevant or possible) answers to it. But this makes the meaning of a question just a set of statements.

J. L. Austin once claimed that a good deal of natural-language vocabulary has meanings whose job is to signal that one is, and is only, performing a (nonassertive) speech act. For example, on Austin's view, to utter "I promise to meet you at 5:00" is not to assert anything, but to make a promise. Austin (1962) gives a lengthy catalog of verbs (part of) whose conventional meaning, he claims, is to signal (when used in the first-person present) that a particular speech act is being performed, representative examples being "acquit," "nominate," "bet," "toast," and "concede." He suggests that the number of such verbs contained in English is "of the third order of the power of 10."

There are arguably many expressions whose purpose is in part or in whole to signal that, whatever else the speaker might be doing, he is performing a particular nonassertive speech act, though exactly which expressions do this is a matter of controversy. "Just between you and me" (as in "Just between you and me, the provost hates the president") might be a conventional means to warn or ask one's audience not to divulge the information imparted by the rest of the sentence. Racial slurs are, inter alia, conventional means of insulting and displaying contempt for their targets, as are the merely obscene or insulting things we may call someone in the course of commenting on them. Presumably, though, to utter something like "That jerk Smith is at the door" is to say something true or false, depending (only) on whether Smith is at the door.

CONVENTIONAL IMPLICATURE

Grice (1967/1989) drew a distinction between what the use of a sentence "strictly" says and what it implies. Both what is said and what is implicated are statements. Indeed, what a sentence use says, in Grice's sense, seems to be the statement that a semantic theory (of the second sort discussed above) aims to assign to the use. According to Grice, it is what a sentence strictly says, and *only* what it strictly says, that is relevant to the question of whether the use of the sentence is true.

What, then, is the role of what is implicated by the use of a sentence? Some such implication is a one-off affair, as when one says, "There's an umbrella in the closet," expecting one's auditor to work out that rain is in the offing. Implication of this sort exploits facts obvious to all—for example, that speakers generally try to say helpful and relevant things—to efficiently convey information; it allows us to convey much more than our words literally mean.

Grice distinguished this sort of implication—*conversational implicature*, as he called it—from cases in which "the conventional meaning of the words used ... determine[s] what is implicated, besides helping to determine what is said" (Grice 1967/1989, p. 25). Grice's examples were the words "therefore" and "but." In uttering "*A*; therefore *B*," Grice claimed, I say that *A*, say that *B*, commit myself to *B*'s following from *A*, but I have not "*said* (in the favored sense)" that *B* follows from *A*: "I do not want to say that my utterance ... would be, *strictly speaking*, false should the consequence in question [fail] to hold" (Grice 1967/1989, pp. 25–26). In uttering "He is *F* but *G*," one speaks truly, Grice said, just in case the relevant individual is *F* and *G*, though one clearly conveys some sort of contrast between being *F* and being *G*. To use "therefore" or "but" is to commit to these implications. Since the implications are carried by the very words used, they are not one-off conversational implicatures but *conventional implicatures*.

A rather large class of expressions have been said to give rise to conventional implicatures. Karttunen and Peters (1979) suggest that words and constructions often said to give rise to presuppositions in fact give rise to conventional implicature. Here are some examples, with the word purportedly carrying the conventional implicature italicized and the implicature roughly indicated in parentheses:

Even John understands it. (John is unlikely to understand it.)

Martin *still* loves her. (Martin loved her in the past.)

Jed *failed* to pass. (Jed tried to pass.)

Other examples of purported conventional implicatures are nonrestrictive relative clauses and appositives. "Martina, a yogi, hunts bears" commits the speaker to Martina's being a yogi, but arguably would be true even if she is not one, so long as she does hunt bears.

It is controversial whether there is such a thing as conventional implicature. Bach (1999) argued that a complete report of Bob's utterance of "Even Mo likes Jo" is given with "Bob said that even Mo likes Jo"; simply saying, "Bob said that Mo likes Jo" is not giving a complete report. Since "that even Mo likes Jo" is here specifying what Bob said, Bach concluded, part of what Bob's utterance says must be (something like the claim) that Mo's liking Jo is unexpected. But if that is part of what is said, then the utterance is true only if it is unexpected that Mo likes Jo. According to Bach, this sort of argument shows that pretty much every expression alleged to carry a conventional implicature in fact does not.

It is not clear that this argument succeeds in showing that conventional implicatures are a fiction. "What is said (by utterance *u*)," as used by Grice, is a technical term. The phrase and its cousins have an everyday use as well. It is not at all clear that Grice assumed that if an utterance would naturally and correctly be reported as saying that *p*, then *p* must be part of what it says *in the technical sense*. We are, after all, pretty loose in how we report indirect speech.

One might hold that conventional implicatures are just as much *said by* a use of a sentence as anything, but have properties and relations to sentence uses that make it worthwhile to distinguish them from other claims literally made by sentence uses. Christopher Potts (2005) distinguished what he called "at issue" claims made by a sentence use (roughly, what Grice had in mind by "what is said") from conventional implicatures. (However, Potts's view, unlike Grice's, is apparently that conventional implicatures are relevant to truth conditions. He takes conventional implicatures to be "entailments," and holds that sentences carrying such implicatures can typically be paraphrased by conjunctions, one conjunct of which is the implicature.)

For Potts, one putative difference between conventional implicature and at-issue content is that even when a speaker embeds an expression carrying a conventional implicature, the speaker becomes committed to the implicature; this is not so with at-issue content. To see the point, consider "Bob, a linguist, likes clams," where the at-issue content is that Bob likes clams and the conventional implicature is that Bob is a linguist. When one embeds the sentence under negation or an attitude verb (as in "It is false that Bob, a linguist, likes clams," or "Mary said that Bob, a linguist, likes clams"), use of the resulting sentence seems to commit the user to the conventional implicature, but not to the at-issue content.

A conventional implication is like a presupposition in this regard. Potts argues that conventional implicatures are not presuppositions, since false conventional implicatures and false presuppositions have different effects. When a presupposition of a sentence is false, the assertion of its at-issue content is unfelicitous, perhaps without truth value; this is not so with conventional implicature. In the case of conventional implicature, that Bob is not a linguist does not impugn or cast doubt on the claim that Bob likes clams. Knowledge that the presupposition of "It was Bob who stole the book (namely, that someone stole it) is false makes the assertion that it was Bob who did it unacceptable.

NONPROPOSITIONAL MEANING

What is conventionally implicated has truth conditions. A non-truth-conditional conventional implicature does not enter into the truth conditions of the use of a sentence; its truth or falsity is not relevant to the truth or falsity of the sentence use implicating it. Other alleged sorts of non-truth-conditional meanings, however, are non-truth-conditional in the sense that they simply are not the sort of thing that can be true or false—they are, as it is sometimes said, not truth-apt.

One (alleged) example of such a meaning is presented by those who hold that linguistic meaning, or an aspect thereof, is to be identified with one or another psychological role associated with an expression. It has been proposed that the meaning of a sentence as used by a particular speaker is or involves one or more of: its inferential role (reflected by the speaker's dispositions to make inferences from and to the sentence), its evidential role (reflected in what observations and experiences incline the speaker to accept or reject the sentence), and its probabilistic role (the function that sends a sentence S and a collection C of sentences to the subjective probability the speaker would assign S if he held all of C true). (Developments of such views are in Boer and Lycan 1986, Field 1977, Sellars 1954.) None of these things can sensibly be evaluated for truth or falsity. Those who champion such psychological accounts of meaning often hold that meaning is a two-factor affair, the other factor being truth-conditional. Typically, though not invariably, the two factors are held to be independent.

In part, the appeal of adding psychological role to truth conditions in an account of meaning is that it seems to reflect a genuine tension in our pretheoretic conception of meaning. Consider Putnam's fantasy (in 1975) that there is a Twin Earth as much like Earth as possible, save that something other than H_2O, call it XYZ, plays the role that H_2O plays on Earth: XYZ has all the sensible properties of H_2O; it is XYZ, not H_2O, that fills the seas, that people drink and wash with, etc. Putnam holds, and many concur, that "water" means different things on Earth and on Twin Earth, for here it refers to H_2O, while there it refers to XYZ. But many think that in some very important sense the word has the same meaning in both places, for someone transported to Twin Earth who was innocent of chemistry, it is felt, would not mean anything different by "water" there than he means here. If there are two factors to the meaning of "water"—a truth-conditional one (which varies between Earth and Twin Earth) and a psychological one (which is constant), both intuitions are partially vindicated.

A different kind of nonpropositional meaning is what is sometimes called "expressive" meaning. The idea of such meaning has its roots in the work of emotivists like A. J. Ayer and Charles Stevenson. According to Ayer, the role of ethical discourse is completely noncognitive. Utterances of sentences such as "Stealing is wrong" and "Friendship is good" are not assertions and do not express beliefs. Rather, they are expressions of attitudes of approval or disapproval. Uttering "Stealing is wrong" is doing the sort of thing one does when one shouts "Down with stealing!" or accompanies utterance of the word "stealing" with a disapproving shake of the head. Stevenson's somewhat more sophisticated take on such sentences is that uttering them both expresses a distinctive sort of approval and exhorts (or at least attempts to bring) the audience to share this approval.

Sentences whose role is clearly exhausted by the expression of attitude—"Boo!" "Liver—yuck!" "Damn!"—are not candidates for combining with connectives and quantifiers to form larger sentences. "If liver—yuck, then I won't make dinner" does not have a meaning, for it is not even a sentence. But sentences such as "Stealing is bad" quite obviously do combine with connectives and other sentences, and the results certainly do seem to be meaningful. It seems incumbent on any account of semantics to explain what the meaning of a sentence such as "Stealing is bad only if it causes pain to someone."

Geach (1965), expanding on points in Frege (1918/1952), objects that the emotivist cannot make any sense of the use of normative vocabulary in complex sentences, of embedded uses, as is sometimes said. Someone who utters "If failing Mary will make her sad, you shouldn't do it" need not be expressing disapproval of anything. Even if there is a way around this—one might invoke some sort of "conditional disapproval"—emotivist views make the fact that we give normative arguments an utter mystery. The argument "Borrowing and not returning something is bad; if that is bad, so is stealing; so stealing is bad" is valid—its conclusion follows from its premises. But it seems to be nonsense to think that a feeling of disapproval for stealing *follows* from a feeling of disapproval for borrowing and not returning and whatever attitude might be associated with the conditional above. "Following from," after all, is a relation normally defined in terms of preserving truth. But if this makes no sense, the idea that the argument is valid makes no sense in emotivist terms.

These considerations, incidentally, bear on the view of Austin mentioned above. The argument "If I promise to meet you, I will meet you; I promise to meet you; so I will meet you" seems obviously valid. But there is a sort of ambiguity, on Austin's view, in "I promise to meet you." Embedded in the antecedent of a conditional, it presumably does nothing but express the *statement* that its user promises to meet the addressee. Unembedded, it apparently does not do this, as one, in uttering the sentence, does not *assert* that one promises, on Austin's view; one simply promises. It thus seems like the sense of "I promise to meet you" varies across the two premises of the argument, and thus the argument is not valid.

Expressivists such as Simon Blackburn and Alan Gibbard have recently tried to respond to this sort of objection, giving accounts that (more or less) agree with the emotivist line about simple sentences like "Hooking up is good" and attempting to derive therefrom meanings for complex sentences in which normative vocabulary occurs. Blackburn (1993) agrees with the emotivist that sentences like "Stealing is bad" express motivational states such as attitudes of disapproval. But he aspires to give an account of the meanings of the full range of uses of normative vocabulary, including such sentences as "Mary believes that stealing is bad" and "It's true that stealing is bad." The account is to be one that systematically assigns, to complex sentences, complex attitudes—typically in one or another way compounded out of the attitudes expressed by simple sentences. The sentence "If borrowing and not returning something is bad, then so is stealing it," for example, expresses a commitment to either tolerating borrowing and not returning, or to disapprov-

ing stealing. Such a view would allow us to characterize validity in terms of preservation of commitment—an argument is valid just in case it is impossible to fulfill the commitments associated with premises without fulfilling those associated with the conclusion.

Gibbard (1992, a recast of 1990) suggested that normative sentences—not just sentences from morality, but sentences about what is or is not rational—absorb their meanings holistically from their relations to "immediate motivations," that is, to the states one expresses if one thinks to oneself "Do/Don't do that now!" The idea, roughly put, is that just as complex statements get their truth-conditional content from their inferential relations to sentences expressing observations, so normative statements absorb their content from inferential relations to sentences expressing immediate motivations. Gibbard suggests that the meaning of a normative sentence (including complex combinations of normative and nonnormative elements) can be represented as a set of "factual-normative" worlds, which are pairs of possible worlds and systems of norms. The idea, again roughly, is this. A simple factual statement holds at world w and norm n if it is true there. A simple normative statement such as "That is bad" (whose connection with "Don't do that!" is obvious) holds at w and n provided that n forbids the act referred to. With this as a basis, one can use standard techniques to assign sets of factual-normative worlds to compound sentences.

One might argue with Blackburn and Gibbard about the details of their approaches, worrying, for example, that Blackburn helps himself without justification to the idea that there is a distinctive sort of moral disapproval. Yet it would seem that something along the lines of Blackburn's or Gibbard's story *must* be correct. Here is why.

Forget about claims about morality, rationality, or other obviously normative concerns. Think instead about what is going on when we talk about talk that obviously aspires to be true or false—about what happens when one person says "Jo is bald" and another says "That's not true," or when someone says "The sentence on the board isn't true." It seems obvious that such talk can get it right without being true. If the sentence on the board is a liar sentence, one thing that we *know* about it is that it is not true. We can, after all, *prove* that it is not. But paradox ensues if we take this thing we know—that the sentence is not true—to be true. After all, if what we know—that the sentence is not true—is true, then, since the sentence *says* just that—that it is not true—what the sentence says is true. So what we know is false. But one cannot know something that is false. Similarly, if vague predicates are neither true nor false of their borderline cases (and surely this is the most plausible thing to say about them) and Jo is borderline-bald, then while the person who utters "Jo is bald" says something, what he says is *not* true. But if it is *true* that the sentence is not true, then (since what is not true is false), "Jo is bald" must be false. But since Jo is borderline bald, "Jo is bald" cannot be false either.

What should we make of this? Well, for one thing, when we say, referring to the liar, "That is not true," we should not be understood as *asserting* something, that is, committing to its truth. Rather, we are performing the sui generis speech act of *denial*, where (roughly put) denying a potential truth bearer is the appropriate thing to do if it is *not* true ("not" being used here to deny). This sort of thing applies quite generally to uses of other logical connectives. Sometimes, for example, when someone utters "*A* if and only if (iff) *B*," they are to be understood as asserting the material equivalence of *A* and *B*. But when we say things with the form " '*S*' is true iff *S*" and *S* happens to be a liar sentence, we are not to be understood as *asserting* anything. Rather, we are performing an act that is apt if the claims connected by "iff" have the same (perhaps non-truth-conditional) status.

When we utter sentences, we perform different sorts of speech acts. Sometimes we assert, sometimes we deny, sometimes we perform the sort of act just mentioned. And when we perform such acts, we incur various commitments. For example, assertion commits us to the truth of what is asserted; denial of a potential truth bearer commits us to the nontruth thereof. Sentence-compounding devices, at least on some occasions, contribute not to *sense*, by (for example) expressing truth-functional negation, but to *force*. In the case of "not," for example, one sometimes signals that one is denying, where to deny *S* is to commit to the inaptness of whatever commitment is associated with uttering *S*.

Think of the simplest sentences of one's language as vehicles for performing speech acts, each such act involving its own distinctive kind of commitment, each commitment having its own conditions of appropriateness and inappropriateness. Annexing words like "not" and "if" to sentences yields (when the connectives signal force) sentences that are vehicles for performing speech acts with their own distinctive kinds of commitments, their own aptness conditions. Compounding sentences with several connectives playing the role of force indicators produces a sentence that can serve as a vehicle for performing a complex speech act determined by the meanings of the constituent sentences and the force-indicating meanings of the connectives. Uttering "If *S* is a liar sentence, then it is not true," for example, performs an apt speech act if it is apt either to deny that *S* is a liar sentence or to deny that *S* is true.

Beyond an account of sense or reference, a theory of meaning for a language—at least one component of such a theory—must tell the story of how the acts and commitments associated with the parts of a complex sentence determine the act for which the complex sentence is a vehicle, the commitments one incurs with the act, and the aptness conditions of such commitments. (For the beginning of such a story, see Richard 2006.) Such a story generalizes the sort of ideas Blackburn had. With such a story, one can see that logical validity, in its most basic sense, is preservation of commitment: An argument is valid provided that whenever the commitments associated with the premises are apt, so are those associated with the conclusion.

It was mentioned above that there was something importantly right about Gibbard's and Blackburn's accounts of normative discourse. What is important and surely right is not their view of the nature of the acts performed and commitments incurred in normative utterances. Perhaps those accounts are on the right track, because normative discourse is expressive, not truth-apt. Perhaps they are wrong, and normative discourse is no less truth-evaluable than a stock-price quotation. What is important is the insight that validity (and the other properties we associate with rational discourse) are not the exclusive property of truth-conditional discourse. Sometimes meaning and validity are to be explained in terms of truth conditions. But this is not the only case—it is but a special case.

See also Meaning.

Bibliography

Austin, J. L. *How to Do Things with Words*. 2nd ed. Cambridge, MA: Harvard University Press, 1962.

Ayer, A. J. *Language, Truth, and Logic*. London: Victor Gollancz, 1936.

Bach, Kent. "The Myth of Conventional Implicature." *Linguistics and Philosophy* 22 (4) (1999): 367–421.

Blackburn, Simon. *Essays in Quasi-Realism*. New York: Oxford University Press, 1993.

Boer, Stephen, and William Lycan. *Knowing Who*. Cambridge, MA: MIT Press, 1986.

Field, Hartry. "Logic, Meaning, and Conceptual Role." *Journal of Philosophy* 74 (1977): 379–409.

Frege, Gottlob. "Negation" (1918). In *Translations from the Philosophical Writings of Gottlob Frege*, edited by Peter Geach and Max Black. Oxford, U.K.: Blackwell, 1952.

Geach, Peter. "Assertion." *Philosophical Review* 74 (1965): 449–465.

Gibbard, Alan. "Reply to Blackburn, Carson, Hill, and Railton." *Philosophy and Phenomenological Research* 52 (4) (1992): 969–980.

Gibbard, Alan. *Wise Choices, Apt Feelings*. Cambridge, MA: Harvard University Press, 1990.

Grice, H. P. "Logic and Conversation" (1967). In his *Studies in the Ways of Words*. Cambridge, MA: Harvard University Press, 1989.

Karttunen, Lauri, and Stanley Peters. "Conventional Implicature." In *Presupposition*, edited by Choon-Kyu Oh and David Dinneen. New York: Academic Press, 1979.

Potts, Christopher. *The Logic of Conventional Implicatures*. Oxford, U.K.: Oxford University Press, 2005.

Putnam, Hilary. "The Meaning of 'Meaning.'" In his *Mind, Language, and Reality*. New York: Cambridge University Press, 1975.

Richard, Mark. *Beside Truth*. Oxford: Oxford University Press, 2006.

Sellars, Wilfred. "Some Remarks on Language Games." *Philosophy of Science* 21 (1954): 204–228.

Stevenson, Charles. *Ethics and Language*. New Haven, CT: Yale University Press, 1944.

Mark Richard (2005)

NONVIOLENCE

See *Violence*

NORMATIVE ETHICS

See *Ethics, History of; Normativity*

NORRIS, JOHN
(1657–1711)

John Norris, the English philosopher and disciple of Nicolas Malebranche, was associated with the Cambridge Platonists. Norris was born in Collingbourne-Kingston, Wiltshire. His father was a clergyman and at that time a Puritan. Educated at Winchester and at Exeter College, Oxford, which he entered in 1676, Norris was appointed a fellow of All Souls in 1680. During his nine years at All Souls, he was ordained (1684) and began to write, mostly in a Platonic vein and often in verse. In 1683 he published *Tractatus adversus Reprobationis absolutae Decretum*, in which he attacked the Calvinist doctrine of predestination. His Platonism and anti-Calvinism naturally attracted Norris to the Cambridge Platonists; in 1684 he began to correspond with Henry More and Damaris Cudworth, the daughter of Ralph Cudworth.

The philosophical essays included in *Poems and Discourses* (1684)—renamed *A Collection of Miscellanies* in the 1687 and subsequent editions—could, indeed, have been written by a Cambridge Platonist. Their main argument is that since truth is by its nature eternal and immutable, it must relate ideas which are also eternal and immutable; this condition, according to Norris, can be fulfilled only by ideas which are "in the mind of God"— that is, manifestations of God's essence. Thus, the existence of God is deducible from the very nature of truth; the atheist is involved in a self-contradictory skepticism.

In Norris's *The Theory and Regulation of Love* (1688)—for all that Norris dedicated it to the former Damaris Cudworth, now Lady Masham, and included as an appendix his correspondence with More—the influence of Malebranche began to predominate. At first, it reinforced rather than weakened Norris's sympathy with Cambridge Platonism. Norris followed Malebranche in distinguishing two kinds of love—desire, which seeks to unify itself with the good it pursues, and benevolence, which seeks good for others. But, as also in *Reason and Religion* (1689), Norris explicitly rejected Malebranche's view that the only proper object of desire is God. The objects of desire, Norris said, form a hierarchy—God, the good of the community, intellectual pleasures, and sensual pleasures are all in some measure good. God is the highest but not the only good.

In 1689, Norris married and resigned his fellowship to become rector of Newton St. Loe in Somerset. In his *Reflections on the Conduct of Human Life* (1690), addressed to Lady Masham and intended as an admonition to her, he condemned the life he had lived at Oxford on the ground that he had interested himself in public affairs and in intellectual pursuits; in the future he proposed to dedicate himself in retirement to the "moral improvement of my mind and the regulation of my life." This is Malebranche's, not the Cambridge Platonists', ideal of conduct; even the pursuit of knowledge is conceived of as a worldly enticement.

In 1691, as a result of John Locke's influence, Norris became rector of Bemerton, near Salisbury, where he died on February 5, 1711. He did not win the approval of his Cambridge Platonist bishop, Gilbert Burnet, who would certainly not have appreciated Norris's attack on toleration in *The Charge of Schism continued* (1691). Norris's *Discourse concerning the Measures of Divine Love* (*Practical Discourses*, Vol. III, 1693) and *Letters concerning the Love of God* (1695) reveal the complete disciple of Malebranche; we ought, Norris now said, to love nobody but God. Substantially reversing Immanuel Kant's dictum, he argued that we should treat other human beings as means—occasions of happiness to us—and never as ends. Lady Masham was naturally indignant; in her anonymous *Discourse concerning the Love of God* (1696), a reply to Norris, she argued that men are "made for a sociable life" and should love their fellow men in the same way they love God.

THOUGHT

Norris's metaphysical views, sketched in *Reason and Religion*, are set out in detail in his *Essay towards the Theory of the Ideal and the Sensible World* (Vol. I, 1701; Vol. II, 1704), which fully justifies his nickname "the English Malebranche." Yet the argument of the first volume of the *Essay* would still entitle Norris to be described as a Platonist—or as a Thomist or an Augustinian. Plato, the "Platonic father" Augustine, Francisco Suárez, and Thomas Aquinas all taught, he tried to show, the same lesson as Malebranche—that knowledge is of the eternal and, therefore, of God.

In the second volume, however, when Norris came to consider in more detail how our knowledge of "the world of sense" is related to our knowledge of "the intelligible world," his break with the Platonist tradition, arising out of his allegiance to Malebranche, is at once apparent. It is true that when he did (mildly) criticize Malebranche, it is on the Platonic ground that his theory of the imagination allows too much to sensation; Malebranche's phrase "We see all things in God," he also thought, might suggest to the careless reader that sensation is our analogue for knowledge. "Divine ideas," Norris preferred to say, "are the immediate objects of our thought in the perception of things." But these are minor reformulations. Of much greater significance is the fact that he agreed with the Cartesians that "the world is a great mechanism and goes like a clock" and even accepted, although with some little hesitation, the Cartesian doctrine of animal mechanism. He did not even bother to refer to the Platonist theory of "plastic powers" or to More's criticism of René Descartes's extension-thought dualism. He is a Platonist only where Malebranche is a Platonist—for example, in his rejection of the Thomas-Locke account of abstraction.

Norris's philosophy might properly be described, in the phrase commonly applied to Benedict de Spinoza, as "God-intoxicated." God, for him as for Malebranche, is the efficient cause of all happenings, the only good, the only object of knowledge. We know God directly; everything else is known by way of our apprehension of God's nature as revealed in the ideas that emanate from him. Norris could not explain, he confessed, how spiritual

ideas can represent a material world; the material world is, indeed, an embarrassment to him, fading into the empty concept of "that which occasions our apprehensions" that George Berkeley criticized. He was so concerned to leave nothing lovable in the world, nothing that could be a source of happiness to us, that he reduced it to a nonentity; it exists only as something to be shunned. The relation between our mind and God's is left in equal obscurity.

In 1692 Locke and Norris quarreled on a matter involving Lady Masham; Locke came to be very impatient with Norris's views, which probably provoked his *Examination of Malebranche* (first published in *Posthumous Works*, edited by Peter King, London, 1706); he directly criticized Norris in an essay first published in *A Collection of Several Pieces of Mr. John Locke* (1720). In general, Locke thought of Norris as a completely reactionary thinker.

Other of Norris's works deserving mention are *An Account of Reason and faith in relation to the Mysteries of Christianity* (1697), in which he argued—in reply to John Toland's deistic *Christianity not Mysterious* (1696)—that it is not unreasonable to believe the incomprehensible, and *A Philosophical Discourse concerning the Natural Immortality of the Soul* (1708), which makes use of Platonic-scholastic arguments against Henry Dodwell's *Epistolary Discourse proving … that the Soul is naturally Mortal* (1706). Many of his works, although not *The Ideal World*, were extremely popular, but it is usually impossible to distinguish his influence from Malebranche's. One of the least original of philosophers, he nevertheless displays considerable powers of criticism and exposition. He had a direct influence on Arthur Collier.

See also Cambridge Platonists.

Bibliography

There is no modern edition of Norris. Norris brought together several of his minor works, including *Reason and Religion*, as *Treatises upon Several Subjects* (London, 1697). For his *Poems* see the edition by Alexander Balloch Grosart in the *Fuller Worthies' Library*, Vol. III (Blackburn, U.K., 1871), pp. 147–348; John Wesley included an abbreviated version of *Treatise on Christian Prudence* and *Reflections upon the Conduct of Human Life* in his *Christian Library*, Vol. XXX (London, 1827).

See also Frederick James Powicke, *A Dissertation on John Norris* (London, 1894); Ernest Trafford Campagnac, *The Cambridge Platonists* (Oxford: Clarendon Press, 1901); Flora Isabel MacKinnon, *The Philosophy of John Norris of Bemerton, Philosophical Monographs*, No. 2 of the *Psychological Review* (October 1910); John Henry Muirhead, *The Platonic Tradition in Anglo-Saxon Philosophy* (London,

1931); John K. Ryan, "John Norris, a Seventeenth Century Thomist," in *New Scholasticism* 14 (2) (1940): 109–145; Charlotte Johnston, "Locke's *Examination of Malebranche* and John Norris," in *Journal of the History of Ideas* 19 (4) (1958): 551–558; Richard Acworth, *The Philosophy of John Norris of Bemerton (1657–1712)* (Hildesheim, NY: Olms, 1979); Richard Acworth, "Locke's First Reply to John Norris," *Locke Newsletter* 2 (1971): 7–11; and Charles J. McCracken, *Malebranche and British Philosophy* (Oxford: Clarendon Press, 1983).

John Passmore (1967)
Bibliography updated by Tamra Frei (2005)

NOTHING

"Nothing" is an awe-inspiring yet essentially undigested concept, highly esteemed by writers of a mystical or existentialist tendency, but by most others regarded with anxiety, nausea, or panic. Nobody seems to know how to deal with it (he would, of course), and plain persons generally are reported to have little difficulty in saying, seeing, hearing, and doing nothing. Philosophers, however, have never felt easy on the matter. Ever since Parmenides laid it down that it is impossible to speak of what is not, broke his own rule in the act of stating it, and deduced himself into a world where all that ever happened was nothing, the impression has persisted that the narrow path between sense and nonsense on this subject is a difficult one to tread and that altogether the less said of it the better.

This escape, however, is not so easy as it looks. Plato, in pursuing it, reversed the Parmenidean dictum by insisting, in effect, that anything a philosopher *can* find to talk about must somehow be there to be discussed, and so let loose upon the world that unseemly rabble of centaurs and unicorns, carnivorous cows, republican monarchs and wife-burdened bachelors, which has plagued ontology from that day to this. Nothing (of which they are all aliases) can apparently get rid of these absurdities, but for fairly obvious reasons has not been invited to do so. Logic has attempted the task, but with sadly limited success. Of some, though not all, nonentities, even a logician knows that they do not exist, since their properties defy the law of contradiction; the remainder, however, are not so readily dismissed. Whatever Bertrand Russell may have said of it, the harmless if unnecessary unicorn cannot be driven out of logic as it can out of zoology, unless by desperate measures that exclude all manner of reputable entities as well. Such remedies have been attempted, and their effects are worse than the disease. Russell himself, in eliminating the present king of France, inadvertently deposed

the present queen of England. W. V. Quine, the sorcerer's apprentice, contrived to liquidate both Pegasus and President Harry Truman in the same fell swoop. The old logicians, who allowed all entities subsistence while conceding existence, as wanted, to an accredited selection of them, at least brought a certain tolerant inefficiency to their task. Of the new it can only be said that *solitudinem faciunt et pacem appellant*—they make a desert and call it peace. Whole realms of being have been abolished without warning, at the mere nonquantifying of a variable. The poetry of Earth has been parsed out of existence— and what has become of its prose? There is little need for an answer. Writers to whom nothing is sacred, and who accordingly stop thereat, have no occasion for surprise on finding, at the end of their operations, that nothing is all they have left.

The logicians, of course, will have nothing of all this. Nothing, they say, is not a thing, nor is it the name of anything, being merely a short way of saying of anything that it is not something else. *Nothing* means "not-anything"; appearances to the contrary are due merely to the error of supposing that a grammatical subject must necessarily be a name. Asked, however, to prove that nothing is *not* the name of anything, they fall back on the claim that nothing *is* the name of anything (since according to them there are no names anyway). Those who can make nothing of such an argument are welcome to the attempt. When logic falls out with itself, honest men come into their own, and it will take more than this to persuade them that there are not better cures for this particular headache than the old and now discredited method of cutting off the patient's head.

The friends of nothing may be divided into two distinct though not exclusive classes: the know-nothings, who claim a phenomenological acquaintance with nothing in particular, and the fear-nothings, who, believing, with Macbeth, that "nothing is but what is not," are thereby launched into dialectical encounter with nullity in general. For the first, nothing, so far from being a mere grammatical illusion, is a genuine, even positive, feature of experience. We are all familiar with, and have a vocabulary for, holes and gaps, lacks and losses, absences, silences, impalpabilities, insipidities, and the like. Voids and vacancies of one sort or another are sought after, dealt in and advertised in the newspapers. And what are these, it is asked, but perceived fragments of nothingness, experiential blanks, which command, nonetheless, their share of attention and therefore deserve recognition?

Jean-Paul Sartre, for one, has given currency to such arguments, and so, in effect, have the upholders of "negative facts"—an improvident sect, whose refrigerators are full of nonexistent butter and cheese, absentee elephants and so on, which they claim to detect therein. If existence indeed precedes essence, there is certainly reason of a sort for maintaining that nonexistence is also anterior to, and not a mere product of, the essentially parasitic activity of negation; that the nothing precedes the not. But, verbal refutations apart, the short answer to this view, as given, for instance, by Henri Bergson, is that these are but petty and partial nothings, themselves parasitic on what already exists. Absence is a mere privation, and a privation of something at that. A hole is always a hole *in* something: take away the thing, and the hole goes too; more precisely, it is replaced by a bigger if not better hole, itself relative to its surroundings, and so tributary to something else. Nothing, in short, is given only in relation to what is, and even the idea of nothing requires a thinker to sustain it. If we want to encounter it *an sich,* we have to try harder than that.

Better things, or rather nothings, are promised on the alternative theory, whereby it is argued, so to speak, not that holes are in things but that things are in holes or, more generally, that *everything* (and everybody) is in a hole. To be anything (or anybody) is to be bounded, hemmed in, defined, and separated by a circumambient frame of vacuity, and what is true of the individual is equally true of the collective. The universe at large is fringed with nothingness, from which indeed (how else?) it must have been created, if created it was; and its beginning and end, like that of all change within it, must similarly be viewed as a passage from one nothing to another, with an interlude of being in between. Such thoughts, or others like them, have haunted the speculations of nullophile metaphysicians from Pythagoras to Blaise Pascal and from G. W. F. Hegel and his followers to Martin Heidegger, Paul Tillich and Sartre. Being and nonbeing, as they see it, are complementary notions, dialectically entwined, and of equal status and importance; although Heidegger alone has extended their symmetry to the point of equipping *Das Nichts* with a correlative (if nugatory) activity of nothing, or nihilating, whereby it produces *Angst* in its votaries and untimely hilarity in those, such as Rudolf Carnap and A. J. Ayer, who have difficulty in parsing *nothing* as a present participle of the verb "to noth."

Nothing, whether it noths or not, and whether or not the being of anything entails it, clearly does not entail that anything should be. Like Benedict de Spinoza's substance, it is *causa sui*; nothing (except more of the same) can come of it; *ex nihilo, nihil fit.* That conceded, it remains a question to some why anything, rather than nothing, should exist. This is either the deepest conundrum in metaphysics or the most childish, and though many must have felt the force of it at one time or another, it is equally common to conclude, on reflection, that it is no question at all. The hypothesis of theism may be said to take it seriously and to offer a provisional answer. The alternative is to argue that the dilemma is self-resolved in the mere possibility of stating it. If nothing whatsoever existed, there would be no problem and no answer, and the anxieties even of existential philosophers would be permanently laid to rest. Since they are not, there is evidently *nothing to worry about.* But that itself should be enough to keep an existentialist happy. Unless the solution be, as some have suspected, that it is not nothing that has been worrying them, but they who have been worrying it.

See also Atheism; Ayer, Alfred Jules; Bergson, Henri; Carnap, Rudolf; Hegel, Georg Wilhelm Friedrich; Heidegger, Martin; Logic, History of; Nihilism; Parmenides of Elea; Plato; Quine, Willard Van Orman; Russell, Bertrand Arthur William; Sartre, Jean-Paul; Spinoza, Benedict (Baruch) de; Tillich, Paul.

Bibliography

Modern writers who have had something to say about nothing include:

Barrett, William. *Irrational Man.* Garden City, NY: Doubleday, 1958.

Bergson, Henri. *L'évolution créatrice.* Paris: F. Alcan, 1907. Translated by Arthur Mitchell as *Creative Evolution.* London: Macmillan, 1911.

Carnap, Rudolf. "The Elimination of Metaphysics." In *Logical Positivism,* edited by A. J. Ayer, 69–73. Glencoe, IL: Free Press, 1959.

Edwards, Paul. "Professor Tillich's Confusions." *Mind,* n.s., 74 (1965): 192–214.

Findlay, J. N. *Meinong's Theory of Objects and Values.* 2nd ed. Oxford: Clarendon Press, 1963.

Heidegger, Martin. *Einführung in die Metaphysik.* Tübingen: Niemeyer, 1953. Translated by Ralph Manheim as *An Introduction to Metaphysics.* New Haven, CT: Yale University Press, 1959.

Heidegger, Martin. *Sein und Zeit.* Halle: Niemeyer, 1927. Translated by John Macquarrie and Edward Robinson as *Being and Time.* New York: Harper, 1962.

Heidegger, Martin. *Was ist Metaphysik?* Bonn: Cohen, 1929; 4th ed., Frankfurt, 1943. Translated by R. F. C. Hull and Alan Crick as "What Is Metaphysics?," in *Existence and Being,* edited by W. Brock. Chicago: Regnery, 1949.

Lazerowitz, Morris. *Structure of Metaphysics.* London: Routledge and Paul, 1955.

Munitz, M. K. *Mystery of Existence.* New York: Appleton-Century-Crofts, 1965.

Prior, A. N. "Non-entities." In *Analytical Philosophy I*, edited by R. J. Butler. New York: Barnes and Noble, 1962.

Quine, W. V. *From a Logical Point of View.* Cambridge, MA: Harvard University Press, 1953.

Russell, Bertrand. "On Denoting." *Mind,* n.s., 14 (1905): 479–493.

Sartre, Jean-Paul. *L'être et le néant.* Paris: Gallimard, 1943. Translated by Hazel E. Barnes as *Being and Nothingness.* London: Methuen, 1957.

Taylor, Richard. "Negative Things." *Journal of Philosophy* 49 (13) (1952): 433–448.

Tillich, Paul. *The Courage to Be.* New Haven, CT: Yale University Press, 1952.

Toms, Eric. *Being, Negation and Logic.* Oxford: Blackwell, 1962.

P. L. Heath (1967)

NOUNS, MASS AND COUNT

Many languages mark a grammatical distinction that is commonly referred to as the "mass/count-distinction"; for example, the distinction between the occurrences of "hair" as a mass-noun in "There is hair in my soup," on the one hand, and its occurrences as a singular and plural count-noun in "There is a hair in my soup" or "There are hairs in my soup," on the other. Awareness of this linguistic contrast may, in the Western tradition, date as far back as the pre-Socratics, Plato, and Aristotle; in modern times, however, the first explicit formulation of it is usually credited to Otto Jespersen (1924).

1. THE PROBLEM OF CLASSIFICATION

Almost every aspect of the mass/count-distinction is unclear and contested, including the question of how it is to be drawn:

The Problem of Classification:

(i) Between what sorts of entities is the mass/count-distinction to be drawn?

(ii) By means of what sorts of criteria is the mass/count-distinction to be drawn?

What underlies question (i), for one thing, is a certain ambivalence as to whether the contrast concerns uses or occurrences of expressions or expressions themselves (and, if the former, we face the further question as to what a "use" or an "occurrence" of an expression really is; that is, how, for example, occurrences contrast with types and tokens of expressions). (In what follows, for reasons of convenience, we will speak of both uses or occurrences as well as of expressions themselves as being mass or count.) Moreover, question (i) also encompasses the issue of whether the contrast in question can be properly drawn only with respect to nouns and noun-phrases or whether it can be sensibly extended to other categories, such as adjectives (e.g., with "red" on the mass-side and "circular" on the count-side) as well as verbs and verb-phrases (e.g., with atelic activity-verbs such as "run in circles" being classified as mass and telic achievement- or accomplishment-verbs such as "recognize" or "grow up" being classified as count; see Hoepelman 1976, Taylor 1977, Mourelatos 1978).

Question (ii), on the other hand, asks whether the distinction in question is best drawn, for example, by means of syntactic, morphological, semantic, or pragmatic criteria. To illustrate—restricting ourselves, as is customary, to the category of nouns and noun-phrases, and to such purely syntactic criteria (exhibited overtly in English) as the admissibility of plural-morphology as well as the licensing of "bare" (i.e., unquantified) occurrences or particular kinds of determiners and quantifiers (e.g., "much" versus "many")—we arrive at the following sort of classification:

(M)	*Mass*:	"air," "water," "mud," "sand," "dust," "snow," "gravel," "asparagus," "traffic," …
(C)	*Count*:	"beach," "cloud," "chair," "piece of furniture," "virus," "bacteria," "sheep," "university," "hurricane," "football game," …
(D)	*Dual-Use*:	"hair," "chicken," "carrot," "apple," "cloth," "pain," "disease," …

The nouns in the first list permit "bare" occurrences (as in "Water is wet"); they do not, in their use as mass-nouns, permit pluralization; and they can occur together with such quantifiers as "much" or "little" (as in "much air" and "little air"). The nouns in the second list do not permit (singular) "bare" occurrences (as in "*Beach is sandy"); but they can, in their use as count-nouns, be accompanied by plural morphology; and they are found together with such quantifiers as "many" or "few" (as in "many beaches" and "few beaches"). The nouns in the third list standardly have both sorts of occurrences. A list of this kind, however, masks several potential sources of trouble, which an adequate treatment of the problem of classification would need to address.

AMBIGUITIES. First, some grammatical contexts are at least at first sight ambiguous, in that the most obvious syntactic criteria such as those just cited do not by themselves clearly differentiate a given noun-occurrence as mass or count: examples include the occurrences of "lamb," "apple," and "fish" in "Mary had a little lamb," "The apple in the dessert is moldy," and "Fish floated in the water"; the occurrence of "home" in "at home"; as well as the occurrence of "tape" in such compound expressions as "tape recorder."

TRICKY CASES. Secondly, while the syntactic criteria mentioned above involving plural morphology and quantification do speak to most of the following cases, we may wonder whether they do not in fact misclassify at least some of them:

Collective Mass:	"furniture," "jewelry," "silverware," "clothing," …
Collective Plural:	"spaghetti," "groceries," "news," "clothes," …
Collective Singular:	"crew," "crowd," "mob," "committee," …
Irregular Plural:	"scissors," "pants," "tweezers," "goggles," …
Proper Names:	"Bertrand Russell," "the Holy Roman Empire," "the sixties," …

Thus, we may feel, for example, that "clothing" and "clothes" are sufficiently similar in their semantic contribution that they should be classified together, even though one occurs standardly as a mass-noun in English, whereas the other standardly occurs as an invariably plural count-noun.

ABSTRACT NOUNS. Thirdly, the syntactic criteria mentioned above also apply to nouns and noun-phrases whose denotations are either abstract or at least not straightforwardly concrete, such as the following:

Abstract Mass:	"knowledge," "evidence," "poetry," "money," "information," …
Abstract Count:	"belief," "mistake," "rendition," "symphony," "discovery," …
Abstract Dual-Use:	"logic," "truth," "justification," "science," "theory," …

It has, however, been questioned whether the mass/count-distinction can be sensibly drawn for such nouns and noun-phrases, possibly because the semantic and ontological vocabulary, which will feature prominently below, may not easily extend to their case.

NEW USES FOR OLD NOUNS. Fourthly, it should be noted that the examples given so far attest only to the way in which these nouns are currently and standardly used in English. However, it is relatively straightforward to introduce new uses for old nouns, or even to use a noun in a nonstandard way without much setup. For example, the noun "email" has effortlessly acquired a count-use, even though it was initially used only as a mass-noun; moreover, the use of "car" in "A BMW 300-series is not much car for the money," while deliberately nonstandard, is, as far as issues of grammar are concerned, not completely out of the question. Thus, the mass/count-distinction cannot be viewed as written in stone even within a particular language; expressions can change their status, if speakers of the language, for whatever reasons, so desire.

CROSS-LINGUISTIC VARIATION. Finally, there is considerable cross-linguistic variation in how particular languages pattern with respect to the mass/count-distinction. For one thing, specific nouns that belong to different languages but intuitively have the same meaning can be classified as mass in one language and count in another; for example, the German word for hair ("Haare") is, except for poetic contexts (such as "Rapunzel, let your hair down!"), standardly used only as a singular or plural count-noun, whereas the English noun "hair" standardly has both mass- and count-uses. Furthermore, different languages can differ in how they mark the mass/count-distinction or, indeed, in whether they do so in any obviously visible way at all. In this context, it has been observed that Asian classifier-languages such as Mandarin Chinese and Japanese are of special interest, because they require that every noun be preceded by a classifier reminiscent of the sort of "reference-dividing" relations we observe in English primarily in connection with mass-nouns and plural count-nouns ("basket of," "bouquet of," "bucket of," …). This has motivated some writers, such as R. Sharvy (1978) to speculate that perhaps all nouns are at bottom mass not only in these overt classifier-languages, but across the board, on the theory that such classifiers may be present covertly in every language.

2. THE PROBLEM OF LOGICAL FORM

While consideration of the problem of classification is often regarded only as a means to an end—namely, as a way of clarifying the nature of the subject-matter beyond the clear cases—its importance should not be underestimated, especially given its role in deciding whether or not a specific, more or less tricky, case should be viewed as a counterexample to a particular analysis. Most of the attention surrounding the mass/count-distinction, however, has been focused on the question of what (if any) its semantic and ontological significance might be. Thus, the mass/count-distinction, more so perhaps than any other comparable issue, has provided fertile soil on which to debate questions concerning our most central semantic notions—those of meaning and truth, reference, and quantification—as well as ontological questions concerning the basic categories of what there is; and therein, surely, lies its central interest for linguists and philosophers. Among the wealth of semantic issues that are debated in this connection, the following may be singled out as particularly prominent.

Semantic Role

(iii) What is the semantic role played by mass-nouns and count-nouns?

At least as far as singular count-nouns are concerned, this question is thought to have a straightforward answer; in fact, traditional accounts of meaning, truth, reference, and quantification, with their frequent appeals to the predicate-calculus and the apparatus of set-theory, seem to be in many ways specifically tailored to the semantic needs of singular count-nouns. Such nouns are typically analyzed as playing the semantic role of a predicate whose extension consists of objects, each of which (or so it seems) could at least in principle be referred to as a such-and-such (for some appropriate substantival phrase). These objects, in turn, are thought to compose the domain of values over which variables and quantifiers are interpreted as ranging; and they are taken to enter into set-theoretic relationships with one another.

Mass-nouns and plural count-nouns, on the other hand, have for a variety of reasons resisted straightforward assimilation into this familiar vocabulary. The former in particular have appeared puzzling, for one thing, because they seem to lead, in W. V. O. Quine's words, a "semantic double-life of sorts" (1960, p. 97), in some of their occurrences (e.g., "Snow is white") apparently playing the role of a name or singular term, in others (e.g., "Most snow is white") that of a predicate or general term. This appearance of a "semantic double-life" led Quine to conclude that mass-nouns can play both roles, that of a name and that of a predicate, depending on their position within the statement (see also Ter Meulen [1981] for another version of what may be called the "mixed view"). Others have thought it necessary to choose between these two semantic categories, by defending either a version of the "name view" or the "predicate view." (For examples of the name view, see Parsons 1970, Moravcsik 1973, Bunt 1979, 1985, Chierchia 1982, Link 1983, Lønning 1987, and Zimmerman 1995; for examples of the predicate view, see Burge 1972, and Koslicki 1999; as well as, arguably, Cartwright 1963, 1965, 1970; Montague 1973;

Pelletier 1974; Bennett 1977; Sharvy 1980; Roeper 1983; Pelletier and Schubert 1989; and Higginbotham 1994; though some of these writers are difficult to place.)

Finally, an influential attitude toward the apparently schizophrenic semantic behavior of mass-nouns has also been to detect here a category that resists this sort of classification into either name or predicate, because it harks back somehow to a more "primitive," "pre-individuative," "pre-reference-dividing," "merely feature-placing," "non-objectual," "pre-particular level of thought," one which predates the dichotomy of singular term and general term (see especially Strawson 1953–1954, Quine 1960, Evans 1975, and Laycock 1972, 1975, 1989, 1998 for expressions of this attitude). It is not obvious, however, what to make of this somewhat ambivalent sentiment, because apparently the mode of expression associated with the use of mass-nouns fits comfortably into our present usage and we do not currently inhabit this supposed "archaic" time.

As argued convincingly in Burge (1972), all three views—the mixed view, the name view, and the predicate view—give rise to potential difficulties. The mixed view has trouble capturing inferences which turn on the common semantic core apparently shared by both namelike and predicative occurrences of mass-nouns (e.g., "Snow is white; this stuff is snow; therefore, this stuff is white"). The name view, on the other hand, is forced to invoke an arguably question-begging "reference-dividing" relation, of the form "is a ... of" (e.g., "is a quantity of"), to account for those cases in which mass-nouns play an apparently predicative role (e.g., "most snow," on this view, becomes something along the lines of "most quantities of snow"). Moreover, as noted in Koslicki (1999), the supposed evidence for the name view (and, hence, for one half of the mixed view, as well) is shaky to begin with, because it is drawn from the class of so-called generic sentences; but genericity is not a phenomenon peculiar to mass-nouns and is exhibited to an equal extent by singular and plural count-nouns.

Finally, the predicate view, given our familiar way of thinking about predication as involving domains of objects, threatens to do away completely with the intuitive contrast between the different kinds of noun-occurrences. Whether this threatened obliteration should be taken as cause for alarm, however, depends in part on one's reaction to the kind of skeptical attitude displayed in Burge (1972), according to which the mass/count-distinction seems ultimately to be a pragmatic phenomenon, the grammatical manifestation of the contrast between cases in which, for whatever reasons, standards (though not necessarily clear ones) are already available for what is to count as a such-and-such (for some appropriate substantival phrase) and cases in which there has not been any comparable pressure to clarify or supplement our current practice.

This skeptical outlook takes the linguistic distinction in itself to be a relatively superficial phenomenon, at least from the point of view of semantics and ontology, though there might be a good deal of interest to be said about it, for example, from the perspective of epistemology, philosophy of science, philosophy of mathematics, and psychology especially concerning our practices of counting and measuring (see for example Frege 1884, Carnap 1926, Carey 1985, 1994, Xu 1997). Some of the considerations raised above in Section 1, especially the striking heterogeneity of class of expressions at issue noted in (b) and (c), as well as the flexibility of current usage and the cross-linguistic variation noted in (d) and (e), might in fact be thought to count as prima facie evidence in favor of such a skeptical approach.

In addition to the apparent "semantic double-life" that has been ascribed to mass-nouns by writers such as Quine, this mode of expression has also seemed to pose special challenges with respect to the following question:

Mass-Logic and Mass-Quantification:

(iv) How do mass-nouns behave under quantification and in combination with logical connectives such as negation, disjunction, and others?

As R. Sharvy (1980), P. Roeper (1983), J. T. Lønning (1987), and J. Higginbotham (1994) in particular have discussed in detail, it seems that such statements as "The hot coffee did not disappear" or "All phosphorus is either red or black" cannot be understood straightforwardly in terms of quantification over quantities of coffee or phosphorus and in terms of such set-theoretic notions as membership, subset, union, intersection or complement. For example, it has been argued that "All phosphorus is either red or black" does not mean the same as "Every quantity of phosphorus is either red or black," because, of those quantities of phosphorus that include both red phosphorus and black phosphorus, it is neither true to say that they are red nor that they are black (Roeper 1983, p. 254). Statements of this kind have been taken to provide motivation for thinking that, as in the case of predication, our familiar approach to quantification and other logical operations, as involving domains of objects that can be interpreted as standing in set-theoretic relations to one another, does not do justice to the semantic properties of mass-nouns and the system of determiners that accompanies them.

The suspected failure of the traditional apparatus to yield a fully general logic has commonly been traced to a certain combination of mereological characteristics exhibited by mass-nouns (or their denotations, or the concepts expressed by them). Thus, from the beginning, writers have been struck because not only do sums of, say, mud yield more mud (as of course do sums of, say, people), but because divisions of mud generally (i.e., with the exception of small and not readily accessible parts) also yield more mud (see, for example, Leonard and Goodman 1940, Goodman 1951, Quine 1960, Burge 1972, Laycock 1972, Cheng 1973, Bunt 1979, 1985, Ter Meulen 1981, Roeper 1983, Simons 1987, Higginbotham 1994, and Zimmerman 1995). The first of these properties is known as "cumulativity," the second as "distributivity," and their conjunction is often called "homogeneity"; the semantic relevance (if any) of "parts that are too small" (Quine 1960, p. 98) has given rise to what is known as the "problem of minimal parts."

Moreover, while divisions of mud into more mud, as we now know from empirical inquiry, cannot go on forever, it has been said that, at the very least, it is not part of the meaning of the term "mud" that there are atoms of mud, in the mereological sense of "atom" (i.e., quantities of mud that have no proper parts that are themselves mud), while apparently it does follow from the meaning of such terms as "person" or "people," or at least from the fact that they are standardly used as count-nouns, that their extensions do consist of such atoms, with each single person counting as one of them.

Thus, if these observations are correct, they would lead to the following tripartite division: (i) singular count-nouns are neither cumulative nor distributive, but they are atomic; (ii) plural count-nouns are cumulative and atomic, but not distributive; and (iii) mass-nouns are homogeneous (i.e., both cumulative and distributive), but nonatomic (i.e., uncommitted as between the properties of atomicity and full-fledged atomlessness). And where there are no atoms, so it has seemed to many writers, there set-theoretic operations and the associated approaches to quantification can take no hold; instead, nonatomic, algebraically characterizable systems (such as Boolean algebra or lattice theory) have seemed more appropriate in light of the semantic peculiarities of mass-nouns (see especially Cartwright 1963, for the first fully developed, but unpublished, algebraic account; later analyses in the same style include Bunt 1979, 1985, Roeper 1983, Link 1983, Simons 1987, Landman 1991, and Higginbotham 1994).

Despite the popularity of this style of approach, however, it is at least debatable, first, whether mass-nouns in fact are homogeneous, given the problem of minimal parts; and, secondly, whether the question of atomicity can in fact carry the semantic weight ascribed to it, given that, for example, we can without difficulty refer to something as a building, even when the object in question has proper parts that are themselves buildings (see Koslicki 1999 for a skeptical voice). Also relevant in this connection is the debate in contemporary metaphysics concerning the so-called "problem of the many" (see, e.g., Unger 1981), which concerns the question of whether each region of space-time occupied by something we would ordinarily refer to as, say, "one person" is in fact occupied by indefinitely many numerically distinct, but largely overlapping, persons: however exactly this debate in metaphysics ought to be resolved, at the very least we cannot accuse the philosophers involved in it of not being competent speakers of English!

3. OTHER PURPORTED DIFFERENCES

In addition to the apparent mereological differences as well as the purported differences in semantic role just cited, the following considerations are frequently also thought to bear some relevance to the mass/count-distinction.

CONSTITUTION AND THE (ALLEGED) "STUFF"/ "THING" DICHOTOMY. Exaggerated emphasis on a relatively small class of examples, such as "mud" versus "chair," has led to the idea that the linguistic mass/count-distinction maps straightforwardly onto an alleged metaphysical distinction between "stuff" and "things." A related misconception is that the denotations of mass-nouns constitute the denotations of count-nouns, because it is thought that mass-nouns denote "stuff" and count-nouns denote "things," and that the former constitutes the latter. Whatever exactly the notion of "stuff" comes to, however, it is simply not true that the constitution-relation connects mass- and count-noun denotations in this one-directional way (because, for example, particular virtues may constitute someone's virtue and particular pieces of furniture constitute furniture).

Moreover, as it stands, allusions to the notion of "stuff" are, in the absence of further elucidation, not particularly helpful. According to our ordinary usage, the term, "stuff," is employed in an extremely wide and varied range of contexts and is, in fact, often intersubstitutable with the term, "thing," as in "the stuff/things you've written," "the stuff/things in your attic," and so on. Thus,

unless it can be clarified, for example, whether such mass-noun denotations as asparagus, trash, jewelry or traffic should be considered "stuff," and whether such count-noun denotations as clouds, bacteria or viruses should not be considered "stuff," and, if so, why, this notion is simply too hazy to be of much theoretical use. Moreover, given the heterogeneity of the class of expressions at issue, the flexibility of current usage and the cross-linguistic variation noted in considerations (b) through (e) of Section 1, it is highly questionable whether any single metaphysical distinction can be found to underlie this linguistic contrast.

SHAPE-, STRUCTURE- AND SPACE-OCCUPANCY PROPERTIES. Relatedly, one often finds the mass/count-distinction described as involving a contrast between "units" that are "discrete," "delineated," and "definite," have a "certain shape" or "precise limits," on the one hand, and something that is more "undifferentiated," "continuous," "nondelineated," or "unstructured," on the other hand (see for example Pelletier 1991, Jespersen 1924 for representative formulations). It is difficult to tease apart how much of this vocabulary is intended to be understood epistemically (as terms such as "definite" and "precise" intimate) and how much of it is to be understood metaphysically; in either case, however, it is difficult to discern here anything more than what is already contained in either consideration (a) above or consideration (c) below.

DIVIDED REFERENCE/CRITERIA OF IDENTITY AND INDIVIDUATION. The mass/count-distinction is almost universally conceived of as involving a contrast between expressions that "carry within themselves" criteria of identity and individuation and ones that fail to supply at least one or possibly both sorts of criteria. Thus, Quine famously remarks that, while "shoe," "pair of shoes," and "footwear" all range over the same "scattered stuff," they differ in that the first two "divide their reference" in different ways and the third not at all (1960, p. 91); and P. F. Strawson comments, equally notoriously, that "the general question of the criteria of distinctness and identity of individual instances of snow or gold cannot be raised or, if raised, be satisfactorily answered," because, in his view, "we have to wait until we know whether we are talking of veins, pieces or quantities of gold, or of falls, drifts or expanses of snow" (Strawson 1953–1954, p. 242; see also Laycock 1972, pp. 31–32).

However, as Helen Cartwright has argued forcefully in a series of early papers (especially Cartwright 1965, 1970), if "individuation" is what goes on when a noun has a paradigmatically predicative occurrence (e.g., one that appears next to such determiners such as "all," "some," "most," "the," "this," "much," and "little"), then the mass/count-distinction does not point to a general contrast in whether an expression "individuates," only arguably in how it does so; moreover, the question of identity is an equally moot point, because, as Cartwright points out, there are as many clear or tricky cases on the count-side as on the mass-side (e.g., compare "word" with "work," to use Cartwright's example). Finally, considerations that turn on the phenomenon of change over time, as when we speak for example of something's being the same water from one time to another, even while the water in question is slowly evaporating, also fail to isolate a feature that is peculiar to the denotations of any one class of expressions (see Laycock 1972, 1975, 1989, 1998).

COUNTING AND MEASURING. Finally, we come to a more promising area to explore in connection with the mass/count-distinction, namely the distinction between counting and measuring, that is, the distinction, on the one hand, between the practice of counting and measuring, and that between what we count and what we measure, that is, the subject-matter to which these practice are directed, on the other hand (see for example Parsons [1970] and Cartwright [1975a] for discussion of amounts and measures of amounts). Simply put, the contrast in this area is taken to be the following: whereas mass-noun denotations can only be measured, count-noun denotations can also be counted: thus, in the former case, only the vocabulary of amounts and measures of amount is appropriate, whereas the latter also admits of the apparatus of number and cardinality.

However, even in this area, matters are less clear than is often supposed. For, as it stands, the contrast between what we can and cannot measure really only marks off the sorts of magnitudes discussed by the physicist (e.g., temperature, mass, velocity, distance, and the like) from those entities which, in some way, exhibit these magnitudes; and while it is true that such magnitudes tend to be referred to by means of mass-nouns, the class of mass-nouns is of course thought to be much wider than simply what is encompassed by these magnitude-denoting terms. The area of counting as well is still radically under-explored, at least from the point of view of philosophy, though much interesting work has been done on the subject by psychologists (see for example Carey [1985, 1994] and the references cited therein). If counting involves, as Frege would put it, an association between a concept and a cardinal number, then the key question that arises in this context is just the question G. Frege himself was concerned to answer in Section 54 of the *Grundlagen,* namely

what sorts of requirements must be met by a concept to admit association with number (for discussion, see for example Geach 1962, Dummett 1973, Koslicki 1997, Blanchette 1999). If what has been suggested in the previous paragraph is correct and no general contrast exists between mass- and count-nouns at least in whether they provide criteria of individuation and identity, then the answer to Frege's question concerning counting must lie elsewhere; and what this answer is, it is fair to say, is still an open question.

IV. CONCLUSION

As sobering as we might find this outcome to be, it may be that, at the end of the day, the only absolutely general and incontestable truism that can be stated in connection with the mass/count-distinction is that a true statement containing a singular or plural count-noun, as in "There is a hair in my soup" or "There are hairs in my soup," insures the presence of either exactly one whole hair, or exactly two whole hairs, and so forth, whatever precisely this comes to in metaphysical terms; whereas a true statement of the form "There is hair in my soup" is compatible with there not being exactly one whole hair, or exactly two whole hairs, and so forth, because what is present may be parts of hairs or sums of parts of hairs or sums of hairs. And while this truth-conditional difference, stated in this stark and austere form, without the usual accompaniment of highly metaphorical and generally unhelpful vocabulary, might at first glance strike us as entirely trivial, its semantic and ontological significance, as can be gleaned among other things from the sorts of inferences that are licensed by it, should not be underestimated. Even if hair, perhaps, is no more "stufflike" than hairs, there is still an interesting story to be told as to what makes something one whole hair, or, for that matter, one whole anything (see Fine 1994, 1999, Harte 2002).

See also Aristotle; Frege, Gottlob; Plato; Pre-Socratic Philosophy; Proper Names and Descriptions; Properties; Quine, Willard Van Orman; Semantics; Strawson, Peter Frederick.

Bibliography

Bennett, M. "Mass Nouns and Mass Terms in Montague Grammar." In *Linguistics, Philosophy, and Montague Grammar,* In edited by S. Davis and M. Mithun, 263–285. Austin: University of Texas Press, 1977.

Blanchette, P. "Relative Identity and Cardinality." *Canadian Journal of Philosophy* 29 (1999): 205–224.

Bunt, H. C. "Ensembles and the Formal Semantic Properties of Mass Terms." In *Mass Terms: Some Philosophical Problems,* edited by Francis Jeffry Pelletier, 249–277. Dordrecht, Netherlands: D. Reidel, 1979.

Bunt, H. C. *Mass Terms and Model-Theoretic Semantics.* Cambridge, U.K.: Cambridge University Press, 1985.

Burge, T. "Truth and Mass Terms." *Journal of Philosophy* 69 (1972): 263–282.

Carey, S. *Conceptual Change in Childhood.* Cambridge, MA: MIT Press, 1985.

Carey, S. "Does Learning a Language Require the Child to Reconceptualize the World?" *Lingua* 92 (1994): 143–167.

Carnap, R. "Physikalische Begriffsbildung." In *Wissen und Werken* 39. Karlsruhe, Germany: G. Braun, 1926.

Cartwright, H. M. "Amounts and Measures of Amounts." *Nous* 9 (1975a): 143–164.

Cartwright, H. M. *Classes, Quantities and Non-Singular Reference.* Unpublished Ph.D. diss. University of Michigan, Ann Arbor, 1963.

Cartwright, H. M. "Heraclitus and the Bath Water." *Philosophical Review* 74 (1965): 466–485.

Cartwright, H. M. "Quantities." *Philosophical Review* 79 (1970): 25–42.

Cartwright, H. M. "Some Remarks About Mass Nouns and Plurality." *Synthese* 31 (1975b): 395–410.

Cheng, C.-Y. "Comments on Moravcsik's Paper." In *Approaches To Natural Language,* edited by K. J. J. Hintikka, J. M. E. Moravcsik, and P. Suppes, 286–288. Dordrecht, Netherlands: D. Reidel, 1973.

Chierchia, G. "On Plural and Mass Nominals." *Proceedings of the West Coast Conference on Formal Linguistics* 1 (1982): 243–255.

Dummett, M. *Frege: Philosophy of Language.* Cambridge, MA: Harvard University Press, 1973.

Evans, G. "Identity and Predication." *Journal of Philosophy* 72 (1975): 343–363.

Fine, K. "Compounds and Aggregates." *Nous* 28 (1994): 137–158.

Fine, K. "Things and Their Parts." *Midwest Studies in Philosophy* 23 (1999): 61–74.

Frege, G. *The Foundations of Arithmetic: A Logico-Mathematical Enquiry into the Concept of Number.* Translated by J. L. Austin. Evanston, IL: Northwestern University Press, 1980.

Geach, P. T. *Reference and Generality.* Ithaca, NY: Cornell University Press, 1962.

Gillon, B. S. "Towards a Common Semantics for English Count and Mass Nouns." *Linguistics and Philosophy* 15 (1992): 597–639.

Goodman, N. *The Structure of Appearance.* Dordrecht, Netherlands: D. Reidel, 1951.

Harte, V. *Plato on Parts and Wholes: The Metaphysics of Structure.* Oxford, U.K.: Clarendon Press, 2002.

Higginbotham, J. "Mass and Count Quantifiers." *Linguistics and Philosophy* 17 (1994): 447–480.

Hoepelman, J. "Mass Nouns and Aspect, or: Why We Can't Eat Gingercake in an Hour." *Amsterdam Papers in Formal Grammar* 1, edited by J. Groenendijk and M. Stokhoff, 132–153. 1976.

Jespersen, Otto. *The Philosophy of Grammar.* London: Allen and Unwin, 1924.

Koslicki, K. "Isolation and Non-Arbitrary Division: Frege's Two Criteria for Counting." *Synthese* 112 (1997): 403–430.

Koslicki, K. "The Semantics of Mass-Predicates." *Nous* 33 (1999): 46–91.

Koslicki, K. *Talk about Stuffs and Things: The Logic of Mass and Count Nouns.* Unpublished Ph.D. diss. Cambridge, MA: MIT, 1995.

Landman, F. *Structures for Semantics.* Dordrecht, Netherlands: Kluwer, 1991.

Laycock, H. "Matter and Objecthood Disentangled." *Dialogue* 28 (1989): 17–21.

Laycock, H. "Some Questions of Ontology." *Philosophical Review* 81 (1972): 3–42.

Laycock, H. "Theories of Matter." *Synthese* 31 (1975): 411–442.

Laycock, H. "Words without Objects." *Principia* 2 (1998): 147–182.

Leonard, H., and N. Goodman. "The Calculus of Individuals and Its Uses." *Journal of Symbolic Logic* 5 (1940): 45–55.

Link, G. "The Logical Analysis of Plurals and Mass Terms: A Lattice-Theoretical Approach." In *Meaning, Use, and Interpretation of Language,* edited by R. Bäuerle, C. Schwarze, and A. Stechow, 302–323. Berlin: Walter de Gruyter, 1983.

Lønning, J. T. "Mass Terms and Quantification." *Linguistics and Philosophy* 10 (1987): 1–52.

Montague, R. "Comments on Moravcsik's Paper." In *Approaches To Natural Language,* edited by K. J. J. Hintikka, J. M. E. Moravcsik, and P. Suppes, 289–294. Dordrecht, Netherlands: D. Reidel, 1973.

Moravcsik, J. "Mass Terms in English." In *Approaches To Natural Language,* edited by K. J. J. Hintikka, J. M. E. Moravcsik, and P. Suppes, 263–285. Dordrecht, Netherlands: D. Reidel, 1973.

Mourelatos, A. "Events, Processes and States." *Linguistics and Philosophy* 2 (1978): 415–434.

Parsons, T. "An Analysis of Mass Terms and Amount Terms." *Foundations of Language* 6 (1970): 362–388.

Pelletier, F. J. "Mass Terms." In *Handbook of Metaphysics and Ontology,* edited by H. Burkhardt and B. Smith, 1, 495–499. Munich: Philosophia Verlag, 1991.

Pelletier, F. J., ed. *Mass Terms: Some Philosophical Problems.* Dordrecht, Netherlands: D. Reidel, 1979.

Pelletier, F. J. "Non-Singular Reference: Some Preliminaries." *Philosophia* 5 (1975): 451–465.

Pelletier, F. J. "On Some Proposals for the Semantics of Mass Terms." *Journal of Philosophical Logic* 3 (1974): 87–108.

Pelletier, F. J., and L. K. Schubert. "Mass Expressions." In *Handbook of Philosophical Logic.* Vol. 4, edited by D. Gabbay and F. Guenthner, 327–407. Dordrecht, Netherlands: D. Reidel, 1989.

Quine, W. V. O. *Word and Object.* Cambridge, MA: MIT Press, 1960.

Roeper, P. "Semantics for Mass Terms with Quantifiers." *Nous* 17 (1983): 251–265.

Schubert, L., and F. J. Pelletier. "Problems in the Representation of the Logical Form of Generics, Plurals and Mass Nouns." In *New Directions in Semantics,* edited by E. LePore, 385–451. London: Academic Press, 1987.

Sharvy, R. "Maybe English Has No Count Nouns: Notes on Chinese Semantics." *Studies in Language* 2 (1978): 345–365.

Sharvy, R. "A More General Theory of Definite Descriptions." *Philsophical Review* 89 (1980): 607–624.

Simons, P. *Parts: A Study in Ontology.* Oxford, U.K.: Clarendon Press, 1987.

Strawson, P. F. "Particular and General." *Proceedings of the Aristotelian Society* 54 (1953–1954): 233–260.

Taylor, B. "Tense and Continuity." *Linguistics and Philosophy* 1 (1977): 199–220.

Ter Meulen, A. "An Intensional Logic for Mass Terms." *Philosophical Studies* 40 (1981): 105–125.

Ter Meulen, A. *Substance, Quantities and Individuals.* PhD Thesis, Stanford University, 1980.

Unger, P. "The Problem of the Many." In *Studies in Epistemology,* edited by P. French, T. Uehling, and H. Wettstein, 411–468. Midwest Studies in Philosophy 5. Minneapolis: University of Minnesota Press, 1981.

Ware, R. X. "Some Bits and Pieces." *Synthese* 31 (1975): 379–393.

Xu, Fei. "From Lot's Wife to a Pillar of Salt: Evidence that *Physical Object* is a Sortal Concept." *Mind and Language* 12 (1997): 365–392.

Zimmerman, D. W. "Theories of Masses and Problems of Constitution." *Philosophical Review* 104 (1995): 53–110.

Kathrin Koslicki (2005)

NOUS

Nous is most likely derived from the root *snu,* meaning "to sniff." Homer uses *nous* to mark the realization or understanding of a situation or state of affairs. *Nous* penetrates beyond the surface features of a situation and reveals the underlying truth of the matter. It is not divorced from perception and its most primitive function is that of apprehending or "smelling" danger. In Homer *nous* is also linked to the visualization of a plan of action that is immediately prompted by the awareness of a situation possessing emotional impact.

In Parmenides *nous* maintains its Homeric function as that which reveals ultimate truth. However, it also serves as the source of logical reasoning. In Parmenides *nous* is divorced from perception and it is best understood to mean "thought" or "intellect." In accordance with his rather austere ontology, Parmenides may well hold that that which exists is also that which thinks (i.e., no thing that exists fails to be a thing that thinks).

Anaxagoras treats *nous* as a mass term, like water or air (as opposed to a count term, like man or leaf). He appears to treat *nous,* not as "intellect," but as "reason" or "the virtue of rationality." *Nous,* for Anaxagoras, is the ultimate source of order and motion in the cosmos. By both initiating and governing a vortex, *nous* brings order to an otherwise static primordial chaos. Anaxagoras

asserts that *nous* is the lightest and purest thing. In so doing, he may well be attempting to articulate the idea that *nous* is an immaterial substance.

Plato incorporates elements from Parmenides, Homer, and Anaxagoras into his treatment of *nous.* First, following Parmenides, Plato considers *nous* to be an intellectual faculty that is wholly divorced from perception. Second, following Homer, Plato considers *nous* to be a source of insight or intuition. Still, for Plato, intuition is a nonempirically based grasp of unchanging and eternal truth. Finally, following Anaxagoras, Plato considers *nous* to be the source of order and motion in the cosmos. *Nous,* as rationality itself, is the substance that orders the heavens for the sake of the best. It is the cause of regular celestial motion and it is the cause of rationality in humans.

Aristotle, in his treatment of *nous,* displays acute awareness of views advanced by his predecessors. First, Aristotle takes *nous* to be a source of insight. *Nous* is a grasp of the salient features of a situation, but it is also a grasp of universal scientific principles. *Nous,* even in its later role, is not divorced from perception. It is the grasp of principles that are acquired by induction from perceived cases. Second, Aristotle uses *nous* to mean "intellect." He asserts that one's *nous* is separate from the body. In so doing, Aristotle is likely to be advancing the view that human intellect is an immaterial faculty. Finally, Aristotle's God, the Prime Mover, is *nous.* It is a separately existing and fully actualized rationality. This *nous* is the chief cause of motion, order, and goodness in the cosmos.

See also Anaxagoras of Clazomenae; Aristotle; Homer; Parmenides of Elea; Perception; Plato; Thinking.

Bibliography

Lesher, James H. "The Meaning of *Nous* in the Posterior Analytics." *Phronesis* 18 (1973): 44–68.

Menn, Stephen. *Plato on God as Nous.* Carbondale: Southern Illinois University Press, 1995.

Von Fritz, Kurt. "*Noos* and *Noein* in the Homeric Poems." *Classical Philology* 38 (1943): 79–93.

Von Fritz, Kurt. "*Nous, Noein,* and Their Derivatives in Pre-Socratic Philosophy (excluding Anaxagoras)." *Classical Philology* 40 (1945): 223–242 and 41 (1946): 12–34.

John E. Sisko (2005)

NOVALIS
(1772–1801)

Novalis was the pseudonym of Friedrich Leopold Freiherr von Hardenberg, the lyric poet and leader of the early German romanticists. Novalis was born of Pietistic parents on the family estate, Oberwiederstedt, in Saxony. In preparation for a civil service career, he studied jurisprudence, philosophy, chemistry, and mathematics at Jena, Leipzig, and finally at Wittenberg, where he completed his studies in 1794. In Jena, Novalis came under the influence of Johann Wolfgang von Goethe, Friedrich Schiller, and especially Johann Gottlieb Fichte. Soon afterward he became friendly with Friedrich and August Wilhelm von Schlegel, Ludwig Tieck, Friedrich von Schelling, and Johann Wilhelm Ritter. While apprenticed to a local official in Tennstedt, Novalis became engaged to thirteen-year-old Sophie von Kühn in 1795. Her death in 1797 reinforced his romantic mysticism and culminated in a poetic transfiguration of his loss, in which his love and his desire to follow her into death are mingled (*Hymnen an die Nacht,* first published in 1800). From 1796 on, Novalis worked in the administration of the Saxon salt works at Weissenfels. From 1797 to 1799 he studied mining at Freiburg, where he became engaged to Julie von Charpentier. He died at Weissenfels.

With Friedrich Schlegel, Novalis is the most characteristic spokesman of early romanticism. In opposition to the ideals of the Enlightenment and early classicism he presented his vision of the romantic life. In his novelistic fragment *Heinrich von Ofterdingen,* which was written in opposition to Goethe's *Wilhelm Meister,* he furnished the age with a poetic description of the poet. The self-consciousness implicit in such an undertaking is characteristic of Novalis. Thinking about his own situation, the poet tries to answer the more general question of the destiny of humankind; the poet is a seer who leads man home. The homelessness presupposed in this theme is also manifest in Novalis's characterization of the modern age as fragmented. By contrast, according to Novalis's idealized picture, the Middle Ages was a time of unity.

These ideas are further developed in *Die Christenheit oder Europa* (1799), an essay on the history of Western civilization, in which Novalis attacks the Protestant Reformation and the Enlightenment for having destroyed medieval unity. Also, he proposes that the most important reason for the homelessness of man is simply that he is a finite being. To be finite is to be in search of the infinite, which can be recovered in the depths of the human soul, a concept which develops ideas derived from Fichte's *Wissenschaftslehre.* Meaning, being, and truth are identified with the absolute ego. When the adept in *Die Lehrlinge zu Sais* (1798) lifts the veil of Isis that hides the meaning of human existence, he discovers only his true self. At the same time, this discovery is an escape from all that separates man from nature and from others.

The poet, through knowledge of his true self, is intuitively able to grasp the meaning of the world, which is veiled by mechanistic explanations, and to reveal this meaning to others. Poetry is an attempt to draw away the veil of the finite, which hides the mysterious meaning of everything. It thus has an apparently negative effect. The claims of the finite must be destroyed for the sake of the infinite. Romantic irony negates the ordinary significance of things and paves the way for a magic transformation of reality. Novalis's magic idealism may be described as an esoteric game in which relationships are suggested that may seem fantastic but are designed to reveal a higher meaning. The best example of this is *Heinrich von Ofterdingen,* in which past and present, fairy tale and everyday reality, mingle in such a way that the reader loses his bearings. This loss liberates his imagination. The world reveals its meaning when it is transformed into something man has freely chosen, and the opposition between man and nature is thereby overcome. Salvation lies in the godlike freedom of the artist.

Meaning escapes adequate conceptualization; it can only be hinted at. Fragment and aphorism (*Blütenstaub,* published in 1798) lend themselves particularly well to this purpose, as they point to meanings beyond themselves which must remain unstated. The romantic's refusal to mediate between the finite and the infinite, his assertion that there is no relationship between mere facts and transcendent meanings, makes it impossible to give any definite content to that reality which is said to be the goal of man's search. The movement toward salvation becomes indistinguishable from a flight into nothingness. Thus, in his *Hymnen an die Nacht* Novalis celebrates the night, in which all polarities are reconciled, and opposes it to more shallow day—a theme taken up by Arthur Schopenhauer, Friedrich Nietzsche, and their more recent followers.

See also Enlightenment; Fichte, Johann Gottlieb; Goethe, Johann Wolfgang von; Nietzsche, Friedrich; Reformation; Romanticism; Schelling, Friedrich Wilhelm Joseph von; Schiller, Friedrich; Schlegel, Friedrich von; Schopenhauer, Arthur.

Bibliography

WORKS BY NOVALIS

German Editions

Editions of Novalis's collected works are Ludwig Tieck and Friedrich Schlegel, eds., 2 vols. (Berlin, 1802); Paul

Kluckhohn and Richard Samuel, eds., 4 vols. (Leipzig, 1929; 2nd ed., Stuttgart, 1960–); C. Seeling, ed., 5 vols. (Zürich: Bühl, 1945); and E. Wasmuth, ed., 4 vols. (Heidelberg, 1953–1957).

For Novalis's philosophical works, see *Das philosophische Werke*, Richard Samuel, ed., Vol. I (Stuttgart, 1965), the first volume of a projected four-volume critical edition.

English Translations

The Devotional Songs of Novalis. Edited by Bernard Pick. Chicago, 1910. Also contains German text.

Henry of Ofterdingen: A Romance. Cambridge, MA: Owen, 1842.

Hymns to the Night and Other Selected Writings. Translated by C. E. Passage. New York, 1960.

The Novices of Sais. Translated by R. Manheim. New York, 1949.

WORKS ON NOVALIS

Biser, E. *Abstieg und Auferstehung, Die geistige Welt in Novalis Hymnen an die Nacht.* Heidelberg, 1954.

Carlyle, Thomas. "Novalis." In *Critical and Miscellaneous Essays,* in *Works,* edited by H. D. Trail. London, 1896–1899; New York, 1896–1901.

Dilthey, W. *Das Erlebnis und die Dichtung: Lessing, Goethe, Novalis, Hölderlin,* 3rd ed. Leipzig, 1910.

Friedell, E. *Novalis als Philosoph.* Munich, 1904.

Kuhn, H. "Poetische Synthesis oder ein kritischer Versuch über romantische Philosophic und Poesie aus Novalis Fragmenten." *Zeitschrift für Philosophische Forschung* (1950–1951): 161–178; 358–384.

Küpper, P. *Die Zeit als Erlebnis des Novalis.* Cologne: Böhlau, 1959.

Rehm, W. *Orpheus, Der Dichter und die Toten.* Düsseldorf: L. Schwann, 1950.

Karsten Harries (1967)

NOZICK, ROBERT
(1938–2002)

Robert Nozick was born in Brooklyn, New York, graduated from Columbia University in 1959, and received a PhD from Princeton University in 1963. After stints at Princeton University and the Rockefeller University, Nozick went to Harvard University in 1969, at age thirty, as full professor. There he was named Arthur Kingsley Porter Professor of Philosophy in 1985, then Joseph Pellegrino University Professor in 1998. He was a fellow of the American Academy of Arts and Sciences and served as president of the Eastern Division of the American Philosophical Association.

Nozick and his Harvard colleague John Rawls were the giants of twentieth-century political philosophy. Where Rawls stuck to one task, elaborating and defending his magisterial *Theory of Justice,* Nozick was notably rest-

less and interested in everything. He once said, "I didn't want to spend my life writing *Son of Anarchy, State, and Utopia, Return of the Son,* and so on" (Socratic Puzzles 1997, p. 2). In an age of subspecialization, the range of Nozick's contributions is shocking.

POLITICAL PHILOSOPHY

In *A Theory of Justice,* Rawls described himself as working toward a theory of pure procedural justice. He proposed as a test of distributive justice that inequalities are just only if they offer the greatest possible benefit to the worst-off. In *Anarchy, State, and Utopia* (1974), Nozick's departure was to develop a *genuinely* procedural theory, aimed at no particular end state. Indeed, Nozick's product was less a theory of just distribution than a theory of just transfer. A transfer from one person to another is truly just, according to Nozick, if truly voluntary.

Nozick's argument sometimes is said to lack foundations, to merely postulate rights. More charitably, Nozick's bold claims about rights are his conclusions rather than his premises. Starting from Rawls's foundation—individuals are separate and may not be sacrificed for others—Nozick, in the process arguing for this premise, carries it to its logical conclusion. Part 1 of *Anarchy, State, and Utopia* argues that a world where persons are respected as separate entities within a minimal state is a *possible* world. Part 3 argues that this is an *attractive* world. Part 2 argues that a world where our separateness is *not* taken to its logical conclusion—not taken to culminate in some more or less literal interpretation of Rawls's call for the "most extensive system of liberty compatible with like liberty for all" (1971, p. 302)—is neither attractive nor just.

In one of the century's more influential philosophical examples, Nozick asks us to suppose that we are in a situation as perfectly just and equal as we can imagine. Then someone offers Wilt Chamberlain a dollar for the privilege of watching him play basketball. Before we know it, thousands of people happily are paying Wilt a dollar each every time he puts on a show. Wilt gets rich. The distribution is no longer equal, but no one is complaining. Nozick's question: If we assume for argument's sake that justice is a pattern of equality achievable at a given moment, what happens if we achieve the ideal? Must we then prohibit everything—consuming, creating, trading, giving—that upsets perfect equality? Recent egalitarian work is an evolving response to the problem Nozick's story revealed. In part due to Nozick's argument, egalitarians at the beginning of the twenty-first century realize that any equality worthy of aspiring to will focus

ENCYCLOPEDIA OF PHILOSOPHY
2nd edition

less on equality as a time-slice property of economic distribution of wealth and more on how people are treated: how they are rewarded for their contributions and *enabled* over time to make contributions worth rewarding.

METAPHYSICS AND EPISTEMOLOGY

Nozick's last book, *Invariances* (2001), spans a range of topics including truth, objectivity, and consciousness, and his second book, *Philosophical Explanations* (1981), offers fresh ideas on free will, personal identity, and knowledge. For example, philosophers for millennia had analyzed knowledge as justified true belief. That is, *S* knows that *p* just in case *p* is true, *S* believes that *p*, and *S*'s belief is justified. Since 1963, though, philosophy had been reeling from Edmund Gettier's refutation of this seemingly straightforward analysis. Nozick's response is among the most creative. The problem with justification, as Gettier construed it, is that a belief can be justified, in virtue of coinciding with the facts, without being properly *sensitive* to the facts. Nozick, instead of refining or supplementing the justification condition, *replaced* it with a pair of *tracking* conditions:

If it were not true that *p*, *S* would not believe that *p*.

If it were true that *p*, *S* would believe that *p*.

DECISION THEORY

Nozick's *Socratic Puzzles* (1997), a collection of essays, includes his essay "Newcomb's Problem and Two Principles of Choice." In it Nozick introduced a class of puzzles for prevailing formulas for maximizing expected utility. For example, the devout go to heaven, according to John Calvin, but why? *Because* they are devout? If so, expected utility would suggest that we ought to be devout. Or because of predetermined grace, a side effect of which is an urge to be devout? In this second case, since it is more fun not to be devout, expected utility would suggest that we ought not to be devout. The crucial issue is not whether the outcome is probabilistically linked to one's action but whether it is *affected* by one's action. Therefore, rational choice cannot be entirely captured by any probabilistic formula. Even at its most formulaic, rational choice would have to begin with the problem of choosing a formula to govern subsequent choices, soothe choosing begins prior to having the formula. The chosen formula will be a way of processing information not only about probabilities and utilities but also about causal connections between actions and outcomes. Nozick's essay spawned hundreds of responses.

NONCOERCIVE PHILOSOPHY

One of Nozick's biggest contributions to philosophy was to reflect on, and poke fun at, the competitiveness of philosophical discourse. Nozick returned to this theme in the introductions to each of his major works; it was the only topic that occupied Nozick continuously. "Philosophical training molds arguers. ... A philosophical argument is an attempt to get someone to believe something, whether he wants to believe it or not. ... To argue with someone is to attempt to push him around verbally. ... Perhaps philosophers need arguments so powerful they set up reverberations in the brain: if the person refuses to accept the conclusion, he *dies*" (1981, p. 4). Nozick's remarks on the ideal of "coercive philosophy" led to a generation of self-deprecating humor in seminars across the United States and eventually to a widespread relaxing of what had been a more confrontational, less cooperative disciplinary style.

See also Calvin, John; Decision Theory; Justice; Personal Identity; Rawls, John; Rights.

Bibliography

WORKS BY NOZICK

Anarchy, State, and Utopia. New York: Basic Books, 1974.

Philosophical Explanations. Cambridge, MA: Harvard University Press, 1981.

The Examined Life. New York: Simon and Schuster, 1989.

The Nature of Rationality. Princeton, NJ: Princeton University Press, 1993.

Socratic Puzzles. Cambridge, MA: Harvard University Press, 1997.

Invariances: The Structure of the Objective World. Cambridge, MA: Harvard University Press, 2001.

WORKS ON NOZICK

Feser, Edward. *On Nozick.* Toronto: Thomson Wadsworth, 2004. An accessible discussion of *Anarchy, State, and Utopia.*

Lacey, A. R. *Robert Nozick.* Princeton, NJ: Princeton University Press, 2001. Discusses the range of Nozick's thought.

Paul, Ellen, Jeffrey Paul, and Fred D. Miller Jr., eds. *Natural Rights Liberalism from Locke to Nozick: Essays in Honor of Robert Nozick.* New York: Cambridge University Press, 2005.

Paul, Jeffrey, ed. *Reading Nozick.* Oxford, U.K.: Blackwell, 1982. A collection of responses to *Anarchy, State, and Utopia.*

Rawls, John. *A Theory of Justice.* Cambridge, MA: The Belknap Press of Harvard University Press, 1971.

Schmidtz, David. *Robert Nozick.* New York: Cambridge University Press, 2002. A collection of essays by specialists in the various fields to which Nozick contributed.

Schmidtz, David, and Sarah Wright. "What Nozick Did for Decision Theory." In *The American Philosophers*, Peter French and Howard K. Wettstein, eds. Oxford, U.K.: Blackwell, 2004.

Wolff, Jonathan. *Robert Nozick: Property, Justice, and the Minimal State*. Stanford, CA: Stanford University Press, 1991. The first book-length critique of *Anarchy, State, and Utopia*.

David Schmidtz (2005)

NUMBER

Numbers are central to science. They underlie what Galileo Galilei and Isaac Newton called the primary properties of things, the properties that can be measured (John Locke listed these as number, motion and rest, size, figure, and impenetrability). These underlie secondary properties (like colors and musical harmonies and discords), which in turn underlie the tertiary properties, like beauty, which make life worth living.

The centrality of numbers to science indirectly confers on them philosophical significance, but they have also played a direct role in metaphysics. Plato's theory of universals begins from the problem of the One over Many. Behind the superficial diversity of things in the world, it is often the case that there is one thing that many numerically distinct individuals share in common. For instance, when one doubles the length of the string on a lyre or the length of a column of air in a flute, the note it sounds is always lowered by the same musical interval, an octave. The things that distinct individuals share in common are called universals, and "Platonism" is used as a name for a broad and loose family of theories that affirm the existence of universals.

The existence of numbers has always been central to the history of Platonism, from ancient times to the present. In the nineteenth and twentieth centuries foundational work in the philosophy of mathematics, especially by Gottlob Frege and Bertrand Russell, affirmed the existence of numbers. Following them, Willard Van Orman Quine affirmed the existence of numbers, and he rightly called this doctrine "Platonism". Quine argued that it is reasonable to believe in the existence of numbers because numbers are central to mathematics, which in turn is central to science. This reason for believing in numbers is close to the guiding Pythagorean and Platonist idea that to understand the world we must find the unified mathematical patterns that lie behind the diversities of appearances.

EARLY HISTORY OF NUMBERS

The history of numbers in India, China, and elsewhere is deep and diverse, but it is still not properly understood.

In ancient and modern histories of ideas in Europe, the origin of geometry was traditionally traced to ancient Egypt; and relatively sophisticated advances in arithmetic and algebra have been recognized as having emerged in Mesopotamia; and both these sources entered European traditions through ancient Greece. Knowledge of this ancient history is improving, but it is still incomplete.

The early mathematical advances of ancient Greece are better known, though even here the evidence is sparse. Almost no written records survive from the Pythagorean oral traditions before Plato. What survives from before Euclid's *Elements* consists in little more than hints in Plato and Aristotle.

Euclid's *Elements*, the first systematic presentation of geometry and arithmetic, is magnificent, but little is known of its sources and motivations. It is relatively apparent, however, that some of his theorems consist in translations of algebraic results, known in Mesopotamia, into geometric counterparts. For instance, an algebraic thesis, like $(a + b)^2 = (a^2 + 2ab + b^2)$, would become a theorem concerned with the division of a square into two smaller squares and two rectangles. For some reason, the mathematicians of Plato's Academy emphasized geometry rather than arithmetic, and arithmetic was subsumed under geometry.

PROLIFERATION OF KINDS OF NUMBERS

Besides the whole numbers (or natural numbers) the Greeks also recognized relationships of ratio between numbers. For example, the numbers 9 and 6 stand in the same ratio as 3 to 2, and one can call this ratio (3:2). This same relationship of ratio that holds between any two numbers will also hold between two possible geometrical lengths.

However, among the relationships of ratio that hold between various magnitudes, as for instance between lengths of lines, there are some that do not hold between any two whole numbers. Plato and Aristotle allude, many times, to a proof that no ratio between whole numbers will match the relationship of proportion that holds between the diagonal and the side of a perfect square. This fact would now be expressed by saying that $\sqrt{2}$ is an irrational number, which means that there are no whole numbers a and b such that $a / b = \sqrt{2}$.

The ancient Greeks thought of ratios among lines as forming a domain distinct from the domain of numbers. Numbers consisted simply of whole numbers. As the centuries advanced, the term *number* gradually expanded to include the entire domain of what are now called the positive real numbers. This domain includes all the irrational numbers, such as $\sqrt{2}$ and π, that can be represented as nonterminating decimals (such as 3.1415926 …). This domain includes, as a subdomain, the rational numbers, which are the ratios that hold between whole numbers; and, as a smaller subdomain, the integers, which correspond to just the rational ratios to the unit measure. The domain of number did not initially, however, include the number zero or the negative numbers.

Over several centuries the domain of things that were included as numbers expanded to include zero and negative numbers. First, there was an expansion to include a symbol "0" that was at first to be thought of not as signifying any number, but just as a place holder in the system of Arabic notation that is used today. In the notation "12," the "1" is placed in the second column from the right, and this means that it signifies one group of ten. Take 2 away from 12 and the result is written "10" with the "0" not referring to anything at all, but just serving to keep the "1" in the second column, so that it continues to signify one group of ten.

As time went by, however, the symbol "0" did come to be thought of as standing for something that might be called "the number zero", trusting that there was some suitable thing for this symbol to refer to. It was only gradually that any clear conception began to arise of what kind of thing this number zero might be.

Likewise, negative numbers began as notation that did not refer to any extra numbers, but just told one what to do with ordinary, positive whole numbers. With time, however, this notation came to be thought of as referring to new numbers, and eventually a conception emerged about what kinds of things these new numbers might be.

There was also a tentative expansion, with deep philosophical misgivings, to include what are now known as imaginary and complex numbers. Briefly, the imaginary number i—assuming there is such a thing, and calling it a number—is defined to be that mathematical object that is such that the ratio of 1 to it is the same as the ratio of it to minus 1. That is, $i / 1 = -1 / i$, so that $i^2 = -1$. Complex numbers consist of all the numbers that can be obtained from i by taking multiples of it and adding the result to other numbers.

There was also a tentative expansion, with deep philosophical misgivings, to include infinitesimal magnitudes. These extra entities seemed to be indispensable in the new mathematical theory of physical magnitudes like velocity and acceleration, invented by Newton and Got-

tfried Wilhelm Leibniz and referred to as "calculus" or, in its most general form, "analysis".

Despite the immense success of the calculus in science, the concept of an infinitesimal—a magnitude greater than zero, but less than any finite magnitude—was viewed with some suspicion. In the nineteenth century, through the work of Augustine-Louis Cauchy and Karl Weierstrass, the concept of an infinitesimal was replaced by the concept of the limit of a sequence of numbers. An infinite sequence of numbers s_1, s_2, s_3, … approaches the limit l if the difference between l and s_n can be made as small as one likes by taking sufficiently large values of n. That is, given any positive number d, no matter how small, there is some number N such that the difference between l and s_n is less than d, for every n (N.

Using this concept, the nineteenth-century mathematicians showed how the concepts of continuity, convergence, differential, and integral could all be precisely defined. In this way, it was shown how talk of infinitesimals could be dispensed with entirely.

A further nineteenth-century development was the introduction by Georg Cantor of the concept of a transfinite number. The transfinite numbers can be thought of as measuring the size of infinite sets. Cantor introduced the symbol $\aleph_0$ (pronounced "aleph-null") for the number measuring the size of the set of all positive whole numbers and the symbol c for the transfinite number measuring the size of the set of all real numbers. By a simple, yet ingenious argument (the celebrated diagonal argument), Cantor was able to show that there are more real numbers than whole numbers: $c > \aleph_0$.

Cantor proved that there are always more subsets of a given set than elements of that set (so there are more sets of natural numbers than natural numbers for example). Hence, given any transfinite number measuring the size of an infinite set, there is a larger transfinite number, which measures the size of the set of all subsets of that set.

Cantor developed a transfinite arithmetic for these new numbers, showing how operations corresponding to addition and exponentiation could be defined for them. Again, the new numbers were viewed initially with the deepest suspicion by the mathematical community.

FREGE AND THE PARADOXES

The work of the nineteenth-century mathematicians had begun a reverse process of defining one kind of number in terms of simpler kinds. The complex numbers, it had been shown, could be defined as pairs of real numbers (like the x-y coordinates of Cartesian geometry) along with special rules for adding and multiplying these pairs. The real numbers had been shown by Julius Dedekind and Cauchy to be definable as infinite sequences or sets of rational numbers, while the rational numbers themselves can be identified with sets of pairs of natural numbers.

What of the natural numbers themselves? Frege's work can be seen as an attempt to complete this reverse process of rigorization by providing a firm foundation for the fundamental theory of the natural numbers. Dedekind and Giuseppe Peano had independently specified some simple axioms for that theory (called number theory or arithmetic). However, Frege wanted to answer the questions: What are the natural numbers? How may they be defined? The Dedekind-Peano axioms specify the laws governing the numbers, but do not provide a definition of them.

Imagine if one thought that the number of soldiers in an army was one of the army's most significant properties. One might then think of whole numbers as properties of aggregates. However, as Frege pointed out, if one points to the things on a desk and asks how many there are, one has not yet asked a complete question. There may be two decks of cards; and if so, then there are also 106 cards; and there are a great many molecules; and so on.

This suggests that number is a property of properties. The property of "being a deck of cards on the table" has the property of having one instance; the property of "being a card on the table" has the property of having 106 instances; and so on. The property of "being a unicorn" has the property of having no instances. That higher-order property, the property of having no instances, might aptly be called the number zero.

Consider, then, the theory that the number 2 is a property of a property, namely the property of having two instances, that the number 3 is the property of having three instances, and so on. Frege turned decisively aside from this theory. He argued that numbers could not be universals or concepts, but had to be objects.

For Frege, the fundamental kind of expression used to ascribe numbers to things are expressions like "the number of cards on the desk" or "the number of planets in the solar system." The expression "the number of Fs" is a singular term, purporting to pick out an object, in just the same way as "the brother of John" is a singular term, purporting to pick out a certain individual. So for Frege, ascriptions of number depend for their truth on the existence of objects, which are the referents of expressions of the form "the number of Fs."

Is it legitimate to suppose that given any general term F, there is also an object corresponding to the "the number of Fs"? Frege held that it is legitimate to speak of objects of a certain kind, provided there is a criterion of identity for them. What is the criterion of identity for numbers? The answer is given by the following principle, known as Hume's principle: "The number of Fs = the number of Gs if and only if (iff) there is a one-to-one correspondence between the Fs and the Gs."

A one-to-one correspondence is a relation that pairs each F with exactly one G and each G with exactly one F. So, for example, the number of knives on the table is equal to the number of forks provided that each fork can be paired with a unique knife and each knife with a unique fork.

Frege demonstrated that all the Dedekind-Peano axioms for number theory can be proved from Hume's principle alone, given appropriate definitions that he devised; a fact now known as Frege's theorem.

Frege attempted to go further by giving an explicit definition of "the number of Fs," from which Hume's principle itself could be proved. He defined "the number of Fs" as the set of all properties that can be put in one-to-one correspondence with the Fs. That is, the number n is identified with the extension of the second-order property of having n-members.

This was a disaster. The principle concerning sets that Frege appealed to in his derivation of Hume's principle states that every predicate has an extension. The extension of a predicate is the set of all (and only) those objects that satisfy the predicate. As Russell's paradox shows, however, this principle is inconsistent. If every predicate has an extension, then the predicate "is not a member of itself" has an extension, which would be the set of all (and only) the objects that are not members of themselves. Call this set R. It follows that R is a member of R iff R is not a member of R, a contradiction. Frege's logical system had turned out to be inconsistent. This was the first of a number of paradoxes of set theory that were to have a formative influence on subsequent work in the foundations of mathematics.

There were varying responses to Russell's paradox. Russell and Alfred North Whitehead took one approach: the theory of types. Ernst Zermelo and others took a different approach: that of axiomatic set theory. Given the now standard axioms for set theory, the Frege-Russell definition of the numbers will not work; the assumption that there is a nonempty set of all three-membered sets, for example, leads to a contradiction. A different approach to the definition of the numbers is required. Instead of taking the numeral *n* to refer to the set of all *n*-membered sets, it can be taken to refer to some particular, paradigm example of an *n*-membered set.

John von Neumann provided an effective sequence of paradigm *n*-membered sets. The number zero is the paradigm zero-membered set: the empty set, ∅. The number 1 is the set whose only member is zero. The number 2 is the paradigm two-membered set whose members are 0 and 1. And in general, each number *n* is the *n*-membered set whose members consist of all and only the whole numbers from 0 up to $(n - 1)$.

One can then say that there are *n* members of a particular set iff that set can be placed into a one-to-one correlation with the paradigm *n*-membered set. For instance, there are two decks of cards on the table iff the members of the set of decks of cards on the table can be placed into a one-to-one correspondence with the members of the paradigm two-membered set {∅, {∅}}.

PHILOSOPHIES OF NUMBER

Philosophical accounts of number (and mathematics more generally) can be divided into two broad categories: realist and antirealist.

A realist about number holds that statements concerning numbers are objectively true or false. On this view, statements such as "there are nine planets in the solar system," "there are infinitely many prime numbers," "34957 + 70764 = 105621," or "every even number greater than two is the sum of two primes" (Goldbach's conjecture), say something that is objectively either true or false, even if no one knows which it is. In addition, the realist claims that some such statements are indeed true. That is, the realist typically accepts as true most, or all, of accepted mathematics.

By contrast, an antirealist denies one or both of the two realist claims. That is, the antirealist will deny that there is an objective fact of the matter about the truth value of all statements concerning number or that all currently accepted mathematical statements concerning number are actually true.

THE ARGUMENT FOR PLATONISM

Platonism, as that term is used in modern philosophy of mathematics, is the view that mathematics is the study of an objective realm of independently existing objects. In addition, the platonist holds that these objects are abstract, rather than physical objects. A physical object is something that (if it exists) has a location in space and

time, can undergo changes of state, and can interact causally with other spatiotemporally located objects. Cups and saucers, stars and planets, plants and animals, and atoms and photons are all examples of physical objects. By contrast, an abstract object is something that (if it exists) lacks some or all of these properties. Abstract objects have no location in space and time, they have no state and no history, and they do not interact causally with other objects.

The main philosophical argument for platonism in modern philosophy proceeds as follows. Many statements of arithmetic appear to make existential claims. For example, the statement "there is a prime number greater than three" asserts the existence of an object having certain properties. Since many such arithmetical statements are true, it follows that numbers exist. This does not yet show that numbers must be abstract, but various arguments can be given against the alternatives. For example, every physical object has a location in space and exists for a certain time. Numbers have neither of these properties. Then again, there are infinitely many numbers, but perhaps a finite number of physical objects. It follows that numbers, if they exist, must be nonphysical, abstract objects.

The argument for platonism can be summarized as follows:

P1. Arithmetical sentences express statements that are objectively true or false

P2. Some arithmetical statements are true

P3. Arithmetical statements quantify over certain objects (numbers)

Therefore:

C1: Numbers exist.

However:

P4: Numbers, if they exist, must be abstract (nonphysical, nonmental) objects.

Therefore:

C: Numbers are abstract objects.

THE EPISTEMOLOGICAL PROBLEM

The central problem facing a platonist philosophy of number is epistemological. Abstract objects cannot be directly perceived, nor can they have any effects on objects or processes that can be directly perceived. How then is it possible for us to know anything at all about such objects? The causal isolation of abstract objects appears to make them unknowable. Hence either we have no mathematical knowledge, or platonism is not the correct view of mathematics.

Before Frege, philosophers had postulated that human beings have some kind of direct cognitive access to mathematical objects, through perception or some rational faculty analogous to perception, or (for Immanuel Kant) through an *a priori* intuition or construction.

According to Frege our our only access to numbers is through our knowledge of the truth-values of arithmetical statements. Certain sentences of our language contain terms standing for numbers and quantifiers that range over numbers. If it can be shown that some of those sentences are true (and Frege hoped to show that they are logically true), then we will have explained how we can know about numbers, even though we have no direct perceptual or causal contact with them.

If the reduction of arithmetic to logic could be carried out, our knowledge of numbers would have been shown to be based on our knowledge of the truth of the basic laws of logic. Frege thought there was no real problem about how we know that the laws of logic are true; we can just see that they are. Explaining the psychological mechanisms that give us this ability is outside the scope of philosophy and can be left to the psychologists. The discovery of the paradoxes ruined this comfortable picture, showing that we have no infallible insight into the fundamental truths of logic after all. The reduction of arithmetic to set theory does not resolve this problem. Our knowledge of the basic laws of set theory cannot be any more certain or secure than our knowledge of the fundamental laws of arithmetic.

REALIST ALTERNATIVES TO PLATONISM

In view of the epistemological problem for platonism, many philosophers of mathematics have sought to avoid the conclusion that numbers are abstract objects. However, if that conclusion should be rejected, the argument for platonism given earlier must be unsound. Alternatives to platonism can be usefully classified according to which of the premises of that argument are rejected.

An obvious point at which that argument might be attacked is at premise P4. That is, one could deny that numbers, if they exist, must be abstract. Along these lines are various attempts to provide a physicalist account of mathematical objects such as numbers and sets. Such accounts differ from platonism only in denying that numbers are entirely nonphysical and abstract. The payoff is epistemological. If, for example, numbers are properties or relations that can be instantiated by ordinary physical objects, then some basic knowledge of numbers could be acquired by ordinary perception.

Another realist alternative is to accept P1 and P2, but deny P3; the claim that mathematical statements quantify over a domain of special objects of some kind. One strategy is to think of arithmetic as the theory, not of a special realm of objects, but of a certain pattern or structure. In the case of arithmetic the structure in question is that shared by any infinite progression of objects (also called an ω-sequence) in which (1) there is a unique first element and (2) for any given element there is a distinct, unique next element in the sequence, called the successor of the given element.

According to one variety of structuralism, the truths of arithmetic are simply those that hold in every system of objects that form an ω-sequence. An equation such as $2 + 1 = 3$ is interpreted as elliptical for the generalization; "If S is any system of objects that form an ω-sequence, then the successor of the successor of the first element of S added to the successor of the first element of S is equal to the successor of the successor of the successor of the first element of S."

Structuralism is often motivated by a certain ontological problem for platonism. According to the platonist, sets and numbers are abstract objects. What is the relationship between them? We have already described one way in which the natural numbers can be defined as sets. This is the definition of the natural numbers as the von Neumann numbers: $0 = \emptyset$, $1 = \{0\}$, $2 = \{0,1\}$, and $3 = \{0,1,2\}$ and in general, $N+1 = \{0, 1, ..., N\}$. This is not the only possible set-theoretic definition of the natural numbers, however. Zermelo, for example, defined the sequence as follows: $0 = \emptyset$, $1 = \{0\}$, $2 = \{1\}$, and $3 = \{2\}$ and in general, $N+1 = \{N\}$.

From a purely mathematical point of view the definitions seem equally valid, since they both validate exactly the same theorems of arithmetic. However, the two definitions are certainly not equivalent, since they identify some numbers with distinct sets; on von Neumann's definition $2 = \{\emptyset, \{\emptyset\}\}$ (a set with two members), while on Zermelo's definition $2 = \{\{\emptyset\}\}$ (a set with just one member).

From a platonist perspective there is something puzzling about this. If numbers are independently existing objects, then there must be a fact of the matter about which set, if any, the number 2 is identical with. It cannot be that there are two equally correct definitions of the number 2 that identify it with different sets, but this is exactly what one seems to have in the case of the von Neumann and Zermelo definitions: two equally correct accounts of the number 2 that assign it to distinct sets.

A generalization of this line of argument yields the conclusion that numbers cannot be objects of any kind. Any definition of numbers in terms of particular mathematical objects of some other kind is arbitrary, in the sense that equivalent, but distinct alternative definitions will always be available. However, if, as the platonist holds, numbers are objects, there must be a fact of the matter about which objects the numbers really are. So there must be something wrong with platonism.

From a structuralist perspective, however, this kind of ontological relativity is readily explicable. For on that account, arithmetic is not concerned with a domain of specific objects, but only with what holds good in all ω-sequences. The sequences of sets defined by von Neumann and Zermelo are both examples of ω-sequences, so both systems have the required structure. Any system of objects (sets or otherwise) having the same structure will do just as well, for arithmetic is just the theory of the properties shared by all ω-sequences.

CONVENTIONALISM

A different approach, long popular with empiricists, is to say that mathematics is concerned not with objects, but with relations between concepts. A good example is the account of mathematics associated with the philosophical movement known as logical positivism, which had its heyday in the 1930s and 1940s. According to the positivists, the truths of logic and mathematics are alike in being analytic, by which they meant that they are true solely in virtue of the meanings of the symbols they contain, meanings that are established by linguistic convention.

On this view, 2 + 2 = 4 is true because of the stipulations we have laid down governing the use of the symbols "2," "4," "+," and "=." As such it is completely without empirical content and this explains the irrelevance of empirical evidence to mathematics. No fact about the world can contradict the statement 2 + 2 = 4, because its truth does not depend on facts about the world, but only on facts about what the mathematical symbols occurring in it mean. What our symbols mean is a matter of arbitrary linguistic convention. We can simply stipulate that our symbols are going to have certain meanings and then the truth of various statements involving them will follow. The truths of arithmetic on this view are records of the stipulations we have laid down governing the use of the arithmetical symbols.

Largely as a result of criticisms developed by Quine and others, conventionalism is no longer widely accepted. One difficulty is that even if it were possible simply to stipulate that the terms of a mathematical theory are to be assigned whatever meaning makes all the axioms turn out true, the stipulation will backfire if the axioms are inconsistent. Whether the axioms are consistent or not is itself a mathematical fact which is independent of our stipulations and conventions. If so, then not all mathematical facts can be purely conventional or true in virtue of meaning.

The specific objections to conventionalism are however, less significant than the alternative account of the epistemology of mathematics developed by Quine, which if correct, would undermine the main epistemological motivation for conventionalism. Quine's alternative account is described in the final section of this article.

NOMINALISM

Nominalism is the philosophical thesis that there are no abstract objects that is, everything that exists is a concrete, physical particular. In interpreting mathematics and science then, the nominalist has two options. One option is to say that despite appearances, mathematical and scientific theories do not involve reference to abstract objects after all. The other option is to say that they do and are therefore literally false. The nominalist may then seek to provide a positive account of mathematical and scientific theories, showing how they can be reformulated so as to avoid any reference to abstract objects. The result would be an error theory of science and mathematics.

This second approach is the one taken by the nominalist philosopher Hartry Field, who has attempted to demonstrate that reference to abstract objects can be eliminated from science by showing how nominalistic versions of physical theories might be constructed: versions which do not presuppose the existence of abstract objects such as numbers or functions. The interested reader is referred to the bibliography for further details of the construction and the philosophical debate surrounding it.

FORMALISM

This type of nominalist antirealism concerning numbers and other abstract objects consists in a denial only of the second premise (P2) of the argument for platonism given earlier. On such a view, mathematical sentences express statements which can be true or false, but it is argued that there is no good reason for thinking that any mathematical statements involving quantification over abstract objects are literally true.

More radical types of antirealism deny the first premise (P1) of the argument for platonism. One way of denying that premise is to say that mathematical sentences do not express statements that could be true or false at all, objectively or otherwise. This is the approach taken by the formalist account of mathematics. On this view, mathematics is not a body of statements that can be true or false. Instead, mathematics is thought of as analogous to a game, like chess. It is a game played with symbols according to certain rules.

The most sophisticated version of the formalist account of mathematics is that proposed by the mathematician David Hilbert in the 1920s and early 1930s. According to Hilbert mathematics has a meaningful part and a purely formal part. The meaningful part consists of finitary statements. These are decidable statements concerning only perceptible concrete symbols, such as the numerals 0, S0, SS0, SSS0. The purely formal component consists of ideal statements, statements that involve unbounded quantification over infinite domains such as the natural numbers. All such statements are strictly meaningless, according to Hilbert. Their introduction into mathematical theories was to be justified on purely instrumental grounds. They provide the mathematician with an extremely powerful, but in principle dispensable, means of proving facts about the real finitary subject matter of mathematics.

Hilbert's program was to show, using only finitary methods, that the introduction of such ideal statements into arithmetic could never lead to any false finitary statement becoming derivable. This is equivalent to proving using only finitary methods that classical arithmetic is consistent. He hoped to establish the same result for set theory, thereby establishing that the threat of inconsistency implied by the paradoxes could be guaranteed not to arise there either. "No one," wrote Hilbert, "shall drive us out from the paradise that Cantor has created for us" (Benacerraf and Putnam [1983], p. 191).

There is a fairly broad consensus that Kurt Gödel's second incompleteness theorem shows that Hilbert's program is unachievable, even at the level of arithmetic. Let T be any standard formal system for arithmetic. Suppose there was a finitary consistency proof for T. Then that proof could be formalized as a derivation in T of a formula expressing the consistency of T. However, by Gödel's second incompleteness theorem, no consistent

formal system for arithmetic can contain such a derivation. It follows that the goal of Hilbert's program is unachievable for arithmetic and so also for set theory.

INTUITIONISM

A different response to the paradoxes, current at the time Hilbert was writing, was the intuitionist account of mathematics, proposed by the mathematician Luitzen Egbertus Jan Brouwer and developed by Arend Heyting. Intuitionism can be thought of as denying the first premise of the argument for platonism by claiming that although mathematics does constitute a body of statements that can be true or false, the truth or falsity of a mathematical statement is not independent of human beings.

The platonist thinks of the natural numbers as an infinite domain of objects that exist independently of human thought and that make arithmetical statements objectively true or false. By contrast, intuitionists such as Brouwer and Heyting think of the natural numbers as mental constructions, objects that are created by the human mind. On this view, what makes a mathematical statement true or false is not the existence of objects that are independent of human beings, but the existence of a certain kind of mental construction, a proof (though not a proof in a formal system).

This conception of mathematical truth led the intuitionists to reject the law of excluded middle, as applied to mathematics. That is, they denied the universal validity of the logical schema "Either A or not-A." For on the intuitionist view, a mathematical conjecture for which neither proof nor disproof has yet been constructed, cannot be said to be either true or false.

Although paradox may be avoided in the intuitionistic reconstruction of mathematics, many contemporary philosophers would reject it. One reason is the apparent truncation of classical mathematics necessitated by intuitionism; many theorems of classical analysis and set theory are false when interpreted intuitionistically. A deeper reason may be a distrust of the reforming nature of the intuitionism. The role of philosophy, it is thought, should be to provide an account or interpretation of mathematics as it actually is, not to reformulate or remake mathematics in a new image.

An exception to this general trend is Michael Dummett. A widely accepted philosophical thesis has it that the meaning of a statement is given by its truth conditions. Dummett argues that this is empty, unless accompanied by a substantive account of truth; an account which goes beyond the mere equivalence of 'P is true' with P. But meaning cannot be explained in terms of a concept of truth according to which truth is something that may apply to a statement quite independently of whether it is possible to know that it does, for then our knowledge of the meaning of a statement would not always be capable of being made manifest by publicly observable behaviour—a condition which is necessary for meaning to be communicable. Instead, meaning must be explained in terms of verification conditions; to know the meaning of a mathematical statement is to know what would count as a proof of it. Thus the argument leads to a version of intuitionism; to say that a mathematical statement is true is to say that we have a proof, while to say that it is false is to say that we have a disproof.

Dummett's argument depends only on very general considerations concerning the communicability of meaning. If valid, the argument would apply to statements of any kind whatsoever and not just to mathematical ones. For example, it would be a consequence that perfectly ordinary statements about the past which can no longer be verified or refuted could not be considered either true or false, unless it could be shown that there is some special feature of our use of such statements which makes a verification transcendent account of their meaning possible.

THE INDISPENSABILITY ARGUMENT

The epistemological objection to platonism is one aspect of a more general problem for empiricism. Mathematics appears to be highly non-empirical, in both its subject-matter and its methodology. Empirical evidence does not appear relevant to mathematics. However if, as the empiricist asserts, all our knowledge is ultimately empirical, there seems to be no good reason for thinking that mathematics is true at all. The logical positivist's claim that mathematics is analytic, or true only in virtue of meaning, was an attempt to solve this problem by showing how mathematical statements could be true, though independent of all empirical evidence.

In a now classic series of papers written in the late 1940s and early 1950s, Quine launched a major critique of this conventionalist solution to the problem, while also developing a significant alternative account of the structure of empirical knowledge and the place of mathematics within that structure. Quine argued that the mistake made by earlier empiricists was to think that individual statements can be tested empirically in isolation from each other. Instead, it must be recognized that our scientific beliefs form an interlocked system or web that "faces

the tribunal of experience as a corporate body." (Quine, 'Two Dogmas of Empiricism', in 'From a logical point of view', p. 41). Mathematical beliefs form an indispensable part of this system and are therefore justified to the extent that they contribute to the goals of scientific prediction and explanation. In Quine's view the mathematics used in a successfully confirmed scientific theory is confirmed along with the rest of that theory. Mathematical objects, like numbers and sets, are theoretical posits, epistemologically on a par with electrons and photons.

Quine draws a further conclusion. If mathematics can be supported by empirical evidence, it can also be undermined by it. Our mathematical beliefs are open to empirical falsification and revision, in just the same way as our scientific beliefs. The illusion of a difference between mathematical and other scientific statements is generated, according to Quine, by pragmatic considerations. We are far more reluctant to revise the mathematical and logical components of our scientific theories because these are so deeply embedded in the system of total science that altering them would result in a major restructuring of the entire system. But if the result of such a restructuring was an overall simplification or improvement in the total system of science, then it would be perfectly rationally justified.

Quine's epistemology is significant because it provides a solution, consistent with empiricism, to the epistemological problem for platonism. Quine can accept all the premises in the argument for platonism given earlier. Mathematical statements can be taken to refer, as they appear to refer, to abstract objects such as numbers and sets. But the epistemological problem is resolved. Numbers and sets cannot be perceived, either directly or indirectly, but their utility in enabling us to predict and explain the world provides us with all the justification for their existence we need or could ever be entitled to.

The indispensability of mathematics in science has two aspects: one emphasized by Quine, the other by Hilary Putnam. Quine argues from the indispensability of mathematics in the derivation of the observation statements that confirm or disconfirm scientific theories and hypotheses. Putnam emphases a different aspect of the indispensability of mathematics in science. Mathematics is used in science, not only in deriving predictions from theories but also in formulating the empirical hypotheses of those theories. Consider Boyle's law, for example, which states the relationship between the pressure, temperature, and volume of a fixed quantity of gas enclosed in some container. The law states that the pressure of the gas is equal to a constant multiplied by the temperature of the gas, divided by the volume.

$$P = kT / V$$

Pressure, temperature, and volume are all numerical quantities. The pressure of the gas in kilopascals at a certain time is a real number, as are the volume in cubic centimeters and the temperature in degrees Celsius at a time. The law states that a certain mathematical relationship always holds between these real numbers. Boyle's law is therefore just as much committed to the existence of real numbers and functions as it is to the existence of gases. In this way, realism about physical theory leads to realism about mathematical objects such as numbers.

The Quine-Putnam argument allows for the empirical justification not only of the often highly specific mathematical statements (such as numerical equations) used to derive predictions from a theory but also of any more general mathematical statements, such as set-theoretic axioms, which imply them. Boyle's law can be derived from the more fundamental laws of thermodynamics. Hence any empirical confirmation of Boyle's law accrues also to the thermodynamic laws used to derive it. In just the same way, since arithmetic can be reduced to set theory, the numerical equations used to derive predictions from Boyle's law can be derived from the axioms of set theory. Hence any empirical confirmation of those equations accrues also to the axioms of set theory. In this way, it might be hoped that a great deal of even abstract mathematics can be justified by means of the Quine-Putnam argument.

See also Frege, Gottlob; Mathematics, Foundations of; Platonism and the Platonic Tradition; Quine, Willard Van Orman; Russell, Bertrand Arthur William.

Bibliography

On the historical development of the mathematics of number, see Morris Kline, *Mathematical Thought from Ancient to Modern Times* (New York: Oxford University Press, 1972).

For Euclid's *Elements*, the standard reference is T. L Heath, *The Thirteen Books of Euclid's Elements* (New York: Dover Publications, 1956).

Collections of mathematical papers by Frege, Cantor, Gödel, Zermelo, and others can be found in D. E. Smith, ed. *A Source Book in Mathematics* (New York: Dover Publications, 1959) and J. van Heijenoort, ed. *From Frege to Gödel: A Source Book in Mathematical Logic, 1879–1931* (Cambridge, MA: Harvard University Press, 1967).

For the philosophy of mathematics, the standard collection of papers is Paul Benacerraf and Hilary Putnam, eds. *Philosophy of Mathematics: Selected Readings* (2nd ed. New York: Cambridge University Press, 1983). Also useful is W.

D. Hart, ed. *The Philosophy of Mathematics* (New York: Oxford University Press, 1996).

Frege's classic *Die Grundlagen der Arithmetic* (Breslau, Poland: Koebner, 1884) is translated by J. L Austin as *The Foundations of Arithmetic* (Oxford, U.K.: Basil Blackwell, 1953).

For philosophical expositions of Frege's work, see Michael Dummett, *Frege Philosophy of Mathematics* (London: Duckworth, 1991) and Crispin Wright, *Frege's Conception of Numbers as Objects* (Aberdeen, Scotland: Aberdeen University Press, 1983). W. Demopoulos, ed. *Frege's Philosophy of Mathematics* (Cambridge, MA: Harvard University Press, 1995) provides an excellent collection of papers on the technical aspects of Frege's work.

On the epistemological problem for platonism, see Paul Benacerraf, "Mathematical Truth," *Journal of Philosophy* 70 (1973): 661–679.

For a survey of work on physicalist accounts of mathematical, see A. D. Irvine, ed. *Physicalism in Mathematics*. Dordrecht, Netherlands: Kluwer Academic, 1990.

On structuralism and the ontological problem for platonism, see Paul Benacerraf, "What Numbers Could Not Be," *Philosophical Review* 74 (1965): 47–73; Hilary Putnam, "Mathematics without Foundations," *Journal of Philosophy* 64 (1965): 5–22; and Charles Parsons, "The Structuralist View of Mathematical Objects," *Synthese* 90 (1990): 303–346.

On the conventionalist account of mathematics and logic, see A. J. Ayer, *Language, Truth, and Logic* (London: V. Gollancz, 1946); Rudolf Carnap, "Empiricism, Semantics, and Ontology" (1956) and Carl Gustav Hempel, "On the Nature of Mathematical Truth," *American Mathematical Monthly* 52 (1954), both reprinted in Paul Benacerraf and Hilary Putnam, eds. *Philosophy of Mathematics: Selected Readings* (2nd ed. New York: Cambridge University Press, 1983).

Quine's critiques of conventionalism can be found in "Truth by Convention" and "Carnap and Logical Truth" in Quine, *Ways of Paradox and Other Essays* (Cambridge, MA: Harvard University Press, 1976).

For the indispensability argument, see Quine, "Two Dogmas of Empiricism" and "On What There Is" in his *From a Logical Point of View* (2nd ed. Cambridge, MA: Harvard University Press, 1980). See also Quine, *Word and Object* (Cambridge, MA: MIT Press, 1960).

Putnam's exposition of Quine's argument is to be found in Hilary Putnam, *Philosophy of Logic* (London: Allen and Unwin, 1971).

On Field's program, see Hartry Field, *Science without Numbers: A Defence of Nominalism* (Princeton, NJ: Princeton University Press, 1980). For a critical analysis, see Stewart Shapiro, "Conservativeness and Incompleteness," *Journal of Philosophy* 80 (1983): 521–531. A. D. Irvine, ed. *Physicalism in Mathematics* (Dordrecht, Netherlands: Kluwer Academic, 1990) also contains a number of relevant articles on nominalism.

David Hilbert's formalist program is outlined in a readable way in his "On the Infinite" (1926), which is reprinted in Paul Benacerraf and Hilary Putnam, eds. *Philosophy of Mathematics: Selected Readings* (2nd ed. New York: Cambridge University Press, 1983, pp. 83–201). A scholarly exposition of this and other foundational programs can be found in Marcus Giaquinto, *The Search for Certainty: A Philosophical Account of Foundations of Mathematics* (Oxford, U.K.: Clarendon Press, 2002).

On intuitionism, see the papers by Brouwer and Heyting in Paul Benacerraf and Hilary Putnam, eds. *Philosophy of Mathematics: Selected Readings* (2nd ed. New York: Cambridge University Press, 1982). Michael Dummett's *Elements of Intuitionism* (Oxford, U.K.: Clarendon Press, 1977) is a standard reference work on intuitionistic mathematics and philosophy. Dummett's own argument for an intuitionistic interpretation of mathematics can be found in "The Philosophical Basis of Intuitionistic Logic" in his *Truth and Other Enigmas* (London: Duckworth, 1975).

John Bigelow (2005)
Sam Butchart (2005)

NUMENIUS OF APAMEA

Numenius of Apamea, the second-century Greek philosopher perhaps best known for his description of Plato as an Atticizing Moses, was a precursor of Plotinus and Neoplatonism and also had affinities with Gnosticism and the Hermetic tradition. Of his life practically nothing is known, and even the approximate dates of his birth and death are uncertain. Since his description of Plato is quoted by Clement of Alexandria (*Stromateis* i, 22.93), he cannot have survived much later than 200 CE, while the latest writers cited in the fragments of his works belong to the time of Nero (37–68 CE). He may have been of non-Greek origin, and his name, like that of Porphyry, may have been a Greek translation of a Semitic original. Our sources commonly describe him as a Pythagorean, but Iamblichus and Proclus call him a Platonist, which comes to much the same thing in an age when Plato was considered a disciple of Pythagoras. Certainly Numenius is best grouped with such Middle Platonists as Albinus. His work was based primarily upon exegesis of Plato and presents a systematization of Plato's thought with a dualist emphasis. It is possible that he had some knowledge of Christianity, but what is truly remarkable is his knowledge of Judaism. It has been suggested that he himself was a Jew, but this is far from certain. What is clear is that he sought to go back before Plato and Pythagoras to the teachings of the ancient East, the Brahmins, the Jews, the Magi, and the Egyptians. In this respect there are links with the Hermetic books and with the *prisca theologia* of such Renaissance writers as Marsilio Ficino and Giovanni Pico della Mirandola, although scholars differ as to the extent to which Numenius's philosophy was actually influenced by Oriental ideas and the extent to which it was purely Greek.

A notable feature of his thought is his doctrine of the Demiurge. He postulates two opposed principles, God and matter, the monad and the dyad, but whereas the Pythagoreans adhered to monism by making the dyad emanate from the monad, Numenius developed a dualistic theory. Matter is evil, and the supreme God can therefore have no contact with it; hence the need for a second god, the Demiurge, who is of dual nature, an *anima mundi* related both to God and to matter (cf. the Philonic Logos). There are also two souls in the world, one good and one evil, and two souls in man, a rational and an irrational; and the only escape from this dualism is by deliverance from the prison of the body. Astrological elements in Numenius's anthropology suggest an attempt to give astrology a rational basis.

Numenius is important for his influence on later Neoplatonists, although some of his views were to be rejected by them. The allegation that Plotinus merely plagiarized Numenius prompted Plotinus's disciple Amelius to write a book pointing out the differences between them (Porphyry, *Vita Plotini* 17). The hierarchy of three gods, for example, appears to be similar to Plotinus's hierarchy of being, but the three entities in each case do not correspond exactly in detail. Moreover, Plotinus rejected Numenius's dualistic and Gnosticizing tendencies.

See also Platonism and the Platonic Tradition; Pythagoras and Pythagoreanism.

Bibliography

FRAGMENTS

des Places, Édouard, ed. and tr. *Numénius, Fragments.* Paris: Belles Lettres, 1973. (Includes French translation.)

STUDIES

Armstrong, A. H. *The Architecture of the Intelligible Universe in the Philosophy of Plotinus.* Cambridge, U.K.: Cambridge University Press, 1940.

Beutler, R. "Numenios." In Pauly-Wissowa, *Real-Encyclopaedie.* Supp. VII (1940), pp. 664ff.

Burnyeat, Myles F. "Platonism in the Bible: Numenius of Apamea on *Exodus* and Eternity." In *Metaphysics, Soul, and Ethics. Themes from the Work of Richard Sorabji,* edited by Ricardo Salles. Oxford: Oxford University Press, 2004.

Dillon, John. *The Middle Platonists. A Study of Platonism, 80 B.C. to A.D. 220,* 2nd ed. London: Duckworth, 1996.

Dodds, Eric R. (1960). "Numenius and Ammonius." In *Les sources de Plotin = Entretiens sur l'Antiquité Classique.* Vol. 5. Geneva: Fondation Hardt, 1957.

Festugière, A. J. *La révélation d'Hermes Trismégiste.* Vol. III: *Les doctrines de l'âme.* Paris: Lecoffre, 1953. Vol. IV: *Le dieu inconnu.* Paris: Lecoffre, 1954.

Frede, Michael. "Numenius." In *Aufstieg und Niedergang der römischen Welt,* Vol. II.36.2, edited by H. Temporini and W. Haase. Berlin: de Gruyter, 1987.

Leemans, E. A. *Studie over den Wijsgeer Numenius van Apamea.* Mémoires de l'Académie Royale de Belgique. Vol. 37. Brussels, 1937. Includes fragments and testimonia.

Puech, H. C. *Mélanges Bidez.* Vol. II. Brussels, 1934.

Vogel, C. J. de. *Greek Philosophy.* Vol. III, 421ff. Leiden: Brill, 1959.

R. McL. Wilson (1967)
Bibliography updated by G. R. Boys-Stones (2005)

NUSSBAUM, MARTHA
(1947–)

Martha Nussbaum has contributed to ethics, political theory, classics, philosophy of mind, legal theory, educational theory, public policy, and gender studies. Educated at New York University (BA, 1969) and Harvard University (MA, 1971; PhD, 1975), she has taught at Harvard, Brown University, Oxford University, and the University of Chicago.

Nussbaum's work ranges widely, but she has consistently returned to such themes as: the nature of emotion and its role in philosophical argument, the extension and application of the "capabilities approach" in the theory of justice, the role of philosophical argument and reflection in the public sphere, and the relationship between philosophy and art and literature. Her work can be helpfully characterized as a sustained critique of Platonism. *The Fragility of Goodness* (1986), her first major book, argued that the Platonic view of the good life marks "an aspiration to rational self-sufficiency through the 'trapping' and 'binding' of unreliable features of the world." Such self-sufficiency omits "a kind of human worth that is inseparable from vulnerability, an excellence that is in its nature other-related and social, a rationality whose nature it is *not* to attempt to seize, hold, trap, and control, in whose values openness, receptivity, and wonder play an important part" (pp. 19–20).

Nussbaum has consistently defended the latter. Against the Platonic-Christian view that transcendent Good or God is at the heart of morality, she advances her own comprehensive, Aristotelian-Kantian-Jewish view that religion highlights the largely autonomous, primary domain of human moral effort. The highest moral paradigms are not such figures as the saints or Gandhi, but those who, like Nehru, found the good life in human finitude and limitation. For Nussbaum, rigorist or ascetic moralism, whether in Gandhi or Plato, betrays a violence toward the self that may undermine morality and compassion.

Upheavals of Thought: The Intelligence of Emotions (2001) develops the moral psychology that figures in Nussbaum's ethical and political work. The Platonic ascent of love is criticized for having the lover climb to such heights as to be beyond compassion and human need, beyond even altruistic contact with actual human beings. Christian and Romantic views fail in the same way, and can reinforce developmental tendencies positively inimical to morality—childhood emotions of shame, disgust, and envy. Nussbaum works out a highly qualified "neo-Stoic" view of the emotions, according to which "once one has formed attachments to unstable things not fully under one's control, once one has made these part of one's notion of one's flourishing, one has emotions of a background kind toward them—on my view, judgments that acknowledge their enormous worth—that persist in the fabric of one's life, and are crucial to the explanation of one's actions" (p. 71). Thus, emotions are a type of evaluative judgment, construed in a way broad enough to allow that nonhuman animals and infants, who lack propositional thought, can also be said to have emotions. And they have a narrative structure, found in one's life history. Acknowledging one's neediness, however, and representing the world from the personal point of view and with considerable ambivalence, the emotions so characterized pose problems for moral and political theories stressing mutual respect, dignity, and concern for others.

Nussbaum's account of such emotions as compassion, shame, and disgust, which also receive extended treatment in her *Hiding from Humanity* (2004), is vital for understanding her political philosophy, which draws heavily on Aristotle, Immanuel Kant, John Stuart Mill, Karl Marx, John Rawls, and Amartya Sen. She defends a broadly Rawlsian political liberalism that frames an account of human flourishing adapted to the demands of liberal political theory, respecting the reasonable plurality of views of the good life to be found in the modern world. Her collaboration with Sen, beginning with *The Quality of Life* (1993), has yielded a critique of conventional economic measures of human welfare and pointed up the virtues of instead measuring people's capabilities, what they are capable of doing or being across central areas of human life. Her aim has been to bring her Aristotelianism into harmony with the capabilities approach, adapted to serve as a form of political liberalism that could also undergird the type of universalistic critique required by feminism.

Nussbaum's development of the capabilities approach in connection with feminism has led her to introduce more Kantian and Millian elements into her arguments and to emphasize the recognition of human dignity as a core feature of political liberalism. *Sex and Social Justice* (1999) and *Women and Human Development* (2000) develop the capabilities theory as the philosophical groundwork for basic constitutional standards, applicable to all governments, defining the minimal requirements of respect for human dignity. These works provide a highly developed account of the central human capabilities—life, bodily health, bodily integrity, senses, imagination and thought, emotions, practical reason, affiliation, concern for nature and other species, play, and political and material control over one's environment—and articulate the political liberal demand that all citizens must, as a requirement of justice, enjoy a basic threshold level of each of these capabilities. Her focus on the injustices confronting women, gays, and lesbians, and others suffering from insidious forms of oppression, has widened to cover problems of international justice and justice with respect to nonhuman animals.

Nussbaum has also paid special attention to education. *Cultivating Humanity* (1997) argues for an education (inspired by Plato's earlier, truly Socratic dialogues) that would awaken students to self-scrutiny and to their capabilities for love and imagination. Promoting a greater role for such philosophical reflection in public life has been one of Nussbaum's chief priorities.

See also Aristotelianism; Aristotle; Feminism and the History of Philosophy; Feminist Philosophy; Justice; Kant, Immanuel; Marx, Karl; Mill, John Stuart; Plato; Platonism and the Platonic Tradition; Rawls, John; Sen, Amartya K.; Women in the History of Philosophy.

Bibliography

WORKS BY MARTHA NUSSBAUM

The Fragility of Goodness: Luck and Ethics in Greek Tragedy and Philosophy. New York: Cambridge University Press, 1986.

The Quality of Life, edited by Martha Nussbaum and Amartya Sen. New York: Oxford University Press, 1993.

The Therapy of Desire: Theory and Practice in Hellenistic Ethics. Princeton, NJ: Princeton University Press, 1994.

Cultivating Humanity: A Classical Defense of Reform in Liberal Education. Cambridge, MA: Harvard University Press, 1997.

Sex and Social Justice. New York: Oxford University Press, 1999.

Women and Human Development: The Capabilities Approach. New York: Cambridge University Press, 2000.

Upheavals of Thought: The Intelligence of Emotions. New York: Cambridge University Press, 2001.

Hiding from Humanity: Disgust, Shame, and the Law. Princeton, NJ: Princeton University Press, 2004.

Frontiers of Justice: Disability, Nationality, Species Membership. Cambridge, MA: Harvard University Press, 2005.

WORKS ABOUT MARTHA NUSSBAUM

Goodin, R., and D. Parker, eds. "Symposium on Martha Nussbaum's Political Philosophy." *Ethics* 111 (October 2000). Comprehensive essays by L. Antony, R. Arneson, H. Charlesworth, and R. Mulgan, with responses by Nussbaum.

R. Barton Schultz (2005)